The Psychology of GENDER

THIRD EDITION

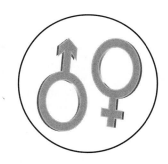

VICKI S. HELGESON

CARNEGIE MELLON UNIVERSITY

PEARSON

Prentice
Hall

UPPER SADDLE RIVER, NEW JERSEY 07458

Library of Congress Cataloging-in-Publication Data

Helgeson, Vicki S.
   The psychology of gender / Vicki S. Helgeson.—3rd ed.
      p. cm.
   Includes bibliographical references and index.
   ISBN-13: 978-0-13-600995-5
   ISBN-10: 0-13-600995-6
1. Sex role. 2. Sex differences (Psychology) I. Title.
   HQ1075.H45 2009
   305.3—dc22

                                                    2007052507

Editorial Director: Leah Jewell
Executive Editor: Jeff Marshall
Project Manager: LeeAnn Doherty
Associate Managing Editor: Maureen Richardson
Full Service Production Liaison: Joanne Hakim
Senior Marketing Manager: Jeanette Koskinas
Marketing Assistant: Laura Kennedy
Senior Operations Supervisor: Sherry Lewis
Cover Art Director: Jayne Conte
Cover Design: Bruce Kenselaar
Cover photo/illustration: Leon Zernitsky/Stock
   Illustration Source/Getty Images

Director, Image Resource Center: Melinda Patelli
Manager, Rights and Permissions: Zina Arabia
Manager, Visual Research: Beth Brenzel
Manager, Cover Visual Research & Permissions:
   Karen Sanatar
Image Permission Coordinator: Fran Toepfer
Full-Service Project Management: Laura Lawrie/
   ICC Macmillan Inc.
Composition: ICC Macmillan Inc.
Printer/Binder: RR Donnelley & Sons Company

Credits and acknowledgments borrowed from other sources and reproduced, with permission, in this textbook appear on appropriate page within text.

Pearson Prentice Hall™ is a trademark of Pearson Education, Inc.
Pearson® is a registered trademark of Pearson plc
Prentice Hall® is a registered trademark of Pearson Education, Inc.

Pearson Education Ltd., London
Pearson Education Singapore, Pte. Ltd
Pearson Education, Canada, Ltd
Pearson Education—Japan
Pearson Education Australia PTY, Limited

Pearson Education North Asia Ltd
Pearson Educación de Mexico, S.A. de C.V.
Pearson Education Malaysia, Pte. Ltd
Pearson Education, Upper Saddle River, New Jersey

10 9 8 7 6 5 4 3 2 1

ISBN 13: 978-0-13-600995-5
ISBN 10:   0-13-600995-6

*To my daughter, Katja, for making me smile
and for providing me with a window into
"gender in action."*

BRIEF CONTENTS

1   Introduction   1

2   Methods and History of Gender Research   29

3   Gender-Role Attitudes   69

4   Sex-Related Comparisons: Observations   100

5   Sex-Related Comparisons: Theory   139

6   Achievement   193

7   Communication   235

8   Friendship   285

9   Romantic Relationships   326

10   Sex Differences in Health: Evidence and Explanations   380

11   Relationships and Health   433

12   Work Roles and Health   495

13   Mental Health   544

CONTENTS

Preface   xvii

Acknowledgments   xxi

1   INTRODUCTION   **1**
Definition of Terms   3
Cultural Differences in the Construal of Gender   10
  Cultures with Multiple Genders   10
  Morocco   11
  The Agta Negrito   12
  Tahiti   12
  Status and Culture   13
Philosophical and Political Issues Surrounding Gender   19
  The Sex Difference Debate   19
  Should We Study Gender?   20
  Social Construction of Gender   20
  Women's Movements   21
  Men's Movements   23
This Book's Approach to the Study of Gender   26
Summary   27
Discussion Questions   27
Suggested Reading   27
Key Terms   28

2   METHODS AND HISTORY OF GENDER RESEARCH   **29**
The Scientific Method   30
  Correlational Study   31
  Experimental Study   33
  Field Experiment   36
  Cross-Sectional Versus Longitudinal Designs   36
Difficulties in Conducting Research on Gender   37
  Experimenter Effects   38
  Participant Effects   43

The Setting: Laboratory Versus Field   44
Variables Confounded with Sex   45
Situational Influences   45
History of the Psychology of Gender   48
1894–1936: Sex Differences in Intelligence   48
1936–1954: M/F as a Global Personality Trait   49
1954–1982: Sex Typing and Androgyny   53
1982–Present: Gender as a Social Category   58
Summary   66
Discussion Questions   67
Suggested Reading   68
Key Terms   68

3   GENDER-ROLE ATTITUDES   69
Attitudes Toward Men's and Women's Roles   70
Affective Component: Sexism   73
Traditional Versus Modern Sexism   73
Hostile Versus Benevolent Sexism   74
Sexism Toward Men   77
Cognitive Component: Gender-Role Stereotyping   78
What Is a Gender-Role Stereotype?   79
Components of Gender-Role Stereotypes   79
The Structure of Gender-Role Stereotypes   83
Subcategories of Gender-Role Stereotypes   85
Do Gender-Role Stereotypes Serve Any Function?   86
Altering Gender-Role Stereotypes   89
Do Stereotypes Reflect Reality?   91
What Is the Status of Stereotypes Today?   92
Behavioral Component: Sex Discrimination   94
Summary   97
Discussion Questions   97
Suggested Reading   98
Key Terms   98

4   SEX-RELATED COMPARISONS: OBSERVATIONS   100
Maccoby and Jacklin's Psychology of Sex Differences   102
Meta-Analysis   104
Sex Comparisons in Cognitive Abilities   106
Spatial Ability   106
Mathematical Ability   110
Verbal Ability   113
Comprehensive Assessment of Cognitive Abilities   116
Sex Comparisons in Social Domains   120

Empathy   120
Helping Behavior   121
Aggression   121
Sexuality   126
Activity   130
General Personality Attributes   131
Sex Comparisons in Moral Development   132
Sex Comparisons in Social Development   135
Sex Similarities Hypothesis Revisited   136
Summary   136
Discussion Questions   137
Suggested Reading   138
Key Terms   138

5 SEX-RELATED COMPARISONS: THEORY   139
Biology   140
Genes   140
Hormones   142
The Brain   145
Psychobiosocial Models   147
Evolutionary Theory and Sociobiology   147
Sexual Behavior   148
Mate Selection   148
Aggression   149
The Hunter-Gatherer Society   150
A Final Note   150
Psychoanalytic Theory   151
Social Learning Theory   152
Observational Learning or Modeling   153
Reinforcement   155
Gender-Role Socialization   157
The Influence of Parents   161
The Influence of Other People   164
Other Features of the Environment   165
Social Role Theory   173
Cognitive Development Theory   177
Gender Schema Theory   178
Considering the Context: Deaux and Major's Model   183
Perceiver   183
Target   185
Situation   185
Constructionist and Postmodern Perspectives   189
Summary   190

Discussion Questions 191
Suggested Reading 191
Key Terms 192

6 ACHIEVEMENT **193**
Individual Difference Factors 195
The Achievement Motive 195
Fear of Achievement 196
Self-Confidence 201
Response to Evaluative Feedback 203
Self-Esteem 206
Stereotype Threat 207
Conceptions of the Self 210
Attributions for Performance 214
Social Factors 218
Expectancy/Value Model of Achievement 219
The Influence of Parents 220
The Influence of Teachers 225
Summary 232
Discussion Questions 233
Suggested Reading 234
Key Terms 234

7 COMMUNICATION **235**
Interaction Styles in Childhood 236
Children's Styles of Play 237
Girls' Difficulty in Influencing Boys 240
Explaining the Different Styles of Play 240
Interaction Styles in Adulthood 242
Qualifiers of Sex Differences 243
Implications of Interaction Styles for Performance 244
Language 245
Qualifiers of Sex Differences 247
Effects of Language on Perception 250
Nonverbal Behavior 251
Smiling 252
Gazing 252
Decoding 253
Sending 253
Touching 253
Influenceability 255
Who Is Influenced? 255
Who Is Influential? 256
Influence Strategies 259

Explanations for Sex Differences in Communication 260
   Sex-Segregated Interactions in Early Life 260
   Status Theory 261
   Social Role Theory 265
Leadership 267
   Who Emerges as a Leader 267
   Leadership Styles 269
   Views of Leaders 270
Emotion 273
   The Experience of Emotion 273
   The Expression of Emotion 275
   Psychological Measures of Emotion 277
   Basis of Emotion 277
Support Provision in Interactions 278
Summary 281
Discussion Questions 283
Suggested Reading 283
Key Terms 284

8 FRIENDSHIP   285

Network Size 286
The Nature of Friendship 287
   Sex Similarities 287
   Sex Differences 288
Closeness of Friendship 292
Barriers to Closeness in Male Friendship 297
   Competition 298
   Homophobia 299
   Emotional Inexpressiveness 300
Self-Disclosure 300
   Sex of Discloser 301
   Sex of Recipient 301
   Situational Variables 301
   Barriers to Male Self-Disclosure 303
Definition of Intimacy 305
Conflict in Friendship 307
Changes Over the Life Span 308
   Early Adulthood: Marriage and Family 308
   Late Adulthood: Retirement and Empty Nest 309
Cross-Sex Friendship 310
   Comparisons to Same-Sex Friendship 310
   Obstacles 312
   Changes Over the Life Span 315

Cross-Race Friendship   316
Friendship at Work   317
Friendships of Lesbians and Gay Men   321
Summary   322
Discussion Questions   324
Suggested Reading   324
Key Terms   324

9   ROMANTIC RELATIONSHIPS   326
Relationship Development   327
    Standards for Relationships   327
    Characteristics Desired in a Mate   329
    Relationship Initiation   336
The Nature of Romantic Relationships   337
    Intimacy   337
    Love   338
    Sexuality   343
Maintaining Relationships   350
    Maintenance Strategies   350
    Marital Satisfaction   352
Conflict   356
    Areas of Conflict   356
    Conflict Management   357
    Demand/Withdraw Pattern   358
    Jealousy   362
Gay and Lesbian Relationships   366
    Relationship Development   367
    Intimacy and Sexuality   369
    Relationship Satisfaction   370
    Conflict   371
    Jealousy   371
    Sex Versus Status   372
Cohabiting Relationships   372
    Who Cohabits   374
    Outcomes of Cohabitation   374
Summary   377
Discussion Questions   378
Suggested Reading   379
Key Terms   379

10   SEX DIFFERENCES IN HEALTH: EVIDENCE AND EXPLANATIONS   380
Sex Differences in Mortality   380
    Life Span   380

Leading Causes of Death 383
Crime Statistics 385
Sex Differences in Morbidity 386
Explanations for Sex Differences in Health 388
Biology 389
Genes 389
Hormones 389
Immune System 390
Cardiovascular Reactivity 390
Artifacts 393
Socioeconomic Status 393
Proxy 394
Physician Bias 394
Health Behaviors 399
Preventive Health Care 399
Smoking 401
Alcohol 407
Drugs 408
Prediction of Smoking, Alcohol Use, and Drug Use 410
Overweight and Obesity 411
Exercise 415
Men's and Women's Social Roles 418
Job Characteristics 418
Driving 419
Risky Behavior 419
Concerns with Health 422
Nurturant Roles 422
Gender-Related Traits 423
Symptom Perception 424
Evidence 424
Explanations 425
Illness Behavior 426
Implications for Morbidity 426
Implications for Mortality 428
Conclusions 429
Summary 430
Discussion Questions 431
Suggested Reading 431
Key Terms 432

11 RELATIONSHIPS AND HEALTH 433
Effects of Marriage on Health 434
Evidence 435
Explanations 437

Effect of Bereavement on Health   441
  Evidence   442
  Explanations   443
Effect of Relationship Dissolution on Health   444
  Breakup of Dating Relationships   444
  Breakup of Marriage: Separation and Divorce   445
  Explanations   446
Effect of Marital Quality on Health   448
  Evidence   448
  Laboratory Studies   450
  Explanations   451
Division of Labor   452
  Who Does What?   452
  What Determines Who Does What?   455
  Satisfaction   458
  Effects on Well-Being   459
Domestic Abuse   460
  Incidence   461
  Characteristics of Perpetrator   467
  Characteristics of Victim   468
  Theories   468
Rape and Other Forms of Sexual Coercion   470
  Definitions   471
  Incidence   472
  Characteristics of Perpetrator   474
  Characteristics of Victim   476
  Theories   477
Parenting and Health   479
  Effects of the Parent Role on Health   480
  Effect of Parenthood on Marriage   484
Effect of Social Support on Health   486
  Sex Comparisons   486
  Evidence: Relations to Health   487
Summary   490
Discussion Questions   492
Suggested Reading   493
Key Terms   493

12 WORK ROLES AND HEALTH   495
Work Role   496
  Women's Employment   497
  Unemployment   503
  Retirement   504

Quality of Work Role   505
  Characteristics of Work   506
  Effects on Health   508
Discrimination   508
  Pay Disparity   510
  Denial of Discrimination   521
Sexual Harassment   524
  Definitions   524
  Incidence   527
  Outcomes of Sexual Harassment   529
  Characteristics of Perpetrator   530
  Characteristics of Victim   531
  Theories   532
The Multiple Roles Question   533
  Does the Work Role Buffer or Exacerbate Family Stress?   536
  Do Family Roles Buffer or Exacerbate Work Stress?   536
  Difficulties in Combining Roles   537
Summary   539
Discussion Questions   541
Suggested Reading   541
Key Terms   542

13 MENTAL HEALTH   **544**
Sex Differences in Depression   545
Methodological Artifacts   549
  Clinician Bias   549
  Response Bias   550
  Different Manifestations of Depression   551
Theories of Depression   553
  Biology   554
  Learned Helplessness   556
  Attributional Styles   557
  Coping   559
  Stressful Life Events   566
  The Female Gender Role   569
  Caregiving   571
Challenges of Adolescence   572
  Gender Intensification   572
  Puberty   574
  Body Image   574
  Self-Esteem   575
  Relations with Parents and Friends   576
  Different Manifestations of Depression   576

Adjustment to Chronic Illness   580
  Male Gender Role   582
  Female Gender Role   584
Eating Disorders   586
  Definitions and Prevalence   586
  Consequences   588
  Etiology   589
Suicide   593
  Incidence   593
  Attempts   595
  The Gender Paradox   595
  Factors Associated with Suicide Among Adults   595
  Factors Associated with Suicide Among Adolescents   597
Summary   598
Discussion Questions   599
Suggested Reading   600
Key Terms   600

References   **602**

Name Index   **670**

Subject Index   **686**

PREFACE

The purpose of this text is to provide a review of the empirical research and conceptual discussions surrounding gender and to examine the implications of gender for relationships and health. The focus of this book goes beyond sex alone—whether one is biologically male or female—to explore the roles that society has assigned to men and women and the other variables that co-occur with sex, such as status and gender-related traits. The implications of social roles, status, and gender-related traits for relationships and health are examined. This is why the book is entitled *The Psychology of Gender* rather than *The Psychology of Sex*. Gender is a term that represents the social and cultural forces that influence men and women in our society. The book discusses the "psychology" of gender because the focus is on the individual in the social context. The primary focus is not on biology and anthropology, although their contributions to the study of gender are included.

Rather than review every single topic related to gender, I examine the implications of gender for two broad domains of research: relationships and health. These domains are chosen, first, because they are central to our lives. Friendships, romantic relationships, and relationships at work have a great impact on our day-to-day functioning. Psychological well-being and physical health are important outcomes in their own right. A second reason for the focus on relationships and health is that these are domains in which clear sex differences have been documented. These sex differences cannot be attributed to biology alone; thus, relationships and health are domains for which gender, the social category, may play a role.

The book is divided into three sections, with each section building on the previous one. First, the nature of gender and the development of gender roles are presented. In the first chapter, I provide a brief overview of the field of gender, including how gender is construed across cultures and some of the philosophical and political controversies in the area. In the next chapter, I review the scientific method that is used to study gender, including the unique difficulties that arise in this field, as well as provide a brief history of the psychology of gender, which includes a review of the various instruments used to study gender (Chapter 2). In Chapter 3, I present research on attitudes toward gender and gender roles, focusing largely on gender-role stereotypes. Then I turn to the research literature to provide the current data (Chapter 4) and theory (Chapter 5) on sex differences in cognitive, emotional, and social domains. In Chapter 5, I discuss different theories of gender-role development, such as evolutionary theory, social learning theory, social role theory, and gender schema theory. In Chapter 6, I discuss the implications of gender and gender roles for achievement. Thus in this first section of the book, I provide important information on the similarities and differences between men and women and the theories that explain any observed differences. The data and the theories are important for understanding the subsequent sections of the book that address the implications of gender for relationships and health.

The second section of the book begins with a discussion of men's and women's communication and interaction styles (Chapter 7). These findings have implications for the specific relationships discussed: friendship (Chapter 8) and romantic relationships (Chapter 9). Recent research on cross-sex friendship, gay and lesbian relationships, and friendships at work are included in these chapters. The role of gender in relationships is critical to understanding the third section of the book, how gender influences health.

The third section begins with an overview chapter documenting sex differences in mental and physical health and theories as to their origins (Chapter 10). Health is broadly construed in this book to reflect physical health problems, such as coronary artery disease, as well as mental health problems, such as depression and eating disorders. In Chapter 11, I investigate the implications of gender as a health resource in relationships, in particular marriage. The effects of marriage and parenting on health are reviewed in Chapter 11, whereas the effects of work on health are reviewed in Chapter 12. The implications of relationships gone awry, domestic abuse, and rape, are discussed in Chapter 11 and sexual harassment in Chapter 12. The final chapter focuses on the implications of gender for mental health, in particular depression, eating disorders, and suicide.

For those of you who are familiar with the previous editions, I would like to highlight some changes that I have made. The basic structure of the book is the same, but all the information has been updated—in particular all the statistics on crime, relationships, and health. I have included more information on different cultures, people of color, and gay and lesbian relationships. There are only two structural changes to the text. First, I reorganized Chapters 1 and 2 into three separate chapters. I created Chapter 2 to focus on methods and history. I expanded on gender-role attitudes and stereotypes from the previous edition (formerly in Chapter 2) to create an entire chapter focused on these issues (Chapter 3). Second, I removed the second edition's Chapter 5 on aggression and incorporated the material into other chapters (gender findings on aggression in Chapter 4; domestic abuse and rape in Chapter 11, and sexual harassment in Chapter 12). Finally, I made the book more visually appealing by increasing the number of visual displays—more figures and more photographs.

Multiple perspectives on the development of differences between men and women are offered, but the primary perspective that I emphasize is a social-psychological one. I examine gender as an individual difference variable but focus on the influence of the context—the situation, the environment, the culture—on gender. I have drawn from research in the areas of psychology, sociology, anthropology, medicine, and public health.

I do not merely itemize sex differences in this text. In many domains, sex differences are more elusive than people believe. I highlight both similarities and differences and remind the reader about the magnitude of differences throughout the chapters. I also point out methodological flaws or difficulties that may bear on the observance of sex differences. The focus of the book is on the *explanations* for men's and women's thoughts, feelings, and behavior—not simply a summary statement of the similarities and differences between men and women.

This text can be used for an undergraduate course on the psychology of gender, preferably for more advanced students. This text also could be supplemented with empirical readings for a graduate-level course. The book should have widespread appeal to students in the sciences and humanities. Students certainly do not have to be psychology majors to read this text, but some knowledge of research methods would be helpful. Because social-psychological theories are so widely discussed in this text, a student who has taken such a course will find the book especially appealing and be able to grasp many of the concepts quite quickly. However, theories are explained in sufficient detail that students without a background in social psychology or psychology should understand the material.

Gender is a topic with which all of us are familiar, regardless of the scientific literature. Thus it is sometimes difficult to mesh personal experiences with the research literature. To help students integrate the two, each of the chapters includes mini-experiments (entitled "Do Gender") for students to test some of the research ideas presented. The results of these experiments will not always work out as intended, partly because the sample sizes will be small, partly

because the samples will not be representative, and partly because the best ideas do not always translate into the best research designs. The purpose of the exercises is to allow students to gain experience with some of the methods used to study gender and to learn firsthand about how people experience gender in their lives. When topics of special interest arise—or what would be referred to as "going off on a tangent" in class—I included sidebars in each chapter, such as "How to Raise a Gender-Aschematic Child" or "The Future of Title IX." Other aids to learning include key terms in boldface throughout the chapters and a summary of key terms and definitions at the end of the chapter; summaries of the main points at the end of the chapter; a list of thought-provoking discussion questions; and a list of suggested readings accompanying each chapter. To make the text more user friendly for students, I have added a section entitled "Take Home Points" at the end of each section of a chapter. Here, I summarize the major points in bullet-point form. This is a new feature of the third edition.

VICKI S. HELGESON

ACKNOWLEDGMENTS

I would like to thank the anonymous reviewers of the first and second editions of this book as well as the people who gave so generously of their time to read and comment on chapters of the book: Rosalind Barnett, Kay Deaux, Alice Eagly, Barbara Gutek, Judith Hall, Susan Sprecher, and Ingrid Waldron. I would like to extend a special thanks to an "anonymous" reviewer who revealed her identity to me, Letitia Anne Peplau. These people's comments and suggestions have greatly enhanced this book.

I owe a great deal of gratitude to the many staff members and students at Carnegie Mellon University who have helped me with each edition of the book. I especially appreciate the efforts of Laura Kiley and Laura Viccaro who spent countless hours on the Web and at libraries helping me to update this book. I feel quite fortunate to have found someone to organize and enter all these references into the book (Gina Durkin), someone to help create the "visuals" that greatly enhanced this edition (Laura Kiley), someone to respond to numerous ancillary requests (Abby Kunz Vaughn), and someone who can carefully proofread for grammar, punctuation, and content all at the same time (Laura Viccaro). I will always be indebted to Denise Janicki, who went through every page of the first volume of this book with a fine-toothed comb, asked questions about statements that were less than sensible, and provided creative ideas to bring the book to life. I also want to thank the students in the Psychology of Gender classes that I have taught over the last 16 years for inspiring me to write this book.

I would like to thank LeeAnn Doherty and Jeff Marshall from Prentice Hall for eagerly lending their assistance and guidance through the process of creating a third edition. I also wish to acknowledge the Prentice Hall reviewers: Rachel Blakock, Ball State University; M. Janelle Cambron, University of Houston; Terri Conley, University of Missouri; Charlene Drake, University of Massachusetts-Lowell; Stefanie Gilbert, Howard University; Shannon K. Gilmartin, Ph.D., California Institute of Technology; William R. Holt, University of Massachusetts-Dartmouth; Becky Muñoz, University of Houston; and Debra H. Zand, University of Missouri-Columbia, Medical School.

Finally, I would like to thank my family: my mother and father for all their love and support over the years; my husband Mark for keeping me in touch with the "real world" outside of academia and for challenging me to think about gender in different ways; and my daughter Katja for teaching me about myself and for providing me with vivid examples of gender-role socialization.

V. S. H.

INTRODUCTION

In 1998, my daughter was born and so was my own personal experience with the psychology of gender. As an advocate of equal opportunities and equal treatment for men and women, I thought this practice should begin with infancy. To start, my husband and I tried not to let gender be the overriding principle by which we chose Katja's toys and clothes. This proved to be far more difficult than we thought. In infancy, there are a fair number of "gender-neutral" clothes and toys. But by 1 year of age, the boys' toys and clothes are in one section, the girls' in another, and there is little common ground. I finally figured out why there are gender-neutral clothes for infants: Many parents-to-be and gift givers make purchases before the baby is born and don't know the sex of the newborn. By age 1, everyone knows.

By dressing Katja in gender-neutral clothes, I learned that the default assumption of others was she must be a boy. Any infant girl in her right mind (or her parents' right mind) would wear pink or ruffles or have bows in her hair (see Figure 1.1) or have her ears pierced! Because I personally hate pink (probably not a coincidence), Katja had a lot of blue, yellow, purple, and red. (This did come back to haunt me around age 4 when pink emerged as her favorite color! However, it only lasted a year and now, at age 9, she detests pink. It must be genetic.) When we carried her around as an infant, people in the grocery store or the shopping mall would comment on what a cute boy we had. When we mentioned he was a she, people often subtly reprimanded us for not providing the appropriate cues: the pink, the ruffles, the hair bows. Some people remarked that of course she was a girl because she had so much hair. I know of no evidence that girls are born with more hair than boys. I found it an interesting paradox that the biological default is female (i.e., at conception, the embryo is destined to become female unless exposed to male hormones), but the social default is male. When in doubt, assume the baby is a boy—unless there are strong social cues indicating

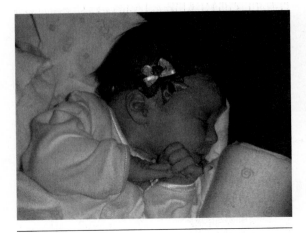

FIGURE 1.1 This infant has a bow in her hair to signal to society that she is female.

the baby is a girl. It is not nearly as offensive to assume a girl is a boy as to assume a boy is a girl. And people do expect you to be offended. When someone did mistake Katja for a boy, I wasn't surprised. How can you tell at that age? But the person who made the remark was always extremely apologetic, as if she had insulted me by assuming Katja was of the other sex.

By age 1, boys' and girls' clothes have little in common. Blue jeans that are plain in the boys' section are decorated with flowers, ruffles, or sequins in the girls' section. A simple pair of shorts in the boys' department is elaborated with a flap in the girls' department so it looks like a skirt. Girls' clothes are covered with an amazing assortment of flowers. Girls also are expected to wear dresses. How practical is it to play in the sand, climb a tree, and run around in a dress? You can't even buy socks that are for both boys and girls; there are boy socks and girl socks. Guess which ones have ruffles?

The point I am trying to convey by my experience is that sex is a very important category to us as a society. In fact, sex is one of the first categories learned by children because (a) sex has only two categories, (b) the categories are mutually exclusive, and (c) we are immediately exposed to members of both categories (Zemore, Fiske, & Kim, 2000). An infant's sex is one of the first things you try to figure out about him or her and one of the first things you notice about a child or an adult. Have you ever found yourself in a situation where you didn't know the sex of a person, or mistook someone for the wrong sex? I remember being with my father-in-law once while a young man with a ponytail changed the oil in my car. My father-in-law was sure that the person was female. I was hushing him as best I could for fear the man would overhear the conversation and replace my oil with wiper fluid. Why are we bothered so much by these situations? Why do you need to know the person's sex to interact with her—or him? A person's sex—really, a person's gender (I explain the distinction in the next section)—has implications for our feelings, our beliefs, and our behavior toward the person. Your own gender has implications for how others feel about you, what others think about you, and how others behave toward you.

Gender has been the subject of scientific scrutiny for over a century. Scientists have debated the similarities as well as the differences between men and women: Are men better at math than women? Are women more emotional than men? Are men more aggressive than women? Do men and women have the same capacities to be nurses, doctors, and lawyers? Scientists also have examined the implications of being male and female for one's relationships and one's health: Are women's relationships closer than those of men? Does marriage provide more health benefits for men compared to women? Are women more depressed than men? Are men less willing than women to seek help for health problems?

You have probably thought about some of these questions. You may be fairly confident you know the answers to some of them. Gender is a topic with which we are all intimately familiar. What woman doubts that men are less likely than women to ask for directions? What man doubts that women are more likely than men to dwell on their problems? We have many experiences we bring to bear on these issues, but our anecdotal observations are not the same as observations gained from well-established scientific methods. In fact, our anecdotal observations may be biased in favor of sex differences when differences do not really exist. When evaluating the literature, you will see the answer to the question of sex differences is usually fairly complicated. The appearance of sex differences depends on myriad factors: the place, time, person, audience, and characteristics of the one making the observation.

In this text, I evaluate the literature on the psychology of gender, paying special attention to the implications that gender has for our relationships and our health. I begin this first chapter by defining the terminology used in the study of gender. Next, I comment on how gender is construed in other cultures. Finally, I conclude the chapter by providing an overview of the various political and philosophical viewpoints that many researchers have taken when studying gender.

DEFINITION OF TERMS

This textbook is called *Psychology of Gender.* Why not *Psychology of Sex?* What is the difference between sex and gender? Is gender just the more politically correct term? One of our first tasks is to define these terms and other sex-related and gender-related ideas.

The first distinction to make is between sex and gender. **Sex** refers to the biological categories of male and female, categories distinguished by genes, chromosomes, and hormones. Culture has no influence on one's sex. Sex is a relatively stable category that is not easily changed, although recent technology has allowed people to change their biological sex. **Gender**, by contrast, is a much more fluid category. It refers to the social categories of male and female. These categories are distinguished from one another by a set of psychological features and role attributes that society has assigned to the biological category of sex. What are some of the psychological features we assign to sex in the United States? Emotionality is a trait we ascribe to women and competitiveness is a trait we ascribe to men. These traits are features of gender rather than sex. Whereas sex is defined in the same way across cultures, gender differs because each society has its own prescriptions for how men and women ought to behave. A feature of the male sex category includes the Y chromosome; regardless of whether a male wears a baseball cap or barrettes, is competitive or empathetic, he is of the male sex because he possesses the Y chromosome. Personality and appearance are related to the gender category. In the United States, a feature of the female gender category is nurturance; a person who is nurturant is behaving in a way consistent with the social category for women. Another feature of the female gender category in the United States is to wear a skirt; typically, if you encounter someone in this country wearing a skirt, you can assume the person is psychologically female as well as biologically female. However, in other countries, such as Scotland, wearing a skirt or a kilt is quite normal for a person of the biological male sex; thus we would not want to use wearing a skirt as a feature of the male or female gender category in Scotland. It is American culture that views a kilt as a skirt; a person from Scotland does not view a kilt as feminine attire. The content of gender categories—but not sex categories—is influenced by society, culture, and time.

Now that this important distinction has been made, I must point out the distinction is rarely employed in practice. Laypersons as well as scientists often use the terms interchangeably; articles in the newspaper as well as articles in scientific journals do not use the terms consistently. Even the American Psychological Association is not consistent in its employment of these terms. For example, when submitting an article to be published in a scientific journal, the editor often replaces the phrase "sex differences" with "gender differences." There is a good chance the author is simply referring to differences between people who are biologically male versus biologically female without any thought to their psychological attributes; that being the case, the correct term would be sex differences. However, some people believe that the phrase "sex differences" implies the basis of the difference is biological. Yet, if you conduct a study of men and women and find that men outperform women on a video game or that women have better recall on a memory task than men, do you have any evidence that the difference is biological? No. A better term to describe these differences is **sex-related behavior**. This term implies the behavior corresponds to sex, but it does not say anything about the cause or the etiology of the difference.

A term that better captures society's influence on the biologically based categories of male and female is **gender role** rather than gender. A **role** is a social position accompanied by a set of norms or expectations. For example, one role you most certainly possess is the role of student. What are some of the expectations that

go along with this role? One expectation is that you study for class; another might be that you socialize and stay up late at night with friends. In this instance, a conflict may exist between the expectations within a given role.

Gender role refers to the expectations that go along with being male versus female. We typically expect men to be strong, independent, competitive, and to keep their emotions hidden. These are features of the male gender role. By contrast, we typically expect women to be caring, emotionally expressive, polite, and helpful: features of the female gender role. In other words, we expect men to be **masculine** and we expect women to be **feminine**. Masculinity includes the traits, behaviors, and interests that society has assigned to the male gender role. A masculine trait is self-confidence; a masculine behavior is aggression; and a masculine interest is watching sports. Femininity includes the traits, behaviors, and interests assigned to the female gender role. A feminine trait is emotional; a feminine behavior is helping someone; and a feminine interest is cooking. In Chapter 2, we discuss the content of masculinity and femininity in more detail.

When expectations within a role conflict, such as in my example of the student, we experience **intrarole conflict**. How might women experience intrarole conflict within their gender role? Women are expected to be emotional and express their feelings but also to be sensitive to the needs of others. So, should a woman who is unhappy with her marriage express those feelings to her husband? If she expresses her feelings, she is adhering to the expectancy that she express emotion, but she is contradicting the expectancy that she not hurt someone's feelings. How might men experience intrarole conflict within their gender role? One expectation of the male gender role is to achieve; another is to be independent and not ask for help. What should a man who desires to adhere to his gender role do if he can't figure out how to put something together by himself? If he asks for help, he will further his achievement goal but at the expense of another goal: appearing independent. College men who are required to work with one another in groups may suffer intrarole conflict. Just because a given role has a set of guidelines does not mean those guidelines might not conflict with one another from time to time. Gender roles are no exception.

When the expectations of one role conflict with the expectations of another role, we experience **interrole conflict**. You possess other roles besides your gender role. What roles conflict with your gender role? At times the expectations of the role of student may conflict with both the male gender role and the female gender role. In a large lecture class, the expectation of a student is to sit quietly in the class and listen, a passive role that may conflict with the active aspects of the male gender role. In a small seminar, the expectation of a student is to participate actively in class discussion, which may include some debate; this active, possibly argumentative role may conflict with the female gender role. Think about some of your relationship roles. Does your role as a friend, son or daughter, boyfriend or girlfriend ever conflict with your gender role? A male student involved in a group project may experience conflict between the male gender role norm to be independent and the student role norm to work together with classmates on group projects. The difficulty here is that the norms for the two different roles clash.

Sometimes we violate the norms associated with our roles, partly due to role conflict. What are the consequences of behaving in ways that violate norms? The consequences could be minor or severe; it will depend on how central that norm is to the role and how strongly the situation calls for adherence to the role. The consequences for a male asking for help are

probably minor. However, the consequences for a male wearing a dress—unless it is a costume party—are likely to be severe. A central feature of the male gender role is to not appear feminine. What are the consequences for a female not being emotional? It will depend on the situation. A female who fails to express feelings at an emotional event, such as a funeral, may be judged quite harshly, whereas a female who fails to express emotions in the context of the classroom will not suffer any negative repercussions.

Think about the consequences for violating the norms that go along with your gender role. Examine the effects of norm violation in Do Gender 1.1.

DO GENDER 1.1
Engaging in Gender-Role Incongruent Behavior

Try adopting some behavior that does not fit your gender role and see how people respond—verbally and nonverbally.

For example, if you are male, try

> Wearing a dress.
> Wearing makeup.
> Calling for an escort service when you walk across campus in the dark.
> Going into a salon and having your fingernails painted.

If you are female, try

> Chewing tobacco in public.
> Joining a group of guys to play football or basketball.
> Working on your car with a man standing by (changing the oil, changing a tire).
> Going into a barbershop and getting your hair cut.

How did you feel?

How did others respond?

Who do you think suffers more for violating gender role norms, men or women? Many people maintain it is men who suffer more. Today, women who behave "like men" are often accepted and even applauded. It is acceptable for women to dress like men by wearing pants, suits, and even ties; it is acceptable for women to have jobs that were traditionally held by men, such as doctor, lawyer, even construction worker. And, it is more acceptable for women to participate in sports (see Figure 1.2). But is it acceptable for men to dress like women by wearing a dress or pantyhose? Are men who possess jobs traditionally held by women, such as nurse or secretary, encouraged or applauded? It is interesting that a little girl who behaves like a boy is called a "tomboy," but a little boy who behaves like a girl is called a "sissy." Sissy has more negative connotations than tomboy. Today, parents have no problem giving their little girls trucks to play with and encouraging girls to play sports. But how do parents feel about giving their little boys dolls and encouraging them to play "house"?

FIGURE 1.2 It is common for girls to participate in sports today, especially soccer.

Most scientists believe men suffer more negative consequences for gender-role violations than women. The reason? Status. Women who take on characteristics of the male gender role are moving toward a higher status, whereas men who take on characteristics of the female gender role are moving toward a lower status. We applaud the move up but not the move down. The relation of gender to status is elaborated on later in the chapter.

The term *gender role* is used interchangeably with the term *sex role*. Personally, I do not know what to make of the latter term. Sex role really does not make sense because it confuses a biological category, sex, with a social category, role. Thus it is peculiar that one of the leading scientific journals in this area is called *Sex Roles* instead of "Gender Roles." I prefer to use the term *sex* when referring to the biological categories of male and female, and to use the terms *gender* and *gender role* when referring to the psychological attributes and expectations we have for those categories.

Now we can ask whether people accept the psychological category that accompanies their biological sex. **Gender identity** or **gender-role identity** is our perception of the self as psychologically male or female. You have probably heard of people who are biologically male but feel as if they are female and wish they were female, or vice versa. **Transgendered** individuals are said to have a gender identity problem, meaning their biological sex is incongruent with their psychological sex (Cole et al., 2000). A transgendered person may be biologically female but feel psychologically like a male and choose to live a life as a male. This transgendered individual may dress and behave like a man, that is, take on the male gender role. In some cases, transgendered people seek to have surgery to change them biologically to the other sex. A person whose sex has been biologically changed is a **transsexual** (Cole et al., 2000).

Do not confuse gender identity with **sexual orientation**, which refers to whether people prefer to have other-sex or same-sex persons as partners for love, affection, and sex. **Heterosexuals** prefer other-sex partners; **homosexuals** prefer same-sex partners; and **bisexuals** are accepting of other-sex and same-sex partners.

Sex typing (which really should be referred to as gender typing) is the process by which sex-appropriate preferences, behaviors, skills, and self-concept are acquired. How does a boy become masculine? A girl feminine? We review the different theories of sex typing in Chapter 5. People who adhere to the gender role that society assigned them are sex-typed. A male who thinks, feels, and behaves in masculine ways and a female who thinks, feels, and behaves in feminine ways are each **sex-typed**. A male who acts feminine and a female who acts masculine are each said to be **cross-sex-typed**. Someone who incorporates both masculine and feminine qualities is not sex-typed and is often referred to as **androgynous**. Androgyny is discussed in more detail in Chapters 2 and 5.

Thus far we have been discussing attributes that define a person's sense of self. Gender also comes into play when we think about other people. Our own personal view about how men and women should behave is called a **gender-role attitude**. You might believe women should be caring, nurturant, and have primary responsibility for raising children, whereas men should be independent, assertive, and have primary responsibility for earning money to take care of the family—regardless of whether you possess these characteristics. If you hold these beliefs, you have a traditional gender-role attitude. That is, your view fits the traditional expectations that society has for how men and women should behave. Alternatively, you might believe both men and women should be assertive and caring and that both should be equally responsible for working inside and outside the home.

In this case, you have an egalitarian gender-role attitude. Many people hold what Hochschild (1989) refers to as a "transitional attitude," which fits somewhere between traditional and egalitarian. You may believe both men and women should participate in work inside the home and outside the home, but that women should give the home their primary attention and men should give work their primary attention. This person is striving for an egalitarian philosophy, but some residual traditional gender-role attitudes remain.

Three other terms reflect one's attitude to the category of sex. Each term maps onto one of the three components of an attitude: affect, cognition, and behavior. The affective (feeling) component of our attitude toward the sex category is called **sexism**, or prejudice toward people based on their sex. Typically, we think of sexism as involving a negative attitude or negative affect, but it could entail positive affect. If you dislike the person your wife hired to take care of your children because the person is male, you are showing sexism. Likewise, if you like the person your wife hired merely because she is female, you are also showing sexism. The cognitive component of our attitude toward sex is a **sex stereotype** or **gender-role stereotype**. These terms refer to our beliefs about the features of the biological or psychological categories of male and female. If you believe the male nanny would not be competent because he lacks the required nurturant qualities, you are engaging in gender-role stereotyping. The behavioral component of our attitude toward men and women is **sex discrimination**, which involves the differential treatment of people based on their biological sex. If you fire the male nanny because you dislike men as nannies and you doubt his competence because he is a man, you are engaging in sex discrimination. Sex discrimination is often a result of both sexism and gender-role stereotyping. These attitudes toward sex are the focus of Chapter 3.

Finally, one last term to discuss is **feminism**. What image did that term conjure up for you? The definitions of feminism are vast and varied. At the most fundamental level, a feminist is someone who believes men and women should be treated equally. You are probably thinking, "Is that all there is to feminism? If so, I must be a feminist." In fact, over the years, I have had many students in class tell me they did not realize they were feminists until taking my class. And several students have told me that their parents did not realize they were feminists until the students took my course. In a study of 233 college women, the majority agreed with at least some of the goals of the feminist movement but few labeled themselves as feminists, as shown in Table 1.1 (Liss et al., 2001). In fact, only one woman called herself a feminist and was active in the women's movement.

A defining feature of feminism is a high regard for women. Most people in our society would agree women should be valued. However, even when people have a positive attitude toward women, they are typically reluctant to identify themselves as feminists (Suter & Toller, 2006). Why? First, feminism has negative connotations.

Some people perceive feminists as women who hate men. Second, feminism often includes the belief that society needs to make changes for equality to occur and can include the impetus to take action to make these changes. It is these latter ideas that are more controversial. When feminism is equated with activism, the term becomes less appealing. However, activism alone cannot be the problem, because college women evaluate the women's movement more favorably than feminism (Buschman & Lenart, 1996). The majority of college women can be considered "precarious feminists." These women believe that community effort is needed to promote equality for all women but that their own achievements depend upon themselves rather than group effort. In other words, the typical college female believes that women as a group need societal help but she, herself, doesn't need any help. This set of beliefs is similar to the "denial of disadvantage" (Crosby, 1984) discussed in Chapter 12—the idea that most women perceive that other women suffer from discrimination but that they have not been victims of discrimination.

In a study of 77 academic psychologists who were members of the Psychology of

TABLE 1.1   **PERCENTAGE OF COLLEGE WOMEN ENDORSING DEGREES OF FEMINISM**

	Number	*Percent (%)*
1. I do not consider myself a feminist at all and I believe that feminists are harmful to family life and undermine relations between men and women.	4	2
2. I do not consider myself a feminist.	37	13
3. I agree with some of the objectives.	105	50
4. I agree with most of the objectives of the feminist movement but do not call myself a feminist.	49	23
5. I privately consider myself a feminist but do not call myself a feminist around others.	13	6
6. I call myself a feminist around others.	12	6
7. I call myself a feminist around others and am currently active in the women's movement.	1	.5

Source: Liss et al. (2001).

Women division of the American Psychological Association, women were asked "When you say 'I am a feminist,' what do you mean?" (Crosby, Todd, & Worell, 1996). The most common response was the belief in gender equality. Fewer than half (41%) of the respondents spontaneously mentioned activism as part of the definition. However, when the women were provided with a list of features and asked to check which ones were part of the definition of feminism, 92% checked "works actively to change social structures." The investigators also found that participants who labeled themselves more strongly as feminists spontaneously mentioned activism. Some examples of their activism are shown in Table 1.2. You probably expected to see much more radical behaviors than the ones listed in the table. You can see that the examples of activism shown in Table 1.2 are ones that promote women or ones in which causes important to women, such as day care, are promoted. Do you participate in similar activities? If so, do you identify yourself as a feminist?

Thus it appears the belief in gender equality is the central feature of feminism, but activism is an important feature of feminism for those whose identities are most strongly tied to it. Conduct Do Gender 1.2 to find out how feminism is viewed at your institution.

TABLE 1.2   Examples of Feminist Activism

Working in women's center on campus.
Developing a course on women's studies.
Helping to set up day care programs.
Promoting women's sports.
Taking a leadership role in the university.
Working at a rape crisis center.
Promoting women political candidates.
Donating money to women's organizations.
Increasing awareness of sexual harassment.
Participating in prochoice rally.

Source: Crosby et al. (1996).

DO GENDER 1.2
Defining a Feminist

Ask 10 men and 10 women to describe the first things that come to mind when they think of the term *feminist*. This will tell you a couple of things: First, you will learn whether people view the term favorably or unfavorably; second, you will learn the content of this category. Construct a frequency distribution of the features listed. The features most often listed by these people are those central to the feminist category; the features listed least are often peripheral to the category and probably more reflective of that particular individual. What percentage of features is negative versus positive? Do men or women view a feminist in more positive or negative terms? To address this question, calculate the number of positive and negative features identified by the group of men and the group of women.

Ask these same 20 people two more questions. Ask whether they believe men and women should be treated equally, the defining feature of a feminist. You could ask people to respond on a 5-point scale: 1 = Definitely not, 2 = Probably not, 3 = Unsure, 4 = Probably should, 5 = Definitely should. Then ask whether each person is a feminist. Do answers to these two questions correspond?

TAKE HOME POINTS

- Sex refers to the biological category; gender the psychological category.

- Intrarole conflict is conflict between expectations within a role; interrole conflict is conflict between expectations of different roles.

- Although most people perceive women in favorable terms, feminism is perceived negatively. Women typically believe that equality for women as a group should be promoted (probably by someone else), but they do not need any group efforts to aid their own achievements.

CULTURAL DIFFERENCES IN THE CONSTRUAL OF GENDER

I have defined the terminology used in the psychology of gender. All these terms, however, are construed at least somewhat differently by people of different ethnic backgrounds in the United States and by people from other cultures. Ramet (1996) proposes the idea of a **gender culture**, which reflects "society's understanding of what is possible, proper, and perverse in gender-linked behavior" (p. 2). In other words, each society generates its own standards for gender-linked behavior.

Because the majority of research that has been conducted and examined in this book interprets gender—the roles of men and women in society—in similar terms, it might be interesting to step outside our cultural view and consider how gender is construed in a few different cultures around the world.

Cultures with Multiple Genders

One assumption about gender shared by many cultures is that there are only two of them: male and female. Did it ever occur to you that there could be more than two genders? In several Native American cultures, there are four genders (Lang, 1996). For these cultures, gender does not map onto biological sex; instead, gender is based on people's social roles. The four categories are man, woman, woman-man, and man-woman. A man who is biologically male but adopts many, if not all, of the social role characteristics of a female is known as a woman-man. A woman who is biologically female but adopts many, if not all, of the social role characteristics of a male is known as a man-woman. Because the notion of two genders is so strongly ingrained in us, people often leap to the conclusion that the man-woman and woman-man must be homosexual. This is

not at all true. In fact, a woman-man is likely to marry a woman; he is simply drawn to the social role of women. He may dress like a woman and adopt the language and mannerisms of a woman. Sometimes, the woman-man and man-woman categories stem not from personal choice but from a family's needs. Perhaps a family needs someone to do male work but has only female children; one of the female children may be designated a man-woman so she can adopt the male social role. Note that the woman-man and man-woman genders are not categories inferior to the traditional man and woman genders.

Another example of multiple genders among Native Americans is the *Berdache* (Schnarch, 1992; Williams, 1993). The male Berdache and female Berdache are third and fourth genders. Of the two, the male Berdache is much more common. The male Berdache is biologically male but takes on characteristics of both men and women in appearance and manner. Historically, the Berdache was highly respected and viewed as sacred. The Berdache was believed to be endowed with spiritual powers and had the highest status among the genders. Today, however, the status and respect ascribed to the Berdache have waned. Although the sexuality of the Berdache is highly variable, younger people are more likely to view the Berdache as homosexual. This is the result of Western culture imposing its rigid gender categories on a person who does not easily fit into them.

The appearance of multiple genders also occurs in the Balkans (Ramet, 1996). In this case, people primarily take on the other gender role to serve society's needs. For example, some biological females are raised as males when the society is in need of those functions best served by men. In the Balkans, these women assume a male social identity and perform the work of men. They are not allowed to marry and are sworn to virginity. These people also are highly respected.

In the city of Juchitan, Mexico, the highest status is conferred to a third gender, the muxe—biological males who dress like females and take on women's roles in the community (Sevcik, 2007). They are highly regarded for their excellent design and artistic skills. They rarely marry, often take care of their mothers, and typically make more money than males or females. People in this region are undecided as to whether this gender is genetically or socially determined. It is certainly the case that people could be accused of encouraging a biologically male child to become a muxe, as muxes bring economic prosperity and high status to a family.

In Western cultures, gender is defined by our genitals (Lang, 1996). We have no culturally defined category for people who are uncomfortable with their sex or who would like to combine elements of both male and female gender roles. We are very uncomfortable when we cannot determine someone's sex and we are very uncomfortable with people who try to create new gender categories (e.g., transsexuals).

Morocco

In Morocco, there are only two genders, but the two are very distinct (Hessini, 1994). The distinction between the male gender role and the female gender role manifests itself in terms of physical space. Private space, the space reserved for the family inside a home, is female space. Public space, basically everything outside of the home, is male space. The duties of men and women are distinct and take place in their separate physical spaces. The women fulfill their roles in female space, inside the home, and the men fulfill their roles in male space, outside the home. It is clear that public space is men's space because only men are found in coffee shops and theaters, and only men hang out in public places. If women are in public, they are usually scurrying from one place to the next.

The distinct roles of men and women are not questioned in Morocco (Hessini, 1994). The man is the leader of the family and works outside the home to provide for the family; the woman is responsible for the household, which includes the education and religious training of children. Even in modern Morocco, women are not concerned with equality. The Moroccan people believe the two sexes complement one another. Although the cultural code is for men to support the family financially, economic necessity has led to an increase in the number of women working outside the home. This is creating some tension because both men and women believe that women's primary responsibility lies inside the home and that women should not work outside the home.

One way in which women are able to work and enter into public spaces is by wearing the *hijab* and *djellaba* when they go out in public (Hessini, 1994). The hijab is a large scarf that covers a woman's head, neck, and shoulders so only her face is seen (see Figure 1.3). The hijab provides a sense of Muslim identity

FIGURE 1.3   In this picture, a Muslim woman is dressed in the traditional *hijab*.

and security for women; it is a veil that women view as shielding them from the outside world so they can feel as if they are in their private space. The djellaba is a long, loose-fitting gown, that hides the shape of the body. Women believe these articles of clothing protect them from men and help preserve the social order. A woman who does not wear the hijab and djellaba is viewed as naked. The thought is that other clothing shows the outline of the female body, which provokes and attracts men, leading to adultery. Women are held more responsible for adultery than men; thus, in a sense, the hijab and djellaba are viewed as avenues to freedom for women in that they allow them to go out in public.

People from the West, however, hardly view the hijab as liberating (Hessini, 1994). Instead, the hijab is viewed as an indication of women's oppression and male domination. The hijab perpetuates the stereotype of women as sexual temptresses whom men are unable to resist.

The Agta Negrito

Some people maintain that women's and men's distinct social roles are rooted in biology. As evidence, they cite the distinct roles of men and women in hunter-gatherer societies. Women are biologically predisposed to gather and men are biologically predisposed to hunt. Women cannot hunt because hunting would reduce their ability to bear and take care of children. In most hunter-gatherer societies, the division of labor is as predicted: Men hunt and women gather.

The Agta Negrito is a society in the Phillipines that challenges this idea (Goodman et al., 1985). In this society, women hunt and are as successful as men. Hunting does not impair women's fertility. Women who hunt do not differ from women who do not hunt in age at menarche, age at first pregnancy, or age of the youngest child. Women who hunt are also able to take care of children.

How are women able to hunt in this society? There are two reasons. One is physical, having to do with the Agta terrain: Women can hunt close to home. The second is social: Other people help with child care. Women hunters either take nursing infants with them or leave toddlers at home where they are cared for by other family members. The structure of this culture shows that (1) there is no biological reason that women cannot hunt and (2) the division of labor between the two sexes is not carved in stone.

Tahiti

Evidence indicates that men's and women's roles can be similar. Tahiti is an example of a truly androgynous society (Gilmore, 1990). The social roles of men and women are very much the same. Women have the same status as men and have the same opportunities as men in domestic, occupational, and recreational spheres. Not only are men's and women's roles similar, but men and women share similar personalities. There is no pressure on men and women to behave differently or to behave in accordance with traditional gender roles. Men are not worried about proving their masculinity, for example, and do not feel the need to take risks. This similarity of men and women is even reflected in their language; there is no word for gender in the language and there are no male or female pronouns. The society is based on cooperation rather than competition. Perhaps because resources are available to people, there is no economic reason to compete. There is little aggression, no war, and no hunting; that is, there is nothing for men to defend. Thus there is no basis for an ideology of masculinity to have evolved. The people in this society truly seem to function without thinking about gender.

Status and Culture

With the exception of Tahiti and probably a few other cultures, one commonality in the way gender is construed around the world is that men have higher status than women (Chisholm, 2000). How is this status difference manifested?

There are a number of indices of gender inequality. The higher illiteracy rates of women, less access to medical care for women, a lower earnings ratio of women compared to men, and the legitimization of physical abuse of women in some countries are all manifestations of men's higher status relative to women's (Chisholm, 2000). In India and China, some female fetuses are aborted because they are less valued than males. The one-child policy in China has led to the abortion of female fetuses even though sex-selective abortion is prohibited by the government. In the year 2000, 110 boys were born for every 100 girls; by the year 2005, the ratio was 118 boys for every 100 girls (Associated Press, 2007).

Although we do not have sex-selective abortion in the United States, a slight preference for the firstborn to be a boy still persists (McDougall, DeWit, & Ebanks, 1999). In 1997, a Gallup Poll was conducted of around 1,000 adults in each of 16 countries across Asia, Europe, North America, and Latin America. Respondents were asked which sex they would prefer if they could have only one child. In 13 of the 16 countries, the preference was for a boy over a girl. In the United States, 35% preferred a boy, 23% preferred a girl, and 42% expressed no preference. These preferences are shown in Table 1.3.

Other evidence that males are more highly regarded than females comes from the effect of

TABLE 1.3   PREFERENCE FOR CHILD'S SEX, IN PERCENTAGES

	Boy	Girl	No Opinion
Canada	26	16	58
Colombia	35	27	38
France	41	31	28
Germany	21	19	60
Great Britain	31	26	43
Guatemala	23	13	64
Hungary	25	12	63
Iceland	12	16	72
India	40	27	33
Lithuania	33	34	33
Mexico	31	24	45
Singapore	19	11	70
Spain	20	27	53
Taiwan	29	9	62
Thailand	44	27	29
United States	35	23	42

Source: Gallup News Service (1997).

a child's sex on the structure of the family. In an analysis of census data from the last half of the 20th century, Dahl and Moretti (2005) found that firstborn females are less likely to live with their fathers than firstborn males. Several factors accounted for this difference. First, women whose firstborn was female were less likely to marry the father than women whose firstborn child was male. Second, women whose firstborn child was female were more likely to divorce than women whose firstborn child was male. Finally, upon divorce, fathers were less likely to have custody of firstborn females than males. The investigators noted that families with firstborn females also ended up with a greater number of children than families with firstborn males. Because the research is archival, one cannot discern cause and effect. However, the weight of the evidence suggests that people—especially fathers—prefer sons over daughters.

A more subtle indicator of the status associated with male children may come from a study that examined birth announcements and coded the type of affect displayed. Birth announcements in two Canadian newspapers were coded for evidence of pride and happiness (Gonzalez & Koestner, 2005). Parents reported more happiness than pride overall, but relatively more pride for boys than girls, and relatively more happiness for girls than boys. Feelings of pride are more strongly associated with status than feelings of happiness.

The dominant group in a society has rights and privileges not available to the subordinate group (Ostenson, 1996). In our society, we can talk about male privilege, White privilege, heterosexual privilege, class privilege, and even attractiveness privilege. People who have the privilege are often unaware of it; those who lack the privilege are aware. For example, heterosexual privilege entails the right to marry, to have a public ceremony that entails celebration and gifts from family and friends, and to have children without being questioned. Heterosexuals do not view this as a privilege because it has come to be expected. Homosexuals, however, who do not have these privileges, certainly recognize heterosexual privilege.

What is male privilege? Historically, women were not allowed to vote or own property. At one time only men were allowed to serve in the military. Today, men have greater access than women to certain jobs and to political office. Until 1972, only men could run the Boston Marathon (Rosenbloom, 2000). The first two women who ran the marathon, in 1966 and 1967, disguised themselves, one by dress and one by name; upon recognition, their completion of the race was dismissed, questioned, and not officially recognized. Only within the last decade have women been allowed to enter the all-male military schools the Citadel and the Virginia Military Institute. Shannon Faulkner applied to the Citadel in 1993 by omitting any reference to her gender; she was admitted, but on learning of her gender, the Citadel withdrew their offer of admission. More recently, public attention was drawn to the fact that women are not allowed membership in the Augusta National Golf Club, the club that hosts the premier golfing event, the Masters. Annika Sorenstam, however, did compete in the Colonial, one of the PGA tours in 2003, becoming the first woman to do so in 58 years and causing some men to withdraw from the tournament. In the year 2007, we see the first serious female contender for president of the United States, Hillary Clinton.

Today, great strides have been made in the United States toward gender equality. Obviously, women can vote, run for political office and win elections, and have gained in occupational status. However, women are not nearly as prevalent in government as men, and women rarely are found in the highest occupational statuses, such as chief executive officers of industry. It was not until 2007 that we saw the first female Speaker of the U.S. House of Representatives, Nancy Pelosi. Whereas only 33% of Americans said they would vote for a woman president from their party in 1937 (Simmons, 2001), the figure rose to 77% in 2007 (Newport & Carroll, 2007). The similarities and differences in the treatment and behavior of men and women appear in numerous chapters throughout the book. The important point to keep in mind is whether a sex difference in behavior is due to something inherent about being male or female or to something about status.

Another indication of men's status in our culture is the use of the generic "he" to imply both men and women. See Sidebar 1.1 for a discussion of this issue.

SIDEBAR 1.1: *A Note on Language*

In 1972, an article appeared in *Ms.* magazine that began with the following story:

> On the television screen, a teacher of first-graders who had just won a national award is describing her way of teaching. "You take each child where you find him," she says. "You watch to see what he's interested in, and then you build on his interests." A five-year-old looking at the program asks her mother, "Do only boys go to that school?" "No," her mother begins, "she's talking about girls too, but". . . . (Miller, Swift, & Maggio, 1997, p. 50)

But what? Is it acceptable to use the male pronoun to imply male and female? In 1983, the American Psychological Association proclaimed that scientists must refrain from using sexist language in their writing. This means that we cannot use the generic *he* to mean both men and women in our scientific writing. The statement was issued 25 years ago. Even today, it is common to find the use of the generic *he* in books in other disciplines. I find that many college students use "he" to refer to men and women in their writing. When I correct students' papers (changing he to he/she or they), some are quite offended and cast me as an extremist. Many people will say that everyone knows "he" refers to "he and she," so what's the harm? "He" is more efficient. When you write the word "he" or "him," do you think of both men and women? The answer is clear: No.

The concern with sexist language is that people do not really perceive "he" as representing "he or she." Several studies have shown that this is a legitimate concern. Nancy Henley (1989) reviewed 20 studies in which participants were given sentences with the generic "he" or unbiased language ("he/she" or "they"). All the studies clearly showed that the generic *he* is more likely to call to mind male names, male persons, and male images. Although female participants were less vulnerable to this bias than male participants, women, too, were more likely to think of men when reading the generic *he*. Studies have students read or speak passages that contain sexist or gender-neutral language and find that sexist language leads people to conjure up more images of male than female figures compared to gender-neutral language (Gastil, 1990; Hamilton, 1988). One study showed that the use of man-suffix terms (e.g., chairman) led to the attribution of more masculine traits than person-suffix terms (e.g., chairperson; McConnell & Fazio, 1996). Henley asks, "So, does man embrace woman? According to these findings, man most readily embraces man" (1989, p. 65). See how language influences perception at your school with Do Gender 1.3.

Is there any reason to believe the climate is changing, that nonsexist language is becoming more acceptable and sexist language is becoming more maligned? In one study, a person who used sexist language was perceived negatively (Johnson & Dowling-Guyer, 1996). College students evaluated the transcript of an occupational counseling session in which the counselor used exclusive language (e.g., referring to all secretaries as *she* and all physicians as *he*) versus inclusive language (e.g., using *he* or *she* or *they* to describe persons). Students rated the counselor who used exclusive language as more sexist than the counselor who used inclusive language. In addition, students were less inclined to see the counselor who used exclusive compared to inclusive language. However, this latter finding really applied only to women who had less traditional attitudes toward gender.

More recently, the issue has been taken up by state legislatures because some states, such as Utah, New York, and Rhode Island, have passed legislation to change their state constitutions to use gender-neutral language. However, Wisconsin rejected the change ("Some State," May 21, 2003).

How should one avoid sexist language? One study compared using *he/she* with alternating between *he* and *she* throughout the essay (Madson & Hessling, 1999). Interestingly, the alternate use of *he* and *she* was viewed as more sexist and led students to overestimate the number of female pronouns used. The easiest way to get around the *he/she* issue is to use the plural *they*. Other tips are shown in Table 1.4.

TABLE 1.4 TIPS FOR NONSEXIST WRITING

1. Replace pronouns (he, his, him) with he or she.
   The student should raise his hand. | The student should raise his or her hand.

2. Delete pronouns (he, his, him) by rewriting sentence in the plural.
   The student sits quietly at his desk. | Students sit quietly at their desks.

3. Delete pronouns entirely from the sentence.
   The teacher read the folder on his desk. | The teacher read the folder on the desk.

4. Change pronouns to "you."
   A person should wash his own clothes. | You should wash your own clothes.

5. Change pronouns to "one."
   Tell the student that he can write a letter. | Tell the student that one can write a letter.

6. Replace "man" with "someone" or "no one."
   No man is an island. | No one is an island.

7. Replace "mankind" or "ancient man" with "our ancestors" or "men and women" or "humanity."
   This is a giant step for mankind. | This is a giant step for men and women.
   | This is a giant step for humanity.

   Ancient man developed the . . . | Our ancestors developed the . . .

8. Replace "men" with "humans."
   Men have always . . . | Humans have always . . .

9. Replace "man-made" with "artificial."
   It is a man-made reservoir. | It is an artificial reservoir.

10. Replace "spokesman" with "spokesperson" or "representative."
    The spokesman for the client's family has arrived. | The representative for the client's family has arrived.

11. Replace "chairman" with "chairperson" or "chair."
    The chairman called the meeting to order. | The chair called the meeting to order.

12. Replace "Englishmen" or "Frenchmen" with "the English" or "the French."
    Englishmen always serve tea with scones. | The English always serve tea with scones.

13. Replace "steward" and "stewardess" with "flight attendant."
    The stewardess served the meal. | The flight attendant served the meal.

14. Replace "salesman" with "salesperson," "salespeople," "sales representative," or "sales clerks."
    Mary is a traveling salesman. | Mary is a traveling salesperson.

Source: Adapted from Miller and Swift (1980).

DO GENDER 1.3
**Effects of Sexist Language
on Male and Female Images**

Ask 10 people to read one of two sentences. The sentences must be identical, with the exception that one version uses sexist language (e.g., "A student should place his homework in a notebook") and one version uses gender-neutral language (e.g., "Students should place their homework in a notebook" or "A student should place his or her homework in a notebook"). You could also compare these two gender-neutral conditions. Ask readers to visualize the sentence while reading it. Then ask them to write a paragraph describing their visual image. Have two people unrelated to the study read the paragraphs and record whether the image was male, female, or unclear.

It appears that children are all too aware of the status difference between men and women. In the early 1990s, 160 4th- through 12th-graders in Canada were asked to imagine what it would be like to wake up as the other sex (Lupaschuk & Yewchuk, 1998). Some sample themes and responses are shown in Table 1.5. You can see that the transition for girls to boys is not all bad; girls say they would have more freedom, more career options, and would not have to think as much about appearance. The transition for boys to girls, however, is much more harsh; boys now have to worry about their appearance and have more restrictions. Although both boys and girls had a positive view of their own sex, overall both boys and girls valued being a boy more than a girl.

In the 1990s, I asked over 300 college students to write essays on the same question, and similar themes resulted. Men and women identified positives and negatives in considering the transformation. Women noted several advantages: They would be less afraid, more adventurous, and more independent; but also several disadvantages: They would have more difficulty receiving support, they would have less meaningful conversations. Some aspects of life were considered to have mixed effects. Women said having to work would be a negative, but this would be offset by more opportunities for advancement. On the positive side, women said they would be taken more seriously as men, but on the negative side this meant more would be expected of them. Men noted primarily negatives in their hypothetical transformations to women: becoming more nervous, self-conscious, and concerned about appearance, worrying about men coming on to them, and worrying about walking alone at night. One advantage men noted was similar to the disadvantage women noted: As women, the men said they would have more friends and be more sociable. Conduct your own experiment on this issue with Do Gender 1.4.

TAKE HOME POINTS

- Not all cultures have only two genders. Third genders are distinct from male and female, not tied to homosexuality, and can be afforded high status.

- Throughout the world, men have a higher status than women, but the status differential varies by country. Sex-selective abortion in China is a strong indication that men are regarded more favorably than women. Other indicators of status throughout the world are the number of women in powerful positions in industry and government and the education of women.

- Although great strides have been made by women in the Western world, parity has not been achieved. More subtle indicators of the status differential between men and women lie in our writing (i.e., use of generic "he"), desires for male over female infants, and children's desires to be male rather than female.

TABLE 1.5   FOURTH- THROUGH TWELFTH-GRADERS' PERCEPTIONS OF LIFE AS THE OPPOSITE SEX

Themes

1. *Females have limited career options.*

   "I don't think as many opportunities would be open to me as a woman." (senior high male)

   "People would expect me to do women's work like clean house or be a secretary." (junior high male)

   "I think there would be many better jobs that I could choose to satisfy what I would want with many more opportunities for advancement. Therefore, I think I could get further in life if I was a boy." (senior high female)

2. *Females are valued for their appearance.*

   I would "get dressed and be ready faster." (junior high female)

   "I would be spending more time with my hair, my face, and my clothes." (senior high male)

   "I couldn't leave the house without my hair just right." (junior high male)

3. *Males are more aggressive, fearless, and get into trouble.*

   "Some boys would try to beat you up." (upper elementary female)

   "I wouldn't be scared of mice and other bugs and creatures." (upper elementary female)

   "I would have to kind of get in trouble to avoid being called names." (upper elementary female)

   "All my friends would be boys and we would always get in trouble because the girls would tell on us for something." (upper elementary female)

4. *Males have more freedom.*

   "I'd be able to go out more." (upper elementary female)

5. *Sex-segregated division of labor.*

   "I would do outside work instead of inside work." (upper elementary female)

   "I would take care of the house." (junior high male)

   "I can't drive a tractor and I can't go to the farm." (upper elementary male)

6. *Being male is preferred.*

   "If I were a girl, I would hate it because I wouldn't be as strong and I would have to buy more stuff like bras and stuff like that." (junior high male)

   "I would be weak, stupid, and silly." (upper elementary male)

   "My whole lifestyle would be shot." (senior high male)

   "First of all, I would scream." (senior high male)

   "I would love my life. No more long hair, girls' clothes, earrings, nylons, makeup, girls' shoes, bras, curling irons, etc." (junior high female)

Source: Lupaschuk and Yewchuk (1998)

DO GENDER 1.4
Life as the Other Sex

Select an age group. Ask 10 males and 10 females to answer the following question: "Imagine that you woke up tomorrow and were the other sex. Go through your entire day and describe how your life would be different."

Read through the stories and identify themes, such as the ones shown in Table 1.5. Construct a frequency distribution of those themes.

PHILOSOPHICAL AND POLITICAL ISSUES SURROUNDING GENDER

The last important issue to address in this introductory chapter is the philosophical and political debates that have taken place with respect to gender. The study of gender, in particular the study of sex differences, is a politically charged topic. With gender, scientists are often in one of two camps: those who believe there are important differences between the sexes and those who believe the two sexes are fundamentally the same. There are also investigators who believe we should or should not compare men and women for a variety of reasons. I address each of these debates and then turn to the political movements that have influenced the study of gender: the women's movements and the men's movements.

The Sex Difference Debate

The people who believe the two sexes are fundamentally the same are known as the **minimalists**. The minimalists believe there are very few differences between men and women and if the context was held constant, differences would vanish. That is, any differences in behavior observed between men and women might be due to the roles they hold or the situations in which they find themselves.

By contrast, the **maximalists** believe there are fundamental differences between men and women. However, they argue that "difference" does not mean "deficit." Theorists such as Carol Gilligan and Nancy Chodorow point out that women's views of the world and ways of relating to the world are different from but not inferior to those of men. In 1982, Gilligan published *In a Different Voice,* in which she claimed that men and women have fundamentally different ways of viewing morality, but that women's view of morality is equally valuable to the view held by men. Maximalists argue there are two very different and equally valuable ways of relating to the world.

You may be wondering, "Why should I care about this debate?" The reason you should care is that our political philosophy determines how we interpret a research finding. Take the sex difference in math. There is a sex difference, and the difference is statistically significant. The difference is also small. One group of researchers emphasizes that the size of the effect is small, that most men and women have similar aptitudes in math, and that only a small percentage of highly gifted men account for this difference. These people also might argue we should ignore the difference. Another group of researchers emphasizes the fact that the difference is real and that even small differences can have large effects. These investigators devote time and economic resources to understanding the cause of the difference and how to eliminate the difference.

Whether someone is a minimalist or a maximalist also has implications for whether gender is worth studying. A maximalist would certainly find gender worth studying, whereas not all minimalists would agree.

Should We Study Gender?

Now let us turn to the question of whether comparing men and women is a legitimate domain of study. Quite a debate has emerged over this issue. McHugh, Koeske, and Frieze (1986) argued that sex comparisons could be made, but that results should not be reported unless there is a theoretical rationale to explain them. They believe that sex differences without a theoretical rationale should be replicated before being published. This would eliminate the problem of investigators routinely testing for sex differences without cause and publishing differences when they find them. However, this approach would create another problem. How do you know if you are replicating an effect if the original effect was not able to be published?

Eagly (1987a) disagrees with this approach. Instead, she suggests just the opposite—that investigators routinely report the results of sex comparisons in their research whether they are hypothesized or not. Eagly raises the concern that McHugh and her colleagues' position would bias published research in the direction of upholding rather than challenging existing theories. If an investigator discovered a domain of math ability in which women outperformed men (which turns out to be true, by the way, as we see in Chapter 3), the investigator wouldn't be able to publish the finding because it didn't fit with previous research. Because the finding isn't published, there wouldn't be the opportunity for others to find out about the result and try to replicate it.

McHugh and her colleagues (1986) also suggested that a cautionary note about the small size of the difference should be attached to sex difference reports. Again, Eagly (1995) disagreed, stating that such a note would need to be attached to all psychological research because most effects are small—of the same magnitude as sex differences. Eagly suggests that the minimalists avoid asking the question "Are there sex differences?" because they are afraid the observance of differences will justify the unequal treatment of women.

A completely different position is held by Roy Baumeister (1988). Disagreeing with both Eagly (1987a) and McHugh and her colleagues (1986), he suggests that the entire field of comparing men and women be abandoned. He said the reason the field of sex differences emerged was to raise people's consciousness about the exclusion of women from research. Because women are now routinely included in studies, there is no longer any need to compare men and women. In agreement with McHugh and her colleagues, he is concerned that the study of sex comparisons perpetuates stereotypes and has the potential to legitimize discrimination. Because people are not randomly assigned to sex, the study of sex differences is not about sex per se, according to Baumeister; it is about some other variable related to sex, such as status. Baumeister argued that scientists should spend their energies focused on these other variables rather than sex.

Social Construction of Gender

The **constructionists** no doubt would agree with Baumeister's (1988) position. They maintain that it is fruitless to study gender because gender cannot be divorced from its context (Baker, 2006; Marecek, Crawford, & Popp, 2004). Constructionists maintain that gender is created by the perceiver: Facts about gender do not exist, only interpretations. The constructionists challenge the use of the scientific method to study gender because they maintain you cannot view the world objectively; our history, experiences, and beliefs affect what we observe. Constructivists argue that the empirical method is not untainted by social forces, and that science is not as value free as some expect.

Constructionists argue that psychologists should not study sex differences because such studies assume gender is a static quality of an individual. They maintain that gender is a dynamic social construct that is ever changing, a social category created by society. Bohan (1997) nicely illustrates the difference between the perspective of people who study sex differences and the constructionists. Sex difference researchers would describe a person as friendly; constructionists would describe an interaction as friendly. The people who perceive the interaction as friendly have a shared definition of friendliness. Now, we can translate this line of thinking to making sex comparisons. Researchers who make sex comparisons might describe women as more empathic than men. Constructionists would focus on the empathy involved in the interaction, the factors that contributed to the empathy, and how empathy becomes linked to women more than men. The constructionists would examine the explanations as to why empathy was illustrated more in women in this particular situation.

Constructionists are concerned that the study of sex comparisons ignores the variability within women and within men. The study of sex comparisons also ignores the situations and circumstances that influence men's and women's behavior. Constructionists argue that the question of whether men and women are similar or different is the wrong question to ask. Questions that ought to be asked revolve around how social institutions, culture, and language contribute to gender and to gendered interactions.

In Chapter 4, I review the literature that compares men and women, being careful to point out the size of the effects, the variability within sexes, and the extent to which the situation or context influences sex differences. Many of the concerns raised by the constructionists are addressed in that chapter. As will be described in Chapter 2, there is also a host of research biases that can influence the domain of sex comparisons.

Women's Movements

It is a common misconception that the women's movement in the United States first began in the 1960s (Murstein, 1974). Women's movements first emerged in the 1800s. The issues these women confronted, however, were different from those of contemporary women. These women believed men and women were fundamentally different, and they did not seek to equalize the roles of men and women. Instead, women aimed for greater respect for their domestic role (Murstein, 1974). Women in the 1800s and early 1900s were concerned with abolition, temperance, and child labor laws. These issues became "women's issues" because women were the ones to raise them. But these women discovered that their low-status position in society kept their voices from being heard. By gaining the right to vote in 1920, women could promote their causes. After that time, the women's movement remained fairly silent until the 1960s.

In 1963, Betty Friedan published *The Feminine Mystique,* in which she discussed "the problem that has no name." The problem was that women's delegation to the domestic sphere of life inhibited their opportunities for personal development. Women were not active in the workforce or in the political community. Friedan organized the National Organization for Women, or NOW, in 1966 (see Figure 1.4). The goal of this women's movement differed from the earlier movements. Here, women were concerned with their subordinate position in society and sought to establish equal rights for women. The purpose of NOW was to "take action to bring women into full participation in the mainstream of American society now, exercising all the privileges and responsibilities thereof, in truly equal partnership with men" (Friedan,

FIGURE 1.4 National Organization for Women, the largest women's rights organization in the United States, in the 2000 World March of Women.

1963, p. 384). In the epilogue to *The Feminine Mystique*, Friedan explains that NOW stood for the National Organization *for* Women rather than the National Organization *of* Women because men must be included to accomplish these goals.

NOW is the largest women's rights organization in the United States. To date, it includes more than a half million members and is represented in all states. NOW seeks elimination of sex discrimination, sexual harassment, racism, and homophobia. NOW has taken on issues of economic equality, violence against women, and reproductive rights. Since its formation, NOW has successfully challenged protective labor laws that kept women from high-paying jobs as well as the sex classification of job advertisements in newspapers. Did you know that job advertisements in the newspaper used to feature a "Help Wanted—Men" column and a "Help Wanted—Women" column? See Table 1.6 for some sample advertisements. Can you imagine an advertisement for a receptionist today that requested an "attractive young lady"? Can you imagine an accountant position available only to men? In recognition of the work that women perform inside the home, NOW popularized the phrase

TABLE 1.6   JOB ADVERTISEMENTS

Help Wanted—Female
Assistant to Executive:
Girl Friday.
Asst Bookkeeper-Biller:
Young, some steno preferred, but not essential; bright beginner considered.
Asst. Bookkeeper-Typist:
Expd. all-around girl.
Secty-Steno:
Age 25–35 Girl Friday for busy treasurer's office.
Receptionist, 5 day wk:
Attractive young lady, good typist, knowledge of monitor board.
Help Wanted—Male
Pharmacist:
To manage large chain-type indep. drug store.
Refrigeration:
Shop servicemen, experienced.
Maintenance:
Foreman, mach. shop exp.
Accountant-Sr.:
For medium-sized firm, heavy experience, auditing, audit program preparation, report writing and federal and state income tax.

Source: New York Times, June 11, 1953.

"women who work outside the home." Most of us feel rightly embarrassed when we ask a woman if she works and she says, "Yes, I work at home all day taking care of two kids, a cat, a dog, and a husband." In 1967, NOW endorsed the Equal Rights Amendment (ERA), which was passed by Congress in 1972 but fell 3 states short of the 38 (three-fourths) needed for ratification in 1982. (The ERA was reintroduced to Congress in 2003 by Senators Edward Kennedy (D-MA) and Carolyn Maloney (D-NY) and awaits ratification by 3 more states.) In 1992, NOW organized a campaign to elect women and feminist persons to political office, which helped send a record-breaking number of women to Congress and to state governments.

For the past 20 years, NOW has been pursuing the Freedom of Access to Clinic Entrances Act which would keep organized groups from blocking and intimidating people entering reproductive health clinics. In 1998, NOW met with some success when a federal court, ruling in their favor, issued an injunction to keep people from interfering with women's access to clinics. However, in 2006 this ruling was overturned by the U.S. Supreme Court (Roth, 2006). In 2004, NOW organized the largest mass action in U.S. history, the March for Women's Lives, which brought a record 1.15 million people to Washington, D.C. to advocate for women's reproductive health options, including access to abortion clinics, effective birth control, emergency contraception, and reproductive health services (Reuss & Erickson, 2006). See Sidebar 1.2: "The Morning After" for NOW's advocacy on behalf of Plan B.

The women's movement in the United States has been criticized as a movement of White middle-class women (Margolis, 1993). However, the U.S. women's movement also is perceived to serve a larger portion of women compared to the movements in other countries, which are perceived to be more radical and less cohesive. For example, in India, the women's movement poses a threat to people's national identity because traditional roles are so grounded in culture. Yet, there is a core of commonality to women's movements around the world: They are focused on improving the position of women in society, equality in the labor force, and economic independence for women (Margolis, 1993).

Men's Movements

Over the past couple of decades, a series of men's movements have appeared, partly in response to the women's movement of the 1960s. None of the men's movements, to date, has had the cohesion or impact on society of this women's movement. Some men's movements endorse the women's movement and share some of the concerns the women's movement raised about the harmful aspects of the male gender role. These men refer to themselves as feminists and are likely to agree that society does not treat men and women equally, that men and women should be paid for equal work, and that features of the male gender role,

SIDEBAR 1.2: *The Morning After*

Plan B, also known as the morning-after pill, is a contraceptive but is widely misconstrued as an abortifacient (ACOG, 2006; Bushman, 2006; Reuss & Erickson, 2006). When taken within 72 hours of sexual intercourse, Plan B prevents up to 89% of pregnancies; it is most effective within 24 hours. Plan B interferes with ovulation, fertilization, or implantation. Thus Plan B is similar to a high-dose birth control pill and operates in the same way. People often confuse Plan B with Mifeprix (RU-486), an abortifacient that was widely publicized in the past decade. Plan B was approved by the Federal Drug Administration (FDA) in 1999 with a prescription. It was not until 2006 that the FDA made Plan B available as an over-the-counter drug for women 18 years of age and older. However, it is not clear just exactly how accessible Plan B is. First, there are age restrictions. Second, the lack of knowledge about what Plan B is and what Plan B does may make women leary of taking it. Finally, some pharmacists and emergency rooms fail to stock the drug—again, in part due to the failure to understand how Plan B operates.

such as competitiveness, homophobia, and emotional inhibition, are not good for men's relationships. In a sense, this movement has encouraged men to behave in more communal ways. The National Organization for Men Against Sexism (NOMAS), founded in 1983 (originally known as the National Organization for Changing Men), is just such a movement. These men advocate positive changes in men, are profeminist, supportive of gay rights, and antiracist.

Other men's movements are a reaction against the women's movement and seek to restore traditional male and female roles. These have attracted more men than the profeminist movements. Two recent movements are the mythopoetic movement and the Promise Keepers. Both of these movements view men and women as fundamentally different. Both encourage men to rediscover their masculinity and to reject what they have referred to as "the feminization of men." The movements are referred to as promasculinist.

The mythopoetic movement was organized by Robert Bly (1990), who wrote the national best-selling nonfiction book *Iron John: A Book About Men.* The concern of the mythopoetic movement is that the modernization of society has stripped men of the rituals of tribal society that bound men together. The movement involves rituals, ceremonies, and retreats, with the goal of reconnecting men with one another. Enthusiasm for this movement has waned over the last decade.

The Promise Keepers is a Christian fundamentalist movement. The Bible is used to justify the differences between men and women and the natural state of men's superior position over women. The first meeting of the Promise Keepers was held in 1990, and 72 men attended (*www. promisekeepers.org*). Attendance peaked in 1996 with 1.1 million men participating in 22 cities nationwide. Participation has dropped off more

recently—less than a half million men participated in Promise Keepers gatherings in 1998 and only several thousand in more recent gatherings. The Promise Keepers reject the traditional view that fathers are only providers and encourage greater involvement with children and families (Silverstein et al., 1999). Men also are urged to renounce alcohol and sexual temptations. To accomplish these goals, Promise Keepers encourage men to reclaim their high-status position in society and their position as head of the family household. The traditional nuclear family is endorsed; homosexuality and homosexual households are rejected. One Promise Keeper reported in a local newspaper, "As the man of the house goes, so goes the house" (Levin, 2000). An interesting aspect of the Promise Keepers's conventions is that more than half of the volunteers who put the conferences together are women, yet women are not allowed to attend. This organization is viewed as antifeminist because men and women are not viewed as equals.

A related Christian fundamentalist movement is the recent emergence of GodMen—an "edgier" version of the Promise Keepers. Godmen aims to reassert masculinity into men and into the church in a bold and brash way. The group rejects the meek version of Jesus and traditional Christian music, encouraging men to be more aggressive in their expression of themselves and of their faith.

Other men want to move beyond gender equality for women to gender equality for both sexes. One man, Warren Farrell (1993), began as a feminist, became a masculinist, and then said that neither really apply. He wrote the book *The Myth of Male Power,* in which he outlines the ways in which men lack power in our society. He is in agreement that there are obvious sources of female powerlessness, such as women's lower pay, women's lack of freedom to walk alone at night, and our lack of respect for women as they age. However, he also says there are indicators of male powerlessness in our society that ought to be recognized. For example, men are the ones drafted into the military. In addition, society instills in men the notion that they are the breadwinners of the family, whereas women have the option of working or staying home to raise children if they can afford it. Men also have been socialized to not ask for help, one result of which is that men commit suicide more frequently than women. Men are much more likely to be in prison compared to women. It is well known that men commit more acts of violence than women, but men also are more likely than women to be victims of violence. Farrell argues that violence against women is repudiated by society, but violence against men is accepted, if not glorified, in the form of sports. He claims that films call attention to violence against women but that the vast majority of victims of violence in films are men. See if Farrell's claims about violence in the media are valid with Do Gender 1.5. Finally, and most important, men die 5 years earlier than women. The fact that African Americans die earlier than Caucasians in the United States is taken as evidence of African Americans' powerlessness compared to Caucasians'.

Should we consider men's lower longevity compared to women to be an indicator of men's powerlessness, as Farrell (1993) suggests? According to Michael Messner (1997), it does not make sense to say both men and women are oppressed in society; for oppression to occur, one group must be oppressed and the other must be the oppressor. Instead, Messner argues that the difficulties men face are the price they pay for being the group in power. In either case, we can agree that relational, mental, and physical health hazards are associated with the restrictive aspects of the female and the male gender roles in our society. This is why this book emphasizes the implications of gender and gender roles for relationships and health.

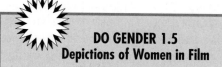

DO GENDER 1.5
Depictions of Women in Film

Warren Farrell (1993) maintains that films call attention to violence against women, but 95% of the people killed are men. He argues that women are not killed in movies, with the exception of a few conditions: (1) when the viewer does not really get to know the woman because she appears in no more than three scenes; (2) when she is not a "real" woman, meaning she is either an alien being or is crazy. Test his hypothesis:

1. Choose a representative sample of movies: comedy, drama, action-adventure, or mystery.

2. Come up with a way to measure violence.

3. Record all acts of violence; include the sex of the perpetrator and the sex of the victim.

4. How did the viewer feel about the victim? Did the viewer "like" him or her, "get to know" him or her (number of scenes)?

5. Can you determine whether the conditions surrounding male violence differ from the conditions surrounding female violence?

TAKE HOME POINTS

- The minimalists believe that men and women are essentially the same, that differences are small, and that those that do exist are likely to be due to social forces.

- The maximalists believe that men and women are fundamentally different in important ways, but that "different" does not mean that one is better than the other.

- The question of whether sex comparisons ought to be routinely made or ought to be made only when there is theoretical justification is a politically charged topic. People who advocate shying away from the study of sex comparisons are often concerned that finding differences between men and women will lead to their unequal treatment. However, others would argue that we can only institute change by knowing whether differences exist.

- Social constructionists argue that science cannot be applied to the study of gender because gender is not a static quality of a person but is a product of society. As the context changes, so does gender.

- Today's women's movements have as their common thread a concern with improving the position of women in society and ensuring equal opportunities for women and men.

- Today's men's movements are varied, some endorsing feminist positions and others advocating a return to traditional male and female roles.

THIS BOOK'S APPROACH TO THE STUDY OF GENDER

According to Deaux (1984), there are three approaches to the study of gender. First, sex is used as a subject variable. This is the most traditional approach to research and represented in the studies of sex comparisons. The idea here is that sex is an attribute of a person; investigators compare the thoughts, feelings, and behaviors of men and women. Deaux (1984) concludes that this approach has shown that most sex differences are qualified by interactions with context; for example, sex differences in conformity appear in some situations (e.g., public) but not others (e.g., private). A second approach has been to study the psychological differences between men and women: masculinity and femininity. This second approach is still an individual differences approach, but the subject is the social category of gender roles rather than the biological category of sex. Here, we examine how gender

roles influence people's thoughts, feelings, and behaviors. Is being female associated with providing help, or is being empathic a better predictor of helping behavior? If the latter is true, both men and women who are high in empathy will be helpful. Third, sex is examined as a stimulus or target variable. Researchers examine how people respond to the categories of male and female. An example of this approach is finding that people rate pictures of infants as more attractive when the infant is thought to be a female and stronger when the infant is thought to be a male. Only with this latter approach can sex be randomly assigned.

All three of these approaches are represented in this text. I examine gender as an individual difference variable but am careful to note how the context influences behavior. I highlight both similarities and differences between men and women. Most important, I focus on the explanations for the source of any observed sex differences, for example, whether other variables that co-occur with sex, such as status or gender-related personality traits, are the causal source of the behavior.

I focus on two domains of behavior: relationships and health. Relationships are an important subject in their own right. Relationships contribute to the quality of our life as well as to our mental and physical health. The impact of relationships on our psychological and physical well-being, the prevalence of violence in relationships, and the high rate of relationship dissolution in the form of divorce in the United States are reasons that relationships require our attention. Health also is an important subject in and of itself. Over the past century, we have extended our life span by decades but now are more likely to live with health problems for longer periods of time. We have been made increasingly aware of the role that psychological and social factors play in our health. Gender has implications for those psychological and social forces.

SUMMARY

First, we reviewed some important terms in the psychological study of gender. Sex, the biological category, was distinguished from gender, the psychological category. An important term is gender role, which refers to the expectations that society has for being male or female; we expect men to be masculine and women to be feminine, in other words, to act in accordance with their gender role. Other terms defined include gender identity, sexual orientation, sex or gender typing, sexism, gender-role stereotype, and sex discrimination. I discussed the multiple meanings of feminism, concluding that equality for men and women was the most central component of the definition and activism a more peripheral component. Because each society has its own definitions of gender and ways of defining male and female roles, I also described several cultures that have alternative ways of constructing gender.

Next, I presented various political and philosophical debates in the study of gender. The minimalists, who emphasize the similarities between men and women, were distinguished from the maximalists, who emphasize the differences. I provided an overview of the issues that have arisen when people discuss whether sex differences should be examined, reported, and/or interpreted. A brief history of the women's movements was provided along with a description of the more recent men's movements.

DISCUSSION QUESTIONS

1. What is the distinction between "sex" and "gender"? How do you think this distinction should be employed in practice?
2. Describe a personal experience of intrarole or interrole conflict with respect to gender.
3. How is gender portrayed in other cultures?
4. What are some of the ways we can determine whether men have higher status than women in a given culture?
5. Do you think we should be comparing men and women? Why or why not?
6. Why hasn't any one men's movement gained the strength of the women's movement?
7. How can the use of sexist language be harmful?

SUGGESTED READING

Eagly, A. (1995). The science and politics of comparing women and men. *American Psychologist, 50,* 145–158.

Marecek, J., Craword, M., & Popp, D. (2004). On the construction of gender, sex, and sexualities. In A. Eagly, A. E. Beall, & R. J. Sternberg (Eds.), *The psychology of gender* (2nd ed.), pp. 192–216. New York: Guilford Press.

Miller, C., & Swift, K. (1988). *The handbook of nonsexist writing.* New York: Harper & Row.

KEY TERMS

Androgynous—Term describing one who incorporates both masculine and feminine qualities.

Bisexual—Individuals who accept other-sex and same-sex individuals as sexual partners.

Constructionist perspective—Perspective that maintains that gender cannot be divorced from its context.

Cross-sex-typed—Condition of possessing the biological traits of one sex but exhibiting the psychological traits that correspond with the other sex.

Feminine—Description of trait, behavior, or interest assigned to the female gender role.

Feminism—Belief that men and women should be treated equally.

Gender—Term used to refer to the social categories of male and female.

Gender culture—Each society's or culture's conceptualization of gender roles.

Gender identity/gender-role identity—One's perception of oneself as psychologically male or female.

Gender role—The expectations that go along with being male or female.

Gender-role attitude—One's personal view about how men and women should behave.

Heterosexuals—Individuals who prefer other-sex sexual partners.

Homosexuals—Individuals who prefer same-sex sexual partners.

Interrole conflict—Experience of conflict between expectations of two or more roles that are assumed simultaneously.

Intrarole conflict—Experience of conflict between expectations within a given role.

Masculine—Description of a trait, behavior, or interest assigned to the male gender role.

Maximalist—Person who maintains there are important differences between the two sexes.

Minimalist—Person who maintains the two sexes are fundamentally the same.

Role—Social position accompanied by a set of norms or expectations.

Sex—Term used to refer to the biological categories of male and female.

Sex discrimination—Behavioral component of one's attitude toward men and women that involves differential treatment of people based on their biological sex.

Sexism—Affective component of one's attitude toward sex characterized by demonstration of prejudice toward people based on their sex.

Sex-related behavior—Behavior that corresponds to sex but is not necessarily caused by sex.

Sex stereotype/gender-role stereotype—Cognitive component of one's attitude toward sex.

Sex-typed—Condition of possessing the biological traits of one sex and exhibiting the psychological traits that correspond with that sex.

Sex typing—Acquisition of sex-appropriate preferences, behaviors, skills, and self-concept (i.e., the acquisition of gender roles).

Sexual orientation—Preference to have other-sex or same-sex persons as sexual partners.

Transgendered—Descriptive term referring to an individual whose psychological sex is not congruent with biological sex.

Transsexual—Person whose biological sex has been changed surgically.

METHODS AND HISTORY OF GENDER RESEARCH

"Poverty after Divorce" (Mann, 1985a)

"Disastrous Divorce Results" (Mann, 1985b)

"Victims of Reform" (Williamson, 1985)

These were some headlines following the publication of Lenore J. Weitzman's (1985) book *The Divorce Revolution, the Unexpected Social and Economic Consequences for Women and Children in America.* She cited statistics that showed women's standard of living drops 73% after divorce, whereas men's standard of living increases by 42%. The study received a great deal of media attention, making headlines of newspapers across the nation. A social scientist and an economist were shocked by these statistics because they did not match their longitudinal data from a representative sample of couples who had divorced in the United States. Their data showed that

women's standard of living fell by only 30% during the first year following divorce, and even men's standard of living declined by 7% (Duncan & Hoffman, 1985). These statistics were subsequently confirmed by the U.S. Bureau of the Census (1991).

Why the discrepancy? Weitzman's data were based on a very small sample—114 men and 114 women who became divorced—and the sample was not representative. The response rate in that study also was low, less than 50%. And, standard of living was calculated from a fairly unreliable source, respondents' self-reports of their finances before and after divorce. The tragedy in all of this is not so much that a methodologically weak study was conducted but that the methodologically weak study attracted so much attention and the methodologically strong refutations received hardly any.

In this text, I review the scientific literature on gender and its implications for relationships and health. I also make reference to some of the more popular literature on gender, which is more likely to make newspaper headlines. You may already be familiar with books such as Deborah Tannen's (1990) *You Just Don't Understand: Women and Men in Conversation* and John Gray's (1992) *Men Are from Mars, Women Are from Venus.* I include these more popularized views of gender because I want you to be familiar with them. You will read about sex differences in the newspaper and hear about sex differences on television, especially on news shows such as *Dateline* and *20/20.* In this text, we evaluate these popularized notions about gender and sex differences from the point of view of the scientific literature. You will be able to judge which differences are real and which are not, which differences are exaggerated, and which comparisons between men and women have not been studied adequately. You will also know what questions to ask when faced with a report on sex differences. In order to do so, you need to be familiar with the scientific method. Thus, in the first section of this chapter, I review the scientific method on which the majority of the research presented in this text is based. Then I examine the unique difficulties that researchers face when studying gender. In the second half of the chapter, I provide an overview of the history of the psychology of gender. In reviewing the history of the field, I examine the different ways that people conceptualize and measure gender roles.

THE SCIENTIFIC METHOD

If you have taken a research methods course, you are familiar with the scientific method and you know that it is difficult to conduct good research. A number of terms are introduced in this section; they are summarized in Table 2.4 at the end of this section.

The scientific method rests on **empiricism**. Empiricism means information is collected via one of our major senses, usually sight. One can touch, feel, hear, or see the information. This information, referred to as **data**, usually takes the form of thoughts, feelings, or behaviors. For example, I examine the way in which men and women think about themselves and the world, the way men and women experience and express emotions, the way men and women interact with other people, and the way men's and women's bodies respond to stress. Statements about these observations, or data, are called **facts**. A collection of facts can be used to generate a **theory**, or an abstract generalization that provides an explanation for the set of facts.

For a theory to be scientific, it must be falsifiable, meaning there must be the possibility it can be disproved. Creationism, for example, is not a scientific theory because there is no way to disprove it. Intelligent design is a new term that has been applied to the study of religion as a way to explain the origin of humankind. Although the term was developed to sound scientific, it also is not a scientific theory because it is not testable—that is, there is no observation or experiment that can be performed to support or refute religion.

A theory is used to generate a **hypothesis**, a prediction that a certain outcome will occur under a specific set of conditions. A hypothesis is tested by creating those conditions and then collecting data. The statements made from the data, or facts, may either support the hypothesis, and thus the theory, or suggest the theory needs to be modified. Each of these steps in the research process is shown in Figure 2.1.

Let's take an example. One theory of the origin of sex differences is social role theory. According to social role theory, any differences in

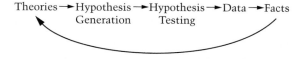

Theories ⟶ Hypothesis ⟶ Hypothesis ⟶ Data ⟶ Facts
Generation   Testing

FIGURE 2.1   Steps in the research process.

behavior we observe between men and women are due to the different social roles they hold in society. We can apply this theory to the behavior of nurturance. One hypothesis would be that women are more nurturant than men because their social roles of mother and caretaker require more nurturant behavior than the social roles men possess. This hypothesis suggests that men and women who are in the same social roles will show similar levels of nurturance. We could test this hypothesis in two ways. We could compare the levels of nurturance among men and women who have similar roles in society—stay-at-home moms and stay-at-home dads. We could measure nurturance by how they interact with babies in a nursery. These observations would be the data. Let's say we find that stay-at-home moms and dads spend the same amount of time holding the babies, talking to the babies, and playing with the babies. These are facts, and they would support our hypothesis that men and women who possess the same social roles behave in similar ways.

Another way we could test our hypothesis would be to assign males and females to one of two social roles in the laboratory, a caretaker or a noncaretaker role, and observe nurturant behavior. In the caretaker condition, we would ask participants to play with and take care of a puppy; in the noncaretaker condition, we would ask participants to teach the puppy some tricks. If both men and women show the same high level of nurturant behavior in the caretaker condition and the same low level of nurturant behavior in the noncaretaker condition, our hypothesis that social role rather than sex leads to differences in nurturance would be supported, and our theory

would be supported. If women are observed to show greater levels of nurturance than men in both conditions, regardless of the instructions received on how to interact with the puppy, we would have to revise our theory. This observation would suggest there is something about being female, aside from the social role, that leads to nurturance.

The two studies just described are quite different in design. The first is a correlational study and the second an experimental study. Most of the studies in this text are either correlational or experimental. Let me describe the differences.

Correlational Study

A **correlational study** is one in which you observe the relation between two variables, usually at a single point in time. For example, we could correlate job characteristics with nurturant behavior. We would probably observe that people who held more people-oriented jobs displayed more nurturance. The problem would be that we would not know if the job caused nurturance or if nurturant people were attracted to those jobs. Does being a social worker lead to nurturance, or do more nurturant people choose social work? We also could correlate sex with job characteristics. We would probably find that women are more likely than men to hold people-oriented jobs. The problem here isn't exactly the same as the one just identified. Here, we know that job characteristics do not cause someone's sex. However, we still do not know if someone's sex caused him or her to have a certain kind of job. There may be a third variable responsible for the relation between sex and people-oriented jobs. That third variable could be salary. Perhaps the pay of people-oriented jobs is lower than that of other jobs and women are more likely to be hired into low-salary positions. Thus the primary weakness of correlational research is that a number of explanations can account for the relation between two variables.

The value of a correlation can range from −1 to +1. Both −1 and +1 are referred to as perfect correlations, which means you can perfectly predict one variable from the other variable. In the examples just cited, there will not be perfect correlations. It will not be the case that all nurturant people are in people-oriented jobs or all women are in people-oriented jobs. An example of a perfect correlation can be found in physics. There is a perfect correlation between how fast you are driving and how far your car takes you. If you drive 60 mph, you will travel 60 miles in one hour or 120 miles in 2 hours. For every 1 mph you increase your speed, you will travel 1 mile farther in an hour. That is, you can perfectly predict distance from speed. As you might guess, we cannot perfectly predict one variable from another in psychological research. Most correlations reported in psychology will fall in the .3 to .4 range.

A **positive correlation** is one in which the levels of both variables increase or decrease at the same time. For example, you might find that women who hold more traditional gender-role attitudes are more likely to perform the majority of household chores; that is, as women's gender-role attitudes become more traditional, the amount of household chores performed increases. This is depicted in the left half of Figure 2.2. A **negative correlation** occurs when the level of one variable increases as the level of the other decreases. This is depicted in the right half of Figure 2.2. An example of a negative correlation would be the amount of household chores performed by a man with traditional gender-role attitudes: The more traditional his attitude, the fewer household chores he performs.

Correlational studies are often conducted with surveys or by making observations of behavior. It is important how you choose the people to complete your survey or to be the subject of observation; they need to be representative of the population to whom you wish to generalize your findings. I once had a student in my class

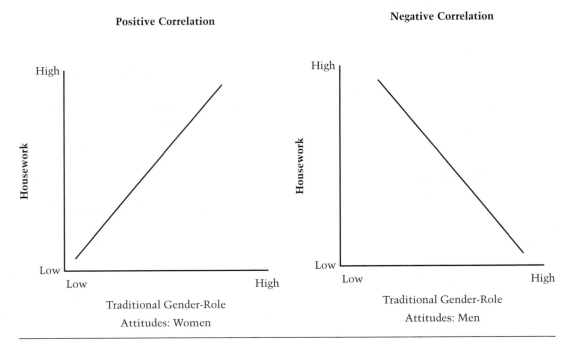

FIGURE 2.2   Examples of correlations.

conduct an observational study to see if sex is related to touching. She conducted the study on the bus and concluded that nobody touches anyone. This study suffered from a **selection bias**; people on the bus are not a representative sample, especially during the morning commute to work. To ensure a representative sample, the researcher should **randomly select** or **randomly sample** the participants from the population of interest. Random selection ensures that each member of the population has an equal chance of being a participant in the study. You could randomly select a sample by putting the names of all the people in the population in a hat and drawing out a sample of names. You could assign every member of the population an identification number and randomly select a set of numbers. Imagine you want a representative sample of 100 adults in your community. If every phone number in your community begins with the same first three digits, you could have a computer generate a series of four-digit random sequences and call those phone numbers with those sequences. Would this procedure result in a random sample? Close—but the sample would be biased in one way: You would not be representing the people in your area who do not have telephones.

Although random selection is important for the validity of correlational research, it is difficult to achieve and rarely employed. Often, we want to make inferences that generalize to the entire population, or at least the population of our country. It would be difficult to place 250 million names in a hat. Instead, we approximate and randomly select from a community we believe is fairly representative of the population. The important point to keep in mind is that we should generalize our findings only to the population it truly represents. This is particularly important in the study of gender because the vast majority of research has been conducted on White middle-class Americans, and findings may not generalize to people of other races, other classes, or other cultures.

You are probably wondering how a research participant pool at a university fits into the random selection process. The answer is, not very well. Do you have a research participant pool at your institution in which you are asked to participate in experiments for credit? Or, are there postings that request volunteers to participate in research? In either case, you are probably choosing to participate in a particular experiment; that is, you were not randomly selected from the entire population of college students. Worse yet, the kinds of people who choose to participate in a certain experiment may not be representative of the entire population of students. We must keep this research limitation in mind when generalizing from the results of our studies.

Experimental Study

The second research method we discuss in this text is the **experimental method**. In an experiment, the investigator manipulates one variable, called the **independent variable**, and observes its effect on another variable, called the **dependent variable**. To keep these two concepts straight, remember that the dependent variable "depends on" the independent variable. In the experiment described previously, the instructions on how to interact with the puppy were the independent variable (caretaker vs. noncaretaker condition) and the behavior of nurturance was the dependent variable. Table 2.1 lists more examples of independent variables and dependent variables.

How do we know that other variables besides the independent variable—the instructions—aren't responsible for the effect on nurturance? Maybe the students in the caretaker condition were more nurturant with the animals

TABLE 2.1 EXAMPLES OF INDEPENDENT AND DEPENDENT VARIABLES

Research Question	Independent Variable	Dependent Variable
Is employment harmful to women's health?	Employment	Health
Does testosterone increase aggression?	Testosterone	Aggression
Is rumination a source of depression?	Rumination	Depression
Which relationships are closer—same-sex or other-sex?	Relationship type	Closeness
Are men or women smarter?	Sex	Intelligence
Does commitment in a relationship decrease power?	Commitment	Power
Are lesbians more masculine than heterosexual women?	Sexual orientation	Gender role
Is touching a function of status?	Status	Touching
Is housework divided more evenly among egalitarian couples?	Egalitarian vs. traditional	Division of labor
Do we smile more at male or at female infants?	Infant sex	Smiling

than students in the noncaretaker condition because they had pets in their homes when they were growing up. This is possible, but unlikely, because participants are randomly assigned to each condition in an experiment. **Random assignment** means each participant has an equal chance of being assigned to each condition. Because of random assignment, on average, the people in one condition will be comparable to the people in the other condition, with the exception of how they are treated with regard to the independent variable. Random assignment is the key feature of the experimental method.

Random assignment can be accomplished by flipping a coin or drawing numbers out of a hat. Random assignment means there is no systematic way of assigning people to conditions. Dividing the classroom in half so people on the right are in one group and people on the left are in another group would not be random. Theoretically, there could be differences between the kinds of people who sit on the right versus the left side of the classroom. In the classroom in which I teach, students who sit on the left side of the seminar table can look out the window, whereas students who sit on the right side have

a view of the wall, so they might as well look at me. Imagine you had asked participants to decide whether they wanted to play with the puppy or teach it tricks. If you let people choose their condition, the people in the two conditions would be different; nurturant people are likely to choose to play with the puppy. Differences in nurturant behavior between the two conditions would be due to a selection bias because people selected their own groups and were not randomly assigned to condition.

In a true experiment, one must be able to manipulate the independent variable to study its effects. Notice that some of the independent variables in Table 2.1 are changeable and some are not; that is, one can manipulate employment, testosterone, rumination, and relationship commitment to study their effects. Other independent variables are not changeable, the most important of which is sex. When sex is a characteristic of a person, as in the research question "Are men or women smarter?" sex is referred to as a **subject variable**. Studies in which sex is a subject variable are not true experiments because someone cannot be randomly assigned to be male or female. The majority of research that compares men and women—evaluating similarities and differences between men's and women's behavior—is not experimental for this reason. We observe in the laboratory or in the real world how men and women think, feel, and behave. This research is correlational because we cannot manipulate a person's sex.

Is there any way we can use an experiment to make sex comparisons? We can make sex a **stimulus** or **target variable**, meaning it is the characteristic of something to which people respond. Let's take the research question "Do we smile more at male or female infants?" One way to answer that question is to compare how often adults smile at male and female infants. However, this would be a correlational study; we would be correlating infant sex with smiling, and sex would be a subject variable. We would not know if infant sex caused the smiling or something else about the infant caused the smiling; for example, infant girls are more likely to wear pink and perhaps pink causes smiling. A better way to address this research question is by conducting an experimental study in which infant sex is a target variable. We could show people pictures of the same child dressed in gender neutral clothes and randomly tell one group the infant is "Joe" and the other group the infant is "Joelle." Then we can tell if people smile more at infants they perceive to be female compared to those they perceive to be male. When sex is a target variable, random assignment can take place and a true experiment can be conducted.

There are advantages and disadvantages of both correlational and experimental methods. The major ones are identified in Table 2.2.

The advantage of the experimental method is that cause and effect can be determined because all other variables in the experiment are held constant except for the independent variable (the cause). Thus any differences in the dependent variable (the effect) can be attributed to the independent variable. One point on which philosophers of science agree about causality is that the cause must precede the effect. In an experiment, the cause, by definition, precedes the effect. The cause cannot always be determined in a correlational study. Thus the strength of the experimental method is **internal validity**, that is, being confident you are measuring the true cause of the effect.

The disadvantage of the experimental method is that experiments are usually conducted in an artificial setting, such as a laboratory, so the experimenter can have control over the environment. Recall the experiment where people were interacting with a puppy. The experiment was set up to observe nurturant behavior. Do interactions with a puppy in a laboratory where people are told how to behave generalize to how adults on the whole interact with their own pets? Or to how they interact with their children? Results from experiments conducted in the laboratory may be less likely to generalize to the real world; that is, they are low in **external validity**. In the real world, men and women may be given very different messages about how to interact with puppies, babies, and adults. In addition, in the real world, people do not think their behavior is being observed by an experimenter.

External validity is a strength of the correlational method. You can observe behavior in a real-world setting so you are studying the true

TABLE 2.2 EXPERIMENTAL METHOD VERSUS CORRELATIONAL METHOD

	Experimental	*Correlational*
Strength	Internal validity	External validity
Weakness	External validity	Internal validity

behavior. You could ask people to report their true nurturant behavior on a questionnaire or you could unobtrusively observe nurturant behavior by studying mothers and fathers with their children at school or during a doctor's visit. Recording the amount of time nurses spend with patients is a good indication of nurturant behavior.

Correlational studies can be easy to conduct. A quick survey allows one to collect a large amount of information at one time on a range of variables. The major disadvantage of the correlational method is that one cannot determine cause and effect because the variables are measured simultaneously. If I find that boys perform better than girls on a spatial skills test, I do not know if sex caused the difference in scores or if something else associated with being male and female is responsible for the difference—such as boys having more experience with sports which fosters spatial skills. The correlational method lacks internal validity.

Field Experiment

On rare occasions the experimental method is taken into the real world, into what we call the *field* where the behavior under investigation naturally occurs. These are **field experiments**, which attempt to maximize both internal and external validity. An example of a field experiment on gender and nurturance is randomly assigning men and women managers in a business organization to receive different instructions on how to interact with their employees: either to teach them new information and technology (noncaretaker condition), or to make sure they all get along with one another and are happy (caretaker condition). The experiment has internal validity because people are randomly assigned to condition. On average, the only difference between the two groups of managers is the instructions they received. The experiment has external validity because we are

observing actual nurturant behavior in a real-world setting: the organization. We could measure nurturant behavior in terms of offers to help the employee or time spent with the employee talking about likes and dislikes about the job. Now, imagine how likely an organization would be to let you randomly assign their managers to have different kinds of interactions with their employees. In addition, imagine how difficult it would be to ensure that only the independent variable differs between the two groups. Many other variables could influence managers' behavior that would be difficult to control: the way the manager is treated by his or her own boss, the nature of the employee's job (whether it involves working with others, whether it involves technology), and the number of employees a single manager has. Would you be able to assign a manager randomly to focus on technology with one employee but focus on relationships with the other employee? Because field experiments do not have the same kind of controls over behavior that laboratory experiments do, they are difficult to conduct.

Cross-Sectional Versus Longitudinal Designs

Aside from conducting a field study, there is another way to enhance the internal validity of correlational studies. Recall that a correlational study usually measures the relation between two variables at a single point in time. This is not always the case. When a single time point is used, we say the study is **cross sectional**. However, we may measure the independent variable at one time and the dependent variable later; this is a **longitudinal** study. In a longitudinal study, there are multiple time points of study. Can we discern cause and effect with a longitudinal study? Remember, a key principle to establishing causality is that the cause precedes the effect. A longitudinal study helps establish causality but does not ensure it. Let's take an example.

We could survey a group of women from the community to see if employment is related to health. If we conduct one survey at a single point in time, we are conducting a cross-sectional study. Let's say we find a correlation: Employment is associated with better health. The problem is that we do not know if employment leads to better health or if healthier people are more likely to be employed. A longitudinal study may help solve this problem. We could measure both employment and health at one time (Time 1) and then 6 months later (Time 2). If employment at Time 1 is associated with a change in health between Time 1 and Time 2, employment is likely to have caused better health. We can be even more confident of this relation if health at Time 1 does not predict change in employment between Time 1 and Time 2.

Longitudinal studies help establish causality and also help distinguish **age effects** from **cohort effects**. A *cohort* refers to a group of people of similar age, such as a generation. In the cross-sectional study previously described, let's say we find a relation between age and employment, such that older women are employed for fewer hours outside the home. Can we conclude that women decrease the amount of hours they spend in employed work as they get older? If so, this would be an age effect. Or, is it the case that older women were raised at a time when women were less likely to be employed? The fact that older women work fewer hours outside the home than younger women might be because older women hold traditionally female jobs that require fewer hours. If so, this finding is a cohort effect, an effect due to the generation of the people. In a cross-sectional design, we cannot distinguish age effects from cohort effects. With a longitudinal design, we would take a single cohort of women (age 20 to 25) and follow them for years to see if their employment and health changed over time.

TAKE HOME POINTS

- The scientific method rests on empiricism, and a key determinant of whether something is a scientific theory is whether it is falsifiable.

- The key feature of the experimental method is random assignment, which helps to isolate the independent variable as the true cause of the effect.

- Experiments are often high in internal validity but may lack external validity if conducted in the laboratory.

- Correlational research is often easier to conduct than experimental research and has high external validity, but low internal validity.

- Most research in the area of sex comparisons is correlational because sex is a subject variable rather than a target variable.

- Field experiments—though difficult to conduct—maximize both internal and external validity.

- Longitudinal studies can help to enhance the internal validity of correlational research.

DIFFICULTIES IN CONDUCTING RESEARCH ON GENDER

Now that you understand the basic components of the research process, we can examine the difficulties that arise when applying this process to the study of gender. The study of gender has some unique difficulties that other research domains do not face. Other difficulties inherent in scientific research are particularly problematic in the study of gender. At each stage of the research process, the researcher, who is sometimes the experimenter, can intentionally or unintentionally influence the outcome. Biases may be detected in the question asked, the way the study is designed, how the data are collected, how the data are interpreted, and how the results are communicated. Participants in experiments also can influence the outcome by their awareness of gender-role stereotypes, their desire to fit or reject gender-role norms, and their concerns with self-presentation. That is, participants care about how they appear to the experimenter and to other participants. In this section, I review the ways the experimenter and then the participant can influence study outcomes.

Experimenter Effects

Experimenter effects refer to the ways the experimenter, or the person conducting the research, can influence the results of a study. A review of studies on sex differences in leadership style showed that the sex of the author influenced the results (van Engen & Willemsen, 2004)! It turned out that male authors were more likely than female authors to report that women used a more conventional style of leadership that involved monitoring subordinates and rewarding behavior. How can this be? One explanation is that people published studies that fit their expectations. Another explanation is that men and women experimenters designed different kinds of studies, with one design showing a sex difference and one not.

The experimenter can influence the outcome of a study at many levels. Each of these is described below and shown in Figure 2.3.

Question Asked and Study Design. First, the experimenter can influence the outcome of a study by the nature of the question asked and the subsequent design of the study. For example, a researcher could be interested in determining the effects of women working outside the home on children's well-being. One researcher may believe it is harmful for women to work outside the home while they have small children. To test this hypothesis, the researcher could design a study in which children in day care are compared to children at home in terms of the number of days sick in a year. Because the children at day care will be exposed to more germs, they will experience more sick days the first year than children at home. In this case, the experimenter's theory about mothers working outside the home being harmful to children will be supported. However, another experimenter may believe mothers working outside the home is beneficial to children. This experimenter examines the reading level of kindergartners and finds that children whose mothers worked outside the home have higher reading levels than children whose mothers did not work outside the home. The problem here: The mothers who worked outside the home were more highly educated than the mothers who worked inside the home, and this education may have been transmitted to the children. In both cases, the experimenter's preexisting

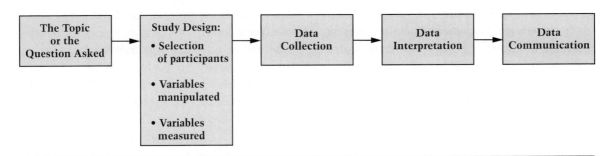

FIGURE 2.3 Stages of the research process that can be influenced by the experimenter.

beliefs influenced the specific question asked and the way the study was designed to answer that question.

Most scientists are very interested in the phenomenon they study and do have expectancies about the results of their work. In an area as controversial as gender, it is difficult to find a scientist who does not have a belief about the outcome of the study. It is all right to have an expectation, or hypothesis, based on scientific theory, but we must be cautious about hunches based on personal experiences and desires. The best situation is one in which the scientist conducting the research does not care about the outcome of the study and has little invested in it. Perhaps scientists should be randomly assigned to topics! Most of us do care about the outcomes of studies and are invested in those outcomes. As a mother who works outside the home, what would I do if I conducted a study and found that children whose mothers worked suffered? The task that the scientist must confront is to set aside preexisting beliefs and biases to conduct a study in as objective a way as possible. **Replication**, or the repeating of a study, by different investigators with different measures of the independent variable and the dependent variable helps enhance our confidence in a finding.

Study Design: Participants. The experimenter can influence the outcome of the study by the specific participants who are chosen. Obviously, experimenters who limit their studies to all males or all females should question whether their findings generalize to the other sex. Experimenters who study both men and women should also be sensitive to other variables besides sex that could distinguish the two groups. For example, several decades ago, an experimenter who compared the mental health of men and women might have been evaluating employed men and nonemployed women because most men worked outside the home and most women did not. If such a study showed women to be more depressed than men, we might wonder whether this finding was attributable to being female or to not having a job outside the home. Today, any studies conducted of men and women would take into consideration employment status. There are other variables that may co-occur with sex and be responsible for any observed sex differences, such as income, occupational status, and even health. Investigators should make sure they are studying comparable groups of men and women.

Study Design: Variables Manipulated and Measured. The experimenter can influence the outcome of a study through the variables that are manipulated and measured. McKenna and Kessler (1977) discovered that the way a variable was manipulated in an experiment differed depending on whether the participants were male or female. They examined studies on aggression and found that aggression as an independent variable took a more passive form among studies of women than among studies of men. Aggression was manipulated in studies of women by having people read about a frustrating situation. Aggression was more likely to be manipulated in studies of men by treating people in a hostile manner. Would it surprise you if these studies showed that males responded more aggressively to being ridiculed than females did to reading about being stuck in a traffic jam?

Dependent measures also can be biased in favor of males or females. A study that compares male and female mathematical ability by asking children to make calculations of baseball averages is biased against females to the extent that boys and girls have different experiences with baseball. A study that evaluates sex differences in helping behavior by measuring how quickly a person responds to an infant's cries is biased against males to the extent that men and women have different experiences with children. A helping situation biased in the direction of males is assisting someone with a flat tire on the side of the road. Here, you may find that men are more likely than women to provide assistance because men may have more experience changing tires than women. It is unlikely men have a "tire-changing" gene that women do not possess, just as it is unlikely women have a "diaper-changing" gene that men do not possess. Men are provided with more opportunities to change tires just as women are provided with more opportunities to console a crying infant. Thus, in generalizing across studies, we have to ensure that the different ways a dependent variable is measured do not account for the findings.

Data Collection.   The experimenter can influence the outcome of a study by how the data are collected. The experimenter may treat men and women differently in a way that supports the hypothesis. Rosenthal (1966) found that male and female experimenters smiled more and glanced more at same-sex participants than other-sex participants while giving the experimental instructions. He concluded that men and women are not in the same experiment when the experimenter is aware of their sex.

The experimenter can influence participants' behavior by giving subtle cues like nodding of the head to indicate the correct response is being given. An experimenter who believes that women self-disclose more than men might unintentionally elicit differences in self-disclosure by revealing more personal information to female than male participants. The experimenter might provide subtle nonverbal cues that encourage female disclosure (e.g., head nodding, open posture, smiling, looking attentive) and subtle cues that discourage male disclosure (e.g., looking bored, not paying attention, shifting around anxiously in one's seat).

The experimenter's beliefs can influence his or her own behavior, which then encourages participants to respond in a way that confirms the experimenter's beliefs. That is, the participant's behavior becomes a self-fulfilling prophecy. In these cases, experimenters are probably not intentionally influencing the outcome, but their beliefs are subtly influencing their own behavior and, consequently, the participant's behavior. It may be difficult for experimenters to treat male and female participants equally because most experimenters are aware of gender-role stereotypes and the norms for male and female behavior. One way to minimize this bias is for the investigator to hire an experimenter who is blind to the purpose of the study, especially the hypotheses. In this situation, your only concern is that the experimenter brings to the study his or her lay perceptions of how men and women differ. A better solution is to have the experimenter blind to the participant's sex. One way to accomplish this, although not always feasible, is to provide standardized instructions or questions to participants via an audiotape or intercom, so the experimenter cannot see the participant.

Data Interpretation.   The experimenter can influence the outcome of the study by the way he or she interprets the data. One problem in the area of gender is that we might interpret the same behavior differently depending on whether the subject is male or female. In many cases, it is difficult to be blind to the participant's sex, especially if you are observing a behavior. Imagine that you observe someone screaming. If the person screaming is female, you may interpret the behavior as hysteria; if the person screaming is male, you may interpret the behavior as anger. The following classic study illustrates how people can interpret the same behavior differently depending on an individual's sex.

A study was conducted in which college students were shown a videotape of an infant playing with a teddy bear, a doll, a buzzer, and a jack-in-the-box (Condry & Condry, 1976). Students were asked to rate the intensity of the infant's emotional responses to each object. Students were randomly assigned to one of two conditions in which they were told the infant was a girl, "Dana," or a boy, "David." The infant's emotional responses to the teddy bear and the doll were rated as consistently positive, and the infant's emotional responses to the buzzer were rated as consistently negative, regardless of whether the infant was seen as Dana or David. Students perceived the infant's response to the jack-in-the-box differently, however, depending on the infant's sex: If the infant was thought to be a male, his crying was viewed as showing anger; if the infant was thought to be a female, her crying was viewed as showing fear. Thus the same behavior—crying—was interpreted as fear in one case and anger in the next. These differences were larger among the male than the female students. The authors concluded that people view behavior similarly when it is clear cut, but that under conditions of ambiguity, such as the situation with the jack-in-the-box, behavior may be interpreted differently depending on whether it is displayed by a male or a female. This study has far-reaching implications for our behavior as adults. Just think how differently you would respond to someone who was afraid versus someone who was angry.

Even when the interpretation of a behavior in an experiment is clear, the overall outcome of an experiment may be subject to different interpretations. For example, one behavior that has received a great deal of attention in the gender literature is conformity. The question is, "Are women more conforming than

TABLE 2.3 CONFORMITY OR INDEPENDENCE?

	Women	Men
Public	8.51	6.92
Private	8.55	8.12

Note: Numbers reflect the extent of agreement with the confederate, with higher numbers indicating more conformity.
Source: Adapted from Eagly, Wood, and Fishbaugh (1981).

men?" But why isn't the question, "Are men more independent than women," or "Are men less compliant than women?" If more women than men agree with a group of people and more men than women disagree with a group of people, are women conforming or are men being independent? A study by Eagly and colleagues manipulated the conditions that surrounded conformity and found that men's being more independent than women was a more accurate statement of the results than women's being more conforming than men (Eagly, Wood, & Fishbaugh, 1981). Eagly manipulated whether participants indicated their agreement or disagreement with other people publicly or privately; the results are shown in Table 2.3. In the public condition, women showed more conformity than men; in the private condition, however, there were no sex differences in conformity, and men's and women's behavior was more like that of women in the public condition. Thus, the deviant cell in this study was when men expressed their opinions publicly. Instead of showing that women are more concerned with appearing agreeable in the presence of other people, the study showed that men are more concerned with appearing independent in the presence of other people.

Communication of Results. Finally, the experimenter can influence the impact of a study by how the findings are communicated.

Experimenters may report only results that support their hypotheses. That is, experimenters who believe there are sex differences may conduct a dozen studies until a difference appears and then report that one difference. Experimenters who believe there are no differences between men and women may conduct a dozen studies, slightly altering the situation in each one, until no difference appears and then report that study. This is a problem for the study of gender because, as noted in Chapter 1, there are different political philosophies about whether there are a few small sex differences or major sex differences that pervade our lives.

Another problem with the communication of results is that sex differences are inherently more interesting than sex similarities; thus studies of differences are more likely to be published. A researcher who designs a study that does not involve issues of gender may routinely compare men's and women's behavior in the hope that no differences are found. In this case, the investigator considers sex to be a nuisance variable. If no differences are found, gender is probably not mentioned in the article, so there is no record of the similarity! If differences are found, gender may become the focus of the study. The scientific bias of publishing differences is perpetuated by the media, who are not likely to pick up a story on a study that shows sex similarities. A study that shows differences is going to gather the attention of the media and will be placed in a prominent place in the newspaper.

Susan Faludi (1991) published a book entitled *Backlash: The Undeclared War Against American Women* in which she describes somewhat questionable research findings that are published by the media even when refuted by other scientific research. (The divorce statistic example at the beginning of this chapter was discussed in her book.) According to Faludi, they are published because they support the culture of the time. For example, a story in the newspaper appeared showing that the chance of a single college-educated woman getting married was 20% at age 30, 5% at age 35, and 1.3% at age 40. The study made front-page news, despite questionable methods and a small sample size. A follow-up study that used actual census data showed quite different statistics: at age 30, 58% to 66%; at age 35, 32% to 41%; and at age 40, 17% to 23%. The follow-up study, however, was not picked up by the media. Faludi reports another example having to do with age and infertility. A study of infertility widely noted in newspapers and on radio and television talk shows showed that women between the ages of 31 and 35 had a 40% chance of becoming infertile. Reporters did not note, however, that this study was based on a very unique sample: women receiving artificial insemination because their husbands were sterile. A subsequent study based on a more representative sample showed that the infertility rate for women between the ages of 30 and 34 was 14%, only 3% more than women in their early 20s.

Faludi's position is that research findings showing adverse effects of the women's movement on women's economics, fertility, and relationships are being highlighted, whereas research findings showing positive effects of the women's movement are stifled. Regardless of whether Faludi's overall claim is correct, these examples show that the media are more likely to sensationalize the more outrageous research findings and are less likely to highlight findings of sex similarities. Sex differences are interesting; sex similarities are not. The media also can distort the explanations for findings of differences between men and women. A recent study showed that the political orientation of a newspaper (as defined by the most recent presidential candidate endorsed) was associated with the explanations provided for sex differences (Brescoll & LaFrance, 2004). More conservative

DO GENDER 2.1
Comparing Media Reports to Scientific Reports

Find a news article on gender, most likely on sex differences, in the newspaper or news-magazines. Find one that refers to the original source of the study; that is, it gives the reference to a scientific journal. Compare the news version of the study to the scientific report of the study. Answer the following questions:

1. Did the news article accurately reflect the findings of the scientific study?

2. What did the news article leave out, if anything?

3. What did the news article exaggerate, if anything?

4. Was there anything in the news article that was misleading?

5. What did you learn by reading the scientific article that you would not have learned by reading the news article?

6. Why did this particular study appear in the news? Was it important? Was the finding "catchy"?

newspapers were more likely to emphasize biological explanations. One of the skills you will gain from reading this text is being able to evaluate reports about sex differences you read in the popular press. Start now with Do Gender 2.1.

In summary, we need to be alert to how experimenter expectancies can shape the results of studies. One remedy is to have a team of scientists with opposing beliefs conduct research on a topic. Why do you think this does not happen very often? Social psychologists have shown that we are attracted to people who share our beliefs and values—people who are like us. Thus it is more likely that we will find ourselves collaborating with people who share our beliefs about the outcome of a study. Replication is another strategy we have built into science as a check on the influence experimenters have on research findings. Before taking a finding seriously, we make sure it has been repeated with different samples, with different measures of both the independent and dependent variables, and by different investigators. We can be more confident of similarities or differences between male and female behavior when we see them emerge repeatedly and across a wide variety of contexts. As shown in Chapter 5, however, changing the context usually alters how men and women behave.

Participant Effects

The ways in which participants of an experiment can influence the outcome of a study are referred to as **demand characteristics**. There are certain demands or expectations about how to behave as a participant in an experiment. Participants often conform to or react against these demands. The **social desirability response bias** is one example of a demand characteristic. That is, people want to behave in socially desirable ways, ways in which they appear normal and likable. In our society, it is socially desirable for men to appear masculine and women to appear feminine. On self-report inventories of masculinity and femininity, men typically rate themselves as high on masculinity and women rate themselves as high on femininity regardless of how they really score on traits that define those concepts. That is, regardless of whether a man rates himself as independent or self-confident (traits we ascribe to masculinity), most men rate themselves as masculine. Thus participants may behave in ways that fit their gender role, especially if they realize the purpose of the experiment.

If I asked the students in my class for a show of hands as to who is emotional, more women than men would raise their hands. If I asked the students for a show of hands as to who is aggressive, more men than women would raise their hands. Does this mean men are more aggressive than women and women more emotional than men? Certainly not—on the basis of that showing of hands. It is socially desirable for men to say they are aggressive and women to say they are emotional. The design of the study is poor because the public behavior increases the chance of introducing a social desirability response bias.

An example of demand characteristics occurred in a study of pain reports. Male and female college students were asked to put their hand in ice-cold water and report the level of pain they felt. Males reported much less pain in the presence of an attractive opposite-sex experimenter than a same-sex experimenter, whereas females reported more pain in the presence of an attractive opposite-sex experimenter than a same-sex experimenter. One precaution that you can take to guard against demand characteristics is to have responses be private—anonymous and confidential—rather than public. Another precaution is to disguise the purpose of the experiment.

In a review of the literature on parents' treatment of children, the review concluded that parents treat sons and daughters the same (Lytton & Romney, 1991). However, a closer inspection of the studies revealed that parents *said* they treated sons and daughters the same, but observational studies showed differences.

One remedy to the problem of participant effects is to have multiple measures of a behavior. For example, if you want to know how men and women compare in terms of assertiveness, you could examine self-reports of assertiveness, you could set up an experiment to elicit assertive behavior, and you could obtain other people's reports of participants' assertive behavior. In studies of aggression among children, a frequently used measure of other people's reports is peer nomination. All the children in the class nominate the most aggressive child, the child most difficult to get along with, or the child who makes them afraid. When one person is named by the majority of the children, we can have a great deal of confidence that the child is exhibiting some kind of behavioral problem.

The Setting: Laboratory Versus Field

Much of our research on gender is conducted in the laboratory rather than the field, or the real world. A number of problems emerge in applying the conclusions from research on gender conducted in the laboratory to our everyday lives, specifically problems with external validity. In the laboratory, everything is held constant except the independent variable, which is usually participant's sex. Thus men and women come into the laboratory and face equal treatment and equal conditions. The problem is that men and women do not face equal conditions in the real world. Thus we might be more likely to find similar behavior in the laboratory than in the real world. If that is the case, the differences in behavior observed in the real world might be due to the different situations in which men and women find themselves.

For example, if you bring men and women into the laboratory and then provoke them, they may display similar levels of anger. However, in the real world, women are more likely than men to hold low-status positions where displays of anger are inappropriate and often punished. In addition, in the real world, men are more often provoked than women. Thus men may display more anger than women in the real world because men are more likely to be provoked and women are more likely to be punished for displays of anger. These ideas were supported in research by Biaggio (1989). In the first study, college students were asked to record all anger-provoking incidents for a 2-week period and how they responded to them. Men not only reported more anger-provoking incidents than women, but men were more likely than women to respond to each incident with physical or verbal antagonism. In the second study, college students were brought into the lab and shown an insulting letter. Men and women responded to the letter with equal levels of anger.

Another difficulty with laboratory research is that it is often conducted on college students. College students differ from the general population in a number of ways. They are more likely to be White, upper to middle class, higher in education, and homogeneous on a number of dimensions. The college experience is one in which the roles of men and women and the statuses of men and women are more similar compared to their situations after college. Thus it is questionable whether we can generalize the similarities observed among college students to the general population.

Variables Confounded with Sex

A fundamental problem for the study of gender is that we cannot randomly assign a person to be male or female. As mentioned earlier, sex is usually a subject variable rather than a true independent variable that can be manipulated. You can manipulate sex when you are leading respondents to believe the sex of a target person is what you want them to believe it is. Here, sex is a target variable. However, when comparing men's and women's feelings, thoughts, and behavior, we cannot be certain any differences found are due to sex alone; men and women come into the laboratory with their own values, histories, and experiences. Most important, sex is confounded with status.

We cannot separate the effects of sex from status. Is it that women smile more than men, or is it that low-status people smile more than high-status people? We will see in Chapter 7 that many of the sex differences observed in verbal and nonverbal communication seem to be due to status. When men and women are randomly assigned to a high-status or low-status position in the laboratory, high-status persons of both sexes typically display so-called male behavior and low-status persons of both sexes typically display so-called female behavior.

Another variable besides status that is confounded with sex is gender role. When we observe a sex difference in a behavior, is it due to the biological category of male or female, or is it due to the psychological category of gender? Too often, we fail to examine whether the difference is due to sex or to gender role. One area of research where there is substantial agreement as to whether a sex difference exists is aggression. Even aggression, however, may be partly due to biological sex and partly due to gender role, that is, our encouragement of aggression among males and discouragement of aggression among females. Features of the male gender role have been linked to aggression. Throughout this book, we are very attentive to the impact that gender roles have in areas of sex differences.

Situational Influences

Even if we examine personality traits in addition to participant's sex, we often find that in some situations we observe a difference and in some situations we do not observe a difference. Some situations are high in behavioral constraints, meaning the behavior required in the situation is clear and not very flexible; in this case, sex may have little to do with behavior. A graduation ceremony is such a situation. Men and women are usually dressed alike in robes, march into the ceremony together, and sit throughout the ceremony quietly until their name is called to receive their diplomas. The behavior in this situation is determined more by the situation than by characteristics of the people, including their sex. Other situations low in behavioral constraints would allow the opportunity for men and women to display different behaviors; informal social gatherings are an example of such a situation.

Certain situations make gender especially salient. As shown in Figure 2.4, a wedding is such a situation. Traditions make sex salient. Here, the norms for men's and women's attire are very different; no one expects men and women to dress the same at a wedding. The dress is formal; it would be unusual for a man to attend a wedding in a dress or a woman to attend a wedding in a tuxedo. The bride does not throw the bouquet to the entire crowd, only to eligible women; likewise, the groom throws the garter to eligible men. This is an occasion that may make differences in the behavior of men and women more likely to appear.

There also may be specific situational pressures to behave in accordance with or in opposition to one's gender role. Being raised in a traditional family, I have often found myself behaving in ways more consistent with the female gender role when I am with my family than when I am at home. When I was growing up, it was customary during large family gatherings for the women to tend to the dishes and the men to tend to the football. Did I help with the dishes? Of course. It would be rude not to. Besides, I don't really like football. Would my dad help with the dishes? Probably not. He likes football and would be shooed out of the kitchen.

There may be other situations in which behaving in opposition to gender roles is attractive. I remember the first time I went to look for a car by myself. The salesperson guided me to the cars with automatic transmissions and made some remark about women not being able to drive cars with a manual transmission. The worst part was he was right; I had tried and could not drive

FIGURE 2.4 Wedding picture, illustrating a situation with high behavioral constraints and a situation in which gender and gender-based norms are salient.

a stick shift. But that incident inspired me. I was determined to learn how to drive a stick shift and to buy a car with a manual transmission—to do my part in disconfirming the stereotype. I now drive a car with a manual transmission and probably always will because of that salesperson's remark. In this case, the situation made gender roles salient, but the effect was to create behavior inconsistent with gender roles.

The situational forces that shape behavior are a dominant theme in this book. We cannot study gender outside of the context in which it occurs, the situations in which men and women find themselves, and the people with whom they interact. This is the social psychological perspective and a perspective emphasized throughout this book.

TABLE 2.4   KEY TERMS USED IN SCIENTIFIC METHOD

Age effect: effect due to the age of the respondent.

Cohort effect: effect due to the cohort or generation of the respondent.

Correlational study: study in which one observes the relation between two variables, often at a single point in time.

Cross-sectional study: study in which the data are collected at one point in time, usually from a cross section of different age groups.

Data: information (e.g., thoughts, feelings, behaviors) collected for the purpose of scientific examination.

Demand characteristics: the ways participants of an experiment can influence the outcome of a study.

Dependent variable: variable that is expected to be influenced by manipulation of the independent variable; the effect.

Empiricism: basis of scientific method that involves the collection of information via one of the major senses (usually sight).

Experimenter effects: ways in which the experimenter can intentionally or unintentionally influence the results of a study.

Experimental method: research method in which the investigator manipulates one variable and observes its effect on another variable.

External validity: the confidence that the results from an experiment generalize to the real world.

Facts: statements made about data.

Field experiments: experiments in which the investigation is taken into the environment where the behavior to be studied naturally occurs.

Hypothesis: prediction that a certain outcome will occur under a specific set of conditions.

Independent variable: variable manipulated during an experiment; the cause.

Internal validity: the confidence that the true cause of the effect is being studied.

Longitudinal study: study in which data are collected at multiple time points.

Negative correlation: correlation in which the level of one variable increases and the level of the other variable decreases.

Positive correlation: correlation in which the levels of both variables increase or the levels of both variables decrease at the same time.

Random assignment: method of assignment in which each participant has an equal chance of being exposed to each condition.

Random selection/random sampling: method of selecting a sample in which each member of the population has an equal chance of being a participant in the study.

Replication: repetition of a study, often with different measures of the independent variable and the dependent variable.

Selection bias: result of participants not being randomly sampled or not being randomly assigned to condition.

Social desirability response bias: a demand characteristic; ways in which participants behave in experiments to give socially desirable answers.

Stimulus/target variable: variable that can be manipulated in an experiment.

Subject variable: variable that is a permanent characteristic of the person (subject) and may affect the person's response to another variable.

Theory: abstract generalization that provides an explanation for a set of facts.

TAKE HOME POINTS

- The experimenter can influence the outcome of a study by the way it is designed and by the way the data are collected, interpreted, and reported. This is one reason that we are more confident in findings that have been replicated by a number of researchers who have used different methods and different measures.

- Participants also can influence the outcome of the study. Especially when the behavior is public, demand characteristics are likely to operate. Ensuring confidentiality and disguising the nature of the research will minimize demand characteristics.

- Differences between men and women are less likely to be found in the laboratory, where men and women face equal conditions, than in the real world, where they do not.

- When finding that men and women differ on some outcome, one must be careful to determine whether the sex difference is due to sex, status, gender role, or something else.

HISTORY OF THE PSYCHOLOGY OF GENDER

In Chapter 1, I provided a very abstract definition of gender roles. Where did this concept come from? What did it mean 100 years ago, and what does it mean today? Is it better to be masculine or feminine? Or does it depend on whether you are male or female? Here, I provide a brief review of the history of the psychology of gender. I examine the different ways that people conceptualized and measured gender roles. I have divided the history of the field into four periods that approximate those identified by Richard Ashmore (1990). Each time period is marked by one or more key figures in the field.

1894–1936: Sex Differences in Intelligence

The first period focused on the differences between men and women and was marked by the publication of a book by Ellis (1894) entitled *Man and Woman*, which called for a scientific approach to the study of the similarities and differences between men and women. No consideration was yet given to personality traits or roles associated with sex. Thus, gender roles were not part of the picture. The primary goal of this era was to examine if (really, to establish that) men were intellectually superior to women. To accomplish this goal, scientists turned to the anatomy of the brain (Shields, 1975).

First, scientists focused on the size of the human brain. Because women's heads and brains are smaller than those of men, there seemed to be conclusive evidence that women were intellectually inferior. However, men were also taller and weighed more than women; when body size was taken into account, the evidence for sex differences in intelligence became less clear. If one computed a ratio of the weight of the brain to the weight of the body, women appeared to have relatively larger brains. If one computed the ratio of the surface area of the brain to the surface area of the body, men appeared to have relatively larger brains. Thus brain size alone could not settle the question of sex differences in intelligence.

Next, researchers turned to specific areas of the brain that could be responsible for higher levels of intellectual functioning. The frontal cortex was first thought to control higher levels of mental functioning, and men were observed to have larger frontal lobes than women. Then it appeared men did not have larger frontal lobes; instead, men had larger parietal lobes. Thus thinking shifted to the parietal lobe as the seat of intellectual functioning. All this research came under sharp methodological criticism because the scientists observing the anatomy of the brain were not blind to the sex associated with the particular brain; that is, the people evaluating the brain knew whether it belonged to a male or a female. This situation was ripe for the kinds of experimenter biases described earlier in the chapter. Obviously, scientists could have developed hypotheses based on what they had already observed to be true. If they found that one part of a brain was larger in men than women, then that part of the brain was assumed to hold the key to intellectual powers.

The period ended with the seminal work of *Sex and Personality* published by Lewis Terman and Catherine Cox Miles in 1936. They concluded there are no sex differences in intellect: "Intelligence tests, for example, have demonstrated for all time the falsity of the once widely prevalent belief that women as a class are appreciably or at all inferior to men in the major aspects of intellect" (p. 1).

TAKE HOME POINTS

- Initial research in the area of gender focused on trying to establish that men were smarter than women by examining the size of the brain.

- The research was unsuccessful. It was not clear that one could link brain size to intellect.

1936–1954: M/F as a Global Personality Trait

During this next period, researchers shifted their focus from sex differences alone to consider the notion of gender roles. The construct of masculinity-femininity, or M/F, was introduced during this period. Terman had concluded that the differences between men's and women's intelligence were small and possibly nonexistent. Instead, he argued that the real mental differences between men and women could be captured by measuring masculinity and femininity.

Researchers developed a 456-item instrument to measure masculinity-femininity. It was called the Attitude Interest Analysis Survey

(AIAS; Terman & Miles, 1936) to disguise the true purpose of the test. The AIAS was the first published M/F scale. The items chosen were based on statistical sex differences observed in elementary, junior high, and high school children. This meant that items on which the average female scored higher than the average male were labeled feminine, and items on which the average male scored higher than the average female were labeled masculine, regardless of the content of those items. The M/F scale was also bipolar, which meant that masculinity and femininity were viewed as opposite ends of a single continuum. The sum of the feminine items was subtracted from the sum of the masculine items to yield a total M/F score.

The instrument was composed of seven subject areas: (1) word association, (2) inkblot interpretation, (3) information, (4) emotional and ethical response, (5) interests (likes and dislikes), (6) admired persons and opinions, and (7) introversion-extroversion, which really measured superiority-subordination. Sample items from each subject area are shown in Table 2.5. Several of these subscales are quite interesting. The information scale was based on the assumption that men have greater knowledge than women about some areas of life, such as sports and politics, and women have greater knowledge about other areas of life, such as gardening and sewing. Thus giving a correct response to an item about which women are supposed to know more than men would be scored as feminine; conversely, giving a correct response to an item about which men are supposed to know more than women would be scored as masculine. For example, consider the first item on the information subscale shown in Table 2.5. Answering that a marigold is a flower would be scored as feminine, whereas answering that a marigold is a stone would be scored as masculine. The emotional and ethical response subscale was scored such that being feminine

TABLE 2.5 SAMPLE ITEMS FROM THE ATTITUDE INTEREST ANALYSIS SURVEY

Responses with a (+) are indicative of masculinity; responses with a (−) are indicative of femininity; responses with a 0 are neutral and not scored as either.

Word Association

Look at the word in capital letters, then look at the four words which follow it. Draw a line under the word that goes best or most naturally with the one in capitals; the word it tends most to make you think of.

1. POLE	barber (0)	cat (+)	North (−)	telephone (+)
2. DATE	appointment (−)	dance (+)	fruit (+)	history (+)

Inkblot Association

Here are some drawings, a little like inkblots. They are not pictures of anything in particular but might suggest almost anything to you, just as shapes in the clouds sometimes do. Beside each drawing four things are mentioned. Underline the one word that tells what the drawing makes you think of most.

1. bush (0)
   lady (+)
   shadow (+)
   mushroom (−)

2. flame (−)
   flower (+)
   snake (−)
   worm (−)

Information

In each sentence draw a line under the word that makes the sentence true.

1. Marigold is a kind of	fabric (+)	flower (−)	grain (−)	stone (+)
2. Tokyo is a city of	China (−)	India (−)	Japan (+)	Russia (0)
3. A loom is used for	cooking (+)	embroidering (+)	sewing (+)	weaving (−)
4. The number of players on a baseball team is	7 (−)	9 (+)	11 (−)	13 (0)

Emotional and Ethical Response

Below is a list of things that sometimes cause anger. After each thing mentioned draw a circle around VM, M, L, or N to show how much anger it causes you.

   VM means VERY MUCH; M means MUCH; L means A LITTLE; N means NONE.

1. Seeing people disfigure library books	VM (−)	M (−)	L (+)	N (+)
2. Seeing someone trying to discredit you with your employer	VM (+)	M (0)	L (+)	N (−)

Below is a list of things that sometimes cause disgust. After each thing mentioned draw a circle around VM, M, L, or N to indicate how much disgust it causes you.

   VM means VERY MUCH; M means MUCH; L means A LITTLE; N means NONE.

1. An unshaven man	VM (−)	M (−)	L (+)	N (+)
2. Gum chewing	VM (−)	M (−)	L (+)	N (+)

Below is a list of acts of various degrees of wickedness or badness. After each thing mentioned draw a circle around 3, 2, 1, or 0 to show how wicked or bad you think it is.

   3 means EXTREMELY WICKED; 2 means DECIDEDLY BAD; 1 means SOMEWHAT BAD; 0 means NOT REALLY BAD.

1. Using slang	3 (−)	2 (−)	1 (+)	0 (+)
2. Excessive drinking	3 (−)	2 (+)	1 (+)	0 (0)

TABLE 2.5   (CONTINUED)

Interests

For each occupation below, ask yourself: Would I like that work or not? If you would like it, draw a circle around L. If you would dislike it, draw a circle around D. If you would neither like nor dislike it, draw a circle around N. In deciding on your answer, think only of the kind of work. Don't consider the pay. Imagine that you have the ability to do the work, that you are the right age for it, and that it is equally open to men and women.

1. Forest ranger	L (+)	D (−)	N (0)
2. Florist	L (−)	D (+)	N (+)

Personalities and Opinion

Below is a list of famous characters. After each name draw a circle around L, D, or N to indicate whether you like that character.

L means LIKE; D means DISLIKE; N means NEITHER LIKE NOR DISLIKE.

1. Daniel Boone	L (+)	D (−)	N (−)
2. Christopher Columbus	L (−)	D (+)	N (+)
3. Florence Nightingale	L (−)	D (+)	N (+)

Read each statement and consider whether it is mostly true or mostly false. If it is mostly TRUE, draw a circle around T. If it is mostly FALSE, draw a circle around F.

1. The world was created in 6 days of 24 hours each.	T (+)	F (0)
2. Love "at first sight" is usually the truest love.	T (+)	F (−)

Introvertive Response

Answer each question as truthfully as you can by drawing a line under YES or NO.

1. Did you ever have imaginary companions?	YES (−)	NO (+)
2. Do you worry much over possible misfortunes?	YES (−)	NO (+)
3. As a child were you extremely disobedient?	YES (+)	NO (−)
4. Do people ever say that you talk too much?	YES (+)	NO (−)

Source: Terman and Miles (1936).

meant getting angry when seeing others treated unfairly and being masculine meant getting angry when being disturbed at work.

There were no assumptions about the basis of these sex differences. Terman and Miles (1936) left the cause of the sex differences—biological, psychological, or cultural—unspecified.

A few years later, Hathaway and McKinley (1940) developed the Minnesota Multiphasic Personality Inventory (MMPI). It eventually included an M/F scale that consisted of items reflecting altruism, emotional sensitivity, sexual preference, liking certain occupations, and gender identity questions. The most notable feature

in the development of this scale is that the femininity items were validated on 13 homosexuals. Homosexual men were compared to heterosexual male soldiers; at that time, heterosexual male soldiers epitomized masculinity and homosexual men were considered feminine. In fact, feminine traits were considered to be a predisposing factor to homosexuality in men (Terman & Miles, 1936). Women were not even involved in research to evaluate femininity. Thus we can see at least two major problems with this instrument: First, women were not involved in the conceptualization of the female gender role; second, only 13 homosexual men were involved in the study, which is hardly sufficient to validate an instrument even if they had been the appropriate population.

Some researchers became concerned about the self-report methodology used to assess M/F. The purpose of the tests might have been obvious, which could lead men and women to give socially desirable rather than truthful responses. The concern focused on demand characteristics. Thus several projective tests of M/F were developed, including one by Franck and Rosen (1949). They developed a test that consisted of incomplete drawings, like the stimuli shown in the first column of Figure 2.5. Franck and Rosen began with 60 stimuli, asked men and women to complete the drawings, and found sex differences in the way that 36 of the

60 were completed. These 36 stimuli then comprised the test. How did men and women differ in their drawings? Men were found to be more likely to close off the stimuli, make sharper edges, include angles, and focus on unifying objects rather than keeping them separate. Women were found to leave a stimulus open, to make round or blunt edges, and to make lines that pointed inward. The content of the objects men and women drew also was found to differ: Men drew nude women, skyscrapers, and dynamic objects, whereas women drew animals, flowers, houses, and static objects.

Interestingly, Franck and Rosen (1949) did not conclude that a male and a female who receive the same score on the test are the same in terms of masculinity and femininity. In fact, they argued that the drawings of a male who receives a feminine score are quite bizarre and very different from the drawings of a female who receives a feminine score. They applied the same logic to a female who receives a masculine score. If the instrument does not measure psychological masculinity and femininity among both men and women, we have to wonder about the purpose of the test. Franck and Rosen suggested their instrument measures acceptance of one's gender role rather than the degree of masculinity and femininity. Males who scored masculine and females who scored feminine were considered to have accepted their gender roles.

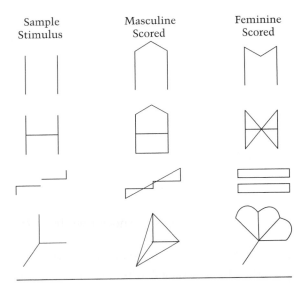

| Sample Stimulus | Masculine Scored | Feminine Scored |

FIGURE 2.5   Examples of the kinds of incomplete drawings that appeared on Franck and Rosen's (1949) projective test of masculinity/femininity. How the drawings were completed was taken as an indication of masculinity or femininity. The second column represents masculine ways of completing the drawings and the third column represents feminine ways of completing the drawings.

Source: Adapted from Franck and Rosen (1949).

TAKE HOME POINTS

- During this period, the concept of masculinity-femininity was introduced. However, it was defined merely by sex differences.

- Because women were rarely included in research, one scale of femininity, from the MMPI, was validated on homosexual men. Homosexuality was thought to be equivalent to femininity.

- Projective tests of masculinity-femininity were developed to reduce demand characteristics. However, these tests were flawed in that sex differences in drawings were taken to be evidence of masculinity and femininity.
- All the M/F scales developed during this period suffered from a number of conceptual weaknesses:

  —The tests did not distinguish between more or less masculine people, nor did they distinguish between more or less feminine people.
  —They merely distinguished men from women, a distinction that did not need to be made.
  —Any item that revealed sex differences was taken as evidence of masculinity and femininity, regardless of its relevance to these constructs (e.g., thinking Tokyo is a city in India is an indicator of femininity).
  —All the scales were bipolar, such that masculinity represented one end and femininity represented the other.
  —Gay men were equated with feminine women.

- There seemed to be some confusion among masculinity, femininity, and sexual orientation. An assumption at the time was that psychologically healthy men were masculine and psychologically healthy women were feminine.

1954–1982: Sex Typing and Androgyny

This period was marked by Eleanor Maccoby's (1966) publication of *The Development of Sex Differences*, which reviewed important theories of sex typing, that is, how boys and girls developed sex-appropriate preferences, personality traits, and behaviors. Many of these theories are reviewed in detail in Chapter 5.

In addition, in 1973, Anne Constantinople published a major critique of the existing M/F instruments. She questioned the use of sex differences as the basis for defining masculinity and femininity; she also questioned whether masculinity-femininity was really a unidimensional construct that could be captured by a single bipolar scale. The latter assumption, in particular, was addressed during this period by the publication of instruments that distinguished masculinity and femininity as independent constructs.

Instrumental Versus Expressive Distinction. A distinction brought to the study of gender roles that helped conceptualize masculinity and femininity as separate dimensions was the distinction between an instrumental and an expressive orientation. In 1955, Parsons, a sociologist, and Bales, a social psychologist, distinguished between instrumental or goal-oriented behavior and expressive or emotional behavior in their studies of male group interactions. The instrumental leader focuses on getting the job done and the expressive leader focuses on maintaining group harmony.

Parsons and Bales (1955) extended the instrumental/expressive distinction to gender. They saw a relation between superior power and instrumentality and a relation between inferior power and expressivity. They believed the distinction between the husband role and the wife role was both an instrumental/expressive distinction as well as a superior/inferior power distinction. The instrumental orientation became linked to the male gender role and the expressive orientation became linked to the female gender role.

Two instruments were developed during this period that linked the instrumental versus expressive orientation to gender role. In 1974, Sandra Bem published the Bem Sex Role Inventory (BSRI) and Spence, Helmreich, and Stapp published the Personal Attributes Questionnaire (PAQ). The BSRI and the PAQ are still the most commonly used inventories to measure masculinity and femininity today. The innovative feature of both instruments is that masculinity and femininity are conceptualized as two independent dimensions rather than a single bipolar scale; thus a person receives a masculinity score and a femininity score. Masculinity and femininity are no longer viewed as opposites.

The BSRI (Bem, 1974) was developed by having undergraduates rate how desirable it is for a man and a woman to possess each of 400 attributes. Items that students rated as more desirable for a male to possess were indicators of masculinity, and items that students rated as more desirable for a female were indicators of femininity. Items were not based on respondents' views of how likely men and women are to have these traits but on their views of how *desirable* it is for men and women to have the traits. The final BSRI consisted of 60 items: 20 masculine, 20 feminine, and 20 neutral items. The neutral items are included in the instrument to disguise the purpose of the scale.

In contrast to the BSRI, the PAQ (Spence et al., 1974) was developed by focusing on the perception of how *likely* men and women are to possess certain traits. College students were asked to rate the typical adult male and female, the typical college male and female, and the ideal male and female. The items on this instrument are shown in the top half of Table 2.6. The masculinity scale included items that students viewed as more characteristic of men than women but also as ideal for both men and women to possess. "Independence" was a masculinity item; the typical college male was viewed as more independent than the typical college female, but independence was perceived as equally desirable in both men and women. The femininity scale included items that were more characteristic of women than men but viewed as ideal in both women and men. "Understanding of others" was a femininity item; the typical college female was rated as more understanding of others than the typical college male, but respondents viewed being understanding of others as a socially desirable trait for both women and men. Spence and colleagues (1974) also created a third scale, called the masculinity-femininity scale. These were items on which college students believed the typical college male and the typical college female differed, but they also were items that students viewed as socially desirable for one sex to

TABLE 2.6 PERSONAL ATTRIBUTES QUESTIONNAIRE

Masculinity (M+)	Femininity (F+)	Masculinity-Femininity (M/F)
Independent	Emotional	Aggressive
Active	Able to devote self to others	Dominant
Competitive	Gentle	Excitable in major crisis
Can make decisions	Helpful to others	Worldly (vs. home-oriented)
Never gives up	Kind	Indifferent to others' approval
Self-confident	Aware of others' feelings	Feelings not easily hurt
Feels superior	Understanding of others	Never cries
Stands up well under pressure	Warm in relations to others	Little need for security

Source: Spence, Helmreich, and Stapp (1974).

Extension of Personal Attributes Questionnaire	
Unmitigated Agency (M–)	
Arrogant	Dictatorial
Boastful	Cynical
Egotistical	Looks out for self
Greedy	Hostile

Source: Spence, Helmreich, and Holahan (1979).

possess but not the other. The masculinity-femininity subscale was a bipolar scale in which one end represented masculinity and the other femininity; for example, the typical college male was viewed as worldly, whereas the typical college female was viewed as home oriented. In addition, respondents viewed it as more socially desirable for men than women to be worldly and more socially desirable for women than men to be home-oriented.

Like the BSRI, the items on the masculinity scale were thought to reflect an instrumental or agentic orientation, and the items on the femininity scale were thought to reflect an expressive or communal orientation. Scores on the masculinity and femininity scales are generally uncorrelated, reflecting the fact that they are two independent dimensions. Because the meaning of the bipolar masculinity-femininity scale was, and still is, unclear, it is seldom included in research. The BSRI and the PAQ masculinity scales are highly correlated, as are the femininity scales.

When these scales were developed, consistent sex differences appeared. Men scored higher than women on the masculinity scales, and women scored higher than men on the femininity scales. But the scales were developed 30 years ago. Do sex differences still appear today? There is some evidence for the current validity of the BSRI in that people still have different views of what is desirable in a woman and in a man (Holt & Ellis, 1998), although the differences are stronger among some subgroups of Americans (e.g., European American men in the Northeast, African American men in the South) than others (e.g., European American woman in the Northeast; Konrad & Harris, 2002). Research that has examined masculinity and femininity scores from the 1970s to the late 1990s shows there are still consistent sex differences on both scales (Lueptow, Garovich-Szabo, & Lueptow, 2001; Spence & Buckner, 2000).

Some evidence indicates that women's masculinity scores have increased over time, however, which has reduced the sex difference in masculinity (Spence & Buckner, 2000). In fact, people view masculine characteristics as more desirable in women today than they did in 1972 (Auster & Ohm, 2000). People's views of what is desirable in men have not changed. These findings reflect the greater changes in the female than the male gender role over the past several decades. There has been more encouragement for women to become agentic than for men to become communal.

Androgyny.   One outgrowth of these two M/F inventories (the BSRI and the PAQ) was the conceptualization of and research on **androgyny**. Androgyny emerged from the operationalization of masculinity and femininity as unipolar, independent dimensions. The androgynous person was someone who displayed both masculine and feminine traits. Androgyny was first measured with the BSRI by subtracting the masculinity score from the femininity score. Positive difference scores reflected femininity, and negative difference scores reflected masculinity. Scores near zero reflected androgyny, signifying that people had a relatively equal amount of both traits. A male who scored masculine and a female who scored feminine were referred to as **sex-typed**. A masculine female and a feminine male were referred to as **cross-sex-typed**. One problem with this measurement of androgyny is that the score did not distinguish between people who endorsed many masculine and feminine qualities from people who endorsed only a few masculine and feminine qualities. Someone who endorsed 10 masculine and 10 feminine traits received the same score (0) as someone who endorsed 2 masculine and 2 feminine traits; both were viewed as androgynous.

Spence and colleagues (1974) had an alternative system for scoring androgyny. They

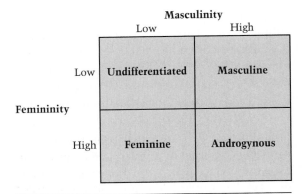

Masculinity

	Low	High
Low	Undifferentiated	Masculine
High	Feminine	Androgynous

Femininity

FIGURE 2.6   This is a sex-typing typology based on people's scores on masculinity and femininity.

divided scores on the masculinity and femininity scales in half to create the four groups shown in Figure 2.6. Someone who possessed a high number of masculine features and a low number of feminine features was designated masculine; someone who possessed a high number of feminine and a low number of masculine features was designated feminine. These people were referred to as sex-typed if their sex corresponded to their gender role. The androgynous person was someone who possessed a high number of both masculine and feminine features. A person who had few masculine or feminine traits was referred to as undifferentiated. To this day, most researchers still do not know the meaning of this last category, yet they often create these four categories when using either the PAQ or BSRI.

Androgyny was put forth by Bem (1974, 1975) as an ideal: The androgynous person was one who embodied the socially desirable features of both masculinity and femininity. It was no longer believed the most psychologically healthy people were masculine men and feminine women; instead, the healthiest people were thought to be those who possessed both attributes. Androgynous people were supposed to have the best of both worlds and to demonstrate the greatest behavioral flexibility and the best

psychological adjustment. Unfortunately, subsequent research revealed that the masculinity scale alone predicts behavioral flexibility and psychological adjustment as well as, and sometimes better than, the androgyny score (e.g., Woo & Oei, 2006). In hindsight, this finding is not so surprising because the traits included on the BSRI and PAQ masculinity scales are those valued by American society. Bem actually conceptualized androgyny to be much more than the sum of masculine and feminine traits. Androgyny had implications for how one thought about the world. This is elaborated on in Chapter 5 in the discussion of gender-schema theory.

Undesirable Aspects of Masculinity and Femininity.   One criticism of the PAQ and of the BSRI is that the vast majority of attributes are socially desirable. In 1979, Spence, Helmreich, and Holahan set out to develop scales that paralleled the original M and F scales in content but differed in social desirability. Conceptually, the masculinity scale, which they referred to as M+, was thought to reflect a positive instrumental or agentic orientation, whereas the femininity scale, which they referred to as F+, was thought to reflect a positive expressive or communal orientation. Spence and colleagues were looking to develop scales that measured socially undesirable aspects of agentic and communal orientations.

They turned to the work of David Bakan (1966), who richly developed the ideas of agency and communion. Bakan argued there are two principles of human existence: an agentic one that focuses on the self and separation, and a communal one that focuses on others and connection. Bakan also suggested that agency is the male principle and communion the female. Bakan argued that it is important for agency to be mitigated by communion and that **unmitigated agency** would be destructive to the self and society. Unmitigated agency reflected a focus on the self to the neglect of others. Drawing on this work, Spence and colleagues (1979) developed a negative masculinity scale that reflected unmitigated agency; the scale included in the Extension of the Personal Attributes Questionnaire (EPAQ) is shown in the bottom of Table 2.6.

The unmitigated agency scale is agentic like the earlier positive masculinity scale, more common in men than women, and socially undesirable in both men and women. Most important, it conceptually reflects the construct of unmitigated agency: a focus on the self to the exclusion of others. It includes a hostile attitude toward others and self-absorption. The scale is positively correlated with the M+ scale, reflecting the focus on the self, and negatively correlated with the F+ scale, reflecting the absence of a focus on others (Helgeson & Fritz, 1999).

Spence and colleagues (1979) also wanted to capture socially undesirable aspects of the female gender role. Turning to Bakan (1966) again, they noted that communion also ought

to be mitigated by agency. Although Bakan never used the term **unmitigated communion**, he noted it would be unhealthy to focus on others to the exclusion of the self. Spence and colleagues had more difficulty coming up with traits that conceptually reflected unmitigated communion. They developed two negative femininity scales, but neither conceptually captured the construct of unmitigated communion (Spence et al., 1979). Later, I developed an unmitigated communion scale (Helgeson, 1993; Helgeson & Fritz, 1998), shown in Table 2.7. The unmitigated communion scale has two components: overinvolvement with others and neglect of the self. It is positively correlated with F+, reflecting the focus on others, and negatively correlated with M+, reflecting the absence of a focus on the self (Helgeson & Fritz, 1999).

Both unmitigated communion and unmitigated agency have been shown to be important constructs in the area of gender and health and account for a number of sex differences in health. This research is discussed in later chapters of the book that focus on health.

TABLE 2.7 UNMITIGATED COMMUNION SCALE

Instructions: Using the scale below, place a number in the blank beside each statement that indicates the extent to which you agree or disagree. Think of the people close to you—friends or family—in responding to each statement.

Strongly Disagree	Slightly Disagree	Neither Agree nor Disagree	Slightly Agree	Strongly Agree
1	2	3	4	5

1. I always place the needs of others above my own.
2. I never find myself getting overly involved in others' problems.*
3. For me to be happy, I need others to be happy.
4. I worry about how other people get along without me when I am not there.
5. I have no trouble getting to sleep at night when other people are upset.*
6. It is impossible for me to satisfy my own needs when they interfere with the needs of others.
7. I can't say no when someone asks me for help.
8. Even when exhausted, I will always help other people.
9. I often worry about others' problems.

Items are reverse scored.
Source: Helgeson and Fritz (1998).

TAKE HOME POINTS

- The period between 1954 and 1982 brought with it major innovations in the conceptualization and measurement of gender roles.

- The distinction between the instrumental and expressive orientation was made and then linked to gender. This led to the development of two instruments, the PAQ and the BSRI, which are the most widely used instruments to measure psychological masculinity and femininity today.

- These two instruments differed from previous instruments in that masculinity and femininity were established as two independent dimensions rather than bipolar ends of a single continuum.

- The use of independent M/F scales led to the development of the androgyny construct. Initially, androgyny was captured by similar scores on masculinity and femininity and later by high scores on masculinity and femininity.

- The most recent advance during this period was the idea that there are socially undesirable aspects of gender roles that ought to be considered and measured. This led to the concepts of unmitigated agency and unmitigated communion.

1982–Present: Gender as a Social Category

Over the past two and a half decades, research on sex and gender has proliferated. There have been two recent trends. The first has been to view gender as a multifaceted or multidimensional construct, meaning that the two-dimensional view of masculinity and femininity is not sufficient to capture gender roles. The development of the unmitigated agency and unmitigated communion scales was a first step in this direction. The second research direction has been to emphasize the social context in which gender occurs. The research on gender diagnosticity addresses this issue. Emphasis on the social context led to research on gender-role constraints, the difficulties people face due to the limits a society places on gender-role-appropriate behavior. I examine each of these research directions.

Gender Role as Multifaceted. In 1985, Spence and Sawin called for the renaming of the PAQ masculinity and femininity scales. They stated that these scales reflect only one aspect of masculinity and femininity—instrumentality or agency and expressiveness or communion—and that the names of the scales should reflect these aspects. They argued that masculinity and femininity are multidimensional constructs that cannot be captured by a single trait instrument. See Sidebar 2.1 for another view of the multidimensional nature of gender.

Sidebar 2.1: *Multiple Masculinities*

Robert Connell argues that there are multiple versions of masculinity—a masculinity for men of color, a masculinity for gay men, a masculinity for working-class men. The dominant form of masculinity, however, is aggressive, not emotional, heterosexual, and *not* feminine. This is referred to as hegemonic masculinity (Connell, 1987; Connell & Messerschmidt, 2005). The main goal of hegemonic masculinity is to legitimize male dominance or patriarchy. Hegemonic masculinity may not be the most common masculinity, but it is still depicted as the ideal masculinity in our culture. Evidence of hegemonic masculinity can be found among white-collar crime involving men, the media's representation of men in sports, war, male risk-taking behavior, and the gender-based hierarchy of most organizations.

What else is involved in masculinity and femininity besides the traits that appear on the BSRI and the PAQ? Researchers began to realize that lay conceptions of masculinity and femininity included more diverse content, such as physical characteristics and role behaviors, in addition to personality traits. In 1994, I adopted a different approach to identify the content of masculinity and femininity (Helgeson, 1994b). Rather than viewing masculinity and femininity as clear-cut categories composed of a set of necessary and sufficient features, I viewed them as fuzzy categories, or prototypes. A **prototype** is an abstract set of features commonly associated with a category, such that features vary in their representativeness of the category.

Before I explain the prototypes of masculinity and femininity, let's take an example of a prototype of another category. Take the category chair. What are some features of this category? One feature is "seat" or "something you sit on." This is a central feature of the category chair. If you can't sit on it, can it be a chair? However, the feature "seat" is not sufficient to define the category chair because you can sit on a sofa or on the floor. Other features of the category chair include arms, legs, and a back. These features are less central to the category chair than seat because a chair, for example, a beanbag chair, can exist without legs or arms. Applying the prototype approach to the categories of masculinity and femininity would provide us with the features that constitute these categories as well as indicators of how central or peripheral the features are to the categories.

In a prototype study, 223 college students and 182 of their parents were asked to describe a masculine man, a masculine woman, a feminine man, or a feminine woman (Helgeson, 1994b). Slightly less than half of the sample was Caucasian; thus the sample was diverse in terms of age as well as ethnicity. The features of

masculinity and femininity fell into one of three categories: personality traits, interests, or physical appearance. The average person identified 5 personality traits, 2 interests, and 3 physical appearance features for each target. In addition, many of the identified personality traits were reflected on conventional M/F inventories, suggesting that lay conceptions of M/F do fit the scientific literature. For example, feminine items identified by at least 10% of the respondents and included on the PAQ are *emotional, passive, not aggressive, cries easily,* and *helpful. Likes kids, soft-spoken,* and *shy* are feminine items that appear on the BSRI. The masculine items *aggressive, competitive,* and *dominant* are included on both the PAQ and the BSRI; *adventurous, ambitious, strong convictions,* and *interested in fitness and sports* are included on the BSRI; *self-confident* is on the PAQ; and *hostile, arrogant,* and *selfish* are on the unmitigated agency scale of the EPAQ. Let's take a closer look at the prototypes of masculinity and femininity.

Features unique to the masculine male were socially desirable (e.g., well dressed), but features unique to the masculine female were socially undesirable (e.g., not caring, ugly). Physical appearance features were named more often in response to a masculine female than a masculine male. What does this mean? When we think of a masculine woman rather than a masculine man, we especially focus on physical appearance. Among the masculine personality traits identified, the ones attributed to a female were negative (aggressive, unsocial, uncaring, hostile). The masculine female was viewed more negatively all around than the masculine male. The traits ascribed to the masculine female were more indicative of unmitigated agency than agency.

With a feminine target, physical appearance features came to mind when thinking of a female more than a male. This is similar to the finding for the masculine targets. Thus physical appearance comes more to mind when thinking of a female than a male, regardless of whether the target is masculine or feminine. Feminine physical appearance features included wears a dress, wears frills, wears heels, wears makeup, and has long hair. Some personality features were distinct to the feminine male; some were positive (e.g., talkative, emotional, creative) and some negative (e.g., insecure, weak).

One limitation of most of this research is that conceptions of masculinity and femininity are limited to the people who have been studied: typically, White middle-class American men and women. It would be interesting to know more about conceptions of masculinity and femininity across people of different races, classes, religions, and more diverse age groups, such as children and the elderly. Try Do Gender 2.2 to see if you can broaden your understanding of people's views of masculinity and femininity.

The Social Context Surrounding Gender.
An emphasis during this period, and today, is on how the social context influences the nature of gender. Social psychologists, in particular Kay Deaux and Brenda Major (1987), have examined gender as a social category by emphasizing the situational forces that influence whether sex differences in behavior are observed. Their model of sex differences is discussed in more detail in Chapter 5. Another approach has been the movement by the **social constructionists**, who argue that gender does not reside inside a person but resides in our interactions with people (Bohan, 1997; Tavris, 1999). According to the constructionist viewpoint, there is no essence to masculinity and femininity; instead, masculinity and femininity are categories constructed by society (Bohan, 1997; Tavris, 1999). Masculinity and femininity reside in the eyes of the perceiver.

Social constructionists distinguish themselves from the **essentialists**, who view gender

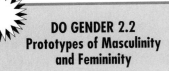

DO GENDER 2.2
Prototypes of Masculinity and Femininity

Construct your own prototypes of masculinity and femininity by asking 20 people, 10 men and 10 women, to describe a masculine and a feminine person and consider the following questions in their descriptions.

1. What does a masculine (feminine) man (woman) look like?

2. What personality traits does a masculine (feminine) man (woman) possess?

3. How does a masculine (feminine) man (woman) behave?

4. What is a masculine (feminine) man (woman) interested in?

5. What does a masculine (feminine) man (woman) think about?

List all the features mentioned, and construct a frequency distribution for each feature. Identify the most frequently named features and indicate what percentage of your respondents named each feature.

To make your study more interesting, focus on a specific group of people you think are underrepresented in this research. You might choose children, the elderly, people of a minority race such as Asian Americans, Hispanic Americans, or African Americans, or people of a unique occupation. Then compare the responses you receive to those described in the text. Use only one target sex, male or female, so you can compare the responses you receive to those in the text.

as an attribute of a person. Constructionists criticize the essentialist viewpoint for leading to false universals. Essentialists compare men and women and make conclusions about differences in general. Social constructionists ask, "Which men? Which women?," emphasizing the diversity of human experience (Bohan, 1997). Another concern that constructionists raise is the assigning of qualities associated with women to the female sex rather than to the context in which women find themselves (Bohan, 1997). For example, should a lack of assertiveness be ascribed to the female sex or to the subordinate role that characterizes women? Constructionists are concerned that qualities resulting from societal forces, such as oppression, are being ascribed to the female gender. They also are concerned that recent essentialists, such as Carol Gilligan, are encouraging women to value qualities that emerge from oppression. Gilligan applauds women's different, but equally important, way of viewing morality: Women focus on relationships. According to Bohan (1997), it is a very effective strategy for the oppressor to encourage the oppressed to value their qualities. The problem in the area of gender is that society does not value the qualities associated with women to the extent that society values the qualities associated with men.

Constructionists are concerned that the experiences women have are being attributed to the women themselves rather than society. As an example, Bohan (1997) makes the point that women today take self-defense classes to prepare themselves for the violence of society. This strategy focuses on women rather than society as the problem. It is easier to change individuals than it is to change social institutions.

There is support for the social constructionist viewpoint. The studies reviewed in Chapter 4 that compare men and women in a number of domains may appear to take an essentialist viewpoint, but the research results in a constructionist conclusion. Most of the reviews of sex comparisons lead to the conclusion that the situation, the context, has a large influence on the size of any differences that appear between men and women.

In conclusion, social constructionists emphasize the diversity of human experience and view gender as the effect of an interaction rather than the cause of the interaction. We, the perceivers, create gender by our expectations, by our behavior, and by what we decide to include in this category.

Gender Diagnosticity.   A newer approach to the study of gender roles takes into consideration both of the issues raised in this section: the multifaceted view of gender and the social context surrounding gender. This approach to the measurement of gender-related individual difference variables is known as **gender diagnosticity** (GD; Lippa & Connelly, 1990). GD estimates the probability that a person is male or female given a set of gender-related indicators (e.g., wears a dress, likes football). Items that discriminate men from women are assigned weights, which depend on the magnitude of the discrimination. GD is a weighted combination of the indicators that discriminate men from women. Indicators may include occupational preferences, personality characteristics, attitudes, cognitive abilities, and leisure interests. Thus GD can be applied to a broad range of gender-related phenomena and is multidimensional.

One advantage of GD over traditional measures of M/F is that it is tailored to the specific population; in one group of people, being achievement oriented may be a construct that discriminates between the sexes, but in another group of people, such as college students, this variable may not discriminate between men and women very well. Because GD is not a static category, it does not "reify" the constructs of masculinity and femininity (Lippa, 1991, 1995). Thus GD pays special attention to the social context. GD also can change over time as gender-related preferences change. For example, wearing earrings used to be diagnostic of the female sex, but not so today; similarly, wanting to be a medical doctor is no longer diagnostic of sex because similar numbers of men and women attend medical school. GD also can be used to examine the extent to which different people distinguish males and females. In a study of adolescents, researchers found that males and females between the ages of 12 and 14 showed the greatest differentiation between the sexes (Loehlin et al., 2005). They also found that GD measures were highly similar across adults in the United States, Australia, and Sweden. It would be interesting to apply this approach to Eastern cultures. Lippa has shown that GD is more strongly related than traditional M/F scores (defined by the PAQ and BSRI) to gender-related behaviors, such as smiling, spatial skills, and SAT scores (Lippa, 1991; Lippa & Connelly, 1990). The major advantage of the GD measure is that it can change with time and place so that new measures of masculinity and femininity do not have to be continually reinvented.

Gender-Role Strain. By viewing gender as a social category, researchers paid greater attention to the influence of society on the nature of gender roles. One outgrowth of this recognition was research on **gender-role strain**, a phenomenon that occurs when gender-role expectations have negative consequences for the individual. Gender-role strain is likely to occur when gender-role expectations conflict with naturally occurring tendencies or personal desires. An uncoordinated male or an athletic female may experience gender-role strain in physical education classes. A male who wants to pursue dance or a woman who does not want to have children also may suffer some gender-role strain.

I asked the undergraduates in my Psychology of Gender class to identify sources of gender-role strain, that is, situations in which

what they wanted to do conflicted with what they were expected to do based on their sex. The women identified three areas of conflict. First, they wanted to be assertive and independent but felt they were expected to be dependent, especially on men. Second, some women said they were expected to be nurturant and to "mother" but were not interested in children. Third, women expressed that they were held to a double standard by society, especially their parents and grandparents: They were expected to get an education but not at the expense of finding a good man to marry.

The men identified four areas of strain. First, some men expressed the desire to talk about inner feelings and problems but felt this conflicted with the male image, especially the fraternity male. Second, some men felt strain because they were not athletic. Third, some men said they felt conflicted during sports when they were expected to be aggressive and competitive but also wanted to be a "good sport." Fourth, men expressed displeasure over the idea that they were expected to be the dominant force in relationships with women, the one to initiate activities and the one to take charge; they would prefer a more equal relationship.

Obviously, these ideas are only a few examples of gender-role strain—and certainly not from a representative sample. The men and women who gave these examples were enrolled in a Psychology of Gender course. How might their ideas differ from those of other college students? Examine sources of gender-role strain at your college in Do Gender 2.3.

Joseph Pleck (1995) describes two theories of gender-role strain. **Self-role discrepancy theory** suggests that strain arises when you fail to live up to the gender role society has constructed. This describes the man who is not athletic, the man who is unemployed, the woman who is not attractive, and the woman who does not have children. **Socialized dysfunctional characteristic**

DO GENDER 2.3
Gender-Role Strain

Interview 10 men and 10 women at your college. Identify common sources of gender-role strain.

1. Think about how men (women) are expected to behave. How does your behavior differ from how men (women) are expected to behave?

2. Think about how men (women) are expected to look. How does your appearance differ from how men (women) are expected to look?

3. Think about the personality characteristics that men (women) are expected to have. How does your personality differ from the personality men (women) are expected to have?

4. Think about the things that are supposed to interest men (women). How do your interests differ from the interests that men (women) are expected to have?

5. Think about the ways in which your behavior matches the behavior that society expects of men (women). Do you feel any of these behaviors are harmful?

6. Think about the ways in which your physical appearance matches the way society expects men (women) to look. Do you feel any of these expectations are harmful?

7. Think about the ways in which your personality matches the personality society expects men (women) to have. Do you feel any of these personality traits are harmful?

8. Think about the interests you have that correspond to the interests society expects men (women) to have. Do you feel it is harmful to have any of these interests?

theory states that strain arises because the gender roles that society instills contain inherently dysfunctional personality characteristics. For example, the male gender role includes the inhibition of emotional expression, which is not healthy; similarly, the female gender role includes dependency, which also may not be adaptive. The first four questions in Do Gender 2.3 assess self-role discrepancies, and the last four questions assess socialized dysfunctional characteristics.

Male Gender-Role Strain.   The concept of gender-role strain has largely been applied to men. The ideas were inspired by popular books on men that appeared in the 1970s and the 1980s, such as Goldberg's (1976) *The Hazards of Being Male*, Nichols's (1975) *Men's Liberation: A New Definition of Masculinity*, Tolson's (1977) *The Limits of Masculinity*, and Naifeh and Smith's (1984) *Why Can't Men Open Up?* These books, based largely on anecdotal evidence collected by men interviewing men, outline how some of the features of the male gender role limit men's relationships and are potentially harmful to men's health. These books largely adopt Pleck's (1995) socialized dysfunctional characteristic theory. Collectively, they identified a number of sources of gender-role strain among men:

1. Homophobia, the fear of homosexuality or being considered a homosexual, limited men's abilities to connect with other men.

2. Competitiveness limited men's relationships with other men by keeping them from revealing vulnerabilities.

3. Emotional inhibition limited men's relationships with both men and women by keeping them from expressing their feelings.

4. Physical strength kept men from admitting pain or seeking help for physical problems.

5. An achievement orientation made men goal oriented at the expense of considering or enjoying the process to reach the goal.

6. Dominance and aggression harmed men's relationships with men and women and with society as a whole.

7. Independence and self-reliance kept men from asking for needed help.

As you can see, each of these aspects of male gender-role strain has implications for men's relationships and men's health, the two emphases of this text. Do the sources of gender-role strain identified by the men you interviewed in Do Gender 2.3 fit into these seven categories?

A variety of instruments measure the kinds of male gender-role strain just described, such as the Masculine Gender Role Stress Scale (Eisler & Skidmore, 1987) and the Gender-Role Conflict Scale (O'Neil et al., 1986). Each instrument has a number of subscales reflecting the different sources of strains. A common subscale is inhibiting emotions, signifying that the inability to express emotions is one of the most prominent sources of strain for men. The achievement orientation and the repercussions that follow when a man fails to achieve also are captured in each of the scales. Concerns with physical strength and elements of homophobia appear on some of the scales. Scores on these instruments have been associated with poor mental and physical health (McCreary et al., 1996; Monk & Ricciardelli, 2003).

Another way to view gender-role strain is to examine the prescriptions that society has for the male gender role. Pleck, Sonenstein, and Ku (1993) argued that society rather than biology is responsible for much of men's behavior. This represents a social constructionist perspective. They created a masculine gender-role ideology scale to represent the extent to which men endorse society's prescriptions for the male gender role. Whereas the PAQ and BSRI masculinity scales measure whether one possesses culturally defined masculine traits, masculine gender-role ideology measures whether one believes the self *should* have masculine traits. The scale includes the ideas that men are always ready to have sex, that men should not have to do housework, that men deserve respect, that men should not self-disclose, that men should be physically tough, and that men should not act like women. In a 1988 national survey of 1,880 adolescent males ages 15 to 19, Pleck and colleagues (1993) linked masculine ideology to a variety of problem behaviors, including difficulties with school, substance abuse, sexual activity, and delinquency. One limitation of this study is that the data were correlational; thus we do not know if masculine ideology led to the problem behavior or the problem behavior led to masculine ideology.

Part of the social constructionist view of gender is that different social forces affect different groups of men—not only men in different cultures, but also men of different age groups and men of different racial backgrounds. Thus the nature of gender-role strain will differ. One ethnic group in which gender-role strain has been studied is the African American community. African American men face a dilemma because in the United States the male gender role is associated with high power and high status, but the African American race is associated with a lack of power and low status. American culture does not provide African American men with legitimate pathways to validate their masculinity. Thus gender-role strain arises among African American men in part due to self-role discrepancy theory, the idea that African American men are not given the opportunity to achieve the male gender-role ideal as articulated by American culture. The central features of the masculine gender role are achievement and success; racism and poverty make it difficult for African American men to be economically successful, and they are more likely to be unemployed and are less educated than Caucasian men. Staples (1978) suggests that African American men's lack of opportunity to pursue legitimate pathways to masculinity leads them to resort to other avenues, in particular, violence.

This issue was depicted in a scene from the 1991 movie *Grand Canyon*. The car of a White man, Kevin Kline, breaks down on the way home from a Lakers game in Los Angeles. No sooner has Kline called a towing company than he is accosted by several young African American men. As the men are about to rob Kline, Danny Glover (another African American man) shows up in a tow truck. Glover tries to talk the leader of the African American men into doing him a "favor" and letting the two of them (Glover and Kline) go on their way. The leader grants the favor but only after getting Glover to admit he was asking for a "favor" rather than making a demand, not out of respect for the man but because he had a gun. The African American leader says, "No gun, no respect—that's why I always got the gun." The threat of violence is one way to get respect.

An avenue that African American men are encouraged to pursue to validate masculinity is athletics; this has been referred to as the "manhood hustle" (Doyle, 1995). A focus on athletics can be healthy, but African American men may neglect their education to spend time on athletics. The reality is that very few African American men, or men in general, will be able to make a living as successful athletes. African American men also may face gender-role strain when the norms for the male gender-role clash with the norms for African American culture. The male role in our society emphasizes "doing, competing, and achieving," whereas the African American role emphasizes "feeling and cooperation" (Harris & Majors, 1993).

One study explored whether African American and Caucasian men face different sources of gender-role strain. Harris, Torres, and Allender (1994) identified 30 messages that American culture provides to men about how they should behave. White men and African American men between the ages of 18 and 74 were asked how much influence each message had on them. More African American men said the message to be a "warrior" had been influential; the warrior message involves identifying with war heroes and risking one's life to prove oneself. More Caucasian men said the message to be "stoic" (i.e., ignore pain, not admit weakness) and the message to be "self-reliant" (i.e., asking for help implies weakness) were influential. These findings for stoicism support the idea that Caucasian men are less likely than African American men to emphasize feelings.

Female Gender-Role Strain. Gender-role strain has rarely been studied in women. In 1992, Gillespie and Eisler identified five areas of strain for women: (1) fear of unemotional relationships (e.g., *feeling pressured to engage in sexual activity*); (2) fear of physical unattractiveness (e.g., *being perceived by others as overweight*); (3) fear of victimization (e.g., *having your car break down on the road*); (4) fear of behaving assertively (e.g., *bargaining with a salesperson when buying a car*); and (5) fear of not being nurturant (e.g., *a very close friend stops speaking to you*). This female gender-role strain scale was associated with depression and was independent from the PAQ femininity scale.

One instance in which gender-role strain may be prevalent among women is when they find themselves in traditionally male settings, such as medical school or law school. McIntosh and colleagues (1994) found that women experienced greater strains than men during law school. Over the course of the first year of law school, women's health declined and levels of depression increased relative to those of men. The investigators identified two major sources of strain among women: sexism, the idea that the women felt they were treated differently, and a lack of free time and a lack of time with one's partner or spouse. The latter source of strain may reflect a conflict that women face between pursuing achievement and tending to their relationships. Partners may be less supportive of women than men putting their personal lives on hold to pursue a career.

TAKE HOME POINTS

- Two shifts occurred in the most recent thinking about gender roles: (1) the realization that gender roles are multifaceted constructs that cannot be fully captured by single trait measures of agency and communion and (2) the idea that gender roles are influenced by the social context, time, place, and culture.

- Masculinity and femininity are now conceptualized as broad categories that include personality traits, physical appearance, occupational interests, and role behaviors.

- Measures of gender diagnosticity are one way to take the changing social context into consideration.

- One outgrowth of the emphasis on the social context in studying gender has been to consider the strains people face from the gender roles society imposes. Strains arise when our behavior is discrepant from the role that society has set forth, and when the behaviors required of the role are not compatible with mental and physical health.

- Gender-role strain among men includes homophobia, competitiveness, emotional inhibition, aggression, and a reluctance to seek help.

- Gender-role strain among women, less studied, includes fear of physical unattractiveness, fear of victimization, difficulties with assertion, and uncertainty about how to behave in traditionally masculine settings.

- The nature of gender-role strain differs across race, ethnicity, and culture.

SUMMARY

First, the scientific method that is used to study gender was reviewed. The scientific method rests on empiricism; it includes the collection of data that are then used to make statements, develop theories, and generate hypotheses. Two scientific methods were discussed: the correlational method and the experimental method. The advantage of the experimental method is internal validity, and the advantage of the correlational method is external validity. The importance of random selection and random assignment was explained. I also described the differences between cross-sectional and longitudinal studies; longitudinal designs may provide stronger tests of causality and are able to distinguish cohort effects from age effects.

We face a number of difficulties in the scientific study of gender. The experimenter can be a source of bias by influencing the question asked, the way a study is designed (including the participants chosen and the way variables are manipulated and measured), the way the data are collected, how the data are interpreted, and whether the data are reported. Participants also can influence the outcome of a study, in particular by demand characteristics and concerns with self-presentation. Other difficulties that researchers encounter when studying gender include the problem of generalizing from the laboratory to the real world, isolating the effects of participant's sex from variables that are confounded with sex such as status and gender role, and considering how the context influences behavior.

In the second half of the chapter, I reviewed the history of the psychology of gender. The field began by addressing the question of whether women were intellectually inferior to men. When there was insufficient evidence to support this claim, the field shifted to focus on the mental or psychological differences between men and women, that is, masculinity and femininity. The first comprehensive measure of masculinity and femininity was the AIAS, but numerous other inventories soon followed. A major shift in the conceptualization and measurement of masculinity and femininity occurred in 1974 with the development of the BSRI and the PAQ. These two instruments challenged the bipolar assumption that masculinity and femininity are opposites and the view that the healthiest

people are masculine men and feminine women. Instead, the model of mental health was embodied in the androgynous person, someone who incorporates both masculine and feminine traits.

The most recent approaches to the conceptualization of masculinity and femininity have emphasized their multiple components. We now realize that masculinity and femininity consist of behaviors, roles, and physical characteristics as well as personality traits. Researchers have also emphasized how the social context influences the display of sex differences and the meaning of gender. Gender diagnosticity is one approach that has taken the social context into account. An area of research that emphasizes the role society plays in shaping gender-role norms is gender-role strain. Gender-role strain is experienced when the norms for our gender role conflict with our naturally occurring tendencies or with what would be psychologically adaptive. This area of research has largely been applied to men.

DISCUSSION QUESTIONS

1. Describe a scientific theory with which you are familiar. It does not have to be from psychology; it could be from biology or physics, for example. Go through the stages of the research process shown in Figure 2.1.
2. What is the difference between random assignment and random sampling? How is each related to internal and external validity?
3. Identify behaviors you think might be interpreted differently when displayed by a male versus a female. For each one, explain why.
4. If you have ever been in an experiment, discuss some of the ways that

just knowing you were in an experiment influenced your behavior.
5. Describe the greatest difficulty you believe researchers face when studying gender. What is the best precaution to take against this difficulty?
6. What are some of the weaknesses and strengths of the instruments that have been used to measure masculinity and femininity?
7. Discuss the concepts of agency, communion, unmitigated agency, and unmitigated communion. How would you expect these constructs to be related to one another?
8. What are some areas of gender-role strain for men and women today?

SUGGESTED READING

Ashmore, R. D. (1990). Sex, gender, and the individual. In L. A. Pervin (Ed.), *Handbook of personality: Theory and research* (pp. 486–526). New York: Guilford Press.

Bakan, D. (1966). *The duality of human existence.* Chicago: Rand McNally.

Spence, J. T., & Helmreich, R. L. (1978). *Masculinity and femininity: The psychological dimensions, correlates, and antecedents.* Austin: University of Texas Press.

Thompson, E. H., Jr., & Pleck, J. H. (1995). Masculine ideologies: A review of research instrumentation on men and masculinities. In R. F. Levant & W. S. Pollack (Eds.), *A new psychology of men* (pp. 129–163). New York: Basic Books.

KEY TERMS

Androgyny—Displaying both masculine and feminine traits.

Cross-sex-typed—Exhibiting gender-role characteristics that correspond with the other sex.

Essentialism—Perspective that gender is a permanent attribute of the person.

Gender diagnosticity (GD)—Estimation of the probability that a person is male or female given a set of gender-related indicators.

Gender-role strain—Tension that develops when the expectations that accompany one's gender role have negative consequences for the individual.

Prototype—Abstract set of features commonly associated with a category, such that features vary in their representativeness of the category.

Self-role discrepancy theory—The strain that arises when we fail to live up to the gender role society has constructed.

Sex-typed—Exhibiting the gender-role characteristics that correspond with our sex.

Social constructionist approach—Suggests that masculinity and femininity are categories constructed by society, and each society may have a different definition of masculinity and femininity.

Socialized dysfunctional characteristics theory—Inherently dysfunctional personality characteristics that are fundamental to the gender roles instilled by society.

Unmitigated agency—Personality orientation characterized by a focus on the self to the exclusion of others.

Unmitigated communion—Personality orientation characterized by a focus on others to the exclusion of the self.

GENDER-ROLE ATTITUDES

In 1977, a group of college men were induced to talk to either an attractive female or an unattractive female. Not surprisingly, men liked the attractive female more than the unattractive female. However, there's a twist—all of the men were talking to the same female by phone—only half were shown a picture of an attractive person and half were shown a picture of an unattractive person. Clearly, the idea that "attractive people are nicer and more likeable" was operating here. The fact that these men's beliefs were influenced by the picture is not surprising. What may be more surprising is the fact that the woman behaved differently toward the men who thought she was attractive versus unattractive. When a set of judges who were blind to condition (i.e., did not know which picture the men saw) listened to the audiotaped phone calls, they rated the woman as warmer and friendlier when she was talking to a male who thought she was attractive than unattractive (Snyder, Tanke, & Berscheid, 1977).

The woman's behavior is an example of the self-fulfilling prophecy. That is, she came to fulfill the expectations that the men had—that attractive women are nicer than unattractive women. This study illustrates the dangers of our expectancies. It is not only that our expectations influence our own behavior, but they also influence the behavior of others so that they confirm our expectancy. Now, imagine what could happen in the case of gender. We have strong expectancies about the differences between men and women. There is clearly an opportunity for those expectations to affect our behavior toward men and women so that they produce the stereotypes we hold.

In the last chapter, I provided a brief history of how gender roles have been conceptualized and measured. This research was devoted to identifying the features of gender roles. In this chapter, I investigate people's attitudes toward gender roles. Do you view the traditional male favorably or unfavorably? How do you behave when confronted with people who do not conform to gender-role expectations? First, I examine research on attitudes toward men's and women's roles, that is, whether you believe men and women should have distinct and separate roles or whether you believe they should have similar and equal roles. Then I review the literature on the three components of attitudes toward the category gender: affect (feelings), cognition (beliefs), and behavior. People's feelings toward gender are described by the term *sexism*; people's beliefs about gender are referred to as *gender-role stereotypes*; and people's behavior toward others based on gender is known as *sex discrimination*.

ATTITUDES TOWARD MEN'S AND WOMEN'S ROLES

Do you find it acceptable for women to work outside the home? To be construction workers (see Figure 3.1)? To serve in the military? Is it acceptable for men to take the same amount of time off from work as women when a child is born? To stay home and take care of children? If you find all these ideas acceptable, then you

FIGURE 3.1 A woman is using a compound miter saw to cut wood for the interior of a house.

have an egalitarian view of gender roles. Most people find they agree with some of these ideas, but not all, or they only agree in part with each of the ideas. For example, most people find it acceptable for women to work outside the home—which is a good thing, because most women do. Fewer people find it acceptable for a woman to work outside the home when she has a 3-month-old child and there is no financial need for her to work.

Attitudes toward men's and women's roles have been referred to as **gender ideologies** (Hochschild, 1989). A **traditional gender ideology** maintains that men's sphere is work and women's sphere is the home. The implicit assumption is that men have greater power than women. An **egalitarian gender ideology** maintains that power is distributed equally between men and women and men and women identify equally with the same spheres. There could be an equal emphasis on home, on work, or on some combination of the two. Most people's attitudes toward men's and women's roles lie somewhere between traditional and egalitarian. Thus Hochschild identified a third gender ideology, **transitional**. A typical transitional attitude toward gender roles is that it is acceptable for women to devote energy to both work and family domains, but women should hold proportionally more responsibility for the home, and men should focus proportionally more of their energy on work.

Perhaps the most widely used instrument to measure attitudes toward gender roles is the Attitudes Toward Women Scale (ATWS; Spence & Helmreich, 1972). The ATWS was developed during the women's movement of the 1960s and assessed beliefs about the behavior of men and women in domains that have traditionally been divided between them, such as raising children, education, and paid employment. Although the scale's title specifies attitudes toward women, many of the items really measure attitudes toward both women's and men's roles.

Here are some sample items from the 15-item scale (Spence & Helmreich, 1972):

- Swearing and obscenity are more repulsive in the speech of a woman than a man.

- Women should worry less about their rights and more about becoming good wives and mothers.

- It is ridiculous for a woman to run a locomotive and for a man to darn socks.

- Sons in a family should be given more encouragement to go to college than daughters.

- There are many jobs in which men should be given preference over women in being hired or promoted.

You probably noticed that some of the items on the ATWS are quite outdated. For example, it is quite common for daughters to go to college and "run a locomotive." Not surprisingly, attitudes toward men's and women's roles using the ATWS have become more liberal over time (Twenge, 1997). Although women's attitudes have always been more egalitarian than men's—even across a variety of cultures (Gibbons, Stiles, & Shkodriani, 1991), the size of the sex difference seems to be getting smaller over time. Today, most people appear to have egalitarian attitudes using the ATWS.

However, the ATWS is not a good measure of contemporary gender-role attitudes. First, there are demand characteristics in responding to this scale. Who wouldn't agree at least on a self-report instrument that men and women should have similar job opportunities? Second, the ATWS fails to capture some of the contemporary issues about men's and women's roles, such as whether women should serve in the military, whether men and women should

participate equally in child care, and whether women have the right to an abortion.

One scale that was developed to reflect issues more relevant to women is the Liberal Feminist Attitude and Ideology Scale (LFAIS; Morgan, 1996). The LFAIS has a gender role subscale that reflects relations between men and women and responsibilities at work versus home. Sample items include "It is insulting to the husband when his wife does not take his last name," and "An employed woman can establish as warm and secure a relationship with her children as a mother who is not employed." This scale may show more variability in gender-role attitudes. See if you can come up with some other domains that reflect contemporary gender-role attitudes in Do Gender 3.1.

DO GENDER 3.1
Creating a Contemporary Gender-Role Attitudes Scale

Decide on some ways in which men and women are not treated equally—at your institution, in your town, in your culture. Create a scale to assess people's beliefs about whether the treatment should be equal. Identify more subtle ways in which differential treatment exists and is often accepted (e.g., If there were a draft, women should be just as likely to men to serve in the military; Mothers are better than fathers at caring for a sick child.)

After you have created the scale, decide on some variables—both personality and situational—that you believe might be related to scores on your scale. What personality characteristics do you think might be associated with more liberal gender-role attitudes? What situational variables (perhaps features of the home environment in which the participant was raised) might contribute to more liberal gender-role attitudes?

There are ethnic and cultural differences in attitudes toward men's and women's roles. In some ways, African Americans seem to be more traditional than Caucasians, and in other ways less traditional than Caucasians. Binion (1990) found that African American women were more likely than Caucasian women to be classified as androgynous and masculine. However, African American women reported more traditional attitudes toward men's and women's roles than Caucasian women. African American women were more likely than Caucasian women to believe that women are responsible for raising the children, that men should not have to do housework, and that men do not take women seriously.

How can this contradiction be resolved? Why do African American women have less traditional gender-role traits but more traditional gender-role attitudes? One reason that African American women possess stereotypical masculine traits is that these traits (e.g., independent, self-reliant, hardworking) are necessary for African American women to survive in American society (Binion, 1990). African American women have been employed outside the home for a longer period of time than Caucasian women due to economic necessity (Sanchez-Hucles, 1997). In fact, African Americans have more positive attitudes toward women working outside the home than Caucasians (Blee & Tickamyer, 1995). However, African Americans have a conservative attitude about women's role in the home, in part so they can get along more easily with African American men. Attempts by African American women to gain equality in the home may be especially threatening to African American men who, unlike Caucasian men, are not viewed as the more powerful group by society. Thus African American women face a predicament in aligning themselves with the women's movement because doing so puts them at odds with men who are their allies in the race movement.

Attitudes toward gender roles also have been studied among the Chinese. Historically, men and women in China have held very traditional roles. The Confucian doctrine of the Chinese culture emphasizes the lower status of women compared to men; one doctrine is "The virtue of a woman lies in three obediences: obedience to the father, husband, and son" (cited in Chia, Allred, & Jerzak, 1997, p. 138). In a study comparing students from Taipei, Taiwan, to students in North Carolina, Chinese students had more conservative attitudes toward marital roles in terms of who should make the decisions within the family (Chia et al., 1994). In addition, Chinese male students thought it more inappropriate for men to express emotion than did American students.

Cross-cultural research on attitudes toward gender can be difficult to conduct because the definition of a traditional gender role differs across cultures. For example, the traditional male in the United States is independent and competent, but the traditional male in China values poetry, reading, rituals, and music, as well as interdependence and cooperation (Chia et al., 1994).

TAKE HOME POINTS

- One's attitudes toward gender can be classified as traditional, egalitarian, or transitional.

- Although gender-role attitudes have become less traditional over time, most people fit into the transitional category, not fully embracing equality for men and women across all domains.

- To understand cultural differences in gender-role attitudes, one needs to understand what the expectations for men and women are in the particular culture.

- African Americans have more traditional attitudes about women's roles in the home but less traditional attitudes about women working outside the home.

AFFECTIVE COMPONENT: SEXISM

Sexism is one's attitude or feeling toward people based on their sex alone. Disliking a doctor because she is female or a nurse because he is male are examples of sexism. Instruments that measure sexism often consist of people's beliefs about men and women but contain an affective component to these beliefs. That is, the beliefs reflect either a high or low regard for someone because of his or her sex.

Traditional Versus Modern Sexism

You might expect that sexism has declined over the past several decades, and perhaps it has. But today there is a more subtle version of sexism. Swim and colleagues (1995) distinguished between traditional and modern sexism. Traditional sexism includes endorsement of traditional roles for men and women, differential treatment of men and women, and the belief that women are less competent than men. Traditional sexism reflects an open disregard for the value of women. Few people today would publicly express such feelings. Modern sexism, by contrast, includes the denial of any existing discrimination toward women, an antagonism to women's demands, and a resentment of any preferential treatment for women. In short, modern sexism implies that one is not sympathetic to women's issues and indirectly endorses the unequal treatment of men and women. The two sexism scales are positively correlated, meaning that people who score high on one scale are likely to score high on the other scale.

Modern sexism is associated with underestimating women's difficulties in obtaining jobs traditionally held by men. Swim et al. (1995) found that modern sexism was correlated with overestimating the percentage of women who hold male-dominated jobs. Modern sexism also is associated with the use of sexist language

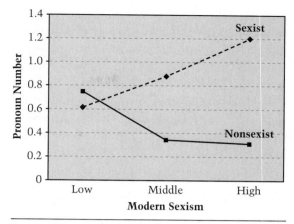

FIGURE 3.2   Students who scored in the upper third of the modern sexism scale used the most pronouns reflecting sexist language and the fewest pronouns reflecting nonsexist language.
Source: Adapted from Swim, Mallett, and Stangor (2004).

and with the inability (or unwillingness) to detect sexist language when asked to do so (Swim, Mallett, & Stangor, 2004). As shown in Figure 3.2, when people were divided into three groups on the modern sexism scale, those who scored highest used the most sexist language and the least nonsexist language when writing a response to a moral dilemma.

An example of modern sexism is the perception that African American women have preferred status in the workforce. Some people believe an African American woman somehow counts twice in terms of affirmative action: once for being female and once for being African American, which gives her a special advantage in acquiring a job. However, African American women are not advantaged (Sanchez-Hucles, 1997). African American women are paid less than White women, African American men, and White men, and they have the lowest status positions in the workforce. Although there has been an increase in the number of African American women who have attained professional positions, the percentage of White women in professional positions is over 10 times that of African American women. According to Sanchez-Hucles (1997), "The myth of African American women's advantage allows privileged individuals to deny their own privilege and minimize the oppression that African American women and others with unprivileged status face in their work lives" (p. 576).

Hostile Versus Benevolent Sexism

You are probably thinking of sexism as a *negative* feeling toward women. But sexism, like any other affective attitude, can consist of negative or positive feelings. This is reflected in the distinction that Glick and Fiske (1996) made between hostile sexism and benevolent sexism in their Ambivalent Sexism Inventory. **Hostile sexism** is just as it sounds: feelings of hostility toward women. It is a negative attitude toward women, in particular those who challenge the traditional female role. **Benevolent sexism**, by contrast, reflects positive feelings toward women, including a prosocial orientation toward women (e.g., the desire to help women). Both hostile sexism and benevolent sexism are rooted in patriarchy, gender differentiation (i.e., different roles and traits ascribed to men and women), and sexual reproduction (Glick & Fiske, 2001). Patriarchy and gender differentiation lead to hostile sexism by exaggerating the differences between men and women and justifying the superiority of the dominant group. Benevolent sexism comes from men's dependence on women for intimacy, sexual reproduction, and gender-differentiated social roles (i.e., domestic labor). The items on the hostile sexism and benevolent sexism scales are shown in Table 3.1.

The ambivalence in attitudes toward women stems from the paradox that women

TABLE 3.1   SAMPLE ITEMS FROM AMBIVALENT SEXISM INVENTORY

Hostile Sexism
Patriarchy
Women seek to gain power by getting control over men.
Many women are actually seeking special favors, such as hiring policies that favor them over men, under the guise of asking for "equality."
Gender Differentiation
Women are too easily offended.
Sexual Reproduction
Many women get a kick out of teasing men by seeming sexually available and then refusing male advances.

Benevolent Sexism
Patriarchy
In a disaster, women ought to be rescued before men.
Women should be cherished and protected by men.
Gender Differentiation
Many women have a quality of purity that few men possess.
Women, as compared to men, tend to have a more refined sense of culture and good taste.
Sexual Reproduction
Every man ought to have a woman he adores.
No matter how accomplished he is, a man is not truly complete as a person unless he has the love of a woman.

Source: Glick and Fiske (1996, 2001).

hold a lower status than men, but that the female stereotype is more positive than the male stereotype. Whereas hostile sexism punishes women who do not conform to traditional roles, benevolent sexism rewards women for doing so. For example, in one study college students who scored high on hostile sexism toward women viewed a female candidate for a managerial position less favorably and were less likely to recommend that she be hired; however, hostile sexism was unrelated to views of a male candidate (Masser & Abrams, 2004). The authors concluded that hostile sexism is harmful to women when they are in contexts that threaten men's status.

The items on the benevolent sexism scale are more palatable to many people. People who endorse benevolent sexism are viewed more favorably than those who endorse hostile sexism and are less likely to be viewed as sexist (Barreto & Ellemers, 2005). However, the negative implications of benevolent sexism are clear. Benevolent sexism is a harmful attitude because it is rooted in the belief that women are less competent than men and are in need of men's help. Benevolent sexism provides a powerful justification for the high-status group to exploit the low-status group. According to Jackman (1994), "the agenda for dominant groups is to create an ideological cocoon whereby they can define their discriminatory actions as benevolent" (p. 14). That is, dominant groups need to develop an ideology that justifies their superior position and is supported by the subordinate group. Benevolent sexism fills this prescription. Benevolent sexism justifies the behavior of the high-status group by casting it in positive terms that the low-status group can endorse: Women need men to take care of them. According to Jackman (1994), benevolence is more effective than hostility in exploiting someone.

Regardless of whether people endorse benevolent sexism, mere exposure to these beliefs can increases people's justification of the differential status of men and women. Jost and Kay (2005) showed that priming people to think about women being communal in one study and priming people with benevolent sexist beliefs in another study increased undergraduate men's and women's endorsement of the way men and women are currently treated in society—or the status quo. By distinguishing women from men in a way that makes stereotypical feminine traits positive, people endorse the differentiation and buy into the current system that supports this differentiation.

A related construct is **benevolent discrimination**, or men providing more help to women than men (Glick & Fiske, 1999b). What is the harm in men holding a door open for a woman? paying for dinner at a restaurant with a woman? Again, the implicit message is that women need help and protection. The behavior appears prosocial but really legitimizes women's inferior position. It is difficult to reject benevolent discrimination because (1) the behavior provides a direct benefit to the recipient, (2) the help provider will be insulted, (3) social norms dictate that one should accept help graciously, and (4) it is difficult to explain why help is being rejected. See Sidebar 3.1 for a discussion of benevolent sexism and female criminals.

Although the benevolent and hostile sexism scales reflect two very different affective states in regard to women, the two are positively correlated, meaning that people who endorse items on one scale also endorse items on the other. This positive correlation underscores the idea that both hostile sexism and benevolent sexism are based on a belief that women are inferior to men. The positive correlation of the benevolent and hostile sexism scales has been shown to exist in 19 countries (Glick et al., 2000). Among those countries, nations that scored higher in hostile and benevolent sexism also scored higher in gender inequality, as measured by the presence of women in politics,

SIDEBAR 3.1: *Benevolent Sexism and Female Criminals*

Are men and women treated equally within the criminal justice system? Some believe that women are treated more leniently than men partly because women are viewed as less of a threat to society than men (weaker) and partly because of a paternalistic need to help and care for women. However, when women commit crimes that violate the female stereotype, they could be treated more harshly. In a study of a local newspaper in Bloomington, Indiana, women who committed violent crimes were treated more harshly than men by the media, whereas women who committed nonviolent crimes were treated more leniently by the media (Grabe et al., 2006). In another study where registered voters posed as mock jurors, women received a lighter sentence than men for a heinous crime unless there was testimony from the victim's family—in which case the female received a more severe sentence than the male (Forsterlee et al., 2004). The authors argue that the testimony made the incongruence between such extreme violence and the female gender role salient.

One example of an extreme violation of the female gender role is killing one's children. In 1966, Myra Hindley tortured and murdered her two children. She was not declared mentally ill and was sentenced to life in prison. When a group of young adults, mostly college students, were presented with this information, those who scored high on benevolent sexism judged Myra more harshly than those who scored lower on the scale (Viki, Massey, & Masser, 2005). Those who scored higher on benevolent sexism also were more likely to say that Myra violated the female gender role, and this gender role violation explained the link between benevolent sexism and the negative evaluation of Myra. Neither sex nor hostile sexism was related to evaluations of Myra. Thus in this case, benevolent sexism was related to a negative judgment rather than a positive judgment of a woman.

the number of women in the workforce, and female literacy rates.

Not surprisingly, men score higher than women on hostile sexism around the world (Glick et al., 2000). The sex difference in benevolent sexism is less reliable. In four countries women scored higher than men on benevolent sexism—Cuba, Nigeria, South Africa, Botswana. These latter four countries also were the most sexist. Why would women in these countries support benevolent sexism? In general, women support benevolent sexism because (1) it does not seem like prejudice because of the "appearance" of positive attributes and (2) women receive rewards from benevolent sexism (i.e., male protection). These rewards may be especially important in sexist countries, where women are most likely to be victims of violence. As stated by Glick and Fiske (2001), "The irony

is that women are forced to seek protection from members of the very group that threatens them, and the greater the threat, the stronger the incentive to accept benevolent sexism's protective ideology" (p. 115).

There is experimental evidence that women rely on benevolent sexism when faced with an environment in which men are hostile toward women (Fischer, 2006). Female college students were randomly assigned to one of three groups: One group was told research shows men have negative attitudes toward women, one group was told men have positive attitudes toward women, and one group was provided with no information about men's attitudes toward women. The women then completed the Ambivalent Sexism Inventory. Benevolent sexism scores increased in the negative attitudes condition relative to the other two conditions, whereas hostile sexism scores were unaffected.

Sexism Toward Men

Although sexism can be exhibited toward both men and women, it is typically studied and measured as feelings toward women. Jokes about female drivers and "dumb blondes" are regularly perceived as examples of sexism. But aren't jokes about men's incompetence at being fathers or men not asking for directions also examples of sexism? I came across the following cartoon in the *New Yorker* (June 5, 2000; see Figure 3.3). Now, imagine that the sex of the characters was reversed: The joke wouldn't be funny, and the cartoon wouldn't be published.

Feelings toward the male sex have been explored in the Ambivalence Toward Men Inventory, which was developed to distinguish feelings of hostility and benevolence toward men (Glick & Fiske, 1999a). This ambivalence also is rooted in patriarchy, gender differentiation, and

"There's an article in here that explains why you're such an idiot."

FIGURE 3.3   People do not always recognize this kind of cartoon as sexism, but if the sexes were reversed, it would easily be labeled as sexism. © The *New Yorker* collection, 2000, William Haefeli from cartoonbank.com. All rights reserved.

TABLE 3.2   Sample Items from Ambivalence Toward Men Inventory

Hostile Sexism
Patriarchy
Men will always fight for greater control in society.
Gender Differentiation
Most men are really like children.
Sexual Reproduction
Men have no morals in what they will do to get sex.

Benevolent Sexism
Patriarchy
Even if both work, the woman should take care of the man at home.
Gender Differentiation
Men are less likely to fall apart in emergencies.
Sexual Reproduction
Every woman ought to have a man she adores.

Source: Glick and Fiske (1999a).

sexual reproduction. Sample items are shown in Table 3.2. The hostility toward men scale consists of negative attitudes surrounding the resentment of patriarchy, a perception of negative attributes in men, and beliefs that men are sexually aggressive. The benevolence scale reflects positive views of men, including the benefits of patriarchy, the positive attributes of men, and women's fulfillment through connections with men.

The Ambivalence Toward Men Inventory was examined in a study of 16 nations (Glick et al., 2004). Like the sexism toward women scales, the benevolent and hostile scales are positively correlated. In addition, hostile and benevolent sexism toward men were higher among nations with less gender equality, as assessed by women's education and the representation of women in government and high status occupations. In 15 of the 16 nations, women scored higher than men on hostile sexism toward men. This sex difference was larger in nations where men endorsed more hostile sexism toward women. Thus it appears that women are more hostile toward men in situations where men are hostile toward women.

However, men scored higher than women on benevolent sexism toward men in 11 of the 16 nations. Why do men endorse benevolent sexism toward men? Benevolent sexism toward men portrays a positive view of men while maintaining their higher status over women. This is unlike women's endorsement of benevolent sexism toward women which is mixed in its effects—on the one hand, it reflects a positive view of women, but on the other hand, it promotes the idea that women have lower status than men.

TAKE HOME POINTS

- Traditional sexism is a blatant disregard for women, whereas modern sexism is a more subtle indicator of devaluing women, for example by denying that women have any disadvantages in society compared to men.

- Hostile sexism reflects a negative feeling toward women, whereas benevolent sexism reflects a positive feeling toward women based on their sex.

- Benevolent sexism is less likely to be regarded as sexist because it focuses on positive beliefs about women and results in prosocial behavior (i.e., men helping women).

- Hostile and benevolent sexism are positively correlated, however, reflecting the fact that both are rooted in the belief that women are less competent than men.

- Women in countries that are more sexist are more likely to endorse benevolent sexism toward women.

- Sexism toward men is less well studied compared to sexism toward women and more accepted in some sense than sexism toward women. Women score higher than men on hostile sexism toward men, whereas men score higher than women on benevolent sexism toward men.

COGNITIVE COMPONENT: GENDER-ROLE STEREOTYPING

The following is a description of a famous person:

> This individual is an accomplished 20th-century political figure who, prior to entering politics, worked as a research chemist and as a tax attorney.

Who do you think this person is? Can you picture the person? Now read the next description of a famous person:

> This internationally recognized public figure was known to be a loving and involved parent, and had gained a reputation for always being well coifed and tastefully dressed.

Who do you think this person is? Can you picture the person? Does this description bring to mind a different image than the first one? Are the traits described in the second passage incompatible with those described in the first passage? You might be surprised to know that both passages refer to the same person—the person depicted in Figure 3.4, Britain's former prime minister, Margaret Thatcher. Gender-role stereotypes probably led you to picture the first person as a man and the second person as a woman.

FIGURE 3.4 Former British prime minister, Margaret Thatcher.

What Is a Gender-Role Stereotype?

A stereotype is a schema or a set of beliefs about a certain group of people. **Gender-role stereotypes** are the features we assign to men and women in our society, features not assigned due to biological sex but due to the social roles that men and women hold. Thus I refer to these stereotypes as gender-role stereotypes rather than sex stereotypes. One reason that it may not have occurred to you that the descriptions in the previous paragraph were of the same person is that the first description fits our male gender-role stereotype and the second fits our female gender-role stereotype.

Stereotypes have descriptive and prescriptive components (Fiske & Stevens, 1993). The descriptive component identifies the features of the stereotype. The trait features of the male and female stereotypes are likely to be those found on the PAQ and BSRI masculinity and femininity inventories. The descriptive aspect of stereotypes is limiting, as we judge feminine women as less competent for leadership positions and masculine men as less capable of nurturing children.

The prescriptive component of a stereotype is how we think people *ought* to behave due to their sex. The prescriptive component of gender-role stereotypes says that men should be masculine and women should be feminine. Other people enforce the prescriptive component of a stereotype. If you are a man who does not want a career but would prefer to stay home and take care of a family, how will other people react? If you are a female who wants a career and does not want to have children, how will others react? There is a great deal of pressure from other people to adhere to gender roles.

Gender-role stereotypes differ from many other stereotypes because gender is a category that is activated immediately upon meeting someone. One of the first things that you notice about a person is his or her sex. Imagine you see a baby, such as the one in Figure 3.5. The baby

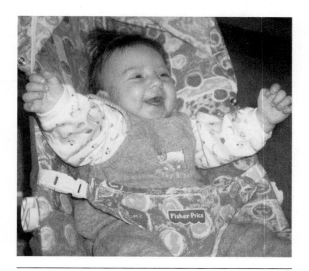

FIGURE 3.5   Photograph of a baby dressed in blue with a lot of hair. Is it a boy or a girl?

has long hair, so it must be a she. If the baby is dressed in blue (as the caption says), it must be a he. You might become extremely uncomfortable because you do not know which pronoun to use. Most people are greatly concerned about referring to a baby by the wrong sex.

Components of Gender-Role Stereotypes

What are the features of the male and female gender-role stereotypes? In 1972, Broverman and colleagues developed a questionnaire to assess people's perceptions of masculine and feminine behavior. They administered this questionnaire to over 1,000 people, and concluded there was a strong consensus as to the characteristics of men and women across age, sex, religion, marital status, and education.

They defined a stereotypical feature as one in which 75% of both males and females agreed the trait described one sex more than the other. This definition rule led to the 41 items shown in Table 3.3. The male characteristics (listed in the right column) focused on competence, rationality, and assertion. The female characteristics (listed in the left column) focused on warmth

TABLE 3.3 Stereotypic Sex-Role Items

Competency Cluster: Masculine Pole Is More Desirable	
Feminine	Masculine
Not at all aggressive	Very aggressive
Not at all independent	Very independent
Very emotional	Not at all emotional
Does not hide emotions at all	Almost always hides emotions
Very subjective	Very objective
Very easily influenced	Not at all easily influenced
Very submissive	Very dominant
Dislikes math and science very much	Likes math and science very much
Very excitable in a minor crisis	Not at all excitable in a minor crisis
Very passive	Very active
Not at all competitive	Very competitive
Very illogical	Very logical
Very home-oriented	Very worldly
Not at all skilled in business	Very skilled in business
Very sneaky	Very direct
Does not know the way of the world	Knows the way of the world
Feelings easily hurt	Feelings not easily hurt
Not at all adventurous	Very adventurous
Has difficulty making decisions	Can make decisions easily
Cries very easily	Never cries
Almost never acts as a leader	Almost always acts as a leader
Not at all self-confident	Very self-confident
Very uncomfortable about being aggressive	Not at all uncomfortable about being aggressive
Not at all ambitious	Very ambitious
Unable to separate feelings from ideas	Easily able to separate feelings from ideas
Very dependent	Not at all dependent
Very conceited about appearance	Never conceited about appearance
Thinks women are always superior to men	Thinks men are always superior to women
Does not talk freely about sex with men	Talks freely about sex with men

Warmth-Expressiveness Cluster: Feminine Pole Is More Desirable	
Feminine	Masculine
Doesn't use harsh language at all	Uses very harsh language
Very talkative	Not at all talkative
Very tactful	Very blunt
Very gentle	Very rough
Very aware of feelings of others	Not at all aware of feelings of others
Very religious	Not at all religious
Very interested in own appearance	Not at all interested in own appearance
Very neat in habits	Very sloppy in habits
Very quiet	Very loud
Very strong need for security	Very little need for security
Enjoys art and literature	Does not enjoy art and literature at all
Easily expresses tender feelings	Does not express tender feelings at all easily

Source: Broverman et al. (1972).

and expressiveness. These traits are similar to the ones found on conventional M/F inventories.

Broverman and colleagues (1972) also found that the male characteristics were more highly valued than the female characteristics. You can see in Table 3.3 that more masculine characteristics are socially desirable (right column in the top half) than feminine characteristics (left column in the bottom half). When the investigators asked men and women to indicate which of these traits are most desirable in an adult, without specifying the adult's sex, more masculine than feminine items were endorsed. Mental health professionals also rated the masculine items as healthier than the feminine items for an adult to possess. In fact, when mental health professionals were asked to identify which items fit a healthy female, a healthy male, and a healthy adult, their ratings of the healthy adult and the healthy male did not significantly differ, but their ratings of the healthy adult and healthy female did. That is, the stereotype of the healthy adult more closely approximated the stereotype of an adult male than an adult female. These findings suggest that characteristics of the male gender role are more highly valued than characteristics of the female gender role. Is this still true today? Answer this question by conducting the experiment in Do Gender 3.2.

Not only is the stereotype of an ideal adult the stereotype of a male, but apparently, the stereotype of an entire country also more closely approximates the stereotype of a male than a female. In one study, college students rated their perceptions of 28 countries, as well as their perceptions of adult men and women from those countries, using 41 agentic and communal traits (Eagly & Kite, 1987). The investigators wanted to determine whether the stereotype of a nation was more similar to the stereotype of the nation's men or the nation's women. College students rated countries with which they would be familiar, such as Iran, Cuba, Israel, Japan, Denmark,

---

DO GENDER 3.2
Comparisons of Ideal Adult with Ideal Male and Ideal Female

List the stereotypical sex-role items in Table 3.3. Place each feature on a 5-point scale, such as:

Not at   1   2   3   4   5   Very
all caring   caring

Ask a sample of your friends to rate the ideal person on each of these features. On the next page, ask the same friends to rate the ideal male on each of these features. On the third page, ask the same friends to rate the ideal female on each of these features. Always make sure the "ideal person" is the first page so as to disguise the nature of the research. Counterbalance the order of the second and third pages. That is, ask half of your participants to rate the ideal male second and the other half to rate the ideal female second.

For each item, examine the mean response for the ideal person, the ideal male, and the ideal female. Does the ideal person more closely resemble the ideal male, the ideal female, or both equally?

---

and India. The investigators predicted that the stereotype of the nation would be more similar to the stereotype of the nation's men than the nation's women to the extent that men and women had unequal roles in that country. In countries where men have a higher status than women, the women are less likely to hold prominent roles in the nation and are less visible to outsiders. Indeed, the authors found that students' perceptions of a country were more similar to their perceptions of the men than the women who inhabited that country. This trend was especially strong in countries that students viewed as not emphasizing equality for men and women.

Gender-role Stereotypes of Older People.
Gender-stereotype research often focuses on younger adults, typically college students. Stereotypes of older men and women may differ. The media would certainly lead to the perception that we have more negative views of older women than older men, at least when it comes to physical appearance. A meta-analysis of the relation of age to gender stereotypes showed that younger adults are rated more favorably than older adults but that the effect of age differs for men and women (Kite et al., 2005). Increased age was more strongly associated with negative evaluations of women than men. However, age was also related to the perception of a decline in competence, and this relation was stronger for men than women. Because competence is such an integral part of the male gender role, it is interesting that people perceive men to decline more than women on this dimension.

Stereotypes of Homosexuals.   Stereotypes of homosexuals are that they possess gender-role characteristics associated with the other sex—especially in the case of gay men (Madon, 1997). People also associate homosexuality in men with a variety of emotional difficulties and gender identity problems (Boysen et al., 2006). Those who have more negative attitudes toward homosexuality are most likely to endorse this stereotype.

Similarly, the possession of cross-sex traits leads to the perception that a person is homosexual (Wong et al., 1999). Again, the link is stronger in men. That is, feminine traits and appearance are more strongly associated with being a gay man than masculine traits and appearance are associated with being lesbian. Thus deviations from one's gender role are more strongly associated with homosexuality in men than women.

Gender-role Stereotypes of People Who Vary in Race and Ethnicity.   One of the problems with research on gender-role stereotypes is that the stereotypes are often generated by middle-class Caucasians about middle-class Caucasians. Do people of different races have the same stereotypes of male and female gender roles?

A major cross-cultural study of gender-role stereotypes was undertaken by Williams and Best (1990). They examined the gender-role stereotypes of people in 30 countries, including Nigeria, England, Spain, Australia, India, Thailand, Bolivia, Peru, and the United States. Williams and Best were surprised at the similarities in gender-role stereotypes across such a diverse set of cultures. In all 30 countries, the male stereotype was more active and stronger than the female stereotype. Men were more likely to be viewed as dominant, critical, logical, and unemotional, whereas women were more likely to be viewed as affectionate, helpful, anxious, and dependent. Men were viewed as more instrumental, and women were viewed as more relationship oriented.

Surprisingly, the difference between men's and women's stereotypes was unrelated to socioeconomic status or the educational level of women in the country. Instead, religion seemed to have a greater influence on stereotype differentiation. Men and women were viewed as more different from one another in predominantly Protestant countries, such as the United States and England, compared to predominantly Catholic countries, such as Ireland and Brazil. Women were also viewed more positively in Catholic than Protestant countries. The authors attributed these findings to the greater prominence that women are given in Catholic compared to Protestant theology; specifically, in the Catholic Church, the Virgin Mary is held in high regard, as are the many female saints. The investigators also compared the Muslim religion in Pakistan, where all significant religious figures are male, to the Hindu religion in India, which includes both gods and goddesses. The people in Pakistan were more likely than the people in India to differentiate between men and women; in addition, Pakistanis viewed women less favorably than Indians.

Views of Men and Women Who Vary in Ethnicity or Culture. People from a wide variety of cultures may share similar gender-role stereotypes, but do people's stereotypes of men and women depend on the ethnic group to which the target person belongs? In one study, 259 college students (half of whom were Caucasian) indicated their perceptions of Anglo American, African American, Asian American, and Mexican American men and women (Niemann et al., 1994). The most frequently generated descriptors for each racial group are shown in Table 3.4.

We can see that race certainly influences the content of male and female stereotypes. Both Anglo and African American males are described as athletic, but Asian American and Mexican American males are not, and African American females are. Anglo and African American men are described as tall, but Asian American and Mexican American men and women are described as short. Sociable is an attribute used to describe all groups of women except Asian American, but sociable also is used to describe Anglo and African American men. Caring is an attribute shared by all four groups of women, but also Anglo American and Asian American men.

We can also find contradictory features within a given gender-role stereotype, which likely reflect individual differences in perceptions. Mexican American women are viewed as attractive yet overweight. Anglo American men are viewed as hard workers yet ambitionless. African American men and women and Mexican American men and women are viewed as antagonistic yet pleasant.

The Structure of Gender-Role Stereotypes

Gender-role stereotypes, like perceptions of masculinity and femininity, consist of role behaviors (e.g., being the head of the household or the primary child caretaker), physical features (e.g., muscular or thin), and occupations (e.g., truck driver or nurse). In addition to describing these diverse features of gender-role stereotypes, researchers have begun to look at how the components of stereotypes are related to one another. If you know someone has a masculine occupation, such as construction worker, do you then infer masculine traits, masculine role behaviors, and masculine physical features? For example, if you discover a woman is an auto mechanic, will you infer she is independent or emotional? Will you assume she is the person in the house who takes care of finances or household chores?

In a series of experiments, Deaux and Lewis (1984) showed that one component of gender-role stereotypes did implicate the other components. More important, the stereotype component was more important than the sex of the person in determining the other judgments. This means that if you know a person is a nurse, you are more likely to infer a feminine trait, such as kind, rather than a masculine trait, such as self-confident, even if the target person is male.

When it came to inferring the target person's sexuality, however, college students used information about both the person's sex and gender-role stereotypes. Homosexuality was most likely to be inferred when one component

TABLE 3.4 MOST FREQUENT FEATURES OF EACH CATEGORY

Anglo-American Males	African American Males	Asian American Males	Mexican American Males
Intelligent	Athletic	Intelligent	Lower class
Egotistical	Antagonistic	Short	Hard worker
Upper class	Dark skin	Achievement oriented	Antagonistic
Light skin	Muscular	Speak softly	Dark skin
Pleasant	Criminal	Hard worker	Noncollege
Racist	Speak loudly	Pleasant	Pleasant
Achievement oriented	Tall	Dark hair	Dark hair
Caring	Intelligent	Good student	Ambitionless
Attractive	Unmannerly	Small build	Family oriented
Athletic	Pleasant	Caring	Short
Sociable	Lower class	Slender	Criminal
Blond hair	Ambitionless	Family oriented	Poorly groomed
Tall	Noncollege	Upper class	Unmannerly
Hard worker	Racist	Shy	Intelligent
Ambitionless	Sociable	Speak with accent	Alcohol user

Anglo-American Females	African American Females	Asian American Females	Mexican American Females
Attractive	Speak loudly	Intelligent	Dark hair
Intelligent	Dark skin	Speak softly	Attractive
Egotistical	Antagonistic	Pleasant	Pleasant
Pleasant	Athletic	Short	Dark skin
Blonde hair	Pleasant	Attractive	Overweight
Sociable	Unmannerly	Small build	Baby makers
Upper class	Sociable	Achievement oriented	Family oriented
Caring	Intelligent	Caring	Caring
Light skin	Attractive	Shy	Intelligent
Achievement oriented	Lower class	Dark hair	Sociable
Fashion conscious	Egotistical	Slender	Noncollege
Light eyes	Ambitionless	Hard worker	Ambitionless
Independent	Caring	Passive	Passive
Passive	Humorous	Good student	Short
	Honest	Well mannered	Antagonistic

Source: Adapted from Niemann et al. (1994).

of gender-role stereotypes, role behavior, was incongruent with the target's sex, for example, a male who decorates the house or a female who climbs mountains.

This research suggests there is cohesion to gender-role stereotypes, and a person's sex is not as important as traits, role behaviors, and physical features in implicating the stereotype.

Thus if you see a female and know nothing about her, you are likely to assume features of the female gender role. However, if you are provided with other gender-role information about this female, for example, that she exhibits masculine role behavior or is in a masculine occupation, you are more likely to use that information than her biological sex to draw inferences about her personality. Thus aspects of gender-role stereotypes hang together, but the person's sex does not have to be part of the stereotype.

To what extent do people rely on stereotypes when other information is available about the person? If you do not know anything about your neighbor's 10-year-old except the child is a girl, you may buy her a doll for her birthday. What if you know that your neighbor's 10-year-old daughter is always climbing trees in the backyard? Would you still buy her a doll, or would something more active seem appropriate? How much you know about a person determines if you use category-based expectancies or target-based expectancies. **Category-based expectancies** occur when you do not know much about a person except the category to which he or she belongs. In that case, you rely on the category to make a judgment. In the absence of any other information aside from sex, you might assume sex-related traits and sex-related preferences. **Target-based expectancies** are the perceptions you have about a person based on individuating information. Once you acquire more information about a specific target, besides the person's sex, you will use that information to make judgments. As evidence of this, Chang and Hitchon (2004) had college students read about either a male or a female political candidate in which information on competence about traditionally masculine issues (e.g., economy, national security) or traditionally feminine issues (e.g., education, health care) was present or absent. In the absence of information, people relied on category-based expectancies and judged the female as more competent on feminine issues and the male candidate as more competent on masculine issues. However, when information was provided, target-based expectancies took over; male and female candidates were judged as equally competent on all issues regardless of whether they were masculine or feminine. The influence of individuating information does not have the same effect on children, however. See Sidebar 3.2 for a discussion of children's stereotypes.

Subcategories of Gender-Role Stereotypes

As men's and women's roles have changed, we have created multiple categories for men and women. That is, there are subcategories of gender-role stereotypes. For example, our stereotype of a male businessman is not the same as our stereotype of a male construction worker; likewise, our stereotype of a female homemaker is not the same as our stereotype of a female doctor. Subtypes of the male stereotype include two tough-minded subtypes: the career man and the cool playboy; and a quieter, softer, philanthropist man (Six & Eckes, 1991). Subtypes of the female stereotype include a traditional category (housewife), a nontraditional category (career woman), and sex object (Six & Eckes, 1991). Another subtype is feminist. See Sidebar 3.3 for an interesting discussion of how this stereotype influences our perceptions of women.

Is having subcategories within one general stereotype helpful? It may seem that subtyping is beneficial because it detracts from the power of the overall stereotype. However, subtyping is merely a way to create an exception and leave the overall stereotype intact (Fiske & Stevens, 1993). How many of you know someone who is extremely prejudiced against African Americans but manages to adore Michael Jordan or Tiger Woods? They are viewed as exceptions to the African American stereotype and members of the subtype "successful African American athlete" or "successful athlete." Thus, subtyping does not necessarily reduce the power of stereotypes.

Sidebar 3.2: *Children's Stereotypes*

Gender-role stereotyping begins at an early age, possibly earlier for girls than boys. There is some evidence that 18-month-olds show a greater preference for gender-stereotyped toys (Serbin et al., 2001). By 18 to 24 months, girls are able to link masculine toys and activities with males and feminine toys and activities with females, whereas boys do not make these associations until 31 months of age (Poulin-Dubois et al., 2002; Serbin et al., 2001). Even 3-year-old girls are more knowledgeable about stereotypes than boys (O'Brien et al., 2000).

Young children have more rigid stereotypes about men and women than do adults (Trautner et al., 2005), probably because children's thinking in general is more rigid. Young children are more likely than adults to rely on target sex than individuating information when making a judgment about a person. That is, children rely more on category-based expectancies than target-based expectancies in comparison with adults. Attention to individuating information appears to increase with age. For example, in one study, children ages 4 through 10 were asked to choose which toy a target child would like to play with (Martin, 1989). Each child was given a description of a boy or a girl who had stereotypical, nonstereotypical, or neutral interests. A stereotypical interest would be a boy who likes to play with airplanes or a girl who likes to play with a makeup kit; a nonstereotypical interest would be a boy who likes to play with an iron or a girl who likes to play baseball. The child was then asked how much the target child wanted to play with the following four sex-typed toys: a car, a train engine, a sewing machine, and a doll. The younger children, on average age 4½, chose the toy that matched the target child's sex, regardless of the target child's interests. For example, when told that the target girl likes to play baseball, younger children still believed the girl would prefer to play with a sewing machine than a car. Older children, on average age 8½, paid attention to both kinds of information, the target child's sex and the target child's interests. They thought a boy who likes to play with an iron would be interested in the train engine because he was a boy but also a doll because of his feminine interests.

At first glance, it may seem that increasing age leads to decreasing use of gender-role stereotypes because people are using the individuating information instead of the target's sex to make judgments. Yet I pointed out earlier that gender-role stereotyping increases with age. How do these two ideas fit together? Older students may be less likely to rely on target sex to infer behavior, but they use their knowledge of gender-role stereotypes to generalize from one aspect of gender-role behavior to another. The older students are taking into consideration the individuating information rather than target sex, but that individuating information comes from gender-role stereotypes. Beliefs about gender roles—masculinity and femininity—may be more rigid than beliefs about sex.

There seem to be three phases of stereotype development in children (Trautner et al., 2005):

— Preschool: acquire information about gender-related characteristics
— Ages 5–6: information is consolidated and applied to male or female (rigid)
— Ages 7–8: information is less rigidly applied to sex

Do Gender-Role Stereotypes Serve Any Function?

A stereotype is a belief about someone based on his or her membership in a category. Categorizing people and objects simplifies our world. Think about when you first meet someone. You place that person into a number of categories, each of which leads you to draw a number of inferences. You notice whether the person is male or female, a student or a professor, Catholic or

SIDEBAR 3.3: *"Feminism Lite"?*

One stereotype of a feminist woman is that she is unattractive. Bullock and Fernald (2003) had a hunch that the feminist message was more convincing to college women when it was delivered by a woman who did not fit this stereotype—that is, a woman who presented herself in a more traditional feminine manner and appearance. They termed this phenomenon "feminism lite." They tested their idea in a study of college women by varying the physical attractiveness of a speaker who delivered either a profeminist or an antifeminist message. The speaker also dressed in either a feminine or masculine style. Much to the researchers' dismay, feminism lite was confirmed. As shown in Figure 3.6, college women who identified themselves as feminists were more persuaded by the feminist message when delivered by a woman who appeared feminine than masculine. Nonfeminist students were not influenced by the speaker's appearance. Feminine appearance also was associated with attitude change. When the speaker delivered a profeminist message, feminine appearance led to a greater increase in egalitarian beliefs than masculine appearance. When the speaker delivered an antifeminist message, feminine appearance led to a greater increase in traditional beliefs than masculine appearance. The speaker's appearance also influenced how likely college women were to say they would hire the speaker. Students said they were more likely to hire the woman who appeared in feminine attire than masculine attire. But, this effect was observed *only* among the women who identified themselves as feminists. The authors of the study suggested that feminist women may be the most threatened by the stereotype of feminists being unattractive and distanced themselves from someone who confirmed that stereotype.

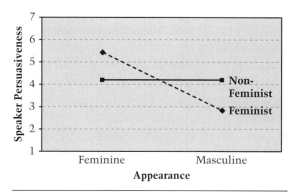

FIGURE 3.6 Paradoxically, feminist women were more influenced by a feminine-appearing speaker than a masculine-appearing speaker delivering a feminist message.
Source: Adapted from Bullock and Fernald (2003).

atheist, athletic or nonathletic. You then use these categories to make certain inferences. For example, you might feel more comfortable swearing in front of an atheist than a Catholic because expletives often have religious connotations. But who is to say the atheist would not be offended or the Catholic does not have a foul mouth? You may assume the student is about 20 years old and the professor about 50. There are exceptions here, too, as you may find a 50-year-old return-to-school student and a 30-year-old professor. Although there are exceptions, categories generally simplify information processing.

The danger of stereotyping is that it influences our perception and recollection of events in a way that can be harmful to men and women. Even if you don't endorse a particular stereotype, the mere knowledge of the stereotype can affect your behavior. Recall the study by Jost and Kay (2005) that showed the activation of the female stereotype encouraged both men and women to believe the current treatment of women and men is fair in society. Gender-role stereotypes also can lead people to perceive men and women differently when they are displaying the same behavior (Aries, 1996). In one study (Newcombe & Arnkoff, 1979), men and women used similar language in a conversation, but respondents perceived female language as less powerful, consistent with the female stereotype. Why is this important? As you will see in Chapter 7, women's language has implications for judgments of their competence. Thus misperceiving women's language can lead to misperceptions of competence.

Another problem with stereotypes is that they can lead us to treat people differently when we should not. That is, we may discriminate against people based on their sex. Stereotyping can also be harmful when our beliefs influence our behavior toward others in such a way that others confirm the stereotype. This is known as a **self-fulfilling prophecy**. For example, if you believe boys are not good at reading and do not like to read, you might not give your male preschooler as many books to read as your female preschooler. If he doesn't have the same opportunities to read as his sister, will it be a surprise that he has more difficulty reading than she does? No, your stereotype will have created a situation that then confirms the stereotype.

An example of this self-fulfilling prophecy was demonstrated with respect to females' performance on a math test. Female high school students were randomly assigned to a condition in which they were told male students performed better than female students on the test in the past (i.e., activation of negative stereotype) or a condition in which no information was given about others' performance (control condition; Keller, 2002). As shown in Figure 3.7, females performed worse when the negative stereotype was activated compared to the control condition, whereas male students' performance was unaffected by the manipulation.

Up to this point, the impact of the self-fulfilling prophecy on stereotypes has sounded

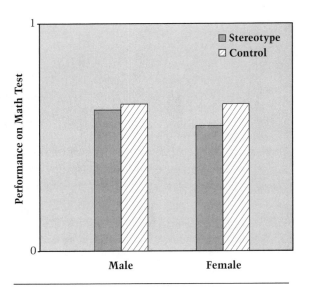

FIGURE 3.7 Females performed worse on a math test after they had received information consistent with the negative stereotype surrounding women and math (experimental condition). Male performance was unaffected by this information. *Source:* Adapted from Keller (2002).

mostly negative. Can the self-fulfilling prophecy ever help performance? If I believe boys are quite skilled at reading and give a boy a lot of books to read, will he develop superior reading skills? Quite possibly. Shih, Pittinsky, and Ambady (1999) investigated whether stereotypes can help as well as hinder performance. They studied quantitative skills among Asian women because of the contradictory stereotypes for Asians and women in this domain: Females are depicted as having inferior quantitative skills, whereas Asians are depicted as having superior quantitative skills. The investigators found that Asian women's performance on a math test improved when their racial identity was made salient but deteriorated when their gender identity was made salient. Thus it appears that stereotypes can influence performance in both positive and negative ways.

Altering Gender-Role Stereotypes

If we make exceptions for cases that do not fit our stereotypes and treat people in ways that will confirm our stereotypes, how can stereotypes ever be altered? Stereotypes are difficult to change. We tend to notice information that confirms our stereotype and ignore information that disconfirms it or create a special subtype for those disconfirming instances. We also make dispositional or trait attributions for behavior that confirms the stereotype but situational attributions for behavior that disconfirms the stereotype. Let's take an example. We expect women to show an interest in children. Therefore, if we see a woman playing with a baby, we are likely to make the dispositional attribution that she is nurturant rather than the situational attribution that she is bored and looking for a way to distract herself. Conversely, if we see a man playing with a baby, we are more likely to decide that situational forces constrained his behavior (e.g., someone told him to play with the baby) because attentiveness to children is not consistent with the male gender-role stereotype. Test this idea yourself in Do Gender 3.3 by coming up with stereotype-consistent and stereotype-inconsistent behaviors and asking people to make attributions for those behaviors.

Sometimes when we cannot ignore stereotype-inconsistent information, we instead view the behavior as more extreme. For example, assertiveness may be viewed as more extreme when displayed by a woman than a man. **Correspondent inference theory** (Jones & Davis, 1965) can explain why this happens. According to this theory, we are more likely to make dispositional attributions for behavior that is not normative, but unique. For example, we are more likely to infer that a person is emotional if he or she cries during a comedy than during a sad movie. Because many people cry during sad movies, this behavior is considered

---

DO GENDER 3.3
Attributions for Stereotype-Consistent and Stereotype-Inconsistent Behavior

Identify a set of five behaviors that are stereotype-consistent for men and five behaviors that are stereotype-inconsistent for men. An example of a stereotype-consistent behavior is "Joe watches football on television." An example of a stereotype-inconsistent behavior is "Joe is washing the dishes." Now, do the same for women. An example of a stereotype-consistent behavior is "Maria is sewing a shirt." An example of a stereotype-inconsistent behavior is "Maria is changing the oil in her car."

Ask 10 men and 10 women to explain each of the behaviors. Categorize each explanation as dispositional (due to something about the person, a trait) or situational (due to something about the environment, such as luck, chance, or the force of an external agent). It is best to be blind to the sex of the person who gave you the response.

---

normative, so crying during a sad movie does not say anything about an individual's personality. Crying during a comedy, however, is not normative and leads to stronger trait attributions for behavior. Thus, we are also more likely to infer aggression in a woman who uses power in her speech than in a man who uses power in his speech because the woman's behavior is more unique.

Another reason that it is difficult to alter stereotypes is the **backlash effect**. When people display counterstereotypical behavior, they may be penalized. In a laboratory study, college students competed against a confederate who either outperformed them in a stereotypical domain (e.g., women categorizing pictures of toddlers) or a counterstereotypical domain (e.g., women categorizing pictures of football players; Rudman & Fairchild, 2004). When losing to someone who succeeded in a counterstereotypical domain, both male and female participants sabotaged the confederate's future performance by providing unhelpful assistance. When losing to someone who succeeded in a stereotypical domain, there was no sabotage. It appears that people are well aware of the backlash effect, as a subsequent experiment showed that participants who succeeded in a counterstereotypical domain tried to conceal their performance. Thus, the backlash effect serves to maintain stereotypes by penalizing people for counterstereotypical behavior, dissuading people from publicizing counterstereotypical behavior, and by undermining performance in counterstereotypical domains.

There are circumstances in which stereotypes can be changed. First, it is easier to disconfirm stereotypical traits when the behavior that reflects the trait is clear rather than ambiguous (Rothbart & John, 1985). For example, it would be easier to disconfirm the stereotype that a woman is talkative rather than the stereotype that a woman is emotional, because it is easier to observe talking or not talking than emotionality. It also is easier to disconfirm positive traits than negative traits (Rothbart & John, 1985). Thus your favorable impressions of people are more easily changed than your unfavorable impressions; it is easier to change people's beliefs that a woman is kind than to change people's beliefs that a woman nags. Rothbart and John (1985) remark, "Favorable traits are difficult to acquire but easy to lose, whereas unfavorable traits are easy to acquire but difficult to lose" (p. 85).

The prototype approach has been applied to stereotyping to understand how stereotypes can be altered (Rothbart & John, 1985). The likelihood of a target being associated with a category depends on how well the target fits the category overall. When faced with a target person, we try to find the closest match between the target person's features and the features of a specific category, or stereotype. How good the match is depends on how prototypical, or how good an example, the target is of the category. Disconfirmation of a feature of a stereotype is more likely to occur if the target person otherwise closely matches the category. That is, we are more likely to change a feature of a stereotype if the disconfirming behavior is in the context of other behavior that fits the stereotype. Let's take an example. The feature "not emotional" is part of the male stereotype. How might we decide that being emotional is acceptable for men? We will be more persuaded by an emotional male who watches football than by an emotional male who reads poetry; similarly, we will be more persuaded by a successful competitive businessman who is emotional than an emotional male hair stylist. What would have to happen for us to view the traditionally masculine occupations, such as lawyer and doctor, as acceptable for women? We will be more convinced by a female doctor who is married and has a family than by a single female doctor with no family in the area. We are more likely to view disconfirming behavior as acceptable if it is displayed by someone who otherwise fits the gender-role stereotype.

Sometimes we do not have to alter our stereotype because a target person calls to mind more than one stereotype; then, we can choose which stereotype to invoke. When thinking of Martina Navratilova, do you apply the category "lesbian" or "successful athlete"? People who like Navratilova, but have a negative stereotype of lesbians, recall the stereotype of successful athlete. For those people, she does not represent a disconfirming instance of the stereotype of lesbians; instead, she is an example of the stereotype for "successful athlete."

Do Stereotypes Reflect Reality?

Stereotypes reflect society's beliefs about the features that men and women possess, about which there is widespread agreement. But do stereotypes reflect reality? Gender-role stereotypes are an exaggeration in that they do not take into consideration any overlap between men and women. It is certainly not the case that all men are independent and all women are emotional. Some women are more independent than the average man, and some men are more emotional than the average woman.

However, there is some research that suggests our gender-role stereotypes are accurate. Swim (1994) compared college students' perceptions of the magnitude of 17 differences in men's and women's personalities to the results of research findings. If people perceived the same size difference on an attribute, such as empathy, as the research found, the stereotype would be accurate. Swim concluded that students typically did *not* overestimate the differences between men and women. Overestimation occurred for only two behaviors, aggression and verbal skills. Students thought the size of the sex differences in aggression and verbal skills was greater than research findings have shown to be true. Hall and Carter (1999) conducted a similar study examining 77 traits and behaviors among five samples of college students. On the whole, students were quite accurate. However, there was some variability in accuracy—the students who viewed themselves as more stereotypical were less accurate in their beliefs about men and women.

In sum, people's beliefs about the differences between men and women are fairly good representations of the actual differences. One problem with this area of research is that it is difficult to test the accuracy of many components of gender-role stereotypes. Obviously, we can determine objectively that men, on average, are taller than women. But how do we determine whether men are truly more independent than women? How do we determine whether women are more empathic than men?

This may be an impossible task because of the **shifting standard** (Biernat, 2003). The shifting standard is the idea that we might have one standard for defining a behavior for one group, but another standard for defining the behavior in another group. Have you ever heard the phrase (or, dare I say, used the phrase) "she hits well, *for a girl*"? The idea is that you hold the same behavior to different standards for males and females. A certain level of skill at baseball may be regarded as good if the person with the bat is female but only average if the person with the bat is male. Just as the standards for female and male athletes may not be the same, the standards for female and male nurturance may not be the same. You might have regarded a man as a "great dad" because he spends some of his leisure time playing with his kids and taking them shopping. That same behavior may not signify a "great mom," however. Thus it is very difficult to compare men and women on a dimension if different standards are used.

Research supports the shifting standard. In one study, college students enacted the role of baseball manager and rated the athletic ability of a set of male and female photographs (Biernat & Vescio, 2002). Among a set of male and female photographs rated as equally athletic, students expected the male players would have better batting averages and make fewer errors than the female players. Participants also reported more enthusiastic reactions to female players getting a hit compared to male players. The authors argue that the same judgment of athleticism is interpreted differently for male and female targets. In another study, college students evaluated men and women who stayed at home to take care of children and men and women who worked full time (Bridges, Etaugh, & Barnes-Farrell, 2002).

Although men and women homemakers were perceived as equally communal (and more communal than full-time employed men and women), women homemakers were perceived to provide more affection and comfort to children and engage in more child care activities than male homemakers. Again, it seems as if the same trait, being communal, is associated with a higher level of behavior for mothers than fathers.

The shifting standard makes it difficult to compare men's and women's behavior because we have different standards for defining a behavior displayed by a man versus a woman. Behavior that is similar may appear to be different because of shifting standards, as in the studies just described. Behavior that actually differs between men and women also may appear similar because of shifting standards. For example, you might believe men are helpful because they stop and help someone with a flat tire. You might also believe women are helpful because people are more likely to seek support from a woman than a man. But the behaviors are different and not necessarily comparable.

Taken collectively, these studies show it is difficult to assess the accuracy of stereotypes. We may perceive men and women to behave differently because sex differences in behavior truly exist. Or it may be that our stereotypes about men and women affect our interpretation of the behavior.

What Is the Status of Stereotypes Today?

Have stereotypes changed over time? Bergen and Williams (1991) investigated this question by comparing the stereotypes of male and female college students in 1972 to those in 1988. At each timepoint, 100 students were asked to rate how frequently each of 300 items was associated with men and women. The correlation of the ratings across the 2 timepoints was high ($r = .90$). More recently, Lueptow et al. (2001) examined college students' perceptions of the

typical male and typical female from 7 separate samples collected over 23 years—1974 through 1997. They found little evidence that stereotyping of men and women had decreased over time and even some evidence of an increase. As shown in Figure 3.8, men's and women's ratings of the typical female became more feminine over time. The typical female's masculinity increased for a time, peaked in 1986, and then decreased so that it was the same in 1997 as it was in 1977. Both men and women perceived the typical male as increasing slightly in masculinity over time but decreasing in femininity over time. Thus, there was not a lot of evidence for changes in college students' perceptions of men and women. However, a recent study of young adults from the United States, Brazil, and Chile showed that stereotypes of women became more masculine and less feminine over time in all countries but especially Brazil and Chile (Diekman et al., 2005). The authors concluded that the political changes that had taken place in Brazil and Chile in the past decade had led to greater participation of women in the public spheres, which accounts for the greater increase in masculine traits. There was little change in stereotypes of men.

The majority of studies on gender stereotypes focus on young adults, often college students. There is evidence that men and women perceive themselves in more similar terms as they grow older. Middle-aged men and women describe themselves in less stereotypical terms than young adults (Huyck, 1999). Other research suggests that as people get older, they describe themselves in less agentic and more communal terms (Diehl, Owen, & Youngblade, 2004).

Another way to learn about whether society's stereotypes of men and women have changed is to examine depictions of men and women on television. Three of the most poplar sitcoms in the 1980s reflected the new emphasis on androgyny: *Family Ties, Growing Pains,* and *The Cosby Show.* All three depicted

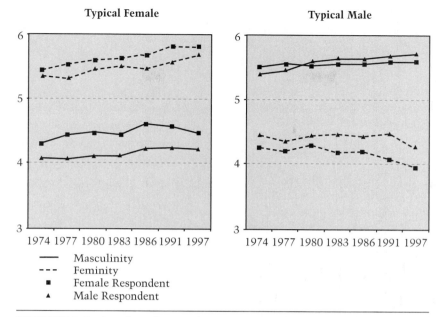

FIGURE 3.8 Men's and women's ratings of the typical female became more feminine over time. Ratings of the typical female's masculinity increased up until 1986 but then decreased somewhat. Men's ratings of the typical male have increased in masculinity and decreased in femininity over time.
Source: Adapted from Lueptow et al. (2001).

feminine-looking, dedicated mothers who were professionals in male-dominated fields (architect, writer, lawyer). The shows also featured devoted fathers who were professionals in fields that required sensitivity and concern for others (educational program producer for a PBS station, psychiatrist, obstetrician). By contrast, more recent television shows reflect a range of roles. The popular sitcom *Everybody Loves Raymond* portrays traditional male/female roles where the husband is a full-time paid employee and the wife stays home with the children, whereas *Friends* portrays nontraditional roles in the form of single parents, professional women, and men heavily involved in family roles. The influence of the media on gender roles is discussed in Chapter 5 when we review gender-role socialization theories of sex differences. Conduct Do Gender 3.4 to see if you think stereotypes have changed.

DO GENDER 3.4
Stereotypes Obtained from Media Portrayals of Men and Women

Examine a set of television shows to see if and how the stereotypes of men and women have changed. You may focus on a particular type of program or sample across a variety of programs (e.g., drama, comedy, cartoon). Then, examine one episode of 10 different programs and record the following for each character:

1. Character's sex.

2. Character's appearance.

3. Character's role (housewife, doctor, detective).

4. Character's personality traits.

5. Character's behavior.

If you are really energetic, conduct the same kind of experiment on a similar set of shows that appeared on television 20 or 30 years ago. Then compare the two sets of stereotypes. A variation of this experiment is to review television commercials or magazine advertisements.

TAKE HOME POINTS

- Gender-role stereotypes are the beliefs that we hold about male and female social roles.

- The descriptive aspects of gender-role stereotypes represent how we believe men and women *are* in our society; the prescriptive aspects of gender-role stereotypes represent how we believe men and women *ought to be* in our society.

- People tend to see a greater correspondence between the mentally healthy person and the mentally healthy male than between the mentally healthy person and the mentally healthy female. This suggests that we attach greater value to the male than the female gender-role stereotype.

- People of different ethnic backgrounds have some commonality in their conceptions of gender-role stereotypes.

- However, gender-role stereotypes appear to depend on the age, race, and class of the target person.

- Stereotypes consist of traits, behaviors, roles, and interests. Knowing people's status on any one of these stereotype dimensions allows us to infer their status on the other dimensions. In fact, people use one stereotype component to infer someone's status on other stereotype components.

- Stereotypes can be thought of as category-based expectancies. We rely on category-based expectancies, in this case gender-role stereotypes, when we have little information about a person. When provided with more information, we rely on target-based expectancies—meaning that we use what we know about the person (target) to draw inferences.

- In one sense, stereotypes are helpful; they simplify information processing.

- In another sense, stereotypes are harmful. Our expectations about people can influence how we behave toward them in such a way that they confirm our initial expectancies. This is called a self-fulfilling prophecy.

- Stereotypes are difficult to alter. When confronted with information that disconfirms a stereotype, we typically ignore the information, fail to recall it, make a situational attribution for it, or create a subtype. In other cases, we view the behavior as more extreme.

- The best way to change a specific aspect of people's gender-role stereotypes is to present them with an example of someone who disconfirms the stereotype on one dimension but otherwise fits the stereotype. This example will be more compelling than someone who departs from the stereotype on a lot of dimensions.

- It is difficult to determine whether our stereotypes of men and women are accurate because of the shifting standard. The shifting standard represents the idea that we view the exact same behavior differently when displayed by a male and a female.

BEHAVIORAL COMPONENT: SEX DISCRIMINATION

In 1993, Shannon Faulkner applied to an all-male military school, the Citadel (Lacayo, 1995). As we noted earlier, she was accepted because she made no reference to her sex on the application. When the Citadel discovered they had admitted a female, they withdrew the offer. A U.S. District Court ruled that the all-male admissions policy was unconstitutional and Faulkner entered the Citadel in August 1995. She lasted 5 days and then withdrew. Whether the fight was lost due to a lack of physical preparation for the Citadel, or to the emotional stress of death threats and classmates clad in T-shirts bearing the slogan "1,952 bulldogs and 1 bitch," no one can be sure (Lacayo, 1995). Her departure was marked by cheers and honking horns.

Several months later, in January 1996, lawyers from the Virginia Military Institute (VMI) argued before the U.S. Supreme Court that the VMI was not suitable for women because a woman's aspirations in the South are largely to marry, women's ethics revolve around care more than justice, even "macho" women cry, and only "bad girls" would want to attend an all-male military school (Carlson, 1996). The Court, however, ruled that the school would have to admit women.

Discrimination is the differential treatment of individuals based on their membership in a category. Sex discrimination, the subject of the cases just cited, is the differential treatment of persons based on their sex. As shown by the remarks made to the Supreme Court, gender-role stereotyping and prejudice or sexism can lead to sex discrimination. Both women and men can be victims of sex discrimination. A recent review of laboratory studies showed that people evaluate male and female applicants for other-sex jobs as less competent than for same-sex jobs (Davison & Burke, 2000). In an archival analysis of new hires in U.S. law firms during the 1990s, Gorman (2005) found that job criteria that were more masculine (e.g., ambitious, independent, logical) were associated with hiring fewer women, and job criteria that were more feminine (e.g., cooperative, friendly, verbally oriented) were associated with hiring fewer men.

The differential evaluation of men and women in the same job led to a widely publicized case on sex discrimination. The case is noteworthy because social psychological testimony on gender-role stereotyping played an instrumental role in the Supreme Court decision. The case involved Ann Hopkins, who was denied partnership at Price Waterhouse, one of the top eight accounting firms in the United States. Hopkins maintained she was denied partnership because of her sex. Price Waterhouse maintained that she had some "interpersonal skills" difficulties: "According to some evaluators, this 'lady partner candidate' was 'macho,' she 'overcompensated' for being a woman, and she needed a 'course at charm school.' A sympathetic colleague advised that Hopkins would improve her chances if she would 'walk more femininely, wear make-up, have her hair styled, and wear jewelry'" (*Hopkins v. Price Waterhouse*, 1985, p. 1117, cited in Fiske et al., 1991).

Susan Fiske, a social psychologist and an expert on stereotyping, presented the conditions that foster stereotyping to the Supreme Court. One condition is when an individual is unique in his or her membership in a given category. A single man in a class of 30 women or a single Asian person in a class of 20 Caucasians is more likely to become a victim of stereotyping. Only 1% of the partners (7 of 662) at Price Waterhouse were female at the time (Fiske & Stevens, 1993). Another condition that fosters stereotyping is when the group to which an individual belongs is incongruent with the person's role, in this case, the person's occupation. For example, male nurses are more likely to be viewed in terms of gender-role stereotypes than female nurses. In the 1980s, Ann Hopkins was in a nontraditional occupation for women, as there were few women who were managers of a Big 8 accounting firm. This is a case in which stereotype-inconsistent behavior which could not be ignored was viewed as more extreme; thus assertive behavior on the part of Hopkins was likely to have been viewed as aggressive. Although some of her clients viewed her aggressive behavior in positive terms—behavior that implied she could get the job done—the partners viewed her aggressive behavior in negative terms—as that of someone who was difficult to get along with. Citing the literature on gender-role stereotyping, Fiske and colleagues (1991) maintained that Hopkins's behavior may have been viewed differently because she was female. Recall the research on the shifting standard.

The Supreme Court took the scientific literature on gender-role stereotyping seriously and found in favor of Hopkins. The Court noted that the situation presented to Hopkins by Price Waterhouse was a no-win situation: The job required the trait of "aggressiveness" in order to succeed, yet the partners objected to women possessing this trait. The Court responded:

> Indeed, we are tempted to say that Dr. Fiske's expert testimony was merely icing on Hopkins's cake. It takes no special training to discern sex stereotyping in a description of an aggressive female employee as requiring "a course in charm school." Nor . . . does it require expertise in psychology to know that, if an employee's flawed "interpersonal skills" can be corrected by a soft-hued suit or a new shade of lipstick, perhaps it is the employee's sex and not her interpersonal skills that has drawn the criticism. (*Price Waterhouse v. Hopkins*, 1989, p. 1793, cited in Fiske et al., 1991)

If we remove gender-role stereotypes, will sex discrimination disappear? Not necessarily. Some research has shown that sex discrimination

SIDEBAR 3.4: *A 50–50 Relationship, the Case of "Wendt vs. Wendt" (Strober, 2002)*

Lorna and Gary Wendt met in high school and married after college. While he completed his M.B.A. at Harvard, Lorna Wendt worked as a music teacher. After they had their first child, Lorna Wendt stopped working outside the home and Gary Wendt rose through the corporate ranks to become chairman and CEO of General Electric Capital Services. After 30 years of marriage, in 1995, Gary Wendt asked his wife for a divorce and offered her $10 million. While Gary Wendt considered this sum of money more than enough for his wife to be "comfortable," Lorna Wendt said that the offer was not equitable. Because the estate was worth $100 million, Lorna Wendt argued that she was entitled to $50 million or half the assets.

In cases where the estate is less than $10–12 million, most courts divide the assets in half upon divorce. However, when the estate exceeds that figure, women often do not receive half the assets. This is when the court tries to figure out how much each party contributed to the marriage. In cases where the husband worked and the wife was a homemaker, it becomes very difficult to identify the value of the unpaid homemaker role. Lorna Wendt started out with the responsibilities of managing the household and taking care of children, but as her husband moved up the career ladder, she took on the added responsibilities of entertaining clients and planning social events. In the end, the court awarded Lorna Wendt $20 million and an additional $250,000 per year in alimony for life.

In 2001, Lorna Wendt was interviewed on National Public Radio Morning Edition (2001). When asked why she contested her husband's initial offer of $10 million, Lorna Wendt said: "My thinking was that I was an equal partner. When I entered this marriage, at that time, we were equal. We were partners in everything we did, every plan we made, even down to the finances. We worked very hard together to get where we were in a position that afforded us this money, and he could not devalue what I had brought to our relationship by putting a number such as that."

Since the divorce and settlement, Lorna Wendt has founded the Institute for Equality of Marriage to provide people with information about managing finances before, during, and after marriage. Lorna Wendt strongly advocates for prenuptial agreements, advising both partners to ask each other before marriage if they are equal partners. She says, "Can you imagine if Gary had said to me, you know, 35 years, ago 'No, I think you're about 10 percent'."

can occur in the absence of gender-role stereo-types. For example, Glick, Zion, and Nelson (1988) found that they could alter managers' and business professionals' perceptions of, but not their behavior toward, male and female job applicants. When they provided professionals with the same information about male and female applicants—that they possessed features of the male gender role—professionals perceived men and women as equally aggressive. However, the professionals still indicated they would be more likely to interview male than female applicants for a masculine job and more likely to interview female than male applicants for a feminine job. Thus regardless of a person's traits, we may still view a receptionist as "female" and a construction worker as "male." It is occupational stereotypes that could lead to sex discrimination.

It is sometimes difficult to evaluate the equal treatment of men and women when they do not have the same positions in society. See Sidebar 3.4 for a controversial case of sex discrimination. When people think of sex discrimination, they typically think of women as being treated unfairly compared to men, especially in regard to employment situations. This topic is reviewed in more depth in Chapter 12. Can you think of any ways we treat men unfairly? When the military draft was still in effect and only men were chosen, was that sex discrimination? When two working parents divorce and custody is automatically awarded to the mother, is that sex discrimination? Remember that sex discrimination refers to the differential treatment of either men or women due to their sex.

SUMMARY

In this chapter, I moved beyond conceptions of gender roles to the study of attitudes toward gender roles and to the category of gender. Attitudes consist of three components: affective, cognitive, and behavioral. With respect to gender, the affective component is sexism, the cognitive component is gender-role stereotyping, and the behavioral component is sex discrimination. I reviewed instruments that measure traditional and modern sexism as well as sexism that includes both favorable and unfavorable attitudes toward women. I presented the components of gender-role stereotypes and dis-

cussed how the components are related to one another. I presented data on the problems with gender-role stereotypes, including how they affect perception and behavior. There are difficulties in changing gender-role stereotypes, in particular because stereotype-inconsistent behavior is often unnoticed, attributed to situational causes, or viewed as more extreme. Sexism and gender-role stereotyping are antecedents to sex discrimination, which I discussed in the context of a recent Supreme Court ruling that utilized data on gender-role stereotyping in reaching its decision.

DISCUSSION QUESTIONS

1. In what areas have attitudes toward men's and women's roles become less traditional over time, and in what areas have they remained unchanged?

2. What is the difference between hostile and benevolent sexism?
3. Who is most likely to hold benevolent sexist beliefs?

4. How do gender-role stereotypes relate to self-perceptions of gender role?
5. Why is it difficult to change gender-role stereotypes? How would you go about trying to change someone's gender-role stereotype?
6. The majority of studies on gender-role stereotypes have been conducted on Caucasian, middle-class adults, typically college students. In what ways

have these samples limited our research?
7. In what ways does it seem that stereotypes of men and women have changed? In what ways, are they the same?
8. How can gender-role stereotypes be harmful?
9. How would our lives be different if gender-role stereotypes were erased from our minds?

SUGGESTED READING

Biernat, M. (2003). Toward a broader view of social stereotyping. *American Psychologist, 58*, 1019–1027.

Deaux, K., & Kite, M. (1993). Gender stereotypes. In F. L. Denmark & M. A. Paludi (Eds.), *Psychology of women: A handbook of issues and theories* (pp. 107–139). Westport, CT: Greenwood Press.

Fiske, S. T., Bersoff, D. N., Borgida, E., Deaux, K., & Heilman, M. E. (1991). Social science research on trial: Use of sex stereotyping

research in *Price Waterhouse v. Hopkins. American Psychologist, 46*, 1049–1060.

Glick, P., & Fiske, S. T. (1996). The Ambivalent Sexism Inventory: Differentiating hostile and benevolent sexism. *Journal of Personality and Social Psychology, 70*, 491–512.

Swann, W. B., Jr., Langlois, J.H., & Gilbert, L. A. (Eds.). (1999). *Sexism and stereotypes in modern society: The gender science of Janet Taylor Spence.* Washington, DC: American Psychological Association.

KEY TERMS

Backlash effect—The penalty that is imposed on people for counterstereotypical behavior.

Benevolent discrimination—Providing more help to women than men with the notion that women are less competent than men and are in need of men's help.

Benevolent sexism—Positive feelings toward women coupled with the notion that women are less competent than men and in need of men's help.

Category-based expectancies—Assumptions about individuals based on characteristics of general categories to which they belong.

Correspondent inference theory—Idea that people are more likely to make dispositional attributions for behavior that is unique or extreme rather than normative.

Egalitarian gender ideology—Maintains that power is distributed equally between men and women and that men and women identify equally with the same spheres.

Gender ideology—Attitudes toward men's and women's roles.

Gender-role stereotypes—Features that individuals assign to men and women in their society; features not assigned due to one's biological sex, but due to the social roles men and women hold.

Hostile sexism—Feelings of hostility toward women reflected by negative assumptions about women.

Self-fulfilling prophecy—Situation in which expectations influence behavior toward someone so the person behaves in a way to confirm our expectations.

Sexism—Feeling toward people based on their sex alone.

Shifting standard—Idea that there is one standard for defining the behavior of one group, but another standard for defining the behavior of another group.

Target-based expectancies—Perceptions of a person based on individual information about that person.

Traditional gender ideology—Maintains that men's sphere is work and women's sphere is home.

Transitional gender ideology—Maintains that it is acceptable for women and men to identify with the same spheres, but women should devote proportionately more time to matters at home and men should devote proportionately more time to work.

CHAPTER 4

SEX-RELATED COMPARISONS: OBSERVATIONS

"Are Boys Better at Math?" (United Press International, *New York Times*, December 7, 1980)

"New Study Shows Boys Outnumber Girls 13 to 1 as Top Math Scorers" (Cowen & Cowen, *Christian Science Monitor*, December 6, 1983)

"Male Hormones Linked to Math Ability in Junior High School Boys, Study Finds" (Associated Press, *Toronto Star*, May 30, 1986)

These are the eye-catching headlines of stories about a study on sex-related differences in math. Differences are interesting. Differences are eye catching. And, as you will see in this chapter, differences are often exaggerated and overinterpreted—especially the one referred to in these headlines.

As mentioned in Chapter 1, the subject of sex comparisons is controversial.

Scientists continue to debate whether sex comparisons should be made. Regardless of our philosophy on this issue, we cannot ignore the fact that a vast literature exists on this topic. Many sex comparisons have been made in cognitive abilities: Who has better spatial abilities? Who has greater aptitude in math? Are men or women better with language? Sex comparisons also have been made in social domains: Is one sex more empathic? Who helps more? Are men really more aggressive than women? The sexes also are compared in terms of moral and social development. I review each of these areas of research in this chapter. Other areas in which sex comparisons have been made, particularly those having to do with relationships and health, are addressed in subsequent chapters. The primary goal of this chapter is to evaluate the results of sex comparisons in cognitive, social, and developmental domains.

Before embarking on this review, you should realize that there are more similarities than differences between men and women. However, there are some obvious, incontestable differences. For example, men, on average, are taller than women; men, on average, are stronger than women; women, by contrast, have a higher proportion of body fat than men. These are biological facts. However, even within the realm of biology, a great number of similarities exist between men and women. Most men and women have two eyes, two arms, and two legs; most men and women have a heart, lungs, and vocal cords with which they can speak. The same logic applies to the cognitive and social domains. Although there may be some differences, by far, men and women have more in common in the way they think and in the way they behave.

If there are so many similarities between men and women, why do we focus on differences? Belle (1985) suggests that we tend to focus on differences when we are confronted with two of anything. For example, parents with two children are more likely than parents of three or more children to emphasize the differences between the children: "Mary is good in math but not geography; Johnny is good in geography but not math." Parents with three children, however, are more likely to describe each child individually without making a comparison to the other children: "Mary is good in math, Johnny is good in geography, Paul is good in English." Belle also reported that the same phenomenon occurs among anthropologists studying two kinds of cultures. Whereas two cultures are often described in comparison to one another, anthropologists who study more than two cultures emphasize the diversity of human nature. Thus we would be less likely to

emphasize sex differences if there were at least three sexes!

If there are more similarities than differences between men and women, why does it seem that men and women are so different? Why is John Gray's (1992) book *Men Are from Mars, Women Are from Venus* a best seller if men and women are not opposites? One reason is that differences are more salient and more eye catching than similarities. I mentioned in Chapter 1 that sex is a very salient attribute of a person. Thus when two people perform differently on a task and we look for an explanation, we can easily draw the inference that sex must be the distinguishing factor. Second, we have stereotypes about men's and women's behavior that are quite strong and quite distinct. We often recall information that confirms our stereotypes and disregard information that disconfirms our stereotypes. This is called **confirmatory hypothesis testing**. We are most likely to do this when we have strong expectations, when the stereotype is about a group, and when the stereotype is about a trait (Stangor & McMillan, 1992). For example, one stereotype about babies is that males are more active than females. Several years ago, my husband and I were visiting some neighbors. There was a male infant and a female infant, both of whom seemed intent on tearing up the house! The mother of the male infant remarked, "Isn't it true about how much more active boys are than girls? Look at Justin compared to Emily." My husband, who thankfully is oblivious to some gender stereotypes, disappointed the mother by failing to confirm her hypothesis. He said, "They both seem pretty active to me!" The mother was clearly disappointed in this response. If a male and a female take a math test and the male outperforms the female, most people will remember this incident. But if the female outperforms the male, we will either forget the incident, decide the female or male was "different" and not representative of the group, or make a situational attribution (e.g., Maria had seen the test before; Matthew didn't get much sleep last night).

As you will see, sex differences have been documented in some domains. Unfortunately, a significant difference in performance between males and females is often misunderstood to mean all males are better at task X than all females, or all females are better at task Y than all males. An example of a significant difference in performance is shown in Figure 4.1. You can see the mean score for men is slightly (and

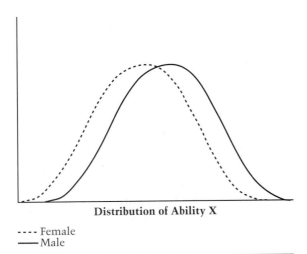

Distribution of Ability X

---- Female
—— Male

FIGURE 4.1   Sample distribution of a hypothetical ability (ability X) for males and females. You can see a great deal of overlap between the two distributions. Yet the average of ability X is slightly higher for males than females. This illustrates the fact that a sex difference in an ability does not mean all men differ from all women. In fact, a statistically significant sex difference can exist even when most of the men and women are similar in their ability level.

could be significantly) higher than the mean score for women. But you should also notice a great deal of overlap in the distributions of men's and women's scores. Only a small number of men are performing better than all of the women, and only a small number of women are performing worse than all of the men. Thus even though a sex difference exists, most men and women are performing about the same. Keep this in mind when you read about a sex difference in this chapter. Also remember that a sex difference does not imply all men differ from all women, which may explain why you will have some personal experiences that do not fit with the research literature.

I begin my review of sex comparison research by discussing the early work of Maccoby and Jacklin, who published the first comprehensive review of sex differences in 1974. Although this book was written a long time ago, it had a great impact on the field. As you will see, it also was subjected to serious criticism. Then I review the more recent work on sex comparisons that have been made in several important cognitive and social domains.

MACCOBY AND JACKLIN'S PSYCHOLOGY OF SEX DIFFERENCES

Maccoby and Jacklin's (1974) *Psychology of Sex Differences* entailed a comprehensive review of the ways men and women differ psychologically. They examined intellectual or cognitive domains as well as social abilities. Their conclusions were surprising to many people: They found that sex differences existed in only a few domains and that many stereotypes had no basis in fact. They identified sex differences in only four domains: verbal ability (advantage girls), visual-spatial ability (advantage boys), mathematical ability (advantage boys), and aggression (greater in boys). They found no sex differences in self-esteem, sociability, analytic ability, or achievement motivation, and it was unclear whether there were sex differences in activity level, competitiveness, dominance, or nurturance.

One limitation of Maccoby and Jacklin's (1974) work is that it was a **narrative review**. In a narrative review, authors decide which studies are included and come to their own conclusions about whether the majority of studies provide evidence for or against a sex difference; basically, a tally is made of the number of studies that report a difference versus no difference. This kind of review presents several difficulties. One problem is that the authors decide how many studies are enough to show a difference does or does not exist. If 12 of 12 studies show a difference, a difference must exist. But what about 10 of 12? Or 8 of 12? Or even 6 of 12? How many is enough? A second difficulty with narrative reviews is that the pattern of results may be disproportionately influenced by findings from small samples. Perhaps the majority of studies show men and women have equal verbal ability, but all of these "no difference" studies have sample sizes under 30, and the few studies that report women have greater verbal skills than men are based on sample sizes of over 100. Should we still conclude there is no sex difference in verbal ability? The power to detect a significant difference between men and women when one truly exists is limited in small samples. Thus a narrative review of an area of research that contains many small sample studies may lead to faulty conclusions.

In 1976, Jeanne Block wrote a response to Maccoby and Jacklin's (1974) review of sex differences that was virtually ignored. Block reviewed the same literature and arrived at conclusions very different from the ones

reached by Maccoby and Jacklin. First, she noted that Maccoby and Jacklin did not censor the studies they included; that is, they averaged across all studies, whether methodologically sound or not. A number of studies had very small samples, a problem just noted. Some studies used unreliable instruments; other studies used instruments that lacked **construct validity**, meaning there was not sufficient evidence that the instruments measured what they were supposed to measure.

Second, Block (1976) noted tremendous age bias in the studies reviewed. She found that 75% of the reviewed studies were limited to people age 12 and under; 40% used preschool children. The reason so many studies were conducted with children is that comparisons between males and females first became popular in developmental psychology. Developmental psychologists compared males and females in their studies, hoping no differences would be found so they could combine boys and girls when analyzing their data. Why is it a problem that Maccoby and Jacklin's (1974) review focused so heavily on children? The problem is that they did not take into consideration the fact that some sex differences might not appear until adolescence and later; in fact, the three cognitive differences that Maccoby and Jacklin noted did not appear until adolescence. Adolescence is sometimes referred to as a time of **gender intensification**, a time when boys and girls are concerned with adhering to gender roles. Thus sex differences that arise as a result of socialization pressures might not appear until adolescence. Even sex differences thought to be influenced by hormones might not appear until puberty. When Block categorized the studies into three age groups (under 4, between 5 and 12, and over 12), she found that sex differences in many domains became larger with increasing age.

In the end, Block agreed with the sex differences that Maccoby and Jacklin found but also found evidence of other sex differences. She concluded that boys, compared to girls, were better on insight problems, showed greater dominance, had a stronger self-concept, were more active, and were more impulsive. Girls, in comparison to boys, expressed more fear, showed more anxiety, had less confidence on tasks, maintained closer contact with friends, sought more help, scored higher on social desirability, and were more compliant with adults.

The conclusions of Maccoby and Jacklin (1974) and of Block (1976) were obviously not the same. Both, however, relied on narrative reviews of the literature. In the 1980s, a new method was developed to review the literature that led to more objective conclusions: meta-analysis. Much of the recent literature on sex comparisons, which is described in this chapter, has relied on meta-analysis.

Meta-Analysis

Meta-analysis is a statistical tool that quantifies the results of a group of studies. In a meta-analysis, we take into consideration not only whether a significant difference is found in a study but also the size of the difference, or the **effect size**. The effect size is calculated by taking the difference between the means of the two groups (in this case, men and women), and dividing this difference by the variability in the scores of the members of these two groups (i.e., the standard deviation), as shown in Figure 4.2. As the size of the sample increases, the estimate

$$d = \frac{M_{males} - M_{females}}{\sqrt{\dfrac{SD^2_{males} + SD^2_{females}}{2}}}$$

Note: SD = Standard Deviation

FIGURE 4.2 The *d* statistic, as calculated by this formula, is used to determine the size of a sex difference.

of the mean becomes more reliable. This means the variability around the mean, the standard deviation, becomes smaller in larger samples. A small difference between the means of two large groups will result in a larger effect size than a small difference between the means of two small groups. Hence a study that shows men score 10 points higher than women on the math SAT will result in a larger effect size if there are 100 women and men in the study than if there are 20 women and men in the study. The size of an effect is measured with the *d* statistic. The rule of thumb used to interpret the *d* statistic is that .2 is a small effect, .5 is a medium effect, and .8 is a large effect (Cohen, 1977). A .2 effect size means that sex accounts for less than 1% of the variance in the outcome; a .5 effect means that sex accounts for 6% of the variance; a .8 effect means that sex accounts for 14% of the variance (Cohen, 1977).

If a large effect accounts for only 14% of the variance, is a small effect even worth discussing? As you will discover in this chapter, many sex differences are small. Whether small means trivial is an issue that continues to be hotly debated. The finding that sex accounts for 1% of the variance in an outcome does not appear to be earth shattering. However, 1% can be quite meaningful (Rosenthal, 1994): It depends on the outcome. For example, small effects in medical studies can have enormous implications. In a study to determine whether aspirin could prevent heart attacks, participants were randomly assigned to receive aspirin or a placebo. The study was called to a halt before it ended because the effects of aspirin were so dramatic (Steering Committee, 1988). The investigators deemed it unethical to withhold aspirin from people. In that study, aspirin accounted for less than 1% of the variance in heart attacks.

What about outcomes that are relevant to gender? Bringing the issue closer to home,

Martell, Lane, and Emrich (1996) used computer simulations to examine the implications of a small amount of sex discrimination on promotions within an organization. They showed that if 1% of the variance in performance ratings were due to employee sex, an equal number of men and women at entry-level positions would result in 65% of men holding the highest level positions over time—assuming promotions were based on performance evaluations. So here, a very small bias had large consequences. Keep this in mind when considering the sizes of the effects in this chapter.

Using meta-analysis rather than narrative reviews to understand an area of research has several advantages. As mentioned previously, meta-analysis takes into consideration the size of the effects; thus all studies showing a significant difference will not be weighted similarly. Another advantage of meta-analysis is that researchers can examine how other variables influence, or moderate, the size of the effect. A **moderating variable** is one that alters the relation between the independent and the dependent variable. I often refer to a moderating variable as an "it depends on" variable. When sex comparisons are made, a difference may "depend on" the age of the respondents, the gender role of the respondents, or the year the study was published. Recall that Block (1976) found that many sex differences were apparent only among older participants; thus age was a moderator variable. Another potential moderating variable is the year of publication. If a sex difference appeared in the 1970s but disappeared by the 1990s, perhaps men's and women's behavior became more similar over time. We can even ask if the results of a sex comparison depend on the sex of the author; men or women may be more likely to publish a certain result. Age, gender role, author sex, and year of publication are frequently tested as moderator variables in the following meta-analyses.

In one way, meta-analysis is limited in the same way narrative reviews are: Researchers still make subjective decisions about what studies to include in the review. Researchers conducting a meta-analysis often come up with a set of criteria to decide whether a study is included in the review. Criteria may be based on sample characteristics (e.g., restrict to English-speaking samples) or on methodological requirements (e.g., participants must be randomly assigned to condition). One difficulty with any kind of review, meta-analytic or narrative, is that studies failing to detect a difference are less likely to be published. In meta-analysis, this is referred to as the **file-drawer problem** (Hyde & McKinley, 1997): Studies that do not find sex differences are not published and end up in investigators' file drawers. Thus the published studies represent a biased sample of the studies that have been conducted. The file drawer problem may not be as significant in studies of sex comparisons as in other research because some of the sex comparison data come from studies whose primary purpose was not to evaluate sex. Investigators may be studying aggression, empathy, or math ability for other reasons aside from sex but report the results of sex comparisons as a matter of routine.

TAKE HOME POINTS

- Men and women are more similar than different, as shown by the overlapping distributions in Figure 4.1.

- The first comprehensive review of sex differences was published by Maccoby and Jacklin and revealed that there were sex differences in only four domains: verbal, spatial, math, aggression.

- That review was a narrative review, which is limited by the fact that it doesn't take into consideration the size of the differences.

■ Meta-analysis provides a way to quantitatively review studies, taking into consideration sample size and effect sizes (*d*'s).

■ Meta-analysis also allows one to consider whether certain variables, known as moderator variables, influence the size of the sex difference.

■ A disadvantage of both narrative and meta-analytic reviews is that studies finding no differences are less likely to be published, a weakness known as the file-drawer problem.

SEX COMPARISONS IN COGNITIVE ABILITIES

Many people assume men have greater spatial and math abilities than women. People also assume women have greater verbal skills than men. As the literature here shows, these assumptions are overly simplistic. This area of research is highly controversial because a sex difference in an area of cognition could lead people to assume one sex is more suitable for a career requiring that ability. This could ultimately lead to sex discrimination. Thus it is important we evaluate this research carefully. For each cognitive ability I discuss, one or more meta-analyses exist. I report the effect size, the *d*, in parentheses for the major findings. As shown in Figure 4.3, a *d* that is positive indicates men outperform women, and a *d* that is negative indicates women outperform men.

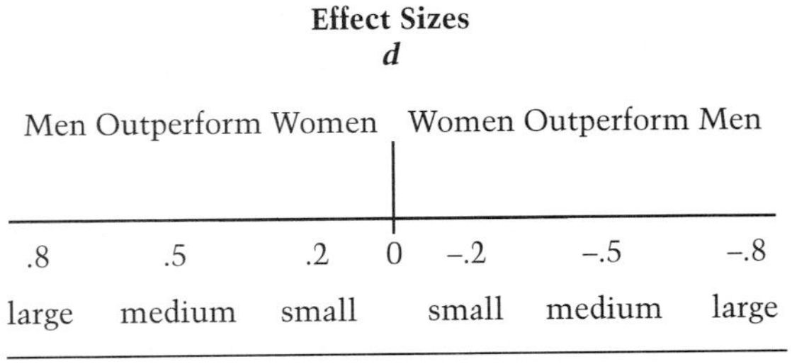

Effect Sizes
d

Men Outperform Women	Women Outperform Men

.8	.5	.2	0	−.2	−.5	−.8
large	medium	small		small	medium	large

FIGURE 4.3   Indication of the strength of effect sizes (*d*).

Spatial Ability

Spatial skills involve the ability to think about and reason using mental pictures rather than words. However, spatial ability is not a single construct. Think of all the activities that involve spatial skills: reading maps, doing jigsaw puzzles, trying to pack all your belongings from school into the trunk of a car, and finding where you put your keys. Given the diversity of tasks that involve spatial skills, it is no surprise that the results of sex comparisons depend on the type of spatial skill.

Voyer, Voyer, and Bryden (1995) conducted a meta-analysis on the three distinct spatial skills shown in Figure 4.4. They found moderate sex differences for spatial perception (*d* = +.44) and mental rotation (*d* = +.56), but only a small difference for spatial visualization (*d* = +.19). Thus the size of the sex difference in spatial skills ranged from very small to medium, depending on the particular skill. Similar findings appeared in a society that supports a gender-egalitarian ideology, Norway, where college males outperformed college females on mental rotation (*d* = +.85) and spatial visualization (*d* = +.48; Nordvik & Amponsah, 1998). The sex difference held even when male and female technology students who had a similar high school background in math and physics were compared. Sex differences in spatial abilities do not appear to be disappearing with time (Halpern & Collaer, 2005).

The meta-analysis showed that the size of the sex difference increased with age. In children under 13, sex differences ranged from zero to small. In children over 18, sex differences ranged from small to large. Findings were averaged across the different spatial tasks when age was examined as a moderator variable.

A very consistent and sizable sex difference exists in one skill that requires spatial ability: aiming at a target (Kimura, 1999). Men are

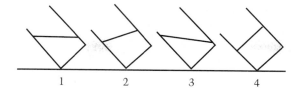

A spatial perception item. Respondents are asked to indicate
which tilted bottle has a horizontal water line.

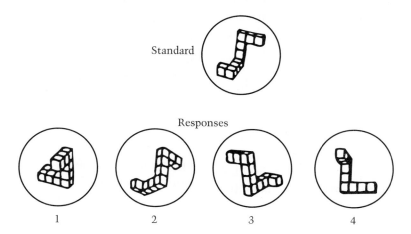

A mental rotation item. Respondents are asked to identify the two responses
that show the standard in a different orientation.

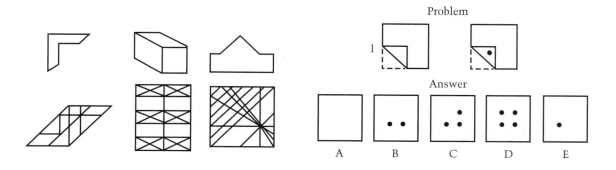

Spatial visualization items. Left, Embedded Figures: Respondents are asked to find the simple
shape shown on the top in the complex shape shown on the bottom. Right, Paper Folding:
Respondents are asked to indicate how the paper would look when unfolded after a hole is punched.

FIGURE 4.4 Sample items from tests that measure spatial perception, mental rotation, and spatial
visualization.
Source: M. C. Linn and A. C. Petersen (1985). Emergence and characterization of sex differences in
spatial ability: A meta-analysis. *Child Development, 56,* 1479–1498. © 1985 Society for Research in Child
Development.

consistently better than women in their accuracy at hitting a target, whether shooting or throwing darts. Physical factors such as reaction time, height, and weight do not account for this sex difference. Differences in experiences with target shooting also do not account for the sex difference (Kimura, 1999). The sex difference can be observed in children as young as 3 years old. Performance on this task seems to be unrelated to performance on other spatial ability tasks, such as mental rotation (Kimura, 1999).

Up to this point, the size of the sex difference in spatial skills has been variable, but the effects have always been in the direction of men. Can we conclude that the direction of the effect is consistent across spatial tasks? No. A spatial domain in which women appear to have greater aptitude than men is spatial location memory (Eals & Silverman, 1994). Women are more likely than men to notice if an object has been moved from its original location, and women are better than men at finding lost objects. If you show men and women a picture that contains a number of objects, such as the one shown in Figure 4.5, and remove or move one object, women will be more likely than men to notice the change. How quickly can you figure out which objects have been moved in the bottom compared to the top of Figure 4.5? If you place men and women in a room with objects, after leaving the room, women will be more accurate than men in recalling which objects were in the room and where those objects were located. Women also seem to excel at a game that requires object location (McBurney et al., 1997). In a memory game, a set of cards is presented with the pictures turned face down. There are pairs of cards with the same picture, and each person may turn over any two cards to try to find a match. Women are better than men at finding the matches. Thus the direction of the sex difference in spatial skills is not consistent across all tasks.

One conclusion is that men are better at manipulating objects in space, and women are

DO GENDER 4.1
Sex Comparisons in Directions

Choose one location that is across the town or city where you live and one location that is not very far away. Ask 10 men and 10 women to give you directions to each of these locations. Then have them write out the directions. Record use of landmarks, estimates of distance, use of street names, and north/south/east/west terminology to see if there are sex differences.

better at locating objects. If true, these differences could lead men and women to give directions differently. Two studies have found that women are more likely to use landmarks, and men are more likely to use distances and north/south/east/west terminology when giving directions (Dabbs et al., 1998; Lawton, 2001). A parallel finding has been shown with rats: Female rats are more likely than male rats to rely on landmarks and male rats are more likely than female rats to use geometric cues when solving problems (Kimura, 1992). Look at the map shown in Figure 4.6. How would you get from the Town Hall to Katja Park? Conduct your own survey on how men and women give directions in Do Gender 4.1 to see if this is true.

TAKE HOME POINTS

- The direction and magnitude of sex differences in spatial abilities depend on the specific task.

- Men may have more skill than women in spatial perception, whereas women may have more skill than men in object location.

- Of all the spatial abilities, the sex difference in mental rotation is the largest, in favor of men.

FIGURE 4.5   Example of a test used to measure spatial location memory. Cover the bottom figure and study the top figure. Now, cover the top figure and examine the bottom figure. Which items are in a different location?

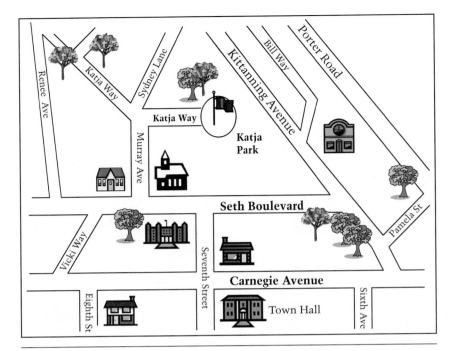

FIGURE 4.6 Research has suggested that men and women give directions differently: Men use north/south/east/west terminology and women use landmarks. How would you get from the Town Hall to Katja Park?

Mathematical Ability

Certainly, math ability is one domain in which sex differences are clear cut, right? Two meta-analytic reviews concluded there was a small sex difference in math ability favoring males. Hyde, Fennema, and Lamon (1990) conducted a meta-analysis of 100 studies on math skills that involved 254 independent samples. The overall effect size was small, $d = +.15$, favoring males over females. Hedges and Nowell (1995) conducted a meta-analysis of large samples of high school students. They found effect sizes that ranged from $+.03$ to $+.26$, with an average of $+.16$. Thus both reviews concluded that there was an overall sex difference in math in favor of males but that the difference was small.

Like spatial skills, math ability also encompasses an array of distinct skills, and results of sex comparisons depend on the specific skill. In a national sample of 12th-graders conducted by the Educational Testing Service (Cole, 1997) males outperformed females on math concepts ($d = -.11$), but females outperformed males on math computation ($d = -.18$). There is cross-cultural support for these differences: Similar trends have been identified in samples from Thailand, Taiwan, and Japan (Kimura, 1999).

Sex differences in math also appear to be influenced by age. A study of kindergarten through third-graders showed that there was no overall sex difference in math skills and no sex difference in the rate of improvement over these four grades (Lachance & Mazzocco, 2006). However, two large nationally representative longitudinal studies showed that boys and girls had similar math scores in elementary school (or, if anything, favoring females), but a small sex difference favoring males appeared by the time they reached 12th grade (Leahey & Guo, 2001). When examining the specific domains of math, one meta-analysis showed that men outperformed women on mathematical problem solving ($d = +.08$), but this difference was limited to older children, specifically high school ($d = +.29$) and college students ($d = +.32$; Hyde et al., 1990). However, in another area, math computation, females outperformed males ($d = -.14$), but this difference was limited to elementary and middle school children ($d = -.20$ and $-.22$, respectively; Hyde et al., 1990). There were no sex differences in understanding of mathematical concepts ($d = -.03$) at any age. Thus the male advantage in math appears to emerge with age.

Sex differences in math skills also appear to be decreasing over time (Hyde et al., 1990). The effect size in studies published before 1974 was $+.31$, whereas the effect size in studies published from 1974 onward was $+.14$. Even sex differences on college admissions tests seem to be getting smaller over time (Leahey & Guo, 2001). Thus as men and women are provided with more similar math-related opportunities and are equally encouraged to pursue math, differences may be diminishing.

The small sex difference in math aptitude certainly challenges prevailing stereotypes. Where does the idea come from that men outperform women in math by leaps and bounds? One source is studies of select samples of individuals who are highly talented in math. In Hyde and colleagues' (1990) meta-analysis, the effect sizes for select samples ranged from $+.33$ to $+.59$. This means that among people who are very talented in math, men have greater ability than women. In fact, when these select samples were excluded from the meta-analysis, the effect size was near zero ($d = +.05$). A major study of talented adolescents showed a sizable advantage for men over women in math. This was the Study of Mathematically Precocious Youth (SMPY) that attracted the headlines at the beginning of the chapter. This study examined nearly ten thousand 12- and 13-year-olds who were talented in math

(Benbow & Stanley, 1980). To be eligible for the study, students had to have scored in the upper 2% to 5% on a national standardized math test. The study involved six separate samples evaluated between 1972 and 1979. These students completed the math and verbal SAT tests. Although there was no sex difference on the verbal portion of the SAT, a medium-size sex difference appeared on the math portion ($d = +.39$). The size of the difference was even larger when the extreme high end of this already highly select sample was examined. Specifically, 2 times as many boys as girls scored above 500, 4 times as many boys as girls scored above 600, and 12 times as many boys as girls scored above 700 on the math SAT (Benbow, 1988). Benbow noted that the size of the sex difference did not seem to be changing over time.

Remember, the findings from the SMPY are not representative of the general population: This was a highly select sample. And the study was conducted a very long time ago. Unfortunately, the results of the study were highly publicized and the selectness of the sample often was not noted or was lost in the content of the news articles. This explains why people seem to believe there is a larger sex difference in math skills than there really is.

There is also a great paradox when it comes to gender and math. Females receive better math grades in school, but males perform better on math achievement tests, including the SAT, the ACT, and the GRE (Royer & Garofoli, 2005). Several explanations have been put forth to explain this discrepancy. (See "Paradox of School: Grades and Standardized Tests: Why Aren't They the Same?" in Sidebar 4.1 for a discussion of this issue.) One possibility is that males and females use different strategies to solve math problems and that the strategies females use are more closely tied to the classroom. This hypothesis was supported by a study of high-math-ability junior and senior high school students who were asked to solve

SIDEBAR 4.1: *Paradox of School Grades and Standardized Tests: Why Aren't They the Same?*

Why do girls outperform boys in the classroom—even in stereotypical masculine subjects, such as math—yet perform worse than boys on standardized tests? One reason why girls perform better than boys in school is that boys and girls approach their schoolwork differently (Kenney-Benson et al., 2006). Girls have a more mastery-oriented style (I do math to improve my skills), whereas boys have a more performance-oriented style (I do math to show my teacher I'm smarter than the other students). In a study of fifth-graders who were followed for 2 years, investigators linked these sex differences in orientation to math grades. In addition, they found that girls were less likely than boys to be disruptive in class. The combination of having a mastery orientation and being less disruptive in the classroom was linked to girls' higher math grades.

But, these different learning styles do not translate into higher achievement scores for girls in math. Thus the different environments of the school and the achievement test setting may contribute to the paradox of women receiving higher math grades in school and males receiving higher math test scores.

math SAT problems out loud (Gallagher & DeLisi, 1994). Although there was no sex difference in overall performance, females performed better on conventional problems that were learned in the classroom, and males performed better on unconventional problems that had not been learned in the classroom. In terms of strategy, females were more likely than males to rely on conventional strategies that had been learned in the classroom, and males were more likely than females to come up with new strategies on their own. It was not that these new or unconventional strategies were more likely than conventional strategies to lead to correct solutions, but unconventional strategies may signify the willingness to try something new when what you have already learned in the classroom doesn't work. The authors suggest that males may be more likely than females to do this because they have greater confidence in math. If these findings generalize beyond high-math-ability males and females, they may explain why females perform better than males in the classroom, and males perform better than females on standardized math tests.

Is nature or nurture responsible for the sex difference in math? Some argue that the sex differences in math that appear among older students occur because women take fewer math and science courses than men in high school and college (Hyde et al., 1990). Benbow and Stanley (1980) argued that the large sex difference in the SMPY that persisted across time suggests a biological basis. They suggested this difference in math could not have come from boys and girls taking different courses, because they have had similar educational backgrounds at this point in their education (seventh and eighth grade). In fact, research has shown that differences in math courses cannot account for men's superior math performance (Bridgeman & Wendler, 1991). However, others argue that men and women never have similar experiences with math because math is more strongly encouraged in boys than girls by parents, teachers, and peers (Eccles & Jacobs, 1986). This point is elaborated in Chapter 6.

Perhaps men and women have different attitudes toward math. A meta-analysis of attitudes toward math revealed that men were much more likely than women to view math as a male domain ($d = +.90$; Hyde et al., 1990). The authors found that the size of the difference in attitudes toward math seemed to increase with age; in particular, there were larger sex differences among high school students compared to elementary school children. Thus if attitudes toward math were to account for sex differences in performance, it would do so only among older students. This fits with the one domain in which a substantial sex difference has been documented in the normal population, problem-solving ability, a difference that appears only among older students. Thus part of the reason men perform better on math tasks compared to women among older students is because men are more confident than women in math.

Have attitudes toward math changed? A recent Gallup Poll (2005) showed that similar numbers of male and female teens aged 13 to 17 said math is their favorite subject (29%). However, more girls than boys said that math was their most difficult subject (44% vs. 31%).

It also is possible that men's greater math ability is linked to men's greater spatial ability, in particular mental rotation. Mental rotation ability is related to scores on math achievement tests (Nuttall, Casey, & Pezaris, 2005). Math ability includes both spatial and verbal skills. One study showed that males performed better on math problems that required spatial solutions, and females performed better on problems that required verbal solutions and memory from textbooks (Gallagher, Levin, & Cahalan, 2002). Another study examined whether men's better spatial skills or women's greater math anxiety contributed to the sex difference in math performance (Casey, Nuttall, & Pezaris, 1997). Among the top third of college-bound students, men had higher SAT math scores than women, men performed better on the mental rotation task, and women had higher math anxiety. Men's mental rotation abilities and women's

anxiety contributed to the sex difference in SAT math scores, but the effect for mental rotation was twice as strong.

TAKE HOME POINTS

- Sex differences in math for the general population are small and may be decreasing over time.

- Sex differences are not consistent across all math domains. Men have higher problem-solving ability, but women have greater computational skills.

- Some sex differences in math appear with increased age, but the explanation for this effect is not clear. Some argue that differential experiences with math among older students account for the increase in the sex difference with age.

- One paradox in math is that females outperform males in the classroom, but males outperform females on standardized tests. Explanations for this paradox have to do with the different test settings, the different factors that play a role in classroom test and achievement tests scores, and the different strategies that males and females use to solve math problems.

- Sex differences in math ability among the highly talented are substantial; these differences may relate to men's advantage in spatial skills, in particular mental rotation.

Verbal Ability

Of all the cognitive domains, sex differences in verbal ability are the first to emerge in children (Halpern, 2000). On average, girls talk earlier than boys and develop larger vocabularies and better grammar than boys. Some of these sex differences diminish with time.

Hyde and Linn (1988) conducted a meta-analysis of 165 studies that evaluated sex differences in verbal ability. They found a very small effect ($d = -.11$), in the direction of women outperforming men. The investigators examined several types of verbal ability, including vocabulary, analogies, reading comprehension, and essay writing. All the effect sizes were small, except for speech production; in that case, there was a moderate effect of female superior performance ($d = -.33$). Sex differences also were consistent across age groups, from 5-year-olds to adults over 26. However, sex differences appeared to decrease over time. In studies published before 1974, the effect size was $d = -.23$; in studies published in 1974 and after, the effect size was $d = -.10$. There also was a trend for articles whose first author was male to report smaller effect sizes than in articles whose first author was female; this reminds us of the potential for investigators to influence their results. More recently, another meta-analysis appeared that was limited to studies of high school students (Hedges & Nowell, 1995); all effects for verbal ability were near zero.

There is one verbal ability in which a large sex difference exists: writing. Until recently, standardized tests did not include a writing component because it is difficult to score. The Educational Testing Service (Cole, 1997) administered a writing proficiency exam to 4th-, 8th-, and 11th-graders in 1984, 1988, 1990, and 1992. Females outperformed males at all ages and at all times of assessment. Thus the sex difference in writing ability has been stable over time.

Like math ability, sex differences in verbal skills also depend on the population studied. Sex differences are larger when people with verbal difficulties are examined (Hyde & McKinley, 1997). Boys are 10 times more likely than girls to have severe dyslexia and 3 to 4 times more likely than girls to stutter (Halpern, 2000). Several people question whether boys have more verbal difficulties than girls or if boys are more likely to be referred for special services than girls. Shaywitz and colleagues (1990) followed 445 kindergartners in the state of Connecticut through third grade. They evaluated the prevalence of reading disabilities among children in second and third grade in two different ways. First, they identified reading disabled children by using objective performance criteria; these were referred to as "research-identified" disabled students. Second, they noted whether teachers referred students for special education services for reading disability; these were referred to as "school-identified" disabled students. As shown in the right half of Figure 4.7, schools were two to four times more likely to identify boys as reading disabled compared to girls—a significant difference. As shown in the left half of Figure 4.7, researchers identified similar percentages of boys and girls as reading disabled using objective criteria. Why the discrepancy? Specifically, why are boys who are not objectively determined to have a reading disability labeled so by teachers? Investigators also had teachers rate students on a host of other characteristics. Teachers viewed reading disabled boys as overactive and having more behavioral problems compared to non-reading-disabled boys. Teachers' views of boys' behavior may have influenced their judgments of the boys' reading ability.

Again, researchers have concluded that sex differences in verbal ability depend on the specific domain. Most differences are small, but some, such as differences in writing ability, are more substantive. The sex difference may be larger when people with verbal difficulties are considered.

TAKE HOME POINTS

- There is a small sex difference in verbal ability, favoring females.

- The size of the sex difference depends on the specific verbal ability; the sex difference is large in the case of writing.

- One reason for the sex difference in verbal ability has to do with the fact that a larger proportion of males than females have verbal difficulties.

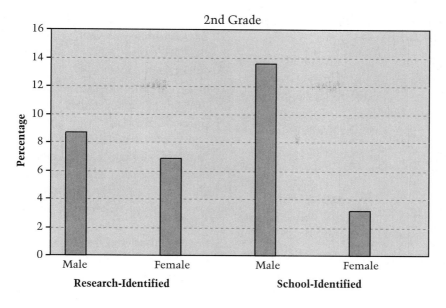

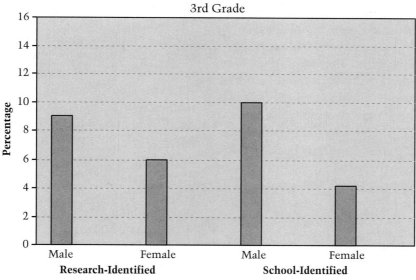

FIGURE 4.7   Identification of reading disability in second- and third-grade boys and girls. Researchers were equally likely to identify boys and girls as having a reading disability using objective criteria. Teachers at the school, however, were more likely to refer boys than girls for a reading disability using their own subjective criteria.

Source: Adapted from Shaywitz et al. (1990).

Comprehensive Assessment of Cognitive Abilities

Before winding up this section, let's look at three major studies, one of which is cross sectional, that evaluate sex differences and similarities for a wide range of cognitive abilities. We will see if they agree with the findings from the previous meta-analyses.

The first is a study conducted by Hedges and Nowell (1995) in which they analyzed data from six nationally representative samples of adolescents and young adults between 1960 and 1992. Between 11,000 and 25,000 people were surveyed in each study. A strength of this report is the representativeness of the samples; too often, studies of sex differences in cognition use select samples, such as highly gifted individuals or even college students. On average, women outperformed men on reading comprehension, perceptual speed, and associative memory, but these effect sizes were small. Men outperformed women on math, social studies, and spatial abilities, but these effect sizes also were small. There were two moderate effects: Women performed better in writing, and men performed better in science. The largest effects were for vocational aptitude domains, such as mechanical reasoning, electronic information, and automobile shop information, where men outperformed women. Although sex differences in math and science narrowed over time, the sex difference in reading and writing appeared to be stable over the 32 years.

Hedges and Nowell (1995) also found that men's scores were more variable than women's on almost all the cognitive domains examined. More men than women were in both the bottom and top 10% of the distributions; this explains why sex differences in math are small in nationally representative samples, but larger in select, talented samples where only the upper portion of the distribution is examined.

The second study on cognitive abilities was conducted by the Educational Testing Service (ETS; Cole, 1997) in 1997. It included over 400 different tests from over 1,500 data sets that involved millions of students from fourth grade through graduate school. The primary conclusion of this study was that sex differences in performance across the different domains were small; most were close to zero. Figure 4.8 shows the size of the differences for 15 domains among 12th-graders. The size of a given difference is again represented by the d statistic. In this figure, a positive d means girls outperformed boys, whereas a negative d means boys outperformed girls. Notice that the vast majority of the differences are small, between $-.2$ and $+.2$. Notice also that the differences within the various kinds of math ability and verbal ability are not consistent. For two verbal abilities (writing and language) there are sizable differences favoring females; the other two verbal skills (reading and vocabulary reasoning) show very small differences in the direction of females. There are two categories of math ability, one of which favors males (concepts) and one females (computation); in both of these cases, the difference is small. Among the other domains, there is a small advantage for boys in geopolitical subjects (e.g., history, economics, and geography) and a large advantage for boys in mechanical/electronic subjects. There are small advantages for girls in perceptual speed and short-term memory.

Consistent with previous reports, differences were more likely to be found among older than younger students. There were virtually no differences in any subject area for fourth-graders. Differences in language abilities began to emerge by grade 8, whereas differences in mathematical abilities began to emerge by grade 12. The study also showed that over the past 30 years, the sex difference in

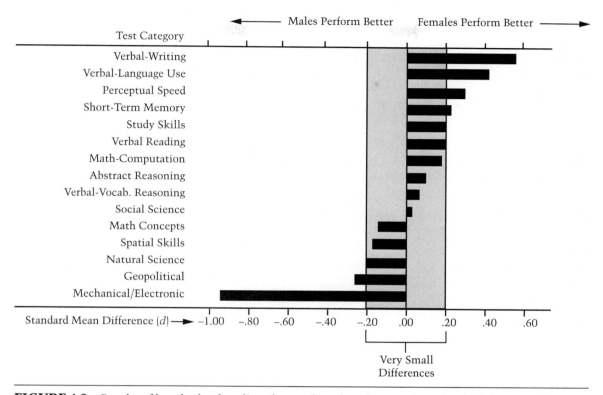

12th-Grade Profile: Gender Difference and Similarity for 15 Types of Tests

FIGURE 4.8 Results of hundreds of studies of tests of men's and women's academic abilities. As shown by the results for 12th-graders, most sex differences are very small.
Source: N. S. Cole (1997). *The ETS gender study: How females and males perform in education settings.* Copyright 1997. Reprinted by permission of Educational Testing Service, the copyright owner.

mathematical ability has decreased, whereas the sex difference in language has remained unchanged.

Like Hedges and Nowell (1995), the ETS (1997) study showed that males have more variability in their distribution of scores than females. This is shown in Figure 4.9. Thus slightly more males than females are at both the higher and lower ends of the distribution. The explanation for this finding is not clear. Again, the greater male compared to female variability

has implications for studies in which select populations are evaluated, such as only those attending college. Those studies may be sampling from the right half of the distribution in Figure 4.9, making it look as if there is more of a male advantage than there really is in the general population.

Finally, the ETS (1997) study noted that, regardless of test scores, females outperform males on nearly all major subject areas when it comes to school grades. High school grades are

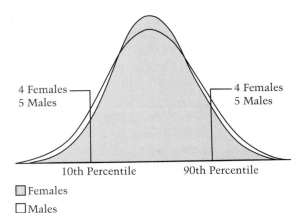

4 Females
5 Males

4 Females
5 Males

10th Percentile   90th Percentile

☐ Females
☐ Males

FIGURE 4.9 Score distributions. On many tests of academic ability, males have more variability in their scores than females, meaning more males are at the high end and low end of the distribution. Below the 10th percentile and above the 90th percentile, there are 4 females for every 5 males. *Source:* N. S. Cole (1997). *The ETS gender study: How females and males perform in education settings.* Copyright 1997. Reprinted by permission of Educational Testing Service, the copyright owner.

important because they predict college performance, even when test scores are taken into consideration. The authors suggest that grades may reflect other domains besides aptitude, such as effort and class participation.

Sex comparisons on cognitive abilities also have been made across 33 countries (National Center for Education Statistics, 2001). As shown in Figure 4.10, females outperformed males in reading across all the countries, males outperformed females in math in the vast majority of countries although the differences are small, and sex differences in science are inconsistent in direction across countries, but uniformly small.

Taken collectively, sex differences in most cognitive domains have decreased over time. It is not clear whether one sex is improving, another sex is deteriorating, or more recent studies are more methodologically sound. Standardized tests may be less biased today than they were 30 years ago. It also is possible that the political climate has contributed to the decrease in sex differences. The atmosphere has shifted from emphasizing to minimizing sex differences. The political climate may be a reaction to a true decline in differences, or this climate may contribute to a greater publication of studies that show no differences.

TAKE HOME POINTS

- The results of large-scale studies are similar to the results of the meta-analyses: Most sex differences are small. However, keep in mind that a small difference may have meaningful implications.

- More important than the size of the difference is the variability of the differences. It is much too simplistic to talk about sex differences in spatial skills, math ability, or verbal skills because each domain consists of a number of distinct skills. For example, in the spatial domain, there is a sizable male advantage for one skill, mental rotation. In the verbal domain, there is a sizable sex difference in writing, favoring females.

- The size of the difference also depends on the sample. There are substantial sex differences in math among highly talented samples and substantial sex differences in verbal skill among those with verbal difficulties.

- Evidence also seems to indicate a greater male compared to female variability in quantitative, spatial, and verbal skills.

- The size of the sex difference in math skills appears to be decreasing, but it is not as clear if the size of the sex difference in verbal skills is decreasing.

- Socialization practices have shifted over time as sex differences in cognitive abilities have diminished. Parents may be more likely to encourage girls to perform well in math and science and to encourage boys to perform well in reading and writing.

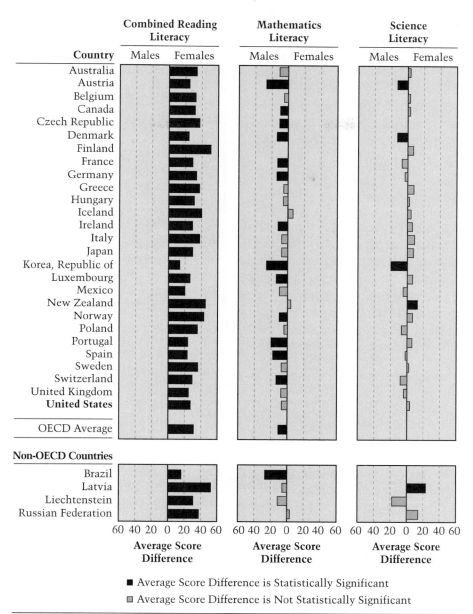

	Combined Reading Literacy		Mathematics Literacy		Science Literacy	
Country	Males	Females	Males	Females	Males	Females
Australia						
Austria						
Belgium						
Canada						
Czech Republic						
Denmark						
Finland						
France						
Germany						
Greece						
Hungary						
Iceland						
Ireland						
Italy						
Japan						
Korea, Republic of						
Luxembourg						
Mexico						
New Zealand						
Norway						
Poland						
Portugal						
Spain						
Sweden						
Switzerland						
United Kingdom						
United States						
OECD Average						

Non-OECD Countries

Brazil
Latvia
Liechtenstein
Russian Federation

60 40 20 0 20 40 60   60 40 20 0 20 40 60   60 40 20 0 20 40 60

Average Score Difference   **Average Score Difference**   **Average Score Difference**

■ Average Score Difference is Statistically Significant
▢ Average Score Difference is Not Statistically Significant

FIGURE 4.10 Among 15-year-olds, females outperform males in reading literacy across all 27 countries; males outperform females in math in the majority of countries, but differences are smaller; and few countries show a sex differences in science literacy. *Source:* National Center for Education Statistics (2001).

Outcomes of Learning: Results From the 2000 Program for International Student Assessment of 15-Year-Olds in Reading, Mathematics, and Science Literacy
National Center for Education Statistics: Mariann Lemke, Laura Lippman & Ghedam Bairu.
Education Statistics Services Institute: Christopher Calsyn & Thea Kruger.
Westat: Leslie Jocelyn, David Kastberg, Yan Yun Liu, Stephen Roey & Trevor Williams.

SEX COMPARISONS IN SOCIAL DOMAINS

Cognitive abilities were easily assessed by standardized tests and measures. Social abilities are a little trickier. How do we judge which sex is more helpful, more sexual, more empathic, or more aggressive? Should we rely on self-report measures? Do people know their own abilities, or will they distort them in the direction of the ability they ought to have? Perhaps observing behavior is a better method to assess social abilities. But are observers truly unbiased in their perceptions and interpretations of a behavior? Each method has its advantages and disadvantages; thus in social domains, we look for consistency in findings across methodologies.

Empathy

Crying at a sad film, saying "I understand" to a friend who has disclosed a problem, and putting yourself in someone else's shoes are all different ways of empathizing. **Empathy** is defined in many ways, but at its core, it seems to involve feeling the same emotion as another person or feeling sympathy or compassion for another person. Sex differences in empathy, like sex differences in cognition, depend on how empathy is measured.

A meta-analysis of 259 studies showed a sex difference in empathy, favoring females ($d = -.18$; Eisenberg & Fabes, 1998). There were several moderator variables, however. First, the sex difference was greater when empathy was measured by self-report than by observation. For measures that are less under the conscious control of the participants, such as parent and teacher observations or facial expressions in response to specific situational cues, sex differences appear in the same direction but of a much smaller magnitude. One concern with self-report measures is demand

---

DO GENDER 4.2
The Effect of Demand Characteristics on Reports of Empathy

Find a standardized empathy self-report scale. Develop two forms of the scale. Name one form "Empathy." Give the second form a title that would be more consistent with the male gender role or at least neutral with respect to gender, like "Environment Accuracy." Randomly distribute one of the two forms to 20 men and 20 women. Do women report more empathy than men on both forms?

---

characteristics. Undoubtedly, men and women realize that women are supposed to be more empathic than men. Thus men and women may distort their self-reports of behavior in the direction of gender-role norms. See if you can find evidence of this problem in Do Gender 4.2.

When physiological measures of empathy are used (e.g., heart rate or skin conductance), there are no clear sex differences. However, it is not clear that physiological responses indicate only empathy. If your heart starts racing when you watch a woman in a film get raped, what does this mean? Is it empathy, the actual experiencing of another person's distress? Is it compassion? Or is it discomfort at witnessing such a violent act?

The second moderator variable was how empathy was measured. Sex differences were larger when measures of kindness and consideration were used rather than measures of instrumental help. (This will help to clarify the finding in the next section on helping.) Third, the sex difference was larger in correlational and naturalistic than experimental studies. Finally, the sex difference was larger if the empathy target was an adult rather than a child, indicating that women and men respond more similarly to children.

At first glance, it appeared that the sex difference in empathy increased with age. However, when the above-mentioned moderator variables were statistically controlled, there was no age effect. Age was confounded with study design. Studies of older children and young adults are more likely to be conducted in naturalistic settings where the sex difference is larger. Thus, the apparent age effect was really a study design effect.

Helping Behavior

Although I have convinced you that the evidence women are more empathic than men is weak, you probably have every confidence that women are more helpful than men. Is this true? Not according to Eagly and Crowley's (1986) meta-analysis of helping behavior. The 172 studies in this review measured actual helping behavior or the self-report of a commitment to engage in a helping behavior; in other words, self-reports of general helpfulness were not included. The effect was in the direction of males helping more than females ($d = +.34$). The direction of this sex difference may seem surprising because helping is central to the female gender role. The sex difference was limited to a certain kind of help, however. That is, the situation was a moderator variable: Males were more likely than females to help in situations of danger.

Another important moderator variable was the sex of the person in need of help. The sex of the recipient influenced whether a male helped but not whether a female helped. Males were more likely to help females than males, whereas females were equally likely to help males and females. There also was a sex difference in receipt of help. Women were more likely than men to receive help in general ($d = -.46$). In addition, women were more likely to receive help from men than women, whereas men were

equally likely to receive help from men or women. Thus men helping women seems to be an especially prevalent kind of helping.

The investigators found many of these sex differences were stronger under public conditions, where others could view the behavior, than under private conditions, where the behavior was anonymous. Males and females may behave differently in the presence of others because they are concerned with adhering to gender-role norms. In situations of danger, we expect men to provide help and women to receive help. In Eagly and Crowley's (1986) review, the publication year was inversely correlated with the size of the effect, indicating the sex difference was getting smaller over time. Perhaps our expectations of men's and women's roles in situations of danger have changed over the years.

One of the limitations of this literature is that most of the situations involved strangers. In the real world, most helping behavior occurs in the context of relationships. Thus the kind of helping central to the female gender role may not have been tapped in these studies. Helping behavior that occurs in relationships is discussed in Chapters 8 and 9. In that context, a great deal of evidence indicates that both men and women turn to women for help.

Aggression

- On April 16, 2007, Cho Seung-Hui killed a woman and a man at 7:15 A.M. in a dormitory at Virginia Polytechnic Institute. Two hours later he proceeded into an academic building and killed another 30 students in offices and classrooms, and then killed himself. Between the first killing and second massacre, he took time to stop at a mailbox and send a news station writings filled with anger and photographs of himself engaging in aggressive behavior.

- On October 2, 2006, Charles Carl Roberts IV, a 32-year-old truck-driver, carried a shotgun, a semiautomatic pistol, a rifle, two knives, and 600 rounds of ammunition into an Amish schoolhouse in Lancaster, Pennsylvania. He told the 15 boys to leave and then lined up the 6 girls before the blackboard and shot them before shooting himself ("Fifth girl dies," 2006).

- On July 29, 1999, Mark Barton, a 44-year-old securities day trader, killed his wife, his 12-year-old son, and his 7-year-old daughter in his home. He then went on a rampage, killing nine other people in two office buildings in Atlanta before killing himself (Sack, 1999).

- On April 20, 1999, Eric Harris and Dylan Klebold, two teenagers, killed 12 classmates and wounded 23 others within 16 minutes and then killed themselves at Columbine High School in Littleton, Colorado. They had intended to kill 488 people in the cafeteria with two bombs. Cho Seung-Hui had referred to Eric and Dylan as martyrs. ("Sheriff Releases," 2000).

- On February 29, 2000, a 6-year-old boy who was living in a crack house brought a gun to school and killed a 6-year-old girl, Kayla Rolland, at an elementary school in Michigan. The boy was determined to be too young to prosecute (Barboza, 2000).

- Between October 2, 2002, and October 22, 2002, 10 random people in the Washington, D.C., area were killed by snipers while pumping gas, getting groceries, cutting grass, and getting into cars in parking lots. John Allen Muhammed, age 41, and his companion, John Lee Malvo, age 17, have been charged with the crimes (Blumenthal, 2002).

- And, of course, on September 11, 2001, 19 men on suicide missions hijacked four American planes in the United States, resulting in the collapse of the World Trade Centers and the loss of thousands of lives. In the aftermath, the war on terrorism ensued while the Israel-Palestinian conflict intensified in the form of increased suicide bombings. As the suicide bombings became almost commonplace, a couple of noteworthy incidents captured public attention: Several female Palestinians completed suicide missions.

- Finally, in the small town where I grew up (Bradley, Illinois), Timothy Buss at age 13 murdered and then mutilated the body of a 5-year-old girl in 1981. Fourteen years later, in 1995, after being released from prison on parole, Buss returned to the area and brutally murdered a 10-year-old boy (Cotliar, 1996).

What do all of these atrocities have in common? They were horrendous acts of violence that received a great deal of media attention, causing us, as a nation, to question the sources of such behavior. Except for the female suicide bombers, they also all involved male perpetrators. The public has taken note of such incidents, especially the Virginia Tech and Columbine massacres, because the perpetrators were so young. In the past decade, books that address the subject of troubled boys who become involved in violence have been best sellers, such as *Lost Boys: Why Our Sons Turn Violent and How We Can Save Them* by James Garbarino (1999), *Raising Cain: Protecting the Emotional Life of Boys* by Dan Kindlon, Michael Thompson, and Teresa Barker (1999), *Real Boys: Rescuing Our Sons from the Myths of Boyhood* by William Pollack (1998), and *The Minds of Boys: Saving Our Sons From Falling Behind in School and Life* by Michael Gurian and Kathy Stevens (2007).

Sex of Perpetrator.   Observational studies of children confirm sex differences in aggression at an early age, and these differences generalize across cultures (Munroe et al., 2000). A survey of over 15,000 sixth- through tenth-graders revealed that boys are more likely than girls to be involved in violent behavior: Boys were more likely than girls to have carried a weapon in the last month (23% vs. 7%), carried a weapon in school (15% vs. 4%), and had four or more physical fights in the last year (13% vs. 6%; Nansel et al., 2003). In addition, boys admit to greater bullying in school than girls (23% vs. 11%). A meta-analytic review of sex comparisons showed that men were more aggressive than women (Bettencourt & Miller, 1996). Sex differences in verbal aggression were less consistent than sex differences in physical aggression. There were no sex differences in verbal aggression in the field ($d = +.03$) and only a small sex difference in the laboratory ($d = +.13$; Bettencourt & Miller, 1996). When more indirect forms of aggression are examined, such as relational aggression (as discussed in Chapter 7), sex differences may disappear. Sex differences in aggression also seem to appear early in life. In a study of 17-month-olds, parents reported that boys were more likely than girls to kick, hit, and bite (Baillargeon et al., 2007). Boys also were 2.5 times more likely than girls to be classified as highly aggressive.

The sex difference in aggression remained the same when children were followed for 1 year.

Like the other domains of sex differences reviewed in this chapter, aggression also is influenced by a variety of situational variables. One important situational factor is provocation, which may release women from the constraints the female gender role places on aggressive behavior. The Bettencourt and Miller (1996) meta-analysis showed that provocation led to greater aggression than nonprovocation, and that provocation altered the size of the sex difference in aggression. The sex difference was smaller under provocation conditions ($d = +.17$) than under neutral conditions ($d = +.33$). In addition, a judge's rating of the intensity of a provocation was negatively correlated with sex differences in aggression; in other words, the stronger the provocation, the smaller the sex difference.

Another situational variable that has been investigated is the emotional arousal generated by the situation. Because males may be more easily aroused than females and less able to regulate their emotions, Knight and colleagues (2002) predicted that sex differences in aggression would be minimal in situations of no or very high emotional arousal and maximal in situations of low or medium emotional arousal. As shown in Figure 4.11, at very low levels of arousal, one would expect sex differences to be small because both men and women can control their behavior. At very high levels of arousal, sex differences also would be small because emotion regulation is disrupted in both males and females. However, at a moderate level of arousal, one would predict larger sex differences because males will experience the arousal more intensely, and males will be less able to regulate the arousal. Their results supported this hypothesis. Sex differences in aggression were significant when there was no arousal ($d = +.30$) but larger when there was a

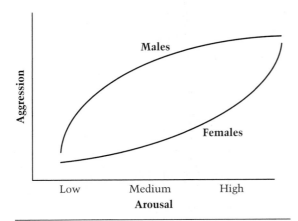

FIGURE 4.11 At low and high levels of arousal, sex differences in aggression are small. At medium levels of arousal, sex differences in aggression are largest.

small or medium amount of arousal (both d's $= +.51$) and not significant when there was high arousal ($d = -.15$). The idea that men are less able to regulate their emotions is consistent with research that shows men are more impulsive than women and less able to delay gratification than women (Campbell, 2006).

Other features of the situation may contribute to sex differences in aggression. The meta-analysis showed that sex differences in aggression were larger when women had greater fears of retaliation (Bettencourt & Miller, 1996). Thus fears of retaliation are stronger deterrents of aggression for women than for men, whereas provocation is more likely to release women's inhibitions to behave aggressively.

Are sex differences in aggression getting smaller over time? As men's and women's roles have become more similar, have rates of aggression become more similar? As women have become more assertive, have they also become more aggressive? One meta-analysis showed that sex differences in aggression seem to be getting larger over time (Knight, Fabes, & Higgins, 1996). However, there is a problem with comparing the early to the later studies—the

research methodologies have changed over time (Knight et al., 1996). Recent studies are more likely to have used nonexperimental methods such as field designs, and these methods show larger sex differences than laboratory studies. In one meta-analysis, the size of the sex difference for nonexperimental studies was larger than that for experimental studies ($d = +.77$ vs. $d = +.37$; Knight et al., 1996). When differences in the research methodologies used in the early and later studies were taken into consideration, the year of publication was unrelated to the size of the sex difference in aggression. In the end, we have no evidence that sex differences in aggression have changed over time. We only know that researchers today are using different methods to study aggression. See Sidebar 4.2 for a discussion of a potential rise in female aggression.

Measuring aggression is not as easy as you might think. The limitations of self-report methods are obvious. Are observations of behavior any more objective? We know from previous chapters that the same behavior may be construed differently when it is observed in a man or a woman. Is aggressive behavior viewed the same when the perpetrator is male versus female? One study showed that we view the same behavior as more aggressive when it is displayed by a male, and we also view the same behavior as more aggressive when it is displayed *toward* a female (Harris & Knight-Bohnhoff, 1996a). In this study, college students and a group of people working on a military base were presented with an aggressive scenario in which the sex of the perpetrator and the sex of the victim were varied. Respondents viewed the same aggressive behavior as more serious when the perpetrator was a man and the victim was a woman. People may perceive aggression to be more serious when committed by a male and more serious when directed toward a female because of the differences in physical strength between the sexes. In other words, people perceive the same

SIDEBAR 4.2: *Is Aggression Increasing Among Women?*

Is aggressive behavior on the rise among females? Juvenile arrests have increased at a faster rate in recent years for girls than boys. In a self-report survey of urban minority middle school students, 66% of sixth-grade girls and 77% of sixth-grade boys reported delinquent behavior (e.g., stealing, destroying property; Nichols et al., 2006). There was no sex difference among seventh-graders: 78% of girls and 80% of boys. Among violent offenders, however, the increase among girls may be more "apparent" than real. In their book *The Female Offender*, Chesney-Lind and Pasko (2004) argue that the media sensationalize female violence in part because it is the exception rather than the rule, but that violent crime among women has not increased in recent years. As shown in Figure 4.12, arrests for violent crime have decreased over the past 13 years for boys, and arrests for violent crime have remained the same for girls—and have remained substantially lower than arrests for boys. The overall arrest rate has increased for both males and females—but the rate of increase has been greater for adolescent and adult women. These arrests, however, are for less serious crimes, such as larceny (shoplifting) and status offenses (e.g., running away from home, curfew violation). When one compares youths' self-report of these crimes to rates of arrest, it appears that girls are more likely than boys to be arrested for the crime. The same pertains to drug offenses. Although boys are much more likely than girls to be arrested for drugs, the rate of arrest has increased much more for girls than boys—despite the fact that the sex difference in usage has remained the same. Among adults, there is an increasing number of women in prisons, but this increase is not due to an increase in violent crime among women but to an increase in less severe crimes, such as drugs and shoplifting. Even among white-collar crime, the typical female perpetrator differs from the typical male perpetrator. With the exception of Martha Stewart, the male who embezzles money is more likely to be a manager or officer of the company, whereas the female who embezzles money is more likely to be a clerical worker or bank teller.

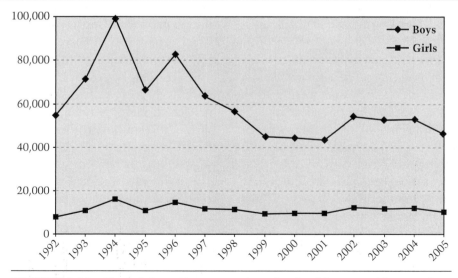

FIGURE 4.12   Total violent crime arrests (murder, forcible rape, robbery, and aggravated assault) for boys and girls under age 18.
Source: Adapted from Federal Bureau of Investigation, Uniform Crime Reports (1995–2005).

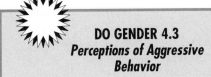

DO GENDER 4.3
Perceptions of Aggressive Behavior

Create two different scenarios of aggressive behavior. For each scenario, manipulate the sex of the perpetrator and the sex of the victim. You will have four different versions. The scenarios should be identical, with the exception that the sex of the perpetrator and victim are different. Ask a group of men and women to rate the aggressive behavior in terms of severity. Does the sex of the perpetrator, sex of the victim, or sex of the respondent influence perceptions?

aggressive act to have different consequences depending on the sex of the perpetrator and sex of the victim. These findings are noteworthy because some of the strongest support for sex differences in aggression comes from studies of children—and here aggression is measured via direct observation. Examine how sex influences the perception of aggressive behavior with Do Gender 4.3.

Sex of Victim   Not only are men more likely than women to be the perpetrators of aggression, but men are also more likely than women to be the victims of aggression. We often lose sight of this latter fact. Men are more likely than women to report being victims of physical aggression. In a study of college students, men were twice as likely to report having been kicked, bitten, hit by a fist, and hit by another object (Harris, 1996). Men were 3 times as likely to report being threatened with a gun or knife. In a survey of over 15,000 sixth- through tenth-graders, more boys than girls reported being bullied in school (16% vs. 11%; Nansel et al., 2003).

The sex of the perpetrator and the sex of the victim may be interrelated. A study of

elementary school children found that boys were more aggressive toward other boys than girls, but that girls were equally aggressive to boys and girls (Russell & Owens, 1999). However, the kind of aggression that girls used with boys and girls differed; girls tended to be physically aggressive with boys but used verbal and indirect aggression with girls.

Sexuality

Are men the more "sexual" sex, or did the sexual revolution and the women's movement place men and women on more equal ground in the sexual arena? Again, the answer depends on how sexuality is defined. Oliver and Hyde (1993) conducted a meta-analysis on sexual attitudes and sexual behaviors. They examined data from 239 independent samples published between 1974 and 1990. Most of the respondents were college students and young adults. Not surprisingly, men were more liberal in their overall attitudes toward sex, but the size of the effect depended on the specific attitude and behavior. Men were more liberal in their attitudes toward premarital sex, especially when it was casual ($d = +.81$). There were small effect sizes on other attitudes toward sex: Men were more accepting of extramarital sex ($d = +.29$), more likely to have had sex ($d = +.33$), and had had a larger number of sexual partners ($d = +.25$). Although there was a very small sex difference in attitudes toward masturbation ($d = +.09$), there were very large sex differences in the incidence of masturbation ($d = +.96$), with men reporting a higher incidence than women. The effect sizes for sexual attitudes and behavior were inversely correlated with the year of publication. Thus many of the sex differences had diminished over time. Sex differences also decreased as the age of the respondent increased, meaning there were fewer sex differences among adults than among younger people. The authors found no sex differences in sexual satisfaction, incidence of kissing, incidence of oral sex, or attitudes toward homosexuality.

This latter finding was later contested. Whitley and Kite (1995) located some additional studies on attitudes toward homosexuality and reported a small sex difference ($d = +.26$), such that males held more negative attitudes than females. The sex of the target was critical: Men were significantly more negative than women about gay men ($d = +.51$), but there was no sex difference in attitudes toward lesbians. This finding was later replicated by Whitley and Egisdottir (2000).

Gender role and gender-role attitudes seem to be more strongly related to attitudes toward homosexuality than sex per se. People who score high on instrumental traits have more favorable attitudes toward homosexuality, whereas people who scored high on hypermasculinity (extreme masculinity) have more negative attitudes toward homosexuality (Whitley, 2001). Gender-role attitudes are even stronger predictors of attitudes toward homosexuality. People who have traditional gender-role attitudes and score high on modern sexism and benevolent sexism possess the most negative attitudes toward homosexuality. This is not surprising because homosexual behavior is a threat to traditional beliefs about men's and women's roles. Men are less tolerant of homosexuality compared to women because the male gender role is more narrowly defined than the female gender role. Violation of the male gender role has more negative consequences because it has a higher status in our society, so there is more to lose by violating it (Kite & Whitley, 2003).

Social dominance orientation is also linked to negative attitudes toward homosexuals (Whitley & Egisdottir, 2000). Social dominance orientation reflects the desire for the ingroup to dominate and be superior to the outgroup (e.g., It's okay if some groups have more of a chance in life than others). As shown in Figure 4.13, men are higher than women in social dominance orientation; social dominance orientation is related to having more traditional gender-role beliefs; and traditional gender-role beliefs are associated with negative attitudes toward homosexuals.

The sex differences in sexual behavior and attitudes have led Baumeister and colleagues (Baumeister, Catanese, & Vohs, 2001) to argue that men have a stronger sex drive than women, despite the fact that this is a "politically incorrect" statement to make. They define sex drive as the frequency and intensity of sexual desire. They note that, compared to women, men think more about sex, desire more sex, desire more sexual partners, masturbate more frequently, initiate more sex, are less willing to forego sex, and have more permissive attitudes toward sex. A greater sex drive among men compared to women appears to be supported

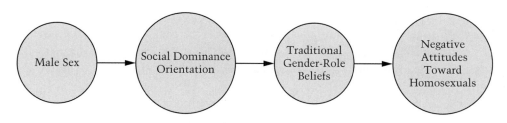

FIGURE 4.13 A pathway by which male sex leads to negative attitudes towards homosexuals.

Studies of sexual behavior are difficult to conduct, and many reports have been based on convenience samples (i.e., people who volunteer to participate in a study or people who are interested in the topic of sexual behavior). In 1992, one of the first national representative studies of sexual behavior, referred to as the National Health and Social Life Survey, was conducted (Laumann et al., 1994; Laumann & Michael, 2000). Over 3,000 people participated. The study is important because a representative sample of adults ages 18 to 59 was obtained to report on their sexual behavior. Some of the findings correspond to the meta-analysis. There were sex differences in the frequency of masturbation over the prior year: Whereas 37% of men said they never masturbated, the corresponding figure for women was 58%; over three times as many men as women reported masturbating in the prior week (27% vs. 8%). One similarity was in the frequency of sex. Men and women reported they had sex equally often during the prior year; however, over half of the men (54%) but only 19% of women reported thinking about sex every day or several times a day. Consistent with the meta-analysis, men reported more sexual partners during the prior year and during the prior 5 years. When respondents were asked how many sexual partners they had had since age 18, over 50% of the men but only 30% of the women identified more than five partners. During the prior year, 23% of men and 12% of women reported having more than one partner.

This study also compared how different races and ethnicities viewed sex. As shown in Table 4.1, the majority of White, African American, and Mexican American men and women do not believe that premarital sex is wrong but do believe that teenage sex is wrong (Mahay, Laumann, & Michaels, 2001). Among the three ethnic groups, Whites were least conservative and Mexican Americans most conservative. It is good that people held positive attitudes toward premarital sex as the majority of people in each ethnic group had engaged in premarital sex. More women than men in all three ethnic groups say that religion influences their sexual behavior, but this view is held strongest by African American women. Women in all three ethnic groups were also more likely than men to hold a relational view of sex (i.e., only have sex if in love with the person). African American men were least likely to hold this view. These findings are interesting because a similar percentage of each group said that they were in love with the first person with whom they had sex. The majority of men and women in all three groups said that any sex between two consenting adults is OK. Whites were less likely than African Americans and Mexican Americans to say that homosexual activity is wrong; the sex difference (men less tolerant) was only significant among Whites.

by the Pfizer Global Study of Sexual Attitudes and Behavior, a survey of over 27,000 men and women aged 40 to 80 from 29 countries around the world (Pfizer, 2002). When asked to rate how important sex was on a 5-point scale, ranging from 1 (not important) to 5 (very important), 83% of men compared to 63% of women gave a rating of 3 or higher, meaning sex was moderately, extremely, or very important to them.

One puzzling finding from the meta-analysis and an in-depth study of sexual behavior (see Sidebar 4.3) is that men have more sexual partners than women. If men and women are having sex with each other, shouldn't they report the same number of partners? What are some of the reasons that men might report more sexual partners than women? Laumann and colleagues (1994) offer some possible explanations. First, there are more women than

TABLE 4.1 MAHAY ET AL. 2001

	Premarital Sex Is Wrong	Did Not Have Premarital Sex	Teenage Sex Is Wrong	Religion Shapes View of Sex	Relational View of Sex	In Love With First Sex Partner	Recreational View of Sex	Homosexual Activity Is Wrong
White								
male	21.6	11.3	73.5	44.4	53.1	42.3	73.2	71.4
female	30.3	22.9	84.6	56.6	76.4	74.8	74.0	63.2
African American								
male	25.5	2.5	67.6	49.5	43.3	33.3	74.4	82.4
female	38.3	7.5	83.2	69.2	77.0	69.8	80.1	83.2
Mexican American								
male	27.7	9.3	75.9	51.8	56.6	42.7	81.9	84.2
female	41.8	21.9	92.4	60.9	78.3	84.2	84.6	85.4

Source: Adapted from Mahay, Laumann, and Michaels, 2001.

men in the United States, so it is possible for men to have more partners than women. The size of the sex ratio in the population, however, is unlikely to account for such a large sex difference in the number of sexual partners. Second, it is possible that a few women are having sex with a large number of men. In fact, some research shows that women with a lot of sexual partners, prostitutes, are underrepresented in research, and their inclusion would diminish the sex difference (Brewer et al., 2000). Third, the homosexual population could account for these findings; if gay men have more partners than do lesbians, there would appear to be an overall sex difference in the number of partners. The explanation that the authors favor and that makes the most sense to me is a response bias: It is socially desirable for men to exaggerate and women to underreport the number of sexual partners.

One problem with research on sexuality is that the data, for obvious reasons, are gathered via self-report rather than observation. Thus the conclusion we reach is that men and women report differences in sexual attitudes and behaviors. We must be cautious in interpreting these

findings because demand characteristics (i.e., men's and women's desire to adhere to their gender roles) may influence the reports. It would be consistent with the male gender role to exaggerate sexual activity and express more liberal attitudes, and it would be consistent with the female gender role to underreport sexual activity and express more conservative attitudes.

Another way to think about sex differences in sexual behavior is to focus on the variability in behavior rather than the average level of behavior. According to Baumeister (2000), women's sexual behavior is more variable than men's and responds to changing circumstances. He refers to this idea as **erotic plasticity**, the extent to which one's sex drive is influenced by social and cultural factors. For example, he points out that the women's movement had a large effect on women's sexual behavior but not much effect on men's sexual behavior. He uses the survey data that Laumann and colleagues (1994) collected to illustrate his point. The percentage of men who had five or more sexual partners by age 30 was similar for the oldest cohort of men (38%) and the youngest cohort of men (49%). The behavior of women, however, had obviously undergone a change: The percentage of women who had five or more sexual partners by age 30 was 2.6% for the oldest cohort and 22.4% for the youngest cohort. A meta-analysis of sexual behavior and attitudes over a 50-year-period (1943 to 1999) supports Baumeister's theory. The meta-analysis showed that sexual behavior and attitudes became more permissive over the years, but the year of publication was a stronger predictor of female compared to male attitudes (Wells & Twenge, 2005).

Baumeister also points out that cultural and social factors have a greater influence on women's sexual behavior compared to men. For example, religion is more closely tied to the sexual behavior of women; a very religious woman may not have sex outside of marriage, whereas a man might be willing to have sex outside of marriage regardless of his religious beliefs. There also is greater variation in women's sexual behavior across cultures. Furthermore, immigration studies show that women's sexual behavior changes as they become more acculturated into their new country, but men's sexual behavior remains the same.

Data on sexual behavior among homosexuals also support Baumeister's theory: Lesbians report more heterosexual sex than gay men; there also are more bisexual women than men. Finally, the last piece of evidence that Baumeister uses to support his theory is the finding that there is less consistency between sexual attitudes and sexual behaviors among women than men. In other words, aspects of the situation or the environment have more of an influence on women's sexual behavior. For example, whether a man uses a condom can be predicted from his attitudes about condoms; whether a woman asks a man to use a condom will be determined by a variety of other factors aside from her attitudes about condom usage, such as the characteristics of the particular man.

Although a great deal of evidence supports women's greater erotic plasticity, the evidence is largely circumstantial. In other words, no study has been conducted to actually test the theory. Instead, Baumeister (2000) looked to the literature and examined whether the results from previous studies fit this theory. The theory is certainly provocative.

Why might women's sexual behavior be more variable than men's? Some argue that the difference is rooted in biology—that women's hormones make them more receptive to societal influences (Anderson, Cyranowski, & Aarestad, 2000). Others suggest the difference is rooted in social factors, specifically that men have more power than women, and it is more adaptive for low-power people (women) to change their behavior to fit the desires of high-power people (men; Hyde & Durik, 2000). Baumeister (2004) argues that a weaker motivation for sex on the part of females leads to greater plasticity. He says that a parallel situation exists with the drive to raise children. Here, women have a stronger motivation than males, and the father role shows greater plasticity or variability.

Activity

When I chased my 2-year-old daughter around the yard for hours, I found it difficult to believe the stereotype that boys are more active than girls. However, when I attended her preschool at age 4 and saw all of the girls seated quietly coloring and most of the boys running in circles around the room, I had to pause. Eaton and Enns (1986) conducted a meta-analysis of 90 articles that included 127 comparisons of boys' and girls' activity levels, typically measured either by an objective instrument or by observation. They found that males were more active than females, and the effect size was moderate ($d = +.49$). The effect size seemed to increase with age: small among infants ($d = +.29$), medium among preschoolers ($d = +.44$), and large among older children ($d = +.64$). The increase in the effect size because of age could be due to biological maturation or differential socialization pressures. The size of the effect also depended on the presence of peers: When peers were present, the effect was larger ($d = +.62$) than when they were absent ($d = +.44$). This finding supports some kind of social influence. Either boys and girls are changing their behavior to fit peers' expectations, or peers are exacerbating boys' and girls' preexisting tendencies.

General Personality Attributes

Up to this point, I have examined sex comparisons of some specific behaviors, but are there general differences in men's and women's personalities? A meta-analysis is available to address this question. Feingold (1994) conducted a meta-analysis on the studies reviewed by Maccoby and Jacklin (1974) and then conducted a meta-analysis that included more recent studies. Both reviews reached the same conclusions. There were no sex differences in self-esteem or locus of control. Men were more assertive than women ($d = +.38$ in the first analysis, $d = +.17$ in the second analysis), and women were more anxious than men ($d = -.29$ in the first analysis, $d = -.15$ in the second analysis). Feingold also examined whether the method of assessing personality affected the results. Most studies of personality rely on self-report measures; as mentioned previously, the problem with those studies is that men and women are aware of gender-role-appropriate behavior and may respond in ways to fit their gender roles. So, are men really more assertive than women? Or, do men know they should be assertive, and women know they should not be so assertive, and so they report behavior that fits their gender roles? Interestingly, an examination of studies that relied on behavioral measures of assertiveness found no sex differences ($d = +.04$), whereas studies that relied on self-report measures showed the expected difference, although it was small ($d = +.23$).

Feingold (1994) conducted a second study that examined markers of the more traditional domains of personality: neuroticism, conscientiousness, agreeableness, extroversion, and openness to experience. Large sex differences appeared on two traits, assertiveness ($d = +.50$) and nurturance ($d = -.97$), the two traits that map onto Bakan's (1966) notions of agency and communion. Men were more assertive than women, and women were more nurturant than men.

A more recent review of sex differences in these personality traits across 26 cultures showed that sex differences in personality were small but consistent in the direction of men being more assertive, women being more submissive, women being more nurturant, and women having more negative affect (Costa, Terracciano, & McCrae, 2001). These findings generalized across cultures. Surprisingly, sex differences were *smaller* among more traditional cultures. We would expect men's and women's behavior and thus their personality traits to differ the most in traditional cultures where male and female roles are most distinct. The authors suggested that traditional cultures may link sex differences in behavior to "roles" rather than "traits." Thus non-Western cultures may not translate behavior differences into trait differences. Indeed, other research has shown that Western cultures are more likely than other cultures to link behavior to traits (Church, 2000), a bias referred to as the *fundamental attribution error*.

Sex differences in personality also may be more strongly linked to gender roles rather than sex. For example, empathy is associated with being female and with psychological femininity, or communion. The sex difference in empathy is completely accounted for by empathy's association with communion (Karniol et al., 1998).

- There is a sex difference in empathy, favoring females. The size of the effect depends on how empathy is measured, with larger differences appearing on self-report measures and smaller differences appearing on observational and behavioral measures.

- A meta-analysis on helping behavior showed that men help more than women, contrary to expectations. However, this sex difference was limited to situations of danger. In addition, the sex of the recipient moderated the effect: Men helping women was the most prevalent kind of helping.

- Men are more likely than women to be the perpetrators and victims of aggression.

- Sex differences in aggression (male more than female) are smaller under conditions of provocation and very low or very high arousal.

- There is no evidence that the sex difference in aggression is changing over time.

- Compared to women, men have more permissive attitudes toward sex, think about sex more, desire more sex, and have more sex—leading some to suggest that men have a stronger sex drive than women.

- Men and those with traditional gender role attitudes have more negative attitudes toward homosexuals, in particular gay men. Homosexuality violates the male gender role, and there are stronger repercussions for violations of the male than the female gender role.

- Differences in men's and women's sexual behavior may be thought of in terms of erotic plasticity, or the notion that women's sexual behavior is more variable than men's.

- Boys are more active than girls, and this sex difference increases with age and with the presence of peers.

- The most robust sex differences in personality traits seem to be that men are more assertive than women, and women are more nurturant than men. Self-report measures show larger sex differences than behavioral observations.

- For all the domains of social behavior, measurement is an important moderator. Self-report measures are influenced by demand characteristics as men and women try to behave in ways that fit their gender roles (e.g., empathy, personality). Consistent with this idea, sex differences for some behaviors were larger under public than private conditions (e.g., helping), and other behaviors were larger when peers were present than absent (e.g., activity).

SEX COMPARISONS IN MORAL DEVELOPMENT

Imagine the following dilemma: Heinz has a wife who is dying, and he is unable to get a drug that would save her life. The only pharmacist who sells the drug is asking an exorbitant amount of money for it, and Heinz is poor.

This is the famous "Heinz dilemma." The question we are faced with is this: Should Heinz steal the drug? It is not the answer to the question that determines the extent of someone's moral development. Rather, it is the reasoning that is used to arrive at an answer that determines one's stage of moral reasoning.

This dilemma was used by Lawrence Kohlberg (1981) in his creation of a six-stage theory of moral development. Kohlberg evaluated people's stages of moral development by presenting them with a series of hypothetical moral dilemmas and coding their responses. The first two stages of moral development are called *preconventional* and emphasize the physical consequences of behavior. In other words, people decide for or against a behavior out of a fear of punishment or a desire to be rewarded. The third and fourth stages are called the *conventional* stages and emphasize the importance of rules and laws; the third stage emphasizes conformity to rules and others' expectations, whereas the fourth stage emphasizes the importance of maintaining law

TABLE 4.2   KOHLBERG'S STAGES OF MORAL DEVELOPMENT

1.	Preconventional	Concern for consequences; focus on punishment; obedience
2.		Concern for consequences; motivated by rewards
3.	Conventional	Conformity to others' expectations; concern with disapproval
4.		Adhere to legitimate authority; emphasize rules and justice
5.	Postconventional	Concern with community respect; focus on law
6.		Developing internal standards; moral principles

Source: Kohlberg (1963).

and order. The fifth and sixth stages are referred to as *postconventional* and involve developing one's own internal standards, separate from those of society.

Kohlberg (1981) based his theory on a longitudinal study of boys, following them from elementary school through adulthood. Because Kohlberg's study excluded females, one questions whether his theory generalizes to girls. In 1982, Carol Gilligan criticized Kohlberg's work, arguing his stages did not fairly represent women's views of moral reasoning. Gilligan said that women often ended up being classified as having a lower stage of moral development than men when using the Kohlberg scheme. Girls often were classified at only the third stage of development, which emphasizes how others feel about the situation, pleasing others, and gaining approval from others. Boys were more likely to be classified at the fourth stage, which emphasizes rules and duties, or the postconventional stage, which emphasizes individual rights and personal standards.

Gilligan (1982) took issue with this classification hierarchy. She argued that women do not have a moral orientation that is inferior to men's but an orientation that is different from men's. She argued that women have a **morality of responsibility** that emphasizes their connection to others, whereas men have a **morality of rights** that emphasizes their separation from others. Women are concerned with their responsibilities to others, others' feelings, and the effect their behavior has on relationships, whereas men are concerned with their rights, rules, and standards of justice. Gilligan stated, "While she places herself in relation to the world . . . he places the world in relation to himself" (p. 35). Kohlberg's stages of moral development emphasize the importance of developing a sense of justice, whereas Gilligan emphasizes the importance of a responsibility or care orientation. Gilligan argued that Kohlberg's theory identified the male way of moral reasoning as superior to the female way.

Do men and women really think about morality differently? A recent meta-analysis of 160 independent samples showed a small sex difference in moral reasoning (Jaffe & Hyde, 2000). Women scored higher than men on a care orientation ($d = -.28$) and men scored higher than women on a justice orientation ($d = +.19$). However, a number of variables moderated these effects. One important moderator was the procedure used to elicit moral reasoning. Sex differences were larger when participants were asked to describe their own personal dilemmas (the procedure used by Gilligan) than when participants responded to standard dilemmas (the procedure used by Kohlberg). Thus it may not be that men and women reason about morality differently; instead, men and women may be faced with different kinds of moral dilemmas. Women face those that require a care orientation and men face those that require a justice orientation.

More recently, other ways to assess moral development have evolved. In one study, 5th-,

DO GENDER 4.4
Experiences of Guilt

Ask 10 men and 10 women to describe a time when they felt guilty. You could have them choose the most recent incident or the most severe incident. Code responses into a justice orientation or a care orientation. Are there sex differences in guilt experiences? Administer the PAQ from Chapter 2 to find out if agency and communion are related to guilt experiences. You also might compile a list of these experiences and ask a second group of students to rate how frequently they have had these experiences. Do men and women engage in different behaviors for which they might feel guilt, or do men and women engage in the same behavior but one sex feels guiltier than the other sex?

8th-, and 11th-graders were asked to describe three situations in which they felt guilty (Williams & Bybee, 1994). The investigators hypothesized that boys would feel more guilt over breaking rules if they emphasize a justice and rule orientation, and girls would feel more guilt over inconsiderate behavior if they emphasize a care orientation. The results showed that boys were more likely than girls to describe situations in which they damaged property, were fighting with others, and victimized animals. Girls were more likely to describe situations of lying and inconsiderate behavior. The authors interpreted these findings as evidence of Gilligan's theory. However, boys and girls may simply engage in different kinds of immoral behavior. Use this methodology in Do Gender 4.4 to see if college students' experiences of guilt correspond to Gilligan's theory.

It is also possible that moral orientation is tied to gender roles rather than sex per se. In one study, adults were asked to describe themselves (Pratt et al., 1988). The descriptions were classified as focusing more on connection (i.e., self in relationship with others) or on individuation (i.e., self as separate from others). People classified as having connection self-concepts were more likely to adopt the care orientation, whereas people classified as having individuation self-concepts were more likely to adopt the justice orientation. In another study, college students responded to three moral dilemmas (an unplanned pregnancy, marital infidelity, caring for a parent) and moral reasoning was classified as self oriented (one's own comfort and discomfort as guiding principle), as other oriented (others' welfare as guiding principle), and self and other oriented (balancing both the needs of self and of others as guiding principle; Sochting, Skoe, & Marcia, 1994). They found that masculinity, as measured by the PAQ, was associated with a self-orientation, femininity was associated with an other-orientation, and androgyny was associated with the combined self- and other-orientation.

Sex differences in morality also are likely to be influenced by ethnicity and culture. For example, Stack (1997) constructed a set of moral dilemmas and gave them to African American adolescents to resolve. Boys' and girls' reasoning were equally likely to be classified as care or justice oriented. Stack argued that African American men and women have more similar views of themselves in relationship to others because they jointly face prejudice and discrimination from the environment.

Morality can be construed in other ways besides Kohlberg's theory. If one views morality in terms of attitudes toward extramarital affairs, divorce, or legalizing marijuana, for example, women hold more traditional views than men according to a survey that has been administered every year between 1973 and 1998 (Eagly et al., 2004). Women's greater religiosity seemed to account for these differences. Women also scored higher on an index of social compassion, which reflected issues such as gun control, racial discrimination, decreasing the income differential between rich and poor, and the death penalty. These sex differences were stable across time.

There is a lot of evidence that women are more religious than men. According to a Gallup Poll conducted between 2002 and 2006 (Gallup Poll, 2007a), women are more likely than men to say that they are religious, and this sex difference persists across the life span. Religiosity also is associated with ethnicity, with more non-Hispanic Blacks saying religion is very important compared to Whites, Asians, and White Hispanics. When it comes to church/synagogue attendance, the sex difference appears to be limited to Whites (Gallup Poll, 2007b). Whereas, equal percentages of Hispanic and Black men and women attend church on a weekly basis, (around 50%) more White women than White men do so (54% vs. 31%).

TAKE HOME POINTS

- Kohlberg's (1981) theory of moral development was criticized for excluding women during its creation; the concern was that women emerged as morally inferior to men.

- More recent data, however, have suggested there really are no sex differences in moral development using Kohlberg's procedure.

- The controversy sparked the concept of two different views of morality, one emphasizing individual rights (justice) and the other emphasizing responsibility to others (care). It is not so much that men and women view morality differently as that men and women face different kinds of moral dilemmas. Men seem to face moral dilemmas that focus on justice, and women seem to face moral dilemmas that focus on relationships.

- Aside from sex, gender roles have been linked to care and justice orientations.

SEX COMPARISONS IN SOCIAL DEVELOPMENT

List 10 responses to the following question: "Who am I?" Your responses to this question indicate how you define yourself, that is, your identity. The achievement of an identity is one of several stages of Erikson's (1950) stages of social development. According to his theory, social development proceeds through a set of stages; the issues of one stage of development must be resolved successfully before proceeding to the next stage. The identity stage precedes the intimacy stage. That is, one must have established a firm identity before one can establish a truly intimate relationship.

People who study gender have taken issue with the sequence set forth by Erikson. If the achievement of an identity precedes the achievement of intimacy, how do we explain the person who achieves his or her identity in part by connection to others? Some researchers have argued that Erikson's sequence may describe men's social development better than women's social development (Gilligan, 1982; Marcia, 1993) because women are more likely to experience identity and intimacy simultaneously. That is, part of women's identity is their relationship with others.

Early research on adolescents supported this theory (Douvan & Adelson, 1966). Boys formed their identities by making concrete occupational plans, whereas girls' future plans were unclear—their identity would be shaped by whom they married. Thus girls' identities were a consequence rather than an antecedent of intimacy. Did this mean boys had reached a higher level of social development than girls? No. At that time, boys and girls were socialized in ways that made for very different identity formations.

Even today, men's and women's social development may follow different courses. Studies have shown a stronger relation between identity and intimacy development in men than in women because intimacy is as likely to precede as to follow identity development in women (Orlofsky, 1993). A recent study of high school students showed that identity issues were more salient than intimacy issues in both male and female decision making (Lacombe & Gay, 1998). However, female students were more likely than male students to merge the two concerns. A study of early adolescents showed that males had a stronger identity development than females, but that identity development increased more with age among females (Montgomery, 2005). Thus we may socialize males to focus on identity development earlier than females, and it may take females longer than males to fully develop their identity.

Again, we can ask whether gender roles rather than sex per se are related to the social stages of development. Research has linked masculinity to identity achievement and femininity to intimacy achievement (Marcia, 1993).

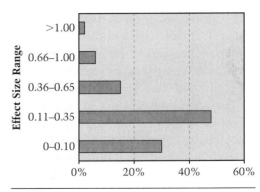

FIGURE 4.14   Effect sizes for sex differences in cognition, communication, social and personality variables, self-esteem, motor skills, activity, and moral reasoning.
Source: Adapted from Hyde (2005).

TAKE HOME POINTS

- According to Erikson's theory of social development, identity achievement precedes intimacy achievement.

- Some research suggests that this theory may apply more to men than to women, as women are more likely to work on the two tasks simultaneously. That is, women are more likely than men to define themselves in part through intimate relationships.

SEX SIMILARITIES HYPOTHESIS REVISITED

Having reviewed all the different sex differences in this chapter, you may feel a bit overwhelmed. Are there sex differences or not? Hopefully, you have reached two conclusions: (1) There are few sizable sex differences, and (2) among the ones that do exist, there is a host of moderator variables. These points have been driven home recently by a review article of 46 meta-analyses on sex differences, many of which are discussed in this chapter. From this review, Hyde (2005a) concludes that it is not the case that "men are from Mars and women are from Venus." As shown in Figure 4.14, the vast majority of effect sizes are quite small.

SUMMARY

I reviewed the evidence for sex differences in cognitive abilities, specifically spatial skills, math skills, and verbal skills. Overall, most of the differences are small. For each domain, the size of the sex difference varies with how the ability is assessed. For example, in the spatial skills domain, there is a more substantial sex difference favoring males for one particular skill, the mental rotation task, but negligible differences for the other spatial skills. In terms of verbal skills, many differences are small, but the female advantage in writing is an exception. The size of the sex difference also depends on the nature of the population. Sex differences in math are minimal among general populations; among individuals highly talented in math, males clearly outperform females. Sex differences in verbal skills also are influenced by the population studied; among children with verbal difficulties, there is a preponderance of boys over girls. For many of these areas of cognition, the differences seem to be getting smaller with time.

I also reviewed the evidence for sex differences in a number of social behaviors. Many domains show larger sex differences when self-report methods are used compared to more objective measures of behavior. For example, self-reports of empathy demonstrate a substantial sex difference favoring women, but observational measures are less clear. Other sex differences in social behavior are influenced by the environment; for example,

boys' higher activity level compared to girls' is exacerbated by the presence of peers, and sex differences in aggression are reduced under conditions of provocation. One limitation of much of this research is a lack of external validity because social behavior is often studied in the laboratory, where the natural context is removed.

Two stage theories of development, moral development and social development, may differ for men and women. Men may define morality in terms of justice and women in terms of responsibility or connection to others. If true, previous theories of moral development may unfairly represent women as inferior. However, it appears that men and women have similar views of morality but face different moral dilemmas that call for construing morality differently. The problem with previous theories of social development is that the sequence of establishing an identity before achieving intimacy may describe men's experiences more than women's.

DISCUSSION QUESTIONS

1. Have each person in the class read one of the meta-analytic reviews of sex comparisons in this chapter and provide more detail on the procedures used and the specific findings.
2. For which of the cognitive domains is there the most evidence of sex differences? Sex similarities?
3. What does the sex difference in "variability" refer to?
4. Which cognitive differences between men and women seem most likely due to environmental factors, and which seem most likely due to biological factors?

5. What are some of the methodological problems in making sex comparisons in social behavior?
6. What are some moderator variables of sex differences in aggression?
7. What is the evidence for women having greater erotic plasticity than men?
8. Do men and women define morality differently?
9. How are identity and intimacy related for men and women today? Should Erikson's theory be modified?

SUGGESTED READING

Gilligan, C. (1982). *In a different voice: Psychological theory and women's development.* Cambridge, MA: Harvard University Press.

Halpern, D. F. (2000). *Sex differences in cognitive abilities* (3rd ed.). Mahwah, NJ: Erlbaum.

Hyde, J. S. (2005a). The gender similarities hypothesis. *American Psychologist, 60,* 581–592.

Kimura, D. (1999). *Sex and cognition.* Cambridge, MA: MIT Press.

Laumann, E. O., & Michael, R. T. (Eds.). (2000). *Sex, love, and health in America: Private choices and public policies.* Chicago: The University of Chicago Press.

(Classic) Maccoby, E. E., & Jacklin, C. N. (1974). *The psychology of sex differences.* Stanford, CA: Stanford University Press.

KEY TERMS

Confirmatory hypothesis testing—Process of noticing information that confirms stereotypes and disregarding information that disconfirms stereotypes.

Construct validity—Evidence that a scientific instrument measures what it was intended to measure.

Effect size—Size of a difference that has been found in a study.

Empathy—Ability to experience the same emotion as another person or feel sympathy or compassion for another person.

Erotic plasticity—Extent to which one's sex drive is influenced by social and cultural factors.

File-drawer problem—Difficulty encountered when compiling a review of scientific literature because studies showing null results are unlikely to be published.

Gender intensification—Concern on the part of girls and boys with adherence to gender roles; applies to adolescence.

Meta-analysis—Statistical tool that quantifies the results of a group of studies.

Moderating variable—Variable that alters the relation between the independent variable and the dependent variable.

Morality of responsibility (care orientation)—Moral reasoning that emphasizes connections to others, responsibilities, and others' feelings.

Morality of rights (justice orientation)—Moral reasoning that emphasizes separation from others, rights, rules, and standards of justice.

Narrative review—Review of scientific literature in which the authors reach their own conclusions about whether the majority of studies provide evidence for or against the topic of the review (e.g., sex differences).

SEX-RELATED COMPARISONS: THEORY

Now the opposite of the male is the female. . . . In human beings the male is much hotter in its nature than the female. On that account, male embryos tend to move about more than female ones, and owing to their moving about they get broken more, since a young creature can easily be destroyed owing to its weakness. And it is due to this self-same cause that the perfecting of female embryos is inferior to that of male ones. . . . We should look upon the female state as being as it were a deformity, though one which occurs in the ordinary course of nature. (Aristotle, 1963; pp. 391, 459, 461)

Aristotle had one theory of sex differences. More recently, John Gray (1992) set forth another in *Men Are from Mars, Women Are from Venus:*

One day long ago the Martians, looking through their telescopes, discovered the Venusians. Just glimpsing the Venusians awakened feelings they had never known. They fell in love and quickly invented space travel and flew to Venus. The Venusians welcomed the Martians with open arms. . . . The love between the Venusians and the Martians was magical. They delighted in being together, doing things together, and sharing together. Though from different worlds, they reveled in their differences. . . . Then they decided to fly to Earth. In the beginning everything was wonderful and beautiful. But the effects of Earth's atmosphere took hold, and one morning everyone woke up with a peculiar kind of amnesia. . . . Both the Martians and Venusians forgot that they were from different planets and were supposed to be different. . . . And since that day men and women have been in conflict. (pp. 9–10)

These two theories about the origin of sex differences are quite different and hardly comparable. But both theories have one thing in common: Men and women are opposites.

In this chapter, I discuss a number of theories that might shed light on the sex-related differences reviewed in Chapter 4. These theories are applicable to the origin of sex differences in cognition and social behavior, and to the development of gender roles. I discuss biology, including the role of genes, hormones, and brain anatomy, and evolutionary theory, an emerging field that applies biological principles to the understanding of social behavior. I examine psychoanalytic theory, social learning theory, cognitive development theory, and a bridge of the latter two theories—gender schema theory. I discuss at length gender-role socialization and a related theory, social role theory. I end the chapter by presenting a premier social psychological theory of sex differences that emphasizes the more immediate (i.e., situational) factors (Deaux & Major, 1987). I conclude with some remarks about the constructionist and postmodern perspectives on this area of research.

As you will see, there is no one correct theory. Each has something to contribute to discussions of the origin of sex differences and the development of gender roles.

BIOLOGY

Biological theories of sex differences identify genes and hormones, as well as the structure and function of the brain, as the causes of observed differences in physical appearance, cognition, behavior, and even gender roles.

Genes

Could gender roles be hardwired? Are there specific genes linked to masculinity and femininity?

The contribution of genes to masculinity and femininity has been examined by comparing monozygotic twins (also known as identical twins) who share 100% of their genes to dizygotic twins (fraternal twins) who share 50% of their genes. The theory behind these kinds of twin studies is that genes explain the greater similarity in behavior between identical twins compared to fraternal twins because the environment for both sets of twins is the same, but the genes differ. Two studies found a greater correspondence in self-reports of masculinity and femininity between identical twins compared to fraternal twins (Lippa & Hershberger, 1999; Mitchell, Baker, & Jackson, 1989). Mitchell and colleagues concluded that genes explain from 20% to 48% of the differences, and environment explains from 52% to 80% of the differences in masculinity and femininity. Thus genes may partly contribute to the development of gender roles.

Twin studies also have been used to examine the heritability of homosexuality. The concordance of homosexuality is considerably higher among monozygotic twins than dizygotic twins—20% to 24% compared to 10% or less (Hyde, 2005b). This difference applies to both gay men and lesbians. If one identical twin is homosexual, note that the chances that the other identical twin is homosexual are far from 100%.

One question to raise about twin studies is whether the environment of identical twins is really the same as the environment of fraternal twins. I have twin nephews who are identical. One of people's first responses to them when they were born was to look for similarities. In fact, people sent them all sorts of newspaper stories depicting bizarre twin coincidences, which encouraged them to look for similarities. Investigate how people respond to identical and fraternal twins with Do Gender 5.1. One study addressed this issue by comparing the correspondence in sex-typed behavior between

DO GENDER 5.1
The Environments of Identical and Fraternal Twins

Can we presume that the greater similarity in behavior of identical twins compared to fraternal twins is due to genes alone because both sets of twins share the same environment? The question you are investigating in this exercise is whether they do share the same environment. Ideally, you should interview a pair of identical twins and a pair of fraternal twins. If you don't have access to both, perhaps you can interview one set and the class can pool the results. Ask the twins, their siblings, and their parents questions such as the following:

1. Do you dress alike?

2. Do you share the same room?

3. Do people refer to you as "the Twins"?

4. Does everyone know you are a twin?

5. Do you share the same friends?

6. Do you play together?

7. Do you play with the same toys?

8. Do people comment on how much alike the two of you are in personality?

9. Do people seem to look for similarities in your behavior?

10. Do people seem to look for differences in your behavior?

11. How are the two of you similar? Different?

The goal of this exercise is to examine similarities and differences in the physical and social environments (i.e., how parents, teachers, and peers respond) of the two kinds of twins. I argue that the environment of identical twins is not the same as the environment of fraternal twins because people expect to see more similarities in identical than in fraternal twins. Recall the power of our expectancies!

monozygotic twins, dizygotic twins, and twins with siblings (Iervolino et al., 2005). There was greater correspondence among monozygotic than dizygotic twins, and greater correspondence between dizygotic twins than siblings. In the end, the authors concluded that both genetics and environment made significant contributions to sex-typed behavior, but that the genetic contribution was stronger for girls than boys. In addition, the study showed that the shared environment of twins compared to siblings also contributes to sex-typed behavior.

Aggression is one social behavior for which there are clear-cut sex differences, and some of this difference has been attributed to biology. Twin studies find a much stronger correlation of aggressive behavior between monozygotic than dizygotic twins. A meta-analysis of 51 twin and adoption studies showed a moderate contribution of genetics to antisocial behavior (accounted for about 40% of the variance), including criminal behavior, delinquency, and behavioral aggression (Rhee & Waldman, 2002). Adoption studies are used to establish the contribution of genes to behavior by comparing the similarity in behavior between adopted siblings to the similarity in behavior between biological siblings who have been reared apart. One such study showed that there was a greater correspondence between parents' reports of family functioning and the rate of antisocial behavior in their biological than in their adopted children.

Sex-related chromosomal abnormalities also have been linked to aggression. An early genetic theory of aggression focused on the role of an extra Y chromosome in men (Manning, 1989). Some studies found a higher than average proportion of men with the XYY configuration in prison than in the normal population. However, more recent studies have called this finding into question. Even if the XYY pattern is linked to aggression, the vast majority of the criminal population does not have this extra Y chromosome, and the vast majority of people with the extra Y chromosome are not prisoners. Studies have shown that boys with the XYY pattern are more irritable and have more temper tantrums than boys without that configuration. However, it also is the case that parents of these children are aware of the extra Y chromosome and the potential link to aggression. These parents may respond to their child's behavior differently, which may further encourage aggressive behavior.

Hormones

Hormones are chemicals produced by the endocrine system that circulate throughout the body. There are two classes of sex-related hormones: **androgens** and **estrogens**. The male sex hormones are androgens (e.g., testosterone), and the female sex hormones are estrogens. This does not mean, however, that males have only androgens and females have only estrogens; men and women have both classes of hormones, but in different amounts. Sex hormones affect the brain, the immune system, and overall health. Undoubtedly, hormones also influence behavior. The question is, to what extent?

How can we evaluate the effects of hormones on men's and women's behavior? Could we randomly assign one group of women to receive testosterone and one group of women to receive a placebo? Clearly, some ethical issues arise in manipulating people's hormone levels. One solution is to study the relation of different levels of hormones across men and women to some behavior. This would be a correlational study. Another solution is to manipulate the hormones of other species, such as rats, and observe their behavior. Indeed, research has shown that if male or female rats are deprived of sex hormones, sex-related behavior is affected (Kimura, 1992, 1999). For example, male rats who are deprived of androgens show less mounting behavior. Can we extrapolate from this research that

human sexual behavior is determined by hormones? Maybe in part, but certainly not exclusively. Many other factors influence the frequency of human sexual behavior.

Has there been any link between hormones and sex-related differences in cognitive abilities? It would certainly be a straightforward theory if we found that androgens were linked to spatial skills and estrogens were linked to verbal skills. However, the relation of hormones to cognition is more complicated than that (Kimura, 2004). One source of information on the role of hormones on cognition and behavior comes from studies of girls with congenital adrenal hyperplasia (CAH), a genetic disorder resulting from a malfunction in the adrenal gland that results in prenatal exposure to high levels of male hormones. These individuals are typically reared as females because they have female sex organs.

Some studies have found that girls with CAH perform better on tasks of spatial abilities compared to girls without CAH (Kimura, 1992). This would seem to be conclusive evidence for a link of male hormones to spatial abilities. However, a study showed that higher levels of testosterone were associated with superior spatial skills among women but inferior skills among men (Kimura, 1987); if testosterone was the key to spatial abilities, men with high levels of testosterone also should have greater spatial ability. In a review of the literature, Collaer and Hines (1998) concluded that very little evidence supports the theory that prenatal exposure to sex hormones influences cognitive abilities.

Perhaps hormones are related to the more social aspects of behavior. Testosterone seems to play a role in sexual attitudes and behavior, but the specific relation is not clear (Baumeister, Catanese, & Vohs, 2001). Again, in their review of the literature, Collaer and Hines (1998) concluded there were effects of hormones on social behavior, but the effects depended on the specific hormone and the specific domain of behavior. There is a clear relation between prenatal exposure to androgens and masculine gender-role behavior among women but not men. For example, researchers have compared girls with CAH to their healthy sisters on gender-related behavior and attitudes. One study found that CAH girls demonstrated more masculine play, activities, and physical appearance than their sisters (Dittmann et al., 1990). Studies also have shown that CAH girls show less interest in infants, less desire to have children, and more desire to have a career (Dittmann et al., 1990; Leveroni & Berenbaum, 1998; Udry, Morris, & Kovenock, 1995). Berenbaum and Hines (1992) found that girls exposed to high levels of prenatal androgens were more likely to play with male toys (e.g., helicopter, cars, blocks) and less likely to play with female toys (e.g., dolls, kitchen equipment, telephone) at ages 3 and 8 than girls who had not been exposed.

There are several problems with this theory. First, exposure to prenatal androgens does not increase masculine behavior in boys. Second, there could be other variables responsible for the link between androgen exposure and more masculine-type behavior, activity being one such variable. Perhaps prenatal androgens make children more active, which then leads them to more masculine-type behavior. A specific social behavior that has been linked to male hormones is aggression. See Sidebar 5.1 for a discussion of the role of hormones in aggression.

SIDEBAR 5.1: *Does Too Much Testosterone Lead to Aggression?*

Hormonal explanations for male violence often center on the male hormone, testosterone, which has been linked to frustration, impatience, high levels of physical activity, and rough-and-tumble play (Miedzian, 1991). Interestingly, testosterone decreases with age, just as aggression decreases with age (Rushton, 1986).

Is there any evidence that testosterone is linked to violence? A meta-analysis of 54 samples showed a weak but positive relation of testosterone to aggression ($d = +.28$; Book, Starzyk, & Quinsey, 2001). For males, the relation decreased with age such that the largest effect was observed among 13- to 20-year-olds ($d = +.58$). Studies of male prisoners have found that testosterone levels are higher among men who committed personal crimes of sex and violence than property crimes of burglary, theft, or drugs (Dabbs et al., 1995) and among men who committed more ruthless crimes (i.e., premeditated; Dabbs, Riad, & Chance, 2001). In addition, prisoners with high testosterone levels were more likely to have violated prison rules. Testosterone also has been linked to aggressive behavior in hockey players (Scaramella & Brown, 1978).

Thus a relation exists between aggression and testosterone, but the evidence is far from clear that testosterone plays any causal role in aggression (Kemper, 1990). This area of research is largely correlational. Does testosterone cause aggression, or does behaving aggressively lead to a rise in testosterone? Aggressive and competitive interactions have been shown to increase levels of testosterone (Archer, 1991). Another problem is that the relation between testosterone and aggression is confounded by dominance. Testosterone is linked to dominance, which may be achieved through aggressive behavior. For example, testosterone rises in monkeys as they establish dominant hierarchies (Kemper, 1990). The fact that the relation of testosterone to aggression is stronger among people of a lower social class may be due to their attempts to acquire dominance. Testosterone also has been linked to other personality traits, such as irritability, sensation seeking, inability to tolerate frustration, and impulsivity, which also could cause aggression (Harris, 1999). Even if hormones are linked to aggressive behavior, it is more likely that hormones interact with situational factors to produce aggression rather than directly causing aggression (Herbert, 1989).

Researchers also have investigated whether exposure to prenatal androgens is linked to sexual orientation or gender identity problems. There appears to be a link between CAH and homosexuality or bisexuality in women (Collaer & Hines, 1998). However, the size of this effect is small, meaning the majority of CAH women are heterosexual. CAH also is more strongly linked to homosexual *fantasy* rather than homosexual behavior in women (Dittmann, 1997; Veniegas & Conley, 2000). CAH does not seem to be associated with significant gender identity problems. In an examination of 250 individuals with CAH reared as females, only 13 reported any gender identity problems, 4 of whom wished to be male (Dessens, Slijper, & Drop, 2005).

The studies of CAH are problematic in their ability to make strong conclusions about hormones and gender-related behavior. Girls with CAH are often born with male genitalia, a condition usually altered with surgery. Thus the parents and the children are aware of the influence of this particular prenatal androgen. Parents might expect the CAH child to exhibit more masculine behavior, provide the child with more masculine toys and masculine

activities, and respond more favorably to masculine behavior displayed by the child. The child herself also might be more comfortable engaging in masculine activities because of her own awareness of the exposure to male hormones. It is difficult to disentangle this issue from the research.

The relation of male hormones to gender-related behavior also has been studied among people who are genetically male (XY chromosome) but have an insensitivity to androgens, the masculinizing hormones. These individuals have what is known as complete androgen insensitivity syndrome (CAIS) and are born with female genitalia. They are typically reared as females. One study compared 22 girls with CAIS to healthy girls and found no differences in gender-related behavior or personality traits that typically show sex differences (Hines, Ahmed, & Hughes, 2003). The authors argue that two X chromosomes are not necessary for female gender-role behavior and that hormones can override biological sex. Historically, many people in the medical community believed hormones could *determine* gender-role behavior. See Sidebar 5.2 for a discussion of a noteworthy case that challenged this perception.

SIDEBAR **5.2**: *Raising a Boy As a Girl—Nature Versus Nurture*

Twin boys, Brian and Bruce Reimer, were born to a couple in Canada in 1965. When Bruce was circumcised at 8 months, the penis was accidentally destroyed. Distraught, the parents turned to Dr. John Money, a noteworthy sex researcher from Johns Hopkins whom they saw on television. Dr. Money had said that you could change a child into a boy or a girl with surgery and hormones, and the child's genetics did not matter. The Reimers visited Dr. Money in 1967. Dr. Money suggested that the Reimers castrate Bruce and raise him as a girl. The parents followed Dr. Money's advice. They changed Bruce's name to Brenda, dressed him in girls' clothes, and gave him girl toys. Dr. Money published numerous articles about this study, citing it as a spectacular example of how a child's sex could be changed. The scientific reports claimed the entire family had adjusted easily to the situation. These results trickled down to the lay community, as evidenced by a *Time* magazine report: "This dramatic case . . . provides strong support . . . that conventional patterns of masculine and feminine behavior can be altered. It also casts doubt on the theory that major sex differences, psychological as well as anatomical, are immutably set by the genes at conception" (Time, January 8, 1973, p. 34).

However, a later report published by Diamond and Sigmundson (1997) in the *Archives of Pediatric and Adolescent Medicine* and a biography of Bruce/Brenda written by John Colapinto (2000) suggested differently. Brenda rejected feminine toys, feminine clothing, and feminine interests right from the start. She had no friends, was socially isolated, and was constantly teased and bullied by peers. She perceived herself as a freak and believed early on she was a boy. When she expressed these concerns to Money during the family's annual visits to Johns Hopkins, they were ignored. During adolescence, Brenda was given hormones to develop breasts. She strongly objected to taking the hormones and often refused. By age 14, she had decided to become a boy and adopt the lifestyle of a boy. Finally, Mr. Reimer broke down and confessed to Brenda what had happened. In the biography, the teenager recalls feelings of anger and disbelief but mostly relief at this revelation. Brenda started taking male hormones, had surgery to remove the breasts, and became David. At age 25, he married.

A short time later, David revealed the full story of his life to John Colapinto who wrote his biography, *As Nature Made Him* (Colapinto, 2000). Unfortunately, the past could not be erased for David. Facing the death of his twin two years earlier, marital difficulties, clinical depression, and unemployment, he took his own life on May 5, 2004. The author of his biography, John Colapinto, said that he was shocked but not surprised by the suicide and lamented that "the real mystery was how he managed to stay alive for 38 years, given the physical and mental torments he suffered in childhood that haunted him the rest of his life" (Colapinto, 2004).

If androgens have a "masculinizing" effect on girls, do estrogens have a "feminizing" effect? Most of the research addressing this question has come from exposure to a synthetic estrogen, diethylstilbestrol (DES), prescribed for pregnant women in the 1960s to prevent miscarriage. Its use was discontinued when it was linked to cancer. In a review of the literature, Collaer and Hines (1998) report that exposure to DES seems to be associated with increased **lateralization** of language (i.e., distinct to one hemisphere of the brain) but has no effect on play behavior or cognitive abilities. DES also is associated with a bisexual or homosexual orientation in women (Collaer & Hines, 1998; Veniegas & Conley, 2000), but again the majority of women exposed to DES are heterosexual. Exposure to DES seems to have little effect on males. Perhaps exposure to DES does not have the same psychosocial consequences as exposure to androgens in CAH because of parental expectancies. The children do not

show physical evidence of the effects of DES as they do with CAH.

With the exception of the CAIS studies, the evidence for the effects of prenatal hormones on girls' gender-role behavior is much stronger than it is for boys' gender-role behavior (Collaer & Hines, 1998). It may be that gender-role behavior is more fluid in society for girls than boys so boys feel stronger pressures to adhere to the male role, overcoming the impact of any prenatal hormone exposure. This would be consistent with the notion of erotic plasticity discussed in Chapter 3.

The Brain

If genes and hormones cannot explain sex differences in cognition and behavior, perhaps the brain can. Isn't it true that women are "right-brained" and men are "left-brained"? Or, is it the reverse? It is true that different areas of the brain are responsible for different cognitive functions. For example, spatial abilities are located in the right hemisphere and verbal abilities in the left hemisphere. Aha! So it must be that males are right-hemisphere-dominant and females are left-hemisphere-dominant. Unfortunately, this theory does not hold up for long. The left hemisphere also is responsible for analytical skills, those required in math; thus, if females are left-hemisphere-dominant, they should be better than males at math.

One theory is that cognitive skills are more strongly located in one part of the brain for men than women. For example, there seems to be greater right hemisphere specialization of visual-spatial skills for men than women, and this specialization difference accounted for the sex difference in mental rotation in one study (Siegel-Hinson & McKeever, 2002). However, there is no corresponding left hemisphere specialization of verbal skills for women (Frost et al., 1999).

Relatedly, another possibility is that women's brains are more bilateral than those of men; that is, women are more likely than men to use either hemisphere of their brain for a specific function. Men, by contrast, are said to be more lateralized, meaning the two hemispheres of the brain have more distinct functions. In support of this theory, some evidence indicates that the size of the corpus callosum, the structure that connects the right and left hemispheres, is larger in women. This may reflect greater opportunity for communication between hemispheres for women compared to men (Kimura, 1992).

To test whether there are sex differences in lateralization, Springer and Deutsch (1981) reviewed the effects of damage to the left versus the right hemisphere of the brain on men's and women's cognitive abilities. They found the particular hemisphere that was damaged had distinct effects on men but not on women. Damage to the right hemisphere affected men's spatial abilities, whereas damage to the left hemisphere affected men's language abilities. The less distinct effects on women led them to conclude that women's abilities could be located in either hemisphere. However, the evidence for sex differences in brain lateralization is not conclusive. In a meta-analytic review of studies that examined sex differences in the lateralization of language, the overall effect size was not significant (Sommer et al., 2004). Hiscock and colleagues (1995) reviewed the evidence on sex differences in brain lateralization for a variety of cognitive tasks and found that the sex difference was small, accounting for between 1% and 2% of the variability in brain lateralization. Most studies do not find a sex difference in brain lateralization, but among the ones that do, men appear to be more lateralized than women.

Some argue that differential brain lateralization contributes to the emotional differences between men and women (Guerrero & Reiter, 1998). There appears to be some evidence that memory for emotionally arousing events is encoded differently in the brain by males and females (Cahill et al., 2004). For females, activity in the left hemisphere of the amygdala is associated with long-term memory for emotion-arousing events; for males, activity in the right hemisphere of the amygdala is associated with long-term memory for emotion-arousing events. Memory in general may be located in different areas of the brain for men and women. One study showed that the left hippocampus was activated in women, whereas the right hippocampus was activated in men during an object location memory task (Frings et al., 2006). The implications of these differences are not yet fully understood.

In total, researchers have investigated the brain by examining differences in the hemispheres used and differences in structures. By examining all of the aspects of the brain, it is not surprising that some sex differences appear.

The question remains as to whether these differences in brain anatomy or structure have any functional significance.

Psychobiosocial Models

A common objection to biological theories of sex differences and gender-related behavior is that any biological differences found between men and women will be used to justify the inferior status of women in society. However, ignoring biological differences between men and women will not help to understand cognition and behavior—nor will it help to remedy any deficits found in one sex compared to the other (Halpern, Wai, & Saw, 2005). Halpern and colleagues propose an alternative theory to the traditional nature versus nurture model of sex differences—the psychobiosocial model. They argue that nature and nurture are not two mutually exclusive categories, but categories that interact with one another. As shown in Figure 5.1, biological factors operate within a social context. Even if biological differences exist, the environ-

ment can still exert an influence and an important one at that!

TAKE HOME POINTS

- Twin and adoption studies conclude that genes play a role in sex differences in cognition and social behavior as well as gender-related behavior, but that role is far from 100%.

- Sex hormones are linked to sex-related behavior. Those links are stronger for social behavior than cognition, and those relations are stronger among women than men. The strongest evidence lies in the relation of prenatal exposure to male hormones (androgens) to male gender-role behavior in women.

- The major problem with studies of the relations of hormones to behavior is that they are correlational; thus cause and effect cannot be established.

- Studies of the brain reveal some sex differences in structure, but the meaning of those differences is unclear.

- In sum, biological theories leave open to explanation much variability in the behavior of men and women.

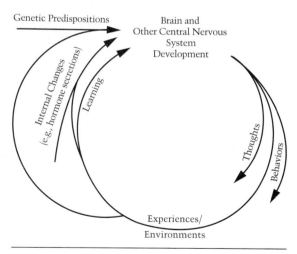

FIGURE 5.1 Psychobiosocial model showing the interrelation between biological, psychological, and social influences.
Source: Halpern, Wai, & Saw (2005).

EVOLUTIONARY THEORY AND SOCIOBIOLOGY

We typically think of evolution as explaining how humans developed from simpler organisms, not why men behave in masculine ways and women in feminine ways. Evolutionary psychology applies the principles of evolution to the study of cognition and behavior. Sociobiology examines the biological origins of social behavior—in other words, how social behavior evolved over time to perpetuate the species. Both evolutionary psychology and sociobiology are extensions of Darwin's theory of evolution, which states that we behave in ways to ensure the survival of our genes. The idea is that different behaviors may have evolved in men and women because it was adaptive for their survival (Kenrick, Trost, & Sundie, 2004).

People often confuse the fields of sociobiology and evolutionary psychology. Although there is a great deal of overlap, there are some distinctions. One is that evolutionary psychology is not limited to the study of social behavior, as is sociobiology. Thus evolutionary psychology might be the more appropriate term to use in the study of gender. There are other, more philosophical distinctions, such as whether the replication of genes is a goal that motivates behavior (sociobiology, yes; evolutionary psychology, no). These distinctions are beyond the scope of this text, but see David Buss's (1999) textbook *Evolutionary Psychology* for an elaboration of these issues.

Evolutionary theory can be applied to several domains of social behavior. Here, I discuss sexual behavior, mate selection, and aggression as examples. Evolutionary theory also is linked to the development of the hunter-gatherer society, which shaped men's and women's roles.

Sexual Behavior

Buss (1995) argues that we can observe sex differences in behaviors that historically presented men and women with different challenges. One such domain is sexual behavior. First, men and women face different challenges during pregnancy. Because conception takes place inside of the female, males face the challenge of establishing paternity. The challenge that females face is to safely get through 9 months of pregnancy and a period of lactation. Thus males will behave in ways to increase their chances of paternity and females in ways to ensure the survival of themselves and their infant. Second, men and women face different challenges to successful reproduction. For men to reproduce successfully, it is in their best interest to have

sexual intercourse with as many women as possible and to mate with women who are more likely to be fertile (i.e., young). For women to reproduce successfully, it is in their best interest to be selective in choosing a man who has the resources to help ensure the survival of the children.

This theory can explain some differences in sexual behavior, for example, why men have a lower threshold for interpreting an ambiguous behavior by a female in sexual terms and more favorable attitudes toward casual sex. The theory conflicts, however, with the finding that the sex difference in number of sexual partners is small (Oliver & Hyde, 1993) and that the vast majority of both men and women prefer a long-term relationship over a short-term sexual relationship (Pedersen et al., 2002).

Cultural factors may have overridden the influence of evolutionary theory on sexual behavior. Today, with the introduction of effective contraceptives, sexual behavior does not always lead to reproduction. The fact that contraceptives are so commonly used suggests that reproduction is often *not* the intention of sex. The sociobiological view of sex differences in sexual behavior assumes sexual intercourse will lead—or is intended to lead—to reproduction. I doubt the majority of men are thinking about establishing paternity and the majority of women are thinking about their partner's ability to support a child when deciding whether or not to engage in sex.

Mate Selection

Evolutionary psychology also can address the issue of mate preferences. Women place a greater value than men on financial success in a partner. This finding has been replicated in 37 cultures around the world (Buss, 1989). Men, by contrast, emphasize reproductive fertility in their selection of mates (Buss, 1989; Buss &

Kenrick, 1998). Men have been found to have a preference for a waist-to-hip ratio in women that is indicative of reproductive capacity and general good health.

Evolutionary theory also can explain why women prefer older men and men prefer younger women. Men's financial resources generally do not diminish and may, in fact, increase with age. However, women's reproductive resources do diminish with age. Men with financial resources may be attracted to women with reproductive resources. In a study of a computer dating service in Germany, men with the highest personal income were the most likely to desire younger partners (Grammer, 1992). However, it is a well-established research finding that people who are similar in attractiveness or similar in economic resources are most likely to be attracted to one another. The young beautiful woman coupled with the older wealthy man is the exception rather than the rule. It is not a surprise, however, that the vividness of couples such as Anna Nicole Smith (now deceased) and J. Howard Marshall, the oil tycoon, attract our attention.

Has culture influenced mate selection as it has sexual behavior? In the 37 cultures studied, the sex difference in mate preference was stronger among cultures where women had less power than men (Eagly & Wood, 1999). You might expect that women today are less likely to desire men with financial resources because they are more likely to have their own source of income. Such changes have been supported by a report of mate preferences from 6 samples accrued between 1936 and 1996 (Buss et al., 2001). Over time, women decreased the value they attached to a mate with ambition. Men increased the value they attached to mates with education and financial assets and decreased the value they placed on domestic skills. Both men and women increased their value of physical attractiveness in a mate over time. In general,

men's and women's mate preferences have become more similar over time.

Aggression

Sociobiologists argue that men are aggressive because they are in competition with each other for women and the opportunity to reproduce. This view is supported by studies that find a large number of violent acts are committed by men who are trying to establish dominance among a group of men (Daly & Wilson, 1988; Wilson & Daly, 1985). A study of the nature of urban homicide in the United States concluded that the most prevalent urban homicides were due to conflicts over status (Daly & Wilson, 1988). These conflicts were often minor, such as one person insulting another (Wilson & Daly, 1985). The men most likely to commit acts of violence were the ones who had not established dominance: young men and poor men. Although these findings suggest status and dominance may play a role in instigating male violence, they do not establish that competition over women is the precipitating factor.

Evolutionary theory also can be used to explain violence in families (Daly & Wilson, 1999). At first glance, familial violence would seem to violate the basic principles of evolutionary theory. However, the majority of homicides within families occur between spouses who are genetically unrelated to each other rather than between blood relatives. Women, but not men, are at greatest risk for being murdered when they try to end the relationship. Consistent with evolutionary theory, the primary motive men have for killing their spouse is sexual jealousy. Also consistent with evolutionary theory is the fact that young wives are most likely to be murdered, perhaps because youth is a sign of fertility, and fertility would make a woman more attractive to male rivals. Although young men are the individuals most likely to commit murder, the wife's age is a better predictor than the husband's age of a wife being murdered. Evolutionary theory also has been applied to the study of violence toward children. Among parents who abuse or kill their children, the incidence is much higher among stepparents than biological parents (Daly & Wilson, 1999). In sum, some patterns of violence are consistent with evolutionary principles.

The Hunter-Gatherer Society

Evolutionary theory suggests that the hunter-gatherer society developed from women's stronger investment in children compared to men. With women caring for children, men were left to hunt. The hunter-gatherer society has been linked to sex differences in both social behavior and cognition (Ecuyer-Dab & Robert, 2004). In terms of social behavior, men behave aggressively because aggression was required to hunt and feed the family; women evidence nurturance because nurturance was required to take care of children. Women became emotionally expressive and sensitive to the emotions in others because they were the primary caretakers of children. Men learned to conceal their emotions because a successful hunter needed to be quiet and maintain a stoic demeanor to avoid being detected by prey. In terms of cognition, men's greater spatial skills and geographic knowledge could have stemmed from their traveling more than women and venturing farther from the home when hunting. Women's greater ability to locate objects could be linked to their having to keep track of objects close to home; foraging for food, in particular, required women to remember the location of objects.

A Final Note

Some people find sociobiology and evolutionary theory distasteful as an explanation for sex-related differences in cognitive and social behavior, in part because these theories make sex-related differences seem unchangeable and view traditional roles as "natural." The concern is that men's and women's different roles must have been—and still are—desirable if they led to survival. Buss and Kenrick (1998) argue against this interpretation. They suggest that evolutionary psychology is not deterministic, but interactionistic: It interacts with the environment. Behavior that evolved for survival reasons can be influenced by the culture, such as the examples of the influence of birth control pills on sexual behavior and the influence of women's increased economic resources on mate selection. Buss and Kenrick suggest that evolutionary psychology is useful for understanding the mechanisms behind behavior. To change behavior, we must understand its causes. There are limitations to evolutionary theory, however, most of which will be discussed in Chapter 9 on relationships.

TAKE HOME POINTS

- Because males and females face different challenges in ensuring the survival of their genes, sex differences in sexual behavior and mate selection have evolved.

- According to evolutionary theory, males prefer to have sex with as many fertile women as possible, and females prefer to have sex with a male who can provide economic resources to ensure the survival of their children.

- Despite the deterministic tone of evolutionary theory, there is evidence that cultural factors can override these tendencies. Today, men and women have similar preferences in terms of sexual partners and mate selection.

- Women's greater investment in children could be one explanation for the evolution of the hunter-gatherer society. The structure of that society has been linked to some sex differences in social behavior and cognition.

PSYCHOANALYTIC THEORY

The first name that comes to mind in response to psychoanalytic theory is Sigmund Freud (see Figure 5.2). Freud (1924, 1925) was a physician and a psychoanalyst who developed a theory of personality, most notable for its emphasis on the unconscious. Although his emphasis on the effects of the unconscious on behavior is one of the most noteworthy tenets of his theory, his reliance on unconscious processes also makes his theory very difficult to test.

Freud articulated a series of psychosexual stages of development, the third of which focused on the development of gender roles. According to Freud, stage 3, the phallic stage, develops between 3 and 6 years of age. It is during this stage of development that boys and girls discover their genitals and become aware that only boys have a penis. This realization leads

FIGURE 5.2 Sigmund Freud, the father of psychoanalytic theory.

boys and girls to view girls as inferior. It is also during this time that boys are sexually attracted to their mothers, view their fathers as rivals for their mother's affections, and fear castration by their fathers because of their attraction to their mother. Boys resolve this castration anxiety, and thus the Oedipal complex, by repressing their feelings toward their mothers, shifting their identification to their fathers, and perceiving women as inferior. This is the basis for the formation of masculine identity.

Girls experience penis envy and thus feel inferior to boys. Girls are sexually attracted to their fathers, jealous of their mothers, and blame their mothers for their lack of a penis. Girls' eventual awareness that they cannot have their fathers leads to a link between pain and pleasure in women, or masochism. Females handle their conflict, known as the Electra complex, by identifying with their mothers and focusing their energies on making themselves sexually attractive to men. Thus self-esteem in women becomes tied to their physical appearance and sexual attractiveness. According to Freud, the Electra complex is not completely resolved in the same way that the Oedipal complex is resolved— partly due to the clearer threat for boys than girls (fear of castration) and partly due to girls having to face a lasting inferior status. According to Freud, how boys and girls resolve all of these issues has implications for their sexuality and future interpersonal relationships.

Several difficulties are inherent in this theory of gender-role acquisition. Most important, there is no way for it to be evaluated from a scientific standpoint because the ideas behind it are unconscious. We must be even more cautious in taking this theory seriously when we realize Freud developed it by studying people who sought him out for therapy.

Freud had many critics. A notable one was Karen Horney (1926, 1973), a feminist psychoanalyst and physician. Like Freud, she placed a great deal of emphasis on the unconscious and the importance of sexual feelings and childhood experiences in personality development. However, Horney believed social forces rather than biology influenced the development of gender identity. She said girls' penis envy did not reflect a literal desire for a penis but reflected a desire for men's power and status in society. She argued that men also experience envy—envy of women's breasts and ability to bear children. She believed men perceive women as inferior as a way to elevate their own status. In fact, she argued that men's feelings of inferiority are responsible for men's need to prove their masculinity through sexual intercourse.

A more modern version of psychoanalytic theory, referred to as object-relations theory, was applied to the acquisition of gender roles by Nancy Chodorow (1978) in her book *The Reproduction of Mothering*. Chodorow's theory emphasizes the importance of early relationships in establishing gender identity. Like other psychoanalytic theorists she stresses the importance of sexuality, but she believes the family structure and the child's early social experiences, rather than unconscious processes, determine sexuality. She believes the fact that women are the primary caretakers of children is responsible for the development of distinct gender roles. Both boys' and girls' first primary relationship is with their mothers, a relationship that affects boys' and girls' sense of self, future relationships, and attitudes toward women.

According to Chodorow (1978), girls acquire their gender identity by connecting with the one person with whom they are already attached: their mother. This explains why females focus on relationships and define themselves through their connection to others. In later years, girls have difficulty finding the same intimate attachment to men. Boys, by contrast, acquire their gender identity by rejecting the one person with whom they have become attached, by separating or individuating themselves from their mother. Thus males learn to repress relationships and define themselves through separation from others. With whom do boys identify? Because fathers are less of a presence than mothers in children's lives, fewer models are available to boys; thus boys come to define masculinity as "not being feminine" or not being like their mother. Whereas girls learn the feminine role by observing their mother on a day-to-day basis, boys may find themselves identifying with cultural images of masculinity to learn their gender role.

Because girls identify with their mother, their tendency to mother "reproduces" itself. Chodorow (1978) argues that women have a greater desire than men to be parents because they are more likely to have identified with a parenting role. According to Chodorow, the fact that women are the primary caretakers of children in our society leads directly to the division of labor (i.e., men working outside the home and women working inside the home) and the subsequent devaluation of women in society. The only way these roles can change, according to Chodorow, is for men to become more involved in raising children. Given the decline of the nuclear family and the greater diversity of family structures today, it is possible to test Chodorow's theory. Conduct Do Gender 5.2 to determine if children have more traditional gender roles when they are raised in a traditional family structure compared to a nontraditional family structure. Like Freud's theory, Chodorow's theory also lacks empirical data.

SOCIAL LEARNING THEORY

We learn behavior in two ways, according to social learning theory (Bandura & Walters, 1963; Mischel, 1966). First, we learn behavior that is

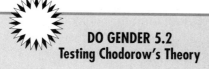

DO GENDER 5.2
Testing Chodorow's Theory

According to Chodorow, male and female gender roles are grounded in the fact that boys and girls are raised by mothers. This leads to the prediction that children's gender roles will be more traditional when they are raised in two-parent families where the father works outside the home and the mother works inside the home. What would you predict if both parents worked? What would you predict in single-parent families—mother only? father only? What would you predict in families where the father stays at home and the mother works outside the home?

Answer one of these questions by comparing two kinds of families: the traditional nuclear family (two parents, father works outside the home, mother works inside the home) and a nontraditional family (your choice).

Have the children in each family complete a measure of gender roles or gender-related attitudes from Chapter 2. Record the child's sex. See if children's gender roles are more traditional in the traditional than the nontraditional families.

modeled; second, we learn behavior that is reinforced. These are the primary principles of social learning theory, and they apply to the acquisition of gender-role behavior as they do to any other domain of behavior (Mischel, 1966).

Observational Learning or Modeling

Children develop gender roles by patterning their behavior after models in the social environment. Modeling, or observational learning, is "the tendency for a person to reproduce the actions, attitudes, and emotional responses exhibited by real-life or symbolic models" (Mischel, 1966, p. 57). Observational learning may occur from exposure to television, books, or people. Gender roles are constructed and altered by exposure to new and different models.

Whom will children imitate? At first, children may not be very discriminating and may model anyone's behavior. Eventually, they pay attention to the way others respond to their imitative behavior. If others reward the behavior, it is likely to be repeated. Thus modeling and reinforcement interact with each other to influence behavior. If a little boy sees someone on television punching another person, he may try out this behavior by punching his sibling or a toy. Although the parent may show disapproval when the boy punches his sibling, the parent may respond to punching the toy with mixed reactions. If everyone in the room laughs because they think the boy's imitation of the television figure is cute, the boy will respond to this reinforcement by repeating the behavior. Observational learning also is more likely to occur if the consequences of the model's behavior are positive rather than negative. Children should be more likely to imitate an aggressor on television who is glorified rather than punished. And many television aggressors are glorified, in cartoons such as *The Simpsons, Pokemon,* and *Dragon Ball-Z,* for example. Some of the conditions that influence observational learning are shown in Table 5.1.

TABLE 5.1   CONDITIONS THAT INFLUENCE OBSERVTIONAL LEARNING

Observational learning increases
   If there is a positive relationship between observer and model.
   If the consequences of model's behavior are positive rather than negative.
   If the model is in a position of power.
   If the model is the same sex and behaves in a gender-role congruent way.

Initially, social learning theory suggested that one way children become sex-typed is by imitating the same sex. But children do not always imitate the same sex (Maccoby & Jacklin, 1974). They are more likely to imitate same-sex behavior that is perceived as typical for the person's sex (Jacklin, 1989; Perry & Bussey, 1979). Children can easily figure out that women are more likely than men to be nurses and men are more likely than women to be construction workers. This explains why a girl is more likely to imitate a mother who is a nurse rather than a mother who is a construction worker. A girl whose mother is a construction worker may still perceive that only men are construction workers because the majority of people in this field are male.

One sex-related behavior that has been examined extensively in terms of social learning theory is aggression. Models of aggression for males abound. Think of the movies *Pulp Fiction, The Terminator, The Departed, Mystic River, The Matrix, Scream, 300,* and *Natural Born Killers.* The last is a movie about a young couple who murder 52 people while on a road trip across the United States. There have been numerous reports of copycat killings based on these movies. One victim was shot and paralyzed by a couple who said they were inspired by *Natural Born Killers* (Swerczek, 1999). The victim even tried to sue Oliver Stone, the film's director. *Scream* is a slasher film about a woman harrassed with phone calls and attacked by a man in a Halloween mask. There are also a slew of copycat killings based on this movie, with the Halloween mask left as the insignia.

Aggression is also modeled in television and video games. A content analysis of popular video games revealed that 80% included violence as part of the strategy, and 50% contained violence directed at specific others (Dietz, 1998). Even toy commercials provide models of aggression, and this modeling is aimed at boys. In one study, 69% of the toy commercials depicting only boys showed physical aggression, verbal aggression, or both (Sobieraj, 1998). Not one of the toy commercials featuring only girls involved either physical or verbal aggression.

Why do examples of aggressive behavior lead people to imitate them? Witnessing another's behavior not only teaches us how to perform the behavior but suggests the behavior is appropriate. Viewing people on television, in video games, or in the home respond to conflict with aggression may lead one to behave aggressively in a situation of conflict because it is the only response that is cognitively available.

The application of social learning theory to sex-related differences suggests that as the norms change and the role models of a culture (e.g., in the media) change, sex differences will change. Think of how the traditional male gender role has been influenced by different models. In the 1950s, a model of the male gender role was John Wayne, a cowboy who smoked cigarettes. It is unlikely this is the aspiration of most young men today. In the 1970s, the macho male gave way to sensitive and caring images like those portrayed by Alan Alda in *MASH* and Michael Landon in *Little House on the Prairie.* In the 1980s, a model was Detective Sonny Crockett (played by Don Johnson) of the television show *Miami Vice,* whose unshaven face became the decade's symbol of masculinity. Today, images of masculinity that come to mind are the slightly chauvinistic physician Dr. House of *House* and the macho mob boss Tony Soprano of *The Sopranos.*

Social learning theory has contributed to the change in occupational aspirations among children, in particular girls. More women have entered the workforce and more women have jobs that were once held only by men. Girls have come to modify their occupational aspirations. In one study, second-graders were asked what kind of job they would want as an adult (Helwig, 1998). They were then asked this same question in fourth and sixth grade. Girls' preferences for stereotypical female occupations (e.g., nurse) decreased over time, and their preferences for stereotypical male occupations (e.g., physicians) increased over time. This no doubt reflects the fact that more women are entering what were once regarded as exclusively male occupations. In addition, the total range of occupations that girls selected increased over time. Boys' behavior, however, became more stereotypical over time: They increased their preference for male-typical occupations. The reality is that the range of occupations has increased more for women than it has for men.

Social learning theory can explain why some of the sex differences in cognition and behavior have diminished over time. A longitudinal study of 10-year-olds showed that involvement in counterstereotypical activities was associated with less traditional attitudes toward gender and better grades in subjects deemed more appropriate for the other sex 2 years later (e.g., math for girls; McHale et al., 2004). These findings were stronger for females than males, however. As men become more involved in child care and more models of men as parents appear, sex differences in empathy and nurturance may be reduced. As women become more involved in sports, sex differences in spatial skills could become smaller.

There is already some support for the role of social learning theory in the development of spatial skills. A meta-analysis revealed that experience with spatial activities is related to spatial ability (Baenninger & Newcombe, 1989). Thus one reason that men have superior spatial skills compared to women might be that boys are more likely than girls to be given toys that require spatial abilities. For example, building blocks, math toys, and sports all require spatial skills, and these activities are encouraged more in boys. The meta-analysis also showed that experimental studies of spatial training improved spatial skills. Spatial training typically involved repeated exposure to a spatial skills task or spe-

cific instructions on how to perform spatial tasks. The effects of training were similar for men and women, meaning men and women were equally likely to benefit from spatial skills training. This meta-analysis pointed a strong finger at the role of the environment in sex differences in spatial skills. Some researchers have called for spatial instructions in the education system because we know it is teachable and we know it is linked to cognitive skills, including math (Halpern & Collaer, 2005).

Reinforcement

Reinforcement theory no doubt sparks images of Pavlov's dog salivating at the bell, the cue that signifies a reward is coming. With respect to gender-role acquisition, the nature of the bell is different for boys and girls. We reward boys and girls for different behaviors, and the consequences of a behavior determine whether the child performs it again. The cartoon "Jump Start" (Figure 5.3) illustrates how parents reinforce behavior. Imagine a girl plays with a doll; a parent may smile, play with her, or buy her another doll. Now imagine a boy plays with a doll; a parent may ignore the behavior, take the doll away, frown, or even scold the boy and say, "Only girls play with dolls." Consequences, however, do not actually have to occur to influence behavior; the child may infer that a consequence is likely to occur. For example, men do not have to paint their fingernails ahead of time to learn that the consequences will be negative.

We are less tolerant of and more likely to punish cross-sex behavior among boys than among girls. We do not mind if women wear ties or suits, but we mind if men wear dresses; we do not mind if daughters are athletic, but we are less enthusiastic about sons who are graceful; we are even less tolerant of attraction to a member of the same sex in men than in women. Homosexuality is viewed as a greater violation of the male gender role than the female gender

FIGURE 5.3 Cartoon illustrating parents reinforcing toughness in boys. Jump Start cartoon by Robb Armstrong, March 7, 1999, "Kiss, Smooch, Smack, Wak . . ." Jump Start reprinted by permission of United Feature Syndicate, Inc.

role; that is, men are more likely than women to be punished for being homosexual.

Aggression is a behavior that is more likely to be reinforced in males than females—by parents, teachers, and peers (Feshbach, 1989). Parents may overtly encourage aggression by telling their sons it is OK to fight with other children as a way to settle arguments. Other parents encourage aggression in subtle ways; they verbally declare that fighting is not appropriate, but at the same time they beam with pride when their child emerges as the victor of a fight. Teachers inadvertently encourage aggression in boys more than girls by reacting more strongly to aggressive behavior in boys than girls. This attention—

whether positive or negative—is reinforcing in and of itself. Aggressive behavior is more likely to decrease when it is ignored by teachers and peers.

TAKE HOME POINTS

- A central tenet of social learning theory is that the child is a passive agent upon whom society impacts.

- Social learning theory states that we acquire gender-related behavior because gender-congruent behavior is modeled and reinforced by society.

- We are more likely to imitate same-sex models, especially when they display gender-congruent behavior, models who are reinforced for their behavior, and models we like.

- Society is filled with models of male aggression—in movies, on television, and in video games—who are reinforced for their behavior.

- As models of appropriate behavior for males and females change, the behavior of males and females may change. This has been demonstrated in terms of how girls' occupational aspirations have changed over the years—more so than those of boys.

- Boys and girls are rewarded for gender-congruent behavior. Boys are more likely than girls to be punished for gender-incongruent behavior, further supporting the rigidity of the male compared to the female role.

- Boys are more likely to be rewarded by parents, teachers, and peers for aggression.

GENDER-ROLE SOCIALIZATION

Social learning theory is believed to be the basis for gender-role socialization theory. According to social learning theory, behavior is a function of rewards and observational learning. According to gender-role socialization, different people and objects in the child's environment provide rewards and models that shape behavior to fit gender-role norms. Agents in the environment encourage men to be agentic and women to be communal, to take on the male and female gender roles. Boys are taught to be assertive and to control their expression of feelings, whereas girls are taught to express concern for others and to control their assertiveness. This encouragement may take the direct form of reinforcement or the indirect form of modeling. See Sidebar 5.3 for an in-depth examination of how gender-role socialization of males in our culture contributes to aggression.

Gender-role socialization may not only contribute to actual sex differences in behavior but could also contribute to the *appearance* of sex differences. Recall that sex differences in empathy were much larger for self-report measures than for more objective measures. Could this be due to the fact that women know they

SIDEBAR 5.3: *The "Masculine Mystique"*

Aggression has been linked to the male gender role by Myriam Miedzian (1991) in her book *Boys Will Be Boys: Breaking the Link Between Masculinity and Violence*. Miedzian argues that we cannot study violence without considering the fact that men are much more likely than women to commit acts of violence. Linking violence to men, however, often makes people feel uncomfortable. Some argue that women commit acts of violence too. According to Miedzian, to study violence without linking it to being male is missing a central piece of the puzzle. Where would AIDS researchers be if they did not consider the fact that the incidence of HIV in Western countries was much higher among gay men and intravenous drug users? To ignore these facts would certainly have impeded research.

It goes without saying that not all men are violent. However, because men are more prone to violence, it is important to identify predisposing factors. Miedzian (1991) argues that the **masculine mystique** plays a major role in criminal and domestic violence. The masculine mystique consists of toughness, dominance, emotional detachment, callousness toward women, eagerness to seek out danger, and competition. Miedzian argues that we not only tolerate violence in males, but we also encourage it. War is an example: We associate war with maleness and we associate avoiding war with a lack of masculinity; we glorify war with toys, books, television, and movies; political leaders affirm their masculinity by engaging in war. Miedzian points out that the media claimed former President George H. Bush proved his manhood and overcame his image as a "wimp" by going to war with Iraq; Bush's approval ratings hit an all-time high during the Persian Gulf War and plummeted after the war was over. Similar claims may be made about President George W. Bush's invasion of Iraq in 2003.

Miedzian (1991) also argues that men grow up in a culture of violence. Hollywood offers an abundance of models of men committing violent acts, and some of these models become heroes (e.g., Sylvester Stallone, Arnold Schwarzenegger). Themes of violence pervade music, sports, video games, and toys geared toward boys. Miedzian says, "He is learning to sacrifice his body unnecessarily and to hide all feelings of fear and vulnerability, however warranted they may be. He is also being taught to sacrifice the bodies of others" (p. 201).

The masculine mystique is more dangerous for lower-class than upper-class boys. Upper-class boys are provided with legitimate pathways to validate their masculinity through achievement; lower-class boys have more difficulty attaining achievement levels that will garner dominance and respect. Black males, in particular, are denied legitimate opportunities to validate their masculinity through achievement and economic success; thus Black men may resort to other means. Staples (1995) argues that higher rates of violence in Black communities may stem from "relative deprivation." In fact, the highest rates of violence occur in communities where the income gap between Blacks and Whites is largest.

An alternative way to view aggression from a gender-role perspective is to consider the facets of the female gender role that might inhibit aggression. Empathy is a primary candidate. Empathy involves taking another person's perspective and being able to experience vicariously another person's feelings. Empathy is inversely related to aggression and has been used as a principle to intervene with aggression. For example, children 7 to 11 years old from Los Angeles who attended an empathy training program showed a decrease in aggression (Feshbach, 1989).

Miedzian (1991) suggests that one way to foster empathy in men is to increase nurturant behavior, such as by having men become more involved in raising children. She suggests an innovative program whereby both boys and girls receive child care training that begins in elementary school and extends through high school. She describes some of these programs, reporting that they are associated with reduced violence, delinquency, and teenage pregnancy. Some schools today provide life skills training in middle school that includes child care. I find it interesting that this is one lifetime duty for which neither men nor women are adequately prepared; women are expected to know how to take care of and raise children (the maternal instinct), and men are excused for not knowing how to do these things. By introducing child care skills early in life, boys and girls would not only gain useful knowledge about how to parent but would also grow up to view child care as an essential element of both men's and women's roles. Taking care of children should promote nurturance and empathy, which would reduce aggression.

are supposed to be empathic and men know they are not supposed to be empathic? The issue is one of response bias. Men and women may be distorting their behavior in ways to make them appear more consistent with traditional gender roles, which would artificially inflate the size of sex differences.

It is not surprising that the response bias issue could exaggerate sex differences in empathy. But could a response bias influence something that would appear to be much less subjective, such as spatial ability? Evidence indicates that when you disguise the nature of a spatial skills task in terms of masculinity and femininity, sex differences in spatial ability disappear. Massa, Mayer, and Bohon (2005) used the embedded figures test to measure spatial ability but described the test as measuring either spatial ability or empathy. As shown in Figure 5.4, females who held the feminine

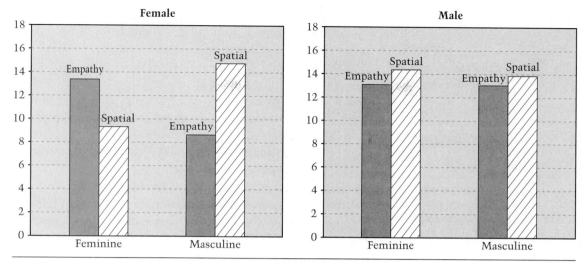

FIGURE 5.4   Score on the embedded figures test. Feminine women performed better when the test was presented as a measure of empathy than spatial ability, whereas masculine women performed better when the test was presented as a measure of spatial ability than empathy. Gender role and test instructions did not affect men's scores.

Source: Adapted from Massa, Mayer, and Bohon (2005).

gender role performed better on the task when it was described as measuring empathy than when it was described as measuring spatial ability. However, females who held the masculine gender role performed better when the task was described as measuring spatial ability than empathy. Neither gender role nor task instructions influenced men's performance on the embedded figures task. To the extent that men and women view a particular task as one in which men or women are expected to excel, participants may respond in a way to confirm this expectation. Test this idea yourself in Do Gender 5.3.

Gender-role socialization may explain sex-related differences in the expression of emotion. Women's concerns with relationships may lead them to express emotions that strengthen relationships and inhibit emotions that could harm relationships (Timmers, Fischer, & Manstead, 1998). Thus women may express sadness to an-

other person because they believe sharing such an experience will increase the closeness of the relationship. Women may be reluctant to express anger directly toward another person because of the potential damage to the relationship. Men, by contrast, are motivated to express emotions that yield power and control and reluctant to express emotions that suggest low power and vulnerability. Sadness and fear are "low-power" emotions, whereas anger and pride are "high-power" emotions.

To test these ideas, college students were presented with vignettes of four different emotions (anger, disappointment, sadness, fear) and asked how they would express these emotions (Timmers et al., 1998). Students were presented with different options for the expression of each emotion (e.g., cry, walk away, yell, be silent). Women were more likely than men to say they would respond to sadness, fear, and disappointment by verbally expressing their

DO GENDER 5.3
Can Perceptions Alter
Sex Differences?

1. Ask 20 people to complete two tasks, one being a test of spatial skills and one being a test of verbal skills. Come up with your own two tasks.

2. Before asking people to complete the tasks, randomly assign them to one of the following two conditions:

Condition 1: This is the control group. Give no particular instructions.
Condition 2: This is the experimental group. Manipulate respondents into perceiving that the spatial task is one in which females excel and the verbal task is one in which males excel. Think about what information you can provide to alter people's perceptions. You might provide fake statistics that show one sex performs better than the other sex. You might describe the type of person who excels on the task in masculine versus feminine terms.

3. After people have completed the task, have them rate how they view each task on a number of scales, two of which are

Not at
all masculine 1 2 3 4 5 Very masculine
Not at all
feminine   1 2 3 4 5 Very feminine

You may include other rating scales so respondents will not detect which items you are really interested in. You also could use other terms besides *masculine* and *feminine,* such as those that appear on the masculinity and femininity scales.

4. Compare male and female performance on the two tasks in the two different conditions.

feelings. Men were more likely to say they would respond to these three emotions by keeping their feelings to themselves. Both men and women are behaving in ways that fit their motivations with regard to relationships. Women's verbal expression of feelings is likely to increase the intimacy of a relationship. Men refrain from such expressions because revealing vulnerabilities would reduce their power in the relationship.

Men's motive to express power and control and women's motive to maintain relationships also can be seen in how students said they would respond to anger. Their responses depended on whether the person with whom they were talking was or was not the target of the anger. Men said they would be more likely to yell if the person was the target of their anger than if the person was not. By contrast, women said they would be more likely to yell if the person was not the target of their anger than was the target of their anger. The authors suggested that men express anger directly to the target because the goal is to change or control the other person's behavior. Women are unlikely to express anger directly to the target of their anger because it could damage the relationship. The goal of expressing anger to someone who is not the target would be to obtain comfort and support, a goal consistent with the female (but not the male) focus on relationship maintenance.

There is evidence that cultural factors can override gender roles in terms of emotion expression. In a study of college students from 37 countries spanning five continents, sex differences in emotion expression were larger in countries with *less* traditional gender roles (Fischer & Manstead, 2000). The authors argue that less traditional countries, such as the United States, have an individualistic orientation; the emphasis is on individual expression of feelings. In an individualistic country, individual differences in terms of gender roles may appear. In collectivist countries such as China or India, which are often more traditional, behavior, including the expression of emotion, is determined more by the environment: the norms of the culture and the other people in the situation. Thus people (men and women) behave more similarly in terms of emotional expression in collectivist cultures.

Now we turn to the question of who or what in the environment is the socializing agent for gender roles.

The Influence of Parents

Differential Treatment of Boys and Girls. Parents are prime candidates for contributing to gender-role socialization. However, evidence for parents treating boys and girls differently has been inconsistent. One of the early studies in this area was conducted by Rubin, Provenzano, and Luria in 1974. They showed that parents stereotyped newborns by perceiving girls as pretty, little, and soft in comparison to boys. They also found that fathers stereotyped their children more than mothers. Twenty years later, investigators tried to replicate these findings and failed (Karraker, Vogel, & Lake, 1995). Parents were asked to freely describe their infant and then rate their infant on a series of dimensions at two different times, postdelivery in the hospital and 1 week later at home. Results showed absolutely no difference in the open-ended descriptions of boys and girls at either time. There were a few differences on the dimensions evaluated: Parents viewed girls as having finer features, as less strong, and as more delicate than boys. Unlike the study by Rubin and colleagues, there was no difference between mothers' and fathers' perceptions of their children.

What about the way parents treat their sons and daughters? Lytton and Romney (1991) conducted a comprehensive meta-analytic review of 172 studies that evaluated parents'

socialization practices with children, and they concluded that parents' overall treatment of boys and girls was similar. In only one way were parents found to treat boys and girls differently: Parents encouraged sex-typed toys ($d = +.34$). There were trends that showed parents encouraged achievement, were more restrictive, and were more strict with boys; by contrast, parents encouraged dependence and were warmer with girls. These effects were small, however, and did not reach statistical significance. They also found that fathers were more likely than mothers to treat sons and daughters differently.

There was a trend in the meta-analysis for parents to use more physical punishment with boys than girls, but the effect size was small. A more recent review of the literature led to the conclusion that boys are physically punished more than girls (Zahn-Waxler & Polanichka, 2004).

Lytton and Romney (1991) examined whether the methodology of a study influenced the results. Studies that included more objective methods, such as experiments and observational studies, showed larger differences in the way parents treated boys and girls than studies that used more subjective methods, such as questionnaires and interviews. In other words, parents did not report treating sons and daughters differently, but their behavior suggested otherwise. In general, the higher quality studies showed larger differences in the way parents treated sons and daughters.

Recent observational studies show that parents play differently with boys and girls. One study showed that parents spent more time playing with masculine than feminine or neutral toys with boys and more time with feminine and neutral than masculine toys with girls (Wood, Desmarais, & Gugula, 2002). Thus parents were more rigid in the toys they selected to play with boys. In another study, preschool boys were more likely than girls to say their dads would object if they played with a toy stereotyped for the other sex (i.e., dishes; Raag & Rackliff, 1998). The authors found that these boys spent less time playing with feminine toys when the stereotype was activated (i.e., they were told "dishes are for girls"). Finally, an observational study showed that both mothers and fathers engaged in more pretend play with girls than boys and fathers engaged in more physical behavior with boys than girls (Lindsey & Mize, 2001). Parents also used more assertive behavior in play with boys and more polite suggestions in their play with girls. The style of play parents used with children was positively correlated with the play children later used with peers during preschool. The authors concluded that parents may be modeling gender-typed play, which children then extend to their relations with peers.

Another reason Lytton and Romney's (1991) meta-analysis did not show stronger sex differences in parents' treatment of children is that some behaviors were overlooked. Parents' different treatment of boys and girls may be subtle. One observational study showed that mothers spent more time watching boys and more time actively involved with girls (Clearfield & Nelson, 2006). The authors concluded that parents could be sending the message that it is OK for boys to be independent whereas girls require assistance. In another observational study, the physical environments parents created for boys and girls ages 5, 13, and 25 months differed vastly (Pomerleau et al., 1990). Children were visited in their home by a trained observer, who noted the children's toys, how the children were dressed, and the decor of the children's rooms. Girls were more likely than boys to have dolls, kitchen appliances, and child's furniture, whereas boys were more likely to have tools, sports equipment, and vehicles. Boys were more likely to wear blue and red

clothing, whereas girls were more likely to wear pink clothing. Boys' rooms were more likely to contain blue bedding and curtains, whereas girls' rooms were more likely to contain yellow curtains.

Lytton and Romney's (1991) meta-analysis also showed that parents' differential treatment of children seemed to decline with the child's age. This is not surprising because parents gain more target-based information as children grow older; thus they are less likely to rely on category-based (stereotypical) information. The question remains as to the impact of these very early differences in boys' and girls' environments and interactions with parents. Exposure to certain classes of toys could lead to later preferences for those toys. Does exposure to some kinds of toys foster particular skills that might advantage one sex over the other? If you think the toys that boys and girls have today are similar, visit a nearby toy store: The aisles of girls' toys are noticeable from 50 feet away because of the blinding pink packaging. Examine boys' and girls' toys by visiting a toy store with Do Gender 5.4.

DO GENDER 5.4
Toy Store Visit

Visit a toy store or the children's section of a department store. Take notes on what you see. Can you tell which are the girls' toys and which are the boys' toys? If so, how? Pay attention to location in the store, packaging, color, and the nature of the toy. How are the toys different? How are the toys similar? Compare these toys to the ones you had during your childhood. Observe the shoppers, particularly as their behavior relates to gender.

Emotion   One area in which parents may treat children differently is emotion. There is a great deal of evidence that parents discuss emotions and use more emotion words with daughters than sons (Brody & Hall, 1993; Malatesta et al., 1989). For example, Kuebli and Fivush (1992) visited parents and children in their homes on three occasions and found that both mothers and fathers used a greater number and a greater variety of emotion words with their daughters than with their sons.

What are the implications of parents using more emotion words with daughters? Several longitudinal studies have demonstrated that parents' language is associated with children's subsequent use of language. In two such studies, parents used more emotion words and a greater variety of emotion words with 40-month-old daughters than sons, despite the lack of sex differences in the children's initial use of emotion words (Adams et al., 1995; Kuebli, Butler, & Fivush, 1995). By 70 months, the girls were responding with a greater variety of emotion words than were the boys.

One possibility is that parents are using more emotion words with girls because they are responding to differences in the language that girls and boys already use. That is, perhaps there is a biological basis to girls' greater use of emotion words, which then prompts parents to respond to them with more emotion words. One study ruled out this hypothesis by showing that children's language did not influence mothers' language over time (Kuebli et al., 1995). Thus parents are not merely responding to inherent differences in children's use of emotion words.

There is also evidence that parents use different emotion words with sons and daughters. When talking about an event the parent and child both experienced (e.g., a holiday, a trip), parents were more likely to recount the sad parts of the event to daughters than to sons.

However, they were equally likely to mention the happy parts of the event with sons and daughters (Kuebli & Fivush, 1992). For example, parents might be more likely to remind their daughter it rained on the day they were supposed to go to the beach or that they had to wait in line for hours at the amusement park. But parents would be equally likely to remind their son and daughter that they won a stuffed animal at the fair. Another study found that a greater proportion of emotion words were positive (happy) with sons than daughters, and a greater proportion of emotion words were negative (sad) with daughters than sons (Kuebli et al., 1995). These differences could have implications for the way men and women cope with stressful events: Mothers are teaching daughters to talk about negative emotions and teaching sons not to dwell on negative emotions. These ideas fit with a finding discussed later in the text concerning men's and women's different styles of coping with negative events: Women cope by ruminating about the event, and men cope by distracting themselves (Nolen-Hoeksema, 1987).

Parents' reactions to emotional expressions also may influence whether children express emotion. Females are socialized to express their emotions, whereas males are socialized to conceal their emotions. In a study of first-, fourth-, and sixth-graders, girls expected more favorable reactions from parents to the expression of sadness compared to boys (Fuchs & Thelen, 1988). Girls were equally likely to express sadness at all three ages, whereas boys expressed less sadness with increasing age. Older boys might have become more aware of others' reactions. The one exception is anger. Parents are more accepting of boys' than girls' expressions of anger (Zahn-Waxler & Polanichka, 2004). In fact, parents are more likely to inhibit the expression of anger and point out the consequences of these actions in girls compared to boys. These differences may lead to the inhibition of aggression in girls compared to boys.

Gender-Role Beliefs.   The last issue I address concerns the impact of parents' gender-role beliefs on children's gender-role socialization. That is, do parents with more egalitarian beliefs have children who are less rigid in their gender roles? A meta-analytic review of the literature showed there was a small effect of parents' gender-role beliefs on children's gender-related cognitions ($d = +.33$; Tenenbaum & Lemper, 2002). The correspondence was greater between parents' beliefs and children's beliefs about others (i.e., stereotypes) rather than children's perceptions of their own masculine and feminine traits. One longitudinal study showed that mothers' gender-role attitudes when their children were young predicted children's gender-role attitudes at age 18 (Cunningham, 2001). Specifically, more egalitarian mothers had children who grew up to believe household chores should be divided equally between men and women. Aside from parents, siblings may have a role in gender-role behavior. One study showed that boys with older brothers and girls with older sisters were more sex-typed than only children (Rust et al., 2000). In addition, boys with older sisters and girls with older brothers were the least sex-typed and most androgynous of all.

The Influence of Other People

If parents treat boys and girls in a fairly similar way, who treats them differently? One possibility is that it is other people, such as relatives, teachers, friends, and neighbors, rather than parents who treat children differently (Jacklin & Baker, 1993). Recall that we are more likely to stereotype people we do not know very well. Thus parents may be less likely than friends or relatives to use category-based information when interacting with their children.

This line of thinking is similar to that of Judith Harris (1998), who concluded that parents have largely no effect on the development of a child's personality. (This was a great relief to me, as the book appeared shortly after my daughter was born.) She wrote a controversial book entitled *The Nurture Assumption: Why Children Turn Out the Way They Do: Parents Matter Less Than You Think and Peers Matter More.* The title says it all. Harris argues that the source of influence on children comes from outside the home, in particular, from the peer group. Her conclusion is partly based on the fact that children raised by the same parents in the same environment often turn out to have very different personalities. However, we can debate whether the same home and the same parents constitute the same environment for each child. Harris's theory is called group socialization and emphasizes the child's experience outside the home. According to her theory, children learn behavior inside the home but then test it on others outside the home to see if it is going to be accepted or rejected. Others' reactions determine if the behavior is repeated.

Is there evidence that peers influence sex differences? The differences in boys' and girls' early peer groups could certainly lead to differences in emotional expression (Brody & Hall, 1993). Boys play in larger groups, which have the potential for conflict and aggression. In boys' groups, the potential for the expression of anger is high, but the potential for the expression of emotions that make us vulnerable to peers, such as fear and sadness, is low. Girls play in small groups, which minimize conflict and emphasize cooperation. In girls' groups, the potential for the expression of emotions that foster relationships, such as sadness and fear, is high. The influence of same-sex social interactions on boys' and girls' behavior is addressed in detail in Chapter 7.

Peers also contribute to aggression through modeling and reinforcement. Whereas aggression in younger children is associated with being rejected by peers, some recent evidence suggests that aggression can confer status among preadolescents and adolescents. One study selected children who were rejected by peers (i.e., peers said they did not like them) and followed their social status for 2 years (Sandstrom & Coie, 1999). The aggressive children were more likely to improve their social status 2 years later. The status improvement of aggressive children was more strongly observed among boys than girls. Another study of inner-city ninth-graders, the majority of whom were ethnic minorities, showed that children who engaged in aggressive and disruptive behavior (e.g., picked on other kids, got into fights, lost temper easily, teased other children) were more popular with their peers than nonaggressive children (Luthar & McMahon, 1996).

Why do aggressive children, in particular boys, gain popularity among their peers? Some social cliques are based on aggression. During adolescence, aggressive behavior may come to be viewed as powerful and glamorous. Particularly among inner-city youth, aggressive behavior may be viewed as an acceptable and effective way to achieve goals (Luthar & McMahon, 1996). The aggressive adolescents who become more popular may be characterized by what has been referred to as **proactive aggression** compared to **reactive aggression** (Poulin & Boivin, 2000b). Reactive aggression is an angry, impulsive response to threat or provocation more clearly tied to the frustration-aggression hypothesis. Proactive aggression, by contrast, is unprovoked, planned, goal directed, and socially motivated. Groups of children form alliances, partly based on their aggressive behavior (Coie et al., 1995). These alliances are based on proactive rather than reactive aggression (Poulin et al., 1997). Proactive aggressive

groups may gang up on and target a specific individual. These children expect to be rewarded for their behavior. Whereas reactive aggression has been associated with peer rejection, proactive aggression has been associated with peer acceptance (Poulin & Boivin, 2000a). Through proactive aggression, peer groups promote and reinforce aggressive behavior. Interestingly, one study showed it is proactive rather than reactive aggression that is more strongly tied to delinquency and violence (Vitaro, Brendgen, & Tremblay, 2002).

There may be cross-cultural differences in peer support of aggression. In a study that compared European American, Chinese American, and Chinese (from Taiwan and China) seventh- and eighth-graders, European American children were more approving of aggressive and antisocial behavior (i.e., fighting, damaging property) than Chinese children (Chen et al., 1998). The Chinese American (Chinese living in California) children's approval of antisocial behavior fell between the two groups, indicating some acculturation into American society. Across all four cultures, boys were more approving than girls.

So, is there anything that parents can do, according to Harris (1998)? Yes: Parents should choose to live in a good neighborhood. This is because it is the peers in the neighborhood who are going to influence the child. But we wonder: What is the cause of the neighborhood children's behavior?

Other Features of the Environment

Toys. When my daughter returned to school from one Christmas vacation, the teacher naturally asked each of the third-graders to name their favorite Christmas present. The most popular gifts were the Nintendo DS and iPods—named by both boys and girls. After that, for the girls it was the American Girl Doll. My daughter, however, proudly announced that her favorite

FIGURE 5.5   A girl surrounded by dinosaurs—far from a stereotypical feminine toy.

FIGURE 5.6   Girls are shown in one of their favorite pastimes, playing in dress-up clothes.

FIGURE 5.7   This is the Little Tikes Push and Ride. The toy is marketed to boys as the Push and Ride Racer and to girls as the Push and Ride Doll Walker. *Source:* Courtesy of Little Tikes.

gift was a giant stuffed triceratops—not a conventional toy for girls (see Figure 5.5).

Boys and girls play with different toys: Boys overwhelmingly play with vehicles, machines and construction sets (e.g., building blocks), whereas girls play with dolls, domestic toys, and dress-up clothes, as shown in Figure 5.6. Toys also are marketed to a specific sex by the color and the packaging. Consider the Little Tikes Push and Ride toy shown in Figure 5.7. It is marketed to boys as the Push and Ride Racer in bold primary colors and marketed to girls as the Push and Ride Doll Walker in pink and blue pastel colors. The advertisement for boys reads: "The high spoiler on this sporty toddler-mobile provides a sturdy handle for a child's first steps." The advertisement for girls reads: "The doll seat on this cute toddler-mobile holds a favorite doll or stuffed toy and provides a sturdy handle for a child's first steps." Thomas the Train, which has been around for 100 years, still features mostly male trains. The Mattel Barbie computer aimed at girls is not equipped with the same educational programs as the Mattel Hotwheels computer aimed at boys, a distinction observed by a nonprofit organization called Dads and Daughters (2000) that monitors the media for advertising that undermines girls. The response from Mattel to this observation was that the fashion program on the Barbie computer did not permit enough space for educational programs. The Dads and Daughters organization remarked that Mattel must think boys need mental stimulation and girls need new outfits. The Dads and Daughters organization also was instrumental in keeping Hasbro Toys from releasing a line of dolls for young girls modeled after a scantily-clad female music group (FOX News, 2006). Unfortunately, the wide-eyed, full-lipped, sexy Bratz dolls are still on the shelves.

Does it matter if boys and girls play with different toys? The toys children play with may influence sex differences in cognition and behavior. Toys may directly reinforce sex differences in cognitive abilities. As recently as 1992, the Mattel Corporation produced the Teen Talk Barbie, who said, among other things, "Math class is tough" (Sadker & Sadker, 1994). Some argue that boys' toys are more likely than girls' toys to foster the development of spatial skills, and girls' toys are more likely than boys' toys to foster the development of verbal skills (Hughes, 1991). Blakemore and Centers (2005) examined people's perceptions of the educational value of 126 toys that had been categorized as strongly feminine, moderately feminine, neutral, moderately masculine, and strongly masculine (see Figure 5.8). Interestingly, the neutral and moderately masculine toys were rated the highest on overall educational value, scientific attributes, cognitive skill development, and physical skill development. However, there is no evidence that playing with boys' toys leads to greater spatial ability or that playing with girls' toys improves verbal skills. If this were true, sex differences in spatial and verbal abilities would be amenable to change. It also is plausible that children with better spatial skills are drawn to boys' toys and children with better verbal skills are attracted to girls' toys (Hughes, 1991).

Books. The books children read also may model and encourage gender-role-appropriate behavior. A writer of children's books, Mem Fox (1993), points out that everything we read, from

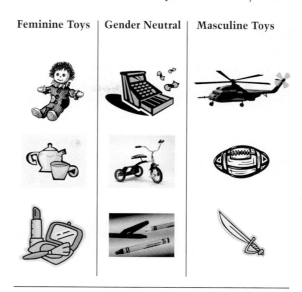

| Feminine Toys | Gender Neutral | Masculine Toys |

FIGURE 5.8 Examples of toys that were categorized by Blakemore and Centers (2005) as extremely feminine, neutral, or extremely masculine.

advertisements to magazines to books, shapes who we are by the images of men and women presented. She comments that if girls can do anything, "Why is it, then, that in children's literature they are still portrayed more often than not as acted upon rather than active? As nurturers rather than adventurers? As sweetness and light rather than thunder and lightning?" (pp. 84–85). The same can be said of boys. Fox remarks, "Why is it that ballet dancing and painting are seen as less fit occupations for them than being machine gunners, for example, or baseball players? Why should they live, as most of them do, with the idea that it is, in the main, their crippling responsibility to provide for a family when they become grown-up boys?" (p. 85).

Consider the classic fairy tales and nursery rhymes that are still read to children. Boys and girls alike learn from Cinderella, Sleeping Beauty, and Snow White that "what is beautiful is good" and clearly rewarded. Specifically, men fall in love with beautiful women; good women are obedient, gullible, vulnerable, and—if

SIDEBAR 5.4: *Mother Goose and Father Gander*

Father Gander alters the traditional Mother Goose nursery rhymes to present a more equal representation of men and women and to show men and women in more egalitarian roles. For example, the old woman in the shoe now has a husband to help her take care of the children and Ms. Muffet brings the spider to the garden to catch insects instead of running away from it. Below are listed two classic Mother Goose Nursery Rhymes along with their updated version by *Father Gander* (Larche, 1985).

Mother Goose	*Father Gander*
Peter, Peter, pumpkin eater	Peter, Peter, pumpkin eater
Had a wife and couldn't keep her	Had a wife and wished to keep her
He put her in a pumpkin shell,	Treated her with fair respect,
And then he kept her very well	She stayed with him and hugged his neck!
Humpty Dumpty sat on a wall	Humpty Dumpty sat on a wall
Humpty Dumpty had a great fall.	Humpty Dumpty had a great fall.
All the king's horses and all the king's men	All of the horses, the women and men
Couldn't put Humpty together again.	Put Humpty Dumpty together again!

In other nursery rhymes, *Father Gander* simply extended the passage to include women. For example,

Mother Goose and Father Gander

Jack be nimble, Jack be quick,
Jack jump over the candlestick!

Father Gander's extension

Jill be nimble, jump it too,
If Jack can do it, so can you!

Father Gander also added some nursery rhymes that depict men and women in more equal roles, for example:

Mandy's Mom stays home to work,
Millie's Mom goes outside.
David's Dad is on the road,
Donald's Dad works inside.

A working Mother's really great,
A working Father, too.
A stay-at-home Mom is first rate,
Or a Dad who stays home with you.

beautiful—will be rescued by men; other women (stepsisters, stepmothers) are evil, competitors for men; and a woman's ultimate dream is to marry a rich, handsome prince. Nursery rhymes depict females as quiet and sweet, as maids, crying, and running away from spiders, whereas males are shown as kings, thieves, butchers, and adventurers. See Sidebar 5.4 for one attempt to create a more egalitarian representation of men and women in nursery rhymes.

Ernst (1995) examined the children's books that appeared in the 1990s and noted that twice as many books were about boys as girls, and two to three times as many biographies were about boys. This pattern even occurred among award-winning children's books. Ernst argued that the prevalence of male characters leads to the conclusion that men are more important than women, and what men do is more worth writing and reading about. In addition, Ernst found that children's books continued to depict men and women in traditional roles. Male characters have an impact on and change the world; female characters follow the lead of others.

A more recent study of 83 "Notable Books" designated as outstanding by the American Library Association showed that males and females were equally likely to be represented as main characters (Gooden & Gooden, 2001). However, more of the illustrations featured males than females. There was a greater diversity in roles for adult male characters than adult female characters. Adult female characters were most likely to hold traditional roles. Adult male characters were seldom depicted as nurturant, as having domestic roles, or as interacting with children—and never depicted performing household chores! Thus gender-role stereotypes still persisted in these children's books, but their prevalence has decreased over time. However, we must realize this is a select group of books being examined. Less is known about the frequency of male and female characters and the portrayal of those characters among books that are not selected as among the best.

Even among children's books that are designated nonsexist, traditional roles for women persist. In one study, the content of children's books that had been identified as sexist or nonsexist by publishers and researchers was examined (Diekman & Murnen, 2004). Although women were more likely to be portrayed as having stereotypically masculine traits and interests

---

DO GENDER 5.5
How Are Men and Women Portrayed in Children's Books?

Review 10 children's storybooks. Record the sex of all the characters and how they are portrayed. What are they doing? Are they good characters or bad characters? What are their personality traits? How do other characters react to them?

---

in the nonsexist compared to the sexist books, there was no difference in the portrayal of women as having stereotypically feminine traits and interests. Thus the nonsexist books seem to portray an image of women as having masculine traits and interests but also retaining the traditionally feminine traits and interests. This finding seems to suggest that women's entry into nontraditional roles is more acceptable if it takes place in the context of retaining traditional feminine roles. As noted in Chapter 3, we are more accepting of stereotype incongruent behavior if it takes place in the context of a person upholding other aspects of the stereotype. Children's books may portray a woman as a physician but also show her as a nurturant parent. Examine portrayals of gender roles in children's books on your own in Do Gender 5.5.

Does it really matter whether the main character of the books that children read is male or female? Ochman (1996) addressed this question by developing a set of stories about a child that meets a dragon. The child was male in one version of the story and female in the other version. Third-graders were read these stories over a 4-week period. She found that children's self-esteem increased at the end of the 4 weeks when they had been read a story about a same-sex character. That is, girls' self-esteem increased more after hearing the story about the female child than the male child, and boys' self-esteem increased more after hearing the story about the male child than the female child.

Television. Television is also a source of information about gender roles. There seems to be a relation between watching television and holding stereotypical beliefs about gender roles. A study of fourth- and fifth-graders showed that television viewing was associated with holding gender-role stereotypes (Signorielli & Lears, 1992). The more children watched television, the more they held stereotypical beliefs about men's and women's roles. A study of Latino adolescents found that those who were less acculturated into the United States watched more television, and watching more television was associated with more traditional gender-role attitudes for females but not males (Rivadeneyra & Ward, 2005).

Some of the most popular television shows today are reality television. Reality dating programs (RDPs) were studied among college students. The frequency of watching RDPs was associated with more traditional attitudes toward men and women in romantic relationships—in particular, greater sexual double standards, viewing men and women in opposition to one another while dating, viewing men as driven by sex, and viewing dating as a game between men and women (Zurbriggen & Morgan, 2006). The cross-sectional nature of the study, however, makes it unclear whether viewing the shows increases sex-role stereotypes or whether those who hold sex-role stereotypes are more likely to be attracted to RDPs.

In some ways, but not all, gender roles are certainly less stereotyped on television today than they were 50 years ago. Depictions of men and women on the most popular sitcoms (as indicated by Nielsen ratings) were examined from 1950 to 1996 (Olson & Douglas, 1997). More recent sitcoms differed from earlier sitcoms in that they showed more variability in men's and women's roles. Although gender roles are somewhat traditional on *King of Queens* or *The Office*, they are less so on *Scrubs* and *Will and Grace*. Roles are less traditional on the popular show *ER*, but the vast majority of doctors are still men and the vast majority of nurses are women. The show *Desperate Housewives* depicts stereotypes of suburban housewives. One of the most popular game shows, *Deal or No Deal*, involves viewers choosing briefcases that contain varying amounts of money from a series of scantily clad women. Some shows actually poke fun at the stereotypes and counterstereotypes of men and women, as in the womanizer and the sensitive chiropractor on *Two and a Half Men*.

Women are clearly more of a presence on television today. In 2006, Katie Couric became the first female evening news anchor, receiving widespread attention. The percentage of women shown as prime-time characters has increased over the years but still remains lower than that of men (Elasmar, Hasegawa, & Brain, 1999). Only 18% of the major characters on prime-time television are women, and the majority of those are depicted in domestic comedies. There are few female main characters on dramas. Conduct your own analysis of recent television shows in Do Gender 5.6.

DO GENDER 5.6
How Men and Women Are Portrayed on Television

Watch one episode each of the 10 most popular television shows. You may limit your analysis to comedies or dramas or compare the two. What is the sex of the main character/characters? Describe the personality characteristics, behavior, and occupation of the characters in the shows. Are roles traditional or nontraditional? In what ways?

Children's cartoons still portray gender roles in quite traditional ways (Leaper et al., 2002). Male characters are more aggressive and more likely to be leaders, whereas female characters are a source of affection and romance, fearful, and polite. With the exception of educational/family cartoons, there are more male than female cartoon characters. Two recent cartoons have emerged with strong female characters—Sandy the **squirrel** on *Spongebob Squarepants* and Dora on *Dora the Explorer* who seeks out interesting destinations with her trusty map and friend Boots the monkey.

Advertisements. Advertisements continue to depict men and women in stereotypical ways (O'Barr, 2006). For babies, pink and blue are the clues to gender. Men are portrayed as athletic, strong, typically outdoors, and often involved in sports when they are young. As they age, they become financially successful rather than physically successful. Ads emphasize appearance and nurturing qualities for women. Even advertisements that depict girls emphasize appearance. One ad depicts a girl playing dress up with the quote "It's never too soon to learn how to accessorize." Whereas females are depicted with big smiles, males are somber—conveying the idea that women are emotionally expressive and men are stoic.

Women also continue to be portrayed as sex objects. Most recently, a group of 24 teenage girls from a variety of backgrounds, races, and neighborhoods in Allegheny County, Pennsylvania, formed what they called a Girlcott to voice their opposition to such portrayals by Abercrombie & Fitch. Abercrombie & Fitch sold T-shirts that had sexist slogans across the front such as "Do I Make You Look Fat?" and "Who Needs Brains When You Have These?" The girls' advocacy and media attention (including an appearance on the *Today Show*) led to a meeting with Abercrombie & Fitch, during which they

successfully persuaded them to remove some of these T-shirts. In 2006, they were honored at a conference of the National Organization for Women (Women and Girls Foundation, 2006).

Television commercials have been the subject of most research on gender and advertising. Although women are almost as likely as men to be portrayed as the main character of prime-time commercials (Stern & Mastro, 2004), they are portrayed in stereotypical ways, and this generalizes across cultures (Furnham & Mak, 1999). Women are younger than men, and more likely than men to represent domestic products. While females are depicted in the home surrounded by domestic products, men are depicted outdoors often engaging in leisure activities. Women are more likely than men to be shown with personal care products and performing household chores. A common image in commercials is women waiting on men because the men are hungry or not satisfied with their meal. Men are more likely to be shown in the context of automobiles, automotive products, or technology-related products. There is little sex-role reversal, and when it does occur, it is usually accompanied by humor.

One recent study examined the extent to which women and men in commercials were shown in stereotypical roles for their own sex, stereotypical roles for the other sex, and in nonstereotypical roles in Japan, Taiwan, Malaysia, and the United States (Bresnahan et al., 2001). Women were more likely to be shown in the female stereotypical role, and men were more likely to be shown in the male stereotypical role across the four cultures. Interestingly, the most common portrayal of both men and women in Japan, Taiwan, and Malaysia was in nonstereotypical roles. The United States was the exception! Another study of commercials in the United States evaluated the specific ways in which Black and White men and women were portrayed (Coltrane & Messineo, 2000). As shown in Figure 5.9, men were portrayed as

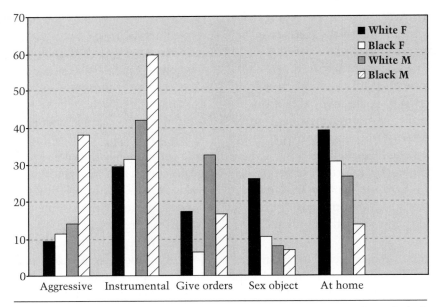

FIGURE 5.9 Percentage of White male, White female, Black male, and Black female characters in commercials depicted as aggressive, instrumental, giving orders, as sex objects, and in the home setting.
Source: Coltrane and Messineo (2000).

more aggressive and more instrumental than women—especially Black men. Men were also more likely to be seen in the dominant role of giving orders, but this pertained only to White men. White and Black women were more likely to be shown at home than men, and Black men were especially unlikely to be shown at home. White women, but not Black women, were more likely to be shown as sex objects.

One way in which television continues to depict men as dominant is in terms of narration of commercials. Men are still much more likely than women to narrate commercials, although there has been a slight decline over time—the percentage was 93% in the 1950s, 91% in the 1980s, 86% in the mid-1990s, and 71% in 1998 (Allan & Coltrane, 1996; Coltrane & Messineo, 2000).

Boys and girls also are shown in traditional roles in commercials directed toward children: Boys appear aggressive, dominant, and active,

whereas girls appear shy, giggling, and deferent (Browne, 1998). The most sex segregation occurs in children's toy advertisements (Rajecki et al., 1993). Only 30% of toy advertisements showed both a male and a female, whereas 76% of food advertisements and 89% of other advertisements showed both sexes. In an analysis of children's toy advertisements in the United States and Australia, no commercials depicted girls playing with traditional "boy toys" such as trucks, and no commercials depicted boys playing with traditional "girl toys" such as dolls (Browne, 1998). In addition, commercials that feature boys or masculine toys are perceived as more aggressive (Klinger, Hamilton, & Cantrell, 2001), suggesting the toy industry is targeting boys with aggressive toys. There is evidence that toy commercials influence how children view toys. In a study of first- and second-graders, children were shown either a traditional toy commercial (i.e., boy playing with a stereotypical boy toy) or a nontraditional toy commercial (i.e., girl playing with a stereotypical boy toy) and later were asked to sort the toys (depicted on cards) into those that are for boys, for girls, and for both boys and girls (Pike & Jennings, 2005). Children exposed to the nontraditional commercial were more likely to classify toys as for both boys and girls.

TAKE HOME POINTS

- Sources of gender-role socialization include parents, teachers, peers, neighbors, and the media.

- One positive aspect of gender-role socialization theory is that if these practices contribute to sex differences, society is then capable of providing the training or skills that men and women require to remedy any deficiencies.

- Averaging across studies, it appears that parents treat sons and daughters in more similar than different ways.

- One way parents treat boys and girls differently is in providing sex-typed toys and sex-typed environments (e.g., clothing, décor of bedrooms). There is debate over the impact of such behavior.

- Parents also communicate differently with sons and daughters, particularly with respect to emotion.

- It is not clear if parents treat sons and daughters differently with respect to other behaviors, such as encouraging nurturance in girls and independence in boys. Differences are more likely to appear on objective (observation) than subjective (parents' self-report) measures.

- Differential treatment of boys and girls is more likely to occur among younger than older children. With age, parents respond to individual characteristics of the child other than sex.

- Because parents have the opportunity to acquire individuating information about their children, it is possible that other people (e.g., neighbors, peers) and other things (e.g., television, books) socialize children to behave in gender stereotypical ways.

- Boys and girls play with different toys. It is more acceptable for girls to play with stereotypical boy toys than it is for boys to play with stereotypical girl toys. As masculine toys have been found to have more educational value than feminine toys, the question is whether the difference in boys' and girls' toys is related to sex differences in cognition.

- The presence of women has increased in all forms of media—books, television, commercials. Females are increasingly portrayed in nonstereotypical roles on television and in books, but not at the expense of giving up traditional roles. There has been less change in the portrayal of men in the media.

SOCIAL ROLE THEORY

According to social role theory, differences in men's and women's behavior are a function of the different roles men and women hold in our society (Eagly, Wood, & Diekman, 2000). This is a variant of gender-role socialization theory. Whereas gender-role socialization theory focuses on the individual and the environmental forces that shape the individual, social role theory focuses on society and how societal role structures shape behavior across groups of people. That is, social role theory focuses on the more abstract social conditions of society rather than the concrete ways that individuals behave toward men and women. According to social role theory, the way labor is divided between men and women in society accounts for why men become agentic and women become communal. Men are primarily responsible for work outside the home, which leads to an agentic orientation. Women, even when employed, are primarily responsible for work inside the home, which leads to a communal orientation. When the roles that men and women hold are similar, sex differences are minimized.

The roles that men and women possess in society, men being agentic and women being communal, have been used to explain sex differences in a variety of social behaviors

(Eagly, 1987b). Women may be more easily influenced or more conforming than men because they want to appear agreeable and maintain group harmony. The nonverbal behaviors in which women engage more than men—smiling, laughing, gazing, and nodding—may reflect women's desire to foster the development of relationships. Finally, women's tendency to be more agreeable in small groups can be construed as behavior that aims to enhance group relations.

Social role theory does not specify that men must be agentic and women must be communal. It simply states that the roles men and women hold in society are responsible for sex differences in behavior. However, most societies have organized men's and women's roles in a way so that men develop agentic characteristics and women develop communal characteristics. As men's and women's roles have become more similar in Western cultures, sex differences have decreased (Larson & Wilson, 2004). When males and females are provided with equal access to education, males and females take on more similar roles in society—females delay marriage and parenthood and take on the work role. Similar levels of education in males and females, however, do not always mean equal, especially if women are educated and oriented toward domestic roles and men are educated for paid employment roles.

One way to determine the contribution of society to gender roles is to examine practices across cultures. One of the most extensive cross-cultural studies of gender roles was conducted by Whiting and Edwards (1988). They observed the way that children ranging in age from a few months to 10 years from 12 different communities (described in Table 5.2) interacted with other children and adults. The investigators' main hypothesis was that the environments of men and women differ and that these different environments contribute to sex differences in behavior. In general, their hypothesis was supported.

Whiting and Edwards (1988) studied several interpersonal behaviors and found sex differences in two of them: nurturance (helping) and egoistic dominance (coercion, competition). In both cases, Whiting and Edwards concluded that differences in behavior were due to the different environments of boys and girls. Different environments provided girls with more practice in nurturance and boys with more practice in egoistic dominance. This interpretation of sex differences is consistent with social role theory.

Nurturance was defined in this study as helping behavior. Examples of nurturant behavior included consoling, smiling, and offerings of toys or food. The investigators discovered that girls interacted more than boys with younger children, and interactions with younger children demanded nurturance. In particular, "lap children," defined as children less than 1 year old, seem to elicit nurturance with their cries, smiles, and vocalizations. Both boys and girls demonstrated more nurturance toward lap children than any other age group of children. There was no evidence that girls were more nurturant than boys when one controlled for the greater amount of time that girls spent with lap children. Because girls did spend more time with lap children, however, they developed the necessary caretaking skills to a greater extent than boys.

Egoistic dominance was defined as attempts to change another person's behavior to suit one's own needs; coercion, insults, and competitive behavior are examples of egoistic dominance. Boys interacted more with peers than did girls, and interactions with peers were characterized by displays of greater egoistic dominance. Boys were especially more likely to interact with older children of the same sex. Older boys are more likely than older girls to behave in egoistic dominant ways with younger

TABLE 5.2   COMMUNITIES WHERE CHILDREN'S SOCIAL INTERACTION WAS OBSERVED

Location	National Affiliation	Linguistic Affiliation	Type of Settlement	Population
New Samples				
Kienn-taa	Liberia	Kpelle, Mende	Section of a town	200
Kowet Western Province	Kenya	Kipsigis, Nilo-Hamitic	Farm homesteads	447
Kisa Western Province	Kenya	Abaluyia	Farm homesteads	3,000
Kariobangi, Nairobi Central Province		Abalyayia	Housing estate in a city	13,000
Ngeca Central Province	Kenya	Kikuyu, Bantu	Village surrounded by farm homesteads	6,000
Bhubaneswar Orissa	India	Oriya	City	50,000
Six Culture Samples				
Nyansongo Western Province	Kenya	Gusii, Bantu	Farm homesteads	208
Juxtlahuacca Oaxaca	Mexico	Mixtecan	Barrio, Indian section of a town	600
Tarong, Luzon	Philippines	Iloco	Scattered hamlets	259
Taira	Okinawa	Hokan and Japanese	Village	700
Khalapur Uttar Pradesh	India	Hindi	Town, clustered	5,000
Orchard Town New England	United States	English	Part of a town	5,000

Source: Adapted from Whiting and Edwards (1988).

children. Thus boys had greater experience than girls with egoistic dominant interactions.

Whiting and Edwards (1988) also observed that parents treated boys and girls differently. Although mothers behaved in equally sociable and nurturant ways to both, they were more likely to assign child care and household chores to girls. Why do mothers ask girls rather than boys to take care of children? Is it because mothers believe girls have a greater capacity for caretaking than boys? Is it because mothers believe girls are more interested in caretaking than boys? Or, is it because mothers believe caretaking is not suitable for boys—is inconsis-

tent with the male gender role? Mothers also were more likely to give commands to girls than to boys. At younger ages, these commands involved how to behave appropriately in terms of hygiene and etiquette; at older ages, these commands involved requests for help with household and child care tasks. Whiting and Edwards remark, "Girls work while boys play" (p. 125). Mothers exerted more controlling behavior over boys in terms of punishments and reprimands for misbehavior, a finding consistent with empirical studies conducted in the United States. The investigators suggest that this difference in treatment of boys and girls was due to boys being less compliant than girls with mothers. Girls were more likely to comply with their mothers' commands perhaps because girls spend more time with their mothers or perhaps because boys are aware of their higher status compared to girls.

The differential treatment of boys and girls was greatest in societies where the status of men and women was most unequal. Physical autonomy of girls—for example, their ability to venture far from the house—was most restricted in communities with the greatest status difference between men and women. Whiting and Edwards (1988) stated, "The power of mothers to assign girls and boys to different settings may be the single most important factor in shaping gender-specific behaviors in childhood" (p. 86).

In conclusion, the authors point out that the different environment of boys and girls does not say anything about the cause of those differences. Are boys and girls genetically hardwired to select different environments? Or, do adults' beliefs about the differences between men and women lead them to place boys and girls in different environments? More specifically, is there a genetic predisposition in girls to interact with lap children and in boys to interact with peers, which then causes these differences in nurturance and egoistic dominance? Or, do societies assign boys and girls to different settings, which then elicit these behavioral differences?

There are other roles that men and women occupy in society besides work and family roles that influence gender-role behavior. For example, men are more likely than women to occupy military roles and athletic roles. These roles may contribute to sex differences in aggression. Men and women also are likely to hold different occupational roles that may contribute to sex differences in aggression. Men hold occupations in the business world that require competitiveness, whereas women hold service occupations such as nursing and teaching, which require nurturance and are incompatible with aggression.

Another difference between men's and women's social roles lies in their differential status. Men and women do not have equal statuses in our society. Thus any differences in behavior observed between men and women may be due to the status differences in their roles rather than the roles per se. For example, men's higher status may explain why men are less influenceable than women. Sex differences in nonverbal behavior also may be due to status; women may smile and gaze more than men because a low-status person needs to appear attentive and agreeable to a high-status person.

Social role theory has been extended to include the biological contributions to roles. According to **biosocial theory**, men's and women's behavior is a function of physiological differences between men and women as well as the social roles they occupy (Wood & Eagly, 2002). A cross-cultural analysis provides support for the theory by showing that women could engage in more masculine behavior, such as hunting, when reproductive functions did not interfere with the role. Recall the Agta Negrito from Chapter 1 in which women were able to hunt because the hunting was nearby and relatives took care of children.

TAKE HOME POINTS

- Social role theory states that the roles that society assigns men and women are responsible for gender roles.

- Men's role to work outside the home fosters agency, whereas women's role to work inside the home fosters communion.

- Cross-cultural research shows that boys and girls are assigned different roles of children and that these roles lead to sex-typed behavior. Specifically, girls' time with "lap" children fosters nurturance, whereas boys' time with older peers fosters egoistic dominance.

COGNITIVE DEVELOPMENT THEORY

Social learning theory, gender-role socialization, and social role theory all emphasize the effect of the environment on the child's skills and behaviors. In contrast, cognitive development theory states that the acquisition of gender roles takes place in the child's head. "It stresses the active nature of the child's thoughts as he organizes his role perceptions and role learnings around his basic conceptions of his body and his world" (Kohlberg, 1966, p. 83). An assumption of cognitive development theory is that the child is an active interpreter of the world. Learning occurs because the child cognitively organizes what he or she sees; learning does not occur from reinforcement or from conditioning. That is, the child is acting on his or her environment; the environment is not acting on the child.

Cognitive development theory suggests there are a series of stages of development that eventually lead to the acquisition of gender roles. First, children develop a **gender identity** (Kohlberg, 1966). By age 2 or 3, children learn the labels "boy" and "girl" and apply these labels to themselves and other people. The labels are based on superficial characteristics of people rather than biology, however. If someone has long hair, she must be a girl; if someone is wearing a suit, he must be a man; and if you put a dress on the man, he becomes a she. That is, children at this age believe a person's sex can change—including their own sex. A boy may believe he can grow up to be a mother.

Upon recognition that there are two groups—males and females—and that the self belongs to one of those groups, evaluative and motivational consequences follow (Martin & Ruble, 2004). The evaluative consequence is a preference for the group to which one belongs. The motivational consequence is to learn about one's own category and identify ways in which the two categories differ.

Children do not use the labels "boy" and "girl" correctly until age 4 and 5. Children learn **gender constancy** by age 5. That is, they can categorize themselves as male or female and realize they cannot change their category. But even at age 5, children may not use biological distinctions as the basis for categorization. They are more likely to classify people as male or female by their size, strength, or physical appearance. I experienced an example of this confusion one day when I was taking my daughter who was 2 years old at the time to day care. Another girl, about 4 or 5 years old, came over and asked, "Is she a boy?" I was a bit surprised because my daughter was wearing a Minnie Mouse outfit. I told the little girl she was a girl. In some frustration, the little girl replied, "Then why is *she* wearing boy shoes?" My daughter was wearing blue sandals. It is during this stage of development that children's gender-related beliefs are most rigid (Martin & Ruble, 2004). Conduct your own experiment with young children to try to identify how they decide someone is male versus female (see Do Gender 5.7). By age 5, children also learn the content of gender categories and become aware of the different roles that men and women possess in society.

According to cognitive development theory, gender identity determines gender-role attitudes and values. Once children acquire their gender identity, they have a high internal motivation to behave in ways consistent with their self-concept. The child identifies the self as male or female and wants to behave in ways consistent with this self category. Their self-concept as male or female expands as they take in new information from the environment.

One limitation of Kohlberg's theory is that he states gender constancy must be achieved before children will value and seek out behavior that fits their gender role. Yet studies have shown that children who have not achieved gender constancy still choose sex-typed behavior (Bussey & Bandura, 1992). Bussey and

DO GENDER 5.7
How Children
Determine Gender

Interview 5 children: a 2-year-old, a 3-year-old, a 4-year-old, a 5-year-old, and a 6-year-old. If the class is involved in this assignment, each of you can pool the results so that you will have more than 5 participants. Try to find out how each child determines whether someone is male or female. You can do this through a set of open-ended interview questions. For example, is the teacher male or female? How do you know? Are you male or female? How do you know? Is Santa Claus male or female? How do you know? You can also do this by presenting each child with a series of pictures, perhaps from storybooks, and ask the child to indicate whether the character is male or female and to explain why. Whichever method you choose, be sure to standardize it so you are using the same procedure for each child.

Bandura (1999) have advanced the notion of **social cognitive theory**, which states that cognitive development is one factor in gender-role acquisition, but there are social influences as well, such as parents and peers. According to social cognitive theory, external sources have the initial influence on behavior. For example, the promise of a reward or the threat of punishment influences behavior. Later, however, children shift from relying on external sources to internal standards to guide behavior. Social cognitive theory emphasizes the interplay between psychological and social influences.

TAKE HOME POINTS

- Cognitive development theory emphasizes the role that the child plays in interpreting the world. The child is an active agent in gender-role acquisition.

- There is a series of stages that children move through to acquire gender roles, starting with gender identity and proceeding to gender constancy.

- Social cognitive theory combines elements of social learning theory and cognitive development theory by recognizing that the child and the environment interact with one another to produce gender roles.

GENDER SCHEMA THEORY

You are probably familiar with the following puzzle: A little boy and his father get into an automobile accident. The father dies, but the little boy is rushed to the hospital. As soon as the boy gets to the emergency room, the doctor looks down at him and says, "I cannot operate. This boy is my son."

How can this be? Didn't the boy's father die in the accident? The solution, of course, is that the physician is the boy's mother. Why is it that we presume the physician is male? Because being male is part of our schema for the category "physician."

A **schema** is a construct that contains information about the features of a category as well as its associations with other categories. We all have schemas for situations (e.g., parties, funerals), for people at school (e.g., the jocks, the nerds), for objects (e.g., animals, vegetables) and for subjects in school (e.g., chemistry, psychology). The content of a schema varies among people. Those of you who are psychology majors have more elaborate schemas for psychology than those of you who are not psychology majors. You know there are differences among clinical psychology, social psychology, and cognitive psychology; a nonpsychology major may not know of these distinctions and may think all fields of psychology are alike. Those of you who are avid football fans have more elaborate football schemas, including all the rules of the game, the players on the different teams, and the current status of each team, compared to those of you who are not interested in football.

Schemas can be helpful in processing information. Whenever you encounter the object or the setting for which you have a schema, you do not have to relearn the information. So, those of you who have rich football schemas can use your knowledge of what happened in last week's playoffs to understand the games being played this coming weekend.

A gender schema includes your knowledge of what being male and female means and what behaviors, cognitions, and emotions are associated with these categories. When buying a gift for a newborn, one of the first questions we ask is if the baby is a boy or a girl. This category guides our choice of clothing or toys. When looking over the personnel at the dry cleaners, we presume the seamstress is the female clerk and not the male clerk because sewing is consistent with the female gender role, not the male gender role. When hiring a secretary, we interview only female applicants because "secretary" is part of our female gender-role schema, not our male gender-role schema. In fact, to have male secretaries, we have come up with a new term: administrative assistant.

What does it mean to be **gender schematic**? Someone who is gender schematic uses the gender category to make decisions about what to wear, how to behave, what career to pursue, what leisure interests to pursue, and what emotions to present to others. Someone who is **gender aschematic** does not consider gender when making these decisions.

To understand this more clearly, let's take an example of another variable on which people vary in terms of schematicity: religion. For some of you, religion is central to your identities and one of the first things you notice about a person: whether the person is religious and, if

so, to which religion he or she belongs. You notice whether a person observes religious practices and has any religious belongings in the home. Religious holidays influence your behavior. That is, you are religious schematic. For others of you, religion is not central to your self-concept, and you are religious aschematic; you will not notice whether a person engages in religious practices ("Did we say prayers before the meal at Joe's house? I really can't recall"), not notice if religious symbols are in a person's home, and fail to notice religious holidays. Being religious aschematic does not mean you are not religious; it just means religion is not something you think about and not something that influences your behavior. A strong atheist can still be religious schematic; an atheist may be well aware of religious practices and go to great lengths to ignore religion. This person is still letting religion influence behavior.

It is likely that all of us are gender schematic, to some extent. Bem (1981) argues that gender is a pervasive dichotomy in society that guides our thinking about what clothes to wear, what toys to play with, and what occupations to pursue. But there is variability among us in how readily we think of gender when processing information. The person who does not rely on male/female categories as a way of organizing the world is gender aschematic. This person is less likely to be concerned with the gender category when deciding how to think, feel, or behave. It does not occur to the person that a secretary cannot be male, that it is not OK for a male to wear a barrette, or that girls should not play with trucks.

Gender schema theory is a theory about the *process* by which we acquire gender roles; it is not a theory that describes the content of those roles. The theory simply states that we divide the world into masculine and feminine categories. The culture defines those categories. Gender schema theory combines elements of both social learning theory and cognitive development theory in describing how we acquire gender roles. Social learning theory explains how we acquire the features of the male and female gender categories and what we associate with those categories. Cognitive development theory describes how we begin to encode new information into these cognitive categories to maintain consistency. The child learns to invoke a gender-role category or schema when processing new information.

A construct you may be more familiar with than gender schema theory is **androgyny**. Recall that the androgynous individual has both masculine and feminine attributes (Bem, 1981). Bem linked gender schematicity to the construct of androgyny. Because the gender aschematic person does not use gender as a guiding principle when thinking about how to behave, Bem suggested this person would incorporate both traditionally masculine and traditionally feminine qualities into his or her self-concept, or be androgynous. Bem presumed the gender aschematic person would have the flexibility to develop both masculine and feminine qualities. By contrast, gender schematic people were thought to be sex-typed, that is, masculine if male and feminine if female. Theoretically, cross-sex-typed people (masculine females, feminine males) are also gender schematic; they would still use gender as an organizing principle but would be concerned with adhering to behavior consistent with the norms for the other sex.

Bem (1984) advanced her gender schema theory by showing that sex-typed people engage in gender schematic processing. For example, in one study, she flashed the 60 attributes of the Bem Sex Role Inventory on a screen. College students were asked to decide whether the attribute described them. The dependent variable in this experiment was how quickly the student made the judgment. Bem hypothesized that sex-typed respondents, compared to androgynous respondents, would decide more quickly that a sex-appropriate attribute described them and that a sex-inappropriate attribute did not describe them. For example, a feminine female could quickly decide that yes, she is "helpful" and no, she is not "loud." Sex-typed respondents were also expected to take longer to reject a sex-appropriate attribute and to take longer to accept a sex-inappropriate attribute compared to androgynous individuals. So that same feminine female would take longer to admit that no, she does not cook and yes, she is competitive. The results confirmed the hypothesis. The left half of Figure 5.10 indicates how quickly people endorsed terms that were consistent with gender-role schemas compared to terms that were neutral. It appears that sex-typed individuals were faster in making schema-consistent judgments than cross-sex-typed, androgynous, and undifferentiated individuals. The right half of Figure 5.10 indicates how quickly people endorsed terms that were inconsistent with gender-role schemas compared to terms that were neutral. Sex-typed individuals were slower in making schema-inconsistent judgments, especially relative to cross-sex-typed, androgynous, and undifferentiated individuals. In other studies, Bem found that sex-typed individuals were more likely to categorize a list of attributes in terms of gender and more likely to organize groups of others in terms of gender compared to androgynous persons.

Bem also found support for her theory by demonstrating that sex-typed individuals prefer to engage in behavior consistent with their gender role. In one study, college students were asked to choose which of two activities they would prefer to perform and then to engage in a gender-role-inconsistent activity (Bem, 1984). Sex-typed individuals were more likely than androgynous individuals to choose behaviors consistent with their gender role and to feel

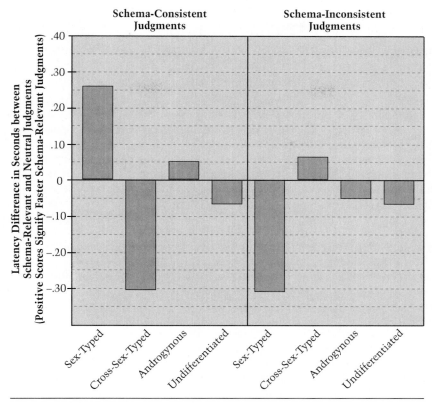

FIGURE 5.10   Sex-typed individuals more quickly endorse information consistent with their gender-role schemas than cross-sex-typed, androgynous, or undifferentiated individuals. Sex-typed individuals are slower to endorse information inconsistent with their gender-role schemas than the other three groups of individuals.
Source: Bem (1981).

more uncomfortable performing the gender-role-inconsistent behavior.

One difficulty with gender schema theory is its relation to androgyny. The androgynous person is supposed to be gender aschematic. Being gender aschematic implies the person does not think of the world in sex-related terms, yet androgyny is defined in terms of gender-related traits. Bem (1981) acknowledges this measure of androgyny may not imply the flexibility in behavior she had hoped. Androgyny can be restrictive in the sense that the person has

two ideals to meet: a masculine one and a feminine one. Androgyny also does not rid society of the two culturally defined gender categories, which was Bem's ultimate aim. Bem really advocated gender aschematicity, not androgyny.

Bem's (1984) gender schema theory obviously has some political overtones. Historically, Bem has advocated the minimization of differences between men and women—basically reducing the differences to biology alone. She has suggested society should rid itself of the social construction of gender associated with

SIDEBAR 5.5: *How to Raise a Gender Aschematic Child*

Bem (1984) suggests how to raise a gender aschematic child using practices she adopted in raising her son and daughter. These ideas are shown in Table 5.3. Her basic position is that you teach your child that sex is only a biological category, and the only way you can know whether someone is male or female is to see the person naked. Because society associates sex with much more than biology, the parent must go to some lengths to make sure prevailing stereotypes are not instilled in the child. This includes altering storybooks so all men are not viewed as having short hair and all women are not viewed as having long hair; all men are not viewed as heroes and all women are not rescued; all men are not depicted in blue and all women in pink. The parent would provide the child with a range of toys and not let the child's gender influence the choice of toys; both boys and girls would be given blocks, trucks, and dolls. There would be no such thing as "girl clothes" and "boy clothes"; both could wear shirts, pants, dresses, and barrettes.

Boys in dresses?! Boys wearing barrettes?! When I first present Bem's (1984) ideas in class, these remarks are the most commonly made. Students are all for letting girls wear any clothes and play with any toys, but someone usually draws the line at seeing a boy in a dress. Because I find dresses fairly uncomfortable, my personal response is to remove dresses from the category of clothing for both men and women. Another common reaction from students is that a child should choose who he or she wants to be and how he or she wants to behave—that parents should not force the child to be gender schematic or gender aschematic. Bem would respond that a child is never "free" to behave as he or she pleases because society will provide clear messages about how to behave, and those messages will be sexist. Thus if parents do not inoculate their children against gender schemas, society will impose those schemas. For those of you who are interested in the results of Bem's child-rearing practices, she has published an autobiography describing her egalitarian marriage and her gender aschematic child rearing (Bem, 1998). At the end of her book, her children comment favorably on the way they were raised. And, yes, Bem's grown son still occasionally wears a dress.

biological sex. In such a culture, there would be no need for the terms *masculinity* and *femininity*; the term *androgyny* would be meaningless. Sex would be viewed as having a very limited influence on us, no more influence then, say, eye color. In fact, Bem encourages the raising of gender aschematic children. See Sidebar 5.5 for a further discussion of this issue.

More recently, Bem (1995) has realized her utopian ideals are not reachable. She has suggested an alternative strategy for minimizing sex differences, or what she now refers to as

TABLE 5.3   BEM'S IDEAS ON HOW TO RAISE A GENDER ASCHEMATIC CHILD

1. Teach what sex is: a biological distinction. (You cannot tell if someone is male or female unless you see the person naked.)
2. Teach what sex is not: get rid of the cultural correlates of sex.
   Provide child with both male and female toys and clothes.
   Censor books and television for depictions of men and women in traditional roles.
   Eliminate own gender-stereotyped behavior. (E.g., only mom washes dishes, only dad washes car.)
3. Counter cultural stereotypes with counterexamples. (E.g., Child: "Only men can be doctors." Parent: "But your Aunt Jean is a doctor.")
4. Teach that society's view of gender is not only different from the one you are teaching but it is also incorrect.

"turning down the volume on sex differences." Her new strategy is to "turn up the volume on sex differences." By this, she means we should have 1,000 categories for sex instead of only 2. She suggests starting with a modest 18 categories, derived from all possible combinations of sex (male, female), gender role (masculine, feminine, androgynous), and sexual orientation (heterosexual, homosexual, bisexual). By having so many categories, it would be difficult to have clear-cut boundaries between any two categories. The categories would become fluid and, ultimately, the distinctions among them less important, if not meaningless.

TAKE HOME POINTS

- Gender schema theory combines elements of both social learning theory and cognitive development theory; social learning theory explains how the content of gender schemas are acquired; cognitive development theory suggests that people use those schemas to guide their behavior.

- People who are gender schematic divide the world into masculine and feminine categories and allow the gender category to influence how they dress, behave, and think.

- A person who is gender aschematic relies on other categories besides gender to interpret the world.

- When Bem first put forth her theory of gender aschematicity, she reasoned that someone who is not constrained by the gender category would be likely to develop both masculine and feminine traits—or what is now referred to as androgyny.

- However, Bem really advocated a gender-aschematic society rather than an androgynous one.

CONSIDERING THE CONTEXT: DEAUX AND MAJOR'S MODEL

All the theories discussed so far emphasize how biological or social forces alone or in conjunction with one another could have led to sex differences in cognition or behavior or could have shaped the traditional male and female gender roles. Descriptions of each of these theories, as well as their key concepts, are presented in Table 5.4. Instead of focusing on how gender-related behavior is acquired, like the other theories reviewed in this chapter, Deaux and Major (1987) focused on the conditions that create the *display* of gender-related behavior. That is, they emphasized the proximal, or more immediate, causes of whether a sex difference is observed rather than the distal, or more distant, factors such as biology and socialization.

From a social psychological perspective, the theories discussed so far in this chapter are fundamentally flawed (Deaux & LaFrance, 1998) because they do not take the situation, the context, into account. Deaux and Major (1987) noted that one reason men's and women's behavior is inconsistent across studies is that the situation has a strong impact on behavior. Thus they incorporated the situation into their model of sex differences.

Deaux and Major's (1987) model emphasizes three determinants of whether a sex difference in behavior is displayed: (1) the perceiver's expectancies, (2) the target's (i.e., person who may or may not display the sex difference) self-concept, and (3) the situation. I review how each of these contributes to the display of sex differences.

Perceiver

The perceiver is the person observing the behavior. The perceiver has an expectation about whether a person, the target, will display a behavior. This expectation is likely to be confirmed by either **cognitive confirmation** or **behavioral confirmation**. Cognitive confirmation is the idea that we see what we want to see; it explains how two people can see the same behavior and interpret it differently. Have you ever watched a baseball game with a person rooting for the other team? What happens during those

TABLE 5.4   THEORIES OF SEX DIFFERENCES

Theory	Description	Key Terms
Biological	Identifies genes and hormones as well as the structure and function of the brain as the cause of observed physical appearance, cognition, behavior, and gender roles.	androgens, estrogens, corpus collosum, lateralization
Evolutionary	An extension of Darwin's theory of evolution that states different social behaviors may have evolved in men and women because it was adaptive for their survival.	adaptive, challenges, maternal investment, interactionism
Psychoanalytic	Original theory suggested that gender roles are acquired by identification with the same-sex parent. Modern versions emphasize the importance of all early relationships.	Oedipal complex, unconscious processes, identification, object-relations theory
Social learning	Contends that all behaviors—including those specifically related to gender role—are learned through reinforcement and/or modeling.	reinforcement, observational learning, environmental influence
Gender-role socialization	States that people and objects in the child's environment shape behavior to fit gender-role norms.	differential socialization, parental influence, sex typing
Social role	Variant of gender-role socialization theory that suggests differences in men's and women's behavior are a function of the different roles that men and women hold in our society.	conformity, differential status, nurturance, egoistic dominance
Cognitive development	Assumes the child is an active interpreter of the world, and observational learning occurs because the perceiver cognitively organizes what he or she sees. Social cognitive theory extends this position by suggesting gender-role acquisition is influenced by social as well as cognitive factors.	gender identity, gender constancy, categorization
Gender schema	Contends that children acquire gender roles due to their propensity to process information into sex-linked categories.	gender-role schema, gender aschematic, androgyny

instant replays? You are sure the person on your team is safe and your friend is sure the person is out. The two of you actually see the same replay but interpret the behavior differently and, not surprisingly, in line with what you hoped to see. Behavior is often subject to multiple interpretations, especially social behavior. Thus the person who believes baby boys are more active than baby girls will probably maintain this belief despite numerous counterexamples because he

or she is free to interpret a wide range of behavior as active or inactive.

Behavioral confirmation is the process by which a perceiver's expectation actually alters the target's behavior. The target then confirms the perceiver's expectancy. Imagine that a mother believes boys are not as capable as girls of taking care of small children. This mother is likely to give her daughter more opportunities to take care of the new baby in the family. Thus it will not be surprising if the daughter becomes more skilled than the son at feeding and entertaining the baby!

Target

The target in an interaction is the person whose behavior is of interest. The target of an interaction influences whether he or she displays behavior consistent with stereotypes about sex differences by two processes: **self-verification** and **self-presentation**. Self-verification is our concern with behaving in ways consistent with our self-concept. If you are a member of the National Rifle Association (NRA), you may not be able to keep yourself from speaking about the importance of the Second Amendment. If you are a very traditional male, it may be important to you not to express emotions in any situation. Self-presentation is our concern with how our behavior appears to others. The NRA member may find it inappropriate to voice concerns about Second Amendment rights to a mother whose child was accidentally killed by a gun. The traditional male may realize certain situations call for emotional expression, such as a funeral.

There are individual differences in concerns with self-presentation and self-verification. **Self-monitoring** is an individual difference variable that describes the extent to which one is more concerned with self-presentation or self-verification (Snyder, 1979). A high self-monitor is someone who changes his or her behavior to fit the situation. This person will be outgoing at a party, yet serious during a study session. This person will be both supportive of a woman's right to an abortion when talking to a group of feminists but sympathetic to the plight of the unborn child when talking to a priest. This person is very much concerned with self-presentation. A low self-monitor typically behaves the same from one situation to the next. If this person is serious, he or she will be serious at a party, serious at a study session, serious at a movie, and serious during a hike. If in favor of reducing social security, this person will state his or her beliefs whether talking to a 30-year-old or a 70-year-old. The low self-monitor is most concerned with self-verification. The situation, however, will also influence whether we are more concerned with self-verification or self-presentation. Now, I turn to the importance of the situation.

Situation

In some situations, you may be more concerned with adhering to your principles and values and want to behave in a way that is consistent with them. What will determine this? The strength of your values is one determinant. If the issue is something you care strongly about, you will stand firm in your beliefs no matter what the situation. If I believe hunting is a valuable sport, I will voice this opinion to a group of people who I expect will disagree with me, such as vegetarians. In other areas, however, I may be less certain about an issue. I may be able to see both the pros and cons of day care for children; thus I will not be outspoken in advocating or rejecting day care in any situation and may tend to agree with both points of view depending on the situation.

In some situations, you will be very much concerned with how you appear to others. These situations include ones in which other people have power over you and situations in which you need something from these other people. If you are a Democrat, and you discover your professor is a Republican, you may decide to conceal your political views. Why? Because you want the professor to like you, especially if you feel grades are going to be subjective. Obviously there are exceptions. If you feel strongly about being a Democrat or are a low self-monitor, you may share your political views with the professor anyway.

The following personal example illustrates how self-verification may operate in some situations and self-presentation may operate in others. In most situations, if someone asked, "Do you mind if I smoke?" I would say yes. I would be behaving true to my self-concept as a nonsmoker and one not very fond of smoke. However, several years ago, I was in a situation where I was surrounded by a half dozen male physicians who I was hoping would refer patients to a study I was conducting. The chief among the group, who was sitting next to me in a nonsmoking building, started the meeting by turning to me and asking, "Do you mind if I smoke?" I found myself quickly replying, "No, I don't mind at all." In this particular situation, self-presentation won out over self-verification; my goal of behaving in ways consistent with my self-concept was not as strong as my goal of not offending the physician so I would receive patient referrals.

Other aspects of the situation will influence behavior. Some situations have high behavioral constraints; they provide strong cues as to how to behave. In these situations, most people will behave in accordance with those cues. For example, church is a situation with high behavioral constraints. Most people, regardless of individual difference variables, will behave in the same way during a church service: sit quietly, listen, try to stay awake, sing when others are singing, and recite passages when others recite passages. There is a set script for behavior. Deviations from these behaviors, such as giggling, are quite noticeable. Other situations are low in behavioral constraints. A party is such a situation. Some people will be loud and mingle with the crowd; others will sit quietly with one other person and talk for hours. Either behavior is acceptable. What situations are high and low in behavioral constraints with respect to gender? A wedding is a situation high in behavioral constraints. Clear guidelines dictate how the bride and groom are to dress and behave, and the guidelines are

quite different for the two of them. The classroom is a situation low in behavioral constraints with respect to gender. There are clear guidelines for behavior (sit quietly, take notes, raise hand to answer a question), but these guidelines do not differ for men and women.

Deaux and Major's (1987) model of sex differences, shown in Figure 5.11, shows how these three components—perceiver, target, and situation—interact to determine whether sex differences appear. Let's go through the model, step by step, with an example. In this example, the perceiver is a father, the target is his 3-year-old daughter, and the situation is that they are playing with toys at a day care.

Box A: This box represents the father's beliefs about men and women, that is, whether he has gender-role stereotypes, specifically about the toys that are appropriate for a girl to play with. As the father gets to know the daughter more, he will be less likely to rely on gender-role stereotypes (category-based information) and more likely to respond to target-based information (the attributes of his daughter).

Box B: This box represents whether a gender schema is activated in the father's mind. A recent event could activate a gender schema. For example, on the way to the day care, the father could have heard a story on the news about differences in social abilities between boys and girls. Attributes of the daughter or the situation could activate a gender schema. Is his daughter dressed quite differently from the boys at the day care? Is she wearing a pink frilly dress? Or is the daughter wearing a shirt and pants that do not distinguish her from the other children? The day care also may make gender salient if the teacher has the boys on one side of the room and the girls on the other side of the room, or if it

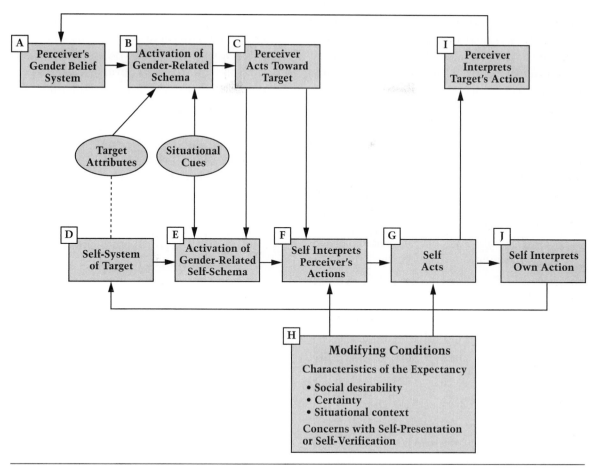

FIGURE 5.11 Deaux and Major's (1987) model of social interaction for gender-related behavior. This model explains how the perceiver, the target, and the situation determine whether sex differences in behavior are displayed in a given situation.
Source: Deaux and Major (1987).

appears that children are playing only with members of their same sex.

Box C: Here the father behaves toward his daughter. If he is highly gender schematic and has had gender schemas recently activated, perhaps he will offer his daughter a doll to play with. If he is gender aschematic and has not had gender schemas activated, he might offer his daughter the toy that looks most interesting to him or the toy he knows will be of most interest to her.

Box D: This box represents the target's self-concept, part of which is whether the daughter is gender schematic. In this example, the daughter is likely to know she is a girl and probably has noticed that boys and girls play with different toys. The daughter, however, has her own unique interests in the toys. Let's imagine her favorite toy is a remote-control car and she does not like playing with dolls.

Box E: The same things that activated the father's gender-related schema in Box B can activate the daughter's gender-related schema in Box E. This also includes how the father behaves toward her. Why did he offer her a doll when she never plays with dolls?

Box F: Here the daughter interprets the father's behavior, which is that he has just offered her a doll when she was about to play with the remote-control car. Now she has to decide whether to play with the doll, which would be behavior consistent with self-presentation (pleasing the father), or to play with the car, which would be behavior consistent with self-verification.

Box G: The daughter behaves. The interesting part of this story is that regardless of whether the daughter plays with the doll or the car, the father's gender belief system (Box A) and the daughter's self-system (Box D) are likely to remain intact. If the daughter plays with the car, she will confirm her belief that she likes cars (Box J), which fits with her self-system (Box D). The father is likely to make a situational attribution for the behavior, such as, "The car is novel, but in time she will return to the dolls" (Box I). Thus the father's belief system (Box A) also remains intact. Alternatively, if the daughter plays with the doll, the father naturally sees that the behavior fits his belief system (Box I). The daughter will realize she is playing with the doll so she can play with her dad and discount her aberrant behavior (Box J). She does not have to alter her self-system either.

Box H: This box has to do with the characteristics of the situation that might influence behavior. Is the behavior socially desirable? In our example, playing with a doll or car is socially desirable behavior.

But what is socially desirable may differ for males and females. Is it socially desirable for a boy to play with a doll? The certainty of the perceiver's and target's self-concepts will influence the outcome. In our example, the 3-year-old is likely to have a quite malleable concept of what toys are appropriate for boys and girls. If the father has spent little time around the daughter, he, too, might be less certain about the toys she will like. Those who have the strongest stereotypes are most likely to have them confirmed. The situation also determines constraints on behavior. Playtime at day care is likely to be a situation with low behavioral constraints. Finally, the extent to which the target is concerned with self-presentation (i.e., pleasing her father) versus adhering to her self-concept (i.e., playing with what she really likes) will influence behavior.

Although the diagram may seem complicated at first glance, the interaction we just described is actually overly simplified. In every interaction, the perceiver is also a target, and the target is also a perceiver. So we could talk about how the daughter influences her father's behavior. We could also talk about how the other children and the teacher influence the father-daughter interaction. Each person has expectancies for self and others. The point is that in any given situation, many proximal variables determine whether a behavior occurs, specifically whether men and women display differences in behavior.

TAKE HOME POINTS

- Unlike the other theories in this chapter, the Deaux and Major (1987) model emphasizes the more proximal causes of sex differences, highlighting the impact of the situation.

- Perceivers influence whether sex differences are observed through cognitive and behavioral confirmation.

- Targets influence whether sex differences are observed through self-verification and self-presentation.

- Features of the situation that influence the observance of sex differences are behavioral constraints, whether the situation calls for self-presentation, and the strength of one's views on the subject of interest.

CONSTRUCTIONIST AND POSTMODERN PERSPECTIVES

The constuctionists have difficulty with the subject of comparing men and women. They view gender as a dynamic force rather than a static, individual difference variable. Questions about sex differences and sex similarities do not make sense because sex cannot be studied apart from its context. Men's and women's behavior does not exist in a vacuum; it always occurs in a specific place and time. Thus the constructionists argue that sex comparisons cannot be made with empirical methods.

Perception is the critical feature of the postmodern perspective. According to the constructionists, we cannot discover reality because we construct it (Hare-Mustin & Marecek, 1988). Empirical methods are based on the idea that reality can be observed and truth and facts can be distinguished from values. Constructionism maintains, however, that values determine reality. Thus the constructionists maintain we cannot truly understand the nature of gender or sex.

As part of the constructionists' perspective, Hare-Mustin and Marecek (1988) make the point that research showing sex differences and research showing sex similarities are both biased. The former line of research is subject to an alpha bias (in which actual similarities are overlooked), and the latter is subject to a beta bias (in which actual differences are overlooked). The maximalists (i.e., people who perceive large differences between men and women) are most likely to fall victim to the alpha bias and the minimalists (i.e., people who perceive small differences between men and women) to fall victim to the beta bias. The constructionists are not in favor of either approach. They state, "All knowledge is influenced by the standpoint of the knower" (p. 427). Instead of arguing which approach is correct (which can never truly be known), the constructionists examine the consequences of each approach for the study of gender.

An important negative consequence of the alpha bias—of emphasizing men and women as fundamentally different—is that the influence of status, power, and the different roles men and women hold in society are neglected. Differences are attributable to biological sex, and the role of environmental variables is ignored. A positive consequence of the alpha bias is that feminine traits are valued. But does valuing women—specifically, their relationship orientation—mean we are affirming the low status and low power of women that led to these characteristics? This presumes, of course, that status and power explain the relationship orientation of women.

An important negative consequence of the beta bias—believing men and women are more similar than they really are—is that treating men and women similarly can be problematic if, in fact, they are different. Hare-Mustin and Marecek (1988) give the example of parental leaves: Should the same parental leave be granted to men and women if the demands on men and women are not the same? In addition, the beta bias would ignore the differential status of men and women in society. A positive consequence of the beta bias is that opportunities for women may increase if people treat men and women equally.

The constructionist perspective and the social psychological perspective share an emphasis on the context. This text takes largely a social psychological perspective rather than a constructionist perspective in understanding sex similarities and differences and the implications of gender for relationships and health.

However, this is not to say the cautions the constructionists make about the limits of our empirical methods should be ignored.

SUMMARY

I reviewed the different theories that explain the origins of the sex differences discussed in Chapter 3 as well as how gender roles are acquired. Biological theories of sex differences focus largely on the role of hormones in gender-related behavior and the effects of the structure of the brain on sex differences in cognition. The evidence for each of these subject areas is fairly controversial. The role of hormones is difficult to study because we cannot manipulate hormone levels in human beings; thus we are left to rely on correlational research among humans and experimental research on animals. Evolutionary psychology and sociobiology are theories that introduce evolutionary principles to explain cognitive and social behavior. Although a number of social behaviors, such as mate selection and sexual behavior, can be explained by sociobiology, it is difficult to test this theory experimentally.

Psychoanalytic theory began with Freud but has been updated by Chodorow. The basis of the theory, whether traditional or modern, is how identifying with the same-sex parent influences the acquisition of gender roles. Social learning theory states that reinforcement and modeling apply to the acquisition of gender-role behavior just as they do to any other behavior. The principles of social learning theory have been applied directly to gender-role acquisition in the form of gender-role socialization theory. Gender-role socialization emphasizes the role that social agents, in particular parents, play in developing children's

gender roles. The evidence for parents' differential treatment of sons and daughters is contradictory; put simply, parents treat sons and daughters more similarly than differently, but the few differences may have a large impact. In particular, parents provide sons and daughters with different toys, ones suitable for their gender. Social role theory is similar to gender-role socialization in that it emphasizes the social forces that shape gender-role behavior. However, social role theory examines those forces at a higher level, for example, by claiming the division of labor between men and women in society (men working, women caring for children) fosters agentic and communal behavior. Interesting cross-cultural research confirms the notion that the different opportunities societies present to boys and girls can lead to the development of gender-distinct behavior. By contrast, cognitive development theory emphasizes the child as an active processor of the environment rather than a passive recipient of modeling and reinforcement. Gender schema theory integrates the principles of social learning theory (and gender-role socialization) with cognitive development theory. The principles of social learning theory are responsible for the content of the gender categories in society, and cognitive development theory is responsible for our acting in accordance with those categories. Gender schema theory is really a theory of process, rather than content; people who are gender schematic behave in ways consistent with the gender schema of a given society;

people who are gender aschematic do not use gender as a guiding principle for behavior.

Finally, Deaux and Major offer a theory that describes the more proximal determinants of men's and women's behavior. According to Deaux and Major, characteristics of the perceiver, the target, and the situation will determine at any given moment how people behave and whether a sex difference is observed. The constructionist perspective also emphasizes the importance of the situation or the context in determining behavior but views gender as a meaningless category that is so subjective and value laden, it cannot be subject to empirical scrutiny.

Obviously, no one theory is correct in terms of explaining all sex differences or in terms of explaining how men and women come to possess male and female gender roles. Some theories have more evidence than others. Some theories are more easily testable than others. Some theories are more relevant to one aspect of gender than others; for example, hormones may play a greater role in aggression than in verbal ability. Each of these theories appears throughout this text, but the predominant theories discussed are ones that focus on social or environmental contributors to the impact of gender on relationships and health.

DISCUSSION QUESTIONS

1. Discuss the strengths and weaknesses of each theory of gender introduced in this chapter.
2. Which theory of gender is most difficult to test? Easiest to test?
3. If you were going to develop a study to determine whether parents treat sons and daughters differently, how would you go about developing this study? In particular, what specific behaviors would you measure?
4. How are gender roles portrayed in the media?
5. Give some specific examples of how our culture models and reinforces violence.
6. What is the masculine mystique?
7. How do the roles men and women hold in society contribute to agentic and communal behavior?
8. Distinguish between social learning theory and cognitive development theory. How does gender schema theory integrate the two?
9. Debate the advantages and disadvantages of raising a gender aschematic child.
10. Apply Deaux and Major's model to a specific behavior. Review each of the steps in the model shown in Figure 5.11.

SUGGESTED READING

Bem, S. L. (1998). *An unconventional family.* New Haven, CT: Yale University Press.

Buss, D. M. (1995). Psychological sex differences: Origins through sexual selection. *American Psychologist, 50*(3), 164–168.

(Classic) Chodorow, N. (1978). *The reproduction of mothering: Psychoanalysis and the sociology of gender.* London: University of California Press.

Deaux, K., & Major, K. (1987). Putting gender into context: An interactive model of gender-related behavior. *Psychological Review, 94,* 369–389.

Eagly, A. H., Wood, W., & Diekman, A. B. (2000). Social role theory of sex differences and similarities: A current appraisal. In T. Eckes & H. M. Trautner (Eds.), *The developmental social psychology of gender* (pp. 123–174). Mahwah, NJ: Erlbaum.

Miedzian, M. (1991). *Boys will be boys: Breaking the link between masculinity and violence.* Thousand Oaks, CA: Sage.

(Classic) Whiting, B. B., & Edwards, C. P. (1988). *Children of different worlds.* Cambridge, MA: Harvard University Press.

KEY TERMS

Androgens—Male sex hormones (e.g., testosterone).

Androgyny—Incorporation of both traditionally masculine and traditionally feminine qualities into one's self-concept.

Behavioral confirmation—Process by which a perceiver's expectation actually alters the target's behavior so the target comes to confirm the perceiver's expectancy.

Biosocial theory—Theory that states sex differences are due to both physiological and role differences between men and women.

Cognitive confirmation—Idea that individuals see what they want to see.

Estrogens—Female sex hormones.

Gender aschematic—Someone who does not use the gender category as a guiding principle in behavior or as a way of processing information about the world.

Gender constancy—Categorization of the self as male or female and the realization that this category cannot be changed.

Gender identity—Label determined by biological sex that is applied either to the self or other people.

Gender schematic—Someone who uses the gender category as a guiding principle in behavior and as a way of processing information about the world.

Lateralization—Localization of an ability (e.g., language) in one hemisphere of the brain.

Masculine mystique—Image of masculinity upheld by society that consists of toughness, dominance, emotional detachment, callousness toward women, eagerness to seek out danger, and competition.

Proactive aggression—Aggressive behavior that is planned and generally socially motivated.

Reactive aggression—Aggressive behavior that takes the form of an angry, impulsive response to threat or provocation.

Schema—Category that contains information about the features of the category as well as its associations with other categories.

Self-monitoring—Variable that describes the extent to which one is more concerned with self-presentation or self-verification.

Self-presentation—Concern individuals have with how their behavior appears to others.

Self-verification—Concern individuals have with behaving in ways consistent with their self-concepts.

Social cognitive theory—States that cognitive development is one factor in gender-role acquisition, but there are social influences as well.

6

ACHIEVEMENT

. . . there is reasonably strong evidence of taste differences between little girls and little boys that are not easy to attribute to socialization. . . . I guess my experience with my two and a half year old twin daughters who were not given dolls and who were given trucks, and found themselves saying to each other, look, daddy truck is carrying the baby truck, tells me something.

Do you recognize this quote? The person who shared this anecdote? This is a story that was told by Larry Summers, at the time president of Harvard University, who was trying to explain to a conference aimed at diversifying the science and engineering workforce why he thought there were gender disparities (Summers, 2005). Summers implied that there was a basic biological difference between men and women that accounted for the disparity, and he dismissed socialization and discrimination as having a minimal impact. He made these remarks in January 2005, tried to clarify them a few days later, and outright apologized one month later. During the intervening month, he was educated about much of the research that you read in Chapters 4 and 5 and some of what you will read in Chapter 6. It was too late, though. He inspired the furor of women's groups all over the country as well as the faculty of Harvard. One year later he resigned. It probably didn't help that the number of women faculty who had received tenure during his 5 years of administration had declined (Bombardieri, 2005).

During elementary school, girls typically receive higher grades than boys, even in the traditionally masculine subjects of math and science. Yet today, women are still less likely than men to pursue careers in these subject areas. Why? Do women have lower math aptitude? If so, why are their math grades higher than or the same as boys' grades prior to high school? Perhaps women are less likely than men to pursue careers that involve math because they are less interested in math. We know that girls are less likely than boys to choose to take extra math courses in high school. Do parents, teachers, and peers influence girls' pursuit of math?

Girls may have different beliefs about the cause of their high math grades than boys. Perhaps, boys believe they have a natural talent, and girls believe they have to work really hard to get those good grades. If so, where do those different beliefs originate? Remember the talking Barbie who said, "Math is hard"?

What exactly is the status of gender and education today? Thirty years ago, more men than women attended and graduated from college. Much has changed. In 2003, 26% of women and 29% of men aged 25 and older held bachelor's degrees (U.S. Census Bureau, 2004a). In that same year, more than half—58%—of bachelor's degrees were awarded to women (U.S. Department of Education, National Center for Education Statistics, 2004). There are currently more women than men enrolled in college. However, men and women pursue different fields. Men are 10 times more likely than women to major in computer science and

6 times more likely than women to major in engineering (National Science Foundation, Division of Science Resources Statistics 2004). As shown in Table 6.1, men are more likely than women to receive bachelor's degrees in computer science and engineering, whereas women are more likely than men to receive degrees in elementary education and nursing. Women are equally as likely as men to receive a science degree, but women tend toward the life sciences whereas men tend toward the physical sciences. The low rates of women in engineering have not changed over the past 10 years.

Women also are more likely than men to be enrolled in graduate school, although women receive fewer advanced degrees than men. Whereas women are equally likely to receive a bachelor's degree in science, they are much less likely than men to earn an advanced science degree. There are some areas where women have made significant progress. In 2004, women received 46% of the degrees in medicine and 49% of the degrees in law (National Center for Education Statistics, 2005). Although women have

TABLE 6.1 PERCENT OF BACHELOR'S DEGREES CONFERRED TO MALES AND FEMALES IN **2001 & 2002**

Field of Study	Percent Male	Percent Female
Agriculture and natural resources	54.9	45.1
Accounting	39.5	60.5
Biological and life sciences	40.5	59.5
Business management and administrative services	50.6	49.4
Computer and information sciences	72.3	27.7
Education	23.3	76.7
Elementary Education	11.0	89.0
Engineering	80.1	19.9
Nursing	9.2	90.8
Mathematics	52.3	47.7
Physical sciences and science technologies	58.8	41.2
Psychology	22.5	77.5
Social sciences and history	48.2	51.8

Source: Adapted from Freeman (2004) and U.S. Department of Education, *National Center for Educational Statistics (2003).*

made substantial gains, they are not achieving as much as men at the highest levels. The correlation between the average GRE score in a discipline and the percentage of male Ph.D.'s in that discipline is .76, suggesting that men are going into the more demanding fields (Templer & Tomeo, 2002). What are some of the reasons women are less likely to realize their achievement potential? This chapter explores answers to this question.

In the first section of the chapter, I describe a number of individual difference explanations for men's and women's choice of different areas of study and levels of achievement. These explanations pertain to characteristics of men and women. Men and women may be motivated to achieve in different domains and may have different beliefs about their abilities, which could influence their motivations. There are a variety of explanations as to why women do not realize their achievement potential, including ideas that women fear success, lack self-confidence, have lower self-esteem, and are faced with stereotype threat.

In the second section of the chapter, I explore social explanations for sex differences in achievement. How do other people's expectations and beliefs—in particular those of parents and teachers—influence men's and women's achievement?

INDIVIDUAL DIFFERENCE FACTORS

The Achievement Motive

Look at the picture of the two acrobats flying through the air depicted in Figure 6.1. What do you see? What kind of story would you write about the two acrobats? If you wrote about how hard the two people had worked to become

acrobats, about all they had given up for their profession, about how successful they were, and about the difficult feats they were trying to accomplish, you might be considered to have a high motive for achievement. At least, this is one way the need for achievement has been measured.

David McClelland and colleagues (McClelland et al., 1953) described the **achievement motive** as a stable personality characteristic that reflects the tendency to strive for success. The achievement motive was measured by people's responses to scenes from Thematic Apperception Test (TAT) cards like the one depicted in Figure 6.1. People would view the scene on the card and write a story about it. The content of the story was then coded for themes related to the achievement motive. Mentions of success, striving, challenge, and accomplishment would reflect themes of achievement. People who scored high in achievement motivation were found to persist longer at tasks and to actually reach higher levels of achievement. Those people were men. Achievement motivation did not predict these same outcomes in women. Some people suggested that women did not have as great a desire or need for achievement.

There were several problems with this conclusion. First, the domains of achievement

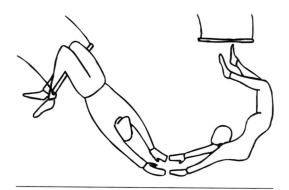

FIGURE 6.1 Adaptation of a Thematic Apperception Test (TAT) card depicting two acrobats flying through the air.

studied (or depicted by the TAT cards) may have been more relevant to men than women, especially in the 1950s and 1960s. For example, viewing a TAT card that depicted two scientists in a laboratory may not have aroused the achievement motive in women because few women worked in science laboratories at the time. Women may not have been able to see themselves as a scientist in a laboratory, or women may not have had any desire to be a scientist in a laboratory. One factor that determines whether someone pursues success in an area is the value the person attaches to success in that area. Women, especially in the 1950s, may not have valued achievement in the sciences.

Another difficulty with the study of achievement motivation in women is that the characteristics that defined the motive (assertiveness, independence, competitiveness) conflicted with the characteristics of the female gender role. Thus another reason women did not fit into the theory of achievement motivation is that women recognized that achievement-related behavior would be inconsistent with their gender role.

What did women do, and what do women do, when they have a high need for achievement but believe achievement conflicts with their gender role? One response is to conceal achievements. Female students may tell their peers they scored lower on an exam than they really did. Another response is to compensate for the threat to the female gender role that achievement poses by adopting extremely feminine dress and manner. Another option is for a woman to master both roles: the role of high achiever and of traditional housewife. Thus high-achievement women may spend enormous amounts of energy both at work and at home to demonstrate that achievement does not conflict with or undermine femininity. One area of research that has addressed how women reconcile a need for achievement with a need to adhere to the female gender role is the fear of achievement or fear of success literature.

Fear of Achievement

Historical Literature. In the early 1970s, one explanation of why women did not reach high levels of achievement was that they suffered from a "fear of success." Matina Horner (1972) noted that competence, independence, and intellectual achievement were inconsistent with the norms for femininity but consistent with the norms for masculinity. Thus women faced a dilemma when achieving. Women might withdraw from achievement behavior because they are concerned with the threat that achievement poses for their gender role.

Horner (1972) defined the **fear of success** as the association of negative consequences with achievement. For women, the negative consequences were feeling unfeminine and experiencing social rejection. A woman who believes graduating at the top of the class will lead people to dislike, tease, or avoid her may have a fear of success, whereas a woman who believes graduating at the top of the class will bring respect from peers and parents does not have a fear of success (Figure 6.2). In order to have a fear of success, however, the individual also must believe achievement is possible. People who realize they have no way of reaching a goal will not be concerned with the negative consequences of reaching the goal. Thus someone may believe getting an A on an exam will alienate friends but also know there is no possible way to get an A on the exam; this person will not worry about the negative consequences of success. By contrast, the person capable of getting an A and who believes this achievement will lead to rejection by peers is likely to have a fear of success. The person could respond to this fear by either decreasing the amount of effort put into the task (i.e., studying less) or by hiding the achievement from peers.

FIGURE 6.2   The historical "fear of success" literature showed that women associated negative social consequences with high achievements, such as graduating at the top of one's class.

To summarize, there are two requirements for a fear of success: First, the person must perceive achievement as possible, if not likely; second, the person must associate achievement with negative consequences. A fear of success is not the same as a desire to fail. The person who fears achievement does not seek out failure; instead the person avoids situations that might lead to high achievement and expends less effort so high achievement is not realized.

What was Horner's (1972) evidence for a fear of achievement among women? She used a projective storytelling method. She gave college students the first sentence of a story and asked them to complete it. For example, female students were told "Anne is at the top of her class in medical school," whereas male students

were told "John is at the top of his class in medical school." Students were then asked to complete the story. Horner reasoned that anyone who wrote a story that showed conflict about the success, denied credit for the success, or associated negative consequences with the success showed a fear of success. The majority of men (90%) wrote positive stories in response to this cue. A substantial portion of the women (65%) wrote troubled stories that showed some conflict or negative consequences associated with Anne's achievement. For example, some women wrote stories about Anne purposely not performing well the next semester or dropping out of medical school. Other women wrote stories about Anne being alienated by friends and family and being very unhappy.

Horner (1972) conducted this first study in 1964 and replicated the findings over the next 6 years with other samples of college students and with high school and junior high school students. Interestingly, she noted a trend over time for the fear of success to increase among *men*. Men began to write stories that associated male achievement with selfishness and egoism. Conceptually, the fear of success is the same in men and women: the association of negative consequences with achievement. However, the fear of success was associated with distinct negative consequences for men and women. For women, the major negative consequence was social rejection; for men, the major negative consequence was self-absorption. Both led to unhappiness.

Interestingly, these two concerns map onto the two negative gender-related traits discussed in Chapter 2: unmitigated communion and unmitigated agency. The fear of success among men seems as though it would characterize someone who possessed the features of unmitigated agency: overly absorbed with the self to the exclusion of others. The fear of success among women seems as though it would characterize someone who possessed the features of unmitigated communion: overly concerned with others and their opinions.

Horner (1972) found other indicators of women's fears of success. She noted that high fear of success women performed worse on a task when working with men than when working with women. These women seemed to perceive achievement in the presence of males as especially aversive. Women who scored high in fear of success admitted they would prefer to tell a male they received a C rather than an A on an exam. Horner found that women who were high in fear of success were more likely than women who were low in fear of success to switch from nontraditional to traditional college majors. For example, high fear of success women who were planning to become physicians or lawyers changed their career paths to become teachers or housewives.

Horner's (1972) work has been criticized on many levels. Some have suggested that her projective test actually indicates a discomfort with gender-role-incongruent behavior rather than a fear of success (Zuckerman & Wheeler, 1975). It turns out that *both* men and women write more negative stories in response to Anne rather than John graduating at the top of the class (Zuckerman & Wheeler, 1975). Both men and women may write negative stories because they are uncomfortable with the idea of women being successful or because they realize that successful women face obstacles.

Contemporary Literature. The studies on fear of success were conducted mostly in the 1960s and the 1970s. Is there any evidence of a residual fear of achievement in women or men today? Do today's college women feel uncomfortable outperforming men? Do women hide their good exam performances from friends, especially male friends? Do women continue to associate achievement with negative interpersonal consequences?

Some studies have attempted to develop more objective measures of the fear of achievement by asking people directly whether they associate success with negative emotional and social consequences. These self-report instruments include items such as "I'd be concerned about making my friends feel threatened if I became a superior student to others," and "If I became one of the best students at school, I'd worry about losing friendly acceptance by my peers" (Ishiyama & Chabassol, 1984). Negative consequences include a concern with negative reactions by peers, social isolation, alienation of others, feelings of pressure to live up to others' expectations, and discomfort with praise. Some studies find that women score higher than men on these kinds of items (Fried-Buchalter, 1997). A study of college students in China showed that women scored higher on this kind of measure compared to men, but that both Chinese men and women scored higher than U.S. samples (Wang & Creedon, 1989). The greater fear of success in China compared to the United States may reflect a greater concern with the effects of individual behavior on relationships on the part of the Chinese.

Some studies of early adolescents suggest that girls still associate success with some negative consequences. Bell (1996) held weekly discussions with elementary school girls to identify barriers to their success. She found that girls felt achievement and affiliation were opposites, that one could not do both. She referred to this as the "smart versus social" dilemma. The girls feared that achievement would jeopardize their relationships. This is exactly the theme that underlies the historical fear of success literature. Girls also identified a second dilemma, "silence versus bragging." The girls said they often hide their success because talking about it is like bragging and might make other people feel bad. Thus a concern for others and relationships keeps the girls from announcing their achievements. This is reminiscent of Horner's (1972) work where she reports that high fear of success girls often hide their good grades from others. The girls also stated they felt uncomfortable being singled out by a success because their concerns were with establishing connections to others, not with differentiating themselves from others. The following exchange between the group leader and one of the girls illustrates these ideas (Bell, 1996, p. 422):

JANE (after receiving a compliment on a science prize): Well, I don't feel that great when you say that to me because I feel like everybody's equal and everybody should have gotten a prize no matter what they did. I think Chris should have gotten it.

MYRA: OK Jane, tell the group why you didn't say "I feel good about winning the prize."

JANE: Well I feel like um, like everybody's looking at me and um saying, "Oh, she shouldn't have won that prize, I should have won" and everybody's gonna be mad at me because um, I won and they didn't.

MYRA: Is there any situation that you could think of where you won an honor that you were deserving of and felt good about?

JANE: If other people won also.

Other studies show that high levels of achievement have negative consequences for girls' self-image. In one study, achievement in math and science predicted an increase in social self-image (i.e., feeling accepted by others) from sixth to seventh grade for both boys and girls, but predicted an increase in social self-image from seventh to eighth grade for boys only (Roberts & Petersen, 1992). Girls' social self-image improved most if they received B's in math rather than C's or even A's. These results especially applied to girls who indicated they valued being popular in school more than they valued getting good grades. Thus the authors concluded that girls feel more accepted if they are not at the top of their math class, especially if the girls are socially oriented.

Similar findings were obtained in another study of sixth- through eighth-graders (Roberts et al., 1990). Achievement, as measured by final course grades, was associated with a positive self-image for both male and female sixth-graders. However, between sixth and seventh grade, the relation between achievement and self-image became weaker for girls, but stronger for boys. The authors proposed that girls begin to feel a conflict between achievement and peer acceptance at this time, so their self-esteem is no longer as closely tied to achievement. Conduct Do Gender 6.1 using Horner's (1972) projective

DO GENDER 6.1
Do Women Fear Achievement, and Do Men Fear Affiliation?

Try out Horner's projective test. Ask a group of students to write a story in response to the following sentence: "_____ is at the top of her (his) class in medical school."

You choose the name. You might try a name that can be perceived as either male or female, such as Pat. Or, you might have half of each sex respond to a male target and half to a female target. After participants have completed the story, have them respond to a few objective items that could measure fear of success, as discussed in the text.

Decide how you want to code the stories. Do you want to code violent imagery, negative imagery, or threat? Be sure to have clear operational definitions of anything that you code. Ideally, you would find another coder and evaluate the stories independently. Make sure the stories are anonymous with respect to sex when you rate them.

Are there sex differences in fears of success on the projective measure? On the objective measure? How do the objective and projective measures compare?

method and some objective questions to test the findings in your own school.

Leaving Traditionally Masculine Pursuits.

One facet of the historical literature on women's fear of success is that high-achievement women switch from traditionally masculine pursuits to traditionally feminine ones. One study examined this issue by comparing college men and women who were in traditionally male or traditionally female fields (i.e., four possible groups). All four groups reported a similar level of attachment to their major, but women in masculine fields were more likely than the other three groups to think about changing their major (Steele, James, & Barnett, 2002). In a nationally representative study of eighth-graders who aspired to have careers in science and engineering, more females than males changed their minds over the next six years (Mau, 2003). Six years later, 22% of males had pursued careers in these areas compared to 12% of females. Among medical school students, women are as likely as men to start careers in internal medicine and surgery, but over time women switch from these fields to gynecology and obstetrics, areas more compatible with the female role (Gjerberg, 2002).

What are women's reasons for switching out of traditionally masculine pursuits? In a study of female 12th-graders who aimed to pursue traditionally masculine fields but switched to neutral or feminine fields 7 years later, three reasons were prominent. First, the women desired a more flexible job; second, the women were concerned with the high time demands of the job; and third, the women had low intrinsic interest in the value of physical sciences (Frome et al., 2006). In an interview study with college women, Seymour (1995) found that women voiced concerns that were first raised by Horner in 1972. Women still seemed concerned that being successful, especially in math and science,

is viewed as not feminine and might have interpersonal costs. Some of these women reported they hid their good grades from their male peers. The women also reported difficulties in working with their male peers. The men who majored in math, science, and engineering validated women's concerns. These men reported that they considered intelligence and physical attractiveness to be mutually incompatible in women. The men viewed women in math, science, and engineering as pursuing majors that were "unnatural." Find out on your own why men and women switch from nontraditional to traditional majors with Do Gender 6.2.

DO GENDER 6.2
Reasons for Switching from Nontraditional to Traditional Majors

Conduct interviews with both men and women who switched from nontraditional to traditional majors and from traditional to nontraditional majors. First, you will have to decide what the traditional majors for men and women are. For example, you might find 5 women who switched from science, math, or engineering to nursing, and 5 men who switched from the liberal arts to business. To gather more data on this issue, this could be used as a class project with the interview format standardized.

Ask a series of open-ended questions to find out why people initially chose their major, why they switched, if they had any difficulties switching, and how others reacted to their switch. Then, you might follow up with some closed-ended questions to make sure the issues you are interested in are addressed. For example, you might have some specific statements about negative peer reactions or fears of negative consequences associated with success.

- People who have a fear of success are capable of high achievement but associate negative consequences with achievement.

- The basic concern is that achievement is inconsistent with the female gender role. Females are concerned that attaining high levels of achievement will have social costs.

- The fear of success literature was, and still is, quite controversial. There is concern with the validity of the projective tests that were first used to identify a fear of success in women. However, self-report instruments still show that women more than men associate success with negative consequences.

- Some women who start out in traditionally masculine fields leave those domains for more traditionally feminine pursuits. Further research with these women will tell how much of this change is due to a fear of success versus a concern with the demands and lack of flexibility of a traditionally masculine career.

Self-Confidence

Do women have less confidence in themselves compared to men? Interestingly, women will defend other women's abilities but not necessarily their own. Collis (1991) refers to this as the "We can but I can't" paradox. In general, women are more likely than men to underestimate their abilities and less likely to expect success. What are the consequences of a lack of self-confidence? When we expect not to succeed in a certain domain, we will choose an easier task, give up more easily on a given task, and pursue activities in other domains.

Nature of Task. Women are not less self-confident than men on all tasks. The *nature of the task* is an important determinant of sex differences in self-confidence. Women are less self-confident than men about their performance on masculine tasks, such as science. In one study,

women perceived that they had less scientific ability than men and perceived their performance on a science test to be worse than men—despite the fact that men's and women's performance on the test was the same (Ehrlinger & Dunning, 2003). Getting back to the consequences of low self-confidence—the women who perceived their performance to be poor were less likely to sign up for a science competition. However, on feminine tasks, such as those that involve social skills or verbal abilities, women are either more self-confident than men, or there are no sex differences in self-confidence. Sex differences in self-confidence also can be influenced by whether a gender-neutral task is presented as one in which men outperform women or one in which women outperform men. Men will be more self-confident in the former case, and women will be more self-confident in the latter case.

The Appearance of Low Self-Confidence. At times, women only *appear* less self-confident than men because they are concerned about how their superior performance will affect another person's self-esteem (Exline & Lobel, 1999). One study showed that women will underestimate their abilities to preserve other people's self-esteem (Heatherington et al., 1993). College students were asked to predict their GPA privately or publicly. Women estimated lower GPAs than men in the public condition but not in the private condition. Thus women were not actually less self-confident than men, but they appeared less self-confident in the presence of men. The issue is more than one of self-presentation. Women are not merely concerned with how others view them. They are concerned that their good performance might make someone else feel bad. In a second study by the same investigators, students predicted their GPA either privately, publicly to a nonvulnerable other, or publicly to a vulnerable other. The vulnerable other was someone who had received a low GPA in college; the GPA of the nonvulnerable other was not mentioned. Men and women gave similar GPA estimates in the private condition and in the public nonvulnerable other condition. However, when faced with a person who had a low GPA (public vulnerable), women estimated lower GPAs than men. Thus women underestimate their performance in public because they don't want to injure another person's self-esteem, not because they are concerned with how others view them. The focus of concern is on others rather than on themselves.

Women's behavior makes sense in light of the fact that women are more likely than men to believe their public expression of achievement affects other people's self-esteem. College students were led to believe they outperformed a peer (scored at the 91st percentile compared to the 42nd percentile) and were asked to either make a modest disclosure (told peer they performed above the 50th percentile) or an immodest disclosure (told peer their specific score; Daubman & Sigall, 1997). Women believed the peer felt better and liked them more when they made a modest compared to an immodest disclosure. The nature of the disclosure did not affect men's impressions of how the peer felt. In a second study, the investigators examined whether women believed an achievement disclosure affected only other women. Female respondents thought that female peers would like them better and feel more confident when they made modest compared to immodest disclosures. However, male respondents thought female peers would like them better when they made immodest compared to modest disclosures. The nature of the disclosure did not affect how males or females thought male peers would react. In sum, women seem to be concerned that revealing a high level of achievement would make other women feel bad about themselves. By contrast, men believe disclosing a high level of achievement would make women feel positive about them.

Women's Underconfidence or Men's Overconfidence?   The literature on self-confidence has typically been interpreted in terms of a female disadvantage: Women's self-confidence is *lower* than that of men. But, do women underestimate their abilities, or do men overestimate their abilities? One way to address this question is to compare men's and women's confidence to their actual performance. If someone expects to receive a 90 on a test and receives an 80, the person is overconfident. If someone expects to receive an 80 and receives a 90, the person is underconfident. When college students' confidence and performance on an exam were evaluated in this way, both men and women were overconfident (Lundeberg, Fox, & Puncochar, 1994). However, when correct and incorrect responses were distinguished, women's confidence levels were more closely tied to their exam performance. In other words, women were more confident on items they answered correctly than on items they answered incorrectly. Men were equally overconfident on correct and incorrect items. More recently, comparisons of exam performance to exam confidence across 25 universities that span five countries confirmed the high rate of overconfidence among men and women in the United States but showed no sex differences in overconfidence (Lundeberg et al., 2000).

Another set of studies examined whether the nature of the task influences men's and women's overconfidence versus underconfidence (Beyer, 1990). Students were asked how many questions on a quiz they expected to answer correctly, and confidence levels were compared to accuracy levels. The quizzes contained masculine questions, feminine questions, or gender-neutral questions. On the masculine task, males were overconfident in one study and accurate in the second study. Females underestimated their performance on the masculine task in both studies. On the feminine and the gender-neutral tasks, males and females were typically equally accurate. In another study, confidence was compared to performance in the domain of math (Lloyd, Walsh, & Yailagh, 2005). Here, females were underconfident. Thus, once again, sex differences in confidence levels are most apparent for the masculine task. And, the sex difference in confidence on masculine tasks is partly due to male overconfidence and partly due to female underconfidence.

TAKE HOME POINTS

- The major factor that influences sex differences in self-confidence is the nature of the task. Sex differences in self-confidence seem to be limited to masculine tasks; it is here that women tend to underestimate their performance and lack self-confidence. Thus, lack of self-confidence could be a contributing factor to the underrepresentation of women in masculine areas of achievement, specifically math and science.

- Part of the sex difference in self-confidence is due to women *appearing* less confident. Women are more reluctant than men to display confidence when they have outperformed another person. Women are more likely than men to believe that others' self-esteem would be threatened by such displays.

Response to Evaluative Feedback

I began college with a major in journalism. I took some psychology classes along the way. Two things happened to make me switch from journalism to psychology: First, I discovered all my journalism assignments—news stories, feature stories, editorials, and investigations—were on psychological topics; second, not one of my journalism professors took me aside and told me I was a gifted writer. Receiving A's on

papers was not enough to make me think I could be a successful journalist; I was waiting for the tap on the shoulder. Ironically, after I switched my major to psychology in my junior year, a journalism professor did take me aside and told me what I had wanted to hear. By then it was too late, and I had already developed a passion for psychology.

Recently, a similar experience occurred, but this time I was the one tapping someone else's shoulder. I had taken aside an undergraduate who was torn between art and psychology, and within psychology, torn between clinical work and research. I told her I thought she had all the skills needed to make a fine researcher: clear conceptual thinking, a strong methodological knowledge base, and creativity in experimental design. I did not think twice about this conversation until she told me the following semester that it had influenced her to switch her focus to research. The interesting part of this story—and here is where it becomes relevant to the chapter—is that she shared the experience with her boyfriend, and he was befuddled. He could not understand why what I had said had made any difference.

Women may be more influenced than men by the feedback they receive from others about their performance. This could stem from a lack of self-confidence on the part of women, or it could stem from an openness to others' opinions; the sex difference can easily be cast in a positive or negative light. In either case, when women are told they have performed poorly or lack ability, they may be more likely than men to take the feedback to heart. Grades in math are more strongly correlated with women's than men's perceived competence in math (Correll, 2001), suggesting that others' opinions have a stronger influence on women than men. Studies of adults and children show that females react more negatively to failure feedback than do males (Roberts, 1991). Women's thoughts about themselves, including beliefs about their abilities, are more influenced by other people's appraisals of their abilities compared to men. The direction of the influence could be positive or negative, depending on whether the feedback is positive or negative.

Evidence for these ideas comes from a series of studies conducted by Tomi-Ann Roberts and Susan Nolen-Hoeksema. In one study, they asked college students to imagine being a manager of an organization and giving a presentation (Roberts & Nolen-Hoeksema, 1989, Study 1). The students were then asked to imagine receiving positive or negative feedback after the presentation. The investigators asked students to report how much they thought the feedback would influence their own evaluations of their performance. As shown in Table 6.2, men reported being more influenced by positive than negative feedback, whereas women reported being equally influenced by positive and negative feedback. In addition, women reported being more influenced than men by negative feedback. Students also were asked how informative they expected such feedback to be. Women found negative feedback to be more informative than men did, but both men and women viewed positive feedback as more informative than negative feedback.

In a follow-up study, the investigators conducted an experimental test of their hypothesis to see if feedback actually influenced women's more than men's perceptions of their abilities (Roberts & Nolen-Hoeksema, 1989, Study 2). Students were asked to solve a series of cognitive tasks and were then provided with positive feedback ("You are doing very well"; "Your performance is above average") or negative feedback ("You are not doing very well"; "Your performance is below average"). Students were asked how confident they were that they could perform the task and how satisfied they were with their performance before and after receiving the feedback. As shown in Figure 6.3, females' confidence clearly changed in the direction of the feedback, whereas males' confidence was largely unaffected by the feedback. Similarly, males' satisfaction with their performance was unaffected by the feedback, whereas females were much less satisfied with their performance after the negative compared to the positive feedback. The investigators also compared the number of correctly solved tasks

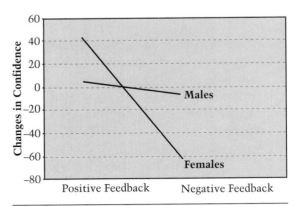

FIGURE 6.3   Effect of feedback on self-confidence. Female college students became more confident about their ability to perform a task after receiving positive feedback and less confident after receiving negative feedback. Male college students' self-confidence did not change and was unaffected by the nature of the feedback that they received.

Source: Adapted from Roberts and Nolen-Hoeksema (1989, Study 2).

TABLE 6.2   DEGREE OF INFLUENCE FEEDBACK WOULD HAVE ON OWN EVALUATION OF PERFORMANCE

	Positive Feedback	*Negative Feedback*
Men	7.60	6.35
Women	7.87	7.58

Source: Adapted from Roberts and Nolen-Hoeksema (1989, Study 1).

to the number of tasks respondents estimated they solved correctly. It appeared that males overestimated their performance, especially in the negative feedback condition, and females underestimated their performance.

Females' greater responsiveness to evaluative feedback was replicated in a subsequent experiment by the same investigators. They asked college students to give a speech to a group of three other students who were confederates of the experimenter (Roberts & Nolen-Hoekema, 1994). One of the confederates provided positive feedback, negative feedback, or gave no feedback. Prior to the feedback, women reported higher performance expectancies compared to men, possibly because giving a speech is considered to be a more feminine task. The results of the study showed that women's evaluations of their speech were more affected by the feedback than those of men. Women's evaluations of their speech became more positive in the positive feedback condition and more negative in the negative feedback condition, whereas men's evaluations were less affected by the feedback. Women were not more responsive to the feedback because they were less confident than men. Recall that women actually had higher initial expectancies than men. Women also were not more responsive to the feedback because they wanted to appear agreeable to the confederates; the evaluations were confidential. However, females indicated that the feedback was more accurate than males did. Thus the authors concluded that women are more responsive to feedback than men because they find the feedback to be more informative about their abilities.

One concern about these studies is that they are all conducted with college students, and the feedback is given by peers rather than authority figures. We would expect people to be more responsive to feedback from those judged to be more knowledgeable. An undergraduate and I tested whether there were sex differences

in responsiveness to feedback in a real-world setting (Johnson & Helgeson, 2002). We measured the self-esteem of bank employees before and after they met with their supervisor for their annual performance evaluation. As shown in Figure 6.4, women's self-esteem improved slightly after receiving a positive evaluation and declined substantially after receiving a negative evaluation, whereas men's self-esteem was largely unaffected by the nature of the feedback. Women also took the evaluation process more seriously, regarded the feedback as more accurate, and viewed their supervisors as credible sources. Men who received negative feedback appeared to prepare themselves psychologically for the upcoming evaluation by derogating the source of the feedback ("My supervisor isn't that smart") and the feedback system ("The evaluation process is not fair"). In general, the results of this study supported the laboratory findings.

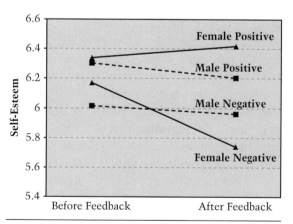

FIGURE 6.4 Women's self-esteem slightly improved after receiving a positive evaluation from their supervisor, and women's self-esteem drastically decreased after receiving a negative evaluation. Men's self-esteem was unaffected by the feedback they received from their supervisor.

Source: Adapted from Johnson and Helgeson (2002).

- Women are more responsive to evaluative feedback than men—meaning that they find the feedback to be more credible and use it to make inferences about their abilities.

- One reason that women are more responsive to feedback is that they view the information as more accurate—as more informative of their abilities.

- Men may discount negative feedback in an effort to protect their self-esteem.

Self-Esteem

Do women's lower self-confidence and greater responsiveness to evaluative feedback reflect a lower level of self-esteem? The answer to that question partly depends on the age of the respondents.

A meta-analysis of sex comparisons in self-esteem found a small difference in favor of males ($d = +.21$; Kling et al., 1999). Effect sizes varied greatly by age, with the largest sex difference emerging during adolescence ($d = +.33$ for 15- to 18-year-olds). Effect sizes were smaller for younger and older respondents. The few studies that examined self-esteem among respondents over age 60 found no sex difference. The effect size was significant in studies of exclusively White samples ($d = +.20$) but not significant among studies of exclusively Black samples ($d = -.04$).

Is the sex difference in self-esteem among adolescents due to a decline in females' self-esteem or an increase in males' self-esteem? One review article concluded that both boys' and girls' self-esteem decreases during early adolescence but that boys' self-esteem rebounds and shows a large increase during high school compared to girls (Twenge & Campbell, 2001). A comparison of White and Black girls showed that Black girls' self-esteem is less likely than White girls' self-esteem to decline over adoles-

cence (Biro et al., 2006). One reason is that Black girls have a stronger racial identity than White girls (DuBois et al., 2002).

What are some of the reasons that females, especially adolescent White females, have lower self-esteem than males? One reason is that these girls have less favorable attitudes than boys toward their gender role. We saw in Chapter 2 that girls were more likely than boys to want to become the other sex and that boys viewed changing their sex as a negative event, whereas girls viewed changing their sex as more of an opportunity. A second reason for girls' lower self-esteem compared to boys is girls' greater emphasis on popularity and increased contact with the opposite sex. Girls, in particular Caucasian girls, place a greater value on popularity than boys do. Being concerned with how others view oneself leads to a fragile self-esteem, because one's self-worth depends on others. In a study of 11th- and 12th-graders, girls' self-esteem was positively correlated with the quality of their other-sex relationships but not the quality of their same-sex relationships (Thomas & Daubman, 2001). Boys' self-esteem was unrelated to other-sex or same-sex relationship quality.

One aspect of self-esteem particularly relevant to adolescents is body image. Males' and females' satisfaction with their body may begin to change with the onset of puberty. In a cross-sectional study of 5th-, 8th-, and 12th-graders, boys and girls were asked how their physical appearance affects their feelings about themselves (Polce-Lynch et al., 1998). Girls were more likely than boys to identify both positive and negative effects. Boys in all grades were most likely to say their physical appearance had no effect on their self-esteem. Eighth-grade girls, who are at the onset of puberty, reported the most negative effects. Body image is more strongly related to overall self-esteem for adolescent girls than boys (Miller & Downey, 1999; Polce-Lynch et al., 2001). Being overweight is especially linked to self-esteem in girls. In one study, normal weight and overweight women either read a story stressing the importance of achievement or not, and then self-esteem was measured (Jambekar, Quinn, & Crocker, 2001). The overweight women who had achievement primed showed the lowest self-esteem. Because appearance is linked to achievement for women, the authors reasoned that the achievement prime made women who did not fit the ideal female body image more distressed. Thus another reason that sex differences in self-esteem emerge during adolescence is that physical appearance is changing, and girls become dissatisfied with their appearance. One study even showed that calling attention to women's appearance interferes with their mental performance (Fredrickson et al., 1998). Men and women were asked to either try on a sweater or a swimsuit before completing a math test. Men and women performed the same after trying on the sweater, but women performed worse than men after trying on the swimsuit. The authors reasoned that the swimsuit induced a state of self-objectification in women that interfered with their concentration and adversely affected performance.

Interestingly, African American girls attach less importance to physical appearance and are more satisfied with their appearance than Caucasian girls (Molloy & Herzberger, 1998). A higher body mass index seems to be more strongly associated with low self-esteem among White than Black adolescent females (Biro et al., 2006). This explains the lack of sex differences in self-esteem among African Americans.

There are multiple aspects of self-esteem in addition to body image. It may be less informative to compare men's and women's overall self-regard if men and women have high self-esteem in different domains. For example, females have higher social self-esteem, and males have higher athletic and appearance self-esteem (Quatman & Watson, 2001).

The relation of gender role to self-esteem is much more clear and consistent than the relation of sex to self-esteem. Masculinity or agency, as measured with the PAQ or BSRI, is strongly positively related to self-esteem. Femininity or communion, by contrast, is not related to one's overall self-regard but may be related to components of self-esteem (see Helgeson, 1994c, for a review). Communion is often related to the social aspects of self-esteem, such as feeling comfortable and competent in social situations. Communion is correlated with self-esteem in domains reflecting honesty, religion, and parental relationships, whereas agency is correlated with self-esteem in domains reflecting physical abilities and problem solving, as well as general self-esteem.

TAKE HOME POINTS

- On some measures of general self-concept, males score higher than females, but the size of the difference is very small.

- Age is an important moderator of sex differences in self-esteem; the difference appears to emerge in adolescence.

- One dimension of self-esteem particularly relevant to adolescent females is body image. Adolescent girls are more unhappy with their body than adolescent boys, which may partly account for adolescent girls' lower levels of self-esteem.

- Gender-related traits, such as agency and communion, seem to show more consistent relations to self-esteem than sex per se.

Stereotype Threat

Regardless of women's self-esteem or self-confidence, they are well aware of the stereotype that women have less aptitude in traditionally masculine domains, such as math and science, compared to men. The theory of **stereotype threat** suggests that making this stereotype salient increases the pressure on women during performance—a pressure that arises due to fears of confirming the stereotype. Studies of stereotype threat show that the activation of such stereotypes adversely affects women's performance. Two studies showed that women performed worse than men on a math test when told there is a sex difference in math performance, but women and men performed the same when provided with no information (Keller, 2002) or when told that there is no sex difference in math performance (Spencer, Steele, & Quinn, 1999). Stereotype threat also appears to extend to politics for women. When men and women college students took a political knowledge survey, women performed the same as men unless they were randomly assigned to a condition where the stereotype of men having more political knowledge than women was activated (McGlone, Aronson, & Kobrynowicz, 2006).

Men are not invulnerable to stereotype threat. When male and female college students completed a social sensitivity test that involved decoding nonverbal cues, men performed more poorly than women when told the test measured social sensitivity but performed the same as women when told the test measured information processing (Koenig & Eagly, 2005). Thus the theory of stereotype threat generalizes to any group of people for whom there are stereotypes.

Clearly the activation of a stereotype affects immediate performance, but are there any other consequences? Two studies showed that the activation of a stereotype led women to show less interest in math activities (Davies et al., 2002). In another study, college women were subliminally primed with words connected to being female (dress, lady, she) or male (uncle, hammer, man) and then asked to rate how pleasant they would find certain activities (Steele & Ambady, 2005). As shown in Figure 6.5, women expressed more interest in the arts than

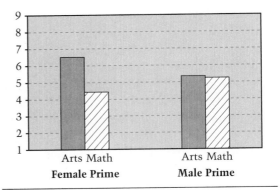

FIGURE 6.5 Women expressed more interest in the arts than in math when they received a female prime and equal interest in the arts and math when they received a male prime.
Source: Adapted from Steele and Ambady (2006).

in math when shown the female prime and equal interest in arts and math when shown the male prime. However, the long-term effects of stereotype threat may be influenced by how strongly people identify with the domain in question. In one study, stereotype threat was induced by having students take a math test for which past research did or did not show men outperformed women (Lesko & Corpus, 2006). Stereotype threat was successfully induced when students were told that sex differences appeared in past research. Interestingly, the women in the stereotype threat condition who perceived themselves to be very good at math (strong math identity) discounted their poor performance by saying the test was not accurate and not reflective of their ability. Thus at least those who identify with a domain may be able to discount poor performance induced by stereotype threat and continue to persist in the area. We should be most concerned about the effects of stereotype threat on people who do not identify with the domain or are trying out something new. They may see their poor performance as diagnostic of their abilities and give up the area of pursuit.

Another way to erase the effects of stereotype threat is to activate images that run counter to the stereotype. For example, in one study male and female undergraduates with high math aptitude who defined math as self-relevant were exposed to a stereotypical or counterstereotypical commercial of women and then given a math test (Davies et al., 2002). Consistent with the theory of stereotype threat, women performed worse than men when they were exposed to the stereotypical commercial. However, women performed similarly to men when exposed to the counterstereotypical commercial. These results are shown in Figure 6.6. Other research shows that exposure to female role models can counter stereotype threat. Men and women performed the same on a math test in the presence of a female experimenter with high math aptitude, but men outperformed women when the female experimenter was low in math aptitude (Marx & Roman, 2002).

If people are educated about stereotype threat, will that nullify its effects? This idea was tested in a study of college students (Johns, Schmader, & Martens, 2005). Students completed a series of math problems after being randomly assigned to one of three groups. In the first condition, the task was described as a problem-solving task. In the second condition, the task was described as a math test. In the third condition, the task was described as a math test, but students were told that stereotype threat could decrease their performance. Results showed that women performed the same as men in the first condition and worse than men in the second condition—the typical stereotype threat effect. However, women performed the same as men in the third condition—when the task was viewed as a math test but information on stereotype threat was provided.

Until recently, it has not been clear *how* stereotype threat affects performance. It has

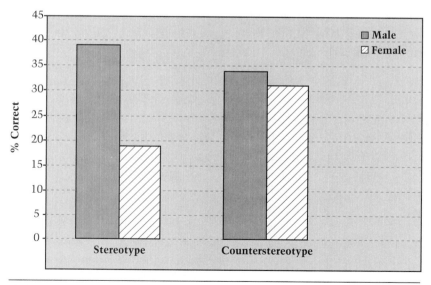

FIGURE 6.6   Effect of stereotype versus counterstereotype commercial on men's and women's math performance. Women performed more poorly when exposed to the stereotype compared to the counterstereotype commercial. Men's performance was unaffected by the commercial.
Source: Adapted from Davies et al. (2002).

been assumed that stereotype threat provokes anxiety which then interferes with performance. But, anxiety is difficult to measure. One study used nonverbal indicators of anxiety to test this hypothesis. Gay and heterosexual men were observed playing with children, and child care skills were coded by observers as well as nonverbal indicators of anxiety (Bosson, Haymovitz, & Pinel, 2004). For half of the men, their sexual preference was primed before the play period, potentially activating stereotype threat among gay men. Gay men displayed poorer child care skills than heterosexual men only when sexual orientation was primed, consistent with stereotype threat. Gay men also displayed more nonverbal signs of anxiety (but did not report more anxiety) than heterosexual men under the priming condition.

Others have suggested that stereotype threat interferes with performance by reducing one's cognitive capacity or one's ability to focus on the task (Koenig & Eagly, 2005). One group of investigators suggested that there should be differential effects of stereotype threat on an easy versus a difficult task (O'Brien & Crandall, 2003). When the task is difficult, the arousal from stereotype threat should be high and interfere with performance; when the task is easy, the arousal from stereotype threat should be low, allowing one to attend more closely to the task and facilitating performance. In support of their hypothesis, women who were told there were sex differences on a math task performed worse than women who were told there were no sex differences when the task was difficult but performed better when the task was easy.

TAKE HOME POINTS

■ Stereotype threat is the idea that activating a stereotype may create a concern with confirming the stereotype and thereby interfere with performance. In the area of gender, it has most often been applied to women's math performance.

■ The effects of stereotype threat on those who strongly identify with a domain may be transient if they discount the validity of a poor performance.

■ It is possible that the effects of stereotype threat may be nullified by teaching people about it.

■ Stereotype threat may interfere with performance by reducing cognitive capacity and/or increasing anxiety.

Conceptions of the Self

Cross and Madson (1997) argue that many of the sex differences we observe in behavior are due to the different ways men and women define themselves: Men maintain an independent sense of self that is separate from others; women, by contrast, maintain an interdependent sense of self in which others are integrated into the self. They note that men are more likely to describe themselves in terms of their independence from others (e.g., emphasizing personal attributes and skills), and women are more likely to describe themselves in terms of their connection to others (e.g., emphasizing roles and relationships to others).

Cross and Madson (1997) report that women think more about other people, pay more attention to others, and have greater recall for information about others. In fact, women (and those high in communion) score higher than men on relational-interdependent self-construal, which is the tendency to define oneself in terms of relationships, and men score higher than women on an independent self-construal (Cross & Morris, 2003; Guimond et al., 2006). One study used "autophotographical essays" to determine whether men defined themselves in independent terms and women defined themselves in interdependent terms. College students were asked to take 12 photographs that described who they were (Clancy & Dollinger, 1993). Women were more likely than men to take pictures that showed other people and that showed themselves with other people. Men were more likely to take pictures that showed themselves alone, showed themselves engaged in some physical activity, and showed themselves with an object, such as a motor vehicle.

Sex differences in self-construal are not universal. Guimond and colleagues (2007) argue that sex differences in self-construal are variable, and that social comparison processes influence these sex differences. When men and women make between-group comparisons (i.e., men compare themselves to women and women compare themselves to men), sex differences in self-construal increase. When men and women make within-group comparisons (i.e., men compare themselves to men and women compare themselves to women), sex differences in self-construal decrease. Guimond and colleagues argue that one reason that sex differences in personality and values are stronger in more egalitarian Western countries than less egalitarian Eastern countries is that Western countries promote between-group comparisons. Eastern countries have such a large status difference between men and women that it makes no sense for them to compare themselves to one another. See if there are sex differences in self-construal at your school with Do Gender 6.3.

How are these different self-definitions related to self-esteem? It is not the case that a relational self-construal is related to low self-esteem (Cross, Bacon, & Morris, 2000). Instead, evidence indicates that agentic self-definitions are related to men's self-esteem, and communal self-definitions are related to women's self-esteem. Men's self-esteem seems to be based on power, differentiating themselves from others, effectiveness, and independent action, whereas women's self-esteem is based on relationships

DO GENDER 6.3
Self-Conceptions

Have a group of students respond to the question "Who am I?" Then, review each of the attributes and categorize them as emphasizing separation from others, connection to others, or neither. Make sure you are blind to the respondent's sex when you categorize the attributes.

Is it true that females define themselves more in terms of connection to others, and males define themselves more in terms of their separation from others?

Administer a measure of gender-related traits and see if agency, communion, unmitigated agency, or unmitigated communion are related to these categories. What would you predict?

and connections (Miller, 1991). In a study of 17- to 19-year-olds, agency, defined as perceived opportunities for the future, predicted increased self-esteem over a 4-year period among men but not women (Stein, Newcomb & Bentler, 1992). Communion, defined as the quality of relationships, predicted increased self-esteem over the same time period among women but not men. Older studies of adolescents showed that being popular was more important to girls' than boys' self-esteem, and being smart was more important to boys' than girls' self-esteem (Rosenberg, 1989). It remains to be seen as to whether those differences still hold today.

One study showed that independence is related to self-esteem in men and interdependence is related to self-esteem in women (Josephs, Markus, & Tafarodi, 1992). College students identified their best skill or ability in four domains (social, athletic, academic, creative) and then estimated the percentage of college students who were as good as they were in those domains. The investigators hypothesized that men's self-esteem would be linked to perceiving themselves as unique—to believing few others were as good as they were in a domain—but women's self-esteem would not. Men were thought to derive their self-esteem from distinguishing or separating themselves from others. In each of the four domains, high-self-esteem males perceived themselves to be more unique than low-self-esteem males, high-self-esteem females, and low-self-esteem females. These results are shown in Figure 6.7a for academic ability and Figure 6.7b for social ability. You can see that the high-self-esteem males estimated that the fewest other students have their level of ability. Women apparently do not need to perceive themselves as different from others in order to feel good about themselves.

By contrast, interdependence was most strongly linked to women's self-esteem. These same investigators showed college students a word and asked them to construct a sentence in which the word interacts with either you, the group with whom you most highly affiliate, your best friend, or Ronald Reagan (Josephs

et al., 1992). The authors hypothesized that women with high self-esteem would be more likely than women with low self-esteem or men in general to later recall words from sentences that referred to the best friend or the group. This is because women's self-concepts are linked to important others. This is exactly what happened. High-self-esteem women recalled more words linked to the best friend (see Figure 6.8a) and to the important group (see Figure 6.8b) than did low-self-esteem women, high-self-esteem men, or low-self-esteem men. The authors reasoned that women have more elaborate knowledge structures about others than men do because they derive their self-worth through their connections to others.

Men's and women's different sources of self-esteem were also examined by asking college students how important each of the following was in terms of making them feel good about themselves: reflected appraisals (e.g., having others think highly of you), social comparisons (e.g., doing a better job than someone else), and self-perceived competence (e.g., getting a lot of work done; Schwalbe & Staples, 1991).

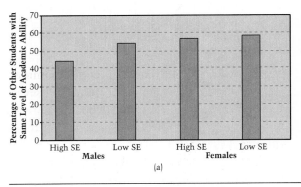

(a)

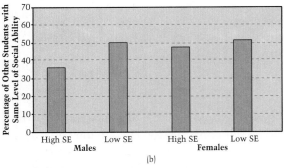

(b)

FIGURE 6.7   Effect of self-esteem (SE) and sex on perception of others' academic and social ability. This study showed that men's self-esteem is linked to feeling distinct from others. High-self-esteem males perceived themselves to be more unique (i.e., they reported fewer other students with their same level of ability) than low-self-esteem males, high-self-esteem females, and low-self-esteem females. Figure 6.7a demonstrates this finding for academic ability and Figure 6.7b demonstrates this finding for social ability.
Source: Adapted from Josephs et al. (1992).

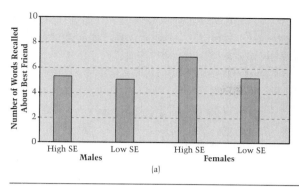

FIGURE 6.8   Effect of self-esteem (SE) and sex on words recalled about best friend and important group. This study showed that women's self-esteem is linked to their connections to others. High-self-esteem women recalled more words related to other people than low-self-esteem women, high-self-esteem men, and low-self-esteem men. Figure 6.8a demonstrates this finding for words recalled about a best friend and Figure 6.8b demonstrates this finding for words recalled about an important group of people.
Source: Adapted from Josephs et al. (1992).

Men found social comparison information more important than women did, which is consistent with the finding from the Josephs and colleagues' (1992) study of men's need for uniqueness. Women found reflected appraisal information more important than men did, indicating women's greater concern with how they appear to others. It is noteworthy that both men and women found self-perceived competence to be important to their self-esteem and equally so.

Thus although the evidence for men basing their self-esteem on independence and women basing their self-esteem on interdependence seems clear, some people have taken issue with this conclusion. The primary criticism is over the definition of interdependence. Baumeister and Sommer (1997) argue that there are two kinds of interdependence: **relational interdependence** and **collective interdependence**. The relational aspects of the self are those that emphasize close relationships with other people. The collective aspects of the self are those derived from group memberships and affiliations. What appears to be men's desire for independence and separation may really be their

desire to form broader social connections with others, such as those achieved by power and status. Baumeister and Sommer argue that men and women are equally social, but they are sociable in different spheres: Women invest in a small number of relationships and men orient themselves toward the broader social structure and embed themselves in larger groups. Men's emphasis on power and status, for example, can be viewed as men separating themselves from others or as men wanting to have a certain relation toward others. Another example of men's interdependence that Baumeister and Sommer cite comes from the helping literature. Recall that the meta-analysis on helping showed that men were more helpful than women (Eagly & Crowley, 1986), but an important moderator was the relationship to the recipient. Men help people they do not know, which is akin to helping society at large, whereas women help people they do know and with whom they have a relationship, such as family and friends.

The association of sex to relational and collective interdependence was examined in a series of studies (Gabriel & Gardner, 1999). In one study, students were asked to respond to the question "Who am I?" Responses showed that men identified more collective aspects of the self (e.g., fraternity member) than did women, and women identified more relational aspects of the self (e.g., daughter) than did men. In another study, students were asked to recall a happy or sad event. For both events, women's recollections were more likely than men's to be relational (e.g., death of family member) and men's recollections were more likely to be collective (e.g., losing an important sporting event).

To this point, I have been emphasizing differences. But there are also similarities in the sources of self-esteem for men and women. For example, feeling accepted by others is associated with feeling good about the self, and feeling rejected by others is associated with feeling bad about the self for both men and women (Leary et al., 1995). However, the associations are stronger for women than men. These ideas have been replicated in a study of undergraduates in China. Both men and women derived their self-esteem from similar sources: family relationships, family responsibilities, and personal goals (Watkins & Yu, 1993). However, women rated family relationships as more important than did men.

It is quite likely that cultural and ethnic factors influence the sources of self-esteem for men and women. Although Western cultures emphasize individualism, achievement, and success, there are people whose opportunities to achieve are limited—by poverty or by discrimination. African Americans, in particular, may derive self-esteem from other domains. Because the family is central to the identity of African Americans, partly as a buffer against racism, African Americans may derive more of their self-esteem from relationships. In one study, school achievement was linked to self-esteem among White adolescents but not among Black

adolescents (Hughes & Demo, 1989). In a study of college students, Black students scored higher on a measure of collectivism than did White students (Oyserman, Gant, & Ager, 1995).

TAKE HOME POINTS

- Men's sense of self is based more on independence, whereas women's sense of self is based more on interdependence.
- These different self-construals have been differentially linked to self-esteem in men and women.
- Interdependence is a broad term, including a relational and a collective component. Women are more likely to emphasize the relational aspect, whereas men are more likely to emphasize the collective aspect.

Attributions for Performance

It is no surprise that I receive comments about an exam only from students who do poorly. The students who do poorly typically complain that the exam questions were unfair, too difficult, too picky, or unclear. The students who do well are more likely to believe that they deserved a good grade for studying hard or for being naturally smart. Why don't the students who do well tell me that I came up with great exam questions? Because that would not be part of the **self-serving bias.** The self-serving bias is the tendency to take credit for our successes and blame other people or other things for our failures. In general, self-serving biases appear to be adaptive, in part because self-esteem is protected in the face of failure.

Dimensions of Causality   The self-serving bias has to do with the attributions that we make for performance. An **attribution** is the cause we assign to a behavior. Attributions can be classified along the two dimensions shown in Figure 6.9 (Weiner et al., 1971). The first

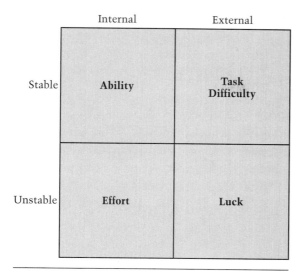

Internal   External

Stable   **Ability**   **Task Difficulty**

Unstable   **Effort**   **Luck**

FIGURE 6.9 Two dimensions on which attributions (causes) can be classified: locus (internal vs. external) and stability (stable vs. unstable).

dimension represents the locus of the cause, internal or external. An **internal attribution** is located within the person, and an **external attribution** is located in the environment. A **stable attribution** is one that does not change across time or situations. An **unstable attribution** is one that does change across time and situations. In the context of performance (as shown in Figure 6.9), an internal, stable attribution would be your ability or lack thereof. An internal, unstable attribution would be how much effort you put into the task, presumably by studying. An external, stable attribution would be the difficulty of the test, an unchangeable, inherent characteristic of the task. An external, unstable attribution would be luck or some transient environmental factor, such as the weather.

The locus of causality dimension has implications for self-esteem. An internal attribution for failure (I am stupid) will decrease self-esteem, whereas an internal attribution for success (I am a brain) will increase self-esteem. An external attribution for failure will preserve self-esteem (It wasn't my fault that my computer crashed), whereas an external attribution for success does not confer any self-esteem (The teacher must not have been paying attention when she graded my essay).

The stability dimension has implications for persistence. An unstable attribution for failure (I did not study) may lead us to try harder or to try to change the environment. A stable attribution for failure (I do not have the ability) may lead us to give up. A stable attribution for success (The teacher is an easy grader) will encourage us to continue with the behavior or to keep the environment the same (e.g., don't switch teachers). An unstable attribution for success (The teacher didn't have her glasses on) merely tells you that the performance may not be repeated, so you will need to continue to exert the same level of effort or keep the environmental conditions the same (e.g., hide the teacher's glasses).

Sex Comparisons.   Do men and women differ in their attributions for success and failure? In 1984, Kay Deaux developed a model of how people's expectancies about men's and women's performance would influence the attributions made. This model is shown in Figure 6.10. The first part of the model states that we attribute behavior to stable and internal causes if it matches our expectancy (i.e., a person fails whom we expect to fail or a person succeeds whom we expect to succeed; Weiner et al., 1971). Thus, if we expect men to perform well on masculine tasks, we should attribute their success to ability; similarly, if we expect women to perform well on feminine tasks, we should attribute their success to ability. In addition, if we expect women to fail at masculine tasks, we should attribute their failure to lack of ability. The second part of the model states that if a behavior violates our expectations, we attribute it to unstable causes. Thus, if we expect women to fail at a masculine task, we should attribute their success

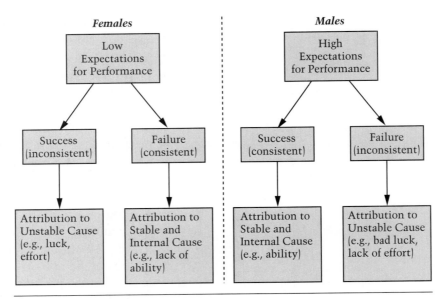

FIGURE 6.10 Expectancy model of attributions: actors. This model shows that when performance fits our expectations (success following high expectations for performance, failure following low expectations for performance), we attribute the cause to stable factors. When performance does not fit our expectations (success following low expectations for performance, failure following high expectations for performance), we attribute the cause to unstable factors. *Source:* K. Deaux (1984). From individual differences to social categories: Analysis of a decade's research on gender. *American Psychologist, 39,* 105–116.

to effort and good luck. If we expect men to succeed at a masculine task, we should attribute their failure to lack of effort and bad luck. This model strongly suggests that the nature of the task should influence the attributions we make for men's and women's performance.

Many of the attribution studies were conducted 20 years ago, and not all of the more recent studies have supported this pattern of sex differences in attributions for performance. A meta-analysis found no sex of perceiver differences in attributions, meaning that men and women tended to make the same attributions for other men's and women's performance (Swim & Sanna, 1996). However, perceivers made different attributions on some tasks, in particular masculine tasks (e.g., those involving

math abilities). On masculine tasks, perceivers attributed women's success to effort and men's success to ability. Thus perceivers are attributing men's success to a stable cause and women's success to an unstable cause, implying that men's success is more likely than women's to be repeated. On masculine tasks, perceivers attributed men's failure to unstable causes, that is, lack of effort and bad luck, whereas perceivers attributed women's failure to the difficulty of the task. Again, perceivers are attributing men's failure to unstable causes that will not necessarily be repeated but women's failure to a stable cause that implies the failure will be repeated. The meta-analysis showed fewer differences in the attributions made for men's and women's performance on feminine tasks (e.g., those involving verbal abilities). To be fair, most studies examined only masculine tasks, and the majority of studies focused on college students.

A more recent study has shown that the subject area influences the attributions that men and women make for performance (Beyer, 1999). Although men made greater ability attributions for success than women in general, and women made greater effort attributions for success than men in general, the specific subject area influenced attributions. For success, women made stronger ability attributions than men in English, whereas men made stronger ability attributions than women in math. For failure, men made greater attributions to effort than women—especially in the case of English—and women made greater attributions to lack of ability compared to men (Beyer, 1999). Thus, men seem to have exhibited more of the self-serving bias compared to women.

A meta-analytic review of the literature on the self-serving bias showed that there was no overall sex difference, but there was a sex by age interaction, meaning that the sex difference depended on the age of the respondents (Mezulis et al., 2004). Among children, girls displayed more of a self-serving bias than boys; among early adolescents, there was no sex difference; and among older adolescents and adults, men displayed more of a self-serving bias than women.

Attributions for performance have been studied among children, in an effort to understand how they perceive their performance. One study of 8- to 9-year-olds showed that boys and girls make different attributions for math performance even when their grades are the same. Girls were less likely than boys to attribute math success to ability but more likely than boys to attribute math failure to lack of ability, despite the fact that girls and boys had the same math grades (Dickhauser & Meyer, 2006). These differences are shown in Figure 6.11. Even more worrisome is that these findings were strongest

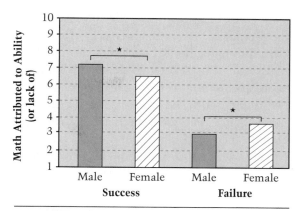

FIGURE 6.11 Boys are more likely than girls to attribute math success to ability, and girls are more likely than boys to attribute math failure to lack of ability.
Source: Adapted from Dickhauser and Meyer (2006).

among the high math ability students. If the girls and boys have the same grades, why are they assigning different causes to performance? It appeared that boys and girls relied on different information to infer their math abilities. Girls relied on teacher evaluations, whereas boys relied on both teacher evaluations and their objective math performance. Despite no difference in objective math performance, teachers perceived that girls had less math ability than boys. Girls assessed their own abilities in terms of these teacher perceptions.

Implications for Achievement. What are the implications of sex differences in attributions for performance? If you fail an exam because you believe you do not have the ability, what do you do? You might give up on the subject, drop the class, and decide not to pursue other classes in that area. If you fail an exam and believe it was due to lack of effort (i.e., you did not try hard enough), what do you do? The answer is obvious: You try harder next time. Thus the difference in attributions for failure can influence whether we persist in an area or give up completely.

One study examined the implications of third-graders' and junior high school students' attributions for performance on an important math exam (Stipek & Gralinski, 1991). Students' expectancies about the exam were assessed before the exam, and students' attributions for performance were measured after the exam. Despite the fact that boys and girls performed equally well on the exam, boys expected higher grades than girls did. In addition, boys and girls made different attributions for their performance. When performance on the exam was good, boys were more likely than girls to attribute their success to ability. When performance on the exam was poor, girls were more likely than boys to attribute their failure to lack of ability. The implications? Despite their similar performances, boys had higher expectations for their performance on the next exam compared to girls, and girls were more likely than boys to say they wish they could avoid math. The differing expectations and intentions undoubtedly reflect the students' beliefs about the cause of their performance.

Attributions for performance may influence the difficulty of the tasks that males and females undertake. One study showed that males chose more difficult goals than females, and that males were more likely to believe ability as opposed to luck contributed to the achievement of this goal (Levy & Baumgardner, 1991). The investigators suggested that girls may choose less difficult goals than boys because they are less confident of their success and believe luck rather than ability determines their performance.

TAKE HOME POINTS

- At least for masculine tasks, which are basically achievement related, males and females make different attributions for their own performance. They also perceive the causes of other males' and females' performance to differ.

- In general, men's success is attributed to internal causes, in particular, ability, and women's success is attributed to internal, unstable causes (e.g., effort) or external causes (e.g., luck). The implications are that men's success will be repeated, but women's will not. By contrast, men's failure is attributed to external causes or internal, unstable causes (e.g., lack of effort), and women's failure is attributed to internal, stable causes (e.g., lack of ability). The implications here are that men's failure will not necessarily be repeated, but women's will.

- These attributions about performance seem to be a function of our expectancies for men's and women's successes and failures.

- People's beliefs about the causes of their performance have implications for their future efforts in that area. If we attribute the cause of a failure to lack of ability, such as the case of females in math or males in English, we are less likely to pursue work in that area. If we attribute the cause of a success to an unstable factor, such as females believing they have to put considerable effort into math to do well, we also are less likely to pursue work in that area. We are more likely to pursue areas of interest in which we believe we have the ability to succeed.

SOCIAL FACTORS

In grade school, there is a paradox between girls' and boys' performance and their beliefs about their performance. Despite the fact that girls either perform better than or equal to boys in areas such as math, girls rate their ability lower and have more negative attitudes toward math compared to boys. What are the reasons for these discrepancies? One answer concerns the beliefs that other people hold about boys' and girls' abilities. Despite the small size of sex differences in most intellectual domains (see Chapter 4), people continue to believe that men and women have different abilities. I begin this next section of the chapter by describing the expectancy/value model of sex differences in achievement. This model rests heavily on gender-role socialization. Then I examine several sources of social influence. First, I examine the role of parents in influencing children's beliefs about their abilities; then I examine the role of teachers in influencing children's beliefs about their abilities. Both parents and teachers may communicate to children that they have different abilities and provide boys and girls with different experiences.

Expectancy/Value Model of Achievement

If girls perform better than boys in math and science at younger ages, why don't more women have careers in math and science? This question puzzled Jacquelynne Eccles and her colleagues, so they developed a theory to account for the discrepancy between men's and women's school performance and career choices. Their **expectancy/value model of achievement** suggests that men's and women's achievement-related choices are a function of their performance expectancies ("Will I succeed?") and the value they attach to the area ("Is this important?"; "Do I care about it?"; Eccles et al., 1999). The two are not independent, as performance expectancies influence values. That is, how much ability a child perceives he or she has in an area affects how much value is attached to the area (Jacobs et al., 2002). Performance expectancies and values influence the decision to engage in an activity, the decision to persist in the activity, and ultimately performance in the activity.

Performance expectancies and values are influenced by gender-role socialization. People in children's environments—parents, teachers, peers—influence males and females to value different areas. Performance expectancies and values also are shaped by the experiences children have and by their interpretations of those

experiences. For example, boys and girls might have the same math grades but interpret them differently. If girls believe their high grades are due to effort and boys believe their high grades are due to inherent ability, boys will be more likely than girls to believe they will succeed in math in the future. It is the *self-perception* of ability rather than the actual ability that predicts whether students pursue a given domain (Updegraff et al., 1996).

Numerous studies have been conducted in support of this theory. In general, males perceive greater competence in math, science, and team sports, whereas females perceive greater competence in reading (Freedman-Doan et al., 2000; Lupart, Cannon, & Telfer, 2004). Males also attach greater value to science than females but show equal interest in math as females (Lupart et al., 2004). The expectancy/value model predicts participation in activities, course selection, and occupational aspirations (Simpkins, Davis-Kean, & Eccles, 2005, 2006). In fact, one study showed that perceptions of competence in math predicted the pursuit of a career in a quantitative field, independent of actual ability (Correll, 2001). In another study, females' competence beliefs in math predicted whether they enrolled in more math courses the next year (Crombie et al., 2005). Thus males may be more likely than females to pursue a career in math not because of differences in actual ability but because of differences in "perceived" ability.

One of the features of the expectancy/value model is that achievement-related behavior is understood as a choice between at least two behaviors (Eccles et al., 1999). In other words, a boy who has equally good grades in all subject areas knows he will pursue a career in only one area. Even if the boy's grades in math and English are the same and he equally values math and English in elementary school, at some point he is likely to choose between the two areas and value one more than the other. Gender-role socialization may lead him to value math over English. Parents, teachers, and counselors all have the opportunity to encourage or discourage pursuits in a given area.

When comparing the effects of competence beliefs and values on outcomes, it appears that competence beliefs are more strongly linked to performance, and values are more strongly linked to what we pursue (Wigfield & Eccles, 2002). In fact, Wigfield and Eccles argue that the reason there are fewer women in math and sciences has more to do with values than competence. Achievement differences between men and women have decreased over time, but the differences in the activities that men and women value have not changed to the same degree.

Plenty of research suggests that men and women continue to value different pursuits. In terms of overall career choices, males value the status and money associated with a job more than females, whereas females value whether a job will make the world a better place more than males and are more interested in people-oriented jobs (Eccles et al., 1999; Lupart et al., 2004). These divergent interests may explain why girls are underrepresented in computer science. Girls are likely to be attracted to occupations that involve interactions with other people, and the computer scientist often is depicted as a nerd who works in isolation from others. In a series of focus groups with middle school and high school girls from 70 different schools, girls expressed a lack of interest in computer science—not because they lacked the ability but because they lacked the desire (American Association of University of Women, 2000). The investigators summarized girls' responses with the phrase "We can, but I don't want to." Girls perceived the computer scientist to be male and antisocial; the career simply did not appeal to them.

Girls and boys also have had different interests in sports and athletics, but the size of that difference has been reduced dramatically with the passage of Title IX. See Sidebar 6.1 for a discussion of the recent challenges to Title IX.

TAKE HOME POINTS

- According to the expectancy/value model of achievement, we pursue areas of achievement in which we expect to succeed and that we value.

- Even when abilities seem to be equal, men and women have different expectancies for success in an area.

- Men and women attach different values to achievement-related pursuits. Women are more interested than men in jobs and careers that involve people.

- In the next sections, we will discuss how the social environment can shape males' and females' expectancies and values.

The Influence of Parents

A great deal of evidence indicates that parents influence children's perceptions of competence, values, and performance. Parents have stereotypes about the subject areas in which boys and girls excel, and parents have opinions about the subject areas in which it is important for boys and girls to excel. Specifically, parents rate girls' math ability as lower than that of boys and believe math is more difficult for girls than for boys—despite equal performance by boys and girls in math during elementary school (Herbert & Stipek, 2005). Parents believe girls are more competent in English and boys are more competent in sports (Eccles, Jacobs, & Harold, 1990). Parents also believe that math and athletics are less important for girls than for boys and that English is less important for boys (Yee & Eccles, 1988). Parents' general sex stereotypes influence their beliefs about their children's

SIDEBAR 6.1: *The Future of Title IX*

Title IX says "No person in the United States shall, on the basis of sex, be excluded from participation in, be denied the benefits of, or be subjected to discrimination under any education program or activity requiring Federal assistance." The law was enacted in 1972 and basically prohibits sex discrimination in educational programs that receive federal assistance. Title IX has made great advances in creating more equal educational opportunities for men and women. The athletic arena is where the greatest strides have been made (U.S. Census Bureau, 2007a). In 1972, 30,000 women participated in college athletics, whereas the figure for 2004 to 2005 was 167,000. Ten times as many women participate in high school athletics today as they did in 1972 (National Federation of High School Associations, 2006).

Institutions can show compliance with Title IX in one of three ways:

1. Provide athletic opportunities to men and women in proportion to their enrollment.

2. Expand programs for the underrepresented sex (i.e., women).

3. Accommodate the interests and abilities of the underrepresented sex (i.e., women).

Recently, Title IX has come under attack. One way that Title IX can be achieved is to eliminate teams; that is, if a school has a men's soccer team and no women's soccer team, it can eliminate the men's team rather than add the women's team. The National Wrestling Coaches Association filed a suit against the Department of Education because some of their teams have been cut. In response, the secretary of education convened a commission in 2002 to offer further guidance in regard to Title IX. The commission made a number of recommendations, nearly all of which would undermine the advances in sex equality that Title IX has made. Two of the commission members, female former Olympic gold medalists, refused to sign the report. In 2003, the secretary of education rejected most of the committee's recommendations (Lochhead, 2003). The reactions were mixed. On the one hand, some of the most devastating challenges to sex equality were rejected. For example, the secretary did *not* approve the use of private donations to fund men's teams. However, there are several recommendations that the secretary did uphold that are cause for concern. One is the use of interest surveys to meet number 3, accommodating the underrepresented sex. If a school can show there is less interest in women's soccer than men's soccer, the school would not have to provide a women's soccer team. The problem is that the existence of a team is what generates interest! The current level of men's and women's interest is also likely to reflect the opportunities they had in the past. The secretary also endorsed another recommendation of the commission, which was that eliminating teams would be looked on unfavorably as a way to achieve Title IX. We will see what the effects of these new guidelines are on men's and women's athletic participation over the coming years.

areas of competence. For example, parents who believe girls are better at reading and boys are better at math perceive that their daughter has higher reading ability and their son has higher math ability—even when the children's objective performance on exams is the same (Tenenbaum & Leaper, 2003).

Rather than assume a bias on the part of parents, is it possible their beliefs about their sons' and daughters' different abilities are accurate? It is difficult to assess whether one person has more inherent ability than another. If a sex difference appears on an objective indicator of performance, does this mean one sex has greater natural talent than the other? Not necessarily. Boys and girls may have had different experiences, which led to different performances. For example, men and women may have equal abilities in math, but different experiences provided by teachers, parents, relatives, and peers may lead boys to outperform girls. Even when more objective indicators of performance are taken into consideration (e.g., test scores, teachers' ratings of students, grades), parents still hold sex-differentiated beliefs about their children's abilities that exceed any observed differences in performance (Eccles et al., 1990). It also turns out that parents who hold stronger stereotypes about men and women are more likely to translate those stereotypes into their beliefs about their individual daughters and sons.

Some of parents' beliefs generalize across cultures. Mothers in Minneapolis, Taiwan, and Japan all indicated that their kindergarten girls were better at reading than their boys and that their boys were better at math than their girls (Lummis & Stevenson, 1990). There were no objective sex differences in ability among these children. It is interesting that parents have sex-differentiated beliefs for children at this early age, because at this age level neither boys nor girls have received any formal instruction in reading or math!

Parents' stereotypes also lead them to make different attributions for boys' and girls' success in different subject areas. Parents are more likely to attribute boys' success in math to talent (an internal, stable attribution) and girls' success in math to effort (an internal, unstable attribution; Räty et al., 2002). Parents also said talent was more important than effort for success in math, which would imply that boys should be more successful at math than girls. Parents attributed math failure to lack of effort for both boys and girls, no doubt to preserve a positive image of their child. However, mothers were more likely to attribute girls' failure to the task being too difficult. In summary, parents appear to be less confident about their girls' than their boys' math abilities.

Are the different attributions for male and female math performance justified? Perhaps girls do have less talent in math compared to boys and compensate by expending more effort. This would explain why boys and girls have similar math grades. However, boys and girls report spending the same amount of time studying math (Eccles et al., 1990).

Another way that parents communicate their perceptions of a child's ability is by how they provide help. Helping a child with homework might seem as if it demonstrates parent involvement and interest to a child. However, it also has the potential to demonstrate to the child that the parent believes the child *needs* help—that is, it can communicate that the child lacks competence in an area. In a study of middle-school children, parents were found to intrude more on homework with sons than daughters (e.g., unsolicited help, remind, monitor), but girls were more responsive to this kind of behavior than sons—and the response was negative (Bhanot & Jovanovic, 2005)! For females only, parents who held stereotypes that girls were not as good in math as boys were more likely to intrude on girls' homework, and these girls perceived that they had less math ability. In another study, parent help with schoolwork was categorized as either "autonomy-granting" (e.g., attributing the behavior to the child, emphasizing mastery of content over performance, communicating to children that they can do it on their own) or "controlling" (e.g., rewarding children for schoolwork, emphasizing that performance standards are important, communicating that children are not capable of solving problems on their own; Pomerantz & Ruble, 1998). Parents were found to use both autonomy-facilitating and controlling behavior with sons but controlling behavior alone with daughters. It is the controlling behavior that could undermine children's perceptions of competence.

We know that parents have different beliefs about their children's abilities. The next question is whether those beliefs influence the children's own perceptions of their ability. Parents' beliefs about children's competence are linked to children's own perceptions of competence, even after taking into account their current performance (Eccles, Freedman-Doan, Frome, Jacobs, Yoon, 2000; Herbert & Stipek, 2005; Tiedemann, 2000). In other words, children seem to base their beliefs about their math, sports, and social ability more on what their parents think than on what their teachers think. These studies were cross-sectional, however, making it difficult to know if parents' beliefs are causing children's beliefs or children's beliefs are causing parents beliefs. This issue has been addressed by several longitudinal studies that have shown parents' beliefs that their sons have greater ability in sports, math and science, and that their daughters have greater ability in music predict children holding these same perceptions of their abilities at a later time (Fredricks, Simpson, & Eccles, 2005; Jacobs, Vernon, & Eccles, 2005). These findings appear to hold even when one controls for the objective grades children receive from teachers (Frome & Eccles, 1998). Parents' beliefs about their children's abilities may affect how children interpret the grades they receive from teachers.

The next question is whether parents' beliefs influence children's actual abilities, not just the children's perceptions of their abilities. In other words, do parents' stereotypes about boys and girls become self-fulfilling prophecies so their sons and daughters differ in their abilities as parents expect? Parents can influence their children's abilities in a myriad of ways. Parents encourage the pursuit of different activities by their emotional reactions to performance (e.g., joy rather than contentment with a child's A on an exam), interest shown in the activity, toys and opportunities provided to pursue an activity, time spent with the child on an activity, and direct advice to pursue an activity (Eccles et al., 2000). For example, parents who believe boys are better than girls at math might buy a son a calculator, play math games with him, or teach him how to calculate baseball averages. They also might work with a son on math homework and express high praise to him for good math performance and great disappointment for poor math performance. These same parents may not provide a daughter with math-related opportunities, not encourage her to spend time on math homework, and show indifference to reports of high or low grades in math. In one study, fathers were found to use more cognitively complex language when talking with sons than daughters about science (e.g., asking more conceptual questions, using more difficult vocabulary), which conveys the importance of science to sons (Tenenbaum & Leaper, 2003). Research has also shown that parents encourage computer usage, math and science, and sports for sons more than daughters by buying sons more items related to those activities and by spending more time with sons than daughters engaged in these activities (Fredericks et al., 2005; Jacobs et al., 2005; Simpkins et al., 2005). Just the opposite occurs for girls compared to boys in the area of music. These behaviors are subsequently linked to children pursuing the activities that parents encourage. To the extent the child pursues the activities, performance is affected. The theoretical model by which parents may influence children's abilities is shown in Figure 6.12.

This area of research has implications for the early findings from the Study of Mathematically Precocious Youth. Benbow and Stanley (1980) argued that the sex differences they found in math performance were due to male natural talent rather than males having different experiences than females. They believed boys and girls had similar backgrounds in math

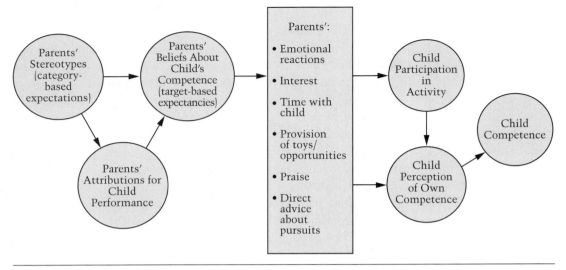

FIGURE 6.12 A model describing how parents' beliefs can influence children's performance.

at that age, meaning boys and girls had taken a similar number of math courses. Given the evidence on how parents' beliefs may influence children's self-perceptions and behavior, could boys and girls really be said to have similar backgrounds in math?

This study of highly talented youth is also of concern because of the media attention it received. Worse yet, the media coverage influenced parents' perceptions of their children's abilities (Eccles & Jacobs, 1986). Mothers who had heard recent media reports about this study were compared to mothers who had not heard of the study. Mothers who had heard the reports said that math was harder for their daughters than for their sons. Mothers who were unaware of the report stated that math was equally difficult for their sons and daughters. This finding was particularly troublesome because the study focused on a very select population: highly talented boys and girls. Thus the findings did not pertain to the children of most of the parents in the study.

There is another way parents can influence their children's achievement. Parents' gender-role attitudes and own career choices influence children's choices of achievement. For example, there is a strong relation between fathers' careers and sons' career choices (Barling, 1991). Mothers' gender-role attitudes are linked to daughters' gender-role attitudes as well as daughters' career choices (Steele & Barling, 1996). Mothers who held nontraditional attitudes about gender roles had daughters who shared these attitudes and who chose careers that were less likely to be pursued by females. These relations were stronger when the daughter identified with the mother.

TAKE HOME POINTS

- Parents have stereotypes that boys are better than girls in math and girls are better than boys in verbal abilities, regardless of actual school performance.

- Parents communicate these stereotypes to children by the activities they encourage, the toys they buy, the time they spend with children, and the attributions they make for performance.

- Parents' communications influence children's ability perceptions and, ultimately, children's performance.

The Influence of Teachers

Teachers can influence children's beliefs about their abilities by the attention and instruction they provide to students and by the nature of the feedback they provide about performance. In 1992, the American Association of University Women (AAUW) published a report, *How Schools Shortchange Girls*, which concluded there is a pervasive gender bias in the classroom in terms of differential attention and differential feedback to boys and girls. Some of this research is addressed below.

Attention.   In 1994, Sadker and Sadker published a book entitled *Failing at Fairness: How America's Schools Cheat Girls*. In this book, they documented the results of extensive observational studies of teacher-student interactions in rural, urban, and suburban settings across the United States. In 1995, Brady and Eisler reviewed the literature on teacher-student interactions in the classroom, examining both observational and self-report studies. Both these sets of investigators reached the same conclusions: From elementary school through graduate school, teachers interact more with

boys than girls and give boys better feedback than girls. Teachers call on boys more often than girls, ask boys higher-level questions, and expand on boys' more than girls' comments. In college, professors give men more nonverbal attention than they give women: making greater eye contact with men and waiting longer for men to answer a question. Girls are interrupted more than boys, and boys receive more criticism from teachers. Teachers, especially male teachers, seem to be reluctant to criticize girls because they fear upsetting them. However, recall there are benefits of criticism. Two more recent observational studies of student-teacher interactions showed that teachers still initiate more interactions with boys than girls. One study suggested that these differences were due to the fact that male students volunteered to answer questions more often than female students (Altermatt, Jovanovic, & Perry, 1998), whereas the other study showed that differences in male and female students' behavior did not account for teachers' behavior (Duffy, Warren, & Walsh, 2001). Teachers' lack of attention to female students is depicted in the cartoon shown in Figure 6.13.

FIGURE 6.13   Cartoon illustrates how teachers pay more attention to boys than girls, referring to the lack of attention to girls as a "girl's education."
Source: DOONESBURY ©1992 G. B. Trudeau. Reprinted with permission of UNIVERSAL PRESS SYNDICATE. All rights reserved.

Brady and Eisler (1995) also noted in their meta-analysis that self-report studies show fewer differences than observational studies; that is, girls and boys do not report being treated very differently by teachers. The one exception is that boys report receiving more negative treatment than girls. In a study of 1st- through 10th-graders, children were asked if they think that boys and girls are treated the same (Myhill & Jones, 2006). The vast majority of students said that boys were treated more negatively than girls, and this observation seemed to increase with age. One investigator compared self-reports to observational data from her own classroom (Lundeberg, 1997). She found a discrepancy between student self-reports and observer ratings: Objective raters noted that boys talked more than girls, but students reported the discussion seemed to be equal. Thus students are unaware of some of the differences in the way teachers treat men and women in the classroom. Conduct your own observational study of a classroom in Do Gender 6.4 to see if gender bias exists.

Feedback.   One reason girls do not receive as much attention as boys is that girls behave well in school and do not demand as much attention as boys do. While the girls are behaving themselves, the teachers are spending time with the "difficult" boys. In other words, these girls suffer from benign neglect. Meanwhile, the boys' bad behavior is reinforced because it receives the teacher's attention. The different kinds of attention boys and girls receive for behavior (girls for good behavior and boys for bad behavior) ends up affecting how boys and girls respond to the feedback they receive from teachers about their academics.

This was shown in an early observational study that has now become a classic in the field (Dweck et al., 1978). Two raters observed instances of evaluative feedback given to children

DO GENDER 6.4
Classroom Behavior

Conduct your own observational study of classroom behavior. Record some or all of the following, noting whether the interaction involved a male or female student. Are there other features of teacher-student interactions worth observing?

1. Teacher calling on student.

2. Teacher giving praise.

3. Teacher criticizing.

4. Length of time teacher waits for a response after calling on student.

5. Nature of teacher's response to a student's response (praise, criticism, expands on, ignores).

6. Number of times teacher interrupts student.

7. Number of times student interrupts teacher or another student.

8. Student raising hand.

9. Student shouting out answer.

After conducting your observational study, you might also administer a questionnaire to the teacher and the students asking whether they observed different frequencies of behavior with male and female students. You can then compare your observational data to the student and teacher self-report data.

and noted whether the feedback was positive or negative and whether it pertained to the children's intellectual performance or to nonintellectual aspects of performance. Feedback about nonintellectual aspects often pertained to conduct, as in "Johnny, please settle down and sit in your chair," or appearance: "Mary, you have a lovely outfit on today." The investigators found no difference in the amount of positive or negative feedback given to boys and girls, but an important difference is whether the feedback pertained to intellectual or nonintellectual aspects of the children's performance. For girls, only 30% of the negative feedback pertained to nonintellectual aspects of performance, whereas 70% pertained to intellectual aspects of performance. For boys, 67% of the negative feedback pertained to nonintellectual aspects of performance, whereas only 33% pertained to intellectual aspects of performance. The authors suggested these differences make negative feedback a very salient indicator of poor performance for girls but an unclear indicator of poor performance for boys. When girls receive negative feedback, it is more likely to be related to their schoolwork than work-irrelevant domains, such as conduct or appearance; thus girls take negative feedback seriously. Boys, by contrast, are able to discount negative feedback because it usually has nothing to do with the intellectual aspects of their performance. Thus when boys receive negative feedback about their work, they can reason, "The teacher doesn't like me. She is always criticizing me. She tells me to dress neater and to be quieter. What does she know about whether or not I can read?"

In the same study, positive feedback typically pertained to intellectual aspects of performance for both boys and girls. However, when compared to the positive feedback boys received, proportionally more of girls' positive feedback concerned nonintellectual aspects of their performance. Thus positive feedback is a clear indicator of good performance for boys but not as meaningful for girls because it sometimes has to do with nonintellectual aspects of their performance. Girls, then, are unsure whether to take positive feedback about their work seriously because teachers are providing positive feedback about other domains not relevant to work, such as their appearance or

behavior. Here, girls may conclude, "The teacher just likes me. She likes how neat I keep my desk and that I don't cause trouble. That's why I received an A on my homework." The investigators also found that teachers made different attributions for boys' and girls' failures: Teachers were more likely to make attributions to motivational factors, such as lack of effort, for boys than for girls.

The investigators conducted an experimental test of their theory by providing typical female and male feedback to students and examining the students' attributions for hypothetical successes and failures. They found that typical male feedback (i.e., negative feedback to both intellectual and nonintellectual areas; positive feedback to intellectual) was tied to attributing failure to effort and typical female feedback (i.e., negative feedback to intellectual only; positive feedback to both intellectual and nonintellectual) was tied to attributing failure to lack of ability. The researchers concluded that girls take negative feedback seriously because it is more likely to be tied exclusively to work, and boys discount negative feedback because they receive so much negative feedback about areas other than their work. The end result is that boys can maintain a belief in their abilities despite negative feedback from teachers.

What are the implications of these results for how teachers and parents should provide feedback to children? Should we start criticizing girls for behavior unrelated to their work so they can discount negative feedback and make external attributions for failure? That would not seem to be an optimal answer. Alternatively, we could make sure we are providing positive feedback to females about areas relevant only to work, so the positive feedback is salient and directly tied to their performance. The idea here is to eliminate the positive feedback about performance-irrelevant domains such as appearance. If we take Dweck and colleagues'

(1978) results seriously, the idea of complimenting or praising a person about something unrelated to their work to soften the blow before providing negative work-related feedback is doing them a disservice.

The study by Dweck and colleagues is 30 years old. Is there any more recent evidence on this issue? Unfortunately, no one has tried to replicate these exact findings in recent years. Research still shows that boys receive more negative feedback than girls in the classroom—especially about their conduct (Foote, 2002). One study showed that this kind of negative feedback affects children's attitudes toward schoolwork and school in general (Morgan, 2001). Boys and girls were randomly assigned to receive positive competence feedback with or without negative feedback about the neatness and organization of their work. Both boys and girls who received the negative behavioral feedback expressed less interest in the project and liked the teacher less than boys and girls who received only the positive competence feedback. In contrast to the Dweck and colleagues' (1978) study, boys and girls who received the negative behavioral feedback also rated their competence on the task as lower. These findings suggest that the effects of negative behavioral feedback in the classroom may be far reaching and may explain why boys have less positive relationships with teachers and less favorable attitudes toward school compared to girls.

There are also hazards associated with girls' receipt of positive feedback for work-irrelevant domains that may extend beyond the classroom. Girls may be more vulnerable than boys to other situations in which positive feedback undermines attributing success to ability. One such situation is flirting. Satterfield and Muehlenhard (1997) examined the impact of flirting on college students' perceptions of their abilities. They were concerned that an authority figure who provides positive feedback in the context of flirting could change someone's attribution for success from internal to external. That is, flirting detracts from the sincerity of feedback. The individual reasons, "This person is praising my skill in this area only because he or she likes me."

In a study to test these ideas, college women and men were exposed to an experimenter and an authority figure confederate who praised the students' creative abilities. The authority figure provided this feedback in either a nonflirtatious or flirtatious manner. The flirtatious condition included winking, eye contact, and compliments about the student's appearance. In the flirtatious condition, women's ratings of their creativity decreased from before to after the feedback. In the nonflirtatious condition, women's creativity ratings were unchanged. Thus positive feedback from a flirtatious authority figure was discounted and actually led women to lower their perceptions of their abilities. Men's ratings of their creativity were unaffected by whether the positive feedback was provided by a flirtatious or a nonflirtatious authority figure. In either case, men's ratings did not change from before to after the feedback. The reason women's beliefs about their abilities were affected by the flirtatious confederate and men's were not may have to do with women having a greater history of receiving praise for domains unrelated to ability (e.g., Dweck et al., 1978).

Effects on Performance. Teachers' beliefs about students' abilities have been shown to influence student performance. In one study, sixth-grade students were followed over the course of a year to determine the effect of teachers' initial expectations on students' subsequent performance in math (Jussim & Eccles, 1992). The investigators studied 98 teachers and 1,731 students. Although boys and girls performed equally well in math, teachers perceived that girls performed better and tried harder, but that boys had more talent. In other words, the teachers attributed girls' performance to effort and boys' performance to ability. Teachers' attributions to effort appeared to be erroneous because girls did not report expending greater effort on math than boys did. What is important is that teachers' perceptions of students' math ability predicted the change in math achievement from fifth to sixth grades. In other words, a student's math achievement improved between fifth and sixth grade when teachers started out believing the student had high math ability—which was the case for boys more than girls.

Teachers also have different expectations for the performance of different racial groups, which may influence performance. Teachers have especially low expectations for Black males' performance (Simms, Knight, & Dawes, 1993). This is a problem because teachers' expectancies predict students' academic behavior. Thus one reason Black males have a negative view of school is that teachers' low expectations have been communicated to them. Black males receive more negative feedback and more mixed (positive and negative) feedback than Black females or White students. Although teachers attribute failure to external causes for White males, they attribute failure to internal causes for Black males (Simms et al., 1993).

One solution to the different experiences that girls and boys have in the classroom is single-sex education. The evidence as to whether single-sex education provides a solution to the problems discussed in this chapter is mixed, as discussed in Sidebar 6.2.

SIDEBAR 6.2: *The Single-Sex Classroom Debate*

The rationale for placing males and females in single-sex classrooms is that somehow one sex suffers from being combined with the other. At younger ages, some argue that boys are at a disadvantage compared to girls because of the difference in physical maturity. Boys are more likely than girls to get into trouble at school and boys receive lower grades than girls. Ironically, the inferior performance of boys could have an adverse effect on girls. For girls, the issues are that they may decrease their academic effort to ensure their popularity with boys, that they may not receive the same attention by teachers that boys receive, and that they are subtly discouraged from pursuing nontraditional careers.

In 1998, the American Association of University Women (AAUW) published a report that evaluated the effects of single-sex education and surprisingly concluded that there is little evidence for its benefits. Although female students rate single-sex classes favorably and report that such classes help them learn, there does not appear to be any evidence that single-sex classes influence achievement; in fact, there are some indications of adverse effects. There does seem to be some evidence that single-sex schools are beneficial for females of a lower socioeconomic status (SES). The researchers concluded that the single-sex school requires that lower SES females focus more on academics than they normally would if they were attending a coeducational school. Coeducational schools place a relatively high value on sports and recreation, which might be more distracting to girls with a lesser academic interest.

The AAUW, however, noted that the topic is difficult to study. First, single-sex education can take various forms, ranging from single-sex schools to single-sex classes within a coeducational school. Even single-sex classes are varied, ranging from one single-sex class that meets five days a week to one or two full days of single-sex classes. This variability in single-sex format makes it difficult to compare findings across studies.

Second, there are few single-sex schools. Because of legal difficulties in instituting a single-sex school in the United States, few exist and most that do are private. Thus, a major difficulty in evaluating single-sex education is that there is a selection bias in who attends single-sex schools. A rigorous test of single-sex education would require a control group, but there are few opportunities to randomly assign a student to have a single-sex versus coeducational school experience. Instead, investigators compare the people who attend single-sex schools to the people who attend coeducational schools. But the two groups of students are not the same. In cases where females who attend a single-sex school attain higher levels of achievement than females who attend a coeducational school, the difference disappears when socioeconomic status is taken into consideration (AAUW, 1998). In other words, the higher level of achievement of females who attend single-sex schools is accounted for by the fact that these females come from more educated and wealthier families. Girls who attend single-sex schools have higher achievement aspirations, making them more achievement oriented than girls who attend coeducational schools (Watson, Quatman, & Edler, 2002).

More recently, the state of California conducted the largest field experiment of single-sex education (Datnow, Hubbard, & Woody, 2001). Single-sex education was offered in six different school districts. The goal was to provide diversity in educational choice to families while also providing equal access to males and females. The pilot program failed miserably. The results suggested that neither goal was met. Instead, program evaluators found that teachers taught in ways that reinforced gender stereotypes and ignored the extent to which the classroom might have shaped boys' and girls' behavior in coeducational environments. The teachers assumed that boys needed discipline and taught boys in a regimented and harsh style. By contrast, the teachers assumed that girls were well behaved and sensitive and taught girls in a more cooperative and nurturing way. Separating the sexes seemed to make gender a more prominent feature of the classroom. Girls were taught that "you can do anything" as long as you look pretty and wear makeup, whereas boys were taught that it is okay to express emotion as long as you appear strong and take care of your wife. There was no evidence that disruptive behavior declined in single-sex classrooms. Similar to the AAUW report, the researchers concluded that academics are most strongly influenced by the teacher, the curriculum, and the availability of resources and that single-sex education is not the solution.

In 2005, the U.S. Department of Education conducted a review of existing studies on single-sex education. They concluded that the results are not clear. For some outcomes, there is the suggestion that single-sex education might be helpful; for many outcomes, there is no evidence. The most common finding is one of "no difference" between single-sex and coeducational schooling. The U.S. Department of Education also cautioned that (a) few studies examine moderators to determine if there are a certain group of individuals who benefit from single-sex education, such as low socioeconomic status individuals, and (b) few studies are methodologically strong.

Here are four fairly recent studies of single-sex education, which give you a flavor of the variety of methodologies used to address this issue. Taken collectively, the support for single-sex education is modest at best. It is interesting that two of the studies suggest that single-sex classrooms are associated with more rather than fewer behavioral problems.

1. One school randomly assigned students to either single-sex or coed classrooms for their entire sixth grade (Belcher, Frey, & Yankeelov, 2006). The single-sex students were more attentive and more interested in class and thought the classroom was more orderly than the coed students. However, there were no differences in academic test scores.

2. A study of a coeducational school that introduced single-sex classes for math found that the majority of women perceived single-sex classes favorably, citing greater feelings of confidence, less embarrassment over wrong answers, and greater support (Jackson, 2002). By contrast, men did not report the same benefits. The majority of men said that the single-sex classes were not helpful,

and one third said they were less confident. Single-sex classes for men were associated with an increase in misbehavior, competition, and aggression. Although women were once considered a distraction for men, this study concluded that men may be more distracted by each other.

3. One study provided some validity to the claim that single-sex schools are more apt to support nontraditional careers. Male alumni who had attended single-sex versus coeducational schools were compared on their interests and careers (James & Richards, 2003). Men who attended single-sex schools were more likely than men who attended coed schools to have positive attitudes toward English, history, and reading; to have majored in the humanities; and to have careers that involve the humanities. Although it is possible that the single-sex environment reduced the pressure on men to conform to traditional male norms, it also is possible that there were differences in the kinds of men who went to single-sex versus coed schools—perhaps the former were more interested in the humanities.

4. A naturalistic study of the social impact of single-sex education was undertaken by examining males and females who transitioned from coeducational classes in fourth grade to single-sex classes in fifth grade (Barton & Cohen, 2004). Whereas boys gained more friends with the transition, there was an increase in relational aggression, rejection, and victimization among girls.

One problem with the study of single-sex education is how to define effectiveness or success. Success is typically defined by grades and by scores on standardized tests. But, there may be other outcomes in which we should be interested, such as teenage pregnancy and bullying. What about how an individual functions as a member of society? subsequent career success, job performance, and leadership? These kinds of outcomes are much more difficult to assess, but they may be the outcomes for which single-sex education provides an advantage.

Even when single-sex education is successful, investigators suggest that the factors responsible for the positive effects are ones that could be applied to coeducational schools. For example, single-sex schools may have teachers with higher qualifications and smaller classrooms compared to coeducational schools.

Despite the equivocal empirical support for single-sex education, in January 2002 President Bush signed into law the "No Child Left Behind Act," which permits the use of single-sex public education, provided there are comparable resources for men and women. The law also made single-sex schools eligible for a large pot of federal funds. Because most people had interpreted Title IX as prohibiting single-sex education, the U.S. Department of Education amended it in October 2006 to give local schools the right to create single-sex classrooms for academic subjects as long as similar coeducational classes are offered and males and females receive equal treatment. These new regulations have been met with disapproval by the AAUW, NOW, and many others, all of whom cite concerns that "separate is not equal" and that stereotypes about gender are being used to justify single-sex classrooms without evidence that they are helpful.

TAKE HOME POINTS

- Teachers give boys more attention than girls in school.

- Teachers are especially more likely to criticize boys than girls in school—but criticism can be helpful as it provides feedback about how to change behavior.

- Teachers also provide more negative behavioral feedback to boys than girls which ends up reinforcing the behavior and allowing boys to discount negative feedback about their classwork.

- Teachers provide more positive behavioral feedback to girls than boys which ends up diluting the positive feedback that girls receive about their classwork and potentially leads females to attribute positive feedback that they receive in the real world to extraneous factors.

- ■ Teachers have different beliefs about boys' and girls' abilities which translate into how they spend time with boys

and girls as well as the nature of the feedback they provide. Like parents, teachers attribute boys' success in math to ability and girls' success in math to effort.

- ■ Teacher expectations have been shown to affect student performance.

SUMMARY

In the first part of the chapter, I examined a number of individual difference variables that might explain men's and women's different levels of achievement. The early work in this area suggested women have a lower need for achievement compared to men. This hypothesis was later dismissed by suggesting that women's lack of achievement compared to men stems from women's "fear of success." The fear of success literature was and continues to be fairly controversial, in part due to the projective nature of the fear of success measures. Recent studies, however, suggest there is still a concern among some women that success may have negative implications for relationships. Another reason women are thought to achieve less than men is that women have lower levels of self-confidence compared to men or even lower levels of general self-esteem. Women's lower self-confidence and lower self-esteem are limited to certain circumstances, specifically when the task is in a masculine domain. Women also seem to take feedback more to heart than men, which means that their self-esteem is affected by others' positive and negative evaluations of their performance. In areas where women are presumed to be inferior to men, making those stereotypes salient adversely affects women's performance. In regard to self-esteem, it is more accurate to say men and women have different beliefs about their strong points and derive their self-esteem from different sources. Evidence suggests that men derive self-esteem more from individuating

themselves from others (i.e., feeling unique in comparison to others), whereas women derive self-esteem from their connection to others.

A final individual difference factor that may have implications for men's and women's achievement has to do with the way they explain their successes and failures. Women are more likely than men to attribute success to effort or luck (unstable causes), whereas men are more likely to attribute success to ability (an internal, stable cause). Women are more likely to attribute failure to stable causes, such as lack of ability or task difficulty, whereas men are more likely to attribute failure to unstable causes, such as lack of effort or bad luck. These differences in attributions, however, are largely limited to masculine tasks. Sex differences in attributions for performance on feminine tasks are less clear. Importantly, the different attributions men and women make for performance may have implications for the decisions they make about how hard to try in an area or even whether to pursue a particular area of achievement.

In the second half of the chapter, I explored social factors that might contribute to men's and women's beliefs about their abilities as well as their attributions for performance. According to the expectancy/value model, people pursue achievement in an area in which they expect to succeed and they regard as important and interesting. Children's expectancies and values, however, are a function of gender-role socialization. One source of socialization is parents. Parents often have stereotyped views of boys' and girls' abilities, believing boys have greater math ability and girls have greater verbal ability, which they translate into beliefs about their specific sons' and daughters' abilities. Parents seem to hold these sex-differentiated beliefs even when boys and girls receive the same grades in school. Some evidence indicates that parents' beliefs about their children's abilities influence children's own self-perceptions and children's actual abilities. In other words, parents' stereotypes about boys' and girls' abilities may become self-fulfilling prophecies. The feedback and experiences that parents provide to their children may lead the children to develop the different abilities parents initially expected.

A second source of influence on children's beliefs about their abilities is teachers.

Teachers pay more attention to boys than girls in the classroom. This may be due, in part, to boys' misbehavior demanding more attention. Teachers are more likely to criticize boys than girls; interestingly, criticism is linked to greater self-confidence. More important, the nature of the feedback that teachers provide to boys and girls differs. Boys seem to receive a great deal of negative feedback about work-irrelevant domains, which then leads boys to discount negative feedback about their work and maintain a belief in their abilities. This type of negative feedback also may undermine boys' interest in school. Girls, by contrast, seem to receive more positive feedback about work-irrelevant domains, which, unfortunately, leads girls to discount positive feedback about their work and make more unstable attributions for success.

DISCUSSION QUESTIONS

1. Discuss the evidence in favor of and against a "fear of success" in women. What would be a good way to examine this issue today?
2. Of all the ideas discussed in this chapter, which do you find to be most convincing as an explanation of why women have not reached the same level of achievement in society as men?
3. Which is more adaptive: men's or women's response to evaluative feedback?
4. Under what circumstances would you expect men and women to make similar versus different attributions for their performance?
5. Considering the results from the studies on evaluative feedback and the work by Dweck on teachers' attributions for performance, what is the best way to provide feedback to children? To adults?
6. Given what you have learned about the different ways men and women define their core selves, what would you predict would influence men's versus women's self-esteem?
7. What are the two components of the expectancy/value model of achievement?
8. What are some of the specific ways in which parents' beliefs about their children's abilities could influence their children's actual abilities?
9. What do you believe are the major advantages and disadvantages of single-sex classrooms?
10. What could be done to reduce gender bias in the classroom?

Suggested Reading

Cross, S. E., & Madson, L. (1997). Models of the self: Self-construals and gender. *Psychological Bulletin, 122,* 5–37.

Classic Dweck, C. S., Davidson, W., Nelson, S., & Enna, B. (1978). Sex differences in learned helplessness: II. The contingencies of evaluative feedback in the classroom; III. An experimental analysis. *Developmental Psychology, 14,* 268–276.

Jacobs, J. E., Davis-Kean, P., Bleeker, M., Eccles, J. S., & Malanchuk, O. (2005). "I can, but I don't want to": The impact of parents, interests, and activities on gender differences in math. In A. M. Gallagher & J. C. Kaufman (Eds.), *Gender differences in mathematics: An integrative psychological approach* (pp. 246–263). New York: Cambridge University Press.

Roberts, T-A. (1991). Gender and the influence of evaluations on self-assessments in achievement settings. *Psychological Bulletin, 109,* 297–308.

Sadker, M., & Sadker, D. (1994). *Failing at fairness: How America's schools cheat girls.* New York: Scribner's.

Key Terms

Achievement motive—Stable personality characteristic that reflects the tendency to strive for success.

Attribution—Cause assigned to a behavior.

Collective interdependence—Connection to others derived from group membership.

Expectancy/value model of achievement—Theory that achievement-related choices are a function of our expectancy for success and our value of the area.

External attribution—Cause assigned to a behavior that originates in the environment.

Fear of success—Association of negative consequences with achievement.

Internal attribution—Cause assigned to a behavior that originates within the person.

Relational interdependence—Emphasis on close relationships.

Self-serving bias—The tendency to assign internal attributions for success and external attributions for failure.

Stable attribution—Cause for a behavior that does not change over time.

Stereotype threat—Theory that activating the female stereotype hinders women's performance.

Unstable attribution—Cause for a behavior that may change with time, day, or place.

7

COMMUNICATION

"What 'I Love You' Really Means" (*Glamour*)

"99 Ways to Read a Man" (*Glamour*)

"Decoding Guy-Speak" (*Ladies' Home Journal*)

"What Men Still Don't Understand" (*Redbook*)

"What He's Really Thinking" (*Cosmopolitan*)

"Why Women Can't Communicate Clearly" (*AskMen.com*)

These are a few of the headlines in recent years that suggest men and women have difficulties communicating with each other. In 1990, Deborah Tannen wrote a popular book entitled *You Just Don't Understand: Women and Men in Conversation*. From this book, it would appear that men and women have completely different styles of conversation, completely different styles of nonverbal communication, and completely different styles of interacting with one another. Indeed, many of the conversational excerpts provided in her book ring true. But the book is largely based on anecdotal evidence of men's and women's interactions. The stories ring true because they are consistent with our schemas about how men and women interact and because it is easier to recall schema-consistent information than schema-inconsistent information. The research evidence, however, shows that men's and women's communication patterns are much more varied. Many more variables than the person's sex influence communication, for example, the sex of the person with whom one is interacting, the situation in which people find themselves, the goal or purpose of the interaction, and the status of the interaction partners. Kathryn Dindia (2006), a gender and communications scholar, concludes that men and women are not from different planets or cultures and do not speak different languages. Instead of men being from Mars and women being from Venus, Dindia (2006) argues that a better metaphor would be that men are from North Dakota and women are from South Dakota—meaning that there are some slight differences in communication, but many more similarities.

This is the first chapter in the section on gender and relationships. Before discussing specific aspects of men's and women's friendships, romantic relationships, and work relationships in the next chapters, here I review the literature on how men and women communicate. This chapter focuses on both verbal and nonverbal communication. I begin by describing the research on men's and women's interaction styles in childhood and adulthood and the variables that influence those styles. I then turn to the literatures on verbal behavior—the language men and women use—and nonverbal behavior, such as touching, gazing, and smiling. Next, I examine a particular interaction style, one in which one person is trying to influence another. Who is more likely to influence and be influenced? Then I review several theories that might explain the previously discussed differences in interaction patterns, verbal and nonverbal behavior, and influenceability: sex-segregated interactions in early life, status or power, and social role theory. Next I examine emotion—experience, expression, and bases. I briefly address the topic of leadership by examining who is likely to become a leader, what style the person uses, and how he or she is evaluated. Finally, I conclude the chapter with a discussion of a particular form of communication between men and women—the exchange of support.

INTERACTION STYLES IN CHILDHOOD

Two children are sitting quietly at a table in the family room coloring and talking about being best friends. A group of children are playing soccer in the backyard, shouting at one another to get to the ball. Who are the children at the table? In the backyard? Boys? Girls? Both? Can you tell?

There are certainly some differences in the ways boys and girls play. For example, girls are likely to play in dyads and boys are likely to play in groups. They are also likely to be playing with the same sex. A primary determinant of how boys and girls interact with one another is their peer group (Maccoby, 1998). From very early on, children tend to prefer and seek out interactions with same-sex peers. Thus same-sex play, in and of itself, becomes a socializing agent that ultimately leads males and females to have different interaction styles.

What is the evidence for same-sex play preferences? Do you recall playing with children of the same sex or children of the other sex? At what age? At ages 1 and 2, there are no preferences for same- or other-sex peers, but by age 3 there is a clear same-sex preference in girls (Maccoby, 1998). A year later, boys' same-sex preference emerges. The preference to interact with same-sex peers peaks between the ages of 8 and 11 (Maccoby, 1998). The same-sex play preference even extends to engaging in gender-neutral activities. The same-sex play preference also appears across very different cultures (Munroe & Romney, 2006).

Even though girls initiate the same-sex play preference, by age 5, the preference is stronger in boys than girls. Boys' groups are more exclusionary of the other sex than are girls' groups. Boys view other boys who play with girls as feminine, and boys do not tolerate feminine behavior in another boy. It is important for boys' sense of masculinity to demonstrate that they are not feminine and to reject all associations with femininity. Girls, however, do not feel the same need to reject masculinity. Girls are more accepting of masculine behavior in another girl (Maccoby, 1998). Children also believe others like them more if they play with the same sex than the other sex. In one study, children who said that others approved of other-sex play were, in fact, more likely to engage in other-sex play (Martin et al., 1999).

Why do children prefer to play with others of the same sex? Maccoby (1998) provides two reasons. First, she argues that children have different styles of play that are not very compatible. Second, she argues that girls find it difficult to influence boys, which makes interactions with boys less desirable. I discuss the evidence for each of these reasons.

Children's Styles of Play

Boys' play and girls' play are very different (Maccoby, 1998; Rose & Rudolph, 2006). Boys play in large groups, whereas girls are more likely to play with only one or two friends. Boys' play is rough, competitive, and emphasizes dominance; girls' play is quiet, often conversational, and involves more structured activities (e.g., drawing or painting; see Figure 7.1). Boys' play is boisterous, activity oriented, and takes up a good deal of space (i.e., the street, the entire yard). Boys are more likely to play outdoors, whereas girls are more likely to play inside the house or stay within their yards. These sex differences emerge in childhood and persist or increase during middle childhood and adolescence. Even boys' and girls' fantasy play differs. Girls are more likely to pretend to play house or school, where one person enacts the role of teacher or parent and the other enacts the role of student or child; boys, by contrast,

are more likely to emulate heroic characters, such as Superman. No wonder Maccoby (1998) argued that the two play styles are not very compatible.

Boys and girls also have different conversational styles, which map onto their distinct styles of play (Maccoby, 1998). Boys' conversation is motivated to establish dominance, whereas girls' conversation serves to foster connection. Boys interrupt each other, threaten each other, refuse to comply with one another, try to top one another's stories, and call each other names; girls express agreement with one another, take turns when speaking, and acknowledge one another's feelings. Boys are more likely to order someone to do something ("Pick up the ball!"), whereas girls are more likely to make a polite suggestion ("Could you pick up the ball, please?").

These differences in conversational style were demonstrated in a study of third-graders playing checkers with either first-graders or other third-graders who were the same sex (McCloskey, 1996). The study showed that boys

FIGURE 7.1 This is a common form of play among girls—dyadic and quiet, with the opportunity for conversation.

TABLE 7.1   RELATIONAL AGGRESSION ITEMS

1. When angry, gives others the "silent treatment."
2. When mad, tries to damage others' reputations by passing on negative information.
3. When mad, retaliates by excluding others from activities.
4. Intentionally ignores others until they agree to do something for him or her.
5. Makes it clear to his or her friends that he or she will think less of them unless they do what he or she wants.
6. Threatens to share private information with others in order to get them to comply with his or her wishes.
7. When angry with same-sex peer, tries to steal that person's dating partner.

Source: Werner and Crick, (1999).

brag to and insult their partner, a behavior McCloskey labeled **egoistic dominance**. By contrast, girls were more likely to instruct their partner on how to play the game, especially when the partner was a first-grader. McCloskey labeled this behavior **prosocial dominance**. These findings are consistent with the cross-cultural research discussed in Chapter 4 that showed boys and girls hold distinct roles (Whiting & Edwards, 1988). See Sidebar 7.1 for a discussion of the different ways boys and girls manage conflict with peers.

Yet, there is some evidence that different play styles do not completely account for the same-sex play preference. In one study, children ages 2½ to 5 who had more and less sex-typed

SIDEBAR 7.1: *Mean Girls? Relational Aggression*

It is not the case that girls' play is free from social conflict: It is just that conflict takes a different form among girls than boys. Among boys, conflict is overt and can become physically aggressive; conversely, conflict may be more subtle with girls. Boys may shout at one another, argue, or become physical, whereas girls use social alienation or **relational aggression** (Crick & Grotpeter, 1995; Crick et al., 1999). Relational aggression is hurting or threatening to hurt a relationship with another person. That is, girls display aggression by spreading rumors about someone, excluding someone from an activity, or threatening not to be the person's friend anymore. Some examples of relational aggression are shown in Table 7.1.

Crick and Grotpeter (1995) found evidence of boys' and girls' different expressions of conflict in a study of aggressive behavior among third- through sixth-graders. Children nominated classmates who displayed different kinds of aggressive behavior. Boys were found to use more overt aggression than girls, such as hitting and yelling. Girls were found to use more relational aggression than boys, such as excluding people from their group and threatening not to like someone. This sex difference in the kind of aggression boys and girls use has been replicated in other studies, including children as young as preschool (Crick et al., 2006). Cross-cultural studies in Russia, China, Finland, and Indonesia also provide support for sex differences in relational aggression (Crick et al., 1999; French, Jansen, & Pidada, 2002). There is some evidence that the intimate dyadic nature of girls' friendships contributes to relational aggression. Because girls have intimate knowledge about their friends, they can use this knowledge in an adverse way. In a study of fourth-graders, relationship aggression increased over the year for girls as did intimate disclosure to friends. The increase in relational aggression was associated with the increase in intimate disclosure (Murray-Close, Ostrov, & Crick, 2007). Even among preschoolers, relational aggression is associated with teacher reports of children being exclusive (i.e., wanting to be only with each other) and intimate (i.e., telling each other secrets; Sebanc, 2003).

Although relational aggression is perceived as hurtful and harmful by children, girls evaluate relational aggression as a better strategy to use than do boys, and boys evaluate overt aggression as a better strategy to use than do girls (Crick & Werner, 1998). Both boys and girls view relational aggression as less harmful than physical aggression (Murray-Close, Crick, & Galotti, 2006). Longitudinal studies have shown that relational aggression is a risk factor for subsequent personal difficulties—both internalizing (e.g, depression) and externalizing (e.g., acting out) problems—especially when it is combined with physical aggression (Crick, Ostrov, & Werner, 2006). Some evidence suggests that relational aggression has greater negative consequences for girls than for boys (Crick et al., 1999; Werner & Crick, 1999). A study of preschoolers showed that relational aggression predicted peer rejection 18 months later for girls but not boys (Crick et al., 2006). In addition, preschool girls without friends were more relationally aggressive than preschool girls with friends, but this was not the case for boys (Sebanc, 2003).

The effects of relational aggression are not all negative. A study of preschoolers showed that relational aggression was associated with having more reciprocal friendships (i.e., both persons nominate each other as friends; Burr et al., 2005). The authors suggested that children were attracted to those who displayed relational aggression because they were highly visible and socially dominant in class. Relational aggression has distinct effects on popularity when one distinguishes between sociometric popularity, which is measured by having all the people in the class rate whom they like and dislike, and perceived popularity, which entails having people nominate whom they perceive to be popular. The two are positively correlated but become less strongly related as children grow older. Relational aggression is associated with lower sociometric popularity but greater perceived popularity—especially for girls (Andreou, 2006; Cillessen & Borch, 2006).

What is the origin of relational aggression? Unlike physical aggression, the environment plays a much larger role than genetics (Brendgen et al., 2005). One social role theory is that girls are just as aggressive as boys, but that it is inconsistent with the female role to express aggression in an overt way. Therefore, girls conceal their hostility and end up manifesting it as relational aggression. Exposure to television also has been associated with relational aggression in girls (Ostrov, Gentile, & Crick, 2006). Relational aggression also may be acquired from modeling. One study showed that older siblings' relational aggression in the fall predicted younger siblings' relational aggression the following spring (Ostrov, Crick, & Stauffacher, 2006). Just like physical aggression, relational aggression has been linked to cognitive biases (Crick et al., 2004). The bias is in the interpretation of ambiguous relationship situations. Children who are relationally aggressive are more likely to make hostile attributions for ambiguous relationship situations (Leff, Kupersmidt, & Power, 2003).

play styles were equally likely to play with the same sex (Hoffmann & Powlishta, 2001). It is also possible that same-sex play leads to different play styles rather than different play styles leading to same-sex play. In a study of preschool and kindergarten children, greater same-sex play in the fall predicted an increase in sex-typed play for both boys and girls in the spring (Martin & Fabes, 2001). Specifically, same-sex play in girls predicted a decrease in activity and aggression over the year, whereas same-sex play in boys predicted an increase in activity, aggression, and Rough-and-tumble play over the year.

If same-sex play increases stereotypical play styles, does cross-sex play reduce stereotypical play styles? There is some evidence that

FIGURE 7.2 A boy and girl playing together; cross-sex play is not the norm, especially dyadic cross-sex play.

this may be the case. Mixed-sex play accounts for about 30% of children's interactions (Fabes, Martin, & Hanish, 2004) but is typically not dyadic (see Figure 7.2 for an exception; Fabes, Martin, & Hanish, 2003). There seems to be some accommodation of play styles when boys and girls are together. Studies of preschoolers show that boys are less active, less forceful, and more agreeable with females than males, and females are more active, more forceful, more controlling, and less agreeable with males than females (Fabes et al., 2003; Holmes-Lonergan, 2003). Accommodation of interaction styles also has been observed among fifth- and sixth-graders playing computer games (Calvert et al., 2003). Boys engaged in more fast-moving play, whereas girls engaged in more language-based play, but these differences decreased when interacting with the other sex. Thus same-sex play seems to be the most stereotyped, and cross-sex play has the potential to decrease stereotypes. There is some evidence that greater time in same-sex play is associated with more sex-stereotyped play over time (Fabes et al., 2004).

Girls' Difficulty in Influencing Boys

A second reason children prefer to play with same-sex peers is that girls find it difficult to influence boys. According to Maccoby (1998), girls attempt to influence others by making polite suggestions, whereas boys are more likely to make demands. Boys are not responsive to girls' polite suggestions; thus girls' tactics are effective with other girls and with adults, but not with boys. The question is—why are boys unresponsive to girls?

The differences in interaction styles and influence styles explain why it appears that girls spend more time in close proximity to authority figures (e.g., teachers) than boys do. It was first thought that girls stayed closer to teachers because of the affiliative nature of their gender role. However, girls stand near teachers only in the presence of boys. Girls likely believe that an adult authority figure will temper boys' dominant behavior.

Explaining the Different Styles of Play

The different ways boys and girls play, interact, and attempt to influence one another might explain why boys and girls prefer to play with peers of their own sex. But what is the source of boys' and girls' divergent play styles? Why is boys' play louder and more aggressive than girls' play? Maccoby (1998) discusses three primary reasons.

First, she suggests that *biology* may play an important role in shaping children's play behavior. She notes that boys' rough-and-tumble play and girls' interest in caretaking can be observed in other nonhuman primates, such as monkeys. She also suggests that sex differences in brain maturation might lead females to develop language abilities and to regulate emotions earlier than males. If true, this could explain why girls' relationships focus more on language and are more emotionally controlled (i.e., less noisy and less volatile).

Maccoby (1998) suggests that sex hormones might be linked to play styles. However, she acknowledges that a hormonal explanation cannot fully account for the differences in play styles because boys' and girls' play is also influenced by the situation. Many of the differences in boys' and girls' play stem from the people with whom they are interacting. For example, boys are more active than girls in the presence of other boys but not alone. If hormones influence play styles, they would have to predispose boys to behave differently with other boys than when alone. Of course, there could be a synergistic effect of hormones so that different play styles become exaggerated in the presence of same-sex peers.

Second, Maccoby (1998) takes up the *socialization* hypothesis. She believes socialization has little to offer in the way of explaining why boys and girls have different styles of play. Maccoby states that children do not learn same-sex play from parents because most of parents' interactions are with each other—the other sex. However, if children distinguish friendship from romantic relationships, they may notice that Mom and Dad are "friends" with people of the same sex. Maccoby (1998) acknowledges that the way parents treat children might have something to do with why boys and girls develop different interaction styles. Parents handle girls more gently, talk more about emotions with girls, are more tolerant of fighting among boys, and are more likely to use physical punishment with boys. In addition, parents give children sex-typed toys and reinforce sex-typed behavior. These "small" differences in behavior could lead boys' play to be rougher and girls' play to center more on emotions. The question is whether parents' differential treatment of boys and girls leads to different play styles, or whether the different play styles of boys and girls lead parents to treat them differently.

Maccoby argues that adults do not encourage children to play with the same sex; however, there is no evidence on this issue. It seems quite likely that parents select same-sex neighborhood playmates for their children. That is, parents may simply provide a greater opportunity for same-sex play. Think about who is usually invited to a 4- or 5-year-old's birthday party. It is usually the same sex—especially in the case of girls. The question is: Do parents seek out same-sex peers for their children to play with before the children are old enough to have strong preferences?

Perhaps it isn't parents who encourage same-sex play. Perhaps it is other people in the child's environment. I remember when we first moved into our current neighborhood that the neighbors remarked on how lucky we were because there were a lot of other girls for our daughter to play with. Teachers also may reinforce the gender dichotomy. I observed a group of 8- to 10-year-olds playing Red Rover at an after-school program. The teachers were distraught because the girls kept losing to the boys. There were about 7 girls on one team and 12 boys on the other. It just did not occur to the teachers that boys and girls could be on the same team. Instead, the teachers tried to find ways to give the girls advantages to "even out" the teams.

However, if same-sex play were due entirely to adult socialization, we should find greater same-sex play in the presence of adults. However, just the opposite is found. Same-sex play is more common in unstructured than adult structured activities (Fabes et al., 2004). In addition, reinforcement for cross-sex play seems to have its effects only in the presence of the reinforcer. When reinforcement is withdrawn, children revert back to same-sex play. In a study of children from 10 different cultures, sex segregation was found to be largest among cultures that provide children with the greatest freedom to choose playmates—cultures that allow children to range farther from the home (Whiting & Edwards, 1988). In cultures where children are required to stay closer to home, there is less sex segregation, presumably because there are fewer choices of playmates. These findings suggest that children *prefer* to play with same-sex peers. In sum, the jury is still out on how much sex segregation is actually shaped by society.

Third, Maccoby (1998) addresses the question of whether *cognitive differences* between boys and girls lead to differences in play styles. Cognitive-developmental theory suggests that as children acquire a gender identity, they begin to prefer similar others, which would consist of same-sex children. Children learn to behave in ways appropriate for their sex and to interact with others who are behaving in a similar way.

Little research has tried to differentiate boys and girls who have stronger and weaker same-sex peer preferences. This may shed some light on the origin of same-sex play preferences. Conduct your own research on the issue with Do Gender 7.1.

TAKE HOME POINTS

- Both boys and girls develop a strong preference to play with members of the same sex.

- The same-sex preference appears first among girls but becomes stronger among boys.

- Reasons for the same-sex play preference include the fact that girls and boys have different play styles and girls have difficulty in influencing boys.

- Same-sex play is more gender stereotyped than mixed-sex play, and mixed-sex play has the potential to reduce stereotyped play.

- The different styles of play may be due to biology, cognition, or socialization.

DO GENDER 7.1
Which Boys Play with Girls and Which Girls Play with Boys?

Visit a local day care or preschool. Choose 10 children to observe, 5 boys and 5 girls. It would be preferable if you could choose these children randomly from a list of the children in the class. Each day observe a different one of the children, recording how much time he or she spends in same-sex play and mixed-sex play.

Now, see if you can distinguish the children who engage in more or less mixed-sex play. Does the type of play differ? How do they speak to one another? If you can find out information about their families, you could determine if they come from different backgrounds—parent gender roles, presence of siblings in the household. You might also interview the children to measure variables that could distinguish those who play more or less frequently with the same sex, such as gender-role attitudes and parents' traditionality. Ask Johnny why he plays with Joan, but not Marcus. Ask Tisha why she plays with Hannah, but not Paul.

Unless you follow the children over time, this cross-sectional study will not be able to distinguish cause and effect. That is, you will not know if individual difference variables led the children to become involved in more same-sex play or whether same-sex play shaped the children in some ways.

INTERACTION STYLES IN ADULTHOOD

There are parallels between the sex differences in interaction styles observed among children and adults. Much of the research on adult interaction styles comes from studies of how people behave in small groups. This research shows that men's behavior is more directive, more dominant, more hierarchical, and more task focused; by contrast, women's behavior is more supportive, cooperative, and egalitarian. Studies of group interactions show that females engage in more **positive social behavior**, such as agreeing with others, showing group solidarity, encouraging others to talk, and making positive comments (Smith-Lovin & Robinson, 1992; Wood & Rhodes, 1992). Women are also likely to reciprocate positive social acts. In other words, women help escalate positive social behavior. Men talk more in groups compared to women (Smith-Lovin & Robinson, 1992), and men engage in more **task behavior**, such as asking for and offering opinions and suggestions (Wood & Rhodes, 1992). Men even respond to positive social acts with task behavior rather than a reciprocation of positive social behavior (Wood & Rhodes, 1992). Men also engage in more **negative social behavior**, such as disagreement and antagonism, and help escalate negative social behavior (i.e., respond to negative social behavior with more negative social behavior; Wood & Rhodes, 1992).

Given this brief summary of quite distinct interaction styles, I now must caution you that sex differences in interaction styles are not that clear cut. The way men and women behave with one another is qualified by a host of other variables. As noted by Aries (2006), "we need to move beyond the conception that the interaction styles of men and women reside within individuals." The context is important.

Qualifiers of Sex Differences

One determinant of sex differences in interaction styles is the nature of the task. Men are more task oriented in masculine situations, whereas women are more task oriented in feminine situations. A task orientation includes making suggestions and providing information. Thus a certain degree of confidence in or knowledge of the situation is required before we engage in task behavior. Men and women are likely to be more confident in situations relevant to their own sex, which enables them to make suggestions and provide information. Because masculine situations are studied more often, it may only appear that men are more task oriented than women.

Another major determinant of men's and women's interaction styles is the sex of the person with whom they are interacting. For example, Carli (1989) found that women displayed more positive social behavior (e.g., agreeing with their partner) and men displayed more task-oriented behavior and disagreement when they were interacting with members of the same sex. However, Carli also found that both men and women used more feminine behavior (e.g., agreement) with female partners and more masculine behavior (e.g., disagreement) with male partners. In other words, just as in the studies of children, men and women accommodated to each other. As shown in Figure 7.3a, both men and women engaged in more masculine behavior (task behavior) when they were paired with men than with women. As shown in Figure 7.3b, both men and women engaged in more feminine behavior (positive social behavior) when they were paired with women than men. Thus men and women behave most differently from each other when they are with members of their same sex.

Sex differences in interaction styles also tend to be greater when the interaction is brief and among strangers (Aries, 2006). This is the typical laboratory study. When we have little information about others besides their sex, we rely more on that information when making judgments or deciding how to behave. As people get to know one another and understand each other's abilities, sex becomes less important as a determinant of interaction behavior. This is the distinction made in Chapter 3 between category-based and target-based expectancies.

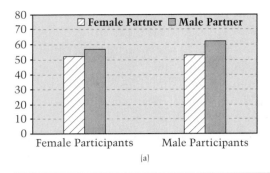
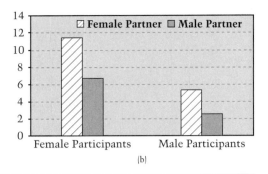

FIGURE 7.3   (a) Both men and women display more task behavior when they interact with a male than a female. (b) Both men and women display more positive social behavior when they interact with a female than a male. Numbers represent the percentage of all behaviors displayed in a particular dyad.
Source: Adapted from Carli (1989).

One limitation of this line of research is that many of the studies have been conducted on White middle-class people, often college students. The homogeneity of the people studied may make men as a group look more similar to each other than they really are and may make women as a group look more similar to each other than they really are. When we examine people of different races, ages, and socioeconomic statuses, there is likely to be greater variability in male and female interaction styles.

Implications of Interaction Styles for Performance

To the extent that men and women do have different interaction styles, what are the implications for performance? A group's performance may depend on the match between the members' interaction styles and the task with which the group is faced (Hutson-Comeaux & Kelly, 1996). Groups that have task-oriented goals will perform better when members show task-oriented behavior. Groups focused on a social activity or an activity that requires consensus will perform better if members display more positive social behavior. Consistent with this idea, one study found that male groups outperformed female groups when the task required the generation of ideas, and female groups outperformed male groups when the task required the group to reach consensus (Hutson-Comeaux & Kelly, 1996). One limitation of these studies is that sex—but not sex-specific interaction styles—is being linked to group performance. We assume male groups are performing better on task outcomes because they are displaying task-oriented behavior and female groups are performing better on social outcomes because they are displaying more positive social behavior. It would be more helpful to know that task behavior contributes to better outcomes in groups where the mission is to solve a problem and that positive social behavior contributes to better outcomes in groups that require members to come to an agreement.

TAKE HOME POINTS

- There are differences in the styles men and women exhibit when interacting in small groups. Women engage in more positive social behavior (e.g., agreement), and men engage in more task behavior (e.g., providing or asking for information) and negative behavior (e.g., disagreement).

- These differences are influenced by whether the group is composed of same-sex or other-sex persons. In the presence of the other sex, men and women accommodate to each other.

- These differences also are a function of the nature of the task. Both men and women exhibit more task-oriented behavior in areas in which they have expertise.

- These differences also have largely been found among laboratory studies of people who do not know each other. Interaction styles among people in ongoing relationships may be influenced by factors other than sex.

LANGUAGE

Imagine the following interaction:

PERSON A: I haven't talked to you in so long. What's up?

PERSON B: I've been really stressed out lately. Things are kind of weird at home.

PERSON A: What's been going on?

PERSON B: It's my brother.

PERSON A: Uh-huh.

PERSON B: It's never anything specific, but he's just really, really annoying me and there's nothing I can do about it. You know?

PERSON A: That sounds tough.

PERSON B: I've even been having dreams where he's doing something really awful.

PERSON A: It's probably a good thing that you don't have to live with him anymore, don't you think? But it seems like it still haunts you. It must still bother you if you have dreams about him a lot and stuff.

Now consider the following interaction:

PERSON A: Pat still hasn't given me back that money I lent him.

PERSON B: I never would have lent it to him in the first place.

PERSON A: Normally I wouldn't have, but he was in a bind and . . .

PERSON B: Man, you just don't get it. I told you a long time ago: You never lend money to that guy. Never. I've known him twice as long as you have, so I know all about it.

The two interactions are both same-sex interactions. Can you tell which one is between two women and which is between two men? How? There are aspects of language that distinguish men's and women's speech—but usually only when they interact with the same sex. The language used in mixed-sex interactions is much harder to distinguish. The two same-sex interactions above are very stereotypical. The first interaction was between two women, and the second was between two men. The speaking styles differed on a number of dimensions discussed in this section.

One of the most common perceptions we have about the differences between men's and women's language is that women use more of it! That is, women talk more than men. In the interactions just described, the women's conversation was longer than the men's. Does this stereotype have a basis in reality? In a meta-analytic review of the literature on children's language, girls were found to talk more than boys (Leaper & Smith, 2004). However, the effect size was small ($d = -.11$), sex differences were larger among younger children, and sex differences were larger when children interacted with adults compared to peers.

Among adults, just the opposite sex difference was found. James and Drakich (1993) reviewed 56 studies on talking among adults and discovered that 24 showed men talked more than women, 10 showed men talked more on some measures, 16 showed no sex differences in talking, 4 revealed mixed findings, and only 2 showed that women talked more than men.

Why do men talk more than women? The traditional explanation is based on status theory: Men have a higher status than women, so they are able to be the more dominant force in conversation. James and Drakich (1993) offered a different explanation. They argued that men's task behavior involves more talking than women's socioemotional behavior. For example, giving advice to someone is likely to take longer than agreeing with someone. In fact, James and Drakich found that many studies showed men and women spoke the same number of times or had the same number of turns in talking but that men's turns took longer.

If men talk more than women, why do people perceive that women talk more? One answer has to do with the setting in which talking is examined. James and Drakich (1993) found that men were especially more likely than women to talk when the setting was structured or formal. In informal conversations, men's talking advantage appears to be smaller. Informal conversations often involve more socioemotional behavior and less task behavior. In addition, to whom one is talking influences the length of conversation. Our images of women in conversation depict women talking to other *women*. Although our perceptions of sex differences in talking are based on same-sex interactions, much of the research is based on mixed-sex interactions. Try Do Gender 7.2 to figure out the conditions under which people *perceive* that men and women talk equally, men talk more, or women talk more.

Aside from general amount of talking, what are the specific differences in the language men and women use? Written language was examined among a group of college students who were asked to write or e-mail about how they spent the past summer (Colley et al., 2004). Women wrote longer than men and used more intensive adverbs (e.g., really), exclamations, and emotion than men; men used more offensive

DO GENDER 7.2
Perceptions of Talking

Develop a survey about perceptions of talking and administer it to a group of people. The class could divide into groups so each group administers the survey to a different age group: children (10 to 12), early adolescents (13 to 15), later adolescents (16 to 18), college students, middle-aged adults, the elderly. Ask about people's perceptions of who talks more (men or women) across a variety of settings, for example, conversations at work, informal conversations among friends, discussions of male problems, discussions of female problems, conversations with strangers, conversations about politics, conversations about family. Come up with a set of variables that might influence talking: sex composition of dyad (same sex vs. mixed sex), nature of relationship (friend vs. relative), topic of conversation (current events, work), setting (work vs. school). You could ask about either other people's perceptions or people's personal experiences.

language than women. E-mail language was more informal than written letters for both men and women. Language also was examined in an online discussion for introductory psychology students (Guiller & Durndell, 2006). Postings by women contained more personal opinion, more qualifiers, more intensive adverbs (e.g., I "totally" agree), and more general agreement, whereas postings by men were more authoritative, containing more assertions and disagreements.

Features of language that have been studied are shown in Table 7.2 (Mulac, 2006). Men are more likely than women to refer to quantity in language (e.g., "That house is as large as a football field"; "I had to walk four times as far to school as my son does"); to use directives; to make reference to themselves (i.e., use "I"); and

TABLE 7.2   FEATURES OF LANGUAGE

Feature	Example	Sex Difference
Self-reference	"I"	Male
Directive/imperative	"Close the door"	Male
Quantity terms	"Five miles"	Male
Intensive adverb	"so"; "really"	Female
Use emotions	"afraid"; "loved"	Female
Ask questions	"Why?"	Female
Hedges	"sort of"; "kind of"; "maybe"	Female
Sentence length	longer sentences	Female
Judgment adjectives	"good"; "stupid"	Male
Minimal response	"OK"; "uh-huh"	Female
Qualifiers	"unless"	Female

to use judgment adjectives (e.g, "This is a ridiculous assignment"). Women are more likely than men to use intensive adverbs (e.g., so, really), refer to emotions in language, use longer sentences, ask questions, and use hedges (e.g., sort of, kind of, maybe). Women also are more likely than men to use the **minimal response**, such as saying "uh-huh," "okay," or nodding, while someone is speaking. Some of these differences can be found in the example interactions I provided. However, I do not want to overstate the differences. The fact of the matter is that when communications written by men and women are examined, people typically cannot guess the sex of the writer or speaker (Mulac, 2006). Thus again, there must be more similarities than differences in the language used by men and women.

To better understand the language men and women use, we can classify it along three dimensions (Mulac, Bradac & Gibbons, 2001). First, language is direct or indirect. Men's language is more direct because they use directives; women's language is more indirect because they ask questions and use hedges. Second, language can be succinct or elaborative. Women's longer sentences and use of intensive adverbs make their language more elaborative. Third, language can be instrumental

or affective. Men's reference to quantity is instrumental, and women's use of emotion words is affective. Thus men's language can be said to be instrumental, succinct, and directive, whereas women's language is affective, elaborative, and indirect. Even among children, girls' language is more affiliative and boys' more assertive (Leaper & Smith, 2004).

Qualifiers of Sex Differences

These conclusions about sex differences in language are overly simplistic. Sex differences in language use are not always consistent. One factor that influences the language men and women use is the sex of the person with whom one is talking. Women's greater use of "polite" language, for example, may take place only in their interactions with men. One study found that women used more disclaimers, tag questions, and hedges with men than with women (Carli, 1990).

Language also can serve different purposes. Take interruptions as an example. Most people believe men interrupt more than women, but it may depend on the context. Maltz and Borker (1982) contend that men interrupt to assert themselves and gain the floor, whereas women interrupt to request elaboration or clarification from the speaker. The setting also influences interruptive behavior (Aries, 1996). During informal conversations, women interrupt more than men. Women also often talk at the same time as one another, completing each other's sentences and agreeing with one another. These interruptions convey enthusiasm and involvement in the conversation rather than dominance. Thus interruptions have a different meaning in informal settings. In more formal conversations that have a task focus (which are often the situations in the laboratory), men interrupt more than women. These may be the kinds of interruptions that convey dominance; for example, one person interrupts another to change the subject.

The difference in the meaning of interruptive behavior is illustrated in a study of patient-physician interactions (Hall et al., 1994). Interruptions were associated with lower patient satisfaction when either patient or physician was male but greater patient satisfaction when both patient and physician were female. The investigators concluded that interruptions conveyed dominance when a male was involved in the interaction and enthusiasm when the interaction took place between two women. It may be that the setting was viewed as more formal for men than women, or it may be that the nature of interruptive behavior is different among men and women.

Language also may be more strongly influenced by gender roles than by sex. What we have referred to as female language—the minimal response, hedges, intensive adverbs—is really communal language. What we have referred to as male language—directives and imperatives—is really agentic language. One study showed that psychological gender (i.e., BSRI agency and communion) did a better job of predicting language than biological sex (Janssen & Murachver, 2004).

Another reason for sex differences in language may have to do with the topic of conversation. Men and women speak about different topics that requires different language. In one study, titled "Girls Don't Talk About Garages," college students could accurately predict the sex composition of a dyad talking—not because of the language used but because of the differences in topics (Martin, 1997). Male same-sex dyads talked about sports, women, being trapped in relationships, and drinking; female same-sex dyads talked about relationships, men, clothes, and feelings. Recall the interactions described at the beginning of this section. How did you know the first interaction was between two women and the second was between two men? One way you distinguished the conversations may have been the topic. The topic of the first interaction was a relationship problem and the topic of the second was money. In the study of college students, perceivers were more accurate in identifying same-sex dyads than cross-sex dyads. The greatest confusion was between female-female dyads and cross-sex dyads. The conversations and language used in cross-sex dyads may be more similar to those used in female same-sex dyads. As you will see in Chapter 8, men are more likely than women to change their behavior when interacting with the other sex. Find out for yourself if your classmates can identify the storyteller with Do Gender 7.3.

The same concern I raised about the brevity of interactions for the study of interaction styles applies to the study of language. Sex differences in language are more likely to be found in shorter interactions. In experimental settings, participants are strangers and interactions are brief. This is just the kind of situation in which sex is salient and stereotypes are likely to operate. Sex differences in communication disappear when longer interactions are examined. A study that supported this idea involved

DO GENDER 7.3
Sex Differences in Lanugage Use

Have 5 male friends and 5 female friends write stories about a specific topic—but the same topic (current relationship problem, how they feel about school, relationships with parents, earliest memory). See if your classmates can guess the sex of the writer better than chance (i.e., more than 50%). Ask what information they used to identify the sex of the speaker. Also ask them to rate the stories on the use of the language features shown in Table 7.2. Compare the accurate guesses to the inaccurate guesses to see which information was more diagnostic.

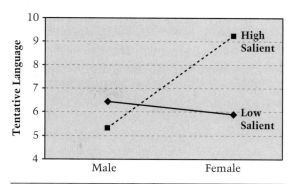

FIGURE 7.4 Women used more tentative language than men when gender was made salient, but women used the same amount of tentative language as men when gender was not salient.
Source: Adapted from Reid et al. (2003).

same-sex and mixed-sex dyads meeting for three or four 90-minute sessions (Wheelan & Verdi, 1992). During the first session, the investigators found sex differences in communication consistent with previous research; after that, however, sex differences disappeared. Thus, as men and women become familiar with each other, their speech may become similar.

One reason that sex differences in language may disappear as people get to know one another is that sex is a less salient feature of the interaction. Gender salience has been found to affect sex differences in language. In a study of college students, either their gender was made salient or their student status was made salient before they engaged in a 10-minute dyadic discussion of a gender-neutral topic (Reid, Keerie, & Palomares, 2003). As shown in Figure 7.4, women used more tentative language than men when gender was salient, but there were no sex differences in tentative language when the student status was made salient. Another study showed that gender salience affected only the language use of gender schematic people—that is, people who are

sensitive to gender (Palomares, 2004). Gender schematic women used more feminine language and less masculine language, but only if gender was made salient. The salience manipulation had similar effects on men's language, but the effects were not as strong. The language of gender aschematic men and women was not affected by the salience manipulation.

An important determinant of sex differences in language use is the sex of the interaction partner—or more importantly the language used by the interaction partner. In a study of e-mail exchanges among college students, men and women were found to use different language but also to use the language that was used by their interaction partner (Thomson, Murachver, & Green, 2001). Thus the most sex differences in language occurred in same-sex exchanges. But when men and women talked to one another, they used the language of their partner, which ended up revealing an overall less gendered language style.

To the extent that sex differences in language are due to socialization, these differences may not generalize to other cultures with different socialization practices. There is a fairly large literature comparing U.S. communication to communication in Japan (Waldron & DiMare, 1998). Many of the sex differences in language found in this chapter do not generalize to Japan. For example, sex differences in assertive language found in the United States are not found in Japan (Thompson, Klopf, & Ishii, 1991). In general, the language that the Japanese use is more similar to the language used by women in Western cultures (e.g., the United States; Wetzel, 1988). Parallels have been drawn between Japanese versus Western language and female versus male language. The Japanese as a culture value language that communicates sensitivity to others' needs, language that includes empathy and agreement. Whereas people from Western cultures would view this language as powerless language, the Japanese do not. Power, in and of itself, is viewed differently by the two cultures. Americans, for example, view power as an attribute of a person, so a person can use more or less powerful language; the Japanese view power as an attribute of a social role or a position. Thus the position confers power, regardless of the language used. It does not make sense to talk about powerful language in Japan. In fact, language viewed as dominant in the United States—being assertive, interrupting someone, challenging someone—is viewed as childish in Japan.

Effects of Language on Perception

Regardless of whether men and women speak differently, people interpret the same speech as different if displayed by a man versus a woman. Some evidence suggests that language influences perceptions of women more than men. In one study, men liked more, and were more influenced by, a woman who used tentative rather than assertive speech, whereas men's speech did not affect men's or women's liking or influenceability (Carli, 1990). Men also viewed the woman who used tentative speech as less competent than the woman who used assertive speech. Does this mean men like less competent women? Thus women are presented with an interesting dilemma when facing a male audience. Women are viewed more favorably in terms of likability when they use so-called "feminine" speech but at the expense of being viewed as competent. This issue is discussed more fully in the section on influence.

See Sidebar 7.2 for a discussion of sex differences in language when sex goes against status—the female versus the male physician.

SIDEBAR 7.2: *Physician-Patient Interactions*

One particularly interesting interaction to study from a gender perspective is the interaction between a patient and a physician. The physician-patient interaction is by definition one of unequal status. When the physician is male and the patient is female, the status difference in roles (physician vs. patient) is congruent with the status difference in sex (male vs. female). But today, it is no longer the case that the physician is always male. Because physician and patient roles are highly structured, with a clearly established hierarchy, male and female physicians might communicate similarly and male and female patients might respond similarly. In other words, the clear-cut demands of these roles may override any sex differences in communication style previously discussed. The research, however, does not support this idea.

Roter, Hall, and Aoki (2002) conducted a meta-analysis of patient-physician interactions, most of which were based on observational studies. They found that female physicians made more active partnership statements (i.e., enlisting patient input, working together on a problem), asked more questions about psychosocial issues, had more emotion-focused talking, and used more positive talk (i.e., reassurance, encouragement, agreement). In other words, as the authors conclude, female primary care physicians engaged in more "patient-centered" communication. Visits with female physicians also lasted 2 minutes longer, which was 10% of the visit. There was no sex difference in the number of general questions asked or the amount of biomedical information provided. Recent studies have confirmed these findings (Zaharias, Piterman, & Liddell, 2004; Zandbelt et al., 2006). The latter study involved videotaped patient-physician interactions and found that female physicians displayed more encouragement, were more attentive, made more summary statements, and reflected on patient comments more than male physicians—all of which can be considered patient-centered communication. The sex of the patient did not affect the interaction.

What are the implications of the differences between male and female physicians' communications? A meta-analysis of patient responses (Hall & Roter, 2002) showed that patients talk more, make more positive statements, discuss more psychosocial issues, and—most importantly—provide more biomedical information to female than male physicians. Thus female physicians may be more successful than male physicians at making patients feel comfortable and eliciting information. The extent to which these differences influence patient health outcomes, however, is unknown.

TAKE HOME POINTS

- Men's language is more direct, succinct, and instrumental, whereas women's language is more indirect, elaborative, and affective.

- Sex differences in language are moderated by a host of variables, including the sex of the interaction partner and the length of the interaction.

- Men's and women's language become more similar in mixed-sex than same-sex dyads, evidence of some accommodation.

- The best way to distinguish male versus female conversation is from the topic rather than any particular feature of language.

- Language influences our perceptions of people; the same language style leads to different inferences when displayed by women versus men.

NONVERBAL BEHAVIOR

Recall the two interactions described in the previous section on language. Now, imagine you can see the people talking. What aspects of their behavior—other than their language—provide you with information about the interaction? Is it only people's verbal response that indicates whether they are listening? What about eye contact? What about posture? Do you feel people are really paying attention when they yawn?

A lot more information is contained in an interaction besides the language used. Aspects of communication that do not include words are referred to as *nonverbal behavior*. The domains of nonverbal behavior that scientists have investigated, especially with respect to gender, are smiling, gazing, accuracy in interpreting emotion (decoding), accuracy in conveying emotion (sending), and touching.

In 2000, Hall, Carter, and Horgan conducted a meta-analytic review of the literature on nonverbal behavior. They concluded that (1) females smile and gaze more than males; (2) females stand closer to others, face others more directly, and are more likely to touch other people; (3) males have more expansive body movements (i.e., take up more space) than females; (4) females are more accurate in interpreting others' emotional expressions and are better able to convey emotions than males. Interestingly, college students' perceptions of sex differences in nonverbal behavior correspond with the sex differences found in the meta-analytic reviews (Briton & Hall, 1995). Thus people's beliefs about sex differences in nonverbal behavior appear to be fairly accurate. Most recently, Hall (2006) concluded that sex differences in nonverbal behavior, in particular smiling and decoding, are larger than most sex differences and larger than most social psychological effects.

Like the other behaviors we have examined in this chapter, sex differences in nonverbal behavior cannot be fully understood without considering the sex of the person with whom one is interacting. Again, men and women accommodate to each other. The sex difference in smiling, gazing, distance, and touch is much larger when comparing same-sex dyads to mixed-sex dyads. For example, the most smiling will be observed between two women, and the least smiling will be observed between two men. Two females will stand closest to one another, two males will stand farthest from one another, and a male/female dyad will fall somewhere in between.

It is possible that gender role rather than sex per se is related to nonverbal behavior. In 1992, Gallaher had college students observe their friends' nonverbal behavior over several days. Gender roles were related to nonverbal behavior, such that femininity was associated with being more expressive and masculinity was associated with being more expansive.

Smiling

Several meta-analyses indicate that females smile more than males (Hall et al., 2000; LaFrance & Hecht, 2000; LaFrance, Hecht, & Paluck, 2003). The effect size seems to be moderate, in the $d = -.40$ range. The sex difference appears to be largest among teenagers (LaFrance et al., 2003) and not consistent among children (Kolaric & Galambos, 1995). An interesting study of yearbook pictures of males and females from 14 different schools in kindergarten through college showed that the sex difference in smiling became significant by second grade, peaked in fourth grade, and persisted through college (Dodd, Russell, & Jenkins, 1999). These findings are cross sectional, however, making it difficult to determine if the effect is due to age or cohort. Students from one of the schools were followed over time. The results were the same, suggesting the sex difference emerges over time.

There are several situational variables that influence the sex difference in smiling. First, the sex difference in smiling seems to be limited to social settings and is especially large when people know they are being observed (LaFrance et al., 2003). Second, there is cross-cultural variation in the sex difference, with the largest difference appearing in Canada ($d = -.59$) and the smallest difference appearing in Britain ($d = -.13$; LaFrance et al., 2003). Finally, smiling seems to be more strongly correlated with personality variables associated with sex, such as sociability, nurturance, and femininity, rather than sex per se (Hall, 1998).

Gazing

Gazing is a difficult nonverbal behavior to interpret. In general, gazing is thought to convey interest and attention; thus it is not surprising that sex differences in gazing have been found in the direction of women gazing more than men. Furthermore, sex differences in gazing (female more than male) are typically larger when the situation evaluated is a friendly one. Yet, in other situations, gazing can convey a different message, in particular, a message related to status. A high-status person, for example, may gaze intently at the person to whom he or she is speaking. To confuse matters even more, sex differences in gazing do not generalize to all other cultures. For example, in Japan, it appears women make less eye contact than men, especially during interactions with other women (Bond & Young Ho, 1978). Eye contact here may convey dominance.

Decoding

Females seem to be more sensitive than males to nonverbal cues, meaning they can more accurately interpret the meaning of nonverbal behavior (Rosip & Hall, 2004). Females are better able to understand the meaning behind such nonverbal cues as facial expression, vocal intonation, and body position. This finding seems to generalize to people in other countries, such as Malaysia, Japan, Hungary, Mexico, New Zealand, Hong Kong, and Israel (Hall et al., 2000). It also generalizes to infants, children, and adolescents (McClure, 2000). Furthermore, the sex of the target does not make a difference in decoding accuracy; that is, females are more accurate than males in decoding both men's and women's emotions. The female advantage is stronger for nonverbal facial behavior than for nonverbal body movements or auditory cues.

One exception to females' decoding accuracy is deception. Females are not more accurate than males at detecting deception unless language is involved, in which case women are better than men at detecting deception (Forrest & Feldman, 2000). If females' decoding ability has to do with their orientation toward facilitating relationships, it is not a surprise that females are not as good as males at detecting deception. Detecting deception would not necessarily foster relationship development, whereas accurately interpreting another's emotions certainly would.

Sending

The counterpart to understanding another's emotions is the ability to convey one's own emotions accurately. Sending reflects the capacity to convey emotions without intentionally doing so. Because emotional expressiveness is central to the female gender role, it is not surprising that women are better senders than men (Hall et al., 2000). That is, others are better able to judge the emotions of a woman than of a man. Again, the difference is larger when judging facial expressions than vocal cues. It is not clear whether a sex difference in sending occurs among children.

Touching

There is not a clear sex difference in touch because the nature of the touch and the context have such a strong influence on whether touch occurs. The sex composition of the dyad is a strong determinant of touch. In an observational study of touch across a variety of settings, women were significantly more likely than men to receive touching, and there was a trend for men to be more likely than women to initiate touch (Major, Schmidlin, & Williams, 1990). Both of these findings are misleading, however, because touching was best understood by considering both the sex of the initiator and the sex of the recipient. As shown in Figure 7.5a, there was greater cross-sex than same-sex touch. Within cross-sex dyads, males were more likely to touch females than females were to touch males. Males initiated more touch—but only toward females; females received more touch—but only when initiated by males.

Other contextual factors, such as age and relationship status, have been investigated in regard to touch. In contrast to interactions among adults, interactions among children show greater same-sex than cross-sex touch (see Figure 7.5b). Among children, it appeared

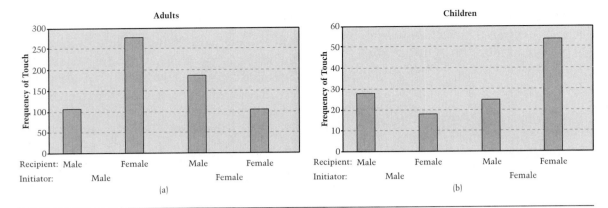

FIGURE 7.5 Among adults, there is greater cross-sex than same-sex touching. Among children, there is greater same-sex than cross-sex touching. Adults are shown in Figure 7.5a and children are shown in Figure 7.5b.
Source: Adapted from Major, Schmidlin, and William (1990).

that females were more likely to initiate touch, but this was due to the high proportion of touching in the female-female dyad compared to the other three dyads. In an observational study of touch among teenagers and adults, men initiated touch toward women among the younger group, but women initiated touch toward men among the older group (Hall & Veccia, 1990). In that study, age is confounded with relationship status, such that younger people have less developed relationships than older people. Among the younger people, men may initiate touch to indicate their control of a newly formed relationship. Among older people, women may initiate touch as an expression of the intimacy of the more developed relationship. Two other observational studies confirmed the fact that men initiate touch more during the early stages of a relationship (dating), and women initiate touch more during the later stages of a relationship (marriage; Guerrero & Andersen, 1994; Willis & Briggs, 1992). An evolutionary explanation for this behavior is that men use touch to seduce a woman into a sexual relationship during the early stages, and women use touch to preserve the intimacy of the relationship during the later stages.

One interesting arena in which to explore touch is sports. Here it is more acceptable for men to touch one another. When male baseball and female softball teams were observed over 20 games, there were no sex differences for the majority of the 32 kinds of same-sex touch coded (Kneidinger, Maple, & Tross, 2001). Among the sex differences that did appear, they were typically in the direction of females engaging in more touching. Specifically, females were more likely to engage in intimate forms of touch with one another, such as group embraces. The outcome of the event also influenced sex differences in touch. After a positive event, men and women were equally likely to touch. However, after a negative event, women were more likely than men to touch—probably reflective of women conveying greater sympathy for one another.

Conduct your own observational study of touch in Do Gender 7.4 to see what variables influence touch.

DO GENDER 7.4
Observational Study
of Touching

Conduct an observational study of touching. Choose a setting, for example, the cafeteria, an airport, the mall, a bar. Have the class break into groups so each group can observe a different setting. Record instances of touch. Record sex of initiator and sex of recipient. Come up with a list of other variables to record that may help you understand touching, such as type of touch, intention of touch, length of touch, age of participants, and relationship status.

TAKE HOME POINTS

- There are fairly robust sex differences in nonverbal behavior.

- Women smile more, gaze more, are better able to express an emotion, and are better able to read another person's emotions.

- The sex difference in touch depends on many factors, including the target of the touch, the age of the participant, and the relationship between the two people. One reason findings are so variable is that touch has many meanings; it can be used to indicate status or to express intimacy.

INFLUENCEABILITY

An important behavior that occurs in the context of social interactions is interpersonal influence. Recall that one reason children play with members of the same sex is that girls find it difficult to influence boys. Does this difficulty hold up among adults? Are men more influential than women? Are men or women more susceptible to influence? Do men or women exert influence in the same ways?

Who Is Influenced?

The situation plays an important role in who is influenced. It turns out that dispositional characteristics do not predict who is easily influenced as well as situational characteristics. Women may be more easily influenced than men, but it is because they find themselves in different situations than those of men. People interact differently with women than with men, and the interaction style used with women leads to influence.

This idea was shown in a dyadic interaction study conducted by Carli (1989). Men and women were placed in same-sex or mixed-sex dyads and asked to talk about an issue with which they disagreed. Participants' opinions on lowering the drinking age and providing free day care for working parents were obtained prior to creating the dyads so that disagreement on the issue could be assured. The pair then discussed the topic for 10 minutes. One of the partners in each dyad was randomly assigned to try to persuade the partner. The discussion was videotaped and later coded for number of task contributions (giving suggestions or opinions), agreements, disagreements, questions, negative social behaviors (showing negative affect), and positive social behaviors (showing positive affect; see Table 7.3 for examples of codes). After the discussion, each member of the dyad indicated privately what his or her opinion was on the topic. The change in opinion from before to after the discussion was the measure of influence.

Neither task behavior nor positive social behavior was related to attitude change. Disagreement was related to *less* attitude change, or less influence. The only interaction style associated with greater influence was agreement. People who interacted with a partner who expressed at least some agreement were more likely to change their attitudes in the direction of

TABLE 7.3   SAMPLE INTERACTION STYLES

Task Behavior
   "You should ask your roommate not to drink in your room."
Agreement
   "I agree that alcoholism is an important problem in our society."
Disagreement
   "I disagree that lowering the drinking age will solve any of our problems."
Questions
   "Why do you think lowering the drinking age would decrease rates of alcoholism?"
Negative Social Behaviors
   "If you think it is OK to drink any alcohol and drive, then you are an idiot."
Positive Social Behavior
   "We all have to figure out how to deal with people who drink and drive."

Q: Why are women more easily influenced than men?

A: Because people (both men and women) agree more
   with women and agreement facilitates influence.

Being female ⟶ Others express agreement ⟶ Influence

FIGURE 7.6   Model of influence process.

the partner than people who interacted with a partner who expressed complete disagreement.

It makes sense that we are more receptive to the ideas of someone who finds a way to agree with us; disagreement puts us on the defensive. However, our intuition is to disagree with someone to change the person's mind. When people were randomly assigned to the persuade condition, they used more disagreement, less agreement, and more task behavior—but only with males, not with females. Unfortunately, this is exactly opposite of the kind of behavior that is persuasive. Thus it is not surprising that men and women were more successful in persuading females than males; men and women were more likely to agree with females.

Thus women are not more easily influenced than men due to some fundamental female trait, but due to the fact that people feel more comfortable in interactions with women and thus display agreeable behavior. Women are more easily influenced than men because of the way people behave toward men and women. People use ineffective influence strategies with men (e.g., disagreement) but express agreement with women, and agreement leads to influence. Figure 7.6 illustrates the process by which women come to be more easily influenced than men.

Who Is Influential?

Men are more influential than women, partly because men are viewed as more credible sources. Would women be as influential as, or more influential than, men if their credibility were enhanced? A great deal of evidence suggests that women who adopt more masculine language or communication styles or who are made to appear more competent are actually *less* influential, at least when the target audience is male. In one study, U.S. managers were sent an application packet that included an interview transcript containing assertive, rational, or flexible influence strategies (Buttner & McEnally, 1996). The managers, mostly male, were most likely to hire the male who displayed the assertive style and least likely to hire the female who displayed the assertive style. Another study showed that masculine language used by women increased their influence when the audience was female but decreased their

influence when the audience was male. Carli (1990) instructed college students to listen to a speech that was either assertive or tentative and given by either a male or female confederate. The tentative version of the speech included tag questions, hedges, and disclaimers, whereas the assertive version did not. In the speech, the confederate argued that the college bus should begin charging a fare, an issue with which all participants disagreed. As shown in the left half of Figure 7.7, female speakers had a greater influence on female respondents when the speech was assertive rather than tentative; however, female speakers had a greater influence on male respondents when their speech was tentative rather than assertive. As shown in the right half

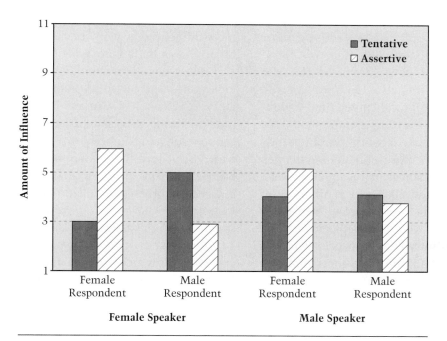

FIGURE 7.7   Female speakers were more effective in influencing females when they used assertive rather than tentative language. However, female speakers were more effective in influencing males when they used tentative rather than assertive language. Male speakers' ability to influence was not affected by the nature of the language they used toward either a male or a female audience.

Source: Adapted from Carli (1990).

of Figure 7.7, male speakers had a similar influence on respondents regardless of the style of their speech.

Interestingly, both male and female respondents rated the female tentative speaker as less competent and less knowledgeable than the female assertive speaker. Why were male respondents more influenced by a less competent speaker? Carli (1990) suggests the first thing a person of lower status must convey to a person of higher status is that he or she is not trying to compete for status. Using tentative language communicates this. Thus male respondents may have been more receptive to the female tentative speaker's arguments because they did not have to be concerned with status issues. The female assertive speaker might have been perceived as challenging the men's higher status. Thus women may have to adopt a more stereotypical style to influence men.

Other studies have supported the idea that men are more influenced by a woman who behaves in a stereotypical rather than a non-stereotypical way—even though the stereotype for females is lacking credibility. One study showed that men are more influenced by women who use tentative than assertive language (Reid, Keerie, & Palomares, 2003). In another study, male college students were more influenced by a female speaker who was depicted as very traditional than by a female speaker who was depicted as nontraditional—even though the traditional female was judged as *less* competent (Matschiner & Murnen, 1999). The male students liked the traditional more than the nontraditional female, and liking leads to influence. In a second study, college students were asked to view a videotape of either a male or a female speaker who discussed a position on an issue in either a sociable or task-oriented style (Carli, LaFleur, & Loeber, 1995). After the speech, students rated how much they liked the speaker and how much

they agreed with the speaker's position on the issue. As in the previous study, male students were more influenced by the female speaker with a sociable style than the female speaker with a task-oriented style. Male students were also more influenced by the male speaker with a task-oriented style than the female speaker with a task-oriented style. Female students' influenceability was not affected by speaker style or speaker sex. For male students, likability was strongly related to influence when the speaker was female but not when the speaker was male. And, male students liked sociable female speakers more than task-oriented female speakers. Thus again, for male students, the likability of a female speaker led to influence, and a sociable style but not a task-oriented style was associated with likability and influence. Again, men are more influenced by women who use a feminine rather than a masculine style of speaking.

Even among preschoolers, dominance in a female is not perceived favorably (Sebanc et al., 2003). Preschoolers worked in groups on a movie-viewing task that had the potential for cooperation and competition. Peers liked dominant boys more than nondominant boys but liked dominant girls less than nondominant girls. Thus women face a dilemma when they are expected to behave in a submissive way but the situation requires assertive skills to succeed.

Even when men and women have equal expertise in an area, women may exert less influence than men—especially if the task is masculine in nature. In one study, 40 teams of 3 to 5 students were assembled to work on a decision-making task (Thomas-Hunt & Phillips, 2004)—a task that was determined to be masculine in nature. Each group contained a male or a female expert; expertise was established by individual performance on the task prior to group discussion. Men and women were equally likely to be defined as experts in these groups, meaning there was no sex difference on individual performance. How did the groups respond when there was a male or a female expert in their midst? First, the female experts were judged as having less knowledge about the task than the male experts. Second, female experts had less influence on the group's overall performance. Finally, groups that contained a female expert had a poorer outcome compared to groups that contained a male expert. How can we explain these findings? When an expert disagrees with the group or offers an opinion that differs from that of the group, it is possible that the consequences are more negative for women than men. To the extent women are aware of this possibility, the female experts may have been less likely to assert themselves. Thus as shown in Figure 7.8, the minimal contribution of the female expert could have accounted for the poor outcomes. Negative stereotypes of assertive females may lead female experts to be more tentative, to minimize their contributions, and censor their remarks. The cumulative effect of these behaviors is that the female expert has less influence on the group outcome, and the group

perceives her to have less expertise. In the end, the group is not able to take advantage of the expertise of the female compared to the male expert.

Influence Strategies

Another reason women are more easily influenced and less influential than men may have to do with the ways men and women try to influence others. Some studies have found that men and women use different influence strategies. In a study of dating couples who discussed a problem in their relationship, females were more likely than males to use coercion, and males were more likely than females to use logic and reason (Oriña, Wood, & Simpson, 2002). Logic did not have any impact on influence, but coercion was related to *less* influence. That study focused on a previously unexplored influence strategy, referred to as "relationship referencing." This occurs when we remind our partner about the importance of the relationship in the course of exerting influence. Men and women were equally likely to use this strategy, and it was the most effective strategy in terms of changing the partner's opinion.

The Lack of Female Experts' Influence on Groups

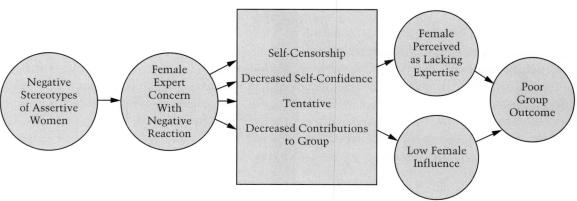

FIGURE 7.8   Model of how groups are not able to take advantage of female expertise.
Source: Adapted from Thomas-Hunt and Phillips (2004).

- Women are more easily influenced than men because people adopt a more agreeable interaction style with women than men. And, agreement leads to influence.

- Men are more influential than women because they are viewed as more credible sources of information.

- A woman's language may enhance her credibility, but whether it enhances her ability to influence depends on the sex of the audience.

- Men react negatively to women who use an assertive influence style. Men are more influenced by a woman who uses a traditional, more feminine style of speaking, largely because she is more likable and less threatening to men's status. For men, likability leads to influence—when the speaker is female.

- Women are faced with a dilemma when interacting with men: If they behave in a way that enhances their competence in the eyes of men, it may also reduce men's liking for them and receptivity to their ideas.

EXPLANATIONS FOR SEX DIFFERENCES IN COMMUNICATION

A variety of explanations are available for the differences I have discussed in this chapter on male and female communication. Here I discuss three of them. The first explanation states that differences in communication evolve from children's tendencies to play with same-sex peers. The second theory, status theory, suggests any differences in communication between men and women are due to their unequal status. Once one controls for the status or power differential between men and women, sex differences in communication disappear. Third is social role theory, which argues that the roles men and women hold in society are responsible for sex differences in

communication. In particular, the female role emphasizes connections to others, whereas the male role emphasizes separation from others. These are not the only theories of sex differences in communication, as biological and evolutionary explanations also have been advanced for sex differences in nonverbal behavior (Andersen, 2006; Ellis, 2006), but they are the three that have received the most attention in the literature.

Sex-Segregated Interactions in Early Life

Interaction Styles.   Maccoby (1998) suggests that children's style of interacting with same-sex peers is responsible for the sex differences in interaction styles that emerge in adulthood. Boys' interactions are hierarchical, oriented toward establishing dominance. Girls' interactions are more lateral, oriented toward providing mutual support. These differences could account for the task-oriented style of men and the socioemotional style of women.

Language.   Men and women may use different language because different kinds of language were functional during same-sex play in childhood. Maltz and Borker (1982) argue that boys and girls grow up in different cultures, and these cultures contribute to sex differences in language. It is not that boys and girls are socialized to talk in different ways; rather, different kinds of conversation have evolved in same-sex girls' groups compared to same-sex boys' groups. Recall that boys play in larger groups, often outdoors, and with a background of noise and a tone of competition. This kind of play requires assertive language and the use of demands rather than requests. Girls' play is often quieter, more cooperative, nonhierarchical, and takes place in smaller groups. This kind of play is more consistent with the use of polite suggestions. According to Maltz and Borker, sex differences in language are larger among children than adults. As adults, we learn how to interact with the other sex and accommodate our behavior accordingly.

Status Theory

Sex is inherently confounded with status. Men have a higher status and more power than women. Status theory has been used to explain sex differences in interaction styles, in language, in nonverbal behavior, and in influence-ability.

Interaction Styles. One theory of how status influences behavior is **expectations states theory**. According to this theory, group members form expectations about their own and others' abilities, which are based on the value they assign to people in the group. We expect the high-status person to contribute more and the low-status person to facilitate the contributions of the high-status person (Smith-Lovin & Robinson, 1992). Because men have a higher status than women, we have higher expectations of men's abilities compared to women's abilities. This theory suggests that sex differ-

ences in interaction styles stem from our more positive evaluation of men's abilities compared to women's. In other words, in the absence of any other information about men's and women's abilities, sex will be interpreted as status during a group interaction.

A classic study that supported this theory was conducted by Wood and Karten (1986). College students were assigned to four-person mixed-sex groups which met to discuss a task. In half of the groups, one male and one female were randomly assigned to have a high-status position and the other male and female to have a low-status position. Status was manipulated by revealing either high or low scores on a fake aptitude test. The other half of the groups did not have status manipulated, and group members were aware only of each other's sex. Group members were asked to discuss a dilemma and resolve it. When status was not manipulated, group members perceived men as more competent than women, as talking more than women, and as engaged in more task behavior than women. As shown in Figure 7.9a, when status was manipulated, high-status people

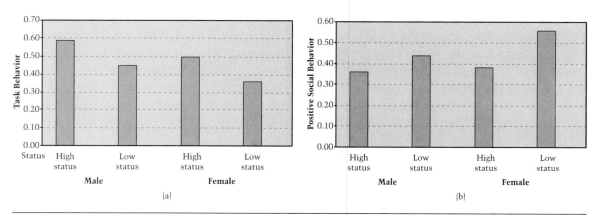

FIGURE 7.9 (a) Effect of sex and status on task behavior. When status was manipulated, the high-status person, male or female, was more likely to engage in task behavior than the low-status person. (b) Effect of sex and status on social behavior. When status was manipulated, the low-status person, male or female, was more likely to engage in positive social behavior than the high-status person.
Source: Adapted from Wood and Karten (1986).

engaged in more task behavior than low-status people regardless of sex. Further, group members perceived high-status people, regardless of sex, as more competent than low-status people. As shown in Figure 7.9b, low-status people engaged in more positive social behavior than high-status people. However, when status was not manipulated, women engaged in more positive social behavior than men did. This study shows that status is responsible both for people's tendency to perceive men as more competent than women and for some of the sex differences in interaction styles.

Status theory also was tested by a field study of adults in the community (Moskowitz, Suh, & Desaulniers, 1994). Participants monitored their interactions with their boss, coworkers, and subordinates over 20 days. For each interaction, respondents rated whether dominant versus submissive behavior and agreeable versus quarrelsome behavior occurred. The former category of behavior was referred to as *agency* and the latter as *communion*. The status of the work role (whether the person was a supervisor or subordinate or coworker) but not sex predicted agentic behaviors. People were more dominant when they were supervisors and more submissive when they were supervisees, regardless of sex. However, sex, but not the status of the work role, predicted communal behavior: Women behaved more communally than men regardless of the status of their interaction partners. Thus this study partly supported status theory and partly supported social role theory, discussed in the next section.

Expectations states theory says we have higher expectations for the contributions of the high-status person. However, the relevance of the task to men and women may alter people's expectations about capabilities. We expect men to be more competent than women on masculine tasks, and we expect women to be more competent on feminine tasks. Yet the sex difference in interaction styles does not necessarily disappear or reverse itself when feminine tasks are studied. Thus status based on expectations states theory alone cannot explain sex differences in interaction styles.

Language. Parallels can be drawn between powerful language and male communication and powerless language and female communication (Kalbfleisch & Herold, 2006). If a male talks more, interrupts more, and uses fewer hedges in an interaction with a female, we cannot discern whether the difference is due to sex or status. The more powerful person is more likely to interrupt, to give directives, to talk more in groups, and to show anger—language often attributed to men. The less powerful person inhibits, uses tentative and deferential language, uses other-directed language, displays sadness, and censors one's remarks—language often attributed to women.

One study compared the effects of sex and status on language and found that status accounted for differences in verbal communication, but that sex accounted for differences in nonverbal communication (Johnson, 1994). Undergraduates role-played three-person organizations, in which one member was assigned to be a leader and two were assigned to be employees. Four groups were examined: male manager with male employees, male manager with female employees, female manager with male employees, and female manager with female employees. Overall, managers engaged in more talking, used less back-channel communication, and used fewer qualifiers compared to employees—regardless of manager's sex, employees' sex, or the sex composition of the group. (**Back-channel responses** include sentence completion, brief questions of clarification, and the minimal response.) Thus status rather than sex was linked to differences in

SIDEBAR 7.3: *Is It Dr. X? Professor X? or Janet?*

Several studies show that college students are more likely to address male professors by titles and female professors by first names. This is *not* due to the fact that male and female professors request different forms of address. What are the implications of calling your professor Dr. Smith or Janet, Dr. Jones or Jim? Several studies have shown that people associate a teacher who is referred to by a title as opposed to a first name with higher status (Stewart et al., 2003). In one of these, college students read a transcript of a class session in which the male or female instructor was addressed by first name or title by the students (Takiff, Sanchez, & Stewart, 2001). Students perceived the professor as having a higher status (i.e., higher salary, more likely to have tenure) when addressed by title rather than first name. However, the title was associated with perceiving the female professor as less accessible to students and the male professor as more accessible to students. Thus female professors may have to choose between status and accessibility.

language. Nonverbal behavior, specifically, smiling and laughing, was not predicted by status but was predicted by sex: In general, females laughed more than males, regardless of their position in the organization. Surprisingly, the most smiling was by males in mixed-sex groups regardless of whether they were managers or employees; the least smiling occurred among males in same-sex groups. See Sidebar 7.3 for an interesting discussion of status and language that you encounter daily.

Nonverbal Behavior.   Henley (1977) was one of the first to argue that differences in nonverbal behavior imply power or status. She argued that the greater social sensitivity of women was due to their low status. She suggested that women would have better decoding skills than men and engage in some nonverbal behaviors more frequently than men (e.g., smiling) because women are in a lower-status position in society. It is important for low-status people to monitor the environment because other people have influence over them.

Status theory has been tested as an explanation of women's greater interpersonal sensitivity compared to men. In a study of dyadic interactions between convenience store employees, researchers examined sex and status differences in nonverbal behaviors (Hall & Friedman, 1999). Videotapes of the interaction showed that women smiled more, nodded more, and used less dominant vocal language. However, the status of the employees—as determined by the employees themselves, the CEO, and Human Resources—was not linked to any of these differences.

Even if low status were related to greater interpersonal sensitivity, one would not know if this finding were due to low-status people being more accurate decoders or high-status people providing more cues about their feelings. A study that examined both possibilities found that subordinates more accurately detected the leader's feelings *not* because of the subordinate's abilities, but because the leader was more expressive (Snodgrass, Hecht, & Ploutz-Snyder, 1998). Therefore, subordinate sensitivity is due to leaders being more expressive of feelings rather than subordinates being more aware of those feelings. In sum, little evidence suggests that subordinates are more skilled than leaders in accurately decoding the other person's feelings.

Status clearly cannot account for the sex difference in smiling (Hall, Horgan, & Carter, 2002). In experimental studies where status is manipulated, there is no effect of status manipulations or people's perceptions of status on smiling. Interestingly, people have stereotypes that low-status people smile more than high-status people, but this stereotype has not been confirmed by the data. Hecht and LaFrance (1998) assigned undergraduates to interact in dyads in which members were either equal or unequal in power. The status of the person did not predict smiling. There was more total smiling in the equal power condition than the unequal power condition. In terms of sex differences, females engaged in more smiling than males, but only in the equal power condition. Status was related to the *freedom to smile* rather than the tendency to smile, meaning that the high-status person could smile whenever he or she was in a good mood but the low-status person could not. The investigators suggested that people in positions of low power have constraints imposed on them in terms of how they behave; they are not as free as those in higher-power positions to express their feelings.

The relation of status to touch is not clear. One variable that may shed light on the issue is the nature of touch. In an observational study of people at an academic conference, status was related to different kinds of touch (Hall, 1996). Status was measured in terms of age, rank at the institution, reputation of the institution, and number of articles published in the previous few years. High-status people were observed to engage in more affectionate touching, such as touching an arm or shoulder, whereas low-status people were more likely to engage in formal touching, such as a handshake. The authors concluded that high- and low-status persons may be equally likely to engage in touching, but that they initiate touch for different reasons: High-status people may

touch to display their power, whereas low-status people may touch to gain power.

From these and other studies, there is growing evidence that status cannot account for sex differences in nonverbal behavior. A meta-analytic review of the literature examined whether status was related to perceptions of nonverbal behavior as well as to actual nonverbal behavior (Hall, Coats, & LeBeau, 2005). Status was described as the "vertical dimension of relationships" and included power, dominance, and hierarchy. Although people perceived a relation between the vertical dimension of relationships and less smiling, more gazing, more touch, more interruptions, less interpersonal distance, and more expressive faces, in actuality there was little relation between the vertical dimension of relationships and nonverbal behavior.

Influenceability. Sex differences in influenceability may be due to status. Drawing on expectations states theory, Lockheed and Zelditch (1985) argued that the high-status person is more influential because we have higher expectations for this person's performance. If the task is masculine or gender neutral, we will have higher expectations for men's performance and confer men greater status. If the task is feminine, we will have higher expectations for women's performance and confer women greater status. In a review of 64 studies on influenceability in mixed-sex groups, 45 showed men to have greater influence, 11 showed no difference, and 8 showed women to have greater influence (Lockheed & Zelditch, 1985). Sex differences in influenceability were strongest when the task was masculine, when we presumably assign men a high status. On feminine tasks, there was typically no sex difference in influenceability, but some studies showed a female advantage.

Status may also explain who is more susceptible to influence during an interaction.

Eagly and Wood (1982) had college students read vignettes in which one person was trying to influence another. In the experimental condition, information about the dyad members' respective statuses was manipulated by providing job titles. In the control condition, no information except the dyad members' sex was given. In the control condition, students perceived females as lower in status and more susceptible to influence than males. In the experimental condition, students perceived the low-status person as being more susceptible to influence than the high-status person regardless of sex.

Status or power may explain sex differences in influence strategies. In one study, college students imagined they were interacting with a same-sex or other-sex person and had more power (an expert), less power (a novice), or power similar to the person (Sagrestano, 1992). Students were asked how they would influence their partner. Men and women reported similar influence strategies regardless of whether their partner was male or female. Both men and women were most likely to use direct and bilateral strategies (e.g., bargaining). However, the power relation between participant and partner affected influence strategies; direct and unilateral strategies (e.g., telling person what you want) were used more often by participants who had high power, and bilateral strategies were used more often by participants who were equal in power to their partner.

Cross-cultural evidence indicates that power is a stronger predictor of influence strategies than sex. Influence strategies were investigated among U.S., Japanese, and Korean students attending a U.S. college (Steil & Hillman, 1993). The three most frequently used strategies by all three groups were direct influence strategies: stating the importance of one's position, reasoning, and convincing the partner. The three least frequently used strategies by

all three groups were indirect influence strategies: acquiescing, evading, and using an advocate. The investigators found that power, but not sex, was associated with strategy use. People who said they had greater power in their relationships were less likely to use indirect influence tactics. There were minor cultural differences in that Japanese and Korean students tended to endorse more polite tactics than U.S. students. For example, Japanese and Korean students said they were more likely to acquiesce and less likely to try to convince their partner compared to U.S. students.

TAKE HOME POINTS

- Status theory suggests that sex differences in communication are due to the status differences between men and women.

- The best tests of this theory have been laboratory studies in which men and women are randomly assigned to high- and low-status positions.

- These kinds of studies have made a convincing case that sex differences in interaction styles, language, and influence are largely due to status.

- Status theory does not seem to be a good explanation of sex differences in nonverbal behavior.

Social Role Theory

Social role theory suggests that our expectations about male and female behavior stem from our stereotypes about the different social roles men and women hold in society. Women are more likely than men to hold domestic roles, for example. Even within the work setting, men and women are likely to hold different roles; for example, men are more likely to be the leaders and the supervisors, whereas women are more likely to be the subordinates. Gender roles are an important social role that men and women hold, leading men to behave in agentic or instrumental ways and women to behave in communal or relationship-maintaining ways. To the extent that other roles become more salient than gender roles, people's behavior will be more influenced by other roles than gender roles.

Interaction Styles.   Parsons and Bales (1955) applied social role theory to sex differences in interaction style. They first observed that small group interactions were characterized by two forms of group behavior: task behavior and social behavior. They argued that both kinds of behavior were important to the viability of the group, but that the two were incompatible. In other words, different people were needed to serve the two distinct functions. This idea was confirmed by Bales and Slater (1955), who observed that the best liked person in the group was not the person considered to have the best ideas. The person with the best ideas gave suggestions and opinions: task-oriented behavior. The person who was best liked made statements indicating group solidarity, made statements that relieved group tension, and asked for opinions and suggestions: socioemotional behavior.

Parsons and Bales (1955) suggested that families were small groups, and that husbands and wives held different roles within the family. The father is responsible for task behavior, such as providing for the family, whereas the mother is responsible for socioemotional behavior, such as raising children. Parsons and Bales linked men's and women's traditional family roles to group interactions. They suggested that all groups had two functions: to accomplish the goals of the group and to preserve the group as a unit. They suggested that the first function fit with men's instrumental roles and the second fit with women's socioemotional roles.

Other people have argued more directly that men and women display different interaction styles because of the way they are socialized in our society (Wood & Rhodes, 1992). Females are socialized to be communal, whereas males are socialized to be agentic. A communal person is likely to engage in positive social behavior during group interactions, whereas an agentic person is likely to engage in instrumental social behavior during group interactions.

The study previously described by Carli (1989) supports a social role rather than a status interpretation of interaction styles. She found that men displayed the most task behavior and women displayed the most social behavior when men and women were compared in same-sex dyads rather than mixed-sex dyads. If sex differences in interaction style were due to status, we would find larger differences in interaction styles in mixed-sex or unequal status dyads as opposed to same-sex dyads.

Language.   The differences in the language that men and women use may be considered to reflect different emphases on relationships. Women are said to talk in ways that maintain relationships; they encourage others to communicate by asking questions and making responses that encourage conversation. Men's language is less facilitative of relationships. Men interrupt others, challenge others, disagree, ignore others' comments by delayed use of the minimal response or giving no response, and make declarations of fact and opinion.

However, the research has shown that it is not clear whether women's language is related to their lower status or to their gender role's greater emphasis on relationships. Some aspects of women's language are related to status and some are related to relationship maintenance. For example, hedges and disclaimers may reflect women's lower status compared to men, but intensifiers and verbal reinforcers may reflect women's socioemotional orientation. These ideas were examined in a study of same-sex and mixed-sex dyads' discussions of a topic on which the partners disagreed (Carli, 1990). Women used more disclaimers and hedges in mixed-sex than in same-sex dyads, which suggests that status played a role in the behavior. However, women used more intensifiers and verbal reinforcers compared to men in same-sex dyads, which is the kind of language that serves to maintain relationships.

Nonverbal Behavior.   Many of the nonverbal behaviors in which women engage can be viewed as behaviors that promote and foster good relationships. Smiling at others, gazing at others, and standing close to others can all be viewed as affiliative behavior. Recall that the study conducted by Johnson (1994) showed that sex rather than status was related to nonverbal behavior, such as smiling and laughing. A study of social interactions among groups of college students showed that smiling was unrelated to each person's status in the group but was related to the likability of group members (Cashdan, 1998). The previously mentioned study by Hall and Friedman (1999) showed that status could not explain sex differences in nonverbal behavior. Videotapes of employee interactions showed that women were warmer, more expressive, smiled more, nodded more, and interrupted less compared to men. The individual's status within the organization or relative to the partner did not explain these sex differences.

Influence.   Is it also possible that personality characteristics correlated with sex determine influence strategies? Steil and Weltman (1992) examined whether personality variables (e.g., nurturance and dominance) were associated with influence strategies. They found that

women engaged in more indirect bilateral strategies (e.g., displaying positive affect, smiling) than men, but that personality characteristics accounted for this sex difference. Greater nurturance and less dominance were associated with the use of indirect bilateral strategies.

TAKE HOME POINTS

- Social role theory states that the differences in men's and women's communication styles have to do with the different social roles men and women hold in our society, the male role being agentic and the female role being communal.

- Men's task behavior and women's positive social behavior fit their social roles.

- Some aspects of language fit men's goal of gaining control over the interaction (e.g., directives) and some aspects fit women's goal of encouraging communication (e.g., back-channel responses).

- Social role theory is most helpful in explaining sex differences in nonverbal behavior. Women's smiling, touching (in some contexts), decoding ability, and expressions of emotions are all aimed at fostering relationships.

- Women's greater use of indirect influence strategies compared to men has been explained by higher levels of nurturance and lower levels of dominance.

LEADERSHIP

Who Emerges as a Leader

Who is more likely to emerge as a leader—a man or a woman? Although male and female students view leadership roles in organizations as equally desirable, women perceive that they are less likely to attain these positions compared to men (Killeen, Lopez-Zatra, & Eagly, 2006). A meta-analysis of group interaction studies evaluated who emerged as the leader in the group

(Eagly & Karau, 1991). Leadership was measured by both objective indicators of group participation as well as respondents' reports of who appeared to be the group leader. Across laboratory and field studies and across both measures of leadership, men were more likely than women to emerge as leaders. Men contributed more to the group and were more likely to be perceived and chosen as leaders. The nature of the leadership role influenced who emerged as a leader. Men were especially likely to emerge as leaders when task leadership was needed ($d = +.41$). When the nature of the task was not specified, men also were more likely to emerge as leaders, but the effect was smaller ($d = +.29$). When social leadership was necessary, there was a small effect for women to be more likely to emerge as leaders ($d = -.18$).

There are two methodological limitations of this research. First, the majority of the studies were conducted with college students in the laboratory. More studies are needed in the field to see who actually emerges as a leader in an organization. Second, laboratory interactions are brief; in the real world, we usually have more than 30 minutes to determine who will be the chairperson of an organization. In their meta-analytic review, Eagly and Karau (1991) found that the length of the interaction influenced who emerged as a leader: Males were more likely to emerge as leaders when the group interaction lasted less than 20 minutes ($d = +.58$), but there was no sex difference if the group lasted longer than one session ($d = +.09$). Again, when people have little information about one another, gender-role stereotypes or category-based expectancies influence behavior. With more time, and presumably more information, stereotypes have less impact on behavior.

Gender-related traits may be more important than sex in predicting who emerges as the leader in a group. In a study of college students enrolled in a business course, agency, but not communion (as measured with the BSRI), was associated with self-perceptions and others' perceptions of leadership (Kent & Moss, 1994). Self-esteem, dominance, and other traits related to masculinity also seem to predict leadership (Aries, 1996). However, it is unclear whether these same traits predict leadership in women. Masculine traits are a stronger predictor of leadership in men because the traits are congruent with men's gender role.

One masculine trait associated with leadership is dominance. Men may be more likely than women to emerge as leaders because they behave in a more dominant manner. Nyquist and Spence (1986) paired high- and low-dominant persons together in same-sex and cross-sex dyads. The dyad was first asked to decide who would be the leader on a gender-neutral task (a board game). In same-sex dyads, the high-dominant person was chosen to be the leader 73% of the time. In dyads where the male was high in dominance and the female was low in dominance, the high-dominant male was chosen to be the leader in 90% of the cases. Yet in dyads where the female was high in dominance and the male was low in dominance, the high-dominant female was chosen to be the leader only 35% of the time. Thus when the role of dominance was congruent with sex, the choice of leader was clear: male. But was the male chosen because of his sex or because of his dominance? When the female was high in dominance and the male was low in dominance, the male was still chosen. In this case, sex appeared to be more important than dominance in establishing who was to be the leader.

This finding was examined more closely by Davis and Gilbert (1989) who wondered if men were chosen as leaders in these dyads because the dyad members did not know each other very well and had little information to use to select a leader. Thus, Davis and Gilbert conducted a similar experiment but first had dyad members work together on a task that would reveal the personality trait of dominance before selecting a leader. When participants were asked to choose a leader for a subsequent task, the high-dominant person was chosen to be the leader regardless of sex. In dyads with a high-dominant male and a low-dominant female, the high-dominant male was chosen to be leader 75% of the time. In dyads with a high-dominant female and a low-dominant male, the high-dominant female was chosen to be leader 71% of the time.

Taken together, these two studies show we are more likely to rely on stereotypes in the absence of other information about people. But once we obtain more information, we are likely to use that information when deciding how to behave. Again, this is the distinction between category-based expectancies and target-based expectancies.

Leadership Styles

Do men and women have different styles of leadership? Social role theory suggests that men and women behave similarly when occupying similar roles. However, because gender roles may still be operating on the part of the leader as well as on the part of perceivers, men's and women's behavior is likely to differ in the leadership role (Eagly & Johannesen-Schmidt, 2001). Women face a conflict between the characteristics of the leadership role and the female gender role.

Eagly and Johnson (1990) conducted a meta-analytic review of sex differences in leadership style. Three leadership styles were evaluated: task oriented, socioemotional, and democratic/autocratic. The task-oriented leader lays out plans, articulates rules, and organizes how a task will be accomplished. The socioemotional leader is focused on maintaining group harmony, concentrates on helping people in the group, and explains problems in a friendly

manner. The democratic leader encourages others to participate in the group's decisions, whereas the autocratic leader discourages others' participation. Eagly and Johnson found no sex difference in task orientation ($d = .00$) or interpersonal orientation ($d = +.04$). Females, however, were found to be more democratic than males ($d = -.22$). The investigators examined the setting in which each study was conducted. They reasoned that sex differences in leadership style would be minimal in organizational settings where participants know one another, their roles are clear, and the nature of the task is clear. By contrast, the authors predicted that sex differences would appear in laboratory studies where participants are strangers and the task is ambiguous, a context in which gender roles would be salient. The results supported the hypothesis. Men and women did have different leadership styles in laboratory studies (men task oriented and women socioemotional) but not in organizational studies. However, the sex difference in democratic leadership was consistent across the two types of studies.

More recently, leadership styles have been described as transactional, transformational, or laissez-faire. A transformational style involves inspiration, motivation, providing a role model, and motivating subordinates. A transactional style of leadership is a more conventional style that involves monitoring subordinates, rewarding behavior, and intervening. Descriptors of each are shown in Table 7.4 (Powell & Graves, 2006). A meta-analysis of these three leadership styles showed that women had a more transformational style than men ($d = -.10$; Eagly, Johannesen-Schmidt, & van Engen, 2003). Women also were more likely than men to display the contingent reward aspect of the transactional style ($d = -.13$), whereas men were more likely to display the two other components of the transactional style—active

TABLE 7.4 CONTEMPORARY LEADERSHIP STYLES

Transformational
- **charismatic**—provide role model
- **inspiring**—display optimism and excitement about mission
- **intellectually stimulating**—encourage new perspectives
- **mentoring**—provide individualized attention

Transactional
- **contingent reward**—rewards if achieve goals
- **management by exception**—intervening to correct problem
  - **active management by exception**—monitor performance
  - **passive management by exception**—wait for someone to report problem

management by exception ($d = +.12$) and passive management by exception ($d = +.27$). Men also were more likely to use laissez-faire leadership than women ($d = +.16$). A second meta-analysis revealed similar results (van Engen & Willemsen, 2004). That meta-analysis showed that the sex difference in the transformational style is larger in more recent than older studies. Interestingly, studies authored by males (compared to females) were more likely to show that women had a transactional style of leadership.

Which leader and style of leadership is most effective? A meta-analytic review found absolutely no sex difference in leader effectivenss (Eagly, Karau & Makhijani, 1995). Instead, the most effective leader held a gender-congruent role. When the leadership role was congruent with the male gender role (high task ability, more typical of males), men engaged in more task behavior and were more effective than women. When the leadership role was congruent with the female gender role (high interpersonal ability, cooperation required), women engaged in more task behavior and were more effective than men. It appears that those who occupy gender-incongruent roles are perceived to lack the skill necessary to execute task behavior.

A meta-analytic review that compared the transactional to the transformational style of leadership showed that the transformational style of leadership is most effective (Lowe, Kroeck, & Sivasubramaniam, 1996). The way in which effectiveness was measured influenced the size of this effect. The transformational style of leadership was related to both subordinates' perceptions of the leader's effectiveness and to more objective organizational measures, but the former effects were larger than the latter. Both men and women perceive passive management by exception as negative but active management by exception, contingent reward, and transformational leadership as positive (Walumbwa, Wu, & Ojode, 2004).

Views of Leaders

"Think manager—think male" is the name given to the phenomenon that people still perceive the successful manager to resemble the typical male rather than the typical female (Schein, 2001). Although this view has declined among women, it has persisted among men over the past 3 decades and generalizes to other countries, such as China, Japan, and Germany. If the leadership role is incongruent with the female gender role, how do people view women as leaders? Do people judge women leaders less harshly because they have overcome gender-role stereotypes? Or, do people evaluate women leaders more negatively because they are behaving in a way inconsistent with gender-role norms?

There are two kinds of prejudice against female leaders (Eagly & Karau, 2002). First, due to descriptive stereotypes, people may evaluate a woman leader less favorably than a man leader because she lacks the agentic qualities needed for leadership. Second, due to prescriptive stereotypes, people may evaluate a woman leader less favorably *if* she possesses agentic leadership qualities because those qualities conflict with the female gender role. Eagly and colleagues (1992) conducted a meta-analysis on studies that evaluated leaders to determine if people were biased for or against women. These studies typically presented people (often college students) either with written vignettes that manipulated the sex of a described leader or with confederates who enacted a leadership role. The meta-analysis found a very small effect indicating a bias against female leaders. People perceived female leaders to be less competent than male leaders ($d = +.09$) and were less satisfied with female compared to male leaders ($d = +.10$). The bias against female leaders was larger when they used a more masculine style of leadership (i.e., autocratic and directive). In addition, male respondents judged female leaders more harshly than female respondents did. A more recent laboratory study confirmed the finding that female leaders are viewed more negatively than male leaders. Students who inferred that the masked leader on a video was female rated her as more dominant, more assertive, and less warm compared to those who inferred that the leader was male (Koch, 2004).

These findings fit with other research reported in this chapter that women are not viewed favorably, especially by men, when they behave in ways inconsistent with the female gender role. Agentic traits in women are viewed as implying a lack of communal traits (Heilman, 2001). In one study, college students viewed a high-agency man as more qualified for a job that required social skills than a high-agency woman (Rudman & Glick, 2001). Thus a high-agency woman may be viewed as less qualified for a leadership position than a high-agency man because she is thought to lack social skills. There is evidence that women leaders are perceived more favorably when agentic traits are complemented by communal traits (Eagly & Karau, 2002).

In the laboratory, sex is often salient. In the field, there may be a host of other variables that influence people's perceptions of a leader other than his or her sex. In fact, studies of people in the workforce do not support a bias against female leaders. Three studies of employees' evaluations of their managers in business, industry, government, and health care found no bias against female leaders (Bass, Avolio, & Atwater, 1996). Subordinates were either more satisfied with female managers or equally satisfied with male and female managers. Across the three studies, female managers were rated as more charismatic, or as better role models, compared to male leaders. In a study of 2,482 managers from 459 organizations across the United States, women managers were perceived by their bosses and their employees to be better leaders in terms of communal characteristics (e.g., communication, feedback, and empowerment) as well as agentic characteristics (e.g., goal setting, decisiveness, and planning; Pfaff, 1999). In some occupations, a feminine leadership style is the most highly valued. For example, international managers are most effective if they have strong interpersonal and cooperative skills. Ironically, few women hold those positions (2% to 15%; Harris, 1998).

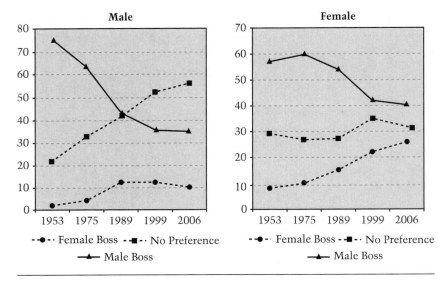

FIGURE 7.10 Preference for a male boss has substantially declined over time and having no preference has substantially increased over time—both especially for men. Preference for a female boss has slightly increased, more so for women.

Source: Adapted from Carroll (2006).

One way to tap people's perceptions of leaders is to ask whether they would prefer to work for a man or a woman. A Gallup Poll conducted since 1953 shows that preference for a male boss has declined—especially among men (Carroll, 2006a). In 1953, both men and women preferred a male boss: sixty-six percent preferred a male, 5% preferred a female, and 25% had no preference. Today, as shown in Figure 7.10, the preference for a male boss has declined and having no preference has increased—especially for men. The preference for a female boss increased slightly, more so among women. In 2006, 34% of males said they would prefer a male boss, 10% a female boss, but the majority—56%—had no preference. Among females, 40% said they would prefer a male boss, 26% a female boss, and 37% had no preference.

How do we reconcile the different findings from the laboratory and the field? Perhaps we should dismiss the laboratory studies because the tasks are not realistic. However, we should also realize that men and women who are leaders in organizations are not necessarily a representative sample of men and women. It may take a certain kind of woman to emerge in a leadership role in the real world.

TAKE HOME POINTS

- Gender and leadership is one area of research where the findings from laboratory studies may not generalize to the field.

- Men are more likely than women to emerge as leaders in laboratory studies where participants are often strangers and have only a brief opportunity to interact.

- More important than sex may be personality traits that go along with sex, such as dominance. In the real world, it is more likely that the dominant person will emerge as the leader regardless of sex. Of course, men are more likely than women to be dominant.

- Women are more likely to display a transformational style of leadership, whereas men are more likely to display a transactional style of leadership. The transformational style is most effective.

- Laboratory studies have found a small but consistent negative bias against female leaders. The bias is especially strong among men. In the field, however, people view women leaders favorably, sometimes even more favorably than men.

- Leadership is one area of research where it is especially important that we maximize the external validity of our controlled laboratory studies.

EMOTION

Two people receive news that an accident has caused a neighbor to lose her baby. One cries; the other does not. You probably imagine that the one who cries is female, the more emotional sex. Two people witness some teenagers soaping their car on Halloween. One yells at the teenagers and chases them down the street; the other ignores the incident. You probably imagine the one yelling is male, the more . . . the more what? Yes, anger, too, is an emotion. So, who is the more emotional sex?

Certainly the stereotype claims women are more emotional than men. In fact, one of the items on the PAQ femininity scale is "very emotional." However, the femininity scale is really a measure of communion or expressiveness rather than emotionality. How should we decide whether men or women are more emotional or whether the sexes are equally emotional? Researchers have examined three primary sources of information to address this issue: people's self-reports of their experience of emotion, people's nonverbal expressions of emotion, and people's physiological responses to emotion stimuli. Unfortunately, there is not

a consistent pattern of findings across these three modalities as to whether one sex is more emotional than the other. I review each source of information.

The Experience of Emotion

First, we can ask whether men and women experience emotions similarly. Many investigators argue that men and women have similar emotional experiences. Ekman (1992) points out there is a universal set of emotions that both men and women experience and common facial expressions that generalize across the two sexes as well as across different cultures.

Do men and women experience emotions with the same frequency? We typically address this question by asking men and women to provide direct reports as to how often they experience a particular emotion. Studies that use this method typically reveal that women report greater emotion than men (LaFrance & Banaji, 1992). Women say that they experience emotions more intensely than men and that they let emotions influence their decisions (van Middendorp et al., 2005). In a nationally representative sample, participants were asked how often they felt a variety of emotions (Simon & Nath, 2004). Although there was no sex difference in the frequency of emotions experienced, men were more likely than women to report positive emotions and women were more likely than men to report negative emotions. The latter sex difference disappeared when income was statistically controlled, implying that the reason women experience more negative emotions than men is due to their lower status.

Other studies measure emotionality indirectly through self-report. For example, participants might be asked to describe an emotional experience, or conversations of participants could be recorded; these verbalizations are then coded for the number of emotion words used,

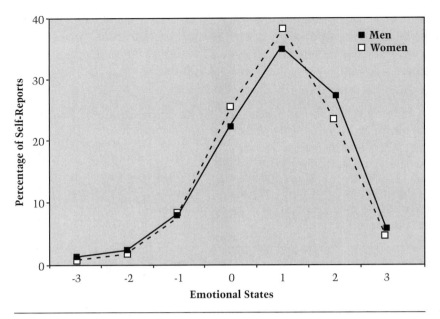

FIGURE 7.11 Men and women report similar frequencies of both positive and negative emotions throughout the day.

which is taken to be an index of emotionality. Such indirect self-report methods typically do not reveal sex differences (LaFrance & Banaji, 1992). In other words, men and women use the same amount of emotion words when describing an emotional event.

One concern about research showing sex differences in the frequency or amount of emotion is that these reports are susceptible to a recall bias (Larson & Pleck, 1999). Much of the data that show women experience more emotion than men come from self-report studies where men and women recall their emotions over a period of time. Possibly women are simply better than men at recalling their emotions. To address this issue, Larson and Pleck (1999) had married couples carry electronic pagers and beeped them periodically throughout the day so they could report their current emotional state. These online reports revealed that men and women experience similar emotions. The frequencies of both positive and negative

emotions are shown in Figure 7.11. Other studies have used this same methodology with college students and adults and confirmed the finding (Larson & Pleck, 1999).

What accounts for the discrepancy in findings between retrospective reports and online measures of emotion? Some suggest that women report more emotion than men on retrospective measures because women encode emotion in greater detail than men. For example, one study showed that women were better able to recall more positive and more negative life events than men (Seidlitz & Diener, 1998). Women also used more words to describe both positive and negative events than men, which the authors interpreted as reflecting a sex difference in encoding emotion. Furthermore, this sex difference in encoding accounted for the sex difference in number of events recalled. Another study showed that across seven samples, women scored higher than men on a test of emotion complexity and differentiation, which suggests women have more complicated representations of emotion (Feldman, Sussman, & Zigler, 2000).

The next question is why women encode emotion in greater detail than men. It may be that women pay more attention to emotional events than men because emotions occur within the context of relationships, and relationships are more central to women's than men's self-concepts. Richards and Gross (2000) suggested an alternative explanation: Men are more likely than women to suppress emotion, which interferes with the memory for emotional events. In support of their hypotheses, they found that people who were randomly assigned to suppress their emotion while watching a film (i.e., told not to let any feelings show that they experience during the film) had poorer memories for the film than those who were simply told to watch the film. As you will see in Chapter 9, among married couples, men are more likely than women to suppress emotion during discussions of relationship conflict.

Cross-cultural research also has examined whether there are sex differences in the experience of emotion. Across 37 countries, there was no sex difference in the experience of the powerful emotions (e.g., anger; Fischer et al., 2004). However, women around the world were more likely than men to report the powerless emotions—namely, fear, sadness, shame, and guilt. Women's status in the particular country did not affect women's reports of emotions but did affect men's reports of emotions. In countries where women held a higher status, such as the United States, men reported less intense powerless emotions. The authors suggested that power is more strongly associated with the male role in Western than non-Western countries. However, it appears that the higher status of women in Western countries does not translate into men and women experiencing similar emotions.

The Expression of Emotion

Despite men's and women's similar experiences of emotion, considerable evidence supports sex differences in the expression of emotion (Simon & Nath, 2004). Women report they are more emotionally expressive than men. For example, female undergraduates rated themselves higher on spontaneous expressions of emotions and emotional sensitivity (recognizing and responding to others' emotions), whereas male undergraduates rated themselves higher on emotional control (i.e., regulating emotions; Guerrero & Reiter, 1998). Self-report data are hardly convincing, however, because men and women are clearly aware of the stereotypes that women are emotional and expressive and men are not emotional and inexpressive.

Observational data also support the claim that women are more expressive than men. Sex differences in the expression of emotion have been found as early as infancy. A study of 2-year-olds showed that girls were more expressive than boys during play (Malatesta et al., 1989). Observational data are not without their limitations, however. Coders are typically not blind to respondent sex and may rate the same face as more expressive if believed to be female than male. Try Do Gender 7.5 to see how

DO GENDER 7.5
Perception of Emotion
in Boys and Girls

Videotape an infant or child playing. Make sure the sex of the child is not obvious. Tell 10 people the child is male and 10 people the child is female. Ask them to rate how emotional the child is, how expressive the child is, and what emotion the child is experiencing. Does the sex of the child influence these reports?

knowledge of sex can influence perceptions of emotion. However, other observational and physiological data are more compelling. Both men and women can more easily identify the emotion of a female than of a male (LaFrance & Banaji, 1992), suggesting that women's faces are more emotionally expressive than men's faces. When men and women experience similar emotions, physiological measures reveal greater facial activity in the female face (Thunberg & Dimberg, 2000).

Females are not more likely than males to express all emotions. Women are more likely to express emotions such as happiness, sadness, fear, guilt, and shame, whereas men are more likely to express anger, pride, and contempt (Brody & Hall, 1993).

The expression of anger may be influenced by sex. How do men and women respond when they become angry? Women report that they are more likely than men to cry and to express hurt feelings when angry (Fehr et al., 1999). In the laboratory, men and women responded the same to an anger-provoking incident (Biaggio, 1989). However, when men and women recorded how they responded to anger-provoking incidents in their daily lives over a 2-week period, men were more likely to respond with physical and verbal antagonism, whereas women reported more passive responses. Recall that one limitation of laboratory research is that men and women have a similar status and are treated the same, which may limit the extent to which findings generalize to the real world.

Crying is one behavior in which sex differences in emotional expression are thought to exist. There are sex similarities and differences with respect to crying. College women report being more likely than college men to cry in response to anger, fear, sadness, and disappointment (Timmers et al., 1998). Women also report crying more often and with more intensity than men (Lombardo et al., 1983). And, women are more likely to cry across a variety of situations than men (e.g., wedding, breakup of a relationship). However, men and women are equally likely to cry when a close other dies. Men and women also rank order the situations that would evoke the most and least crying similarly.

Gender roles have been related to the expression of emotion and often show stronger relations than respondent's sex. Femininity or communion, specifically, has been associated with emotional expression (Brody & Hall, 1993). Two studies have associated androgyny with emotional expression. In a study that compared androgynous, masculine, and feminine persons, androgynous persons were found to be more emotionally expressive than masculine persons, and feminine persons fell between the two groups (Kring & Gordon, 1998). The relation of androgyny to the expression of such a variety of emotions may have to do with the fact that androgyny incorporates both femininity and masculinity, which are each linked to the expression of different emotions: Androgyny includes femininity, which is associated with expressions of love, happiness, and sadness, along with masculinity, which is associated with expressions of anger and hate. In another study, dominance and affiliation explained the sex difference in displays of anger and disgust (Hess, Adams, & Kleck, 2005). That is, students thought the more dominant and less affiliative person would display more anger and disgust. In a follow-up, students were asked what emotion should be displayed in response to an anger-provoking event by a person who was either described as dominant or submissive. The high-dominant male and female were expected to react with anger. However, the low-dominant person was expected to react differently depending on sex: Females were expected to react with sadness, whereas males were expected to react with anger. The authors concluded that dominance can override our stereotypes with respect to expressions of anger, but when someone is not dominant, we revert back to our stereotypes about the acceptability of anger expression.

Physiological Measures of Emotion

Given the limitations of self-report methods of measuring emotion, we might hope that physiological methods would provide a more definitive answer to the issue of sex differences in emotions. Unfortunately, physiological indicators of emotionality are controversial. Researchers find it difficult to agree on which physiological measure best taps emotion: heart rate, blood pressure, galvanic skin response? Even within a given physiological measure, findings are inconsistent across studies. For example, studies that examine galvanic skin response show that sometimes males and sometimes females are more responsive to emotional stimuli (LaFrance & Banaji, 1992). When multiple measures of physiological reactivity are used, findings within a study are often inconsistent across measures. Despite these difficulties, a couple of findings have emerged. One consistent finding is that women show greater facial activity compared to men, as measured by electromyograph (EMG) responses. EMG response is a facial muscle movement especially sensitive to negative emotion. With the exception of EMG responses, it appears there is slightly more evidence that men are more physiologically reactive to emotions than women (LaFrance & Banaji, 1992).

How do we reconcile the different conclusions reached by self-report and physiological data? One answer is that women are more outwardly expressive and men are more internally reactive to emotional stimuli. This idea was supported by a study in which college students viewed a film depicting one of three emotions (sadness, fear, happiness; Kring & Gordon, 1998). There were no sex differences in the self-report of an emotion. However, videotaped documentation showed that women were more emotionally expressive than men, and physiological measures evidenced that men were more reactive to some of the films. The investigators suggested men were more likely to be internalizers with respect to emotions, by experiencing them physiologically but not expressing them, and women were more likely to be externalizers with respect to emotions, by expressing them outwardly but not reacting physiologically.

Basis of Emotion

The idea that women express emotions outwardly and men express emotions inwardly suggests the basis of an emotion may differ for men and women. That is, men and women may base their emotions on different sources of information. Pennebaker and Roberts (1992) have made a compelling case that men infer their emotion from internal physiology and women infer their emotion from environmental cues. Men seem to be more sensitive to internal physiology than women. In the real world, information from internal physiology and external stimuli are both available. When men and women have been brought into the laboratory where external cues are held constant and physiological cues are manipulated, men are better than women at predicting the physiological changes within their body.

For example, Pennebaker and Watson (1988) asked people with normal-range blood pressure to come into the laboratory and carry out a series of tasks. Blood pressure was measured throughout the tasks and estimated by participants. Respondents also carried a portable blood pressure monitor at home and estimated their blood pressure once a day over a period of 2 weeks. Men and women were equally accurate in estimating their blood pressure at home, where internal and external information was available. Men and women also were more accurate at home than in the laboratory. However, in the laboratory, where the external cues were held constant and only internal physiological information was available, men were more accurate than women.

In an old but classic study, Cox and colleagues (1985) asked a group of insulin-dependent diabetics to estimate their blood glucose levels about 4 times a day for 10 days at home, and about 54 times over a 24-hour period in the hospital, where blood glucose levels were manipulated. Men and women were equally accurate in estimating their blood glucose levels at home and more accurate at home than in the laboratory. However, men were more accurate than women in the laboratory. Again, in the natural environment, two sources of information are available to people with diabetes: how they are feeling physiologically and environmental information, such as time of day, nature of food eaten, time of last insulin injection, and stressfulness of current circumstances. These studies suggest that in the natural environment, women attend to environmental cues and men attend to internal cues.

Pennebaker and Roberts (1992) offer a variety of explanations for this phenomenon, but they do not favor any particular one. Possibly biological differences between men and women make physiological information more available to men. Perhaps the lower status of women leads them to pay more attention to their environment, even in the case of determining their own emotions.

TAKE HOME POINTS

- Much of the research that shows men experience less emotion or less intense emotion than women is based on retrospective measures.

- Larson and colleagues' studies of online emotion show no sex differences in the experience of emotion, suggesting that men and women are equally likely to experience emotion.

- One reason that women recall more emotion than men is that women encode emotional events in greater detail than men.

- Women are more likely than men to express the majority of emotions; the one exception is anger, which men express more than women.

- Men seem to be more physiologically reactive to emotion than women.

- The bases of emotion also may differ for men and women, such that women attend more to the environment and men attend more to internal physiology.

SUPPORT PROVISION IN INTERACTIONS

Deborah Tannen (1990) begins one section of her popular book *You Just Don't Understand* by relaying the following interaction (p. 49):

> Eve had a lump removed from her breast. Shortly after the operation, talking to her sister, she said that she found it upsetting to have been cut into, and that looking at the stitches was distressing because they left a seam that had changed the contour of her breast. Her sister said, "I know. When I had my operation I felt the same way." Eve made the same observation to her friend Karen, who said, "I know. It's like your body has been violated." But when she told her husband, Mark, how she felt, he said, "You can have plastic surgery to cover up the scar and restore the shape of your breast."

Eve did not find her husband's remarks reassuring. Of course, Mark was not trying to offer reassurance. He was offering her advice, which he thought would make her feel better.

One important communication between men and women involves the discussion of problems and the exchange of support. According to Tannen (1990), men are more likely to respond to problems by providing advice and women by providing sympathy. Women do not wish to receive advice any more than men wish to receive sympathy. Women inquire about a person's problems to show their concern, whereas men do not inquire about a person's problems out of respect for the person's privacy. According to Tannen, these differences in support provision and support expectancies make for a great deal of conflict between men and women.

Is there evidence behind Tannen's (1990) thinking? One study seemed to provide evidence for most of Tannen's assertions. Men and women stated how they would respond to a series of hypothetical problems (Basow & Rubenfeld, 2003). Men were more likely than

women to change the subject, and women were more likely than men to express sympathy. However, there was no sex difference in the provision of advice.

That study was criticized by MacGeorge and colleagues (2004) on several grounds. First, MacGeorge and colleagues noted that the similarities in men's and women's responses were greatly overlooked. As shown in Figure 7.12, men and women are both much more likely to offer sympathy than joke around or change the subject. Yet the interpretation of the findings brought much more attention to the differences between men and women. Second, the methodology used may be vulnerable to demand characteristics. Men and women may be reporting how they are expected to respond rather than as to how they would actually respond. Thus MacGeorge and colleagues undertook their own study by having adults respond out loud as to what they would say in response to a series of hypothetical same-sex friend problems. Responses were then coded

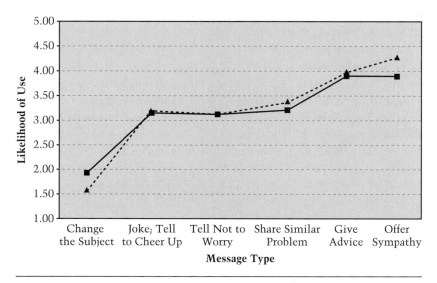

FIGURE 7.12 Men's and women's responses to a friend's problems in the Basow & Rubenfeld (2003) study.
Source: MacGeorge et al. (2004).

into different categories. Similar proportions of men's and women's responses were coded as sympathy, sharing a similar problem, asking questions, or minimization, but proportionally more of men's responses could be classified as advice compared to women. Here the similarities in support provision greatly outweighed the differences.

Support provision also has been examined in the laboratory by studying how men and women actually respond to problems. There are some inconsistencies in the results across studies, but one thing is clear: There is little support for the claim that men provide more advice, and only modest support for the idea that women provide more empathy.

I was involved in a study that examined support exchanges between strangers in the laboratory (Mickelson, Helgeson, & Weiner, 1995). One member of the dyad shared a problem with the other, and the other had the opportunity to respond. Objective coders rated these responses from transcripts of the audio-taped conversations. Dyad members also indicated what kind of support they provided and received. According to coders, male participants received more negative responses (i.e., minimization, changing the subject) than did female participants; that is, both men and women responded negatively to men sharing a problem. (No wonder men choose not to share their problems!) There was no evidence that men provided more advice than women according to coders' ratings or self-reports. Female listeners reported that they provided more emotional support than male listeners, but coders did not confirm this difference; in other words, women reported providing more emotional support than men did, but outside observers did not agree. Knowledge of gender-role stereotypes and norms may have influenced participants' reports. As suggested by MacGeorge

and colleagues (2004), participants may be responding according to how they expect themselves to behave rather than according to how they actually behave. It is also possible that women are truly providing more emotional support than men, but that objective coders cannot code such subjective behavior accurately.

Sex differences in supportive interactions also have been examined in the context of ongoing relationships. In a laboratory-based study of college students, same-sex and cross-sex friends shared a problem with one another (Fritz, Nagurney, & Helgeson, 2003). The participants and objective coders agreed that women provided more emotional support than men—to both men and women. Men, in general, did not provide more advice than women, but men provided more advice to other men; that is, the greatest amount of advice occurred in the context of the male-male dyad. In another study, pairs of same-sex and cross-sex friends discussed how their relationship had changed since college (Leaper et al., 1995). Conversations were audiotaped and transcribed, and the responses of the listener were coded. There were twice as many "active understanding" responses in the female-female dyad than any other dyad. Active understanding reflects emotional support, specifically, acknowledging the speaker's feelings and encouraging the speaker to reflect on issues. There were no dyad differences in advice giving. Finally, a study of newlywed couples showed no sex differences in instrumental behavior (advice) or emotional behavior (reassurance, encouragement) during problem disclosure (Pasch, Bradbury, & Davila, 1997).

Thus, despite people's perceptions, there is not much evidence that men and women respond differently to problems; there is some evidence that women provide more emotional support, but little evidence for sex differences in advice sharing. McWilliams and Howard (1993), however, point out that men's and women's advice may be perceived differently. Specifically, male advice may be interpreted as instrumental and female advice as communal. The gist of this is that men's advice would be taken as a serious attempt to tell someone what to do and women's advice would be viewed as an attempt to help or convey concern about the problem. The bottom line is that there are many more similarities (as shown in Figure 7.12) than differences in the way that men and women respond to problems.

It is also possible that gender roles rather than sex may be more strongly related to support provision. In the laboratory study of friends sharing problems just discussed (Fritz et al., 2003), the gender-related traits of the partner were associated with the kind of support he or she provided. Communal partners provided more emotional support, and agentic partners provided more advice. In this study, communion and agency were better predictors of support provision than sex. Other studies have shown that communion is related to expressions of sympathy, less advice, and less changing the subject, whereas agency is related to minimizing the problem (Basow & Rubenfeld, 2003; MacGeorge et al., 2004).

SUMMARY

Boys and girls clearly have different styles of interacting with one another. Boys play in groups that are loud, boisterous, and hierarchical, whereas girls play in dyads that are quiet, conversational, and egalitarian. A strong preference to play with same-sex peers likely exacerbates the difference in play styles. The source of the different styles—biology versus socialization and cognition—is not clear. The distinct play styles map onto the differences in adult interaction styles. In general, studies of small groups show that men are more task oriented and women are more socioemotional. However, these general findings are qualified by a number of variables: the nature of the task, the sex of the interaction partner, and the length of the interaction. Sex differences are strongest for gender-typed tasks, for interactions with same-sex people, and when interactions are brief.

Men and women differ in their use of some features of language. Men's language is more instrumental, succinct, and directive, whereas women's language is more affective, elaborative, and indirect. Women's language has been described as promoting relationships but also as being unassertive. Women's style of speaking appears to have negative implications when used by women but not men. In particular, men like—but view as less competent—a woman who uses feminine rather than masculine language.

There are a number of sex differences in nonverbal behavior: Women smile more, gaze more, are better at conveying emotion, and are better at decoding others' emotions compared to men. Sex differences in touch are more complicated. Among children, touch is more frequent among same-sex peers than cross-sex peers. Among adults, touch is more frequent among cross-sex dyads than same-sex dyads. Within adult cross-sex dyads, touch is determined by relationship status: Men initiate touch during the early stages of a relationship, and women initiate touch during the later stages. In general, sex differences in nonverbal behavior are more frequently observed among same-sex dyads than cross-sex dyads.

In addition to sex, gender roles may influence nonverbal behavior. However, these effects have rarely been explored.

There are three primary explanations for sex differences in communication: sex-segregated interactions in early life, status, and social role. Boys' and girls' tendencies to interact with same-sex peers leads to divergent play styles that include different forms of communication. According to status theory, men's communication is a function of their higher status, and women's communication is a function of their lower status. A number of compelling studies show that men and women behave the same when status is held constant. Evidence for status theory is especially strong in studies of group interactions. According to social role theory, men's communication is a function of their instrumental orientation, and women's communication is a function of their expressive orientation. Support for this theory comes largely from studies showing that nonverbal differences between men and women persist across situations, including different statuses.

Research on social influence generally shows that men are more influential and women are more easily influenced. Men are more influential partly due to their being viewed as more credible sources of information. Some evidence suggests that women are more influential when they adopt a feminine, less assertive way of speaking than when they adopt a more masculine, self-confident style—at least when the audience is male. Studies have shown that susceptibility to influence depends on the nature of the task and the interaction style used. A primary reason that women are more easily influenced than men is that people are nicer to women and more agreeable; people argue with men. Agreement leads to influence, but disagreement does not. Do sex differences in influence have anything

to do with the styles men and women use? Early studies indicated that men use more direct influence tactics compared to women. However, more recent studies show that other variables, such as the personality trait of dominance and relationship characteristics, are better predictors of influence strategies.

If men are more influential, it follows that men are more likely to assume the role of leader in a group. Men are more likely to emerge as leaders, especially when the task is masculine, when interactions are brief, and when men behave in ways congruent with their gender role (i.e., dominant). Despite the fact that men are more likely than women to be leaders, women leaders are more likely than men leaders to use the transformational style of leadership which has been determined to be the most effective style. People's views of male and female leaders depend on whether the study is conducted in the laboratory or the field. Whereas laboratory studies indicate a bias against women, field studies indicate a bias in favor of women. Some research shows the same style may be viewed differently when displayed by a man versus a woman. Again, women seem to benefit from using a more gender-congruent, socioemotional style than a gender-incongruent, task-oriented style of leadership.

In general, men and women seem to experience emotion similarly, although women are more emotionally expressive than men. Sex differences in emotional expression depend on the specific emotion: Women are more likely to express sadness, love, and fear, whereas men are more likely to express anger and pride. There is some evidence that emotion for women has a more external focus; women express emotion externally and use cues from the environment to determine emotional states. By contrast, emotion for men has a more internal focus; they react to emotion physiologically but do not necessarily express it outwardly. Men also rely on internal states rather than external cues to determine feelings.

Finally, there is a pervasive conception that men and women provide different kinds of support when sharing problems. Men are thought to provide advice and women to provide sympathy. Laboratory studies, however, have revealed more support for the latter than the former.

DISCUSSION QUESTIONS

1. Compare laboratory and field research on sex differences in communication. In which areas of communication do you expect laboratory research and field research to come to different conclusions?
2. Discuss boys' and girls' different play styles and explanations of their origins.
3. What are some of the factors that influence men's and women's interaction styles?
4. Which sex differences in language and nonverbal behavior are best explained by status theory, and which are best explained by social role theory?
5. Imagine you are studying patient-physician communication. What other variables would be important to know besides the sex of the participants?
6. What trait variables and what situational variables lead to being influenced?
7. Is there a sex difference in emotionality?
8. How does the social environment influence men's and women's expression of emotion?
9. What is the best leadership style for women to adopt? Under what circumstances?
10. Do men and women respond to other people's problems differently?

SUGGESTED READING

Aries, E. (1996). *Men and women in interaction.* New York: Oxford University Press.

Carli, L. L. (1989). Gender differences in interaction style and influence. *Journal of Personality and Social Psychology, 56,* 565–576.

Dindia, K., & Canary, D. J. (2006) (Eds.). *Sex differences and similarities in communication: Critical essays and empirical investigations of sex and gender in interaction* (2nd ed.). Mahwah, NJ: Erlbaum.

Fischer, A. H. (1997). *Gender and emotion.* New York: Cambridge University Press.

Maccoby, E. E. (1998). *The two sexes: Growing up apart, coming together.* Cambridge, MA: Harvard University Press.

Underwood, M. K. (2003). *Social aggression among girls.* New York: The Guilford Press.

KEY TERMS

Back-channel response—Response that facilitates communication, including sentence completion and use of the minimal response.

Egoistic dominance—Interaction style characterized by verbal aggression that intends to demonstrate superiority over other participants in the interaction.

Expectations states theory—States that group members form expectations about their own and others' abilities which influence the nature of interactions.

Minimal response—Response that encourages the speaker to continue, such as "uh-huh" or "OK."

Negative social behavior—Behavior during group interaction that could harm a relationship, such as disagreement and provoking conflict.

Positive social behavior—Social behaviors engaged in during group interactions that are intended to maintain group harmony.

Prosocial dominance—Interaction style characterized by providing instruction or assistance that intends to foster connection between those involved in the interaction.

Relational aggression—Aggressive interaction behavior usually expressed by girls that is characterized by social alienation tactics such as excluding someone from an activity or threatening not to be a person's friend anymore.

Task behavior—Social behavior, such as asking questions and offering suggestions, that is directed toward achieving a specific goal.

FRIENDSHIP

Batman and Robin, Sherlock Holmes and Watson, Tom Sawyer and Huckleberry Finn, Butch Cassidy and the Sundance Kid, the Lone Ranger and Tonto. Who symbolizes friendship to you? What are some famous pairs of friends? What do all these pairs of friends have in common? They are men (see Figure 8.1). When I asked some students if they could think of a famous pair of female friends, the best anyone could come up with was Laverne and Shirley—or maybe Thelma and Louise. Does the bond between two men epitomize friendship? As you will see in this chapter, it depends on what constitutes friendship.

Much of this chapter focuses on friendships between men and friendships between women, or same-sex friends. Although romantic partners can certainly be friends (in fact, I hope they are!), studies on friendship typically focus on platonic, non-romantic relationships. However, platonic friendship does exist between men and women. This area of research is referred to as cross-sex friendship, and I discuss it toward the end of the chapter. Today, one arena in which cross-sex friendships are likely to form is in the workplace. Because women are almost as likely as men to work outside the home and because women are more likely to work in jobs once held exclusively by men, men and women are more likely to come into contact with one another at work. I examine the scant literature on friendships at work. The literature on same-sex friendship and cross-sex friendship typically assumes heterosexuality. Therefore, I also review the research on friendship among gay men and lesbians.

There are at least two levels of analyses to the study of gender and friendship (Wright, 2006). First, there is the **dispositional level of analysis**, which emphasizes the characteristics of the person as a determinant of friendship. What characteristics of a person predict friendship? One attribute of a person is his or her sex; another is his or her gender role. An example of a dispositional analysis

FIGURE 8.1   Batman and Robin are a famous pair of same-sex friends.

detail the quality of friendship. *Quantity* refers to the number of friends or the size of the network. *Quality* refers to the nature of the friendship. Is it close? Is it intimate? What functions does the friendship serve? I discuss specific aspects of friendship such as self-disclosure, intimacy, and conflict. The structural level of analysis appears as I describe how friendship changes across the life span. Then I turn to the literature on cross-sex friendship. I compare cross-sex friendship to same-sex friendship, describe the unique features of cross-sex friendship, and discuss changes in the structure of cross-sex friendship across the life span. The literature on cross-sex friendship leads into the literature on friendship at work. Finally, I conclude the chapter with a discussion of the nature of friendship among gay men and lesbians.

NETWORK SIZE

Do males and females have the same number of friends? The answer is unclear. Most studies show that boys and girls have a network of friends similar in size and structure (Belle, 1989; Urberg et al., 1995). As described in the previous chapter, there are some structural differences in boys' play versus girls' play that may lead boys to have slightly larger social networks than girls. Girls are more likely to interact in dyads and to spend time talking to one another, whereas boys are more likely to spend time in large groups that are focused on some activity. Girls are more likely to have a best friend (Golombok & Fivush, 1994; Urberg et al., 1995) and to distinguish between a friend and a nonfriend. In fact, girls' relationships are more exclusive than boys' (Brown, Way, & Duff, 1999). That is, it is more difficult to join a girls' group than a boys' group, perhaps because girls' groups are smaller and more intimate. In a study of sixth- through

is the research showing that women's relationships are more intimate than those of men because women are more likely than men to self-disclose. The analysis focuses on a characteristic of women as a determinant of friendship closeness: their tendency to self-disclose. There is also a **structural level of analysis** that emphasizes the different positions of men and women in society. One position or role in society that men traditionally have held more than women is the work role. An example of a structural level of analysis is the research showing that men have more cross-sex friendships than women because men are more likely than women to work outside the home. The structural level of analysis also calls attention to the impact of situational variables on gender and friendship.

In reviewing research on friendship, I begin with an examination of the quantity of friendships and then describe in more twelfth-graders, girls were more likely than boys to be in a clique (Urberg et al., 1995).

Among adults, some studies show that women have more friends, some studies show that men have more friends, and other studies show no sex difference in number of friends (Wright, 1999). One reason that it is difficult to determine if there are sex differences in the size of friendship networks is that the *concept* of friend may differ for men and women. Now, we discuss the nature of men's and women's friendship.

TAKE HOME POINTS

- It is unlikely that network size differs vastly between boys and girls or men and women.

- It may appear at times that boys have more friends than girls, just because boys play in larger groups than girls.

THE NATURE OF FRIENDSHIP

Friendship is another area of research where the differences between males and females are overemphasized compared to the similarities. There are numerous ways in which men's and women's friendships are quite similar. Yet it is true that women's friendships are closer than those of men and friendships with women are closer than friendships with men. There are some important differences in the nature of men's and women's friendship that may explain these sex differences. First, I review the similarities, and then I turn to the differences.

Sex Similarities

There are important similarities between men's and women's friendships. One way in which men's and women's friendships are similar is in terms of what men and women want from a friend. Both rate trust and authenticity as

the most important dimensions of friendship (Parker & de Vries, 1993). Although men and women may differ in how important they perceive a feature of a friendship to be, they often agree on which attributes of a relationship are more or less important. For example, women may self-disclose in same-sex relationships more than men or view self-disclosure as more important in relationships, but both men and women may still rate self-disclosure as a more important feature of friendship than spending time sharing activities. This idea was supported in a study in which men and women rated how important eight different communication skills were to same-sex friendship (Burleson et al., 1996). Some of the skills reflected the affective aspects of relationships (comforting one another, making a person feel good about himself or herself), whereas other skills reflected the instrumental aspects of communication (entertaining one another, casual conversations, conveying information). Women rated the affective aspects as more important than men did, and men rated the instrumental aspects as more important than women did. Aha, differences again! But both men and women agreed the affective aspects of friendship were more important than the instrumental aspects of friendship.

Despite the fact that women engage in more self-disclosure with friends compared to men (a sex difference that will be discussed in more depth in a few pages), both men and women spend a substantial amount of time in casual conversation with their friends (Wright, 2006). When asked about the purpose of meeting with a same-sex friend, both men and women say that meeting to talk is the primary purpose of getting together with a friend (Duck & Wright, 1993).

It also seems to be the case that the same characteristics of a friendship predict satisfaction in both men and women (Reisman, 1990). For example, although men's same-sex friendships are less intimate and less support-ive than women's, intimacy and support are equally associated with how much men and women enjoy spending time with their friends (Bank & Hansford, 2000).

Egalitarianism is another important fea-ture of friendship for both men and women. Friendship by definition implies equal status. It stands to reason that people would find friend-ships more satisfying when they are of equal rather than unequal status. In one study, college students described a same-sex friendship in which the power distribution was equal and one in which the power distribution was un-equal (Veniegas & Peplau, 1997). Both men and women evaluated the equal power relationship more favorably.

Finally, another important but often-overlooked aspect of friendship is fun and relax-ation (Fehr, 2000). This is a feature of friendship that is equally valued by both males and females.

Males and females also seem to be equally knowledgeable about their friends, at least at younger ages. A study of third- through sixth-graders compared boys' and girls' perceptions of their friendships to that of their friends (Simpkins et al., 2006). Although one might have predicted that girls would be more in tune with their relationships than boys, perceptions were quite similar for both boys and girls. The authors argued that boys and girls may have the same knowledge about their relationships but acquire the knowledge from different sources. Whereas girls obtain information about their relationship directly through self-disclosure, boys may obtain the same information more indirectly through shared activities.

Sex Differences

If there are all these similarities in friendship, are there really any differences? During childhood, the nature of male and female friendship be-comes more distinct with increasing age. That is, boys and girls spend time with their friends in different ways. In a study of second-, fifth-, and eighth-graders, there were no differences between the amount of time that second grade boys and girls spent talking and sharing feelings with friends, but by fifth grade girls spent significantly more time than boys talking and sharing feelings, and the difference became even larger by eighth grade (Buhrmester & Furman, 1987). During adolescence, this differ-ence in the nature of male and female friend-ship remains. Girls spend time talking with their friends, and boys spend time sharing ac-tivities (McNelles & Connolly, 1999). Boys view friendship as instrumental: A friend is someone with whom you do things. Girls view friend-ship as more emotional: A friend is someone with whom you connect. Adolescent girls also spend more time than boys do with friends and rate their friendships as more satisfying than boys do (Brown et al., 1999; Verkuyten & Masson, 1996). Adolescent girls rate their same-sex and cross-sex friendships (which could have been romantic) as more intimate, a greater source of companionship, and a greater source of emotional and instrumental support compared to adolescent boys (Kuttler, LaGreca, & Prinstein, 1999; Lempers & Clark-Lempers, 1993).

Although similarity between friends is an important feature of friendship for both boys and girls, the amount and nature of the similar-ity may differ. In a study of 15- to 18-year-olds in the Netherlands, boys reported they were less similar to their friends than girls did (Verkuyten & Masson, 1996). When asked to provide a description of their best friend, boys were more likely to identify social characteristics (e.g., nationality, group affiliations) and girls to identify personal characteristics (e.g., honest, understanding).

During adolescence, boys and girls also begin to interact more with each other and to form friendships with the other sex. Some of those friendships will evolve into romantic relationships, and some will remain platonic. Adolescent boys' friendships with males and females are very different, whereas adolescent girls' friendships with males and females are quite similar. Friendship with females involves conversation and self-disclosure whether the partner is male or female; thus the partner's sex does not lead females to alter their friendship style. However, males do alter their friendship style when with females. Adolescent boys' friendships with males involve more shared activities, whereas their friendships with females involve more self-disclosure.

The female emphasis on self-disclosure and the male emphasis on shared activities persist in adulthood. In a study of college students from the United States and Russia (Sheets & Lugar, 2005), females shared more personal information with friends compared to males, and males shared more activities with friends compared to females, as shown in Figure 8.2. In addition, college students from the United States shared more intimate information with

their friends compared to Russian students, and Russian students shared more activities with friends than U.S. students.

The research is clear in indicating that women's friendships are more communal than those of men, largely due to the emphasis on self-disclosure. However, the sex difference in agency or instrumentality has been more heavily debated (Wright, 2006). For example, a study of ninth-graders showed that girls rated their close friendships higher on emotional closeness and self-disclosure than boys, but there were no sex differences in shared activities (Camarena, Sarigiani & Peterson, 1990). Sex differences in shared activities appear to be more likely to be found in studies that rely on retrospective measures than in studies that use more online techniques, such as daily diaries where behavior is recorded more closely to the time that it occurs (Wright, 2006).

Even if males and females engage in the same amount of shared activities with their friends, it may be the case that the nature of the shared activities differs for males and females (Wright, 2006). It has been assumed that shared activities are not an intimate way to spend time with a friend. However, some

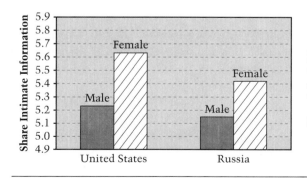 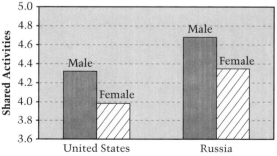

FIGURE 8.2 Sex differences in sharing intimate information and shared activities appeared for both U.S. and Russian college students. Females shared more personal information than males, and males shared more activities with friends than females.
Source: Adapted from Sheets and Lugar (2005).

shared activities can be considered more intimate than others. Is going to a movie with friends the same as going to a book club with friends or cooking dinner with friends? Some activities are more conducive to self-disclosure than others. Even the same activity may be performed differently by men and women. When I first came across Wright's point that men and women may share activities in different ways, I reflected on my own friendships. I play racquetball once a week with a very good friend. We have the court for 60 minutes, but we play for only 45 minutes—we talk about family, friends, and politics in between games while we are catching our breath—not to mention the time we spend catching up on the way to and from the court. There are a lot of activities—golf, biking, hiking—that may or may not include more intimate exchanges.

Cross-cultural research on friendship has confirmed a number of findings on gender and friendship already discussed in this chapter. In a study in New Zealand, college women emphasized self-disclosure, and men emphasized shared activities as the basis of their friendship (Aukett, Ritchie, & Mill, 1988). In addition, women reported more emotional support from their same-sex than cross-sex friends, whereas men reported more emotional support from their cross-sex friends. Both men and women said they discuss personal problems with women. A study of college students in Hungary also revealed that men said it was easier to talk to and feel close to women than men (Reisman, 1990).

Within the United States, however, there are ethnic differences in friendship that have often been overlooked in the literature. Much of the research on friendship in the United States has focused on White middle-class children, college students, and adults. Sex differences seem to be larger among White men's and women's friendships compared to those of other races. One study compared Asian American,

African American, and European White American college students' (all living in California) goals in helping a friend with a problem (Samter et al., 1997). Emotion-focused goals involved talking and letting the other person express himself or herself, and problem-focused goals involved helping the person solve the problem and giving advice. Although men and women in all three ethnic groups rated emotion-focused goals as more important than problem-focused goals, Asian American men rated emotion-focused goals as more important than did African American men, with Caucasian men scoring in the middle. Caucasian women rated emotion-focused goals as more important than did African American women, with Asian American women scoring in the middle. The authors suggested that providing emotional support to friends is more central to White women's than African-American women's same-sex friendships.

Another study showed that support plays a larger role in African American men's friendship than the friendships of men of other races (Way, Becker, & Greene, 2006). That study showed that there were fewer sex differences in friendship among African American and Asian American adolescents compared to White and Latino adolescents.

Finally, a longitudinal study of ethnic minority (African American, Latino, Asian American) children showed that sex differences in support from friends disappeared with age (Way & Greene, 2006). As shown in Figure 8.3, among the younger adolescents, girls reported higher friendship quality (friendship quality was defined as support) than boys. With age, friendship quality increased for both boys and girls, but the rate of change was higher for boys. By age 18, males and females reported equal support in their friendships. The rate of increase was the same for all three ethnic groups: African Americans, Latinos, and Asian Americans.

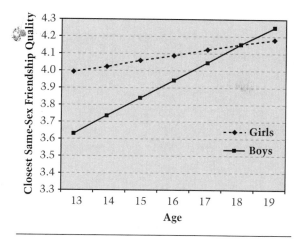

FIGURE 8.3 At younger ages, girls report higher quality same-sex friendships than boys. With time, friendship quality increases—more so for boys than girls, so that no sex difference in friendship quality appears by the end of adolescence.
Source: Way and Greene (2006).

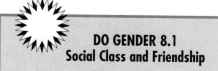

DO GENDER 8.1
Social Class and Friendship

First, decide what dimensions of friendship might vary by social class (e.g., self-disclosure, shared activities, trust, competition). Develop questions to measure these aspects of friendship. Have your friends' parents complete the questionnaire with respect to their current friendships. Record whether the parent is a blue-collar worker or a white-collar worker to see if there are class differences in friendship.

Within the African American community, Franklin (1992) concluded that the friendships of working-class Black men differ from the friendships of more upwardly mobile Black men. The friendships of upwardly mobile Black men are similar to White men's friendships: activity based, lacking in self-disclosure, and work focused. Franklin argued that upwardly mobile Black men discover the way to get ahead is to behave like successful White men, which means that relationships with other men are competitive, and friends are kept at a distance. The friendships of working-class Black men, however, are closer because of shared feelings of oppression and victimization. They seem to understand each other in ways that White men and upper-class Black men do not. They have a "stick together—it is us against them"—mentality. Because these friendships involve a great deal of trust and loyalty, working-class Black men react harshly toward a friend who violates these principles. The relation of social class to friendship is a topic worth more investigation. Start with Do Gender 8.1.

Women also may be more likely than men to have reciprocal relationships. A study of college students showed that female friends have a greater *mutual* exchange of self-disclosure and empathy than male friends do (Parker & de Vries, 1993). That is, support was both provided and received in the context of female-female relationships. A reciprocal relationship also can be defined as one in which both people define the relationship similarly; that is, they agree there is a friendship. A nonreciprocal relationship is one in which only one person identifies the other as a friend. Using this definition, a study of junior high school students and a study of 6th- through 12th-graders found that boys were less likely than girls to have reciprocal relationships (Clark & Ayers, 1992; Urberg et al., 1995).

Finally, differences between men's and women's friendships may be exaggerated by the respondents themselves. In an interview study with working-class and professional men and women, respondents gave stereotypical descriptions of their friends early in the interview when they were talking about friends in the abstract—men said they shared activities with friends and women said they shared feelings with friends (Walker, 1994). However, when respondents were asked to describe specific friends, men's and women's responses were quite similar. Both men and women shared feelings with friends. Thus on questionnaires where one is merely asked to describe friendships in general, men and women may be providing stereotypical responses either because they think this is how they are supposed to respond (i.e., response bias) or because they think that their relationships fit the stereotypes when in actuality they may not.

TAKE HOME POINTS

- Both men and women want the same things from friendship and view self-disclosure, empathy, trust, and expressions of support as the most important features of a friendship.

- Both men and women equally engage in casual conversation with friends, view egalitarianism as central to friendship, and believe fun and relaxation are important aspects of friendship.

- The primary difference in the nature of men's and women's friendships is that an activity is the focus of men's interactions and conversation is the focus of women's interactions. This difference first appears during childhood and then persists through adolescence and adulthood.

- When interacting with the other sex, however, males modify their style more than females. It appears that both males and females turn to females to self-disclose and share confidences.

- Taken collectively, it is clear that female friendships are more communal than those of males, but the sex difference in the instrumentality of friendship is less clear. Regardless of whether there is a sex difference in shared activities, men and women may spend time sharing activities in different ways so that shared activities are more intimate for women than for men.

- Although some of these findings generalize to different cultures, there are ethnic differences in friendship within the

United States. The female emphasis on self-disclosure is not as strong in Black women's friendship as it is in White women's friendships, and the male lack of self-disclosure in friendship is more strongly associated with White than Black male friendship.

CLOSENESS OF FRIENDSHIP

At one time, men's friendships were regarded as stronger than women's friendships. In 1969, Lionel Tiger maintained that men were biologically predisposed to develop superior friendships compared to women. Tiger suggested the male-male bond was as important to the survival of the species as the male-female bond was for reproduction. Men depended on other men for defense of their territory, for gathering food, and for maintaining social order in the community. In support of his claim, Tiger cites another author, who says,

> Woman is an eminently unsociable being and refrains from forming unions on the basis of like interest, remaining centered in the kinship group based on sexual relations and the reproductive function. Associations created or even joined by women on equal terms with the men are rare and must be considered weak imitations of the exclusively male association. (Schurtz, cited in Tiger, 1969, p. 128)

Perhaps these ideas are why the friendships that have been depicted in the media (identified at the beginning of the chapter) involve men.

The more recent consensus has been that women's relationships are closer than those of men. Starting in middle school, girls begin to report that their friendships are more intimate than boys' (Rubin et al., 2004; Zarbatany, McDougall, & Hymel, 2000). Girls report greater validation, caring, and self-disclosure in

TABLE 8.1   Scales from Acquaintance Description Form

Friendship Strength
Voluntary interdependence: Degree to which one commits free time to another.
Person-qua-person: Viewing one person as unique and genuine.
Relationship Values or Rewards
Utility value: Friend uses time and resources to provide assistance.
Ego support value: Friend regards one as competent.
Stimulation value: Friend is interesting, stimulating, expands one's knowledge.
Self-affirmation: Friend recognizes valued attributes.
Security value: Regards friend as safe and nonthreatening.
Relationship Stress or Conflict
Maintenance difficulty: Time spent resolving conflicts.
Relationship Differentiation
Exclusion: Claim access to interactions with friend.
Permanence: Difficult to dissolve, permanently binding.
Salience of emotional expression: Expression of positive affect central to relationship.
Degree of social regulation: Relationship influenced by social norms.
General Favorability
Tendency to respond to friendship favorably.

Source: Wright (1985).

same-sex friendships compared to boys. Women report that their relationships are more intimate than men's relationships (Aukett et al., 1988; Veniegas & Peplau, 1997); women characterize their friendships as involving more self-disclosure, appreciation, empathy, and authenticity compared to men (Parker & de Vries, 1993); and women are more satisfied than men with their friendships (Reisman, 1990; Wright, 1999).

One way that friendship closeness has been studied is with the Acquaintance Description Form, which assesses different dimensions of friendship (ADF; Wright, 1985). These dimensions are shown in Table 8.1. Two scales measure friendship strength, five scales assess rewards we receive from friendship, one scale assesses conflict, and four scales assess variables expected to differ across different relationships. The instrument also contains a general favorability scale that assesses our tendency to view a relationship positively across all dimensions.

In a study of 11th- and 12th-graders using the ADF, girls rated both same-sex and other-sex friendships as higher in friendship strength and relationship rewards compared to boys (Thomas & Daubman, 2001). However, girls also rated their friendships as higher in maintenance difficulty than males. In a study of college students, women reported an overall more positive view of their same-sex friendships than men (Duck & Wright, 1993). A study of 10th-graders, 12th-graders, and first-year college students showed that females rated their same-sex friendships as closer and more cohesive than those of males in all three groups (Johnson, 2004).

Thus studies using the ADF seem to show women have closer friendships than men and that friendships with women are closer than friendships with men. We must consider the nature of the dimensions reflected on the ADF. Are they biased in the direction of tapping female aspects of friendship? Males may rate their same-sex friendships as lower on these dimensions compared to females, but are males less satisfied with their same-sex friendships?

One way to address this question is to examine men's and women's conceptions of an ideal friend using the ADF. Elkins and Peterson (1993) had college students rate their actual as well as their ideal same-sex friend and cross-sex (nonromantic) friend on each of the dimensions of the ADF. The male-male friendship received the lowest actual and lowest ideal ratings, as shown in Figure 8.4. Although the male-male friendship was the least close as measured by the ADF, males were *not* dissatisfied with this state of affairs. The discrepancy between actual and ideal friendship was the same for males and females in same-sex and cross-sex friendships. Thus men perceive their same-sex friendships as less close than other relationships, but men have lower expectations for the closeness of those friendships.

Another way that researchers have examined the closeness of men's and women's friendships is with a method called the Rochester Interaction Record (RIR). Researchers from the University of Rochester developed the RIR to describe the nature of social interactions on a day-to-day or moment-to-moment basis (Wheeler, Reis, & Nezlek, 1983). Participants complete an RIR for every 10-minute interaction they have over the course of a day. This may seem quite cumbersome, but many of our daily interactions

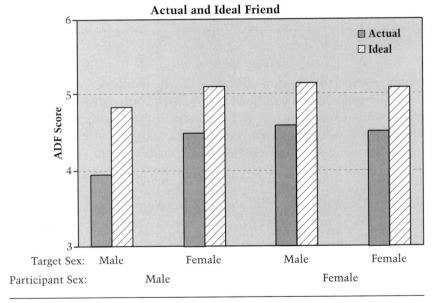

FIGURE 8.4   Ratings of ideal friend and actual friend on measure of relationship strength (ADF). Men rated their ideal male friend lower than they rated their ideal female friend or than women rated their ideal male or female friend. Men also rated their actual male friend lower than they rated their actual female friend or than women rated their actual male or female friend. Although the male-male friendship is less close than other friendships, it is held to a lower standard.

Source: Adapted from Elkins and Peterson (1993).

LONELINESS

Date _____ Time _____ AM ___ Length _____ Hrs ___ Mins ___			
	PM ___		
Initials _____	If More Than 3 Others:		
Sex _____	# Of Females _____	# Of Males _____	
Intimacy:	Superficial 1 2 3 4 5 6 7 Meaningful		
I Disclosed:	Very Little 1 2 3 4 5 6 7 A Great Deal		
Other Disclosed:	Very Little 1 2 3 4 5 6 7 A Great Deal		
Quality:	Unpleasant 1 2 3 4 5 6 7 Pleasant		
Satisfaction:	Less Than Expected 1 2 3 4 5 6 7 More Than Expected		
Initiation:	I Initiated 1 2 3 4 5 6 7 Other Initiated		
Influence:	I Influenced More 1 2 3 4 5 6 7 Other Influenced More		
Nature:	Work Task Pastime Conversation Date		

FIGURE 8.5   Rochester Interaction Record.

Source: L. Wheeler, H. Reis, and J. Nezlek (1983). Loneliness, social interaction, and sex roles. *Journal of Personality and Social Psychology, 45,* 943–953.

are much briefer, lasting only a minute or two. People typically report about seven or eight 10-minute interactions during an average day. The RIR, shown in Figure 8.5, contains questions about who was involved in the interaction as well as rating scales of the quality of the interaction.

In a now classic study, college students completed the RIR for every 10-minute interaction they had every day for 2 consecutive weeks (Wheeler et al., 1983). As shown in Figure 8.6a, they found a consistent sex difference in the meaningfulness of interactions, measured as the average of each interaction's intimacy, self-disclosure, other-disclosure, pleasantness, and satisfaction (i.e., the first five ratings scales shown in Figure 8.5). Men's same-sex interactions were significantly less meaningful than women's, even when interactions with a best friend were examined. All interactions involving at least one female (female-female, male-female)

were equally meaningful, and they were more meaningful than those involving only males. This study showed that friendship closeness is due not only to a dispositional variable, sex of the person, but also to a structural difference, the sex of the friend with whom one is interacting. Men do not always display less intimacy than women in their interactions with friends. In fact, when men's interactions involve a woman, they can be just as intimate as women's interactions. Men's interactions are less intimate than women's only when they involve another man. Other research has shown that male-male friendships score lower on appreciation, empathy, responsibility, and connectedness compared to female-female and male-female friendships (Parker & de Vries, 1993).

The finding that men's interactions with other men are the least meaningful was replicated by a study that explored several explanations for it (see Figure 8.6b; Reis, Senchak,

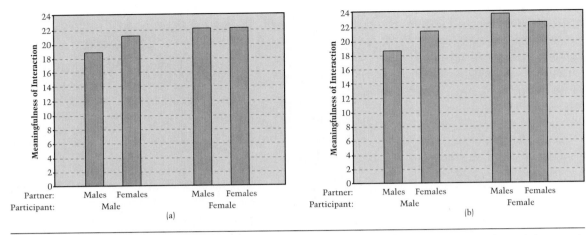

FIGURE 8.6 Meaningfulness of interactions with men and women. A daily diary study showed that men's interactions with men were rated as less meaningful than men's interactions with women or women's interactions with men or women. The results of the study by Wheeler et al. (1983) are depicted in Figure 8.6a. The results were replicated by Reis et al. (1985) and are shown in Figure 8.6b.
Sources: Adapted from Wheeler et al. (1983) and Reis et al. (1985).

& Solomon, 1985). First, the investigators examined whether men were simply more selective than women about the people with whom they are intimate. As in the previous study, RIR interactions with the best friend only were examined. Women rated their interactions with their best friend as more meaningful compared to men. Students also provided a written account of their most recent meaningful conversation with their same-sex best friend. Judges reviewed the narratives and determined that women's accounts were more intimate than those of men. Thus it did not appear men were being more selective than women.

Second, Reis and colleagues (1985) asked whether men's friendships lacked intimacy because men were not *capable* of intimacy or because men *preferred* not to behave in intimate ways. Students and their best same-sex friends were asked to engage spontaneously in a conversation about something that was important to them. A female graduate student rated videotapes of these interactions and

found men's interactions were as intimate as women's, as demonstrated by men and women self-disclosing at similar levels. However, a panel of undergraduates found that males discussed less intimate topics than females did. The authors concluded that men and women are equally capable of intimacy, but men *prefer* not to behave as intimately as women.

There may be a downside to the greater closeness of female compared to male friendship. It has been suggested that females' friendships are more fragile than those of males. In a study of sixth-graders making the transition to seventh grade, females were less likely than males to maintain the same friends over the transition (Hardy, Bukowski, & Sippola, 2002). Seventh grade males and females had the same number of friends, but proportionally more of the females' friends were new and not the same as those they had in sixth grade. In studies of college students, females' closest friendship seem to be of shorter duration than males' closest friendship (Benenson & Christakos, 2003;

Johnson, 2004). In one study, females were more likely than males to say that their closest friends had done something to hurt the friendship, and females had more friendships that had ended compared to males (Benenson & Christakos, 2003). The authors suggest that females may have poorer conflict resolution skills than males. Because females are more concerned with directly hurting a relationship, they may express their distress in more covert ways. The intimate information gained about a friend can be used in gossiping or other forms of relational aggression. As noted in Chapter 7, relational aggression is more common in female than male friendship. Thus the greater closeness of female compared to male friendship does not mean that female friendships are without difficulties.

An individual difference variable related to sex that predicts friendship closeness is gender role. Femininity, or expressiveness, is related to social self-esteem, friendship quality, and friendship satisfaction (Helgeson, 1994c; Jones & Costin, 1995; Zarbatany, Conley, & Pepper, 2004).

Cross-cultural research suggests that some of the sex differences in intimacy are a Western phenomenon. The intimacy of college students' friendships in the United States were compared to those in Germany, the Netherlands, Hong Kong, and Jordan (Reis, 1998). The size of the sex difference in intimacy (female greater than male) varied by culture. The difference was largest in the United States ($d = -.95$), followed by Germany ($d = -.70$) and then the Netherlands ($d = -.39$) and Hong Kong ($d = -.34$). In Jordan, there was no sex difference in intimacy ($d = +.12$). In the three Western cultures, men were more intimate with women than with men. In Jordan and Hong Kong, men were equally intimate with men and women. Thus the link of intimacy to women appears to be a facet of Western culture.

TAKE HOME POINTS

- Females have closer same-sex friendships than males.

- Friendships with females are closer than friendships with males.

- The lack of closeness in male same-sex friendships is not due to men being incapable of intimacy; instead, men prefer not to behave intimately with their same-sex friends.

- The downside of the closeness of female friendship is that the friendships may be more fragile. The information gained from intimate exchanges may be turned into relational aggression when conflict arises.

BARRIERS TO CLOSENESS IN MALE FRIENDSHIP

Why are male same-sex friendships less intimate and sometimes less satisfying than female same-sex friendships? Mazur and Olver (1987) suggested that men see danger in affiliations with other men. Drawing on Pollak and Gilligan's (1982) work with the TAT pictures (recall Chapter 6), they demonstrated that men fear affiliation with men. They presented undergraduates with a series of situations involving same-sex characters. Each situation had a structured and unstructured version. For example, an unstructured situation was two men (or women) sitting together on a bench; a structured situation was two men (or women) sitting together on a bench waiting for their turn at bat. The investigators suggested that men would feel more comfortable in a structured situation in which an activity (in this case, playing baseball) serves as the basis for the interaction. They hypothesized that men would either respond negatively to the unstructured situation or impose structure on the situation to reduce the potential for closeness. The results showed that men were more likely than women to respond to the unstructured cue by writing stories that contained negative affect and by imposing structure (i.e., came up with a reason the people were sitting together on the bench). There was no sex difference in response to the structured cue. Mazur and Olver argued that men's emphasis on shared activities is a way to impose structure on a relationship and reduce the potential for closeness.

There are a number of barriers to closeness in men's same-sex friendships. We discuss three: competition, homophobia, and emotional inexpressiveness.

Competition

One barrier to male friendship is competition. Men's friendships are more overtly competitive than women's friendships. Competition limits intimacy because it is difficult to be close to someone with whom you are in competition; we would not reveal weaknesses, inadequacies, or difficulties to a competitor. Competition among men makes them feel threatened by one another's achievements. In general, men are more sensitive than women to status features in relationships. In a meta-analytic review of the literature, Feingold (1988) found greater matching on physical attractiveness among male-male friendships than female-female friendships. Feingold argued that physical attractiveness is a status cue, so it was important for men to match on this variable. Similarly, a study of junior high school students found that male friends were more similar to one another on status cues (e.g., niceness of clothes) than were female friends (Clark & Ayers, 1992).

Note that I said that male friendships were more *overtly* competitive than female friendships. Competition, however, is not limited to male friendship. Female friendships can be competitive but the competition is not as

direct or overt. Females are more uncomfortable than males with overt competition (Benenson et al., 2002). The overt expression of competition in relationships is viewed as unfeminine, so women resort to more subtle tactics. For example, a friend of mine told me of an occasion when her aunt was so concerned about being the best dressed person at a party that she refused to tell her friends what she intended to wear. My mother was once accused of leaving out a key ingredient of a dessert recipe she passed on to a friend. Both of these situations are examples of covert competition. Thus competition may undermine friendships for both men and women but in different ways. Investigate this issue with Do Gender 8.2.

Aside from direct versus indirect, there are other distinctions that can be made in regard to competition. A number of different kinds of competition have been distinguished from one another, as shown in Table 8.2. One study examined three kinds of competition among 7th-graders from Canada, Costa Rica, and Cuba (Schneider et al., 2005): hypercompetition,

DO GENDER 8.2
Male Versus Female Competition

Interview your friends to find out how competition manifests itself in their friendships. Ask for examples of competitive behavior in their friendships with men and their friendships with women. Over what things do people compete: money? status? physical attractiveness? grades? romantic partners? Are the behaviors that men identify different from the behaviors that women identify? Are the behaviors that people identify about men different from the behaviors that people identify about women?

TABLE 8.2   THE NATURE OF COMPETITION

Hypercompetition	intense desire to win, associated with hostility; disregard for opponent "I get upset when X wins." "Winning makes me feel powerful."
Nonhostile social comparison	comparison of achievement without hostility "I like to play X to see who is better."
Enjoyment of competition	intense involvement in activity "I like to play *X* for the fun of it."
Personal development competition	competition for self-improvement "Competition helps me to be the best I can be."

nonhostile social comparison, and enjoyment of competition. Hypercompetition involves an intense desire to win at all costs, without any regard to the effects on the opponent. Nonhostile social comparison occurs when we compare our achievement to that of another, but without anger, hostility, or jealousy. Enjoyment of competition reflects an intense engagement in a competitive activity. Overall, boys' friendships contained more competition than girls' friendships. However, the implications of competition for the friendship depended on the nature of the competition. Hypercompetition was related to more conflict and less closeness in friendships. Enjoyment of competition was unrelated to friendship closeness but was related to more companionship in friendship for boys. Finally, nonhostile social comparison was related to more friendship closeness for boys. Thus the distinctions among the different kinds of competition mattered more for boys' than girls' friendships.

Another kind of competition that has been studied is personal development competitiveness, which is aimed at using competition for self-improvement. Personal development competition appears to be a healthy kind of competition for both males and females. One study of college students differentiated hypercompetitiveness from personal development competitiveness (Ryckman et al., 1997). Students who scored high on either hypercompetitiveness or personal development competition placed a high value on achievement. Students who scored high on hypercompetitiveness also scored high on desire for power or control over others, whereas students who scored high on personal development competition scored high on a social concern scale. The distinction between these two kinds of competition also was examined in a study of college women (Burckle et al., 1999). Hypercompetitiveness was related to disturbed eating behavior, but personal development competition was not. The authors focused on disturbed eating behavior because society places a high value on women's appearance; thus, appearance might be a domain in which women are competitive.

Homophobia

Another reason men are uncomfortable with closeness in their same-sex friendships is **homophobia**, defined as the fear of homosexuality or the fear of appearing homosexual. Because men do not want to appear to be homosexual, they limit their physical contact and their emotional closeness with other men, reserving those kinds of contacts for romantic relationships with women. Men who score higher in homophobia report less trust, less understanding, fewer expressions of caring, and less empathy in their relationships with other men (Devlin & Cowan, 1985).

A study of college students demonstrated how men limit their physical contact with other men and how both men and women view physical contact between two men as abnormal (Derlega et al., 1989). Students were asked to role-play a situation in which they were greeted either by a same-sex friend, a cross-sex friend, or a romantic partner at the airport (Derlega et al., 1989). Four levels of tactile intimacy were coded: 0 = No touch; 1 = Handshake, or touch on head, arm, back; 2 = Light hug, hold hands; and 3 = Solid hug, kiss. Men were less intimate greeting men than they were greeting women. Men also were less intimate greeting men than were women greeting women. In a second study, the investigators examined college students' attitudes toward different levels of touch between same-sex and cross-sex dyads. Students were shown a picture of a pair of people either not touching, hugging, or putting their arms around each other's waist. They were told the pair consisted of two men, two women, or a man and a woman. Students rated increasing levels of touch as less normal when they thought the pair was two men. All forms of touch were rated as normal when the pair was depicted as a man and a woman. When the photo was thought to consist of two women, level of touch partly affected perceptions of normalcy. Women with arms around each other's waist was rated as abnormal, but women hugging each other was rated as normal. Students also indicated that an arm around another's waist was an indication of a sexual relationship in all three dyads. Hugging, however, was an indicator of a sexual relationship only in the male-male dyad.

Emotional Inexpressiveness

A third barrier to closeness in men's same-sex relationships is emotional inexpressiveness. Men tend to express less emotion in relationships

compared to women. Inexpressiveness may help to maintain power, but at the expense of closeness.

A recent study compared the different explanations for the lack of intimacy in men's relationships (Bank & Hansford, 2000). Homophobia and emotional restraint seemed to explain why college men had less intimate and less supportive same-sex friendships than college women. In this study, men and women scored similarly on measures of competition, so competition could not explain why men's friendships were less close than those of women.

TAKE HOME POINTS

- Male friendship is more overtly competitive than female friendship. Competition among females is more likely to be covert.

- There are different kinds of competition, only some of which may be barriers to intimacy among men. Hypercompetitiveness is one such form of competition.

- Males may score higher than females on other kinds of competition, such as competition for social comparison or personal development competitoin, but these kinds of competition are not likely to inhibit intimacy.

- Homophobia also limits intimacy among men's same-sex friendships. Men do not want to appear to be homosexual and infer homosexuality from expressions of affection between men.

- Men refrain from expressing emotion in their relationships with other men, because expressing emotion is viewed as weakness and as feminine. It is difficult to be close to someone when you keep your feelings to yourselves.

SELF-DISCLOSURE

The primary reason that women's friendships are viewed as closer than men's friendships is because women self-disclose more than men.

Let's take a more in-depth look at the literature on self-disclosure. Do women self-disclose more than men about everything? To whom do people self-disclose—women or men? Are there any situational factors that influence self-disclosure?

Sex of Discloser

Dindia and Allen (1992) conducted a meta-analysis on sex differences in self-disclosure. They found a small effect ($d = -.18$) indicating that women self-disclose more than men. The size of the sex difference was similar across self-report ($d = -.17$) and observational ($d = -.22$) studies. However, the sex difference was larger for studies that relied on other people's reports of someone's behavior ($d = -.44$). That is, other people view the difference between men's and women's self-disclosure to be larger than it really is. Gender-role stereotypes may be influencing people's reports of others' behavior.

Sex differences in self-disclosure may be more apparent when the nature of the topic is examined. Several studies show that women are especially more likely than men to self-disclose about personal issues, such as relationship problems or areas of personal weakness. One study found that women were more likely than men to discuss intimate topics and problems with their same-sex friends, but no sex differences in self-disclosure were found about less intimate topics (Tschann, 1988).

Females also engage in a form of self-disclosure with friends that is referred to as **co-rumination** (Rose, 2002): repeatedly discussing problems, including the causes, the consequences, and the negative feelings, with a friend. Although corumination is linked to higher friendship quality and partly explains why women have higher quality friendships than men, corumination is also linked to depression (see Chapter 13).

Sex of Recipient

Who is more likely to be on the receiving end of self-disclosure? The answer depends in part on who is disclosing. Women are clearly more likely than men to be the recipients of female disclosure. The question is: To whom do men self-disclose?

Dindia and Allen's (1992) meta-analytic review showed two sex of target effects. One indicated that people are more likely to self-disclose to women than to men. The other effect showed that people are more likely to self-disclose to the same sex than to the other sex. For women, a same-sex target is another woman, so the result is clear: Women are more likely to self-disclose to women than to men. For men, a same-sex target is not a woman; thus the recipient of male self-disclosure is not always clear. There may be some topics that men discuss with men and others that men discuss with women. Evidence suggests that men and women prefer to talk to men about task-oriented problems and to women about relationship problems (Derlega, Barbee, & Winstead, 1994). For example, one study showed that males disclosed equally to males and females on a variety of topics but discussed personal finances with men more than with women (Dolgin, Meyer, & Schwartz, 1991). These preferences likely have to do with the support people expect men and women to provide. Task-oriented problems may require more advice, and relationship problems may require emotional support. Explore this issue with Do Gender 8.3.

Situational Variables

Situational variables also affect self-disclosure. Studies have shown that men's levels of self-disclosure can be increased if they are motivated to self-disclose. In one study, researchers manipulated whether participants believed there was the possibility of a future interaction with

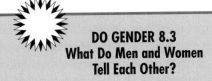

DO GENDER 8.3
What Do Men and Women Tell Each Other?

Come up with a list of topics. Ask a group of men and women to report how frequently they discuss each topic with their same-sex friends and cross-sex friends. You could have them pick their best same-sex friend and best cross-sex friend. Divide the topics into two groups: more intimate and less intimate. Is there a sex of participant difference in self-disclosure? Is there a sex of target difference? Does it depend on the topic?

the other person in the experiment (Shaffer, Pegalis, & Bazzini, 1996). The investigators predicted that men would be especially likely to self-disclose to women if they believed there was the possibility of a future interaction. They also expected this effect would be strongest for traditionally masculine men.

Shaffer and colleagues (1996) had undergraduates work on a first task with a partner and then led them to believe they would be working on a second task with or without their partner. This was the manipulation of future interaction. The initial task was discussing four different topics (the most important decision I ever made, sacrifices I made for others, aspects of personality I dislike, past and present things of which I am ashamed) with a stranger who was really a confederate. Conversations were audiotaped and evaluated by two raters for intimacy of self-disclosure. Women were more intimate when they disclosed to female than male targets. Men's self-disclosure was influenced by their masculinity scores, the sex of the target, and the possibility of future interaction. As shown in the right panel of Figure 8.7, men

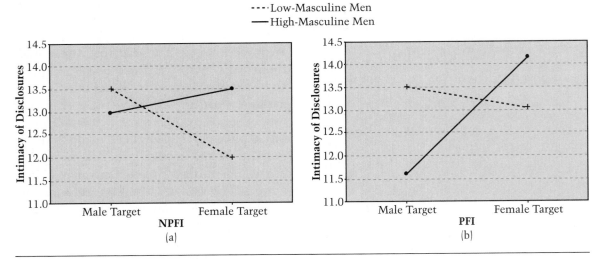

FIGURE 8.7 Men who score high on masculinity are motivated to self-disclose to a female they have just met and with whom they have the possibility of forming a relationship. High-masculine men self-disclosed more intimately to a female than a male target, only when there was the possibility of a future interaction (PFI). Where there was no possibility of a future interaction (NPFI), high-masculine men's disclosures were equally intimate toward a male or female target.
Source: Shaffer, Pegalis, and Bazzini (1996).

who scored high on masculinity self-disclosed more to female than male targets when there was the possibility of a future interaction (PFI). When there was no possibility of a future interaction (NPFI; left panel of Figure 8.7), high-masculine men self-disclosed equally to male and female targets.

Are highly masculine men increasing their self-disclosure to female targets when they expect to interact with them again? Or are highly masculine men decreasing their self-disclosure to male targets when they expect to interact with them again? Highly masculine men may be especially uncomfortable disclosing to other men if they think they will see them again. Indeed, comfort level did explain the results from this study. High-masculine men reported greater comfort and were more interested in establishing a relationship with the female than the male target when there was the potential for future interaction. In general, female respondents were more comfortable and more interested in establishing a relationship with the female than the male target. Thus it appears both women and masculine men self-disclosed most to female targets when there was the possibility of a future interaction because they felt comfortable and wanted to establish a relationship.

Other situational variables affect sex differences in self-disclosure. Age is one. For example, in one study, females self-disclosed more to women than men among adolescents, but females disclosed equally to men and women among young adults (Reisman, 1990). Adolescent men self-disclosed equally to men and women, but by young adulthood they disclosed more to women than men. Thus with age, both males and females increased their disclosure to the other sex.

Marital status also affects men's and women's self-disclosure to friends, but not in the same way. Marriage inhibits men but not women from self-disclosing to friends. In one study, married men were less likely than married women or unmarried persons of either sex to discuss intimate topics or personal problems with same-sex friends (Tschann, 1988). Married women were more likely than married men to disclose to friends, and they were equally likely to self-disclose to a friend and to a spouse. Married men reserve their intimate disclosures for their spouse.

We might expect men's friendships in countries with a less individualistic focus to differ from men's friendships in the United States in terms of self-disclosure. The friendships of college students in the United States were compared to those of students in India (Berman, Murphy-Berman, & Pachauri, 1988). Students in both countries were asked to complete a self-disclosure scale in regard to their same-sex best friend. In the United States, women reported greater disclosure than men; in India, there was no sex difference in self-disclosure. In the United States, women spent more time than men in private conversations; there were no differences in how men and women spent time with their same-sex friends in India. Thus, in societies that emphasize interdependence, men's and women's friendships are more similar. This may be due to the fact that the ideal male in India is viewed quite differently from that in the United States. The ideal male in India is social, interdependent, and expressive, rather than competitive, independent, and nonexpressive; these differences may have implications for men's friendships with other men.

Barriers to Male Self-Disclosure

Men may be less likely to self-disclose than women because self-disclosure involves revealing weaknesses and vulnerabilities, which is inconsistent with the male gender role. Two aspects of the male gender role—inhibiting affection and restricting emotions—have been associated with less self-disclosure of emotion among male and female college students (Snell et al., 1989).

Another reason men may not self-disclose as much as women has nothing to do with men's personalities but has to do with society's expectations of men. Men are not viewed as favorably as women when they self-disclose. A meta-analysis of the studies that examined the relation of self-disclosure to liking showed the relation was stronger for female disclosers ($d = +.30$) than male disclosers ($d = +.11$; Collins & Miller, 1994). This finding held for both male and female respondents. In other words, both men and women liked a woman who disclosed more than a man who disclosed.

Men who self-disclose might be viewed as having more problems than women who self-disclose. This idea was supported by a study conducted a very long time ago in which college students read several vignettes in which one person either did or did not disclose a personal problem (a mental illness or a car accident; Derlega & Chaikin, 1976). The sex of the discloser and the sex of the recipient were varied. Men were rated as better adjusted under nondisclosure than disclosure conditions, whereas women were rated as better adjusted under disclosure than nondisclosure conditions. The sex of the disclosure recipient did not influence the results. In addition, participants liked the female discloser better than the female nondiscloser but liked the male discloser and nondiscloser equally. Regardless of sex, the discloser was rated as more feminine than the nondiscloser. Thus self-disclosure was viewed as part of the female gender role. Try Do Gender 8.4 to see if men are still viewed less favorably than women today when they self-disclose.

☀ DO GENDER 8.4
Do You Want to Be Friends with a Guy Who Discloses a Personal Problem?

Create two vignettes that contain a story about someone disclosing a problem. In one vignette, make the disclosure more personal than the other vignette. Now, vary the sex of the person engaging in self-disclosure across the two vignettes so that you have two versions of each vignette. Randomly assign a group of college students to read one of the vignettes and then answer some questions about how they viewed the person in the story. Did they view male and female disclosures differently in terms of personality traits? in terms of likeability and desirability for friendship? in mental health?

If you want to make the design more complicated, you can also take the opportunity to vary the recipient of disclosure. Are people more accepting of a male who reveals a personal problem to a female than a male?

TAKE HOME POINTS

- Women engage in more self-disclosure than men.

- Women are especially likely to disclose to women over men. It is unclear whether men disclose more to women or men; it may depend on the topic of disclosure.

- Men are clearly capable of self-disclosure (just as they are capable of intimacy) but seem to prefer not to engage in it. Men can be motivated to self-disclose to women when they are interested in establishing a relationship.

- Men do not disclose as much as women because revealing weaknesses is inconsistent with the male gender role and because people do not respond as favorably to self-disclosure by men compared to women. If people have negative views of men who disclose their problems, it is not surprising that men are reluctant to ask for help.

DEFINITION OF INTIMACY

I have reviewed research showing that women's friendships are closer than those of men. I also have shown that women self-disclose more than men. Because the intimacy of a relationship is often measured by self-disclosure, the logical conclusion is that women's relationships are more intimate than those of men. However, some have suggested that self-disclosure is a "feminine" definition of intimacy and that men and women may define intimacy differently. Women may be more likely to express intimacy through self-disclosure, and men may be more likely to express intimacy through participation in shared activities. To the extent that is the case, there would be less evidence for women's friendships being more intimate than those of men.

Do men and women define intimacy differently? Swain (1989) found that the vast majority of men mentioned activities rather than self-disclosure when describing their most meaningful experience with a friend. He documents a "covert intimacy" in men, which he defines as "behavior in the context of a friendship that connotes a positive and mutual sense of meaning and importance to the participants" (p. 72). This covert intimacy reflects the comfort that men feel in each other's presence, a comfort that stems from shared experiences and mutual understandings. He suggests that intimacy for men comes from action rather than self-disclosure: Men feel connected to other men who choose them to share an activity, who provide them with assistance, and who joke around about ideas or histories common to only the pair.

Yet plenty of other research has shown that men and women agree that self-disclosure is more central to intimacy than shared activities. In one study, college students were asked to define the terms *closeness* and *intimacy* in the context of their current same-sex and cross-sex (nonromantic) relationships (Parks & Floyd, 1996). The most frequently cited definition of closeness for both men and women was self-disclosure, although females were more likely than males to mention self-disclosure (76% vs. 64%). The second definition was support provision; again, females identified this feature (45%) more than males (27%). Sharing activities was the third most frequent definition, and it was identified by an equal number of males (35%) and females (28%). A study of college students and community residents found that both men and women were more likely to identify interactions that represented intimacy as containing self-disclosure and emotional support than shared activities and practical support (Fehr, 2004). However, women viewed self-disclosure as more central to intimacy than men.

Although self-disclosure is the most central feature of intimacy for both men and women, self-disclosure may contribute more to intimacy for women than men, and shared activities may contribute more to intimacy for men than women (Wright, 2006). A study of two cohorts of eighth-graders demonstrated that self-disclosure and shared experiences predicted emotional closeness for boys, whereas only self-disclosure predicted emotional closeness for girls (Camarena et al., 1990). Yet, even for boys, the relation of self-disclosure to emotional closeness was much stronger than the relation of shared experiences to emotional closeness. More recently, a group of seventh- and eighth-graders and first-year college students were asked to describe a time when they felt especially close to a friend, and responses were coded into categories (Radmacher & Azmitia, 2006). First, the results overall revealed more support for similarities than differences in conceptualizations of intimacy among males and females. The most frequent pathway to intimacy for both males and females involved self-disclosure. Second, college students were more likely to define intimacy in terms of self-disclosure and less likely to define intimacy in terms of shared activities compared to adolescents. Third, among the college students, men and women were equally likely to define intimacy in terms of self-disclosure, but women were more likely to include emotional support in their definitions, and men were more likely to include shared activities in their definitions. Overall, the authors found that self-disclosure predicted intimacy for males and females, but shared activities additionally predicted intimacy for males, replicating the results reported by Camerena and colleagues (1990) above.

Although men and women have different experiences of intimacy (women's being more affective and men's being more instrumental), the two sexes seem to agree on the definition of intimacy. As shown in Figure 8.8, self-disclosure is an important, if not the most important, feature of intimacy for both men and women.

However, men are more likely than women to incorporate shared experiences into their conceptualizations of intimacy. Studies of intimacy have neglected the fact that we can be engaged in self-disclosure and shared activities simultaneously. Two men may be discussing problems with their girlfriends while fixing a car: How are these episodes classified—as self disclosure or as shared activities? How do men and women classify this experience?

According to Reis and Shaver (1988), intimacy involves revealing one's innermost self, which can be accomplished via self-disclosure or shared activities. Intimacy is not a static state but a process. This means that self-disclosure alone is not sufficient to establish intimacy. The partner's response to the self-disclosure is just as important as the self-disclosure itself to the intimacy of an interaction. Reis and Shaver suggest that intimate interactions are ones that lead to feeling understood, validated, and cared for. Both self-disclosure and shared activities could accomplish this.

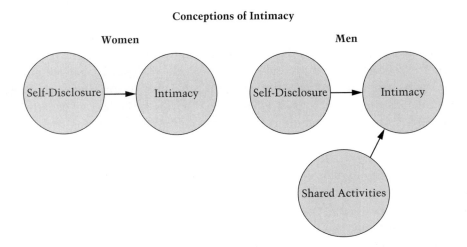

FIGURE 8.8 Self-disclosure is the most important determinant of intimacy for women and men. However, self-disclosure is relatively more important to women than men, and men's definitions of intimacy include shared activities.

CONFLICT IN FRIENDSHIP

I have focused on the positive aspects of friendships. But relationships do not always run smoothly. What produces conflict in men's and women's friendships? Quite a while ago, my colleagues and I conducted a study that investigated people's conceptions of distance, a time when they felt detached from their friends (Helgeson, Shaver, & Dyer, 1987). Feelings of distance may stem from conflict. The primary feature of distance for both men and women was disapproval of a partner's behavior. Students reported feeling distant from their friends when their friends betrayed them, engaged in immoral behavior, or embarrassed them. Other notable features of distance were not spending time together and feeling as if the partner did not understand when there was a problem. Thus distance was partly defined as the opposite of intimacy: a lack of understanding. Overall, men and women had similar conceptions of distance. Moreover, both sexes reported feelings of anger more often than feelings of hurt.

Although the same events may lead to conflict for men and women, do they respond to conflict in similar ways? In a study of fourth- and fifth-graders, boys and girls reported they would respond to hypothetical conflicts quite differently (Rose & Asher, 1999). Girls were more likely than boys to say they would accommodate and compromise. Boys were more likely than girls to say they would respond by asserting their own interest and using more hostile strategies (e.g., verbal aggression, walk away from situation). Another study of children showed that males and females are equally likely to confront conflict, but do so in different ways. Third- and fourth-graders played a game with someone from class (Hartup et al., 1993). Conflict was instigated by providing each member of the dyad with different rules about how to play the game. (This could be really fun to do with adults!) Conflict was coded from videotapes and defined as one person objecting to the other person's behavior. Results showed no sex differences in the amount of conflict; that is, conflict was equally likely to be observed among boys and girls. Girls were more likely to respond to the conflict by asserting themselves and providing a rationale, whereas boys were more likely to respond to the conflict by asserting themselves without providing a rationale. In other words, girls would say, "You can't move that piece because . . ." and boys would leave it at "You can't move that piece!" The authors concluded that males issue orders without providing justification because they are concerned with their status in relationships: High status alone should be enough to justify an order. Females provide justification because they are concerned with maintaining the relationship and acquiring their partner's agreement. In this study, boys and girls were equally likely to acquiesce to their partner and equally likely to compromise.

Studies of adults show that women are more direct than men in bringing up conflict and discussing it with their same-sex friends. (As you will see in Chapter 9, this finding also holds for romantic relationships.) Although men are not direct in the sense of bringing up an issue, men are direct in terms of how they discuss conflict when it is brought up. For example, men are more likely than women to express anger to their friends. In the study just reported (Helgeson et al., 1987), men were more likely than women to report having argued with their partners. Women may be more concerned than men with the threat that such expressions bring to relationships.

TAKE HOME POINTS

- Men and women experience similar kinds of conflict in their friendships.

- However, men and women respond to conflict in different ways. Men are more likely to be direct in the confrontation and express anger; women are more likely to confront the conflict by discussing the issue and accommodating.

CHANGES OVER THE LIFE SPAN

More than chronological age, life events affect friendship. Getting married, becoming a parent, building a career, retiring, and widowhood are all examples of structural issues that may influence friendships for men and women. Some of these life events are more likely to be experienced by one sex than the other or are more likely to have an effect on the friendships of one sex than the other. For example, widowhood is more likely to affect women than men because women live longer than men. However, widowhood may have a stronger effect on men's friendships than women's friendships because wives are often the sole source of support and connection to other relationships for men. Retirement may have a stronger impact on men's friendships than women's friendships because men's friends are more likely than

women's to be found in the workplace. Here, I examine some of the structural factors that influence men's and women's friendships in early and later adulthood.

Early Adulthood: Marriage and Family

Historically, men's friendships were based at work and women's were based at home (Wellman, 1992). Women were the social organizers of the couple's friendships, often arranging social activities with other couples. In an early study, Fischer (1979) found that young married men had a larger social network than young married women because men had opportunities to meet people at work, whereas women's opportunities to meet people were restricted by having to stay home with children. Women who became parents had fewer friendships than men, presumably because child care took up a larger portion of women's than men's free time.

However, today the majority of women work outside the home, even when they have children. Would you predict that these earlier findings still hold today? Are men's friends at work and women's at home? Are men more likely than women to have friends during the early years of marriage and parenthood? One reason that the earlier findings may still hold today is that women who work outside the home are often responsible for housework and child care, which would leave little time for friends. Work also is less likely to lead to friendships for women who work in male-dominated professions because there would be fewer potential female friends available. Contemporary research shows that the number of friends and the frequency of interaction with friends decrease for both men and women during adulthood due to career development and increased time spent with family. Men spend less time with friends after they get married, in part because they have more familial obligations and in part because friends perceive they should not spend time with them now that they are married (Cohen, 1992). Thus both family and work obligations limit friendship. However, career development seems to have a greater effect on men's decreased contact with friends, and parenthood seems to have a greater effect on women's decreased contact with friends (Wright, 1989). The different positions held by men and women at work and in the family create unique opportunities for and place specific constraints on friendship formation.

Late Adulthood: Retirement and Empty Nest

The elderly value the same things from friendship as do younger people—similar values, similar lifestyles, and same sex, race, and marital status (Rawlins, 2004). The similarity is based less on age and more on capabilities. A major barrier to friendship among the elderly is increased health problems (Rawlins, 2004). Health problems may reduce mobility, may prevent reciprocity of support (a key component of friendship), may pose difficulties for communication, and can lead to increased health complaints, which often drive network members away. Although friends are a major source of companionship for the elderly, friends are less likely than family to provide assistance with health problems. Friendship seems to be free from the obligations of familial relationships to provide that kind of support.

With advancing age, friendships may increase for women and decrease for men due to differences in the opportunities for friendship. As women get older, they experience the departure of their children from home, which leads to a decrease in their household responsibilities. Thus older women are left with more time for friends. For men, increased age brings retirement, which may be associated with a loss of friends if many of their connections are made through work. With retirement, the number of friends often decreases for men, and men's dependence on wives for support and social contacts increases. In addition, women are more likely than men to maintain friendships from their youth in old age (Rawlins, 2004).

Marital status has a great impact on friendship among the elderly (Akiyama, Elliott, & Antonucci, 1996), especially elderly men. Married men have more people in their social network compared to unmarried men. For men, women are often their link to social relationships. Marital status has no effect on the number of friends that women have because women maintain a network of friends outside their marital relationship. Among the elderly, both men and women have more women friends than men friends (Akiyama et al., 1996). Because men die younger than women, elderly women are more available as friends (see Figure 8.9).

FIGURE 8.9 Picture of two elderly women friends. Partly because women outlive men, and partly because women maintain friendships from youth more than men, friendships among elderly women are strong.

A major source of friendship for the elderly, especially women, is the senior center. Elderly women who live alone are more likely than married women to use senior centers, and participation in senior centers is related to better mental health and good health behavior for these women (Aday, Kehoe, & Farney, 2006).

TAKE HOME POINTS

- The role of friendship in men's and women's lives decreases during early adulthood because family and work roles take up much of people's free time.

- With the departure of children from the home and retirement, friendship takes on an increasingly important role in women's lives.

- Elderly men have difficulty maintaing social ties if friendships were tied to work.

- Widowhood poses more of a problem for men than women because social connections are often maintained by wives.

CROSS-SEX FRIENDSHIP

Can men and women be friends? This is the question taken up by the characters played by Meg Ryan and Billy Crystal in the movie *When Harry Met Sally*. Sally told Harry they would just be friends. Harry, however, insisted they could not be friends because men and women can never be friends—sex always gets in the way. Even when Sally said she had a number of male friends, Harry argued that sex is somehow involved in the relationship—if not on her part, then on the part of the men. Of course, as you might imagine, a friendship emerges between Harry and Sally that then blossoms into a romantic relationship, confirming the stereotype that men and women cannot be *just* friends.

Many people today, especially college students, would disagree with Harry. In a study in which college students in the United States and Russia were asked to identify up to their eight closest friends, 27% of those friends were of the other sex for U.S. men and women (Sheets & Lugar, 2005). Among the Russian students, 26% of women had included an other-sex friend, but only 17% of men's friends included one of the other sex. Even noncollege samples show on average that 40% of men and 30% of women are able to identify at least one cross-sex friend (Wright, 1989). However, Harry may have a point about sex interfering with friendship. I elaborate on this later.

Most relationship research either focuses on same-sex friendship or romantic relationships. Cross-sex friendship is a relatively new area of research. A cross-sex friendship is typically defined as a friendship with someone of the other sex that is not romantic, sexual, or familial. Cross-sex friendships are not uncommon, but they are much less common than same-sex friendships (Monsour, 2002). Historically, cross-sex friendships among adults were rare; the traditional division of labor in society did not provide many opportunities for men and women to interact with one another. The changing nature of male and female roles in society has made members of the other sex more available as potential friends.

Comparisons to Same-Sex Friendship

The first studies of cross-sex friendship appeared in the 1980s. Most of those studies focused on comparing cross-sex friends to same-sex friends. Thus we know quite a bit about how the two types of friendships compare.

On average, cross-sex friendships are less intimate than same-sex friendships (Lempers & Clark-Lempers, 1993; Werking, 1997a). This description is more accurate for women than it is for men, however. Women are closer to their same-sex friends than their cross-sex friends, but it is not clear if this is the case for men.

Studies of adolescents, college students, and other adults show that males seem to benefit more from cross-sex friendship. A study of adolescents showed that girls reported similar levels of esteem support from same-sex and cross-sex friends, but boys reported more esteem support from cross-sex than same-sex friends (Kuttler et al., 1999). In a study of 11th- and 12th-graders, boys rated cross-sex friendship as more rewarding than same-sex friendship (Thomas & Daubman, 2001). A study of college students showed that both men and women were closer to their female friends than their male friends (Reeder, 2003). Men clearly self-disclose more to cross-sex than same-sex friends (Werking, 1997b).

Using the ADF (see Table 8.1), Wright and Scanlon (1991) found that women were closer to same-sex than cross-sex friends, but men were equally close to both types of friends. They asked adults in their twenties through fifties to complete the ADF for their best same-sex and best cross-sex friend. Women's friendships with women were closer than either women's friendships with men or men's friendships with either men or women. Women rated their same-sex friendship as higher on almost all of the dimensions on the ADF compared to their cross-sex friendship. Men, by contrast, gave equivalent ratings to their same-sex and cross-sex friendships on all of the dimensions except one: Men rated their male friendship as higher in voluntary interdependence than their female friendship. Voluntary interdependence, one of the two measures of relationship strength, reflects a willingness to commit time to the friend.

Cross-sex friendship takes on increasing importance with age. A study of 8th-, 10th-, and 12th-graders along with first-year college students showed that 8th- and 10th-graders rated

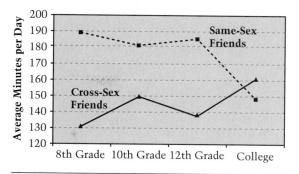

FIGURE 8.10 Among the younger grades, students spent more time with same-sex friends than cross-sex friends. By college, students spent more time with cross-sex than same-sex friends.
Source: Adapted from Johnson (2004).

their same-sex friendships as closer than their cross-sex friendships, but 12th-graders and first-year college students rated their cross-sex friendships as closer than their same-sex friendships (Johnson, 2004). Cross-sex friends were not supposed to include romantic partners in this study. Although females spent more time with friends overall than males, both males and females spent an increasing amount of time with cross-sex friends as they grew older, as shown in Figure 8.10.

What do people look for in a cross-sex friendship? As in our selection of same-sex friends, the similarity principle of attraction applies. That is, "Birds of a feather flock together." Cross-sex friends, like same-sex friends, have a great deal of demographic similarity. They are similar in age, education, marital status, and parental status. They also are similar in terms of personality traits (e.g., locus of control), behaviors (e.g., self-disclosure), and relationship beliefs (e.g., how to resolve conflicts; Morry, 2007). And, greater similarity predicts more satisfying friendships. However, there may be more subtle ways in which differences exist. College students said it was easier to relate to same-sex friends and they discussed and did different things with same-sex and cross-sex friends (Parks & Floyd, 1996).

Cross-sex friends might serve different functions for men and women compared to same-sex friends. As described in Chapter 7, having cross-sex friends during childhood provides opportunities to learn new styles of play and decreases sex-typed behavior (Fabes et al., 2004). Children who have cross-sex friends also may find it easier to interact with the other sex during adolescence, when such encounters are more frequent. Cross-sex friends can give insight into the other sex and can validate one's attractiveness to the other sex (Monsour, 2002). Some studies have found that men derive more emotional support from cross-sex friends than same-sex friends (Werking, 1997b). For women, cross-sex friendship provides companionship and a sense of relief from the intensity of their same-sex friendships. Women have more conflict with their same-sex friends than their cross-sex friends (Werking, 1997b). Women also suggest cross-sex friends provide a resource for physical protection (Bleske-Rechek & Buss, 2001). Thus it appears that both men and women are deriving emotional support from their friendships with women and companionship from their friendships with men.

Who has cross-sex friends? Gender roles may be one determinant. In a study of college students, feminine or expressive men had more cross-sex friendships than masculine men (Reeder, 2003). Similarly, masculine or agentic women had more cross-sex friendships than

feminine women. In other words, feminine men and women had more friendships with women, and masculine men and women had more friendships with men. Recall the results from the study on self-disclosure (Shaffer et al., 1996), which were depicted in Figure 8.7: Highly masculine men self-disclosed more to women than men. It may be that masculine men are inhibited in relationships with men, but not in relationships with women. Androgynous people may relate more similarly to cross-sex friends and same-sex friends because the friend's sex does not exert as much of an influence on their behavior.

Obstacles

O'Meara (1989) identified five challenges that cross-sex friendships face; these are listed in Table 8.3. First is the **emotional bond challenge**, in which friends question the nature of the relationship. Is the closeness called friendship or romantic love? This is the question that was taken up by the movie *When Harry Met Sally*. According to the movie, cross-sex friendship cannot really exist; even their friendship ultimately evolved into a romantic relationship. Second is the **sexual challenge**. We are socialized to view members of the other sex as potential romantic and sexual partners. Is there sexual attraction? This is the issue with which Harry was initially most concerned. Third is the **equality challenge**. Equality is central to friendship, and men and women have an unequal

TABLE 8.3 CHALLENGES OF CROSS-SEX FRIENDSHIP

Emotional bond	Is this friendship or romantic love?
Sexual	Is there sexual attraction?
Equality	Is this relationship equal?
Audience	How is this relationship viewed by others—and do I care?
Opportunity	Are there cross-sex people in my life available as friends?

Source: O'Meara (1989).

status. Will the relationship be equal? Fourth is the **audience challenge**. Friends may be concerned with the public's perception of their relationship. In fact, people often view cross-sex friendships with suspicion and wonder if they are not in fact romantic relationships. Fifth is the **opportunity challenge**. Cross-sex friendships are less common and more difficult to establish than same-sex friendships because women and men are often not together in situations that would allow them to become friends.

The prevalence of these challenges in college students' good and casual cross-sex friendships was examined with a series of open-ended questions and closed-ended questions that reflected these challenges (Monsour et al., 1994). The primary conclusion was that the majority of relationships did not suffer from any of these strains. The greatest challenge was the emotional bond challenge, and it was more of a problem with good relationships than with casual relationships. There were no sex differences in the sexual challenge, although more men than women admitted they thought about sex. The sexual challenge was mentioned more often by students who were single compared to students who were involved in a romantic relationship. The fewest problems were reported regarding the equality challenge. Theoretically, the equality challenge should be a major issue for cross-sex friends because friendship by definition is based on equality, and there may be an imbalance of power in cross-sex friendship. People are more satisfied with friendships that are equal in power (Veniegas & Peplau, 1997).

Although there was little support for the audience challenge, another study did show that women are more concerned with how people view their cross-sex friendships than their same-sex friendships (Wright & Scanlon, 1991). Monsour and colleagues. (1994) found that the audience challenge was related to students' scores on a personality variable known as

self-monitoring. Recall from Chapter 5 that high self-monitors are very aware of their environment and concerned about the impression they make on others. High self-monitors reported more audience challenge problems.

The authors concluded that researchers have overestimated the degree to which cross-sex friendships face these challenges. However, it is also possible that respondents described only the cross-sex friendships that did not suffer from these challenges. A cross-sex friendship facing any one of these challenges might not be the one that comes to mind when researchers ask about friendship. Cross-sex friendships that do face these challenges may be less close than ones that do not. In addition, it would be important for future research to obtain both persons' perceptions of a cross-sex friendship; one person may not be facing the emotional bond challenge or sexual challenge, but the other may.

In one study in which both friends' views of the relationship were elicited, one person's romantic interest in the cross-sex friendship was uncorrelated with the other person's romantic interest in the friendship (Afifi & Burgoon, 1998). If the emotional bond challenge truly did not exist, there would be substantial agreement between friends (and a correlation) as to feelings toward the relationship.

The one challenge that has received the most research attention, especially in recent studies, is the sexual challenge. Despite Monsour and colleagues' (1994) results, evidence indicates that sexual tension is a problem in cross-sex friendship, especially for men (Parks & Floyd, 1996). Men are more likely than women to report sexual attraction and a desire for sex with cross-sex friends compared to women (Bleske-Rechek & Buss, 2001; Bleske & Buss, 2000).

However, a study of college students showed that most did not report either romantic or sexual attraction to cross-sex friends (Reeder, 2000). Instead, the most prevalent kind of attraction was friendship attraction—liking or loving each other as friends. Only 28% reported being physically or sexually attracted to their friend, and 14% expressed an interest in a romantic relationship with the friend. However, among those who were sexually attracted to their friend, less than half were also romantically attracted to the friend. Thus it is important to distinguish the sexual challenge from the emotional bond challenge. The authors also noted that romantic and sexual attraction seemed to dissipate with time, as these kinds of attraction were less prevalent in cross-sex friendships of longer duration. Because the study was cross-sectional, it is not clear whether romantic and sexual attraction actually decreased as the relationship lengthened or whether relationships with romantic and/or sexual attraction eventually dissolved or changed into romantic relationships.

Men appear to make less of a distinction between cross-sex friends and romantic partners compared to women. One-sided attraction occurs on the part of males more than females (Bleske & Buss, 2000). However, one-sided attraction on the part of women is more likely to lead to sex than one-sided attraction on the part of men, suggesting that men are more likely than women to take advantage of sexual opportunities (Bleske & Buss, 2000).

Not only do people express sexual interest in cross-sex friends, but a number of people report having had sex with cross-sex friends. Some research shows that half (51%) of college students have had sex in the past with a platonic cross-sex friend whom they were not dating nor had any intention of dating (Afifi & Faulkner, 2000). Of those, 56% had sex with more than one cross-sex friend. Cultural norms would suggest that having sex with a friend would have a devastating effect on a relationship. Indeed, this happens on occasion. But the majority (67%) of people said the quality of the relationship improved after having sex. Of those, only half said

the relationship evolved into a romantic one. Thus sex enhanced the quality of many *friendships*. According to Baumgarte (2002), we lack a cultural script for cross-sex friendship. We shouldn't assume sex is bad for a friendship—it depends on how sex is interpreted by both partners.

Although the prevalence of sexual and romantic attraction in cross-sex friendships is debatable, the research clearly shows that these challenges exist for some cross-sex friendships. Thus one might ask, "What keeps cross-sex friendships from developing into romantic relationships?" The number one reason for keeping a cross-sex friendship platonic seems to be the desire to preserve the relationship and avoid any kind of breakup (Messman, Canary, & Hause, 2000). People may perceive that romantic relationships have the potential to end. By keeping a relationship as a friendship, we can feel more secure in maintaining that relationship. Other reasons that college students give for keeping a cross-sex friendship platonic include not being attracted to the person, believing that one's social network would disapprove of the relationship (the audience challenge), and being afraid of getting involved romantically with anyone because of the risk of getting hurt.

Thus how do people maintain cross-sex friendships? How do they keep these friendships from developing into romantic relationships? They avoid discussing the relationship, they avoid flirting, and they discuss other romantic relationships (Guerrero & Chavez, 2005).

Little longitudinal data exists on cross-sex friendships. It would be interesting to know how likely they are to develop into romantic relationships, how likely they are to dissolve, and what instigates their termination. Does getting married or becoming involved in a romantic relationship interfere with cross-sex friendship? A local radio station in Pittsburgh invited listeners to call in and share how they would feel

**DO GENDER 8.5
What Happens When Men
and Women Become Friends?**

Interview 10 of your fellow students about their current and past cross-sex friendships. Find out what happened to the past relationships: Did they end? Did any of them evolve into romantic relationships? Examine the reasons for the relationship ending, including O'Meara's (1989) challenges.

Examine how certain life events influenced these friendships, such as the development of a romantic relationship. In other words, when one person developed a romantic relationship, did that alter the cross-sex friendship? How did the romantic partner view the cross-sex friendship? Are men and women equally accepting of their partner's cross-sex friends?

if a future husband or wife had a cross-sex friend stand up for them at their wedding. Listeners, especially women, were appalled. However, the listeners to this radio station were hardly a representative sample. Today, men do stand up for women as the "man of honor" or "person of honor," and women do stand up for men as the "best woman" or "best person." These people are sometimes friends and sometimes siblings. Explore the future of cross-sex friendship in Do Gender 8.5.

Changes Over the Life Span

Age has a curvilinear relation to cross-sex friendship. Cross-sex friendship is rare in childhood, peaks during later adolescence and young adulthood, and becomes rare in old age (Werking, 1997a; Winstead, Derlega, & Rose, 1997).

From early to middle childhood, cross-sex friendship and cross-sex play decrease as the social network becomes more discouraging of such behavior (Monsour, 2002). Children may not have the opportunity to make friends with members of the other sex because boys and girls are often pitted against each other. In school, there may be the boys' lunch line and the girls' lunch line. Often teams are formed by having the girls compete against the boys. In addition, children, especially boys, are often teased if they play with the other sex. However, having cross-sex friends as children increases the likelihood of having cross-sex friends later in life (Monsour, 2002).

Cross-sex friendships are more common in adolescence and young adulthood (Winstead et al., 1997). In a study of 10th- through 12th-graders, 47% reported a cross-sex friend as one of their closest friends, and males and females were equally likely to identify a cross-sex friend (Kuttler et al., 1999). In college, there is more opportunity for cross-sex friendships due to the availability of potential friends and the similar status that men and women hold in college. Furthermore, cross-sex friendships likely lead to dating relationships.

Among adults, marital status influences cross-sex friendship. Marriage may be a deterrent from friendly relations with the other sex. A number of studies have shown that married people are less likely than unmarried people to have cross-sex friends (Werking, 1997a). However, recall that married people also have fewer same-sex friends than unmarried people.

Cross-sex friendship declines with age among adults (Winstead et al., 1997). The elderly are more likely than younger people to associate cross-sex friendship with romantic interest (Rawlins, 2004), and there is a strong norm among the elderly against dating. Thus cross-sex friendships are most likely to occur among the elderly in the context of an organized social event involving a lot of other people. Elderly women, in particular, avoid cross-sex friendships. The following example illustrates just how foreign the concept of cross-sex friendship is to an elderly woman. My mother-in-law lived in an apartment building that housed mostly senior citizens after she was widowed. I often saw a single elderly man sitting by himself at a picnic table outside the building. Even though my mother-in-law was an extremely friendly and sociable person, she did not feel comfortable talking to a man unless she was in the company of other women. If the person at the picnic table were a woman, I have no doubt my mother-in-law would have been sitting right beside her in a minute. It's especially unfortunate for men that the norms against cross-sex interaction are so strong because older men tend to have lost more of their same-sex friends.

The question is whether the norm prohibiting cross-sex friendship is an age effect or a cohort effect. When today's college students reach senior citizen status, will they also find strong norms against cross-sex friendships?

TAKE HOME POINTS

- For women, same-sex friendships are closer than cross-sex friendships.

- Men, by contrast, seem to gain more from cross-sex friendships in terms of emotional support and intimacy.

- Cross-sex friendships serve some important functions that same-sex friendships do not serve, such as emotional support for men, companionship for women, and the perspective of the other sex for both men and women.

- Cross-sex friendships face a number of challenges: emotional bond, sexual, equality, audience, and opportunity.

- There is debate over how much romantic and sexual interest pervade cross-sex friendships. Sexual interest seems to be more common among men than women.

- Cross-sex friendships are rare among children, peak during adolescence and young adulthood, and diminish substantially among the elderly.

CROSS-RACE FRIENDSHIP

Race is a powerful determinant of friendship. It is one of the demographic variables upon which friends tend to match. However, cross-race friendship does exist—but more so among children than adults. Even among children, cross-race friendship appears to decline with age and seems to be less stable than same-race friendships (Aboud, Mendelson, & Purdy, 2003). Cross-race friendships are rated as less intimate than same-race friendships, but as similar in terms of loyalty.

One factor that influences cross-race friendship is the diversity of the schools that children attend. Cross-race friendships are more common among racially diverse schools (Quillan & Campbell, 2003). Children who are in the racial minority of a school that has a small number of minority students are more likely to have only same-race friends. One study of first- and fourth-grade children showed that the racial diversity of the school influenced children's perceptions of similarity and feelings toward cross-race friendship (McGlothin & Killen, 2005). Children who attended more racially diverse schools evaluated same-race and cross-race peers as equally likely to become friends. However, White children who attended more racially homogenous schools viewed cross-race peers as less likely to become friends than same-race peers—especially if the cross-race peers did not share the same activity interests. It is noteworthy that students judged friendship as most likely to occur between two people when there were shared activity interests—regardless of the racial composition of the dyad. Thus shared interests seems to be a more important factor than race in determining friendship for children.

Why do cross-race friendships decline with age? Although children do not express overt prejudice—that is, they do not identify race as a factor in selecting a friend—more subtle forms of prejudice may begin to emerge. One study showed that the **outgroup homogeneity effect** begins to emerge with age (McGlothin, Killen & Edmonds, 2005). With increased age, White children began to perceive Black children as more similar to one another—and thus more different from themselves.

Which children have cross-race friends? First, boys are more likely than girls to have cross-race friends (Scott, 2004). Second, social status may be associated with more cross-race friendship. In a study of Black and White children, those who were well-liked, popular in school, perceived to be smart, and leaders had more cross-race friends (Lease & Blake, 2005). The authors concluded that the same set of social skills that leads to friendship also leads to crossing racial barriers. The findings of that study did not hold as well for Black boys. In the case of Black boys, those with cross-race friends were perceived to be nice and good listeners, but not leaders or outstanding athletes.

Cross-race friendships are more problematic between Blacks and Whites than between two people of other races (Scott, 2004). White people are more likely to have cross-race friends who are Hispanic or Asian than Black (Quillan & Campbell, 2003). Cross-race friendships also are less common among Whites than among African Americans, largely because African Americans are more likely to be in the minority in their environment, which means more Whites are available for friendship. In a study of junior high school students, 25% of the White students had cross-race friendships, whereas 50% of the Black students had cross-race friendships (Clark & Ayers, 1992). Cross-race friendships were more common than cross-sex friendships.

The largest barrier to cross-race friendship is prejudice (S. Rose, 1996). Prejudice is associated with fewer cross-race friendships (Aboud et al., 2003). Friendship by definition involves an equal-status relationship; thus one reason African Americans may be leery of friendships with White people is that they are not typically treated by Whites as peers (S. Rose, 1996). Although people today are less overtly prejudiced than in past decades, there are more covert forms of prejudice, such as preferring not to live in a neighborhood with people of another race and preferring not to have your child marry a person of another race.

FRIENDSHIP AT WORK

Because men and women spend so much time at work and because work is so central to our lives, it is not surprising that some of our friendships are based at work. Friendships at work serve multiple functions, all of which can help one to make work more successful (Elsesser & Peplau, 2006). Same-level friendships can provide access to information and assistance with work, promote team building, and provide emotional support. Friendships with mentors can provide advice, protection, and access to promotion. Despite companies' concerns that friendships at work can be disruptive and distracting, there is evidence that having friends at work may enhance performance. A 2001 Gallup Poll found that people who had a best friend at work were more likely to be engaged in their work (Jones, 2004). Over half of the adults polled who strongly agreed that they had a best friend at work said they were engaged in their work, whereas only 8% who strongly disagreed with that statement were engaged in their work. A study of a telecommunications company found that workers who developed reciprocal relations at work, in which they did favors for and received favors from one another at work, were more productive (Flynn, 2003). Although friendships with a boss are rare, those friendships are associated with job satisfaction (Rath, 2006)

Friendships at work usually follow a developmental course. Relations at work begin on an instrumental level: Both people are working on a task. One person then chooses whether to make the relationship more affective. "Friendly relations at work" must be distinguished from friendship at work (Bridge & Baxter, 1992). Friendly relations are people at work with whom one is sociable. Being friendly with each other at work promotes cooperation and getting the job done. Friendly relations lack the intimacy of friendship and do not involve the obligations of friendship.

Friendships at work are common. In survey studies that have involved over 500 full-time workers, Marks (1994) found that 50% of respondents identified at least one coworker who was a close friend, 48% said they discussed important matters with at least one coworker, and 50% said they get together outside of work with at least one coworker. There were no sex differences in these measures of coworker friendship. There was a strong preference, however, for coworkers to be same-sex friends, especially among men. The same-sex preference for friendship at work can be disadvantageous to women—especially women who work in an all-male environment or women who work in an environment where the higher status people are all men.

Work is a good setting to study cross-sex friendships. Although the workplace is still sex segregated, there is increasing opportunity for men and women to work together. A study in Helsinki found that engineers, teachers, factory workers, and secretaries had more cross-sex friendships when their jobs were not sex segregated (Haavio-Mannila, Kauppinen-Toropainen, & Kandolin, 1988). Cross-sex friendships also were more likely to form among people who were doing the same kind of work. Thus men and women are more likely to develop cross-sex friendships at work if they actually perform similar jobs.

There are barriers to cross-sex friendship at work (Elsesser & Peplau, 2006). Men and women may be concerned that friendliness at work will be misinterpreted as romantic or sexual interest—or, worse yet, as sexual harassment. Even if the recipient of the friendly overture does not misinterpret the behavior, men and women may be concerned that coworkers will! In other words, the audience challenge of cross-sex friendship may be especially relevant in the work environment. In a study of men and women professionals at work, men and women were equally likely to voice these concerns about cross-sex friendship at work (Elsesser & Peplau, 2006). However, married employees expressed fewer concerns about cross-sex friendship than unmarried employees, and more concerns were expressed about cross-sex friendships with supervisors or subordinates than peers.

Bridge and Baxter (1992) refer to friendships at work as "blended friendships" because they require the merging of two roles: coworker and friend. Because a friendship at work involves two roles, it is vulnerable to **role conflict**, which occurs when the demands of one role are inconsistent with the demands of another role. You might have found yourself suffering from role conflict when your role as student required that you study for an upcoming exam and your role as a member of some organization (band, fraternity/sorority) required that you work on the upcoming festivities at your school. Bridge and Baxter interviewed nonacademic university employees as well as adult students and found evidence for four different kinds of role conflict among friends at work. They did not examine the issue of gender, however, so I will speculate as to whether gender ought to be an important factor in these kinds of conflicts. You can test these ideas in Do Gender 8.6.

Impartiality versus favoritism: As a friend, we expect special treatment and favoritism, but the workplace typically requires treating people equally. Is there any

DO GENDER 8.6
Role Conflict at Work

Develop items to measure the forms of role conflict discussed by Bridge and Baxter (1992). Administer the items to men and women who have a close friend at work. Determine if there are sex differences. Also, develop a set of open-ended questions to assess role conflict at work.

reason to believe men or women would be more likely to suffer from this role conflict?

Openness versus closedness: Friendships require open, honest communication. At work, we may be expected to hold confidences. Because the literature shows that women self-disclose to friends more than men do, we might predict that women would be more likely than men to suffer from this role conflict. However, sex differences in self-disclosure are clearer when the topic is a personal one. It is not clear if there would be sex differences in refraining from self-disclosure when the topic is work related.

Autonomy versus connectedness: Work provides a way of connecting to one another, which should foster friendship. Difficulties arise when we feel a lack of autonomy in a friendship because we spend so much time with a friend (i.e., seeing the person daily at work). Because autonomy is central to the male gender role, we might expect that men are more likely than women to suffer from this form of role conflict.

Judgment versus acceptance: An important attribute of friendship is mutual acceptance. The work role might require one person to critically evaluate the other.

The literature on women's responsiveness to evaluative feedback suggests that women take feedback to heart more than men do, which could lead to more conflict in women's than men's friendships. Women supervisors may become nervous when providing feedback to women. One reason could be that some of these supervisor-supervisee relationships are friendships. Alternatively, we might predict that men suffer from this form of role conflict more than women because criticizing someone or evaluating someone creates a status differential in a relationship, and men are more sensitive than women to status in friendship.

Unlike friendships outside of work, women may be less desirable as friends at work. According to Ibarra (1993), women may not be selected as friends because (1) they are in the minority in terms of numbers at the upper level, (2) they are in lower-status positions at work, and (3) sex-role stereotypes lead to unfavorable attributions for their performance. Markiewicz, Devine, and Kausilas (2000) studied the friendships of men and women information technologists, lawyers, and middle managers. As predicted, there was no evidence that friendships with women were more satisfying. It was the quality of friendships with men that predicted work outcomes. For example, greater conflict with the closest male friend was associated with less job satisfaction, and a stronger relationship with a male friend was associated with a higher salary. Of course, the study is cross-sectional, so it is not clear whether relationships with men influenced the job outcomes or the job outcomes influenced the relationships.

Friendships at work are usually formed among peers, people who are working at similar job levels (Winstead et al., 1995). In fact, if only one person in a friendship is promoted, the friendship may disintegrate (Wright, 1999). Another kind of friendship at work is an unequal status one, the friendship between one person and his or her mentor. There is a benefit and a cost to friendships between a supervisor and a supervisee. On the downside, such friendships make disciplinary action more difficult for the supervisor; on the upside, such friendships may encourage greater cooperation and facilitate getting the job done. If the subordinate is female and the supervisor is male, people are often suspicious of the nature of the relationship.

There has been some research on women's friendships with other women at work. When few women were in the workplace and women were considered tokens, women viewed other women with suspicion and often participated in the derogation of women (O'Leary, 1988). Women may have been competitive with one another for what they viewed as the few women positions.

Historically, relationships with a female boss were viewed as especially problematic, as evidenced by an entire book devoted to the issue: *How to Work for a Woman Boss* (Bern, 1987). This book provides employees with dozens of strategies on how to work for a female boss. Some are quite humorous today, and others seem as though they would be equally useful when working for a male boss (see Table 8.4 for sample strategies). Recall from Chapter 7 that today most men and women do not have clear preferences for a male or female boss. However, at times women prefer to work for male bosses because men typically have more power and can acquire more resources. But there is also evidence that women prefer to work for female bosses because women typically treat them with

TABLE 8.4 TIPS ON HOW TO WORK FOR A WOMAN BOSS

1. Forget your anger and quit demanding that your boss have qualities that she doesn't possess at the present time. If she's astute, she's going to realize her deficiencies pretty quickly and overcome the problem.

2. Assuming that you have a good relationship with your woman superior, tactfully suggest that a few workshops might be helpful for achieving greater understanding between her and the men and women in her department. She may view this as a fine idea and present it to the president. Many excellent training programs are available and are quite effective for lessening a tension-filled workplace atmosphere.

3. Be enthusiastic and optimistic. These two personality traits will take you very far with little effort on your part. Moreover, they will make you visible, especially when your passive boss practices being invisible.

4. If your boss is the token woman manager within the company, practice patience. She might be acting passive deliberately in order not to make waves or call attention to herself. If you are a woman, remember an important point: Businesses that have appointed one female manager are often slow to promote another woman to an equal position. Play it cool; otherwise, you will threaten not only your woman boss but her male superiors as well.

5. And most important, don't discuss your weaknesses with her, for she'll never let you forget them and will continually use them to further intimidate you.

6. Let her open the door and hold it for you if she reaches it first.

7. Let her light her own cigarette, pour her own drink, and carry her own packages.

8. Allow her to put on her own coat, but help her if she's overburdened with papers and briefcase. In the reverse situation, allow her to help you.

Source: Bern (1987).

more respect and more often involve them in decisions.

FRIENDSHIPS OF LESBIANS AND GAY MEN

The nature of friendship as typically defined by heterosexuals is similar for homosexuals. However, friendship holds a different place in the lives of homosexuals. Friendships often replace or take greater precedence over familial relationships among homosexuals because homosexuals have less support from family than heterosexuals do (Nardi & Sherrod, 1994; Shippy, Cantor, & Brennan, 2004). A study of older gay men (ages 50 to 87) showed that men maintain contact with their biological families but call upon friends for assistance (Shippy et al., 2004). There is surprisingly little research on friendships among homosexuals.

We do know that the friendships of gay men and lesbians parallel those of heterosexuals in terms of matching on an array of demographic variables. That is, gay men and lesbians are likely to be friends with people who share the same sex, race, age, relationship status, and parental status (Galupo, 2007; Weinstock, 1998). However, matching on sexual orientation differs between gay men/lesbian women and bisexuals. As shown in Figure 8.11, gay men and lesbians have more friends who are gay or lesbian than heterosexual or bisexual, whereas bisexual men and women are more likely to have heterosexual friends than gay, lesbian, or bisexual friends (Galupo, 2007).

One question is whether gay men's and lesbians' friendships differ in the same way that heterosexual men's and women's friendships do. Do gay men focus on shared activities? Do lesbians focus on self-disclosure? Nardi and Sherrod (1994) addressed these questions by sending out a survey on friendship to men and women who participated in gay and lesbian

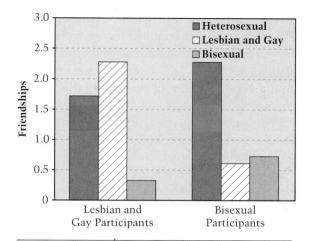

FIGURE 8.11 Lesbian and gay men are more likely to have friends of the same sexual orientation, whereas bisexual men and women are more likely to have heterosexual friends than gay, lesbian, or bisexual friends. Adapted from Galupo (2007)

organizations. The sample was predominantly White, educated, and professional. Respondents were asked to evaluate three kinds of friends: casual (more than an acquaintance but not a close friend), close (mutual commitment to one another, talk openly with one another), and best friend (greatest commitment to one another, talk the most openly with one another, accepts you as you are). The best friend could not be the respondent's partner.

First, Nardi and Sherrod (1994) found there were no sex differences in number of friends: Gay men and lesbians named the same number of people in each of the three categories. They also found no sex differences in self-disclosure, activities shared over the previous 2 months, or social support. Thus, unlike studies of friendship among heterosexuals, homosexual men's and women's friendships were more similar in terms of how they spent their time together. These data suggest that the agentic/communal distinction that characterizes sex differences in the heterosexual friendship literature does not reflect sex alone. In the friendships of gay men and lesbians, the male/female distinction does not apply.

There were no differences in the amount of conflict gay men and lesbians reported in their friendships. However, there were sex differences in how important it was to resolve conflict. Lesbians said it was more important to resolve conflict and were more bothered by conflict than gay men were. This difference is consistent with the heterosexual literature. In addition, lesbians were more likely than gay men to report expressing emotion when resolving conflict, but lesbians and gay men were equally likely to talk about or ignore the conflict.

One way in which gay and lesbian friendship differs from heterosexual friendship is that the line between friend and lover is more often blurred. Nardi and Sherrod (1994) found that 71% of gay men and 84% of lesbians considered their lover to be their best friend. Lesbians, in particular, are likely to remain friends with former lovers. Because homosexuals' romantic partners are of the same sex as their friends, homosexual same-sex friendship may be more similar to heterosexual cross-sex friendship. Thus homosexual friendship may face some of the same challenges as heterosexual cross-sex friendship.

Nardi and Sherrod (1994) suggested that sexuality will be more integral to gay men's friendships than to lesbians' friendships because men in general are more likely to use sex to achieve intimacy. They found that the majority of gay men (62%) reported having had sex with one or more of their casual friends, whereas a minority of lesbians (34%) reported having had sex with one or more of their casual friends (Nardi, 1992). The discrepancy was not as large for close friends: Seventy-six percent of gay men reported having had sex with one or more of their close friends, whereas 59% of lesbians reported having had sex with one or more of their close friends (Nardi, 1992). For gay men, sex is likely to precede friendship, whereas for lesbians, friendship precedes sex. This is parallel to the findings on the relation between sex and intimacy among heterosexual men and women.

SUMMARY

Studies on children and adult friendship do not reveal consistent differences in the number of friends that males and females have. However, female's friendships seem to be closer than those of males. One reason for this is the nature of male and female friendship: Men's relationships are agentic—activity focused—and women's relationships are communal—emotion focused. Sex differences in the nature of friendship emerge with age. Boys emphasize the instrumental aspects of friendship (shared activities) and girls emphasize the emotional aspects of friendship (self-disclosure). These differences persist into adulthood. Partly because of self-disclosure, girls' and women's friendships are closer than those of males. The closeness of male friendships is restricted by homophobia and emotional inhibition.

Do women self-disclose more than men? The answer is yes, and the sex difference increases as the topic of disclosure becomes more personal. One reason for this sex difference is that both men and women view self-disclosure as a feminine activity and view men who self-disclose less favorably than women who self-disclose. Women are more likely to self-disclose to women, whereas men reserve some disclosures for women and some for men. Aside from sex, a host of other variables influence self-disclosure, such as gender roles, situational variables, age, and marital status.

Does self-disclosure equal intimacy? Traditionally, intimacy has been defined by self-disclosure, but this has been a subject of contention. Some people maintain that self-disclosure is a feminine version of intimacy and men define intimacy through shared experiences. Research shows that self-disclosure is important to both men's and women's conceptions of intimacy, but men's conceptions may also include shared activities. For both men and women, an intimate interaction is one in which they feel understood, cared for, and appreciated. These feelings may come from self-disclosure, shared activities, or some combination of the two.

Friendships are not only a source of affection, intimacy, and support but also can be a source of conflict. Men and women report similar sources of conflict in their friendships but handle conflict somewhat differently. Women are more likely to confront conflict directly with the intent of resolution and in a way that does not harm the relationship; men raise the issue of conflict, but with less concern about its effect on the relationship.

The study of friendship is greatly limited by its focus on middle-class White people. Interesting differences appear in the nature of friendship due to ethnicity, social class, and cultural ideology. Friendship also is affected by age and by stage in the life cycle—being married, having children, working. All these factors influence the availability of friends as well as the place of friendship in life.

An emerging area of research is on cross-sex friendship. Although cross-sex friends are not as common as same-sex friends, cross-sex friendship is not unusual. Women still rate same-sex friends as closer than cross-sex friends. However, men are sometimes closer to cross-sex friends. Cross-sex friendship can serve important functions for men and women, such as insight into the other sex, a source of emotional support for men, and relief from the intensity and conflict of same-sex friendship for women. A number of barriers to cross-sex friendship have been postulated, but little empirical evidence indicates these barriers actually pose serious difficulties. One controversial area is sexual attraction. Some evidence suggests this is more of a problem for men than for women in cross-sex friendship. Data are meager on the outcome of cross-sex friendships: Do they last, dissolve, or evolve into romantic relationships? Cross-sex friendship is most common among young adults and least common among children and older adults. Social norms and structural barriers discourage children from playing with the other sex, discourage married adults from spending time with the other sex, and inhibit the elderly from developing relationships with the other sex.

Cross-race friendships are more common among children than adults. Prejudice and school diversity are related to cross-race friendship. Boys may have more cross-race friends than girls.

One arena in which cross-sex friendship can arise is the workplace. Friends at work are becoming increasingly common, especially among people who are peers and have similar job responsibilities. Despite the concerns that organizations often have for fraternization among employees, there is evidence that friendship at work is good for productivity. I discussed several difficulties that friendships at work face due to the inherent conflict between the roles of friend and coworker.

I conclude the chapter by discussing friendships among gay men and lesbians. The communal/agentic dimensions of friendship used to evaluate heterosexual friendship do not apply to homosexual friendship. Sexuality plays a greater role among the friendships of gay men. Because of the potential for sexual attraction, studies of friendship among gay men and lesbians may benefit from comparisons to cross-sex friendship among heterosexuals.

DISCUSSION QUESTIONS

1. Whose relationships are closer: men's or women's? Why?
2. How should we determine the answer to the previous question? How would you define a friend?
3. What role do self-disclosure and shared activities play in men's and women's friendship?
4. What person and situation variables influence self-disclosure?
5. What inhibits men's self-disclosure to other men?
6. Why are females' relationships considered to be more fragile than those of males'?
7. Discuss competition in the context of friendship. Do you believe that it is healthy or unhealthy?
8. What are some critical normative life events that affect friendship? Are the effects for men and women the same?
9. Describe how the way a culture construes the roles of men and women could affect their friendships.
10. In what ways are cross-sex friendships similar to and different from same-sex friendships?
11. What are the challenges that cross-sex friendship face?
12. What does the research on same-sex friendship and cross-sex friendship lead you to predict about friendship among gay men and lesbians?
13. How do marriage and work affect men's and women's friendship?

SUGGESTED READING

Dindia, K., & Allen, M. (1992). Sex differences in self-disclosure: A meta-analysis. *Psychological Bulletin, 112,* 106–124.

Elsesser, K., & Peplau, L. A. (2006). The glass partition: Obstacles to cross-sex friendships at work. *Human Relations, 59,* 1077–1100.

Monsour, M. (2002). *Women and men as friends: Relationships across the life span in the 21st century.* Mahwah, NJ: Erlbaum.

Nardi, P. M., & Sherrod, D. (1994). Friendship in the lives of gay men and lesbians. *Journal of Social and Personal Relationships, 11,* 185–199.

Winstead, B., Derlega, V. J., & Rose, S. (1997). *Gender and close relationships.* Thousand Oaks, CA: Sage.

Wright, P. H. (2006). Toward an expanded orientation to the comparative study of women's and men's same-sex friendships. In K. Dindia & D. J. Canary (Eds.), *Sex differences and similarities in communication* (2nd Ed.) (pp. 37–57). Mahwah, NJ: Erlbaum.

KEY TERMS

Audience challenge—Concern that cross-sex friends have about how their relationship is viewed by others.

Autonomy versus connectedness—Conflict encountered by friends at work when the regular exposure to one another required by the work relationship begins to interfere with individual feelings of autonomy.

Corumination—Discussing problems repeatedly in the context of a relationship.

Dispositional level of analysis—Emphasizes the characteristics of the person as a determinant of friendship.

Emotional bond challenge—Challenge faced by cross-sex friendship whereby the friends must decide if the closeness they feel toward one another is friendship or romantic love.

Equality challenge—Challenge faced by cross-sex friendships because the equality central to friendship conflicts with the status hierarchy typically associated with male/female relationships.

Homophobia—Fear of homosexuality or fear of appearing homosexual.

Impartiality versus favoritism—Situation encountered by friends at work when the desire to give a friend special treatment conflicts with the necessity to treat all workers the same.

Judgment versus acceptance—Difficulty experienced by friends at work when the mutual acceptance expected of friendship conflicts with the requirement that one friend critically evaluate the other.

Openness versus closedness—Situation encountered by friends at work when the expectation of the honest communication central to friendship conflicts with the necessity to keep professional confidences.

Opportunity challenge—Difficulty experienced when attempting to establish a cross-sex friendship that results from the fact that members of the same sex are generally more accessible.

Outgroup homogeneity effect—The tendency to see members of the outgroup as all alike, more similar than different, as compared to the ingroup, to which one attributes greater diversity.

Role conflict—Situation that occurs when the demands of one role are inconsistent with the demands of another role.

Sexual challenge—Challenge faced by cross-sex friendship whereby the friends must ask themselves if there is a sexual attraction between them that could lead to a romantic relationship.

Structural level of analysis——Emphasizes the different positions or roles men and women hold in society as a determinant of friendship.

CHAPTER 9

ROMANTIC RELATIONSHIPS

My husband had a number of friends from work with whom we occasionally got together. One of these friends was Bill. My husband had known Bill for about a year, and to his knowledge (or anyone else's), Bill was not romantically involved with anyone. Bill was from India and had gone home for a 2-week vacation. When Bill returned, he was married.

This was an arranged marriage, a concept foreign to people in the Western world. Marriage without love? Without romance? It may surprise you to know that romantic relationships are a relatively recent phenomenon even in the United States (Murstein, 1974). Historically, people turned to friends and relatives rather than a spouse for love and emotional support. The functions of marriage were specific: economic security and procreation. Love was not among these functions. One reason love did not play a significant role in marriage is that it was thought to threaten family bonds, which were more important for position in society at that time.

Even a few hundred years ago, love was largely independent of and antithetical to marriage. When two people fell in love, it was regarded as a problem. Parents were concerned about controlling this "dangerous passion." In the 19th century, spouses were polite to one another and, ideally, compatible, but they led largely separate lives. Even by the mid–19th century, love was not a prerequisite to marriage. Love was expected to follow rather than precede marriage. When individual choice did emerge in the 19th century, people generally chose their partner based on character, health, religious morals, and financial stability. These were the same factors that guided parents' choices. Choosing a partner based on physical passion was not at all acceptable.

During the latter part of the 19th century and in the 20th century, the idea of marriage based on love developed. This coincided with American women's increase in freedom and status. It is the 20th century that is really known as the century of the "love marriage." Today, the practical functions of marriage have been replaced with more emotional functions. We have very high expectations of marriage. Marriage is expected to be a "SuperRelationship" that fulfills spiritual, sexual, romantic, and emotional needs rather than social, economic, or religious requirements (Whitehead & Popenoe, 2001).

This chapter focuses on romantic relationships, what men and women want from relationships, and how men and women behave in relationships. I discuss how men and women construe the positive aspects of romantic relationships, such as intimacy, love, and sexuality, and also how men and women manage the conflict in their relationships. Research focuses on dating couples, often college students, as well as married couples.

The majority of research focuses on heterosexual relationships. However, there is a growing literature on homosexual relationships. Studying homosexual relationships not only allows us to test whether our existing theories about relationships generalize to homosexuals but also provides us with insight into gender. Are differences in heterosexual men's and women's behavior in relationships due to the structure of the relationship (i.e., it consists of a male and a female) or due to inherent differences between men's and women's personalities? Examining same-sex romantic relationships allows us to address this question.

RELATIONSHIP DEVELOPMENT

Men and women are definitely interested in romantic relationships. In a survey of over 2,000 freshmen from 101 colleges and universities in the United States, 96% said they expected to marry (Steinberg, 1998). Among people over 30 who have not yet married, men indicate a greater desire to marry than women (Frazier et al., 1996). One reason may have to do with men's lack of support relative to women. In this study, men reported less social support than women, and lacking social support was associated with greater interest in marriage.

Standards for Relationships

In general, men and women have similar reasons for entering romantic relationships. Support and companionship are the primary motivating factors. But when involved in a romantic relationship, do men and women have different expectations of what the relationship should provide or use different standards to measure a good relationship? As you will discover later in the chapter, women are less satisfied with their romantic relationships, including marriage, than men. Different expectations have been postulated as an explanation for women's greater unhappiness with relationships. Women may have higher relationship standards than men, which could result in relationships being less likely to meet women's standards. Alternatively, men and women may have the same standards, but relationships could provide more resources to men than to women. If true, men are more likely to have their standards met because they get more out of relationships than women. The first reason focuses on women: women having higher relationship standards. The second reason focuses on the relationship: how its characteristics meet more of men's than women's needs. Evidence supports both views.

Tornstam (1992) concluded that women have higher expectations than men for romantic relationships. In a study of approximately 3,000 men and women in Sweden, ages 18 to 80, younger women (under 50) had higher expectations for intimacy (defined as mutual trust, openness, and understanding) compared to men.

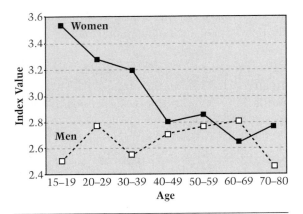

FIGURE 9.1 Expectations of intimacy. Among younger people, women have higher expectations for intimacy than men. Among adults age 50 and over, men and women have similar expectations for intimacy.
Source: L. Tornstam (1992). Loneliness in marriage. *Journal of Social and Personal Relationships, 9,* 197–217. Copyright 1992. Reprinted by permission of Sage Publications, Ltd.

This is shown in Figure 9.1. The sex difference decreased with age. Among adults 50 and over, there was no sex difference in intimacy expectations; with increasing age, women's expectations for intimacy declined over time to match those of men. Interestingly, married women under 50 were lonelier than married men in that same age group. Tornstam reasoned that these women were lonelier than men because they expected their relationships to provide more intimacy.

Do women change their intimacy expectations as they grow older? Because this is a cross-sectional study, we do not know if women adjust their expectations for marriage downward over time or whether the women in the older cohort are different in some way from the women in the younger cohort. The older cohort could consist of a more traditional group of women who had lower expectations from the start. It is also possible that the young women

with high expectations for intimacy divorce before reaching the older cohort.

Vangelisti and Daly (1997) reached conclusions opposite to Tornstam's (1992). They found that women do not have different standards for relationships than men, but women's standards are less likely than men's to be met. They asked 122 adults enrolled in continuing education courses to rate how important 30 standards were to successful relationships and how much their current relationship met each standard. These 30 standards were grouped into seven categories: (1) relational identity (spending time together, being known as a couple); (2) integration (accepting each other's weaknesses, recognizing there is conflict in relationships); (3) affective accessibility (self-disclosure, expressing feelings); (4) trust (being faithful, committed, honest); (5) future orientation (sharing similar plans for the future); (6) role fulfillment (each person fulfills his or her roles); and (7) flexibility (adapting to one another).

There was a sex difference in the importance of only one of the seven standards, trust, which women regarded as more important than did men. There were no sex differences in the importance of the other six standards, suggesting that men and women held similar expectations for relationships. For all the standards except trust, women reported that their current relationship was less likely to have fulfilled their standards compared to men. These results are shown in Figure 9.2; the top line indicates the importance of the standard and the bottom line indicates whether the standard is fulfilled in the current relationship. You can see a large discrepancy between the two lines for women, but a small discrepancy for men. The size of the discrepancy between the importance of the standard and the relationship having met the standard was strongly associated with marital dissatisfaction for both men and women. This study suggests that men and women have similar

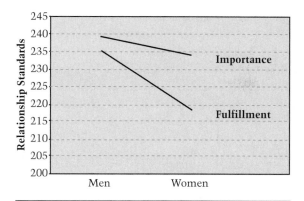

FIGURE 9.2 Sex differences in importance of and fulfillment of relationship standards. Men and women report that a set of relationship standards are similarly important to them. However, women perceive that their relationships are less likely to have fulfilled these standards compared to men. *Source:* Adapted from Vangelisti and Daly (1997).

views of what is important for a relationship and are equally unhappy when their relationship does not meet their expectations, but women's expectations are less likely than men's to be met.

Characteristics Desired in a Mate

Read the following personal ads taken from a local newspaper (MacDowell, 1999):

Women Seeking Men

Educated, attractive, creative SWF, 29, 5′ 5″, 120 lbs., long brown hair, seeks handsome, articulate *SWPM, 29–39, 6′ +*, gentleman, *higher education (Doctorate/Master's a must)*, who enjoys politics, arts, medicine. Multilingual a plus.

SF, 5′ 3″, 135 lbs., blonde/brown, enjoys reading, music, concerts, movies, hanging out with friends. *Seeking SM, with good work ethic*, but can also be romantic, spontaneous, for LTR.

Men Seeking Women

SM, 29, 6′ 1″, 190 lbs., enjoys all outdoor athletic activities, stimulating conversation. *Seeking well-built lady, 30–40, with sense of humor. Redheads a plus.*

Seeking attractive, down-to-earth, emotionally well-adjusted (the elusive criterion) SWF, late 20–30s, independent not disinterested, sense of humor (shares mine). Me: attractive, tall, fit, *educated (master's)*, *employed*, *condo/car-owning* SWM, 32.

Affectionate, loving, honest, compliant, *hardworking*, handsome WM, 39, enjoys affection, music, clubbing, chats, movies. Seeking the perfect lady to share eternity and dreams, romance, passion; for lasting, loving relationship.

Not surprisingly, the women seeking men are providing information about their personal attractiveness and seeking men with education and a good work ethic. The men seeking women are interested in finding an attractive mate and providing information about their financial status and work ethic. Now consider the following ad:

Extremely good-looking SWM, 24, blond/blue, seeks financially stable female, age/race open for possible LTR.

As you can see, there are exceptions to the stereotype. If you review all the ads carefully, you will see there are other qualities besides physical attractiveness and work status that are desired in a mate. What else are people seeking? They are looking for someone who shares their interests, has a sense of humor, is affectionate, and is romantic.

Evidence.   Despite the previous personal ads, research shows that in general, men and women desire the same characteristics in their partners: honesty, warmth, affection, kindness, and someone to share activities. However, some sex differences in desires also appear that are consistent with stereotypes. As indicated in the personal ads, men desire physical attractiveness in a partner, whereas women desire intelligence or occupational status. Men and women are quite aware of these differences.

Feingold (1992) conducted a meta-analysis of the studies that evaluated sex differences in the characteristics desired in a mate. He found that females were substantially more likely than males to emphasize socioeconomic status ($d = -.69$) and ambition ($d = -.67$), but only somewhat more likely to emphasize intelligence ($d = -.30$) and character ($d = -.35$). There was no sex difference in the value attached to personality. Feingold (1990) also conducted a meta-analysis of sex differences in the importance attached to a mate's physical attractiveness. Across five different methodologies, Feingold found that men were more likely than women to emphasize physical attractiveness in a mate. The size of the effect was much larger in studies that used self-report methods (d's in the +.50 range) than in those that examined behavior (d's in the +.30 range).

There is cross-cultural support for these sex differences. In a cross-cultural study of mate preferences, women were more likely than men to prefer a mate who had money, ambition, and high social status in 27 of the 37 cultures, including the United States (Shackelford, Schmitt, & Buss, 2005). Men were more likely than women to prefer a physically attractive mate in 30 of the 37 cultures, also including the United States.

A national survey of adults ages 19 to 35 showed that men focus on youth and attractiveness in mate selection, and women focus on status and earning potential (Sprecher, Sullivan, & Hatfield, 1994). Participants were asked how willing they would be to marry someone who

had 1 of 12 characteristics. Women were more likely than men to say they would marry someone 5 years older, someone who earned more money than they, someone who was more educated than they, someone who was not attractive, and someone who already had children. Men were more likely than women to say they would marry someone who was 5 years younger, someone who did not have a steady job, someone who earned less than they, someone who was less educated, and someone of a different race. There were no sex differences in willingness to marry someone who was previously married or of a different religion. These results again show that women are more concerned with financial security than physical attractiveness, and men are more concerned with physical attractiveness than financial assets.

Some of these sex differences varied by race. As shown in Figure 9.3a, both Black and White women were less likely than Black or White men to marry someone who did not have a steady job. However, this sex difference was stronger among White respondents because White women were especially unlikely to marry someone without a steady job. Black women may be more tolerant of a mate not holding a steady job because Black men are, in fact, less likely to have steady jobs compared to White men. By contrast, as shown in Figure 9.3b, White women were the most willing to marry someone who was unattractive.

Men and women are well aware of sex differences in mate selection. College students in the United States, Netherlands, and Korea were asked how distressed they would be if their partner became interested in someone else who outperformed them on a number of dimensions (Buss et al., 2000). Across all three countries, males said they would be more distressed than females at rivals who outperformed them in terms of job prospects, physical strength, and financial prospects. By contrast, females said

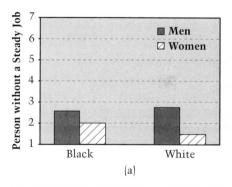 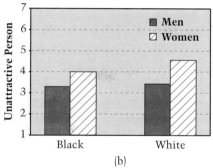

FIGURE 9.3   (a) Black and White women said they would be less willing to marry someone without a steady job than Black and White men. (b) Black and White women said they would be more willing to marry someone who was unattractive than Black and White men. The sex difference for both of these characteristics was stronger among White respondents because White women were especially unwilling to marry someone without a steady job and especially willing to marry an unattractive person.
Source: Adapted from Sprecher, Sullivan, et al. (1994).

they would be more distressed than males at rivals who were physically more attractive.

All these studies show sex differences in preferences for a mate to be physically attractive and to have high status, but they do not address how important either of these two characteristics are to men's and women's mate preferences. Studies that have evaluated the importance of a variety of characteristics show physical attractiveness and status to be relatively *unimportant*. For example, a 2001 national survey of women ages 20 to 29 showed that 80% believe it is more important that a husband can communicate his innermost feelings than make a good living (Whitehead & Popenoe, 2001). Hatfield and Sprecher (1995) had students from the United States, Russia, and Japan rate how much they cared whether their partner possessed the 12 positive traits shown in Figure 9.4. They found that students in all three countries, men and women alike, valued internal characteristics about a person (e.g., kind

and understanding, sense of humor, expressive and open) more than external (e.g., athletic, physically attractive, status). The rank order of the characteristics, as shown in Figure 9.4, was quite similar for men and women. When a specific trait was compared between men and women, however, differences emerged for 7 of the 12 traits. Across the three cultures, men valued physical attractiveness more than women did. Women valued resources, such as ambition, potential for success, money, and intelligence, more than men did, but also traits such as kindness and expressivity. In fact, across the three countries, there was a sex difference in "choosiness," such that women rated all the traits, on average, as more important than did men. Thus women appear to be more selective about the characteristics of a mate compared to men. In addition, students from the United States were choosier than students from Russia, who were choosier than students from Japan.

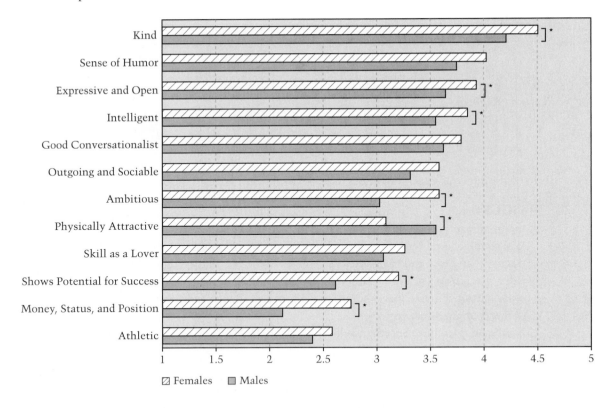

FIGURE 9.4 Trait preferences in men and women. Students from the United States, Russia, and Japan rated how important these characteristics were in a mate. Across the three cultures, women were the "choosier" sex, meaning they valued almost all of the traits more than men did. The one exception was physical attractiveness, which men regarded as more important than women did.

Source: Adapted from Hatfield and Sprecher (1995).

*Means for men and women are significantly different.

Some of the studies ask people about characteristics that they would desire in a potential marriage partner, whereas other studies do not specify the nature of the relationship. It is certainly possible that the characteristics we desire in a mate are not the same as the characteristics we desire in someone with whom we will have a single date. One study compared men's and women's mate preferences for a one-night stand, for a single date, for a steady date, and for marriage (Kenrick et al., 1993). Undergraduates reported the minimum acceptable level of 24 traits (e.g., kind, physically attractive) for each relationship. Overall, women required higher levels of each of the traits compared to men regardless of the relationship, confirming the "choosiness" finding reported above. The characteristics most highly valued by both men and women were emotional stability and agreeableness. Again, the expected sex differences appeared on items deemed less important: Women held higher standards for status-related characteristics, such as ambition and earning capacity, and men held higher standards for physical attractiveness. Importantly, the most sex differences in mate preferences occurred for the one-night stand, and the fewest sex differences occurred for dating and marriage. Thus, in terms of serious relationships, men's and women's mate preferences are quite similar. This shows how important it is to consider the nature of the relationship when evaluating sex differences.

One limitation of all these studies is that people are asked to evaluate a single mate characteristic at a time. However, in real relationships, there are trade-offs. Having people rate an entire list of traits doesn't reveal the trade-offs. Maybe you would prefer an attractive mate but not a hostile attractive mate—if that were the case, you would be much more favorably predisposed to a kind, trustworthy, average-looking mate. The trade-offs in mate selection were addressed by having people choose between pairs of traits (Fletcher et al., 2004). When people had to choose between attractiveness and warmth, men were more likely than women to choose attractiveness, but this was limited to short-term encounters. In long-term relationships, men were much more likely to choose warmth over attractiveness. When the trade-off was between warmth and status, both men and women chose warmth—in both short-term and long-term relationships. Another study examined the trade-off issue by giving men and women varying "budgets" for mate selection (Li & Kenrick, 2006). That is, participants were asked to design the ideal mate and given various amounts of "mate dollars" to purchase these characteristics. With a small budget, the typical sex differences prevailed, with women emphasizing a mate's resources and men emphasizing a mate's physical attractiveness. With a larger budget, men's and women's preferences became more similar. This was especially the case in long-term relationships. In short-term relationships, men were less choosy than women, and both men and women valued physical attractiveness.

In conclusion, it appears that men and women agree on the most important characteristics a partner should possess, especially for a serious relationship such as marriage. Physical attractiveness and earning potential are less important characteristics in a mate but ones that men and women emphasize differentially, especially for dating relationships.

Explanations. What is the explanation for men's preference for physically attractive women and women's preference for financially secure men? One explanation comes from evolutionary theory, which states that men and women behave in ways that will maximize the survival of their genes. Men value physical attractiveness and youth in their mates because these are indicators of fertility. In fact, there is some evidence that both men and women are better able to recall attractive than unattractive female faces, suggesting that physical attractiveness in women has evolved as a cue to reproductive fertility (Becker et al., 2005). There is no difference in the recall of attractive and unattractive male faces. Women prefer mates who have a high occupational status because financial resources will help ensure the survival of their offspring. These ideas are based on the parental investment model (Buss, 1989), which states that women will invest more in their offspring than will men because they have less opportunity than men to reproduce.

If evolutionary theory explains sex differences in mate selection, women who are physically attractive should be more likely than women who are physically unattractive to secure a mate who is financially stable. There are vivid instances of young attractive women paired with wealthy older men; Hugh Hefner and

Donald Trump are examples of wealthy men who have attracted numerous younger and attractive women. Anna Nicole Smith is an example of an attractive woman who at age 26 married a wealthy 90-year-old man. The idea that attractive women will be linked to wealthy and high-status men and wealthy and high-status men will be linked to attractive women is known as the "potentials-attract hypothesis." This hypothesis was tested by having young adults rate themselves on 10 attributes and then rate how much they desired those attributes in a mate (Buston & Emlen, 2003). There was no evidence to support the potentials-attract hypothesis for either men or women; instead, the similarity-attraction hypothesis prevailed. People's self-ratings on an attribute predicted a greater desire for that attribute in a partner. When examining who people actually end up with as mates, there also does not appear to be any support for the potentials-attract hypothesis. A study of 129 newlywed couples showed no evidence that physically attractive women were more likely than physically unattractive women to be paired with a financially well-off mate (Stevens, Owens, & Schaefer, 1990). Instead, there was strong support that mates matched on physical attractiveness and education.

Eagly and Wood (1999) have argued that social role theory provides a better explanation than evolutionary theory for sex differences in mate selection. They suggest that a society's emphasis on a distinct division of labor between the sexes will be directly linked to sex differences in mate selection. In other words, females will value a mate with high earning capacity and males will value a mate with domestic skills in societies where men's role is to work outside the home and women's role is to work inside the home. Eagly and Wood tested this hypothesis by linking the gender equality of a culture to the size of the sex difference in mate preferences. They reanalyzed the data that Buss and colleagues (1990) had collected on mate selection preferences from 37 cultures around the world. First, they confirmed Buss and colleagues' finding that women were more likely than men to value a mate with high earning capacity and men were more likely than women to value a mate who was physically attractive. However, they also pointed out that men were more likely to value a mate who was a good cook and a good housekeeper. This sex difference was as large as the previous two. Evolutionary theory would not lead to this prediction, but social role theory would. Second, sex differences in preferences for a mate with high earning capacity were highly correlated with sex differences in preferences for good domestic skills. Therefore, cultures in which high earning capacity is valued more by women are the same cultures in which domestic skills are valued more by men. Finally, the gender equality of a culture (as measured by the percentage of women in administrative, technical, and professional positions; the percentage of women in political office; and the percentage of men's salary the average woman earns) was inversely related to the size of the sex difference in earning capacity preference and domestic skill preference, but not physical attractiveness preference. That is, sex differences in earning capacity and domestic skill preference were higher in more traditional cultures. The traditionality of a culture did not have anything to do with the sex difference in the value attached to physical attractiveness. Another study related traditional gender-role ideology to sex-typed mate preferences across nine nations (Eastwick et al., 2006). Men with more traditional gender-role beliefs showed a greater preference for younger mates with domestic skills, and women with more traditional gender-role beliefs showed a greater preference for older mates with financial resources.

A third theory of mate preferences is social construction theory, which argues that social norms dictate what is desirable in a mate. A study of American and Israeli college students supported this theory (Pines, 2001). Students were interviewed about their most significant romantic relationship and asked why they had fallen in love. Consistent with evolutionary theory, 80% of men and 53% of women mentioned physical appearance. However, 89% of men and 97% of women mentioned personality, so physical appearance was not the most important feature named. Only 4% of men and women mentioned status, contradicting evolutionary theory. The primary finding of the study, however, was that there were more cultural differences than sex differences in mate preferences, emphasizing how norms shape what is attractive in a mate. Americans were more influenced by status and similarity than Israelis. A study of mate preferences in the United States and the People's Republic of China also supported social construction theory (Toro-Morn & Sprecher, 2003). The most important preferences in a mate were the same for both countries: honest, trustworthy, warm, kind, healthy, sense of humor. The least important preferences also were the same: age, popularity, wealth, and social status. There were more sex differences in China than in the United States. In both countries, men preferred a younger mate and a physically attractive mate compared to women, whereas women preferred a mate with high social status compared to men. These differences, however, were larger in China than in the United States. In addition, only in China did men value a mate who was a good housekeeper more than women. It is not a surprise that the sex differences in mate preferences were larger in a culture where men's and women's roles are more distinct and there is a greater status differential between men and women. When women have less access to economic resources, it is not surprising that they value a mate's access to economic resources.

One limitation of many of these studies is that people, usually college students, are asked to *imagine* what features are important in a relationship. Our preferences in the abstract for a hypothetical mate may not be the same as our preferences in an actual mate. More useful information is gained by examining people's actual choices for romantic partners. As noted above, studies of married couples tend to show similarity on a range of characteristics (Stevens et al., 1990). Feingold (1988) conducted a meta-analysis of 34 samples that evaluated the similarity of a couple's physical attractiveness. He found evidence for matching, meaning that partners were similar in their levels of physical attractiveness. Explore preferences for a hypothetical versus an actual mate further in Do Gender 9.1.

DO GENDER 9.1
Differences in Preferences
for Hypothetical and Actual Mates

Identify 10 characteristics of a potential mate. Make sure half are internal characteristics (e.g., trustworthy) and half are external (e.g., physically attractive). Have 10 friends who are not seriously involved with someone rate how important each characteristic is in a potential mate ("the hypothetical mate"). Then have 10 friends who are involved in a serious relationship rate the extent to which their partner possesses these characteristics. Is there a difference between what people desire in a hypothetical mate and what they have found in an actual mate? You might find more sex differences (e.g., men valuing physical attractiveness) among the people who do not have partners and are thinking of hypothetical mates.

Relationship Initiation

Do you remember your first date? How did it come about? Did one person call the other person? Who decided what to do? How do men and women become involved in romantic relationships?

Traditionally, the male has taken the initiative in romantic relationships. Today, it is more acceptable for women to invite men on a date, and there are more forums set up for female initiation; there are dances in high school and parties in college where females are intended to initiate. Yet these forums are distinct because they focus on the female as the initiator. Female initiation is not normative. There is evidence that when females initiate first dates, men expect greater sexual involvement—although, in actuality, there is no evidence that more sexual behavior occurs when females initiate (Mongeau et al., 2006).

Men still shoulder more of the responsibility for relationship initiation. In a study of college students, both men and women said they were equally capable of and successful in initiating a romantic relationship, but men recalled doing so more frequently than women (Clark, Shaver, & Abrahams, 1999). Men and women also reported different strategies for relationship initiation. Men used more direct strategies, such as asking the person for a date or making physical contact with the person; women used more indirect strategies, such as hinting or waiting for the other person to make the first move. Gender roles may be more strongly tied to relationship initiation than sex. In the study of college students, masculinity was related to the use of direct initiation strategies (Clark et al., 1999); femininity, however, was not related to the use of direct or indirect strategies.

One way to examine the nature of relationship development is to examine the first date. There are clear first date **scripts**. A script is a schema or cognitive representation of a sequence of events. These scripts are gender based. In essence, the male is proactive and the female is reactive (Mongeau, Serewicz, Henningsen, Miller, & Davis, 2006). The male initiates the date, decides what to do on the date, arranges transportation, pays for the date, and initiates sexual contact. By contrast, the female accepts or rejects the invitation, the plans for the date, and sexual advances (Honeycutt & Cantrill, 2001). Men's first date scripts consist of more gender-stereotypical behavior (e.g., asking for date, initiating sex) than women's first date scripts, which may indicate the script for a first date is more rigid for men than for women (Rose & Frieze, 1993). There is quite a bit of agreement between men and women about how the course of a first date unfolds.

It is interesting that the burden of initiation rests on males when adolescent males today report more awkward communication in romantic relationships and say they are less confident in their romantic relationships compared to females (Giordano, Longmore, & Manning, 2006). In fact, adolescent males are more likely than adolescent females to report that their partner influences them. Thus, compared to the discussion of self-esteem and self-confidence in Chapter 6, the early stages of romantic relationships may be one arena in which men are less confident and influential than women.

TAKE HOME POINTS

- There is evidence that women have higher standards for romantic relationships than men—especially younger women—and there is also evidence that women's relationship standards are less likely to be met than those of men. Either could explain why women are less satisfied in marriage compared to men.

- Men and women agree on the most important characteristics of a mate—kind, understanding, honest, trustworthy, sense of humor, open and expressive.

- There are consistent sex differences on traits that are relatively unimportant in choosing a mate: Men weigh physical attractiveness more heavily than do women, and women weigh economic resources more heavily. These differences are consistent across cultures and across time, meaning they persist today.

- The nature of the relationship influences mate preferences. Sex differences are more likely to appear when the relationship is less serious; men's and women's preferences are most similar in serious relationships.

- People make trade-offs when choosing mates. Again, when trade-offs have to be made, sex differences are minimized, and men and women choose more similar mates.

- The sex differences in mate preferences that do exist can be explained by evolutionary theory, social role theory, and social construction theory.

- The weakness of evolutionary theory is that it cannot explain men's preferences for women with domestic skills; the weakness of social role theory is that it cannot explain men's preferences for attractive mates. Both theories, however, can explain why women prefer a mate with greater economic resources.

- Social construction theory of mate preferences is supported by cultural differences in mate preferences. Sex differences in mate preferences may be larger in more traditional cultures where men's and women's roles are distinct and women have less access to economic resources.

- Historically, and still today, society expects men to initiate romantic relationships. Despite this expectation, men may be relatively uncomfortable having this responsibility.

THE NATURE OF ROMANTIC RELATIONSHIPS

Romantic relationships are expected to provide closeness or intimacy, love, and sexual exclusivity. I examine each aspect of romantic relationships.

Intimacy

I remember interviewing a couple several months after the husband had suffered a heart attack. I spoke to the two individuals. During the course of the separate conversations, I learned that each person had a different conceptualization of "closeness." The wife told me of an occasion when the two of them were sitting together in the living room and watching television. She was not very interested in the television program and he was not talking to her. Because he wasn't paying any attention to her, she went into the other room and called a friend. The husband told me about the same interaction, but it held a different meaning for him. He told me that the two of them were sitting comfortably together watching television, something he defined as a moment of closeness. Then, all of a sudden, she disrupted this moment by leaving the room and calling a friend. They were both upset by the sequence of events, but for different reasons. These two people had different definitions of intimacy. She defined intimacy by talking or self-disclosure; because the two of them were not talking, she didn't consider the interaction very meaningful, so she called a friend. He defined intimacy more as a feeling of comfort in the other's presence and physical proximity. She disrupted this connection by leaving the room.

Although my anecdote suggests differences in men's and women's conceptualizations of intimacy, empirical research has not suggested that overall conceptualizations of intimacy differ for men and women. My colleagues and I investigated sex differences in intimacy by asking college students to recall a time when they felt intimate or close to a person of the other sex (Helgeson, et al., 1987). We constructed frequency distributions of all the features identified in these episodes. In general, men's and women's experiences of intimacy were quite similar. For both men and women, intimacy episodes largely revolved around feelings and expressions of love and appreciation, feelings of happiness and contentment, and self-disclosure. There was some indication that men regarded physical contact as more central to intimacy than women did. Men were more likely than women to include physical contact and sex in their intimacy episodes, but these were not prominent features of intimacy even for men. Thus as in the research on mate selection, on the whole men and women agree on how they define an intimate relationship. However, men and women differ on the more peripheral features required in an intimate encounter.

This study is limited in two ways. The first is the self-report nature of the methodology; both men and women may have been concerned about how the experimenter would view their conceptions of intimacy if their stories had revolved around sex. A second limitation is the age and education of the sample; perhaps conceptions of intimacy are different among older men and women. I recall sitting in an airplane reviewing these intimacy episodes when an older man sitting next to me inquired about what I was doing. When I explained I was trying to find out how people define intimacy by asking them about times they felt intimate or close to another person, he remarked, "You mean sex? You are asking people to describe sex?" Although hours and hours of coding did not support this claim, it is possible that definitions of intimacy vary among younger and older respondents. When I reported the results of this study to students in my gender course, one man made a very interesting comment: "If intimacy doesn't mean sex, then why do they call it 'intimate apparel'?" I thought he had a very good point.

There is some evidence that the relation between intimacy and passion differs for men and women (Vohs & Baumeister, 2004). The same increase in intimacy seems to be associated with a greater increase in passion among males than females. And, females seem to require greater intimacy than males to develop passion. One way to increase the intimacy of a relationship is to express feelings of love or commitment. Metts (2004) showed that such expressions (e.g., saying "I love you") prior to sex predicted less regret over sex and greater confirmation of the relationship. However, these relations were stronger for females than males, supporting the idea that intimacy is more of a prerequisite for sex for women than men.

One feature of intimacy that seems to be more relevant to women than men is self-disclosure. In the prototype study, women were more likely than men to identify self-disclosure as a feature of intimacy (Helgeson et al., 1987). Among married couples, women self-disclose more than men (Hendrick, 1981). However, this sex difference may be less applicable to African American couples. In a study of Black and White married couples, White men were less likely than White women to self-disclose, but there were no sex differences in self-disclosure among Black couples (Oggins, Veroff, & Leber, 1993). Black men appear to feel more comfortable self-disclosing to spouses than White men do.

Love

What is love? Many people have shared poetic thoughts ("Beauty and Love Quotes," 2000):

> "To love a thing means wanting it to live." (Confucious, *Analects*, 6th century B.C., 12.10, translated by Ch'u Chai and Winberg Chai)

> "As selfishness and complaint pervert and cloud the mind, so love with its joy clears

and sharpens the vision." (Helen Keller, *My Religion*, 1927)

"The simple lack of her is more to me than others' presence." (Edward Thomas, 1878–1917, English poet)

Even second-graders have strong opinions about love. Here are a few comments they made (Noel, 1997):

> "When someone comes over, or you're hanging around someone, you know when you're in love. After you love someone, you play with the person you love for a long time." (male)

> "When you're in love, you're very nervous. When he or she is very nice and sweet to you for a long time and you are never fighting, you know you're going to be in love and hope it will last a long time." (female)

> "When a girl hugs you or kisses you, you know when you're in love. When the girl gives a ring to a boy and the girls says 'I love you.' Then you go out to dinner." (male)

> "When you meet someone who likes you, and you like them, then you know you're in love. Then you go on dates. Then it's marriage time, and you might have a baby." (female)

From distinguished poets to second-graders, the ideas of love for men and women have been adequately captured. All the elements are there: wanting to spend time together (a very long time), feeling nervous, showing affection, and putting the other person first.

When it comes to matters of the heart, who is more romantic: men or women? One way that this question has been addressed is by asking people whether they would marry someone with whom they were not in love. In a study conducted several decades ago, Kephart (1967) asked over 1,000 college students, "If a boy (girl) had all the other qualities you desired, would you marry this person if you were not in love with him (her)?" The majority of the men (65%) but only a small portion of the women (24%) said no. In fact, one of the women remarked, "I'm undecided. It's rather hard to give a 'yes' or 'no' answer to this question. If a boy had all the other qualities I desired, and I was not in love with him—well, I think I could talk myself into falling in love!" (p. 473). This study concluded that men view love as more central to marriage than women do. In this sense, men could be considered the more romantic sex.

One reason men were more romantic than women had to do with the historical relationship between the sexes. Women were marrying not just a man, but a way of life; thus women were taught to be practical in mate selection. Men could "afford" to fall in love. Today, women are more likely to be economically independent than they were 30 years ago. Do Kephart's findings still apply?

More recent studies of the Kephart question have suggested that men and women are equally romantic when it comes to marriage. In a study of college students in the United States, Japan, and Russia, men's and women's responses were similar in the United States and Japan (Sprecher, Aron, et al., 1994). As shown in Figure 9.5, over 80% of both men and women said they would *not* marry the person if they were not in love with him or her. In Russia, the sex difference appeared. Women were less likely than men to view love as a basis for marriage. Russians, in general, had less romantic ideals than the Japanese or Americans.

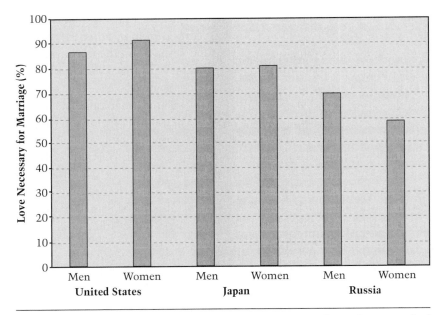

FIGURE 9.5 Students in the United States, Japan, and Russia were asked the "Kephart question" (whether they would marry someone who had all the qualities they desired in a mate but they were not in love with the person). Men and women in the United States and Japan were equally likely to say they would not marry the person, that love was the basis for marriage. Only in Russia were women less likely than men to view love as necessary for marriage. *Source:* Adapted from Sprecher, Aron, et al. (1994).

Do Gender 9.2 at your college to see if the findings hold.

Despite the fact that we view women as more relationship-oriented than men, research suggests that men are more likely than women to have romantic notions about love. Sprecher and Metts (1989) developed a romanticism scale that consists of four beliefs: (1) love finds a way or conquers all; (2) there is only one true love for a person; (3) one's partner is ideal; and (4) one can fall in love at first sight. Sample items measuring each of these beliefs are shown in Table 9.1. Men score higher than women on this romantic beliefs scale (Hendrick & Hendrick, 2002). Men fall in love more quickly compared to women. By contrast, women are more likely to have a practical view of

DO GENDER 9.2
Who Is More Romantic in Love?

Ask 10 men and 10 women the following question: "If a man (woman) had all the other qualities you desired, would you marry this person if you were not in love with him (her)?"

Either have a scale of response options (yes, no, unsure) or create a 5-point scale ranging from 1, definitely no, to 5, definitely yes. What other variables besides sex might be associated with responses? Does age matter? Does ethnicity? What about parents' marital status? Gender roles?

TABLE 9.1 ROMANTIC BELIEFS SCALE

Love Finds a Way

1. If I love someone, I will find a way for us to be together regardless of the opposition to the relationship, physical distance, or any other barrier.
2. If a relationship I have was meant to be, any obstacle (e.g., lack of money, physical distance, career conflicts) can be overcome.
3. I expect that in my relationship, romantic love will really last; it won't fade with time.
4. I believe if another person and I love each other we can overcome any differences and problems that may arise.

One and Only True Love

1. Once I experience "true love," I could never experience it again, to the same degree, with another person.
2. I believe that to be truly in love is to be in love forever.
3. There will be only one real love for me.

Idealization of Partner

1. I'm sure that every new thing I learn about the person I choose for a long-term commitment will please me.
2. The relationship I will have with my "true love" will be nearly perfect.
3. The person I love will make a perfect romantic partner; for example, he or she will be completely accepting, loving, and understanding.

Love at First Sight

1. I am likely to fall in love almost immediately if I meet the right person.
2. When I find my "true love" I will probably know it soon after we meet.
3. I need to know someone for a period of time before I fall in love with him or her.

Source: Adapted from Sprecher and Metts (1989).

relationships, believing that it is possible to love more than one person and that economic security is more important than passion to a relationship (Frazier & Esterly, 1990). Thus men may still hold more romantic ideals than women. Although women have achieved greater economic independence over the past several decades, most women expect that they will not be the sole income provider. Thus women may still have some reason to be more practical when it comes to love.

Another way that men's and women's approaches to love have been addressed is by examining "styles" of loving. Hendrick and Hendrick (1986) developed a typology of love styles based on Lee's (1973) theory of love.

According to Lee, there are three primary love styles: **eros**, or romantic love; **storge**, or friendship love; and **ludus**, or game-playing love. There are also three blends of these love styles: **mania**, or manic love, is a blend of eros and ludus; **pragma**, or practical love, is a blend of storge and ludus; **agape**, or pure love, is a blend of eros and storge. The love styles are depicted in Figure 9.6, and sample items are shown in Table 9.2.

Sex differences appear on some of these love styles. Women typically score higher than men on pragma and storge, and men score higher on ludus and sometimes agape (Lacey et al., 2004; Hendrick & Hendrick, 2002). The sex difference in pragma is consistent with the

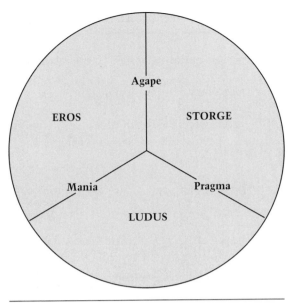

FIGURE 9.6 Love styles.

Source: J. A. Lee (1973).

previously reviewed research showing women are more practical than men when it comes to love. The sex difference in ludus is certainly consistent with our stereotypes that men are less willing than women to commit to a relationship. One study compared love styles among college students in the United States, Russia, and Japan (Sprecher, Aron, et al., 1994). Again men scored higher on ludus and women scored higher on pragma—but only in the U.S. sample. Women scored higher than men on mania in the United States and Russia, but men scored higher on mania in Japan. In addition, students from the United States were more likely to endorse eros and storge and less likely to endorse ludus and mania than students from Russia or Japan. One limitation of this research is that most of it has been conducted with college students. It would be interesting to see how people's love styles change with age.

TABLE 9.2 LOVE STYLES

Eros
My lover and I have the right physical "chemistry" between us.
I feel that my lover and I were meant for each other.

Ludus
I try to keep my lover a little uncertain about my commitment to him or her.
I enjoy playing the "game of love" with a number of different partners.

Storge
It is hard to say exactly where friendship ends and love begins.
The best kind of love grows out of a long friendship.

Pragma
I consider what a person is going to become in life before I commit myself to him or her.
An important factor in choosing a partner is whether or not he or she will be a good parent.

Mania
When my lover doesn't pay attention to me, I feel sick all over.
When I am in love, I have trouble concentrating on anything else.

Agape
I would endure all things for the sake of my lover.
I cannot be happy unless I place my lover's happiness before my own.

Source: Hendrick and Hendrick (1986).

Sexuality

Men seem to be more satisfied with their sexual relationships than women. In a study of adults in 29 countries, men reported higher sexual well-being compared to women (Laumann et al., 2006). The sex difference was larger in countries that were considered male-centered where there was a greater status differential between men and women, such as Brazil, Korea, and Morocco. Perhaps one reason that men are more satisfied than women is that men are more likely to take the initative when it comes to sex and more likely to disclose their sexual desires. In a study of college dating couples, males were more likely than females to discuss sex, including their sexual desires, while females were more likely than males to report that they had difficulty getting their partner to do what they wanted during sex (Greene & Faulkner, 2005). Thus here is one

arena where men seem to communicate more effectively than women.

Attitudes Toward Sex.   Sexual behavior and attitudes have become more permissive over the years, and the changes have been greater among women than men. In a review of 530 studies of young people (typically high school age) conducted between 1949 and 1999, the year the study was published correlated with more permissive sexual behavior (Wells & Twenge, 2005). This correlation was stronger for women than men, supporting Baumeister's idea of erotic plasticity mentioned in Chapter 4. Figure 9.7 shows how the year of publication is associated with a greater percentage of sexually active women. In the 1950s, 13% of young women were sexually active, compared to 47% by the late 1990s.

Today, the majority of men and women find sex between an unmarried man and woman

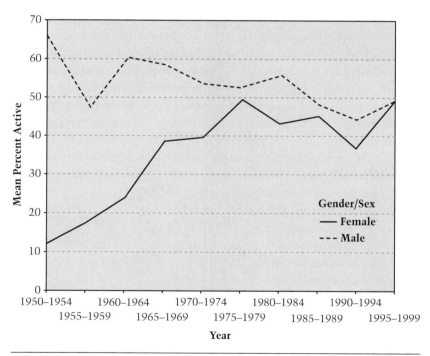

FIGURE 9.7   The relation of study year of publication and the percent of sexually active young people (high school age).
Source: Wells and Twenge (2005).

acceptable, men slightly more so (61%) than women (55%; Gallup Jr., 2003). In a survey of over 2,000 college students from 201 colleges and universities in the United States, 68% said sex before marriage was acceptable if the two people loved each other (Steinberg, 1998).

There are some differences between men's and women's attitudes about sex. First, women have more negative attitudes toward sex compared to men (Geer & Robertson, 2005). Even at younger ages, this seems to be true. A study of adolescents showed that males identify more benefits from having sex compared to females (e.g., physical pleasure, reduced loneliness, respect from friends), whereas females identify more costs associated with sex compared to males (e.g., lose respect from friends, guilt, embarrassment; Deptula et al., 2006).

Second, men have more permissive standards compared to women, meaning men find sex to be more acceptable in general. However, sex differences in attitudes toward sex depend on the degree of commitment in the relationship. College students in the United States, Russia, and Japan were asked how acceptable it was to have intercourse on a first date, a casual date, when seriously dating, when preengaged, and when engaged (Sprecher & Hatfield, 1996). Students rated acceptability for themselves, for a typical male, and for a typical female. Not surprisingly, students in all three countries rated sexual intercourse as more acceptable as the commitment of the relationship increased. People in all three cultures agreed sexual intercourse was not acceptable during the early stages of a relationship. As shown in Figure 9.8, in all countries, men viewed sexual intercourse as more acceptable than women did during the early stages of the relationship, but there were no sex differences in acceptability during the later stages of the relationship. When engaged, about 90% of respondents gave at least some approval to sexual intercourse. Americans were more permissive than the

Japanese, and Russians fell between the two groups. These cultural differences were strongest among the more committed relationships.

This study also showed that men hold a double standard regarding the acceptability of engaging in sex, at least during the early stages of a relationship. Men said that sexual intercourse is more acceptable for men than women during the early stages of a relationship. By the later stages, men viewed sexual intercourse as equally acceptable for men and women. Whereas Russian and Japanese women held this double standard, women in the United States showed no evidence of the double standard. Other research has shown that men are more likely than women to hold a sexual double standard (Greene & Faulkner, 2005). Does a double standard exist in your school? Find out with Do Gender 9.3.

Men not only have more permissive attitudes toward sex, but men also find it more acceptable to try to attract someone else's mate, a phenomenon referred to as "mate poaching." In a study of nearly 17,000 people across 53 countries, more men than women admitted to engaging in mate poaching and to succumbing to mate poaching—meaning that they became involved with other women when they were in a committed relationship (Schmitt, 2004). Consistent with social role theory, the sex difference in

DO GENDER 9.3
Sexual Double Standard

Ask a group of men and women to rate the acceptability of sexual intercourse for a man and a woman involved in various levels of relationship commitment (e.g., met at a party, dating for six months, engaged). Do men or women hold a double standard (i.e., believe sex is more acceptable for men than for women) at any particular stage of a relationship?

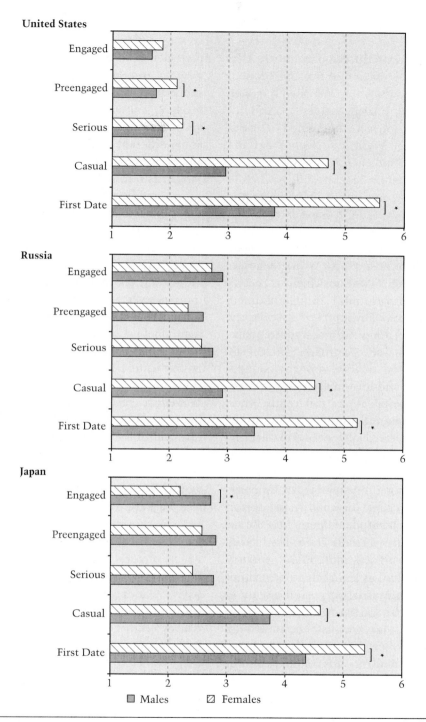

FIGURE 9.8 Sexual standards. Among students from the United States, Russia, and Japan, men have more permissive standards for sexual intercourse than women do when the relationship is more casual. In serious relationships, men and women view sexual intercourse as equally acceptable.

Source: Adapted from Sprecher and Hatfield (1996).

Note: Higher numbers mean less permissive; ˙indicates a sex difference.

mate-poaching was reduced in countries that provided greater access to resources for women.

Men seem to draw the line when the mate is already married. That is, the vast majority of both men and women in the United States as well as many other countries disapprove of extramarital affairs (Sprecher, 2006). Although attitudes toward sex in general and sex before marriage have become more liberal over the past few decades, attitudes toward extramarital affairs have not changed and remained negative. Among women, 93% believe that extramarital sex is wrong or almost always wrong, whereas the corresponding figure for men is nearly as high—89% (Thornton & Young-DeMarco, 2001). Yet, in a nationally representative survey, 25% of men and 15% of women reported having had extramarital sex (Laumann et al., 1994).

Because of the way we view the connection between sex and love in men and women, we view extramarital affairs differently when committed by men and women. In one study, college students viewed a hypothetical relationship between a single friend and a married person (Sprecher, Regan, & McKinney, 1998). Students' perception of the married person having the affair depended on whether the person was male or female. Students perceived the female married person as more committed to the affair, as more in love, as more likely to marry the single friend, and as less likely to have other affairs than the male married person. Men and women had similar views on this issue. These findings suggest that people believe women have affairs only when they are in love with another person but that men have affairs without necessarily loving the person. It is also possible that people perceive male extramarital affairs as more common than female extramarital affairs and, thus, less meaningful. In fact, as noted above, men are more likely than women to have extramarital affairs (Laumann et al., 1994).

The research on perceptions of extramarital affairs provides some support for the idea that men separate sex from love, and women view sex and love as occurring together. Further support comes from a study that shows married men and women perceive different justifications for extramarital affairs (Glass & Wright, 1992). Four different justifications for extramarital affairs were examined: sexual pleasure and excitement, romantic love, emotional intimacy (understanding, companionship, mutual respect), and extrinsic reasons (career advancement, revenge on spouse). Nearly a third (30%) of women and 20% of men said that none of these reasons justified an extramarital affair, indicating an overall intolerance for the behavior. However, when justified, men and women disagreed as to the reasons. Women rated romantic love as a greater justification compared to men, and men rated sexual pleasure as a greater justification than women. Women found romantic love to be the strongest justification for extramarital affairs and sexual pleasure to be the weakest justification. Men did not rate one justification more strongly than another.

Motives for Sex. If men are more likely than women to separate sex from love, do men and women have different motives for engaging in sex? DeLameter (1987) concluded that men have a recreational orientation toward sex in which physical gratification is the goal and a relationship is not required. By contrast, women have a relational orientation toward sex in which sex is integrated into the relationship as a way to convey intimacy. Research, largely based on college students, suggests that men are more likely than women to engage in sexual intercourse for reasons having to do with physical pleasure, and women are more likely than men to engage in sexual intercourse for emotional intimacy and love (Regan & Berscheid, 1999). In one study, college men and women were asked what caused sexual desire in men and women (Regan & Berscheid, 1999). Love was cited as a cause of sexual desire in women by 42% of respondents and in men by 10% of respondents. Respondents also thought the physical environment, such as a romantic setting, was more likely to lead to sexual desire in women than in men. By contrast, sexual desire in men was viewed as being affected less by the interpersonal aspects of the situation and more by internal motivations. Whereas 66% of respondents identified personal causes of sexual desire in men, such as physical need, hormones, and alcohol, only 33% identified these factors as causes of sexual desire in women.

Research among older adults (ages 22 through 57) confirms different motives for sex (Sprague & Quadagno, 1989). Men and women were asked about their primary reason for engaging in sexual intercourse. Responses were categorized into physical (i.e., tension release) versus emotional (i.e., to show love). Overall, women's reasons were more likely to be emotional than physical, and men's reasons were more likely to be physical than emotional. However, the age of the respondent influenced the results. As age increased, sex differences in the reasons for engaging in sex disappeared and almost reversed themselves; some evidence indicated that older women emphasized physical motives and older men emphasized emotional motives for sexual intercourse. Thus the idea that men separate sex from love may be a better descriptor of younger men.

These sex differences have been replicated among homosexuals. In one study, heterosexual and homosexual men were more interested in having sex for pure pleasure, to relieve sexual tension, and to please their partner than heterosexual and homosexual women (Leigh, 1989). Heterosexual and homosexual women were more interested than men in having sex to express emotional closeness. Thus the difference in motives for sex is a function of people's sex rather than sexual orientation.

Men's and women's motives for sex also can be examined in their motives for infidelity.

College students who had been in an exclusive relationship and reported being emotionally or sexually unfaithful to their partner responded to a set of reasons for the infidelity (Barta & Kiene, 2005). The number one reason for both men and women was being dissatisfied with the current relationship, although women endorsed this option more than men. The second and third reasons were partner neglect and revenge, for which there were no sex differences. The least endorsed reason was interest in sex and sexual variety, which men endorsed more than women—again supporting the idea that younger men have a more recreational view of sex than younger women.

First Sexual Experiences. The age of first intercourse has declined over the years, more so for women than men (Wells & Twenge, 2005). In the late 1960s, the average age of first intercourse was 19 for women and 18 for men. By the late 1990s, the average was 15 for both men and women. The age may be getting even younger, however. As shown in Figure 9.9, the

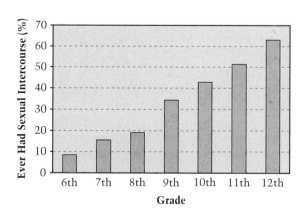

FIGURE 9.9 Percentage of students who have ever had sexual intercourse. Note that the figures for middle school reflect median rather than mean. Middle school figures taken from U.S. Department of Health and Human Services (2005a); High school figures taken from Centers for Disease Control and Prevention (2006b).

SIDEBAR 9.1: *Does Abstinence Only Work?*

During the last decade, the federal government allocated large amounts of money to support abstinence only education among upper elementary and middle-school children. There are a number of tenets of abstinence only education, the most notable of which are (1) abstinence of sex until marriage is the expected standard, and (2) sexual intercourse outside of marriage is associated with harmful psychological and physical consequences. In 1997, Congress mandated a scientific evaluation of abstinence only programs. In 2005 to 2006, 4- to 6-year follow-up data were evaluated from programs in Virginia, Florida, Wisconsin, and Mississippi that had randomized students to the abstinence only education or a control group that did not receive this program (Trenholm et al., 2007). Results showed no group differences in sexual behavior—49% of students in both groups had remained abstinent. The age of sexual initiation was the same in both groups. There was also no group difference in unprotected sex, which was surprising given that other research has shown that those who pledge abstinence are less likely to use contraception when they break their pledges. It is noteworthy that there is little evidence that premarital sex is associated with poor health outcomes, unless the sex was forced, prepubertal, or with a relative (Else-Quest, Hyde, & DeLamater, 2005). In a nationally representative survey, 83% of adults (ages 18 to 59) said that their first sexual intercourse was before marriage. Given the high rates of sexual activity before marriage, abstinence only education without information on effective contraceptive use seems to be a fairly irresponsible approach.

rate of sexual intercourse is increasing among middle school and high school students, such that nearly two thirds of 12th-graders have had sexual intercourse. Across the different grades, more boys than girls have had sex. I would have to say that the "abstinence only" campaign is not working. (See Sidebar 9.1 for an expanded discussion of that issue.)

There are both similarities and differences in the reasons that males and females choose to have sex and choose to refrain from sex. Boys' and girls' reasons for having sex are similar: love for their partner, curiosity, and sexual desire (Albert, Brown, & Flanigan, 2003). Half of the boys and girls said having sex increases a boy's popularity, whereas fewer boys (36%) and girls (20%) said having sex increases a girl's popularity. In terms of not having sex, college students said that one of the most important reasons that they remained a virgin was that they had not found the right partner (Sprecher & Regan, 1996). Women rated this reason as

more important than men did. The next most important category of reasons concerned fears: Men and women were equally likely to cite fears of AIDS and sexually transmitted diseases as a deterrent to sex, but women were more likely than men to mention fears of pregnancy. Men and women were equally likely to endorse religious or moral beliefs as reasons for sexual abstinence. The only reason that men endorsed more than women was feeling shy or embarrassed to initiate sex. A lack of desire for sex was identified as the least important reason by both. Overall, women are more likely to report pride in their virginity, whereas men are more likely to report embarrassment (Sprecher & Regan, 1996).

Perhaps in response to the abstinence only campaign in recent years, some young people have taken a pledge of virginity. Does it work? Yes, and no. Yes, it works in the sense that people who make a public or written commitment to refrain from sex until marriage delay sex compared to those who do not make a pledge. (In this case, sex is defined as sexual intercourse. It turns out that pledgers are more likely to have oral and anal sex than non-pledgers.) No, it does not work in that the vast majority of people who make this pledge have sex before marriage. One study followed 7th through 12th grade pledgers and nonpledgers for 5 to 6 years and showed that 88% of pledgers had sex before marriage compared to 99% of nonpledgers (Bruckner & Bearman, 2005). One cause for concern is that pledgers were less likely than nonpledgers to use condoms during the first sexual intercourse, replicating an earlier study (Berman & Bruckner, 2001). Although the rate of sexually transmitted diseases (STD) was the same for the two groups, pledgers were less likely than non-pledgers to be tested for STDs. There are important methodological differences between virginity pledge studies and abstinence only programs. People are choosing to engage in a virginity pledge rather than being randomly assigned to take such as pledge, as is the case with the research on abstinence only programs.

When men and women do have their first sexual experience, how do they respond? Men report more positive reactions compared to women. In one study, college students rated the amount of pleasure, anxiety, and guilt they felt during their first sexual experience (Sprecher, Barbee, & Schwartz, 1995). Both men and women agreed they experienced more anxiety than pleasure or guilt; however, men indicated they experienced more pleasure than women did, and women indicated they experienced more guilt than men did. One factor that accounted for the sex difference in pleasure was that men were more likely than women to experience orgasm during their first sexual experience. In addition, both men and women reported more pleasure if the relationship was serious rather than casual. Men and especially women recalled more pleasure if that relationship was still intact at the time of the study (which was true in fewer than 25% of the cases). This finding could be due to a recall bias, however; men and women may be recalling more pleasure from their first sexual experience *because* the relationship lasted.

Another study suggested that women experience more positive feelings than men *after* their first sexual experience with a partner. College students were asked to recall their feelings of attraction before and after having had sex with a partner (Haselton & Buss, 2001). Women reported an increase in attraction, and men reported a decrease in attraction. The finding for men was limited to men who had had a larger number of sexual partners. The authors refer to their findings as an "affective shift" and link it to evolutionary theories of mating strategies. The male strategy is to terminate a relationship after sex, which would be facilitated by a decrease in attraction to one's sexual partner. The female strategy is to secure the relationship after sex, which would be facilitated by an increase in attraction to one's sexual partner.

TAKE HOME POINTS

- On the whole, men and women conceptualize intimacy in the same ways. Intimacy includes expressions of love and appreciation, feelings of happiness and contentment, and self-disclosure.

- Sex may be a more important component of intimacy for men than women, but it is still not the most important feature of intimacy for men.

- Historically, women had a more practical view of love and men had a more romantic view. Today, the sex differences are smaller, but men still tend to hold more romantic ideals than women.

- Men and women are equally accepting of sex in serious relationships. In more casual relationships, men are more accepting of sex.

- A double standard exists regarding sex in casual relationships, such that it is more acceptable for a man than a woman to engage in premarital sex. In other cultures, both men and women share the double standard, but in the United States, only men hold the double standard.

- Both men and women are disapproving of extramarital sex, but women show stronger disapproval than men do.

- There is some evidence that sex may have different meanings for men and women, especially among younger people. Men have a more recreational view of sex and women a more relational view.

- This difference may explain why both men and women perceive that a woman who has an extramarital affair is more serious about the relationship partner than a man who has an extramarital affair.

- The age of first sexual experience is lowering, and the majority of young people have sex before marriage despite abstinence only education and pledges of virginity.

- Abstinence only education and pledges of virginity seem to delay sex but do not postpone sex to marriage and may be associated with less contraceptive use.

- Women rate their first sexual experience less positively than men do, but women's feelings of attraction toward their partner may increase after sex.

MAINTAINING RELATIONSHIPS

Consider the following book titles that appeared in the past decade:

Ten Lessons to Transform Your Marriage: America's Love Lab Experts Share Their Strategies for Strengthening Your Relationship (Gottman, Gottman, & Declaire, 2006)

Couple Skills: Making Your Relationship Work (McKay, Fanning, & Paleg, 2006)

Communication Miracles for Couples: Easy and Effective Tools to Create More Love and Less Conflict (Jonathan Robinson, 1997)

How One of You Can Bring the Two of You Together: Breakthrough Strategies to Resolve Your Conflicts and Reignite Your Love (Sue Ellen Page, 1998)

What do these books have in common? First and foremost, they are all geared toward the preservation or maintenance of relationships. Second, toward whom are these books directed? Survey the sex of the people browsing through this section of your local bookstore. In *How One of You Can Bring the Two of You Together*, my bet is that the "one of you" is a woman. As you will see in this section of the chapter, women are typically regarded as the caretakers of relationships.

Maintenance Strategies

What do people do to keep a relationship going? Five now classic maintenance strategies have been identified (Canary & Stafford, 1992). They are (1) positivity (acting in a positive manner toward the spouse); (2) openness (self-disclosure); (3) assurance (assure partner of commitment to relationship); (4) network (involve family and friends in relationship); and (5) tasks (sharing household chores). Sample items from each of these strategies are shown in Table 9.3. When married couples spent 2 weeks keeping a daily record of how frequently they employed these relationship-maintenance strategies, the relative order of the strategies used was the same for men and women (Canary & Stafford, 1992). That is, both men and women used strategies in the following order, from most frequent to least frequent: tasks, positivity, assurance, network, and openness. However, women were found to use more maintenance strategies than men; specifically, wives recorded more openness,

TABLE 9.3   MAINTENANCE STRATEGIES

Positivity
Attempt to make our interactions very enjoyable.
Try to build up spouse's self-esteem, including giving him or her compliments, and the like.
Do not criticize spouse.

Openness
Encourage spouse to disclose thoughts and feelings to me.
Simply tell spouse how I feel about the relationship.
Like to have periodic talks about our relationship.

Assurances
Stress my commitment to spouse.
Imply that our relationship has a future.
Show my love for spouse.

Network
Focus on common friends and affiliations.
Show that I am willing to do things with spouse's friends or family.
Include our friends or family in our activities.

Tasks
Help equally with tasks that need to be done.
Share in the joint responsibilities that face us.
Do my fair share of work we have to do.

Source: Adapted from Canary and Stafford (1992).

networks, and shared tasks than men. Wife assurance was the strongest predictor of husband and wife commitment to the relationship. These results underscore the idea that wives more than husbands are responsible for maintaining relationships. No wonder the popular books are aimed toward women.

Other research has shown that wife maintenance behaviors are more strongly related to the couple's love, commitment, and satisfaction than husband maintenance behaviors (Canary & Wahba, 2006). The most maintenance behaviors occur in a relationship that the wife perceives as equitable, and the least maintenance behaviors occur in a relationship in which the wife feels underbenefited—that she receives less from the relationship than her partner. The husband's perception of relationship equity seems to be less related to maintenance behavior.

What do wives do to maintain relationships? One way that wives maintain relationships is by taking on more than their share of the division of labor in the family, the "tasks" category in Table 9.3. This topic will be discussed in more depth in Chapter 11. A second way is by sacrificing personal leisure time. Women report having less leisure time at home than men (Canary & Wahba, 2006). For example, at the end of the day when both husband and wife are sitting down watching television, the wife is likely to be folding laundry or creating a grocery list at the same time. Another way that wives maintain relationships is to accommodate their own preferences to match those of their husband. In a study of newly married couples, men's and women's preferences for who participates in child care activities were uncorrelated shortly after marriage but were highly correlated 2 years later after parenthood (Johnson & Huston, 1998). Who changed? Husbands' later preferences were largely a function of their earlier preferences and were not affected much by wives' early preferences. By contrast, wives' later preferences were a function of husbands' early preferences, but only under one condition: when she reported high levels of love toward her spouse. Thus one way that wives who are very much in love reduce conflict is to adjust their preferences to match those of their husbands.

Another way that couples maintain relationships is by altering their views of the male-female relationship to match those of their partner. Attitude alignment occurs in both married and cohabiting couples; that is, when one partner is traditional, the other partner is more likely to become traditional and when one partner is egalitarian, the other partner is more likely to become egalitarian (Kalmijn, 2005). The effect of men on women is similar to the effect of women on men, but the effects partly depend on the nature of the view. Wives' egalitarian views have a stronger effect on husbands than wives' traditional views. And, husbands' traditional views have a stronger effect on wives than husbands' egalitarian views.

It is not only wives who maintain relationships. Partners of either sex who score high on expressivity or psychological femininity are likely to be concerned with relationship maintenance. Both husbands and wives who score higher on expressivity put more effort into improving the relationship (Huston & Houts, 1998). Femininity also is more strongly related than sex to the five relationship maintenance strategies shown in Table 9.3 (Canary & Wahba, 2006).

Marital Satisfaction

What predicts how satisfied men and women are with their romantic relationships? One predictor is relationship talk—the extent to which the couple talks about the state of the relationship. Relationship talk is more strongly related to women's than men's marital satisfaction (Badr & Acitelli, 2005). There are a variety of other characteristics that are linked to marital satisfaction, including personality characteristics (gender roles) and relationship characteristics (power distribution, equity). Here I discuss each of these.

Gender Roles. If men are socialized to be masculine and women to be feminine, do the happiest couples consist of a masculine husband and a feminine wife? The literature on this issue is clear: Couples with traditional gender roles have the least relationship satisfaction (Ickes, 1993). Instead, the happiest and longest lasting relationships are ones in which one partner is either androgynous or feminine, regardless of the partner's gender role (Antill, 1983). This is also true for gay and lesbian relationships (Kurdek & Schmitt, 1986) as well as dating couples (Steiner-Pappalardo & Gurung, 2002). Thus it is femininity rather than masculinity that is most strongly tied to relationship satisfaction. This is not surprising because femininity reflects a focus on others, involving warmth, caring, and understanding—all attributes we would expect to foster good relationships. If one person in the couple has sufficient feminine attributes, it means one person is paying attention to and taking care of the relationship. The following studies illustrate this point.

People recognize the value of feminine traits in relationships. In a study of college students, men and women perceived a potential mate to be more desirable if he or she was androgynous (possessed both masculine and feminine characteristics) as opposed to sex-typed or undifferentiated (Green & Kenrick, 1994). Students also rated the feminine characteristics as more important than the masculine characteristics. Vonk and van Nobelen (1993) found that both men and women rated themselves as behaving in a more feminine way and a less masculine way when they were with their partner than when they were by themselves. This indicates that both men and women recognize the importance of femininity to relationships. Moreover, people who behaved in feminine ways with their partner also reported the highest relationship satisfaction.

One way that femininity may be linked to relationship satisfaction is through interpersonal skills. In a study of college students, femininity was associated with greater competence in providing support and self-disclosing (Lamke et al., 1994). These domains of expressive competence accounted for the relation of femininity to relationship satisfaction.

Is there a role for masculinity in relationship satisfaction? In the previous study, masculinity was associated with domains of instrumental competence, such as initiating relationships and bringing up issues of conflict (Lamke et al., 1994). However, instrumental competence was not associated with relationship satisfaction. Two studies of married couples examined the implications of both positive and negative masculine and feminine attributes for marital satisfaction (Bradbury, Campbell, & Fincham, 1995). In the first study, both positive masculine attributes (i.e., agency) and positive feminine attributes in the husband predicted an increase in the wife's marital satisfaction over the year. In the second study, negative masculine attributes in the husband (i.e., unmitigated agency, which includes being hostile, greedy, and arrogant) predicted a decline in the wife's marital satisfaction. Attributes of the wife did not influence the husband's marital satisfaction in either study. These findings underscore the importance of distinguishing positive from negative masculine traits. They also support the idea that characteristics of the husband influence the wife's psychological well-being, but the reverse is not true. This finding is discussed in more detail in a later section of the chapter.

Power Distribution. One way gender-role attitudes manifest themselves in marriage is in how power is distributed between husband and wife. What is the difference in the power that men and women hold in relationships? One would expect that younger men and women should have more equal power in relationships because they are less likely to adhere to traditional roles. College men and women in particular have a similar status and similar access to resources. Thus there is reason to predict that power will be distributed equally in college relationships. However, most dating couples report an imbalance of power in their relationship, usually in the direction of the male having more power (Sprecher & Felmlee, 1997).

One of the difficulties with studies of the distribution of power in relationships is that they are based on self-report. A more creative methodology to assess power in relationships was developed and examined across several cultures (Wagner et al., 1990). The investigators asked men and women in Austria, the United States, India, and Turkey to imagine they bought a fairly expensive product and their spouse either approved or disapproved of the purchase. Respondents were asked to rate how good or bad they would feel in each situation. The discrepancy between how the person felt when the spouse disapproved versus approved represented "dependence on the other's agreement," which would reflect low power. In other words, if you feel really good when you buy something of which your spouse approves and really bad when you buy something of which your spouse disapproves, you have low power in the relationship. By contrast, if your feelings are relatively unaffected by whether your spouse approves or disapproves of your purchase, you have high power in the relationship.

As expected, in families in which the husband was dominant, men were less dependent than women. This means that men were less affected than women by whether their spouse approved or disapproved of their purchase. In egalitarian families, men and women were equally dependent. Interestingly, these findings held for only the two Western cultures, Austria and the United States. There was actually less dependence in the traditional patriarchal cultures of India and Turkey. If the families are more patriarchal, meaning husbands are dominant, why aren't wives more affected by their husband's approval versus disapproval? The authors explain that the traditional gender roles in India and Turkey are independent roles: Men's and women's roles are distinct from one another and they function in those roles independent of one another. This means that each person has great control over his or her domain but little control over the spouse's domain. They grant each other this power. If one person makes a purchase, the other would have little to say about it. Determine the level of "dependence" in your own and your peers' relationships with Do Gender 9.4.

Thus far, the evidence is that power is most likely to be shared between husbands and wives across a variety of ethnic groups. However, there is a problem in the way an equal power relationship has been conceptualized in these studies. People can report an equal power relationship in two ways. First, power can be equal because the two people share responsibility for all domains; this is the definition of a true egalitarian relationship. Second, power can be equal such that one person has exclusive power in some domains and the other person has exclusive power in other domains; thus there is an *average* balance of power. This is the situation that characterized the Turkish and Indian marriages. But, are these egalitarian relationships? They can be, but often they are not. If the domains of power are divided along traditional gender-role lines, such that women have power

DO GENDER 9.4
Economic Independence

One way to determine whether your relationship is egalitarian is to examine economic independence. How much can you spend without asking your partner? How much can your partner spend without asking you? What is the most you have ever spent without asking your partner? What is the most your partner has ever spent without asking you?

Now try the Wagner and colleagues' (1990) experiment. Ask each member of a couple to imagine making a fairly expensive purchase. Ask them to imagine that their spouse approves and to rate how they would feel: 1 = Feel very bad and 5 = Feel very good. Then ask them to imagine that their spouse disapproves and to rate how they would feel: 1 = Feel very bad and 5 = Feel very good. To determine power, evaluate the discrepancy in ratings for spouse approval versus disapproval (higher discrepancies equal less power).

over child care matters and men have power over economic resources, it is unlikely the relationship is truly egalitarian.

One determinant of relationship satisfaction for both men and women is **equity** (Cahn, 1992). An equitable relationship is one in which a person feels that what he or she puts into and gets out of a relationship is equal to what the partner puts into and gets out of the relationship. People who report they are overbenefited (receive more from the relationship than their partner) or underbenefited (receive less from the relationship than their partner) are dissatisfied in relationships, whether male or female (Cahn, 1992). See Sidebar 9.2 for Hugh Hefner's version of equity and egalitarianism in relationships.

Characteristics of Him But Not Her. Although there are common characteristics of people (e.g., femininity) and relationships

SIDEBAR 9.2: *Equity in Relationships According to Hugh Hefner*

In 1999, Hugh Hefner claimed his relationships with his four girlfriends are equal. Here is an excerpt from an interview with Hugh Hefner (by Terry Gross) on National Public Radio (November 29, 1999):

GROSS: Now, here's something I sometimes wonder about couples in which there is a really big age disparity between them. . . . Like, if you're 52 years older than the woman you're seeing, she. . . . In some ways, she couldn't possibly be your equal because you've lived a long time, you've been very successful, you've amassed a fortune, and published this world-renowned magazine, whereas they're not even out of college yet. So, it just wouldn't be possible for them to function as your equal.

HEFNER: Is that of some importance?

GROSS: Well, if I was the woman in the relationship, it would be important to me.

HEFNER: Well, I think—quite frankly—that people are attracted to one another for a variety of reasons. There is more than one kind of equality. And in my relationship with the women that I am seeing right now, there is a very real equality in terms of who makes the decisions in the relationship in what we do and how we spend our time, etc. But, I would say that the relationships are more complementary than equal. Each of us brings something different to the relationship. I bring the experience and the years and the wisdom and whatever. And they bring a very special joy, [they] relate to life that is not so sophisticated, not so cynical, and very refreshing.

(e.g., equity) that influence both husband and wife marital satisfaction, there also is evidence that the husband influences the wife's marital satisfaction more than the reverse. For example, Blum and Mehrabian (1999) examined the relation of temperament to marital satisfaction. A positive temperament included feeling affectionate and excited, whereas a negative temperament included feeling nasty and enraged. They found that men's marital satisfaction was linked more to their own temperament than their wife's temperament. By contrast, women's marital satisfaction was equally influenced by their own and their husband's temperament. Men's emotional communication skills are associated with wives' marital satisfaction, but women's emotional communication skills are not related to husbands' marital satisfaction (Cordova, Gee, & Warren, 2005).

Wives are also more influenced than husbands by their spouse's psychological state. In a study where husbands and wives recorded their emotions periodically throughout the day, the husband's emotions influenced the wife's emotions, but the wife's emotions had no impact on the husband's emotions (Larson & Pleck, 1999). In another study, husbands' depression was associated with low marital satisfaction for both husbands and wives, but wives' depression was not associated with husband or wife marital satisfaction (Thompson, Whiffen, & Blain, 1995). In general, there is more evidence of **emotional transmission** from husbands to wives than wives to husbands (Larson & Almeida, 1999).

Even in the domain of sexual relations, characteristics of the husband predict the wife's sexual satisfaction, but the reverse is not true. In one study, the extent to which husbands understood their wife's sexual preferences predicted higher wife sexual satisfaction and fewer wife sexual difficulties (Purnine & Carey, 1997). However, the extent to which wives understood their husband's sexual preferences was unrelated to husband sexual satisfaction or sexual difficulties.

Why are women affected by what is happening with men—their temperament, their emotional communication skills, their well-being, their understanding of sexual preferences—but men are relatively unaffected by these same characteristics of women? Aspects of the male and female gender roles provide some clues. Women are socialized to focus on others, which may explain why others' feelings and behavior influence women's feelings and behavior. By contrast, men are socialized to focus on the self, which may explain why it is only attributes of the self that determine men's feelings and behavior. In addition, women may have greater skills than men in detecting another's emotions, which makes them more responsive to others' emotions (Larson & Pleck, 1999).

TAKE HOME POINTS

- There are five classic relationship maintenance strategies: positivity, openness, assurances, network, and tasks.

- Women engage in more relationship maintenance than do men.

- Women's maintenance behaviors are more strongly related to relationship outcomes than men's maintenance behaviors.

- Femininity or communion is a better predictor of relationship maintenance than sex.

- Features of the person (dispositional level of analysis) and features of the environment or situation (structural level of analysis) influence marital satisfaction.

- One feature of the person is the level of femininity. Femininity rather than masculinity is most strongly related to relationship satisfaction. Femininity is related to providing support, self-disclosure, and managing conflict effectively in relationships.

- Another factor that influences relationship satisfaction is the power balance of the relationship. In general, more

egalitarian relationships are associated with relationship satisfaction for both men and women.

- There are different ways of conceptualizing egalitarianism: joint participation or separate but equal participation. The latter may not be a truly egalitarian philosophy.

- Psychological femininity or a communal orientation may be responsible for women being more affected by the psychological and physical state of their partner.

CONFLICT

Areas of Conflict

Popular books suggest that men and women experience a good deal of conflict. John Gray's best-seller *Men Are from Mars, Women Are from Venus* (1992) suggests that men's and women's relationships are destined to be full of conflict because the two sexes have completely different styles of relating to people. The title of Lillian Rubin's (1983) popular book *Intimate Strangers* certainly implies that men and women face considerable conflict. In my opinion, both these books, as well as many others, exaggerate the difference between men and women as well as their potential for conflict. However, as is often the case, there is a kernel of truth to some of these ideas.

Rubin (1983) describes why men and women have relationship problems, largely based on the ideas of Nancy Chodorow (1978). Recall Chodorow's psychoanalytic theory of gender-role development from Chapter 5. According to Chodorow and Rubin, men's and women's difficulties in relating to each other stem from their earliest relationship to their primary caretaker, usually the mother. Because girls grow up identifying with the person who is their primary attachment, girls find it easy to make connections to one another but find it difficult to separate from one another. Conversely, because boys grow up being forced to reject the person with whom they have identified (mother) in favor of someone who plays a smaller role in the home (father), boys are adept at separation and have difficulty with connection.

Is there any evidence that men and women report distinct areas of conflict in romantic relationships that map onto these ideas? In general, men and women identify similar areas of conflict in relationships. In the prototype study that I conducted with college students, I found that the nature of conflict was largely the same for men and women (Helgeson et al., 1987). College students were asked to recall times when they felt distant from their romantic partner. The core feature of distance episodes for both men and women was disapproval of a partner's behavior. The disapproval was often in response to behaviors that threatened the relationship, such as a partner showing interest in or dating others. Other precursors to feelings of distance were lack of communication and physical separation.

Yet some studies have found that women identify problems over independence more often than men (Cochran & Peplau, 1985). Women's problems with autonomy may come from their difficulty at achieving it. Women may be concerned that asserting their independence detracts from the relationship. Whereas men are expected to pursue independent activities outside of the relationship, the expectations for women are not that clear. For these reasons, women may desire more autonomy in relationships.

One source of conflict that bothers men and women equally is deception. However, evolutionary theory suggests that men and women will differ in the kinds of deception that upset them. Across several studies, women were found to be more upset than men about a partner's deception about resources (e.g., lie about income), whereas men were found to be more upset than women about a partner's deception about sex (e.g., lying about a desire for sex; Haselton et al., 2005).

Conflict Management

When conflict arises, how do men and women handle it? A meta-analysis on conflict resolution strategies showed that women are more likely than men to compromise across most cultures (Holt & DeVore, 2005). Men are more likely than women to use a forceful style, which means being goal-oriented rather than concerned with the effect on relationships, but only among individualistic cultures. Whereas these strategies may be more applicable to how men and women respond in organizations, the way men and women respond to conflict within a personal relationship could differ. Studies of relationships show that men are more likely than women to avoid conflict. In one study, high school students were asked how often they engaged in a series of tactics when they had an important conflict with their romantic partner (Feldman & Gowen, 1998). Men were more likely than women to use distraction. However, if men are engaged in conflict, they tend to use more coercion, aggression, and control tactics compared to women (Cahn, 1992). These findings are consistent with the differences in conflict management among friends described in Chapter 8.

One way conflict management has been studied is by observing couples' behavior in the laboratory as they discuss a conflict. Distressed spouses in general display more disagreement and more criticism than nondistressed spouses, but this difference is more apparent among women than men (Baucom et al., 1990). Women display more emotion, in particular more negative affect, than men during conflict discussions—but again, this difference seems to be limited to unhappy couples. In a study of middle-aged and older couples, there were no sex differences in the emotion displayed by men and women in happy couples. However, women displayed more emotion than men in unhappy couples. This finding was especially salient for negative emotion, (Carstensen, Gottman, & Levenson, 2004). This is one reason that women have been referred to as the "emotional barometer" of relationships (Floyd & Markman, 1983): If the woman is displaying high negativity, the relationship is likely to be in distress.

The display of negative affect in women may not reflect distress as much as their approach to managing the conflict. Whereas women are more likely to confront the conflict, men are more likely to withdraw or be defensive (Carstensen et al., 2004). In addition, men are more likely to try to deescalate the conflict by neutralizing the atmosphere—that is, they respond to negative behavior with neutral behavior, at least among distressed couples. Whereas nondistressed women are able to resist negative reciprocity (i.e., responding to negative affect with more negative affect), distressed women seem to have a difficult time doing so (Notarius et al., 1989). When distressed couples come into the laboratory, the wife often sees it as an opportunity to resolve a conflict; thus she confronts the conflict, which includes displays of negative affect. The husband's goal, by contrast, is to keep the conflict from escalating; thus he responds to her negative affect with displays of either neutral or positive affect: He tries to smooth things over. Rather than perceiving his response as a positive one, she is frustrated that he is not becoming engaged in this conflict. In other words, she perceives her husband's lack of negative affect as a sign that he is not engaged in the interaction. Women then respond by intensifying their negative behavior, in essence escalating the conflict.

The following exchange illustrates this sequence of events:

WIFE: Let's talk about why you don't help out more with the children. (confrontation of conflict with negative affect)

HUSBAND: You do such a good job with the children that it doesn't seem like this is really an issue of conflict. (attempt to neutralize the affect with positive statement)

WIFE: You just don't get it, do you? If you spent more time with the children, you could do a good job too. (more negative affect, or reciprocity of negative affect)

Demand/Withdraw Pattern

Here's another interaction between husband and wife. Read this and decide what is going on here.

PERSON A: Why don't you spend a little more time working inside the house?

PERSON B: What? What do you mean?

PERSON A: You are never at home and when you are at home, you spend all of your time reading. I have to clean up everything.

(silence)

PERSON A: You could at least read Mandy a bedtime story.

(still no response; in fact, the sound of a newspaper opening up can be heard)

Links to Gender.   Man or woman? Who do you believe is more likely to be Person A? Person B? This episode is an example of the **demand/withdraw pattern**. It is characterized by one person demanding, if not nagging, and the other person not responding, or withdrawing. The demander is more likely to initiate problem discussion, whereas the withdrawer is more likely to avoid problem discussion (Christensen & Heavey, 1993). Among distressed and nondistressed couples, the demander is more likely to be a woman and the withdrawer to be a man (Christensen & Heavey, 1993; Gottman, 1994). This demand/withdraw pattern has been present in marriage since the early part of the 20th century (Gottman & Carrere, 1994). In public, women are more likely to appear deferential and polite, but in the private sphere of marriage, women confront and demand (Gottman & Carrere, 1994).

Christensen and Heavey (1993) have conducted numerous studies of married couples that rely on either couples' self-reports of demand and withdraw behavior or on coders' observations of such behavior while couples discuss problems. There is a great deal of agreement between the two measures of demand and withdraw behavior. Apparently couples know who demands and who withdraws. Across their studies, Christensen and Heavey conclude that about 60% of couples are characterized by wife demand/husband withdraw, 30% by husband demand/wife withdraw, and 10% by an equal proportion of both demanding and withdrawing.

Explanations.   Why do wives tend to be the demanders and husbands tend to be the withdrawers? Christensen and Heavey (1993) suggest that husbands and wives have a fundamental conflict: Women prefer closeness and men prefer independence. This is the basic dilemma identified by Rubin (1983) and Chodorow (1978). Men can achieve independence on their own, but women require the support of their partner to achieve closeness. This fundamental conflict leads men and women to employ different strategies in relationships. Women need to demand to obtain closeness, whereas men can withdraw to achieve independence. Christensen and Heavey measured conflict over closeness versus independence and found this type of conflict is associated with greater demand/withdraw behavior. In addition, the person who wanted greater closeness (usually the woman) was more likely to be the demander, and the person who wanted greater independence (usually the man) was more likely to be the withdrawer.

Another explanation for the wife demand/husband withdraw pattern is that it is wives who most often want change in the relationship. If this explanation is true, one should observe more husband demanding when the husband wants change in the relationship. To test this idea, Christensen and Heavey (1993) had married couples with children talk about an area in which the mother wanted a change and an area in which the father wanted a change. The two interactions were videotaped. Self-reports and observer ratings of demand/withdraw behavior showed that the typical wife demand/husband withdraw pattern was found when the issue was one in which the mother desired a change. This is shown on the left side of each of the figures in Figure 9.10. When the issue was one in which the father desired a change (the right half of the figures), there was less mother demanding and more father demanding, but the pattern did not completely reverse itself. Instead, for the father issue, there was no sex difference in the demand/withdraw pattern. Thus the previous literature could be overestimating the female demand/male withdraw pattern because the conflicts most often discussed in the laboratory are probably "wife issues": issues in which the wife wants the change (Christensen & Heavy, 1990).

One criticism of the Christensen and Heavey (1993) study is that the issues mothers and fathers chose were in the domain of parenting. Thus even the husband's issue could be viewed as one in which the wife was highly invested. The findings were replicated in two other studies in which the husband and wife were able to choose among a number of issues, not all of which had to do with parenting (Heavey, Layne, & Christensen, 1993; Vogel & Karney, 2002). The findings from both studies paralleled those shown in Figure 9.10: For the wife issue, there was greater female demand and male withdrawal; the pattern changed but did not reverse itself for the husband issue. In one of these studies, the demand/withdrawal pattern was associated with how important the

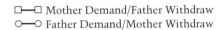

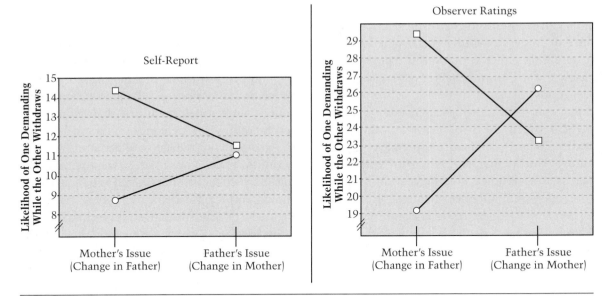

FIGURE 9.10   Demand/withdraw pattern. When the issue being discussed is one in which mothers are concerned, the typical wife demand/husband withdraw pattern is observed. There is little husband demand/wife withdrawal. When the issue being discussed is one in which fathers are concerned, wife demand/husband withdrawal decreases and husband demand/wife withdrawal increases. However, the pattern does not completely reverse itself. Thus the wife demand/husband withdraw pattern is not only a function of wives having more concerns in the relationship.

Source: A. Christensen and C. L. Heavy (1993). Gender differences in marital conflict: The demand/withdraw interaction pattern. In S. Oskamp and M. Constanzo (Eds.), *Gender issues in contemporary society* (Vol. 6, pp. 113–141). Beverly Hills, CA: Sage.

topic was to the person (Vogel & Karney, 2002). For example, the more important the husband's topic was to him, the less he withdrew. The more important the wife's topic was to her, the more she demanded and the less she withdrew. Examine the demand/withdraw pattern in couples you know in Do Gender 9.5.

When husbands want change, why isn't there more evidence that husbands demand and wives withdraw? Christensen and Heavey (1990, 1993) suggest that couples are likely to have a history of resolving men's issues compared to women's issues in marriage. This occurs for two

reasons. First, men desire less change in relationships; thus men raise fewer issues. Second, men have greater power in relationships; thus the issues that men raise are addressed. Because men's issues are addressed, there is less likelihood of getting into any kind of demand/withdraw cycle. Women's issues are less likely to be resolved than men's issues, so there is more opportunity for conflict. This may lead to a propensity on the part of women to demand and a propensity on the part of men to withdraw. The demand/withdraw cycle is self-perpetuating. The more one person demands, the more the other

DO GENDER 9.5
Who Demands and Who Withdraws?

Come up with your own self-report measure of demand and withdraw behavior. Some sample items adapted from Christensen and Heavey (1993) are shown here. Measure the frequency with which such behavior occurs among dating couples you know by asking them to complete your survey. Is there evidence that women demand more? Men withdraw more? Is relationship satisfaction related to demand/withdraw? Do you find that the less satisfied person engages in more demand behavior? What other predictions would you make based on the literature reviewed in this chapter?

Sample Demand/Withdraw Items

One person nags and the other person refuses to discuss the topic.
One person makes demands and the other person is silent.
One person criticizes and the other person withdraws.
One person tries to start a conversation about a problem and the other person tries to avoid the topic.

withdraws; the more one withdraws, the more the other demands. Thus the female demand/male withdraw pattern can be explained partly in terms of men's and women's personality predispositions and partly in terms of the situations in which men and women find themselves in marriage (e.g., women have lower power, women perceive more problems).

Another argument as to why women demand and men withdraw is that women have a greater tolerance for the physiological arousal that conflict produces (Gottman, 1994; Levenson, Carstensen, & Gottman, 1994).

Gottman has suggested that men may avoid situations that produce an increase in physiological arousal because their bodies recover more slowly from arousal than women's bodies. Recall from Chapter 7 that men are more in touch with their internal physiology than women are. Thus men may find the physiological arousal that conflict produces more aversive than women do and withdraw from it. One study found a greater correspondence between negative affect and physiological arousal among men than women (Levenson et al., 1994). The investigators had 156 couples discuss a conflict while their physiological arousal was measured. Physiological measures included heart rate, skin conductance, and body temperature; interactions were videotaped. Each member of the couple viewed the videotape and used a rating dial to indicate their affect over the course of the discussion. As predicted, men's physiological arousal was correlated with their self-reports of negative affect during the conflict discussion. For women, physiological arousal was unrelated to their reports of affect.

One problem with the arousal explanation for male withdraw behavior is that numerous studies show that women become more physiologically aroused than men during discussion of conflict. This is explored in more detail in Chapter 11. Gottman's (1994) response to this might be that men's withdraw behavior is effective in that it keeps men from becoming aroused.

There are also cultural reasons for the demand/withdraw pattern (Noller, 1993). In the United States, men withdraw because they are socialized to resist pressure and maintain their independence; withdrawing maintains a position of power. Women are socialized to be relationship experts. Because women have experience managing conflict, they are less disturbed by it. The link of demand behavior to being female and withdraw behavior to being male has been replicated across Brazil, Italy, and Taiwan

(Christensen et al., 2006). However, other cross-cultural research on the demand/withdraw pattern has shown that it is linked to the structure of marriage more than sex, per se. In a study of American and Pakistani couples, female demand/male withdraw was greater among Americans than Pakistanis, and male demand/female withdraw was greater among Pakistanis than Americans (Rehman & Holtzworth-Munroe, 2006). The nature of demand and withdraw behavior, however, differed between the two countries. Whereas Americans conceptualize withdraw behavior as reflecting resistance to change, withdraw behavior in Pakistan may reflect a less powerful position—resigned acceptance. Demands on the part of American women were more dominant and aggressive, whereas the demands of Pakistani women were more unassertive and pleading. Thus the greater power differential between men and women in Pakistan compared to the United States may explain why Pakistani women engage in more withdrawal and less assertive demands.

Implications for Relationships. What are the implications of the demand/withdraw pattern for marital satisfaction? Not surprisingly, high rates of demand/withdraw behavior are associated with reports of lower marital satisfaction across a variety of cultures (Christensen et al., 2006; Rehman & Holtzworth-Munroe, 2006). However, the negative effect of demand/withdrawal behavior appears to be buffered by the expression of affection in marriage (Caughlin & Huston, 2002). In other words, demanding and withdrawing are less likely to be linked to low marital satisfaction if couples are affectionate toward one another.

The effect of the demand/withdraw pattern on marital satisfaction also appears to depend on who is engaging in the demanding and who is engaging in the withdrawing. One study found that wife demand/husband withdraw behavior was

associated with declines in wife satisfaction over a year, but husband demand/wife withdraw behavior was associated with *improvements* in wife satisfaction over the year (Heavey et al., 1993). These findings were replicated in a second study (Heavey, Christensen, & Malamuth, 1995). Why would husband demand behavior be associated with an improvement in wife marital satisfaction? One theory is that demanding behavior reflects engagement in the relationship, and wives are happy that husbands are engaged. In both studies, demand/withdraw behavior did not predict changes in husbands' marital satisfaction, which is consistent with previous research on the predictors of marital satisfaction. Characteristics of the spouse or relationship affect wives more than husbands.

There also has been research on the demand/withdraw pattern in abusive relationships, and it appears the pattern is exacerbated in these couples. One study compared demand and withdraw behavior among couples in which the husband was and was not abusive (Berns, Jacobson, & Gottman, 1999). There was greater wife demand behavior and greater husband withdraw behavior in abusive than nonabusive couples. However, there also was greater husband demand behavior in abusive than nonabusive couples. The investigators suggested the high level of demand behavior among husbands reflected their dissatisfaction with the relationship and attempts to control their wife's behavior. Although the abusive husbands demanded change in their wife, husbands were withdrawing from any attempts their wife made to change the husband's behavior.

Jealousy

In the context of romantic relationships, jealousy is the concern that there is a rival for the other's affections. Are men or women more jealous? There is little evidence for sex differences in jealousy (Wright, 1999). When a difference is found, it is usually in the direction of women being more jealous than men. One concern with this research is that men may be less likely than women to admit jealousy. Research that has examined different dimensions of jealousy supports this idea. In a study of 66 married couples, men and women were equally likely to have jealous thoughts and to experience jealous feelings, but women were more likely to communicate jealousy (Guerrero et al., 1993). Men have been socialized to keep jealous feelings to themselves; admitting jealousy implies weakness and vulnerability. Women may be more likely than men to communicate their feelings about jealousy because they are concerned with preserving the relationship.

Different events may inspire jealousy in men and women. According to evolutionary theory, different situations should provoke jealousy in women and men. Because men are uncertain of the paternity of their offspring, they should be extremely upset by sexual infidelity: Sexual infidelity not only jeopardizes the chance of a man's genes surviving but also means that a man could be investing his resources into raising a child that is not genetically related to him. Sexual infidelity should be less disturbing to women because it does not threaten her genetic link to offspring. Instead, women should be more upset by their partner falling in love with someone else, or emotional infidelity. Emotional infidelity could lead the husband to take his resources elsewhere and invest in children with someone else; thus in that sense emotional infidelity threatens the viability of the female's offspring.

To test this idea, Buss and colleagues (1992) asked college students whether they would be more disturbed by sexual or emotional infidelity. The exact wording of the questions is contained in Table 9.4. As shown in Figure 9.11, they found that women were more distressed by emotional than sexual infidelity, and men were more distressed by sexual than emotional infidelity. In a subsequent experiment, the investigators also found physiological effects that paralleled the self-reports of distress. Men were more physiologically reactive when they imagined their partner being sexually unfaithful rather than emotionally unfaithful, whereas women were more physiologically reactive when they imagined their partner being emotionally rather than sexually unfaithful.

However, these results were not replicated in another study in the United States, a study in the Netherlands, or a study in Germany (Buunk et al., 1996). These three other studies did confirm that men were more distressed than women by sexual infidelity. However, the majority of men in Germany and the Netherlands and about half the men in the United States said emotional infidelity was more distressing than sexual infidelity. Thus men are more distressed

TABLE 9.4 EMOTIONAL VERSUS SEXUAL INFIDELITY

Imagine you discover that the person with whom you've been seriously involved became interested in someone else. What would upset or distress you more (please circle only one in each set):

Set A
(A) Imagining your partner forming a deep emotional attachment to that person.
(B) Imagining your partner enjoying passionate sexual intercourse with that other person.

Set B
(A) Imagining your partner trying different sexual positions with that other person.
(B) Imagining your partner falling in love with that other person.

Source: Buss et al. (1992).

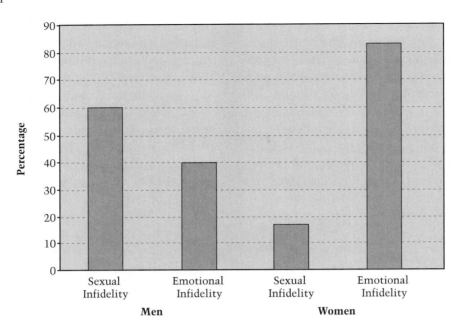

FIGURE 9.11 Sex differences in cues for sexual jealousy. When asked to choose which of two situations would be more upsetting, more men choose sexual infidelity than emotional infidelity. More women choose emotional infidelity than sexual infidelity.

Source: Adapted from Buss et al. (1992).

than women by sexual infidelity, but men also are more distressed by emotional infidelity than sexual infidelity. Thus the comparison referent is important!

One difficulty with this area of research is the extent to which sexual infidelity and emotional infidelity are intertwined. Perhaps men view sexual infidelity as implying emotional infidelity. Men might think, "If my wife was unfaithful, she must *really* be in love with someone else." Recall that both men and women perceive that women connect sex with love. If that is the case, men are comparing the combination of sexual and emotional infidelity to emotional infidelity alone. Women, by contrast, may perceive that emotional infidelity implies sexual infidelity. They may believe that if their husbands are emotionally unfaithful, they must also be having sex with the person. In other words, wives are comparing sexual infidelity to

the combination of emotional and sexual infidelity. Explore the link between emotional and sexual infidelity in Do Gender 9.6.

Another concern with the findings on sex differences in jealousy is the use of the forced-choice method. Respondents have to choose which of the two scenarios is more distressing. DeSteno and colleagues (2002) found that sex differences did not appear when respondents rated how upset they were by each scenario or used a checklist of emotions in response to each scenario. To determine which method revealed the accurate response, the investigators conducted a second study in which respondents were given the forced-choice question under a cognitive load condition (i.e., simultaneously engaging in a memory task) or not. They reasoned that the true response would emerge under the cognitive load condition because thought processes would be more automatic and less censored. In the

DO GENDER 9.6
Relations Between Sexual and Emotional Infidelity

Ask a group of people who are in a steady dating relationship to imagine their partner has become interested in someone else. Read the first item under Set A in Table 9.4 (the item that indicates emotional infidelity). Now have these people rate how likely they would be to think their partner had sexual relations with the other person.

Similarly, have another group of people read the second item under Set A in Table 9.4 (the item that indicates sexual infidelity). Have the people rate how likely they would be to think their partner had fallen in love with the other person.

1. Is sexual infidelity linked to emotional infidelity?

2. Is emotional infidelity linked to sexual infidelity?

3. Do the answers to these questions depend on the sex of the respondent?

no-load condition, the typical sex difference emerged. Under cognitive load, however, both men and women were more likely to choose sexual infidelity than emotional infidelity as more upsetting.

Thus although there are patterns of jealousy that are consistent with evolutionary theory, the evidence in favor of an evolutionary theory of sex differences in jealousy is not clear. A recent review of the literature found little evidence for sex differences in sexual jealousy (Harris, 2003). Sex differences are reduced under cognitive load; the majority of studies show that men are more upset by emotional than sexual infidelity; and fewer sex differences appear on continuous measures compared to forced-choice measures (Green & Sabini, 2006).

TAKE HOME POINTS

- Men and women identify similar areas of conflict in relationships. There is some suggestion that women report more conflict over achieving autonomy in the context of relationships than men.

- In marital interaction studies, women display more negative affect than men and are more likely to reciprocate negative affect than men in distressed couples—leading to the suggestion that women are the *emotional barometers* in relationships.

- The demand/withdraw behavior pattern has been linked to gender. Women are more likely to demand, and husbands are more likely to withdraw.

- There are several explanations for this pattern:

  a. Men and women have a basic conflict in that women want connection, which requires cooperation from a partner, and men want autonomy, which they can achieve on their own.

  b. Women identify more problems in a relationship than men do. To resolve problems, confrontation or demanding behavior may be necessary. In fact, evidence indicates that when husbands have problems in a relationship, their rate of demand behavior increases and their rate of withdraw behavior decreases.

  c. The demand/withdraw pattern may be related to the power structure in relationships and the lower status of women. Demanding behavior may be an attempt to improve one's status, whereas withdraw behavior may be an attempt to maintain the status quo.

- The demand/withdraw pattern is associated with lower levels of marital satisfaction. This pattern is more pronounced in abusive relationships.

- There seems to be some modest evidence that husband demand behavior has positive implications for women's marital satisfaction. Demand behavior relative to withdraw behavior shows involvement in the relationship, and women want men to be involved.

- Men and women seem to experience jealousy with equal frequency.

■ Evolutionary theory predicts that men will be more distressed by sexual infidelity than emotional infidelity, whereas women will be more distressed by emotional infidelity than sexual infidelity. Support for this position is limited.

GAY AND LESBIAN RELATIONSHIPS

There are three major reasons for studying gay and lesbian relationships. First, gay men and lesbians are an important population in their own right. Second, studying homosexual relationships enables us to test relationship theories that were largely established on heterosexual relationships; it is important to know whether relationship theories generalize across a variety of relationships. Third, and most important to this book, studying gay men and lesbians can increase knowledge about how gender roles operate in relationships. As Kurdek (2003) describes, gay and lesbian couples are "natural experiments" of relationships without men's paternalistic power and women's maternalistic care. One can ask, for example, whether men have more power than women in heterosexual relationships because they are male or because they often make more money than women. By examining power distributions in homosexual relationships, we can answer these questions.

There has been much less research on gay and lesbian relationships compared to heterosexual relationships. Instead, target issues have been the origins of homosexuality and its pathology (Peplau, 1991). One reason for the lack of attention to homosexual relationships is the number of myths about them. People tend to believe that homosexual relationships are unhappy, dysfunctional, deviant, and transient. Research shows that these beliefs are not true (Peplau & Spalding, 2000). Homosexual relationships can be long lasting. In Eldridge and Gilbert's (1990) study, 90% of lesbian couples

lived together, and the average relationship lasted 5.4 years, with some lasting as long as 20 years. A study of over 700 homosexual Black men and women who were involved in relationships also disconfirmed the myth of transient homosexual relationships, as the average relationship lasted over 2 years and ranged from several months to 35 years (Peplau, Cochran, & Mays, 1997). Studies also have shown that the majority of gay and lesbian relationships are close and mutually satisfying. In fact, one reason that gay and lesbian people seek marriage is to establish the legitimacy of their relationships to the heterosexual world (Lewin, 2002).

Another myth about gay men and lesbians is that they are unhappy people and have low self-esteem. This hardly characterizes the majority of gay men and lesbians. However, there is a higher prevalence of some mental health problems among gay and lesbian people compared to heterosexuals. In a nationally representative survey, gay and bisexual men had an elevated rate of major depressive disorder, and lesbian and bisexual women had an elevated rate of generalized anxiety disorder compared to heterosexuals (Cochran, Sullivan, & Mays, 2003). The difference between the male groups was larger than the difference between the female groups. One reason for elevated mental health problems among homosexuals is the impact of discrimination (Mays & Cochran, 2001). One would expect discrimination to be greater for gay men than lesbians because people have more tolerant attitudes toward lesbians than gay men. In fact, mental health problems are elevated more for gay men than lesbians.

Another reason for the lack of research on gay and lesbian relationships is that the gay and lesbian community has been reluctant to participate in psychological research. Historically, there has been good reason for homosexuals to mistrust psychologists: Up until 1973, the American Psychological Association classified homosexuality as a mental disorder (Conger, 1975).

It is difficult to study gay and lesbian relationships because all homosexuals are not open about their sexual orientation. Many of the studies of gay men and lesbians described in this chapter were conducted by recruiting participants from advertisements in college newspapers, from gay and lesbian publications, from contacting gay and lesbian organizations, and by word of mouth from one study participant to another. Obviously, the participants in these studies are not representative of the population; gay men and lesbians who are less open about their sexuality or less involved in the homosexual community are underrepresented.

Research on gay and lesbian relationships became more visible with the development of AIDS. AIDS increased the awareness of homosexuality, and the loss of life through AIDS increased awareness of the closeness of homosexual relationships. Gay and lesbian relationships have received more recent attention over the past few years as the subject of same-sex marriage has emerged. In 2000, Vermont became the first state in the nation to permit civil unions between gay men and lesbians. These civil unions provide most of the rights and responsibilities of marriage. Today, Connecticut and New Jersey also allow civil unions. In 2004, Massachusetts became the first state to allow same-sex marriage, and in 2005, Canada legalized same-sex marriage. These recent actions have aroused a furor in many states, leading the vast majority of states to develop laws or constitutional amendments to ban same-sex marriage. To date, every state except six (Connecticut, Massachusetts, New Jersey, New Mexico, New York, and Rhode Island) has prohibited same-sex marriage (Stateline, 2007). Thus legal certificates that allow same-sex marriage or civil unions in other states or countries will not be recognized by the majority of the United States.

Consistent with U.S. politics, a 2006 Gallup Poll showed that the majority of Americans oppose gay marriage and, in fact,

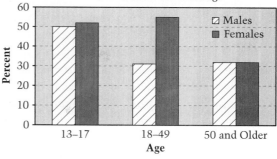

Teenagers' and Adults' Favorability Toward Same-Sex Marriage

FIGURE 9.12 Americans' views on same-sex marriage. The majority of people oppose same-sex marriage, with the exception of teenagers and women between the ages of 18–49.
Source: Adapted from Newport (2006) and Saad (2006a).

half are in favor of a constitutional amendment to define marriage as between a man and a woman (Newport, 2006; Saad, 2006a; Gallup Poll, 2006.) Teenagers have more favorable views of gay marriage, with half voicing approval—the rate being the same for males (50%) and females (52%). As shown in Figure 9.12, among adults, the only group that favors gay marriage is women between the ages of 18 to 49—55% support gay marriage. Support for gay marriage is much lower among men between the ages of 18 to 49 (31%), men 50 and older (32%), and women 50 and older (32%).

Let's review some of the research on gay and lesbian relationships.

Relationship Development

Characteristics Desired in a Mate. Do gay men and lesbians show the same differences in mate preferences as heterosexual men and women? To address this question, Gonzales and Meyers (1993) compared the personal advertisements of heterosexual and homosexual men and women. They found that gay men were most likely to emphasize the importance of a partner's physical appearance in their advertisements, and lesbians were least likely to emphasize physical appearance. Heterosexual women indicated stronger preferences for attractiveness and were more likely to emphasize their own attractiveness compared to homosexual women. In another study of personal advertisements, gay men were more likely than lesbians to indicate a preference for a physically attractive partner, whereas lesbians were more likely to indicate personality preferences (e.g., sense of humor) than were gay men (Hatala & Prehodka, 1996). A third study of personal advertisements of heterosexual, bisexual, and lesbian women found that lesbians placed the least importance on physical appearance and bisexuals the most emphasis, with heterosexual women falling between the two groups (Smith & Stillman, 2002). Thus the finding that men emphasize physical attractiveness more than women in heterosexual relationships seems to be even more extreme in homosexual relationships. This suggests the attractiveness preference is linked to being male: Men prefer attractive partners, whether the partner is male or female.

By contrast, the sex difference in preference for financial security is exaggerated in heterosexual compared to homosexual relationships (Gonzales & Meyers, 1993). Heterosexual men were more likely than homosexual men to offer financial security in their advertisements. Heterosexual women were more likely than homosexual women to express a desire for financial security. Another study found that heterosexual women are more concerned with their partner's status than either homosexual women or both groups of men (Bailey et al., 1994).

Just as one should not generalize from studies of White heterosexuals to all heterosexuals, one also should not generalize from studies of White homosexuals to all homosexuals. Studies of minority homosexual relationships are

exceedingly rare. One exception is a study of desired mate characteristics among Black homosexuals (Peplau et al., 1997). Like studies of heterosexuals, respondents rated internal characteristics (e.g., honesty, kindness) as more important than external characteristics (e.g., physical attractiveness, income). There was no sex difference in the importance assigned to a partner's physical attractiveness or income, unlike the findings for heterosexuals. These findings even contradict the research just reviewed showing that gay men are more likely than lesbians to ascribe importance to physical attractiveness. With respect to partner income, it is not surprising that White and Black homosexuals find it less important than do heterosexuals; both partners are more likely to be working outside the home in homosexual relationships compared to heterosexual relationships, in part because homosexuals are less likely to have children at home. Whereas research on heterosexuals finds that men are more satisfied than women and research on White homosexuals finds no sex difference in relationship satisfaction, this study of Black homosexuals found that women were more satisfied than men with their relationships.

Like heterosexuals, homosexuals may prefer mates who are similar to them. Because the pool of possible mates is smaller for homosexuals, matching may be less possible. One study showed a striking degree of correspondence between homosexual partners on demographic characteristics, but less correspondence on personality traits (Kurdek, 2003). Lesbians were more likely than gay men to have similar personality traits.

Relationship Initiation. The initiation of a relationship may be more awkward for homosexuals than heterosexuals (Peplau & Spalding, 2000). One way that a relationship may develop is out of friendship. Lesbian relationships, in particular, are likely to develop out of friendship (Rose, Zand, & Cini, 1993). However, the progression from friendship to romantic partners may be difficult for lesbians (Rose et al., 1993). Traditionally, women are not used to taking the initiative in the development of romantic relationships. Thus it may take time for the relationship to move beyond friendship to a romantic relationship. Lesbian friendships may face the emotional bond challenge that confronts cross-sex friendship among heterosexuals: When does the relationship cross over from friendship to romantic love, and are the feelings mutual?

Relationship formation among homosexuals has been studied by examining first date scripts (Klinkenberg & Rose, 1994). Homosexual scripts for a first date show that gay men place a greater emphasis on sexuality and lesbians place a greater emphasis on intimacy. More men than women expected sex on a first date. Nearly half of men (48%) but only a small portion of women (12%) had sex on a recent first date. Lesbian scripts were more likely to emphasize the affective aspects of the date, such as thinking about how one felt about the person.

Thus many of the sex differences in first date scripts observed among heterosexuals appeared in the study of homosexuals (Rose & Frieze, 1993). Common features included grooming for the date, discussing plans for the date, initiating physical contact, the actual date activity (movie, dinner), and feelings of nervousness. Another parallel between homosexual and heterosexual first date scripts is that men paid more attention to the physical aspects of intimacy (sex), and women paid more attention to the emotional aspects of intimacy. These similarities suggest that sex differences in emphasis on physical versus emotional intimacy are truly related to being male versus female because they generalize across heterosexual and homosexual relationships. Another way in which homosexual first date scripts were similar to heterosexual

scripts is that men were more proactive than women: Gay men were more likely than lesbians to discuss making arrangements for the date. One way that homosexual scripts were quite different from heterosexual scripts is in the lack of attention to physical appearance: Neither gay men nor lesbians included concerns about their own physical appearance. With the exception of men being more proactive than women, homosexual scripts did not have stereotypical gender roles; the features of the first date were equally likely to be tied to either partner in the couple.

Intimacy and Sexuality

If women's friendships are closer than those of men and women are more relationship focused than men, it seems likely that a romantic relationship between two women will be closer or more intimate than a romantic relationship that involves at least one man. Kurdek (1998) tested this idea by comparing the intimacy level of the relationships of cohabiting lesbians, cohabiting gay men, and heterosexual married people. Intimacy was measured in terms of the amount of time spent together, perception of closeness, and including "partner" in one's self-definition. The hypothesis was confirmed. Lesbians and gay men reported greater intimacy than heterosexual married people. Despite the higher intimacy, lesbians and gay men also reported greater sense of autonomy than heterosexual married couples (e.g., having separate friends from partner, making decisions without checking with partner).

If men are more likely than women to define intimacy through sexuality, we would expect the most sexual behavior to occur among two gay men and the least to occur among two lesbians. This turns out to be true (Herek, 2006). Compared to heterosexual men, homosexual men have fewer exclusive relationships, report more sexual relationships outside of their current relationship in the prior year, and report a greater number of romantic partners (Bringle, 1995). Like heterosexual males, the same level of intimacy is not required for the development of passion among gay men compared to women (Vohs & Baumeister, 2004). Gay men develop passion more quickly than heterosexual females and lesbians.

Sexuality also seems to be more central to Black men's than Black women's homosexual relationships. The study of Black homosexuals showed that men reported being more likely than women to have had sex on the first date with their current partner (31% vs. 18%; Peplau et al., 1997). About half of the men and half of the women said they had agreed to be monogamous in their current relationship, but more men had engaged in sex outside the relationship (65%) than women (46%).

Thus parallels exist between heterosexual and homosexual romantic relationships in terms of women's emphasis on emotional intimacy and men's emphasis on sexual intimacy. This means sexual behavior may not necessarily be the best criterion for distinguishing between friendships and romantic relationships among lesbians. Using a heterosexual definition of sex to distinguish friendships from romantic relationships among lesbians is problematic because lesbians are less likely to engage in genital stimulation compared to gay men and heterosexual couples (Rothblum, 2002). A broader definition of sex may be required to define lesbian romantic relationships. In fact, the extent to which two women identify as a couple might be a better marker of a romantic relationship (Rose et al., 1993).

Relationship Satisfaction

The relative unavailability of marriage to homosexuals makes it difficult to compare gay and lesbian relationships to heterosexual married couples. Despite this research limitation, the vast majority of research shows that gay men and lesbians are as committed and satisfied with their relationships as heterosexuals (Herek, 2006; Peplau & Spalding, 2000), and that satisfaction with their relationships changes over time similar to that of heterosexuals. Although studies of heterosexual relationships often find men are more satisfied than women, a study of gay and lesbian couples without children found no sex difference in relationship satisfaction (Kurdek, 1996). Thus the sex difference in marital satisfaction among heterosexuals pertains more to the nature of male-female relationships than to sex (i.e., being male or female).

In general, the same kinds of variables that are associated with relationship satisfaction among heterosexuals also are associated with relationship satisfaction among homosexuals (Herek, 2006; Kurdek, 2006). Moreover, the same relationship theories that apply to heterosexual relationships apply to homosexual relationships. Commitment to a relationship is typically a function of the positive forces that attract one to a relationship and the barriers to leaving a relationship. This commitment process functions the same among heterosexuals and homosexuals. Kurdek (1992) found that relationship satisfaction increased over a 4-year period to the extent that gay men and lesbians derived more rewards, perceived fewer costs, and increased their emotional investment in the relationship. There seem to be no differences between heterosexuals and homosexuals in the forces that attract them to a relationship. However, homosexuals face fewer barriers to relationship dissolution than heterosexuals. For example, homosexual marriage is typically not recognized by the law, and homosexuals are less likely to have children. Homosexuals are less likely to have the support of family to maintain the relationship but more likely to have support from friends (Herek, 2006). Thus homosexuals face fewer barriers to leaving a relationship.

Social exchange theory suggests relationship satisfaction is partly determined by the benefits gained and costs incurred in a relationship. Benefits may be love and support as well as the partner's income. Costs may be time, money, and effort in maintaining the relationship. One predictor from social exchange theory is that the person more dependent on the relationship will have less power in the relationship; the person who has greater personal resources (education, income) will have more power in the relationship. This theory seems to hold well across heterosexual and gay men's relationships (Peplau & Spalding, 2000). The link of resources to power among lesbians is less clear.

Equality may be more central to gay and lesbian relationships than heterosexual relationships. Same-sex couples have a more egalitarian division of labor in the home than heterosexuals (Herek, 2006). Equality may be especially important to lesbian couples. One study showed that lesbian couples had more shared decision making and equal power compared to gay male or heterosexual couples (Kurdek, 2003). Equality also seems to be strongly linked to relationship satisfaction among lesbians (Peplau & Beals, 2001). These findings are interesting because we know women are more focused than men on equality in heterosexual relationships. Thus equality may have more to do with being female than with being female in the context of a heterosexual relationship.

Conflict

There is some evidence that gay and lesbian couples may be more effective in addressing conflict than heterosexual couples. In a relationship interaction study, lesbian, gay, and heterosexual couples were videotaped discussing a problem (Gottman, Levenson, Swanson et al., 2003). Homosexual initiators of problem discussion were less belligerent, less dominant, and more likely to maintain a positive tone throughout the interaction compared to their heterosexual counterparts. Homosexual couples used more affection and humor throughout the

interaction compared to heterosexual couples. A survey study showed that gay men and lesbians argued more effectively than heterosexuals (Kurdek, 2004). Gay men and lesbians were less likely than heterosexuals to engage in the demand/withdrawal pattern and more likely to suggest solutions and compromises compared to heterosexual married couples. Another interaction study that involved only gay and lesbian couples supported the research on married couples that shows men's behavior is more likely to affect women than women's behavior is to affect men. In this study, one partner's emotion during conflict discussion was related to the other partner's relationship satisfaction among lesbian couples but not gay male couples (Gottman, Levenson, Gross et al., 2003). Similarly, one partner's sadness while discussing the events of the day was related to lower relationship satisfaction for the other partner among lesbian couples, but not gay male couples.

Jealousy

Because sexual exclusivity does not seem to be as central to homosexual men's relationships, it is not surprising that homosexual men experience and express less sexual jealousy compared to heterosexual men (Bringle, 1995). In one study, homosexual men were more likely than heterosexual men to act as if nothing had happened after their partner had a sexual encounter. Homosexual men were less likely than heterosexual men to confront their partner.

With respect to the motives for jealousy, findings for homosexual couples are similar to those for heterosexual couples. In one study, heterosexual and homosexual men and women were given the forced-choice emotional versus sexual infidelity task and asked how much more distressing the one they chose would be (Sheets & Wolfe, 2001). Heterosexual women, gay men, and lesbians all said emotional infidelity was much more distressing than sexual infidelity. Heterosexual men said the two kinds of infidelity were equally distressing. Thus gay men and lesbians, like heterosexual women, are relatively less upset by sexual infidelity compared to heterosexual men. The authors suggest these findings argue against a biological basis for sex differences in jealousy.

Sex Versus Status

Sex and status are confounded in a heterosexual relationship. Research on homosexual relationships can help tease apart sex differences from status differences. For example, is the sex difference in influence tactics due to sex or power? One study found that the person who had less power in the relationship used weaker influence tactics than the person who had more power, across heterosexual, gay, and lesbian relationships (Howard et al., 1986). There also appear to be no sex differences in conflict engagement or withdrawal behavior among gay men and lesbians (Kurdek, 2003). Thus the demand/withdrawal pattern found in heterosexual relationships is likely due to the status differences between men and women rather than their sex.

By contrast, some domains of behavior seem to be more strongly linked to sex than to status or power. Sexuality is one of those (Peplau & Garnets, 2000). In heterosexual and homosexual relationships, men place greater emphasis on sex compared to women (Peplau, 1991). Both homosexual and heterosexual men express more interest in casual sex and greater frequency of casual sex than do heterosexual and homosexual women (Bailey et al., 1994). Sexual exclusivity is least common among gay males.

TAKE HOME POINTS

- Myths that gay relationships are transient and less satisfying than heterosexual relationships have been dispelled by research.

- Gay men and lesbians are attracted to a similar set of characteristics in potential mates as heterosexuals. Gay men, like heterosexual men, are interested in a mate's physical attractiveness—more so than lesbians. However, lesbians, unlike heterosexual women, are not attracted to a potential mate's financial resources.

- The script for relationship initiation among homosexuals is similar to the script for heterosexuals. Just as heterosexual men take the proactive role in relationships more than heterosexual women, gay men are more proactive than lesbians.

- Relationship initiation for lesbians is compounded by the fact that sexuality is not as central to their relationships as it is to gay men's relationships.

- The idea that men define intimacy in terms of sexuality more so than women extends to homosexual relationships.

- The same variables that predict relationship satisfaction among heterosexuals predict relationship satisfaction among homosexuals.

- When sex differences found in heterosexual relationships also are found in homosexual relationships, there is support for the idea that the difference is due to something inherent about being male and female in our culture.

- When sex differences found in heterosexual relationships are not found in homosexual relationships, there is the possibility that the differential status of men and women contributes to the difference in a heterosexual relationship.

COHABITING RELATIONSHIPS

Cohabitation is becoming increasingly common, and attitudes toward cohabitation are becoming increasingly favorable. In 2002, half of women between the ages of 15 and 44 had cohabited at some point in their lives (U.S. Department of Health and Human Services, 2005b). In the 2004 Census, just over 5 million men and women cohabited, whereas in 1980 the figure was just over 1.5 million (U.S. Census

TABLE 9.5   PATTERNS OF COHABITATION

	Example country	Description
Marginal	Italy	**lowest rate**
Prelude to marriage	Belgium	**relatively low rate**, short duration, **high proportion ending in marriage**, very low incidence of children
Stage in marriage	Austria	moderate rate, short duration, **high proportion ending in marriage**, low incidence of children
Alternative to single	United States	moderate rate, short duration, **moderate proportion ending in marriage**, low incidence of children
Alternative to marriage	France	**high rate**, long duration, **low proportion ending in marriage**, low incidence of children
Indistinguishable from marriage	Sweden	**high rate**, long duration, **high proportion ending in marriage, high rate of marriage after children**

Source: Heuveline and Timberlake (2004).

Bureau, 2004b). Cohabitation has even increased among the elderly (Brown, Lee, & Bulanda, 2006).

There are racial differences in cohabitation. Black people are less likely than White people to marry or cohabit, but Black people are proportionally more likely than White people to choose cohabitation over marriage. To be more specific, Black women are twice as likely as White women to have their first union be cohabitation as opposed to marriage (Raley, 1996). Some have argued that White people generally view cohabitation as a prelude to marriage, whereas Black people view cohabitation as an alternative to marriage (Fein et al., 2003).

This conclusion would be consistent with the findings of Heuveline and Timberlake (2004), who examined cultural differences in cohabitation. They identified six distinct patterns of cohabitation across a number of European countries, New Zealand, and the United States, as shown in Table 9.5, and determined that the United States was quite variable in its conceptualization of cohabitation. Cohabitation in Sweden was considered "indistinguishable from marriage" because of the high rates of cohabitation (67%), the long duration of cohabitation, the high incidence of having children while cohabiting, and the high likelihood of getting married after having children (82%). In France, cohabitation was considered an "alternative to marriage" because of the very high rates of cohabitation (83%), the long duration of cohabitation, and the relative low likelihood of getting married even if children are born (24%). Cohabitation seemed to reflect just one "stage in the marriage process" for a number of countries, of which Austria is a good example. Here the rates of cohabitation are moderate (58%), the duration relatively short, the proportion ending in marriage very high (77%), and the likelihood of having children while cohabiting low (18%). For Belgium, cohabitation was viewed as a "prelude to marriage" as the frequency of cohabitation is relatively low (28%), the duration relatively short, and the proportion ending in marriage high (75%). Cohabitation played a "marginal role" in relation to marriage in several countries, including Italy where the frequency of cohabitation is extremely low (9%). Finally, the United States was considered to be more variable in terms of its pattern of cohabitation. The authors described it as conceptualizing cohabitation as an "alternative to being single" because the rate was moderate (47%), the duration relatively short, the proportion ending in marriage moderate

(48%), and the incidence of children relatively low (20%).

The increase in cohabitation accounts for most of the decline in marriage rates in the United States. However, cohabitation has merely delayed rather than replaced marriage. In 1970, the median age of marriage for men was 23; it was 21 for women. In 2005, the median age of marriage for men was 27; it was 25.5 for women (U.S. Census Bureau, 2005a). When first cohabitation and first marriage are conceptualized as first unions, the age at first union has not changed much (Bumpass, Sweet, & Cherlin, 1991).

Cohabitation is not only more common today, it is also much more widely accepted, especially among younger people (Cunningham & Antill, 1995). The majority of today's high school seniors have positive attitudes toward cohabitation (Lye & Waldron, 1997). A study of 9th- through 12th-graders showed that half said that they would *want* to live with someone before marriage (Martin et al., 2003). Cohabitation is partly more accepted because premarital sex is more widely accepted. Cohabitation also may be more common because people are leery of the high divorce rate (Popenoe & Whitehead, 1999). People who cohabit are more likely to have experienced parental divorce (Cunningham & Antill, 1995). Cohabitation is often viewed as a way to test a relationship before marriage; the most common reason that men and women report for cohabiting is to see if they are compatible before marriage (Bumpass et al., 1991). The development of the women's movement and the increased number of women in the workforce also may account for some of the rise in cohabitation. Women are less likely to rely on marriage for economic support and may associate marriage with traditional gender roles. A cohabiting relationship may seem like a more egalitarian alternative.

Who Cohabits

People often associate cohabitation with the college experience. However, cohabitation is more common among less educated people and poorer people (Seltzer, 2000). Cohabitation is especially likely if the male has a low income. A common reason for cohabiting is to share living expenses; people who have financial constraints may view cohabitation as an alternative to marriage. Economic reasons are undoubtedly responsible for the increase in cohabitation among the elderly (Chevan, 1996). Marriage increases income taxes and reduces social security payments. Elderly people, who are often on a fixed income, do not want to become involved in an arrangement that will reduce their income. Further evidence for the role of income in cohabitation comes from research that shows higher income people who cohabit are more likely to have plans to marry (Bumpass et al., 1991).

Cohabitation also is more common among previously married persons than never-married persons (Bumpass & Sweet, 1989; Bumpass et al., 1991). In a study of people in their early thirties, half of never-married people had cohabited, whereas two thirds of previously married people had cohabited (Bumpass & Sweet, 1989). In fact, previously married couples are slightly more likely than never-married couples to enter cohabitation without any plans of marriage. Thus the decline in rates of remarriage is partly due to an increase in cohabitation.

People assume cohabiting couples are childless. This is not the case, especially when one of the persons has been previously married. In fact, 11% of births are to unmarried women cohabiting with a partner (Bumpass & Lu, 2000).

Outcomes of Cohabitation

Cohabiting relationships are usually of short duration; most cohabiting couples marry or terminate their relationship rather than remain in a long-term cohabiting relationship. Bumpass and Lu (2000) reported that half of cohabiting relationships ended within a year due to marriage or breakup. The majority of cohabiting relationships end in marriage, although this is less true today than it was in the 1970s (Seltzer, 2000). Thirty percent of cohabiting relationships end in marriage after 1 year, 58% after 3 years, and 70% after 5 years (Bramlett & Mosher, 2002). These figures are higher for Hispanics and considerably lower for Blacks. Most cohabiting couples expect to marry. In one study, 47% of people said they have definite marriage plans (Bumpass et al., 1991). In another study, 75% reported some plans to marry (Brown & Booth, 1996). Interestingly, women were less likely than men to expect to marry their partner. High income and religious affiliation predict marriage following cohabitation (Bramlett & Mosher, 2002).

Remember that people view cohabitation as a way to test the relationship before marriage. Does it work? Is cohabitation the solution to the rising divorce rates? The evidence suggests not. Married couples who cohabited before marriage are more likely to break up and report lower marital satisfaction than married couples who did not cohabit (Stanley, Rhoades, & Markman, 2006). In one study, people who cohabited before marriage were 50% more likely to become divorced (Bumpass & Sweet, 1989). In another study, people who cohabited before marriage were over 200% as likely to divorce (Krishnan, 1998). Even cohabitation after divorce is associated with lower happiness upon remarriage and less stable remarriage relationships (Xu, Hudspeth, & Bartkowski, 2006).

Why does cohabiting appear to lead to less successful marriages? One answer lies in the kind of people who choose to cohabit. There is a selection bias in comparing marriages among people who did and did not cohabit; after all, people are not randomly assigned to cohabit or not. The kind of person who cohabits has less traditional views of gender roles, less traditional views of marriage, is more accepting of divorce, and is less religious (Clarkberg, Stolzenberg, &

Waite, 1995; Cunningham & Antill, 1995; Hill & Peplau, 1998). Each of these factors is associated with divorce.

Women who cohabit before marriage are more likely to be career oriented and less reliant on marriage for economic support than women who do not (Clarkberg et al., 1995). By contrast, men who cohabit are less financially successful than men who do not. People who cohabit before marriage also are less attached to their families than people who do not (Clarkberg et al., 1995). Thus a number of differences between those who do and do not cohabit could explain the higher divorce rate among former cohabitors.

Cohabitation also may be construed differently by men and women. Men may be less likely than women to perceive cohabitation as a prelude to marriage. In one study of married people, men who had cohabited were less committed to the marital relationship than men who had not, whereas there was no difference in women's commitment based on cohabitation history (Stanley, Whitton, & Markman, 2004). In another study, men who had cohabited prior to engagement were less committed during marriage than men who had cohabited after engagement or had not cohabited at all, whereas no commitment differences appeared among the groups of women (Rhoades, Stanley, & Markman, 2006).

In addition to the difference in the kinds of people who enter into cohabiting relationships, cohabiting relationships may differ qualitatively from marital relationships. It is possible that people enter cohabiting relationships instead of marriage because they are more tentative about the relationship; that tentativeness could be a sign of a less well-functioning relationship. A great deal of evidence suggests cohabiting relationships are not as healthy as marital relationships; cohabiting heterosexual couples are less committed to their relationship, less satisfied with their relationship, and report more problems in their relationship compared to married couples (Stanley et al., 2006) and gay and lesbian couples (Kurdek & Schmitt, 1986). Similar to the data for marriage, women are more likely than men to cite difficulties in cohabiting relationships (Bumpass et al., 1991). There is also a higher incidence of domestic violence and child abuse in cohabiting compared to marital relationships (Cunningham & Antill, 1995; Popenoe & Whitehead, 1999). The lower quality of cohabiting relationships may extend into marriage. People who cohabited before marriage report lower marital quality than people who did not cohabit before marriage (Booth & Johnson, 1988). These effects remain throughout the duration of the marriage.

Finally, a third reason cohabitation may have adverse effects on marriage is the possibility that the cohabitation experience alters the people or the relationship in ways that make it less viable after marriage. First, cohabitation may make people more accepting of divorce (Cunningham & Antill, 1995). Second, people who cohabit have a more egalitarian division of labor, which may be difficult to sustain in marriage due to outside pressures to enact traditional sex roles (Seltzer, 2000). Third, people who cohabit experience less commitment to their relationship and a greater degree of freedom in their activities (Popenoe & Whitehead, 1999). Upon marriage, the low commitment level and high freedom level may persist and cause difficulties. Cohabiting relations are more ambiguous than marriage in terms of the nature of the relationship and the future of the relationship. Some people may just "slide" into marriage from cohabitation without making a serious decision, an effect that has been referred to as "sliding versus deciding" (Stanley et al., 2006). Thus some evidence suggests cohabitation alters people and their relationships in ways that create problems in marriage.

The outlook for cohabiting relationships is not entirely gloomy. Researchers have failed to consider the possibility that the divorce rate would be even higher if all people who cohabited had married (Cunningham & Antill, 1995). Cohabiting relationships are heterogeneous, and a subset of couples may be successful. Some people cohabit as a prelude to marriage, whereas others cohabit as an alternative to marriage; the negative effects of cohabiting may characterize the latter more than the former. Couples who cohabit as a prelude to marriage and do so for a very short time may be less vulnerable to the negative effects of cohabitation (Brown, 2004). Studies have compared couples who cohabited before or after engagement on their marital outcomes. A marital interaction study showed that couples who had cohabited prior to engagement displayed more negative interactions, less supportive behavior, and poorer problem-solving skills compared to those who had cohabited after engagement or those who had not cohabited at all (Kline et al., 2004). Another study found that cohabitation with only the person who ended up becoming one's spouse was not related to marital breakup, but multiple cohabitations prior to marriage were related to marital breakup (Teachman, 2003). People who cohabit for longer periods of time end up having the least successful marriages (Cunningham & Antill, 1995).

TAKE HOME POINTS

- Cohabitation is becoming more widely accepted, especially among younger people but even among the elderly.

- Despite the rise in cohabitation, cohabitation is associated with poor marital outcomes. That is, those who cohabit prior to marriage are less satisfied and more likely to break up after marriage than those who did not cohabit. There are three explanations for this finding:

  1. There is a selection bias; that is, the kind of people who enter into cohabiting relationships are the kind of people who are more prone to divorce.

2. Cohabiting relationships are qualitatively different from marital relationships, especially in terms of commitment level.
3. Cohabitation may change the nature of a relationship in a way that makes it less viable upon marriage.

■ Cohabitation is less likely to be associated with poor marital outcomes if the couple had marriage plans prior to cohabitation.

SUMMARY

Men and women are equally interested in romantic relationships and generally expect to get the same things out of a romantic relationship: love, companionship, intimacy, and sex. Men and women also have fairly similar standards for romantic relationships, but it appears women's standards are less likely than men's to be met. This is not surprising because women voice more dissatisfaction with relationships compared to men. Men and women also desire similar characteristics in a partner; both value internal characteristics, such as trustworthiness and kindness, more than external characteristics, such as money and physical appearance. There is an overall sex difference such that women attach more importance to most characteristics compared to men, which implies that women are choosier. There also are consistent sex differences in preferences for some of the less important characteristics; across cultures, men attach greater importance to the physical appearance of their partner and women attach greater importance to the financial status of their partner. Evolutionary theory and social role theory provide explanations for these differences.

Romantic relationships are characterized by intimacy, expressions of love and caring, self-disclosure, and sexuality for both men and women. There is little evidence that men and women define intimacy in their relationship differently. Some evidence suggests that men hold more romantic beliefs about relationships compared to women, and there are some sex differences in styles of love. Men tend to adopt a more game-playing strategy of love, whereas women tend to adopt a more practical and friendship-based approach.

Men have more permissive attitudes toward sex, but these differences are limited to less serious relationships. Men can separate sex from love, but women are more likely to see the two as co-occurring. In fact, men are more likely than women to seek sex for physical pleasure, whereas women are more likely to seek sex for emotional intimacy.

Who are the happiest couples? Research on gender roles shows a clear link between femininity and relationship satisfaction. As long as one member of the couple possesses feminine traits, someone is attending to the relationship. Research on power shows that couples who share power and couples in which the man is dominant are satisfied with the relationship. The least happy couples are ones in which the wife is dominant. Regardless of what one puts into a relationship, men and women are most happy when they perceive their contributions as equitable. It also turns out that characteristics of men (gender roles, personality traits, well-being) are related to women's relationship satisfaction, whereas characteristics of women have little impact on men's relationship satisfaction.

Connection versus separation is a source of conflict for men and women. Women express more concerns about autonomy in a relationship, and men complain that women are too dependent on them. Women also express concerns about a lack of communication with men. The primary way conflict has been examined is in laboratory studies of conflict discussions; these studies show quite divergent styles of interactions among distressed couples: Women are more negative than men and remain engaged in the conflict, whereas men withdraw from the conflict and try to deescalate it with positive behavior. Because the behavior of women is so different in distressed versus nondistressed relationships, women have been referred to as the "emotional barometers" of relationships. Much research has focused on a particular pattern of conflict behavior known as the demand/withdraw pattern. Research suggests that women are more likely to demand and men to withdraw, largely because women desire more change in relationships than men do.

Jealousy is equally likely to be evoked in men and women. Research has examined jealousy over sexual infidelity versus emotional infidelity, arguing that men are more upset by the former and women by the latter. However, methodological issues suggest that the sex difference may be overstated.

The majority of research in this chapter is limited to White middle-class adults and college students. Relationships in other cultures may operate differently depending on the values of the culture and the way gender roles are arranged in the relationship. Studies of gay male and lesbian relationships have shown that many features of relationships span both heterosexual and homosexual relationships (e.g., how relationships develop, the forces that attract one to a relationship, and how relationships dissolve). These studies also have shown that (1) some of the sex differences in behavior in heterosexual relationships are more likely to be a function of status than of sex; (2) some mate preferences and ways of behaving in relationships are a function of both sex and sexual orientation; and (3) men's greater emphasis on sex in relationships pervades both heterosexual and homosexual relationships.

Finally, the chapter concludes with a discussion of cohabiting relationships. Cohabiting relationships are of a lower quality than marital relationships, and cohabitation prior to marriage is predictive of divorce. The negative outcomes of cohabitation may be due to the kinds of people who enter into cohabitation, the nature of the cohabiting relationship itself, or to actual adverse effects of cohabitation on people's relationships.

DISCUSSION QUESTIONS

1. What are the similarities and differences in men's and women's mate preferences?
2. How do men and women view the relation of sex to love?
3. Which sex is more romantic? Why?
4. Why do women demand and men withdraw?
5. Knowing what you do about gender roles in relationships, how would you predict that gay men's relationships would differ from lesbians' relationships?
6. What kinds of problems might be unique to homosexual couples? Heterosexual couples?
7. If the majority of men held the male gender role and the majority of women held the female gender role, regardless of sexual orientation,

describe the nature of lesbian relationships, gay relationships, and heterosexual relationships.

8. What are the differences in the way men and women interact when discussing conflict?

9. What does it mean that women are the "emotional barometer" in a relationship?

SUGGESTED READING

Christensen, A., & Heavy, C. L. (1993). Gender differences in marital conflict: The demand/withdraw interaction pattern. In S. Oskamp & M. Constanzo (Eds.), *Gender issues in contemporary society* (Vol. 6, pp. 113–141). New York: Sage.

Gottman, J. M. (1994). *What predicts divorce? The relationship between marital processes and marital outcomes.* Hillsdale, NJ: Erlbaum.

Kurdek, L. A. (2003). Differences between gay and lesbian cohabiting couples. *Journal of Social and Personal Relationships, 20,* 411–436.

Peplau, L. A., & Spalding, L. R. (2000). The close relationships of lesbians, gay men, and bisexuals. In C. Hendrick & S. S. Hendrick (Eds.), *Close relationships: A sourcebook* (pp. 111–123). Thousand Oaks, CA: Sage.

Seltzer, J. A. (2000). Families formed outside of marriage. *Journal of Marriage and the Family, 62,* 1247–1268.

Wells, B. E., & Twenge, J. M. (2005). Changes in young people's sexual behavior and attitudes, 1943–1999: A cross-temporal meta-analysis. *Review of General Psychology, 9,* 249–261.

Winstead, B. A., Derlega, V .J., & Rose, S. (1997). *Gender and close relationships.* Thousand Oaks, CA: Sage.

KEY TERMS

Agape—Pure love, a blend of eros and storge.

Demand/withdraw pattern—Interaction episode characterized by one person demanding and the other person not responding or withdrawing.

Equity—State of a relationship in which the ratio of what one puts in and gets out of a relationship equals that of the partner.

Emotion transmission—Situation in which one person's emotions influence another person's emotions.

Eros—Romantic love.

Ludus—Game-playing love.

Mania—Manic love, a blend of eros and ludus.

Pragma—Practical love, a blend of storge and ludus.

Script—Schema or cognitive representation for a sequence of events.

Social exchange theory—Theory that relationship satisfaction is partly a function of the rewards and costs in the relationship.

Storge—Friendship love.

SEX DIFFERENCES IN HEALTH: EVIDENCE AND EXPLANATIONS

Women are sicker than men. They report spending more days in bed during the year due to illness compared to men, report more pain, are more depressed, perceive their health as less good, and report more physical symptoms than men. Yet women live longer than men! In fact, men are more likely than women to die from 9 of the 10 leading causes of death in the United States. This is the great paradox of gender and health. Women have higher rates of **morbidity** (i.e., illness), but men have higher rates of **mortality**.

This chapter begins the final section of the book, which focuses on the implications of gender for health, one domain in which there are pervasive and sizable sex differences, such as those just described. I construe health broadly, as both emotional well-being (psychological distress, life satisfaction,

happiness) and physical problems (physical symptoms, coronary heart disease). This chapter provides an overview of sex differences in health as well as the common classes of explanations for these sex differences. First, I describe the sex differences in mortality rates and then differences in morbidity rates. Then, I review numerous explanations for these differences.

SEX DIFFERENCES IN MORTALITY

Life Span

Men die younger than women throughout the life span. Although 105 boys are born for every 100 girls in the United States (Matthews & Hamilton, 2005), more boys than girls die at every age. There is not an equal number of males

TABLE 10.1   NUMBER OF DEATHS PER 100,000 IN 2005

Age	Male	Female	Male:Female Ratio
01–4	32	28	1.14
05–14	19	14	1.36
15–24	113	43	2.63
25–34	137	63	2.17
35–44	240	142	1.69
45–54	539	311	1.73
55–64	1,121	706	1.59
65–74	2,647	1,761	1.50
75–84	6,409	4,539	1.41
85 and over	15,100	13,355	1.13

Source: Adapted from U.S. Census Bureau (2007b).

and females in the United States until age 18. After that, there is a greater number of females than males. The ratio of male to female mortality for each age group is shown in Table 10.1. For every 28 girls who die between the ages of 1 and 4, 32 boys die, resulting in a male to female ratio of 1.14. You can see that the sex difference peaks during adolescence and young adulthood.

Some claim that males are more likely than females to die even before birth. Researchers have suggested that 120 to 160 boys are conceived for every 100 girls (Stillion, 1995), which would imply a high death rate for boys if only 105 boys to 100 girls are actually born. However, Waldron (1998) contends that the number of males and females conceived is unknown because we do not have any idea of the number of males and females who die during the first 8 weeks after conception. We know more male fetuses die compared to female fetuses, but the term *fetus* is not applied until after the 8th week of gestation, and by far the highest mortality rate before birth occurs during those first 8 weeks. Technically, it is plausible that more females than males are conceived, but a very high proportion of those females die during the first 8 weeks of pregnancy, resulting in a higher male:female ratio of infants.

After birth, it is certain males have higher death rates than females at all ages. Thus it comes as no surprise that women live longer than men. In 2004, people in the United States reached a record long life expectancy of 78 years (U.S. Census Bureau, 2007b). However, men did not live as long as women. In 2004, life expectancy at birth for White women was 81 and for White men was 76. Life expectancies at birth for Black people lagged behind, but the sex difference persisted: 77 for Black women and 70 for Black men. The 2000 census showed that the life expectancies for Hispanics in the United States exceeded those for Blacks and Whites, with Latina women outliving men by 6 years (women 83.7; men 77.2; Andalo, 2004). On average, women outlive men by 5 years in the United States.

Sex differences in longevity have existed throughout the 20th century, but their size has varied. The average length of life for men and women during each decade of the 20th century is shown in Table 10.2. In 1900, the average man lived to be 46 and the average woman 48; the sex difference in mortality was only 2 years. Life spans lengthened for both men and women over the course of the century due to better nutrition, better health care, and the development

TABLE 10.2 **LIFE EXPECTANCIES OVER THE 20TH CENTURY**

	Men	*Women*	*White Men*	*White Women*	*Black Men*	*Black Women*
2004	75.2	80.4	75.7	80.8	69.8	76.5
2000	74.1	79.5	74.8	80.0	67.2	74.7
1990	71.8	78.8	72.7	79.4	64.5	73.6
1980	70.0	77.5	70.7	78.1	63.8	72.5
1970	67.1	74.7	68.0	75.6	60.0	68.3
1960	66.6	73.1	67.4	74.1	61.1	66.3
1950	65.6	71.1	66.5	72.2	59.1	62.9
1940	60.8	65.2	62.1	66.6	51.5	54.9
1930	58.1	61.6	59.7	63.5	47.3	49.2
1920	53.6	54.6	54.4	55.6	45.5	45.2
1910	48.4	51.8	48.6	52.0	33.8	37.5
1900	46.3	48.3	46.6	48.7	32.5	33.5

Note: The figures from 1900 to 1960 for Black people reflect "Black and other" people.
Source: U.S. Census Bureau (2007c).

of vaccines. The sex difference in longevity widened during the middle of the century, peaking in 1979 (U.S. Census Bureau, 2007c), when women outlived men by nearly 7.8 years. The increased sex difference was due to the reduction in women's mortality during childbirth and the increase in men's mortality from heart disease and lung cancer. The increase in men's lung cancer can be directly tied to smoking.

More recently, the sex gap in mortality has narrowed. In the 1980s and 1990s, sex differences in life expectancy grew smaller. Today, the gap is the smallest it has been since 1948. The narrowing has been attributed to a greater proportionate decrease in heart disease and cancer mortality among men than women and to a greater increase in the incidence of lung cancer among women than men (Rieker & Bird, 2005). Between 1979 and 1986, lung cancer increased 7% for men and 44% for women (Rodin & Ickovics, 1990). These statistics can be directly tied to changes in smoking patterns. Women's smoking rates increased during the second half of the 20th century, and women were less likely than men to quit smoking (Waldron, 1995).

Sex differences in mortality are largest for those with less education. The rate of male to female mortality is 1.84 for those with less than 12 years of education and 1.56 for those with 13 or more years of education (Williams, 2003). As you can see in Table 10.2, there also are large race differences in mortality, and the size of the sex difference in mortality is greater for Black than White people. This is largely due to the high mortality rate of Black men. Black men are the only group whose life expectancy remained relatively unchanged for the 10-year period from 1985 to 1995. The poor health of Black men is partly a function of education and partly a function of their minority status. There are large differences in pay and employment between college-educated White and Black men, and this difference has increased over the past 20 years (Williams, 2003). I always remember that the famous tennis player, Arthur Ashe—who was Black and had HIV from a blood transfusion—said it was more difficult being Black than having AIDS (Deford, 1993). Although this was an era in which HIV was highly stigmatized, he suffered much greater discrimination due to his race than his HIV status, even as a famous athlete. Although Black people constitute only 13% of the population, they make up 47% of murder victims (Bureau of Justice Statistics, 2006a). Among males ages 18 to 24, Black men are over 8 times more likely than White men to become a victim of murder.

African American women suffer health disparities due to both gender and race discrimination (Geiger, 2006). AIDS is the leading cause of death among African American women ages 25 to 44. African American women have a much higher risk of HIV infection than White women.

Sex differences in life expectancy exist in other nations of the world. Table 10.3 shows sex differences in life expectancies in Western and Eastern Europe and developing countries. The sex difference is larger in Eastern than Western Europe. The sex difference is more variable in developing countries where the life span is much shorter. In developing countries the status differential between men and women is even greater, leading to high rates of female infanticide, pregnancy-related deaths, and poverty-related mortality (Murphy, 2003).

One country that saw a dramatic decline in life expectancy toward the end of the 20th century is Russia (Notzon et al., 1998). While life expectancy was increasing in the United States during the 1990s, life expectancy declined in Russia. In 1990, Russian men lived to be 64 years old and Russian women 74 years old. Only 4 years later in 1994, the life expectancy for men had declined to 58 and for women to 71; the decline for men was twice that for women. By 2006 (see Table 10.3), some gains in life expectancy had been made for men and women, but the large sex difference remains. This 14-year sex difference is the largest among industrialized nations. Three quarters of the decline in life expectancy in the 1990s was due to the increase in death from heart disease, injuries, suicide, and homicide among people ages 25 to 64. The

TABLE 10.3   ESTIMATES OF **2006** LIFE EXPECTANCIES AROUND THE WORLD

	Male	Female	F:M Difference
East			
Bulgaria	68.7	76.1	7.4
Poland	71.0	79.2	8.2
Romania	66.6	74.4	8.0
Russia	60.5	74.1	13.6
West			
Denmark	75.5	80.2	4.7
France	76.1	83.5	7.4
Ireland	75.1	80.5	5.4
Netherlands	76.4	81.7	5.3
Portugal	74.4	81.2	6.8
Developing Countries			
Botswana	33.9	35.6	1.7
Cambodia	57.4	61.3	3.9
Haiti	51.9	54.6	2.7
Laos	53.5	57.6	4.1
Madagascar	54.9	59.8	4.9
Nepal	60.4	59.9	−.5
Rwanda	46.3	48.4	2.1
Somalia	46.7	50.3	3.6
Zimbabwe	40.4	38.2	−2.2

Source: The World Factbook (2007).

primary reason for the decline in life expectancy was the economic and social instability that resulted from the breakup of the Soviet Union. This led to an increase in poverty, a decline in income, an increase in stress, and a rise in alcohol intake. All these factors are more relevant to men and threatening to the male gender role, which could account for the greater impact on men's mortality rates.

Leading Causes of Death

At the turn of the 20th century, men and women were most likely to die from infectious diseases,

TABLE 10.4   AGE-ADJUSTED DEATH RATES (PER 100,000) FOR THE LEADING CAUSES OF DEATH IN 2003

Cause of Death	All	M/F	B/W	H/W
Heart disease	232.3	1.4	1.3	.8
Cancer	190.1	1.5	1.2	.7
Cerebrovascular disease	53.5	1.0	1.5	.8
Chronic lower respiratory disease	43.3	1.4	.7	.4
Accidents	37.3	2.2	1.0	.8
Diabetes mellitus	25.3	1.3	2.1	1.6
Pneumonia and influenza	22.0	1.4	1.1	.8
Alzheimer's disease	21.4	.8	.8	.6
Kidney disease	14.4	1.4	2.3	1.0
Septicemia	11.6	1.2	2.3	.8
Suicide	10.8	4.3	.4	.4
Liver disease	9.3	2.2	.9	1.6
Hypertension and renal disease	7.4	1.0	2.8	1.0
Parkinson's disease	6.2	2.2	.4	.5
Homicide	6.0	3.6	5.7	2.9

M/F = Male to female ratio; B/W = Black to White ratio; H/W = Hispanic to non-Hispanic White ratio.
Source: Hoyert et al. (2006).

such as tuberculosis, influenza, pneumonia, and diphtheria. Today, with the exception of AIDS and some recent infection epidemics (e.g., SARS), people are less likely to die from communicable diseases. Instead, people die from diseases in which lifestyle factors play a role. The leading causes of death in the United States are shown in Table 10.4. The leading cause of death for both men and women, White, Black, and Hispanic, is coronary heart disease. See Sidebar 10.1 for an elaboration on heart disease. The second leading cause of death is cancer, followed by cerebrovascular disease (i.e., stroke), chronic lower respiratory disease (i.e., emphysema), and then accidents. The etiology of these diseases is much more complicated than the etiology of an infectious disease. There are a variety of factors that play a role in the top five leading causes of death, many of which include behavioral factors, such as smoking, diet, drinking, and driving while intoxicated. The most noteworthy feature

of Table 10.4 is that the death rates for 12 of the top 15 causes are higher in males than females. Alzheimer's disease is the only cause of death that has a higher mortality rate for women across Whites, Blacks, and Hispanics. The largest sex differences appear for accidents, Parkinson's disease, suicide, homicide, and liver disease. In the case of diabetes, the direction of the sex difference depends on race: Men have higher rates than women among Whites, but women have higher rates than men among Blacks and Hispanics. This is likely due to the high rate of obesity among Black and Hispanic women. Note that HIV did not make the list of the leading causes of death; it has not been on the top 15 list since 1997. However, HIV is in the top 10 for Black men.

The leading causes of death are influenced by age, race, and sex. The leading cause of death for younger people (ages 15 to 24) is accidents for Hispanic men and women, White men and

SIDEBAR 10.1: *Is Heart Disease Only For Men?*

Cardiovascular disease is the leading cause of death in the United States. In 2003, 911,000 people died from heart disease, and heart disease accounted for 37% of the deaths in the United States (National Institutes of Health, 2006). In fact, there were more deaths from heart disease than from the next five leading causes of death combined. Death rates from heart disease have declined since 1980, which greatly contributed to the overall increase in life expectancy.

Heart disease is often viewed as a disease of men. There is good reason for this. Under age 45, White men have 6 times the risk of heart disease as White women, and Black men have 2 times the risk of heart disease as Black women (Ho, Paultre, & Mosca, 2005). It is not until age 95 that the risks are equal for men and women among Whites and Blacks. However, heart disease is not limited to men. It is the leading cause of death for *both* men and women. In fact, because women live longer than men, more women than men ultimately die of heart disease (Rieker & Bird, 2005). The death rate from heart disease has declined in recent years, but the decline has been greater for men than women, greatest for White males, and least for Black females (National Institutes of Health, 2006). In terms of absolute numbers, more women than men die from heart disease in a given year, which has been the case since 1984. This fact is due to a greater number of women than men in the population, especially among the elderly—and heart disease is a disease of the elderly.

Although women have lower rates of heart disease than men, when heart disease strikes women they often have a worse prognosis compared to men. In a study of heart attack survivors, women were more likely than men to have a second heart attack and to continue to have cardiac symptoms a year later (Young & Kahana, 1993). Women have more complications after **myocardial infarction** (MI), or heart attack, than men (Fetters et al., 1996; Young & Kahana, 1993), and women are more likely than men to die after an MI (Young & Kahana, 1993).

women, and Black women. For Black men ages 15 to 24, the leading cause of death is homicide. Although HIV is not in the top 10 causes of overall mortality, it is among the top 5 for some subgroups of people ages 25 to 44: White men, Black men, Hispanic women, and Black women. Sex differences in accidents, suicide, and homicide account for most of the sex difference in mortality among younger people. Among older people, heart disease and cancer account for most of the sex difference in mortality.

Another noteworthy feature of Table 10.4 is that the mortality rate for Black people is higher than that for White people for 9 of the 15 leading causes of death. The largest differences appear for homicide, hypertension, kidney disease, septicemia, and diabetes. Black people have less than half the rate of suicide and

Parkinson's disease as White people. By contrast, the mortality rate for Hispanics is less than that of non-Hispanic Whites, with the exception of diabetes, homicide, and liver disease.

Crime Statistics

Men are more likely than women to commit violent crimes, and men are more likely than women to be the victims of violent crimes, with the exception of rape. That is, men are more likely than women to be assaulted, robbed, threatened with violence, and killed. For homicide, both perpetrator and victim are male in 65% of the cases. In the year 2004, men were nearly 4 times as likely as women to be murdered and 10 times as likely as women to commit murder (Federal Bureau of Investigation, 2006). It is rare that women commit murder. Imagine how society would have reacted if the two teenagers at Columbine High School were girls instead of boys or the college student at Virginia Tech was female instead of male. When women are victims, they are almost 10 times as likely to be killed by a male as a female. However, women are almost 4 times as likely to kill men as to kill women. The female perpetrator/female victim category is a rare one.

We often imagine murder as involving a stranger. Many of the mass killings we hear about in the media draw a great deal of publicity and involve a person killing strangers. However, statistics show that only 14% of victims were murdered by strangers, 51% knew the perpetrator, and the relationship was unknown in 35% of the cases (Federal Bureau of Investigation, 2006). The perpetrator's relationship to the victim differs for men and women. Women are more likely than men to be killed by someone they know across all age groups. In 2004, 33% of women murdered were killed by husbands or boyfriends, whereas only 3% of the men murdered were killed by wives or girlfriends (Federal Bureau of Investigation, 2006). Across the United States in the year 2004, more women than men were killed by a spouse, former spouse, or boyfriend/girlfriend (1,159 vs. 385; Federal Bureau of Investigation, 2006).

Although men are more likely than women to be victims of violence, the association of violence with poor health seems to be stronger for women than men (Sundaram et al., 2004). In a national survey in Denmark, a history of violence was more strongly associated with self-ratings of poor health, anxiety, depression, and stomach problems in women than men. The authors suggested that the reason for these findings probably has to do with the fact that violence is more likely to take place in the context of relationships for women compared to men.

TAKE HOME POINTS

- Men die younger than women at all ages of the life span.

- The sex difference in longevity increased over the 20th century to a record 7.8 years in 1979 but more recently has decreased. Today, women outlive men by 5 years.

- The leading causes of death are heart disease, cancer, cerebrovascular disease, chronic lower respiratory disease, and accidents — all causes for which lifestyle factors play a role.

- Men are more likely than women to die of most of the leading causes of death.

- Men are more likely than women to commit violent crimes and to be victims of violent crimes, including homicide.

- Women are more likely than men to be killed by someone they know.

SEX DIFFERENCES IN MORBIDITY

Morbidity reflects illness. Whereas mortality rates have decreased and the life span has lengthened, morbidity rates have increased. People are living longer, but partly because they are living with diseases rather than dying from them. During the early part of the 20th century, the leading causes of death were from infectious diseases. The causes of these diseases were relatively simple to understand; typically, there was a single causal agent, the germ. With the development of penicillin and vaccinations, people began to live longer; thus they had more time to develop and subsequently die from chronic diseases. Whereas an acute illness lasts a short time and is either fatal (a possibility in the case of tuberculosis or pneumonia) or non-fatal (the common cold), a **chronic illness** is long lasting and typically does not disappear.

A chronic illness can be fatal or nonfatal; rheumatoid arthritis is an example of a nonfatal chronic illness, and cancer and heart disease are examples of chronic illnesses that can be fatal—in fact, they are the two leading causes of death. The increase in chronic disease accounts for the increase in morbidity, that is, the increase in illness, disability, and activity restriction among the U.S. population.

Women have higher morbidity rates than men. In fact, the morbidity-free life expectancy (i.e., life without chronic disease) has declined for both men and women but more so for women than men (Perenboom et al., 2005). In 1989, women had 55.3 morbidity-free years, whereas men had 54.7. By 2000, women had declined to 51 morbidity-free years, and men had declined to 53.9. Although men have higher incident rates (i.e., men contract the diseases more than women do) and death rates from the two leading causes of death (heart disease and cancer), women suffer from more acute illnesses and more nonfatal chronic illnesses compared to men (Case & Paxson, 2005). Women suffer higher rates of arthritis, immune disorders, and digestive conditions compared to men. Women suffer from more painful disorders compared to men, such as migraines, tension headaches, musculoskeletal pain, back pain, abdominal pain, carpal tunnel syndrome, irritable bowel syndrome, rheumatoid arthritis, multiple sclerosis, and Raynaud's disease (LeResche, 2000). Thus at any given point in time, women are more likely than men to be ill and to be living with a chronic disease.

Women also report more psychological and physical symptoms than men (Gijsbers van Wijk, Huisman, & Kolk, 1999). This difference first appears during adolescence. In a study of 11- to 15-year-olds across 29 European and North American countries, girls reported more health complaints (e.g., headache, stomachache, depression, dizziness) than boys (Torsheim et al.,

TABLE 10.5   ODDS RATIO OF WOMEN HAVING MORE HEALTH SYMPTOMS THAN MEN

	Low GDI	Medium GDI	High GDI
11-year-olds	1.56	1.17	1.18
13-year-olds	1.88	1.70	1.56
15-year-olds	2.27	1.91	1.88

Note: GDI = Gender Development Index, high GDI signifies women have higher education and income.
Source: Torsheim (2006).

2006). The difference appeared for all countries and for each of the 9 health complaints. As shown in Table 10.5, the sex difference (i.e., odds ratio, such that higher numbers mean more females than males) increased with age and decreased in countries where women had more education and income (i.e., higher gender development index).

Women perceive their health to be worse than men's. Subjective health perceptions are typically measured by a single item that asks respondents to rate their health as poor, fair, good, very good, or excellent. A 1998 nationwide survey of adults in the United States revealed that men were more likely than women to report their health was excellent (Division of Adult and Community Health, 1998). However, the sex difference in subjective health perceptions decreases with age (Gorman & Read, 2006).

Women also report more **illness behavior** than men, that is, behaviors that signify illness. For example, women report more days in bed due to illness, more days in which they restricted their activities due to illness, and greater use of prescription drugs. Women report greater disability and greater functional limitations than men, and this difference persists throughout adulthood and increases with age (Gorman & Read, 2006).

One aspect of illness behavior is seeking medical care. Women report a greater use of health services compared to men (Green & Pope, 1999), which is often taken as an indication of women being sicker than men. Sex differences in the use of health care services peak during women's childbearing years. When reproductive-related reasons are taken into consideration, sex differences in hospitalization become more similar, but women still receive greater outpatient care than men. One reason women use more health care is that women have a greater number of chronic conditions. Some of women's higher morbidity rates are related to gynecological problems, but even when these problems are taken into consideration, women have higher rates of morbidity than men.

Interestingly, sex differences in morbidity do not appear until adolescence. For example, chronic illnesses, such as asthma and migraine headaches, are more prevalent among boys than girls during childhood; by early adolescence, however, this sex difference reverses itself (Sweeting, 1995). Not only does depression increase among girls during adolescence (discussed in Chapter 13), but physical symptoms such as stomach problems and headache also increase among adolescent girls (Sweeting & West, 2003). Health care utilization rates reflect these changes. During childhood, boys visit health care professionals more frequently than girls do, but during adolescence, girls visit health care professionals more than boys. It is difficult to link health care utilization in childhood to children's behavior, however, because adults are more likely than children to be making the decision to seek health care. Thus it may be that parents, in particular mothers, are more likely to take boys than girls to see a doctor when they are young. Parents might take boys' complaints more seriously because they expect boys to be less likely than girls to complain of symptoms; admitting illness violates gender-role norms for boys.

TAKE HOME POINTS

- Women have higher rates of morbidity than men.

- Whereas men are more likely to suffer from fatal chronic illnesses, women are more likely than men to suffer from nonfatal chronic illnesses and painful disorders—meaning that at any point in time women are more likely than men to be ill.

- Women also report more symptoms, perceive their health to be worse, restrict their activities due to illness, and seek medical care more than men.

- These sex differences in morbidity first appear during adolescence.

EXPLANATIONS FOR SEX DIFFERENCES IN HEALTH

Next, I examine six classes of explanations for sex differences in morbidity and mortality. First, I examine biological factors that might contribute to sex differences in health. Second, I consider the role of artifacts in sex differences in health. **Artifacts** are factors that cause sex differences to appear that do not really exist. For example, men have a higher socioeconomic status than women, and socioeconomic status is related to health. Is women's poor health a function of their lower income? Physician bias is another example of an artifact; perhaps physicians treat men and women differently so it appears women are sicker, but men and women are actually equally healthy or unhealthy. Third, I consider the role of health behaviors, such as preventive health care, smoking, drinking, drug use, diet, and exercise; there are sex differences for most of these behaviors. Fourth, I consider aspects of the male and female gender roles that might influence health. Aspects of the male gender role can be linked to specific health behaviors and to general risk-taking behavior; aspects of the female gender role can be related to greater concerns with health, but also to risks associated with involvement in relationships. Fifth, I discuss whether men and women perceive symptoms similarly or whether women have a lower threshold for symptoms, which makes it appear women are sicker than men. Finally, I consider whether men and women respond to symptoms in similar ways in terms of taking care of themselves and seeking medical attention.

BIOLOGY

Genes

Women may have a greater genetic resistance to some diseases compared to men. Women may be genetically predisposed to better health because they have a second X chromosome. The X chromosome carries more information on it than the Y chromosome. In females, an abnormality on an X chromosome is not necessarily a problem because a second X chromosome is there to suppress it; the abnormality is usually recessive. Thus a female will simply be a carrier of the abnormality but will not manifest it. The male, however, has a Y chromosome, which cannot override an abnormality on an X chromosome. This may explain why more males than females suffer some congenital disorders, such as hemophilia, meningitis, muscular dystrophy, and mental retardation.

Hormones

Estrogen plays a significant role in women's health. One reason men have a higher incidence of heart disease than women is that women are protected from heart disease by estrogen, at least at younger ages. The sex difference in rates of heart disease is much larger at younger ages before women reach menopause.

After menopause, women's rates of heart disease increase dramatically.

Why does heart disease increase in women after menopause? One theory is that women are protected from heart disease before menopause because of their higher levels of estrogen. With menopause, estrogen levels drop. Although the decline in estrogen that accompanies menopause does not influence blood pressure, diabetes, or body mass index (Fetters et al., 1996), it may lead to changes in cholesterol (i.e., decreasing the good cholesterol and increasing the bad cholesterol) and it may alter the blood clotting process (Fetters et al., 1996).

Researchers were so confident of the link between estrogen and heart disease that many women were put on hormone replacement therapy (HRT) after menopause to reduce their risk of heart disease. Many of the studies linking HRT to lower rates of heart disease, however, were correlational, meaning it was difficult to discern cause and effect. Use of HRT could have been confounded with some other variable, like socioeconomic status, to influence rates of heart disease. That is, women of a higher socioeconomic status could have been more likely to use hormone replacement therapy, and women with a higher socioeconomic status have better health. Finally, a randomized trial of over 16,000 postmenopausal women was conducted to determine the effect of HRT on the prevention of heart disease (Writing Group for the Women's Health Initiative Investigators, 2002). The trial was stopped early in 2002 because the effects of HRT were so dramatic. Unfortunately, the effects were not as predicted. Women on HRT had a significant increased risk of breast cancer and an increased risk of heart attack. Subsequent trials have linked HRT with an increased risk of heart disease and stroke (Lowe, 2004). This is a significant example of how important it is to conduct experimental research to test theories developed from correlational data. We also have learned that higher SES women were, in fact, more likely to use HRT (Lawlor, Smith, & Ebrahim, 2004).

Thus a clear link between high levels of estrogen and low levels of heart disease has not been established. Another problem for the theory is that oral contraceptives, which often contain estrogen, increase risk factors for heart disease. Oral contraceptives increase blood pressure, cholesterol levels, and blood glucose levels. Using oral contraceptives in combination with smoking is a particularly lethal combination, increasing the risk of a heart attack 20-fold (Fetters et al., 1996).

Estrogen also plays a hazardous role in the development of some cancers (breast cancer, endometrial cancer) and may be linked to osteoarthritis. Estrogens may play a role in autoimmune diseases, but whether the links are protective or harmful is not clear (Schuurs & Verheul, 1990). Thus hormones certainly play a role in men's and women's health, but which hormones are responsible for the effects and the direction of the effects are not clear.

Immune System

Recently, it has been suggested that the nature of men's and women's immune systems differ (Bouman et al., 2004), but the effects seem to be paradoxical. Women's immune systems may respond to viruses better than men's (Whitacre et al., 1999), and women seem to have a greater immune response to infection than men (Rieker & Bird, 2005). However, this immune response could explain why women's immune systems end up attacking their own bodies resulting in a higher rate of autoimmune diseases. Women are more vulnerable than men to diseases specific to the immune system, such as lupus and rheumatoid arthritis. Among humans, men have lower rates of immunoglobulin M (a protein involved in immune function), which may be a source of men's greater vulnerability to disease (Schuurs & Verheul, 1990).

Cardiovascular Reactivity

Cardiovascular reactivity refers to the increase in blood pressure and heart rate that occurs when engaging in a challenging or stressful task. You may experience cardiovascular reactivity when taking an exam, when thinking an exam, or when receiving a graded exam. You are also likely to experience cardiovascular reactivity during an argument, a traffic jam, or when your computer screen freezes. Yet we all do not experience the same level of reactivity to the same stressors. The theory behind studying cardiovascular reactivity is that people who exhibit heightened physiological responses to stressful events might be damaging their arteries on a daily basis, making them more vulnerable to heart disease. There is evidence that cardiovascular reactivity is related to indicators of heart disease (Treiber et al., 2003).

To the extent that cardiovascular reactivity is linked to heart disease, sex differences in reactivity become an important topic. Numerous studies have shown that men exhibit greater cardiovascular reactivity than women, which could explain a portion of men's higher rates of heart disease. Cardiovascular reactivity is typically studied in the laboratory by exposing participants to a stressful or challenging task and observing changes in blood pressure or heart rate. Men are more reactive than women to the majority of laboratory stressors studied (Matthews, Gump, & Owens, 2001).

However, researchers soon realized that men may show greater reactivity than women to laboratory tasks because the tasks are more relevant to men than women. Laboratory tasks that reveal men to be more reactive than women are often achievement oriented. The real-world stressors that show men to be more reactive than women are typically exams and work, which are also achievement oriented. Some evidence suggests that women exhibit greater reactivity than men when the domain is more relevant to women, such as a discussion of relationship conflict (e.g., Kiecolt-Glaser et al., 1996). As you will see in Chapter 11, women exhibit greater cardiovascular, neuroendocrine, and immune reactivity than men when discussing a relationship conflict.

Several studies have examined the idea that men react to stressors relevant to the male gender role and women react to stressors relevant to the female gender role. In one study, men were more reactive than women to two masculine tasks, serial subtraction and a handgrip squeeze, whereas women were more reactive than men to a feminine task, giving a speech on likes and dislikes about one's physical appearance (Stroud, Niaura, & Salovey, 2000). In another study, college males' and females' reactions to either an achievement (math, verbal memorization) or interpersonal (rejection) challenge were examined (Stroud, Salovey, & Epel, 2002). As shown in Figure 10.1, men exhibited greater cortisol increases than women in response to

achievement stressors, and women exhibited greater cortisol increases than men in response to the interpersonal stressor.

Another way to examine whether the nature of the task influences sex differences in cardiovascular reactivity is to use the same stressor and make it more relevant to men or women. In one such study, college students were either assigned to enact the role of a submissive or a dominant job applicant (Smith et al., 1996). Men showed greater cardiovascular reactivity than women when they played the dominant role, whereas women showed greater cardiovascular reactivity than men when they played the submissive role. Thus men and women showed heightened reactivity to stressors that are consistent with their gender role. Reactions to gender-related tasks also may be influenced by whether the participant holds traditional views about gender. In one study, men who scored higher on a measure of male gender role stress (i.e., viewed threats to the male role as stressful) showed greater cardiovascular reactivity as well

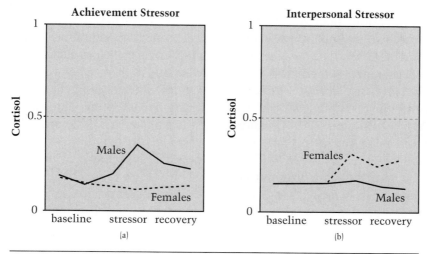

FIGURE 10.1   (a) Men show elevated cortisol reactivity to an achievement stressor compared to women; (b) Women show elevated cortisol reactivity to an interpersonal stressor compared to men.
Source: Adapted from Stroud et al. (2002).

as poorer performance on a cognitive task when it was described as relevant to the male role compared to when it was not relevant to the male role (Cosenzo et al., 2004). Men who scored low on gender role stress did not behave differently in the two conditions.

In total, these studies seem to provide a fair amount of evidence that men are more reactive to masculine tasks or tasks relevant to the male role and women are more reactive to feminine tasks or tasks relevant to the female role. Thus the case would seem to be closed on sex differences in cardiovascular reactivity. However, one study found just the opposite results—masculine people were more reactive to a feminine stressor, and feminine people were more reactive to a masculine stressor (Davis & Matthews, 1996). Participants who scored high on masculinity or femininity were randomly assigned to either persuade or empathize with their partner. Masculine people were more reactive when they had to empathize with rather than persuade their partner, whereas feminine people were more reactive when they had to persuade rather than empathize with their partner.

What is the bottom line? Are men and women more reactive to gender-congruent or gender-incongruent tasks? One resolution to this issue is to determine whether a task is perceived as a challenge or a threat, which may influence whether the tasks are low or high in difficulty. Wright and colleagues (1997) predicted that people would evidence greater reactivity to a gender-congruent task only when difficulty was high. In that case, the thought of not performing well on a task consistent with one's gender role might be perceived as a threat. When the task is easy, people whose gender role is congruent with the task expect to perform well and are not threatened by the task. People whose gender role is incongruent with the task are likely to perceive the task as more of a challenge—in a sense, a higher difficulty level. These people feel less capable and expend more

effort. In a test of this hypothesis, college students participated in a memory task in which good performance would allow them to avoid a noise stressor. The experimenter told half of the participants that men have greater ability on the task and typically outperform women and the other half that women have greater ability and typically outperform men. The difficulty of the task was also manipulated. The investigators' predictions were confirmed. When the task was low in difficulty, women showed greater reactivity than men to the masculine task, and men showed greater reactivity than women to the feminine task. When the task was high in difficulty, women showed greater reactivity than men to the feminine task, and men showed greater reactivity than women to the masculine task. Thus sex differences in reactivity not only depend on the relevance of the task to gender roles but also on the difficulty of the task. The difficulty of a gender-role congruent task may determine whether the person feels comfortable and competent or threatened by the possibility of failure.

This discussion has presumed that tasks can be categorized as either masculine or feminine, as either communal or agentic, and that tasks are not equally relevant to both men and women. As men's and women's roles change, are sex differences in the stressors that evoke reactions in men and women changing? Frankenhaueser (1991) argued that sex differences in reactivity have substantially decreased over the past couple of decades in Sweden as gender roles have become less rigid. The decrease in sex differences in reactivity is largely due to women becoming more reactive to achievement stressors. Frankenhaeuser (1991) showed that women in nontraditional roles (e.g., bus driver, engineer, lawyer) demonstrate reactivity levels similar to those of men. In one study, Frankenhaeuser and colleagues (1989) found that men and women who were in similar jobs (middle managers) showed similar physiological reactivity levels during the day at work. However, when men and women returned home where roles were less similar, differences in physiology appeared. Men's blood pressure and catecholamines dropped after 5 P.M., whereas women's blood pressure remained high and catecholamines either did not drop as much or actually increased. As will be described in more detail in Chapter 11, the demands of home life are different for men and women.

■ The fact that women have a second X chromosome may protect women from some genetically based diseases.

■ Estrogens clearly play a role in women's greater resistance and vulnerability to disease. The nature of this relation is complicated.

■ There is a paradox in immune function for men and women. It appears that women's immune systems may be more responsive to infection, but also more vulnerable to autoimmune disease.

■ Historically, research showed that men exhibited greater cardiovascular reactivity to stressful tasks compared to women, which was thought to provide an explanation for men's greater vulnerability to heart disease.

■ More recent research has shown that sex differences in cardiovascular reactivity are dependent on the nature of the stressor. Men's and women's reactivity may be quite similar when they feel similarly challenged or threatened.

ARTIFACTS

One class of explanations for sex differences in health is that the differences are not real but are due to artifacts. Recall that artifacts are methodological variables that might lead to the appearance of sex differences in health even when differences do not exist. A confounding variable, such as socioeconomic status, could be an artifact of the relation between gender and health. Other artifactual explanations have to do with the way that health is measured. Although mortality is an objective index of health, many of the indexes of morbidity are subjective and may be influenced by the way they are assessed. Thus sex differences in morbidity may be especially vulnerable to artifacts.

Socioeconomic Status

Socioeconomic status (SES) clearly is related to health. With every increase in income, even among people who are middle to upper class, health improves. If SES is measured by earnings, men have a higher status than women. If SES is measured by education, today men and women have a relatively equal status. It does not appear that differences in men's and women's SES can explain sex differences in either mortality or morbidity.

Another question is whether SES shows the same relation to health for men and women. The answer to this question is not clear. In a group of young adults, the relation of SES to health was similar for men and women (Matthews, Manor, & Power, 1999), whereas in another study SES was more strongly related to men's than women's health (Arber & Ginn, 1993).

One reason that the relation of SES to women's health has been inconsistent across studies may have to do with how SES is measured in women. Some studies use the woman's occupation and income to represent SES, whereas other studies use the husband's occupation and income to represent the woman's SES. In a study that followed people for nearly 20 years, SES was associated with reduced mortality among women regardless of how it was measured (McDonough et al., 1999). Both own income and spouse income predicted reduced mortality among women.

Among men, however, it is not clear whose income is more important to their health. The previous study showed that men's income was associated with reduced mortality for men, but spouse income was associated with *increased* mortality. This finding is consistent with some research reviewed in Chapter 12 that shows men's mental health may be adversely affected by wives with a high income. A woman's high contribution to family income may threaten the man's role as family provider, causing an increase in men's distress. In addition, men who are married to women with high incomes might also suffer because the women are not tending to men's health care needs (McDonough et al., 1999). As discussed in Chapter 11, one reason men benefit from marriage is that wives take care of the family's health. A wife who works full time in a high-powered job is going to be less likely than other wives to make physician appointments for her husband, remind him of physician appointments, buy healthy food for him, or cook healthy meals.

Women's status, as measured in other ways besides income, has been associated with both men's and women's health. The status of women in each of the 50 states, as measured by the number of women in politics and the number of women who worked outside the home, has been associated with lower mortality rates for both men and women (Kawachi et al., 1999). In a study in Hungary, the social status, education, and income of women predicted male mortality more so than the same SES indicators of men (Kopp et al., 2005). Thus in a country where there is a greater status differential between men and women, women's gains in status appear to be good for both male and female mortality.

Proxy

One very uninteresting reason women may report greater morbidity than men is that respondents in surveys are more likely to be women than men; that is, women report on behalf of

themselves and their spouse. Respondents, whether male or female, report greater symptoms for themselves than for others. Each of us is certainly more aware of our own health idiosyncracies than we are of another person's. Thus survey research may underestimate men's illness if women are allowed to report on behalf of men. Today, people are aware of this bias, so more recent studies do not permit proxy responses.

Physician Bias

Physicians may respond to men and women differently, contributing to sex differences in health. Two areas in which this issue has been well investigated are heart disease and mental health.

Heart Disease.   Women have a worse prognosis from heart disease compared to men possibly because women are treated less aggressively than men for heart disease, as shown in Table 10.6. Why would this be?

One reason women are disadvantaged compared to men is that diagnostic tests and treatments have largely been developed on men. Major clinical trials that have made important contributions to the treatment of heart disease have historically included only men. For example, the Multiple Risk Factor Intervention Trial Research Group (1983) was conducted to reduce risk factors of heart disease. The study included

TABLE 10.6   STAGES OF TREATMENT FOR CORONARY HEART DISEASE

	Women are less likely than men to:
Prevention	have cholesterol checked receive cholesterol lowering drugs
Response to symptoms	be referred to a cardiologist receive diagnostic tests for heart disease
Treatment	be treated with drugs that dissolve clots be treated with angioplasty be treated with bypass surgery

12,866 men and 0 women. In the Physicians Health Study, physicians were randomly assigned to receive aspirin or placebo to see if aspirin protected against heart disease (Steering Committee, 1988). The study was terminated early because the benefits of aspirin were so large that it was unethical to withhold this information from the public. No female physicians were included in the study. In response to this concern, the National Institutes of Health made a major commitment to women's health in the 1990s, first by requiring clinical trials to report the number of men and women in studies and second by developing the Women's Health Initiative. The Women's Health Initiative is a longitudinal study of about 164,000 women to evaluate the effects of diet, vitamins, and hormone replacement therapy on heart disease, cancer, and osteoporosis. The study began in 1992 and is nearing completion, although the HRT portion ended early as described previously.

The fact that diagnostic tests and treatments were developed on men poses two problems for women. First, because men's and women's anatomy differs, it is quite likely that a test developed on men's bodies is not as accurate in detecting disease in women's bodies. Second, a treatment developed for men may not be as effective among women.

Substantial evidence indicates that men and women are treated differently by the health care system with respect to heart disease. In terms of prevention, women are less likely than men to have a fasting cholesterol test taken and are less likely to be placed on lipid-lowering drugs than men, despite the fact that women have higher total cholesterol levels and these drugs have been shown to be equally effective in men and women (Hippisley-Cox et al., 2001). Once symptoms of heart disease develop, women are less likely than men to be referred to cardiologists (McKinlay, 1996). One recent study showed that women with heart problems were more likely then men with heart problems to be

mistakenly discharged from hospital emergency rooms (Pope et al., 2000). All patients who presented to the emergency room with complaints of cardiac symptoms and were discharged were reevaluated 24 to 72 hours later to determine if they had in fact sustained heart damage. Missed diagnoses were more common in women than men, which may result in a higher mortality for women than men.

Women also are less likely than men to receive diagnostic tests for heart disease (McKinlay, 1996). One of the major diagnostic tests is cardiac catheterization. A catheter is inserted through a person's arm or groin and threaded through the arteries until it reaches the coronary arteries. (Coronary arteries are the vessels that carry blood to the heart muscle.) A dye is injected so blockages are illuminated. Other tests may be indicative of blockages, but only a coronary catheterization conclusively reveals the presence of blockages. Women are less likely than men to be referred for such a procedure (Gan et al., 2000). In one study, women were referred for cardiac catheterization at just over half the rate of men (15% versus 27%), despite the fact that women reported greater difficulties in functioning due to chest pain (Steingart et al., 1991). This referral bias cannot be attributed to male physicians. Both male and female physicians are more likely to refer men than women for catheterizations, and male physicians are more likely than female physicians to refer both men and women (Rathore et al., 2001). Thus the male treated by a male is most likely to be referred, and the female treated by a female is least likely to be referred.

Once diagnosed with heart disease, women are less likely than men to receive each of the three major treatments for heart disease (Kattainen et al., 2005). One treatment is drug therapy. Few studies of drugs for heart disease have been conducted with women, so it is difficult to know if heart medications have the same effects on women as they do on men. A specific type of drug therapy used in the treatment of heart disease is **thrombolytic therapy**. Thrombolytic drugs are administered during the course of a heart attack with the hope of opening the arteries, increasing blood flow, and reducing the amount of heart damage. Among those who sustain a heart attack, women are less likely than men to receive thrombolytic therapy (Gan et al., 2000).

A second treatment for heart disease is **percutaneous transluminal coronary angioplasty (PTCA)**. With PTCA, a balloon is placed on the tip of a catheter, which is then threaded through the coronary arteries. At the site of the blockage, the balloon is inflated in an effort to increase the diameter of the artery and thus increase blood flow. Women are less likely than men to be referred for coronary angioplasty. What is not clear is if the differential referral rates are appropriate. On the one hand, angioplasty is a fairly simple procedure with a high success rate. On the other hand, women have been shown to have a higher mortality rate than men during or shortly after PTCA (Fetters et al., 1996). Yet long-term outcomes following angioplasty seem to be similar for men and women (Fetters et al., 1996).

The third major treatment for heart disease is **coronary artery bypass surgery**. Arteries are taken from the person's leg or chest wall and used to bypass the blockages of the arteries that supply blood to the heart. This is a major surgical procedure. Women are less likely than men to be referred for bypass surgery even when they have comparable medical profiles (Travis, 2005).

Again the question is asked: Is it appropriate for there to be sex differences in referral rates for bypass surgery? Earlier studies suggested that women were less likely than men to benefit from bypass surgery in terms of reduced chest pain (Fetters et al., 1996), and women were more likely than men to die during bypass surgery (Wenger, 1998). However, more recent studies suggest that the sex difference in mortality following bypass surgery may be disappearing (Travis, 2005).

One study showed that not only were women treated less aggressively for heart disease than men but also that older women with heart disease were more likely than older men with heart disease to have "Do not resuscitate" (DNR) orders included in their charts (Gan et al., 2000). Among the people who had DNR orders, women were less ill than men. The reason for this discrepancy is unclear. We do not know if women were more likely than men to request the DNR order or if health care professionals were more likely to offer the DNR order to women than men.

Some of these sex differences in the management of heart disease are interrelated. Studies have demonstrated that the reason women were less likely than men to receive PTCA or bypass surgery is that women were less likely to have had the definitive diagnostic test: cardiac catheterization (Gan et al., 2000). Among those who received this test, an equal proportion of men and women were recommended for PTCA and bypass surgery. Bernadine Healy, former director of the National Institutes of Health, referred to the idea that men and women receive the same treatment for heart disease once they have a catheterization or a heart attack as the **Yentl syndrome**. Healy (1991) stated, "once a woman showed that she was just like a man, by having severe coronary artery disease or a myocardial infarction, then she was treated as a man would be" (p. 274). Although women are still less likely than men to be referred for diagnostic procedures and treatment procedures, the sex difference appears to be decreasing (Wenger, 1998).

Another reason for women's poorer prognosis is that women have more ambiguous symptoms of heart disease compared to men, which may go undetected. Men are more likely to have classic chest pain, and women are more likely to have ambiguous symptoms. In one study, men and women with coronary artery disease were asked to provide a written description of their symptoms (Philpott et al., 2001). Women described more pain in their throat, jaw, and neck than men, as well as more shortness of breath.

However, even when symptoms are the same, physicians appear less likely to diagnose heart disease in women than men. In one study, male internists were presented with a videotape of a patient with symptoms of heart disease (McKinlay, 1996). Internists were less likely to diagnose heart disease when the video depicted a female than a male. In another study, 192 physicians were presented with a case of a hypothetical smoker with a cough and breathlessness. Physicians diagnosed chronic obstructive pulmonary disease in 65% of the cases if the patient was male and 49% of the cases if the patient was female (Chapman, Tashkin, & Pye, 2001). However, the sex difference decreased as more information was provided about the case, such as the results of diagnostic tests.

Women's complaints of cardiac symptoms may be mistaken for signs of psychological distress. Because women are more depressed than men, women's symptoms may more likely be interpreted as depression or anxiety. In fact, chest pain can signify stress and anxiety. When patients report feelings of psychological distress along with cardiac symptoms, the psychosocial complaints may distract the physician from the cardiac symptoms—at least when the patient is female. In one study, undergraduates, community residents, and physicians were given vignettes in which a person had clear symptoms of heart problems (chest pain, shortness of breath, sweating) or ambiguous symptoms of heart problems (jaw pain, being out of breath, and indigestion; Martin, Gordon, & Lounsbury, 1998). The target person was assigned either a male name or a female name and depicted as undergoing high stress or low stress. Respondents rated the female under high stress as less likely than the female under low stress or either of the males to be having cardiac symptoms. Whether the symptoms were clear or ambiguous did not influence responses. What influenced the response was the combination of being female and being under high stress.

Similar findings appeared in a study of medical students and residents. When provided with a vignette of a person with clear cardiac symptoms (e.g., chest pain, shortness of breath) who was or was not experiencing stress (Chiaramonte & Friend, 2006), men and women were treated differently only under conditions of high stress. As shown in Figure 10.2a, coronary

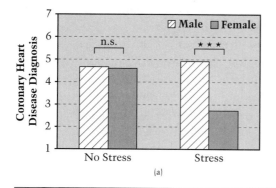
(a)

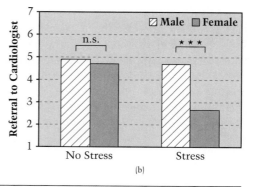
(b)

FIGURE 10.2   Medical students and residents were equally likely to (a) diagnose heart disease in men and women and (b) refer men and women to a cardiologist when the patient had no stress but less likely to diagnose heart disease in women and less likely to refer women to a cardiologist compared to men under conditions of stress.
Source: Adapted from Chiaramonte and Friend (2006).

heart disease was equally likely to be diagnosed among men and women in the no stress condition but less likely to be diagnosed among women in the high stress condition. In addition, men and women in the no stress condition were equally likely to be referred to a cardiologist, but women were less likely than men to be referred to a cardiologist in the high stress condition (see Figure 10.2b). The authors found that symptoms of women in the high stress condition were less likely to be attributed to organic causes compared to the symptoms of the targets in the other three conditions. Thus, stress may distract physicians from diagnosing heart disease in women.

Taken collectively, heart disease in women may not be diagnosed as quickly as it is in men because women's signs of heart disease are more ambiguous and because health care professionals associate heart disease with being male rather than female. See if the men and women with heart disease you encounter have different experiences with the health care system with Do Gender 10.1.

Mental Health. In general, health care providers spend less time with men, provide men with fewer services, and provide less health information and advice to men (Courtenay, 2000a). In terms of mental health, women are more likely than men to receive prescriptions for psychotropic drugs, such as tranquilizers, antidepressants, and sedatives, following a visit to a hospital clinic (Morabia, Fabre, & Dunand, 1992). There are a number of possible reasons for this difference. First, it is possible that women are more psychologically distressed than men; support is provided for this hypothesis in Chapter 13. It also is possible that psychotropic drugs are overprescribed to women because women's symptoms are more likely attributed to psychological causes.

Some evidence suggests physicians are more likely to attribute problems to psychological causes in women than in men. One reason that women with an immune disorder take so long to receive definitive diagnoses may be that the vague symptoms accompanying these illnesses are attributed to emotional problems (Chrisler & O'Hea, 2000). This kind of bias has implications for the kinds of treatment men and women receive. Women's greater use of medication compared to men may reflect physicians overprescribing antidepressants and tranquilizers to women. An examination of medical records across the nation revealed that women were more likely than men to receive antidepressants and antianxiety drugs, even when they had similar symptoms as men (Hohmann, 1989). These differences in prescribed medication could be due to physician bias or to female patients being more likely than male patients to request medication for anxiety and depression.

Physician bias has been applied not only to the diagnosis of psychiatric disorders, such as depression, but also to alcohol usage. According to Bickel (1997), alcohol problems are underdiagnosed in women compared to men because the criteria used to identify such problems are more relevant to men. Common signs of alcohol

---

DO GENDER 10.1
Men's and Women's Experiences with Heart Problems

Interview one adult man and one adult woman who has had a heart problem, such as a heart attack. Ask them what their symptoms of the heart problem were, when they first noticed symptoms, and how they responded to those symptoms. How long did they wait before going to the doctor? How did the physician respond? Did the physician know right away the symptoms were cardiac in nature? How were they treated for their heart problem?

problems in men are difficulties with the law, problems at work, and general disruptive behavior. Women with alcohol problems may be less likely to show symptoms that are disruptive to society. Thus alcohol problems in women may be less easily detected by others.

TAKE HOME POINTS

- Artifactual explanations for sex differences in health include men's higher socioeconomic status compared to women, women as proxy reports for men's health, and physicians' differential treatment of men and women.

- Although men have a higher SES than women and SES is clearly related to health, SES does not appear to account for sex differences in health.

- Men have higher rates of heart disease than women, but women's disease is more advanced at diagnosis compared to men. Reasons include the more ambiguous nature of women's symptoms compared to those of men and the attribution of cardiac symptoms to psychological causes in the presence of stress among women.

- Women are treated less aggressively than men for cardiac disease, but there is some evidence that the major treatments for heart disease are less effective and riskier for women than men. Thus, it is not clear that physician bias is responsible for the differential treatment of men and women.

- Physicians are more likely to prescribe medication for psychological disorders to women than men, but it is not clear if this is due to physician bias or female patients requesting more medication compared to male patients.

- Physicians are more likely to attribute ambiguous symptoms to psychological causes in women than men.

HEALTH BEHAVIORS

One class of variables that may explain sex differences in mortality and morbidity are **health behaviors**. These include risky behaviors, such as smoking, alcohol abuse, and drug abuse, as well as healthy behaviors, such as preventive health care, exercise, and diet. Waldron (1995) argues that sex differences in behavior are the major reason men die younger than women, and these behavioral factors contribute to sex differences in the leading causes of death. Behaviors are implicated in heart disease, lung cancer, chronic lower respiratory disease, accidents, suicides, homicides, liver disease, and AIDS. Now that people are living longer and dying of chronic disease, behavioral factors may play a larger role than biology in sex differences in mortality.

Preventive Health Care

Women are more likely than men to believe in the value of preventive health care. Women are more likely to take vitamins (Slesinski, Subar, & Kahle, 1996) and attach greater importance to healthy eating than men (Wardle et al., 2004). Across 23 different countries, women were more likely than men to report that they avoided high-fat foods, ate more fruit, ate more fiber, and limited salt (Wardle et al., 2004). Among college students in the United States, females report a better diet than males among all ethnic groups except Hispanics, in which case there is no sex difference (Courtenay, McCreary, & Merighi, 2002). There is a downside to the female emphasis on dieting, however. Females also are more likely than males to practice unhealthy forms of dieting, such as fasting and using laxatives (Wu, Rose, & Bancroft, 2006).

Women are more likely to perform regular self-exams, to have a regular physician, and to have regular check-ups (Courtenay et al., 2002). Women are also more likely to take prescriptions as recommended and to return to the doctor's office for follow-up care. Conduct Do Gender 10.2 to find out if your male and female peers have a physician and examine their reasons.

DO GENDER 10.2
Do You Have a Doctor?

Interview 10 male and 10 female college students to find out if they have a regular doctor. You might ask, "If you become sick, is there a specific doctor you would call?" To really be certain that people have a physician, you might even ask for the physician's name. If a person does not have a physician, ask why.

Then, interview 20 older adults (10 male, 10 female) and ask the same question. You might interview the same students' parents, university staff, or faculty.

Are there sex differences in having a physician? Does it depend on age? What are the reasons for not having a physician? Do men and women provide different reasons?

One reason women have a regular physician and have better preventive care habits centers on reproductive issues. Women regularly visit the doctor for pap smears, mammograms, birth control, pregnancy, and postmenopausal symptoms. Men do not have the same regular life events or health issues early in life that require establishing a regular physician or routine physician visits. However, even when reproductive visits are excluded from analyses, women still visit the doctor more frequently than do men. In a sense, it is difficult to account completely for reproductive reasons when examining sex differences in the use of health care services. We can certainly count the number of visits attributed to reproductive issues, such as pregnancy or contraception, but we must consider that women are more likely than men to become involved in the health care system in the first place because of reproductive issues. Thus, when it comes to getting a flu shot, getting a regular physical, and seeking medical attention in response to a complaint, women are more likely

to have a resource available and to be familiar with turning to that resource. Thus in a sense, reproductive issues could still explain why women are more likely than men to visit a physician.

One group of women do not receive greater health care compared to men: lesbians. Both lesbians and gay men may be underserved by the health care system (Mann, 1996). Lesbians are less likely than heterosexual women to have health insurance from a spouse's employment. Lesbian households also have lower income, associated with lower use of health services, in particular lower rates of screening for breast cancer (Rankow & Tessaro, 1998b). Despite the fact that lesbians have just as high a risk for cervical cancer as heterosexual women, they are less likely to obtain pap smears (Rankow & Tessaro, 1998a). Although rates of screening have increased in recent years for lesbians, screening rates are still lower than rates for heterosexual women (Roberts et al., 2004). Both lesbians and gay men report feeling uncomfortable dealing with a health care system that is not sensitive to homosexuality (Mann, 1996; Rankow & Tessaro, 1998a). Over the last decade, lesbians have become more likely to disclose their sexual orientation to health care providers (Roberts et al., 2004). Gay men are stigmatized by the association of homosexuality with AIDS, and this association may make them unwilling to deal with the health care system.

What are the implications of heterosexual women's greater use of medical services for prevention compared to men? Theoretically, if women visit the doctor more frequently than men do, women's illnesses should be diagnosed at an earlier stage than men's. Early intervention may keep minor illnesses from developing into fatal ones. Routine office visits provide physicians with an opportunity to detect disease and provide patients with an opportunity to disclose problems. Although this is a compelling explanation for sex differences in mortality, there is no evidence to show that women's greater use of health services leads to earlier detection of disease. In fact, heart disease is detected later in women than men, and women delay longer in seeking treatment for symptoms of heart disease. Women wait longer than men before seeking help for symptoms of chest pain (Dracup et al., 1995), perhaps because they are less familiar with the symptoms of heart disease compared to men.

Smoking

Smoking has been referred to as the single most preventable cause of death (American Cancer Society, 2007). Tobacco accounts for almost one in five deaths in the United States. Smoking is associated with an increased risk of heart disease and stroke and an increased risk of at least 15 different kinds of cancer, including lip, oral, lung, esophagus, pancreas, kidney, and stomach. Among men, smoking is associated with slightly less than a 1 in 2 chance of developing cancer at some point in life; among women, the rate is slightly more than 1 in 3. There also are a number of chronic conditions associated with smoking such as chronic bronchitis and emphysema.

Smoking reveals a dose-response relation to heart disease, meaning the more one smokes, the greater the risk of heart disease (Rich-Edwards et al., 1995). When people quit smoking, the risk of heart disease decreases dramatically. Within 3 to 5 years after quitting, heart disease rates are similar to those of a nonsmoker. Smoking also is more strongly linked to heart disease in women than in men. In a prospective study of healthy men and women, smoking predicted the incidence of a heart attack 12 years later for both men and women, but the relation was stronger in women (Prescott et al., 1998). Women who smoked had 2.24 times the risk of a heart attack as women who did not smoke, whereas the relative risk for men was 1.43. These findings held even when the number of cigarettes smoked was taken into consideration.

Smoking is most strongly linked to lung cancer. The risk of lung cancer decreases as the length of smoking cessation increases (U.S. Department of Health and Human Services, 2004). However, the risk of lung cancer remains higher among former smokers than nonsmokers, no matter how long the cessation period. The increased rates of men smoking in the middle of the 20th century can be directly tied to the dramatic rise in lung cancer and heart disease among men and the subsequent widening of the sex difference in mortality at that time (Waldron, 2000). The increased rates of smoking among women in the 1960s and 1970s can be directly tied to the increased rate of lung cancer that emerged among women 20 to 30 years later. In 1987, lung cancer surpassed breast cancer as the leading cause of cancer death among women. The increase in smoking among women and the lower quit rates among women contributed to the recent narrowing of the sex gap in longevity. Although rates of lung cancer have decreased since 1984 in men, rates of lung cancer increased among women until leveling off in the past few years. Smoking is also riskier for women than men in terms of lung cancer. Given the same level of smoking, women are more susceptible than men to lung cancer (Ernster, 1996). Women may have a genetic predisposition to develop lung cancer, making smoking especially harmful to women (Shriver et al., 2000).

Besides heart disease and lung cancer, smoking poses a variety of other health problems for men and women. Women who smoke are vulnerable to osteoporosis, early menopause, decreased fertility, and complications during pregnancy. Men and women who smoke are at increased risk for other cancers, such as cancer of the mouth, pancreas, bladder, and kidneys (Berman & Gritz, 1991).

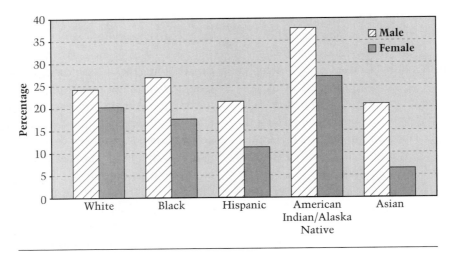

FIGURE 10.3 Current smoking among adults in the United States. These are the percentages of adults who report they currently smoke. In all ethnic groups, more men than women smoke.

Source: Adapted from Centers for Disease Control and Prevention (2006a).

Prevalence Among Adults. The most recent data from a national health survey of people in the United States show that 21% of adults smoke (Centers for Disease Control and Prevention, 2006a). As shown in Figure 10.3, men are more likely than women to smoke across ethnic groups in the United States. The sex difference is largest for Asians and Hispanics and smallest for Whites. Among the 50 states, the lowest rate of smoking is 12% in Utah and the highest rate is 29% in Kentucky (Centers for Disease Control and Prevention, 2005).

Sex differences in smoking changed over the latter half of the 20th century (Waldron, 2000). In the early part of the century, men smoked more than women because smoking was not viewed as socially acceptable among women. In 1955, 25% of women smoked compared to 52% of men (Chesney & Nealey, 1996). In the 1960s and 1970s, the health hazards of smoking became publicized, but smoking also became more socially acceptable for women (Waldron, 2000). Smoking among women increased with the development of the women's movement and

came to be associated with women's fight for equality. Thus, in the 1960s and 1970s, men's rates of smoking initiation were lower than those of women, and more men than women began to quit smoking. Today, men still have higher quit rates than women. The sex difference in smoking has decreased over time.

Along with the sex difference in smoking patterns, the sex difference in lung cancer shifted. In 1950, the male:female ratio of lung cancer was 4.6; in 1960, it was 6.7; in 1990, it was 2.3; in 1999 to 2003, it was 1.6 (American Cancer Society, 2007). The sex ratios are closer to 2 among African Americans, Asians, and Hispanics. Because lung cancer occurs 2 to 3 decades following smoking, the changes in men's and women's rates of lung cancer can be directly tied to the changes in their rates of smoking. The rate of smoking has declined since 1965, more so for men—especially White men.

Prevalence Among Adolescents and Children. Smoking is particularly important to study among children and adolescents. First, the majority of smokers begin to smoke during adolescence or early adulthood; 63.4% of new smokers in 2005 started smoking before the age of 18 (Substance Abuse and Mental Health Services Administration, 2006). Second, some evidence suggests that smoking slows lung development among adolescents (Gold et al., 1996). These effects are stronger among females than males.

Among high school students in 2005, 23% of both girls and boys reported they currently smoked, which was defined as having smoked one or more cigarettes in the past 30 days. As shown in Figure 10.4, the rate of smoking increased among children in the early 1990s, decreased since 1997 and now appears to have leveled off or may be increasing in some groups (Centers for Disease Control and Prevention, 2006d). In the 1990s, smoking among Black

males increased dramatically, but those rates have decreased in recent years. Among Whites, slightly more girls smoke than boys, whereas among Blacks and Hispanics, more boys than girls smoke. Data collected on younger children reveal no sex or race differences in smoking. The first national survey of middle school children (grades 6 through 8) showed that 9.2% of children smoke, and these rates were similar for boys and girls and for White, Black, and Hispanic students (Centers for Disease Control and Prevention, 2000b).

Do boys and girls have different concerns about smoking? Although both are equally aware of the disadvantages of smoking, they are differentially concerned with specific disadvantages. Both boys and girls perceive health consequences as the major disadvantage, but this is regarded as

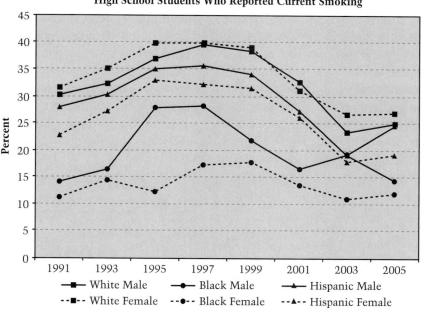

High School Students Who Reported Current Smoking

FIGURE 10.4   Prevalence of current cigarette smoking among high school students over time. Smoking rates increased among White, Black, and Hispanic high school students in the early 1990s, decreased since 1997, and seem to have leveled off.

Source: Adapted from Centers for Disease Control and Prevention (2006d).

more important by boys (Taylor et al., 1999). Girls focus more on the moral (i.e., smoking is wrong) and the aesthetic consequences of smoking (e.g., yellow teeth, bad breath), whereas boys are more concerned with the effects of smoking on athletic performance (Taylor et al., 1999). Black children are more likely than White children to be concerned about the ethics of smoking. Black children also are more likely than White children to perceive parents as a deterrent to smoking.

Smoking Cessation.   More men than women have quit smoking. There is also evidence that when both men and women try to quit smoking, men's attempts are more often successful. In three randomized clinical trials to test the effectiveness of the nicotine patch, men were more successful than women in quitting smoking regardless of whether they received the real nicotine patch or the placebo patch (Wetter et al., 1999b). At the end of treatment, 45% of men had quit compared to 29% of women. At 6-month follow-up, 25% of men had remained quitters compared to 12% of women. In an intervention program using nicotine gum, men were more likely than women to have quit at 12 months (29% vs. 25%) and at 36 months (22% vs. 18%; Bjornson et al., 1995). Perhaps physicians are aware of this difference, as physicians are less likely to prescribe smoking cessation medication to women than men (Steinberg et al., 2006). Although the majority of the evidence suggests men are more successful in quitting, adolescent males and females are equally confident they can quit (Sussman et al., 1998).

Several theories attempt to explain why it may be more difficult for women to quit smoking. One theory is that smoking is associated with negative affect and depression (Covey, 1999; Wetter et al., 1999b), and women are more likely than men to be depressed. People with a history of depression or anxiety disorders are more likely to smoke than are people without

such histories (Covey, 1999). Even among adolescents, depression has been linked to smoking (Simons-Morton et al., 1999). Depression also is associated with being less able to quit smoking (Zhu et al., 1999). In one study, depressed people were 40% less likely to quit smoking than nondepressed people (Anda et al., 1990). Depression is not only associated with difficulty quitting, but when people with a history of depression quit, their depression increases (Glass, 1990). To recap, one reason women may be less able to quit smoking is that depression interferes with cessation and women are more likely than men to be depressed.

Another theory as to why women might have more difficulty quitting smoking is that women are more likely to be physiologically addicted to smoking. Female smokers are more likely than male smokers to report behaviors indicative of physiological addiction, including smoking a cigarette within 10 minutes of waking, smoking when sick, being upset about having to go a whole day without a cigarette, and reporting "not feeling right" if one goes too long without smoking (Royce et al., 1997; Sussman et al., 1998). The Fagerstrom Tolerance Questionnaire, shown in Table 10.7, is a widely used measure of physiological addiction to nicotine (Heatherton et al., 1991). If you have friends who smoke, conduct Do Gender 10.3 to see who

---

DO GENDER 10.3
Who Is More Physiologically Addicted to Smoking?

Administer the Fagerstrom Tolerance Questionnaire shown in Table 10.7 to 10 male and 10 female smokers. Is one sex more addicted than the other? Can you predict addiction from any other variables, such as age or depression?

TABLE 10.7   REVISED FAGERSTROM TOLERANCE QUESTIONNAIRE

1. How soon after you wake up do you smoke your first cigarette?
   a. After 60 minutes.
   b. 31–60 minutes.
   c. 6–30 minutes.
   d. Within 5 minutes.

2. Do you find it difficult to refrain from smoking in places where it is forbidden?
   No   Yes

3. Which cigarette would you hate to give up?
   a. The first one in the morning.
   b. Any other.

4. How many cigarettes per day do you smoke?
   a. 10 or fewer
   b. 11–20
   c. 21–30
   d. 31 or more

5. Do you smoke more frequently during the first hours after waking than during the rest of the day?
   No   Yes

6. Do you smoke if you are so ill that you are in bed most of the day?
   No   Yes

Source: T. F. Heatherton et al. (1991). Copyright 1991. Reprinted by permission of Taylor and Francis.

is more strongly addicted to smoking. Also see Sidebar 10.2 for a discussion of how methodology affects reporting of withdrawal symptoms.

Perkins and colleagues (1996; Perkins, Donny, & Caggiula, 1999), however, have argued that women are *less* likely than men to be physiologically addicted to nicotine. They base their argument on research that shows nicotine replacement therapies are less effective for women (Perkins et al., 1999). In one study, nicotine replacement therapy influenced a physiological recording of sleep quality, an objective measure of withdrawal symptoms, among men but not women (Wetter et al., 1999a). Men and women who had quit smoking were randomly assigned to receive a nicotine patch or a placebo patch, and their sleep quality was measured physiologically. Men who received the nicotine patch had better sleep quality, as indicated by physiological recordings of sleep duration and sleep awakenings, than men who did not receive the patch. The patch did not influence women's sleep quality. Thus the nicotine patch was effective in helping men sleep but had no effect on women's sleep quality. Wetter and colleagues concluded that their findings supported Perkins's theory that men are more physiologically addicted to nicotine.

In general, research on people who quit smoking shows that men choose to use more nicotine replacement therapies (e.g., nicotine sprays) than women do (Perkins et al., 1999). These findings suggest that men find nicotine more rewarding and more relieving of withdrawal symptoms. Men are also better than women at discriminating different doses of

SIDEBAR 10.2: *How Methodology Affects Self-Report of Withdrawal Symptoms*

Another way physiological addiction is measured is by self-reports of withdrawal symptoms when quitting smoking. Withdrawal symptoms include depressed mood, insomnia, irritability, anxiety, difficulty concentrating, restlessness, decreased heart rate, and increased appetite (American Psychiatric Association, 2000). It is not clear whether men or women report more withdrawal symptoms. The methodology of a study influences whether sex differences in withdrawal symptoms appear. Prospective studies (conducted during cessation) show no sex differences, whereas retrospective studies (conducted after cessation) show that women recall more symptoms than men. What is the source of this discrepancy? Is it that women recall more symptoms than they actually experience, or that men recall fewer symptoms? The latter seems to be the case. Pomerleau and colleagues (1994) compared prospective and retrospective reports of withdrawal symptoms. They asked men and women first to recall their experience of four common withdrawal symptoms (anxiety, anger/irritation, difficulty in concentrating, hunger) from previous attempts to quit smoking and then to report prospectively their experience of these symptoms over the first few days that they quit smoking. Men recalled fewer symptoms in the past than they actually experienced during their present attempt; in other words, men's recall of symptoms underestimated the extent to which they actually experienced symptoms. For example, only 5% of men said they experienced difficulty concentrating during past attempts to quit smoking, but 58% reported this symptom during the present attempt. Women's retrospective reports of difficulty concentrating were more similar to their prospective reports (40% vs. 56%). There were no sex differences in any of the prospective reports of symptoms. Thus retrospective methodologies may suggest that women experience more withdrawal symptoms due to men's tendency to recall fewer symptoms than they actually experienced. According to self-reports of current withdrawal symptoms, men and women experience similar withdrawal symptoms, which means similar levels of physiological addiction.

nicotine (Perkins, 1999). In one study, women were either given a cigarette that did or did not contain nicotine (Perkins et al., 2006). When they were provided with no information about whether the cigarette contained nicotine, women in the two conditions found the cigarettes equally satisfying. When they were told which cigarette contained nicotine, the women who had the nicotine cigarette found it more satisfying than the women who had the cigarette without nicotine. Thus women who were blind to the content of the cigarette did not find the one with nicotine to be more rewarding.

If women are not as physiologically addicted to nicotine, what is the basis of women's addiction? Perkins and colleagues suggest that smoking is more of a sensory experience for women than for men: Women enjoy the visual

and olfactory experiences of smoking more than men do.

A third theory as to why women have greater difficulty quitting smoking is that women are more concerned with the potential for weight gain. Fear of weight gain is a deterrent to smoking cessation especially among women (Jeffery et al., 2000). In a study of men and women 1 to 2 years out of high school, women smokers were more likely to express concerns about weight gain if they quit smoking (Pirie, Murray, & Luepker, 1991). In fact, women were more likely than men to say they experienced weight gain and a desire to eat when they tried to quit smoking. However, after quitting, no evidence indicates that weight gain predicts relapse in women (Borrelli et al., 2001; Perkins et al., 2001).

Quitting smoking does lead to weight gain, but not as much as people think, partly because people underestimate how much they weighed before they quit smoking (Peterson, 1999). According to the U.S. Surgeon General (Centers for Disease Control and Prevention, 2007b), women gain between 6 and 12 pounds during the first year after they quit smoking. In subsequent years, the weight gain diminishes. The weight gain associated with smoking cessation is far less hazardous to health then the hazards associated with smoking.

Men and women quit smoking for different reasons (Waldron, 1997). Men quit smoking for physical fitness reasons, whereas women are likely to quit smoking when they become pregnant. The percentage of women who quit smoking during pregnancy increased from 37% in 1993 to 46% in 1999 (Colman & Joyce, 2003). However, most of these women resume smoking after childbirth. Half of women resume smoking within 6 months of delivery and over two thirds resume smoking by 1 year (Centers for Disease Control and Prevention, 2007b; Colman & Joyce, 2003).

Thus various theories have been put forth to explain why women have more difficulty than men when they try to quit smoking. One theory is that women are more depressed and depression interferes with smoking cessation. Some evidence supports this. Another theory is that women are more physiologically addicted to smoking, but the evidence in support of this theory is completely contradictory. On some self-report measures of physiological addiction, women appear more dependent than men on nicotine; on others, there are no sex differences; yet another group of investigators suggests men are more physiologically addicted because nicotine patches are more effective in relieving men's withdrawal symptoms than those of women. A third theory is that women are more concerned than men with the weight gain that

follows smoking cessation. This concern may interfere with initial cessation efforts but does not predict relapse. People do gain weight when they quit smoking but probably not as much as they expect.

Alcohol

The relation of moderate alcohol intake to health is mixed. On the one hand, alcohol in moderation is protective against heart disease and appears to provide immunity from the common cold (Rich-Edwards et al., 1995). However, alcohol in moderation may also be associated with breast cancer (American Cancer Society, 2003).

Large quantities of alcohol are clearly harmful to health. Heavy use of alcohol is associated with increased risk of heart disease, cancer, cirrhosis of the liver, accidents, suicide, homicide, and male impotence (American Cancer Society, 2003; Waldron, 1995). Alcohol is linked to motor vehicle accidents; in 2005, 24% of drivers in fatal crashes has been drinking alcohol (U.S. Department of Transportation, 2005b). Alcohol use also has been associated with accidents more generally, especially among men. In a national sample, moderate to heavy drinking was associated with injuries in men but not women (Cherpitel, 1993). Alcohol abuse also has economic and social consequences. It has been linked to loss of jobs as well as loss of relationships (Lex, 1991) and is associated with antisocial behaviors, such as aggression (Hull & Bond, 1986).

Alcohol has different consequences for men and women (Nolen-Hoeksema & Hilt, 2006). Although women have a lower genetic risk for alcohol-use disorders, the physiological consequences of alcohol are more damaging to women. It takes proportionally less alcohol to have the same effect on a woman as a man; even if a man and a woman of similar weight drink the same amount of alcohol, the woman will have a higher blood-alcohol level. The ratio of fat to water in a woman's body is greater than that in a man's body; in other words, men have more water available in their systems to dilute consumed alcohol. In addition, more of the alcohol is metabolized by enzymes in the stomach for men compared to women. Thus, men and women who drink the same amount of alcohol in proportion to their body weight will not have the same blood-alcohol levels. This may be one reason why alcohol is more strongly associated with cirrhosis of the liver in women than in men. The progression from the first drink to an alcohol-related problem is faster among women than men, a process referred to as "telescoping." Thus, women are more vulnerable than men to both acute and chronic (long-lasting) effects of alcohol.

Prevalence. The prevalence of alcohol usage was examined in the 2005 National Survey of Drug Abuse, which is a national survey of over 8,000 persons ages 12 and over (Substance Abuse and Mental Health Services Administration, 2006). This representative survey revealed that 58% of males and 46% of females have used alcohol in the past month. Among those 12 to 17 years old, rates were similar for males (16%) and females (17%), whereas among those 18 to 25 years old, males exceeded females (66% vs. 55%). Across the entire sample, the rate of binge drinking, defined as 5 or more drinks on one occasion in the past month, was over twice as high for males as females (31% vs. 15%). And the rate of heavy alcohol usage, defined as 5 or more drinks on one occasion for 5 of the last 30 days, was over three times higher among males than females (10% vs. 3%). Several nationally representative surveys have shown that men have twice the rate of alcohol abuse as women (Nolen-Hoeksema & Hilt, 2006). There is cross-cultural support for these findings. In a study of 10 countries (Australia, Canada, Czech Republic, Estonia, Finland, Israel, Russia,

Sweden, Netherlands, United States), men drank alcohol more frequently, consumed higher amounts of alcohol at one time, had more episodes of heavy drinking, and were more likely to suffer adverse consequences of drinking (e.g., health problems, criticism by others, losing control; Wilsnack et al., 2000).

Consistent with this survey, the 2005 Monitoring the Future Study revealed similar rates of alcohol usage in the past 30 days among male and female 8th-graders (16% vs. 18%) and male and female 10th-graders (33% and 34%) but higher rates of alcohol use among male than female 12th-graders (51% vs. 43%; Johnston et al., 2006a). Among college students and young adults (ages 19 to 30), more males than females used alcohol (74% vs. 64%; Johnston et al., 2006b). The sex difference in daily use of alcohol was even more dramatic—8% of males compared to 3% of females said they drank alcohol every day. And, the sex difference in binge drinking was large—47% of males compared to 28% of females.

One reason adult women drink less heavily than men has to do with society's attitudes toward drinking (Nolen-Hoeksema & Hilt, 2006). Society disapproves of heavy drinking in women, which is thought to interfere with the female role of being responsible for children. Another reason women drink less than men is that women are more involved in religion, which deters drinking. Sex differences in drinking have decreased over the last 50 years, and no sex differences appear among adolescents. Is this because society now views drinking as equally acceptable in men and women? Find out about your peers' attitudes toward men and women drinking in Do Gender 10.4.

Drugs

The health consequences of substance abuse can be severe; the most severe consequence is death. However, substance abuse also can lead to other problems, such as complications with pregnancy,

DO GENDER 10.4
Attitudes Toward Men
and Women Drinking

Create several scenarios of a person at a party drinking varying amounts of alcohol, ranging from none to moderate to a lot (i.e., so much that he or she gets sick or blacks out). Create two versions of these scenarios by using a male name and a female name. Develop a set of items to measure people's attitudes toward the person in the scenario. Are men and women who do not use alcohol viewed similarly? Are men and women who drink alcohol viewed similarly? Does it depend on the level? Finally, do the answers to these questions depend on the sex of the respondent?

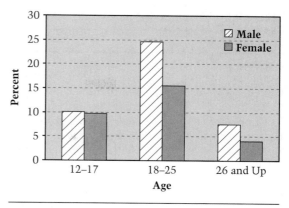

FIGURE 10.5   Percentage of people using illicit drugs in prior month 2005.
Source: Adapted from Substance Abuse and Mental Health Services Administration (2006).

health problems in children born to addicted mothers and fathers, and sexual difficulties (Griffin, Weiss, & Mirin, 1989). Use of intravenous drugs has been linked to AIDS (Waldron, 1995).

Prevalence.   Men use more drugs than women do. According to findings from the 2005 National Household Survey on Drug Abuse, the rate of drug use has declined for both men and women since the late 1970s, stabilized in the 1990s, and shown a slight increase recently (Substance Abuse and Mental Health Services Administration, 2006). These findings are based on persons age 12 and over using illicit drugs within the prior month. Figure 10.5 shows the rates of drug use for males and females in different age groups in 2005. Males have nearly twice the rate of drug use as females except between the ages of 12 and 17, when rates are similar. The sex difference holds for Whites, Blacks, and Hispanics. Men are also twice as likely as women to be classified as dependent on drugs or alcohol (10% vs. 4.9%), although women become more easily addicted to drugs than men (Roth, Cosgrove, &

Carroll, 2004). There is no sex difference in substance dependence in the 12- to 17-year-old range (7.6% males; 8.0% females). Rates of substance dependence are lower among Blacks (6.2%) than Whites (7.5%) or Hispanics (7.8%). Although men are more likely than women to use illicit drugs, women are more likely than men to receive treatment. Homosexuals use more drugs than heterosexuals (Cochran et al., 2004).

A study that provides substantial information about drug usage among adolescents is the Monitoring the Future Study (Johnston et al., 2006c). This study has tracked drug use among thousands of high school seniors since 1975 and among thousands of 8th- and 10th-grade students since 1991. Between the late 1970s and 1990, drug usage declined dramatically among adolescents, but drug usage increased during the 1990s. Since the late 1990s, drug usage has leveled off and more recently shown a slight decline. For example, among 12th-graders, marijuana use over the past year increased in the 1960s, peaked at 51% in 1979, decreased to 22% in 1992, rose in the 1990s to near 40% and has declined a bit in recent years. Similar trends were observed for other illicit drugs. There has been a very slight decline during the past few

TABLE 10.8 **SEX DIFFERENCES IN SUBSTANCE ABUSE**

Substance	Abuse Ratio
Alcohol	Males higher (5:1)
Amphetamine	Males higher (3–4:1)
Caffeine	Males higher
Cannabis	Males higher
Cocaine	Males higher (1.5–2.0:1)
Hallucinogens	Males higher (3:1)
Heroin	Males higher (3:1)
Inhalants	Males higher
Nicotine	Males higher
Sedatives	Females higher

Source: Adapted from the American Psychiatric Association (2000).

years. Sex differences in illicit drug use appear to increase with age. There are no sex differences in illicit drug use among 8th-graders, but sex differences appear with age such that 12th-grade boys are more likely than girls to use illicit drugs. A similar pattern of findings holds for marijuana.

Males use more of almost all kinds of drugs compared to females. The only drug that females tend to use more than males is sedatives; this finding holds for all age groups. Averaging across studies, sex differences in the use of specific drugs are shown in Table 10.8. Men are more likely than women to use illegal drugs, but women are more likely to use prescription tranquilizers and sedatives.

Prediction of Smoking, Alcohol Use, and Drug Use

Demographic characteristics are associated with each of these problem behaviors. For example, lower levels of education and income are associated with greater smoking among adults for Whites but not among Blacks or Hispanics (Barbeau, Krieger, & Soobader, 2004). More educated and higher income people are less likely to start smoking and more likely to quit if they start. Education seems to be more strongly related to a decline in smoking among men than women. Sexual orientation also has been associated with these high-risk behaviors. Lesbians are more likely than heterosexual women to drink and smoke (Fassinger & Arseneau, 2007).

The family environment has been strongly linked to problem behaviors. First, family environments in which smoking, alcohol use, and drug use are modeled are more likely to produce teenagers who engage in these same problem behaviors. Parents' attitudes toward problem behaviors are associated with children's engagement in them (Flay, Hu, & Richardson, 1998). Living with a parent who smokes is associated with the onset of smoking (Flay et al., 1998), the frequency of smoking (Simons-Morton et al., 1999), and lower rates of quitting smoking (Zhu et al., 1999). Family members' use of alcohol and drugs also are associated with children's usage and subsequent development of alcohol and drug problems (Abdelrahman et al., 1998). Children of alcoholics are 4 to 5 times more likely to become alcoholics (Lex, 1991). Easy access to cigarettes, alcohol, and drugs and lack of rules about substance use in the home predict usage among children (Abdelrahman et al., 1998; Resnick et al., 1997).

Family support is linked to less use of cigarettes, alcohol, and drugs (Resnick et al., 1997), whereas family conflict is associated with greater alcohol and drug usage (Abdelrahman et al., 1998; Hops, Davis, & Lewin, 1999). It is not clear, however, whether conflict leads to usage or usage leads to family conflict. One study, however, showed that family conflict among children ages 7 to 9 predicted drug usage 7 years later (Hops et al., 1999).

During adolescence, it is peers rather than the family who have the strongest influence on problem behavior (Abdelrahman et al., 1998). Friends' attitudes toward smoking are associated with teens smoking (Flay et al., 1998; Simons-Morton et al., 1999). Adolescents are more likely to smoke if their friends smoke (Abdelrahman et al., 1998), and the more friends who smoke, the greater likelihood the adolescent will smoke (Flay et al., 1998). Peer usage of alcohol and drugs is also associated with adolescents' usage (Abdelrahman et al., 1998).

There is some evidence that girls are more susceptible to the influence of others when it comes to these problem behaviors (Griffin et al., 1999; Siddiqui et al., 1999). One reason for stronger links of friends' behavior to girls' behavior may have to do with popularity. In a study in Britain, smoking was linked to popularity among girls, but not boys. Girls who were in the most popular cliques smoked (Michell & Amos, 1997). Popular boys were reluctant to smoke because it conflicted with involvement in sports. The family also plays a larger role in problem behaviors for girls than boys. Adolescent girls who abuse drugs have high family conflict and low family cohesion (Dakof, 2000). These factors do not distinguish boys who do and do not use drugs. Even among adults, relationships have a stronger impact on drinking alcohol among women than men (Skaff, Finney, & Moos, 1999).

The effect of parents and peers on problem behavior also depends on race. Parental attitudes are more strongly linked to smoking among Black and Hispanic than White adolescents, whereas peers' attitudes toward smoking have a stronger effect on White than minority adolescents (Siddiqui et al., 1999). Compared to White persons, minority persons place greater importance on family than peers.

Problem behaviors also seem to be related to one another. First, cigarette use, alcohol use, and substance abuse are interrelated. Second, poor grades in school are associated with all three problem behaviors (Abdelrahman et al., 1998; Hops et al., 1999; Resnick et al., 1997). Third, all of these problem behaviors are associated with depression among adolescents and adults (Berger & Adesso, 1991; Horwitz & White, 1991).

Of the three problem behaviors, alcohol is most strongly linked to gender roles. The traditional male not only drinks alcohol but also prides himself on being able to drink large quantities without losing control. McCreary, Newcomb, and Sadava (1999) distinguished among several male gender-role characteristics to see which were associated with drinking alcohol among a group of recently graduated college students. Masculine gender-role stress, which reflects distress when facing situations inconsistent with the male gender role, was associated with more alcohol-related problems. Agency, however, as measured by the PAQ, was associated with fewer alcohol-related problems. Having traditional attitudes about men was associated with reports of greater alcohol consumption. Studies of adolescents also have linked traditional gender-role attitudes to the use and abuse of alcohol (Huselid & Cooper, 1992; Pleck et al., 1993). More traditional attitudes are associated with greater usage for males, but less usage for females. Alcohol use is consistent with traditional masculinity but inconsistent with traditional femininity. Thus it appears there are characteristics of the male gender role that are advantageous and disadvantageous with respect to drinking alcohol. Masculine traits that reflect a healthy sense of self (i.e., agency) are associated with fewer alcohol problems. However, having traditional attitudes toward gender roles is associated with greater alcohol problems in males.

Overweight and Obesity

Obesity is a risk factor for all causes of mortality, heart disease, Type 2 diabetes, hypertension (high blood pressure), high cholesterol, and some cancers. Obesity takes different forms in men and women. Men are more likely to have **android obesity**: the apple shape, which consists of extra weight collected around the abdomen. Android obesity is measured by the ratio of waist to hip size. A ratio of more than 1.0 is a significant risk factor for men and a ratio of more than .8 is a significant risk for women (Wing & Klem, 1997). Women are more likely to have **gynoid obesity**: the pear shape, which consists of extra weight around the hips. Android obesity poses greater risks to health than gynoid obesity, meaning that obesity poses a greater risk for men than for women. Among those 45 years old and younger, obesity has a stronger relation to mortality for men, but among those over 45, overweight and obesity have a stronger relation to mortality for women (Muennig et al., 2006).

Aside from physical health problems, there are implications of obesity for quality of life. The social, psychological, and economic consequences of obesity are more severe for women than for men (Muennig et al., 2006). In a longitudinal study of 370 people, overweight women were less likely to marry, completed fewer years of school, had lower incomes, and were more likely to live in poverty 7 years later than women who were not overweight (Gortmaker et al., 1993). Similar consequences were detected among men, but the effects were not as strong. The investigators of this study compared the effects of being overweight to the effects of having other chronic health conditions, such as asthma, diabetes, and arthritis. They found these other conditions had none of the social or economic consequences that obesity had. Obesity also is related to depression in White, Black, and Hispanic women (Heo et al., 2006). The relation of obesity to depression for men is less consistent.

Definition.   Obesity is typically determined by a combination of height and weight, or the **body mass index** (BMI), the calculation for which is shown in Table 10.9. A BMI between 25 and 29.9

TABLE 10.9   BODY MASS INDEX (BMI)

BMI calculation: $\dfrac{\text{Weight (kilograms)}}{\text{Height}^2 \text{ (meters)}}$

is classified as overweight, and a BMI over 30 is classified as obese.

Prevalence.   As indicated by the Surgeon General's call to action in 2001, obesity has become an epidemic in the United States. In the 2003 to 2004 National Health and Nutrition Examination Survey, 34% of adults over 20 years old were overweight and an additional 32% were obese (Ogden et al., 2006). The rate of obesity has doubled since the 1976 to 1980 survey. The increase in overweight and obesity is due in part to an increase in weight among the most obese (i.e., the heaviest people are becoming heavier) and in part to an increase in weight for all age and sex groups (i.e., the entire distribution of weight has shifted). Men are more likely than women to be overweight, but women are more likely than men to be obese. Among Whites, the rate of obesity is the same for men and women (31% men; 30% women), whereas the rate of obesity is much higher among females than males among Blacks (54% vs. 34%) and Hispanics (42% vs. 32%).

Obesity also has increased dramatically among children. The increased rates for children ages 12 to 19 are shown in Figure 10.6. Overweight among children is defined as a BMI at or above the 95th percentile for one's age and sex. The percentage of overweight children in the 2003 to 2004 survey was 18% for boys and 16% for girls (Ogden et al., 2006). The size and direction of the sex difference depends on race. Among Hispanics, more males are overweight compared to females (22% vs. 16%); among Whites, slightly more males are overweight compared to females (18% vs. 15%); but among Blacks, more females are overweight compared to males (24% vs. 16%). Obesity is especially problematic in children because dietary and exercise habits instilled in childhood are difficult to change. In addition, obesity is accompanied by metabolic changes in children that are difficult to reverse (Centers for Disease Control and

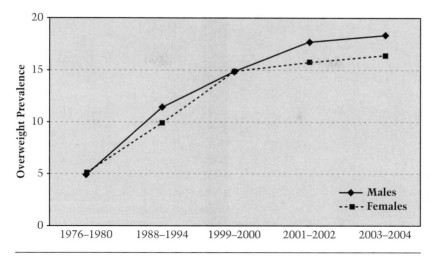

FIGURE 10.6   The rate of overweight children and adolescents has dramatically risen over the past 30 years.
Source: Adapted from Ogden et al. (2002) and Ogden et al. (2006).

Prevention, 2000a). One result of the increase in obesity among children is the increase in Type 2 diabetes—formerly a disease thought to characterize older people. Type 2 diabetes is an endocrine disorder in which the body is not as capable of using insulin to metabolize food. Of children diagnosed with Type 2 diabetes, 80% are overweight (Centers for Disease Control and Prevention, 2003).

Obesity is more common among those with a lower SES (Zhang & Wang, 2004), partly because low SES is associated with poorer diets and less exercise. However, obesity is not clearly related to socioeconomic status among all ethnic groups. Obesity is related to higher SES among White men, White women, and Black women; lower SES among Black and Hispanic men; and unrelated to SES among Hispanic women. Ethnic groups may vary in their attitudes toward food and obesity. Because weight symbolized wealth historically, minority groups may have a less negative view of being overweight.

Views of obesity have been studied among White and Black women. When Black and White women view the same image of a person's body, Black women view the image as slimmer than White women do (Flynn & Fitzgibbon, 1998). That is, Black women are less influenced than White women by society's association of attractiveness with thinness. Black women view these images as applying to White women. Black women are more satisfied with their bodies than White women are, even when they are overweight (Flynn & Fitzgibbon, 1998). Across a range of studies, between 0% and 60% of overweight Black women say they have a normal weight; the comparable figure for White women is between 0 and 8%.

The differences between how Black and White women perceive their weight have both a positive and negative consequence for Black women. On the negative side, Black women are more likely than White women to be obese, which poses a serious risk factor to physical health. Furthermore, obese Black women are less likely than obese White women to view their weight as a problem. On the positive side, Black women are less likely than White women to

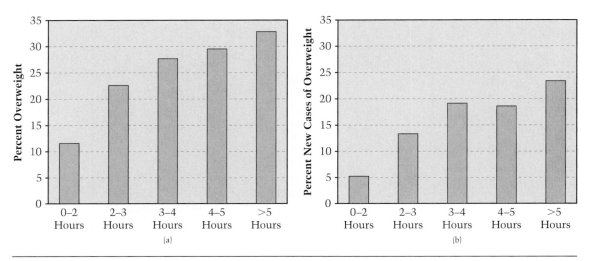

FIGURE 10.7 (a) The more hours that children and adolescents watched television in an average day, the more likely they were to be overweight. (b) The more hours that children and adolescents watched television predicted an increasing number of new cases of overweight four years later.
Source: Adapted from Gortmaker et al. (1996).

be diagnosed with eating disorders, although this race difference is getting smaller (Flynn & Fitzgibbon, 1998).

Etiology. There are genetic predispositions to obesity, but societal and behavioral factors also are involved. Because the increase in obesity has been so dramatic and has affected the entire population of people, some explanations must focus on societal changes. Among these are the increased availability of food, the increase in food consumption, and the decrease in physical activity (Flegal & Troiano, 2000). In a study that examined societal changes over the late 1970s, 1980s, and 1990s, trends were found for greater consumption of food away from home and a greater increase in calories from salty snacks, soft drinks, and pizza (Nielsen, Siega-Riz, & Popkin, 2002).

The increase in obesity among children has been attributed to poor diet and lack of physical activity—both of which are influenced by heavy television viewing. In a longitudinal study that followed children and adolescents for 4 years,

television viewing was linked to obesity at study start in a dose-response fashion as shown in Figure 10.7a (Gortmaker et al., 1996). In addition, television viewing predicted an increase in new onsets of obesity over the 4 years (see Figure 10.7b). To test the possibility that overweight children were more attracted to television, the investigators examined whether obesity at study start predicted an increase in television viewing. It did not. Other studies have found links of television and computer usage to obesity. In a study of 9- to 14-year-olds, television watching and video and computer game usage were associated with increases in BMI over a 1-year period (Berkey et al., 2000).

Why are women more likely than men to suffer from obesity? First, women engage in a lower level of physical activity than men (Wing & Klem, 1997). Second, there are life events associated with obesity in women: Women are most likely to gain weight when they get married, when they have a child, and during menopause (Wing & Klem, 1997).

Exercise

Physical activity has been related to lower mortality rates (U.S. Department of Health and Human Services, 1996), and a lack of physical activity is clearly linked to the increase in obesity. Specifically, physical activity is associated with reduced heart disease, hypertension, some cancers (e.g., colon cancer), and Type 2 diabetes. Exercise may be associated with a reduced incidence of osteoporosis in women.

Among adults, rates of leisure exercise increased in the 1970s and 1980s but then decreased in the 1990s and after the turn of the century. In 2005, 31% of men and 28% of women engaged in regular leisure-time physical activity, defined as vigorous exercise 3 times a week or moderate/light exercise 5 times a week (Centers for Disease Control and Prevention, 2007a). An additional 39% of men and 41% of women engaged in no leisure-time physical activity. Across all age groups, men are more likely than women to engage in leisure-time physical activity (see Figure 10.8 for an exception). White people also are more likely to engage in physical activity than Black or Hispanic people.

Whereas the earlier guidelines encouraged adults to engage in moderate activity on a daily basis, more recent guidelines have suggested that vigorous activity provides additional benefits to health (Tanasescu et al., 2002; Dietary Guidelines for Americans, 2005). Vigorous activity is defined as 20 minutes of activity that causes sustained increases in breathing or heart rate. These new guidelines are a problem for older women. A Gallup Poll showed that women are less likely to engage in vigorous exercise than men (27% versus 31%; Brooks, 2003). Older females compensate partly by engaging in more light or moderate activity.

The kind of exercise in which men and women engage differs (Jacobs et al., 2005). Men are more likely to be involved in team sports,

FIGURE 10.8 Adult women exercising. Adult women are less likely than adult men to exercise, and even less likely to be involved in competitive exercise.

whereas women are more likely to be involved in individual sports and noncompetitive exercise. The motives for exercise also differ (Waldron, 1997); men are motivated by competition, whereas women are motivated by concerns about appearance and weight control. Unfortunately, a study of adult women showed that body shape motives for physical activity are associated with *lower* levels of physical activity compared to other motives for exercise (such as health and intrinsic interest in exercise; Segar, Spruijt-Metz, & Nolen-Hoeksema, 2006).

Rates of physical activity among children have decreased dramatically. In 1984, 62% of children engaged in vigorous activity, whereas in 1990, only 37% of children did so (Centers for Disease Control and Prevention, 1992).

Vigorous activity was defined as exercising for a minimum of 20 minutes 3 times a week, such that breathing was heavy and heart rate increased. Rates of vigorous activity differed by race: 39% White, 35% Hispanic, and 29% Black. There is also a sex difference in physical activity: Boys are more active than girls. In the 1990 national survey of high school children, 50% of boys and 25% of girls said they engaged in vigorous activity (Centers for Disease Control and Prevention, 1992). One reason boys get more exercise is that boys are more likely to participate in sports, especially team sports (Centers for Disease Control and Prevention, 2006c), although this trend is decreasing. In 2005, 62% of boys and 50% of girls in grades 9 through 12 participated in team sports. The sex difference was smaller for Whites (62% vs. 54%) than Blacks (65% vs. 44%) and Hispanics (62% vs. 44%). As shown in Figure 10.9, the number of girls who

participated in high school athletic programs has dramatically increased over the past 30 years. During the 2005 to 2006 school year, the four sports that had the most boys participate were football, basketball, track and field, and baseball; the leading sports for girls were basketball, track and field, volleyball, and softball. The fifth leading sport was the same for boys and girls—soccer—with nearly the same number of male and female participants.

One reason for the reduced rates of physical activity among children is that technological advances have made sedentary activities more appealing; these include television, video games, and the computer. In a nationally representative sample of children ages 8 through 16, watching television was inversely associated with exercise and positively associated with obesity (Andersen et al., 1998). Children who watched more than 4 hours of television a day were at particular

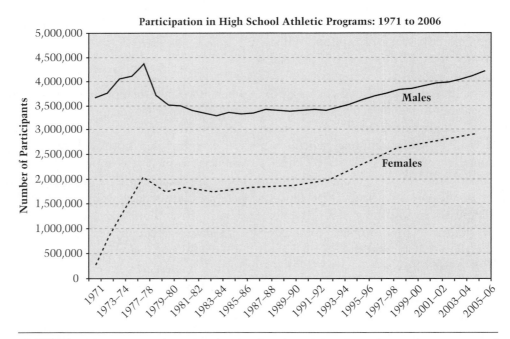

FIGURE 10.9 The number of high school male and female students who participated in team sports between 1971 and 2006. Female participation has dramatically increased. *Source:* Adapted from National Federation of State High School Associations (2006).

risk for obesity and lack of exercise. The relation of television to lack of exercise was especially strong among non-Hispanic Black persons and Mexican Americans. The authors suggest that one reason rates of exercise are low in these ethnic groups is that children do not go outside to play because parents are concerned about the safety of their neighborhood.

Physical activity in childhood is important because these patterns persist into adulthood. Among high school students, participation in athletics has been associated with lower rates of alcohol and drug usage, and these relations are stronger for males than females (Fredricks & Eccles, 2006). In other ways, physical activity is especially important to adolescent girls. First, physical activity has been linked to an improved body image, which may reduce the risk of eating disorders in females (Richards et al., 1990). One study showed that adolescent girls who were physically active and involved in sports were less depressed, in part because they had a more positive view of their bodies (Dishman et al., 2006). Second, physical activity is a deterrent to sexual behavior among girls. A study of college women found that those who participated in team sports during high school engaged in less sexual risk taking and had better sexual and reproductive health (Lehman & Koerner, 2004). A sense of empowerment appeared to explain these relations. Another study of 13- to 16-year-old adolescents showed that girls who participated in athletics were less sexually active, but boys who participated in athletics showed a trend toward greater sexual activity (Miller et al., 1998). The investigators suggested that gender roles might explain the different associations of athletic activity to sexual behavior among boys and girls. For males, athletic behavior is part of the male gender role, as is sexual activity; for females, athletic behavior signifies independence and is inconsistent with the passive nature of the female gender role. Thus girls who participate

in athletics may be better able to resist sexual pressures, which is consistent with the empowerment explanation for the benefits of athletics.

TAKE HOME POINTS

- Women practice better preventive health care than men by taking vitamins, watching their diet, and visiting the physician on a regular basis. Reproductive issues do not clearly account for this sex difference.

- Smoking is the health behavior that can be most strongly tied to the leading causes of death, and smoking contributes greatly to sex differences in mortality.

- Among adults, men smoke more than women but are quitting at higher rates; among children and adolescents, there are fewer sex differences in smoking.

- Lung cancer is the best illustration of how changes in smoking have influenced changes in mortality rates. Men smoke more than women, have higher rates of lung cancer than women, and die younger than women. However, more men also have quit smoking, and women's rates of smoking have not decreased to the extent that men's have, resulting in an increase in lung cancer among women and a reduction in the sex difference in longevity.

- There are a variety of reasons why women may have more difficulty with smoking cessation compared to men: links of smoking to depression, greater physiological addiction in women (a hotly debated issue), and a concern with weight gain after smoking cessation.

- Men drink more than women, but the same amount of alcohol per body weight has more hazardous health consequences for women than men.

- Men use more drugs than women, and the sex difference increases with age during adolescence.

- The family environment and peers influence rates of smoking, alcohol, and drug use among children and adolescents. These environmental factors seem to have stronger links to girls' than boys' behavior.

- The increase in obesity in the United States is now considered an epidemic. Women have higher rates of obesity than men among African Americans and Hispanics, but the same rate among Caucasians.

- There are socioeconomic and cultural explanations for ethnic differences in obesity. Black and Hispanic groups have a lower income, and low income is generally associated with obesity. Culturally, however, being thin is not as valued among the African American as the Caucasian community.

- Physical activity is related to health in general, including obesity. The decline in physical activity is one contributor to the increase in obesity.

- Television, video games, and computers have been linked to both the decline in physical activity and the increase in obesity.

- Boys are more active than girls, but the sex difference has decreased in recent years as athletics have become more available to girls.

MEN'S AND WOMEN'S SOCIAL ROLES

If gender roles contribute to sex differences in health, fewer sex differences should exist when roles are more similar. Leviatan and Cohen (1985) tested this hypothesis by studying men and women in a kibbutz setting where their roles were more equal. A kibbutz is a community in Israel characterized by a collective lifestyle whereby everyone contributes to the welfare of the community. On a kibbutz, there is equal access to health care, all men and women work inside and outside of the home, and all participate in community decisions. However, roles are not perfectly equal even on a kibbutz. It is still true that women tend to take care of household chores more than men, and the kinds of jobs men and women hold are different and sex-stereotypical. Women are more likely to be employed in education and service industries,

whereas men are more likely to be employed in agriculture and industry. Nonetheless, Leviatan and Cohen found that sex differences in life expectancies on the kibbutz were smaller than those in the general population, largely due to an increase in men's life expectancy. Leviatan and Cohen suggest men may have had more social support on the kibbutz and may have been faced with fewer sources of male gender-role strain.

The same hypothesis was tested in a second study of people on a kibbutz (Anson, Levenson, & Bonneh, 1990). A wide array of health outcomes were examined, and sex differences appeared on only two of them—in the direction opposite to that previously observed. Women rated their subjective health as higher than men, and women were less disabled than men. There were no sex differences in psychological distress, physical symptoms, health behaviors, chronic illnesses, restricted activity days, doctor visits, or use of medication. These two studies suggest that when men's and women's social roles are more similar, sex differences in health diminish.

What are some specific features of men's and women's social roles that might be linked to health? Men's social roles include risky behavior, such as working at hazardous jobs and driving. Risk-taking behavior, in general, is part of the male gender role. The female social role includes attending to one's own health concerns. However, the female gender role also is associated with taking care of others, which could have negative implications for health. In this next section, I review some aspects of the male and female social roles, including gender-related traits, that have implications for health.

Job Characteristics

One social role that men and women occupy is their work role. Men work at more hazardous jobs compared to women. According to the Bureau of Labor Statistics (2005), only 7% of job-related fatalities reported in 2005 were women, despite the fact that women comprise 46% of the workforce. The sex difference in fatalities likely reflects men working in riskier jobs than women. Because men are more likely than women to be employed in manual labor positions, men are also more likely to sustain physical injuries in the form of accidents at work. Men, especially Black men, are more likely to be exposed to hazardous substances at work, such as asbestos that has been linked to lung cancer (Waldron, 1995). A study of adults in England and Wales found that the sex difference in life expectancy was smaller for professionals and managerial workers than manual unskilled workers (Donkin, Goldblatt, & Lynch, 2002).

Men's labor at home also includes more risks than women's labor at home. For example, men are more likely to be the ones who repair electrical problems and climb on the roof to fix a leak.

Driving

In 2005, 43,443 people were killed in motor vehicle accidents, which is a decline since the peak of 54,589 in 1972 (U.S. Department of Transportation, 2005b). The decline in motor vehicle accidents and motor vehicle fatalities has been linked to improved safety measures, including the use of seat belts and lower rates of drinking and driving.

Driving is part of men's social role. Men drive more than women, and when men and women are together, the man typically drives the car. Men drive faster and take more risks while driving. Thus it is not surprising that men have 3 times the rate of fatal automobile accidents as women (U.S. Department of Transportation, 2005b). Women also are more likely than men to wear a seatbelt (83% vs. 77%), although this sex difference has decreased over the past decade, largely due to increased usage among men (U.S. Department of Transportation, 2005a).

One link to motor vehicle fatalities and an explanation for the sex difference in fatalities is alcohol. The percentage of drivers in fatal crashes who had been drinking alcohol has declined from 41% in 1982 to 24% in 2005 (U.S. Department of Transportation, 2005b). The highest rates occur among 21- to 24-year-old drivers. Among fatal crashes, 27% of male drivers and 15% of female drivers were in crashes that involved alcohol.

The sex difference in mortality from motor vehicle accidents has declined over time (U.S. Department of Transportation, 2005b). In 1950, men were 3.4 times as likely as women to die in a motor vehicle accident; in 2005, the figure was 2.3. In 1950, men were 5.8 times as likely as women to die as the driver of a motor vehicle; in 2005, the figure was 3.2. The primary reason for the decrease in the size of the sex difference is a modification of the female gender role: Women increased their rates of driving.

Risky Behavior

Many differences in health can be explained by a single aspect of the male gender role: risk-taking behavior (Waldron, 1997). Men's activities are inherently riskier than women's, and men take more risks than women during these activities. Because of men's risk-taking behavior, men have higher rates of all kinds of accidents compared to women, including driving, work, and recreational (Waldron, 1997). We have seen that men's jobs are more hazardous than those of women. We also have seen that men are more likely to find themselves in the driver's seat of a car and to take more risks when driving. Men also are more likely to engage in risky leisure activities such as downhill skiing, skydiving, and mountain climbing (see Figure 10.10). Men are more likely to drown from swimming and boating; men are more likely to own guns and the greater use of guns contributes to a greater number of fatal gun accidents (Waldron, 1995). Until recently, only men participated in the armed services, risking death from combat. Men engage in riskier sexual

FIGURE 10.10   Men have riskier leisure activities compared to women.

behavior than women, in terms of inconsistent condom use and sex with multiple partners (Beadnell et al., 2005). See Sidebar 10.3 for a discussion of this issue.

A number of studies have been conducted on risk-taking behaviors. In a study of high school and college students, men reported being more likely than women to engage in risky behavior, such as jumping off a moving vehicle (Langhinrichsen-Rohling et al., 1998). A meta-analysis of 150 risk-taking behavior studies revealed that men were higher risk takers than women ($d = .13$; Byrnes, Miller, & Schafer, 1999). This effect held across a range of behaviors that included sex, drinking, using drugs,

SIDEBAR 10.3: *Condom Use*

Although there is no known cure for AIDS, there are prevention strategies. Condoms limit the spread of HIV through sexual transmission (Hein, 1998). The percentage of women who had ever had a male partner use a condom increased from 52% in 1980 to 90% in 2002 (Mosher et al., 2004). Among sexually active teens ages 15 to 19, 45% reported regular use of condoms. However, condom usage is not consistent. In a national representative survey of heterosexuals, only 17% of those with multiple sexual partners reported they always used a condom (Catania et al., 1992).

Although the prevention effort for men and women is the same (i.e., using a condom), the behavior is different. Prevention efforts targeted toward men aim at getting men to wear condoms. Prevention efforts targeted toward women aim at women getting men to wear condoms. The nature of male and female roles may make the behavior required of women more difficult. Women are concerned that having a condom available means they will be perceived as promiscuous (Leary, Tchividjian, & Kraxberger, 1994) and that asking a partner to use a condom raises issues of trust and fidelity (Williams et al., 2001). A study of Mexican adolescents revealed that both men and women believe that the male should initiate condom use (Martinez-Donate et al., 2004). On average, women have less power in their relationships compared to men, making them less assertive in sexual matters. Women are also socialized to be the more passive sexual partner. These aspects of the female gender role may make it more difficult for women to ensure their partner uses a condom. Only 5% to 26% of women report always using a condom during sexual intercourse (Morokoff, Harlow, & Quina, 1995). Women who possess more traditional gender roles may find it especially difficult to get their partner to use a condom. In a study that involved focus groups with Latina women, issues revolving around gender roles, status, and power arose in 71% of the groups (Amaro & Gornemann, 1992). Women suggested that feelings of powerlessness kept them from influencing their partners to use condoms. A focus group study with Haitian men and women showed that the use of condoms is associated with HIV and infidelity (Ulin, Cayemittes, & Metellus, 1993). Although men were more willing to use condoms with younger girls to prevent pregnancy, men did not believe women who were wives or in long-term relationships had the right to ask a man to use a condom. Women are expected to overlook extramarital behavior in husbands. It is men's rather than women's attitudes toward condom usage that predicts whether condoms are used (Sheeran, Abraham, & Orbell, 1999).

Traditional roles may also prevent men from using condoms. In a study of adolescent males, those who scored high in masculine ideology (i.e., endorsed traditional beliefs about the male role) had a greater number of sexual partners, had negative attitudes toward the use of condoms, and were less likely to wear condoms (Pleck et al., 1993). Traditional beliefs about male and female roles are also associated with risky beliefs about condoms, such as an association of condom use with less enjoyment of sex (Shearer et al., 2005). Gay men may also be concerned about maintaining a masculine self-image and fail to use condoms (Leary et al., 1994). Using a condom implies safety and therefore, less masculinity because it is masculine to take risks.

risky driving, risky physical activities, and gambling. The authors also found that the size of the sex difference had decreased over time. Men score higher than women on sensation seeking (Zuckerman, 1994), which is the tendency to seek novel and stimulating experiences. Sensation seeking is associated with a number of risky health behaviors among adolescents, such as drinking alcohol, smoking, and having a greater number of sexual partners (Kraft & Rise, 1994). Try Do Gender 10.5 to see if there are sex differences in risky leisure activities

DO GENDER 10.5
Risky Leisure Activities

Develop a list of leisure activities that vary in their level of risk. Ask a group of men and women if they have ever engaged in the activity and, if so, how often. You might also ask respondents how willing they would be to engage in each activity. Also administer a measure of gender roles. Agency, communion, unmitigated agency, and traditional gender-role attitudes are good candidates.

Is there a sex difference in willingness to engage in risky activities? Is there a sex difference in having engaged in risky activities? Are differences in risky behavior linked to gender roles?

among your peers and if risky activities can be linked to gender roles.

Participation in violent sports is a risky behavior consistent with the traditional male gender role. Masculinity is not only connected to sports but also to playing sports while in pain or while injured (White, Young, & McTeer, 1995). Playing through pain and injury in sports is not only tolerated but also encouraged among men. Playing while injured is a sign of emotional toughness and physical strength; in fact, taking care of oneself after an injury is viewed as weak behavior that undermines masculinity. The athlete who continues to play while injured is afforded high status.

Risk-taking behavior has been evaluated in children by examining accidents and injuries. Boys sustain more injuries than girls, and boys' injuries are more severe than those of girls (Rosen & Peterson, 1990). Interestingly, children by the age of 6 perceive girls as more vulnerable to injury than boys (Morrongiello, Midgett, & Stanton, 2000). When children were shown pictures of a boy or a girl engaged in varying degrees of risky behavior on a swing set or a bike, children said girls were more likely than boys to get injured. This perception may lead girls to be more cautious than boys.

One reason boys are more likely to be injured than girls may be that boys are encouraged to take greater risks than girls. In one study, parents were shown a video of children on a playground and asked what they would say (Morrongiello & Dawber, 2000). Mothers of girls were more likely to warn of injury risk and were more likely to intervene and to do so quickly. In another study, parents were observed teaching their 2- to 4-year-old children how to climb down a fire pole (Morrongiello & Dawber, 1999). Both mothers and fathers provided boys with more instructive information than girls, less physical assistance than girls, and were more likely to reject boys' requests for physical assistance. Thus parents are more likely to encourage risk-taking behavior in boys.

Concerns with Health

So far, we have discussed a number of characteristics of the male gender role that might account for men's higher mortality rates: hazardous jobs, driving, and risky behavior in general. What aspects of the female gender role relate to women's lower mortality rates and higher morbidity rates? One aspect of the female gender role that may be related to both is women's concern with health (Waldron, 1997). More frequent visits to the physician might be counted as higher morbidity, but—if effective—could reduce mortality.

Studies have shown that women are more interested than men in health matters (Green & Pope, 1999). For example, women report they think about health and read about health in newspapers and magazines more often than men do. Women are designated as the persons responsible for the family's health care. However, it is not the case that women's concerns with health lead them to engage in all health-promoting behaviors; for example, women exercise less than men and have been more reluctant than men to quit smoking.

By contrast, men are typically unconcerned with health matters and associate preventive health care with undermining masculinity (Courtenay, 2000a). In fact, men may brag about not having seen a doctor, about not taking time off from work when sick, and about engaging in risky activities that undermine health. At times, there can be serious health consequences for adhering to the male gender role. For example, men are less likely to use sunscreen than women and more likely than women to get skin cancer.

Nurturant Roles

One aspect of the female gender role poses a risk to women's health and may account for some of women's higher morbidity rates compared to men: women's nurturant role (see Figure 10.11). Women are socialized to take care of others, and taking care of others has its costs. Although there are obvious health benefits to involvement in social networks, reviewed in detail in Chapter 11, there is a downside to such involvement for women. For one, social networks increase exposure to infectious disease; thus women may sustain more minor illnesses than men, such as colds and flu, because they spend more time around people, in particular children, compared to men.

A specific hypothesis about how women's involvement in relationships could be hazardous to their health is the **nurturant role hypothesis**

FIGURE 10.11 Women traditionally hold more nurturant roles than men.

(Gove, 1984; Gove & Hughes, 1979). According to the nurturant role hypothesis, women's roles require them to attend to the needs of others, and taking care of others interferes with taking care of oneself. First, the nurturant role leads to caretaking behavior, which results in fatigue and vulnerability to illness. Second, the nurturant role leads to greater exposure to communicable diseases. Finally, once sick, the nurturant role prevents one from taking care of oneself.

In a classic study, Gove and Hughes (1979) found that women suffered greater health problems than men due to their nurturant roles. Specifically, women were more likely than men to say they did not get enough sleep and did not eat properly when taking care of others. Women also reported they were more likely to catch others' illnesses and did not take care of themselves when they were ill (i.e., continued with chores, did not get proper rest). Married women suffered more of these problems than married men, and the differences were even greater when the people had children. This is because married women, especially mothers, have greater nurturant role obligations. Among married couples without children, 14% of men and 21% of women said they were unable to rest when they were sick; among married couples with children, 16% of men and 44% of women said they were unable to rest when they were sick. Among unmarried individuals who lived alone, there were no sex differences in these nurturant role problems. Nurturant role problems, in particular the inability to rest when ill, were associated with poor physical health and accounted for most of the sex differences in physical health.

The nurturant role hypothesis has not gone without criticism. For example, as you will see in Chapter 11, married women are healthier than single women, which would seem to contradict the nurturant role hypothesis because married women have more nurturant roles. Women with seemingly more role obligations, such as women who work and women who have children, report less illness and less disability.

How can these contradictory ideas be reconciled? Are nurturant roles related to less illness or more illness among women? One possibility is that nurturant roles lead to more illness but also to less *reporting* of illness. People who have more nurturant role responsibilities may be less able to restrict activities and seek health care. Thus the nurturant role hypothesis is a viable explanation for women's higher rates of morbidity compared to men. As you will see in Chapter 11, marriage and social networks confer fewer health benefits to women than to men, and one reason is there are health costs to involvement in social networks for women.

Gender-Related Traits

The last social role explanation for sex differences in morbidity and mortality involves gender-related traits. Gender-related traits include agency, unmitigated agency, communion, and unmitigated communion. These traits could be linked to some of the previously mentioned social role explanations. For example, unmitigated agency is related to feelings of superiority and invulnerability, which would promote risky behavior, whereas unmitigated communion would be related to having overly nurturant roles.

A body of research has linked gender-related traits to health (Helgeson, 1994c). Although the hope was that androgyny, the combination of agency and communion, would be the best predictor of health, research has shown that agency alone is the best predictor of psychological well-being. Overall, agency has been associated with greater perceived health, fewer physical symptoms, reduced psychological distress, reduced psychiatric problems, and better physical health (Ghaed & Gallo, 2006; Helgeson, 1994c). Agency also has been linked to a variety of good health practices, including physical activity, healthy eating, and good dental hygiene (Danoff-Burg, Mosher, & Grant, 2006). By contrast, communion is typically unrelated to psychological or physical health (Ghaed & Gallo, 2006; Helgeson, 1994c). Thus, some of men's lower morbidity rates compared to women may be explained by the male gender-related trait of agency, but women's higher morbidity rates cannot be linked to the female gender-related trait of communion.

The distinctions between agency and unmitigated agency and between communion and unmitigated communion are important. In my dissertation research with survivors of a first heart attack, I distinguished agency from unmitigated agency and found that unmitigated agency was associated with more severe heart attacks, whereas agency was associated with less severe heart attacks (Helgeson, 1990). Unmitigated agency has been associated with reckless driving, substance use, binge eating, and psychological distress (Danoff-Burg et al., 2006; Ghaed & Gallo, 2006). Traditional masculinity in the form of masculine occupational preferences predicted increased mortality over 50 years later in a study of gifted children (Lippa, Martin, & Friedman, 2000). Although communion is typically unrelated to health, unmitigated communion is associated with poor health, especially greater psychological distress, and poor health behavior (Gahed & Gallo, 2006; Helgeson, 1994c; Helgeson & Fritz, 1996, 1998).

TAKE HOME POINTS

- When men's and women's social roles become more equal, sex differences in health diminish.

- One reason for men's higher mortality rates compared to women—especially from accidents—is men's greater job hazards, greater driving, and greater risk-taking behavior. Men take greater risks during work, driving, and leisure activities. And, risk-taking behavior is encouraged among males.

- One reason for women's greater morbidity rates compared to men is that women are more concerned with health and more likely to seek the care of a physician.

- A second reason for women's greater morbidity rates compared to men is that women are socialized to take care of others—or to have nurturant roles. Nurturant roles lead to exposure to illness, to fatigue, and to taking care of others instead of the self.

- Among the gender-related traits, agency is related to good health behavior and less psychological distress, whereas unmitigated agency is related to risk-taking behavior. Communion is unrelated to health, but unmitigated communion is related to poor health behavior and psychological distress, possibly due to nurturant roles.

SYMPTOM PERCEPTION

One explanation of why women suffer greater morbidity compared to men is that women are more sensitive to changes within their body. That is, women have a lower threshold for noticing and reporting symptoms.

Evidence

One study concluded that, if anything, women underreport their symptoms (Macintyre, Ford, & Hunt, 1999). When men and women are asked a general question as to whether they have any long-standing illness or disability, they give similar responses; that is, an equal number of men and women admit to a condition. The illnesses reported are also similar in severity. However, when men and women are provided with a list of conditions and asked if they have any of these, women report more conditions. In other words, women need more prompting than men to report an illness. This suggests that women underreport illness when asked open-ended questions.

Research also has directly challenged the idea that women are more in touch with their bodies compared to men. Recall the research discussed in Chapter 7 about the basis of men's and women's emotions. Those studies (Cox et al., 1985; Pennebaker & Watson, 1988) showed that men were more accurate in predicting their physiological state when environmental cues were removed from the situation. That line of research would suggest men are more sensitive than women to symptoms.

Thus no hard evidence indicates that women are more able than men to perceive symptoms. However, it is important, though difficult, to distinguish symptom perception from symptom reporting. Women may be more likely to report a symptom once it is perceived. During childhood, girls are socialized to report symptoms and boys are socialized to withhold symptoms. A study of fourth- and fifth-graders showed that boys and girls liked a hypothetical other boy and girl equally if they had stomach symptoms with evidence of a disease, but girls liked the boy less than the girl who had stomach symptoms without any evidence of disease (Guite et al., 2000). Symptoms in the absence of disease may be viewed as a sign of emotional distress—and expressions of distress are less accepted in males than females.

One area of research aimed at addressing symptom perception is pain research. There are sex differences in pain perception (Fillingim, 2003). The sex differences are most clear in response to experimentally induced pain. In laboratory studies, a pain stimulus is applied to the respondent at a very low level, and intensity is gradually increased. These studies tend to show that women have lower thresholds of pain, report greater intensity of pain, have lower tolerance levels for pain, and are better able to discriminate different levels of pain. Another piece of evidence that pain is linked to sex is the fact that so many pain disorders are more prevalent in women than men—fibromyalgia, rheumatoid arthritis, temporomandibular disorder, and migraines (LeResche, 2000). When men and women present with these disorders, women often report more severe pain than men (Fillingim, 2003). Even among adolescents (ages 11 to 19), a study of those who sought treatment for pain revealed that females reported more severe pain than males but did not report more depression or disability than males (Keogh & Eccleston, 2006).

Explanations

Although sex differences in pain perception are far from clear, this has not stopped investigators from speculating on the cause of differences. One reason biological factors have been thought to play a role in sex differences in pain perceptions is that women are more responsive than men to some classes of painkillers. In one study, analgesics were more effective in reducing pain from wisdom teeth removal among women than men (Gear et al., 1999). Men and women were randomly assigned to receive either a placebo or an analgesic. There was no sex difference in pain reports among patients who received the placebo, but men reported greater pain than women when receiving some of the analgesics. Sex differences in pain also have been linked to different parts of the brain being activated in men and women (Derbyshire et al., 2002). The fact that women are more likely to suffer from painful disorders is also evidence for a biological basis to the sex difference in pain.

Psychological factors also have been linked to sex differences in pain. There appear to be sex differences in coping with pain. Whereas men are more likely than women to try to distract themselves from pain, women are more likely than men to seek support when in pain (Keogh & Eccleston, 2006). Women also are more likely than men to catastrophize or magnify the problem in response to pain, and catastrophic thinking (i.e., feeling helpless, pessimistic) has accounted for some sex differences in pain reports (Edwards et al., 2004; Keogh & Eccleston, 2006). In a laboratory study using the cold pressor test (putting hand in ice water), women's lower self-efficacy beliefs accounted for the sex difference in pain (Jackson et al., 2002). Among those who suffer from painful disorders, anxiety seems to be more strongly related to pain in men than women, and treatment is more effective among anxious men than anxious women (Edwards, Augustson, & Fillingim, 2003; Robinson et al., 2005).

Social factors, too, may influence reports of pain. Family members who experience and frequently express pain may serve as "pain models" for children. In one study, women reported a greater number of pain models than men, and pain models were associated with reports of greater pain symptoms (Koutantji, Pearce, & Oakley, 1998). Reports of pain are also vulnerable to the demand characteristics of the situation. In one study, the sex of the experimenter was manipulated and influenced pain reports (Levine & de Simone, 1991). Men reported less pain in response to the cold pressor test (i.e., putting a hand in ice water) when the experimenter was an attractive female rather than an attractive male. Women reported similar amounts of pain to male and female experimenters. In fact, women tended to report more pain to male than to female experimenters. Thus men were less likely and women were more likely to admit pain when gender was made salient, that is, when the experimenter was of the other sex.

Gender roles may influence pain reports. The male gender role is associated with strength and emotional inhibition, both of which are consistent with minimizing reports of pain. During childhood, boys learn they are to be tough and not admit pain. We applaud the male athlete who "plays through the pain." Aspects of the male gender role and sex stereotypic beliefs about pain have been linked to higher pain thresholds and pain tolerance among men (Wise et al., 2002). One study showed that gender stereotypes regarding men's and women's willingness to express pain (i.e., the idea that men are less willing than women) accounted for women's greater reports of pain compared to men in response to a laboratory pain stimulus (Robinson et al., 2004). Gender roles also may explain why women's pain reports are associated with their facial expressions of pain, whereas men's are not (Kunz, Gruber, & Lautenbacher, 2006). The male gender role encourages the inhibition of emotion, whereas the female gender role encourages the expression of emotion.

TAKE HOME POINTS

- There is no evidence that women suffer greater morbidity than men because they over-report symptoms or are in greater touch with their body compared to men.

- One symptom that is more common among women than men is pain. Women have a lower threshold and tolerance for pain, report more pain, report more severe pain, and suffer from more painful disorders than men.

- Explanations for sex differences in pain include biology, psychological factors such as coping, and social factors, such as gender-role norms.

ILLNESS BEHAVIOR

Illness behavior is often referred to as adopting the "sick role," or labeling a symptom as illness and responding to it. Sick role behavior includes restricting activities, getting bed rest, taking medication, and seeking the help of health care professionals. These are all activities that women do more than men.

Implications for Morbidity

These sick role behaviors are frequently included in indexes of morbidity. Thus one reason women have higher rates of morbidity compared to men is that women are more likely to adopt the sick role (Nathanson, 1978). The **sick role hypothesis** suggests sex differences in medical care utilization are due to women's greater tendency to adopt the sick role. If men and women are equally ill, but women are more likely to seek help for symptoms, sex differences in morbidity are really artifactual. One study showed that women were more likely than men to have restricted their activities for at least half of a day in response to headache pain (14% vs. 8%; Celentano, Linet, & Stewart, 1990). Even when the severity of pain was taken into consideration, the sex difference in activity restriction remained. The authors argue it is more socially acceptable for women than men to reduce their activities when ill.

One reason women may be more willing to adopt the sick role is that women have fewer **fixed role obligations** than men (Marcus & Seeman, 1981). A fixed role is one that is structured and difficult to reschedule (Gove, 1984). Men are likely to have two fixed roles: worker and head of household. Performance in these roles is visible. Historically, women were likely to have only one role, that of housewife, a role relatively unstructured and invisible. A housewife has few deadlines and can easily put chores off from one day to the next; thus women have fewer constraints on their time and are freer to restrict their activities and take care of themselves when ill. In other words, women's social role can accommodate illness. Support for this idea came from a study that showed adopting the sick role (e.g., restricted activity days, days in bed, taking medication, visiting a doctor) was associated with symptoms among women but not among men (Gijsbers van Wijk et al., 1999). The authors concluded that women's roles are more flexible, allowing them to respond to symptoms. One tenet of the fixed role obligations hypothesis is that men's fixed roles keep them task focused, whereas women's lack of fixed roles allows them time to ruminate about their problems. This would explain why women perceive their health as worse than men and why women report more symptoms than men.

In a test of the fixed role hypothesis, Marcus and Seeman (1981) examined the relation of role obligations to health problems. Fixed role obligations were measured in terms of financial responsibility (how much the person contributes to family income), status as head of household, and employment status. They found that men had greater fixed role obligations than women, and women had greater restricted activity days and more chronic illnesses than men. In addition, fixed role obligations were associated with fewer restricted activity days and fewer chronic illnesses. Fixed role obligations accounted for the sex differences in restricted activity days, suggesting women had more restricted activities than men because they had fewer fixed roles. One interpretation of this study is that men's higher number of fixed roles prevented them from adopting the sick role. However, it also is possible that good health allowed men to have more fixed roles. Because the study is correlational, the causal relation between fixed roles and health cannot be determined.

Other research findings are consistent with the fixed role hypothesis. In one study, sex differences in physician visits were reduced when fixed roles (employment status and contribution to family income) were taken into consideration (Marcus & Siegel, 1982). Men were less likely than women to visit physicians, possibly because they were employed and their jobs contributed substantially to the household income. The finding that unemployed people report greater physical and psychological distress is consistent with the fixed role obligations hypothesis (Klonoff & Landrine, 1992).

Today, however, it is not the case that men necessarily have more fixed roles than women. The implication of the fixed role hypothesis is that women who have a large number of role obligations, such as women with children or women who work, would be less likely to adopt the sick role. Are changes in women's roles associated with changes in their health? If women now have more fixed roles, there should be fewer sex differences in morbidity. This hypothesis was tested by examining whether sex differences in morbidity changed as women's roles changed in Denmark, Finland, Norway, and Sweden (Haavio-Mannila, 1986). Consistent with the fixed role hypothesis, women had higher morbidity rates than men in countries where a greater proportion of women were staying at home. Morbidity was measured in terms of illness rates and hospitalization rates. In addition, sex differences in morbidity were larger during periods of history when a greater proportion of women stayed at home. It may be that women who stay home have fewer fixed roles and are thus able to take on the sick role. However, it also is possible that women with fewer roles are less healthy.

Illness behavior may be encouraged in women and discouraged in men. Boys become socialized not to complain about illness and not to seek help for illness or injury. Who encourages these different responses to illness? Parents are an obvious choice. Walker and Zeman (1992) found that girls were more likely than boys to say that parents encouraged illness behaviors, such as missing school and taking medication. The parents, however, reported that they encouraged these behaviors equally in sons and daughters. In a study of 3rd- through 12th-graders, females were more likely than males to say their family thought and talked about health matters (Cohen, Brownell, & Felix, 1990).

Implications for Mortality

Just as women's illness behaviors may account for their greater morbidity compared to men, these same illness behaviors may account for women's longer life span. Perhaps women respond to acute symptoms of illness more quickly, which makes it appear at a given point in time that women are sicker than men. However, women's early response to symptoms could prevent a minor illness from developing into a more serious one.

Once a symptom is perceived, is there evidence that men and women respond to the symptom differently? Help-seeking behavior is inconsistent with the male gender role; admitting illness may be construed as admitting weakness or vulnerability. Thus, men may be less likely to admit they are ill.

Studies show that there are some similarities and some differences in how men and women respond to symptoms. One study found that women reported more physical symptoms than men did, but that men and women were equally likely to have visited a physician in the prior month in response to each symptom (Wyke, Hunt, & Ford, 1998). However, a daily diary study of elderly people (ages 62 through 94) found that women were more likely than men to take action in response to symptoms they experienced over 2 weeks by seeking the attention of medical professionals, by restricting activities, or by self-medication (Rakowski et al., 1988). In addition, a study of people with headache pain showed that women were more likely than men to have consulted a doctor about the pain in the prior year (Celentano et al., 1990).

One way to reconcile these contradictory findings is to take into consideration the severity of the symptom. Research suggests that men's and women's help-seeking responses are more similar when symptoms are severe. Women are more likely than men to visit the doctor for minor conditions, but there are no sex differences in visits to the doctor for serious illness (Dracup et al., 1995; Waldron, 1995, 1997). Women may visit the physician more frequently than men for minor symptoms because they have a lower tolerance for symptoms or feel more comfortable seeking help for minor illness. It is not clear whether men or women delay longer before seeking help for symptoms of a serious illness. Studies of people who have had heart attacks find there is a tendency for women to delay longer than men before seeking help for symptoms (Dracup et al., 1995; Moscucci et al., 2004). By contrast, men appear to delay longer

DO GENDER 10.6
Responses to Symptoms

Develop a list of responses to illness. Your list should include visiting a physician, taking medication, and restricting activities. Ask 10 men and 10 women to recall the last time they were ill and have them indicate how they responded to their illness by checking the responses that apply from your list. Also, ask them to state the nature of the illness or injury so you can determine its severity. Do men and women respond to illness in similar ways? Does it depend on the severity of the illness or symptom?

than women before seeking help for symptoms of cancer (Evans et al., 2005). The findings from both of these studies may be explained by men's and women's lack of knowledge about specific diseases. Women may associate heart disease with being male and be less sensitive to heart disease symptoms. The study of people with cancer showed that men were less knowledgeable than women about cancer and its warning signs. Find out if your male and female peers respond similarly to symptoms in Do Gender 10.6.

TAKE HOME POINTS

- One reason that women have higher morbidity rates than men is that women are more likely than men to adopt the sick role.

- Women are more likely to adopt the sick role because illness is more inconsistent with the male than the female gender role and because women's traditional social roles are more flexible than those of men; in other words, women have fewer "fixed role" obligations which provides them with time to take care of themselves and seek help for symptoms.

- Women's lower mortality rates compared to those of men could be explained by women seeking help for symptoms,

which may keep a minor illness from developing into a serious one.

- The evidence that men and women respond differently to symptoms, however, is contradictory. Women may be more likely than men to respond to minor symptoms, but there are fewer sex differences in response to severe symptoms. There is not a consistent sex difference in the time it takes to seek help for symptoms of serious disease, such as cancer and heart disease.

CONCLUSIONS

I have reviewed a number of classes of explanations for sex differences in morbidity and mortality. Which has the greatest explanatory power? A number of investigators have reviewed the literature and compared different classes of explanations. Over two decades ago, Verbrugge (1985) came to the conclusion that sex differences in health behaviors are a major—if not the major—cause of sex differences in mortality. Courtenay (2000b) certainly agrees; he compiled a list of 30 behaviors—ranging from diet, sleep, and substance abuse to weapon use—that are linked to men's greater mortality than women.

Health behaviors are limited in their ability to explain sex differences in morbidity (Verbrugge, 1989). Men have worse health behaviors than women, yet women have higher morbidity rates. When health behaviors are taken into consideration, sex differences in morbidity actually increase (Verbrugge, 1985). Health behaviors also cannot account in total for the sex difference in mortality. Men may smoke and drink more than women, but women exercise less and have a greater incidence of obesity than men.

It may be that different classes of explanations affect men's and women's health. Denton and Walters (1999) argue that health behaviors play a greater role in men's health, whereas social structural factors play a greater role in women's health. In terms of subjective health status and physical functioning, behavioral factors, such as smoking and drinking, contribute to men's poor health. Social structural factors, such as support from network members and caretaking responsibilities, contribute to women's health. Support is an advantage, whereas caretaking responsibilities are a disadvantage for women. Thus the class of explanations that describe men's health and women's health may differ.

SUMMARY

Men have higher mortality rates than women, but women have higher morbidity rates than men. In this chapter, I reviewed the different classes of explanations for this paradox. Although biological factors certainly contribute to health, biology alone cannot explain the increase in the size of the sex difference in life expectancy that occurred over the 20th century and the changes in the size of the sex difference in life expectancy that have occurred more recently. SES factors contribute to health but are unable to explain sex differences in health. Sex differences in morbidity may be overestimated to the extent that women report on men's health and to the extent that physicians overdiagnose psychiatric problems in women.

A major contributor to sex differences in morbidity and mortality is health behavior. Women engage in more preventive health care compared to men. Although this difference should theoretically lead to women's lower mortality rates, no evidence supports this conjecture. Instead, women's preventive behavior gets counted as physician visits in indexes of morbidity. Smoking is a major contributor to mortality. That men smoke more than women accounts for a portion of the sex difference in mortality as well as the sex difference in specific diseases (e.g., coronary heart disease, lung cancer). That women have increased their rates of smoking during the last half of the 20th century accounts for the fact that the sex difference in life expectancy has narrowed. Men also have higher rates of alcohol and drug usage compared to women. All three risk factors for early mortality (smoking, alcohol, and drugs) are interrelated and associated with other problems, such as depression.

Other health behaviors pose greater risks to women's than men's health: obesity and lack of exercise. More women than men are obese in the United States, and the sex difference is particularly striking among Blacks and Hispanics. Women also exercise less than men, although more girls are becoming involved in sports during childhood.

Another explanation for sex differences in mortality and morbidity focused on the contribution of men's and women's social roles. One of men's social roles is working outside the home, and men are exposed to more hazards at work compared to women. It also is men's social role to drive: Men drive more than women, drive less safely, and are involved in more driving accidents. In general, many of the behaviors that pose dangers for men's health can be conceptualized as general risk-taking behavior. Men's work, home, and leisure activities are riskier than those of women, which undoubtedly contributes to men's higher death rates from accidents.

The female social role has the advantage of making women more concerned with health matters, but the disadvantage of making women the caretakers of other people's health. The nurturant role exposes women to more illness, is a source of fatigue among women, making them more susceptible to illness, and prevents women from taking care of themselves when they are ill.

Other explanations for sex differences in morbidity have to do with women being more sensitive than men to symptoms, more likely to enact the sick role, and more likely to seek medical care. Women appear to have a lower threshold and tolerance for pain in experimental studies of pain perception. The explanation for this sex difference is not clear. It does not appear that women are more sensitive than men to changes within their bodies. However, women are more likely to respond to symptoms by restricting their activities and taking care of themselves, in other words, enacting the sick role. One explanation for this sex difference is that women have fewer fixed role obligations than men, and fewer role obligations are associated with a greater willingness to respond to health problems. Women use health services more frequently than men, but the sex difference is limited to minor symptoms. In the case of serious illness, there is less evidence that either men or women are more likely to seek the attention of a health care professional.

Taken collectively, different explanations are more and less relevant to men and women. A few health behaviors explain a good portion of men's higher mortality rates compared to women. These health behaviors can be construed in terms of a larger framework reflecting men's risk-taking behavior. Women's higher morbidity rates are more likely to reflect women's social roles than their health behaviors.

DISCUSSION QUESTIONS

1. How do sex and race influence the leading causes of death?
2. When examining the relation of SES to health, whose SES should be used? That of the husband? The wife? Both? Why? What are the advantages and disadvantages?
3. Under what conditions do you believe physicians are more or less likely to make a similar diagnosis in a male and a female who present with the same symptoms?
4. In what ways are men and women treated differently for heart disease? Why? Is the differential treatment justified?
5. Discuss how sex differences in smoking, drinking alcohol, and drug usage have changed over time.
6. Given our culture's increasing health consciousness, in particular, the emphasis on diet and exercise, why do you think rates of obesity have increased?
7. Which health behaviors are more strongly related to health in men, and which are more strongly related to health in women?
8. In what ways are men's behaviors riskier than women's? What are the specific health implications?
9. Why are nurturant roles hazardous to health?
10. Discuss how to determine if men and women actually perceive symptoms differently.
11. In what ways are men's and women's responses to illness similar and different?

SUGGESTED READING

Courtenay, W. H. (2000a). Constructions of masculinity and their influence on men's well-being. A theory of gender and health. *Social Science and Medicine, 50,* 1385–1401.

Fillingim, R. B. (2000). *Sex, gender, and pain* (Vol. 17). Seattle: IASP Press.

(Classic) Gove, W. R., & Hughes, M. (1979). Possible causes of the apparent sex differences in physical health: An empirical investigation. *American Sociological Review, 44,* 126–146.

Helgeson, V. S. (1994c). Relation of agency and communion to well-being: Evidence and potential explanations. *Psychological Bulletin, 116,* 412–428.

Nolen-Hoeksema, S., & Hilt, L. (2006). Possible contributors to the gender differences in alcohol use and problems. *The Journal of General Psychology, 133,* 357–374.

Travis, C. B. (2005). 2004 Carolyn Sherif award address: Heart disease and gender inequity. *Psychology of Women Quarterly, 29,* 15–23.

(Classic) Verbrugge, L. M. (1989). The twain meet: Empirical explanations of sex differences in health and mortality. *Journal of Health and Social Behavior, 30,* 282–304.

KEY TERMS

Android obesity—Extra weight around the abdomen.

Artifact—Confounding variable that leads an effect to appear that does not really exist.

Body mass index (BMI)—Measure of obesity that takes into consideration the ratio of weight to height.

Cardiovascular reactivity—Increase in blood pressure and heart rate that occurs when engaging in a challenging or stressful task.

Chronic illness—Disease or condition characterized by persistent health problems that may be treated or controlled but not cured.

Coronary artery bypass surgery—Treatment for heart disease in which arteries taken from a person's leg or chest are used to bypass blockages in the arteries that supply blood to the heart.

Fixed role obligations—Responsibilities specific to one's defining role that are structured and difficult to reschedule.

Gynoid obesity—Extra weight around the hips.

Health behavior—Any activity that either promotes good health (e.g., preventive health care, exercise, healthy diet) or contributes to bad health (e.g., smoking, alcohol, and drug use).

Illness behavior—Condition of labeling a symptom as illness and responding to it as such; adopting the "sick role."

Morbidity—Presence of illness or disease.

Mortality—Death rate.

Myocardial infarction (MI)—Irreversible injury to the heart muscle; heart attack.

Nurturant role hypothesis—Supposition that women's roles require them to attend to the needs of others, which results in fatigue, exposure to illness, and not taking care of oneself when sick.

Percutaneous transluminal coronary angioplasty (PTCA)—Procedure in which a catheter with a balloon attached to it is inserted into a diseased blood vessel. As the balloon is inflated, the plaque is pressed against the walls of the artery allowing for improved blood flow.

Sick role hypothesis—Suggestion that sex differences in using medical care are due to women's greater tendency than men to adopt the "sick role."

Thrombolytic therapy—Treatment of heart disease employing drugs that dissolve blood clots and reestablish blood flow.

Yentl syndrome—Label given to the idea that men and women receive the same treatment for heart disease once women appear like men.

CHAPTER 11

RELATIONSHIPS AND HEALTH

In 1977, James Lynch wrote *The Broken Heart*. The title was a metaphor for the effects of relationships on health, specifically coronary heart disease. Lynch claimed there are

> few conditions in life that do not involve some type of human contact, and so in one sense it would be remarkable if human contact did not influence our hearts. Like the air we breathe, it envelops every aspect of our lives. A simple visit to your doctor, arguments, reassurance and praise, sexual activity, social gatherings, competitive sports, the loss of a friend or loved one, jealousies, humiliations, human triumphs, the cuddling of a child in your lap, the silent hand-holding between two lovers, the quiet comforting of a dying patient—all these affect the heart. (p. 12)

Lynch noted an association between markers of social isolation (e.g., high mobility) and high mortality rates from heart disease. Since then, numerous studies have demonstrated links between aspects of social relationships and health.

This chapter examines the implications of relationships for men's and women's health. We know the female gender role involves a relationship orientation. Does this mean women benefit more than men from social relationships? Or does men's lack of a relationship orientation make relationships all the more important to their health? In the first part of the chapter, I focus on the implications of a primary social relationship for health: marriage. I focus on marriage because quite a bit of evidence suggests that marriage affects men's and women's health in different ways. I also focus on marriage because it is one of the most important relationships (if not the most important relationship) to men and women. I also explore the health implications of the loss of this relationship through death and relationship dissolution (e.g., divorce). Next, I examine the health implications of the quality of marriage for men's and women's health. One central aspect of quality is how household chores and child care are divided in the family. Thus I describe the division of labor, examine predictors of the division of labor, and discuss the implications of the division of labor for relationship satisfaction and well-being. Relationships also can go awry. I briefly describe the research on domestic abuse and rape and examine their implications for health.

Other relationships also influence health. An important familial relationship is parenthood. I discuss how men and women construe parenthood and describe its effects on their health. In the last section of the chapter, I describe the influence of relationships more generally on health—a body of work referred to as social support.

EFFECTS OF MARRIAGE ON HEALTH

"I now pronounce you man and wife." Those are the words of the traditional marriage ceremony. Historically, marriage for women meant they became defined by their relationship to their husband; marriage for men meant they had someone to take care of the home and the children. Today, however, marriage may have a more similar meaning for men and women: gaining a partner, a person with whom to share one's life. Today, the minister or officiator is more likely to say, "I now pronounce you husband and wife," reflecting the similarity of marriage for men and women.

One characteristic of modern marriage is that it is less likely to last. A 2006 Gallup Poll showed that 30% of adults said that they had been divorced; the rate in 1985 was 23% (Carroll, 2006b). There has been a shift in cultural values toward marriage over the last several decades.

Today, there is a greater emphasis on individual and personal fulfillment, which means people may be less likely to tolerate unsatisfying relationships. There also are greater expectations for relationships: Marriage is expected to provide a source of intimacy, sexuality, and companionship. Thus people have increasing expectations of marriage, and marriage may be less likely to meet those expectations. It is also much easier to dissolve a marriage today than it was 30 years ago, and society is more tolerant of marital breakups.

The divorce rate increased dramatically during the 1960s and 1970s but then leveled off in the 1980s. One reason that divorce rates have stabilized is that men and women wait longer before they marry, and older age at first marriage is less likely to result in divorce (Heaton, 2002). Today, the median age of marriage is 27 for men and 25.5 for women (U.S. Census Bureau, 2005a), although the ages differ somewhat by race (White men 27, women 25; Black men 29, women 29; Asian men 29, women 26; Hispanic men 26, women 24).

The divorce rate varies by race and ethnicity. Nearly half (47%) of Black women's marriages end within 10 years, but the corresponding figures are lower for Whites (32%), Hispanics (34%), and Asians (20%; Bramlett & Mosher, 2002). See Table 11.1 for a list of factors that decrease one's risk of divorce.

The increased divorce rate and the increased tendency to have children outside of marriage have led to a decline in the two-parent family—especially among African Americans. In 2005, 55% of Black children lived only with their mothers compared to 29% of Hispanic children and 22% of non-Hispanic White children (U.S. Census Bureau, 2006a). In 2006, nearly twice as many Black adults reported being raised primarily by their mothers than White adults (29% versus 15%; Saad, 2006b).

TABLE 11.1   Factors that Protect Against Divorce During the First 10 Years of Marriage

- higher income
- having a baby 7 months or more after marriage (as compared to before marriage)
- at least age 25 at marriage
- parents married (rather than divorced)
- religious affiliation
- higher education

Source: Bramlett and Mosher (2002).

The marriage rate also has declined in recent years, in part due to increased cohabitation and in part due to people waiting longer before getting married. In 2005, 55% of males and 52% of females over 15 in the United States were married (U.S. Census Bureau, 2006b), although the rate was much lower among Blacks (38% male, 30% female) than Whites (58% male, 55% female). By age 30, 81% of White people, 77% of Hispanic people, and 77% of Asian people have married, compared to 52% of Black people (Bramlett & Mosher, 2002). Most adolescents say that they expect to marry one day, although African American boys and girls have lower expectations than Whites and Mexican Americans (Crissey, 2005). The percentage of the population marrying has decreased while the percentage of people who are divorced and never married has increased. In 1970, 28% of men and 22% of women over 15 years old were never married. The corresponding figures in 2005 were 33% of men and 26% of women (U.S. Census Bureau, 2006b).

Despite the decline in marriage rates and increase in divorce rates, the majority of people in the population continue to opt for marriage. What do men and women get out of marriage? And, do they benefit equally?

Evidence

In 1957, Hannah Lees wrote the book *How to Help Your Husband Stay Alive*. She expressed concern over the fact that men die younger than women and the sex difference in longevity was widening. She argued it was the duty of women to help lengthen the life span of their husband. Lees pointed out "a hundred different ways" a woman could contribute to a man's happiness and asked, "What is it men need in their marriages that not enough women are giving them today?" Lees said wives should provide support to husbands, make husbands' lives easier, help husbands cope with the pressures and frustrations they face in the working world, provide opportunities for husbands to relax, and help husbands take care of their health.

Lees (1957) may have been too critical of wives. It turns out that women do help men live longer. Numerous studies have shown that being married is advantageous to psychological and physical health and that men reap greater rewards from marriage than women do. The importance of marriage to men was best articulated by Bernard in 1972. He said the proportion of men who are married in a society is a social indicator of how the society is operating, just as the unemployment rate is an economic indicator of how the society is operating.

The greater health benefits of marriage for men compared to women come from large epidemiological studies in which men's and women's marital status and health status are measured and then followed for many years. In three such studies, men who were married were less likely to die than men who were unmarried over the 9 to 15 years they were followed (Berkman & Syme, 1979; House, Robbins, & Metzner, 1982; Shye et al., 1995). Marital status did not predict mortality among women in any of these studies. A recent 8-year longitudinal study showed that never-married persons had a 158% increase in mortality compared to married persons, but the difference between the two groups was larger for men than women (Kaplan & Kronick, 2006). Never-married men had especially high rates of mortality from infectious disease and accidents if young and heart disease if older. Marriage not only affects mortality but also affects overall mental health. A study of adults in Japan showed that married people had less depression than unmarried people, but the difference was greater for men than women (Inaba et al., 2005). Taken collectively, across a wide array of indices of well-being, marriage is more beneficial to men than women.

Cross-cultural research supports the idea that marriage confers greater benefits to men's than women's health. In a study of 17 countries (e.g., France, Netherlands, Japan, Norway, Australia), marriage was associated with decreased loneliness and greater perceived health in 16 of the nations (Stack, 1998b). Overall, these effects were stronger for men than women. Most of these nations were Western cultures, however. In a study that compared the health benefits of marriage in India and the United States, marriage was associated with decreased distress among people from the United States (especially men) but was unrelated to distress among people from India (Sastry, 1999). There may be cultural differences in how marriage is construed that explain why marriage is associated with health benefits in the United States but not India. In the United States, marriage is based on love and mutual support, whereas in India, marriage is based on tradition and family obligations; the family rather than the spouse is the primary source of support in India.

Is marriage less beneficial for women than men because marriage is associated with relatively more distress for women or because being unmarried is associated with relatively more distress for men? There is some support for both ideas. One study showed that the rate of psychiatric disorders was higher among married women than married men, but similar among unmarried men and women (Sachs-Ericsson & Ciarlo, 2000). However, another study showed that the state of being unmarried was more distressing for men. In a study of over 4,000 adults in Germany, the three groups of unmarried men were more lonely than the three groups of unmarried women (divorced, widowed, never married), whereas there was no sex difference in loneliness among the married (see Figure 11.1; Pinquart, 2003).

Is it marriage per se that leads to health benefits, or is it the presence of a partner in the household? Several studies have examined the effects of cohabitation on health. A study of people over 50 years old showed that cohabitation did not provide the same benefits as marriage (Brown, Bulanda, & Lee, 2005). Those in cohabiting relationships were more depressed than those who were married but had better mental health than those who were widowed and divorced and comparable mental health to the never married. Two cross-cultural studies, one of 42 nations and one of 17 nations, showed marriage is more strongly related than cohabitation alone to psychological well-being for both men and women (Diener et al., 2000; Stack & Eshleman, 1998). Two longitudinal studies have examined how health changes when one begins a cohabiting relationship compared to a marriage. One tracked alcohol problems and showed that alcohol problems increased over time among those who began a cohabiting relationship compared to those who married—especially among men—despite similar levels of alcohol problems across the two groups at the start of the study (Horwitz &

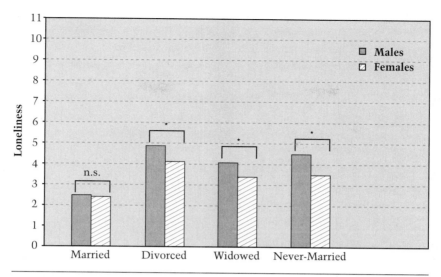

FIGURE 11.1   Among married people, men and women report equal levels of loneliness. Among divorced, widowed, and never-married people, men report more loneliness than women.
Source: Adapted from Pinquart (2003).

White, 1998). Thus, marriage reduced the incidence of alcohol problems over time, but cohabitation did not. The second study showed that those who married showed a decline in depression within a 5-year period, whereas depression did not change among those who started a cohabiting relationship (Kim & McKenry, 2002). However, having a partner is still better than not having a partner. An epidemiological study showed that people who were unmarried had 1.25 times the risk of mortality, whereas people who were unpartnered (which included unmarried) had 1.31 times the risk of mortality (Lund et al., 2002). In general, it appears cohabitation has benefits on health, but the effects are stronger for marriage.

Explanations

Many theories address why marriage benefits health. Marriage is presumed to affect health through a set of physiological processes. Two categories of variables might affect physiology: psychological and behavioral. Marriage may provide one with a sense of identity, a source of self-esteem, and a companion to share activities, all of which should promote a positive psychological state. Marriage also may promote good health behavior (e.g., exercising), decrease risk behavior (e.g., smoking), and promote early detection of disease (e.g., routine physical exam). These effects of marriage on health are referred to as direct effects, or **main effects** (Cohen & Wills, 1985). In each case, marriage is directly linked to a psychological state or behavior that influences health.

An alternative hypothesis is that marriage indirectly affects health by providing resources to cope with stress. These effects are referred to as **buffering effects**; marriage is buffering one against the negative effects of stressors (Cohen & Wills, 1985). During times of stress, marriage may help us perceive a stressful event as less troublesome and may provide resources to

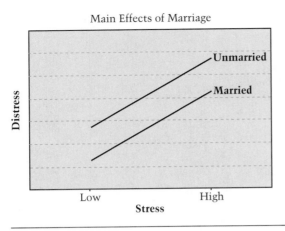

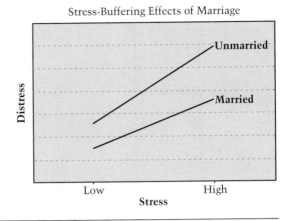

FIGURE 11.2 Main effects of marriage (left panel): Married people are less distressed than unmarried people, regardless of their levels of stress. Stress-buffering effects of marriage (right panel): Married people are especially less distressed than unmarried people when they face high levels of stress. In other words, marriage buffers people from the deleterious effects of stress.

cope with stress (e.g., emotional support, financial support). In the face of an illness, marriage may help us make the health behavior changes necessary for a successful recovery.

The distinction between the main effects and buffering effects hypotheses is shown in Figure 11.2. In the left half of Figure 11.2, the main effects hypothesis shows that married people are less distressed than unmarried people, regardless of the level of stress. The magnitude of the difference between the two lines is the same across low and high stress. Of course, stress leads to an increase in distress among both married and unmarried people. In the right half of Figure 11.2, the stress-buffering hypothesis shows that stress is associated with a larger increase in distress among unmarried people than married people. That is, married people who face high levels of stress are protected from the large increase in distress that unmarried people suffer. Here, the magnitude of the difference between the two lines is greater under high levels of stress. Next, I review some of the research on these psychological and behavioral links of marriage to health.

Social Support. One explanation for the effects of marriage on health involves social support. Married men and women report higher levels of support than unmarried persons, but men may have more of an advantage than women. Wives provide more support than do husbands (Cutrona, 1996). This is especially the case for emotional support. Husbands are more likely than wives to name their spouse as their primary confidant (Tower & Kasl, 1996). Women are more likely than men to name someone else as their primary confidant. Thus marriage may be a greater source of emotional support for men.

However, observational studies of marital interactions and daily diary studies in which men and women record their behavior on a more momentary basis seem to show that men and women are equally likely to provide their spouses with social support (Neff & Karney, 2005). Yet all support is not the same. Women may provide more effective support than men. One study showed that men and women provided the same amount of support, but women's support was better timed than men's.

At the end of each day for 7 days, husbands and wives reported their level of stress, the support they provided, and the support they received. Wives were more likely than husbands to provide support when their partners were stressed. In an observational study where each spouse took turns describing a personal problem, wives provided more support when husbands were describing more severe problems. However, there was no relation between the support husbands provided and the severity of the wife's problem.

The kind of support that we have been discussing is emotional support. There is one kind of support that women are more likely than men to receive from marriage—financial support. In one study, the only women whose health improved from marriage were unemployed women (Waldron, Hughes, & Brooks, 1996). The increase in family income that marriage brought to these women accounted for part of this health benefit. Another study found that the decreased psychological distress of mothers who were married compared to unmarried (either never married or divorced) was associated with fewer financial difficulties (Hope, Power, & Rodgers, 1999).

Stressful Life Events.   Another reason for the differences in distress among people of different marital statuses has to do with the occurrence of negative life events. The state of being unmarried is associated with stressful life events. Separation, divorce, and widowhood are often experienced as negative life events in and of themselves, but they also can lead to other negative life events, such as changes in one's social network. It is these negative life events that may be producing an increase in distress rather than marriage being responsible for a lowered level of distress. As you will see in the sections on widowhood and divorce, some argue that the benefits of marriage are really

not due to marriage per se but due to the stressfulness of the loss of marriage.

Marriage is not only related to the occurrence of fewer stressful life events but is also a buffer against the stress from life events. This buffer appears to be stronger for men than for women. Siegel and Kuykendall (1990) examined the effect of the death of a close family member (not a spouse) on depression among elderly men and women. Marriage protected men, but not women against the depression associated with the loss. Widowed men who suffered the loss of a close family member were especially depressed.

Health Behavior.   Marriage has a positive effect on both men's and women's health behavior, but the effects are particularly strong for men (Schone & Weinick, 1998). Wives take more responsibility for their husband's health than husbands take for their wife's health. Marriage has a stronger beneficial effect on the eating and sleeping patterns of men and is a greater deterrent to drinking and drug problems for men than for women (Umberson, 1987). In a study of over 4,000 married and widowed senior citizens, married men were more likely to have had their blood pressure checked in the prior year, were more likely to engage in physical activities, and were less likely to smoke than widowed men. Marriage benefited women in that married women were more likely to eat breakfast and more likely to use seat belts than widowed women. In a study of people who visited a family medicine clinic, men were twice as likely as women to say they visited the clinic because someone of the other sex encouraged them to do so (Norcross, Ramirez, & Palinkas, 1996); this person was typically a spouse. Married men are more likely to endorse proactive health beliefs, including preventive health care and the tendency to take care of oneself when sick, compared to single men, whereas there are no differences in proactive health beliefs between married and single women (Markey et al., 2005).

Marital Satisfaction.   Another reason marriage may be more health beneficial for men than women is that women are more dissatisfied with their marriages. Women report more problems in marriage, more negative feelings about marriage, and more frequent thoughts of divorce. In a study of the first 4 years of marriage, marital satisfaction decreased over time for both men and women, but the decrease was larger among women than men (Kurdek, 2005).

Men also are more optimistic about marriage than women. A study of college students in Taiwan showed that men were more likely to say that they would have a happy marriage compared to others as shown in Figure 11.3 (Lin & Raghubir, 2005). Women also rated the likelihood of their own happiness as higher than that of others, but the difference was not as large. The figure also shows that men underestimated their chances of getting divorced compared to others more so than women.

One reason marriage may present more problems for women is that women's roles change more after marriage compared to those of men. Historically, women conformed more than men to what their spouse expected of them (Bernard, 1972). Because women were more dependent than men on marriage for financial security, women had more at stake in maintaining the marriage. Thus women were more motivated to accommodate to their spouse's wishes. In addition, the traditional housewife role is inherently frustrating: It lacks status, structure, and recognition because "accomplishments" often go unnoticed (Gove & Tudor, 1973). Today, however, women are more likely to take on other roles besides housewife and are better equipped to take care of themselves financially. Thus men's and women's roles are now more similar in marriage. If the difference in roles is the explanation for why marriage is more health beneficial for men, we should see more similar effects of marriage on men's and women's health in the future.

Selection Hypothesis.   I have been discussing ways in which marriage could influence health,

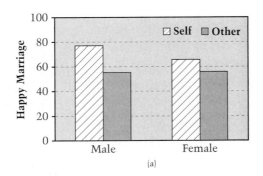

(a)

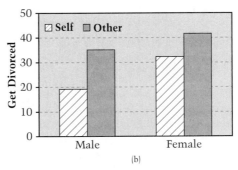

(b)

FIGURE 11.3   (a) College students estimated that they would be more likely to have a happy marriage than others, but the difference for males was greater than females. (b) College students also estimated that they would be less likely to get divorced than others, but this difference was greater for males than females.
Source: Adapted from Lin and Raghubir (2005).

but it also is possible that health influences marriage. This is the **marital selection hypothesis**, the idea that healthier people are "selected" into marriage. To examine the marital selection hypothesis, a longitudinal study must be conducted to determine whether initial health influences subsequent marital status and whether initial marital status influences subsequent health.

Evidence for the selection hypothesis comes from a 10-year longitudinal study of people who were single at the start of the study and either remained single or married (Hope et al., 1999). Those who began the study with lower levels of distress were more likely to get married. This was especially the case for men. Thus, psychological health predicted marital status. In this study, there was no evidence that marriage influenced health; 10 years later, those who married and those who remained single reported similar changes in distress.

However, a longitudinal study of women provided evidence for a reciprocal relation between marriage and health (Waldron et al., 1996). Married women had better health over time compared to unmarried women, and women with health problems were less likely to get married and more likely to divorce over time.

TAKE HOME POINTS

- The benefits of marriage to health are stronger for men than women.

- There are a number of reasons for this: Marriage is a greater source of emotional support, is more likely to alleviate stress, and encourages better health behavior for men than for women. In addition, men are more satisfied with marriage compared to women, partly due to the receipt of more social support resources.

- The relation between marriage and health is bidirectional. Healthier people are more likely to get married, and married people have better health over time.

EFFECT OF BEREAVEMENT ON HEALTH

If marriage is good for health, presumably losing a spouse has negative effects on health. These negative effects could stem from the loss of resources that the deceased spouse provided as well as the general experience of bereavement. Determining the effects of bereavement on health is not easy. Two kinds of studies have been conducted to address this issue: cross sectional and longitudinal. Cross-sectional studies evaluate people who are widowed at a single point in time. The advantage of this methodology is that large representative samples can be studied. There are three disadvantages. First, people will have been widowed for varying lengths of time, and the length of time since widowhood is bound to influence health. Second, the healthiest people are more likely to remarry after widowhood. Thus the people who remain widowed are not representative of all widowed people and may be more unhealthy than the widowed who have remarried. Third, causality cannot be inferred. In other words, we will not know if widowhood caused the decline in health or if unhealthy people were more likely to be widowed. At first glance, this latter possibility may seem unlikely. However, recall that people are attracted to similar others and marry people who are similar to themselves. One characteristic on which matching could occur is health. It is possible, then, that less healthy people are more likely to lose a spouse.

An important methodological issue to keep in mind when evaluating cross-sectional studies of the effect of widowhood on health is whether an appropriate comparison group of nonwidowed persons was used. This is especially important when evaluating sex differences in the effects of widowhood on health. Why? If widowed men and widowed women show equal health profiles, can we conclude that widowhood has the same effects on the health of men and women? No, because men and women who are not widowed differ in health. For example, married women are more depressed than married men. A study that shows no sex differences in depression among widowed men and women could imply that widowhood increased men's distress levels to those of women or lowered women's distress levels to those of men. In other words, widowhood could have very different effects on men's and women's distress. Let's take another example. In general, men have higher suicide rates compared to women. A study that shows no sex differences in suicide rates among the widowed could imply that widowhood increased women's suicide rates to those of men or decreased men's suicide rates to those of women. The most appropriate comparison group to use in a study of widowhood is married men and women because both widowed and married people share the experience of having entered into marriage. It would not be appropriate to compare widowed persons to never-married persons because we know there are differences between the kinds of people who do and do not get married.

The second way to examine the effects of widowhood on health is to conduct a longitudinal study. Longitudinal studies typically examine people shortly after widowhood and then follow them over time to assess changes in their health. The disadvantage of this methodology is that we do not know people's level of health before widowhood. The advantage, however, is that we know people's initial health status immediately after widowhood so we can truly examine changes in health over time.

The ideal study of widowhood would use a **prospective design** in which people's health is examined before and after widowhood. Imagine how difficult this study would be to conduct.

One would have to enroll a large number of people into a study and then follow them for a long time so a sufficient number of people lose a spouse. Thus you can imagine there are few prospective studies on widowhood. One way to conduct a prospective study is to identify people who are at risk for losing a spouse or a partner. One such group of people is partnered men who have HIV. Indeed, prospective studies of gay men have shown negative health effects of bereavement (Reed et al., 1999).

Evidence

Over 20 years ago, Stroebe and Stroebe (1983) reviewed the literature on the impact of widowhood on a wide range of health indicators among men and women. This literature was largely cross sectional; they evaluated only studies that compared widowed men and women to married men and women. With respect to depression, studies either showed that men are more depressed than women after widowhood or there is no sex difference in depression. Both of these findings contrast with the sex differences in depression among married men and women: Married women are more depressed than married men. Thus the authors concluded that widowhood was associated with relatively greater increases in distress for men than women. Similar results appeared for rates of mental and physical illness. Widowed persons suffered poorer health compared to married persons, but the differences were larger among men than women. Widowhood had even stronger effects on the mortality of men compared to women. Although men have higher mortality rates in general, widowhood was associated with a much higher increase in mortality among men than among women. Widowhood also was associated with sharper increases in the suicide rate of men compared to women.

Recent studies confirm the finding that men are more distressed than women following widowhood and show that the sex difference becomes larger over time. One study showed that small sex differences appeared among recently widowed persons, but large sex differences emerged among those who had been widowed more than 4 years (van Grootheest et al., 1999). Similarly, Lee, Willetts, and Seccombe et al. (1998) found that sex differences in depression were not significant among those who had been widowed less than 3 years but were significant among those who had been widowed more than 3 years. Thus women may recover more easily from widowhood than men. In a test of this idea, one study found that widowed women initially had worse mental health than married women (Wilcox et al., 2003), but with time the mental health of widowed women improved and ended up exceeding that of the married women.

Other studies have shown that the sex difference in effects of widowhood disappear with time. A nationally representative survey showed that the transition to widowhood was associated with a decline in health for men but not women, but the negative effects for men were short-lived (Williams & Umberson, 2004). Within 3 to 5 years, these men's health had substantially improved. A 2-year longitudinal study showed that the consistently married had the same level of distress as the consistently widowed (Strohschein et al., 2005), but distress increased among those who were widowed during the 2 years. These findings also support the idea that the negative effects of widowhood may be short-lived.

Explanations

Strains. One explanation for sex differences in health following the loss of a spouse is that men and women face different strains or stressors

from widowhood. Women suffer financial strains, whereas men suffer strains from having to keep up with household chores. The sex difference in depression after widowhood (men greater than women) has been primarily accounted for by household strains (Umberson, Wortman, & Kessler, 1992). That is, one reason men are more distressed than women after widowhood is that they have to cope with household chores. Women's increased distress upon widowhood is mostly accounted for by enhanced financial strains.

Social Support. A major loss associated with widowhood is the loss of social support. **Interpersonal protection theory** has been used to explain why men suffer more than women upon widowhood (Stroebe & Stroebe, 1983). Interpersonal protection theory implies there are differences in social support across the marital statuses, and social support provides a buffer against distress. There are five support-related explanations for greater negative effects of widowhood on men than women. First, because marriage increases men's more than women's social support, widowhood results in a greater loss of support among men than women, especially emotional support (Stroebe & Stroebe, 1983; Umberson et al., 1992). Recall that men are more likely than women to rely on their spouse as the sole source of emotional support; women, by contrast, receive less support from marriage compared to men and often obtain support from other network members. Second, family and friends provide more support to women than men following widowhood (Lee et al., 1998; van Grootheest et al., 1999), in part because women are more likely than men to seek help from others. Third, men suffer a greater loss of support from other network members after widowhood because it is typically the wife who arranges social affairs and maintains contacts with friends and family.

Fourth, widowed men have a smaller reference group compared to widowed women. Because women outlive men, widowed women have a larger peer group available than widowed men do. Thus men lose more in terms of receiving support from a spouse and support from other network members following widowhood.

Finally, widowhood relieves women of the burden associated with support provision. Because women are often the sole providers of emotional support to men, marriage may be associated with some support burden for women. Widowhood relieves this burden. In an interview study with recently widowed men and women, women mentioned a freedom from having to look after someone as a deterrent to remarriage, whereas men did not express this concern (Davidson, 2001). Thus marriage is a greater source of social support for men for multiple reasons.

TAKE HOME POINTS

- There are a number of methodological difficulties when studying the effects of widowhood on health:

  - An appropriate comparison group must be selected as men and women have different health prior to widowhood. The most appropriate group is married people, as both married and widowed people have selected into marriage.

  - Cross-sectional studies, while easy to conduct, pose several difficulties, including the inability to determine causation, the fact that the healthiest people might have remarried, and the varying time frames since widowhood.

- Studies generally show that widowhood is associated with greater adverse effects on men's than women's health across an array of health indicators.

- The reasons for this sex difference have to do with the different strains men and women face and the greater loss of support that a spouse's death poses for men compared to women.

EFFECT OF RELATIONSHIP DISSOLUTION ON HEALTH

The evidence clearly suggests that marriage is associated with greater health benefits for men than for women and the loss of marriage through widowhood is associated with greater harm to men's than women's health. Can we conclude the breakup of marriage or other significant relationships has more adverse effects on men's than women's health? The answer is not as clear. First, I examine the breakup of dating relationships and then the breakup of marital relationships.

Breakup of Dating Relationships

In general, women seem to adjust better than men to the breakup of dating relationships (Choo, Levine, & Hatfield, 1996). One of the first noteworthy studies to shed light on men's and women's perspectives of how relationships dissolve is the Boston Couples Study. In 1972, just over 200 couples who were juniors and seniors in college enrolled in the study (Hill et al., 1976). Two years later, 45% of the couples had broken up. Some evidence suggests that men were more distressed by the breakup compared to women.

Later these findings were replicated in a study of long-distance college student dating relationships (Helgeson, 1994a). Just over 100 students enrolled in the study at the beginning of the school year and were followed for one semester. At the end of the semester, 36% of the couples had broken up. Across an array of measures, women showed better adjustment to the breakup compared to men. As shown in Figure 11.4, at the beginning of the study, when the couples were together (Time 1), women were more distressed than men. At the end of the semester, when a third of the couples had broken up (Time 2), there was no sex difference

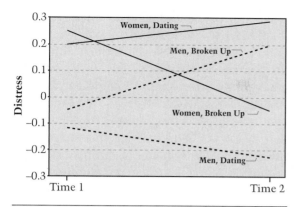

FIGURE 11.4   At the beginning of the semester, when relationships were intact (Time 1), women were more distressed than men. By the end of the semester, when a third of couples had broken up (Time 2), women's distress levels did not significantly differ from those of men. This is because women were more distressed than men among couples who remained together but were less distressed than men among couples who had broken up. Women's distress level decreased following breakup, whereas men's distress level increased following breakup.
Source: V. S. Helgeson (1994). Long distance romantic relationships: Sex differences in adjustment and breakup. *Personality and Social Psychology Bulletin, 20,* 254–265.

in distress among people who had broken up, but women were more distressed than men when the relationship still existed. An alternative way of viewing these findings is that men who broke up became more distressed, whereas women who broke up became less distressed. Women also reported better adjustment to the breakup than men did.

Breakup of Marriage: Separation and Divorce

One indicator that women may adjust better to the breakup of a marriage is that women are less likely than men to remarry after divorce. In

2001, 55% of men compared to 44% of women who had divorced were currently remarried (U.S. Census Bureau, 2005b). It is not clear whether one sex suffers more than the other following separation and divorce. One study measured depression and problem drinking in adolescents who were 12, 15, or 18 years old and then followed them for 13 years (Horwitz, White, & Howell-White, 1996). Taking initial levels of depression and alcohol use into consideration, separation and divorce increased depression and alcohol use for men and women alike. However, another longitudinal study of people who remained married versus people who divorced over 10 years showed that divorced men and women had greater distress than those who remained married, but the difference was larger for women than men (Hope, Rodgers, & Power, 1999).

There are a number of factors that might influence the sex difference in response to separation and divorce. One is the presence of children. If there are no children, women suffer fewer ill effects of separation and divorce (Elliott & Umberson, 2004). When children are involved, strains associated with raising children alone arise. Thus, income and parenthood are important moderators of the effects of divorce on men and women.

Cross-cultural research shows clear health effects of separation and divorce, with more negative effects for men. In a study of nine countries (United States, Canada, Puerto Rico, Germany, Taiwan, Korea, Lebanon, France, New Zealand), separated and divorced individuals were 2 to 4 times more likely to have major depression than married individuals, but the difference was greater for men than women in all of the countries except Canada and Taiwan (Weissman et al., 1996). This is not to say divorce is without consequences for women. In a study that compared Anglo, Chicana, and Mexicana women's reaction to separation and divorce, Chicana women experienced the highest levels of distress (Parra et al., 1995). The Chicana women had a Mexican heritage but were living in the United States. Thus the impact of divorce on women may be particularly stressful when living in a different culture.

Explanations

Strains.   Separation and divorce are associated with a number of strains, including the change in roles that accompanies divorce, single parenthood if children are involved, and the potential for conflict with an ex-spouse (Whisman, Weinstock, & Tolejko, 2006). These strains may differ for men and women. Relationship dissolution may be associated with greater social strains for men and greater economic strains for women. Marital dissolution results in a loss of men's primary confidant. For women, the economic strain associated with marital dissolution is especially large if they retain custody of children. The one study that found greater adverse effects of divorce on women than men (Hope, Rodgers, & Power, 1999) showed the primary explanation had to do with socioeconomic factors. The women most adversely affected were those with parental responsibilities and those who experienced a decline in SES. Even in cohabiting relationships, the economic strains associated with relationship dissolution are greater for women than men. One study showed that men's income declined by 10%, whereas women's declined by 33% after the relationships dissolved (Avellar & Smock, 2005). The greater strains for women partly had to do with the presence of children, which are increasingly common in cohabiting unions.

The strain explanation for the negative health effects of separation and divorce is most appealing when one realizes that there are greater differences in depression between married people and divorced/separated people than married people and unmarried people (Whisman et al., 2006). Thus the health benefits of marriage may have less to do with the benefits of marriage per se, but more to do with the strains associated with the breakup of a relationship. If the health advantage of marriage was due to marriage per se, married people should have better health than all other groups. However, an 8-year longitudinal study that examined the effects of relationship stability and relationship transitions showed that the health of the continually divorced and never married was the same as the continually married (Williams & Umberson, 2004). Transitions out of marriage through divorce or widowhood were associated with adverse effects on health, and these effects were stronger for men than women. The negative effects were also stronger for older men, which supports the role strain argument as older men are probably less prepared to assume household chores than younger men. Another longitudinal study found that the consistently married and the consistently unmarried lived longer than those who had experienced any kind of breakup over 30 years (Tucker et al., 1996). In addition, mortality rates were similar between those who were currently separated/divorced and those who had separated/divorced and remarried. Thus the health detriment was due to the dissolution of the relationship itself, and these effects were stronger for men than women.

If differential strains experienced by men and women following separation/divorce is the explanation for the effects of relationship dissolution on health, one would expect the dissolution of traditional marriages to have stronger negative effects on men and women than the dissolution of egalitarian marriages. In egalitarian marriages, women are less likely to depend on their spouse for financial support and men are less likely to depend on their spouse to take care of the house and to be the sole source of emotional support. Research has yet to investigate this possibility.

Social Selection. The social selection hypothesis could also explain why those who separate and divorce have worse health than those who remain married. Perhaps, poor health precedes rather than follows relationship dissolution. A 9-year longitudinal study of adults in England tried to disentangle the two (Wade & Pevalin, 2004). It turned out that separation and divorce were associated with poor mental health and poor mental health was associated with marital dissolution.

Women Initiate Breakup.   One explanation for why women might adjust better to the breakup of a dating relationship or the dissolution of a marriage might be that women are more likely to initiate relationship dissolution. Women are more likely than men to consider separation and divorce and to initiate the breakup of dating relationships and marriages (Levenson, Carstensen, & Gottman, 1993; Helgeson, 1994a).

We might expect the person who initiates a breakup to adjust better because he or she is the one who wanted the relationship to end. This scenario may be the case for men but is not necessarily the case for women. In a study of dating couples, men adjusted better to the breakup when they initiated it than when their partner initiated it, but who initiated the breakup was unrelated to women's adjustment. As shown in Figure 11.5, women were equally well off, regardless of who initiated the breakup (Helgeson, 1994a). One reason that men were better off when they initiated a breakup is that these men were less happy with the relationship. Women, however, were unhappy with the relationship, regardless of who initiated it.

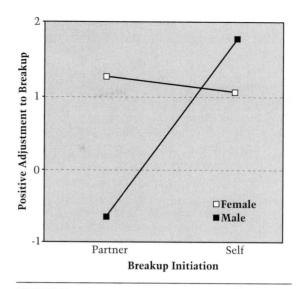

FIGURE 11.5   Women adjusted positively to the breakup regardless of who initiated it. Men adjusted positively to the breakup only when they initiated it. *Source:* Adapted from Helgeson (1994a).

Thus one reason that women adjust well to a breakup whether they or their partner initiate it might be that women are more aware than men of problems in a relationship and more prepared for the relationship to end. In the above-mentioned study, women reported they had thought about and talked about the possibility of a breakup, regardless of who ultimately initiated it (Helgeson, 1994a). Men thought about and talked about the possibility of a breakup only when they ended up initiating it. Thus women seem to have been more psychologically prepared for the breakup than men. These findings are consistent with a study of distressed couples seeking marital therapy that showed women were more aware of problems in the relationship than men (Doss, Atkins, & Christensen, 2003). Both men and women agreed that women were the first to recognize that there was a problem in the relationship, the first to consider seeking help, and the first to initiate treatment. Thus women may adjust better than men to the dissolution of a relationship.

EFFECT OF MARITAL QUALITY ON HEALTH

I have been discussing the effects of marital status—whether one is single, married, widowed, or divorced—on health. Does marital status alone determine our health? Surely, all marriages are not the same or provide the same health benefits. Is a distressed marriage better for health than no marriage at all? Research suggests that the answer is no. For example, a study of the elderly showed that married people were less distressed than unmarried people, but married people who were not happy with the way their spouse treated them were more distressed than unmarried people (Hagedoorn et al., 2006). Thus it is important to consider the quality of the relationship when evaluating the health implications of marriage.

Many of the explanations of why marriage benefits men's health more than women's pertain to the quality of the marital relationship. For example, a primary explanation for sex differences in the effects of marriage and widowhood on health has to do with marriage providing relatively more social support to men. This explanation suggests the quality of the marital relationship is different for men and women. Perhaps marriage benefits men's health more because the relationship is more satisfying to men than to women. In fact, we know men are more satisfied in marriage than women are. To understand thoroughly the effects of marriage on health, we need to examine the quality of the relationship.

Two types of studies examine the nature of marital relationships. In survey studies, men and women complete various marital satisfaction or marital strain inventories. The relation of these self-report measures of marital quality to men's and women's health is then examined. In laboratory studies, men and women engage in some sort of marital interaction (usually, a discussion of a conflict) that is videotaped, recorded, and analyzed. The relation of specific interaction patterns to health is examined. I review both kinds of studies.

Evidence

Survey Studies. Numerous survey studies have found that the quality of the marital relationship is more strongly related to women's than men's health. In a study of married and cohabiting couples, relationship satisfaction was associated with less psychological distress, but the effects were stronger for women than men (Whisman & Uebelacker, 2006). In a longitudinal study of 300 dual-earner couples, a rewarding marriage was associated with a reduction in distress for both men and women, but the effect was stronger among women

(Barnett et al., 1995). Marital quality is more strongly related to women than men's *physical* health in studies that span periodontal disease, rheumatoid arthritis, blood pressure, and cardiac problems (Kiecolt-Glaser & Newton, 2001). In a study of middle-aged women, marital quality predicted less atherosclerosis (i.e., less buildup of placque in the coronary arteries) 11 and 14 years later (Gallo et al., 2003). Those who were happily married had less atherosclerosis than those who were unhappily married, with the unmarried women falling between the two groups. There are exceptions to these findings, however. Two studies showed that marital quality was associated with better subjective health perceptions among both men and women (Umberson & Williams, 2005; Umberson et al., 2006). The authors point out that these findings can still be understood in terms of there being greater health implications for women than men because women report lower marital quality than men throughout marriage. To the extent that poor marital quality translates into health difficulties, women will suffer more problems than men.

A couple of studies have focused on the negative (i.e., conflict) rather than the positive aspects (i.e., social support) of marital relationships. One study showed that conflict with the spouse had a greater effect on women's than men's psychological well-being (Horowitz, McLaughlin, & White, 1998). In that study, conflict with family and friends also was evaluated and found to be more strongly related to women's than men's psychological well-being. Another study showed the quality of marriage was more strongly related to depression in women than men following a major stressful life event. Edwards, Nazroo, and Brown (1998) compared good and poor marriages to good marriages in which the person had been "let down" by the spouse during a crisis. Both men and women were more depressed in poor than

good marriages, but only women were more depressed in "let down" good than poor marriages. Thus women were more sensitive than men to adverse changes in the quality of the relationship. Conflict also has been associated with psychological distress among lesbian couples (Otis, Riggle, & Rostosky, 2006).

To recap, it appears that what is important for men is the mere presence of a spouse, but what is important for women is the support of the spouse or the quality of the relationship. This may be because women are more adept than men at providing the features of social interactions that benefit health. In particular, women may be more effective support providers. A recent study supported this conclusion (Glynn, Christenfeld, & Gerin, 1999). College students underwent a stressful task (giving a speech) in the presence of either a supportive or nonsupportive confederate. The confederate was either male or female. Support from a female decreased both men's and women's cardiovascular reactivity (i.e., increases in blood pressure), whereas support from a male had no effect. Thus the mere existence of a relationship with a woman is health protective, whereas the nature of the relationship with a man must be considered for health benefits to occur.

Many of the studies relating marital quality to health are cross sectional; thus we must be concerned about the direction of causality: Does marital quality influence health, or does health influence marital quality? In a study of newlyweds, the reciprocal relation between marital satisfaction and depression was examined over 18 months (Fincham et al., 1997). Initial marital satisfaction had no impact on subsequent depression for men but predicted depression in women. This fits with previous research showing the quality of marriage affects women's but not men's health. By contrast, initial depression predicted a decline in marital satisfaction among men but did not predict changes in marital satisfaction among women. Thus men's rather than women's initial psychological state seems to influence the quality of marriage. The authors suggested that men respond to depression by withdrawing from relationships and having a negative attitude toward relationships, which ultimately affects the quality of their marriage. Women's depression, however, appears not to affect their relationships. Women may be more likely to hide their depression and keep it from interfering with attending to the relationship.

It is not only the woman's perception of her marriage that influences her health, but her husband's perception of the marriage also affects her well-being. We know from Chapter 9 that characteristics of husbands influence wives' relationships, but characteristics of wives do not have the same influence on husbands' relationships. Is the same true for husbands' and wives' health? Some evidence suggests that husbands' marital satisfaction influences wives' well-being more than wives' marital satisfaction influences husbands' well-being (Quirouette & Gold, 1992).

Laboratory Studies

The studies I reviewed on marital quality and health rely on people's self-reports of marital satisfaction or distress. Another way to examine the link between features of the marital relationship and health is to examine the health consequences of specific behaviors that occur during marital interactions. Because communication is central to the quality of a relationship, numerous studies have couples come into the laboratory and observe how they communicate. Topics of conflict are usually the subject matter. Health is measured in terms of physiological responses to the interactions, such as blood pressure, heart rate, hormone production, and immune function.

These studies tend to show that women are more physiologically reactive to conflict discussions than men are. In one study, patients with hypertension discussed an area of disagreement with their partner for 10 minutes (Ewart et al., 1991). Female patients' blood pressure increased more than male patients' blood pressure. In addition, only women's blood pressure was influenced by the quality of the communication; hostile interactions (e.g., criticism, disagreement) were associated with an increase in blood pressure for women. In another study of personal conflict discussions, the amount of negative interaction influenced wives' but not husbands' physiological reactivity (Gottman & Levenson, 1992).

Immune and endocrine changes during conflict discussion also have been examined. Ninety newlywed couples engaged in a 30-minute conflict discussion (Kiecolt-Glaser et al., 1993). Negative and hostile behavior during the interaction was associated with changes in immune function and elevations in blood pressure in both men and women, but women showed more negative immune changes than men. Endocrine function was later examined in these same couples (Kiecolt-Glaser et al., 1996). Husbands' behavior during the interaction influenced the production of hormones in wives; for example, when husbands withdrew from conflict, wives' cortisol increased, and when husbands provided validation, wives' stress hormones decreased. The behavior of wives was not related to men's hormone levels. All these findings are consistent with Floyd and Markman's (1983) idea that women are the emotional barometers of relationships. Women's bodies are responding physiologically to the nature of marital interactions, whereas men's are not.

Disagreement in general seems to affect women's, but not necessarily men's physiology. In one study, the disagreement was not even about the relationship. Married couples were

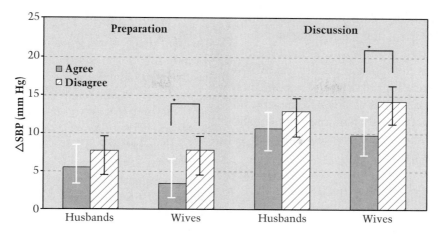

FIGURE 11.6 Effects of disagreement on systolic blood pressure (SBP) reactivity. Men and women were brought into the lab and randomized to take similar sides (agreement) or opposing sides (disagreement) of an issue. During the preparation for the discussion and during the discussion, women's blood pressure reactivity increased more when they disagreed with their husband than when they agreed. Men's reactivity was not affected by whether they disagreed or agreed with their wife.
Source: T. Smith, L. C. Gallo, L. Goble, L. Q. Ngu, and K. A. Stark (1998). Agency, communion and cardiovascular reactivity during marital interaction. *Health Psychology, 17*(6), 537–545.

brought into the lab and assigned to take the same side or opposing sides of an issue (Smith et al., 1998). The latter was expected to provoke disagreement. The issues concerned rent control in the city and university admission standards. Disagreement increased the cardiovascular reactivity of women, but not men. As shown in Figure 11.6, wives had higher reactivity when they disagreed rather than agreed at two different time periods: preparation for the task and during the task discussion. Disagreement did not influence husbands' reactivity.

The greater physiological responsiveness of women compared to men in these studies directly contradicts Gottman's (1994) explanation for why men withdraw from discussions of conflict. Recall from Chapter 9 that he argued

men withdraw because they are more physiologically reactive to stress and less able than women to tolerate such physiological changes. These studies suggest it is women who are more physiologically reactive.

Explanations

One reason that discussions about conflict produce greater physiological changes in women compared to men is that such discussions may be more threatening to women. Relationships are central to the female gender role, and conflict is a threat to relationships. As men's and women's roles become more equal, we might expect future studies to show similar effects of marital quality on men's and women's health. In a study of young dual-earner couples (ages 25 to 40), men and women derived similar positive effects from having a high-quality marital role, and marital role quality was related to reduced psychological distress for both men and women (Barnett et al., 1994). Barnett and colleagues concluded that marriage is equally important to men's and women's identity in dual-earner couples.

TAKE HOME POINTS

- Whereas simply being married influences men's more than women's health, the quality of marriage has a greater effect on women's health.

- The evidence that supports the latter claim is based on surveys of self-reported marital quality as well as laboratory studies of actual marital interactions.

- The nature of marital interactions is more strongly associated with physiological changes in women than men.

- Explanations for these findings have to do with relationships being more central to women's than men's roles.

DIVISION OF LABOR

Traditional roles are enacted by a sex-segregated division of labor: men working outside the home and women working inside the home. Who does what in the family, or the division of labor, is an important aspect of marital relationships that has effects on psychological and physical health. The way work inside and outside the home is divided affects the quality of the marital relationship as well as general psychological distress. I examine the literature on who does what in the family and show how the division of labor is associated with marital satisfaction and well-being.

Who Does What?

"A man may work from sun to sun, but a woman's work is never done." Is there any truth to this old adage? According to Hochschild (1989), there is. She refers to employed women's work at home as "the second shift": Women work one shift at work and a second shift at home. Hochschild interviewed 50 couples and found that women worked on average 15 hours a week longer than men, including paid employment, household chores, and child care. Over the course of a year, she remarked this extra time added up to a full month.

Even when women are employed, they contribute more to household labor than men do. Household labor includes preparing meals, cleaning, yard work, household repairs, grocery shopping, washing clothes, paying bills, automobile maintenance, and running errands. A national survey of over 3,000 couples showed that women spent twice as much time as men on household chores (Blair & Lichter, 1991). Men's and women's participation in specific household chores is shown in Figure 11.7. Women spent 33 hours a week on household labor, and 66% of that time was devoted to meal preparation and household cleaning; men spent 14 hours a week on household labor, and 33% of that time was devoted to outdoor tasks. As you can see, with the exception of auto maintenance and outdoor tasks, women spent more time than men on household chores. In a more recent survey study of U.S. couples who each worked at least 30 hours outside of the home, wives spent 34 hours on household labor and husbands spent 21 hours on household labor per week (Bartley, Blanton, & Gilliard, 2005).

The size of the sex difference in household labor and child care has drastically decreased over the past 4 decades, mostly due to women spending less time on such activities

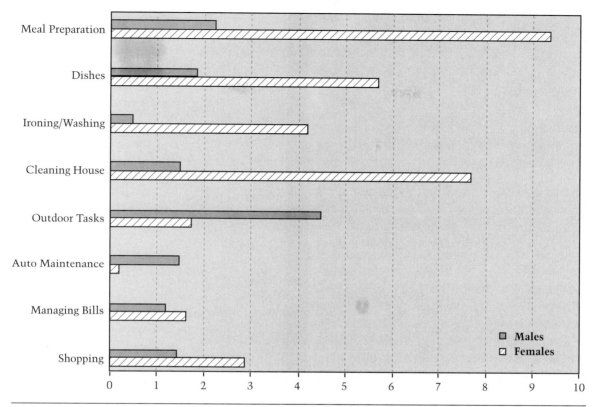

FIGURE 11.7   Mean hours per week spent on household tasks by sex. Women spend more time than men on all household tasks except auto maintenance and outdoor tasks.
Source: Adapted from Blair and Lichter (1991).

and partly due to men spending more time on such activities (Coltrane, 2000). Despite these changes, women still shoulder the responsibility for the majority of household labor. In 1965, women spent almost 4 times the number of hours on household labor and child care as men (Robinson & Godbey, 1999). By 1995, the sex difference was closer to twofold. The fewer hours women spend on family chores is largely accounted for by the increase in women's employment; in 1995, women who were employed spent 7 hours less on household chores and child care than women who were not employed.

Do women spend more time than men on household chores only when married? No, but the largest sex difference in division of labor occurs among married individuals. Whereas cohabiting women perform fewer household chores than married women, cohabiting men perform more household chores than married men (Coltrane, 2000). Men and women come to have more traditional attitudes toward gender roles after marriage, regardless of whether they become parents (MacDermid, Huston, & McHale, 1990). A national survey of over 13,000 families examined the division of household labor among men and women

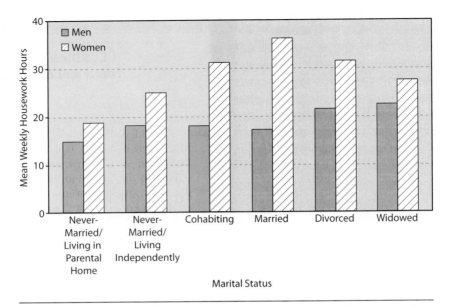

FIGURE 11.8 Across all five marital statuses, women spend more time than men on household labor. The largest sex difference appears among married men and women.

Source: S. J. South and G. Spitze (1994). Housework in marital and nonmarital households. *American Sociological Review, 59,* 327–347. Copyright 1994 by the American Sociological Association. Reprinted by permission.

across a variety of marital statuses: never married, cohabiting, married, divorced, and widowed (South & Spitze, 1994). As shown in Figure 11.8, across all five statuses, women spent more time than men on household labor. Women spent an average of 33 hours per week on household tasks, whereas men spent an average of 18 hours per week. However, the largest sex difference appeared in the married group: Married women spent substantially more time on household labor than unmarried women. In fact, among women, the highest rate of household labor was among the married, followed by cohabiting and then divorced persons. Widowed and never-married women spent the least time on household labor. The amount of time men spent on household labor did not vary as much by marital status. Cohab-

iting, married, and never-married men spent similar amounts of time on household labor; divorced and widowed men spent the largest amount of time on household labor.

The presence of children in the home is associated with a more traditional division of labor (Stevens et al., 2006). About half of the sex difference in the division of labor among married respondents was accounted for by the presence of children in the home and by women working fewer hours than men outside the home (18 compared to 32 hours; South & Spitze, 1994). The other half of the sex difference in division of labor was unexplained. The authors maintain that men and women "do gender" when they marry. This means that marriage leads men and women to enact traditional gender roles.

How do people from different ethnic groups divide the household labor in the family? A national survey of over 13,000 households examined ethnic differences in the division of labor (John, Shelton, & Luschen, 1995). White men reported spending less time on household tasks compared to Black men. White men also were more likely than Black men to say the division of labor in their household was unfair to their wives. Thus White men seem to be aware of their lack of participation in household labor. The sex difference in division of labor is typically larger in Hispanic than non-Hispanic couples. Hispanic women and men are less likely than White or Black women and men to espouse egalitarian views of the division of labor (John et al., 1995). Hispanic women and men are more likely to believe men should support the family and women should support the home.

The fact that women shoulder more of the division of labor at home than men generalizes across countries, suggesting that there are macro-level social forces operating. In a study of 6 countries across Europe and North America, women's domestic labor decreased by 1 hour per day between 1960 and 1997, whereas men's increased by 20 minutes (Sullivan, 2004). Fuwa (2004) hypothesized that the extent of gender equality achieved in a country would predict a more egalitarian division of labor and that individual difference variables, such as income and gender-role attitudes, would only predict the division of labor in countries that achieved some level of gender equality. Both hypotheses were supported. Across 22 countries, those in which women had made greater achievements (e.g., Canada, United States), as measured by income and political and economic representation in the country, had a more egalitarian division of labor than countries in which women had made fewer achievements (e.g., Japan, Italy). Individual difference variables, such as a

woman's work status and gender-role attitudes, were more strongly related to the division of labor in more egalitarian countries. In less egalitarian countries, there are such large differences in political and economic power between men and women that individual difference variables do not have the opportunity to have any effect on the division of labor.

One aspect of household labor in which men have become more involved is child care. Black men are more likely than White men to be involved in child care (Sanderson & Thompson, 2002). Yet father involvement in child care is less than people's ideals. In a 1999 national sample of 234 married couples, over 90% of couples said both parents should be equally involved in four of six child care domains (Milkie et al., 2002). Financial support of the child was one exception. The couples' actual behavior, however, indicated that mothers were primarily responsible for child care and fathers were primarily responsible for financial support. Thus people's hopes and expectations have changed more than their behavior. The discrepancy between ideal and actual father participation in child care was associated with stress in women, but not men.

What Determines Who Does What?

Gender-Role Attitudes.   We would expect that whether the couple endorses traditional versus egalitarian views of marriage would influence the household division of labor. Husbands' gender-role attitudes are more predictive of the division of labor than wives' gender-role attitudes (Cunningham, 2005; Stevens et al., 2006). When the husband has an egalitarian view of marriage, he contributes more and she contributes less compared to other couples. Wives' egalitarian scores seem to be unrelated to either husbands' or wives' household contributions.

There are different facets of gender-role attitudes. Attitudes toward behavior in one domain may not predict behavior in another domain. For example, a man who appears to have an egalitarian gender-role ideology may support his wife working outside the home but strongly object to her mowing the lawn and his having to cook dinner.

Rabin (1998) points out that men's and women's gender-role attitudes are changing and undergoing some negotiation. She refers to the **gender tension line** as the point at which people feel uncomfortable with further change: "The gender tension line is that point beyond which the person can no longer change in terms of gender role and still feel masculine or feminine enough" (p. 182). For example, a man may have egalitarian views and believe both mothers and fathers should change a child's diapers. When at home, the man is willing to change the child's diaper; when in public, however, the man is not willing to take the child into the men's room to change the diaper. Public displays of such behavior cross the line for this man. Similarly, a woman may have egalitarian views of her marriage and work full time; however, when it comes to deciding who retrieves a sick child from school, the woman feels more comfortable having the school contact her than her husband. See if you can determine what your own gender tension lines are in Do Gender 11.1.

Power. There are indicators of power in the marital relationship that may affect the division of labor in the family. Two such indicators are education and income. Several studies have shown that husbands contribute more to household labor when either they have lower income or wives have higher income (Blair & Lichter, 1991; Erickson, 2005). As the income gap increases (men more than women), women spend more time on child care and household chores; a

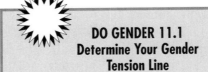

DO GENDER 11.1
Determine Your Gender Tension Line

This exercise involves some in-depth self-analysis. First, think carefully about the behaviors that characterize the other sex in which you would be willing to engage. Start with a domain of behavior, such as appearance. For example, "I am a woman and I would be willing to wear a suit." Then, keep upping the stakes until you find a domain of behavior that "crosses the line" for you. For example, "I would be unwilling to be a stay-at-home parent." Do the same for at least two other domains, such as leisure interests, how you behave in relationships with friends or with a romantic partner, how you would divide the household chores in your family, and so on.

more equal contribution to income is associated with a more egalitarian division of labor (Stevens et al., 2006). The income gap influences men's participation rates more than women's. In other words, high-income men are especially unlikely to spend time on household labor.

One study showed that the effect of income disparity on men's participation in household chores depended on the nature of men's jobs (Arrighi & Maume, 2000). When men's and women's earnings were similar, men who held subordinate positions at work were especially unlikely to participate in household chores. When the nature of men's jobs threatens their masculinity (i.e., low status), they may be reluctant to perform tasks at home that are viewed as part of the female role. When men had much higher income than women (affirming their masculinity), the nature of the job had less effect on participation in household chores.

Women's income seems to be a better predictor of her household labor than her husband's income (Gupta, 2006). When her income increases, her housework decreases. Women's income may provide her with greater power in the relationship to negotiate household labor and also may provide her with the resources to "buy out of household labor" by going out to eat or hiring a housekeeper.

Even among the most highly educated couples and among couples in which the wife has a high income, division of labor is still sex segregated (Blair & Lichter, 1991). Thus other societal bases of power differences between men and women may explain why the division of labor at home is unequal when employment, income, and education are equal.

Work Outside the Home.

Who does what inside the home is bound to be influenced by who does what outside the home. If one partner works full time (usually the husband) and one works part time or not at all (usually the wife), would a 50/50 split on household chores really be an equitable arrangement? Several studies have found that the number of hours people work outside the home influences the division of labor at home. The more hours husbands work outside the home, the fewer hours they work inside the home and the more hours wives work inside the home (Coltrane, 2000; Erickson, 2005). In addition, the more hours wives work outside the home, the more hours husbands work inside the home and the fewer hours wives work inside the home. Wives' employment, however, is a better predictor of the division of labor in the family than husbands' employment (Coltrane, 2000). That is, wives' employment most definitely decreases her contributions to household labor and often increases his contributions to household labor. However, the number of hours that husbands are employed outside the home is not a consistent predictor of men's contribution to household labor.

Sexual Orientation.

One way to understand whether there are universal gender roles with respect to the division of labor is to study homosexual couples. Is it always the case that one person performs the traditionally masculine chores (e.g., mow the lawn, take out the garbage) and one person performs the traditionally feminine chores (e.g., prepare the meal, wash the dishes)?

Division of labor does not appear to be divided into those two distinct roles among lesbian and gay couples (Peplau & Beals, 2001). The traditional husband/wife roles in regard to the division of labor do not apply to homosexual couples. Each partner may specialize in a set of tasks, but those tasks are divided by personal preference rather than gender roles. That is, it is unlikely that one person performs all of the traditionally masculine tasks and one person performs all the traditionally feminine tasks. If that were true, we would expect a high negative correlation between the two domains which turns out not to be true.

There seems to be a more equal division of labor for household chores among homosexual than heterosexual couples. Gay and lesbian couples are more likely than heterosexual couples to share tasks by evenly dividing the chores (Kurdek, 2007). However, lesbians are more likely to share tasks, for example by going grocery shopping together, whereas gay men are more likely to have each person specialize in different tasks. A study of lesbian couples with children showed that biological mothers spent more time on child care than nonbiological mothers, and nonbiological mothers spend more time on paid employment than biological mothers (Patterson, 2003). As in heterosexual couples, the extent to which the division of labor is perceived as unfair is associated with low relationship satisfaction.

The research on the division of labor in homosexual couples suggests that the differential status of men and women in heterosexual couples may contribute to the uneven division of labor. In homosexual couples, there is no differential status based on gender and the division of labor is more evenly divided. In a comparison of heterosexual and homosexual couples, men's and women's income was associated with lower participation in household chores among heterosexual couples but was unrelated to household chores among homosexual couples (Kurdek, 1993). Insofar as income implies status, status seems to have a greater influence on the division of labor in heterosexual than homosexual couples.

Relationship commitment. Some have suggested that men's commitment to the relationship is associated with their contribution to the division of labor. A study of cohabiting couples showed that men who had planned to marry their partner spent more time on household chores than men who did not have marriage plans (Ciabattari, 2004). Women's relationship commitment was unrelated to their contribution to household chores. A study of married couples showed that men's dedication to the relationship was associated with wife satisfaction with the division of labor (Rhoades et al., 2006).

Satisfaction

Are men and women satisfied with an unfair division of labor? Despite the fact that both men and women agree that women contribute more to the division of labor, women are less satisfied than men with this state of affairs (Erickson, 2005; Stevens et al., 2006). Studies suggest that an equal division of labor and men's involvement in child care is more important to women's than men's marital satisfaction (Hoffman & Youngblade, 1999; Rabin & Shapira-Berman, 1997). The amount of housework conducted by men is directly related to women's

marital commitment (Canary & Stafford, 1992) and marital conflict (Perry-Jenkins & Folk, 1994). Hochschild (1989) found that couples were happier when men participated more in household labor, regardless of couples' gender-role ideology.

Wife perception of inequity in the division of labor also is associated with divorce (Frisco & Williams, 2003). There is some evidence that equity is more important to the viability of a relationship among couples who had once cohabited. One study showed that disagreement over the division of labor predicted relationship dissolution among cohabiting couples and among married couples who had cohabited first, but not among married couples without a history of cohabitation (Hohmann-Marriott, 2006). The effects were strongest among those who were currently cohabiting, suggesting that agreement on the division of labor in cohabiting relationships is essential to their viability.

Not all women value an equal division of labor. Socioeconomic status, egalitarian attitudes, and women's employment status all influence how an inequitable division of labor is perceived. In one study, middle-class women had more conflict if they perceived the division of labor as unfair, but working-class women reported *less* conflict in their relationship when they performed more household chores (Perry-Jenkins & Folk, 1994). Another study of working-class women showed that those whose expectations about the division of labor were violated after the birth of a child were more distressed—but the violation was opposite of the direction one would expect (Goldberg & Perry-Jenkins, 2004). Women who spent *less* time on child care than they expected and whose husbands spent more time on child care than they expected were more distressed. This was especially the case for women with a traditional gender-role ideology. There is other research that shows women with traditional gender-role attitudes are not upset by an unfair division of labor, even when they work outside the home (Pina & Bengston, 1993). In fact, a more equal division of labor is associated with conflict in families where husband and wife have traditional attitudes (MacDermid et al., 1990). Thus working-class women and women with traditional gender-role attitudes may not be as upset by an unequal division of labor.

Among women who do value equity in the division of labor, men do not have to perform half of the chores for women to be satisfied. In fact, rarely is household labor divided 50/50, even when men and women work equally outside the home. Why are women satisfied with a less than equitable division of labor? One answer has to do with to whom women compare themselves, that is, their comparison referents. Women compare their own household participation rate to those of other women rather than to that of their husband. Some women compare themselves to the "superwoman," the woman who does it all, who works full time without disrupting family and household responsibilities (Thompson, 1991). Women compare their husband's participation rate to those of other men. They may be satisfied that their husband performs 25% of the household chores because the neighbor's husband does not participate in any household chores. Wives' evaluations of husbands' assistance at home may become even more favorable if the comparison referents become men of previous generations: fathers or grandfathers. Thus one reason women are not as dissatisfied with the division of labor as we would expect is that they do not directly compare themselves to men.

A more recent study suggests that comparison referents may be changing—at least for women. Women compared their contribution to the division of labor to that of their husbands as well as other women, whereas men only compared their contribution to that of

DO GENDER 11.2
Is It Fair? To Whom
Do You Compare?

Interview a few college students who are involved in a romantic relationship with someone they live with. These people can be married or cohabiting. First, try to find out who does what in the relationship. Second, try to find out the rationale for this division of labor. Third, ask about their perceptions of fairness: Is the division of labor fair? How do they decide if it is fair? Ask about comparison referents; that is, to whom do they compare themselves when judging the fairness of how much time they spend on household tasks?

other men (Gager & Hohmann-Marriott, 2006). Thus women may be more unsatisfied with the division of labor today compared to men because they use different comparison referents to evaluate fairness. When women are forced to compare their own participation rate to that of their husband, satisfaction decreases (Hawkins, Marshall, & Meiners, 1995). Find out to whom your peers compare their contributions to household labor in Do Gender 11.2.

Effects on Well-Being

There are two contrasting views on how the division of labor should be related to psychological well-being. One view says the more power we have, the less depressed we are. If that is the case, we should be happiest and least distressed when we use our power to make 100% of the decisions and avoid all household chores. An alternative view that may make more sense in the context of relationships is that an equitable or fair distribution of power is related to less distress.

If the division of labor has stronger implications for women's marital satisfaction, we would expect that the division of labor also would have stronger implications for women's health. There is some evidence that suggests this is true. Hochschild (1989) suggests that women suffer from the "second shift" in terms of fatigue, sickness, and emotional exhaustion. Women's greater participation in household labor compared to men is associated with more depression for women (Coltrane, 2000) and accounts for part of women's higher rates of depression compared to men (Bird, 1999). Yet the amount of time women spend on housework is not as strongly related to depression as women's perception of equity (Bird, 1999; Glass & Fujimoto, 1994). What is important to women is not an equal division of labor, but the perception of an equitable or fair division of labor.

If men do not contribute to household chores, they pay a price for women conducting the second shift (Hochschild, 1989). The price may take the form of wives' resentment, of negative effects on the marital relationship, and of husbands being shut out from relationships with children.

TAKE HOME POINTS

- The sex difference in the division of labor has decreased over the past 40 years, largely due to the increase of women in the employed labor force.

- Even when women hold full-time jobs outside the home, they spend more time than men on household labor and child care.

- One determinant of the division of labor is people's gender-role attitudes; the husband's attitude is a stronger predictor than the wife's. For the division of labor to be more equal, the husband must have an egalitarian gender-role attitude.

- Power is a major determinant of the division of labor. The person who makes more money, works more hours outside the home, and has a higher education typically participates less in household labor.

- The linking of the division of labor to gender roles occurs in heterosexual couples but not homosexual couples; homosexual couples adopt a more egalitarian division of labor and do not divide tasks along gender lines.

- In general, men's contribution to the division of labor is influenced more by their gender-role attitudes than women's contribution to the division of labor. Women's contribution to the division of labor is influenced more by practical issues, such as the number of children in the home and the number of hours that they work.

- Women do not necessarily want an equal division of labor; they want an equitable or fair division of labor, and a 50/50 split may not be necessary for women to perceive fairness.

- One reason that women are more accepting of a less than equal contribution to the division of labor is that they do not compare their own contributions to those of their husbands; instead women compare themselves to other women and compare their husbands to other men. This kind of comparison usually results in a more favorable view of husbands and leaves women more satisfied.

- The inequity in the division of labor is a prominent source of marital distress for women and may be a source of ill health. What is surprising is that women are not more dissatisfied with this state of affairs.

DOMESTIC ABUSE

Historically, men were permitted to hit their wives without sanction from the community, let alone the legal system. In fact, folklore claims that the phrase "rule of thumb" came out of legal reform in the area of wife beating: Husbands were prohibited from hitting their wives with an instrument that was thicker in diameter than their thumb (Kelly, 1994). Today, "rule of thumb" has no meaning because men are not legally permitted to abuse their wives.

This does not mean, however, that violence does not occur in families.

The subject of domestic abuse really came to the public's attention in the 1970s with the development of the women's movement. Shelters for battered women appeared in the 1970s and 1980s. In 1985, Surgeon General C. Everett Koop proclaimed that violence against women was the number-one health problem afflicting women. More attention was brought to the subject of battered women by the 1994 to 1995 trial of O. J. Simpson for the murder of his wife, Nicole Brown Simpson. Although Simpson was acquitted of the murder, the evidence was clear there had been a history of domestic violence in the relationship.

Domestic abuse has been associated with physical, mental, and financial consequences (Wallace, 1999). Domestic abuse results in physical symptoms and physical injuries. Psychological distress may take the form of anxiety and depression. In more severe cases, domestic abuse has been associated with suicide among women (Krane, 1996). The economic costs of domestic abuse are observed in terms of lost days of work, legal fees, and health care.

I entitled this section "Domestic Abuse" rather than "Battered Women," in recognition of the fact that both husbands and wives can be abused. Isn't it true, though, that women are more likely than men to be the subjects of violence in families? Some people argue that adopting gender-neutral language ("domestic abuse" vs. "battered woman") ignores the linking of gender and power to the occurrence of violence in families (e.g., Kurz, 1998). The subject is politically charged. I begin this section by examining the incidence of spousal abuse. Then I examine characteristics of people likely to engage in spousal abuse as well as characteristics of people who suffer abuse. I conclude by reviewing theories of domestic violence. Some common myths about domestic abuse are shown in Table 11.2.

Incidence

It is difficult to calculate the incidence of domestic abuse, in part because abuse can be

TABLE 11.2 Myths About Domestic Abuse

1. "A woman is beaten every _____ seconds in the United States. "

   Fill in the blank with the statistic that you have heard. Regardless, there is no governmental agency that keeps records of domestic abuse.
2. " _____ million women are abused each year in the United States."
   Same limitation as number 1.
3. "Women who kill their abusers receive more severe sentences than men who kill their abusers."
   The Bureau of Justice Statistics shows just the opposite.
4. "Domestic abuse always escalates."
   As you will see in this section of the text, that pertains to only a small subset of domestic abuse.
5. "Only men are the perpetrators of domestic abuse."
   Again, as you will see in this section of the text, this is not at all the case. The most common cases of domestic abuse involve both partners.

Source: Gelles (2007).

physical or verbal. In keeping with the theme of this chapter, I focus more on physical abuse. Yet even estimates of physical abuse are difficult to obtain. Researchers have relied on surveys and police and physician reports to estimate abuse. Obviously, police and physicians underestimate the incidence of abuse because they will be made aware of only the most extreme cases. In a phone survey of 16,000 people, only one fourth of physical assaults by former or current partners were reported to the police (Tjaden & Thoennes, 2000). The most common explanation for failing to report the assault was the belief that the police would not do anything. However, even surveys may underestimate abuse because poor people and non–English-speaking people are underrepresented in surveys.

The first national survey of domestic violence was conducted in 1976 and involved 2,143 families (Straus, Gelles, & Steinmetz, 1980). Rates of violence were so high that the phrase "the marriage license as a hitting license" was coined. The investigators found that 28% of families had engaged in at least one incident of violence over the course of their relationship, and 16% of families had done so in the prior year. Violent acts include punching, kicking, biting, hitting, beating, shooting, and stabbing. The items used to measure violence in this study are from the Conflict Tactics Scale (CTS) and are shown in Table 11.3. This defini-

tion of violence has been used in many subsequent studies. In 1985, a second national survey of 6,002 families revealed the annual incidence of abuse to be 16% (Straus & Gelles, 1990a). The investigators estimated that domestic violence occurs in 8.7 million families per year (Straus & Gelles, 1990a). In a randomized sample of women surveyed from the San Francisco area, a slightly higher figure was reported: Twenty-one percent of women reported their husband had been violent with them (Russell, 1990).

The rates for some acts of violence declined slightly between the 1976 and 1985 national surveys (Straus & Gelles, 1990b). This decline may have been due to the development of women's shelters, the increased public attention the problem received, and the development of policies to handle the abusive person (Straus & Gelles, 1990b; Wallace, 1999). Yet statistics from the late 1990s show an increase in violence; rates were between 28% and 33% (Johnson & Sacco, 1995; Klein et al., 1997; White & Kowalski, 1998). The rate of violence in marriages that ultimately dissolve may be even higher. In a study of 129 divorced mothers, 66% reported experiencing violence at some time during their marriage (Kurz, 1998).

Physical violence among dating couples appears to be equally prevalent, about 32% (White & Kowalski, 1998). A study that examined

---

TABLE 11.3   INDICATORS OF VIOLENCE FROM THE CONFLICT TACTICS SCALE

- threw something at the other one.
- pushed, grabbed, or shoved the other one.
- slapped the other one.
- kicked, bit, or hit with a fist.
- hit or tried to hit with something.
- beat up the other one.
- threatened with a knife or gun.
- used a knife or gun.

Source: Adapted from Straus et al. (1980).

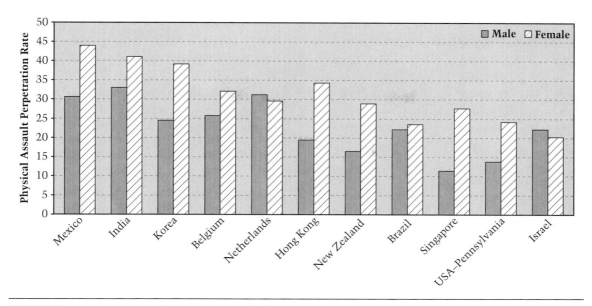

FIGURE 11.9   Sample of countries in which rates of physical assault were examined among dating couples. In most countries, the rate of female perpetration exceeded the rate of male perpetration, but differences were small.
Source: Adapted from Straus (2004).

physical assault among students from 31 colleges that spanned 16 countries showed that the median (50th percentile) percentage of physical assaults among dating couples over the last year was 29%, ranging from a low of 17% to a high of 45%, which was detected in a university in the United States (Straus, 2004). The incidence of physical assault in some of the countries is shown in Figure 11.9.

Are men and women equally likely to engage in domestic violence? In 1998, Currie reviewed 30 studies and showed that men and women were equally violent against their partner. The two nationally representative studies I described, one conducted in 1976 (Straus et al., 1980) and one in 1985 (Straus & Gelles, 1990a), showed that both men and women were violent 50% of the time, only the male was violent 25% of the time, and only the female was violent 25% of the time. In those studies, acts of violence were defined as throwing, pushing,

grabbing, shoving, and slapping, as well as more severe aggressive acts such as kicking, biting, punching, and beating (see Table 11.3). A fairly recent meta-analysis of sex differences in physical aggression in heterosexual romantic relationships showed a small effect in the direction of females being more aggressive than males ($d = -.05$; Archer, 2000). However, the age of the sample was an important moderator of sex differences in physical aggression, with females perpetrating more aggression than males in younger samples (age 22 and younger, $d = -.12$), and males perpetrating more aggression than females in older samples (age over 22, $d = +.12$). This fits with the cross-cultural study of college students, which showed that female perpetration rates were higher than male perpetration rates in 21 of the 31 universities (Straus, 2004). A recent nationally representative survey showed that women reported receiving and perpetrating more violence than men, but in half the relationships the violence seemed to be mutual (Williams & Frieze, 2005).

The picture of sex differences in physical assault has become even more confusing with the National Violence Against Women phone survey of a nationally representative sample of 8,000 men and 8,000 women (Tjaden & Thoennes, 2000). A substantially higher percentage of women than men (22% compared to 7%) reported having ever been a victim of physical assault by a former or current partner. It is difficult to reconcile these findings with previous research because this was a methodologically strong study.

Violence in gay and lesbian relationships has also been contradictory. A nationally representative study of adolescents in same-sex relationships revealed an overall violence rate of 24% using the Conflict Tactics Scale, with slightly higher rates for females than males (Halpern et al., 2004). Violence in same-sex romantic relationships was half the rate of violence in opposite-sex romantic relationships for males, but rates were comparable across same-sex and opposite-sex relationships for females. By contrast, the National Violence Against Women phone survey revealed that males in same-sex relationships were more likely to be assaulted by their partner (15%) than males in opposite-sex relationships (7%), whereas females in same-sex relationships were less likely to be assaulted by their partner (11%) than females in opposite-sex relationships (22%; Tjaden, Thoennes, & Allison, 1999).

One explanation for the contradictory findings may be that women experience more severe violence compared to men. The study of dating high school students revealed females reported more severe violence than males (Molidor & Tolman, 1998). An indicator of the severity of physical assault is injury. The meta-analytic review revealed that females sustain more injuries than males ($d = +.15$; Archer, 2000). This conclusion was confirmed by a more recent study of married adults (Bookwala, Sobin, & Zdaniuk, 2005) and the cross-cultural study of college students (Straus, 2004). Males reported higher rates of injury infliction than females in 18 of the 31 universities.

In addition to injury, violence is associated with greater distress among women than men (Williams & Frieze, 2005). When the consequences of violence from the 1985 national survey were examined, the degree of violence was more strongly associated with psychological symptoms (i.e., depression, stress), physical injury (i.e., need for medical care), and time off from work for women than for men (Stets & Straus, 1990). A study of high school dating relationships showed that when asked to think about the worst incident of violence, 90% of the males said it did not hurt or hurt a little compared to 28% of females (Molidor & Tolman, 1998). In response to this episode of violence, 54% of males said they laughed compared to 10% of females. Although there are certainly demand characteristics operating here that may lead males to minimize the effects of female violence, demand characteristics are unlikely to account for these large differences.

Another reason for the higher than expected rates of female violence toward men has to do with less public disapproval of this kind of violence. Male-female violence is judged more serious than female-male violence (Seelau & Seelau, 2005). In 1968, just over 20% of people said they could imagine a time when it was acceptable for a man to slap his wife, and the same number said they could imagine a time when it was acceptable for a woman to slap her husband. Subsequent surveys carried out in 1985, 1992, and 1994 showed that people's approval of husbands slapping wives had decreased sharply over time to 10% in 1994, but there was no change in approval of wives slapping husbands (Straus, 1995). A cross-cultural survey of dating couples showed that students were more approving of women slapping men than men slapping women in all 31 universities from 16 countries (Straus, 2004). Across the 31 universities, 76% found it acceptable for a woman to slap a man, whereas only 42% found it acceptable for a man to slap a woman. A study of college students showed that both males and females thought it was more acceptable for a woman to hit a man than a man to hit a woman after being betrayed (Forbes et al., 2005).

Men's and women's reports of violence may be influenced by what Currie (1998) refers to as "gendered expectations about appropriate behavior." Women expect men to be aggressive, and men expect women to be passive. Thus women may be less likely to interpret a man's behavior as violent, and men may be more likely to interpret a woman's behavior as violent. A study of college students supports this idea (Currie, 1998). Both men and women minimized violent acts committed by men. Women often justified men's violence and even blamed themselves. Men, by contrast, exaggerated violent acts committed by women. Recall from previous research that the sex of the person engaging in a behavior determines how it is interpreted. Thus, men and women may be equally likely to report that their partners commit violent acts when in actuality men are more violent than women. Violent acts of men may be underreported and violent acts of women may be overreported.

Finally, another distinction that might help shed light on why rates of violence appear to be equal among men and women is the distinction between **common couple violence** and **patriarchal terrorism** (or what is more recently referred to as intimate terrorism; Johnson, 2004). This distinction may help explain why statistics showing equal rates of victimization among men and women do not fit with our intuition that women are more likely than men to be the victim. Patriarchal terrorism refers to violence on the part of men that stems from their attempts to control women. It involves the systematic repetition of violence. Common couple violence, by contrast, refers to the occasional episodes of violent behavior on the part of husbands and wives precipitated by stressful events; it is not linked to the power imbalance between men and women. Common couple violence occurs in an attempt to control the particular situation, whereas patriarchal terrorism is a response to control the relationship more generally. Whereas patriarchal terrorism escalates, common couple violence does not. The control tactics involved in patriarchal terrorism are depicted in Figure 11.10. Johnson (1995) argues that this distinction may help us understand why large-scale surveys have found similar incidences of violence on the part of husbands and wives despite the fact that the people who appear at shelters are predominantly women: The surveys do not distinguish patriarchal terrorism from common couple violence.

More recent studies have tried to distinguish patriarchal terrorism from common couple violence. In one study, adults were administered both the Conflict Tactics Scale and a nonviolent control scale (e.g., limiting partner's contacts, making partner feel inadequate, keeping track of partner's whereabouts, being possessive; Johnson & Leone, 2005). Patriarchal terrorism was defined as the combination of violence and control, whereas common couple violence was defined as violence without control. Patriarchal terrorism included more frequent violence and more severe violence, and resulted in more injuries, greater days of missed work, greater number of times leaving the spouse, and greater symptoms of distress. Patriarchal terrorism also was

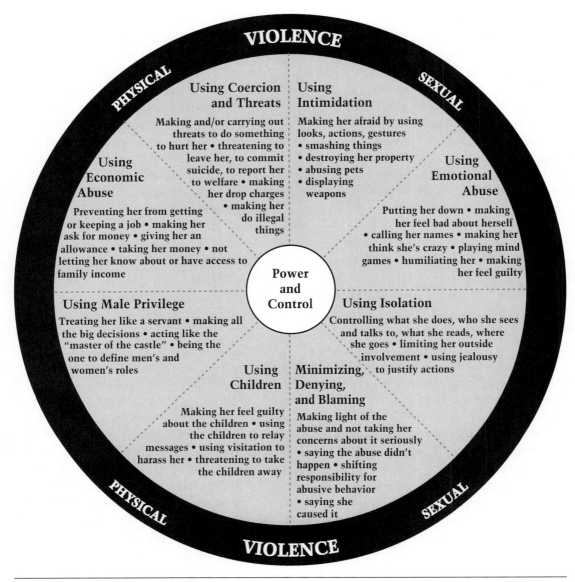

FIGURE 11.10   Control tactics involved in patriarchal terrorism.
Source: E. Pence and M. Paymar (1993). Education groups for men who batter: The Duluth model.
Copyright 1993. Reprinted by permission of Springer Publishing Co.

distinguished from common couple violence in a study of low income minority women (Leone et al., 2004). The women who were victims of patriarchal terrorism reported worse health as indicated by subjective health perceptions, greater psychological distress, and greater numbers of doctor visits than women who were victims of common couple violence.

There are distinct features of patriarchal terrorism. First, abuse is often accompanied by

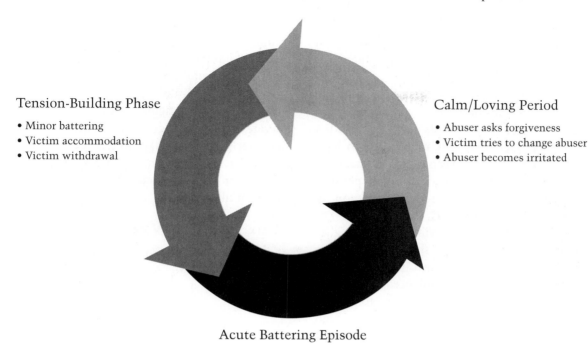

Tension-Building Phase

- Minor battering
- Victim accommodation
- Victim withdrawal

Calm/Loving Period

- Abuser asks forgiveness
- Victim tries to change abuser
- Abuser becomes irritated

Acute Battering Episode

FIGURE 11.11   Cycle of domestic abuse.
Source: Adapted from Walker (1979).

attempts to isolate the victim socially from family and friends, so the victim cannot gain feedback from others about the abuse. Second, the victim is typically economically dependent on the abuser. Third, alcohol is often associated with abuse. However, despite the link between alcohol and violence, alcohol alone is not sufficient to provoke violence (National Institute on Alcohol Abuse and Alcoholism, 1997). Finally, there is a cycle to the abuse (Walker, 1979), as shown in Figure 11.11. There is a tension-building phase, characterized by minor battering in which the victim tries to calm the abuser and accommodate her behavior to him but eventually withdraws. This phase is followed by an explosion, or acute battering episode, which is then followed by a calm and loving period in which the abuser tries to make amends, asks forgiveness, and promises to never hurt the

victim again. It is this positive period that convinces the victim she can change the abuser's behavior. Ultimately, however, the abuser becomes irritated, the victim again engages in accommodation, and then the victim withdraws. The tension escalates until another violent episode is precipitated.

Characteristics of Perpetrator

The person who engages in domestic abuse can be identified by a number of characteristics (Wallace, 1999). Abusive men are more likely to have a lower SES, to be young, and to be unemployed. Abusers typically have stereotypical views of men and women and have authoritarian personalities. They also score higher on hostile sexism (Glick et al., 2002). Abusers often have low self-esteem and use violence as a means to elevate their self-esteem (Gondolf & Hanneken, 1987). In addition, abusers often have a deficit in verbal skills, using violence as one way to handle disagreements.

People who engage in domestic abuse are often exposed to violence as a child, as either the subject of or a witness to violence. Men who abuse their wives are more likely to have witnessed violence between their parents, been abused by their parents, or suffered physical punishment by their parents (Hampton & Gelles, 1994; Straus, 1990a).

Rates of domestic violence are higher among Hispanic families than among other families in the United States. In the 1985 national survey, domestic violence occurred in 25% of Hispanic families compared to 16% of all families (Straus & Smith, 1990). The high rate of violence in Hispanic families was linked to their lower income, younger age, and tendency to live in urban areas. When these three factors were taken into consideration, there were no differences in rates of violence between Hispanic and non-Hispanic families.

Rates of violence are also higher in Black families than White families, as evidenced in both the 1976 national survey (Straus et al., 1980) and the 1985 national survey (Hampton & Gelles, 1994). In the latter survey, Black women were more than twice as likely as White women to experience severe violence. Although low income was associated with violence and accounted for some of the racial differences in violence, domestic abuse remained higher in Black families compared to White families with similar incomes.

Domestic abuse is also more common among younger couples (Capaldi, Kim, & Shortt, 2004). Recall that the meta-analysis noted that the sex difference in abuse (female greater than male) was limited to younger couples. We may know less about how it is that females become violent in the context of intimate relationships because we do not pay much attention to aggression among females during childhood and adolescence. Because girls are less physically aggressive than boys, we pay less attention to aggression in girls. We also tolerate relational aggression (which is more characteristic of girls) more than physical aggression. However, antisocial and aggressive behavior in girls predicts physical aggression among adult women.

Characteristics of Victim

Women who are abused tend to be younger, less educated, and have a lower income (Birns, 1998; Leone et al., 2004). No personality characteristics have been associated with being a victim of abuse (Wallace, 1999). No evidence indicates that the experience of abuse or witnessing abuse as a child is associated with becoming a victim of abuse (Hampton & Gelles, 1994).

An often asked question is why women who are abused remain in the relationship. The answer depends more on features of the situation than characteristics of the victim. A good predictor of whether someone stays in or leaves a relationship is not how satisfied the person is with the relationship but whether the person has alternatives to that relationship. In one study, women who had experienced violence from their husband said they stayed in the relationship because they did not have anywhere to go and did not have a job (Kurz, 1998). Women who are more financially dependent on their husband are more tolerant of abuse in their relationship (Wallace, 1999).

Theories

Some researchers view men's abuse of women as an extreme form of the stereotypical relationship that exists between men and women (Goldner et al., 1990). Spousal abuse is viewed as men's attempt to establish control and to restore dominance to their relationships with women (Birns, 1998; Browne & Williams, 1993). In support of this theory, women who are abused report that violence seemed to occur when they acted independently. Women say their husband tried to control their behavior by isolating them from friends and family. Thus control and dominance seem to be the primary motivations behind abuse. This description of abuse is consistent with the definition of patriarchal terrorism (Johnson, 1995). The theory that spousal abuse is a form of power and a way to exert dominance is supported by data showing that the lowest levels of violence occur in families where power and decision making are shared (Straus et al., 1980; Wallace, 1999). A cross-cultural study of domestic violence in 90 societies revealed that the lowest rates of domestic violence occurred in the more egalitarian societies (Levinson, 1989).

Spousal abuse also could be linked to a distorted perception of male/female interactions. In one study, married men watched three videotapes of women discussing personal problems with a therapist (these were actual sessions) and were asked to rate at various points in the videotape whether the women were critical and/or rejecting of their husbands (Schweinle, Ickes, & Bernstein, 2002). In comparison to a panel of neutral judges, the men who scored higher on a measure of tendency toward spousal abuse were more likely to infer critical/rejecting feelings. Thus men who abuse their wives may be more likely to perceive interactions with women in negative terms. These findings suggest that abuse in men is not necessarily linked to features or behavior of a particular woman, but that abusive men perceive all women in more negative terms.

A personality characteristic, Masculine Gender-Role Stress (MGRS), has been linked to this biased perception of interactions between men and women. Men who score high on MGRS are more likely to perceive situations that challenge traditional male/female roles as stressful. In one study, men listened to vignettes of male/female dating partners having a conflict and were asked to imagine themselves in each situation (Eisler et al., 2000). Men who scored higher on MGRS became angrier, perceived their partners more negatively, and said they would respond to the conflict with greater verbal and physical aggression. In another study of men who were in a substance abuse treatment program, those who scored higher on MGRS reported more abusive behavior toward their female partners (Copenhaver, Lash, & Eisler, 2000).

Consistent with the idea of common couple violence, abuse has been linked to stress. The 1985 national survey showed that the number of stressful life events recently experienced was associated with violence among both men and women (Straus, 1990b). Stress also interacts with personality variables to predict abuse. Straus found that men who believed husbands should be dominant in the family were 1.5 to 3 times more likely to assault their wife than other men if they were under high stress. In addition, men who were socially isolated were more likely to assault their wife if they were under high stress. Thus stressful circumstances might combine with other factors, such as personality traits or environmental conditions, to produce family violence.

See Sidebar 11.1 for a discussion of a particular type of abuse that has received attention—stalking.

Sidebar 11.1: *Stalking*

Stalking has been defined as the "willful, malicious and repeated following and harassing of another person" (National Institute of Justice, 1993, p. 13). An essential aspect of the definition of stalking is repetition. It is not defined as a single behavior, but a pattern of behavior. In fact, the average stalking episode lasts nearly 2 years (Spitzberg & Cupach, 2007).

A recent meta-analysis of stalking showed that females are much more likely than males to be victims—29% versus 11% (Spitzberg & Cupach, 2007). Stalking behaviors can be divided into those that are violent, such as the threat of harm and the infliction of harm, and those that are harassing, such as being watched, being followed, and receiving unwanted phone calls. In the meta-analysis, just over half of stalking (54%) involved threat, 32% involved physical violence, and 12% involved sexual violence. The majority of victims (79%) know the stalker; one half appear to involve a former romantic partner.

There is some overlap among physical abuse, emotional abuse, and stalking. Of women who are stalked by former partners, the majority reported a history of abuse in the relationship (Mechanic, Weaver, & Resick, 2002). However, stalking is more strongly linked to a history of emotional than physical abuse. Like other forms of sexual and physical abuse, stalking appears to stem from a need to control and intimidate a person (Mechanic et al., 2002). These attempts increase in the presence of a threat to the relationship. This is why stalking behavior is so strongly linked to the breakup of relationships. The stereotype of stalking is that it stems from mental illness and involves celebrities. The truth seems to be that stalking is a more normative behavior that stems from romantic relationships gone awry or distorted perceptions of relationships. One possibility is that there are two different kinds of stalking just as there are two different kinds of domestic abuse—one of which may be highly dangerous and the other more stressful and annoying than dangerous.

TAKE HOME POINTS

- The majority of research shows that men and women are equally likely to engage in physical violence in the context of intimate relationships, but methodological issues may distort violence reports.

- "Gendered expectations" may lead people to underreport male violence and overreport female violence.

- People are more accepting of female violence toward men than male violence toward women.

- Women are more likely than men to be injured by violence, and violence has more negative effects on women than men.

- One way to reconcile the large-scale survey studies that show men and women are equally likely to commit violence with the greater attention given to female victims of violence is to distinguish between patriarchal terrorism and common couple violence.

- Patriarchal terrorism is violence that stems from a need to control, escalates, and targets women.

- Common couple violence is the kind of violence that erupts in families in response to stress, does not escalate, and characterizes both men and women. Violence that occurs in the context of stress supports this theory.

RAPE AND OTHER FORMS OF SEXUAL COERCION

In 2006, Duke Lacrosse players invited two exotic female dancers over for a party. The next day, three of those players were charged with rape. Perhaps because the players were White and from privileged backgrounds attending an elite school and the woman was minority, the public expressed little sympathy for the players and most believed the charges were true—especially women (Carroll, 2006c). A year later, the players were cleared of the charges.

Rape is an act of violence with numerous physical and mental health consequences. Physical injuries range from minor bruises to life-threatening injuries to death. Mental health consequences range from fear, anxiety, and depression, to post-traumatic stress syndrome (Koss, Bailey, Yuan, Herrera, & Lichter, 2003). Rape also has been associated with impairments in sexual functioning (Wallace, 1999). A history of sexual assault, especially repeated assault, has been linked to physical disease (Stein & Barrett-Connor, 2000). One study found greater symptoms of anxiety, depression, and sexual concerns among people who experienced a sexual assault 14 years earlier than people who had not (Elliott, Mok, & Briere, 2004). The consequences were more severe for men than women (see Figure 11.12).

In this section, I first define rape and then report studies that examine the incidence of rape and other forms of sexual coercion. I devote a specific section to studies among college students because the findings may differ from those of the general population. I discuss characteristics of the perpetrator and victim: Who rapes and who is likely to be raped? Finally, I discuss theories of rape.

Definitions

You might expect that rape is a straightforward concept with a straightforward definition. However, there are many definitions of rape (Russell, 1990). Definitions vary regarding the specific behavior that distinguishes rape from other sexual acts. The most conservative definition of rape restricts the behavior to penile-vaginal penetration. More liberal definitions include other forms of sexual contact, such as kissing, fondling, oral sex, and anal sex. Definitions also vary in how *nonconsent* to engage in sexual behavior is determined. What is an adequate indicator of nonconsent? Some

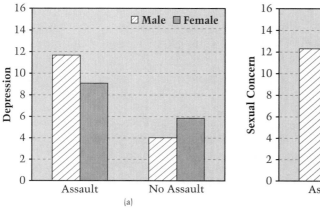
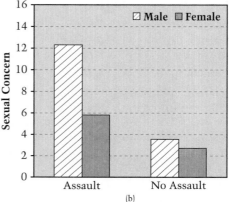

FIGURE 11.12 Sexual assault victims reported more symptoms of depression (a) and sexual concerns (b) than nonvictims 14 years after the assault. Male victims reported more symptoms than female victims.
Source: Adapted from Elliott et al. (2004).

definitions refer to rape as sexual behaviors that are undesired by the victim. Other definitions require evidence of victim resistance. There are other situations in which a person is unable to give informed consent, such as being under age, mentally ill, or intoxicated. Consent also may be obtained under duress. Many definitions refer to the sexual behavior as being forced on the recipient, but defining force is difficult. Does there have to be evidence of physical injury? Are verbal threats sufficient?

In addition, men and women may have different definitions of rape. In vignette studies with college students, men are less likely to perceive that a rape occurred (McLendon et al., 1994), more likely to blame the victim when a rape did occur (Workman & Freeburg, 1999), and more likely to minimize the severity of rape (Ben-David & Schneider, 2005).

One kind of rape that especially suffers from these definitional issues is spousal rape. Some people still believe rape cannot occur in marriage, because sexual intercourse between husband and wife is a right of marriage (Russell, 1990). Historically, rape laws in the United States contained in their definitions of rape what is known as the **marital rape exemption clause.** This exemption can be found in the following definition of rape: "the forcible penetration of the body of a woman, not the wife of the perpetrator" (Russell, 1990, p. 17). It was not until 1993 that all 50 states had deleted the marital rape exemption clause. However, some other countries still employ some form of marital rape exemption.

The definitions of sexual assault or sexual coercion are even more varied. Sexual coercion has been defined as pressure or force to have sexual contact (George, Winfield, & Blazer, 1992; Sorenson & Siegel, 1992), pressure or force to have sexual relations (Struckman-Johnson & Struckman-Johnson, 1994), and, even more broadly, as engaging in sexual activi-ties against one's wishes (Muehlenhard & Cook, 1988). Lower rates of sexual coercion are reported when people are asked if sexual contact was "forced" rather than "unwanted" (Hamby & Koss, 2003). What behaviors constitute sexual coercion? How are force, pressure, and nonconsent determined?

Incidence

Population Studies.   In 2005, 127,430 cases of rape or attempted rape were reported (Bureau of Justice Statistics, 2006a). Lifetime prevalence of rape is 15% for females and 2% for males (Rozee & Koss, 2001). In a community sample of just over 1,000 women, 17% said they had been raped (Testa et al., 2004). Estimating the prevalence of rape is difficult because it is underreported. Many victims do not report rape because they feel guilty, feel a sense of shame, doubt that people will believe them, and/or do not want to share their personal sexual history with strangers. Even surveys of rape may underestimate its incidence (Koss, 1993). The majority of surveys ask individuals a single question about whether they have been raped and use only the term *rape*. However, some individuals do not apply the label of rape to experiences that would qualify as rape; people often do not include oral sex or anal penetration when thinking of rape. In addition, people may not include rape attempts as rape. When multiple questions about rape are asked in surveys, the incidence of rape increases (Koss, 1993).

Estimates of the prevalence of sexual assault among women vary even more than estimates of rape, from 15% to 50% (George et al., 1992). In an interview study of over 3,000 persons in the Los Angeles area, 17% said they had been sexually assaulted (Sorenson & Siegel, 1992). In that study, sexual assault was defined as someone pressuring or forcing them to have sexual contact. More women than men reported sexual assault (17% vs. 9%), and the rate was much higher among non-Hispanic White people (20%) than Hispanic people (8%).

What is the incidence of spousal rape? In a random sample of adults from the San Francisco area, 14% of people who had ever been married reported being a victim of spousal rape or attempted spousal rape (Russell, 1990). In that study, rape was defined as forced oral, anal, digital, or penile-vaginal penetration. In the majority of cases (85%), the rape was penile-vaginal penetration. In 31% of the cases, the rape was isolated, occurring only once. In 37% of the cases, rape occurred between 2 and 20 times; in 31% of the cases, rape occurred more than 20 times. Alcohol was involved in 20% to 25% of the incidents.

An extreme view of the incidence of rape was offered by Griffin (1971). She maintains that all women are victims of rape in a sense—not necessarily because someone has attempted to rape them but because all women have to deal with the fear of rape. Women's day-to-day behavior reflects this fear. Women are more fearful than men of living alone, of walking alone at night, and of leaving a window open or doors unlocked. People chastise women for walking alone at night but do not think twice about men being by themselves. In Chapter 1, I mentioned a study in which I asked college students to imagine a typical day if they were of the other sex; one of the most frequent remarks that men made was that they would have to call campus security to get to their dorm because they would be afraid to walk alone at night. By contrast, women reported that as men they felt a sense of freedom in being able to go where they want when they want. These findings suggest that both men and women are well aware that women are more fearful than men of rape.

Studies of College Students. Studies of college students report higher incidences of

sexual assault, but definitions are often more liberal. In a national survey of female college students, 54% of the 3,187 women reported some form of sexual victimization: 16% rape, 12% attempted rape, 11% sexual coercion, and 15% sexual contact (Ullman, Karabatsos, & Koss, 1999). In over half of the cases (53%), women said the offender used alcohol; in 42% of the cases, the women reported using alcohol. Use of alcohol was not only common during sexual assault but was also associated with the severity of the assault. The more severe cases of assault (i.e., rape, attempted rape) were associated with alcohol usage by both offender and victim. Forty percent of the sexual assaults occurred during a date.

We typically think of women as the victims of rape and sexual assault; in fact, criminal statistics define rape as something that occurs only to women. Although rape may be rare among men, sexual coercion may not. Men may find it difficult to refuse sex because the expectation of the male gender role is that men are always ready and willing to have sex. One study of college men found that 34% reported at least one "forced sexual experience" (Struckman-Johnson & Struckman-Johnson, 1994), defined as the use of pressure or force to have sexual contact or sexual intercourse. Most of these forced sexual experiences involved women and occurred with an acquaintance or a friend rather than a stranger. When women initiated these coercive episodes, men reported that the women typically used persuasion or alcohol. When other men initiated these coercive episodes, men reported that the men used persuasion, bribery, alcohol, or physical threats and restraints. Men rated sexual coercion by men more negatively than sexual coercion by women.

Even among students as young as 10th grade, males have more difficulty than females saying no to sex. In one study, 10th grade boys and girls were asked how confident they were that they could refuse sex if someone tried to pressure them (Zimmerman et al., 1995). Whereas 61% of females said they "definitely" could say no, only 32% of males gave this response. Males cited peer pressure as their primary reason for having difficulty refusing sex.

It is difficult to evaluate what these episodes of sexual coercion mean to men. In one study, their occurrence was unrelated to men's current well-being (Struckman-Johnson & Struckman-Johnson, 1994). In that study, 50% of the men said a female coercive episode had no impact on them at all; in only 23% of the cases was there a strong negative impact. By contrast, the impact of coercion initiated by a male had a strong negative impact on men nearly 50% of the time.

Thus it appears that both men and women college students may be victims of sexual coercion. However, sexual coercion seems to mean something different to men and women. Men feel less able to refuse sex, so they don't— but they also typically do not suffer serious consequences; women feel more able to refuse, so when victimization occurs, they suffer more serious consequences.

Characteristics of Perpetrator

Most of us tend to perceive rape as occurring by a stranger, but in the majority of cases the two people know each other. In 2005, only 35% of women reported being raped by a stranger (Bureau of Justice Statistics, 2006c). One reason rape is underreported and not given more serious attention is that people have more sympathy for victims who do not know their attackers.

Gender-related attitudes affect whether people make a distinction between acquaintance rape and stranger rape. People who score high on benevolent sexism are especially

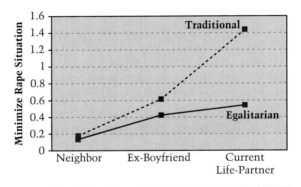

FIGURE 11.13 College students who held more traditional gender-role attitudes were more likely than those with egalitarian attitudes to minimize the severity of rape when committed by an ex-boyfriend or a current life-partner than a neighbor.
Source: Adapted from Ben-David & Schneider (2005).

unsympathetic to victims of acquaintance rape compared to stranger rape (Abrams et al., 2003; Viki, Abrams, & Masser, 2004). Benevolent sexism includes the belief that women should be protected by men but also the belief that women should behave in ways to elicit men's protection. Among acquaintances, the closeness of the relationship also influences people's perceptions of rape. As shown in Figure 11.13, people who have traditional gender-role attitudes are more likely to minimize the severity of rape when it is committed by an ex-boyfriend or a current partner compared to a neighbor; people with egalitarian attitudes do not make this distinction (Ben-David & Schneider, 2005).

We also perceive rape as involving physical force, but rape often involves verbal threats (Ward, 1995). We have less sympathy for victims who do not show physical signs of abuse. To make matters worse, strangers are more likely to use physical force, and known others are more likely to use verbal threats (Cleveland, Koss, & Lyons, 1999). Thus the most common occurrence of rape—a known other who uses verbal threats—evokes the least

TABLE 11.4   SAMPLE ITEMS FROM RAPE MYTH ACCEPTANCE SCALE

1. Any healthy woman can successfully resist a rapist if she really wants to.

2. When women go around braless or wearing short skirts and tight tops, they are just asking for trouble.

3. In the majority of rapes, the victim is promiscuous or has a bad reputation.

4. Women who get raped while hitchhiking get what they deserve.

5. Many women have an unconscious wish to be raped and may then unconsciously set up a situation in which they are likely to be attacked.

Source: Burt (1980).

sympathy from the community. In general, women are more sympathetic than men toward rape victims (Nagel et al., 2005).

Perpetrators have been found to have two primary motives for rape (Groth, Burgess, & Holmstrom, 1977). **Power rape** occurs when the person is seeking to control and exert power over the victim. The rapist with this motive may be more likely to suffer from low self-esteem and, if male, to feel inadequate in his gender role. Traditional masculine beliefs have been directly linked to sexual aggression. In a meta-analytic review of the literature, 11 different measures of masculine ideology were linked to sexual aggression (Murnen, Wright, & Kaluzny, 2002). The strongest relations appeared with measures that reflected acceptance of violence and dominance over women.

Anger rape occurs when the perpetrator is expressing hostility or hate toward the victim; the motivation here is to harm the victim. Anger rape among men may be viewed as revenge against a particular woman or all women in general. Men who rape and behave in sexually aggressive ways toward women typically are more likely to hold hostile attitudes toward women (Lisak, 1991). These men are more likely to report being hurt by women through deception, betrayal, or manipulation, and to feel put down and belittled by women (Lisak & Roth, 1988).

Perpetrators often hold myths about women and rape. Brownmiller (1975) identified four basic rape myths: (1) All women want to be raped; (2) a woman cannot be raped against her will; (3) a woman who is raped is asking for it; and (4) if a woman is going to be raped, she might as well enjoy it. Numerous scales have emerged to measure acceptance of rape myths. Items from one of the most widely used scales (Burt, 1980) are shown in Table 11.4. See how many people today endorse these myths with Do Gender 11.3.

Rape myths are likely to be endorsed by people who have strong gender-role stereotypes,

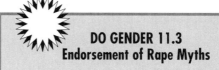

DO GENDER 11.3
Endorsement of Rape Myths

Administer the items in Table 11.4 to a group of men and women to establish the prevalence of rape myths. Feel free to add a few items of your own. What other variables do you expect to be associated with rape myths: traditional attitudes toward gender roles, gender-related traits (agency, communion, unmitigated agency, unmitigated communion), socioeconomic status? Measure one of these other variables and see if it is associated with rape myths in men and women.

people who are more accepting of interpersonal violence, and people who are less educated (Burt, 1980). People who endorse rape myths are more likely to blame the victim and less likely to blame the perpetrator (Kopper, 1996). Women are less likely than men to endorse rape myths (Kopper, 1996; Ward, 1995). In a study of college students, men who were in fraternities and men who were athletes were more likely to endorse rape myths, such as, "Women pretend not to want sex but want to be forced," and, "Women secretly want to be raped" (Boeringer, 1999). Fraternity membership also has been directly linked to sexual aggression (Lackie & de Man, 1997).

However, women also subscribe to some rape myths, and the extent to which they endorse these myths influences their likelihood of admitting to rape. College women who met the legal definition of rape but did not define themselves as having been raped were more likely to endorse rape myths (Peterson & Muehlenhard, 2004). For example, women who did not physically fight off the person who raped them and who subscribed to the rape myth that "it can't be rape if a woman doesn't fight back" were less likely to acknowledge that they had been raped.

Characteristics of Victim

In general, victims of rape and sexual assault span all age ranges and all educational backgrounds. However, rape and sexual assault are more likely to occur among younger people (i.e., ages 13 to 24), Black people, people of a lower SES, and people who have been sexually abused as a child (George et al., 1992; Elliott et al., 2004). By contrast, more educated people report a higher incidence of sexual assault (George et al., 1992). This latter finding is difficult to interpret because definitions of sexual assault vary; more educated people may define sexual assault in more liberal terms or be more likely

to report sexual assault. One variable that may predict victimization is one's relationship orientation. In one study, college women who were more anxious about their relationships and feared losing their partner reported being more willing to engage in unwanted sex (Impett & Peplau, 2002).

Demographic variables, such as social class, ethnicity, and age, are generally not associated with being a victim of spousal rape (Russell, 1990). Attitudes toward gender roles also are not associated with being a victim of spousal rape. However, attitudes toward gender roles are associated with one's response to spousal rape. Women with more traditional attitudes are more likely to blame themselves and to stay in the relationship than women with more egalitarian attitudes. In one study, 22% of wives stayed with their husbands after rape (Russell, 1990). The women who stayed were more likely to have minimized the trauma of the rape, to report it was an isolated occurrence, to have fewer economic resources, and to blame themselves for the rape. Of these variables, the strongest predictor of staying in the relationship was self-blame. Race also was a predictor of staying in the relationship. Whereas 13% of White women remained in the relationship, 42% of Black, Asian, and Latina women stayed in the relationship. Members of minority groups may have lacked economic resources.

Another topic relevant to victims of rape is resistance strategies (Ullman, 1997). Whether or not women resist rape influences how they are viewed by others, and evidence of resistance may be used as proof of the rape. There is an upside and a downside to focusing on rape resistance strategies. The upside is that resistance reduces the likelihood of a completed rape. The downside is that focusing on resistance strategies places the burden on women. A concern that people have with rape resistance strategies is that employing them may threaten one's life.

In a review of the literature (Ullman, 1997), forceful physical resistance strategies decreased the likelihood of a completed rape and were associated with a slight increase in physical injury; nonforceful physical strategies (fleeing, shielding oneself) decreased the likelihood of a completed rape and were not associated with an increase in physical injury; and forceful verbal strategies (screaming) decreased the likelihood of a completed rape. There was not enough information to determine the effect of forceful verbal strategies on physical injuries. Nonforceful resistance strategies (pleading) were ineffective with respect to rape completion.

See Sidebar 11.2 for a discussion of rape prevention strategies.

Theories

The early theories of rape focused on characteristics of the perpetrator (Donat & D'Emilio, 1992). The rapist was considered to be mentally ill and sexually perverted. Thus in a sense, researchers focused on the plight of the perpetrator rather than the plight of the victim. In addition, rape was considered a form of sexually deviant behavior and thus tied to sex rather than aggression. Later, theorists began to focus on characteristics of the victim. As women's

SIDEBAR 11.2: *Rape Prevention Strategies*

Rozee and Koss (2001) developed a strategy for women to resist rape, referred to as the AAA strategy: assess, acknowledge, and act:

1. After saying "no" to sex, ASSESS the situation to see if it is dangerous.

2. If dangerous, ACKNOWLEDGE this and label the situation as a dangerous one.

3. ACT, employ rape resistance strategies:

   a. Leave the situation if possible.

   b. If not, use verbal strategies.

   c. If verbal strategies are not effective, employ physical tactics (self-defense).

People commonly perceive that resisting rape will increase the likelihood of further injury. However, no evidence supports this belief. Attempts to resist rape are more likely to prevent a rape from occurring. In addition, rape resistance strategies increase women's sense of empowerment.

In recognition of the fact that rape is as much a man's problem as a woman's problem, Rozee and Koss (2001) also developed a comparable rape prevention strategy for men, also referred to as the AAA strategy: ask, acknowledge, and act. The strategy is depicted below:

1: ASK oneself if the woman is capable of consenting

If yes → ask if she wants to have sex   If no → ACKNOWLEDGE the fact and ACT (stop)
              ↓   ↓
If yes, ACT (sex is OK)   If no → ACKNOWLEDGE the fact and ACT (stop)

sexuality became more accepted during the middle of the 20th century, people came to wonder what role women played in rape. People asked what the woman could have done to cause or prevent the rape: What was she wearing? Did she fight back? Was there evidence of physical harm? Even today, certain characteristics of women are associated with more blame for rape. Both men and women assign greater blame to women who wear more revealing clothing and have less respectable characters (Whatley, 1996). The next phase in history appeared with the development of the women's movement. Rape was reconceptualized as an act of violence rather than an act of sex. Feminists maintained that rape was a "means of enforcing gender roles in society and maintaining the hierarchy in which men retained control" (Donat & D'Emilio, 1992, p. 14). In her best-selling book *Against Our Will: Men, Women, and Rape,* Susan Brownmiller (1975) defined rape as "a conscious process of intimidation by which all men keep all women in a state of fear" (p. 15).

Today, people generally regard rape as an act of violence rather than sex (Wallace, 1999). Men are socialized to be aggressive, to be dominant over women, and to view women as sexual conquests. However, rape also may be related to an important situational variable: misperceptions of sexual intentions and behavior.

Men interpret sexual behavior differently than women, perhaps because men are more likely than women to assume others are interested in sex. Several studies of college students have demonstrated that men are more likely than women to interpret neutral behavior in more sexual terms. However, it may be a subgroup of men who are more likely to view a female's behavior as sexual. One study of college students showed that only men who endorsed a high number of rape myths overinterpreted behavior as sexual (Abbey & Harnish, 1995). Another study directly linked the overinterpretation of neutral behavior in sexual terms to sexual aggression among men (Bondurant & Donat, 1999). Thus rape may be a function of the person and the situation: Rape may be more likely to occur in certain situations among people who have predisposing characteristics.

Because our stereotype of sexual assault involves a male perpetrator and a female victim, we are also more likely to infer sexual assault when the same act is committed by a male than a female. Male college students were asked to rate the extent to which 14 behaviors were indicative of sexual assault when the perpetrator was male and female (Lev-Wiesel & Besser, 2006). The list contained 8 sexual assault behaviors and 6 neutral behaviors. Students were more likely to rate the sexual assault behaviors as indicative of sexual assault if the perpetrator was male than female.

It also has been argued that our culture's scripts for heterosexual dating sets up opportunities for miscommunication and the potential for sexual aggression (Krahé, 2000). Despite changes in men's and women's roles, dating scripts have retained traditional male and female relations. It is still the case that women are not supposed to initiate sexual interactions and that men have the burden of deciphering the subtle cues of sexual interest that women convey. The expectation is that sexual interest is conveyed with implicit nonverbal behavior rather than explicit verbal behavior. Another feature of the heterosexual dating script is that women should initially reject sexual advances, even when desired. This is referred to as "token resistance." Studies of undergraduates reveal that 40% have used token resistance at least once in a relationship. Thus the heterosexual dating script sets the stage for miscommunication.

- It is difficult to measure the frequency of rape and sexual coercion due to a variety of definitional issues, including the specific act and the determination of consent.

- Although women are much more likely than men to be victims of rape, studies of college students report similar levels of sexual coercion among males and females.

- Similar to the findings for domestic abuse, being a victim of sexual coercion is associated with more negative consequences for females than males unless it is a male coercing a male.

- People are less sympathetic to victims of rape when the rape is committed by a known other and there is no evidence of physical injury, which is unfortunate because it is the most typical rape scenario. Rape is most often committed by someone who is known and with the use of verbal rather than physical threats.

- There are two motives for rape: power, or the seeking of control over the person, and anger, or the expression of hostility toward the person.

- Perpetrators of rape are more likely to hold rape myths. People who hold rape myths express less sympathy for victims.

- Most recent theories conceptualize rape as an act of violence rather than an act of sex.

- Situational forces contribute to rape and sexual coercion. Men are more likely than women to perceive neutral behaviors in sexual terms.

- Sexual scripts for male-female relationships contribute to these misperceptions, as men are expected to initiate sexual interactions and women are expected to dismiss men's advances.

PARENTING AND HEALTH

During the 18th and 19th centuries, men were regarded as the ultimate source of moral influence on children (Pleck, 1987). If marriages dissolved, men retained custody of the children. Fathers' custody of children was partly due to the fact that fathers were in greater proximity to work and children were involved in work. This connection was especially strong with sons. During the 19th and 20th centuries, the role of mother in the family expanded. Women were regarded as pure and innocent, thus possessing the ideal qualities to raise children. In addition, society began to regard infancy and childhood as critical times of development, times in which a mother's role was especially important. It was at this time that it became the norm to award mothers custody of children in the event of divorce. Fathers were still regarded as the moral authority but became more far removed from children, in part due to industrialization shifting fathers' work farther from home.

Family roles again shifted in the middle of the 20th century, specifically after World War II, when women moved into the workforce. The roles of mothers and fathers in the family are not as clearly distinct as they once were. As mentioned previously (and shown in Figure 11.14),

FIGURE 11.14 Photograph of father and child spending time together at the beach.

fathers are more involved in families. Fathers, however, are still typically regarded as the economic providers of a family and mothers are regarded as the primary caretakers of children. For example, the arrival of children in the family is more likely to bring maternity leave than paternity leave.

The traditional family has changed quite a lot over the years. In 1970, 87% of households with children consisted of two parents (U.S. Census Bureau, 2006a). In 2005, the corresponding figure was 67%, due to the increase in divorce and the increase in single people having families. In 2004, the percentage of births to unmarried women was 25% for White women, 24% for Asian women, 32% for Hispanic women, and 62% to African American women. In 2006, 96% of White adults said that their parents were married when they were born compared to 85% of Hispanics and 74% of African Americans (Saad, 2006b).

Today, fewer women are having children. In 1976, only 10% of women did not have children; in 2004, 19% of women between the ages of 40 and 44 did not have children (Dye, 2005). In the late 1950s, there were 3.5 births per woman. In the middle of the 1970s the rate had declined to 1.8. During the past decade, the rate has hovered around 2. The stereotype is that couples who choose not to have children dislike children. However, the most common reasons for not having children are valuing freedom, placing high importance on education/careers, and believing children detract from marriage. As you will see in a subsequent section, there is some truth to the latter point.

With the increase in the number of women working outside the home, many people believe that parents don't spend as much time with children today as they did years ago. This turns out not to be the case. Parents are spending just as much time with children as they did 20 years ago (Galinsky, 2005). But today there is less of a separation between work and family, as more parents work at home and bring work home. Children perceive parents today as stressed and fatigued.

Another change in the traditional family is the increase in number of stay-at-home dads, or men whose primary responsibility in the family is child care. In 2003, 71% of women and 96% of men in married couples participated in the labor force, defined as working at least one week during the past year. Among those who were not in the labor force, 88% of women and 16% of men said their primary responsibility was to take care of the home and family (U.S. Census Bureau, 2004c).

In this section, I examine the implications of the parent role for health. All this research is based on heterosexual couples. Because parenting is a subject of controversy in the gay and lesbian community, a discussion of parenting among homosexuals is presented in Sidebar 11.3.

Effects of the Parent Role on Health

In general, we tend to believe having children is good for our overall life satisfaction and well-being. However, there is little evidence that the presence of children in the home improves psychological well-being or physical health (Ross, Mirowsky, & Goldstein, 1990). A study of employed married men in dual-earner families (Barnett, Marshall, & Pleck, 1992), a study of working women (Barnett & Marshall, 1991), and a study of working men and women (Bond, Galinsky & Swanberg, 1998) all concluded that parental status is unrelated to psychological well-being. One study of dual-earner couples showed that parents were less distressed than nonparents (Barnett et al., 1994), but other studies have shown that the presence of children at home may be detrimental to health. In a nationally representative study of adults, there was a trend for the presence of children in the home to be associated with greater depression (Ross, 1995). In a survey in

Sidebar 11.3: *Parenting Among Homosexuals*

More and more children are being raised by gay and lesbian parents. It is difficult to determine the exact number of children because it is difficult to estimate the number of gay and lesbian people. Parents who are homosexual may also be less likely to report their sexual orientation because they are concerned about losing custody or contact with their children. A national poll showed that nearly half of gay men and lesbians who did not have children said that they would like to have children (Kaiser Family Foundation, 2001).

There are two groups of homosexual parents. The first and largest group consists of homosexual persons who were once married, had children, and then divorced, often due to the discovery or acceptance of homosexuality. A second growing group of parents consists of homosexual couples who choose to have children. In the case of lesbian couples, one partner may become pregnant through the use of a sperm donor. In the case of a gay couple, the most likely avenue is adoption. Alternatively, a lesbian and gay man may decide to have a child together. As shown in Table 11.5, there are few states that expressly permit gay and lesbian adoption but also few states that expressly prohibit it. Most states have not taken a clear position on the issue.

Issues about parenting have arisen for homosexuals that do not arise for heterosexuals. The first issue concerns whether homosexual persons are fit to be parents. The second issue concerns the effects of a parent's homosexuality on children: effects on the children's psychological adjustment, gender-role development, and sexual orientation. Each of these issues has been raised during custody disputes over whether children should be allowed to reside with a homosexual parent. As you will see, there is no evidence to support any of these concerns.

Are homosexuals any less fit to be parents? No evidence suggests that homosexual parents differ from heterosexual parents in levels of self-esteem, psychological distress, or emotional stability (Golombok et al., 2003; Patterson, 2000). Among people who have divorced, one advantage that homosexual parents seem to have over heterosexual parents is that they have fewer difficulties with their divorced partner. This means children of a homosexual parent have more contact with both parents than other children whose parents have divorced. In terms of actual parenting skills, one study found that lesbian parents were better than heterosexual mothers at coming up with solutions to hypothetical child difficulties (Flaks et al., 1995). Another study showed that lesbian mothers were less likely to hit their children and more likely to engage in imaginative play with children (Golombok et al., 2003). Few studies have compared gay fathers to heterosexual fathers; one reason may be that custody disputes typically revolve around whether a lesbian mother rather than a gay father is a fit parent. The woman's sexual orientation is more in question because the norm is for women to retain custody of children.

Are there any adverse effects of homosexual parents on children's psychological well-being? One of the best studies that has been conducted to answer this question selected a group of adolescents from a national survey who were raised by heterosexual and homosexual parents and compared them (Wainright, Russell, & Patterson, 2004). This is a methodologically strong study because the adolescents were participating in a national survey on health. That is, adolescents raised by same-sex parents were not a select group of people who responded to a study on homosexual parenting. The two groups were matched on a number of demographic variables. There were no differences between adolescents raised by heterosexual or homosexual parents on psychological well-being. There were no group differences in academics, such as problems at school or GPA—with the exception that adolescents raised by same-sex parents felt *more* connected to school. There were no group differences in family relationship variables, such as warmth and facilitation of autonomy. There also were no group differences in adolescents' romantic relationships, such as whether they had had a romantic relationship and whether they had had sex. Other studies have concurred with this report and shown no differences in developmental outcomes, psychosocial outcomes, and peer relationships between children raised by heterosexual and homosexual parents (Tasker, 2005).

It is difficult to study the effects of being raised by a homosexual parent on children's psychological well-being because many of these children also come from divorced families. Thus adjustment difficulties could stem from the divorce rather than from the parent's sexual orientation. When children being raised by a homosexual parent are compared to children whose parents are divorced, no differences are found in cognitive functioning, self-esteem, psychological distress, psychiatric disorders, or quality of friendships (Golombok et al., 2003).

One concern that some people have about being raised by homosexual parents is over the nature of gender roles that children will develop. One study addressed this issue by comparing children raised by lesbian parents to children raised by two heterosexual parents and single heterosexual mothers (MacCallum & Golombok, 2004). In this way, the effects of the presence of a father could be examined. There were no differences among the three groups in boys' or girls' masculinity or girls' femininity. However, boys raised in families without a father (single heterosexual mothers and lesbian parents) scored higher on femininity than boys raised by two heterosexual parents. One might expect children raised by homosexual parents to have less traditional gender roles than children raised by heterosexual parents, but both groups of children seem to be equally likely to develop traditional roles and sex-typed activities (Golombok et al., 2003).

Finally, one of the greatest concerns people have expressed is that children raised by gay and lesbian parents will become homosexual. Many studies have now shown that there is no effect of being raised by same-sex parents on sexual orientation (Patterson, 2003). Children raised by heterosexual and homosexual parents report similar levels of attraction to persons of the same sex (Patterson, 2000).

Thus there seems to be no evidence that heterosexual and homosexual parents differ in their adjustment levels or parenting abilities. There is also no evidence that a parent's sexual orientation influences children's psychological adjustment, relationships with peers, gender-role development, or sexual orientation. This field of research challenges psychoanalytic theory and social learning theory, which maintain it is important for children to be raised by both a male and a female. Psychoanalytic theory would suggest that children's gender-role development will be impeded without a mother and father in the home because both parents are necessary for the successful resolution of the Oedipal conflict. Social learning theory suggests that children model their parents' sexual orientation, which does not appear to be true; otherwise, there would be no homosexual children with heterosexual parents.

TABLE 11.5   STATES' STANDING ON GAY AND LESBIAN ADOPTION

Gay and Lesbian Adoption

Statutes permit	California, Connecticut, New York
Highest court ruling permits	Massachusetts, Pennsylvania, Vermont
Statutes prohibit	Florida, Mississippi, Utah

Second-Parent Gay and Lesbian Adoption

Statutes permit	California, Connecticut, Vermont
Highest court ruling permits	Massachusetts, Pennsylvania
Statutes prohibit	Florida, Mississippi, Utah
Highest court ruling prohibits	Nebraska, Wisconsin

Source: Blanks, Dockwell, and Wallance (2007).

Sweden, people with children reported a lower quality of life than people without children (Willen & Montgomery, 1996). The benefits of parenting that do occur seem to appear after children leave the home (Ross et al., 1990).

The effect of parental status on health also may differ across cultures. In a cross-cultural study of representative samples from 17 nations around the world, being a parent was associated with less loneliness but was unrelated to health (Stack, 1998b). The effects on loneliness were stronger for men than for women. In a comparison of the United States and India, the presence of children in the home was associated with lower satisfaction with home life among U.S. women but higher satisfaction with home life among Indian women (Sastry, 1999). The author suggested that having children is more closely tied to a woman's identity in India than in the United States. In addition, the presence of children often leads to role conflict in the United States because women assume other roles.

One reason that the relation of the parent role to health is unclear may have to do with the fact that parents are a heterogeneous group, consisting of those with children at home, those whose children have left home, those who live with biological children, step-children, or a combination of the two, and those who do not have custody of their children. The effect of parenthood on depression was examined in a national survey where the different kinds of parents could be distinguished from one another (Evenson & Simon, 2005). There were no differences in depression between nonparents and all groups of parents until demographic variables were statistically controlled. Then, parents were more depressed than nonparents. This speaks to the issue of the heterogeneity of parenthood. The different groups of parents differed from one another demographically. Several interesting distinctions among parents

emerged. First, there was no group of parents who were better off than nonparents. Parents with children at home were more depressed than nonparents, but there was no difference between parents whose children had left home and nonparents. Second, there were several groups of parents who were more depressed than parents with minor children at home— noncustodial parents and parents with adult children living at home, for example. Third, single parents were more depressed than married parents. The authors concluded that there was no single group of parents whose mental health was better than nonparents, but also that there were some groups of parents who had more mental health problems than other groups. In general, all these findings were similar for both men and women.

What are some of the reasons that having children has negative effects on health? First, children are a financial strain (Ross, Mirowsky, & Goldstein, 1990). One study found that the adverse effects of parenthood on health were accounted for by the increased economic strains that children present (Ross, 1995). Second, children detract from the emotional support available to a spouse. The latter argument is elaborated later in the chapter when I examine how parental status influences the quality of marriage. Third, there are selection effect issues to consider when evaluating the effect of parental status on health. Healthier people are more likely than less healthy people to become parents.

One way in which parenthood benefits health is by discouraging poor health behavior. One study found that the presence of children in the home was associated with lower rates of substance abuse (e.g., marijuana, alcohol) among both mothers and fathers (Umberson, 1987). Thus parenthood, like marriage, may encourage good health behavior.

Becoming a parent may have different consequences for men's and women's health to the extent that it has different consequences for men's and women's other roles. Research suggests that parenthood is accompanied by more changes in women's than men's lives (McBride, 1990), due in part to the fact that women assume more responsibilities for child care and adjust their work schedules accordingly. Thus we may understand more about the effects of parenthood on health when we consider it in the context of other roles. This issue is addressed more fully in the next chapter on work and health, but here I address the implications of parenthood for marriage.

Effect of Parenthood on Marriage

A meta-analytic review of 90 studies revealed that parents have lower levels of marital satisfaction than nonparents ($d = -.19$; Twenge, Campbell, & Foster, 2003). The association also seems to be stronger for women ($d = -.19$) than men ($d = -.13$). Marital satisfaction is inversely related to the number of children couples have, such that more children translates into lower marital satisfaction. There are a number of variables that moderate the relation of parenthood to marital satisfaction. One is the age of the child—at least for women. The difference in marital satisfaction between women with infants and women without children was large ($d = -.50$), whereas the difference between women with older children and women without children was small ($d = -.14$). The age of the child had no influence on the relation of parental status to men's marital satisfaction. In addition, the negative effects of parenthood were stronger among higher SES couples and higher in more recent years.

There are several explanations for the association of parenthood to a decline in marital satisfaction. First, there are economic costs associated with children which could translate into financial problems in marriages. However, if that were the primary explanation, the parent status difference in marital satisfaction would be smaller rather than larger in high SES couples. One also would have predicted the parent status difference in marital satisfaction to be higher among couples with older children because older children cost more money; as noted above, this was not the case.

A second possibility is that the presence of children contributes to a decline in opportunities for sex and sexual satisfaction in marriage declines. If that were the case, one would probably expect larger parent status differences for men than women. Just the opposite was the case.

The third explanation has to do with the restriction on freedom associated with parenting and the role conflict that parenthood brings. This explanation provides a good fit for the data from the meta-analysis. The finding that parenthood has more adverse effects among higher SES families is consistent with the restriction of freedom theory as higher SES families would be more distressed at having to give up the freedom that money can buy (e.g., extensive travel and expensive leisure activities). The finding that parenting effects were stronger for women than men, and especially in the case of women with small children, also fits the restriction of freedom and role conflict hypothesis. Parenthood leads to greater changes in women's than men's roles as women take on more of the responsibility associated with the parent role. Child care is a greater restriction on women's than men's freedom in the family. The fact that the parenthood status findings are larger in more recent years also fits with the role conflict explanation as women face more conflict in juggling family and work roles today than ever before.

Part of the reason that women suffer more role conflict than men with the arrival of children is that the division of labor becomes more traditional with the arrival of children (Kalmijn, 2005). Regardless of the division of labor prior to the arrival of children, women increase their contributions to household tasks when they become parents. This change may increase marital conflict and decrease women's marital satisfaction. When fathers become involved in child care, there seem to be fewer negative consequences for marital satisfaction (Ozer et al., 1998). The move to a more traditional division of labor is not associated with distress among couples who have traditional views of gender roles. In fact, a nontraditional division of labor causes conflict in couples who have traditional gender-role attitudes (Mac-Dermid et al., 1990). This situation occurs among couples who believe wives should take care of the home and family and husbands should be economic providers, but the wife works out of economic necessity and the husband shares household responsibilities because the wife is not always available.

Another reason parenthood is associated with a decline in marital satisfaction is that the couple simply spends less time together (Ross et al., 1990). The time that is spent together is often child focused. Thus, there is less time for the couple to engage in mutually supportive activities. In a longitudinal study of married couples, those who ultimately became parents spent less time together (that was not child focused) than nonparents (MacDermid et al., 1990). All couples reported a decline in the amount of leisure time they spent with their spouse, but this decline was greater among parents than nonparents. Parents spent a large proportion of their time together in child-focused activities rather than in leisure activities.

Most of the studies that have linked parenthood to marital satisfaction are cross sectional. This creates two problems for interpretation. First, there may be a selection bias. Perhaps people who are less happy with their marriage are more likely to have children (or people who are more happy with their marriage refrain from becoming parents). Second, it may be that couples who have children are less likely to divorce, meaning that the parenting couples contain a greater number of unhappy marriages than the nonparenting couples.

Some evidence indicates the quality of the parent-child relationship has stronger effects on men's than women's marital satisfaction. In a study in which 100 couples recorded their daily interactions over 42 days, only among men did tension with children on one day predict subsequent tension with a spouse the next day (Almeida, Wethington, & Chandler, 1999). Thus parenthood strains affected marital strains only among men. This is consistent with other research that shows men's relationships with their children are more strongly tied to the quality of their marriage than are women's relationships with their children (Rogers & White, 1998).

TAKE HOME POINTS

- The effects of the parent role on men's and women's health are unclear. There is little research to show any benefits.

- The mixed effects are due to the fact that so many factors qualify the effect of parenthood on health: ages and number of children, whether the children live in the home, income, and other roles that parents possess.

- Women report more strains in the parent role and greater commitment to the parent role than men do. The quality of this role influences both men's and women's health, but the relation may be stronger among women.

- Becoming parents is associated with a decline in marital satisfaction, and the decline is larger among women.

- The negative effects of parenting on marital satisfaction are due to restrictions on freedom, to a move toward a more traditional division of labor, and to less time that spouses spend together in non–child-focused activities.

EFFECT OF SOCIAL SUPPORT ON HEALTH

In this chapter we have examined the relation of marriage and parenthood to health. However, people have relationships with individuals other than their spouse or children, such as family, friends, and neighbors. These relationships act as sources of social support. Do men and women differ in the amount of support they receive from these other network members? Does support from network members lead to the same health benefits for men and women? First, I review the literature that compares the amount and nature of men's and women's social support. Then, I turn to the question of how support is related to health for men and women.

Sex Comparisons

Social support has a wide variety of meanings. To compare men's and women's social support, we need to distinguish among these different meanings. First, there are quantitative dimensions of support and qualitative dimensions of support. Quantitative dimensions are referred to as **structural measures (of support)**; these measures typically assess the size of a social network or the number of social relations. Qualitative dimensions are referred to as **functional measures (of support)** because they address the question of what functions networks serve. Network members may provide emotional support (love, caring, concern), instrumental support (concrete assistance, such as running an errand), or informational support (guidance, advice). In a review of the literature on gender and support, Belle (1987) concluded that women's networks were more "intensive" but men's networks were more "extensive." This would suggest that women come out ahead on the functional aspects of support, but men come out ahead on the structural aspects of support.

Structural vs. Functional Support. It is unclear whether there are sex differences in structural measures of support. Some studies show that men have larger social networks compared to women (Berkman, Vaccarino, & Seeman, 1993), but other studies show just the opposite (Pugliesi & Shook, 1998).

Sex differences in support functions are more clear. Women are more likely than men to receive support (Belle, 1987) and to perceive that support is available from network members (Kendler, Myers, & Prescott, 2005). These findings generalize across many cultures (Okamoto & Tanaka, 2004). Women also are more satisfied than men with the support they receive from network members (Belle, 1987). Sex differences in the functional aspects of support seem to be notably strong for emotional support. Men are especially less likely than women to have someone available to talk to when they are distressed (Matthews et al., 1999). Even among the elderly, women report greater emotional support (Seeman et al., 1994).

Sex differences in perceptions of, receipt of, and satisfaction with support may have to do with the female gender role more than female sex. Femininity, or communion, has been related to perceived support (Helgeson & Fritz, 1996). Femininity also has been shown to be a better predictor of support than sex (Reevy & Maslach, 2001).

Seeking Support. Women of all ages are more likely than men to seek support during times of stress (Belle, 1987). Support from network members may offset a lack of spousal support for women. In one study, women with a poor quality marriage were less distressed following a severe life event if they sought support from other network members (Edwards et al., 1998). For men, seeking support outside the marriage was associated with an increase in depression (Edwards et al., 1998); thus men seem to suffer if they have to turn to others for support aside from their spouse. This is consistent with other research that shows men in happy marriages self-disclose to their spouse, but men in unhappy marriages self-disclose to no one (Gottman, 1994). Wives, by contrast, self-disclose to others aside from their spouse despite their level of marital satisfaction. Thus women have other sources of support available to them besides their spouse.

When men do seek support, it is most likely to be from a woman. In married couples, men are more likely than women to name their spouse as a primary confidant, whereas women are more likely than men to turn to family and friends for support (Berkman et al., 1993). If both men and women are turning to women for support, it is not surprising that women are more likely than men to report they provide support to others (Belle, 1987; Wethington, McLeod, & Kessler, 1987).

Explanations.   Why don't men have as much support available to them compared to women? One reason is that men are more reluctant to ask for help. The male gender role's emphasis on independence and invulnerability may inhibit men from asking for help when they need it. Another reason men may receive less support may have to do with the perceptions that others hold about men's and women's needs for support. Men and women may assume men do not want or need support and be less likely to offer support to men (Barbee et al., 1993). Thus women may be more likely than men to receive unsolicited support. Men also may lack support compared to women because they are less skilled in activating support (Barbee et al., 1993). Because men have been reluctant to ask for help in the past, they may be unsure about how

DO GENDER 11.4
Social Support Seeking

Is it true that men are less likely than women to seek support when they are having problems? If so, why? Have a group of men and women recall the last time they experienced a stressful event. Then ask them to rate how much they sought the help of others. If they check a response that indicates they did not seek help or did not seek much help, ask why. Tally your responses to see if men's and women's reasons for not seeking help differ.

to obtain help when they really need it. Determine why men and women at your school do not seek support in Do Gender 11.4.

Evidence: Relations to Health

Structural Indexes.   A number of large epidemiological studies have evaluated the relation of social network indexes to health. These studies typically evaluate men's and women's initial health status, measure aspects of their social networks (group membership, church attendance, frequency of contact with neighbors, and sometimes marital status), and then measure physical health years later. A number of these studies show stronger health benefits of social networks for men than women. For example, in a study of 2,754 men and women from Tecumseh County, Michigan, men who reported more social relationships and more activities (e.g., attending voluntary associations and going out to social events) were less likely to die 9 to 12 years later (House et al., 1982). There were weak trends in the same direction for women, but they were not significant. Other studies have found social network indexes predict mortality among men but not women (Kaplan et al., 1988; Schoenbach et al., 1986).

Some studies even show adverse effects of social networks on women's health. For example, Schoenbach and colleagues (1986) found that their social network index was associated with *greater* mortality among White women under 60. In a study in Sweden, a social network index was related to reduced mortality for both men and women with one exception: For women between the ages of 65 and 74, the social network index was associated with heightened mortality (Orth-Gomer & Johnson, 1987). In another study, a greater number of social ties and contacts was associated with worse mental health for Italian and Polish women living in the United States (Cohler & Lieberman, 1980). Finally, one study showed that women were more distressed when they lived with another person than when they lived alone, whereas men were more distressed when they lived alone than when they lived with another person (Page & Cole, 1992).

Explanations. The explanations for the lack of effects and adverse effects of structural support on women's health often revolve around women's social roles. The presence of a social network for women is a double-edged sword (Belle, 1982): It means more people are available to help women but also that more people will turn to women for help. For example, what happens in marriage when one person has a chronic illness? Women are expected to take care of the family whether they are the caregiver or the patient (Revenson, 1994).

Social networks also may expose women to additional sources of stress (Belle, 1982). Women are more likely than men to report stressful life events that involve other people. For example, both a husband and a wife may have a neighbor with cancer; the event occurs to both of them, but when asked about recent stressors, the wife is more likely than the husband to identify the neighbor's illness as a per-

DO GENDER 11.5
The Nature of Stress

Find out if women are more likely than men to report stressful events that involve other network members. Create a stressful events checklist (e.g., failed an exam, got into a car accident, mother became ill, pet died, sister divorced). Ask a group of people to circle all of the events that happened to them over the past year. Divide the stressful events into ones that the individuals experienced themselves (e.g., car accident) and ones that other people experienced but that affected the individuals (sister divorced). Is there a sex difference?

sonal stressor. One study showed that both men and women were affected by stressors that afflicted their spouse and children, but women were more likely than men to be affected by stressors that affected other network members (Wethington et al., 1987). Find out if women are more likely than men to report stressors that involve others in Do Gender 11.5.

Thus it appears that women are more likely than men to reap the benefits of a social network but also to suffer the costs of network involvement. Women are not only more likely to have social support available but are also more likely to have problematic social relations and conflict. The positive and negative effects of social networks for women may cancel each other out in terms of health: Supportive relations decrease depression, but unsupportive relations and caregiver burden increase depression.

Functional Indexes. Some evidence suggests the functional aspects of support are more strongly related to health among women than men. Support has been more strongly related to reduced psychological distress among women than men (Bird, 1999), better perceived health, and less functional disability among women than men (Denton & Walters, 1999), and good health practices among women than men (Jackson, 2006). A study of elderly in Hong Kong showed that social support was more strongly related to positive health perceptions among women than men (Cheng & Chan, 2006). A study of opposite-sex dizygotic twins showed that social support predicted a reduction in the onset of major depression over the next year among females but not males (Kendler et al., 2005). Two studies show links of emotional support to mortality among women but not men (Ell et al., 1992; Reynolds & Kaplan, 1990).

There are exceptions, however. A study of people with heart disease showed social support was equally related to life satisfaction and mood for men and women (Rueda & Perez-Garcia, 2006). A study of elderly people in Japan showed that social support was more strongly related to positive health perceptions among men than women (Okamoto & Tanaka, 2004).

Another way that the effect of functional support on health has been examined is in the

Sidebar 11.4: *Manipulation of Social Support in the Laboratory*

Because survey studies on support and health cannot distinguish cause and effect, a number of laboratory studies have been conducted in which social support is manipulated while the participant undergoes some kind of stress, such as giving a speech or performing a difficult math task. Health is measured in terms of cardiovascular reactivity (e.g., change in blood pressure and heart rate), immune function, or the production of stress hormones (e.g., cortisol). Studies have shown that support provided by a same-sex confederate reduces reactivity (Lepore, Allen, & Evans, 1993) and support provided by a same-sex friend reduces reactivity (Kamarck, Annunziato, & Amateau, 1995). In addition, friend support seems to be more effective than support from a stranger (Christenfeld et al., 1997). However, most of these studies have examined only female participants. One study examined both males and females and found stronger effects of support on reactivity for females than males (Smith, Ruiz, & Uchino, 2004).

The sex of the support provider also might influence how males and females respond. One study manipulated the sex of the support provider and found that support provided by a female confederate was effective in reducing blood pressure for both male and female participants, but support from a male confederate was ineffective for both male and female participants (Glynn et al., 1999). In fact, there was a slight tendency for male participants to show increased reactivity in response to support from a male confederate. The difference between male and female confederates is interesting, given that the support manipulation was standardized. Thus it is not only that women may provide more support than men, but also support from women may actually be more health beneficial. The same behavior may be interpreted differently when displayed by a male versus a female. This would certainly explain why men benefit more from marriage compared to women.

The kind of support manipulated in the vast majority of these laboratory studies, including the last one, is emotional support. Thus the extent to which other kinds of support may be effective in reducing reactivity to stress is unknown. It is also not known whether men and women benefit from different kinds of support in terms of reduced reactivity to stress. Dawn Wilson and her colleagues have examined both emotional support and instrumental support (e.g., advice, concrete assistance) in several studies of African American adolescents. In a study that aimed to enhance a low-sodium diet to prevent hypertension, Black boys did not benefit as much from family emotional support as Black girls in terms of dietary compliance (Wilson & Ampey-Thornhill, 2001). In a laboratory study in which Black boys and girls were asked to role-play several stressful encounters, boys showed higher levels of reactivity when provided with emotional support and lower reactivity in response to instrumental support (Wilson et al., 1999).

Thus the laboratory studies of social support leave several questions unanswered. Is support provided by women more effective than support provided by men, or does this pertain only to emotional support? Do men and women benefit more from emotional support compared to other kinds of support, or does the kind of support that is beneficial depend on the sex of the support provider? For example, perhaps instrumental support from men is effective and emotional support from women is effective.

context of stressor reactivity studies. See Sidebar 11.4 for a discussion of this area of research.

Explanations. The evidence from survey research suggests the qualitative dimensions of support are more strongly related to women's than men's health. Why would this be? The explanation may be similar to the one that explains why marital quality is more strongly related to women's than men's health. Women's identities more than men's are based on their connection to others. Thus variability in an identity-relevant domain is more likely to have implications for health. It may also be that supportive networks benefit women more than men because they facilitate women's coping with distress. Women are more likely to seek support during times of stress; thus if others are supportive, women's needs are met.

TAKE HOME POINTS

- Women have more support available to them compared to men, and women provide more support to others than men.

- Quantitative, or structural, measures of relationships seem to have a stronger effect on men's than women's health.

- One reason for these findings is that relationships are a double-edged sword for women—a source of support and a source of stress.

- Qualitative, or functional, measures of relationships seem to have a stronger effect on women's than men's health.

SUMMARY

Marriage is associated with better health for both men and women. Longitudinal research shows that initial health also influences the likelihood of getting married; however, even adjusting for these selection effects, marriage benefits health. The effect of marriage on health is stronger among men, because marriage is a greater source of support for men, because marriage promotes better health behavior in men, and because men are more satisfied with the state of marriage compared to women.

The loss of marriage through widowhood seems to have more adverse effects on men's than women's health. The effects of widowhood on health can be understood in terms of the different strains men and women suffer when they lose their spouse. The primary reason widowhood has stronger effects on men's health has to do with men's loss of support; women have alternative sources of support available after widowhood. Men are more likely than women to remarry after widowhood and to do so sooner, and remarriage is associated with health benefits for men.

Both men's and women's health suffers upon relationship dissolution. There is some evidence that men suffer greater ill effects than women. Marital dissolution seems to be associated with different strains for men and women and to have different consequences for men's and women's social networks. The exact timing of the ill effects of marital dissolution on men's and women's health is not clear. However, it is clear that women are more distressed than men prior to the relationship breakup and that women are more likely to have thought about the breakup and to actually initiate it. Women's greater mental preparation for the breakup may explain why some studies show women adjust more easily to the dissolution of a relationship.

Although consistent evidence indicates that marital status benefits men more than women, when the quality of marriage is examined, women are more strongly affected than men. Studies consistently show that reports of marital satisfaction and marital conflict have greater implications for women's than men's health. Marital interaction studies also show that communication patterns influence women's more than men's physiology, especially when those communications have to do with discussing a marital conflict.

One important aspect of the marital relationship that has implications for relationship satisfaction as well as health is how labor is divided in the family. In general, women contribute more to household labor regardless of their employment status. Sex differences in the division of labor are greatest among married couples. Factors that influence how labor

is divided are based on power and status, such as gender, income, education, and hours worked outside the home. Gender-role attitudes also influence the division of labor within the family. In general, all these factors have stronger implications for household labor when they characterize men; that is, it is men's gender-role attitudes, income, and hours worked outside the home that influence how much they participate in tasks inside the home. Women's gender-role attitudes, income, education, and hours of work outside the home come into play only in the context of more egalitarian relationships. Further evidence that status and power influence the division of labor in the heterosexual family comes from studies of homosexual couples, where household labor is divided more equally.

In general, the more men contribute to household labor, the more satisfied women are. In fact, the division of labor in the family has a stronger effect on women's than men's marital satisfaction and well-being. However, men do not have to participate equally in household chores for women to be satisfied. It is perhaps remarkable that more women are not dissatisfied with the current state of affairs. A primary reason has to do with the fact that women make within-sex rather than between-sex social comparisons.

More serious threats to relationships include domestic abuse and rape. Women and men seem equally likely to be involved in domestic abuse. When the severity of violence is taken into consideration or injuries are examined, women are more likely than men to be victims. One reason that the literature on domestic abuse does not fit with people's perceptions that women are the primary victim is that there are two kinds of intimate violence: common couple violence and patriarchal terrorism. Patriarchal terrorism is the kind of violence that is characterized by domination and control on the part of males over females. Patriarchal terrorism escalates and poses serious threats to women's health. Common couple violence is the kind of violence that erupts from stress, does not escalate, and equally characterizes women and men.

Rape and sexual coercion are difficult to define. Although women are clearly more likely than men to be victims of rape, reports of sexual coercion are more similar between men and women. Yet, like domestic abuse, women report more severe consequences of sexual coercion compared to men. Perpetrators of rape are more likely to hold rape myths. Both rape and sexual coercion are influenced by situational factors, such as the tendency to interpret neutral behaviors in sexual terms.

Aside from marriage, the other relationship role held by many adults is the parent role. Unlike the marital role, there is no clear evidence that the parent role benefits men's and women's health. The mixed effects are due to the fact that so many factors qualify the effect of parenthood on health: ages and number of children, whether the children live in the home, income, and other roles that parents possess. Women report more strains in the parent role and greater commitment to the parent role than men do. The quality of this role influences both men's and women's health, but the relation may be stronger among women. Parenthood has a negative effect on marital satisfaction. These effects are stronger for women than men, largely due to the greater restrictions on freedom and the greater role changes for women. The quality of parenting has become an important issue for homosexuals, especially lesbian mothers. However, research shows few differences between heterosexual and homosexual parents and few differences among the children they raise.

Other relationships besides marriage and parenthood influence health, such as relationships with family and friends. I distinguished between the structural and functional dimensions of support. It is not clear if there are sex differences in the structural dimensions of support, but women perceive and receive greater support functions. Supportive relations are a double-edged sword for women: The mere existence of social relationships means women have more support available to them but also that women have greater caregiving burdens. This is a likely explanation for why structural measures of support are more consistently related to men's health than women's health. However, the functional aspects of support seem to be more strongly related to women's than men's health.

Taken collectively, the findings on sex differences in the association of marriage to health and sex differences in the association of other social relationships to health are quite similar. Simply being married and having social ties is more beneficial to men than women. For women, the quality of marriage and the quality of support derived from other network members is more strongly tied to health.

DISCUSSION QUESTIONS

1. What is the marital selection hypothesis?
2. Why does marriage have a stronger effect on men's than women's health?
3. What are some of the methodological issues to consider when examining the effect of widowhood on men's and women's health?
4. Given what you know about how men and women behave in marriage and what men and women get out of

marriage, what predictions would you make about how men and women adjust to separation and divorce?

5. What determines household division of labor?

6. What is the gender tension line, and how has it changed over the past 20 years?

7. Are men and women equally likely to be victims of abuse?

8. What are the differences between common couple violence and patriarchal terrorism?

9. What do you think would be the best way to measure the prevalence of sexual coercion? How would you define it?

10. To the extent that parenthood has a negative effect on marriage, what are the explanations?

11. Why are structural indexes of support more strongly related to men's health than women's health?

SUGGESTED READING

(Classic) Brownmiller, S. (1975). *Against our will: Men, Women, and Rape.* New York: Bantam Books.

Gager, C. T., & Hohmann-Marriott, B. (2006). Distributive justice in the household: A comparison of alternative models. *Marriage and Family Review, 40,* 5–42.

(Classic) Hochschild, A. R. (1989). *The second shift.* New York: Avon Books.

Johnson, M. P. (2004). Patriarchal terrorism and common couple violence. Two forms of violence against women. In H. T. Reis & C. E. Rusbult (Eds.), *Close relationships: Key readings* (pp. 471–482). New York: Psychology Press.

Kiecolt-Glaser, J. K., & Newton, T. L. (2001). Marriage and health: His and hers. *Psychological Bulletin, 127,* 472–503.

Rozee, P. D., & Koss, M. P. (2001). Rape: A century of resistance. *Psychology of Women Quarterly, 25,* 295–311.

Tasker, F. (2005). Lesbian mothers, gay fathers, and their children: A review. *Journal of Developmental and Behavioral Pediatrics, 26,* 224–240.

KEY TERMS

Anger rape—Type of rape that occurs when the perpetrator is expressing hostility or hate toward the victim.

Buffering effects—Link of social support to health only under conditions of high stress.

Common couple violence—Occasional episodes of violent behavior on the part of husbands and wives that are precipitated by stressful events.

Functional measures (of support)—Qualitative dimensions of support, such as the type of support offered by network members.

Gender tension line—Point at which one feels uncomfortable with the adoption of some aspect of the other gender role.

Interpersonal protection theory—Suggests that social support differs across marital statuses and that social support buffers us from distress.

Main effects—Direct link of social support to health, regardless of level of stress.

Marital rape exemption clause—Clause that once appeared in state definitions of rape that excluded forced intercourse with one's wife.

Marital selection hypothesis—Suggestion that healthier people are "selected" into marriage.

Patriarchal terrorism—Violence on the part of men that stems from their attempts to control women.

Power rape—Type of rape that occurs when the perpetrator is seeking to control and exert power over the victim.

Prospective design—Research method in which the dependent variable (e.g., health) is measured before and after exposure to the independent variable (e.g., widowhood).

Structural measures (of support)—Quantitative dimensions of support, such as the size of a social network or the number of social relations.

WORK ROLES AND HEALTH

Life was pretty simple for June and Ward Cleaver of *Leave It to Beaver.* Every morning, Ward, dressed in a suit, kissed his wife, and left for work. June, in a dress, took care of the children and had a hot meal waiting for Ward's return from work. The routine was the same for Margaret and Jim Anderson, the married couple on *Father Knows Best.* These two popular television shows from the late 1950s depicted the traditional nuclear family, where men worked outside the home and women worked inside the home.

Contrast that scenario with today's single-parent families where a woman might be responsible for the emotional, practical, and economic support of her children. Television shows of the 1980s and 1990s reflected this changing state of the family by offering alternatives to the traditional families of the 1950s, such as in the sitcom *Grace Under Fire,* where a divorced woman raises three children and works full time in an oil refinery with all male coworkers. Even the media images of two-parent families reflect a move

from the traditional. Consider two shows from the 1980s, *The Cosby Show* and *Growing Pains,* in which mothers have jobs and fathers are very involved with the children. Today, more and more, families are sharing responsibilities. Women, even mothers, often work outside the home and men are more involved in parenting. There are societal signs of this shift. For example, even the U.S. Congress, traditionally all male, finally installed women's restrooms; public places have "family restrooms" where both men and women can change children's diapers. Both men and women juggle multiple roles, in particular the roles of spouse, paid employee, and parent.

A **role** is defined as a position in society governed by a set of **norms**, which are expectations for behavior. One role you have is the role of student. A set of norms dictates how a student should behave. What are these norms? One norm is to study; another norm is to attend class; still another norm is to socialize with your peers. A person may have only a couple of roles or many roles.

495

Other roles you might possess are daughter/son, boyfriend/girlfriend, friend, worker, volunteer, and organizational member. In the literature on men's and women's health, three primary roles have been studied: the spouse role, the parent role, and the worker role. In Chapter 11, I discussed how the presence of the spouse role and the parent role and the quality of the spouse and parent roles are associated with health. In this chapter, I focus on the implications of the work role for men's and women's health. Regardless of whether men and women stay home with children or receive monetary compensation for employment, I realize they work. For simplicity, in this chapter the work role refers to paid employment.

First, I discuss how the mere possession of the work role influences health; then I discuss how the quality of the work role affects health. One important aspect of this role that pertains to gender is discrimination, including the pay disparity between men and women. I discuss a variety of factors that contribute to the pay disparity. Another gender-related aspect of the work role is sexual harassment. I define sexual harassment, discuss its incidence and effects on the worker, and describe theories of sexual harassment. An important question that the literature on roles has tried to address is whether having more roles or fewer roles is better for health. This is the multiple roles question. I conclude the chapter by discussing whether multiple roles are good for health, and which combinations of roles are most beneficial. The benefits of one role can be used to offset the costs of another role (role buffering), but problems in one role can exacerbate difficulties in another role. Evidence for both role buffering and role exacerbation is presented.

One reason it is important to study the effects of different roles on men's and women's health is that sex differences in the possession of roles may explain some of the sex differences in health discussed in Chapter 10. Are women more depressed than men because they hold fewer roles, hold different roles, or value different roles? The **differential exposure hypothesis** states that differences in the kinds of roles men and women possess explain sex differences in health. For example, to the extent that men are more likely than women to possess the work role, and the work role is associated with good mental health, women may suffer poorer mental health compared to men. The **differential vulnerability hypothesis** states that roles have different effects on health for men and women. For example, if parenthood is more central to men's than women's self-concepts, difficulties with children may be more strongly related to women's than men's health.

WORK ROLE

Over the course of the 20th century, women have made greater progress in terms of education and participation in the labor force, although that progress varies by income and race (American Association of University Women, 2003). In 1948, 33% of women age 16 and over worked; in 1970, the rate was 43%, and in 2005, the rate was 59% (see Figure 12.1; U.S. Department of Labor, 2006).

Whereas women's labor force participation has increased since 1975, the participation rate for men has decreased. The reason is unemployment: Not enough jobs are available to accommodate the number of men who wish to work. Historically, women had higher unemployment rates than men, but by 2005, the rates were comparable for men (3.8%) and women (4.2%; U.S. Census Bureau, 2007d). The unemployment rate for Blacks is higher (7.5%) than that for Whites

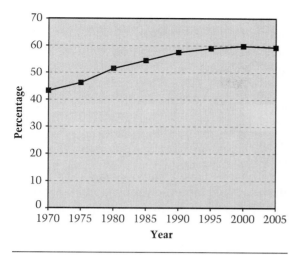

FIGURE 12.1 Percentage of women who participate in the civilian labor force.
Source: Adapted from U.S. Department of Labor (2006).

(3.5%), Asians (3.5%), and Hispanics (4.8%). However, the racial disparity really applies only to men. In June 2007, the percentage of men 20 years and over who were employed was 74% for Whites, 81% for Hispanics, and 65% for Blacks (U.S. Department of Labor, 2007a). The percentage of women 20 years and over who were employed was more equal for Whites, Hispanics, and Blacks (58%, 55%, 60%).

What is the effect of paid employment on men's and women's health? There is reason to assume that both the differential exposure and differential vulnerability hypotheses explain sex differences in the effects of the work role on health. Men are more likely to possess this role than women, especially if the work role is limited to those who are employed full time. To the extent the work role is associated with good health, men are more likely than women to reap the benefits. This is the differential exposure hypothesis. As a society, we attach greater importance to men working outside the home compared to women; thus the effect of the work role on health may be stronger

for men. This is the differential vulnerability hypothesis.

Strong evidence suggests the work role influences the health of both men and women. In general, paid employment is associated with better health for both (Ross et al., 1990). It is difficult to compare the effects of employment on men's and women's health because it is more normative for men than women to work outside the home. When we compare working men to nonworking men, we are typically studying the effect of unemployment on health. When we compare working women to nonworking women, we are comparing employed women to two groups of nonworking women—women who are unemployed and women who choose to be housewives. The two groups are not the same.

The effect of employment on health is a topic that necessarily focuses on women because there is more variability in women's than men's employment. In this first section of the chapter, I focus mostly on the effects of women's employment on their health. I also examine the effect of women working on men's health and on marriage. In the subsequent sections, I evaluate the effect of work on men's health by briefly describing the literatures on unemployment and retirement. After evaluating the effects of the mere possession of the work role on health, I turn to the implications of the more qualitative aspects of the work role for health.

Women's Employment

A historical explanation of why women were more distressed and had worse health than men was that women were less likely to possess the work role (Gove & Tudor, 1973). Work was associated with a number of resources, not the least of which was economic, and women had less access to this resource. However, when women entered the workforce, people began to consider the negative effects of employment on health. People were concerned that women who combined work and family roles would suffer role strain and role overload. People also were concerned that women working would detract from the time women spent taking care of their husbands and family. Thus, in this section, I examine the implications of women working for their own health, the implications of women working for men's health, and then the implications of women working for marriage.

Effects on Women's Health. There are multiple ways to evaluate the effects of work on women's health. Some studies compare the health of employed women to employed men. It is difficult to evaluate the outcome of such a comparison because women, in general, are more distressed than men. Studies that have made this comparison show contradictory findings.

Some studies have compared the health of men and women who work outside the home to men and women who do not work outside the home, to evaluate whether work has similar effects on men's and women's health. These studies tend to show the work role is associated with health for men and women, but the effects are stronger for men. For example, Thoits (1992) found that the work role was more strongly related to symptoms for men than for women. However, this kind of study is problematic because employed men are being compared to unemployed men. It is likely that more of the nonworking men than the nonworking women wish to be employed.

Another way the effect of work on health has been evaluated is to compare women who are employed outside the home to those who are housewives. When working women are compared to housewives, a wealth of evidence indicates that employed women report better psychological and physical health (Fokkema, 2002; Khlat, Sermet, & Le Pape, 2000), even in traditional societies like Spain (Artazcoz, Borrell et al., 2004). Even among women with children,

the weight of the evidence is that employed mothers are healthier than nonemployed mothers, but more so if children are older (Fokkema, 2002). There are cultural differences in the benefits of work for women. For example, a study in India found no differences in psychological well-being between women who did and did not work outside the home (Andrade, Postma, & Abraham, 1999).

One problem with studies that compare the health of employed women to housewives is that they are often cross sectional, meaning the people are studied at a single point in time. Thus we do not know if employment leads to an improvement in health or if healthier people are more likely to be employed. This is the basis of the **selection effect**. Longitudinal studies in which both employment and health are tracked over time enable us to determine whether health leads to employment or employment leads to health. There is evidence for the selection effect—physically healthier people are more likely to be employed—at least when they are seeking employment, which is not the case with homemakers (Ross & Mirowsky, 1995). However, longitudinal studies have also clearly shown that employment leads to better health for women (Klumb & Lampert, 2004).

Explanations. The employee role benefits women's health for a number of reasons. Employment increases self-esteem, instills a sense of accomplishment, and provides more social contacts. Employment also can affect one's sense of control (Rosenfield, 1989). To the extent that employment increases one's sense of control, it should be helpful. However, if employment decreases one's sense of control, it may be harmful. Employment may enhance women's feelings of control by increasing women's economic resources and thus power within the family. However, employment may detract from women's sense of control by making it more difficult for

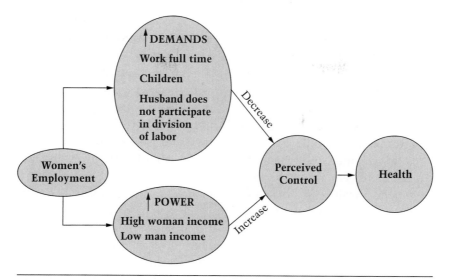

FIGURE 12.2   Model of how employment influences women's health. To the extent that employment increases women's household demands, employment reduces perceptions of control and harms health. To the extent that employment increases women's relative income in the family, employment increases perceptions of control and benefits health.

Source: Adapted from Rosenfield (1989).

women to manage household responsibilities. Thus work has the potential to increase resources for women in one area but decrease resources in another. Each of these resources has implications for control. This model is shown in Figure 12.2.

This model has been supported by three different studies (Rosenfield, 1989). In all three, women who were susceptible to high family demands (i.e., women employed full time with children) were more distressed than men, whereas women with fewer demands (women employed part time with children or women employed full time without children) had levels of distress similar to men's. If demands were low, employed women were less distressed than housewives. Employment also increased women's perceptions of control when it increased their relative income in the family. Women with higher relative incomes had a heightened sense of control

and, subsequently, reduced distress. In total, the healthiest women in this study were those who had children and were employed part time. These women gained some advantage from an increase in relative income that was not offset by an increase in demands.

Support for this model also comes from a study of women in Spain (Artazcoz, Borrell et al., 2004). Women who worked had better health than housewives, but this association was influenced by the education level of the worker and family demands. Family demands had negative effects on health among low educated workers but not among high educated workers, presumably because high educated workers had more resources available to cope with those demands.

The debate between the effects of part-time and full-time work on women's health is unclear. One study showed that part-time employment does not provide the same health benefit that full-time employment does for women (Wethington & Kessler, 1989), whereas a study of women with children under 5 showed that part-time but not full-time work improved health compared to not working (Fokkema, 2002). The effects of part-time and full-time work on women's health are undoubtedly a function of demands and power in the family. Full-time work contributes much more to economic income than part-time work and should be more beneficial to women's health *if* household demands can be met. If demands cannot be met, part-time work may be more adaptive for women's health.

According to this model, the best way for full-time employed women to manage their psychological health is to offset the increase in family demands by having husbands involved in household labor. Alternatively, full-time employed women may be able to pay someone to perform household chores. One study showed that the work role was beneficial to women's health only when they could afford services to assist them with child care and household labor (Khlat et al., 2000). Thus the work role may be more beneficial to middle-class than lower-class women because middle-class women are more able to pay for such services. In addition, lower-class women are more likely to be married to husbands who are unwilling to participate in household labor (Arrighi & Maume, 2000).

Effects on Men's Health. It would probably not occur to us to investigate the effects of men working on women's health. The vast majority of men work and society clearly agrees that working is a good thing for men to do. In addition, men working clearly provides women with economic resources. However, there may be costs to women in terms of men's employment when the work hours are long and when work detracts from family time. These issues have rarely been explored.

Nonetheless, there has been much interest in the effects of women working on men's health. First, do men support their wife working? In general, yes. In fact, men are more likely to support their wife participating in the labor force than they are to support an egalitarian division of labor at home (Kane & Sanchez, 1994). Many men and women still believe women's primary responsibility is child care and men's primary responsibility is paid employment. In a 1997 study of dual-earner couples, 41% agreed that "it is much better for everyone involved if the man earns the money and the woman takes care of the home and children" (Bond et al., 1998). Two decades earlier, in 1977, the corresponding figure was 64%. There are likely to be individual difference characteristics that distinguish men who are more and less supportive of wives working outside the home. One study found that men with high self-esteem supported women working, whereas men with low self-esteem opposed it (Valentine, 1998). Men with low self-esteem may feel their sense of masculinity is threatened when wives work. Conduct Do Gender 12.1 to find out men's attitudes toward married women working at your college.

Even if husbands support their wife working, do they reap any rewards from it? The effect of women working on men's health is unclear. Several older studies found negative effects. For example, Rosenfield (1992) found that women were more depressed than men when wives did not work, but men were more depressed than women when wives worked. Wives working may be particularly distressing to couples who have traditional gender-role attitudes. A study conducted in India, where sex roles are more traditional than they are in the United States, showed that men whose wives worked perceived their health to be worse than men whose wives did not work (Andrade et al., 1999). There are several reasons why traditional couples might not benefit from wives working. First, a wife

DO GENDER 12.1
Men's Support of Working Wives

Interview a group of men about whether they would be in favor of their wife working. Start out by asking the very simple question, "If you get married, how much would you want or not want your wife to work?" Use a scale such as 1 = I really do *not* want my wife to work; 5 = I really *do* want my wife to work.

    Then, see if you can figure out what conditions influence these men's responses. Are there characteristics of men that influence their support for wives working, such as whether their mothers worked or whether they have traditional gender-role attitudes? Are there characteristics of the situation that influence support, such as the presence of children, the number of children, the age of children? What if she worked more than 40 hours per week? What if she made more money than her husband did? Come up with some of your own qualifications. The goal is to try to describe how supportive men are today of wives working and what limitations there are to men's support.

working detracts from the husband's role as family breadwinner. Second, wives in traditional couples may be working out of economic necessity rather than desire. Finally, a wife working is inconsistent with traditional family roles—those wives will be more likely to shoulder the burden of household labor.

    The control theory depicted in Figure 12.2 that was used to explain the effect of work on women's health also can be used to explain the effect of women working on men's health (Rosenfield, 1992). A wife working will increase a husband's distress to the extent it decreases his resources (relative income) and increases his family demands (household responsibilities).

According to this theory, a wife working presents the twofold dilemma for men and women depicted in Figure 12.3. If wife employment increases the husband's family demands and decreases the wife's family demands, husbands will be more distressed and wives will be less distressed—because family demands are associated with increased distress. To the extent that wife employment decreases the husband's relative income and increases the wife's relative income, husbands will be more distressed and wives will be less distressed—because relative income is associated with reduced distress.

    To test the theoretical model shown in Figure 12.3, Rosenfield (1992) examined psychological distress in 172 married couples. Women were more distressed than men. There were no differences in the distress levels of husbands whose wife worked versus husbands whose wife did not work. Thus, wife employment per se did not affect men's distress. However, to the extent that wives' employment decreased husbands' relative income, men's distress levels increased. Men's distress levels also increased if they shared household chores. The effect of family demands was greater than the effect of reduced relative income on men's distress. Thus, wives' employment alone did not influence husbands' distress, but husbands' distress increased to the extent that wives' employment decreased husbands' relative income and increased husbands' family demands. Rosenfield also noted that relative income and household demands were inversely related, meaning that those who had more power (i.e., higher relative income) probably used that power to avoid household tasks.

    By contrast, another study supported the model but emphasized the importance of income: An increase in women's relative income over time was associated with an increase in women's psychological well-being, but a

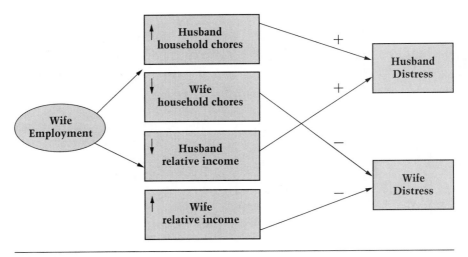

FIGURE 12.3 The dilemma behind women's employment. At the same time that women's employment reduces household demands for women, it increases them for men. Because household demands are associated with increased distress, women benefit and men suffer. At the same time that women's employment increases women's relative income in the family, it decreases men's relative income and power. Because relative income is associated with a decrease in distress, women benefit and men suffer.

decrease in men's psychological well-being (Rogers & DeBoer, 2001). The findings for relative income are interesting because this is a dimension of couples that seems to be changing. Although men are still more likely than women to be the sole wage earner or to earn more money than women, it is no longer unusual for women to make more money than men. A 2003 Gallup Poll showed that men made all or most of the income in 61% of households with children under age 18 (Saad, 2003). However, income was relatively equal in 29% of households, and women made all or most of the income in 9% of households.

Effects on Marriage.   The effect of wife employment on marriage also has been studied. Women's employment seems to benefit marriage when there are fewer children in the home and detract from marriage when there are more

children in the home (Rogers, 1996). When women work more than 40 hours a week, there can be negative effects on marriage (Hyde, DeLamater, & Hewitt, 1998; Rogers, 1996). A noteworthy exception to these findings occurred in a study of female physicians (Barnett & Gareis, 2002). Working more hours was associated with *higher* marital quality for women. The reason seemed to be that their husbands were more involved in household labor when these women worked longer hours. However, this study did not assess men's marital quality, and we know men are not typically happy participating in household labor.

One aspect of marriage that has been studied with respect to the effects of work is sexual functioning. The sexual functioning of couples was studied among women who were housewives, employed part time, employed full time, or employed "high" full time (i.e., 45 or more hours a week; Hyde et al., 1998). Husbands of women employed high full time reported less sexual satisfaction and less frequency of sex than husbands of the other three groups of women. However, there were no differences among the sexual functioning of couples in which women worked full time, part time, or did not work outside the home. In addition, the quality of women's work role was a stronger predictor of sexual outcomes for men and women than the sheer number of hours women worked. Men had the highest sexual satisfaction when both husband and wife had rewarding jobs.

Another feature of women's work that has implications for the marriage is whether the couple wants the woman to be working. Women's employment has a negative effect on marital satisfaction when the couple has traditional values about gender roles, but the wife is required to work outside the home due to the family's financial situation (Ross et al., 1990). Women are unhappy with their marriages if they are employed out of economic necessity rather than choice (Perry-Jenkins, Seery, & Crouter, 1992). However, women are also unhappy with their marriage when they are not employed, wish to be employed, but their husbands do not want them to be employed (Feinauer & Williams-Evans, 1989). Thus, marriages may suffer when employed women do not wish to work and when housewives prefer to be employed.

A feature of women's employment that has implications for marital satisfaction just as it had implications for men's and women's health is the wife's income—especially relative to the husband's income. One study showed that the changes in the income disparity between husband and wife over a 2-year period had no implications for wives' marital satisfaction, but strong implications for husbands' marital satisfaction (Brennan, Barnett, & Gareis, 2001). A decrease in the disparity in income (men higher than women) was associated with a decrease in men's

marital satisfaction, especially among men who said they valued the monetary aspects of their jobs. Thus the implications of women's salaries for men's marital satisfaction appear to depend on whether men identify with the traditional breadwinner role.

In sum, there are features of women's work that can have a negative impact on marriage: long work hours, high income relative to husbands, and greater number of children in the home. A major determinant of women working on marital satisfaction is whether the couple has traditional or egalitarian gender-role attitudes.

Unemployment

A meta-analytic review of 16 longitudinal studies (Murphy & Athanasou, 1999) showed that losing one's job has negative effects on mental health ($d = +.36$) and becoming employed has positive effects on mental health ($d = +.54$). Unemployment may lead to physical health problems, in part because prolonged unemployment has lasting negative effects on health behaviors, such as diet, exercise, and smoking (Wadsworth, Montgomery, & Bartley, 1999). Unemployment seems to have more adverse effects on men's mental health—especially if men are married (Artazcoz, Benach et al., 2004). By contrast, marriage (and children) buffers women from the adverse effects of unemployment.

Not only does unemployment affect health, but health also influences unemployment and reemployment. In a 4-year longitudinal study in Norway, mental health but not physical health in 1989 predicted unemployment in 1993 (Mastekaasa, 1996). Men who were more psychologically distressed in 1989 were more likely to lose their job by 1993. However, it is possible that some people expected to be laid off in 1989, which increased their distress before unemployment. There was also some suggestive evidence that the psychological and physical health of the unemployed influenced reemployment, such that the healthiest people were most likely to become reemployed.

Retirement

Imagine you are 55 years old, work full time, and make $100,000 a year. Your boss calls you into her office and says you can stop working, keep your salary for 2 years, and then earn two thirds of your salary for the rest of your life. Would you retire? The incentives to retire can be strong in some industries.

As a greater portion of our population moves into retirement, this period of life is receiving more attention. Retirement can take a variety of forms. Some people phase in their retirement by reducing the hours they work, whereas others engage in an abrupt retirement. The most common form of retirement today is an abrupt end to the job at age 65 (Shaw et al., 1998). Yet because people are living longer, elderly people can consider working after age 65. A greater proportion of the elderly in the workforce, however, reduces the number of jobs available to younger people. This is one reason many organizations have offered incentives to retire early. In 1930, 5.4% of the population was over 65; in 2005, 12% of the population was over 65.

If work is associated with good health, what is the effect of retirement on health? One determinant will be whether the person chooses to retire or feels forced to retire. The force to retire may come from the employer but could also come from family obligations. Voluntary retirement is associated with more positive attitudes toward retirement (Reitzes & Mutran, 2004), and an abrupt retirement, forced retirement, or retirement viewed as too early are associated with more psychological distress (Szinovacz & Davey, 2004). These effects seem to be stronger for women than men. One reason is that an involuntary retirement for women is likely to be linked to caregiving responsibilities—ill spouse, parent,

or other relative. Further evidence for this possibility comes from a study that showed women and men were more satisfied with a wife's retirement if the spouse was not involved in the decision than if the spouse was involved in the decision (Smith & Moen, 2004). Spouse involvement in the decision could signify an ill spouse. That study showed just the opposite finding for men—couples were more satisfied with a man's retirement when the spouse was involved in the decision than when the spouse was not involved in the decision. Thus spouse involvement may signify something different for husband and wife retirees.

Many couples enjoy more leisure time together after retirement. The actual retirement transition seems to disrupt marital quality, but marital quality improves after a couple of years of adjustment (Moen, Kim, & Hofmaistar, 2001). The one situation in which retirement seems to have negative implications for the quality of marriage is when the spouse continues to work. Although this is the case for both men and women (Moen et al., 2001), the effect may be stronger when the working spouse is the wife. In one study, the husband's retirement had a negative effect on marriage if the wife worked many hours outside the home or had a higher income (Myers & Booth, 1996). That is, when retirement resulted in role reversal—the woman becoming the breadwinner of the family—retirement had a negative effect on marriage. Yet marital satisfaction suffers even more when wives continue to work and husbands fail to participate in household labor (Myers & Booth, 1996).

Much of the early work on retirement focused on men, as men historically made up the larger portion of the workforce. Studies conducted in the 1970s showed that women were more satisfied than men with retirement (Quick & Moen, 1998). These women had been in the labor force for a shorter period of time and in a less steady fashion compared to men. Because the male gender role was so heavily tied to work, one concern that men faced when retiring was a loss of masculinity (Gradman, 1994). To the extent that work is tied to the masculine role, retirement might be viewed as a threat to that role. Gradman examined this issue in a study of men who had retired from a large company. Contrary to expectations, he found the men who best adjusted to retirement were the ones who most strongly identified with their jobs. Thus it appears that men adjust successfully to retirement by maintaining their work role as a part of their self-concept.

More recent research shows that men are more satisfied with retirement compared to women (Quick & Moen, 1998). One reason is that retirement today takes place in a different context for men and women (Szinovacz & Washo, 1992). Retirement is more likely to take place in the context of other life events for women, such as the death of a spouse, a personal illness, or the illness of a family member. These life events have also a stronger effect on women's than men's adjustment to retirement, probably because the life events are more strongly linked to caregiving responsibilities for women. Women who retire to meet family needs at the expense of being able to pursue leisure activities are dissatisfied with retirement (Szinovacz, 1987).

TAKE HOME POINTS

- Paid employment has a positive effect on both men's and women's health.

- The effects may be stronger among men, supporting the differential vulnerability hypothesis, but this difference may be due to the fact that the two groups of nonworking men and women are not alike. Nonworking men are likely to be unemployed, whereas nonworking women are likely to be homemakers.

- Although there is a selection effect, meaning that the healthiest people are likely to become employed, longitudinal studies show that employment leads to good health.

- Whether women work outside the home, in and of itself, is not associated with men's health, but there are conditions under which men may be adversely affected.

- Control theory explains how women's paid employment can influence both men's and women's health: Increased relative income has a positive effect on health, whereas increased family demands have a negative effect on health.

- The effect of retirement on health depends on whether the person chooses to retire.

- Retirement seems to be a less pleasant experience for women, but that is largely because retirement takes place in the context of other life stressors that entail caregiving responsibilities for women.

QUALITY OF WORK ROLE

One reason it is difficult to evaluate the effects of work on men's and women's health is that the nature of the work role differs for men and women. For example, men and women are not employed in the same kinds of jobs. Table 12.1 shows the percentage of women employed in a number of jobs in 1983 and over 20 years later in 2005. Whereas the percentage of women in some occupations has not changed much over the years (dental assistant, registered nurse, elementary school teacher), women are more likely to be found in other professions, such as accountant, architect, dentist, engineer, lawyer, physician, and police officer.

Women also are more likely than men to be employed in part-time positions. In 2005, 75% of employed women held full-time jobs compared to 89% of men (U.S. Department of Labor, 2006). However, this figure really represents a comparison of White women (74%) to White men (90%); Black women are almost equally

TABLE 12.1 WOMEN AS A PERCENTAGE OF WORKERS IN SELECTED OCCUPATIONS IN **1983** AND **2005**

Occupation	1983	2005
Accountants/Auditors	38.7	61.9
Airplane pilots and navigators	2.1	5.2
Architects	12.7	24.4
Auto mechanics	0.5	1.9
Carpenter	1.4	1.9
Clergy	5.6	15.5
Computer programmers	32.5	26.0
Dental assistants	98.1	96.1
Dentists	6.7	22.5
Engineers	5.8	13.8
Financial managers	38.6	51.7
Firefighters	1.0	3.3
Lawyers	15.3	30.2
Mail carriers	17.1	39.1
Photographers	20.7	39.0
Physicians	15.8	32.3
Police/detective	5.7	14.3
Psychologist	57.1	67.3
Registered nurses	95.8	92.3
Social workers	64.3	80.1
Teachers, college and university	36.3	44.4
Teachers, elementary school	83.3	82.2
Truck drivers	3.1	4.5
Typists	95.6	95.0

Source: Adapted from U.S. Census Bureau (2007e).

likely to be employed full time (83%) as Black men (89%; U.S. Department of Labor, 2007b). Men and women also report different job conditions. Thus to compare employed men and women, we need to know more about the characteristics of their jobs to see if the two groups are really comparable. In the following section, I examine the characteristics of work that men and women value as well as face.

Characteristics of Work

Do men and women value the same characteristics of work? A meta-analytic review of studies that included all age groups, ranging from children to adults, revealed that males value a high income, autonomy, challenge, recognition, prestige, and power more than females (see Figure 12.4; Konrad et al., 2000). By contrast, females value easy commute, the physical environment, relations with coworkers and supervisor, job benefits, opportunity to work with people, and task enjoyment more than males.

Sex differences in ratings of job attributes can be misleading, however, because the rank order of job attributes may be similar for men and women. Studies of college students show that women value family considerations (e.g., child care availability) more than men (Heckert et al., 2002), and men value a high salary more than women (Morgan, Isaac, & Sansone, 2001). However, both men and women rated family time as one of the most important features of a job and a high salary as one of the least important features.

The work environments of men and women differ, and status plays a role in these differences. Women report having less job opportunity and less job mobility compared to men (Matthews et al., 1998). Women are less likely than men to have mentoring relationships at work, and mentors can lead to career advancement (Nelson & Burke, 2000). Women also complain of sexual harassment and discrimination (Bond et al., 2004), both of which are reviewed in more detail later in the chapter. Women are especially likely to report these latter sources of strain in work environments that are predominately male (Gardiner & Tiggemann, 1999). Yet work provides women with a resource that it does not equally provide men: Women receive more support at work compared to men (Bond et al., 2004).

Given these differences, do men or women work under more stressful conditions? If the measure of stress is the sheer number of hours worked, then men are under more stress than women because men work more hours compared to women. However, on a variety of other indicators of job strain, women fare poorly compared to men. Compared to men, women report that their jobs require less skill (Hughes & Galinsky, 1994a), are more monotonous

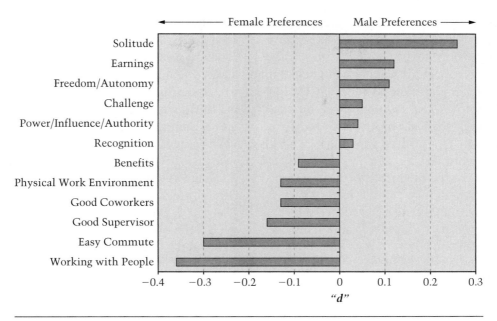

FIGURE 12.4   Sex differences in preferences for a number of job characteristics. The effect sizes ("d" statistic) are shown here.
Source: Adapted from Konrad et al. (2000)

(Matthews et al., 1998), and are less controllable (Hibbard & Pope, 1993; Hughes & Galinsky, 1994a). Among these work conditions, job monotony seems to show the strongest relations to psychological distress in women (Matthews & Power, 2002). Thus one reason work may not always have clear benefits for women's health is that women are more likely than men to face negative work conditions.

I have focused on the different conditions men and women face in paid employment, but how does the work environment of employed women differ from that of housewives? Can the differences in the paid work environment and the home environment explain why employed women are healthier than housewives? Housewives report less support (Matthews, Stansfeld & Power, 1999) and greater stress than employed women (Baruch, Biener, & Barnett, 1987). Housewives' work lacks structure and control. The traditional female role is to see to it that others in the family (husbands, children) are

happy; it is difficult to have control over another individual's happiness. Housewives also complain of a greater burden in taking care of children (Goldsteen & Ross, 1989). This may be surprising because housewives spend more time with children than employed women do. However, the expectations differ for a housewife's and a working woman's time with children. Housewives are always available to children and children know that. Goldsteen and Ross found that women who did not work outside the home said their children made more demands of them and they had less privacy than women who were employed. Because housewives are better integrated into the neighborhood than employed women, neighbors also are more likely to expect housewives than employed women to help out with their children (Goldsteen & Ross, 1989).

The housewife role is not entirely negative, however. There are advantages and disadvantages compared to employment. In a national survey, housewives reported greater job autonomy, fewer time pressures, and less responsibility for things outside of their control (e.g., being held responsible for others' behavior) compared to women who held paid positions of employment (Lennon, 1994). However, housewives also reported more interruptions, more physical effort, and more job routinization. Housewives' psychological health benefited from having less responsibility for things outside of their control but worsened from job routinization. Thus it is not a surprise that no overall difference in depression was found between housewives and employed women in this study.

Effects on Health

Does the quality of one's work role have the same implications for men's and women's health? It may depend upon the aspect of work examined. One study showed that high job demands were associated with lower job satisfaction and greater distress for men but not women (Bond et al., 2004). Yet interpersonal conflict at work (Appelberg et al., 1996) and perceptions of control at work (Muhonen & Torkelson, 2004) seem to be more strongly related to job and health outcomes for women than men.

It is difficult to compare the impact of job quality on men's and women's health because the men and women being compared to one another may differ in the other roles they possess. Perhaps work is less related to women's than men's health because more of the women in the study work part time compared to the men. Or the women in the study were more likely than the men to have family roles (spouse, parent). Studies of dual-earner couples can address this issue because the men and women have similar roles—worker, spouse, and sometimes parent. Four studies of dual-earner couples concluded that job role quality had equal effects on men's and women's health. Two of these were cross sectional and showed that job role quality was equally associated with

decreased psychological distress for both men and women (Barnett et al., 1993, 1994). A longitudinal study of 300 dual-earner couples showed that job role quality predicted changes in distress for both men and women (Barnett et al., 1995). Finally, a fourth investigation of dual-earner couples showed that aspects of the work environment had similar effects on men's and women's health cross sectionally (Barnett & Brennan, 1995) and were equally likely to predict changes in health over a 3-year period (Barnett & Brennan, 1997). In this last investigation, the two aspects of work associated with men's and women's health were job monotony and job strain. Having a challenging, as opposed to a monotonous, job was associated with health benefits, whereas role overload and role conflict were associated with health declines. These four studies focused on men and women who possessed both work and family roles. The findings from these studies support social role theory—that when men's and women's roles are more similar (both married and work full time), the relation between the quality of those roles and health is similar. In actuality, however, men and women do not always have similar roles; thus aspects of work may be more strongly related to men's health.

DISCRIMINATION

One important work condition with implications for men's and women's psychological and physical well-being is discrimination. There are two kind of discrimination: **access discrimination** and **treatment discrimination**. Access discrimination occurs when hiring decisions are made. If men or women are not offered a job or are offered a lesser job because of their sex, this is access discrimination. Access discrimination is more likely to occur when the qualifications for a job are ambiguous (Martell, 1996). If a person of either sex is clearly well qualified for a job,

FIGURE 12.5   Nancy Pelosi was elected the first woman speaker of the U.S. House of Representatives in 2006.

access discrimination is unlikely to occur. Yet some high-status jobs are less accessible to women than to men. For example, women are less represented than men in the legislative branch of government, although important strides have been made (see Nancy Pelosi in Figure 12.5). In 1979, 3% of the U.S. Congress was women; nearly 30 years later in 2007, the figure was 16.3%: 16 of 100 U.S. senators were female, and 71 of 435 (16%) U.S. representatives were women. Nine of the 50 state governors (18%) were women. The occupations in Table 12.1 show that the proportion of women in some jobs has remained the same over time. For example, nearly all dental assistants were women and nearly all firefighters were men in both 1983 and 2005. By contrast, the percentage of women who are accountants and physicians has increased over time.

Access discrimination was the subject of a 2002 nationwide sex discrimination case against Rent-A-Center (Grossman, 2002). It resulted in the awarding of a $47 million settlement. This was the largest national sex discrimination case in the history of the United States for a company of this size (13,000 employees; 2,300 stores). Rent-A-Center was charged with not hiring applicants because they were women and firing employees who were female. The class action suit was brought on behalf of 5,300 women and thousands of rejected job applicants.

Treatment discrimination occurs after the person has the job and takes the form of reduced salary or reduced opportunities for promotion. In 1999, the Massachusetts Institute of Technology released a report admitting treatment discrimination (Koerner, 1999). The report concluded that female faculty received lower pay and fewer resources than male faculty. Women were allocated only half the office space of men. In this rare case, the women did not sue MIT; instead, the school responded to the accusations by conducting their own investigation and substantiating the women's claims.

The **glass ceiling** is a form of treatment discrimination that refers to barriers to advancement of women and minorities in organizations. The glass ceiling is illustrated by the fact that only 10 Fortune 500 companies and 20 Fortune 1000 companies were run by women in 2006. One reason that women do not advance at the rate of men is that women are less likely than men to have mentors (Gutek, 2001). There are fewer women in high-powered positions available to mentor, and men are uncomfortable mentoring young women. The **glass escalator** is another form of treatment discrimination. It refers to the ability of men to be promoted quickly when they take positions in traditionally female fields, such as nursing, social work, or education (Williams, 1998).

Another form of treatment discrimination is holding different standards for men's and women's performance. Laboratory studies have shown that there is a double standard in judging the competence of men's and women's performance (Foschi, 2000). Women are held to higher standards than men even when their performance is the same—especially when the task is masculine in nature. Men's and women's performance evaluations also are influenced by whether the job is congruent with the person's sex (Davison & Burke, 2000). For masculine jobs, the same performance is evaluated more favorably if people believe the employee is male rather than female. For feminine jobs, performance is evaluated more favorably when the employee is female rather than male. The problem is that high-powered leadership positions are viewed as masculine domains. In field studies, which are far fewer and more difficult to conduct, it is not as clear if there is a bias against women (Bowen, Swim, & Jacobs, 2000). The only time that males were evaluated more favorably than females was when all the raters were male. However, men and women were evaluated favorably on different dimensions. Women were judged as more competent than men on interpersonal domains, and men were judged as more competent than women on agentic domains. The question is which domain leads to pay increases and promotions. See Sidebar 12.1 for a humorous essay that illustrates how men's and women's behavior at work may be perceived differently.

Pay Disparity

One form of treatment discrimination that receives a great deal of attention is **pay disparity**. In 2005, women who worked full time earned 81% of men's median salary (U.S. Department of Labor, 2006). In 1979, the comparable figure was 62%. The wage gap has historically been and, as shown in Figure 12.6, is still smaller among Black (89%) and Hispanic (88%) persons than White (80%) and Asian persons (81%). It is also much smaller among younger (ages 16 to 24) than older persons. The wage gap has become smaller over time and is smallest for people just entering the workforce (Stanley & Jarrell, 1998).

Calculating the wage gap is difficult: Using weekly salaries neglects the fact that women's work week is shorter than men's, and using annual salaries neglects the fact that women work fewer weeks per year than men. In 1995, among those employed over 20 hours per week, men

SIDEBAR 12.1: *Perceptions of Men & Women at Work*

The family picture is on HIS desk.
Ah, a solid, responsible family man.
    The family picture is on HER desk.
    Umm, her family will come before her career.

HE is talking with his coworkers.
He must be discussing the latest deal.
    SHE is talking with her coworkers.
    She must be gossiping.

HE's not in the office.
He's meeting customers.
    SHE's not in the office.
    She must be out shopping.

HE's having lunch with the boss.
He's on his way up.
    SHE's having lunch with the boss.
    They must be having an affair.

HE got an unfair deal.
Did he get angry?
    SHE got an unfair deal.
    Did she cry?

HE's getting married.
He'll get more settled.
    SHE's getting married.
    She'll get pregnant and leave.

HE's having a baby.
He'll need a raise.
    SHE's having a baby.
    She'll cost the company money in maternity benefits.

HE's leaving for a better job.
He knows how to recognize a good opportunity.
    SHE's leaving for a better job.
    Women are not dependable.

Source: Gardenswartz and Rowe (1994).

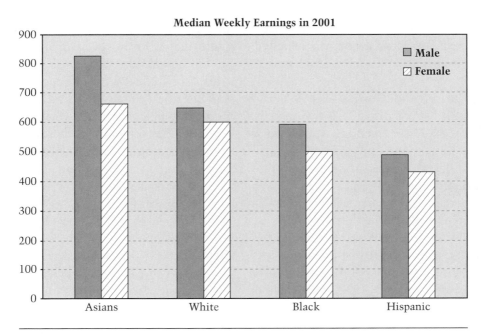

FIGURE 12.6   Men earn more than women across all three ethnic groups, but the gap is larger for Asians and Whites.
Source: U.S. Department of Labor (2006).

worked on average 42 hours per week and women worked on average 37 hours per week (Robinson & Godbey, 1999). A study of men and women who worked at least 35 hours per week also showed a 4-hour discrepancy (men 51 hours, women 47 hours; Bond et al., 1998).

Different theories explain the wage gap. **Supply-side theory**, or human capital theory, emphasizes the difference characteristics of workers that may contribute to the wage gap (Dunn, 1996); thus the focus is on the person. Today men and women tend to have more similar job qualifications, such as education and experience. The other explanation for the wage gap is referred to as **demand-side theory**, or discrimination, which emphasizes the different ways men and women are treated (Dunn, 1996); the focus here is on the environment. The effects of discrimination are typically estimated by the proportion of the wage gap that cannot be explained by all the personal characteristics that distinguish men and women (i.e., supply-side theory). Discrimination is difficult to estimate, and its accuracy fully depends on whether all of those other factors are taken into consideration.

Sex Segregation and Comparable Worth. One reason for the pay disparity is that work is segregated by sex. That is, men and women work in different occupations, and different occupations have different salaries. Many factors contribute to occupational segregation. One is that men and women select different jobs, and another is employer discrimination. In a study of college graduates, college major accounted for about half of the pay disparity between men and women because it was related to occupational choice (Brown & Corcoran, 1997). Men entered occupations that paid more than women. Another analysis showed that occupational segregation accounted for almost all the sex difference in pay (Cotter et al., 1997). That analysis also showed that integration of occupations would increase women's salaries but decrease men's salaries. Sex segregation of occupations declined in the 1970s as women moved into occupations that had traditionally been inhabited by men, such as medicine and law. However, there has been less change in occupational segregation in the 1980s, 1990s, or after the turn of the century. Occupational integration does not solve all the problems. Even if similar numbers of men and women are in a particular occupation, they often hold different positions.

Why do the occupations men enter pay more than the occupations women enter? One theory is that sex is used as a factor to determine the wage of an occupation. The proportion of women in a given occupation is directly and inversely related to the wage (Dunn, 1996). In other words, a job is worth less if women are more likely than men to hold it. If that is the case, there must be a way to compare what men and women do in different occupations to determine the appropriate wage. This idea is reflected in the **comparable worth policy**, which states that men and women in different jobs should be paid the same wage for comparable work. The difficulty comes in identifying comparable work. Some of the factors considered in developing comparable worth standards are job activities, responsibilities, environmental conditions/hazards, knowledge required, education required, skill involved, and experience needed (Barker, 1996).

A comparable worth measure of occupations was developed in the Netherlands (De Ruijter, Schippers, & Van Doorne-Huiskes, 2004). Experts who were job evaluators, vocational advisors, and social scientists evaluated the education, training, responsibility, physical and mental effort, and the cognitive, physical, and social skills required by a number of jobs. They concluded that differences in occupational worth accounted for the pay disparity between male-dominated and female-dominated

DO GENDER 12.2
Development of Comparable Worth Standards

Identify features of a job you think should influence the salary of that job. Then, choose 10 jobs, including some that are sex segregated (e.g., truck drivers, nurses). Rate each of the jobs on the features you have identified. For example, one feature of a job might be education required; rate each of the jobs on this dimension (1 = No education required; 5 = A lot of education required). Come up with a score based on your ratings for each job. In the end, you should have a rank order of which jobs should be paid the most and the least. Comment on how you think your rank order fits with the real-world salaries of those jobs.

occupations. However, they also concluded that people in female-dominant occupations are underpaid relative to their worth.

Many of the features of a job used in developing comparable worth policies are quite subjective, making it difficult to develop rigorous guidelines. In addition, it is not clear that each aspect of a job should be weighted the same as all the others. Try to develop your own comparable worth standards in Do Gender 12.2 to see if you can identify comparable jobs.

When jobs are comparable, do men and women receive similar pay? The statistics in Table 12.2 show that women still receive less money than men when they have similar jobs. Of the 127 jobs compiled by the Department of Labor Statistics (U.S. Department of Labor, 2006) for which there are enough men and women to calculate median weekly earnings, only 4 out of 127 show women with a higher salary than men. A number of studies have directly compared the salaries of men and women with the same jobs. In a study of men and

women business managers, women were paid less than men (Tsui, 1998). There were reasons for men's higher salaries, however: Men were more likely to have graduated from a selective college, had higher SAT scores, and were more likely to hold a graduate degree. Women, however, earned higher grades in college. When all these factors were taken into consideration (supply-side theory), a pay disparity still emerged between men and women. A nationally representative sample of men and women who received bachelors degrees in 1999 to 2000 were followed for the first year after graduation to examine their salaries (Dey & Hill, 2007). Among full-time workers, women's salary was 80% of men's salary. However, a major portion of that gap had to do with the different fields men and women entered. Women were more likely than men to enter lower paying fields, such as education and health. However, even within the same major, men made more money than women, and the wage gap increased each year following graduation. During the first year after graduation, the proportion of men's salary made by women was 81% for business majors, 75% for biology majors, 76% for math majors, and 95% for engineering majors. The first year after graduation is an important year to examine because both men and women are less likely to be married and have families—thus, their roles are quite similar.

By contrast, a study of young physicians showed a pay disparity between men and women that was accounted for by supply-side factors (Baker, 1996). In 1991, male physicians under age 45 made 41% more than their female counterparts. However, this sex difference in salary completely disappeared when medical specialty, practice setting, number of hours worked, education, experience, and the characteristics of the community were considered. This is certainly optimistic news for the issue of pay disparity. Among older physicians (i.e., those

TABLE 12.2 WEEKLY EARNINGS IN DOLLARS FOR FULL-TIME EMPLOYEES

	Men	Women
Accountant/auditor	1072	784
Administrative assistant	654	559
Art Designer	920	653
Baker	480	357
College/university teacher	1173	924
Computer programmer	1129	1014
Elementary school teacher	909	813
Financial manager	1347	853
Janitor	363	441
Lawyer	1748	1354
Mail carrier	874	733
Physician/surgeon	1862	1134
Police detective/sheriff	849	739
Real estate sales	989	716
Registered nurse	1011	930
Social worker	780	682
Truck/driver	631	473
Waiter/waitress	384	332

Source: U.S. Department of Labor (2006).

with more than 10 years of experience), however, men earned more than women even when the previously mentioned factors were taken into consideration. In some specialties, such as internal medicine, men earned more than women regardless of age.

A study of Canadian lawyers also found a pay disparity that was accounted for by supply-side factors (Robson & Wallace, 2001). A 1994 survey of Canadian lawyers revealed that females earned less than males ($73,000 vs. $118,000). This pay disparity was accounted for by women's less experience practicing law, shorter work hours, less likelihood of being employed in a firm, and employment in less prestigious areas of law. It is unclear whether these differences in work situations were products of women's choices or environmental constraints. Interestingly, women were also less likely than men to have "family capital," which includes being married and having children; family capital was associated with higher incomes—although you will see later that this is really only the case for men.

The gender pay gap may interact with the race pay gap. A study of men and women who graduated from historically Black compared to historically White institutions showed that the sex difference in pay was smaller among graduates from historically Black than historically White institutions (Renzulli, Grant, & Kathuria, 2006). Is it because there is less gender discrimination among Black people? Probably not. It is not the case that Black women made relatively more than White women. Instead, men from historically Black institutions made less than men from historically White institutions.

Negotiation. Another explanation for the pay disparity is that men negotiate higher starting salaries than women. A meta-analytic review of the literature showed that women were more cooperative than men during negotiation and received poorer outcomes ($d = +.09$; Walters, Stuhlmacher, & Meyer, 1998). In a study of over 200 students who recently received their M.B.A.'s, men and women were equally likely to negotiate for a higher salary when offered a position, but women received less from the negotiation than men (Gerhart & Rynes, 1991). Men's negotiations led to a 4.3% salary increase, whereas women's negotiations led to a 2.7% salary increase. This may not sound like much of a difference to you, but a small difference based on a percentage can become large over time. As shown in Figure 12.7, if a man and woman were offered an initial salary of $50,000 at age 25 and the above-mentioned difference in salary increase occurred each year, his salary would be nearly double hers by age 65—a phenomenon Babcock and Laschever (2003) refer to as the "accumulation of disadvantage."

In their book *Women Don't Ask: Negotiation and the Gender Divide*, Babcock and

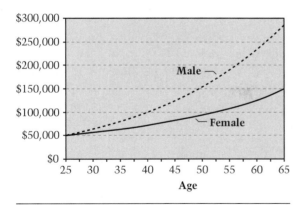

FIGURE 12.7 Hypothetical salary of a male and a female over the ages of 25 through 65 if the male received a 4.3% increase and the female received a 2.7% increase each year.

Laschever (2003) point out that women are less likely to negotiate salaries, ask for less when they do negotiate, and concede earlier than men. The fact that men make a larger initial request than women is important because the initial request is strongly correlated with the final outcome.

Women don't ask for higher salaries, women don't ask for raises or promotions, and women don't ask for better jobs—compared to men. Why do women negotiate less than men? There are a number of reasons. One reason is that men feel like they deserve more than women. In a study of M.B.A. students negotiating a job offer, men negotiated a higher salary than women (Barron, 2003). Men were more likely than women to say they knew their worth, and women were more likely than men to say that they were unsure of their worth. In addition, men were more likely to say that they deserved more than others, whereas women perceived that they were entitled to the same as others. A second reason that women negotiate less than men is that women are more concerned that negotiation will lead to conflict and concerned that conflict will jeopardize the relationship with the

negotiator. Third, women are more likely than men to believe in a meritocracy—that hard work will bring success without having to ask for it. Finally, for all these reasons, women are more anxious than men during negotiations, and anxiety is likely to interfere with women's performance.

Is there a situation in which women are more assertive in negotiation? Yes—when they are asking on behalf of others (Babcock & Laschever, 2003). Because seeing that others' needs are met is part of women's gender role, women are actually more assertive on behalf of others than themselves. Laboratory studies have shown that women will make larger requests when they are made on behalf of others than themselves, whereas men make larger requests for themselves than for others.

Is the solution to teach women better negotiation strategies? The solution may not be that simple. Employers may be more receptive to negotiation among men than women (Wade, 2001). Negotiation takes place in a social context, and women's negotiations are viewed differently from those of men. Recall from Chapter 7 that women who behave in assertive, agentic ways are not liked—especially by men—and thus are not influential. Women may have to find a way to negotiate that does not compromise perceptions of femininity.

Family Ties. A final reason for the wage gap between the sexes that we will explore is the implications of having a family for women compared to men. Employers believe they can pay women less than men because women are less likely to leave their position for more money. Women are less mobile than men because family ties keep women in the area. In a phone survey of married couples, Bielby and Bielby (1992) asked men and women how willing they would be to take a much better job in a city that was 100 miles away; more women (89%) than men (57%)

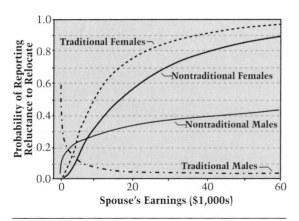

FIGURE 12.8 Women were more reluctant than men to move if they were offered a better job. Women's reluctance was a function of how much money their husband earned and of how traditional they were. The more money the husband earned, the more reluctant women were to relocate if they were offered a better job. This was especially the case for women who held traditional beliefs about gender roles. Men's reluctance to move was not influenced at all by their wife's earnings if they held traditional views of gender roles. Nontraditional males' reluctance to move was modestly affected by how much money their wife earned.
Source: W. T. Bielby and D. D. Bielby (1992). I will follow him: Family ties, gender-role beliefs, and reluctance to relocate for a better job. *American Journal of Sociology, 97*(5), 1241–1267. Copyright 1992. Reprinted by permission of the University of Chicago Press.

expressed some reluctance to move. The majority of women's reasons concerned family ties (56%), whereas only 16% of men named family as a reason for their reluctance. As shown in Figure 12.8, as spouses' earnings increased, people expressed more concerns about moving due to family reasons. This was especially the case for women. Women married to men with high incomes expressed a great reluctance to move for their own job. Women with traditional beliefs

about gender roles were especially unlikely to move for their own job if their husband had a substantial income. Traditional men, however, were willing to relocate for their own job, regardless of how much their wife made. (The spike when spouse earnings is 0 is a statistical anomaly from the logarithmic transformation used to calculate these lines.)

The presence of children, in and of itself, also contributes to the pay gap. In her book *The Price of Motherhood: Why the Most Important Job in the World Is Still the Least Valued,* Crittenden (2001) states "motherhood is now the single greatest obstacle left in the path to economic equality for women" (p. 87). She argues that motherhood is the worst economic decision a woman can make. When women have children, they may experience the **maternal wall**, which means that employers view them as less desirable employees and provide them with fewer resources and opportunities (Williams, 1999). A 10-year follow-up study of college graduates in 2003 showed that the pay gap between men and women was much larger for those with children than those without children (see Figure 12.9; Dey & Hill, 2007).

Some of the effects of parental status on women's salaries are tangible, in that women lose experience and time from work when they have children. A study of currently employed 25- to 64-year-olds examined the extent to which men and women made concessions at work to address child care responsibilities (Carr, 2002). There were three options: (1) stop working to care for children, (2) reduce hours to care for children, and (3) switch to less demanding or more flexible jobs to accommodate children. Of nearly 2,500 surveyed, more women (53%) than men (14%) reported they had made these trade-offs. Younger men were more likely than older men to have made trade-offs. Men made more subtle trade-offs (numbers 2 and 3 as opposed to number 1). The younger women in the sample

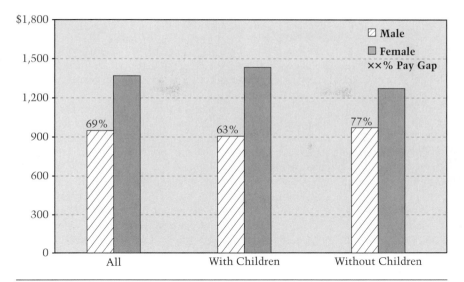

FIGURE 12.9   The difference between men's and women's pay is larger for parents than nonparents.
Source: Dey & Hill (2007).

were increasingly switching to these more subtle trade-offs. Interestingly, whether or not men made trade-offs was unrelated to their incomes, but women who had made trade-offs had lower incomes. See Sidebar 12.2 for a discussion of family-supportive work environments.

Yet, even when the money lost from taking time off is taken into consideration,

Sidebar 12.2: *Family-Supportive Work Environment*

Because there is the potential for both role overload and role conflict when work and family roles are combined, many employers have taken action to support families. There are ways that work can provide resources to cope with family issues (Pleck, 1993). First, employers can provide child care support, in terms of on-site day care or monetary subsidies. Second, employers can provide flexible hours. One organization instituted flexible work hours and found that similar numbers of men and women took advantage of this opportunity (Pleck, 1993). Flextime may be one unrecognized way that men accommodate work schedules to family needs. Pleck points out that employers and coworkers assume men are adjusting their work hours out of personal preference rather than to accommodate family needs, and men allow others to maintain this belief. In other words, men do not advertise that family roles are responsible for the changes they make in their work schedule.

A third policy that employers can institute is family leave. Most developed countries provide some kind of leave for parents with children and hold their job until they return (Moss & Deven, 2006; Sadar, 2006). Among parents who take leaves, longer maternity and paternity leaves are associated with better mental health and higher marital satisfaction (Feldman, Sussman, & Zigler, 2004). The most extensive leave policies are found in the Nordic countries. Iceland has a 9-month leave: 3 months maternity, 3 months paternity, and 3 months to be shared, with up to 80% of salary paid. In Sweden, national paternity leave has been in existence since 1974 (Seward, Yeatts, & Zottarelli, 2002). Today, both parents are provided with a total of 450 days of leave, 360 days for which they receive 80% of their salary and 90 days for which they receive a fixed amount. They can take this leave at any time until the child reaches 8 years old. Mothers and fathers can distribute the leave between themselves in any way that they wish. Typically, mothers take the first part of the leave and fathers take the second part. During the first year that paternity leave was provided in Sweden, only 3% of the people taking leave were men; by 1998, the figure was 32%. Mothers still take more days of leave than fathers.

In the United States, there is no national paternity leave policy and, in fact, there is no national paid leave. In 1993 President Clinton signed into law the Family and Medical Leave Act (FMLA). The FMLA allows employees to take a 12-week unpaid leave of absence from work to care for a child or an ill relative without fear of losing their job. A longitudinal study of over 8,000 men and women who had a child between 1991 and 1999 showed that the FMLA had no effect on men taking a leave or men's length of leave but had a small effect on women's leave taking (Han & Waldfogel, 2003).

Why don't more men in the United States take advantage of paternity leave? A major difference between the policies in the United States and other countries, such as Sweden, is that paternity leave is unpaid in the United States but paid in Sweden. In the United States, men typically use their vacation days or personal days to cover any leave that they take for child care. One study showed that the primary reason men did not take longer leaves was loss of salary; half the men said they would take a longer leave if they received 50% of their salary (Hyde, 1995). Men with more egalitarian gender-role attitudes took longer leaves.

Pleck (1993) argues that there are other, perhaps more important reasons why men in the United States do not take paternity leave: Employers and coworkers have a negative attitude toward paternity leave; men who take advantage of paternity leave are viewed as unmasculine and lacking a commitment to work; there seems to be an unwritten policy not to take paternity leave. Often, organizations provide for paternity leave to avoid sex discrimination charges but do not expect or encourage men to take advantage of it. In fact, after the FMLA became law in 1993, two lawsuits were filed by fathers who said they were discriminated against when they tried to take a family leave to care for a newborn. In 1999, Kevin Knussman, a former Maryland state trooper, was awarded $375,000 in the first sex discrimination case associated with the act (Morse, 1999). Knussman requested an extended leave because his wife had a complicated pregnancy and was not able to take care of the baby. Knussman claimed his request was denied. In 1999, a second suit was filed by David Roberts, a former South Carolina state trooper, who complained he was fired for requesting family leave to care for his newborn daughter (American Civil Liberties Union, 2000). He requested family leave because his wife had not worked long enough to accrue paid leave and he wanted to offer her the opportunity to advance in her position. His supervisor responded by telling him it was a mother's duty to take care of the children. The sharp criticism he received from his supervisors made him withdraw the request, but 3 months later he was terminated. The state of South Carolina is asking the federal court to invalidate the FMLA for state employees. Although the outcome of the case is still pending, this tactic is unlikely to work because in 2003 the U.S. Supreme Court held that state government employees are protected by the FMLA (American Civil Liberties Union, 2003).

parenthood still has a negative effect on women's salaries (Waldfogel, 1997). One reason mothers have a lower hourly wage than nonmothers is that mothers are more likely to be employed in part-time positions, which are associated with lower hourly wages (Waldfogel, 1997).

A study of graduates from a prestigious law school demonstrated the dramatic effect that having children has on women's wages (Wood, Corcoran & Courant, 1993). Women earned 93% of men's wages during the first year after graduation. Fifteen years later, however, women received 62% of men's wages. Nearly half of the pay disparity was accounted for by women's time off from work to have and take care of children. Again, the cost of having children was not accounted for by the sheer amount of time lost at work. Having children had some indirect effects on women's salaries; for example, women change jobs more often than men, which has negative effects on their earnings, and women may choose positions more accommodating to families (more flexible hours, less travel) at the expense of higher salaries. Although few men reduced their full-time status to have children, the wage penalty was actually costlier for men than for women.

Other effects of motherhood on the pay gap are not so tangible. Motherhood is conceived as a low-status characteristic, meaning that it undermines perceptions of women's competence and commitment in the workforce (Ridgeway & Correll, 2004). A number of laboratory studies have shown the negative effects motherhood has on perceptions of women's competence. When college students read a vignette of either a male or a female with or without a child, they judged women as warmer but less competent when they had a child compared to no child (Cuddy, Fiske, & Glick, 2004). Men were perceived as warmer when they had a child, but the presence of a child had no influence on their competence. In addition, students said they would prefer to promote and train a women without a child than a women with a child but preferred to promote and train a man with a child than without a child.

Other research has shown that women suffer and men benefit in the workplace from the presence of family ties. When asked to identify the standards needed to hire a hypothetical person, the standards college students derived for a female with children were higher than those for a female without children, whereas the standards derived for a male with children were more lenient than those for a male without children (Fuegen et al., 2004). The pattern of findings is not limited to vignette studies of hypothetical persons. A study of male and female employees showed that men who were married were more likely than men who were unmarried to receive a promotion, whereas women who were married were less likely than women who were unmarried to receive a promotion (Cobb-Clark & Dunlop, 1999). It is possible that there are differences in the work behavior of married and unmarried men and women. However, it may also be the case that employers believe it is more worthwhile to reward single women than married women because single women are less likely to let family obligations interfere with work and are more likely to seek a job elsewhere that pays more money. Employers may also believe it is more worthwhile to reward married men because they have a family to support. Recall the study of Canadian lawyers in which family capital was associated with higher incomes for men (Robson & Wallace, 2001). This phenomenon has been referred to as the **marital bonus** for men. One study found the marital bonus applied only to men in traditional families where wives did not work (Schneer & Reitman, 1993); the marital bonus disappeared when wives were employed.

One group of women who may not suffer from the wage gap is lesbians. One might expect that gay men and lesbians earn less money for comparable work than their heterosexual counterparts because of discrimination. This is true in the case of gay men, but lesbians earn more than heterosexual women (Black et al., 1998; Peplau & Fingerhut, 2004). One explanation is based on **human capital accumulation**

theory (Black et al., 1998). Heterosexual women limit their market skills more than lesbians because they expect to be part of a traditional family where a second income will exist. Lesbians do not limit their market skills because they are less certain of a second income. Lesbians are more educated than heterosexual women and more likely than heterosexual women to have full-time jobs. Lesbians also are more likely than heterosexual women to have nontraditional jobs, which are associated with higher salaries. Lesbians have greater freedom to pursue their career because they do not have the constraints of a husband and are less likely to have children. However, even when lesbians have children (which is increasingly common), motherhood does not detract from perceptions of competence as it does for heterosexual women. As shown in Figure 12.10, heterosexual college students rated a heterosexual woman as

less competent and less career oriented when she was a parent than a nonparent, rated a heterosexual man as more competent and more career oriented when he was a parent than a nonparent, and rated lesbians as equally competent and career oriented regardless of whether she was a parent or not. Just because lesbians have higher incomes than heterosexual women does not mean that they do not suffer from access or treatment discrimination. To the extent that discrimination does exist, lesbians should have even higher salaries.

Evolutionary Theory. Human capital theory argues that once all the known factors that contribute to pay, such as education and field of study, are taken into consideration, any remaining sex difference in pay is due to discrimination. Evolutionary theory argues the remaining sex difference in pay is due to men's greater

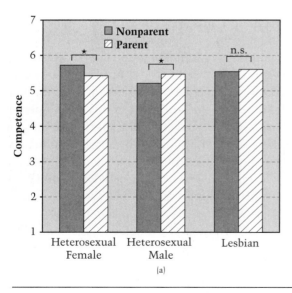
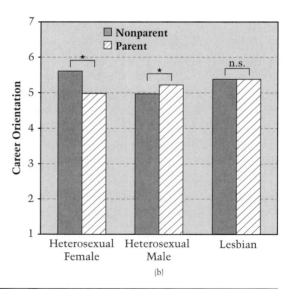

FIGURE 12.10 Heterosexual women were rated as less competent and less career oriented when they were a parent compared to a nonparent; heterosexual men were rated as more competent and more career oriented when they were a parent compared to a nonparent. Lesbians were rated as equally competent (a) and equally career oriented (b) regardless of parental status.
Source: Adapted from Peplau and Fingerhut (2004).

desire to make more money compared to women (Kanazawa, 2005). The argument is that money is central to men's but not women's reproductive success as money is used to ensure the survival of children. Evidence for the theory comes from the fact that men typically rate income as a more important factor in a job compared to women. In addition, the sex difference in the value attached to personal income is larger among people who are married and have children. Men and women who are unmarried without children tend to equally value the income associated with a job.

Denial of Discrimination

It is perhaps surprising that women do not seem more unhappy with the difference in pay between men and women. A 2005 Gallup Poll revealed that 55% of women and 39% of men said that men and women do not have equal job opportunities. Women, on average, perceive that other women are victims of discrimination, but not themselves. Faye Crosby (1984) asked women the following three questions in several studies (p. 371):

1. Do you currently receive the benefits from your job that you deserve to receive?

2. Are you at present the victim of sex discrimination?

3. Are women discriminated against?

The vast majority of women say yes to questions 1 and 3, but no to question 2. They believe they receive the benefits they deserve, that they do not suffer personal discrimination, but that other women are victims of discrimination. Crosby argues that women are denying their disadvantage. She demonstrated this denial in a study of men and women who reported equal satisfaction with their salary but actually

received quite different salaries. Although the men and women were matched to each other in terms of the prestige of their job, their education, their job experience, the number of hours worked, their age, and their marital status, the women received between $5,000 and $8,000 less than the men. Despite their **denial of disadvantage**, the vast majority of the women (and men) agreed that women in general are subject to discrimination and women do not receive the same salary as men for comparable work. The women in this study suffered discrimination, perceived that discrimination existed, but denied they were victims of discrimination. See if this phenomenon appears among your peers in Do Gender 12.3.

DO GENDER 12.3
Denial of Personal Discrimination

You probably will not be able to measure actual discrimination in this exercise, but you can determine the extent to which women perceive that others compared to themselves are subject to discrimination. Ask a group of men and women Crosby's (1984) three questions:

1. Do you currently receive the benefits from your job that you deserve to receive?

2. Are you at present the victim of sex discrimination?

3. Are women discriminated against?

For interest, ask an additional question:

4. Are men discriminated against?

What percentage of men and women perceive that women are victims of discrimination? That men are victims of discrimination? What percentage of men and women perceive they are victims of sex discrimination?

Why do women deny personal discrimination? Crosby (1984) offers a couple of explanations. First, she suggests it is difficult for a person to infer discrimination on the basis of a single case. We can always find another reason why we did not receive the job, the promotion, or the salary increase: Other people had more experience, education, or knowledge. It is difficult for a single person to compare himself or herself to a group of individuals. Second, perceiving discrimination arouses discomfort. If an individual suffers discrimination, someone specific is to blame. Perceiving that a group of people suffer discrimination (i.e., all women) does not cause as much discomfort because the source of the discrimination is more diffuse: society as a whole.

Another reason women do not perceive personal discrimination is that women feel entitled to less pay than men. In two laboratory studies, female college students paid themselves less for the same task than male college students (Desmarais & Curtis, 1997). One reason women feel less entitled to equal pay is because they compare their earnings to those of other women rather than those of other men (Major, 1989). Because work is often segregated by sex, women find other women more suitable sources of comparison. A basic principle of social comparison theory is that we compare ourselves with "similar others." Women perceive similar others to be women in general rather than men—even if the men are in the same job. However, when women do compare themselves to men, they become less satisfied. Recall from Chapter 11 that the tendency of women to compare themselves to women rather than men was also used to explain why women are satisfied with an unequal division of household responsibilities.

This tendency to make **in-group** (within-sex) rather than **out-group** (between-sex) **social comparisons** when evaluating wages was demonstrated in an experimental study by Bylsma and Major (1994). Groups of 6 college students participated in an experiment that involved reviewing college applicants and predicting who would be successful. Participants were told they would be paid based on their performance. The groups were assigned to one of three conditions: a condition in which same-sex peers were paid more than other-sex peers, a condition in which other-sex peers were paid more than same-sex peers, and a condition in which no comparison information was available. In the first two conditions, the social comparison information was made available by a set of receipts that were left on the table. Participants were asked to rate their performance and indicate how much they thought they should be paid. As shown in Figure 12.11, participants gave estimates of higher pay when they thought same-sex peers were paid more than other-sex peers, and

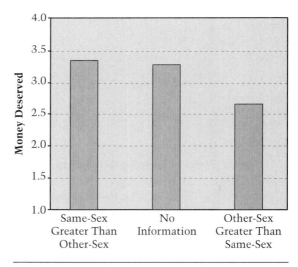

FIGURE 12.11 Men's and women's entitlement to pay as a function of social comparison information. Both male and female participants in an experiment said they should receive more pay when they thought that same-sex people were paid more compared to when they thought other-sex people were paid more. *Source:* Adapted from Bylsma and Major (1994).

lesser pay when they thought other-sex peers were paid more than same-sex peers. Pay ratings of the people in the no social comparison condition fell between the two groups. These findings held for both men and women. Women also rated their performance as superior when they thought same-sex peers were paid more compared to when they thought other-sex peers were paid more. Men's ratings of their performance were not affected by the social comparison information. On average, men rated their performance across the conditions as better than women did.

Thus both men's and women's judgments of entitlement were determined by what the in-group had received. Women's actual ratings of their performance also were influenced by what the in-group was paid. This latter finding is consistent with research that shows women's perceptions of their abilities are responsive to feedback and other environmental information. The implications of these findings are that members of disadvantaged groups, in this case women, will be satisfied with unfair treatment and may even judge they deserve it. A study of college students showed that women expected a lower pay than men and this expectation accounted for about a third of the difference in the actual salaries of the jobs students aimed to find (Heckert et al., 2002). The authors argue that women's expectations of a lower salary become self-fulfilling prophecies. Women expect lower pay and are thus satisfied with lower pay. For women to be dissatisfied with less pay than men, comparisons to men need to be made salient and relevant.

Another reason women may feel entitled to less pay than men reflects how women view their jobs. Thompson (1991) points out that women may place a greater value on their husband's job than their own. Even when women work, they typically perceive their husband as the breadwinner. It is only when women perceive their job

as essential to the economic status of the family that women might become dissatisfied with unequal pay at work and an unequal division of labor at home.

Thus far we have discussed discrimination as a *lack* of opportunity for one sex. The flip side of the coin is preferential treatment based on sex. Preferential treatment in job selection is associated with negative self-views among women, but not men (Gutek, 2001). This fits with the research reviewed in Chapter 6 showing that women's self-perceptions are more vulnerable to others' opinions compared to men. The remedy to the adverse effects of preferential treatment on women is simple—let women know they are competent *before* they are selected for the position.

TAKE HOME POINTS

- Women suffer from both access discrimination and treatment discrimination.

- Treatment discrimination can take the form of the glass ceiling, the glass escalator, and pay disparity.

- The pay disparity between men and women can be accounted for both by factors that distinguish men and women workers (supply-side theory) and the differences in the ways that men and women are treated (demand-side theory).

- One factor that distinguishes male and female workers and accounts for a large portion of the pay disparity is that men enter occupations associated with higher salaries than women. Sex differences in wages still appear among men and women in the same occupation, although the size of the disparity is smaller.

- The fact that women negotiate less than men and women's negotiations are less successful than those of men also contributes to the pay gap.

- Another factor that contributes to the pay gap is children. Women take more time off from work for children, and this differential work experience accounts for a sizable difference in earnings. The presence of children also indirectly contributes to the pay gap as it undermines perceptions of competence for women but not men. In fact, men's salaries seem to benefit from the presence of children, whereas women's suffer.

■ Women are not as dissatisfied with the pay disparity as one might expect. Part of the reason is that women do not perceive themselves as victims of discrimination, although they perceive that *other women* are victims of discrimination.

■ One reason that women do not recognize a personal pay disparity is that women compare their salary to that of other women rather than that of men. When comparisons to men are made salient, women become less satisfied with their pay.

SEXUAL HARASSMENT

In 1991, the Tailhook Association, an organization for Navy aviators, convened at the Hilton Hotel in Las Vegas for their annual convention. The convention was known for its memorable parties and rowdy behavior, but this year things got out of hand—or this year people got caught. Women who were on vacation, as well as women who were members of the association, walked in on the third-floor party to find the halls lined with men (known as the "Banister") who proceeded to grab and fondle various body parts and remove clothing despite the women's screams and attempts to fight the men off. The final report sent to the Navy contained incidents of verbal abuse, physical abuse, and sexual molestation (Ballingrud, 1992).

Not nearly as famous as Tailhook, but equally as devastating, was the Eveleth Mines case (Tevlin, 1998). In 1993, 16 female mine workers successfully sued Oglebay Norton Corp. in the first ever hostile sexual work environment class-action lawsuit in the United States. The mine was decorated with pornography, obscene

graffiti, and sexual objects. One woman went to discuss these issues with her supervisor but found a picture of a vagina on his desk. The women were subjected to dirty jokes, sexual propositions, fondling, and groping on a daily basis. One woman even found semen on the clothes in her locker. Although the courts agreed the women suffered sexual harassment, it took 5 years to settle the case. Monetary awards were provided to the women, but the company did not apologize.

In this section of the chapter, I define sexual harassment, examine its incidence, and describe characteristics of perpetrators and victims. Then, I review some theories of sexual harassment.

Definitions

The following is the Equal Employment Opportunity Commission's (EEOC, 1980, p. 74677) definition of sexual harassment:

> Unwelcome sexual advances, requests for sexual favors, and other verbal or physical conduct of a sexual nature constitute sexual harassment when (1) submission to such conduct is made either explicitly or implicitly a term or condition of an individual's employment, (2) submission to or rejection of such conduct by an individual is used as the basis for employment decisions affecting such individual, or (3) such conduct has the purpose or effect of unreasonably interfering with an individual's work performance or creating an intimidating, hostile, or offensive working environment.

The EEOC defines two types of sexual harassment: (1) **quid pro quo**, which means one person offers work benefits (e.g., promotion) or threatens work repercussions (e.g., loss of job) in exchange for sexual favors, and (2) **hostile environment**, which means the person is faced with a hostile, intimidating work environment. Quid pro quo, which can be translated as "this for that," is likely to occur among two people of different status. Hostile environment sexual harassment, which frequently consists of pervasive pornographic material, sexual language, and displays of sexual behavior, is more likely to occur among coworkers; this type of harassment was the subject of the Eveleth Mines case.

It is difficult to define sexual harassment exclusively in terms of behavior because a given behavior can be construed as harassment in some instances and not others. Although some behaviors can clearly be defined as sexual harassment, such as a sexual bribe, others cannot be objectively classified as harassment in an absolute sense. How can you tell whether a comment or a look is flirting or harassment? Paludi and Barickman (1998) have suggested that one way to determine whether a behavior is harassment is to examine whether the recipient has the freedom to pursue the relationship. If the person feels free to pursue or not pursue the relationship, the behavior is not harassment; if the person feels he or she has no choice, the behavior is harassment. A second way to determine whether a behavior is harassment is to examine the effect of the behavior on the person. If the behavior makes one feel good and even attractive, the behavior is not harassment; if the behavior makes one feel uncomfortable, the behavior is harassment. These definitional distinctions are problematic because they rely on the recipient's interpretation of the behavior. One recipient may feel uncomfortable when a person whistles at her, whereas another recipient may feel attractive.

Much of this discussion has focused on the psychological rather than the legal definition of sexual harassment. In defining hostile environment harassment, the U.S. Supreme Court has set forth guidelines that both the alleged victim and a "reasonable person" must perceive the behavior as hostile (Weiner & Gutek, 1999). Not surprisingly, this standard has been difficult to implement.

There is consensus across studies of undergraduates and adult populations that some behaviors are clearly sexual harassment and some are not (Frazier, Cochran, & Olson, 1995). Sexual propositions, sexual coercion, and sexual touching are viewed as sexual harassment by most everyone. Sexist comments, jokes, coarse language, flirting, and staring, however, are typically not viewed as harassment. There is more agreement that harassment has occurred when behaviors are physical (e.g., petting, pinching) rather than verbal (e.g., sexual comments, innuendoes). Undergraduates are less likely than other adults to view behaviors as sexual harassment.

There are three levels of sexual harassment (Fitzgerald, Gelfand, & Drasgow, 1995). They are shown in Table 12.3, in order from least to most severe. The first two levels are more similar to hostile environment sexual harassment, whereas the third reflects quid pro quo sexual harassment. There is more agreement that harassment has occurred at the most severe levels.

TABLE 12.3   LEVELS OF SEXUAL HARASSMENT

1. Gender harassment (e.g., sexist comments, suggestive stories)
2. Unwanted sexual attention (e.g., leering, attempts at touching, repeated requests for dates)
3. Sexual coercion (e.g., bribes and threats involving sex, negative consequences for refusals to have sex).

Source: Fitzgerald et al. (1995).

TABLE 12.4   Samples Items from the Sexual Experiences Questionnaire

Gender harassment:	Crude sexist remarks
Seductive behavior:	Propositions
Sexual bribery:	Direct offers of reward
Sexual coercion:	Direct threats
Sexual imposition:	Unwanted attempts to touch or fondle

Source: Fitzgerald et al. (1988).

One common instrument used to measure sexual harassment, especially in college students, is the Sexual Experiences Survey (Fitzgerald et al., 1988, 1995). Sample items are shown in Table 12.4.

Do men and women define sexual harassment in the same way? There is clearly a difference. Women are more likely than men to perceive a behavior as harassment (Golden, Johnson, & Lopez, 2001) and to view sexual harassment as a problem in the workplace (Gutek & O'Connor, 1995). A meta-analysis showed that women were more likely to define a situation as harassing, but the effect size was small to moderate ($d = +.35$; Blumenthal, 1998). Differences between men's and women's interpretations of a behavior are most likely to emerge for more ambiguous behaviors, such as staring or sexist remarks. Men and women clearly agree that a sexual proposition is sexual harassment.

Sex differences in perceptions of sexual harassment are not universal. College students from the United States, Australia, Germany, and Brazil read a story about a college professor who invited a student from his seminar to dinner (Pryor et al., 1997). Only in the United States were women more likely than men to view the behavior as sexual harassment. As shown in Figure 12.12, in Brazil, men were more likely than women to view the behavior as harassment, there were no sex differences in perception of harassment in Australia and Germany, and in the United States, women were more likely than men to view the behavior as harassment.

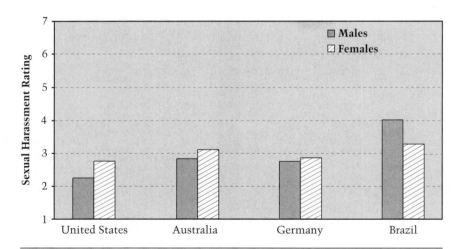

FIGURE 12.12   College students' perceptions of sexual harassment. In the United States, women were more likely than men to interpret a behavior as sexual harassment. In Australia and Germany, there were no sex differences in perceptions of sexual harassment. In Brazil, men were more likely than women to interpret a behavior as sexual harassment.
Source: Adapted from Pryor et al. (1997).

Notice that the sex difference in the United States was not due to U.S. women being more likely than women in other countries to interpret a behavior as harassment but was due to U.S. men being *less* likely than men from other countries to perceive the behavior as harassment. In a cross-cultural study of college students, those from individualistic cultures (e.g., United States, Germany) were more likely to perceive a behavior as sexual harassment, to assign more responsibility to the perpetrator, and to assign less responsibility to the victim than those from collectivist cultures (e.g., India, Taiwan; Sigal et al., 2005).

One characteristic of both the harasser and the harassee that influences people's perceptions is physical attractiveness. In a vignette study, male and female college students perceived the same situation as less harassing when the male perpetrator was attractive compared to unattractive and as more harassing when the female victim was attractive compared to unattractive (Golden et al., 2002).

The status difference between the two people also influences whether a behavior is interpreted as sexual harassment. In quid pro quo sexual harassment, the harasser has a higher status than the person being harassed. Thus we might perceive the same behavior as harassment if the harasser has a high rather than a low status. Research has shown this to be true. A meta-analysis revealed a medium effect for status on perceptions of harassment ($d = +.65$; Blumenthal, 1998), such that a behavior was more likely to be labeled harassment when there was a status difference between perpetrator and target.

However, one study showed that status has a more complicated relation to perceptions of harassment. Although status is associated with power, which leads to a behavior being interpreted as harassment, status is also associated with perceiving the person in more favorable terms, which leads to a behavior not being interpreted

as harassment (Sheets & Braver, 1999). Thus if a high-status person engages in an ambiguous behavior, such as making sexual innuendoes, we will be less likely to interpret the behavior as harassment if we know and like the person than if we do not know and/or do not like the person. This fits with the previous finding that attractive men are judged less harshly than unattractive men for harassment (Golden et al., 2002).

Incidence

In 1992, 10,532 charges of sexual harassment were filed with the EEOC. By 1997, there was an increase of 50%, with 15,889 charges filed. By 2006, the number of charges filed decreased to 12,025 (Equal Opportunity Employment Commission, 2007). The majority of charges are filed by women, but the number of charges filed by men is increasing. In 1992, 9% of charges filed were by men, and in 2006, 15% of charges filed were by men.

How many people have experienced sexual harassment during their working history? The prevalence of sexual harassment is typically measured with surveys. One methodological difficulty with the survey method is that all the respondents do not complete them. The people who complete the survey could differ from the people who choose not to complete the survey. The kind of person who responds to a survey is likely to be interested in the topic, and it makes sense that the people who will be most interested in the topic of sexual harassment are those who have experienced it. There is evidence that such a response bias exists. Gruber (1990) found that studies with low response rates (i.e., a smaller percentage of people returning the survey) revealed higher rates of sexual harassment. This finding suggests that the people who do not respond to surveys are less likely to have been harassed. Thus to obtain a good estimate of the frequency of sexual harassment, it is very important to have a representative sample of participants and a high response rate.

Good studies with representative samples show that the incidence of female sexual harassment ranges between 42% and 53% (White & Kowalski, 1998), with an average of 44% (Gruber, 1990). Higher percentages occur for milder forms of sexual harassment, such as sexual remarks. An older methodologically strong study of sexual harassment among federal employees showed that 42% of women reported being sexually harassed within the prior 2 years (U.S. Merit Systems Protection Board, 1981). The study was repeated in 1987 and in 1994, and similar results were found (U.S. Merit System Protection Board, 1988, 1995). In a survey of 5,225 randomly selected navy personnel (with women oversampled), sexual harassment was reported by 44% of enlisted women, 33% of women officers, 8% of enlisted men, and 2% of men officers (Newell, Rosenfeld, & Culbertson, 1995). Few of these people filed a complaint: only 8% of enlisted women and 6% of women officers. Again, the most frequent types of sexual harassment were the milder forms, such as unwanted looks and sexual jokes. People typically responded to harassment by either avoiding the perpetrator or confronting the perpetrator and asking him or her to stop.

The prevalence of sexual harassment is influenced by the way the question is asked. When men and women are asked about specific behaviors at work, they report comparable levels of sexual harassment (Gutek, 1985). For example, in a study of 1,000 working people, similar percentages of men and women reported that a person of the other sex had made insulting comments (19% men, 23% women), given insulting looks (19% men, 20% women), touched them sexually (33% men, 33% women), and made socializing or dating part of their job (8% men, 12% women). The only exception was that twice as many women as men said they were required to have sex with someone at work as part of their job (8% vs. 4%).

Although men and women reported similar rates of most specific behaviors, when asked if they had been sexually harassed, more women than men said yes (53% vs. 37%). To examine further whether the behaviors men and women reported could be construed as harassment, independent coders rated the behaviors and classified them as definitely sexual harassment, probably sexual harassment, uncertain, probably not sexual harassment, and definitely not sexual harassment. The coders largely agreed with participants' own perceptions; coders said sexual harassment had definitely or probably occurred among 59% of women and 28% of men.

What does the discrepancy between reports of specific behaviors and perceptions of sexual harassment mean? Are the categories of behaviors too broad to capture whether a behavior is harassment? Does the context within which a behavior takes place affect whether a behavior is interpreted as harassment? If so, part of that context may be the sex of the perpetrator, that is, being male. Both men and women assign harsher penalties for the same behavior if the perpetrator is male than female (Cummings & Armenta, 2002).

What is the incidence of sexual harassment among men? The U.S. Merit Systems Protection Board surveys (1981, 1988, 1995) showed that between 14% and 19% of men had experienced sexual harassment in the prior 24 months. In her review of the literature, Gutek (1985) concluded that between 9% and 35% of men experience sexual harassment (depending on the definition) by women at some point in their working life. Men may be even less likely than women to report sexual harassment. Men are expected to handle these kinds of situations on their own; admitting to harassment means admitting to victim status, which is inconsistent with the male gender role. Being the subject of harassment by another man would be especially threatening to men. Thus it is not surprising that men are even less likely to report sexual harassment by other men (Dziech & Hawkins, 1998).

What is the incidence of sexual harassment on college campuses? A 2005 nationally representative survey of undergraduates showed that sexual harassment is prevalent, with two thirds of students reporting some kind of harassment (Hill & Silva, 2005), which is consistent with another recent report of 57% (Huerta et al., 2006). The majority of harassment incidents consist of verbal behaviors, such as lewd comments, jokes, sexual innuendoes, and remarks about body parts. Male and female students are equally likely to be harassed, but females are more bothered than male students by the harassment. Lesbian, gay, and bisexual students were more likely than heterosexuals to experience harassment. Both males and females report that men are more likely to harass them than women. Interestingly, when students were asked why they engaged in sexual harassment, the most common response was because they thought it was funny. Only 17% did so because they wanted to date the person. Conduct your own study of sexual harassment on campus with Do Gender 12.4.

DO GENDER 12.4
Prevalence of Sexual Harassment on Campus

First, you must decide on a definition of sexual harassment. Then, you must decide on the behaviors that constitute sexual harassment. Administer a survey to 10 men and 10 women on campus and ask them how frequently they have experienced each behavior. After the frequency ratings are made, you might ask the respondents to evaluate whether they perceive each of these behaviors as sexual harassment.

Outcomes of Sexual Harassment

Sexual harassment is associated with adverse effects on work quality and on health (Gutek & Done, 2000; Harned & Fitzgerald, 2002; Rederstorff, Buchanan, & Settles, 2007). In terms of work quality, people who are harassed are unhappy with their job, have more difficulty performing their job, and are less committed to their job. People who are harassed may quit their job, be fired, or lose career opportunities. Health outcomes range from psychological distress, such as loss of self-esteem, anxiety, and depression, to physical symptoms, such as headaches and gastrointestinal problems, and even eating disturbances. Sexual harassment also may affect people's ability to trust others. People who are harassed may withdraw from social interactions. Among college students, sexual harassment has been associated with increased distress, eating disturbances, academic disengagement, and poor academic performance (Huerta et al., 2006).

The pervasiveness of harassment seems to be more important than the type of harassment. In a survey of 13,743 women from the U.S. Armed Forces who had experienced sexual harassment, sexual harassment was related to greater psychological distress, less job satisfaction, and lower perceived health. Pervasiveness was a stronger predictor of these outcomes than whether the harassment took the form of sexual coercion, sexual hostility, or unwanted attention. Harassment by higher status perpetrators also was associated with greater distress.

There is no indication that reporting sexual harassment leads to better outcomes (Bergman et al., 2002). The outcome depends on the organization's response, and a typical response is retaliation of some sort. Retaliation and minimization of sexual harassment lead to lower job satisfaction.

Most research on the outcomes of sexual harassment come from survey studies. The problem with survey studies is that both the independent variable (sexual harassment) and the dependent variable (distress) rely on self-report. Laboratory studies in which sexual harassment is manipulated can provide more definitive evidence of its effects. One such study showed that sexual harassment during the interview process impaired women's performance (Woodzicka & LaFrance, 2005). Young adult females were interviewed for a job by a male and randomly assigned to receive one of two sets of interviewer questions. Both sets of questions were out of the ordinary (to control for the surprise element of the questions), but only one set of questions could be construed as sexual harassment. For example, in the control condition, women were asked if they had a best friend and if they thought it was important for people to believe in God. In the sexual harassment condition, women were asked if they had a boyfriend and if they thought it was important for women to wear a bra to work. The interview was videotaped and transcribed and rated by coders who were blind to condition. Women in the sexual harassment condition spoke less fluently, gave lower quality answers to questions, and asked fewer relevant questions during the interview than women in the control condition. Interestingly, women's perception of being harassed was not related to these outcomes. Thus the objective measure of harassment hurt performance, whereas the subjective perception of harassment did not.

In another laboratory study, the effects of sexual harassment were studied by observing the effects of dominant nonverbal behavior (e.g., open posture, look directly at person), an expected correlate of sexual harassment, on performance (Kelly et al., 2005). When college women were exposed to a dominant male confederate compared to a nondominant male confederate, they performed worse on a series of cognitive tasks. In a subsequent experiment, the authors found that high dominant behavior was associated with sexual harassment.

Characteristics of the victim also influence responses to sexual harassment. A study of college students showed that nontraditional/feminist attitudes buffered the effects of sexual harassment for White women but exacerbated the effects of sexual harassment for Black women (Rederstorff et al., 2007). The authors argued that feminist attitudes provided White women with an external attribution for the harassment—societal problems at large. Black women, however, face oppression from both race and gender, and sexual harassment may make this double victimization salient, leading to psychological distress.

Characteristics of Perpetrator

There are few distinctive demographic characteristics of men who sexually harass women. Sexual harassment is usually not related to a man's age, marital status, physical attractiveness, or occupation (Paludi & Barickman, 1998). If anything, men who harass are more likely to be married and are older (Gutek, 1985; U.S. Merit Systems Protection Board, 1981). Harassers are more likely to be coworkers than supervisors (Bondurant & White, 1996), in part because people have more coworkers than supervisors, which means hostile environment harassment is more common than quid pro quo harassment.

Although male harassers cannot be distinguished by demographic characteristics, psychological characteristics are linked to those who may harass. People who score higher on hostile and benevolent sexism are more tolerant of sexual harassment (Russell & Trigg, 2004). Pryor (1998) has developed the *Likelihood to Sexually Harass (LSH)* scale to identify the person most likely to engage in sexual harassment. This scale consists of a series of situations that

TABLE 12.5   LIKELIHOOD TO SEXUALLY HARASS SCENARIO

Imagine you are a college professor. You are 38 years old; you teach in a large Midwestern university; you are a full professor with tenure; you are renowned in your field (abnormal psychology) and have numerous offers for other jobs. One day, following the return of an examination to a class, a female student stops in your office. She tells you that her score is one point away from an A and asks you if she can do an extra credit project to raise her score. She tells you that she may not have a sufficient grade to get into graduate school without the A. Several other students have asked you to do extra credit assignments and you have declined to let them. This particular woman is a stunning blonde. She sits in the front row of the class every day and always wears short skirts. You find her extremely sexy. How likely are you to do the following things in this situation?

  a. Would you let her carry out a project for extra credit (e.g., write a paper)?
      Not at all likely   1   2   3   4   5   Very likely
  b. Assuming that you are very secure in your job and the university has always tolerated professors who make passes at students, would you offer the student a chance to earn extra credit in return for sexual favors?
      Not at all likely   1   2   3   4   5   Very likely
  c. Given the same assumptions as in the question above, would you ask her to join you for dinner to discuss the possible extra credit assignments?
      Not at all likely   1   2   3   4   5   Very likely

Source: Pryor (1998).

create the opportunity for quid pro quo sexual harassment to occur. Following each scenario, respondents are asked how likely they would be to engage in a number of behaviors. A sample scenario is shown in Table 12.5. Men who score high on this scale say they would respond to the series of scenarios by engaging in sexual behavior. Men who score high on this scale endorse stereotypical masculine beliefs and have traditional attitudes toward women (Paludi & Barickman, 1998; Pryor, Giedd, & Williams, 1995). These men equate masculinity with high status, appearing tough, and being dominant. You might expect that men who sexually harass women are likely to interpret neutral behavior in sexual terms. Some research shows this to be true (Deaux & LaFrance, 1998), but other research has strongly refuted this idea (Saal, 1996).

It is not surprising that personality characteristics can be linked to the person who engages in sexual harassment because incidents of harassment are usually not isolated. The male harasser usually approaches more than one woman and the women are aware of this (Gutek, 1985).

Characteristics of Victim

Younger and unmarried women are more likely to be harassed than older and married women (Gutek & Done, 2000). Unmarried men also are more likely than married men to be sexually harassed (Gutek, 1985).

Women's occupations also are linked to sexual harassment. Women employed in male-dominated positions are more likely to be harassed than women employed in traditional occupations (Bondurant & White, 1996), in part because these women have greater contact with men. For example, in a 1988 survey of sexual harassment among active duty military, 64% of women reported an incident of sexual harassment in the prior year (Martindale, 1990). This is a much higher incidence than that reported in nationally representative samples.

Ethnicity is also related to sexual harassment, but it depends on assimilation into

American culture. A study of women working in a food processing company showed that 23% of low-acculturated Hispanic women had been sexually harassed, in contrast to 61% of high-acculturated Hispanic women and 77% of non-Hispanic White women (Shupe et al., 2002). The investigators suggested that the higher rate of sexual harassment among high-acculturated women had to do with the greater threat they posed to traditional roles compared to low-acculturated women. Low-acculturated women retained the traditional male/females roles that are rooted in Hispanic culture.

Women's occupations also influence the type of sexual harassment. Women in traditional occupations are likely to suffer quid pro quo sexual harassment, whereas women in nontraditional occupations are likely to suffer from hostile environment harassment (Lach & Gwartney-Gibbs, 1993). When women are in nontraditional jobs, they are perceived by male peers as a threat to their job. Sexual harassment is most likely to occur in situations where women reject the traditional female role. According to Burgess and Borgida (1999), sexual harassment is a way of punishing women who do not adhere to the prescriptive component of stereotypes. Sexual harassment is used to maintain the status differential between women who threaten the status quo and men.

Theories

One theory of sexual harassment is that it is a natural and normal part of male/female relationships (Tangri & Hayes, 1997). Sexual harassment may be viewed as the product of male hormones or as a normal part of male courting behavior. One motive for sexual harassment may be to seek sexual intimacy. The behavior becomes a problem, however, when it is not desired on the part of the female.

Another theory of sexual harassment is that it is a manifestation of patriarchy—men's dominance over women. According to this view, harassment is a form of men asserting their power over women and has more to do with power than sex (Sandler & Shoop, 1997; Tangri & Hayes, 1997). With quid pro quo harassment, power is certainly an important factor. However, even with hostile environment harassment between coworkers, some would argue that assertion of power is the underlying motivation.

A social psychological perspective conceptualizes sexual harassment as the product of both person factors and situational factors. Sexual harassment is a behavior that occurs among some of the people some of the time (Pryor et al., 1995). Characteristics of people who harass are addressed with Pryor's (1998) LSH scale. What are the environmental conditions that foster sexual harassment? In one study, priming men with a sexist film was associated with gender harassment (i.e., number of sexist questions asked of a female during a mock job interview; Pryor et al., 2000). In another study, men whose masculinity was threatened by being outperformed by a female on a masculine task were more likely to engage in the same form of sexual harassment (Pryor et al., 2000).

Sexual harassment is most likely to occur in situations where it is perceived as acceptable or tolerated (Pryor et al., 1995). In organizations where management condones sexual harassment, the frequency increases. A study conducted by the Department of Defense (Martindale, 1990) nicely illustrates this finding. They compared women's reports of sexual harassment to men's reports of the commanding officers' attitudes toward sexual harassment. Thus estimates of sexual harassment and environmental acceptability were derived from separate sources. In locations where men said the atmosphere was more accepting of sexual harassment, women reported more harassment.

Another theory of sexual harassment that emphasizes the contribution of situational variables is the **sex-role spillover theory**, which suggests that expectations about men's and women's roles carry over to the workplace when they are not appropriate or relevant (Tangri & Hayes, 1997). This theory implies that sexual harassment is more likely to occur when gender is salient (Gutek & Done, 2000), when men are in the clear majority and women are in the minority (Gutek, 1985): Because of women's minority status in male-dominated occupations, their gender role rather than their work role becomes salient. Sexual harassment is also more likely to occur to women whose occupation is consistent with the female gender role, such as waitresses and secretaries, because their sex is salient (Gutek & Done, 2000). This theory also applies to men: Men who work with a large number of women are more likely to experience sexual harassment (Gutek & Done, 2000).

According to Gutek (1985), work conditions are conducive to the sexual harassment of women in two ways. First, attractiveness is valued in female workers more than male workers. In a study of over 1,000 working persons, 50% of the women said physical attractiveness was at least somewhat important in their job; 20% said their attractiveness was very important to their job. Second, women are often in lower job positions than men.

TAKE HOME POINTS

- There are two kinds of sexual harassment: quid pro quo and hostile environment.

- Sexual harassment is difficult to define because it rests in part on how the recipient perceives the behavior.

- Sexual harassment ranges in severity from lewd comments to sexual coercion; there is more agreement that a behavior constitutes harassment when it is more severe.

- Sexual harassment appears to be fairly common; the most common forms are the less severe forms.

- A psychological instrument, the Likelihood to Sexually Harass Scale, has been developed to distinguish between men who are more and less likely to harass.

- Women in traditionally male occupations are more likely to be harassed, perhaps because their presence represents a threat to men.

- Social psychological theories of sexual harassment emphasize that the behavior is a product of both individual difference variables (such as the LSH scale) and situational variables (when the male role is threatened, when women's sex is made salient).

THE MULTIPLE ROLES QUESTION

Historically, men have easily combined the roles of worker, spouse, and parent. Today, more women are combining all three of these roles. The labor force participation rates of married women are as high as, or even higher than, those of unmarried women. In 2005, 68% of married women with children were employed; 73% of women with children between the ages of 6 and 13, and 60% of women with children under 6 (U.S. Census Bureau, 2007f). Women with children are not necessarily employed full time, however. More married than unmarried women work part time, especially if they have children. Many reasons account for the sharp increase in the number of married working women since 1960. Desire for more income is one reason, but there are other important factors, such as birth control, women's increase in education, and the decline in the wage gap. In fact, the increase in employment among married women is larger among those whose husbands are in the top half rather than the bottom half of the income distribution. As shown in Figure 12.13, as of 2005, 56% of White women and 66% of Black women with children 1 year old and younger worked. In

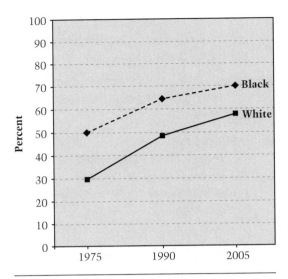

FIGURE 12.13 Changes in the percentage of women with children under age 1 who are employed.

Source: Adapted from U.S. Census Bureau (2007f).

1975, the comparable figures were 29% for White women and 50% for Black women. In 1974, 60% of women said they would prefer to stay home and take care of the house and family, whereas the figure in 1997 reached an all-time low of 42% (Moore, 2005). Since that time, more traditional values have reemerged: In 2005, 53% of women said they would prefer to stay home and take care of the family.

The question is, are multiple roles good for health? The two main hypotheses about the effects of multiple roles on health make opposite predictions. The **role scarcity hypothesis** suggests multiple roles have a negative effect on health because time and resources are limited and additional roles tap resources. The scarcity hypothesis predicts two kinds of strain that stem from the possession of multiple roles: **Role overload** refers to the difficulties in fulfilling obligations for all of one's roles because time is limited; **role conflict** refers to the demands of one role conflicting with the demands from another role. You are suffering from role overload

when you feel stressed because you have three exams on Monday, a party to plan for Saturday, and a fund-raising event to attend on Sunday. You suffer from role conflict when your grandmother turns 90 and your best friend turns 21 on the same Saturday, and family obligations prevent you from celebrating the occasion with your best friend. In either case, having more roles is problematic because it is difficult to meet all the demands of multiple roles.

By contrast, the **role expansion hypothesis** suggests benefits are to be gained from having diverse roles. The additional resources gained by multiple roles outweigh the increase in strains that might arise from more roles. In the early 1970s, when women were just beginning to move into the workforce, Gove and Tudor (1973) used the expansion hypothesis to explain why men were psychologically healthier than women. At that time, women were less likely than men to hold multiple roles. Gove and Tudor argued work would provide women with resources that would reduce their distress. A more specific version of the expansion hypothesis is the **stress-buffering hypothesis**, which articulates the exact benefits of multiple roles: Resources from one role are used to buffer the strains arising from another role. For example, social support from coworkers may help alleviate distress arising from family problems.

What is the evidence for the scarcity and expansion hypotheses? Are multiple roles healthful or harmful? The preponderance of evidence shows that multiple roles are good for men's and women's health (Barnett, 2004). A number of studies have shown that the healthiest people, men or women, are the ones who possess all three roles: spouse, parent, and worker (McMunn, Bartley, & Kuh, 2006). The most distressed people possess none of these roles. A longitudinal study of Swedish adults supported the role expansion hypothesis by showing that a greater number of roles was associated with less physical illness, and an increase in roles over an

8-year period reduced the risk of health problems (Nordenmark, 2004).

It may not be the mere accumulation of roles, but the particular combination of roles that is beneficial. One role may enhance the effects of another role; for example, the parent role may be adaptive only if we possess the worker role. The worker role is critical in the presence of children because financial needs are greater (Thoits, 1992). The parent role also appears to be beneficial to health only if one possesses the spouse role, at least for women (Fokkema, 2002; Khlat et al., 2000). A wealth of evidence suggests that unmarried mothers have the worst psychological and physical health in the United States (Sachs-Ericsson & Ciarlo, 2000) as well as in Britain and Finland (Lahelma et al., 2002). Unmarried mothers may feel overwhelmed with raising children because they lack the emotional and financial support of a spouse.

Some research suggests the added benefits of a work or family role have a stronger effect on women's health when they lack other roles. Several studies have shown that employment has stronger effects on women's health if they lack family roles (spouse, parent; Waldron, Weiss, & Hughes, 1998). Similarly, marriage has a stronger benefit on women's health when they are unemployed than employed (Waldron et al., 1998). Thus the work role is more beneficial to women who lack family roles, and a family role is more beneficial to women who lack the work role. Both these effects can be explained by income: Marriage provides unemployed women with increased income, and employment provides unmarried women with increased income.

Thus far, all hands point to role enhancement. Is there any evidence for the role scarcity hypothesis? There is in terms of exercise. Men and women who have both work and family roles exercise less than those who have fewer roles, and the effects are stronger for men than women (Nomaguchi & Bianchi, 2004). As shown in Figure 12.14, marriage reduces exercise

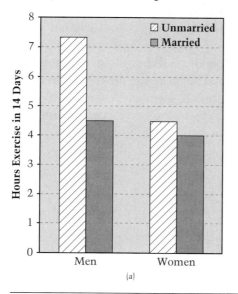

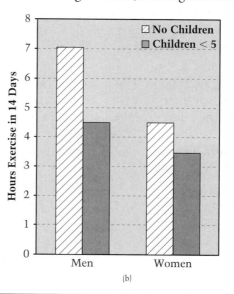

FIGURE 12.14   (a) Married men and women exercise less than their unmarried counterparts, but the effects are stronger for men. (b) The presence of children under age 5 is associated with less exercise for men and women, but the effects are stronger for men.

Source: Adapted from Nomaguchi and Bianchi (2004).

more for men than women (a), as does the presence of children (b).

Does the Work Role Buffer or Exacerbate Family Stress?

A primary explanation for why multiple roles benefit health is that the resources gained by one role can be used to buffer us from the distress associated with strains in another role. Is this true? Do work roles buffer men and women from the strains of family roles? Or, does work stress make us less able to tolerate difficulties with children?

A number of studies have shown that the work role buffers us from stressors at home. A longitudinal study of caregivers found that work buffers the psychological distress associated with caregiving (Pavalko & Woodbury, 2000). Caregivers' health declined more if they were not working than if they were working. Positive aspects of work also can enhance family life. One study showed that having an enriching job (high skill, high authority) was associated with a more positive mood at home and less marital tension (Hughes & Galinsky, 1994b).

However, strains at work can spill over into family life. A study of dual-earner couples showed that men and women were equally likely to perceive that their own work demands interfered with their relationship, but women were more likely than men to perceive that their spouses' work demands interfered with their relationship (Matthews et al., 2006). However, when wives' work demands intruded into the family, there were greater relationship problems. When husbands' work demands intruded into the family, there was no effect on the marital relationship, perhaps because it is more normative for men's work to spill over into the family. Several studies have shown that strains at work are associated with marital distress (Hughes & Galinsky, 1994b; Santos, Bohon, & Sanchez-Sosa, 1998). Stress at work seems to lead to withdrawal behavior at home, especially among men (Schulz et al., 2004).

Thus it appears that the work role, in and of itself, buffers men and women from family stressors. In this way, work can be viewed as a resource. Stressors at work also can exacerbate strains in the family for both men and women.

Do Family Roles Buffer or Exacerbate Work Stress?

The stress-buffering hypothesis also suggests that the presence of family roles buffers one from the distress associated with job difficulties. Two studies showed that either family role—spouse or parent—buffers men and women from the deleterious effects of work-related stress. In a longitudinal study of employed women, being a spouse or a parent buffered women from the impact of stress at work on mental health (Barnett, Marshall, & Singer, 1992). Changes in job role quality over time were more strongly associated with distress for women who did not have partners than women who had partners and for women who did not have children than women who had children. In fact, the subgroup of women who showed the strongest relation between changes in job role quality and changes in distress were women who did not have partners or children. These findings are consistent with the stress-buffering hypothesis that access to resources in one role buffers one from the distress of another role.

Not only the presence of family roles, but also the quality of family roles may buffer distress from the work role. In a study of working women, the quality of the job was more strongly related to distress among women who reported unhappy marriages and among women who had a poor relationship with their children (Barnett, 1994). The same results were found for men (Barnett et al., 1992). In fact, when the two samples were combined, high marital quality and high parental quality equally buffered men and women from distress arising from jobs (Barnett, 1994). In another study, good relationships with children buffered women from the adverse effects of high work demands on psychological distress (Gareis & Barnett, 2002).

Thus family roles buffer strains at work for men and women but also have the potential to exacerbate strain at work for men and women.

Difficulties in Combining Roles

Simon (1995) argues that to understand the effect of multiple roles on well-being, we need to understand what the individual roles mean to men and women. The same role places different demands on men and women. Historically, there have been greater interrelations between work and family roles for men than for women. A man's family role is to provide economic support, an obligation he can fulfill through paid employment. A woman's family role is to provide emotional support, a function not served by paid employment. Thus, men's work and family roles are intertwined: They serve the same function. By contrast, women's work and family roles are independent: The woman's work role does not facilitate the function of her family role and may even detract from it. See Sidebar 12.3 for a

SIDEBAR 12.3: *Working Mothers*

One reason the effects of multiple roles on women's health seem to be more complicated than they are for men's health is that women suffer more role conflict than men when they combine work and parenting roles. Society provides women with mixed messages about whether they should work when they have children. Working mothers receive the message that it is acceptable to work and to be a parent—as long as parenting is the number-one priority. That is, work should never interfere with parenting. In fact, women are more likely than men to take time off from work to take care of children. This means the parenting role has the potential to interfere with the work role for women. Women who opt not to work while raising children, however, may receive a different message from society. Today, these mothers often feel the need to justify why they are not working outside the home. Here, I examine whether paid employment benefits mothers.

Whether working outside the home is beneficial for women with children depends on a number of factors, including salary earned, number of children, availability of child care, and husband's participation in household and child care activities (Ross et al., 1990). A greater number of children in the home may detract from the benefits of employment, but this depends on what resources are available to assist the woman in caring for her children. Access to resources, such as income, child care, or a supportive husband, influences whether mothers benefit from work. In one study, mothers who worked outside the home were distressed when they had difficulty with childcare arrangements and received no help with household labor from husbands (Ross & Mirowsky, 1995). Other studies have shown that employment benefits women's health when husbands share childcare responsibilities (Ozer, 1995).

Another factor that may influence the effect of combining work and family roles on women's health is the traditionality of the field in which women work. It may be easier for women to combine work and family roles if they are employed in a field that by tradition is inhabited by women rather than men. A study of women who were either librarians (traditionally female occupation) or held M.B.A.'s (traditionally male occupation) found that librarians had an easier time combining the two roles (Olson, Frieze, & Detlefson, 1990). However, traditional jobs for women, such as nurses, secretaries, and teachers, may have less flexibility than higher status positions to accommodate family needs. One of the attributes of a high-status position is that the person often sets his or her own hours.

Thus the optimal conditions for work to benefit mothers' health include a husband who helps out at home, an income that can provide for high-quality child care, and a job that accommodates family responsibilities.

DO GENDER 12.5
Combining Roles

Interview a group of men and women who have combined work and family roles—preferably, people who have children and work outside the home. Ask questions similar to the ones Simon (1995) asked. Come up with some of your own questions to determine the unique difficulties men and women face.

discussion of the effect of combining parenthood and work for women. Then conduct Do Gender 12.5 to find out for yourself what difficulties men and women face when combining work and family roles.

To examine these issues, Simon (1995) interviewed 40 couples about how they experienced the relations between their work and family roles. More men than women defined their family role in terms of economic support, and more women than men defined their family roles in terms of emotional support. Women indicated they felt guilty combining work and family roles, whereas no man in the study mentioned guilt. This is an indication that combining roles is more difficult for women. Another indication that work and family roles were less intertwined for women is that women suffered greater interrole conflict than men: Women were more likely than men to report conflicts in combining work with family. The nature of the conflicts men and women reported also differed. Women were more likely to report vague and diffuse conflicts such as "not being there," whereas men reported specific conflicts, such as missing a child's soccer game. More women than men were concerned they neglected the marital relationship. Although women were concerned they did not pay enough attention to their spouse, women were not concerned their

husband did not pay enough attention to them. Men agreed. In other words, both men and women were concerned that wives' employment caused the women to neglect the marriage, yet neither was concerned that men's employment led men to neglect the marriage. A third indication that work and family roles were more independent for women is differences in satisfaction at combining roles. Whereas 90% of the men felt adequate in their family roles as husbands and fathers, 70% of women felt inadequate as mothers and wives. The one situation in which men felt inadequate was when their wife worked but both wished she did not have to work; in this instance, men's work role did not completely fulfill the family role of economic provider.

A number of difficulties arise in families where both men and women work. Hochschild (1989) identified three kinds of tension in dual-earner couples. The first tension exists when men and women have different views about who should do what work outside the home and inside the home. I discussed in Chapter 11 how disagreement about the division of labor in the family is associated with marital unhappiness, especially for women. The second tension occurs when men and women have the desire for traditional roles but their economic status does not permit them to enact those roles. In other words, both husband and wife prefer that the wife takes care of the home and the husband is employed outside of the home, but lack of financial resources requires the woman to be employed outside the home. In this instance, the husband may contribute to household chores, but neither the husband nor the wife is satisfied with this arrangement.

The third tension is one that pervades egalitarian couples who are heavily involved in work outside the home. Husbands and wives in these couples jointly devalue family responsibilities to justify spending more time on their careers. The egalitarian philosophy leads such couples to share responsibilities such that less time is devoted to home and family—less time on housework, less time with children, less time with each other—and someone is hired to take care of most household tasks (cooking, cleaning, and child care). The ideas about what a family needs change to accommodate the couple's egalitarian focus on careers. This issue reminds me of a dual-earner couple I know who adopted two children. After the first child was in preschool, the husband proudly remarked to me that he had never even met the preschool teacher or attended any of the preschool programs for parents because the nanny took care of all of this. After the second child, the couple asked the nanny to move in with them. The husband shared that they slept downstairs while the nanny slept in a room upstairs with the children, which was wonderful because the nanny could console the children at night. Hochschild (1989) calls it a hollow victory "if the work of raising a family becomes devalued because women have become equal to men on traditionally male terms" (p. 211). The homemaker role is now being devalued by both men and women. Hochschild suggests that a primary way to increase the value of this role is for men to become more involved in household labor and child care.

Although a great many changes have been made over the past several decades in terms of work and family roles, in some ways our fundamental way of thinking about men and women has not changed. According to Valian (1998), "... the usual solutions proffered to solve 'women's' problems are higher-quality, more affordable, more widely available childcare; flexible work hours; and family-leave policies. All those improvements are needed, but they fail to question the way the problem is framed. They do not ask why combining work and family is a female problem rather than a human problem, and thus do not address it as a human problem." (p. 45).

TAKE HOME POINTS

- Multiple roles are good for both men's and women's health.

- There is greater support for the role expansion hypothesis than the role scarcity hypothesis. Roles provide resources, and having more roles buffers us from the strains that arise in any one role. The fewer roles we have, the greater the effect that strain in any one role will have on health.

- Although evidence indicates that "more is better" in terms of roles, it also is the case that one role has a stronger effect on well-being when the person lacks other roles: Employment has a stronger effect on the health of men and women who lack family roles, and family roles have a stronger effect on the health of women who lack employment.

- Work and family roles can both buffer one from the distress associated with the other role as well as exacerbate stressors that are associated with other roles.

- Employment benefits women's health even in the presence of children, but the presence of children adds to the complexity of understanding the conditions under which work is beneficial to women.

- To understand the interactive effects among roles, we need to consider what roles mean to men and women and what the demands are in each of the roles.

SUMMARY

In this chapter, I evaluated the effect of work roles on men's and women's health. The work role is associated with health benefits for both men and women. There is no overall effect of women working on men's health, but there may be some conditions under which it has negative implications for men. A primary way in which women working influences both men's and women's health has to do with its effect on resources and demands. To the extent that women working increases women's economic resources and detracts from men's economic resources, women benefit and men suffer. To the extent that women's work increases men's and decreases women's participation in household chores, women benefit and men suffer. Thus it is not the case that men are necessarily worse off if their wife works—it is only under certain conditions that men may suffer. This presents a challenge for couples in which husbands and wives both work.

One reason it is difficult to compare the effect of work on health for men and women is that men and women have different work experiences. Women report more strains in their job role, which may explain why work is not always associated with good health for women. In some studies, aspects of the work role have a stronger relation to men's than women's health. When men's and women's roles are similar (i.e., dual-earner couples), the association of job role quality to health is similar for both.

One aspect of the work role with consequences for women's well-being is discrimination. I distinguished between access and treatment discrimination: Access discrimination reflects the differential opportunities men and women have to hold certain jobs; once hired, treatment discrimination occurs in the form of the glass ceiling and pay disparity. There is still evidence that women make less money than men when characteristics of men and women such as education and experience are taken into consideration. However, the wage gap is closing. Factors that contribute to the wage gap include sex segregation of occupations and parenthood. Women with children earn less than women without children, and both concrete and abstract explanations account for this difference. Interestingly, women

are not as dissatisfied with pay disparity as we would expect. Although women believe other women suffer discrimination, the majority of women deny any personal discrimination; this phenomenon is referred to as the denial of personal disadvantage. One theory of why women deny disadvantage involves social comparison theory: Women compare themselves to other women rather than to men.

Another aspect of work that has consequences for well-being is sexual harassment. Women are more likely to be harassed than men, and sexual harassment is more strongly associated with adverse outcomes among women. There are a variety of forms of sexual harassment, with men and women being most likely to agree that the more severe forms constitute harassment. Both person factors and situational factors combine to produce sexual harassment.

There are contrasting theories as to whether multiple roles are associated with health benefits or health hazards, particularly with respect to women. The role-scarcity hypothesis suggests that additional roles tap resources, which are finite. The role-expansion hypothesis suggests that additional roles provide more resources, in particular, resources that can be used to buffer us from the strains that occur in a particular role (i.e., stress-buffering hypothesis). Taken collectively, more evidence supports the role-expansion hypothesis than the role-scarcity hypothesis. More roles seem to be associated with better health for men and women, but this does not mean role strains do not occur. Women, in particular, face difficulties combining work and family roles when children are at home. These women do not necessarily suffer, however, when they have resources to cope with the increased demands—resources in terms of a high income or a husband who shares household responsibilities. There is also evidence that the addition of a role has a stronger influence on health when people lack other roles; thus multiple roles may be especially beneficial at the lower end of the continuum of roles. As the number of roles increases, additional roles have less incremental benefits.

One way multiple roles are associated with health is that the resources provided by one role buffer us from the strains in another role. Good evidence suggests that work buffers men and women from the strains of family roles and that family roles buffer men and women from the strains of work roles. Yet the positive aspects of one role can not only offset the negative aspects of another role, but the negative aspects of one role can also exacerbate the negative aspects of another role. Difficulties at work can lead to increased strains at home, and demanding family roles can exacerbate strains at work.

DISCUSSION QUESTIONS

1. Is there evidence that work roles have a stronger effect on men's health and family roles have a stronger effect on women's health?
2. Under what conditions is employment most strongly related to good health for women? To poor health for women?
3. What is the difference between access discrimination and treatment discrimination?
4. Why do women deny personal discrimination?
5. Do men and women define sexual harassment differently?
6. Describe sexual harassment from a social psychological perspective: Offer an explanation that takes into consideration both dispositional and situational factors.
7. Distinguish between the role-expansion and role-scarcity hypotheses.
8. What are some of the difficulties men and women face when combining work and family roles? How could these be alleviated?
9. Give an example of the role-buffering hypothesis with respect to work and family roles.

SUGGESTED READING

Babcock, L., & Laschever, S. (2003). *Women don't ask: Negotiation and the gender divide.* Princeton, NJ: Princeton University Press.

Biernat, M., Crosby, F., & Williams, J. (Eds.). (2004). The maternal wall: Research and policy perspectives on discrimination against mothers. *Journal of Social Issues, 60,* 675–682.

Crosby, F. (1991). *Juggling.* New York: Free Press.

Gutek, B. A., & Done, R. S. (2000). Sexual harassment. In R. K. Unger (Ed.), *Handbook of the psychology of women and gender* (pp. 1–61). New York: Wiley.

Klumb, P. L., & Lampert, T. (2004). Women, work, and well-being 1950–2000: A review and methodological critique. *Social Science and Medicine, 58,* 1007–1024.

Nelson, D. L., & Burke, R. J. (Eds.). (2002). *Gender, work stress, and health.* Washington, DC: American Psychological Association.

Simon, R. W. (1995). Gender, multiple roles, role meaning, and mental health. *Journal of Health and Social Behavior, 36,* 182–194.

KEY TERMS

Access discrimination—Situation in which an individual is not offered a given job or is offered a lesser job because of some defining characteristic (e.g., sex).

Comparable worth policy—States that men and women in different jobs should be paid the same wage for comparable work.

Demand-side theory—Explanation for the wage gap that emphasizes the different ways men and women are treated.

Denial of disadvantage—Condition in which women perceive that discrimination exists but deny that they personally are victims of it.

Differential exposure hypothesis—Proposition that men and women possess different roles, which are associated with different stressors and different resources.

Differential vulnerability hypothesis—Proposition that a specific role has different effects on men's and women's health.

Glass ceiling—Label applied to barriers to the advancement of women and minorities in organizations.

Glass escalator—Term referring to the ability of men to be promoted quickly when they take positions in traditionally female fields.

Hostile environment—Type of sexual harassment in which one person is creating a hostile, intimidating work environment for another.

Human capital accumulation theory—A job and the salary associated with the job are functions of the person's characteristics or "human capital," such as skills, experience, and education (see supply-side theory).

In-group comparison—Evaluation of oneself based on the condition of similar others (e.g., within-sex comparison).

Marital bonus—Increase in income granted to men who are married and/or have children compared to men who are single.

Maternal wall—Employer's devaluation and limitation of job opportunities of female employees when they become parents.

Norms—Expectations for behavior.

Out-group comparison—Evaluation of oneself based on the condition of dissimilar others (e.g., between-sex comparison).

Pay disparity—Type of treatment discrimination in which women are paid less than men for doing comparable work.

Quid pro quo—Type of sexual harassment in which one person offers work benefits or threatens work repercussions in exchange for sexual favors.

Role—Position in a society governed by a set of norms.

Role conflict—Condition in which the demands of one role are at odds with the demands of another role.

Role-expansion hypothesis—Idea that benefits are to be gained from having diverse roles.

Role overload—Condition that arises when time limitations create difficulties in fulfilling obligations for one's roles.

Role-scarcity hypothesis—Idea that multiple roles will have a negative effect on health because time and resources are limited and additional roles tap resources.

Selection effect—Potential for healthier people to choose certain roles, which then leads to difficulties in determining whether those roles influence health.

Sex-role spillover theory—Suggestion that expectations about men's and women's roles carry over to the workplace when they are not appropriate or are irrelevant.

Stress-buffering hypothesis—Proposition that resources from one role can be used to buffer one from the strains arising from another role; a more specific version of the role expansion hypothesis.

Supply-side theory—Explanation for the wage gap that emphasizes the different characteristics of male and female workers.

Treatment discrimination—Situation in which an individual receives a reduced salary or reduced opportunities for promotion compared to other individuals having the same job.

MENTAL HEALTH

In 2005, 118 million prescriptions for antidepressants were written, making antidepressants the most commonly prescribed drugs in the United States (Cohen, 2007). Between 1988 to 1994 and 1999 to 2000, the use of antidepressants tripled. One out of 10 women and one out of 25 men 18 years of age and older are currently taking antidepressants (Centers for Disease Control and Prevention, 2004).

Mental health, in particular depression, is clearly an important problem in our country. Some important public figures have brought attention to mental health problems, with the effect of reducing their stigma and permitting more people to seek help for them. Tipper Gore, for example, publicly declared her battle with depression and championed mental health during her tenure as spouse of Vice President Al Gore. Great Britain's Princess Diana acknowledged depression and an eating disorder before her death. Tina Turner (1986) admitted in her autobiography that she tried to kill herself with an overdose of Valium. Mental health problems do not afflict men and women equally. Substantial evidence indicates that women are more likely than men to suffer from depression and to have an eating disorder.

There seems to be a large and pervasive sex difference in depression, such that women suffer more depression than men. Critics, however, argue that definitional and methodological problems make this difference less clear. I begin this chapter by reviewing the evidence for sex differences in depression. Then I examine the extent to which methodological artifacts can account for this difference. The rest of my discussion is devoted to theoretical explanations for the sex difference in depression. These theories have biological, psychological, social, and cultural underpinnings. No one theory can completely account for women being more depressed than men. It is most likely a combination of theories that synergistically interact to explain the sex difference in depression. Many theories have female gender-role socialization at their core.

Theories differentially emphasize the following ideas: (1) Women are led to perceive less control over their environment than men; (2) women adopt a pessimistic way of explaining events; (3) women and men cope differently with stress; (4) women and men face different stressors; and (5) women are more vulnerable to different classes of stressors. One reason gender-role explanations are so viable is that sex differences in depression emerge during adolescence when gender-role norms become salient. Thus I conclude with some remarks about the challenges of adolescence and how they might spark the sex difference in depression.

In addition to reviewing research on depression, I also examine how men and women respond to the onset of a chronic illness, an event that could evoke depression. Aside from depression, I examine two other mental health problems relevant to gender: eating disorders and suicide. Suicide has a paradoxical link to gender; although women attempt suicide more often than men, more men kill themselves than women.

SEX DIFFERENCES IN DEPRESSION

Before we examine the incidence of depression in men and women, we must distinguish between depressive symptoms, which all of us experience to some extent at one time or another, and major depressive disorder or clinical depression, which is a diagnosable mental health problem. Instruments that measure depressive symptoms include items such as feeling sad or blue, feeling depressed, having crying spells, difficulty concentrating, and loss of interest in things. Perhaps you have completed such an instrument during college. A widely used self-report measure of depression, the Center for

TABLE 13.1 CENTER FOR EPIDEMIOLOGICAL STUDIES IN DEPRESSION SCALE (CES-D)

1. I was bothered by things that usually don't bother me.
2. I did not feel like eating; my appetite was poor.
3. I felt that I could not shake off the blues even with the help of my family or friends.
4. I felt that I was just as good as other people.*
5. I had trouble keeping my mind on what I was doing.
6. I felt depressed.
7. I felt that everything I did was an effort.
8. I felt hopeful about the future.*
9. I thought my life had been a failure.
10. I felt fearful.
11. My sleep was restless.
12. I was happy.*
13. I talked less than usual.
14. I felt lonely.
15. People were unfriendly.
16. I enjoyed life.*
17. I had crying spells.
18. I felt sad.
19. I felt that people disliked me.
20. I could not get "going."

*These items are reverse scored so that lower endorsement indicates more depression.
Source: Radloff (1977).

Epidemiological Studies in Depression scale (CES-D; Radloff, 1977), is shown in Table 13.1.

The criteria for a major depressive disorder, as diagnosed by the *Diagnostic and Statistical Manual of Mental Disorders (DSM-IV-TR)* (American Psychiatric Association, 2000), are shown in Table 13.2. The critical feature of a major depressive disorder is the experience of a set of depressive symptoms for a period no shorter than 2 weeks. Major depressive disorder is often referred to as **clinical depression**.

How do we determine the frequency of depressive symptoms or the incidence of clinical depression? Two different methods are used. Depressive symptoms are typically evaluated

TABLE 13.2 MAJOR DEPRESSIVE EPISODE CRITERIA FROM *DSM-IV-TR*

Five or more of these symptoms present for 2 weeks.

- Depressed mood most of the day, nearly every day.*
- Markedly diminished interests in activities.*
- Significant weight loss.
- Insomnia.
- Psychomotor agitation or retardation.
- Fatigue or loss of energy.
- Feelings of worthlessness.
- Diminished ability to think or concentrate or indecisiveness.
- Recurrent thoughts of death.

* One of the five symptoms must include one of these.
Source: American Psychiatric Association (2000).

with community surveys. The strength of this methodology is that large representative samples of men and women can be obtained to identify the frequency of depression. The weakness of this methodology is that depression is measured by self-report instruments which are vulnerable to demand characteristics. If men are less willing than women to report depression, community surveys may underestimate men's levels of depression. Information on clinical depression is typically obtained from treatment facilities. The strength of this methodology is that depression can be evaluated with more sophisticated measures employed by trained clinicians. The weakness is that respondents are not representative of the population. To the extent that men are less likely than women to seek help for depression, studies of people in clinics also may underestimate men's rates of depression.

These two methodologies have provided a wealth of evidence that women experience more depressive symptoms than men in the general population and women are more likely than men to be diagnosed with clinical depression. Epidemiological studies have found the rate of depressive symptoms to be twice as high among women as men (Culbertson, 1997; Nolen-Hoeksema, 1987). The sex difference in major depressive disorder is even higher, on the order of 4 to 1 (Culbertson, 1997). Findings among adolescents are comparable (Compas et al., 1997). Females are also more vulnerable than males to a depression-related disorder, seasonal affective disorder (Lee & Chan, 1998). However, there is no sex difference in bipolar disorder (more commonly known as manic-depressive illness). See Sidebar 13.1 for a brief discussion.

SIDEBAR 13.1: *Bipolar Disorder*

Bipolar disorder includes both manic and depressive symptoms. The disorder takes different forms in men and women. Men are more likely than women to have mania at onset (Carter et al., 2005). Depressive symptoms predominate in women, whereas manic symptoms predominate in men. Women have equal numbers of episodes of depression and mania, whereas men have twice the number of manic as depressive episodes (Robb et al., 1998). In effect, men have more of the manic component than women. Bipolar disorder is also more likely to take place in the context of alcohol abuse, drug abuse, and conduct disorders among males, and more likely to take place in the context of eating disorders among females (Baldassano et al., 2005; Carter et al., 2005). The disorder also appears to be associated with greater impairments in physical functioning for women than men (Robb et al., 1998). The incidence of bipolar disorder peaks during the ages of 16 to 25, during which time it is more common among males than females (Kennedy et al., 2005). After age 25, bipolar disorder decreases among both males and females, but the decrease is larger for males. Thus throughout adulthood, females have higher rates of bipolar disorder than males.

Previously I noted the advantages and disadvantages of surveying the general population versus studying the clinic population. It was not until the early 1990s that the two methods were combined. In an extensive undertaking, clinical interviews were conducted with a representative sample of over 8,000 people ages 15 to 54 in the United States (Kessler, McGonagle, Zhao et al., 1994). The sex difference in major depressive disorder confirmed previous research. The findings, shown in Figure 13.1, revealed a 2:1 sex difference. Women were nearly twice as likely as men to report a history of major depressive disorder and to report the occurrence of major depression over the prior year. The sex difference in depression was similar across the different age ranges

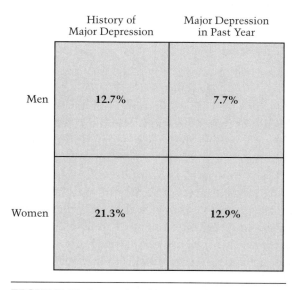

FIGURE 13.1   National survey of major depression. Clinical interviews of a representative sample of over 8,000 people ages 15 to 54 in the United States revealed that women are more likely than men to report a history of major depression and to have had an episode of major depression in the past year. The sex difference is on the order of 2:1.
Source: Adapted from Kessler, McGonagle, Zhao, et al. (1994).

(Kessler et al., 1993; Kessler, McGonagle, Nelson et al., 1994).

Sex differences in depression are found not only in the United States. There is a great deal of cross-cultural support for sex differences in depression. Women are between 2 and 3 times more likely than men to be depressed in countries such as Sweden, Germany, Canada, New Zealand, Puerto Rico, and Korea (Klerman & Weissman, 1989) and in the majority of Islamic countries (Alansari, 2006). One study evaluated the incidence of lifetime depression (i.e., an experience of clinical depression at any time during one's life) across 10 countries (Weissman et al., 1996). As shown in Figure 13.2, rates of lifetime depression were higher among women than men in every country. Females are only 1.6 times more likely than males to be depressed in Lebanon and Taiwan, but 3.1 times more likely to be depressed than males in West Germany. The rate in the United States was 2.6.

In some populations, sex differences in depression are less likely to be found. Although the sex difference in depression consistently appears in developed countries, sex differences in depression do not appear in developing countries (Nolen-Hoeksema, 1990). In addition, sex differences in depression are often not found in homogeneous populations, such as college students (Grant et al., 2002). There also appear to be no sex differences in depression among the Amish. Depression was examined in the Amish community by interviewing residents to see if there was a consensus that certain people in the community appeared "disturbed" (Egeland & Hostetter, 1983). No difference was noted in the number of men and women who were identified as depressed. However, the methodology of the study is somewhat troublesome. Only people who *appeared* depressed were referred to the investigator. People who suffered from less observable forms of depression would not have been identified. Another population that shows no sex

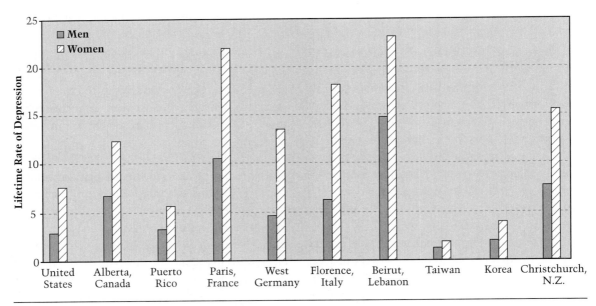

FIGURE 13.2 Incidence of major depression across cultures. Across a variety of cultures, women are more likely than men to have experienced an episode of major depression in their lifetime.
Source: Adapted from Weissman et al. (1996).

difference in depression is the widowed. As discussed in Chapter 11, this is largely because rates of depression increase among men more than women following widowhood.

The sex difference in depression emerges during adolescence and is fairly consistent across the life span (Nolen-Hoeksema, 2004). Thus we may wonder whether the same men and women remain depressed throughout their lives or if, at any given point, women are twice as likely as men to become depressed. No evidence suggests depression is more chronic in women or depression is more likely to recur in women than men (Kessler, 2000; Nolen-Hoeksema, 2004). Once men and women sustain an episode of major depression, they are equally likely to experience a recurrence. In one large-scale study of adults ages 48 to 79, 60% of both men and women who had had one episode of depression experienced a recurrence (Wainwright & Surtees, 2002). Thus among

those without a history of depression, women are more likely than men to become depressed at any given point in time, but no evidence indicates that depression is more likely to recur among women than men among those with a history of depression.

Although the sex difference in depression is consistent across a variety of samples and a variety of methodologies, the size of the difference in the United States appears to have decreased in recent years, largely due to a rise in male depression rather than a decline in female depression (Kessler, 2000). A study in Scotland also found a decrease in the sex difference in depression. The sex difference in hospital admission rates for depression (female: male) decreased from 9:1 in 1980 to 5:1 in 1995 (Shajahan & Cavanagh, 1998). However, in Scotland, the change was due to both an increase in male depression and a decrease in female depression.

■ Females are more likely than males to report depressive symptoms as well as major depressive disorder.

■ The sex difference in depression is on the order of 2:1 (female to male) in the United States.

■ The sex difference is larger among clinic studies than community surveys.

■ Sex differences persist across a variety of cultures but are not observed in some homogenous populations, such as college students and the Amish.

METHODOLOGICAL ARTIFACTS

Some investigators have contested these seemingly indisputable data that a sex difference in depression exists. Three sets of methodological problems or artifacts could explain why women "appear" to be more depressed. First, there may be a bias on the part of clinicians, such that depression is overdiagnosed among women and underdiagnosed among men. Second, there may be a response bias on the part of depressed persons; men may be less likely than women to admit depression or to seek help for depression. Third, men and women may manifest depression in different ways, and instruments are biased in the direction of tapping female depression.

Clinician Bias

One source of bias is the clinician's judgment. Perhaps clinicians are more likely to interpret a set of symptoms as depression when the patient is female than male. Why might this be? First, clinicians are undoubtedly aware of the sex difference in depression. Thus clinicians' mental illness schema for a female patient is more likely to contain depression than their mental illness schema for a male patient. When a female patient comes into the office, depression-related schemas are more likely to be activated. Ambiguous symptoms such as feeling tired or lacking energy can be indicators of a variety of health problems. Clinicians may be more likely to interpret such symptoms as depression in a female patient and cardiac disease in a male patient.

The evidence for clinician bias is equivocal. A study of primary care physicians showed they were less likely to detect depression in men compared to women, and in African Americans and Hispanics compared to Caucasians (Borowsky et al., 2000). In that study, physicians' detection of mental health problems among over 19,000 patients was compared to independent screening of depression. The comparison showed that more of men's than women's depression went undetected by physicians. Another study showed that clinicians view depression as more severe among men who hold nontraditional roles (primary caretaker) than traditional roles (primary breadwinner; Robertson & Fitzgerald, 1990). Research also has shown that physicians are more likely to prescribe antidepressants and antianxiety drugs to women than to men, even when they have similar diagnoses (Simoni-Wastila, 1998). However, it is not clear whether the differential distribution of medication is due to physician or patient behavior. Female patients may be more likely than male patients to request antidepressants. Physician prescription of antidepressants is heavily influenced by patient requests (Kravitz et al., 2005).

More recent studies suggest clinician bias may be weakening. A fairly recent study asked primary care physicians to review vignettes of elderly patients with depression and showed that physicians correctly classified the patients as depressed in 85% of the cases, and equally so for males and females (Kales et al., 2005). Psychiatrists may be even less vulnerable than primary care physicians to biases. One study showed that

DO GENDER 13.1
Is This Depression?

Create a description of a depressed person. Make the symptoms subtle. Do not say the person is depressed. Use items from Tables 13.1 and 13.2 to help you. Create two versions of this description, one with a male name and one with a female name. Randomly distribute one of the two versions to 20 people. Ask each respondent to identify the person's problem.

Compare the percentages of people who identify depression in the female and male vignettes.

psychiatrists were equally likely to diagnose similar symptoms as depression in men and women and prescribed drugs and psychotherapy with equal frequency to men and women (Olfson, Zarin, Mittman, & McIntyre, 2001). Conduct Do Gender 13.1 to see if your peers are predisposed to identify depression in a female more than a male.

Response Bias

People can distort their reports of depression in a number of ways. A common concern is that men may be less likely than women to report depression because depression is inconsistent with the male gender role. The term *depression* has feminine connotations; it implies a lack of self-confidence, a lack of control, and passivity—all of which contradict the traditional male gender role. Sex differences in attitudes toward depression appear by early adolescence. A study of eighth-graders showed that boys said that they would be less willing than girls to use mental health services for emotional problems and viewed people who sought mental health services as weird and weak (Chandra & Minkovitz, 2006). Attitudes towards the use of mental

health services becomes more positive with age, but the sex difference remains (Gonzales, Alegria, & Prihoda, 2005; MacKenzie, Gekoski, & Knox, 2006). The sex difference among adults seems to be limited to White people; Hispanic and African American males and females have more similar attitudes to mental health problems (Gonzales et al., 2005).

One reason that men might be less willing than women to report depression is that they are concerned that others will view them negatively. This concern has some basis in fact. In a study of roommates, depressed men were evaluated more negatively than depressed women by their roommates (Siegel & Alloy, 1990). In addition, roommates of depressed men reported more negative affect than roommates of depressed women, suggesting depression in men was more likely than depression in women to evoke adverse emotional reactions. In a national survey, both men and women reported they were less willing to interact with a male than a female with mental health problems, including depression (Schnittker, 2000). However, there are also reasons to believe that females might be more penalized than males when depressed. A study of depressed adolescents showed that girls showed more social skills deficits than boys (van Beek, van Dolderen, & Demon Dubas, 2006). People might react more adversely to females than males who fail to focus on others because attending only to the self violates female gender-role norms.

I have suggested a couple of reasons why men might want to deny being depressed. Is there evidence that men do, in fact, underreport depression? One study showed that men are leery of admitting depressive symptoms. Men were more likely to endorse depressive items on an instrument labeled "hassles" than an instrument labeled "depression" (Page & Bennesch, 1993). As shown in Figure 13.3, the label did not affect women's reports of depression.

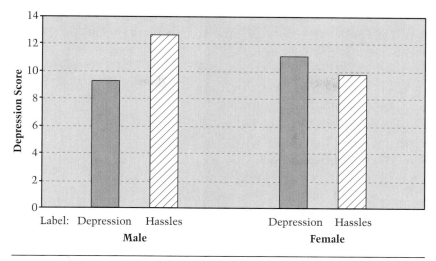

FIGURE 13.3 Effects of questionnaire label on self-report of depression. Men were more likely to report symptoms of depression on a questionnaire that was labeled "hassles" rather than "depression." The label attached to the questionnaire did not influence women's reports of depressive symptoms. *Source:* Adapted from S. Page and Bennesch (1993).

A response bias related to men's unwillingness to report depression is men's unwillingness to seek help for depression. This issue is important to studies of depression conducted in clinics. Even if men and women are equally willing to admit depression on an inventory, men may be less likely than women to seek help for depression (Hartung & Widiger, 1998). Recall that the size of the sex difference in major depressive disorder in clinic populations is larger than that found in surveys of the general population.

A more subtle response bias on the part of men is that they may be less likely than women to realize they are depressed or to interpret their symptoms as depression. In other words, men may fall victim to the same kind of clinician bias just discussed. Men might perceive depression as a female problem and be unlikely to associate ambiguous symptoms with depression. I once interviewed a man following coronary bypass surgery who complained of a lack of energy, a loss of interest in leisure activities, and a desire to stay in bed all day. He was perplexed by these symptoms but completely denied any feelings of depression on a questionnaire I administered. One study showed that men were less likely than women to recognize depression depicted in a series of vignettes (Yoder, Shute, & Tryban, 1990). Thus men may underreport their depression because they do not recognize depressive symptoms. There is also some evidence of a recall bias, such that men underreport depression more than women in an attempt to minimize their past experiences of depression (Kessler, 2000).

Different Manifestations of Depression

One difficulty in examining sex differences in depression, or any other disorder, is that symptoms of depression may differ for men and women. This is a general problem associated with the classification of many mental illnesses (Winstead & Sanchez, 2005). Most mental health problems seem to be more prevalent in one sex than the other, raising concerns about whether there is an actual sex difference in prevalence or if the disorder is described in ways that make it seem one sex is more likely to experience it than the other. If one eliminated disorders from the *DSM-IV* for which there are sex differences in prevalence, 84% of the disorders would be removed. For example, histrionic personality disorder is more common among women than men (Hartung & Widiger, 1998). In an earlier version of the manual used to diagnosis this disorder (the *DSM-III-R*), a feature of the disorder was "overconcern with physical attractiveness." There was some concern that this feature biased the disorder in favor of women. In the most recent version of the manual (*DSM-IV-TR*), this feature was changed to "physical appearance draws attention to the self." Undoubtedly, this change in wording reduced the extent to which the disorder was linked to women. However, the change in wording also altered the actual feature of the disorder. If a feature of a disorder is linked to male or female gender roles, should it be altered so it is equally endorsed by both sexes? We certainly would not change the features of medical illnesses such as prostate cancer or breast cancer so they are equally represented among both men and women. You may recall from Chapter 10 that heart disease is manifested differently among men and women. Men are more likely than women to experience classic chest pain, and women are more likely than men to experience shortness of breath. However, as Winstead and Sanchez (2005) point out, in this case, the underlying disease—heart disease—is the same among men and women. With psychiatric disorders there is no underlying disease that can be objectively measured independently of symptoms.

With respect to depression, some people argue that men and women are equally "distressed" but manifest it in different ways. A study of male and female twins showed their symptoms of depression differed (Khan et al., 2002). Females reported more fatigue, excessive sleepiness, slowed speech and body movements, and males reported more insomnia and agitation. A study of depressed adolescents showed that females reported more guilt, body dissatisfaction, self-blame, feelings of failure, and difficulties concentrating compared to males (Bennett et al., 2005). The latter items could be linked to rumination (discussed later in the chapter), whereas the other items seem to reflect greater links to self-esteem difficulties in females. Find out if your peers perceive depression differently among men and women in Do Gender 13.2.

The idea that some items are more likely to be associated with a trait, such as depression, among men versus women is referred to as **differential item functioning**. Crying is a depression item that may be susceptible to differential item functioning. Crying is a symptom of depression that characterizes women more than men, even among women and men who are equally depressed. This item could cause depression to be overdiagnosed in women.

Other investigators argue that men and women manifest depressive symptoms in

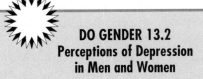

DO GENDER 13.2
Perceptions of Depression in Men and Women

Interview 5 people. Ask each of them to describe how they identify depression in a series of people, for example, their partner, a parent, a sibling, a friend, a work associate, and a stranger. Be sure to record the sex of each of these target people. On average, do people perceive depression differently when it is displayed by a male versus a female?

completely different ways and that male depression is not tapped by existing instruments. Supporters of this view argue that women display symptoms of depression, such as sadness, lethargy, and crying, whereas men are more likely to turn to alcohol when depressed. A study of people diagnosed with major depressive disorder found that depressed men were more likely than depressed women to have a history of alcohol and drug abuse (Kornstein et al., 1995).

The idea that alcohol and drug problems are manifestations of depression in men is not easily refuted. In some sense, the reasoning is circular because depression ends up being defined as whatever mental health problems that men and women exhibit. Even if men and women do manifest distress in different ways, we can still ask why women are more depressed than men and why men have more problems with alcohol than women. I now turn to the different theories that have been developed to account for sex differences in depression.

TAKE HOME POINTS

- Sex differences in depression among clinic populations may be exaggerated to the extent that physicians overdiagnose depression in women and underdiagnose depression in men.

- Sex differences in depression among community populations may be exaggerated to the extent that men are less willing than women to admit or recognize symptoms of depression.

- There is some evidence that people respond more negatively to depression in men than women.

- It is possible that men and women are equally distressed, but that men and women manifest distress in different ways. Women may show symptoms of depression, and men may have alcohol problems.

THEORIES OF DEPRESSION

Sex differences in depression can be understood by distinguishing between two sets of factors: susceptibility factors and precipitating factors (Radloff & Rae, 1979). **Susceptibility factors** are innate, usually biological factors that place women at greater risk for depression than men. Hormones or genes unique to women would be susceptibility factors. Gender-role socialization, however, also could be a susceptibility factor. If we learn women are socialized in different ways than men that make them more at risk for depression, their learning history would be a susceptibility factor. **Precipitating factors** are environmental events that trigger depression. If certain environmental factors induce depression—and women face them more than men—such as poverty or high relationship strain, depression might be triggered more in women than in men.

One fact that any theory of sex differences in depression must take into consideration is that sex differences in depression do not appear until adolescence. Before age 13 or 14, boys and girls are equally depressed or boys are more likely than girls to be depressed (Twenge & Nolen-Hoeksema, 2002). This fact suggests that any theory of sex differences in depression must take one of three forms (Nolen-Hoeksema & Girgus, 1994). These three perspectives are depicted in Figure 13.4.

The **same cause theory** suggests that the same factor causes depression in both males and females, but that factor must increase during adolescence for women only. For example, imagine that a poor body image was equally associated with depression in boys and girls, but a poor body image increased among girls but not boys during adolescence.

The **different cause theory** says there are different causes of girls' and boys' depression, and only the cause of girls' depression increases

Theory	Before Adolescence	After Adolescence	Summary Statement

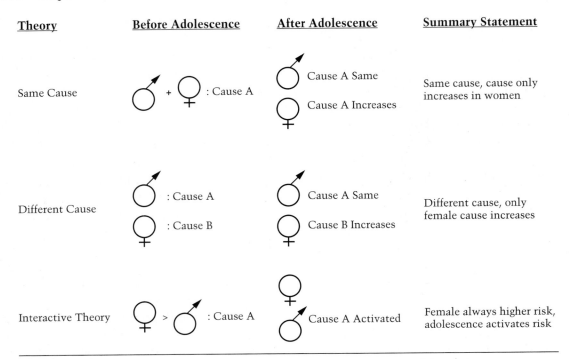

FIGURE 13.4 The same cause, different cause, and interactive theories of depression.
Source: Adapted from Nolen-Hoeksema and Girgus (1994).

during adolescence. For example, imagine a poor body image is associated with depression among girls and being a poor athlete is associated with depression among boys. This theory could explain the emergence of sex differences in depression during adolescence if it were true that a negative body image (i.e., women's risk factor for depression) becomes more prevalent during adolescence, but poor athletic ability (i.e., men's risk factor for depression) does not change over time.

The **interactive theory** suggests being female always poses a risk for depression, but the events of adolescence activate that risk factor. For example, imagine females are more concerned than males with their relationships, and that unsatisfying relationships are more strongly related to girls' than boys' distress. Concern with relationships would be the "female risk factor." This concern could interact with events

likely to occur during adolescence such as interpersonal conflict. Because females are more relationship focused than males, girls will be more likely than boys to react to interpersonal conflict with depression.

In sum, these theories suggest either that the cause of depression is the same for men and women, that there are different causes for male and female depression, or that environmental factors interact with predisposing factors to predict depression. Each of the theories that follow supports one of these perspectives.

Biology

Genes If there is a genetic explanation for the sex difference in depression, we would expect the depression risk factor to lie on the X chromosome. That being the case, we would predict that depressed fathers would be more likely to pass on their depressive gene to daughters than sons because fathers give daughters their X chromosome and sons their Y chromosome. However, more father-son pairs are depressed than father-daughter pairs (Nolen-Hoeksema, 1987). It is also the case that females have higher rates of depression than males among other-sex twins (Takkinen et al., 2004). Thus, sex-linked genes alone cannot explain depression.

Because genes are present at birth, a genetic theory of depression has difficulty explaining the emergence of depression in females during adolescence. Genetic theories could only suggest that women are at risk for depression and the events of adolescence interact with that risk. At least one study supports this theory. A study of 8- to 16-year-old twins found a higher concordance rate of depression in monozygotic than dizygotic twins but only among females who had reached puberty (Silberg et al., 1999). The investigators suggested a latent genetic factor may be involved in women's depression that is activated at puberty.

Hormones In contrast to genes, hormones change over the life span, and there is a great deal of hormonal fluctuation during adolescence when sex differences in depression emerge. Thus hormones would seem to be an ideal explanation for the sex difference in depression. However, no consistent evidence supports the theory that the changes in hormones during puberty are associated with the onset of depression in adolescent females (Brooks-Gunn & Warren, 1989; Nolen-Hoeksema & Girgus, 1994). In one study of 10- to 14-year-old girls, negative affect was associated with rapid rises in hormone levels, but even that association was weak (Brooks-Gunn & Warren, 1989). Hormones may interact with other environmental factors, supporting the interactive theory of depression. Some research has suggested that hormonal changes during puberty alter the way the body responds to stress in females (Stroud et al., 2004).

Aside from the hormonal changes that occur during puberty, researchers have attempted to link hormonal changes at other times in women's lives to depression. Fluctuations in women's hormones, in particular estrogen, prior to menstruation and after the birth of a child are related to depression, but these effects are not nearly large enough to account for the sex difference in depression. One study observed that depression increased as women transitioned through menopause and then decreased after menopause (Freeman et al., 2007). These changes in hormones were associated with the increase in depression that occurred during menopause (Freeman et al., 2006). However, another study was unable to link the decline in estrogen in the elderly to depression (Erdincler et al., 2004). In sum, it has been difficult to link increases in female hormones to depression. It seems more likely that a general pattern of hormonal fluctuation is related to depression.

Some research has focused on the protective effects of male hormones, specifically testosterone, in regard to depression. However, even that relation is not a simple one. In one study, testosterone showed a curvilinear relation to depression, such that people with extremely low or extremely high levels of testosterone were depressed (Booth, Johnson, & Granger, 1999). The relation of high testosterone to depression appeared to be accounted for by its relation to antisocial behavior. High-testosterone men were more likely to engage in antisocial behavior, which was linked to depression. This research is consistent with the idea that men and women manifest depression in different ways. In this study, low testosterone levels were associated with the more stereotypical female form of depression, whereas high levels were associated with the more stereotypical male form of distress: acting-out behavior.

A more recent theory of hormonal influences on depression has focused on oxytocin

(Turner et al., 1999). Oxytocin increases during puberty and has been shown to promote affiliative behavior in women (Frank & Young, 2000). In addition, displays of affiliative behavior have been associated with the release of oxytocin (Gonzaga et al., 2006). Affiliative behavior, in and of itself, should not lead to depression, however. Affiliative behavior might interact with some of the events during adolescence to place women at risk for depression. Specifically, changes in oxytocin regulation during puberty may cause females to be more reactive to interpersonal stressors (Klein, Corwin, & Ceballos, 2006). High levels of oxytocin have been associated with greater interpersonal problems among women (Turner et al., 1999; Taylor et al., 2006). However, there is also some evidence that oxytocin may reduce women's reactivity to stress and explain why social support is related to better health among women (Grewen et al., 2005). In one study, women who reported hugging their partner more often had higher levels of oxytocin and lower levels of resting blood pressure (Light, Grewen, & Amico, 2005). Oxytocin accounted for part of the relation between hugs and blood pressure.

Taken collectively, biological factors alone are not sufficient to explain sex differences in depression. However, much more research is needed on this issue. Hormones, in particular, may play a role, but their effect is not a direct one. The role of oxytocin in depression is a promising avenue of research. Hormones probably have their greatest explanatory power when they are examined within the context of environmental events.

Learned Helplessness

Learned helplessness is the sense of giving up because we perceive that nothing can be done to alter a situation. If you have ever studied long hours for a class without improving your grade, you might have experienced learned helplessness. Learned helplessness is the product of three events (Seligman, 1992). First, we learn an outcome is beyond our control; second, we respond by giving up or ceasing to respond; third, we generalize this response to new situations—perceive that future responses cannot influence future outcomes. A model of learned helplessness is shown in Figure 13.5. According to the

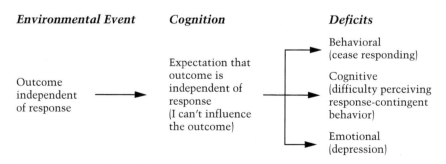

FIGURE 13.5 A model of learned helplessness. An environmental event leads to a cognition, which produces behavioral, cognitive, and emotional deficits.
Source: Adapted from Seligman (1992).

DO GENDER 13.3
Personal Experience of
Learned Helplessness

Review the model of learned helplessness in Figure 13.5. Think about a time when you exerted a response over and over again and found it had no effect on the outcome. Did you give up? After how long? Why? What were the effects of this experience? Specifically, did this lead you to give up on subsequent tasks—related or unrelated to the present one? What were the short-term effects? The long-term effects?

model, the chain of events is instigated by an environmental event rather than by a characteristic of the perceiver. That is, something in the environment leads to the perception of uncontrollability. For example, you exercise daily and eat a healthy diet for 6 months without losing any weight. Your word processing program will not work and after 4 hours of trying different tactics, your computer will not turn on. After the environmental event occurs, it is the cognitive expectation that future responses will not influence outcomes that leads to the behavior of giving up. Recall your own experiences of learned helplessness in Do Gender 13.3.

Is there any evidence that women are more susceptible than men to learned helplessness? Some evidence suggests women receive more "helplessness training" than men. Women are more likely to find themselves in situations in which they do not have control, partly due to their lower status. During childhood, girls learn they cannot influence boys, which is one reason girls play with other girls rather than boys (Maccoby, 1998). Girls receive less attention from teachers, which may teach them that they can do little to influence their environment. In

a study of 1,000 community residents, women scored lower on feelings of control than men did, and reduced feelings of control were associated with depression (Nolen-Hoeksema, Larson, & Grayson, 1999). The female stereotype includes passivity, dependence, and needing others' protection, all of which undermine feelings of personal control. Susceptibility to learned helplessness has been linked to gender roles. In a laboratory study, women who scored high in femininity were less likely to exert control when given the opportunity and to feel depressed after being faced with a control task (Sayers, Baucom, & Tierney, 1993).

The learned helplessness theory of depression is supported by the fact that other demographic variables associated with a lack of control are associated with depression, such as education. The relation of low education to higher depression is stronger among women than men (Ross & Mirowsky, 2006). As shown in Figure 13.6, the sex difference in depression is much larger among those with lower levels of education and disappears among those with a college degree and higher. One factor that female sex and low education have in common is a lack of control or helplessness in influencing the environment. That is, one reason that increased education decreases women's rates of depression is that it enhances their sense of control. The relation of low control to depression appears to be stronger among women than men, and feelings of control explain why sex differences in depression disappear at higher levels of education (Ross & Mirowsky, 2006). Thus the learned helplessness theory of depression is appealing, but there are not good studies that test whether this theory accounts for sex differences in depression. The evidence is largely circumstantial.

Attributional Styles

Recall from Chapter 6 that there are times when men and women make different attributions for

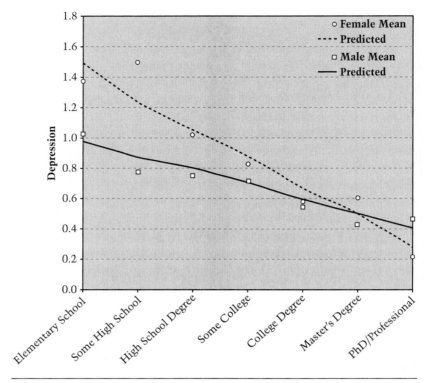

FIGURE 13.6 Rates of depression for men and women across educational level. The sex difference in depression is large among those with lower levels of education and disappears among those with a college degree and higher. Source: Ross and Mirowsky, 2006.

success and failure. One particular attributional style has been linked to learned helplessness and depression: a pessimistic attributional style. A **pessimistic (or depressive) attributional style** occurs when we make internal, stable, and global attributions for negative events (Abramson, Seligman, & Teasdale, 1978). For example, a man who responds to his girlfriend breaking up with him by saying, "I am not a very interesting, attractive, or worthwhile companion, partner, or friend anyway and I never will be" is displaying a pessimistic attributional style. You can certainly see why someone who had this response would be depressed! This person is clearly making internal attributions for the event by blam-

ing himself. The attributions are global because he is generalizing across an array of traits and an array of relationships (friend, partner, companion). The attributions are stable because he says there is no hope for change. A person who responds to a success experience, such as receiving an A on an exam, by saying, "I just got lucky. My luck will wear out. It is only one exam. I am sure I will flunk the rest of them" is also exhibiting a depressive attributional style. This person is attributing the success to outside forces (luck) that are unstable (will wear out) and specific (only this exam).

Each dimension of the pessimistic attributional style—internality, stability, globality—

has been linked to depression (Peterson & Villanova, 1988; Whitley, 1991). It turns out that using a pessimistic attributional style for the interpretation of negative events is more strongly related to depression than using it to interpret positive events (Whitley, Michael, & Tremont, 1991).

One reason that a pessimistic attributional style might lead to depression is that this style of thinking leads to the occurrence of stressful events. In a cross-sectional study, a pessimistic attributional style was unrelated to the occurrence of "independent" stressful events but was related to reporting more "dependent" stressful life events (Simons et al., 1993). A dependent stressful event is one in which our own behavior might have brought about the event, such as the loss of a job. An independent stressful event is one that occurs independent of behavior, such as the death of a relative. Thus people who have a pessimistic way of interpreting the world may create more stress for themselves which then causes them to be depressed.

Are women more likely than men to exhibit the pessimistic attributional style? A meta-analysis addressed this question by examining a related construct, the **self-serving bias**. A self-serving bias is when one makes more internal, stable, and global attributions for positive than negative events—that is, when one takes credit for successes and blames others for failures. The meta-analysis of 266 studies revealed no overall sex difference in the self-serving bias (Mezulis et al., 2004). However, the age of the participants was an important moderator. Among children, girls showed a greater self-serving bias than boys, among adolescents the sex difference disappeared, and among adults men showed a greater self-serving bias than women. Thus attributional style may explain why sex differences in depression appear after puberty.

Coping

General Coping Strategies   Coping refers to the different strategies that we use to manage stressful events and the accompanying distress associated with them. If your girlfriend breaks up with you, you may go talk to a friend about it, you may wallow in self-pity, you may try to figure out what happened, or you may decide to go swimming to take your mind off things. All of these represent different ways of coping.

One distinction that has been made in the literature is between emotion-focused coping and problem-focused coping (Lazarus & Folkman, 1984). **Problem-focused coping** refers to attempts to alter the stressor itself. Finding a solution to the problem, seeking the advice of others as to how to solve the problem, and coming up with a plan to approach the problem are all problem-solving methods. **Emotion-focused coping** refers to ways in which we accommodate ourselves to the stressor. There are a variety of emotion-focused coping strategies that are quite distinct from one another. Distracting oneself from the stressor, avoiding the problem, and denying the problem exists are all ways we change our reaction to the stressor rather than altering the stressor itself. Talking about the problem to relieve distress, accepting the problem, and putting a positive spin on the problem are also emotion-focused ways of coping.

Investigators frequently suggest that women cope with stressful events by engaging in emotion-focused strategies and men cope by engaging in problem-focused strategies. Although the conceptual distinction between problem-focused coping and emotion-focusing coping is a useful one for the area of coping, this distinction may be less useful when studying gender. When coping strategies are placed into these two broad categories, sometimes expected sex differences appear (i.e., women more emotion focused, men more problem focused), sometimes no sex differences appear, and sometimes sex differences appear in the opposite direction (i.e., women are more problem focused). The broad categories of emotion-focused coping and problem-focused coping collapse across distinct coping strategies, and only some of these may show sex differences. For example, researchers often hypothesize that men are more likely than women to engage in problem-focused coping. Yet one primary problem-focused coping strategy is to seek the advice of others, and we know women are more likely than men to seek out others for help. People can seek different kinds of help, however. If people seek others' advice, they are engaging in problem-focused coping; if people seek others in order to express feelings, they are engaging in emotion-focused coping. In the latter case, the person is trying to reduce distress rather than alter the stressor. Researchers do not always distinguish between these two kinds of support-seeking strategies. However, it is possible that women are more likely than men to do both.

Thus to evaluate sex differences in coping, it is important to turn to specific coping strategies. Examples of specific kinds of coping are shown in Table 13.3.

TABLE 13.3 Sample Coping Strategies

Avoidance	I read a book or watch TV to think less about the problem.
Self-blame	I blame myself for what happened.
Wishful thinking	I wish the problem would go away.
Seek social support	I find someone to talk to about the problem.
Active coping	I figure out what to do to solve the problem.
Positive reappraisal	I try to find the good in the situation.

Specific Coping Strategies. Partly in response to the issues raised above—specifically that people seem to think men engaged in problem-focused coping and women engaged in emotion-focused coping—my colleagues and I conducted a meta-analytic review of the literature on sex comparisons in coping (Tamres, Janicki, & Helgeson, 2002). We showed that women were more likely than men to engage in nearly all the coping strategies, those that were problem focused and emotion focused. The sizes of these sex differences were small, however. The largest differences appeared for positive self-talk (i.e., encouraging oneself), seeking support, and rumination (women more than men). Notice that all these strategies involve the expression of feelings, either to oneself or to someone else.

One difficulty in interpreting the literature on gender and coping is that women may report more of all kinds of coping simply because women are more distressed than men and more distressed people try a greater range of strategies. We found some support for this idea in the meta-analysis. We argued that sex differences in coping would be better understood by an examination of **relative coping**, which refers to how likely men or women are to use one strategy compared to another. Instead of comparing the frequency with which men and women engage in a specific kind of coping, we compare the frequency with which men engage in one coping strategy compared to another strategy and the frequency with which women engage in one coping strategy compared to another strategy. Within the range of coping responses, are men relatively more likely to use a strategy compared to women? For example, imagine both men and women report engaging in problem-focused coping with equal frequency: "some of the time." For men, this may be the most frequently employed strategy, whereas women may report engaging in other strategies "almost all of the time." In that case, men would engage in problem-focused coping relatively more often than women. Our meta-analysis showed that men engage in *relatively* more active coping strategies, and women engage in *relatively* more support seeking.

Tend and Befriend.   One team of researchers has argued that women's general response to stress is different from that of men. Historically, the general response to stress has been described as "fight or flight." However, Taylor and colleagues (2000) argued that this response may apply only to men, and women's response to stress may be better understood as "tend and befriend." Is this true? We have seen so far that one of the most consistent sex differences in coping is that women seek the support of others, which is consistent with the tend and befriend idea. We also have some evidence that men may engage in more avoidant coping or distraction, consistent with "flight," and it is clear that men are more physically aggressive than women, consistent with "fight."

Taylor and colleagues (2000) argue that women's response to stress may have biological underpinnings. In particular, they emphasize the role of oxytocin, which may inhibit the flight response and encourage the tending to relationships in women. Oxytocin helps calm us down during times of stress (Light et al., 2000) and promotes affiliative behavior. Positive physical contact, in the form of touch or hugging, releases oxytocin, which then reduces the stress response (Uvnas-Moberg, 1997). The amount of oxytocin released during stress is greater in women than men (Jezova et al., 1996), which may explain why women respond to stress by seeking rather than withdrawing from others.

Although this theory explains why women may cope differently with stress than men, it does not explain why women are more depressed than men. The tend and befriend idea, however, does suggest women will be more involved in relationships than men. To the extent that relationships are a source of stress (an idea expanded on later in the chapter), women's tendency to tend and befriend may have some negative outcomes.

Rumination.   A large program of research on sex differences in depression has focused on two specific kinds of coping strategies: rumination and distraction. Susan Nolen-Hoeksema (1987, 1994) has argued that women are more depressed than men because women ruminate about their feelings after negative events and men distract themselves. She argues that rumination increases depression in three ways, each of which is depicted in Figure 13.7. First, rumination interferes with instrumental behavior, which might reduce depression. For example, if you are dwelling on a poor grade from a first exam, your distress may keep you from studying for the next exam—which ultimately will lead to another failure experience and further depression. Second, rumination about negative feelings makes other negative feelings and negative memories more salient, which will reinforce depression. After failing an exam, other failure experiences may become increasingly vivid. Third, rumination leads people to make pessimistic explanations for negative events, such as the ones characterized by the pessimistic attributional style. In a study of bereaved adults, rumination was associated with an increase in pessimistic thinking (Nolen-Hoeksema, Parker, & Larson, 1994). In a study of college students, rumination was associated with cognitive inflexibility, which means perseverance of thinking and being unable to respond to feedback. This explains why the cycle of rumination and depression is so difficult to break. Sample rumination and distraction items from Nolen-Hoeksema's Responses to Depression Questionnaire are shown in Table 13.4.

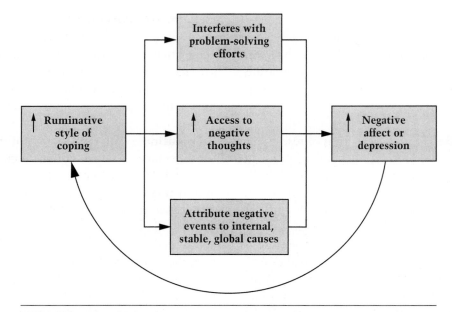

FIGURE 13.7 Nolen-Hoeksema's rumination and depression model. A ruminative style of coping leads to interference with problem-solving efforts, increased access to negative thoughts, and a pessimistic style of thinking (i.e., attribute negative events to internal, stable, global causes)—all of which increase negative affect or depressive symptoms. Negative affect or depressive symptoms also lead to more ruminative coping.

TABLE 13.4 NOLEN-HOEKSEMA'S RESPONSES TO DEPRESSION QUESTIONNAIRE

Sample Rumination Scale Items
1. Think about how alone you feel.
2. Think "I won't be able to do my job/work because I feel so badly."
3. Think about your feelings of fatigue and achiness.
4. Think about how sad you feel.
5. Go away by yourself and think about why you feel this way.
6. Write down what you are thinking about and analyze it.
7. Analyze your personality and try to understand why you are depressed.
8. Think "Why do I have problems other people don't have?"
9. Think "What am I doing to deserve this?"
10. Think "Why do I always react this way?"

Sample Distraction Scale Items
1. Help someone else with something in order to distract yourself.
2. Remind yourself that these feelings won't last.
3. Go to a favorite place to get your mind off your feelings.
4. Concentrate on your work.
5. Do something you enjoy.

Source: Nolen-Hoeksema and Morrow (1991).

DO GENDER 13.4
Sex Differences in Rumination and Distraction

Ask 10 men and women to think about how they respond when they are depressed about an achievement-related failure (e.g., failing an exam) and a relationship-related failure (e.g., relationship breakup). You choose the two specific failure experiences. Then ask people how they responded to each failure experience by having them answer the items in Table 13.4.

Is there a sex difference in rumination and distraction? Does it depend on the situation? Is there another personality variable related to sex that is linked to rumination and distraction?

In a number of studies, Nolen-Hoeksema (1987) has shown that women are more likely than men to respond to depression by talking about and trying to figure out their negative feelings: rumination. By contrast, men are more likely than women to respond to depression by playing sports and by avoiding thoughts about the reasons for their depression: distraction. The sex difference in rumination is more consistent than the sex difference in distraction (Nolen-Hoeksema & Davis, 1999; Strauss et al., 1997). See if there are sex differences in rumination and distraction at your school with Do Gender 13.4

What is the evidence that rumination leads to depression? Numerous studies have shown that people who tend to ruminate in response to a stressful event end up more distressed. In a study of people in San Francisco just after the 1989 earthquake, ruminators were more depressed 7 weeks after the earthquake than non-ruminators (Nolen-Hoeksema & Morrow, 1991). In a 1-year longitudinal study of over 1,000 community residents (Nolen-Hoeksema et al., 1999), women reported a greater tendency than men to ruminate and rumination explained women's increased depression.

Nolen-Hoeksema and colleagues (2004) argue that individuals get involved in a cycle of rumination and depression. This cycle is depicted in Figure 13.7. Rumination increases depression, which then increases rumination. The reciprocal relation between rumination and depression has been demonstrated in longitudinal studies of bereaved adults (Nolen-Hoeksema et al., 1994) and community residents (Nolen-Hoeksema et al., 1999). Rumination also leads episodes of depression to last longer (Nolen-Hoeksema, Morrow, & Fredrickson, 1993).

Another reason for the link of rumination to depression has to do with interpersonal resources. In a study of people who had lost a loved one, ruminators reported less emotional support and more social conflict over the next 18 months (Nolen-Hoeksema & Davis, 1999). The authors reasoned that ruminators dwell on the negative event longer than the norm, and the social network responds negatively. Interestingly, the link of emotional support to decreased depression and social conflict to increased depression was stronger for high than low ruminators. This means ruminators have less of a social resource that has more of an impact on them.

One concern that has been raised about the relation of rumination to depression is that some of the rumination items are confounded with depression. If you review the items in Table 13.4, you will see that the first four items involve ruminating about depression. This makes the theory somewhat circular. Of course, thinking about negative feelings means that you have negative feelings. When the items that overlapped with depression were removed from the scale, the remaining items formed two constellations of traits: (1) reflective pondering (as indicated by items 5, 6, and 7) and (2) brooding (as indicated by items 7, 8, and 9; Treynor, Gonzales, & Nolen-Hoeksema, 2003). The brooding items were more predictive of depression than the reflective items, and brooding appears to explain the sex difference in depression.

Much of this research is quite compelling because it has been conducted in the field with people facing actual stressful life events; thus the research has good external validity. However, recall that the cost of field research is often a loss of internal validity. Is rumination an actual cause of depression? The reciprocal nature of the relation between rumination and depression shows that depression also causes rumination. One way to address the causal issue is to conduct an experiment in a controlled laboratory setting.

Just such an experiment was conducted and showed that inducing depressed people to ruminate increases their depression and inducing depressed people to distract reduces their depression (Lyubomirsky & Nolen-Hoeksema, 1993). Rumination and distraction were manipulated in the laboratory by having depressed and nondepressed college students either think about their feelings and why they are the kind of person they are (rumination condition) or think about external events (distraction condition). Among depressed students, rumination increased depressed mood and distraction reduced depressed mood. However, rumination and distraction had no effect on nondepressed students' moods. There was also evidence that the rumination manipulation interfered with the potential for instrumental behavior among depressed students. Depressed students who were induced to ruminate about themselves reported they were less likely to engage in a list of pleasant activities (e.g., go to dinner with friends, play favorite sport) than the other students.

Why are women more likely than men to ruminate in response to stressful events? One possibility is that people encourage women to ruminate more than men. One study showed that college students gave more ruminative advice (i.e., figure out why you are depressed) to women than to men (Ali & Toner, 1996). Students were equally likely to give distracting advice to men and women. In another study, sixth-, seventh-, and eighth-graders responded to vignettes of men and women ruminating or distracting (Broderick & Korteland, 2002). Distraction was viewed as more appropriate for males than females, and rumination was viewed as more appropriate for females than males. People might encourage women to ruminate because they do not believe it is maladaptive—at least for women. In fact, college students perceive rumination strategies (e.g., talking with someone, determining the cause of one's feelings) as more effective in alleviating depression than distraction strategies (Strauss et al., 1997). When I ask students in my classes why they think that women live longer than men, one of the first responses (usually from a female) is that women think about their feelings and talk about their feelings while men keep their emotions bottled up inside. This answer may be partially correct, but it is also incorrect in a very important way. When thinking about your feelings becomes brooding, there are costs to health for women.

Does a ruminative response style explain why depression emerges only among women during adolescence? Nolen-Hoeksema (1994) views rumination as an interactive cause of sex differences in depression. She argues that females are more likely than males to ruminate even before adolescence, but the negative events that occur to females during adolescence make their ruminative response more detrimental. These negative events include troublesome body changes, difficulties in relationships, and awareness of the limits of the female gender role (i.e., role inconsistent with independence and achievement). These difficulties are addressed in the section on adolescence and depression.

Private Self-Consciousness. Private self-consciousness, or attending to one's inner thoughts and feelings, is typically considered a personality trait rather than a way of coping. Because self-awareness or self-consciousness is so closely linked to rumination, I discuss it here. Sample items from the private self-consciousness scale are "I'm always trying to figure myself out" and "I generally pay attention to my inner feelings" (Fenigstein, Scheier, & Buss, 1975). Private self-consciousness has been linked to depression cross-sectionally in adolescents (Allgood-Merten, Lewinsohn, & Hops, 1990) and longitudinally in a study of middle-age women (Bromberger & Matthews, 1996).

One way private self-consciousness could explain sex differences in depression is if women score higher than men on private self-consciousness. The early studies in this area showed no sex differences in private self-consciousness (Fenigstein et al., 1975). However, two more recent studies of adolescents suggest that girls focus more on their inner feelings than boys do (Allgood-Merten et al., 1990; Sethi & Nolen-Hoeksema, 1997). In one of the studies, children were asked to write down whatever came to mind (Sethi & Nolen-Hoeksema, 1997). Girls' statements contained more references to the self and to relationships, whereas boys' statements contained more references to external stimuli, such as movies, music, and sports. The authors concluded that girls engaged in more internal focusing and relationship focusing, whereas boys engaged in more external focusing. It may be this dispositional difference in styles of thinking that then leads women to ruminate and men to distract when depressed.

Even if there is not an overall sex difference in private self-consciousness, there could be a sex difference in the tendency to react to environmental events by engaging in private self-consciousness. That is, private self-consciousness could be an interactive theory of depression. In the study of middle-age women, private self-consciousness interacted with chronic strains, such that women who were high in private self-consciousness and high in chronic strains were especially distressed (Bromberger & Matthews, 1996). In other words, private self-consciousness was linked to depression among women only when stressful circumstances existed about which they could ruminate. In an experience sampling study where men and women were beeped periodically via palm pilots, private self-consciousness was more strongly associated with negative affect after negative social interactions for women than men (Flory et al., 2000).

Other research has shown that women may be more vulnerable than men to situational cues that evoke private self-consciousness. A meta-analysis of self-report studies of private self-consciousness and mirror manipulations to induce private self-consciousness showed that the link of private self-consciousness to negative affect and self-blame was stronger for women than men (Fejfar & Hoyle, 2000). In one study, women's levels of private self-consciousness increased in response to a self-focusing cue, a mirror, whereas men's levels of private self-consciousness decreased in response to the same cue (Ingram et al., 1988). These findings are shown in Figure 13.8. Unexpectedly, women's levels of private self-consciousness also increased in response to a quite different cue, a video of another person. Because women define themselves partly through their connections to others, seeing another person may have led women to think of themselves and their connections to others.

In sum, the tendency to engage in private self-consciousness provides an explanation for sex differences in depression, partly due to its overlap with rumination. It is also an interactive theory of depression because it predicts that women are more likely than men to respond to certain cues by becoming introspective.

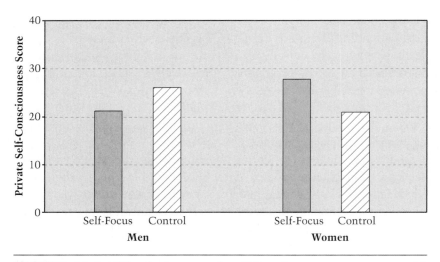

FIGURE 13.8 Effects of sex and self-focusing cue on private self-consciousness. Women's private self-consciousness increased in response to a self-focusing cue, a mirror, whereas men's private self-consciousness decreased in response to the same cue.
Source: Adapted from Ingram et al. (1988).

Stressful Life Events

One reason that women may be more depressed than men is that women experience more traumatic or stressful life events. Although women suffer higher rates of post-traumatic stress disorder than men (Olff et al., 2007), this does not mean that women face more trauma than men. A meta-analysis of sex differences in traumatic events found that men experienced more trauma than women (Tolin & Foa, 2006). This sex difference depended greatly on the nature of the trauma. Whereas women were 6 times as likely as men to report adult sexual assault and 2.5 times as likely as men to report child sexual assault, men were 3.5 times as likely to experience combat/war/terrorism and over 1.5 times as likely to experience nonsexual assault.

Just as we distinguished between major depressive disorder and depressive symptoms, we can also distinguish between traumatic life events (e.g., sexual assault, disaster) and stressful life events (e.g., job loss, divorce, relationship problems, financial difficulties). A meta-analytic review of the literature on sex differences in stressful life events showed that across 119 studies there was a small tendency for females to report more stressful events than males ($d = +.12$; Davis, Matthews, & Twamley, 1999). The size of this effect is extremely small, and a number of variables influenced the size of the relation. One factor that influenced the effect size was how stress was measured. Researchers who study stressful life events typically ask respondents to indicate whether an event happened and/or to rate the level of stress associated with an event. That is, ratings are made of *stress exposure* or *stress impact*. When these two kinds of ratings were distinguished from one another in the meta-analysis, the sex difference in exposure was smaller than the sex difference in impact ($d = +.08$ vs. $d = +.18$). Thus, women may appraise stressors as more severe than men, but women and men do not necessarily experience a different number of stressors. The age of the sample also influenced the size of the relation. The sex difference in stress was larger among adolescent samples compared to children and adult samples, supporting Nolen-Hoeksema's (1994) claim that adolescent females face more stress than adolescent males.

One reason the overall sex difference in exposure to stress is small may be that women and men experience stressors in different domains, just as they experience trauma in different domains. The meta-analysis examined whether sex differences appeared for different kinds of stressors. The sex difference for interpersonal stressors was larger than the sex difference for noninterpersonal stressors ($d = +.17$ vs. $d = +.07$). There was no category of stressor on which men scored higher than women.

A great deal of research on adolescents supports the meta-analysis finding that females report greater interpersonal stress than males. In a study of preadolescent (ages 8 to 12) and adolescent (ages 13 to 18) boys and girls, there was no sex difference in the total number of stressful events reported, but females reported greater interpersonal stress and males reported greater noninterpersonal stress (Rudolph & Hammen, 1999). As shown in the left half of Figure 13.9, adolescent girls reported higher levels of interpersonal stress than preadolescent girls, preadolescent boys, or adolescent boys. As shown in the right half of Figure 13.9, adolescent boys experienced greater noninterpersonal stress than the other three groups. Other studies have shown that adolescent females report more relationship stressors, and adolescent males report more personal stressors (Murberg & Bru, 2004; Shih et al., 2006).

Studies of noncollege adult populations confirm these findings. In a study of married couples, men reported more negative events involving work and finances, whereas women

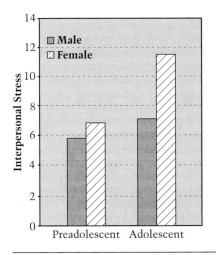 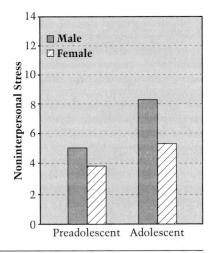

FIGURE 13.9 Sex comparisons of interpersonal and noninterpersonal stress among preadolescents and adolescents. Adolescent females reported higher levels of interpersonal stress compared to adolescent males and either group of preadolescents. Adolescent males reported higher noninterpersonal stress compared to adolescent females and either group of preadolescents.
Source: Adapted from Rudolph and Hammen (1999).

reported more negative events that involved relationships (Conger et al., 1993). In addition, men reported greater distress than women in response to work and financial stressors, whereas women reported greater distress than men in response to relationship stressors. A study of physically disabled people found no difference in the number of stressful events that happened to the self but found women were more likely than men to report events that occurred to others (Turner & Avison, 1989).

Thus it appears that the link of gender to trauma and stress has more to do with men and women experiencing different kinds of traumas and stressors rather than one sex experiencing more trauma or stress than the other. Women are more likely than men to report stressful events that involve relationships and actually occur to others. Although both of these events are sometimes referred to as relationship stressors, there is a difference. In the first case, investigators are finding that women are more likely to report problems within relationships, such as conflicts, breakups, or losses. In the second case, research is showing that women are more likely than men to perceive stressful events that occur to others as their own personal stressors. Further investigate the distinction between these two kinds of stressors with Do Gender 13.5.

Investigators have asked whether sex differences in depression are due to **differential exposure** to stressful events or **differential vulnerability** to stressful events. Differential exposure suggests that women are more depressed than men because they experience more of a certain kind of stressful event. Some major stressors that women experience more than men, such as poverty and sexual abuse, are associated with depression (Nolen-Hoeksema & Keita, 2003). Controlling for these events reduces the sex difference in depression, but does not eliminate it (Kessler, 2000). In fact, if all the stressful events were statistically controlled (not

DO GENDER 13.5
Sex Differences in
Stressful Life Events

Develop a list of stressful life events that are relevant to the population you are sampling. Classify these events into categories, such as personal events and relationship events. Have 10 men and 10 women

1. Indicate if the event occurred to them in the previous year.

2. If the event occurred, have them rate how much the event affected them (none, a little bit, a lot).

3. Indicate if the event happened to someone they know in the previous year.

4. If the event occurred to someone else, rate how much the event personally affected them (none, a little bit, a lot).

Are there sex differences in exposure to different kinds of life events? Are there sex differences in exposure to events that occur to others? Are there sex differences in the magnitude of response to (impact of) personal events? Others' events?

just the ones that affect women more than men), the sex difference in depression would be unchanged. Thus women are not more depressed than men because they simply experience more stressful events. Differential vulnerability implies that certain stressful events are more strongly associated with distress among women than men. For example, one study showed that conflict with friends was a stronger predictor of depression over the course of a year for women than men (Skaff et al., 1999). The distinction between differential exposure and differential vulnerability is partly captured by the difference between stress exposure and stress impact ratings. Turner and Avison (1989) stated the distinction nicely: "Women may care about more people or care more about the people they know, or both" (p. 450). The first part of the sentence pertains to exposure, and the second part pertains to vulnerability.

Studies have compared the differential exposure and differential vulnerability hypotheses and come in on the side of vulnerability. A study of adolescents showed that interpersonal stressors were more strongly associated with depression in females than males, whereas non-interpersonal stressors had similar effects on males and females (Shih et al., 2006). A review of five epidemiological studies showed that men and women were exposed to different kinds of stressors, but stress exposure did not explain sex differences in depression to the extent that sex differences in vulnerability did (Kessler & McLeod, 1984). Men reported more life events in the categories of income loss and ill health, and women reported more life events in the categories of death of a loved one and other network events. Events that involved social networks were more strongly related to depression for women than men. When the effect of women's exposure to network events was compared to the effect of women's vulnerability to network events, vulnerability appeared to account for more of women's depression.

Three more recent studies supported this conclusion. A study of couples showed that women were at greater risk for depression than men only when stressors were network-related (Nazroo, Edwards, & Brown, 1997). A study of adults from the community showed that women were 3 times as likely as men to experience depression in response to stressful events, especially when the events involved network members (Maciejewski, Prigerson, & Mazure, 2001). A study of adults showed that events that happened to the self were equally associated with depression in men and women, but stressful events that happened to others were more strongly associated with depression in women than men (Turner & Avison, 1989).

Taken collectively, these studies show that the reason women are more depressed than men has less to do with the stressful events they face and more to do with how strongly they respond to those events. Women are especially affected by stressors that involve others. Why? This question is addressed next, when I examine the female gender role as an explanation of sex differences in depression.

The Female Gender Role

Communion and Agency.   The female gender role is typically measured with communion scales of the BSRI or PAQ, which reflect a positive focus on others. These scales include traits such as being helpful, kind, and caring. Communion, however, is unrelated to depression. Two meta-analytic reviews of the literature show that communion is virtually unrelated to depression, and agency is associated with a lack of depression (Bassoff & Glass, 1982; Whitley, 1984). Recall that agency reflects a positive focus on the self. One reason for the link of agency to lower depression is problem-solving ability (Marcotte, Alain, & Gosselin, 1999). High-agency people perceive they can solve problems. Longitudinal data reveal protective effects of agency and null effects of communion. In a longitudinal study of middle-age women, a lack of agency predicted an increase in depression 3 years later (Bromberger & Matthews, 1996). Communion did not predict depression.

Thus there appear to be no data linking the female gender role trait of communion to depression. Instead, it seems that features of the male gender role (agency) protect against depression. However, gender roles are multifaceted. I argue there is an aspect of the female gender role related to depression: unmitigated communion.

Unmitigated Communion.   Recall that unmitigated communion is defined as a focus on others to the exclusion of the self (Helgeson, 1994c; Helgeson & Fritz, 1998). Unmitigated communion has been associated with depression in studies of college students, cardiac patients, healthy adolescents, adolescents with diabetes, and healthy adults (Helgeson & Fritz, 1998). In addition, unmitigated communion accounts for sex differences in depression. For example, in a study of adolescents with diabetes, unmitigated communion was more strongly related to depression than respondent's sex, and no sex differences in depression were noted once levels of unmitigated communion were considered (Helgeson & Fritz, 1996). People who score high on unmitigated communion rely on others for self-esteem and internalize others' views of themselves. This external focus is critical to the link of unmitigated communion to depression (Dear & Roberts, 2002).

As shown in Figure 13.10, there are two explanations for the link of unmitigated communion to depression: self-neglect and overinvolvement in others' problems (Fritz & Helgeson, 1998). First, individuals who score high on unmitigated communion are afraid to assert their own needs, inhibit self-expression to avoid conflict, and don't take care of themselves when they are ill—all indicators of self-neglect. Second, people characterized by unmitigated communion become overly involved in others' problems and take on others' problems as their own. Recall from the section on stressful life events that women are more likely than men to report stressful events that occur to other people. Unmitigated communion also has been linked to reporting stressful events that occurred to others. Unmitigated communion may be associated with exposure to others' problems because such individuals seek out others to help. However, the person who scores high on unmitigated communion also may be more likely than others to interpret another person's problem as his or her own. For example, two people may both be exposed to a neighbor going through a divorce, but only the unmitigated communion person defines this stressful event as his or her own personal stressor.

Self-neglect and overinvolvement are interrelated. In a study of adolescents with diabetes, older adolescents (ages 15 to 18) who scored high on unmitigated communion reported being more upset by stressful events that involved others. These stressors explained the link of unmitigated communion to depression and poor control over their diabetes, presumably because they weren't taking care of themselves (Helgeson & Fritz, 1996).

Unmitigated communion also is associated with worrying about other people's problems. Thus unmitigated communion is associated with rumination, consistent with Nolen-Hoeksema's (1994) theory—but the rumination is not about one's own problems, but about other people's problems. Two laboratory studies showed that people high in unmitigated communion ruminate about others' problems (Fritz & Helgeson, 1998). In each study, one person disclosed a problem to another. In one study, the two people discussing the problem were friends. In the other study, a confederate of the experimenter

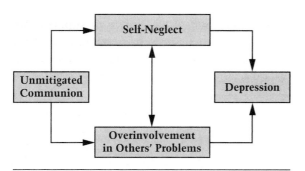

FIGURE 13.10   Model of the relation between unmitigated communion and depression.
Source: Adapted from Fritz and Helgeson (1998).

disclosed a problem to the research participant. Listeners who scored high on unmitigated communion reported more intrusive thoughts about the discloser's problem 2 days later, whether the discloser was a friend or a stranger.

Some evidence suggests that unmitigated communion people are more reactive to interpersonal stress. In a study of college students that involved nightly phone interviews for 7 days, daily interpersonal conflict was associated with daily distress for individuals high and low on unmitigated communion (Reynolds et al., 2006). However, conflict was associated with distress the following day only for individuals high in unmitigated communion. These findings suggest that unmitigated communion individuals' reaction to interpersonal stress is more prolonged. Similar findings appeared in a study that measured a construct related to unmitigated communion, interpersonal sensitivity (how much feelings and behavior of others affect the self). In a study that involved 12 weekly phone calls with adult women who had osteoarthritis or rheumatoid arthritis, the relation of interpersonal stress to negative affect was stronger for those who scored high on interpersonal sensitivity (Smith & Zautra, 2002).

Caregiving

Aside from the personality trait of unmitigated communion, the caregiving aspect of the female gender role may be linked to depression. People characterized by unmitigated communion may be more likely to be caregivers; however, people can end up in the caregiver role regardless of their level of unmitigated communion. Events such as a spouse becoming ill, parents growing older and needing care, and children becoming sick can happen to anyone. Women traditionally shoulder more of the burden of these caregiving responsibilities than men. Caregiving is also more likely to lead to distress in women than in

men. A longitudinal study of dual-earner couples who transitioned into caregiving showed that the transition led to a greater increase in distress among men than women (Chesley & Moen, 2006). One reason may be that some women decrease or cease employment when they become caregivers (Pavalko & Woodbury, 2000), whereas men are more likely to obtain assistance with caregiving (Yee & Schulz, 2000). In a meta-analytic review of the caregiving literature, women reported greater burden than men ($d = +.34$), greater depression than men ($d = +.34$), and a greater number of caregiving tasks than men ($d = +.20$; Pinquart & Sorensen, 2006). The sex difference in depression among caregivers was larger than the sex difference found in noncaregiving populations. The effects of caregiving on men and women may depend in part on their relationship to the person needing care. One study found that female caregivers of spouses, children, or parents were more likely to be distressed than female noncaregivers, but male caregivers were more distressed than male noncaregivers only when the person they were taking care of was a spouse (Marks, 1998).

It is the caregiving role that may explain why social ties are not as protective against depression among women as they are among men. Recall from Chapter 11 that social relations are a double-edged sword for women. Social ties are not only a source of support, but also a source of stress for women. One study showed that the number of social roles was directly related to fewer mental health problems among men but showed a curvilinear relation to mental health problems among women (Weich, Sloggett, & Lewis, 1998). That is, women with the fewest social roles and women with the most social roles had higher levels of mental distress. Women who have many social roles may find that the stressors to which they are exposed outweigh the support they receive.

- Biological factors, including genes and hormones, most certainly contribute to depression but cannot alone explain the sex difference in depression.

- Females' low status in society may lead to lower perceptions of control. A lack of control could contribute to perceptions of helplessness, a precipitant of depression.

- After adolescence, females may be more likely than males to exhibit a pessimistic attributional style and less likely than males to exhibit a self-serving bias, thought processes that have been linked to depression.

- It is not the case that men exhibit more problem-focused coping, and women exhibit more emotion-focused coping. Instead, there are specific coping styles related to sex. Women seek support and ruminate in response to stress more than men.

- Women's tendency to ruminate interferes with instrumental behavior, increases access to other negative cognitions, and increases the pessimistic attributional style, all of which have been linked to depression.

- Women may be more likely than men to respond to stressful events by becoming introspective—that is, privately self-conscious, a construct related to rumination.

- Women are more likely than men to experience relationship events and more vulnerable than men to the negative effects of relationship stressors. It is the latter that is most strongly linked to sex differences in depression.

- There are multiple aspects of the female gender role. Although communion is not related to depression, unmitigated communion is.

- People who score high on unmitigated communion become involved in others' problems to the neglect of themselves, both of which may increase women's risk for depression.

- Aside from unmitigated communion, women are more likely than men to find themselves in the caregiving role. Women report greater caregiver burden than men, increasing their risk of depression.

CHALLENGES OF ADOLESCENCE

Sex differences in depression begin to appear at around age 13, the time of transition from middle school to high school. A meta-analytic review of scores on the Child Depression Inventory showed that boys had slightly higher depression scores than girls below age 13, but that girls had higher scores than boys at age 13 and over (Twenge & Nolen-Hoeksema, 2002). Boys' depression scores remained the same from ages 8 through 16, whereas girls' scores increased between the ages of 12 and 16. Thus something must occur during adolescence to spark this sex difference in depression. Cyranowski and colleagues (2000) state, "Pubertal maturation sensitizes females to the depressogenic effects of negative life events" (p. 22). In this section of the chapter, I examine some of the challenges of adolescence that might lead to an increase in depression among young women.

Gender Intensification

During adolescence, gender roles become salient for males and females. Adolescence has been referred to as a time of **gender intensification** (Hill & Lynch, 1983). During adolescence, boys become increasingly concerned with adhering to the male gender role and girls become increasingly concerned with adhering to the female gender role. These concerns arise in part from outside forces: Adolescents feel increasing pressure from society to adhere to their gender roles.

Gender intensification theory was partly supported in one study that examined changes in gender roles and gender-role attitudes from sixth to eighth grade (Galambos, Almeida, & Petersen, 1990). At all ages, boys scored higher than girls on masculinity, or agency, but the largest sex difference appeared in the oldest group (e.g., eighth-graders). Boys' agency scores

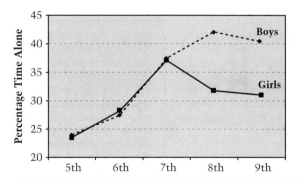
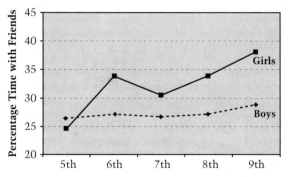

FIGURE 13.11   Girls spend an increasing amount of time with friends as they get older, whereas boys spend an increasing amount of time alone as they get older.
Source: Adapted from Larson and Richards (1991).

increased more than girls' with age. Girls always scored higher than boys on femininity, or communion, but these scores did not change with age. Sex differences in gender-role attitudes increased with age: Girls became more egalitarian and boys became more traditional.

Other evidence for gender intensification comes from studies that show females' interpersonal orientation increases during adolescence. As shown in Figure 13.11, a study of 9- to 15-year-olds showed that older girls spent increasingly more time with friends than younger girls did, whereas time with friends did not change with age among boys (Larson & Richards, 1991). By contrast, older boys spent more time alone than younger boys did. In a study of 5th- through 9th-graders, older girls spent more time in social activities, on the phone with friends, and talking with friends than younger girls did. In addition, girls' conversations began to have a more interpersonal focus as they grew older (Raffaelli & Duckett, 1989). These same behavioral differences were not observed between older and younger boys. A study of 5th-, 8th-, and 12th-graders showed that boys found it more difficult to share their feelings with others as age increased, whereas girls found it easier to share their feelings with

others as age increased (Polce-Lynch et al., 1998). Thus there is some evidence for gender intensification during adolescence.

Why would gender intensification lead to depression? Depression might be heightened among women who realize the limiting value of the female gender role. Although intelligence and achievement orientation in childhood or adolescence exert protective effects on men's mental health, these qualities may pose risks for women's mental health. IQ scores have been associated with ambition, productivity, persistence, and self-satisfaction in young adult men (ages 18 and 23), but introspection, anxiety, rumination, and guilt among young adult women (Block & Kremen, 1996). A longitudinal study showed that higher IQ scores during preschool predicted greater depression among female 18-year-olds, but less depression among male 18-year-olds (Block, Gjerde, & Block, 1991). Five years later, similar results were obtained when predicting depression among the 23-year-olds (Gjerde, 1995).

Other evidence is consistent with the idea that high achievement has positive mental health consequences for men but not women. In a 6-year longitudinal study of people without a history of mental illness, men who attended college were less likely to become depressed than men who did not attend college. By contrast, women who attended college were more likely to become depressed than women who did not (Coryell, Endicott, & Keller, 1992). In a study of patients hospitalized for depression, a high achievement orientation was associated with recovery from depression among men but a lack of recovery from depression among women (Veiel et al., 1992).

Thus adolescence is a time when gender roles become salient for men and women. This is troublesome for some women because they realize the female gender role is inconsistent with achievement.

Puberty

Because the emergence of sex differences in depression coincides with puberty, researchers have investigated whether the physical changes that accompany puberty are associated with depression in women. Some research has shown that reaching puberty is associated with the sex difference in depression (Angold, Costello, & Worthman, 1998), whereas other research has shown that it is the timing of puberty. Reaching puberty early for one's age has been associated with depression in girls (Graber, Brooks-Gunn, & Warren, 2006). One way in which pubertal changes may be associated with depression is through their impact on adolescents' body image.

Body Image

A negative body image is associated with depression in both males and females (Allgood-Merten et al., 1990). However, women have a more negative body image than men, which may make them more vulnerable to depression.

In a study of 9th- through 12th-graders, girls had lower self-esteem and a more negative body image than boys in all grades (Allgood-Merten et al., 1990). Girls' low self-esteem and negative body image accounted for a large portion of the sex difference in depression. Body image also was more strongly associated with self-esteem among girls than boys. Thus the impact of a negative body image on girls' depression may operate through adverse effects on their overall feelings of self-worth.

Girls are not only more dissatisfied with their bodies than boys, but girls also have a more distorted body image compared to boys. One study showed that boys were accurate in identifying the size of the male figure desired by girls, whereas girls identified a thinner female figure than what was actually desired by boys (Safir, Flaisher-Kellner, & Rosenmann, 2005).

Body image is not only influenced by sex but also by race and ethnicity. A study of undergraduates in Canada showed that those with Asian descent—especially Chinese—were less satisfied with their bodies than those with European descent. A meta-analysis of ethnic differences in body image among women revealed that White females are more dissatisfied with their bodies than females from other ethnic groups ($d = +.29$; Grabe & Hyde, 2006). However, the difference in body image depends upon which ethnic group is the subject of comparison. White and Hispanic women are more dissatisfied with their bodies than African American women, with Asian women falling in between. The largest Black/White differences in body image occur during adolescence and young adulthood. It also appears that the size of these ethnic differences has decreased in recent years. In fact, two more recent studies have documented sex differences in body image among African American adolescents (Grant et al., 1999; Gross et al., 2005). Thus a negative body image may play a greater role in African American girls' depression than previously thought. Historically, Black women have been less

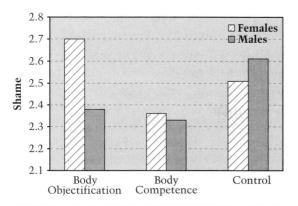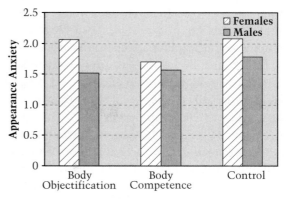

FIGURE 13.12   Women's feelings of shame and appearance anxiety increased relative to those of men in response to the body objectification prime compared to the body competence prime.
Source: Adapted from Roberts and Gettman (2004).

concerned with their weight than White women, but more recent findings suggest these racial differences are disappearing. The increased dissatisfaction with body image among young Black women may be due to the acculturation of Black women into the middle class and to the increased availability of thin Black models in the media (Grant et al., 1999).

It is not only body image but **body objectification** that is also related to depression. Objectification theory states that there are social and cultural forces that sexually objectify women which lead women to evaluate themselves based on their appearance (Fredrickson & Roberts, 1997). Body objectification has been associated with depression among adolescent females (Tolman et al., 2006). The negative effects of body objectification have been demonstrated in experimental research. For example, in one study, college students were asked to unscramble a series of words to form sentences under one of three conditions (Roberts & Gettman, 2004). In one condition, some of the words reflected body competence (e.g., fitness, health, stamina); in a second condition, some of the words reflected body objectification (e.g., attractive, shapely, sexiness), and in the last

condition, the words were neutral (e.g., honesty, music, interesting). As shown in Figure 13.12, women's feelings of shame and appearance anxiety increased in the body objectification condition compared to the body competence condition.

Self-Esteem

Sex differences in self-esteem were reviewed in Chapter 6 and led to the conclusion that there were few overall sex differences among adults, but measurable differences among adolescents. A study of high school students found girls had lower self-esteem than boys and were more depressed than boys (Avison & McAlpine, 1992). Furthermore, self-esteem accounted for sex differences in depression. A study of high school students found girls had greater discrepancies between their ideal self and actual self than boys, and this discrepancy accounted for the sex difference in depression (Hankin, Roberts, & Gotlib, 1997). A study of sixth- and seventh-graders showed that girls received lower scores on a variety of domains of self-esteem: global self-worth, physical appearance, and athletic ability (Ohannessian et al., 1999). Because there was no sex difference in depression among sixth-graders but a sex difference in depression among seventh-graders, the authors argued the sex difference in self-esteem preceded the sex difference in depression. In addition, sex differences in these domains of self-esteem accounted for the sex difference in depression.

The self-concepts that adolescent males and females are expected to develop may have different implications for their mental health. Men are expected to develop an achievement-oriented self-concept, whereas women are expected to develop an interdependent self-concept (Gore & Colten, 1991). The former can be achieved on one's own, whereas the latter can be achieved only with the help of others. This may make women's self-esteem and overall mental health more vulnerable to environmental factors, which may explain why women are more vulnerable than men to stressful events that happen to others.

Relations with Parents and Friends

The move from childhood to adulthood involves changes in relationships with parents and peers. There is evidence that relationships with parents are more strongly associated with depression among adolescent females than males (Leadbeater et al., 1999; Murberg & Bru, 2004). In one study, support from mother influenced the relation of stressful life events to depression for adolescent girls but not adolescent boys (Ge et al., 1994). Thus parental relations are strained during adolescence, and these strains have a greater effect on girls.

Relationships with peers are critical in adolescence. One study followed 12- to 17-year-olds for 1 year and found those who became involved in a romantic relationship over the course of the year showed greater increases in depression than those who did not—especially among girls (Joyner & Udry, 2000). Two reasons

for this finding were identified. Those who became involved in romantic relationships had poorer relationships with parents and more academic difficulties.

Different Manifestations of Depression

An artifactual explanation for the sex difference in depression had to do with the possibility that men and women manifest distress in different ways. This difference in manifestation of distress may begin during adolescence. Instead of sex differences in depression emerging during adolescence, boys and girls may begin to *manifest* depression differently by adolescence. One study showed that clinicians viewed depressed male adolescents as aggressive and disagreeable and depressed female adolescents as introspective and ruminating (Gjerde, Block, & Block, 1988). That is, depressed males showed more **externalizing behavior**, and depressed females showed more **internalizing behavior**. However, the depressed adolescents reported views of themselves that were slightly different from the views the clinicians held. Depressed males reported being aggressive but also worrying and feeling vulnerable—internalizing characteristics not recognized by the clinicians. Depressed females reported being aggressive and unrestrained—externalizing characteristics not recognized by the clinicians. Either the adolescents were less likely to manifest the gender-role-incongruent forms of depression to clinicians, or the clinicians were less likely to perceive them.

TAKE HOME POINTS

- Gender intensification suggests that gender-role norms become salient during adolescence. One reason that girls' depression may increase during adolescence is that they become aware of the limitations of the female gender role.

- A variety of events occur during adolescence—body image changes, challenges to relationships with parents and peers—that may pose a greater risk for depression among girls than boys.

■ It is also possible that the sex difference in manifestation of depression emerges during adolescence, with girls' greater internalizing behavior recognized as depression but boys' externalizing behavior construed as another problem behavior.

This concludes our examination of the theories of depression. There are a variety of other mental illnesses that are relevant to gender either because they afflict one sex more than another or because the characteristics of the disorder are relevant to gender roles. See Sidebar 13.2 for a discussion of some of these mental illnesses and Table 13.5 for a list of their gender-related features. Because there is a large sex difference in attention deficit hyperactivity disorder, I elaborate on it in Sidebar 13.3.

SIDEBAR 13.2: *Gender and Other Mental Illnesses*

In general, women are more likely to have higher rates of histrionic and dependent personality disorders, whereas men are more likely to have higher rates of schizoid, antisocial, and compulsive personality disorders (Winstead & Sanchez, 2005). Most of the information in this section is taken from the *Diagnostic and Statistical Manual of Mental Disorders* (4th ed. text revised; APA, 2000).

Schizophrenia is a form of psychopathology. It is a form of psychosis that includes paranoia, delusions, hallucinations, disorganized speech, and flattened affect. There is a slightly higher incidence among men than women. The major symptoms differ for men and women. Women are more likely to show affective disturbances, paranoia, and hallucinations, whereas men are more likely to show flat affect and social withdrawal. The age of onset also differs. Men are at highest risk for schizophrenia between the ages of 18 and 25, whereas women are at highest risk between 25 and 35. The role of hormones may be implicated in female schizophrenia, as there is an increase in late-onset schizophrenia (after menopause) in women (Lewine & Seeman, 1995). The genetic component of schizophrenia is also stronger in women than men. A great deal of attention has focused on the brain to understand sex differences in schizophrenia. Some research shows that different hemispheres of the brain are affected in men and women (Purcell, Lewine, Caudle, & Pries, 1998), and other research shows that there are differences in the brain structure of men and women (Guerguerian & Lewine, 1998).

Antisocial personality disorder is characterized by a disregard for others, breaking the law, aggression, deceit, manipulation, and lack of empathy. It is a diagnosis made among adults, and one feature of the disorder is that the individual must have a history of conduct disorder as a child. Conduct disorder includes aggression toward people or animals, destruction of property, and serious violation of rules. Both antisocial personality disorder and conduct disorder are much more common in men than women. The emphasis on aggression may account for some of its lower prevalence among women. The psychological and behavioral correlates of antisocial personality disorder are similar for men and women (Cale & Lilienfeld, 2002a, 2002b). For example, a history of sexual and physical abuse is predictive for both sexes.

Borderline personality disorder is characterized by unstable interpersonal relationships and maladaptive interpersonal functioning. Symptoms include fear of abandonment, low self-esteem, and impulsivity, including suicide attempts. About three quarters of the people diagnosed with this disorder are women. Among patients with borderline personality disorder, men and women show equal levels of impairment (Zlotnick et al., 2002).

Histrionic personality disorder includes excessive emotionality and attention seeking. People with this disorder may be dramatic, inappropriately sexually seductive, and use physical appearance to draw attention to themselves. Women are diagnosed with this disorder more than men. Clearly, gender-role stereotypes may play a role in this differential diagnosis. The same behavior in men may not be viewed as pathological. There is some support that among personality disorders, histrionic personality disorder is the female version and antisocial personality disorder is the male version. In a study of actors, psychopathology was more strongly correlated with histrionic personality disorder in females and antisocial personality disorder in males (Cale & Lilienfeld, 2002a, 2002b).

Dependent personality disorder is a disorder related to interpersonal functioning. People with this disorder are passive, indecisive without reassurance from others, clingy and insecure in relationships, and want to be taken care of by others. Women are diagnosed with this disorder more than men. It is also one of the most frequently diagnosed personality disorders.

Narcissistic personality disorder is characterized by feelings of self-importance and superiority, inflation of abilities, entitlement, and a lack of empathy. More men than women are diagnosed with this disorder.

One concern with the sex differences in some of these disorders is that features of a particular disorder are perceived as more maladaptive in one sex than another. Borderline personality disorder is a good example. Being overly dependent, demanding, and having high rates of sexual activity may be viewed as more pathological among females than males (Nehls, 1998). To determine the validity of this concern, one study surveyed clinicians from the American Psychological Association (Anderson et al., 2001). Clinicians were provided with a list of features of antisocial personality, borderline personality, histrionic personality, and narcissistic personality disorders and asked to rate either how rare each feature was in a particular person or how maladaptive the feature was in a particular person. Clinicians were randomly assigned to rate either a male, a female, or a person whose sex was not specified. Although there were differences in the frequency with which clinicians ascribed features of personality disorders to males and females, there was no difference in the pathology of a given feature for males and females for any of the disorders. A similar study was performed with college students and showed that students rated dependent, depressive, and borderline symptoms as more maladaptive in females than males (Sprock, Crosby, & Nielsen, 2001). However, of 105 symptoms, only 8 were rated as differentially maladaptive in males versus females. Furthermore, it is probably more important that clinicians rather than college students do not perceive symptoms differently.

SIDEBAR 13.3: *Attention Deficit Hyperactivity Disorder—A Problem for Males Only?*

Males have higher rates of attention deficit hyperactivity disorder (ADHD) than females. The size of the difference depends on how it is measured (Cassidy, 2007). Among clinic samples, the male to female ratio ranges from 9:1 to 6:1. Among community samples, the difference is smaller but still sizable, on the order of 3:1. ADHD manifests itself differently in males and females. A meta-analytic review of the literature showed that females with ADHD have more intellectual impairment than males, but males with ADHD have more hyperactivity, externalizing behavior, and aggression (Gaub & Carlson, 1997). Boys with ADHD are more likely than girls to have problems at school and to have conduct disorders (Biederman et al., 2002). More recently, three types of ADHD have been delineated: (1) inattentive, (2) hyperactive, and (3) combined—inattentive plus hyperactive. It turns out that females are more likely than males to have the inattentive type (Cassidy, 2007). Thus one reason that males might be more likely to be referred to clinics for ADHD compared to females is that their behavior is more disruptive and attracts attention.

TABLE 13.5   PERSONALITY DISORDERS

Antisocial	Men more than women
—disregard for others	
—breaking the law	
—aggression	
—lack of empathy	
—deceitful	
—impulsive	
—irresponsible	
Borderline	Women more than men
—unstable interpersonal relationships	
—maladaptive interpersonal functioning	
—fear of abandonment	
—low self-esteem	
—impulsivity	
—suicidal behavior	
Histrionic	Women more than men
—excessive emotionality	
—needs to be the center of attention	
—uses physical appearance to get attention	
—overly dramatic	
—inappropriate sexual behavior in interactions with others	
Dependent	Women more than men
—passive	
—can't make decisions without reassurance	
—difficulty doing things on one's own	
—clingy in relationships	
—desire to be taken care of by others	
—high fear of abandonment	
Narcissistic	Men more than women
—feelings of self-importance	
—feelings of superiority	
—high need for admiration	
—inflation of abilities	
—sense of entitlement	
—exploits others	
—lack of empathy	

Source: DSM-IV-TR (American Psychiatric Association, 2000).

ADJUSTMENT TO CHRONIC ILLNESS

This man, let's call him Bill, was 38 years old and had suffered a heart attack. He had a strong family history of heart disease. His father had died when he was in his thirties of heart disease, his mother had recently undergone bypass surgery, and he had already lost a brother to heart disease. Bill smoked a couple of packs of cigarettes a day. He did not have time for exercise or to really think about what he was eating. Bill owned a business and was struggling—not to make ends meet, but to make the business an overwhelming success. He was very stressed by the business. Bill was married and had two young children. How did he respond to his heart attack? He was angry but resigned. He had no intention of changing any of his behaviors. He would continue to smoke, continue to work long hours at work and get little sleep, and had no intention of spending more time with family. The heart attack convinced him he might not live as long as he had hoped, but his response to this fact was to work even harder to ensure the financial security of his family when he passed away. He told me this was the responsibility he had as the "man of the family."

A few days later, I interviewed a woman, let's call her Marie. Marie reluctantly agreed to let me interview her while she was in the hospital recovering from a heart attack. She said she doubted she would have time for the 90-minute interview because she was certain her physician would be in soon to discharge her. (Having experience with the hospital discharge process, I knew we would probably have at least 90 minutes before the physician arrived and the paperwork would be finished!) Marie was anxious to leave the hospital to take care of her husband, who was dying of lung cancer. I asked Marie to recall the earliest signs of her heart problem. She recalled having symptoms of chest pain over a year ago. Her physician had wanted to hospitalize her for some tests, but she refused to leave her ill husband. Instead, she used a nitroglycerin spray daily for the past year to alleviate chest pain. Marie had difficulty answering the questions I asked because she could not keep her mind focused on the interview. She asked me why I was asking so many questions about her when it was her husband who had the real problem. I wondered when Marie left the hospital if she would take care of herself. Somehow, I doubted it.

These two people are among the hundreds of people I have interviewed with a chronic illness, in this case heart disease. I present these two cases, one by a man and one by a woman, to illustrate two very different responses I believe can be tied to traditional gender roles—the man as the breadwinner and the woman as the family caretaker.

In this section of the chapter, I describe how people adjust to chronic illness, with an emphasis on the implications of gender roles. Studies of heart disease show that women adjust more poorly than men. For example, in a review of nine studies, women reported more anxiety and more depression following a heart attack compared to men (Brezinka & Kittel, 1995). In a study of patients who had stents implanted, women reported greater anxiety and more sleep disturbances than men 6 months later (Ladwig et al., 2000). In a study of patients who had cardiac surgery, women had lower physical functioning than men over the course of the entire year following surgery (Jenkins & Gortner, 1998).

Many of these studies comparing men's and women's adjustment to heart disease suffer from an important methodological flaw. They fail to consider differences between men's and women's functioning before the onset of the illness. In the Jenkins and Gortner (1998) study, women had worse functioning than men prior to surgery. Thus women's lower functioning after surgery may be due to a preexisting sex difference in functioning. Another investigator found that women were more depressed than men 1 year after bypass surgery. However, women were also older, were more likely to be widowed, had less income, and had more other health problems compared to men (Ai et al., 1997). When these factors were taken into consideration, the sex difference in depression disappeared. Sex differences in depression following the onset of a chronic illness are especially suspect because of the research just reviewed showing women are more depressed than men among physically healthy samples.

Other research has shown that women adjust better than men to chronic illness. A study of persons with cancer found that females evidenced more positive adjustment than males (Fife, Kennedy & Robinson, 1994). Although men and women reported similar levels of distress, women scored higher on measures of functioning in multiple domains, and women were more likely than men to find meaning in their illness. Women might have more difficulty than men adjusting to chronic illness when they are married because they have difficulty relinquishing the caregiver role. Women who are ill continue to provide support to their spouses, whereas men who are ill focus more on themselves (Revenson et al., 2005). Husbands may not be as supportive as wives when their spouse is ill because they are less familiar with the caregiver role. A study of elderly women with osteoarthritis showed that husbands were less likely to provide support when the women expressed symptoms of pain—suggesting that men may be more likely than women to withdraw from the caregiver role (Stephens et al., 2006).

Are there sex differences in how children adjust to chronic illness? Williams (2000) found that adolescent girls with diabetes and asthma adapted better to their illness than adolescent boys. The girls incorporated their illness into their social identities. They shared their illness with friends. The boys viewed the illness as a threat to their identity, and they hid their illness from friends. The boys compartmentalized the illness so it had little effect on other aspects of their lives. A study of children with diabetes, asthma, leukemia, epilepsy, and cardiac problems reached similar conclusions (Eiser et al., 1992). The investigators found that mothers viewed girls as better adjusted than boys, in terms of their relationships with peers and their coping with schoolwork. However, mothers thought girls had more problems with dependency than boys. Unfortunately, the investigators did not have a comparison group of children without illness. It may be that mothers would perceive these same sex differences among healthy children.

There are really only two ways to determine whether a chronic illness has different effects on men's and women's quality of life. One way would be to conduct a prospective study in which healthy men and women are followed until a chronic illness develops and their adjustment is measured. Second, we could compare the psychological status of men and women with a chronic illness to a control group of healthy men and women. Few studies have used these procedures.

One framework that can be used to understand how men and women adjust to chronic illness is a gender-role perspective. Chronic illness poses different challenges for men and women, in terms of traditional roles. Both the traditional male gender role and the traditional female gender role may make it more difficult to adjust to chronic illness. The reasons for these adverse associations, however, differ. After reading this section, use Do Gender 13.6 to see if a gender-role framework helps you understand how someone adjusts to chronic illness.

DO GENDER 13.6
Gender Roles and Chronic Illness

Interview 2 male and 2 female college students who had a chronic illness as a child. Common chronic illnesses during childhood are diabetes, asthma, and cancer. Ask them a series of open-ended questions to find out how the illness affected their lives—relationships with parents, relationships with friends, leisure activities, schoolwork, self-esteem. After the interview, view the participants' responses from a gender-role perspective. Did any of the effects of the illness seem to be related to gender roles?

Male Gender Role

A number of years ago, an episode of a news program aired that depicted a man who had been diagnosed with a chronic illness—heart disease. The man with heart disease suffered a heart attack but resisted his physician's instructions to reduce his stress, to slow down, and to take life a little easier. Instead, this man reacted against the physician's instructions and against his newfound vulnerability, heart disease, by proving he was just as strong as before and worked even longer hours to maintain his business. He was very concerned about maintaining a macho image. The man then suffered a second, more debilitating heart attack. Ironically, he was so impaired by the second heart attack that he lost the business he was trying so hard to save. If he had followed his physician's instructions the first time, he might not have lost the business or suffered the loss of physical functioning caused by the second heart attack.

The traditional male gender role may be an advantage or a disadvantage in adjusting to chronic illness (see Figure 13.13). On the negative side, characteristics of the traditional male gender role, specifically independence and self-control, are inconsistent with chronic illness. People with a traditional masculine orientation may find it difficult to depend on others for assistance or to ask others for help. This will only be problematic if help is needed. For example, a cardiac patient who refuses to ask for assistance with mowing the lawn or shoveling snow is placing himself or herself at risk for a fatal heart attack.

In addition, the mere existence of a chronic illness may be viewed as a weakness, and vulnerability and weakness are inconsistent with the male gender role. Studies have found that adolescent males feel more stigmatized by chronic illness than adolescent females (Prout, 1989; Williams, 2000). A chronic illness will be especially threatening to men to the extent that it undermines their breadwinner role, which is the case when women go to work, men retire, or men reduce their workloads in response to their illness (Charmaz, 1995).

Because the male gender role is linked to physical strength, men might have more difficulty than women coping with any physical limitations the illness poses. In a study of patients with congestive heart failure, physical limitations were associated with depression for men but not women (Murberg et al., 1998). The authors suggested that men's overall sense of well-being may be more strongly linked to their physical capabilities than women's sense of well-being. That is, men who find it difficult to lift and carry objects, walk, and climb stairs may be more depressed than women with comparable physical limitations. One reason that women may be more accepting of physical limitations than men is that women find it more acceptable to turn to others for assistance (Murberg et al., 1998).

The male gender role also might interfere with general compliance to physician instructions. For example, men with heart disease may

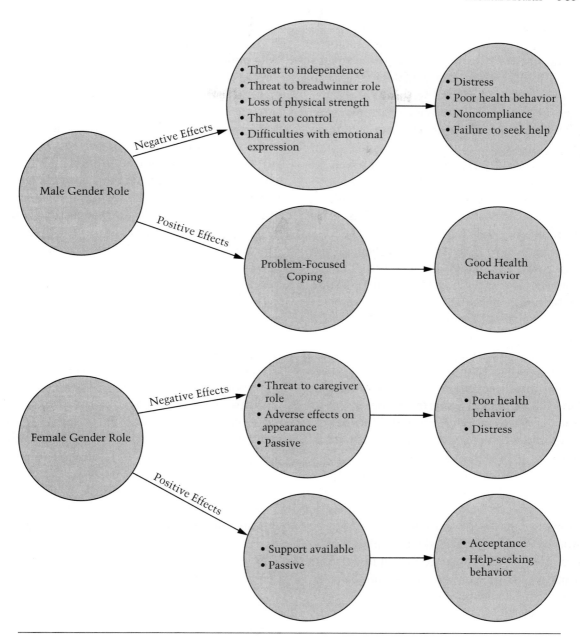

FIGURE 13.13   Implications of Gender Roles for Adjustment to Chronic Illness.

construe a strict diet, exercise regimen, and orders to refrain from physical exertion as interfering with their personal control. Strict orders by physicians to adhere to these behaviors may invoke a state of **psychological reactance** (Brehm, 1966). Psychological reactance occurs when you perceive that someone has taken away your freedom or sense of control by telling you what to do. To restore that freedom, you do just the opposite of what was instructed.

A more familiar term for this idea is "reverse psychology." Think of the times you told someone to do just the opposite of what you wanted so they would react against your instructions and do what you really want. Psychological reactance may be dangerous in the case of patient adherence to physician instructions. In this case, patients' noncompliance restores personal control at the expense of taking care of themselves. People who might be most vulnerable to noncompliance as a result of psychological reactance are those who score high on the gender-related trait unmitigated agency. Unmitigated agency has been associated with poor adjustment to heart disease, in part due to the failure to adhere to physicians' instructions (Helgeson, 1993) and poor health behaviors, in particular smoking (Helgeson & Mickelson, 2000).

Another feature of the male gender role that might impede adjustment to illness is difficulties with emotional expression. The traditional male role requires men to keep feelings and vulnerabilities hidden from others. However, the failure to share feelings and difficulties will keep others from providing needed support. In a study of men with prostate cancer, unmitigated agency was associated with difficulties with emotional expression (Helgeson & Lepore, 1997). It was these emotional expression difficulties that explained the link of unmitigated agency to poor psychological and physical functioning.

On the positive side, characteristics of the male gender role may be quite helpful in coping with chronic illness, which can be construed as a problem meant to be solved. To the extent there are clear-cut behaviors that can solve or "control" the problem, men might be especially likely to engage in those behaviors. A study of patients with heart disease showed that men were more likely than women to attribute the cause of their illness to controllable factors (e.g., diet, overworking, alcohol), whereas women were more likely than men to attribute the cause

of their illness to uncontrollable factors (e.g., heredity; Grace et al., 2005). One behavior that is helpful for managing many illnesses is exercise. Exercise, in and of itself, is consistent with the male gender role. Exercise can also be construed as a problem-focused coping behavior. Adolescent males with diabetes are more likely than adolescent females to use exercise as a way to control their illness (Williams, 2000). In general, male adolescents with chronic illness are more likely to perceive they can control their illness than female adolescents (Williams, 2000). To the extent that control is possible and control behaviors are helpful in regulating the illness, this perspective is a healthy one. Agency is an aspect of the male gender role that may reflect this problem-solving orientation. Agency has been linked to positive adjustment to chronic illnesses, such as heart disease (Helgeson, 1993; Fritz, 2000; Helgeson & Mickelson, 2000), prostate cancer (Helgeson & Lepore, 1997; Helgeson & Lepore, 2004), and rheumatoid arthritis (Trudeau et al., 2003). However, the "chronic" aspect of chronic illness suggests control efforts will be limited in their effects. This aspect of illness could be frustrating to men who focus on control.

Thus the male gender role has links to both successful and problematic adjustment to chronic illness. To the extent the illness threatens masculinity, recovery will be difficult. To the extent masculinity can be used to aid recovery, masculinity will be helpful.

Female Gender Role

When I first started interviewing cardiac patients over 10 years ago, I wondered if the female cardiac patient would have the same "Type A" characteristics as the male cardiac patient—impatience and hostility. The first 20 women I interviewed created quite a different picture of the woman with heart disease. Two of these 20 women had been admitted to the hospital for heart attacks the day after their husbands were admitted for potential heart problems. Interestingly, in each case the husband did not sustain a heart attack, but the wife did. The most noteworthy case was the woman I described previously who had put the health care needs of her husband before her own. A common theme that ran throughout the course of my interviews with these 20 women was that their concern with taking care of others and putting others' needs first had adverse consequences for their own health. Some of these women undoubtedly had difficulty with recovery because they continued to take care of others at the expense of taking care of themselves. However, a few women did view their heart attack as a wake-up call—a chance to shift their priorities and put themselves first.

There are a variety of aspects of the female gender role that have implications for adjustment to chronic illness (see Figure 13.13). One aspect is the extent to which caregiving is central to self-esteem. If the caregiver role is central to one's identity and a chronic illness undermines this role, the person will have difficulty adjusting to the illness. This is the issue that concerned many of the women cardiac patients I first interviewed. When taking care of oneself detracts from taking care of others, these women may neglect their own health. One study of cardiac patients showed that women were more likely than men to resume household responsibilities after they were discharged from the hospital (Rose et al., 1996). Another study of cardiac patients found that women were less likely than men to have assistance with household tasks, such as meal preparation and laundry, regardless of whether or not they were married (Young & Kahana, 1993).

The conflict between receiving assistance and providing assistance to others may be especially difficult for women who are highly invested in the caregiving role, such as those who score high on unmitigated communion. Unmitigated communion has been linked to poor adjustment to chronic illnesses such as heart disease (Helgeson, 1993; Fritz, 2000), breast cancer (Helgeson, 2003), rheumatoid arthritis (Trudeau et al., 2003), and diabetes (Helgeson & Fritz, 1996). One reason seems to be that these women neglect their own health in favor of helping others. In one study of heart disease, people who scored high on unmitigated communion were less likely to follow physicians' instructions to reduce household activities (Helgeson, 1993). In another study of heart disease, people who scored high on unmitigated communion were less likely to adhere to physicians' recommended exercise regimens (Fritz, 2000). A study of adolescents with diabetes showed that those who scored high on unmitigated communion had poor control over their diabetes because they were attending to the needs of others instead of themselves (Helgeson & Fritz, 1996).

The female gender role also is implicated in poor adjustment to illnesses that involve alterations in physical appearance. To the extent that concerns with appearance override concerns with physical health, the female gender role is a disadvantage. In one study, adolescent women with cystic fibrosis were more concerned with their physical appearance than their physical health (Miller, Willis, & Wyn, 1993). In another study, adolescent females with diabetes showed particular difficulties following a diabetic diet because of concerns with weight and body image (Williams, 2000). Dieting in the form of restricting food intake can be very dangerous for people with diabetes.

To the extent that successful recovery from chronic illness requires active attempts at control, women may not adjust as well as men. In a study of adolescents with cystic fibrosis, women were less positive about their illness compared to men (Miller et al., 1993). Women were more passive with respect to their illness and felt powerless compared to men (Miller et al., 1993). These are traits consistent with the female gender role. However, others have argued that the passive aspects of the female gender role may be an advantage because certain aspects of chronic illness are not controllable. Women may be more accepting of such situations than men (Fife et al., 1994).

Aspects of the female gender role may facilitate adjustment to chronic illness. The female gender role permits help seeking and reliance on others for support. Studies of children show that girls are more likely than boys to share their illness with others. In a study of adolescents with cystic fibrosis, girls were more likely than boys to have friends with cystic fibrosis (Miller et al., 1993). In another study of children with chronic illnesses, friends were more likely to visit girls who were sick and absent from school than boys (Prout, 1989). Psychological femininity, or communion, has been associated with perceiving support to be available (Helgeson, 1994c). Thus the female gender role can be adaptive in terms of acquiring needed support resources.

TAKE HOME POINTS

- Clear-cut sex differences in adjustment to chronic illness are not apparent.

- Gender provides an important framework within which we can understand the issues that men and women with a chronic illness face.

- The male gender role is advantageous to the extent a chronic illness is construed as a problem meant to be solved, but disadvantageous to the extent it implies weakness and limits men's feelings of control.

- The female gender role can facilitate adjustment to chronic illness by providing support resources but can impede adjustment when physical attractiveness and caregiving issues interfere with taking proper care of oneself.

EATING DISORDERS

Princess Diana, Jane Fonda, Justine Bateman, Elton John, Paula Abdul, Cathy Rigby, and Mary-Kate Olsen—what do they all have in common? They all have had eating disorders (see Figure 13.14).

Definitions and Prevalence

About 7 million females and 1 million males have an eating disorder (NIMH, 2003). The three major eating disorders are anorexia nervosa, bulimia nervosa, and binge-eating disorder. Although the three disorders can be clearly

FIGURE 13.14 Mary-Kate Olsen, an actress, has had an eating disorder.

defined and distinguished from one another, people can have degrees of any one of them. In fact, various degrees of binge eating exist in the normal population (Attie, Brooks-Gunn, & Petersen, 1990).

Anorexia Nervosa.   Of the three, **anorexia nervosa** is the most life-threatening eating disorder. The primary feature of this disorder is the continual pursuit of thinness. The anorexic person has a distorted body image and refuses to maintain a normal weight. One of the diagnostic features is that the anorexic person weighs less than 85% of what is considered normal for that person's age and height. A common symptom of anorexia in women is amenorrhea (cessation of menstrual cycling).

Ironically, anorexia is more common in industrialized societies, where food is plentiful (America Psychiatric Association, 2000). The majority of cases of anorexia (90%) are found in women, and the lifetime incidence in the female population is 0.5%. The onset of anorexia typically occurs between the ages of 14 and 18.

Bulimia Nervosa.   **Bulimia nervosa.** is characterized by recurrent binge eating followed by inappropriate methods to prevent weight gain, such as vomiting, intense exercising, or the use of laxatives, diuretics, and enemas. By far the most common method of purging is vomiting (America Psychiatric Association, 2000). Although any food can be consumed during a binge, foods typically consist of sweets and fats. During the binge, the person usually feels a loss of control. This person constantly thinks about food and weight control. The typical person with bulimia is of average weight but may have been overweight prior to the onset of the disorder. The low weight of an anorexic person is a feature that distinguishes him or her from the bulimic.

There are two types of bulimia: (1) purging, which involves vomiting and using laxatives, diuretics, and enemas, and (2) nonpurging, which involves dieting and exercise and not the other, more extreme methods. As with anorexia, about 90% of bulimia cases are found among women, and between 1% and 3% of women have bulimia (Pike & Striegel-Moore, 1997). The onset of bulimia is somewhat later than anorexia, during late adolescence to early adulthood (Pike & Striegel-Moore, 1997). The incidence of bulimia has increased over the past several decades, whereas the rate of anorexia has stabilized.

Binge-Eating Disorder.   **Binge-eating disorder** is characterized by recurrent binge eating without purging or fasting (America Psychiatric Association, 2000). Binge eating is accompanied by eating rapidly, eating large amounts of food in the absence of hunger, eating in isolation from others, and feelings of guilt and disgust with oneself for eating. Of the three, binge-eating disorder is the most prevalent, affecting 3.5% of women and 2% of men over their lifetimes (Hudson et al., 2007). Binge eating is more common among women than men, but not to the same extent as anorexia or bulimia. The typical onset of binge-eating disorder is young adulthood.

Disturbed Eating Behavior.   Because the prevalence rate of eating disorders in the general population is so small, investigators often study symptoms of bulimia or anorexia. These symptoms are referred to as *disturbed eating behavior*. One of the most frequently used instruments to assess disturbed eating is the Eating Disorder Inventory (Garner, Olmstead, & Polivy, 1983). Three subscales of this inventory have been linked to eating disorders: drive for thinness, symptoms of bulimia, and body dissatisfaction. The items from each of these scales

TABLE 13.6 **Eating Disorder Inventory**

Drive for Thinness
1. I eat sweets and carbohydrates without feeling nervous. *
2. I think about dieting.
3. I feel extremely guilty after overeating.
4. I am terrified of gaining weight.
5. I exaggerate or magnify the importance of weight.
6. I am preoccupied with the desire to be thinner.
7. If I gain a pound, I worry that I will keep gaining.

Bulimia
1. I eat when I am upset.
2. I stuff myself with food.
3. I have gone on eating binges where I have felt that I could not stop.
4. I think about bingeing (overeating).
5. I eat moderately in front of others and stuff myself when they are gone.
6. I have thought of trying to vomit in order to lose weight.
7. I eat or drink in secrecy.

Body Dissatisfaction
1. I think that my stomach is too big.
2. I think that my thighs are too large.
3. I think that my stomach is just the right size. *
4. I feel satisfied with the shape of my body. *
5. I like the shape of my buttocks. *
6. I think my hips are too big.
7. I think that my thighs are just the right size. *
8. I think that my buttocks are too large.
9. I think that my hips are just the right size. *

* These items are reverse scored meaning less endorsement is indicative of greater problems.
Source: Garner et al. (1983).

are shown in Table 13.6. Many of the studies reviewed in this section have used this instrument or a similar one.

Consequences

The consequences of eating disorders range from minor to severe (Pike & Striegel-Moore, 1997). The average duration of anorexia is 1.7 years, whereas the average duration of bulimia and binge-eating disorder is nearly 8 years (Hudson et al., 2007). Gastrointestinal problems and colon problems may result from repeated use of laxatives. Dental problems may occur from repeated vomiting. Bone problems may occur with anorexia and place one at risk for osteoporosis. Women with eating disorders are likely to have problems getting pregnant. People with anorexia are likely to suffer from hypotension (low blood pressure), which could cause cardiovascular problems. One study reported possible long-term effects of anorexia on the structure of the brain, some of which may not be reversible (Katzman et al., 1997).

With treatment, 60% of people with anorexia recover completely, 20% partly recover, and 20% do not improve (NIMH, 2003). The prognosis is more favorable if anorexia is caught early. Anorexia can result in death due to starvation; the mortality rate is .56% per year or 5.6% per decade, which is by far the highest death rate for any cause of death among females between the ages of 15 to 24 (NIMH, 2001).

Etiology

The etiology of eating disorders is unclear. Eating disorders often co-occur with other disorders, such as depression, anxiety, and substance abuse (Hudson et al., 2007). Researchers have examined genetic links, demographic factors that may predispose one to eating disorders, social factors, and a variety of psychological factors, including difficulties with achievement and lack of control.

Genes.   The heritability component of eating disorders is questionable (Pike & Striegel-Moore, 1997). Some twin studies have found higher rates of eating disorders in monozygotic than dizygotic twins (Klump, Kaye, & Strober, 2001). Because monozygotic twins share 100% of their genes and dizygotic twins share only half of their genes, a higher concordance rate among monozygotic than dizygotic twins is evidence for a genetic influence. However, the correspondence does not occur until puberty, suggesting an interaction between hormones and genes. Twin studies suggest that genes account for 58% to 76% of anorexia and 54% to 83% of bulimia. Eating disorders are more common among women who come from families with a female member who has an eating disorder (Striegel-Moore & Cachelin, 1999). This overlap could be due to shared genes or shared environment.

Demographics.   High socioeconomic status is typically viewed as a protective factor when it comes to mental health. Eating disorders, in particular anorexia, used to be characterized as an upper-class affliction. Today no clear evidence indicates that education or income is related to eating disorders (Striegel-Moore & Cachelin, 1999). Eating disorders are more prevalent among White persons than Black persons (Striegel-Moore et al., 2003), among college students, and among people in certain professions, such as dancers, actors, models, and athletes (Attie et al., 1990; Walters & Kendler, 1995). Among men, eating disorders are especially prevalent among athletes who have strict weight limitations placed on them, such as wrestlers and jockeys (Thompson & Sherman, 1999). In the late 1990s, three college wrestlers died because of the extreme behaviors they used to lose weight before a match (Thompson, 1998); two were working out in rubber suits and one was riding an exercise bike and refused to drink water.

Males and females with eating disorders have a similar age of onset and similar symptoms (Woodside et al., 2001), although men with eating disorders are more likely to attempt suicide than women (Bramon-Bosch, Troop, & Treasure, 2000). One difference is that homosexuality is a risk factor for eating disorders among men. Eating disorders are more common among gay men than heterosexual men (Russell & Keel 2002), partly because of a greater preference for thinness and higher body dissatisfaction among gay men (Boroughs & Thompson, 2002). About 20% of men with eating disorders are gay, compared to 3% to 5% of the general population of men being gay (Andersen, 1999). The rate of eating disorders among gay men appears to be more similar to that of heterosexual women, whereas lesbians have lower rates of eating disorders compared to heterosexual women (Conner, Johnson, & Grogan, 2004).

Much of the research on eating disorders has taken place in the United States, Canada, and England. One study compared the rate of eating disturbances among college women in the United States to Japan. Despite the fact that Japanese women were thinner on average than American women, the rate of eating disturbances was similar (Mukai, Kambara, & Sasaki, 1998). The authors suggested that eating disorders may become more prevalent in countries that internalize Western culture's association of thinness with physical attractiveness.

Female Gender Role. Eating disorders have been linked to features of the female gender role. First, the female gender role places a high value on physical attractiveness. Second, women are interpersonally oriented, so others' opinions are important to them. Both of these concerns play a role in eating disorders.

Gender intensification could provide a framework for understanding eating disorders as it does for depression. Eating disorders first appear during adolescence when gender roles become salient. But, have gender roles been linked to eating disorders? A meta-analytic review of the literature found a small positive relation between psychological femininity, or communion, and disturbed eating behavior ($d = +.14$; Murnen & Smolak, 1997). However, more recent studies have failed to find a relation (e.g., Hepp, Spindler, & Milos, 2005).

There may be other aspects of the female gender role that are more strongly linked to eating disturbances. *Negative femininity* seems to play a role in the development of eating disorders. Negative femininity includes being dependent, weak, timid, and needing others' approval. In studies that examine the positive and negative aspects of femininity, only negative femininity has emerged as a predictor of disordered eating behavior—among both heterosexuals and homosexuals (Lakkis et al., 1999;

Paxton & Sculthorpe, 1991). Unmitigated communion is another gender-related trait that has been implicated in eating disorders (Helgeson et al., 2007). Unmitigated communion individuals have low self-esteem and evaluate themselves based on others' views. Thus they may be more vulnerable to societal pressures to be thin. Unmitigated communion is related to a poor body image (Helgeson, 2003).

Societal Factors. One perspective on eating disorders places the blame on society's obsession with dieting and the pressure for thinness among women. Not surprisingly, dieting appears to be an antecedent to eating disorders (Cogan & Ernsberger, 1999). The majority of women in the United States are currently dieting or have dieted in the past. About 40% of women and 24% of men report they are currently dieting (Wing & Klem, 1997). A 2005 Gallup Poll showed that American women had made an average of 10 serious attempts to lose weight and men had made 5 (Saad, 2005). A national study of high school students found that 46% were currently trying to lose weight, with higher rates for females (62%) than males (30%; Centers for Disease Control and Prevention, 2006b). A sizable number had gone without eating for the previous 24 hours to lose weight: 17% females and 8% males. One problem with dieting is that it causes metabolism to decrease over time, making it increasingly difficult to lose weight. Thus, after initial pounds are shed, more extreme methods are required to achieve the same rate of weight loss.

U.S. society's image of the ideal woman is an extremely thin form, really without shape. Toy models such as Barbie display unrealistic body shapes. When the measurements of Barbie were compared to the actual measurements of a sample of 18- to 35-year-old women, the chances of finding Barbie's measurements in this population were estimated to be less than 1 in 100,000 (Norton et al., 1996). The standards for thinness have grown increasingly strict and have become more unrealistic over the past 3 to 4 decades (Siever, 1996). *Playboy* centerfolds and Miss America contestants became increasingly thin between 1957 and 1978 (Garner et al., 1980). The standards of the ideal male body also have changed. One group of investigators examined changes in male action figures over the past 30 years, in particular, G. I. Joe and Star Wars characters (Pope et al., 1999). Over time, the figures have grown more muscular. Again, if the dimensions of these figures were translated into human beings, only the rare adult male would meet these specifications. The authors contend that changes in these action toys reflect changing standards of the male body image. These changes could be linked to eating disturbances in men.

Today, young women are surrounded by media exposure to thinness through magazines and television. Patients with anorexia and bulimia often recall models in magazines as motivators to lose weight (Levine & Smolak, 1996). During the 20th century, eating disorders rose as the media gave greater attention to thinness (Levine & Smolak, 1996). Exposure to media, including magazines and television, is associated with disordered eating and lower body satisfaction (Levine & Smolak, 1996). However, much of this research is correlational, meaning cause and effect cannot be determined. It is not clear whether the media's attention to thinness increases the prevalence of eating disorders, whether people who have eating disorders pay more attention to the media, or some third variable causes eating disorders and sensitivity to media attention to thinness. One longitudinal study partly addressed this issue by showing that frequent magazine reading was associated with an *increase* in unhealthy weight control measures (e.g., fasting, skipping meals, smoking cigarettes) among female adolescents 5 years later (van den Berg et al., 2007).

Laboratory studies can go further to disentangle cause from effect by observing the effects of brief media exposure on body image. A meta-analysis of these kinds of studies showed a clear adverse effect of exposure to slender female body image ideals on body satisfaction ($d = -.31$; Groesz, Levine, & Murnen, 2002). After exposure to these images, females estimate their bodies are larger, wish they were thinner, and are unhappy with their bodies. Effects were stronger for adolescents than adults.

Concerns about thinness come from sources other than the media, such as family and friends, who are often dieting themselves. Pressure from the media, parents, and peers has been linked to eating disorders in both men and women, but the nature of the pressure differs—girls are pressured to lose weight whereas boys are pressured to gain weight and accrue muscle mass (Ricciardelli & McCabe, 2004). Eating disorders are associated with families who express concerns about weight and with families in which parents are overly critical of weight and appearance (American Psychological Association, 2007). Mothers' attitudes toward their own body and toward their daughter's body have been related to eating disorders among daughters. There may be ethnic differences in mother-daughter communication about weight. In a 3-year longitudinal study of eighth- and ninth-graders, White mothers showed increasing concern with their daughters' physical appearance and encouraged girls to make changes in their physical appearance, whereas Black mothers gave their daughters more favorable feedback about their appearance (Nichter, 2000). Not surprisingly, the Black girls expressed fewer concerns about their weight than the White girls.

Peers also can influence eating behavior. The previously mentioned study of eighth- and ninth-graders showed girls engage in "fat talk" with one another (Nichter, 2000). Fat talk begins with one girl stating, "I'm so fat!" and may be followed up with a friend replying, "No, you're not fat." A dialogue begins in which body weight is the focus of attention. When one person begins engaging in unhealthy eating behavior, friends may follow. A study of sorority members showed that bingeing behaviors were correlated across the girls (Crandall, 1988). Over time, these relations became stronger. As sorority members' relationships strengthened, they grew to have a stronger influence on one another. Friends' bingeing behavior at the beginning of the study predicted participants' subsequent bingeing behavior 1 year later. In one sorority, popularity was directly linked to greater reports of bingeing.

If peers can promote eating disturbances, we would also expect that peers could help one another avoid eating disorders. One set of researchers tried to capitalize on this idea by designing a peer support group intervention to deter eating disorders among college women (Mann et al., 1997). Women were randomly assigned to a control group or an intervention group. In the intervention group, peers who had recovered from an eating disorder shared their experiences and provided information. At the end of the study, much to the investigators' surprise, the intervention group showed more symptoms of eating disorders than the control group. The authors reasoned that listening to peers discuss eating disorders normalized the behavior and reduced the stigma associated with eating disorders. Studies such as this one show the unintended impact that peers can have on eating disorders.

Social factors also might explain why eating disorders are more prevalent among gay than heterosexual men and less prevalent among lesbians than heterosexual women. Gay men report more dissatisfaction with their body compared to heterosexual men, whereas lesbians report greater satisfaction with their body compared to heterosexual women (Lakkis et al., 1999; Williamson & Hartley, 1998). In a study of gay and heterosexual men, body dissatisfaction and low self-esteem were associated with eating disturbances among gay men but not heterosexual men (Williamson & Hartley, 1998). Body image is important to gay men for several reasons. First, the gay community emphasizes youth, thinness, and physical attractiveness (Williamson, 1999). Second, the partners of gay men are also men, and men value physical attractiveness in their partner more than women.

Psychological Factors A general psychological theory of eating disorders is that they stem from feelings of a lack of autonomy, a lack of control, and a lack of a sense of self in combination with a striving for perfection and achievement (Attie et al., 1990). Weight loss is one way to fulfill these needs: Losing weight is a way to gain control over one's body and has the potential to enhance self-esteem. Eating disorders have been linked to a high need for others' approval and a concern with pleasing others (Leary et al., 1994). In a longitudinal study of 12- to 16-year-olds, perfectionism predicted anorexia over the next 2 to 8 years (Tyrka et al., 2002). Many investigators have argued that eating disorders emerge in women during adolescence because it is during this time that girls feel a loss of control, become concerned with others' views of them, and become aware of the limitations of the female gender role with respect to achievement (Attie et al., 1990; Silverstein & Perlick, 1995). One way of responding to these challenges is to exert control over weight.

Eating disorders have been linked to a host of other problems that female adolescents suffer, such as anxiety and depression (Silverstein & Perlick, 1995; Walters & Kendler, 1995), and a history of physical and sexual abuse (Striegel-Moore & Cachelin, 1999). Eating disorders are one way that distress manifests itself among these girls. However, the sex ratio of eating disorders is much larger than the sex difference in depression; thus eating disorders must be more than a manifestation of psychological distress.

TAKE HOME POINTS

- There are three major kinds of eating disorders: anorexia nervosa, bulimia nervosa, and binge-eating disorder. Anorexia is the most lethal of the three.

- Eating disorders tend to emerge during adolescence.

- It is during adolescence that girls experience body changes (in particular, an increase in body fat), become dissatisfied with their bodies, and become increasingly concerned with their appearance and how others view them. During adolescence, girls also recognize limiting factors associated with the female gender role.

- Contributing factors to eating disorders include genes, gender roles, psychological factors (e.g., need for control and perfectionism), and the social environment.

- The media focus on extremely thin images of women has been implicated in eating disorders. Experimental studies have shown that media exposure affects girls' views of their bodies.

SUICIDE

In 1994, Kurt Cobain, 27 years old and lead singer of the popular alternative rock band Nirvana, committed suicide by shooting himself. In 1993, Vince Foster, a White House aide to President Clinton, committed suicide also by shooting himself. Cobain had a history of depression, drug abuse, and suspected suicide attempts. He left a suicide note indicating he lacked the excitement for creating music and felt guilty that the roar of the crowd no longer had an effect on him (Love, 1994). Foster had recently started taking antidepressants. It is

alleged he left a suicide note indicating a sense of failure in his role in Washington (Carlson, 1993). There are some similarities between these two cases: Both used firearms; both had a history of mental health problems; both were men.

Despite the fact that women are more depressed than men, men actually commit suicide more frequently than women. There is an even more interesting paradox: Men commit suicide more frequently than women, but women attempt suicide more frequently than men. In this section of the chapter, I provide statistical information on suicide rates and attempts and then discuss some of the factors associated with suicide and suicide attempts in men and women.

Incidence

Suicide is more common than people think. Did you know more people die from suicide than homicide? Suicide is the third leading cause of death for people between the ages of 15 and 24. The suicide rate is twice as high among White people as Black, Asian, and Hispanic people (National Center for Health Statistics, 2006a). In 2004, 31,647 people committed suicide. As shown in Figure 13.15, the size of sex difference is relatively stable across the life span until old age. Among the elderly, there is a dramatic increase in men's suicide rates, which increases the magnitude of the sex difference. Among persons 65 years and older, men have over 7 times the rate of suicide as women. The sex difference is also a bit larger among the younger cohorts: Among 20- to 24-year-olds, men are nearly 6 times as likely as women to commit suicide. The size of the sex difference is similar among White and non-White persons in the United States.

Sex differences in suicide extend across cultures. The sex difference (male:female ratio) in suicide rates for 18 countries is shown in Table 13.7. In a study of 70 countries, men had

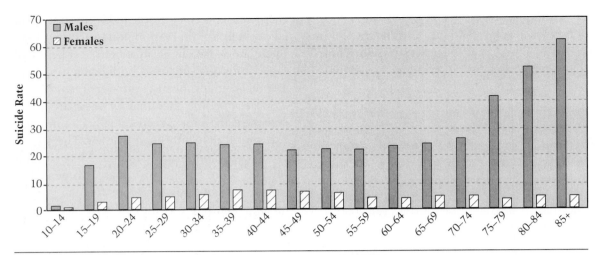

FIGURE 13.15   Suicide rates by sex and age. Men have higher suicide rates than women at all ages. The sex difference is particularly high among young people and the elderly.
Source: Adapted from National Center for Health Statistics (2006a).

TABLE 13.7   **SEX DIFFERENCES IN SUICIDE**

Nation	Male:Female Suicide Ratio
Australia	3.79
Austria	2.91
Belize	13.44
Canada	3.60
Chile	7.29
Denmark	2.81
France	2.92
Germany	2.91
Ireland	5.22
Italy	3.36
Japan	2.75
Luxembourg	5.29
Mexico	5.40
New Zealand	4.71
Sweden	2.33
Thailand	3.16
United Kingdom	3.48
United States	4.29

Source: World Health Organization (2005).

higher suicide rates than women in all countries except China and Papua New Guinea (Canetto & Lester, 1995). The size of the sex difference was smaller in Asian countries. The sex difference in suicide among adolescents also holds across other Western cultures, with the United States having the largest sex difference, a 6 to 1 ratio (Moller-Leimkuhler, 2003).

The most common method of suicide for both men and women is the use of a gun. Interestingly, more deaths by gun are due to suicide than homicide. However, men are more likely than women to use guns. Women are more likely than men to use poisons. The first method is more deadly than the latter. However, the difference in methods does not account for the sex difference in suicide rates. Even within a given method, suicide attempts are more likely to be fatal among men compared to women (Canetto & Lester, 1995).

Pampel (1998) examined suicide rates from 1953 to 1992. Sex differences in suicide decreased from the 1950s to the 1970s but then rose again in the 1980s, due to a greater increase in suicide among men relative to women. The suicide rates of adolescents have decreased from 1990 to 2003 but more recently are on the rise (Centers for Disease Control and Prevention, 2007c). Although the suicide rate is still highest among White males, more recently the greatest rate of increase has been among Black males: Between 1980 and 1995, adolescent Black males' suicide rates doubled. Firearms accounted for two thirds of Black male suicide.

Suicide rates are not as easy to estimate as you might think. The official statistics on suicide rates are likely to be underestimates because some suicides are mistakenly classified as other causes of death. This misclassification may lead to a greater underestimation of female than male suicide. Women are more likely than men to use ambiguous methods, such as poisoning, which are less easily classified as suicide (Canetto & Lester, 1995). Men, by contrast, are more likely to use guns; it is easier to determine that a self-inflicted gunshot was a suicide.

Attempts

Although men commit suicide more frequently than women, women attempt suicide more often than men and express more suicidal thoughts than men. This paradox holds across most Western societies (Canetto & Sakinofsky, 1998). Among adolescents, females also report more suicidal thinking and more suicide attempts than males. Among high school students, females attempt suicide at over twice the rate of males (National Center for Health Statistics, 2005). This sex difference is limited to White and Hispanic students. Among African Americans, the rate is similar for males and females—lower than White females but higher than White males. Suicide attempts are difficult to estimate, however. For example, an overdose of drugs can be interpreted as a suicide attempt or as an accident. Some have suggested that men's suicide attempts are underreported (Canetto & Sakinofsky, 1998). Both attempting suicide and not succeeding are considered weak behaviors inconsistent with the strength and decisiveness of the male gender role; thus men may not admit to making a suicide attempt, and clinicians may be less likely to consider the possibility that a drug overdose in a man was a suicide attempt.

The Gender Paradox

One methodological explanation for the paradox of men's higher suicide rates and women's higher suicide attempts is that men's attempts are underreported and women's actual suicides are underestimated because they are classified as other causes of death (e.g., accidental).

A theoretical explanation behind the gender paradox lies in gender-role socialization. According to Canetto and Sakinofsky (1998), "Women and men will tend to adopt the self-destructive behaviors that are congruent with the gender scripts of their cultures" (p. 17). Suicide is considered masculine behavior, but suicide attempts are considered feminine behavior. Among men, committing suicide is considered to be a powerful response to some kind of failure; attempting but not completing a suicide is often construed as weak behavior and viewed negatively, especially in men. Males are more likely than females to report being concerned with societal disapproval of suicide (Rich et al., 1992), which may explain why their suicide attempts are successful. The gender paradox in suicide attempts and suicide rates is most prominent among adolescents and young adults, the very people who are most concerned with adhering to gender roles (Canetto & Sakinofsky, 1998).

Factors Associated with Suicide Among Adults

Among adults, suicide and suicide attempts have been linked to substance abuse and depression. The link of suicide to depression is problematic, however, because a suicide attempt might lead to a diagnosis of depression. One study of suicide attempters found that depression predicted subsequent suicide within the next 6 years for both men and women (Skogman, Alsen, & Ojehagen, 2004). Evidence in the United States and from other cultures suggests the link between suicide and alcohol abuse is stronger among men than women (Canetto & Lester, 1995).

One antecedent to suicide is the breakup of a relationship. In the United States, the divorce rate is positively correlated with the suicide rate, and the marriage rate is negatively correlated with the suicide rate (Lester & Yang, 1998). In other words, as more people are married, fewer people commit suicide; as more people become divorced, more people commit suicide. In a study of 29 nations, suicide rates were positively associated with divorce rates and negatively associated with marriage rates (Lester & Yang, 1998). In addition, the association with divorce rates was stronger than the association with marriage rates. Divorce rates are also more strongly associated with suicide rates for men than women across a variety of countries (Lester & Yang, 1998). This finding supports the research reviewed in Chapter 11 that marriage is more health protective for men than for women. Suicide rates are higher among single, widowed, and divorced men compared to married men (Canetto & Lester, 1995).

Marital status also influences how people view suicide. Suicide is viewed as less acceptable by married than unmarried people across the United States, Australia, and many European nations (Stack, 1998a). The difference in views of suicide by married and unmarried people is greatest among men, meaning married men find suicide the least acceptable. Views on the acceptability of suicide are important because these views are linked to suicide attempts and suicide completions (Stack, 1998a).

Thus suicide rates in men are linked, in part, to the absence of marriage, which may signify the absence of emotional support. Women's greater integration into social relationships may protect them against suicide. Women not only receive support from network members but provide support to them as well. The fact that women have people to take care of, such as a husband and children, may make them less likely to commit suicide (Canetto & Lester, 1995).

Suicide rates also increase as unemployment increases. This has been shown in the United States as well as in other nations (Lester & Yang, 1998). Suicide rates are more strongly tied to unemployment rates among men than among women. In a study of 15 countries, unemployed people were more accepting of suicide than were employed people (Stack, 1998a).

Among men, suicide is associated with divorce and unemployment; among women, suicide seems to be related to their status. In countries where the status of women is low, such as China, India, and Japan, the suicide rates of women are relatively high (Canetto & Lester, 1995). In countries where women have a low status and are frequently abused by husbands, suicide among women is almost considered acceptable. Suicide by a woman in these societies (such as Papua New Guinea) is construed as an assertive act of rebellion by the woman (Counts, 1987). The husband suffers from public humiliation because her act of assertion undermines his authority and power in the family.

Gender roles have also been implicated in suicide. In a study of the elderly in the United States, the suicide rate of men and women in each state was examined in relation to agentic variables (indicators of financial and social status, such as income and education) and communal variables (indicators of social stability and social environment stress, such as moving and crowding; Coren & Hewitt, 1999). The investigators found that agentic variables more strongly predicted suicide among elderly men than women, and communal variables more strongly predicted suicide among elderly women. Finally, gay, lesbian, and bisexual people are more likely than heterosexual people to report suicidal thinking and attempt suicide (Balsam et al., 2005; Cochran & Mays, 2006).

Factors Associated with Suicide Among Adolescents

Not surprisingly, suicide and suicide attempts in adolescents are associated with other mental disorders, in particular, depression and substance abuse (Lester & Yang, 1998). In one study, 80% of those who attempted suicide could have been classified as having mental disorders, such as major depression, alcohol dependence, drug dependence, or disruptive behavior disorders (Andrews & Lewinsohn, 1992). It is not clear whether suicide and suicidal behavior are more strongly associated with depression in males or females. Two studies showed a stronger link in males (Andrews & Lewinsohn, 1992; Wannan & Fombonne, 1998), and two showed a stronger link in females (Brent, 1995; Prigerson & Slimack, 1999). One longitudinal study of 14- to 18-year-olds showed that a previous suicide attempt predicted a subsequent suicide attempt by age 24 in women but not men (Lewinsohn, Rohde, & Seeley, 2001), suggesting more of a history of suicidal problems in females. One study suggested that depression may be directly linked to suicide in females but indirectly linked to suicide in males through substance abuse (Metha et al., 1998). However, the literature also is not clear as to whether alcohol use is more strongly linked to suicidal behavior in males or females (Brent, 1995; Wannan & Fombonne, 1998) and whether antisocial behavior is more strongly linked to suicidal behavior in males or females (Brent, 1995; Prigerson & Slimack, 1999; Wannan & Fombonne, 1998). In one study, investigators examined suicidal thinking in a high-risk group: adolescents who had a friend

commit suicide in the prior 6 years. Aggressive behavior predicted suicidal thinking among adolescent boys, and depression predicted suicidal thinking among adolescent girls (Prigerson & Slimack, 1999).

Social relationships also play a role in adolescent suicide. In a 1-year longitudinal study of fifth-graders, poor family functioning, as indicated by mothers, was associated with increased suicidal ideation over the year (Garber et al., 1998). Lack of support from and troubled relationships with family and friends have been associated with greater suicidal ideation and more frequent suicide attempts (Dubow et al., 1989; Wannan & Fombonne, 1998). In a study of depressed adolescents, suicide attempts were predicted by a lack of family support and a loss of support over the prior 3 months (Morano, Cisler, & Lemerond, 1993). Loss of support was measured by asking respondents if they had lost anyone in the prior 3 months who had been important to them. Suicide among adolescents has also been associated with the breakup of romantic relationships. In one study, investigators interviewed family members of adolescents who had committed suicide to find out what kinds of life events occurred in the prior year. Compared to a control group of adolescents, family members of suicide victims reported that the adolescents were more likely to have experienced problems in romantic relationships, including breakups (Brent et al., 1993).

TAKE HOME POINTS

- Men commit suicide more than women. This sex difference appears across the life span and persists across cultures.

- Women attempt suicide more than men.

- This gender paradox is partly explained by methodological issues. Suicide in women may be underestimated because women are more likely to use ambiguous methods (e.g., overdose of pills) than men which may be misclassified as accidents. Men's suicide attempts may be underestimated because men are less likely than women to admit to a failed suicide attempt.

- Suicide in both men and women is likely to be associated with other mental health problems, such as depression and substance abuse.

- Among adults, marital breakup and unemployment are linked to suicide—especially in men.

- Among both adolescents and adults, relationship breakups have been linked to suicide.

SUMMARY

A consistent and pervasive sex difference in depression in the U.S. population extends to other cultures. The difference is on the order of 2:1 (female:male), but may be larger in studies of people with major depressive disorder. Sex differences in depression emerge during adolescence and persist over the life span. Sex differences in depression may be affected by a response bias on the part of clinicians and respondents; clinicians may be more likely to recognize or interpret symptoms as depression in women than in men. Because depression is inconsistent with the male gender role, men may be more reluctant than women to admit, report, or seek help for depression.

There are numerous theories of sex differences in depression, tapping biological, psychological, and social factors. Little evidence indicates that genes can explain sex differences in depression. Although hormonal changes have been associated with mood changes, the evidence is inconsistent as to which hormone is protective or harmful at what time. It is more likely that hormonal fluctuation rather than a level of a particular hormone is involved in depression.

Psychological theories of depression suggest women are socialized in ways that lead them to perceive less control than men over their environment. Thus women are more vulnerable to learned helplessness, which can lead to depression. Consistent with this theory, women may be more likely than men to interpret negative events in a pessimistic light. The attributional style theory of depression suggests women are more likely than men to exhibit a pessimistic attributional style and less likely to exhibit the self-serving bias.

Other theories of sex differences in depression focus on the stressors that men and women face and how they cope with them. The coping literature distinguishes between problem-focused and emotion-focused coping, which may not be useful when studying gender. Research suggests that women may be more likely than men to engage in most coping strategies, which may be a result rather than a cause of women's distress. One promising theory of sex differences in depression focuses on a particular maladaptive form of coping, rumination. A great deal of evidence suggests women are more likely than men to respond to stressful events by ruminating about them, and rumination is linked to depression.

There is little evidence that women experience more trauma or stressful life events than men, but women do experience more of a specific kind of trauma or stressor—those that involve relationships. Women report more stressful events that involve relationships, and the association of relationship stressors to distress is stronger for women than for men. It is women's differential vulnerability to stress rather than differential exposure to stress that best explains depression.

The last theory of depression focused on the female gender role. Two aspects of the female gender role must be distinguished: communion and unmitigated communion. Whereas communion is unrelated to depression, unmitigated communion is consistently associated with depression. People characterized by unmitigated communion take on others' problems as their own and become overly involved in helping others. Aside from this specific personality trait, caregiving has been linked more broadly to the female gender role and may be linked to depression.

Regardless of which theory best explains sex difference in depression, the onset during adolescence must be addressed. Several challenges of adolescence were reviewed that might explain this onset, including body image changes and strains in relationships. These events might activate depression in girls who are at risk for depression.

In terms of adjustment to chronic illness, it does not appear that there are clear-cut sex differences. However, gender does provide an important framework within which we can understand the issues that men and women with a chronic illness face. The male gender role is advantageous to the extent a chronic illness is construed as a problem meant to be solved, but disadvantageous to the extent it implies weakness and limits men's feelings of control. The female gender role can facilitate adjustment to chronic illness by providing support resources but can impede adjustment when physical attractiveness and caregiving issues interfere with taking proper care of oneself.

Another mental health problem discussed in this chapter was eating disorders, which are more common in women than in men and more likely to arise during adolescence than at any other time in life. Many of the theories of eating disorders are linked to adolescence. During adolescence, girls' bodies change and girls become more aware of societal pressures to be thin. It is also during adolescence that women recognize the limitations placed on the female gender role and on their control more generally. Eating disorders may be a manifestation of attempts to exert control.

The last mental health problem reviewed was suicide. Men commit suicide more frequently than women at all ages and across most cultures, but women contemplate suicide and attempt suicide more frequently than men. Substance abuse, depression, and impaired social relations all play a role in suicidal behavior among adolescents and adults.

DISCUSSION QUESTIONS

1. Which methodological bias do you believe is most likely to undermine sex differences in depression?
2. What kind of experiences during childhood, adolescence, and adulthood do females face compared to males that might instill learned helplessness?
3. Give an example of a pessimistic attributional explanation for catching a cold.
4. Explain how rumination leads to depression.
5. What is the difference between the differential exposure and the differential vulnerability hypotheses concerning

the relation of stressful events to depression?

6. Which aspects of gender roles are related to depression?

7. What are some of the reasons that sex differences in depression emerge during adolescence?

8. Describe the aspects of the male gender role and the female gender role that hinder and facilitate adjustment to chronic illness.

9. Considering the traits of agency and communion, characterize the couple that would adapt the best to chronic illness.

10. How does society contribute to the development of eating disorders in women?

11. Discuss how the difficulties in documenting suicide rates and suicide attempts might alter the sex difference in suicide and suicide attempts.

12. What social factors are associated with suicide in males and females?

SUGGESTED READING

Canetto, S. S., & Lester, D. (1995). Gender and the primary prevention of suicide mortality. *American Association of Suicidology, 25*(1), 58–69.

Groesz, L. M., Levine, M. P., & Murnen, S. K. (2002). The effect of experimental presentation of thin media images on body satisfaction: A meta-analytic review. *International Journal of Eating Disorders, 31*, 1–16.

Helgeson, V. S., & Fritz, H. L. (1998). A theory of unmitigated communion. *Personality and Social Psychology Review, 2*, 173–183.

Hughes, T. L., Smith, C., & Dan, A. (Eds.). (2003). *Mental health issues for sexual minority women: Redefining women's mental health.* New York: Harrington Park Press.

Nolen-Hoeksema, S. (2004). The etiology of gender differences in depression. In C. M. Mazure & G. Puryear (Eds), *Understanding depression in women: Applying empirical research to practice and policy* (pp. 9–43). Washington, DC: American Psychological Association.

Silverstein B., & Perlick, D. (1995). *The cost of competence: Why inequality causes depression, eating disorders, and illness in women.* New York: Oxford University Press.

Special Issue of *American Psychologist* (2007). Special Issue: Eating Disorders, Vol. 62.

Worell, J., & Goodheart, C. D. (Eds.) (2006). *Handbook of girls' and women's psychological health.* New York: Oxford University Press.

KEY TERMS

Anorexia nervosa—Eating disorder characterized by the continual pursuit of thinness, a distorted body image, and refusal to maintain a weight that is more than 85% of what is considered normal for the person's age and height.

Binge-eating disorder—Eating disorder characterized by recurrent binge eating without purging or fasting.

Body objectification—The experience of one's body being treated as an object to be evaluated and used by others.

Bulimia nervosa—Eating disorder characterized by recurrent binge eating followed by purging via vomiting, laxatives, diuretics, enemas, and/or exercising.

Clinical depression—Another name for major depressive disorder, the critical feature of which is that the person must have experienced a set of depressive symptoms for a period no shorter than 2 weeks.

Different cause theory—Suggestion that there are different causes of girls' and boys' depression and the cause of girls' depression increases during adolescence.

Differential exposure—Idea that men and women are exposed to a different number of or kinds of stressors.

Differential item functioning—Idea that some items are more likely to be associated with a trait, such as depression, among men versus women.

Differential vulnerability—Idea that certain stressors are more strongly linked to distress in one sex than the other.

Emotion-focused coping—Approach to stressful situations in which individuals attempt to accommodate themselves to the stressor.

Externalizing behavior—Aggressive and disagreeable behavior.

Gender intensification—Gender roles becoming salient during adolescence, causing boys and girls to adhere more strongly to these roles.

Interactive theory—Suggestion that being female always poses a risk for depression and the events of adolescence activate that risk.

Internalizing behavior—Introspective and ruminating behavior.

Learned helplessness—Learning that our actions are independent of outcomes, which then leads us to stop responding (give up) in other situations.

Pessimistic (depressive) attributional style—Tendency to make internal, stable, and global attributions for negative events.

Precipitating factors—Environmental events that trigger the emergence of a disorder (e.g., depression).

Problem-focused coping—Approach to stressful situations in which we attempt to alter the stressor itself.

Psychological reactance—Reaction to a perceived threat to control that involves doing the opposite of what is demanded.

Relative coping—Likelihood that men or women use one coping strategy compared to another strategy.

Same cause theory—Suggestion that the same factor could cause depression in both men and women, but the factor increases during adolescence only for girls.

Self-serving bias—Making internal attributions for successes and external attributions for failures.

Susceptibility factors—Innate, usually biological, factors that place one group (e.g., women) at greater risk for a disorder (e.g., depression) than another group.

REFERENCES

Abbey, A., & Harnish, R. J. (1995). Perception of sexual intent: The role of gender, alcohol consumption, and rape supportive attitudes. *Sex Roles, 32,* 297–313.

Abdelrahman, A. I., Rodriguez, G., Ryan, J. A., French, J. F., & Weinbaum, D. (1998). The epidemiology of substance use among middle school students: The impact of school, familial, community and individual risk factors. *Journal of Child and Adolescent Substance Abuse, 8*(1), 55–75.

Aboud, F. E., Mendelson, M. J., & Purdy, K. T. (2003). Cross-race peer relations and friendship quality. *International Journal of Behavioral Development, 27,* 165–173.

Abrams, D., Viki, G. T., Masser, B., & Bohner, G. (2003). Perceptions of stranger and acquaintance rape: The role of benevolent and hostile sexism in victim blame and rape proclivity. *Journal of Personality and Social Psychology, 84,* 111–125.

Abramson, L. Y., Seligman, M. E. P., & Teasdale, J. D. (1978). Learned helplessness in humans: Critique and reformulation. *Journal of Abnormal Psychology, 87,* 49–74.

Adams, S., Kuebli, J., Boyle, P. A., & Fivush, R. (1995). Gender differences in parent-child conversations about past emotions: A longitudinal investigation. *Sex Roles, 33,* 309–323.

Aday, R. H., Kehoe, G. C., & Farney, L. A. (2006). Impact of senior center friendships on aging women who live alone. *Journal of Women & Aging, 18,* 57–73.

Afifi, W. A., & Burgoon, J. K. (1998). "We never talk about that": A comparison of cross-sex friendships and dating relationships on uncertainty and topic avoidance. *Personal Relationships, 5*(3), 255–272.

Afifi, W. A., & Faulkner, S. L. (2000). On being 'just friends': The frequency and impact of sexual activity in cross-sex friendships. *Journal of Social and Personal Relationships, 17,* 205–222.

Ai, A. L., Peterson, C., Dunkle, R. E., Saunders, D. G., Bolling, S. F., & Buchtel, H. A. (1997). How gender affects psychological adjustment one year after coronary artery bypass graft surgery. *Women and Health, 26*(4), 45–65.

Akiyama, H., Elliott, K., & Antonucci, T. C. (1996). Same-sex and cross-sex relationships. *Journal of Gerontology, 51B*(6), 374–382.

Alansari, B. M. (2006). Gender differences in depression among undergraduates from seventeen Islamic countries. *Social Behavior and Personality, 34,* 729–738.

Albert, B., Brown, S., & Flanigan, C. (Eds.). (2003). *14 and younger: The sexual behavior of young adolescents (summary).* Washington, DC: National Campaign to Prevent Teen Pregnancy.

Ali, A., & Toner, B. B. (1996). Gender differences in depressive response: The role of social support. *Sex Roles, 35,* 281–293.

Allan, K., & Coltrane, S. (1996). Gender displaying television commercials: A comparative study of television commercials in the 1950s and 1980s. *Sex Roles, 35,* 185–203.

Allgood-Merten, B., Lewinsohn, P. M., & Hops, H. (1990). Sex differences and adolescent depression. *Journal of Abnormal Psychology, 99,* 53–63.

Almeida, D. M., Wethington, E., & Chandler, A. L. (1999). Daily transmission of tensions between marital dyads and parent-child dyads. *Journal of Marriage and the Family, 61,* 49–61.

Altermatt, E. R., Jovanovic, J., & Perry, M. (1998). Bias or responsivity? Sex and achievement-level effects on teachers' classroom questioning practices. *Journal of Educational Psychology, 90,* 516–527.

Amaro, H., & Gornemann, I. (1992). *HIV/AIDS related knowledge, attitudes, beliefs, and behaviors among Hispanics in the Northeast and Puerto Rico: Report of findings and recommendations.* Boston, MA: Boston University School of Public Health.

American Association of University Women. (1992). *How schools shortchange girls.* Washington, DC: Author.

American Association of University Women. (1998). *Separated by sex: A critical look at single-sex education for girls.* Washington, DC: American Association of University Women Educational Foundation.

American Association of University Women. (2000). *Tech-savvy: Educated girls in the new computer age.* Washington, DC: Author.

American Association of University Women. (2003). *Women at work.* Washington, DC: Author.

American Cancer Society. (2003). *Cancer facts and figures: 2003.* Atlanta: Author.

American Cancer Society. (2007). *Cancer facts & figures 2007*. Atlanta: American Cancer Society.

American Civil Liberties Union. (March 8, 2000). *In blocking father's time off to care for first-born, South Carolina is the "Deadbeat,"* ACLU charges, [news release] Retrieved July 24, 2003, from *www.aclu.org/news/ewsPrint.cfm?ID= 7860&c=182.*

American Civil Liberties Union. (2003). *In victory for working family, high court says states must comply with Family and Medical Leave Act.* [news release]. Retrieved July 24, 2003, from *www.aclu.org/news/NewsPrint.cfm?ID= 12736&c=175.*

American College of Obstetricians and Gynecologists. (2006). ACOG steps up efforts to get emergency contraception to women [Electronic Version]. Retrieved January 23, 2007, from *www.acog.org/from_home/publications/ press_releases/nr05-08-06-1.cfm.*

American Psychiatric Association. (2000). *Diagnostic and statistical manual of mental disorders* (Fourth ed.). Washington, DC: American Psychiatric Association.

American Psychological Association. (2007). *Report of the APA Task Force on the sexualization of girls.* Retrived November 8, 2007, from *www.apa.org/pi/wpo/sexualization.html.*

Anda, R. F., Williamson, D. F., Escobedo, L. G., Mast, E. E., Giovino, G. A., & Remington, P. L. (1990). Depression and the dynamics of smoking: A national perspective. *Journal of the American Medical Association, 264,* 1541–1545.

Andalo, P. (2004). Health for one and all: Latinos in the USA. Retrieved February 26, 2007, from *www.paho.org/English/ DD/PIN/Number19_article01.htm.*

Andersen, A. E. (1999). Eating disorders in gay males. *Psychiatric Annals, 29,* 206–212.

Andersen, B. L., Cyranowski, J. M., & Aarestad, S. (2000). Beyond artificial, sex-linked distinctions to conceptualize female sexuality: Comment on Baumeister (2000). *Psychological Bulletin, 126,* 380–384.

Andersen, P. A. (2006). The evolution of biological sex differences in communication. In K. Dindia & D. J. Canary (Eds.), *Sex differences and similarities in communication* (Second ed.) (pp. 117–135). Mahwah, NJ: Lawrence Erlbaum Associates.

Andersen, R. E., Crespo, C. J., Bartlett, S. J., Cheskin, L. J., & Pratt, M. (1998). Relationship of physical activity and television watching with body weight and level of fatness among children: Results from the Third National Health and Nutrition Examination Survey. *Journal of the American Medical Association, 279,* 938–942.

Anderson, K. G., Sankis, L. M., & Widiger, T. A. (2001). Pathology versus statistical infrequency: Potential sources of gender bias in personality disorder criteria. *Journal of Nervous and Mental Disease, 189,* 661–667.

Andrade, C., Postma, K., & Abraham, K. (1999). Influence of women's work status on the well-being of Indian couples. *International Journal of Social Psychiatry, 45*(1), 65–75.

Andreou, E. (2006). Social preference, perceived popularity and social intelligence: Relations to overt and relational aggression. *School Psychology International, 27,* 339–351.

Andrews, J. A., & Lewinsohn, P. M. (1992). Suicidal attempts among older adolescents: Prevalence and co-occurrence with psychiatric disorders. *Journal of the American Academy of Child Adolescent Psychiatry, 31,* 655–662.

Angold, A., Costello, E. J., & Worthman, C. M. (1998). Puberty and depression: The roles of age, pubertal status and pubertal timing. *Psychological Medicine, 28,* 51–61.

Anson, O., Levenson, A., & Bonneh, D. Y. (1990). Gender and health on the Kibbutz. *Sex Roles, 22,* 213–231.

Antill, J. K. (1983). Sex role complementarity versus similarity in married couples. *Journal of Personality and Social Psychology, 45,* 145–155.

Appelberg, K., Romanov, K., Heikkilä, K., Honkasalo, M.-L., & Koskenvou, M. (1996). Interpersonal conflict as a predictor of work disability: A follow-up study of 15,348 Finnish employees. *Journal of Psychosomatic Research, 40,* 157–167.

Arber, S., & Ginn, J. (1993). Gender and inequalities in health in later life. *Social Science and Medicine, 36*(1), 33–46.

Archer, J. (1991). The influence of testosterone on human aggression. *British Journal of Psychology, 82,* 1–28.

Archer, J. (2000). Sex differences in aggression between heterosexual partners: A meta-analytic review. *Psychological Bulletin, 126,* 651–680.

Aries, E. (1996). *Men and women in interaction: Reconsidering the differences.* New York: Oxford University Press.

Aries, E. (2006). Sex differences in interaction: A reexamination. In K. Dindia & D. J. Canary (Eds.), *Sex differences and similarities in communication* (Second ed.) (pp. 21–36). Mahwah, NJ: Lawrence Erlbaum Associates.

Aristotle. (1963). *Generation of animals* (Rev. ed.). (A. L. Peck, Trans.). Cambridge, MA: Harvard University Press.

Arrighi, B. A., & Maume, D. J., Jr. (2000). Workplace subordination and men's avoidance of housework. *Journal of Family Issues, 21*(4), 464–487.

Artazcoz, L., Benach, J., Borrell, C., & Cortes, I. (2004). Unemployment and mental health: Understanding the interactions among gender, family roles, and social class. *American Journal of Public Health, 94,* 82–88.

Artazcoz, L., Borrell, C., Benach, J., Cortes, I., & Rohlfs, I. (2004). Women, family demands and health: The importance of employment status and socio-economic position. *Social Science & Medicine, 59,* 263–274.

Ashmore, R. D. (1990). Sex, gender, and the individual. In L. A. Pervin (Ed.), *Handbook of personality: Theory and research* (pp. 486–526). New York: Guilford Press.

Associated Press. (2007). *China facing major gender imbalance.* Retrieved January 12, 2007, from *www.msnbc.msn. com/id/16593301/?GT1=8921*

Attie, I., Brooks-Gunn, J., & Petersen, A. C. (1990). A developmental perspective on eating disorders and eating problems. In M. Lewis & S. M. Miller (Eds.), *Handbook of developmental psychopathology* (pp. 409–420). New York: Plenum Press.

Aukett, R., Ritchie, J., & Mill, K. (1988). Gender differences in friendship patterns. *Sex Roles, 19,* 57–66.

Auster, C. J., & Ohm, S. C. (2000). Masculinity and femininity in contemporary American society: A reevaluation using the Bem Sex-Role Inventory. *Sex Roles, 43*(7/8), 499–528.

Avellar, S., & Smock, P. J. (2005). The economic consequences of the dissolution of cohabiting unions. *Journal of Marriage and Family, 67,* 315–327.

Avison, W. R., & McAlpine, D. D. (1992). Gender differences in symptoms of depression among adolescents. *Journal of Health and Social Behavior, 33,* 77–96.

Babcock, L., & Laschever, S. (2003). *Women don't ask: Negotiation and the gender divide.* Princeton, NJ: Princeton University Press.

Badr, H., & Acitelli, L. K. (2005). Dyadic adjustment in chronic illness: Does relationship talk matter? *Journal of Family Psychology, 19,* 465–469.

Baenninger, M., & Newcombe, N. (1989). The role of experience in spatial test performance: A meta-analysis. *Sex Roles, 20,* 327–344.

Bailey, J. M., Gaulin, S., Agyei, Y., & Gladue, B. A. (1994). Effects of gender and sexual orientation on evolutionarily relevant aspects of human mating psychology. *Journal of Personality and Social Psychology, 66,* 1081–1093.

Baillargeon, R. H., Keenan, K., Wu, H. X., Zoccolillo, M., Cote, S., Perusse, D., et al. (2007). Gender differences in physical aggression: A prospective population-based survey of children before and after 2 years of age. *Developmental Psychology, 43,* 13–26.

Bakan, D. (1966). *The duality of human existence.* Chicago: Rand McNally.

Baker, L. C. (1996). Differences in earnings between male and female physicians. *New England Journal of Medicine, 334,* 960–964.

Baker, N. L. (2006). Feminist psychology in the service of women: Staying engaged without getting married. *Psychology of Women Quarterly, 30,* 1–14.

Baldassano, C. F., Marangell, L. B., Gyulai, L., Ghaemi, S. N., Joffe, H., Kim, D. R., et al. (2005). Gender differences in bipolar disorder: Retrospective data from the first 500 STEP-BD participants. *Bipolar Disorders, 7,* 465–470.

Bales, R. F., & Slater, P. E. (1955). Role differentiation in small decision-making groups. In T. Parsons & R. F. Bales (Eds.), *Family, socialization, and interaction process* (pp. 259–306). Glencoe, IL: Free Press.

Ballingrud, D. (1992). Assaults tarnish navy group. *St. Petersburg Times* [Electronic Version]. Retrieved from *proquest. umi.com*

Balsam, K. F., Beauchaine, T. P., Mickey, R. M., & Rothblum, E. D. (2005). Mental health of lesbian, gay, bisexual, and heterosexual siblings: Effects of gender, sexual orientation, and family. *Journal of Abnormal Psychology, 114,* 471–476.

Bandura, A. (1986). *Social foundations of thought and action: A social cognitive theory.* New York: Cambridge University Press.

Bandura, A., & Walters, R. (1963). *Social learning and personality development.* New York: Holt, Rinehart & Winston.

Bank, B. J., & Hansford, S. L. (2000). Gender and friendship: Why are men's best same-sex friendships less intimate and supportive? *Personal Relationships, 7,* 63–78.

Barbeau, E. M., Krieger, N., & Soobader, M. J. (2004). Working class matters: Socioeconomic disadvantage, race/ethnicity, gender, and smoking in NHIS 2000. *American Journal of Public Health, 94,* 269–278.

Barbee, A. P., Cunningham, M. R., Winstead, B. A., Derlega, V. J., Gulley, M. R., Yankeelov, P. A., & Druen, P. B. (1993). Effects of gender role expectations on the social support process. *Journal of Social Issues, 49,* 175–190.

Barboza, D. (2000, March 3). School copes with slain girl, 6-year-old shooter man, 19, charged with giving boy access to his gun. *Times–Picayune,* p. A8.

Barker, M. (1996). Remedying gender-based wage discrimination: The comparable worth approach. In P. J. Dubeck & K. Borman (Eds.), *Women and work: A handbook* (pp. 375–382). New York: Garland.

Barling, J. (1991). Fathers' employment: A neglected influence on children. In J. V. Lerner & N. L. Galambos (Eds.), *Employed mothers and their children* (pp. 181–209). New York: Garland.

Barnett, R. C. (1994). Home-to-work spillover revisited: A study of full-time employed women in dual-earner couples. *Journal of Marriage and the Family, 56,* 647–656.

Barnett, R. C. (2004). Women and multiple roles: Myths and reality. *Harvard Review of Psychiatry, 12,* 158–164.

Barnett, R. C., & Brennan, R. T. (1995). The relationship between job experiences and psychological distress: A structural equation approach. *Journal of Organizational Behavior, 16,* 259–276.

Barnett, R. C., & Brennan, R. T. (1997). Change in job conditions, change in psychological distress, and gender: A longitudinal study of dual-earner couples. *Journal of Organizational Behavior, 18,* 253–274.

Barnett, R. C., & Gareis, K. C. (2002). Full-time and reduced-hours work schedules and marital quality. *Work and Occupations, 29,* 364–379.

Barnett, R. C., & Marshall, N. L. (1991). The relationship between women's work and family roles and their subjective well-being and psychological distress. In M. Frankenhauser (Ed.), *Women, work, and health: Stress and opportunities* (pp. 111–136). New York: Plenum Press.

Barnett, R. C., & Marshall, N. L. (1993). Men, family-role quality, job-role quality, and physical health. *Health Psychology, 12,* 48–55.

Barnett, R. C., Brennan, R. T., Raudenbush, S. W., & Marshall, N. L. (1994). Gender and the relationship between marital-role quality and psychological distress. *Psychology of Women Quarterly, 18*, 105–127.

Barnett, R. C., Marshall, N. L., & Pleck, J. H. (1992). Men's multiple roles and their relationship to men's psychological distress. *Journal of Marriage and the Family, 54*, 358–367.

Barnett, R. C., Marshall, N. L., & Singer, J. D. (1992). Job experiences over time, multiple roles, and women's mental health: A longitudinal study. *Journal of Personality and Social Psychology, 62*, 634–644.

Barnett, R. C., Marshall, N. L., Raudenbush, S. W., & Brennan, R. T. (1993). Gender and the relationship between job experiences and psychological distress: A study of dual-earner couples. *Journal of Personality and Social Psychology, 64*, 794–806.

Barnett, R. C., Raudenbush, S. W., Brennan, R. T., Pleck, J. H., & Marshall, N. L. (1995). Change in job and marital experiences and change in psychological distress: A longitudinal study of dual-earner couples. *Journal of Personality and Social Psychology, 69*, 839–850.

Barr, A., Bryan, A., & Kenrick, D. T. (2002). Sexual peak: Socially shared cognitions about desire, frequency, and satisfaction in men and women. *Personal Relationships, 9*, 287–299.

Barreto, M., & Ellemers, N. (2005). The burden of benevolent sexism: How it contributes to the maintenance of gender inequalities. *European Journal of Social Psychology, 35*, 633–642.

Barrett, L. F., Lane, R. D., Sechrest, L., & Schwartz, G. E. (2000). Sex differences in emotional awareness. *Personality and Social Psychology Bulletin, 26*, 1027–1035.

Barron, L. A. (2003). Ask and you shall receive? Gender differences in negotiators' beliefs about requests for a higher salary. *Human Relations, 56*, 635–662.

Barta, W. D., & Kiene, S. M. (2005). Motivations for infidelity in heterosexual dating couples: The roles of gender, personality differences, and sociosexual orientation. *Journal of Social and Personal Relationships, 22*, 339–360.

Bartley, S. J., Blanton, P. W., & Gilliard, J. L. (2005). Husbands and wives in dual-earner marriages: Decision-making, gender role attitudes, division of household labor, and equity. *Marriage and Family Review, 37*, 69–94.

Barton, B. K., & Cohen, R. (2004). Classroom gender composition and children's peer relations. *Child Study Journal, 34*, 29–45.

Bartsch, R. A., Burnett, T., Diller, T. R., & Rankin-Williams, E. (2000). Gender representation in television commercials: Updating an update. *Sex Roles, 43*, 735–743.

Baruch, G. K., Biener, L., & Barnett, R. C. (1987). Women and gender in research on work and family stress. *American Psychologist, 42*, 130–136.

Basow, S. A., & Rubenfeld, K. (2003). "Troubles talk": Effects of gender and gender-typing. *Sex Roles, 48*, 183–187.

Bass, B. M., Avolio, B. J., & Atwater, L. (1996). The transformational and transactional leadership of men and women. *Applied Psychology: An International Review, 45*(1), 5–34.

Bassoff, E., & Glass, G. (1982). The relationship between sex roles and mental health: A meta-analysis of 26 studies. *Counseling Psychologist, 10*(4), 105–112.

Baucom, D. H., Besch, P. K., & Callahan, S. (1985). Relation between testosterone concentration, sex role identity, and personality among females. *Personality Processes and Individual Differences, 48*(5), 1218–1226.

Baucom, D. H., Notarius, C. I., Burnett, C. K., & Haefner, P. (1990). Gender differences and sex-role identity in marriage. In F. D. Fincham & T. N. Bradbury (Eds.), *The psychology of marriage: Basic issues and applications* (pp. 150–171). New York: Guilford Press.

Baumeister, R. F. (1988). Should we stop studying sex differences altogether? *American Psychologist, 43*, 1092–1095.

Baumeister, R. F. (2000). Gender differences in erotic plasticity: The female sex drive as socially flexible and responsive. *Psychological Bulletin, 126*, 347–374.

Baumeister, R. F. (2004). Gender and erotic plasticity: Sociocultural influences on sex drive. *Sexual and Relationship Therapy, 19*, 133–139.

Baumeister, R. F., & Sommer, K. L. (1997). What do men want? Gender differences and two spheres of belongingness: Comment on Cross and Madson (1997). *Psychological Bulletin, 122*, 38–44.

Baumeister, R. F., Catanese, K. R., & Vohs, K. D. (2001). Is there a gender difference in strength of sex drive? Theoretical views, conceptual distinctions, and a review of relevant evidence. *Personality and Social Psychology Review, 5*, 242–273.

Baumgarte, R. (2002). Cross-gender friendship: The troublesome relationship. In R. Goodwin (Ed.), *Inappropriate relationships: The unconventional, the disapproved, and the forbidden* (pp. 103–124). Mahwah, NJ: Erlbaum.

Beadnell, B., Morrison, D. M., Wilsdon, A., Wells, E. A., Murowchick, E., Hoppe, M., et al. (2005). Condom use, frequency of sex, and number of partners: Multidimensional characterization of adolescent sexual risk-taking. *The Journal of Sex Research, 42*, 192–202.

Bearman, P. S., & Bruckner, H. (2001). Promising the future: Virginity pledges and first intercourse. *American Journal of Sociology, 106*, 859–912.

Beauty and love quotes. (2000). Retrieved June 15, 2000, from *www.cc.gatech.edu/grads/b/Gary.N.Boone/beauty_and_love_quotes.html*.

Becker, D. V., Kenrick, D. T., Guerin, S., & Maner, J. K. (2005). Concentrating on beauty: Sexual selection and sociospatial memory. *Personality and Social Psychology Bulletin, 31*, 1643–1652.

Belcher, C., Frey, A., & Yankeelov, P. (2006). The effects of single-sex classrooms on classroom environment, self-esteem, and standardized test scores. *School Social Work Journal, 31,* 61–75.

Bell, L. A. (1996). In danger of winning: Consciousness raising strategies for empowering girls in the United States. *Women's Studies International Forum, 19*(4), 419–427.

Belle, D. (1982). Social ties and social support. In D. Belle (Ed.), *Lives in stress: Women and depression* (pp. 133–144). Beverly Hills, CA: Sage.

Belle, D. (1985). Ironies in the contemporary study of gender. *Journal of Personality, 53,* 400–405.

Belle, D. (1987). Gender differences in the social moderators of stress. In R. Barnett, L. Beiner, & G. K. Baruch (Eds.), *Gender and stress* (pp. 257–277). New York: Free Press.

Belle, D. (1989). Gender differences in children's social network and supports. In D. Belle (Ed.), *Children's social network and social supports* (pp. 173–188). New York: Wiley.

Bem, S. L. (1974). The measurement of psychological androgyny. *Journal of Consulting and Clinical Psychology, 42*(2), 155–162.

Bem, S. L. (1975). Sex role adaptability: One consequence of psychological androgyny. *Journal of Personality and Social Psychology, 31,* 634–643.

Bem, S. L. (1981). Gender schema theory: A cognitive account of sex typing. *Psychological Review, 88,* 354–364.

Bem, S. L. (1984). Androgyny and gender schema theory: A conceptual and empirical integration. In T. B. Sonderegger (Ed.), *Nebraska symposium on motivation 1984: Psychology and gender* (Vol. 32, pp. 179–226). Lincoln: University of Nebraska Press.

Bem, S. L. (1995). Dismantling gender polarization and compulsory heterosexuality: Should we turn the volume down or up? *Journal of Sex Research, 32*(4), 329–334.

Bem, S. L. (1998). *An unconventional family.* New Haven, CT: Yale University Press.

Benbow, C. P. (1988). Sex differences in mathematical reasoning ability in intellectually talented preadolescents: Their nature, effects, and possible causes. *Behavioral and Brain Sciences, 11,* 169–232.

Benbow, C. P., & Stanley, J. C. (1980). Sex differences in mathematical ability: Fact or artifact? *Science, 210,* 1262–1264.

Ben-David, S., & Schneider, O. (2005). Rape perceptions, gender role attitudes, and victim-perpetrator acquaintance. *Sex Roles, 53,* 385–399.

Benenson, J. F., & Christakos, A. (2003). The greater fragility of females' versus males' closest same-sex friendships. *Child Development, 74,* 1123–1129.

Benenson, J. F., Roy, R., Waite, A., Goldbaum, S., Linders, L., & Simpson, A. (2002). Greater discomfort as a proximate cause of sex differences in competition. *Merrill-Palmer Quarterly, 48,* 225–247.

Bennett, D. S., Ambrosini, P. J., Kudes, D., Metz, C., & Rabinovich, H. (2005). Gender differences in adolescent depression: Do symptoms differ for boys and girls? *Journal of Affective Disorders, 89,* 35–44.

Berenbaum, S. A., & Hines, M. (1992). Early androgens are related to childhood sex-typed toy preferences. *Psychological Science, 3*(3), 203–206.

Bergen, D. J., & Williams, J. E. (1991). Sex stereotypes in the United States revisited: 1972–1988. *Sex Roles, 24,* 413–423.

Berger, B. D., & Adesso, V. J. (1991). Gender differences in using alcohol to cope with depression. *Addictive Behaviors, 16,* 315–327.

Bergman, M. E., Langhout, R. D., Palmieri, P. A., Cortina, L. M., & Fitzgerald, L. F. (2002). The (un)reasonableness of reporting: Antecedents and consequences of reporting sexual harassment. *Journal of Applied Psychology, 87,* 230–242.

Berkey, C. S., Rockett, H. R., Field, A. E., Gillman, M. W., Frazier, A. L., Camargo, C. A. J., & Colditz, G. A. (2000). Activity, dietary intake, and weight changes in a longitudinal study of preadolescent and adolescent boys and girls. *Pediatrics, 105*(4), E56.

Berkman, L. F., & Syme, S. L. (1979). Social networks, host resistance, and mortality: A nine-year follow-up study of Alameda county residents. *American Journal of Epidemiology, 109*(2), 186–204.

Berkman, L. F., Vaccarino, V., & Seeman, T. (1993). Gender differences in cardiovascular morbidity and mortality: The contribution of social networks and support. *Annals of Behavioral Medicine, 15,* 112–118.

Berman, B. A., & Gritz, E. R. (1991). Women and smoking: Current trends and issues for the 1990s. *Journal of Substance Abuse, 3,* 221–238.

Berman, J. J., Murphy-Berman, V., & Pachauri, A. (1988). Sex differences in friendship patterns in India and the United States. *Basic and Applied Social Psychology, 9*(1), 61–71.

Berman, P. W. (1980). Are women more responsive than men to the young? A review of developmental and situational variables. *Psychological Bulletin, 88,* 668–695.

Bern, P. (1987). *How to work for a woman boss: Even if you'd rather not.* New York: Dodd, Mead.

Bernard, J. (1972). *The future of marriage.* New York: World Publishing Co.

Berns, S. B., Jacobson, N. S., & Gottman, J. M. (1999). Demand-withdraw interaction in couples with a violent husband. *Journal of Consulting and Clinical Psychology, 67,* 666–674.

Bettencourt, B. A., & Miller, N. (1996). Gender differences in aggression as a function of provocation: A meta-analysis. *Psychological Bulletin, 119,* 422–447.

Beyer, S. (1990). Gender differences in the accuracy of self-evaluations of performance. *Journal of Personality and Social Psychology, 59,* 960–970.

Beyer, S. (1999). Gender differences in causal attributions by college students of performance on course examinations. *Current Psychology, 17,* 346–358.

Bhanot, R., & Jovanovic, J. (2005). Do parents' academic gender stereotypes influence whether they intrude on their children's homework? *Sex Roles, 52,* 597–607.

Biaggio, M. K. (1989). Sex differences in behavioral reactions to provocation of anger. *Psychological Reports, 64,* 23–26.

Bickel, J. (1997). Gender stereotypes and misconceptions: Unresolved issues in physicians' professional development. *Journal of the American Medical Association, 277,* 1405–1407.

Bickell, N. A., Pieper, K. S., Lee, K. L., Mark, D. B., Glower, D. D., Pryor, D. B., & Califf, R. M. (1992). Referral patterns for coronary artery disease treatment: Gender bias or good clinical judgment? *Annals of Internal Medicine, 116*(10), 791–797.

Biederman, J., Mick, E., Faraone, S. V., Braaten, E., Doyle, A., Spencer, T., et al. (2002). Influence of gender on Attention Deficit Hyperactivity Disorder in children referred to a psychiatric clinic. *The American Journal of Psychiatry, 159,* 36–42.

Bielby, W. T., & Bielby, D. D. (1992). I will follow him: Family ties, gender-role beliefs, and reluctance to relocate for a better job. *American Journal of Sociology, 97*(5), 1241–1267.

Biernat, M. (1991). Gender stereotypes and the relationship between masculinity and femininity: A developmental analysis. *Journal of Personality and Social Psychology, 61,* 351–365.

Biernat, M. (2003). Toward a broader view of social stereotyping. *American Psychologist, 58,* 1019–1027.

Biernat, M., Crosby, F., & Williams, J. (2004). The maternal wall: Research and policy perspectives on discrimination against mothers. *Journal of Social Issues, 60,* 675–682.

Biernat, M., & Vescio, T. K. (2002). She swings, she hits, she's great, she's benched: Implications of gender-based shifting standards for judgment and behavior. *Personality and Social Psychology Bulletin, 28*(1), 66–77.

Binion, V. J. (1990). Psychological androgyny: A Black female perspective. *Sex Roles, 22,* 487–507.

Bird, C. E. (1999). Gender, household labor, and psychological distress: The impact of the amount and division of housework. *Journal of Health and Social Behavior, 40,* 32–45.

Birns, B. (1998). Battered wives: Causes, effects, and social change. In C. Forden, A. E. Hunter, & B. Birns (Eds.), *Readings in the psychology of women: Dimensions of the female experience* (pp. 280–288). Boston: Allyn & Bacon.

Biro, F. M., Striegel-Moore, R. H., Franko, D. L., Padgett, J., & Bean, J. A. (2006). Self-esteem in adolescent females. *Journal of Adolescent Health, 39,* 501–507.

Bjorkqvist, K., & Niemela, P. (1992). New trends in the study of female aggression. In K. Bjorkqvist & P. Niemela (Eds.), *Of mice and women: Aspects of female aggression* (pp. 3–16). San Diego, CA: Academic Press.

Bjornson, W., Rand, C., Connett, J. E., Lindgren, P., Nides, M., Pope, F., Buist, A. S., Hoppe-Ryan, C., & O'Hara, P. (1995). Gender differences in smoking cessation after 3 years in the Lung Health Study. *American Journal of Public Health, 85*(2), 223–230.

Black, D. A., Makar, H. R., Sanders, S. G., & Taylor, L. (1998). *The effects of sexual orientation on earnings.* Unpublished manuscript, Carnegie Mellon University, Pittsburgh, PA.

Blair, S. L., & Lichter, D. T. (1991). Measuring the division of household labor: Gender segregation of housework among American couples. *Journal of Family Issues, 12*(1), 91–113.

Blakemore, J. E. O., & Centers, R. E. (2005). Characteristics of boys' and girls' toys. *Sex Roles, 53,* 619–633.

Blanks, V., Dockwell, B., & Wallance, G. J. (2007). Adoption by gays and lesbians: A survey of the law in the 50 states and the District of Columbia. Retrieved November 8, 2007, from *www.adoptionpolicy.org/pdf/gaysandlesbian.pdf.*

Blee, K. M., & Tickamyer, A. R. (1995). Racial differences in men's attitudes about women's gender role. *Journal of Marriage and the Family, 57,* 21–30.

Bleske, A. L., & Buss, D. M. (2000). Can men and women be just friends? *Personal Relationships, 7,* 131–151.

Bleske-Rechek, A. L., & Buss, D. M. (2001). Opposite-sex friendship: Sex differences and similarities in initiation, selection, and dissolution. *Personality and Social Psychology Bulletin, 27,* 1310–1323.

Block, J. H. (1976). Issues, problems, and pitfalls in assessing sex differences: A critical review of the psychology of sex differences. *Merrill-Palmer Quarterly, 22*(4), 283–308.

Block, J. H., & Kremen, A. M. (1996). IQ and ego-resiliency: Conceptual and empirical connections and separateness. *Journal of Personality and Social Psychology, 70,* 349–361.

Block, J. H., Gjerde, P. F., & Block, J. H. (1991). Personality antecedents of depressive tendencies in 18-year-olds: A prospective study. *Journal of Personality and Social Psychology, 60,* 726–738.

Blum, J. S., & Mehrabian, A. (1999). Personality and temperament correlates of marital satisfaction. *Journal of Personality, 67,* 93–125.

Blumenthal, J. A. (1998). The reasonable woman standard: A meta-analytic review of gender differences in perceptions of sexual harassment. *Law and Human Behavior, 22*(1), 33–57.

Blumenthal, L. (2002). Ex-Tacoman, teen held as D.C. sniper suspect. Retrieved March 25, 2003, from *proquest.umi.com/pqdweb?TS=1048608170&RQT=309&CC=2&Dtp=1&Did=0000. . . .*

Blumstein, P., & Schwartz, P. (1983). *American couples.* New York: William Morrow.

Bly, R. (1990). *Iron John: A book about men.* Reading, MA: Addison-Wesley.

Boeringer, S. B. (1999). Associations of rape-supportive attitudes with fraternal and athletic participation. *Violence Against Women, 5*(1), 81–90.

Bohan, J. S. (1997). Regarding gender: Essentialism, constructionism, and feminist psychology. In M. M. Gergen

& S. N. Davis (Eds.), *Toward a new psychology of gender: A reader* (pp. 31–47). New York: Routledge.

Bolger, N., DeLongis, A., Kessler, R. V., & Wethington, E. (1989). The contagion of stress across multiple roles. *Journal of Marriage and the Family, 51,* 175–183.

Bombardieri, M. (2005). Harvard women's group rips Summers. *The Boston Globe.* Retrieved January 31, 2007, from *www.boston.com/news/education/higher/articles/2005/01/19.*

Bond, J. T., Galinsky, E., & Swanberg, J. E. (1998). *The 1997 National Study of the Changing Workforce.* New York: Families and Work Institute.

Bond, M. A., Punnett, L., Pyle, J. L., Cazeca, D., & Cooperman, M. (2004). Gendered work conditions, health, and work outcomes. *Journal of Occupational Health Psychology, 9,* 28–45.

Bond, M. H., & Young Ho, H. (1978). The effect of relative status and the sex composition of a dyad on cognitive responses and non-verbal behavior of Japanese interviewees. *Psychologia, 21,* 128–136.

Bondurant, B., & Donat, P. L. N. (1999). Perceptions of women's sexual interest and acquaintance rape: The role of sexual overperception and affective attitudes. *Psychology of Women Quarterly, 23,* 691–705.

Bondurant, B., & White, J. W. (1996). Men who sexually harass: An embedded perspective. In D. K. Shrier (Ed.), *Sexual harassment in the work place and academia* (pp. 59–78). Washington, DC: American Psychiatric Press.

Book, A. S., Starzyk, K. B., & Quinsey, V. L. (2001). The relationship between testosterone and aggression: A meta-analysis. *Aggression and Violent Behavior, 6,* 579–599.

Bookwala, J., Sobin, J., & Zdaniuk, B. (2005). Gender and aggression in marital relationships: A life-span perspective. *Sex Roles, 52,* 797–806.

Booth, A., & Johnson, D. (1988). Premarital cohabitation and marital success. *Journal of Family Issues, 9*(2), 255–272.

Booth, A., Johnson, D. R., & Granger, D. A. (1999). Testosterone and men's depression: The role of social behavior. *Journal of Health and Social Behavior, 40,* 130–140.

Boroughs, M., & Thompson, J. K. (2002). Exercise status and sexual orientation as moderators of body image disturbance and eating disorders in males. *International Journal of Eating Disorders, 31,* 307–311.

Borowsky, S. J., Rubenstein, L. V., Meredith, L. S., Camp, P., Jackson-Triche, M., & Wells, K. B. (2000). Who is at risk of nondetection of mental health problems in primary care? *Journal of General Internal Medicine, 15,* 381–388.

Borrelli, B., Niaura, R. S., Hitsman, B., Spring, B., & Papandonatos, G. (2001). Influences of gender and weight gain on short-term relapse to smoking in a cessation trial. *Journal of Consulting and Clinical Psychology, 69,* 511–515.

Bosson, J. K., Haymovitz, E. L., & Pinel, E. C. (2004). When saying and doing diverge: The effects of stereotype threat on self-reported versus non-verbal anxiety. *Journal of Experimental Social Psychology, 40,* 247–255.

Bouman, A., Schipper, M., Heineman, M. J., & Faas, M. M. (2004). Gender difference in the non-specific and specific immune response in humans. *American Journal of Reproductive Immunology, 52,* 19–26.

Bowen, C.-C., Swim, J. K., & Jacobs, R. R. (2000). Evaluating gender biases on actual job performance of real people: A meta-analysis. *Journal of Applied Social Psychology, 30,* 2194–2215.

Boysen, G. A., Vogel, D. L., Madon, S., & Wester, S. R. (2006). Mental health stereotypes about gay men. *Sex Roles, 54,* 69–82.

Bradbury, T. N., Campbell, S. M., & Fincham, F. D. (1995). Longitudinal and behavioral analysis of masculinity and femininity in marriage. *Journal of Personality and Social Psychology, 68,* 328–341.

Brady, K. L., & Eisler, R. M. (1995). Gender bias in the college classroom: A critical review of the literature and implications for future research. *Journal of Research and Development in Education, 29*(1), 9–19.

Bramlett, M. D., & Mosher, W. D. (2002). Cohabitation, marriage, divorce, and remarriage in the United States. *National Center for Health Statistics: Vital Health Statistics, 23*(22), 1–93.

Bramon-Bosch, E., Troop, N. A., & Treasure, J. L. (2000). Eating disorders in males: A comparison with female patients. *European Eating Disorders Review, 8,* 321–328.

Brannon, R., & Juni, S. (1984). A scale for measuring attitudes toward masculinity. *JSAS Catalog of Selected Documents in Psychology, 14,* 6 (Ms. 2012).

Brehm, J. W. (1966). *A theory of psychological reactance.* New York: Academic Press.

Brendgen, M., Girard, A., Dionne, G., Boivin, M., Vitaro, F., & Perusse, D. (2005). Examining genetic and environmental effects on social aggression: A study of 6-year-old twins. *Child Development, 76,* 930–946.

Brennan, R. T., Barnett, R. C., & Gareis, K. C. (2001). When she earns more than he does: A longitudinal study of dual-earner couples. *Journal of Marriage and the Family, 63,* 168–182.

Brent, D. A. (1995). Risk factors for adolescent suicide and suicidal behavior: Mental and substance abuse disorders, family environmental factors, and life stress. *Suicide and Life-Threatening Behavior, 25*(Suppl.), 52–63.

Brent, D. A., Perper, J. A., Moritz, G., Baugher, M., Roth, C., Balach, L., & Schweers, J. (1993). Stressful life events, psychopathology, and adolescent suicide: A case control study. *Suicide and Life-Threatening Behavior, 23*(3), 179–187.

Brescoll, V., & LaFrance, M. (2004). The correlates and consequences of newspaper reports of research on sex differences. *American Psychological Society, 15,* 515–520.

Bresnahan, M. J., Inoue, Y., Liu, W. Y., & Nishida, T. (2001). Changing gender roles in prime-time commercials in

Malaysia, Japan, Taiwan, and the United States. *Sex Roles, 45*, 117–131.

Brewer, D. D., Potterat, J. J., Garrett, S. B., Muth, S. Q., Roberts, J. M., Jr., Kasprzyk, D., Montano, D. E., & Darrow, W. W. (2000). Prostitution and the sex discrepancy in reported number of sexual partners. *Proceedings of the National Academy of Sciences of the United States of America, 97*, 12385–12388.

Brezinka, V., & Kittel, F. (1995). Psychosocial factors of coronary heart disease in women: A review. *Social Science and Medicine, 42*, 1351–1365.

Bridge, K., & Baxter, L. A. (1992). Blended relationships: Friends as work associates. *Western Journal of Communication, 56*, 200–225.

Bridgeman, B., & Wendler, C. (1991). Gender differences in predictors of college mathematics performance and in college mathematics course grades. *Journal of Educational Psychology, 83*(2), 275–284.

Bridges, J. S., Etaugh, C., & Barnes-Farrell, J. (2002). Trait judgments of stay-at-home and employed parents: A function of social role and/or shifting standards? *Psychology of Women Quarterly, 26*, 140–150.

Briere, J., & Lanktree, C. (1983). Sex-role related effects of sex bias in language. *Sex Roles, 9*, 625–632.

Bringle, R. G. (1995). Sexual jealousy in the relationships of homosexual and heterosexual men: 1980 and 1992. *Personal Relationships, 2*, 313–325.

Briton, N. J., & Hall, J. A. (1995). Beliefs about female and male nonverbal communication. *Sex Roles, 32*, 79–90.

Broderick, P. C., & Korteland, C. (2002). Coping style and depression in early adolescence: Relationships to gender, gender role, and implicit beliefs. *Sex Roles, 46*(7/8), 201–213.

Brody, L. R., & Hall, J. A. (1993). Gender and emotion. In M. Lewis & J. M. Haviland (Eds.), *Handbook of emotions* (pp. 447–460). New York: Guilford Press.

Bromberger, J. T., & Matthews, K. A. (1996). A "feminine" model of vulnerability to depressive symptoms: A longitudinal investigation of middle-aged women. *Journal of Personality and Social Psychology, 70*, 591–598.

Brooks, D. J. (2003). Ms. Couch Potato? Gender and exercise. Retrieved January 30, 2007, from *www.galluppoll.com/content/Default.aspx?ci=7669&pg=1&VERSION=p*.

Brooks-Gunn, J., & Warren, M. P. (1989). Biological and social contributions to negative affect in young adolescent girls. *Child Development, 60*, 40–55.

Broverman, I. K., Vogel, S. R., Broverman, D. M., Clarkson, F. E., & Rosenkrantz, P. S. (1972). Sex-role stereotypes: A current appraisal. *Journal of Social Issues, 28*, 59–78.

Brown, C., & Corcoran, M. (1997). Sex-based differences in school content and the male-female wage gap. *Journal of Labor Economics, 15*(3), 431–465.

Brown, L. M., Way, N., & Duff, J. L. (1999). The others in my I: Adolescent girls' friendships and peer relations. In N. G. Johnson, M. C. Roberts, & J. Worell (Eds.), *Beyond appearance: A new look at adolescent girls* (pp. 205–225). Washington, DC: American Psychological Association.

Brown, S. L. (2004). Moving from cohabitation to marriage: Effects on relationship quality. *Social Science Research, 33*, 1–19.

Brown, S. L., & Booth, A. (1996). Cohabitation versus marriage: A comparison of relationship quality. *Journal of Marriage and the Family, 58*, 668–678.

Brown, S. L., Lee, G. R., & Bulanda, J. R. (2006). Cohabitation among older adults: A national portrait. *The Journal of Gerontology, 61B*, S71–S79.

Browne, A., & Williams, K. R. (1993). Gender, intimacy, and lethal violence: Trends from 1976 through 1987. *Gender and Society, 7*(1), 78–98.

Browne, B. A. (1998). Gender stereotypes in advertising on children's television in the 1990s: A cross-national analysis. *Journal of Advertising, 27*(1), 83–96.

Brownmiller, S. (1975). *Against our will: Men, women, and rape.* New York: Bantam Books.

Bruckner, H., & Bearman, P. (2005). After the promise: The STD consequences of adolescent virginity pledges. *Journal of Adolescent Health, 36*, 271–278.

Buhrmester, D., & Furman, W. (1987). The development of companionship and intimacy. *Child Development, 58*, 1101–1113.

Bullock, H. E., & Fernald, J. L. (2003). "Feminism lite?" Feminist identification, speaker appearance, and perceptions of feminist and antifeminist messengers. *Psychology of Women Quarterly, 27*, 291–299.

Bumpass, L. L., & Lu, H. (2000). Trends in cohabitation and implications for children's family contexts in the United States. *Population Studies, 54*, 29–41.

Bumpass, L. L., & Sweet, J. A. (1989). National estimates of cohabitation. *Demography, 26*(4), 615–625.

Bumpass, L. L., Sweet, J. A., & Cherlin, A. (1991). The role of cohabitation in declining rates of marriage. *Journal of Marriage and the Family, 53*, 913–927.

Burckle, M. A., Ryckman, R. M., Gold, J. A., Thornton, B., & Audesse, R. J. (1999). Forms of competitive attitude and achievement orientation in relation to disordered eating. *Sex Roles, 40*, 853–870.

Bureau of Justice Statistics. (2001). *Violent crime rates by gender of victim.* Retrieved May 16, 2003, from *www.ojp.usdoj.gov/bjs/glance/vsx2.htm*.

Bureau of Justice Statistics. (2002, September 9). *Violent victimization rates by gender: 1973–2001.* Retrieved May 16, 2003, from *www.ojp.usdoj.gov/bjs/glance/tables/vsxtab.htm*.

Bureau of Justice Statistics. (2006a). Criminal victimization in the United States-Statistical tables index. Retrieved July 5, 2007, from *www.ojp.usdoj.gov/bjs/abstract/cvus/number_of_incidents745.htm*.

Bureau of Justice Statistics. (2006b). *Homicide trends in the United States.* Retrieved November 8, 2007, from *www.ojp.usdoj.gov/bjs/*.

Bureau of Justice Statistics. (2006c). *Homicide trends in the United States*: U.S. Department of Justice.

Bureau of Labor Statistics. (2005). *Employment and fatality profiles by gender of worker, 2005.* Retrieved November 8, 2007, from *www.bls.gov/iif/oshwc/cfoi/cfch0004.pdf.*

Burgess, D., & Borgida, E. (1999). Who women are, who women should be: Descriptive and prescriptive gender stereotyping in sex discrimination. *Psychology, Public Policy and Law, 5,* 665–692.

Burleson, B. R., Kunkel, A. W., Samter, W., & Werking, K. J. (1996). Men's and women's evaluations of communication skills in personal relationships: When sex differences make a difference and when they don't. *Journal of Social and Personal Relationships, 13,* 201–224.

Burr, J. E., Ostrov, J. M., Jansen, E. A., Cullerton-Sen, C., & Crick, N. R. (2005). Relational aggression and friendship during early childhood: "I won't be your friend!" *Early Education & Development, 16,* 161–183.

Burt, M. R. (1980). Cultural myths and supports for rape. *Journal of Personality and Social Psychology, 38,* 217–230.

Buschman, J. K., & Lenart, S. (1996). "I am not a feminist, but . . .": College women, feminism, and negative experiences. *Political Psychology, 17,* 59–75.

Bushman, S. (2006). Emergency Contraception. Getting medicine's best kept secret into the hands of American women [Electronic Version]. *The Heinz School Review.* Retrieved January 3, 2007, from journal.heinz.cmu.edu/articles/emergency-contraception/.

Buss, D. M. (1989). Sex differences in human mate preferences: Evolutionary hypotheses tested in 37 cultures. *Behavioral and Brain Sciences, 12*(1), 1–49.

Buss, D. M. (1994). *The evolution of desire.* New York: Basic Books.

Buss, D. M. (1995). Psychological sex differences: Origins through sexual selection. *American Psychologist, 50,* 164–168.

Buss, D. M. (1999). *Evolutionary psychology: The new science of mind.* Boston: Allyn & Bacon.

Buss, D. M., & Kenrick, D. T. (1998). Evolutionary social psychology. In D. T. Gilbert, S. T. Fiske, & G. Lindzey (Eds.), *The handbook of social psychology* (pp. 982–1026). New York: Oxford University Press.

Buss, D. M., Abbott, M., Angleitner, A., & Asherian, A. (1990). International preferences in selecting mates: A study of 37 cultures. *Journal of Cross-Cultural Psychology, 21,* 5–47.

Buss, D. M., Larsen, R. J., Westen, D., & Semmelroth, J. (1992). Sex differences in jealousy: Evolution, physiology, and psychology. *Psychological Science, 3*(4), 251–255.

Buss, D. M., Shackelford, T. K., Choe, J., Buunk, B. P., & Dijkstra, P. (2000). Distress about mating rivals. *Personal Relationships, 7,* 235–243.

Buss, D. M., Shackelford, T. K., Kirkpatrick, L. A., & Larsen, R. J. (2001). A half century of mate preferences: The cultural evolution of values. *Journal of Marriage and the Family, 63,* 491–503.

Bussey, K., & Bandura, A. (1992). Self-regulatory mechanisms governing gender development. *Child Development, 63,* 1236–1250.

Bussey, K., & Bandura, A. (1999). Social cognitive theory of gender development and differentiation. *Psychological Review, 106,* 676–713.

Buston, P. M., & Emlen, S. T. (2003). Cognitive processes underlying human mate choice: The relationship between self-perception and mate preference in Western society. *Proceedings of the National Academy of Sciences, 100,* 8805–8810.

Buttner, E. H., & McEnally, M. (1996). The interactive effect of influence tactic, applicant gender, and type of job on hiring recommendations. *Sex Roles, 34,* 581–591.

Buunk, B. P., Angleitner, A., Oubaid, V., & Buss, D. M. (1996). Sex differences in jealousy in evolutionary and cultural perspective: Tests from the Netherlands, Germany, and the United States. *Psychological Science, 7*(6), 359–363.

Bylsma, W. H., & Major, B. (1994). Social comparisons and contentment: Exploring the psychological costs of the gender wage gap. *Psychology of Women Quarterly, 18,* 241–249.

Byrnes, J. P., Miller, D. C., & Schafer, W. D. (1999). Gender differences in risk taking: A meta-analysis. *Psychological Bulletin, 125,* 367–383.

Cahill, L., Uncapher, M., Kilpatrick, L., Alkire, M. T., & Turner, J. (2004). Sex-related hemispheric lateralization of amygdala function in emotionally influenced memory: An fMRI investigation. *Learning and Memory, 11,* 261–266.

Cahn, D. D. (1992). *Conflict in intimate relationships.* New York: Guilford Press.

Cale, E. M., & Lilienfeld, S. O. (2002a). Sex differences in psychopathy and antisocial personality disorder: A review and integration. *Clinical Psychology Review, 22,* 1179–1207.

Cale, E. M., & Lilienfeld, S. O. (2002b). Histrionic personality disorder and antisocial personality disorder: Sex-differentiated manifestations of psychopathy? *Journal of Personality Disorders, 16,* 52–72.

Calvert, S. L., Mahler, B. A., Zehnder, S. M., Jenkins, A., & Lee, M. S. (2003). Gender differences in preadolescent children's online interactions: Symbolic modes of self-presentation and self-expression. *Applied Developmental Psychology, 24,* 627–644.

Camarena, P. M., Sarigiani, P. A., & Petersen, A. C. (1990). Gender-specific pathways to intimacy in early adolescence. *Journal of Youth and Adolescence, 19,* 19–32.

Campbell, A. (2006). Sex differences in direct aggression: What are the psychological mediators? *Aggression and Violent Behavior, 11,* 237–264.

Canary, D. J., & Stafford, L. (1992). Relational maintenance strategies and equity in marriage. *Communication Monographs, 59,* 243–267.

Canary, D. J., & Wahba, J. (2006). Do women work harder than men at maintaining relationships? In K. Dindia & D. J. Canary (Eds.), *Sex differences and similarities in communication* (Second ed.) (pp. 359–377). Mahwah, NJ: Lawrence Erlbaum Associates.

Canetto, S. S., & Lester, D. (1995). Gender and the primary prevention of suicide mortality. *American Association of Suicidology, 25*(1), 58–69.

Canetto, S. S., & Sakinofsky, I. (1998). The gender paradox in suicide. *American Association of Suicidology, 28*(1), 1–23.

Capaldi, D. M., Kim, H. K., & Shortt, J. W. (2004). Women's involvement in aggression in young adult romantic relationships: A developmental systems model. In M. Putallaz & K. L. Bierman (Eds.), *Aggression, antisocial behavior and violence among girls: A developmental perspective* (pp. 223–241). New York: The Guilford Press.

Carli, L. L. (1989). Gender differences in interaction style and influence. *Journal of Personality and Social Psychology, 56,* 565–576.

Carli, L. L. (1990). Gender, language, and influence. *Journal of Personality and Social Psychology, 59,* 941–951.

Carli, L. L., LaFleur, S. J., & Loeber, C. C. (1995). Nonverbal behavior, gender, and influence. *Journal of Personality and Social Psychology, 68,* 1030–1041.

Carlson, M. B. (1993, August 9). Shreds of evidence. *Time,* pp. 26–27.

Carlson, M. B. (1996, January 29). Public eye: The crying game. *Time,* p. 147.

Carr, D. (2002). The psychological consequences of work-family trade-offs for three cohorts of men and women. *Social Psychology Quarterly, 65,* 103–124.

Carroll, J. (2006a). Americans prefer male boss to a female boss. Retrieved January 30, 2007, from *www.galluppoll.com/content/Default.aspx?ci=24346&pg=1&VERSION=p.*

Carroll, J. (2006b). Women more likely than men to say they've been divorced: Overall, 3 in 10 Americans say they've been divorced in their lifetime. Retrieved January 30, 2007, from *www.galluppoll.com/content/Default.aspx?ci=22264&pg=1&VERSION=p.*

Carroll, J. (2006c). Men, women differ in views of Duke lacrosse case. Retrieved January 30, 2007, from *www.galluppoll.com/content/Default.aspx?ci=22696&pg=1&VERSION=p.*

Carstensen, L. L., Gottman, J. M., & Levenson, R. W. (2004). Emotional behavior in long-term marriage. In H. T. Reis & C. E. Rusbult (Eds.), *Close relationships: Key readings* (pp. 457–470). New York: Psychology Press.

Case, A., & Paxson, C. (2005). Sex differences in morbidity and mortality. *Demography, 42,* 189–214.

Casey, M. B. (1996). Understanding individual differences in spatial ability within females: A nature/nurture interactionist framework. *Developmental Review, 16,* 241–260.

Casey, M. B., Nuttall, R. L., & Pezaris, E. (1997). Mediators of gender differences in mathematics college entrance test scores: A comparison of spatial skills with internalized beliefs and anxieties. *Developmental Psychology, 33,* 669–680.

Cashdan, E. (1998). Smiles, speech, and body posture: How women and men display sociometric status and power. *Journal of Nonverbal Behavior, 22,* 209–228.

Casper, L. M. (1997). *My daddy takes care of me: Fathers as care providers* (Current Population Reports, P70-59). Washington, DC: U.S. Census Bureau.

Cassidy, K. W. (2007). Gender differences in cognitive ability, attitudes, and behavior. In D. Sadker & E. S. Silber (Eds.), *Gender in the classroom: Foundations, skills, methods, and strategies across the curriculum* (pp. 33–72). Mahwah, NJ: Lawrence Erlbaum Associates.

Catania, J. A., Coates, T. J., Stall, R., Turner, H., Peterson, J., Hearst, N., et al. (1992). Prevalence of AIDS-related risk factors and condom use in the United States. *Science, 258,* 1101–1106.

Caughlin, J. P., & Huston, T. L. (2002). A contextual analysis of the association between demand/withdraw and marital satisfaction. *Personal Relationships, 9,* 95–119.

Celentano, D. D., Linet, M. S., & Stewart, W. F. (1990). Gender differences in the experience of headache. *Social Science and Medicine, 30*(12), 1289–1295.

Centers for Disease Control and Prevention. (1992). Vigorous physical activity among high school students—United States, 1990. *Morbidity and Mortality Weekly Report, 41*(3), 33–35.

Centers for Disease Control and Prevention. (2000a). Preventing obesity among children. *Chronic Disease Notes and Reports, 13.*

Centers for Disease Control and Prevention. (2000b). Tobacco use among middle and high school students—United States, 1999. *Morbidity and Mortality Weekly Report, 49*(3), 49–53.

Centers for Disease Control and Prevention. (2004). *Almost half of Americans use at least one prescription drug: Annual report on Nation's health shows.* Retrieved August 2, 2007, from *www.cdc.gov/od/oc/media/pressrel/r041202.htm.*

Centers for Disease Control and Prevention. (2005). *Smoking and tobacco use: State tobacco activities, tracking & evaluation (STATE) system.* Retrieved June 25, 2007, from *apps.nccd.cdc.gov/StateSystem/stateSystem.aspx?selectedTopic=100&selectedMeasures.*

Centers for Disease Control and Prevention. (2006a). *Tobacco use among adults—United States, 2005.* Retrieved November 8, 2007, from *www.cdc.gov/MMWR/PDF/wk/mm5542.pdf.*

Centers for Disease Control and Prevention. (2006b). Youth risk behavior surveillance—United States 2005. *Morbidity and Mortality Weekly Report, 55,* 1–107.

Centers for Disease Control and Prevention. (2006c). *High school students engaged in organized physical activity by sex, race and hispanic origin: 2005.* Retrieved November 8, 2007, from *www.cdc.gov/mmwr/preview/mmwrhtml/ss5505a1.htm.*

Centers for Disease Control and Prevention. (2006d). *Homicides and suicides: National violent death reporting system, United States, 2003–2004.* Retrieved November 8, 2007, from *www.cdc.gov/mmwr/PDF/wk/mm5526.pdf*

Centers for Disease Control and Prevention. (2007a). *Physical activity among adults: United States, 2000 and 2005.* Retrieved November 8, 2007, from *www.cdc.gov/nchs/products/pubs/pubd/hestats/physicalactivity/physicalactivity.htm.*

Centers for Disease Control and Prevention. (2007b). *Smoking & tobacco use: 2001 Surgeon General's report—women and smoking.* Retrieved June 25, 2007, from *www.cdc.gov/tobacco/data_statistics/sgr/sgr_2001/sgr_women.*

Centers for Disease Control and Prevention. (2007c). Suicide trends among youths and young adults aged 10–24 years, United States, 1990–2004. *Morbidity and Mortality Weekly Report, 56,* 905–908.

Central Intelligence Agency. (1998). *The world factbook 1999.* Washington, DC: Author.

Chandra, A., & Minkovitz, C. S. (2006). Stigma starts early: Gender differences in teen willingness to use mental health services. *Journal of Adolescent Health, 38,* 754e1–754e8.

Chang, C., & Hitchon, J. C. B. (2004). When does gender count? Further insights into gender schematic processing of female candidates' political advertisements. *Sex Roles, 51,* 197–208.

Chapman, K. R., Tashkin, D. P., & Pye, D. J. (2001). Gender bias in the diagnosis of COPD. *Chest, 119,* 1691–1695.

Charmaz, K. (1995). Identity dilemmas of chronically ill men. In D. Sabo & D. F. Gordon (Eds.), *Men's health and illness: Gender, power, and the body* (pp. 266–291). Thousand Oaks, CA: Sage Publications.

Chen, C., Greenberger, E., Lester, J., Dong, Q., & Guo, M-S. (1998). A cross-cultural study of family and peer correlates of adolescent misconduct. *Developmental Psychology, 34,* 770–781.

Cheng, S. T., & Chan, A. C. M. (2006). Social support and self-rated health revisited: Is there a gender difference in later life? *Social Science & Medicine, 63,* 118–122.

Cherpitel, C. J. (1993). Alcohol, injury, and risk-taking behavior: Data from a national sample. *Alcoholism: Clinical and Experimental Research, 17*(4), 762–766.

Chesley, N., & Moen, P. (2006). When workers care: Dual-earner couples' caregiving strategies, benefit use, and psychological well-being. *American Behavioral Scientist, 49,* 1248–1269.

Chesney, M. A., & Nealey, J. B. (1996). Smoking and cardiovascular disease risk in women: Issues for prevention and women's health. In P. M. Kato & T. Mann (Eds.), *Handbook of diversity issues in health psychology* (pp. 199–218). New York: Plenum Press.

Chesney-Lind, M., & Pasko, L. (2004). *Girls, women, and crime: Selected readings.* Thousand Oaks, CA: Sage.

Chevan, A. (1996). As cheaply as one: Cohabitation in the older population. *Journal of Marriage and the Family, 58,* 656–667.

Chia, R. C., Allred, L. J., & Jerzak, P. A. (1997). Attitudes toward women in Taiwan and China: Current status, problems, and suggestions for future research. *Psychology of Women Quarterly, 21,* 137–150.

Chia, R. C., Moore, J. L., Lam, K. N., Chuang, C. J., & Cheng, B. S. (1994). Cultural differences in gender role attitudes between Chinese and American students. *Sex Roles, 31*(1/2), 23–29.

Chiaramonte, G. R., & Friend, R. (2006). Medical students' and residents' gender bias in the diagnosis, treatment, and interpretation of coronary heart disease symptoms. *Health Psychology, 25,* 255–266.

Chisholm, J. F. (2000). Culture, ethnicity, race, and class. In F. Denmark, V. Rabinowitz, & J. Sechzer (Eds.), *Engendering psychology* (pp. 107–139). Boston: Allyn & Bacon.

Chodorow, N. (1978). *The reproduction of mothering: Psychoanalysis and the sociology of gender.* London: University of California Press.

Choo, P., Levine, T., & Hatfield, E. (1996). Gender, love schemas, and reactions to romantic break-ups. *Journal of Social Behavior and Personality, 11*(5), 143–160.

Chrisler, J. C., & O'Hea, E. L. (2000). Gender, culture, and autoimmune disorders. In R. M. Eisler (Ed.), *Handbook of gender, culture, and health* (pp. 321–342). Mahwah, NJ: Erlbaum.

Christenfeld, N., Gerin, W., Linden, W., Sanders, M., Mathur, J., Deich, J. D., & Pickering, T. G. (1997). Social support effects on cardiovascular reactivity: Is a stranger as effective as a friend? *Psychosomatic Medicine, 59,* 388–398.

Christensen, A., & Heavey, C. L. (1990). Gender and social structure in the demand/withdraw pattern of marital conflict. *Journal of Personality and Social Psychology, 59,* 73–81.

Christensen, A., & Heavey, C. L. (1993). Gender differences in marital conflict: The demand/withdraw interaction pattern. In S. Oskamp & M. Constanzo (Eds.), *Gender issues in contemporary society* (Vol. 6, pp. 113–141). New York: Sage.

Christensen, A., Eldridge, K., Catta-Preta, A. B., Lim, V. R., & Santagata, R. (2006). Cross-cultural consistency of the demand/withdraw interaction pattern in couples. *Journal of Marriage and Family, 68,* 1029–1044.

Christian Science Monitor. (1983). New study shows boys outnumber girls 13 to 1 as top math scorers. Retrieved June 7, 2000, from *web.lexis-nexis.com/universe/docu. . .*

Church, A. T. (2000). Culture and personality: Toward an integrated cultural trait psychology. *Journal of Personality, 68,* 651–703.

Ciabattari, T. (2004). Cohabitation and housework: The effects of marital intentions. *Journal of Marriage and Family, 66,* 118–125.

Cillessen, A. H. N., & Borch, C. (2006). Developmental trajectories of adolescent popularity: A growth curve modelling analysis. *Journal of Adolescence, 29,* 935–959.

Clancy, S. M., & Dollinger, S. J. (1993). Photographic depictions of the self: Gender and age differences in social connectedness. *Sex Roles, 29,* 477–495.

Clark, C. L., Shaver, P. R., & Abrahams, M. F. (1999). Strategic behaviors in romantic relationship initiation. *Personality and Social Psychology Bulletin, 25,* 707–720.

Clark, M. L., & Ayers, M. (1992). Friendship similarity during early adolescence: Gender and racial patterns. *Journal of Psychology, 126,* 393–405.

Clarkberg, M., Stolzenberg, R. M., & Waite, L. J. (1995). Attitudes, values, and entrance into cohabitational versus marital unions. *Social Forces, 74*(2), 609–634.

Clearfield, M. W., & Nelson, N. M. (2006). Sex differences in mothers' speech and play behavior with 6-, 9-, and 14-month-old infants. *Sex Roles, 54,* 127–137.

Cleveland, H. H., Koss, M. P., & Lyons, J. (1999). Rape tactics from the survivors' perspective: Contextual dependence and within-event independence. *Journal of Interpersonal Violence, 14*(5), 532–547.

Clifton, A. K., McGrath, D., & Wick, B. (1976). Stereotypes of woman: A single category? *Sex Roles, 2,* 135–148.

Cobb-Clark, D. A., & Dunlop, Y. (1999). The role of gender in job promotions. *Monthly Labor Review, 122*(12), 32–38.

Cochran, S. D., & Mays, V. M. (2006). Estimating prevalence of mental and substance-using disorders among lesbians and gay men from existing national health data. In A. M. Omoto & H. S. Kurtzman (Eds.), *Sexual orientation and mental health: Examining identity and development in lesbian, gay, and bisexual people* (pp. 143–165). Washington, DC: American Psychological Association.

Cochran, S. D., & Peplau, L. A. (1985). Value orientations in heterosexual relationships. *Psychology of Women Quarterly, 9,* 477–488.

Cochran, S. D., Ackerman, D., Mays, V. M., & Ross, M. W. (2004). Prevalence of non-medical drug use and dependence among homosexually active men and women in the US population. *Addiction, 99,* 989–998.

Cochran, S. D., Sullivan, J. G., & Mays, V. M. (2003). Prevalence of mental disorders, psychological distress, and mental health services use among lesbian, gay, and bisexual adults in the United States. *Journal of Consulting and Clinical Psychology, 71,* 53–61.

Cogan, J. C., & Ernsberger, P. (1999). Dieting, weight, and health: Reconceptualizing research and policy. *Journal of Social Issues, 55*(2), 187–205.

Cohen, E. (2007). *CDC: Antidepressants most prescribed drugs in U.S.* Retrieved August 2, 2007, from *www.cnn.com/2007/HEALTH/07/09/antidepressants/index.html.*

Cohen, J. (1977). *Statistical power analysis for the behavioral sciences.* New York: Academic Press.

Cohen, R. Y., Brownell, K. D., & Felix, M. R. J. (1990). Age and sex differences in health habits and beliefs of school-children. *Health Psychology, 9,* 208–224.

Cohen, S., & Wills, T. A. (1985). Stress, social support, and the buffering hypothesis. *Psychological Bulletin, 98,* 310–357.

Cohen, T. F. (1992). Men's families, men's friends: A structural analysis of constraints on men's social ties. In P. M. Nardi (Ed.), *Men's friendships* (pp. 115–131). Newbury Park, CA: Sage.

Cohler, B. J., & Lieberman, M. A. (1980). Social relations and mental health: Middle-aged and older men and women from three European ethnic groups. *Research on Aging, 2*(4), 445–469.

Coie, J. D., Terry, R., Zakriski, A., & Lochman, J. (1995). Early adolescent social influences on delinquent behavior. In J. McCord (Ed.), *Coercion and punishment in long-term perspectives* (pp. 229–244). New York: Cambridge University Press.

Colapinto, J. (2000). *As nature made him: The boy who was raised as a girl.* New York: HarperCollins.

Colapinto, J. (2004). Gender gap. *Slate.* Retrieved January 22, 2007, from *www.slate.com/id/2101678.*

Cole, N. S. (1997). *The ETS gender study: How females and males perform in educational settings.* Princeton, NJ: Educational Testing Services.

Cole, S. S., Denny, D., Eyler, A. E., & Samons, S. L. (2000). Issues of transgender. In L. T. Szuchman & F. Muscarella (Eds.), *Psychological perspectives on human sexuality* (pp. 149–195). New York: Wiley.

Collaer, M. L., & Hines, M. (1998). Human behavioral sex differences: A role for gonadal hormones during early development. *Psychological Bulletin, 118,* 55–107.

Colley, A., Todd, Z., Bland, M., Holmes, M., Khanom, N., & Pike, H. (2004). Style and content in e-mails and letters to male and female friends. *Journal of Language and Social Psychology, 23,* 369–378.

Collins, N. L., & Miller, L. C. (1994). Self-disclosure and liking: A meta-analytic review. *Psychological Bulletin, 116,* 457–475.

Collis, B. (1991). Adolescent females and computers: Real and perceived barriers. In J. Gaskell & A. McLaren (Eds.), *Women and education: A Canadian perspective* (pp. 147–161). Calgary, Canada: Detselig.

Colman, G. J., & Joyce, T. (2003). Trends in smoking before, during, and after pregnancy in ten states. *American Journal of Preventive Medicine, 24,* 29–35.

Coltrane, S. (2000). Research on household labor: Modeling and measuring the social embeddedness of routine family work. *Journal of Marriage and the Family, 62,* 1208–1233.

Coltrane, S., & Messineo, M. (2000). The perpetuation of subtle prejudice: Race and gender imagery in 1990s television advertising. *Sex Roles, 42,* 363–389.

Compas, B. E., Oppedisano, G., Connor, J. K., Gerhardt, C. A., Hinden, B. R., Achenbach, T. M., & Hammen, C. (1997). Gender differences in depressive symptoms in adolescence: Comparison of national samples of clinically referred and nonreferred youths. *Journal of Consulting and Clinical Psychology, 65,* 617–626.

Condry, J., & Condry, S. (1976). Sex differences: A study of the eye of the beholder. *Child Development, 47,* 812–819.

Conger, J. J. (1975). Proceedings of the American psychological association, incorporated, for the year 1974: Minutes of the annual meeting of the council of representatives. *American Psychologist, 30,* 620–651.

Conger, R. D., Lorenz, F. O., Elder, G. H., Jr., Simons, R. L., & Ge, X. (1993). Husband and wife differences in response to undesirable life events. *Journal of Health and Social Behavior, 34,* 71–88.

Connell, R. W. (1987). *Gender and power.* Sydney, Australia: Allen and Unwin.

Connell, R. W., & Messerschmidt, J. W. (2005). Hegemonic masculinity: Rethinking the concept. *Gender & Society, 19,* 829–859.

Conner, M., Johnson, C., & Grogan, S. (2004). Gender, sexuality, body image and eating behaviours. *Journal of Health Psychology, 9,* 505–515.

Constantinople, A. (1973). Masculinity-femininity: An exception to a famous dictum? *Psychological Bulletin, 80,* 389–407.

Copenhaver, M. M., Lash, S. J., & Eisler, R. M. (2000). Masculine gender-role stress, anger, and male intimate abusiveness: Implications for men's relationships. *Sex Roles, 42,* 405–414.

Cordova, J. V., Gee, C. B., & Warren, L. Z. (2005). Emotional skillfulness in marriage: Intimacy as a mediator of the relationship between emotional skillfulness and marital satisfaction. *Journal of Social and Clinical Psychology, 24,* 218–235.

Coren, S., & Hewitt, P. L. (1999). Sex differences in elderly suicide rates: Some predictive factors. *Aging and Mental Health, 3*(2), 112–118.

Correll, S. J. (2001). Gender and the career choice process: The role of biased self-assessments. *American Journal of Sociology, 106,* 1691–1730.

Coryell, W., Endicott, J., & Keller, M. (1992). Major depression in a nonclinical sample: Demographic and clinical risk factors for first onset. *Archives of General Psychiatry, 49,* 117–125.

Cosenzo, K. A., Franchina, J. J., Eisler, R. M., & Krebs, D. (2004). Effects of masculine gender-relevant task instructions on men's cardiovascular reactivity and mental arithmetic performance. *Psychology of Men and Masculinity, 5,* 103–111.

Costa, P. T., Jr., Terracciano, A., & McCrae, R. R. (2001). Gender differences in personality traits across cultures: Robust and surprising findings. *Journal of Personality and Social Psychology, 81,* 322–331.

Cotliar, S. (1996). Buss gets death in child slaying. *Chicago Sun-Times.* Retrieved from *proquest.umi.com.*

Cotter, D. A., DeFiore, J., Germsen, J. M., Kowalewski, B. M., & Vanneman, R. (1997). All women benefit: The macro-level effect of occupational integration on gender earnings equality. *American Psychological Review, 62,* 714–734.

Counts, D. A. (1987). Female suicide and wife abuse: A cross-cultural perspective. *American Association of Suicidology, 17*(3), 194–204.

Courtenay, W. H. (2000a). Constructions of masculinity and their influence on men's well-being: A theory of gender and health. *Social Science & Medicine, 50,* 1385–1401.

Courtenay, W. H. (2000b). Behavioral factors associated with disease, injury, and death among men: Evidence and implications for prevention. *Journal of Men's Studies, 9,* 81–142.

Courtenay, W. H., McCreary, D. R., & Merighi, J. R. (2002). Gender and ethnic differences in health beliefs and behaviors. *Journal of Health Psychology, 7,* 219–231.

Covey, L. S. (1999). Nicotine dependence and its associations with psychiatric disorders: Research evidence and treatment implications. In D. F. Seidman & L. S. Covey (Eds.), *Helping the hard-core smoker, A clinician's guide* (pp. 23–50). Mahwah, NJ: Erlbaum.

Cox, D. J., Clarke, W. L., Gonder-Frederick, L. A., Pohl, S., Hoover, C., Snyder, A., et al. (1985). Accuracy of perceiving blood glucose in IDDM. *Diabetes Care, 8,* 529–536.

Crandall, C. S. (1988). Social contagion of binge eating. *Journal of Personality and Social Psychology, 55*(4), 588–598.

Crick, N. R., & Grotpeter, J. K. (1995). Relational aggression, gender, and social-psychological adjustment. *Child Development, 66,* 710–722.

Crick, N. R., & Werner, N. E. (1998). Response decision processes in relational and overt aggression. *Child Development, 69,* 1630–1639.

Crick, N. R., Ostrov, J. M., & Werner, N. E. (2006). A longitudinal study of relational aggression, physical aggression, and children's social-psychological adjustment. *Journal of Abnormal Child Psychology, 34,* 131–142.

Crick, N. R., Ostrov, J. M., Appleyard, K., Jansen, E. A., & Casas, J. F. (2004). Relational aggression in early childhood: "You can't come to my birthday party unless . . ." In M. Putallaz & K. L. Bierman (Eds.), *Aggression, antisocial behavior, and violence among girls* (pp. 71–89). New York: The Guilford Press.

Crick, N. R., Ostrov, J. M., Burr, J. E., Cullerton-Sen, C., Jansen-Yeh, E., & Ralston, P. (2006). A longitudinal study of relational and physical aggression in preschool. *Applied Developmental Psychology, 27,* 254–268.

Crick, N. R., Werner, N. E., Casas, J. F., O'Brien, K. M., Nelson, D. A., Grotpeter, J. K., & Markon, K. (1999). Childhood aggression and gender: A new look at an old problem. In D. Bernstein (Ed.), *Nebraska Symposium on*

Motivation and Gender (pp. 75–141). Lincoln: University of Nebraska Press.

Crissey, S. R. (2005). Race/ethnic differences in the marital expectations of adolescents: The role of romantic relationships. *Journal of Marriage and Family, 67,* 697–709.

Crittenden, A. (2001). *The price of motherhood: Why the most important job in the world is still the least valued.* New York: Henry Holt and Company.

Crombie, G., Sinclair, N., Silverthorn, N., Byrne, B. M., DuBois, D. L., & Trinneer, A. (2005). Predictors of young adolescents' math grades and course enrollment intentions: Gender similarities and differences. *Sex Roles, 52,* 351–367.

Crosby, F. (1984). The denial of personal discrimination. *American Behavioral Scientist, 27*(3), 371–386.

Crosby, F. (1991). *Juggling.* New York: Free Press.

Crosby, F. J., Todd, J., & Worell, J. (1996). Have feminists abandoned social activism? Voices from the academy. In L. Montada & M. J. Lerner (Eds.), *Current societal concerns about justice* (pp. 85–102). New York: Plenum Press.

Cross, S. E., & Madson, L. (1997). Models of the self: Self-construals and gender. *Psychological Bulletin, 122,* 5–37.

Cross, S. E., & Morris, M. L. (2003). Getting to know you: The relational self-construal, relational cognition, and well-being. *Personality and Social Psychology Bulletin, 29,* 512–523.

Cross, S. E., Bacon, P. L., & Morris, M. L. (2000). The relational-interdependent self-construal and relationships. *Journal of Personality and Social Psychology, 78,* 791–808.

Cuddy, A. J. C., Fiske, S. T., & Glick, P. (2004). When professionals become mothers, warmth doesn't cut the ice. *Journal of Social Issues, 60,* 701–718.

Culbertson, F. M. (1997). Depression and gender: An international review. *American Psychologist, 52,* 25–31.

Cummings, K. M., & Armenta, M. (2002). Penalties for peer sexual harassment in an academic context: The influence of harasser gender, participant gender, severity of harassment, and the presence of bystanders. *Sex Roles, 47,* 273–280.

Cunningham, J. D., & Antill, J. K. (1995). Current trends in nonmarital cohabitation: In search of the POSSLQ. In J. T. Wood & S. Duck (Eds.), *Under-studied relationships: Off the beaten track* (Vol. 6, pp. 148–172). Thousand Oaks, CA: Sage.

Cunningham, M. (2001). The influence of parental attitudes and behaviors on children's attitudes toward gender and household labor in early adulthood. *Journal of Marriage and the Family, 63,* 111–122.

Cunningham, M. (2005). Gender in cohabitation and marriage: The influence of gender ideology on housework allocation over the life course. *Journal of Family Issues, 26,* 1037–1061.

Currie, D. H. (1998). Violent men or violent women? Whose definition counts? In R. K. Bergen (Ed.), *Issues in intimate violence* (pp. 97–111). Thousand Oaks, CA: Sage.

Cutrona, C. E. (1996). *Social support in couples.* Thousand Oaks, CA: Sage.

Cyranowski, J. M., Frank, E., Young, E., & Shear, M. K. (2000). Adolescent onset of the gender difference in lifetime rates of major depression. *Archives of General Psychiatry, 57,* 21–27.

Dabbs, J. M., & Hargrove, M. F. (1997). Age, testosterone, and behavior among female prison inmates. *Psychosomatic Medicine, 59,* 477–480.

Dabbs, J. M., Jr., Carr, T. S., Frady, R. L., & Riad, J. K. (1995). Testosterone, crime, and misbehavior among 692 male prison inmates. *Personality and Individual Differences, 18,* 627–633.

Dabbs, J. M., Jr., Chang, E-L., Strong, R. A., & Milun, R. (1998). Spatial ability, navigation strategy, and geographic knowledge among men and women. *Evolution and Human Behavior, 19,* 89–98.

Dabbs, J. M., Jr., Riad, J. K., & Chance, S. E. (2001). Testosterone and ruthless homicide. *Personality and Individual Differences, 31,* 599–603.

Dads and Daughters. (1999, December 9). *Dads and Daughters protest halts inappropriate Jewelry.com ad.* Retrieved May 19, 2003, from *www.dadsanddaughters.org/jewelrypr. html.*

Dads and Daughters. (2000, January 24). *Make Mattel put brains over Barbie.* Retrieved from *www.dadsanddaughters.org/barbieact.html.*

Dahl, G. B., & Moretti, E. (2005). *The demand for sons:* Unpublished manuscript, University of California at Berkeley.

Dakof, G. A. (2000). Understanding gender differences in adolescent drug abuse: Issues of comorbidity and family functioning. *Journal of Psychoactive Drugs, 32,* 25–32.

Daly, M., & Wilson, M. (1988). Evolutionary social psychology and family homicide. *Science, 242,* 519–524.

Daly, M., & Wilson, M. (1999). An evolutionary perspective on homicide. In M. Smith & M. A. Zahn (Eds.), *Homicide: A sourcebook of social research* (pp. 58–71). Thousand Oaks, CA: Sage.

Danoff-Burg, S., Mosher, C. E., & Grant, C. A. (2006). Relations of agentic and communal personality traits to health behavior and substance use among college students. *Personality and Individual Differences, 40,* 353–363.

Datnow, A., Hubbard, L., & Woody, E. (2001). Is single gender schooling viable in the public sector? Lessons from California's pilot program. Retrieved May 29, 2007, from *www.oise.utoronto.ca/depts/tps/adatnow/final.pdf.*

Daubman, K. A., & Sigall, H. (1997). Gender differences in perceptions of how others are affected by self-disclosure of achievement. *Sex Roles, 37,* 73–89.

Davidson, K. (2001). Late life widowhood, selfishness and new partnership choices: A gendered perspective. *Ageing and Society, 21,* 297–317.

Davies, P. G., Spencer, S. J., Quinn, D. M., & Gerhardstein, R. (2002). Consuming images: How television commercials that elicit stereotype threat can restrain women academically and professionally. *Personality and Social Psychology Bulletin, 28,* 1615–1628.

Davis, B. M., & Gilbert, L. A. (1989). Effect of dispositional and situational influences on women's dominance expression in mixed-sex dyads. *Journal of Personality and Social Psychology, 57,* 294–300.

Davis, M. C., & Matthews, K. A. (1996). Do gender-relevant characteristics determine cardiovascular reactivity? Match versus mismatch of traits and situation. *Journal of Personality and Social Psychology, 71,* 527–535.

Davis, M. C., Matthews, K. A., & Twamley, E. W. (1999). Is life more difficult on Mars or Venus? A meta-analytic review of sex differences in major and minor life events. *Annals of Behavioral Medicine, 21,* 83–97.

Davison, H. K., & Burke, M. J. (2000). Sex discrimination in simulated employment contexts: A meta-analytic investigation. *Journal of Vocational Behavior, 56,* 225–248.

De Ruijter, J. M. P., Schippers, J. J., & Van Doorne-Huiskes, A. (2004). Comparable worth: Policy and measures. *The Netherlands' Journal of Social Sciences, 40,* 41–67.

Dear, G. E., & Roberts, C. M. (2002). The relationships between codependency and femininity and masculinity. *Sex Roles, 46,* 159–165.

Deaux, K. (1984). From individual differences to social categories: Analysis of a decade's research on gender. *American Psychologist, 39,* 105–116.

Deaux, K., & Kite, M. (1993). Gender stereotypes. In F. L. Denmark & M. A. Paludi (Eds.), *Psychology of women: A handbook of issues and theories* (pp. 107–139). Westport, CT: Greenwood Press.

Deaux, K., & LaFrance, M. (1998). Gender. In D. Gilbert, S. Fiske, & G. Lindzey (Eds.), *Handbook of social psychology* (pp. 788–826). New York: McGraw-Hill.

Deaux, K., & Lewis, L. L. (1983). Assessment of gender stereotypes: Methodology and components. *Psychological Documents, 13,* 25 (MS. No. 2583).

Deaux, K., & Lewis, L. L. (1984). Structure of gender stereotypes: Interrelationships among components and gender label. *Journal of Personality and Social Psychology, 46,* 991–1004.

Deaux, K., & Major, B. (1987). Putting gender into context: An interactive model of gender-related behavior. *Psychological Review, 94,* 369–389.

Deford, F. (1993, February 22). Lessons from a friend. *Newsweek,* pp. 60–61.

DeLamater, J. (1987). Gender difference in sexual scenarios. In K. Kelley (Ed.), *Females, males, and sexuality: Theories and research* (pp. 127–139). Albany: State University of New York Press.

Denton, M., & Walters, V. (1999). Gender differences in structural and behavioral determinants of health: An analysis of the social production of health. *Social Science and Medicine, 48,* 1221–1235.

Deptula, D. P., Henry, D. B., Shoeny, M. E., & Slavick, J. T. (2006). Adolescent sexual behavior and attitudes: A costs and benefits approach. *Journal of Adolescent Health, 38,* 35–43.

Derbyshire, S. W. G., Nichols, T. E., Firestone, L., Townsend, D. W., & Jones, A. K. P. (2002). Gender differences in patterns of cerebral activation during equal experience of painful laser stimulation. *The Journal of Pain, 3,* 401–411.

Derlega, V. J., & Chaikin, A. L. (1976). Norms affecting self-disclosure in men and women. *Journal of Consulting and Clinical Psychology, 44,* 376–380.

Derlega, V. J., Barbee, A. P., & Winstead, B. A. (1994). Friendship, gender, and social support: Laboratory studies of supportive interactions. In B. R. Burleson, T. L. Albrecht, & I. G. Sarason (Eds.), *Communication of social support: Messages, interactions, relationships, and community* (pp. 136–151). Thousand Oaks, CA: Sage.

Derlega, V. J., Lewis, R. J., Harrison, S., Winstead, B. A., & Costanza, R. (1989). Gender differences in the initiation and attribution of tactile intimacy. *Journal of Nonverbal Behavior, 13*(2), 83–96.

Derlega, V. J., Winstead, B. A., Wong, P. T. P., & Hunter, S. (1985). Gender effects in an initial encounter: A case where men exceed women in disclosure. *Journal of Social and Personal Relationships, 2,* 25–44.

Desmarais, S., & Curtis, J. (1997). Gender and perceived pay entitlement: Testing for effects of experience with income. *Journal of Personality and Social Psychology, 72,* 141–150.

Dessens, A. B., Slijper, F. M. E., & Drop, S. L. S. (2005). Gender dysphoria and gender change in chromosomal females with congenital adrenal hyperplasia. *Archives of Sexual Behavior, 34,* 389–397.

DeSteno, D., Bartlett, M. Y., Braverman, J., & Salovey, P. (2002). Sex differences in jealousy: Evolutionary mechanism or artifact of measurement? *Journal of Personality and Social Psychology, 83,* 1103–1116.

Devlin, P. K., & Cowan, G. A. (1985). Homophobia, perceived fathering, and male intimate relationships. *Journal of Personality Assessment, 49*(5), 467–473.

Dey, J. G., & Hill, C. (2007). *Behind the pay gap.* Washington, DC: American Association of University Women Educational Foundation.

Diamond, M., & Sigmundson, H. K. (1997). Sex reassignment at birth: Long-term review and clinical implications. *Archives of Pediatric and Adolescent Medicine, 151,* 298–304.

Dickhauser, O., & Meyer, W. U. (2006). Gender differences in young children's math ability attributions. *Psychological Science, 48,* 3–16.

Diehl, M., Owen, S. K., & Youngblade, L. M. (2004). Agency and communion attributes in adults' spontaneous self-representations. *International Journal of Behavioral Development, 28,* 1–15.

Diekman, A. B., & Murnen, S. K. (2004). Learning to be little women and little men: The inequitable gender equality of nonsexist children's literature. *Sex Roles, 50,* 373–385.

Diekman, A. B., Eagly, A. H., Mladinic, A., & Ferreira, M. C. (2005). Dynamic stereotypes about women and men in Latin America and the United States. *Journal of Cross-Cultural Psychology, 36,* 209–226.

Diener, E., Gohm, C. L., Suh, E., & Oishi, S. (2000). Similarity of the relations between marital status and subjective well-being across cultures. *Journal of Cross-Cultural Psychology, 31,* 419–436.

Dietary Guidelines for Americans. (2005). *Physical activity.* Retrieved November 8, 2007, from *www.healthierus.gov/dietaryguidelines.*

Dietz, T. L. (1998). An examination of violence and gender role portrayals in video games: Implications for gender socialization and aggressive behavior. *Sex Roles, 38,* 425–442.

Dindia, K. (2006). Men are from North Dakota, women are from South Dakota. In K. Dindia & D. J. Canary (Eds.), *Sex differences and similarities in communication* (2nd ed.) (pp. 3–20). Mahwah, NJ: Lawrence Erlbaum Associates.

Dindia, K., & Allen, M. (1992). Sex differences in self-disclosure: A meta-analysis. *Psychological Bulletin, 112,* 106–124.

Dindia, K., & Canary, D. J. (Eds.). (2006). *Sex differences and similarities in communication: Critical essays and empirical investigations of sex and gender in interaction* (2nd ed.). Mahwah, NJ: Lawrence Erlbaum Associates.

Dishman, R. K., Hales, D. P., Pfeiffer, K. A., Felton, G., Saunders, R., Ward, D. S., et al. (2006). Physical self-concept and self-esteem mediate cross-sectional relations of physical activity and sport participation with depression symptoms among adolescent girls. *Health Psychology, 25,* 396–407.

Dittmann, R. W. (1997). Sexual behavior and sexual orientation in females with congenital adrenal hyperplasis. In L. Ellis & L. Ebertz (Eds.), *Sexual orientation: Toward biological understanding* (pp. 53–69). Westport, CT: Praeger.

Dittmann, R. W., Kappes, M. H., Kappes, M. E., Borger, D., Stegner, H., Willig, R. F., & Wallis, H. (1990). Congenital adrenal hyperplasia. I: Gender-related behavior and attitudes in female patients and sisters. *Psychoneuroendocrinology, 15*(5/6), 401–420.

Division of Adult and Community Health. (1998). Behavioral risk factor surveillance system online prevalence data. Retrieved November 1, 2007, from *www.2.cdc.gov/nccdphp/brfss/index.asp.*

Dodd, D. K., Russell, B. L., & Jenkins, C. (1999). Smiling in school yearbook photos: Gender differences from kindergarten to adulthood. *Psychological Record, 49,* 543–554.

Dolgin, K. G., Meyer, L., & Schwartz, J. (1991). Effects of gender, target's gender, topic, and self-esteem on disclosure to best and midling friends. *Sex Roles, 25,* 311–329.

Donaldson, M. (1976). Development of conceptualization. In V. Hamilton & M. D. Vernon (Eds.), *The development of cognitive processes* (pp. 277–303). London: Academic Press.

Donat, P. L. N., & D'Emilio, J. (1992). A feminist redefinition of rape and sexual assault: Historical foundation and change. *Journal of Social Issues, 48*(1), 9–22.

Donkin, A., Goldblatt, P., & Lynch, K. (2002). Inequalities in life expectancy by social class, 1972–1999. *Health Statisitics Quarterly, 15,* 5–15.

Doss, B. D., Atkins, D. C., & Christensen, A. (2003). Who's dragging their feet? Husbands and wives seeking marital therapy. *Journal of Marital and Family Therapy, 29,* 165–177.

Douvan, E., & Adelson, J. (1966). *The adolescent experience.* New York: Wiley.

Doyle, J. A. (1995). *The male experience.* Madison, WI: Brown & Benchmark.

Dracup, K., Moser, D. K., Eisenberg, M., Meischke, H., Alonzo, A. A., & Braslow, A. (1995). Causes of delay in seeking treatment for heart attack symptoms. *Social Science & Medicine, 40*(3), 379–392.

DuBois, D. L., Burk-Braxton, C., Swenson, L. P., Tevendale, H. D., & Hardesty, J. L. (2002). Race and gender influences on adjustment in early adolescence: Investigation of an integrative model. *Child Development, 73,* 1573–1592.

Dubow, E. F., Kausch, D. F., Blum, M. C., Reed, J., & Bush, E. (1989). Correlates of suicidal ideation and attempts in a community sample of junior high and high school students. *Journal of Clinical Child Psychology, 18*(2), 158–166.

Duck, S., & Wright, P. H. (1993). Reexamining gender differences in same-gender friendships: A close look at two kinds of data. *Sex Roles, 28,* 709–727.

Duffy, J., Warren, K., & Walsh, M. (2001). Classroom interactions: Gender of teacher, gender of student, and classroom subject. *Sex Roles, 45,* 579–593.

Duncan, G. J., & Hoffman, S. D. (1985). A reconsideration of the economic consequences of marital dissolution. *Demography, 22,* 485–497.

Dunn, D. (1996). Gender and earnings. In P. J. Dubeck & K. Borman (Eds.), *Women and work: A handbook* (pp. 61–63). New York: Garland.

Dunn, J., Bretherton, I., & Munn, P. (1987). Conversations about feeling states between mothers and their young children. *Developmental Psychology, 23,* 132–139.

Dweck, C. S., Davidson, W., Nelson, S., & Enna, B. (1978). Sex differences in learned helplessness. II: The contingencies of evaluative feedback in the classroom, and III: An experimental analysis. *Developmental Psychology, 14,* 268–276.

Dye, J. L. (2005). Fertility of American women: June 2004. *Current Population Reports* (P20-555). Washington, DC: U.S. Census Bureau.

Dziech, B. W., & Hawkins, M. W. (1998). *Sexual harassment in higher education: Reflection and new perspectives:* New York: Garland Press.

Eagly, A. H. (1987a). Reporting sex differences. *American Psychologist, 42,* 756–757.

Eagly, A. H. (1987b). *Sex differences in social behavior: A social role interpretation.* Hillsdale, NJ: Erlbaum.

Eagly, A. H. (1995). The science and politics of comparing women and men. *American Psychologist, 50,* 145–158.

Eagly, A. H., & Crowley, M. (1986). Gender and helping behavior: A meta-analytic review of the social psychological literature. *Psychological Bulletin, 100,* 283–308.

Eagly, A. H., Diekman, A. B., Johannesen-Schmidt, & Koenig, A. M. (2004). Gender gaps in sociopolitical attitudes: A social psychological analysis. *Journal of Personality and Social Psychology, 87,* 796–816.

Eagly, A. H., & Johannesen-Schmidt, M. C. (2001). The leadership styles of women and men. *Journal of Social Issues, 57,* 781–797.

Eagly, A. H., & Johnson, B. T. (1990). Gender and leadership style: A meta-analysis. *Psychological Bulletin, 108,* 233–256.

Eagly, A. H., & Karau, S. J. (1991). Gender and the emergence of leaders: A meta-analysis. *Journal of Personality and Social Psychology, 60,* 685–710.

Eagly, A. H., & Karau, S. J. (2002). Role congruity theory of prejudice toward female leaders. *Psychological Review, 109,* 573–598.

Eagly, A. H., & Kite, M. E. (1987). Are stereotypes of nationalities applied to both women and men? *Journal of Personality and Social Psychology, 53,* 451–462.

Eagly, A. H., & Steffen, V. J. (1984). Gender stereotypes stem from the distribution of women and men into social roles. *Journal of Personality and Social Psychology, 46,* 735–754.

Eagly, A. H., & Wood, W. (1982). Inferred sex differences in status as a determinant of gender stereotypes about social influence. *Journal of Personality and Social Psychology, 43,* 915–928.

Eagly, A. H., & Wood, W. (1999). The origins of sex differences in human behavior: Evolved dispositions versus social roles. *American Psychologist, 54,* 408–423.

Eagly, A. H., Johannesen-Schmidt, M. C., & van Engen, M. L. (2003). Transformational, transactional, and laissez-faire leadership styles: A meta-analysis comparing women and men. *Psychological Bulletin, 129,* 569–591.

Eagly, A. H., Karau, S. J., & Makhijani, M. G. (1995). Gender and the effectiveness of leaders: A meta-analysis. *Psychological Bulletin, 117,* 125–145.

Eagly, A. H., Makhijani, M. G., & Klonsky, B. G. (1992). Gender and the evaluation of leaders: A meta-analysis. *Psychological Bulletin, 111,* 3–22.

Eagly, A. H., Wood, W., & Diekman, A. B. (2000). Social role theory of sex differences and similiarities: A current appraisal. In T. Eckes & H. M. Trautner (Eds.), *The developmental social psychology of gender* (pp. 123–174). Mahwah, NJ: Erlbaum.

Eagly, A. H., Wood, W., & Fishbaugh, L. (1981). Sex differences in conformity: Surveillance by the group as a determinant of male nonconformity. *Journal of Personality and Social Psychology, 40,* 384–394.

Eals, M., & Silverman, I. (1994). The Hunter-Gatherer theory of spatial sex differences: Proximate factors mediating the female advantage in recall of object arrays. *Ethology and Sociobiology, 15,* 95–105.

Eastwick, P. W., Eagly, A. H., Glick, P., Johannesen-Schmidt, M. C., Fiske, S. T., Freiburger, P., et al. (2006). Is traditional gender ideology associated with sex-typed mate preferences? A test in nine nations. *Sex Roles, 54,* 603–614.

Eaton, W. O., & Enns, L. R. (1986). Sex differences in human motor activity level. *Psychological Bulletin, 100,* 19–28.

Eccles, J. S. (1987). Gender roles and women's achievement-related decisions. *Psychology of Women Quarterly, 11,* 135–172.

Eccles, J. S., & Jacobs, J. E. (1986). Social forces shape math attitudes and performance. *Journal of Women in Culture and Society, 11*(2), 367–380.

Eccles, J. S., Barber, B., & Jozefowicz, D. (1999). Linking gender to educational, occupational, and recreational choices: Applying the Eccles et al. Model of Achievement-Related Choices. In W. B. Swann, Jr., J. H. Langlois, & L. A. Gilbert (Eds.), *Sexism and stereotypes in modern society: The gender-science of Janet Taylor Spence* (pp. 153–192). Washington, DC: American Psychological Association.

Eccles, J. S., Barber, B., Jozefowicz, D., Malenchuk, O., & Vida, M. (1999). Self-evaluations of competence, task values, and self-esteem. In N. Johnson, G. Roberts, & M. C. Roberts (Eds.), *Beyond appearance: A new look at adolescent girls* (pp. 53–83). Washington, DC: American Psychological Association.

Eccles, J. S., Freedman-Doan, C., Frome, P., Jacobs, J. E., & Yoon, K. S. (2000). Gender-role socialization in the family: A longitudinal approach. In T. Eckes & H. M. Trautner (Eds.), *The developmental social psychology of gender* (pp. 333–360). Mahwah, NJ: Lawrence Erlbaum Associates.

Eccles, J. S., Jacobs, J. E., & Harold, R. D. (1990). Gender role stereotypes, expectancy effects, and parents' socialization of gender differences. *Journal of Social Issues, 46,* 183–201.

Ecuyer-Dab, I., & Robert, M. (2004). Have sex differences in spatial ability evolved from male competition for mating and female concern for survival? *Cognition, 91,* 221–257.

Edwards, A. C., Nazroo, J. Y., & Brown, G. W. (1998). Gender differences in marital support following a shared life event. *Social Science & Medicine, 46*(8), 1077–1085.

Edwards, R. R., Haythornthwaite, J. A., Sullivan, M. J., & Fillingim, R. B. (2004). Catastrophizing as a mediator of sex differences in pain: Differential effects for daily pain versus laboratory-induced pain. *Pain, 111,* 335–341.

Edwards, R. R., Augustson, E., & Fillingim, R. (2003). Differential relationships between anxiety and treatment-associated pain reduction among male and female chronic pain patients. *The Clinical Journal of Pain, 19,* 208–216.

Egeland, J. A., & Hostetter, A. M. (1983). Amish Study. I: Affective disorders among the Amish 1976–1980. *American Journal of Psychiatry, 140*, 56–61.

Ehrlinger, J., & Dunning, D. (2003). How chronic self-views influence (and potentially mislead) estimates of performance. *Journal of Personality and Social Psychology, 84*, 5–17.

Eisenberg, N., & Fabes, R. A. (1998). Prosocial development. In W. Damon & N. Eisenberg (Eds.), *Handbook of child psychology* (Vol. 3, pp. 701–757). New York: John Wiley & Sons, Inc.

Eisenberg, N., & Lennon, R. (1983). Sex differences in empathy and related capacities. *Psychological Bulletin, 94*, 100–131.

Eiser, C., Havermans, T., Pancer, M., & Eiser, J. R. (1992). Adjustment to chronic disease in relation to age and gender: Mothers' and fathers' reports of their childrens' behavior. *Journal of Pediatric Psychology, 17*(3), 261–275.

Eisler, R. M., & Skidmore, J. R. (1987). Masculine gender role stress: Scale development and component factors in the appraisal of stressful situations. *Behavior Modification, 11*(2), 123–136.

Eisler, R. M., Franchina, J. J., Moore, T. M., Honeycutt, H. G., & Rhatigan, D. L. (2000). Masculine gender role stress and intimate abuse: Effects of gender relevance of conflict situations on men's attributions and affective responses. *Psychology of Men and Masculinity, 1*(1), 30–36.

Ekman, P. (1992). An argument for basic emotion. *Cognition and Emotion, 6*, 169–200.

Elasmar, M., Hasegawa, K., & Brain, M. (1999). The portrayal of women in U.S. prime time television. *Journal of Broadcasting and Electronic Media, 44*(1), 20–34.

Eldridge, N. S., & Gilbert, L. A. (1990). Correlates of relationship satisfaction in lesbian couples. *Psychology of Women Quarterly, 14*, 43–62.

Elkins, L. E., & Peterson, C. (1993). Gender differences in best friendships. *Sex Roles, 29*, 497–508.

Ell, K., Nishimoto, R., Mediansky, L., Mantell, J., & Hamovitch, M. (1992). Social relations, social support, and survival among patients with cancer. *Journal of Psychosomatic Medicine, 36*, 531–541.

Elliott, D. M., Mok, D. S., & Briere, J. (2004). Adult sexual assault: Prevalence, symptomatology, and sex differences in the general population. *Journal of Traumatic Stress, 17*, 203–211.

Elliott, S., & Umberson, D. (2004). Recent demographic trends in the US and implications for well-being. In J. Scott, J. Treas & M. Richards (Eds.), *The Blackwell companion to the sociology of families* (pp. 34–53). Malden, MA: Blackwell Publishing.

Ellis, H. (1894). *Man and woman.* London: Scott.

Ellis, L. (2006). Gender differences in smiling: An evolutionary neuroandrogenic theory. *Physiology & Behavior, 88*, 303–308.

Else-Quest, N. M., Hyde, J. S., & DeLamater, J. D. (2005). Context counts: Long-term sequelae of premarital intercourse or abstinence. *The Journal of Sex Research, 42*, 102–112.

Elsesser, K., & Peplau, L. A. (2006). The glass partition: Obstacles to cross-sex friendships at work. *Human Relations, 59*, 1077–1100.

Equal Employment Opportunity Commission. (1980). Guidelines on discrimination because of sex (sec. 1604.11). *Federal Register, 45*, 74676–74677.

Equal Employment Opportunity Commission. (2007). *Sexual harassment charges.* EEOC & FEPAs combined (FY1997–FY2006). Retrieved July 10, 2007, from *www.eeoc.gov/stats/harass.html.*

Erdincler, D., Bugay, G., Ertan, T., & Eker, E. (2004). Depression and sex hormones in elderly women. *Archives of Gerontology and Geriatrics, 39*, 239–244.

Erickson, R. J. (2005). Why emotion work matters: Sex, gender, and the division of household labor. *Journal of Marriage and Family, 67*, 337–351.

Erikson, E. H. (1950). *Childhood and society.* New York: Norton.

Ernst, S. B. (1995). Gender issues in books for children and young adults. In S. Lehr (Ed.), *Battling dragons: Issues and controversy in children's literature* (pp. 66–78). Portsmouth, NH: Heinemann.

Ernster, V. L. (1996). Female lung cancer. *Annual Review of Public Health, 17*, 97–114.

Evans, R. E. C., Brotherstone, H., Miles, A., & Wardle, J. (2005). Gender differences in early detection of cancer. *Journal of Men's Health & Gender, 2*, 209–217.

Evenson, R. J., & Simon, R. W. (2005). Clarifying the relationship between parenthood and depression. *Journal of Health and Social Behavior, 46*, 341–358.

Ewart, C. K., Taylor, C. B., Kraemer, H. C., & Agras, W. S. (1991). High blood pressure and marital discord: Not being nasty matters more than being nice. *Health Psychology, 10*, 155–163.

Exline, J. J., & Lobel, M. (1999). The perils of outperformance: Sensitivity about being the target of a threatening upward comparison. *Psychological Bulletin, 125*, 307–337.

Fabes, R. A., Martin, C. L., & Hanish, L. D. (2003). Young children's play qualitites in same-, other-, and mixed-sex peer groups. *Child Development, 74*, 921–932.

Fabes, R. A., Martin, C. L., & Hanish, L. D. (2004). The next 50 years: Considering gender as a context for understanding young children's peer relationships. *Merrill-Palmer Quarterly, 50*, 260–273.

Fagot, B. I., & Hagan, R. (1985). Aggression in toddlers: Responses in the assertive acts of boys and girls. *Sex Roles, 1*, 341–351.

Fagot, B. I., Hagan, R., Leinbach, M. D., & Kronsberg, S. (1985). Differential reactions to assertive and communicative acts of toddler boys and girls. *Child Development, 56*, 1499–1505.

Faludi, S. (1991). *Backlash: The undeclared war against American women.* New York: Crown.

Farrell, W. (1993). *The myth of male power: Why men are the disposable sex.* New York: Simon & Schuster.

Fassinger, R. E., & Arseneau, J. R. (2007). "I'd rather get wet than be under that umbrella": Differentiating the experiences and identities of lesbian, gay, bisexual, and transgender people. In K. J. Bieschke, R. M. Perez & K. A. DeBord (Eds.), *Handbook of counseling and psychotherapy with lesbian, gay, bisexual, and transgender clients* (pp. 19–49). Washington, DC: American Psychological Association.

Federal Bureau of Investigation. (2006). Most victims and perpetrators in homicides are male. Retrieved June 26, 2007, from *www.ojp.usdoj.gov/bjs/homicide/gender. htm#vorelgender.*

Fehr, B. (2000). The life cycle of friendship. In C. H. Hendrick & S. S. Hendrick (Eds.), *Close relationships: A sourcebook* (pp. 71–82). Thousand Oaks, CA: Sage Publications Inc.

Fehr, B. (2004). Intimacy expectations in same-sex friendships: A prototype interaction-pattern model. *Journal of Personality and Social Psychology, 86,* 265–284.

Fehr, B., Baldwin, M., Collins, L., Patterson, S., & Benditt, R. (1999). Anger in close relationships: An interpersonal script analysis. *Personality and Social Psychology Bulletin, 25,* 299–312.

Fein, D. J., Burstein, N. R., Fein, G. G., & Lindberg, L. D. (2003). *The determinants of marriage and cohabitation among disadvantaged Americans: Research findings and needs.* Cambridge, MA: Abt Associates Inc.

Feinauer, L. L., & Williams-Evans, L. (1989). Effects of wife employment preference on marital adjustment. *American Journal of Family Therapy, 17*(3), 208–218.

Feingold, A. (1988). Matching for attractiveness in romantic partners and same-sex friends: A meta-analysis and theoretical critique. *Psychological Bulletin, 104,* 226–235.

Feingold, A. (1990). Gender differences in effects of physical attractiveness on romantic attraction: A comparison across five research paradigms. *Journal of Personality and Social Psychology, 59,* 981–993.

Feingold, A. (1992). Gender differences in mate selection preferences: A test of the parental investment model. *Psychological Bulletin, 112,* 125–139.

Feingold, A. (1994). Gender differences in personality: A meta-analysis. *Psychological Bulletin, 116,* 429–456.

Fejfar, M. C., & Hoyle, R. H. (2000). Effect of private self-awareness on negative affect and self-referent attribution: A quantitative review. *Personality and Social Psychology Review, 4,* 132–142.

Feldman, R., Sussman, A. L., & Zigler, E. (2004). Parental leave and work adaptation at the transition to parenthood: Individual, marital, and social correlates. *Applied Developmental Psychology, 25,* 459–479.

Feldman, S. S., & Gowen, L. K. (1998). Conflict negotiation tactics in romantic relationships in high school students. *Journal of Youth and Adolescence, 27*(6), 691–717.

Fenigstein, A., Scheier, M. F., & Buss, A. H. (1975). Public and private self-consciousness: Assessment and theory. *Journal of Consulting and Clinical Psychology, 43,* 522–527.

Feshbach, S. (1989). The bases and development of individual aggression. In J. Groebel & R. A. Hinde (Eds.), *Aggression and war: Their biological and social bases* (pp. 78–90). New York: Cambridge University Press.

Fetters, J. K., Peterson, E. D., Shaw, L. J., Newby, K., & Califf, R. M. (1996). Sex-specific differences in coronary artery disease risk factors, evaluation, and treatment: Have they been adequately evaluated? *American Heart Journal, 131*(4), 796–813.

Fife, B. L., Kennedy, V. N., & Robinson, L. (1994). Gender and adjustment to cancer: Clinical implications. *Journal of Psychosocial Oncology, 12,* 1–21.

Fifth girl dies. (2006). *Fifth girl dies after Amish school shooting* [Electronic Version]. CNN.com. Retrieved January 22, 2007, from *www.cnn.com/2006/US/10/02/amish.shooting/ index.html.*

Fillingim, R. B. (2000). *Sex, gender, and pain (Vol. 17).* Seattle: IASP Press.

Fillingim, R. B. (2003). Sex-related influences on pain: A review of mechanisms and clinical implications. *Rehabilitation Psychology, 48,* 165–174.

Fincham, F. D., Beach, S. R. H., Harold, G. T., & Osborne, L. N. (1997). Marital satisfaction and depression: Different causal relationships for men and women? *Psychological Science, 8*(5), 351–357.

Fischer, A. H. (1997). *Gender and emotion.* New York: Cambridge University Press.

Fischer, A. H., & Manstead, A. S. R. (2000). The relation between gender and emotions in different cultures. In A. H. Fischer (Ed.), *Gender and emotion: Social psychological perspectives* (pp. 71–94). New York: Cambridge University Press.

Fischer, A. H., Mosquera, P. M. R., van Vianen, A. E. M., & Manstead, A. S. R. (2004). Gender and culture differences in emotion. *Emotion, 4,* 87–94.

Fischer, A. R. (2006). Women's benevolent sexism as reaction to hostility. *Psychology of Women Quarterly, 30,* 410–416.

Fischer, C. S. (1979). *Friendship, gender and the life cycle.* Unpublished manuscript, University of California, Berkeley.

Fiske, S. T., & Stevens, L. E. (1993). What's so special about sex? Gender stereotyping and discrimination. In S. Oskamp & M. Costanzo (Eds.), *Gender issues in contemporary society* (pp. 173–196). Newbury Park, CA: Sage.

Fiske, S. T., & Taylor, S. E. (1991). *Social cognition* (Second ed.). New York: McGraw-Hill.

Fiske, S. T., Bersoff, D. N., Borgida, E., Deaux, K., & Heilman, M. E. (1991). Social science research on trial: Use of sex stereotyping research in *Price Waterhouse v. Hopkins. American Psychologist, 46,* 1049–1060.

Fitzgerald, L. F., Gelfand, M. J., & Drasgow, F. (1995). Measuring sexual harassment: Theoretical and psychometric advances. *Basic and Applied Social Psychology, 17*(4), 425–445.

Fitzgerald, L. F., Shullman, S. L., Bailey, N., Richards, M., Swecker, J., Gold, Y., et al. (1988). The incidence and dimensions of sexual harassment in academia and the workplace. *Journal of Vocational Behavior, 32,* 152–175.

Flaks, D. K., Ficher, I., Masterpasqua, F., & Joseph, G. (1995). Lesbians choosing motherhood: A comparative study of lesbian and heterosexual parents and their children. *Developmental Psychology, 31,* 105–114.

Flay, B. R., Hu, F. B., & Richardson, J. (1998). Psychosocial predictors of different stages of cigarette smoking among high school students. *Preventive Medicine, 27,* A9–A18.

Flegal, K. M., & Troiano, R. P. (2000). Changes in the distribution of body mass index of adults and children in the US population. *International Journal of Obesity, 24,* 807–818.

Fletcher, G. J. O., Tither, J. M., O'Loughlin, C., Friesen, M., & Overall, N. (2004). Warm and homely or cold and beautiful? Sex differences in trading off traits in mate selection. *Personality and Social Psychology Bulletin, 30,* 659–672.

Flory, J. D., Räikkönen, K., Matthews, K. A., & Owens, J. F. (2000). Self-focused attention and mood during everyday social interactions. *Personality and Social Psychology Bulletin, 26,* 875–883.

Floyd, F. J., & Markman, H. J. (1983). Observational biases in spouse observation: Toward a cognitive/behavioral model of marriage. *Journal of Consulting and Clinical Psychology, 51,* 450–457.

Flynn, F. J. (2003). How much should I give and how often? The effects of generosity and frequency of favor exchange on social status and productivity. *Academy of Management Journal, 46,* 539–553.

Flynn, K. J., & Fitzgibbon, M. (1998). Body images and obesity risk among Black females: A review of the literature. *Annals of Behavior Medicine, 20*(1), 13–24.

Fokkema, T. (2002). Combining a job and children: Contrasting the health of married and divorced women in the Netherlands? *Social Science & Medicine, 54,* 741–752.

Foote, C. (2002). Gender differences in attribution feedback in the elementary classroom. *Research in the Schools, 9*(1), 1–8.

Forbes, G. B., Jobe, R. L., White, K. B., Bloesch, E., & Adams-Curtis, L. E. (2005). Perceptions of dating violence following a sexual or nonsexual betrayal of trust: Effects of gender, sexism, acceptance of rape myths, and vengeance motivation. *Sex Roles, 52,* 165–173.

Forrest, J. A., & Feldman, R. S. (2000). Detecting deception and judge's involvement: Lower task involvement leads to better lie detection. *Personality and Social Psychology Bulletin, 26,* 118–125.

Forsterlee, L., Fox, G. B., Forsterlee, R., & Ho, R. (2004). The effects of a victim impact statement and gender on juror information processing in a criminal trial: Does the punishment fit the crime? *Australian Psychologist, 39,* 57–67.

Foschi, M. (2000). Double standards for competence: Theory and research. *Annual Review of Sociology, 26,* 21–42.

Fox, M. (1993). Men who weep, boys who dance: The gender agenda between the lines in children's literature. *Language Arts, 70,* 54–88.

FOX News. (2006, May 25). *Hasbro halts plans for doll based on Pussycat Dolls.* Retrieved January 23, 2007, from *www.foxnews.com/printer_friendly_story/0,3566,196943,00.html.*

Fragoso, J. M., & Kashubeck, S. (2000). Machismo, gender role conflict, and mental health in Mexican American men. *Psychology of Men and Masculinity, 1*(2), 87–97.

Franck, K., & Rosen, E. (1949). A projective test of masculinity-femininity. *Journal of Consulting Psychology, 13,* 247–256.

Frank, E., & Young, E. (2000). Pubertal changes and adolescent challenges. In E. Frank (Ed.), *Gender and its effects on psychopathology* (pp. 85–102). Washington, DC: American Psychiatric Press.

Frankenhaeuser, M. (1991). Mini-series behavioral medicine: An international perspective. *Annals of Behavioral Medicine, 13,* 197–204.

Frankenhaeuser, M., Lundberg, U., Fredrikson, M., Melin, B., Tuomisto, M., Mystern, A.-L., et al. (1989). Stress on and off the job as related to sex and occupational status in white-collar workers. *Journal of Organizational Behavior, 10,* 321–346.

Franklin, C. W., Jr. (1992). Hey home yo, bro: Friendship among Black men. In P. M. Nardi (Ed.), *Men's friendships* (pp. 201–214). Newbury Park, CA: Sage.

Frazier, P. A., & Esterly, E. (1990). Correlates of relationship beliefs: Gender, relationship experience and relationship satisfaction. *Journal of Social and Personal Relationships, 7,* 331–352.

Frazier, P. A., Cochran, C. C., & Olson, A. M. (1995). Social science research on lay definitions of sexual harassment. *Journal of Social Issues, 51*(1), 21–37.

Frazier, P., Arikian, N., Benson, S., Losoff, A., & Maurer, S. (1996). Desire for marriage and life satisfaction among unmarried heterosexual adults. *Journal of Social and Personal Relationships, 13,* 225–239.

Fredricks, J. A., & Eccles, J. S. (2006). Is extracurricular participation associated with beneficial outcomes? Concurrent and longitudinal relations. *Developmental Psychology, 42,* 698–713.

Fredricks, J. A., Simpkins, S., & Eccles, J. S. (2005). Family socialization, gender, and participation in sports and instrumental music. In C. R. Cooper, C. T. G. Coll, W. T. Bartko, H. Davis, & C. Chatman (Eds.), *Developmental pathways through middle childhood* (pp. 41–62). Mahwah, NJ: Lawrence Erlbaum Associates.

Fredrickson, B. L., & Roberts, T.-A. (1997). Objectification Theory: Toward understanding women's lived experiences and mental health risks. *Psychology of Women Quarterly, 21,* 173–206.

Fredrickson, B. L., Roberts, T.-A., Noll, S. M., Quinn, D. M., & Twenge, J. M. (1998). That swimsuit becomes you: Sex differences in self-objectification, restrained eating, and math performance. *Journal of Personality and Social Psychology, 75,* 269–284.

Freedman-Doan, C., Wigfield, A., Eccles, J. S., Blumenfeld, P., Arbreton, A., & Harold, R. D. (2000). What am I best at? Grade and gender differences in children's beliefs about ability improvement. *Journal of Applied Developmental Psychology, 21,* 379–402.

Freeman, C. E. (2004). *Trends in educational equity of girls & women: 2004* (NCES 2005-016). U.S. Department of Education, National Center for Education Statistics. Washington, DC: U.S. Government Printing Office.

Freeman, E. W., Sammel, M. D., Lin, H., & Nelson, D. B. (2006). Associations of hormones and menopausal status with depressed mood in women with no history of depression. *Archives of General Psychiatry, 63,* 375–382.

Freeman, E. W., Sammel, M. D., Liu, L., Gracia, C. R., Nelson, D. B., & Hollander, L. (2004). Hormones and menopausal status as predictors of depression in women in transition to menopause. *Archives of General Psychiatry, 61,* 62–70.

French, D. C., Jansen, E. A., & Pidada, S. (2002). United States and Indonesian children's and adolescents' reports of relational aggression by disliked peers. *Child Development, 73,* 1143–1150.

Freud, S. (1924). The dissolution of the Oedipus complex. *Standard Edition, 19,* 172–179.

Freud, S. (1925). Some physical consequences of the anatomical distinction between the sexes. *Standard Edition, 19,* 243–258.

Friedan, B. (1963). *The feminine mystique.* New York: Norton.

Fried-Buchalter, S. (1997). Fear of success, fear of failure, and the imposter phenomenon among male and female marketing managers. *Sex Roles, 37,* 847–859.

Frings, L., Wagner, K., Unterrainer, J., Spreer, J., Halsband, U., & Schulze-Bonhage, A. (2006). Gender-related differences in lateralization of hippocampal activation and cognitive strategy. *NeuroReport, 17,* 417–421.

Frisco, M. L., & Williams, K. (2003). Perceived housework equity, marital happiness, and divorce in dual-earner households. *Journal of Family Issues, 24,* 51–73.

Fritz, H. L. (2000). Gender-linked personality traits predict mental health and functional status following a first coronary event. *Health Psychology, 19,* 420–428.

Fritz, H. L., & Helgeson, V. S. (1998). Distinctions of unmitigated communion from communion: Self-neglect and overinvolvement with others. *Journal of Personality and Social Psychology, 75,* 121–140.

Fritz, H. L., Nagurney, A., & Helgeson, V. S. (2003). The effects of partner sex, gender-related personality traits, and social support on cardiovascular reactivity during problem disclosure. *Personality and Social Psychology Bulletin, 29,* 713–725.

Frome, P. M., & Eccles, J. S. (1998). Parents' influence on children's achievement-related perceptions. *Journal of Personality and Social Psychology, 74,* 435–452.

Frome, P. M., Alfeld, C. J., Eccles, J. S., & Barber, B. L. (2006). Why don't they want a male-dominated job? An investigation of young women who changed their occupational aspirations. *Educational Research and Evaluation, 12,* 359–372.

Frost, J. A., Binder, J. R., Springer, J. A., Hammeke, T. A., Bellgowan, P. S. F., Rao, S. M., & Cox, R. W. (1999). Language processing is strongly left lateralized in both sexes: Evidence from functional MRI. *Brain, 122,* 199–208.

Fuchs, D., & Thelen, M. H. (1988). Children's expected interpersonal consequences of communicating their affective state and reported likelihood of expression. *Child Development, 59,* 1314–1322.

Fuegen, K., Biernat, M., Haines, E., & Deaux, K. (2004). Mothers and fathers in the workplace: How gender and parental status influence judgements. *Journal of Social Issues, 60,* 737–754.

Furnham, A., & Mak, T. (1999). Sex-role stereotyping in television commercials: A review and comparison of fourteen studies done on five continents over 25 years. *Sex Roles, 41,* 413–437.

Fuwa, M. (2004). Macro-level gender inequality and the division of household labor in 22 countries. *American Sociological Review, 69,* 751–767.

Gabriel, S., & Gardner, W. L. (1999). Are there "his" and "hers" types of interdependence? The implications of gender differences in collective versus relational interdependence for affect, behavior, and cognition. *Journal of Personality and Social Psychology, 77,* 642–655.

Gager, C. T., & Hohmann-Marriott, B. (2006). Distributive justice in the household: A comparison of alternative models. *Marriage and Family Review, 40,* 5–42.

Galambos, N. L., Almeida, D. M., & Petersen, A. C. (1990). Masculinity, femininity, and sex role attitudes in early adolescence: Exploring gender intensification. *Child Development, 61,* 1905–1914.

Galinsky, E. (2005). Children's perspectives of employed mothers and fathers: Closing the gap between public debates and research findings. In D. F. Halpern & S. E. Murphy (Eds.), *From work-family balance to work-family interaction* (pp. 219–236). Mahwah, NJ: Lawrence Erlbaum Associates.

Gallagher, A. M., & DeLisi, R. (1994). Gender differences in scholastic aptitude test—Mathematics problem solving among high-ability students. *Journal of Educational Psychology, 86,* 204–211.

Gallagher, A., Levin, J., & Cahalan, C. (2002). *GRE Research—Cognitive patterns of gender differences on mathematics admissions tests* (No. 02-19 ETS Research Report). Princeton, NJ: Educational Testing Service.

Gallaher, P. E. (1992). Individual differences in nonverbal behavior: Dimensions of style. *Journal of Personality and Social Psychology, 63,* 133–145.

Gallo, L. C., Troxel, W. M., Kuller, L. H., Sutton-Tyrrell, K., Edmundowicz, D., & Matthews, K. A. (2003). Marital status, marital quality, and atherosclerotic burden in postmenopausal women. *Psychosomatic Medicine, 65,* 952–962.

Gallup News Service. (1997, November 7). *Family values differ sharply around the world.* Gallup News Service. Retrieved June 29, 2000, from *web.lexis-nexis.com.*

Gallup Poll. (2005). *Math problematic for U.S. teens. More girls than boys find math, science toughest classes.* Retrieved January 30, 2007, from *www.galluppoll.com/content/Default.aspx?ci=16360&pg=1&VERSION=p.*

Gallup Poll. (2007a). *Religion most important to blacks, women, and older Americans.* Retrieved January 30, 2007, from *www.galluppoll.com:/content/Default.aspx?ci=25585&pg=1&t=XPlyd92h7TRcjZbu.*

Gallup Poll. (2007b). *U.S. churches looking for a few white men.* Retrieved January 20, 2007, from *www.galluppoll.com/content/Default.aspx?ci=12463&pg=1&VERSION=p.*

Gallup, G. H., Jr. (2003). *Current views on premarital, extramarital sex.* Retrieved June 11, 2007, from *www.galluppoll.com/content/Default.aspx?ci=8704&pg=1&VERSION=p.*

Galupo, M. P. (2007). Friendship patterns of sexual minority individuals in adulthood. *Journal of Social and Personal Relationships, 24,* 139–151.

Gan, S. C., Beaver, S. K., Houck, P. M., MacLehose, R. F., Lawson, H. W., & Chan, L. (2000). Treatment of acute myocardial infarction and 30-day mortality among women and men. *New England Journal of Medicine, 343*(1), 8–15.

Garbarino, J. (1999). *Lost boys: Why our sons turn violent and how we can save them.* New York: Free Press.

Garber, J., Little, S., Hilsman, R., & Weaver, K. R. (1998). Family predictors of suicidal symptoms in young adolescents. *Journal of Adolescence, 21,* 445–457.

Gardenswartz, L., & Rowe, A. (1994). *Diverse teams at work: Capitalizing on the power of diversity.* Homewood, IL: Irwin.

Gardiner, M., & Tiggemann, M. (1999). Gender differences in leadership style, job stress and mental health in male- and female-dominated industries. *Journal of Occupational and Organizational Psychology, 72,* 301–315.

Gareis, K. C., & Barnett, R. C. (2002). Under what conditions do long work hours affect psychological distress? *Work and Occupations, 29,* 483–497.

Garner, D. M., Garfinkel, P. E., Schwartz, D., & Thompson, M. (1980). Cultural expectations of thinness in women. *Psychological Reports, 47,* 483–491.

Garner, D. M., Olmstead, M. P., & Polivy, J. (1983). Development and validation of a multidimensional eating disorder inventory for anorexia nervosa and bulimia. *International Journal of Eating Disorders, 2*(2), 15–34.

Gastil, J. (1990). Generic pronouns and sexist language: The oxymoronic character of masculine generics. *Sex Roles, 23,* 629–643.

Gaub, M., & Carlson, C. L. (1997). Gender differences in ADHD: A meta-analysis and critical review. *Journal of the American Academy of Child and Adolescent Psychiatry, 36,* 1036–1045.

Ge, X., Lorenz, F. O., Conger, R. D., Elder, G. H., Jr., & Simons, R. L. (1994). Trajectories of stressful life events and depressive symptoms during adolescence. *Developmental Psychology, 30,* 467–483.

Gear, R. W., Miaskowski, C., Gordon, N. C., Paul, S. M., Heller, P. H., & Levine, J. D. (1999). The kappa opioid nalbuphine produces gender- and dose-dependent analgesia and antianalgesia in patients with postoperative pain. *Pain, 83,* 339–345.

Geer, J. H., & Robertson, G. G. (2005). Implicit attitudes in sexuality: Gender differences. *Archives of Sexual Behavior, 34,* 671–677.

Geiger, H. J. (2006). Health disparities: What do we know? What do we need to know? What should we do? In A. J. Schulz & L. Mullings (Eds.), *Gender, race, class, & health* (pp. 261–288). San Fransisco: Jossey-Bass.

Gelles, R. J. (2007). The politics of research: The use, abuse, and misuse of social science data—The cases of intimate partner abuse. *Family Court Review, 45,* 42–51.

George, L. K., Winfield, I., & Blazer, D. G. (1992). Sociocultural factors in sexual assault: Comparison of two representative samples of women. *Journal of Social Issues, 48*(1), 105–125.

Gerhart, B., & Rynes, S. (1991). Determinants and consequences of salary negotiations by male and female MBA graduates. *Journal of Applied Psychology, 76*(2), 256–262.

Ghaed, S. G., & Gallo, L. C. (2006). Distinctions among agency, communion, and unmitigated agency and communion according to the interpersonal circumplex, five-factor model, and social-emotional correlates. *Journal of Personality Assessment, 86,* 77–88.

Gibbons, J. L., Stiles, D. A., & Shkodriani, G. M. (1991). Adolescents' attitudes toward family and gender roles: An international comparison. *Sex Roles, 25,* 625–643.

Gijsbers van Wijk, C. M. T., Huisman, H., & Kolk, A. M. (1999). Gender differences in physical symptoms and illness behavior: A health diary study. *Social Science and Medicine, 49,* 1061–1074.

Gillespie, B. L., & Eisler, R. M. (1992). Development of the feminine gender role stress scale: A cognitive-behavioral measure of stress, appraisal, and coping for women. *Behavior Modification, 16*(3), 426–438.

Gilligan, C. (1982). *In a different voice.* Cambridge, MA: Harvard University Press.

Gilmore, D. D. (1990). *Manhood in the making: Cultural concepts of masculinity.* New Haven, CT: Yale University Press.

Giordano, P. C., Longmore, M. A., & Manning, W. D. (2006). Gender and meanings of adolescent romantic relationships: A focus on boys. *American Sociological Review, 71,* 260–287.

Gjerberg, E. (2002). Gender similarities in doctors' preferences—and gender differences in final specialisation. *Social Science & Medicine, 54,* 591–605.

Gjerde, P. F. (1995). Alternative pathways to chronic depressive symptoms in young adults: Gender differences in developmental trajectories. *Child Development, 66,* 1277–1300.

Gjerde, P. F., Block, J., & Block, J. H. (1988). Depressive symptoms and personality during late adolescence: Gender differences in the externalization-internalization of symptom expression. *Journal of Abnormal Psychology, 97,* 475–486.

Glass, J., & Fujimoto, T. (1994). Housework, paid work, and depression among husbands and wives. *Journal of Health and Social Behavior, 35,* 179–191.

Glass, R. M. (1990). Blue mood, blackened lungs: Depression and smoking. *Journal of the American Medical Association, 264*(12), 1583–1584.

Glass, S. P., & Wright, T. L. (1992). Justifications for extramarital relationships: The association between attitudes, behaviors, and gender. *Journal of Sex Research, 29*(3), 361–387.

Glick, P., & Fiske, S. T. (1996). The Ambivalent Sexism Inventory: Differentiating hostile and benevolent sexism. *Journal of Personality and Social Psychology, 70,* 491–512.

Glick, P., & Fiske, S. T. (1999a). The Ambivalence Toward Men Inventory. *Psychology of Women Quarterly, 23,* 519–536.

Glick, P., & Fiske, S. T. (1999b). Gender, power dynamics, and social interaction. In M. M. Ferree & J. Lorber (Eds.), *Revisioning gender* (Vol. 5). Thousand Oaks, CA: Sage.

Glick, P., & Fiske, S. T. (2001). An ambivalent alliance: Hostile and benevolent sexism as complementary justifications for gender inequality. *American Psychologist, 56*(2), 109–118.

Glick, P., Fiske, S. T., Masser, B., Manganelli, A. M., Huang, L., Castro, Y. R., et al. (2004). Bad but bold: Ambivalent attitudes toward men predict gender inequality in 16 nations. *Journal of Personality and Social Psychology, 86,* 713–728.

Glick, P., Fiske, S. T., Mladinic, A., Saiz, J. L., Abrams, D., Masser, B., et al. (2000). Beyond prejudice as simple antipathy: Hostile and benevolent sexism across cultures. *Journal of Personality and Social Psychology, 79*(5), 763–775.

Glick, P., Sakalli-Ugurlu, N., Gerreira, M. C., & de Souza, M. A. (2002). Ambivalent sexism and attitudes toward wife abuse in Turkey and Brazil. *Psychology of Women Quarterly, 26,* 292–297.

Glick, P., Zion, C., & Nelson, C. (1988). What mediates sex discrimination in hiring decisions? *Journal of Personality and Social Psychology, 55,* 178–186.

Glynn, L. M., Christenfeld, N., & Gerin, W. (1999). Gender, social support, and cardiovascular responses to stress. *Psychosomatic Medicine, 61,* 234–242.

Gold, D. R., Wang, X., Wypij, D., Speizer, F. E., Ware, J. H., & Dockery, D. W. (1996). Effects of cigarette smoking on lung function in adolescent boys and girls. *New England Journal of Medicine, 335,* 931–937.

Goldberg, A. E., & Perry-Jenkins, M. (2004). Division of labor and working-class women's well-being across the transition to parenthood. *Journal of Family Psychology, 18,* 225–236.

Goldberg, H. (1976). *The hazards of being male.* New York: New American Library.

Golden, J. H. III, Johnson, C., A., & Lopez, R. A. (2001). Sexual harassment in the workplace: Exploring the effects of attractiveness on perception of harassment. *Sex Roles, 45,* 767–784.

Goldner, V., Penn, P., Sheinberg, M., & Walker, G. (1990). Love and violence: Gender paradoxes in volatile attachments. *Family Process, 29*(4), 343–364.

Goldsteen, K., & Ross, C. E. (1989). The perceived burden of children. *Journal of Family Issues, 10*(4), 504–526.

Golombok, S., & Fivush, R. (1994). *Gender development.* New York: Cambridge University Press.

Golombok, S., Perry, B., Burston, A., Murray, C., Mooney-Somers, J., Stevens, M., & Golding, J. (2003). Children with lesbian parents: A community study. *Developmental Psychology, 39,* 20–33.

Gondolf, E. W., & Hanneken, J. (1987). The gender warrior: Reformed batterers on abuse, treatment, and change. *Journal of Family Violence, 2*(2), 177–191.

Gonzaga, G. C., Turner, R. A., Keltner, D., Campos, B., & Altemus, M. (2006). Romantic love and sexual desire in close relationships. *Emotion, 6,* 163–179.

Gonzales, M. H., & Meyers, S. A. (1993). Your mother would like me: Self-presentation in the personal ads of heterosexual and homosexual men and women. *Personality and Social Psychology Bulletin, 19,* 131–142.

Gonzalez, A. Q., & Koestner, R. (2005). Parental preference for sex of newborn as reflected in positive affect in birth announcements. *Sex Roles, 52,* 407–411.

Gonzalez, J. M., Alegria, M., & Prihoda, T. J. (2005). How do attitudes toward mental health treatment vary by age, gender, and ethnicity/race in young adults? *Journal of Community Psychology, 33,* 611–629.

Good, G. E., Dell, D. M., & Mintz, L. B. (1989). Male role and gender role conflict: Relations to help seeking in men. *Journal of Counseling Psychology, 36*(3), 295–300.

Good, G. E., Hepper, M. J., Hillenbrand-Gunn, T., & Wang, L.-F. (1995). Sexual and psychological violence: An exploratory study of predictors in college men. *Journal of Men's Studies, 4*(1), 59–71.

Good, G. E., O'Neil, J. M., Stevens, M., Robertson, J. M., Fitzgerald, L. F., DeBord, K. A., Bartels, K. M., & Braverman, D. G. (1995). Male gender role conflict: Psychometric issues and relations to psychological distress. *Journal of Counseling Psychology, 42*(1), 3–10.

Gooden, A. M., & Gooden, M. A. (2001). Gender representation in notable children's picture books: 1995–1999. *Sex Roles, 45,* 89–101.

Goodman, M. J., Griffin, P. B., Estioko-Griffen, A. A., & Grove, J. S. (1985). The compatibility of hunting among the Agta hunter-gatherers of the Philippines. *Sex Roles, 12,* 1199–1209.

Gore, S., & Colten, M. E. (1991). Gender, stress, and distress: Social-relational influences. In J. Eckenrode (Ed.), *The social context of coping* (pp. 139–163). New York: Plenum Press.

Gorman, B. K., & Read, J. G. (2006). Gender disparities in adult health: An examination of three measures of morbidity. *Journal of Health and Social Behavior, 47,* 95–110.

Gorman, E. H. (2005). Gender stereotypes, same-gender preferences, and organizational variation in the hiring of women: Evidence from law firms. *American Sociological Review, 70,* 702–728.

Gortmaker, S. L., Must, A., Perrin, J. M., Sobol, A. M., & Dietz, W. H. (1993). Social and economic consequences of overweight in adolescence and young adulthood. *New England Journal of Medicine, 329,* 1008–1012.

Gortmaker, S. L., Must, A., Sobol, A. M., Peterson, K., Colditz, G. A., & Dietz, W. H. (1996). Television viewing as a cause of increasing obesity among children in the United States, 1986–1990. *Archives of Pediatrics & Adolescent Medicine, 150,* 356–362.

Gottman, J. M. (1994). *What predicts divorce? The relationship between marital processes and marital outcomes.* Hillsdale, NJ: Erlbaum.

Gottman, J. M., & Carrere, S. (1994). Why can't men and women get along? Developmental roots and marital inequities. In D. J. Canary & L. Stafford (Eds.), *Communication and relational maintenance* (pp. 203–229). London: Academic Press.

Gottman, J. M., & Levenson, R. W. (1992). Marital processes predictive of later dissolution: Behavior, physiology, and health. *Journal of Personality and Social Psychology, 63,* 221–233.

Gottman, J. M., Levenson, R. W., Gross, J., Frederickson, B. L., McCoy, K., Rosenthal, L., et al. (2003). Correlates of gay and lesbian couples' relationship satisfaction and relationship dissolution. *Journal of Homosexuality, 45,* 23–43.

Gottman, J. M., Levenson, R. W., Swanson, C., Swanson, K., Tyson, R., & Yoshimoto, D. (2003). Observing gay, lesbian and heterosexual couples' relationships: Mathematical modeling of conflict interaction. *Journal of Homosexuality, 45,* 65–90.

Gove, W. R. (1984). Gender differences in mental and physical illness: The effects of fixed roles and nurturant roles. *Social Science & Medicine, 19*(2), 77–91.

Gove, W. R., & Hughes, M. (1979). Possible causes of the apparent sex differences in physical health: An empirical investigation. *American Sociological Review, 44,* 126–146.

Gove, W. R., & Tudor, J. F. (1973). Adult sex roles and mental illness. *American Journal of Sociology, 78,* 812–835.

Grabe, M. E., Trager, K. D., Lear, M., & Rauch, J. (2006). Gender in crime news: A case study test of the chivalry hypothesis. *Mass Communication & Society, 9,* 137–163.

Grabe, S., & Hyde, J. S. (2006). Ethnicity and body dissatisfaction among women in the United States: A meta-analysis. *Psychological Bulletin, 132,* 622–640.

Graber, J. A., Brooks-Gunn, J., & Warren, M. P. (2006). Pubertal effects on adjustment in girls: Moving from demonstrating effects to identifying pathways. *Journal of Youth and Adolescence, 35,* 413–423.

Grace, S. L., Krepostman, S., Brooks, D., Arthur, H., Scholey, P., Suskin, N., et al. (2005). Illness perceptions among cardiac patients: Relation to depressive symptomatology and sex. *Journal of Psychosomatic Research, 59,* 153–160.

Gradman, T. J. (1994). Masculine identity from work to retirement. In E. H. Thompson, Jr. (Ed.), *Older men's lives* (pp. 104–121). Thousand Oaks, CA: Sage.

Grammer, K. (1992). Variations on a theme: Age dependent mate selections in humans. *Behavioral and Brain Sciences, 15,* 100–102.

Grant, K., Lyons, A., Landis, D., Cho, M. H., Scudiero, M., Reynolds, L., et al. (1999). Gender, body image, and depressive symptoms among low-income African American adolescents. *Journal of Social Issues, 55*(2), 299–316.

Grant, K., Marsh, P., Syniar, G., Williams, M., Addlesperger, E., Kinzler, M. H., et al. (2002). Gender differences in rates of depression among undergraduates: Measurement matters. *Journal of Adolescence, 25,* 613–617.

Gray, J. (1992). *Men are from Mars, women are from Venus.* New York: HarperCollins.

Green, B. L., & Kenrick, D. T. (1994). The attractiveness of gender-typed traits at different relationship levels: Androgynous characteristics may be desirable after all. *Personality and Social Psychology Bulletin, 20,* 244–253.

Green, C. A., & Pope, C. R. (1999). Gender, psychosocial factors and the use of medical services: A longitudinal analysis. *Social Science and Medicine, 48,* 1363–1372.

Green, M. C., & Sabini, J. (2006). Gender, socioeconomic status, age, and jealousy: Emotional responses to infidelity in a national sample. *Emotion, 6,* 330–334.

Greene, K., & Faulkner, S. L. (2005). Gender, belief in the sexual double standard, and sexual talk in heterosexual dating relationships. *Sex Roles, 53,* 239–251.

Grewen, K. M., Girdler, S. S., Amico, J., & Light, K. C. (2005). Effects of partner support on resting oxytocin, cortisol, norepinephrine, and blood pressure before and after warm partner contact. *Psychosomatic Medicine, 67,* 531–538.

Griffin, K. W., Botvin, G. J., Doyle, M. M., Diaz, T., & Epstein, J. A. (1999). A six-year follow-up study of determinants of heavy cigarette smoking among high-school seniors. *Journal of Behavioral Medicine, 22*(3), 271–285.

Griffin, M. L., Weiss, R. D., & Mirin, S. M. (1989). A comparison of male and female cocaine abusers. *Archives of General Psychiatry, 46,* 122–126.

Griffin, S. (1971). Rape: The all-American crime. *Ramparts, 10,* 26–35.

Groesz, L. M., Levine, M. P., & Murnen, S. K. (2002). The effect of experimental presentation of thin media images on body satisfaction: A meta-analytic review. *International Journal of Eating Disorders, 31,* 1–16.

Gross, S. M., Gary, T. L., Browne, D. C., & LaVeist, T. A. (2005). Gender differences in body image and health perceptions among graduating seniors from a historically black college. *Journal of the National Medical Association, 97,* 1608–1619.

Grossman, R. J. (August, 2002). Paying the price. *Human Resources Magazine.* Retrieved May 8, 2003, from *proquest.umi.com/pqdweb?TS=1052408275&RQT=309 &CC=2&Dtp=1&Did=0000001.*

Groth, A. N., Burgess, A. W., & Holmstrom, L. L. (1977). Rape: Power, anger, and sexuality. *American Journal of Psychiatry, 134*(11), 1239–1243.

Gruber, J. E. (1990). Methodological problems and policy implications in sexual harassment research. *Population Research and Policy Review, 9,* 235–254.

Guerguerian, R., & Lewine, R. R. J. (1998). Brain torque and sex differences in schizophrenia. *Schizophrenia Research, 30,* 175–181.

Guerrero, L. K., & Andersen, P. A. (1994). Patterns of matching and initiation: Touch behavior and touch avoidance across romantic relationship stages. *Journal of Nonverbal Behavior, 18*(2), 137–153.

Guerrero, L. K., & Chavez, A. M. (2005). Relational maintenance in cross-sex friendships characterized by different types of romantic intent: An exploratory study. *Western Journal of Communication, 69,* 339–358.

Guerrero, L. K., & Reiter, R. L. (1998). Expressing emotion: Sex differences in social skills and communicative responses to anger, sadness, and jealousy. In D. J. Canary & K. Dindia (Eds.), *Sex differences and similarities in communication* (pp. 321–350). Mahwah, NJ: Erlbaum.

Guerrero, L. K., Eloy, S. V., Jorgensen, P. F., & Andersen, P. A. (1993). Hers or his? Sex differences in the experience and communication of jealousy in close relationships. In P. J. Kalbfleisch (Ed.), *Interpersonal communication: Evolving interpersonal relationships* (pp. 109–131). Hillsdale, NJ: Erlbaum.

Guiller, J., & Durndell, A. (2006). "I totally agree with you": Gender interactions in educational online discussion groups. *Journal of Computer Assisted Learning, 22,* 368–381.

Guimond, S., Brunot, S., Chatard, A., Garcia, D. M., Martinot, D., Branscombe, N. R., et al. (2007). Culture, gender, and the self: Variations and impact of social comparison processes. *Journal of Personality and Social Psychology, 92,* 1118–1134.

Guimond, S., Chatard, A., Martinot, D., Crisp, R. J., & Redersdorff, S. (2006). Social comparison, self-stereotyping, and gender differences in self-construals. *Journal of Personality and Social Psychology, 90,* 221–242.

Guite, J. W., Walker, L. S., Smith, C. A., & Garber, J. (2000). Children's perceptions of peers with somatic symptoms: The impact of gender, stress, and illness. *Journal of Pediatric Psychology, 25,* 125–135.

Gupta, S. (2006). Her money, her time: Women's earnings and their housework hours. *Social Science Research, 35,* 975–999.

Gurian, M., & Stevens, K. (2007). *The minds of boys: Saving our sons from falling behind in school and life.* San Francisco: Jossey-Bass.

Gutek, B. A. (1985). *Sex and the workplace.* San Francisco: Jossey-Bass.

Gutek, B. A. (2001). Women and paid work. *Psychology of Women Quarterly, 25,* 379–393.

Gutek, B. A., & Done, R. S. (2000). Sexual harassment. In R. K. Unger (Ed.), *Handbook of the psychology of women and gender* (pp. 1–61). New York: Wiley.

Gutek, B. A., & O'Connor, M. (1995). The empirical basis for the reasonable women standard. *Journal of Social Issues, 51*(1), 151–166.

Haavio-Mannila, E. (1986). Inequalities in health and gender. *Social Science and Medicine, 22*(2), 141–149.

Haavio-Mannila, E., Kauppinen-Toropainen, K., & Kandolin, I. (1988). The effect of sex composition of the workplace on friendship, romance, and sex at work. In B. A. Gutek, A. H. Stromberg, & L. Larwood (Eds.), *Women and work: An annual review* (Vol. 3, pp. 123–137). Newbury Park, CA: Sage.

Hagedoorn, M., Van Yperen, N. W., Coyne, J. C., van Jaarsveld, C. H. M., Ranchor, A. V., van Sonderen, E., et al. (2006). Does marriage protect older people from distress? The role of equity and recency of bereavement. *Psychology and Aging, 21,* 611–620.

Hall, J. A. (1996). Touch, status, and gender at professional meetings. *Journal of Nonverbal Behavior, 20*(1), 23–44.

Hall, J. A. (1998). How big are nonverbal sex differences? The case of smiling and sensitivity to nonverbal cues. In D. J. Canary & K. Dindia (Eds.), *Sex differences and similarities in communication* (pp. 155–177). Mahwah, NJ: Erlbaum.

Hall, J. A. (2006). How big are nonverbal sex differences? The case of smiling and nonverbal sensitivity. In K. Dindia & D. J. Canary (Eds.), *Sex differences and similarities in communication* (Second ed.) (pp. 59–81). Mahwah, NJ: Lawrence Erlbaum Associates.

Hall, J. A., & Carter, J. D. (1999). Gender-stereotype accuracy as an individual difference. *Journal of Personality and Social Psychology, 77,* 350–359.

Hall, J. A., & Friedman, G. B. (1999). Status, gender, and nonverbal behavior: A study of structured interactions between employees of a company. *Personality and Social Psychology Bulletin, 25,* 1082–1091.

Hall, J. A., & Roter, D. L. (2002). Do patients talk differently to male and female physicians? A meta-analytic review. *Patient Education and Counseling, 48,* 217–224.

Hall, J. A., & Veccia, E. M. (1990). More "touching" observations: New insights on men, women, and interpersonal touch. *Journal of Personality and Social Psychology, 59,* 1155–1162.

Hall, J. A., Carter, J. D., & Horgan, T. G. (2000). Gender differences in nonverbal communication of emotion. In A. H. Fischer (Ed.), *Gender and emotion: Social and pyschological perspectives* (pp. 97–117). New York: Cambridge University Press.

Hall, J. A., Coats, E. J., & LeBeau, L. S. (2005). Nonverbal behavior and the vertical dimension of social relations: A meta-analysis. *Psychological Bulletin, 131,* 898–924.

Hall, J. A., Horgan, T. G., & Carter, J. D. (2002). Assigned and felt status in relation to observer-coded and participant-reported smiling. *Journal of Nonverbal Behavior, 26*(2), 63–81.

Hall, J. A., Irish, J. T., Roter, D. L., Ehrlich, C. M., & Miller, L. H. (1994). Gender in medical encounters: An analysis of physician and patient communication in a primary care setting. *Health Psychology, 13,* 384–392.

Halpern, C. T., Young, M. L., Waller, M. W., Martin, S. L., & Kupper, L. L. (2004). Prevalence of partner violence in same-sex romantic and sexual relationships in a national sample of adolescents. *Journal of Adolescent Health, 35,* 124–131.

Halpern, D. F. (2000). *Sex differences in cognitive abilities* (Third ed.). Mahwah, NJ: Erlbaum.

Halpern, D. F. (2004). A cognitive-process taxonomy for sex differences in cognitive abilities. *Current Directions in Psychological Science, 13,* 135–139.

Halpern, D. F., & Collaer, M. L. (2005). Sex differences in visuospatial abilities: More than meets the eye. In P. Shah & A. Miyake (Eds.), *The Cambridge handbook of visuospatial thinking* (pp. 170–212). New York: Cambridge University Press.

Halpern, D. F., Wai, J., & Saw, A. (2005). A psychobiosocial model: Why females are sometimes greater than and sometimes less than males in math achievement. In A. M. Gallagher & J. C. Kaufman (Eds.), *Gender differences in mathematics: An integrative psychological approach* (pp. 48–72). New York: Cambridge University Press.

Hamby, S. L., & Koss, M. P. (2003). Shades of gray: A qualitative study of terms used in the measurement of sexual victimization. *Psychology of Women Quarterly, 27,* 243–255.

Hamilton, M. C. (1988). Using masculine generics: Does generic he increase male bias in the user's imagery? *Sex Roles, 19,* 785–799.

Hampton, R. L., & Gelles, R. J. (1994). Violence toward Black women in a nationally representative sample of Black families. *Journal of Comparative Family Studies, 25*(1), 105–119.

Han, W. J., & Waldfogel, J. (2003). Parental leave: The impact of recent legislation on parents' leave taking. *Demography, 40*(1), 191–200.

Hankin, B. L., Roberts, J., & Gotlib, I. H. (1997). Elevated self-standards and emotional distress during adolescence: Emotional specificity and gender differences. *Cognitive Therapy and Research, 21,* 663–679.

Hardy, C. L., Bukowski, W. M., & Sippola, L. K. (2002). Stability and change in peer relationships during the transition to middle-level school. *Journal of Early Adolescence, 22,* 117–142.

Hare-Mustin, R. T., & Marecek, J. (1988). The meaning of difference: Gender theory, postmodernism, and psychology. *American Psychologist, 43,* 455–464.

Hare-Mustin, R. T., & Marecek, J. (1998). Asking the right questions: Feminist psychology and sex differences. In D. L. Anselmi & A. L. Law (Eds.), *Questions of gender: Perspectives and paradoxes* (pp. 104–108). Boston: McGraw-Hill.

Harned, M. S., & Fitzgerald, L. F. (2002). Understanding a link between sexual harassment and eating disorder symptoms: A mediational analysis. *Journal of Consulting and Clinical Psychology, 70,* 1170–1181.

Harris, C. R. (2003). A review of sex differences in sexual jealousy, including self-report data, psychophysiological responses, interpersonal violence, and morbid jealousy. *Personality and Social Psychology Review, 7,* 102–128.

Harris, H. (1998). Women in international management: The times they are a changing? *International Review of Women and Leadership, 4*(2), 6–14.

Harris, I., Torres, J. B., & Allender, D. (1994). The responses of African American men to dominant norms of masculinity within the United States. *Sex Roles, 31,* 703–719.

Harris, J. A. (1999). Review and methodological considerations in research on testosterone and aggression. *Aggression and Violent Behavior, 4,* 273–291.

Harris, J. R. (1998). *The nurture assumption: Why children turn out the way they do; Parents matter less than you think and peers matter more.* New York: Free Press.

Harris, M. B. (1996). Aggressive experiences and aggressiveness: Relationship to ethnicity, gender, and age. *Journal of Applied Social Psychology, 26*(10), 843–870.

Harris, M. B., & Knight-Bohnhoff, K. (1996). Gender and aggression I: Perceptions of aggression. *Sex Roles, 35,* 1–25.

Harris, S. M., & Majors, R. (1993). Cultural value differences: Implications for the experiences of African-American men. *Journal of Men's Studies, 1*(3), 227–238.

Hartung, C. M., & Widiger, T. A. (1998). Gender differences in the diagnosis of mental disorders: Conclusions and controversies of the *DSM-IV. Psychological Bulletin, 123,* 260–278.

Hartup, W. W., French, D. C., Laursen, B., Johnston, M. K., & Ogawa, J. R. (1993). Conflict and friendship relations in middle childhood: Behavior in a closed-field situation. *Child Development, 64,* 445–454.

Haselton, M. G., & Buss, D. M. (2001). The affective shift hypothesis: The functions of emotional changes following sexual intercourse. *Personal Relationships, 8,* 357–369.

Haselton, M. G., Buss, D. M., Oubaid, V., & Angleitner, A. (2005). Sex, lies, and strategic interference: The psychology of deception between the sexes. *Personality and Social Psychology Bulletin, 31,* 3–23.

Hatala, M. N., & Prehodka, J. (1996). Content analysis of gay male and lesbian personal advertisements. *Psychological Reports, 78,* 371–374.

Hatfield, E., & Sprecher, S. (1995). Men's and women's preferences in marital partners in the United States, Russia, and Japan. *Journal of Cross-Cultural Psychology, 26*(6), 728–750.

Hathaway, S. R., & McKinley, J. C. (1940). A multiphasic personality schedule (Minnesota): Construction of the schedule. *Journal of Psychology, 10,* 249–254.

Hawkins, A. J., Marshall, C. M., & Meiners, K. M. (1995). Exploring wives' sense of fairness about family work: An initial test of the distributive justice framework. *Journal of Family Issues, 16*(6), 693–721.

Healy, B. (1991). The Yentl syndrome. *New England Journal of Medicine, 325*(4), 274–276.

Heatherington, L., Daubman, K. A., Bates, C., Ahn, A., Brown, H., & Preston, C. (1993). Two investigations of female modesty in achievement situations. *Sex Roles, 29,* 739–754.

Heatherton, T. F., Kozlowski, L. T., Frecker, R. C., & Fagerstrom, K.-O. (1991). The Fagerstrom test for nicotine dependence: A revision of the Fagerstrom Tolerance Questionnaire. *British Journal of Addiction, 86,* 1119–1127.

Heaton, T. B. (2002). Factors contributing to increasing marital stability in the United States. *Journal of Family Issues, 23,* 392–409.

Heavey, C. L., Christensen, A., & Malamuth, N. M. (1995). The longitudinal impact of demand and withdrawal during marital conflict. *Journal of Consulting and Clinical Psychology, 63,* 797–801.

Heavey, C. L., Layne, C., & Christensen, A. (1993). Gender and conflict structure in marital interaction: A replication and extension. *Journal of Consulting and Clinical Psychology, 61,* 16–27.

Hecht, M. A., & LaFrance, M. (1998). License or obligation to smile: The effect of power and sex on amount and type of smiling. *Personality and Social Psychology Bulletin, 24,* 1332–1342.

Heckert, T. M., Droste, H. E., Adams, P. J., Griffin, C. M., Roberts, L. L., Mueller, M. A., & Wallis, H. A. (2002). Gender differences in anticipated salary: Role of salary estimates for others, job characteristics, career paths, and job inputs. *Sex Roles, 47,* 139–151.

Hedges, L. V., & Nowell, A. (1995). Sex differences in mental test scores, variability, and numbers of high-scoring individuals. *Science, 269,* 41–45.

Heilman, M. E. (2001). Description and prescription: How gender stereotypes prevent women's ascent up the organizational ladder. *Journal of Social Issues, 57,* 657–674.

Hein, K. (1998). Aligning science with politics and policy in HIV prevention. *Science, 280,* 1905–1906.

Helgeson, V. S. (1990). The role of masculinity in a prognostic predictor of heart attack severity. *Sex Roles, 22,* 755–774.

Helgeson, V. S. (1993). Implications of agency and communion for patient and spouse adjustment to a first coronary event. *Journal of Personality and Social Psychology, 64,* 807–816.

Helgeson, V. S. (1994a). Long-distance romantic relationships: Sex differences in adjustment and breakup. *Personality and Social Psychology Bulletin, 20,* 254–265.

Helgeson, V. S. (1994b). Prototypes and dimensions of masculinity and femininity. *Sex Roles, 31,* 653–682.

Helgeson, V. S. (1994c). Relation of agency and communion to well-being: Evidence and potential explanations. *Psychological Bulletin, 116,* 412–428.

Helgeson, V. S. (2003). Unmitigated communion and adjustment to breast cancer: Associations and explanations. *Journal of Applied Social Psychology, 33,* 1643–1661.

Helgeson, V. S., & Fritz, H. L. (1996). Implications of communion and unmitigated communion for adolescent adjustment to Type I diabetes. *Women's Health: Research on Gender, Behavior, and Policy, 2*(3), 169–194.

Helgeson, V. S., & Fritz, H. L. (1998). A theory of unmitigated communion. *Personality and Social Psychology Review, 2,* 173–183.

Helgeson, V. S., & Fritz, H. L. (1999). Unmitigated agency and unmitigated communion: Distinctions from agency and communion. *Journal of Research in Personality, 33,* 131–158.

Helgeson, V. S., & Lepore, S. J. (1997). Men's adjustment to prostate cancer: The role of agency and unmitigated agency. *Sex Roles, 37,* 251–267.

Helgeson, V. S., & Lepore, S. J. (2004). Quality of life following prostate cancer: The role of agency and unmitigated agency. *Journal of Applied Social Psychology, 34,* 2559–2585.

Helgeson, V. S., & Mickelson, K. D. (2000). Coping with chronic illness among the elderly. In S. B. Manuck, R. Jennings, B. S. Rabin, & A. Baum (Eds.), *Behavior, health, and aging* (pp. 153–178). Mahwah, NJ: Lawrence Erlbaum.

Helgeson, V. S., Escobar, O., Siminerio, L., & Becker, D. (2007). Unmitigated communion and health among adolescents with and without diabetes: The mediating role of eating disturbances. *Personality and Social Psychology Bulletin, 33,* 519–536.

Helgeson, V. S., Shaver, P., & Dyer, M. (1987). Prototypes of intimacy and distance in same-sex and opposite-sex relationships. *Journal of Social and Personal Relationships, 4,* 195–233.

Helwig, A. A. (1998). Gender-role stereotyping: Testing theory with a longitudinal sample. *Sex Roles, 38,* 403–423.

Hendrick, C., & Hendrick, S. (1986). A theory and method of love. *Journal of Personality and Social Psychology, 50,* 392–402.

Hendrick, S. S. (1981). Self-disclosure and marital satisfaction. *Journal of Personality and Social Psychology, 40,* 1150–1159.

Hendrick, S. S., & Hendrick, C. (1995). Gender differences and similarities in sex and love. *Personal Relationships, 2,* 55–65.

Hendrick, S. S., & Hendrick, C. (2002). Linking romantic love with sex: Development of the perceptions of love and sex scale. *Journal of Social and Personal Relationships, 19,* 361–378.

Henley, N. M. (1977). *Body politics: Power, sex, and nonverbal communication.* Upper Saddle River, NJ: Prentice-Hall.

Henley, N. M. (1989). Molehill or mountain? What we know and don't know about sex bias in language. In M. Crawford & M. Gentry (Eds.), *Gender and thought: Psychological perspectives* (pp. 59–78). New York: Springer-Verlag.

Heo, M., Pietrobelli, A., Fontaine, K. R., Sirey, J. A., & Faith, M. S. (2006). Depressive mood and obesity in US adults: Comparison and moderation by sex, age, and race. *International Journal of Obesity, 30,* 513–519.

Hepp, U., Spindler, A., & Milos, G. (2005). Eating disorder symptomatology and gender role orientation. *The International Journal of Eating Disorders, 37,* 227–233.

Herbert, J. (1989). The physiology of aggression. In J. Groebel & R. A. Hinde (Eds.), *Aggression and war: Their biological and social bases* (pp. 58–77). New York: Cambridge University Press.

Herbert, J., & Stipek, D. (2005). The emergence of gender differences in children's perceptions of their academic competence. *Applied Developmental Psychology, 26,* 276–295.

Herek, G. M. (2006). Legal recognition of same-sex relationships in the United States: A social science perspective. *American Psychologist, 61,* 607–621.

Hess, U., Adams, R. B., Jr., & Kleck, R. E. (2005). Who may frown and who should smile? Dominance, affiliation, and the display of happiness and anger. *Cognition and Emotion, 19,* 515–536.

Hessini, L. (1994). Wearing the Hijab in contemporary Morocco: Choice and identity. In F. M. Gocek & S. Balaghi (Eds.), *Reconstructing gender in the Middle East* (pp. 40–56). New York: Columbia University Press.

Heuveline, P., & Timberlake, J. M. (2004). The role of cohabitation in family formation: The United States in comparative perspective. *Journal of Marriage and Family, 66,* 1214–1230.

Hibbard, J. H., & Pope, C. R. (1993). The quality of social roles as predictors of morbidity and mortality. *Social Science & Medicine, 36,* 217–225.

Hill, C. T., & Peplau, L. A. (1998). Premarital predictors of relationship outcomes: A 15-year follow-up of the Boston Couples Study. In T. N. Bradbury (Ed.), *The developmental course of marital dysfunction* (pp. 237–278). New York: Cambridge University Press.

Hill, C. T., Rubin, Z., & Peplau, L. A. (1976). Breakups before marriage: The end of 103 affairs. *Journal of Social Issues, 32,* 147–168.

Hill, C., & Silva, E. (2005). *Drawing the line: Sexual harassment on campus.* Washington, DC: American Association of University Women Educational Foundation.

Hill, J. P., & Lynch, M. E. (1983). The intensification of gender-related role expectations during early adolescence. In J. Brooks-Gunn & A. C. Petersen (Eds.), *Girls at puberty* (pp. 201–228). New York: Plenum Press.

Hines, M., Ahmed, S. F., & Hughes, I. A. (2003). Psychological outcomes and gender-related development in complete androgen insensitivity syndrome. *Archives of Sexual Behavior, 32,* 93–101.

Hippisley-Cox, J., Pringle, M., Crown, N., Meal, A., & Wynn, A. (2001). Sex inequalities in ischaemic heart disease in general practice: Cross sectional survey. *British Medical Journal, 322,* 832–834.

Hiscock, M., Israelian, M., Inch, R., Jacek, C., & Hiscock-Kalil, C. (1995). Is there a sex difference in human laterality? II: An exhaustive survey of visual laterality studies from six neuropsychology journals. *Journal of Clinical and Experimental Neuropsychology, 17,* 590–610.

Ho, J. E., Paultre, F., & Mosca, L. (2005). The gender gap in coronary heart disease mortality: Is there a difference between Blacks and Whites? *Journal of Women's Health, 14,* 117–127.

Hochschild, A. R. (1989). *The second shift.* New York: Avon Books.

Hoffman, L. W., & Youngblade, L. M. (1999). *Mothers at work: Effects on children's well-being.* Cambridge: Cambridge University Press.

Hoffmann, M. L., & Powlishta, K. K. (2001). Gender segregation in childhood: A test of the interaction style theory. *The Journal of Genetic Psychology, 162*(3), 298–313.

Hohmann, A. A. (1989). Gender bias in psychotropic drug prescribing in primary care. *Medical Care, 27*(5), 478–490.

Hohmann-Marriott, B. E. (2006). Shared beliefs and the union stability of married and cohabiting couples. *Journal of Marriage and Family, 68,* 1015–1028.

Holmes-Lonergan, H. A. (2003). Preschool children's collaborative problem-solving interactions: The role of gender, pair type, and task. *Sex Roles, 48,* 505–517.

Holt, C. L., & Ellis, J. B. (1998). Assessing the current validity of the Bem Sex-Role Inventory. *Sex Roles, 39,* 929–941.

Holt, J. L., & DeVore, C. J. (2005). Culture, gender, organizational role, and styles of conflict resolution: A meta-analysis. *International Journal of Intercultural Relations, 29,* 165–196.

Honeycutt, J. M., & Cantrill, J. G. (2001). *Cognition, communication, and romantic relationships.* Mahwah, NJ: Lawrence Erlbaum Associates.

Hope, S., Power, C., & Rodgers, B. (1999). Does financial hardship account for elevated psychological distress in lone mothers? *Social Science and Medicine, 49,* 1637–1649.

Hope, S., Rodgers, B., & Power, C. (1999). Marital status transitions and psychological distress: Longitudinal evidence from a national population sample. *Psychological Medicine, 29,* 381–389.

Hops, H., Davis, B., & Lewin, L. M. (1999). The development of alcohol and other substance use: A gender study of family and peer context. *Journal of Studies on Alcohol, 13* (Suppl.), 22–31.

Horner, M. S. (1972). Toward an understanding of achievement-related conflicts in women. *Journal of Social Issues, 28,* 157–175.

Horney, K. (1926). The flight from womanhood: The masculinity-complex in women, as viewed by men and by women. *International Journal of Psycho-Analysis, 7,* 324–339.

Horney, K. (1973). The flight from womanhood. In J. B. Miller (Ed.), *Psychoanalysis and women* (pp. 5–20). Baltimore MD: Penguin Books.

Horwitz, A. V., & White, H. R. (1998). The relationship of cohabitation and mental health: A study of a young adult cohort. *Journal of Marriage and the Family, 60,* 505–514.

Horwitz, A. V., McLaughlin, J., & White, H. R. (1998). How the negative and positive aspects of partner relationships affect the mental health of young married people. *Journal of Health and Social Behavior, 39,* 124–136.

Horwitz, A. V., White, H. R., & Howell-White, S. (1996). Becoming married and mental health: A longitudinal study of a cohort of young adults. *Journal of Marriage and the Family, 58,* 895–907.

Horwitz, A. V., & White, H. R. (1991). Becoming married, depression, and alcohol problems among young adults. *Journal of Health and Social Behavior, 32,* 221–237.

House, J. S., Robbins, C., & Metzner, H. L. (1982). The association of social relationships and activities with mortality: Prospective evidence from the Tecumseh Community health study. *American Journal of Epidemiology, 116*(1), 123–140.

Howard, J. A., Blumstein, P., & Schwartz, P. (1986). Sex, power, and influence tactics in intimate relationships. *Journal of Personality and Social Psychology, 51,* 102–109.

Hoyert, D. L., Heron, M. P., Murphy, S. L., & Kung, H. C. (2006). Deaths: Final data for 2003. *National Vital Statistics Report,* 1–9.

Hudson, J. I., Hiripi, E., Pope, J., H.G., & Kessler, R. C. (2007). The prevalence and correlates of eating disorders in the National Comorbidity Survey Replication. *Biological Psychiatry, 61,* 348–358.

Huerta, M., Cortina, L. M., Pang, J. S., Torges, C. M., & Magley, V. J. (2006). Sex and power in the academy: Modeling sexual harassment in the lives of college women. *Personality and Social Psychology Bulletin, 32,* 616–628.

Hughes, D. L., & Galinsky, E. (1994a). Gender, job, family conditions, and psychological symptoms. *Psychology of Women Quarterly, 18,* 251–270.

Hughes, D. L., & Galinsky, E. (1994b). Work experiences and marital interactions: Elaborating the complexity of work. *Journal of Organizational Behavior, 15,* 423–438.

Hughes, F. P. (1991). *Children, play, and development.* Needham Heights, MA: Allyn & Bacon.

Hughes, M., & Demo, D. H. (1989). Self-perceptions of Black Americans: Self-esteem and personal efficacy. *American Journal of Sociology, 95,* 132–159.

Hughes, T. L., Smith, C., & Dan, A. (Eds.). (2003). *Mental health issues for sexual minority women: Redefining women's mental health.* New York: Harrington Park Press.

Hull, J. G., & Bond, C. F., Jr. (1986). Social and behavioral consequences of alcohol consumption and expectancy: A meta-analysis. *Psychological Bulletin, 99,* 347–360.

Huselid, R. F., & Cooper, M. L. (1992). Gender roles as mediators of sex differences in adolescent alcohol use and abuse. *Journal of Health and Social Behavior, 33,* 348–362.

Huston, T. L., & Houts, R. M. (1998). The psychological infrastructure of courtship and marriage: The role of personality and compatibility in romantic relationships. In T. N. Bradbury (Ed.), *The developmental course of marital dysfunction* (pp. 114–151). New York: Cambridge University Press.

Hutson-Comeaux, S. L., & Kelly, J. R. (1996). Sex differences in interaction style and group task performance: The process-performance relationship. *Journal of Social Behavior and Personality, 11*(5), 255–275.

Huyck, M. H. (1999). Gender roles and gender identity in midlife. In S. L. Willis & J. D. Reid (Eds.), *Life in the middle: Psychological and social development in middle age* (pp. 209–232). San Diego, CA: Academic Press, Inc.

Hyde, J. S. (1984). How large are gender differences in aggression? A developmental meta-analysis. *Developmental Psychology, 20,* 772–736.

Hyde, J. S. (1995). Women and maternity leave: Empirical data and public policy. *Psychology of Women Quarterly, 19,* 299–313.

Hyde, J. S. (2005a). The gender similarities hypothesis. *American Psychologist, 60,* 581–592.

Hyde, J. S. (2005b). The genetics of sexual orientation. In J. Shibley Hyde (Ed.), *Biological substrates of human sexuality* (pp. 9–20). Washington, DC: American Psychological Association.

Hyde, J. S. & Durik, A. M. (2000). Gender differences in erotic plasticity: Evolutionary or sociocultural forces? *Psychological Bulletin, 126,* 375–379.

Hyde, J. S., & Linn, M. C. (1988). Gender differences in verbal ability: A meta-analysis. *Psychological Bulletin, 104*, 53–69.

Hyde, J. S., & McKinley, N. M. (1997). Gender differences in cognition: Results from meta-analysis. In P. J. Caplan, M. Crawford, J. S. Hyde, & J. T. E. Richardson (Eds.), *Gender differences in human cognition* (pp. 30–51). New York: Oxford University Press.

Hyde, J. S., DeLamater, J. D., & Hewitt, E. C. (1998). Sexuality and the dual-earner couple: Multiple roles and sexual functioning. *Journal of Family Psychology, 12*(3), 1–15.

Hyde, J. S., Fennema, E., & Lamon, S. J. (1990). Gender differences in mathematics performance: A meta-analysis. *Psychological Bulletin, 107*, 139–155.

Hyde, J. S., Fennema, E., Ryan, M., Frost, L. A., & Hopp, C. (1990). Gender comparisons of mathematics attitudes and affect. *Psychology of Women Quarterly, 14*, 299–324.

Ibarra, H. (1993). Personal networks of women and minorities in management: A conceptual framework. *Academy of Management Review, 18*, 56–87.

Ickes, W. (1993). Traditional gender roles: Do they make, and then break, our relationships? *Journal of Social Issues, 49*(3), 71–85.

Iervolino, A. C., Hines, M., Golombok, S. E., Rust, J., & Plomin, R. (2005). Genetic and environmental influences on sex-typed behavior during the preschool years. *Child Development, 76*, 826–840.

Impett, E. A., & Peplau, L. A. (2002). Why some women consent to unwanted sex with a dating partner: Insights from attachment theory. *Psychology of Women Quarterly, 26*, 360–370.

Inaba, A., Thoits, P. A., Ueno, K., Gove, W. R., Evenson, R. J., & Sloan, M. (2005). Depression in the United States and Japan: Gender, marital status, and SES patterns. *Social Science & Medicine, 61*, 2280–2292.

Ingram, R. E., Cruet, D., Johnson, B. R., & Wisnicki, K. S. (1988). Self-focused attention, gender, gender role, and vulnerability to negative affect. *Journal of Personality and Social Psychology, 55*, 967–978.

Isenhart, C. E. (1993). Masculine gender role stress in an in-patient sample of alcohol abusers. *Psychology of Addictive Behaviors, 7*(3), 177–184.

Ishiyama, F. I., & Chabassol, D. J. (1984). Fear of success consequence scale: Measurement of fear of social consequences of academic success. *Psychological Reports, 54*, 499–504.

Ishiyama, F. I., & Chabassol, D. J. (1985). Adolescents' fear of social consequences of academic success as a function of age and sex. *Journal of Youth and Adolescence, 14*, 37–46.

Jacklin, C. N. (1989). Female and male: Issues of gender. *American Psychologist, 44*, 127–133.

Jacklin, C. N., & Baker, L. (1993). Early gender development. In S. Oskamp & M. Costanzo (Eds.), *Gender issues in contemporary society* (Vol. 6, pp. 41–57). Newbury Park, CA: Sage.

Jackman, M. R. (1994). *The velvet glove: Paternalism and conflict in gender, class, and race relations*. Berkeley and Los Angeles: University of California Press.

Jackson, C. (2002). Can single-sex classes in co-educational schools enhance the learning experiences of girls and/or boys? An exploration of pupils' perceptions. *British Educational Research Journal, 28*, 37–48.

Jackson, T. (2006). Relationships between perceived close social support and health practices within community samples of American women and men. *The Journal of Psychology, 140*, 229–246.

Jackson, T., Iezzi, T., Gunderson, J., Nagasaka, T., & Fritch, A. (2002). Gender differences in pain perception: The mediating role of self-efficacy beliefs. *Sex Roles, 47*, 561–568.

Jacobs, J. E., Davis-Kean, P., Bleeker, M., Eccles, J. S., & Malanchuk, O. (2005). "I can, but I don't want to": The impact of parents, interests, and activities on gender differences in math. In A. M. Gallagher & J. C. Kaufman (Eds.), *Gender differences in mathematics: An integrative psychological approach* (pp. 246–263). New York: Cambridge University Press.

Jacobs, J. E., Lanza, S., Osgood, D. W., Eccles, J. S., & Wigfield, A. (2002). Changes in children's self-competence and values: Gender and domain differences across grades one through twelve. *Child Development, 73*, 509–527.

Jacobs, J. E., Vernon, M. K., & Eccles, J. (2005). Activity choices in middle childhood: The roles of gender, self-beliefs, and parents' influence. In J. L. Mahoney, R. W. Larson & J. S. Eccles (Eds.), *Organized activities as contexts of development* (pp. 235–254). Mahwah, NJ: Lawrence Erlbaum Associates.

Jaffee, S., & Hyde, J. S. (2000). Gender differences in moral orientation: A meta-analysis. *Psychological Bulletin, 126*, 703–726.

Jambekar, S., Quinn, D. M., & Crocker, J. (2001). The effects of weight and achievement messages on the self-esteem of women. *Psychology of Women Quarterly, 25*, 48–56.

James, A. N., & Richards, H. C. (2003). Escaping stereotypes: Educational attitudes of male alumni of single-sex and coed schools. *Psychology of Men and Masculinity, 4*, 136–148.

James, D., & Drakich, J. (1993). Understanding gender differences in amount of talk: A critical review of research. In D. Tannen (Ed.), *Gender and conversational interaction* (pp. 281–312). New York: Oxford University Press.

Janssen, A., & Murachver, T. (2004). The relationship between gender and topic in gender-preferential language use. *Written Communication, 21*, 344–367.

Jeffery, R. W., Hennrikus, D. J., Lando, H. A., Murray, D. M., & Liu, J. W. (2000). Reconciling conflicting findings regarding postcessation weight concerns and success in smoking cessation. *Health Psychology, 19*, 242–246.

Jenkins, L. S., & Gortner, S. R. (1998). Correlates of self-efficacy expectation and prediction of walking behavior in cardiac surgery elders. *Annals of Behavioral Medicine, 20*(2), 99–103.

Jezova, D., Jurankova, E., Mosnarova, A., Kriska, M., & Skultetyova, I. (1996). Neuroendocrine response during stress with relation to gender differences. *Acta Neurobiologiae Experimentalis, 56,* 779–785.

John, D., Shelton, B. A., & Luschen, K. (1995). Race, ethnicity, gender, and perceptions of fairness. *Journal of Family Issues, 16*(3), 357–379.

Johns, M., Schmader, T., & Martens, A. (2005). Knowing is half the battle: Teaching stereotype threat as a means of improving women's math performance. *Psychological Science, 16,* 175–179.

Johnson, C. (1994). Gender, legitimate authority, and leader-subordinate conversations. *American Sociological Review, 59,* 122–135.

Johnson, E. M., & Huston, T. L. (1998). The perils of love, or why wives adapt to husbands during the transition to parenthood. *Journal of Marriage and the Family, 60,* 195–204.

Johnson, H. D. (2004). Gender, grade, and relationship differences in emotional closeness within adolescent friendships. *Adolescence, 39,* 243–255.

Johnson, H., & Sacco, V. F. (1995). Researching violence against women: Statistics Canada's national survey. *Canadian Journal of Criminology 37,* 281–304.

Johnson, M. E., & Dowling-Guyer, S. (1996). Effects of inclusive vs. exclusive language on evaluations of the counselor. *Sex Roles, 34,* 407–418.

Johnson, M. P. (1995). Patriarchal terrorism and common couple violence: Two forms of violence against women. *Journal of Marriage and the Family, 57,* 283–294.

Johnson, M. P. (2004). Patriarchal terrorism and common couple violence: Two forms of violence against women. In H. T. Reis & C. E. Rusbult (Eds.), *Close relationships: Key readings* (pp. 471–482). New York: Psychology Press.

Johnson, M. P., & Leone, J. M. (2005). The differential effects of intimate terrorism and situational couple violence: Findings from the National Violence against Women Survey. *Journal of Family Issues, 26,* 322–349.

Johnson, M., & Helgeson, V. S. (2002). Sex differences in response to evaluative feedback. A field study. *Psychology of Women Quarterly, 26,* 242–251.

Johnston, L. D., O'Malley, P. M., Bachman, J. G., & Schulenberg, J. E. (2006a). *Monitoring the future: National survey results on drug use, 1975–2005,* Volume 1: *Secondary school students* (NIH Publication No. 06-5883). Bethesda, MD: National Institute on Drug Abuse.

Johnston, L. D., O'Malley, P. M., Bachman, J. G., & Schulenberg, J. E. (2006b). *Monitoring the future: National survey results on drug use, 1975–2005,* Volume II: *College students and adults ages 19–45* (NIH Publication No. 06-5884). Bethesda, MD: National Institute on Drug Abuse.

Johnston, L. D., O'Malley, P. M., Bachman, J. G., & Schulenberg, J. E. (2006c). *Monitoring the future: National results on adolescent drug use: Overview of key findings, 2005* (NIH Publication No. 06-5882). Bethesda, MD: National Institute on Drug Abuse.

Jones, D. (2004). Best friends good for business. *USA TODAY* Retrieved January 31, 2007, from *www.usatoday.com/money/workplace/2004-11-30-best-friends_x.htm.*

Jones, D. C., & Costin, S. E. (1995). Friendship quality during preadolescence and adolescence: The contributions of relationship orientations, instrumentality, and expressivity. *Merrill-Palmer Quarterly, 41,* 517–535.

Jones, E. E., & Davis, K. E. (1965). From acts to dispositions: The attribution process in social psychology. In L. Berkowitz (Ed.), *Advances in experimental social psychology* (Vol. 2, pp. 219–266). New York: Academic Press.

Jones, J. M. (2005). *Gender differences in views of job opportunity: Fifty-three percent of Americans believe opportunities are equal.* Retrieved January 30, 2007, from *www.galluppoll.com/content/Default.aspx?ci=17614&pg=1&VERSION=p.*

Jones, W. H., Chernovetz, M. E. O. C., & Hansson, R. O. (1978). The enigma of androgyny: Differential implications for males and females. *Journal of Consulting and Clinical Psychology, 46,* 298–313.

Josephs, R. A., Markus, H. R., & Tafarodi, R. W. (1992). Gender and self-esteem. *Journal of Personality and Social Psychology, 63,* 391–402.

Jost, J. T., & Kay, A. C. (2005). Exposure to benevolent sexism and complimentary gender stereotypes: Consequences for specific and diffuse forms of system justification. *Journal of Personality and Social Psychology, 88,* 498–509.

Joyner, K., & Laumann, E. O. (2001). Teenage sex and the sexual revolution. In E. O. Laumann & R. T. Michael (Eds.), *Sex, love, and health in America: Private choices and public policies* (pp. 1–27). Chicago: The University of Chicago Press.

Joyner, K., & Udry, J. R. (2000). You don't bring me anything but down: Adolescent romance and depression. *Journal of Health and Social Behavior, 41,* 369–391.

Jussim, L., & Eccles, J. S. (1992). Teacher expectations. II: Construction and reflection of student achievement. *Journal of Personality and Social Psychology, 63,* 947–961.

Kaiser Family Foundation. (2001). *Inside-out: A report on the experiences of lesbians, gays and bisexuals in America and the public's views on issues and policies related to sexual orientation.* Menlo Park, CA. Retrieved November 19, 2007, from *www.kff.org/Kaiserpolls/3193-index.cfm.*

Kalbfleisch, P. J., & Herold, A. L. (2006). Sex, power, and communication. In K. Dindia & D. J. Canary (Eds.), *Sex differences and similarities in communication* (Second ed.) (pp. 299–313). Mahwah, NJ: Lawrence Erlbaum Associates.

Kales, H. C., Neighbors, H. W., Valenstein, M., Blow, F. C., McCarthy, J. F., Ignacio, R. V., et al. (2005). Effect of race and sex on primary care physicians' diagnosis and treatment of late-life depression. *Journal of American Geriatrics, 53*, 777–784.

Kalmijn, M. (2005). Attitude alignment in marriage and cohabitation: The case of sex-role attitudes. *Personal Relationships, 12*, 521–535.

Kamarck, T. W., Annunziato, B., & Amateau, L. M. (1995). Affiliation moderates the effects of social threat on stress-related cardiovascular responses: Boundary conditions for a laboratory model of social support. *Psychosomatic Medicine, 57*, 183–194.

Kanazawa, S. (2005). Is "discrimination" necessary to explain the sex gap in earnings? *Journal of Economic Psychology, 26*, 269–287.

Kane, E. W., & Sanchez, L. (1994). Family status and criticism of gender inequality at home and at work. *Social Forces, 72*(4), 1079–1102.

Kaplan, G. A., Salonen, J. T., Cohen, R. D., Brand, R. J., Syme, S. L., & Puska, P. (1988). Social connections and mortality from all causes and from cardiovascular disease: Prospective evidence from eastern Finland. *American Journal of Epidemiology, 128*(2), 370–380.

Kaplan, R. M., & Kronick, R. G. (2006). Marital status and longevity in the United States. *Journal of Epidemiology and Community Health, 60*, 760–765.

Karniol, R., Gabay, R., Ochion, Y., & Harai, Y. (1998). Is gender or gender-role orientation a better predictor of empathy in adolescence? *Sex Roles, 39*, 45–59.

Karraker, K. H., Vogel, D. A., & Lake, M. A. (1995). Parents' gender-stereotyped perceptions of newborns: The eye of the beholder revisited. *Sex Roles, 33*, 687–701.

Kattainen, A., Salomaa, V., Jula, A., Kesaniemi, Y. A., Kukkonen-Harjula, K., Kahonen, M., et al. (2005). Gender differences in the treatment and secondary prevention of CHD at population level. *Scandinavian Cardiovascular Journal, 39*, 327–333.

Katzman, D. K., Zipursky, R. B., Lambe, E. K., & Mikulis, D. J. (1997). A longitudinal magnetic resonance imaging study of brain changes in adolescents with anorexia nervosa. *Archives of Pediatric Adolescent Medicine, 151*, 793–797.

Kaufman, G. (1999). The portrayal of men's family roles in television commercials. *Sex Roles, 41*, 439–458.

Kawa, I., Carter, J. D., Joyce, P. R., Doughty, C. J., Frampton, C. M., Wells, J. E., et al. (2005). Gender differences in bipolar disorder: Age of onset, course, comorbidity, and symptom presentation. *Bipolar Disorders, 7*, 119–125.

Kawachi, I., Kennedy, B. P., Gupta, V., & Prothrow-Stith, D. (1999). Women's status and the health of women and men: A view from the states. *Social Science & Medicine, 48*, 21–32.

Keller, J. (2002). Blatant stereotype threat and women's math performance: Self-handicapping as a strategic means to cope with obtrusive negative performance expectations. *Sex Roles, 47*, 193–198.

Kelly, H. A. (1994). Rule of thumb and the folklaw of the husband's stick. *Journal of Legal Education, 44*(3), 341–365.

Kelly, J. R., Murphy, J. D., Craig, T. Y., & Driscoll, D. M. (2005). The effect of nonverbal behaviors associated with sexual harassment proclivity on women's performance. *Sex Roles, 53*, 689–701.

Kemper, T. D. (1990). *Social structure and testosterone: Explorations of the socio-bio-social chain.* New Brunswick, NJ: Rutgers University Press.

Kendler, K. S., Myers, J., & Prescott, C. A. (2005). Sex differences in the relationship between social support and risk for major depression: A longitudinal study of opposite-sex twin pairs. *The American Journal of Psychiatry, 162*, 250–256.

Kennedy, M. A., Templeton, L., Gandhi, A., & Gorzalka, B. B. (2004). Asian body image satisfaction: Ethnic and gender differences across Chinese, Indo-Asian, and European-descent students. *Eating Disorders, 12*, 321–336.

Kennedy, N., Boydell, J., Kalidindi, S., Fearon, P., Jones, P. B., van Os, J., et al. (2005). Gender differences in incidence and age at onset of mania and bipolar disorder over a 35-year period in Camberwell, England. *The American Journal of Psychiatry, 162*, 257–262.

Kenney-Benson, G. A., Pomerantz, E. M., Ryan, A. M., & Patrick, H. (2006). Sex differences in math performance: The role of children's approach to schoolwork. *Developmental Psychology, 42*, 11–26.

Kenrick, D. T., Groth, G. E., Trost, M. R., & Sadalla, E. K. (1993). Integrating evolutionary and social exchange perspectives on relationships: Effects of gender, self-appraisal, and involvement level of mate selection criteria. *Journal of Personality and Social Psychology, 64*, 951–969.

Kenrick, D. T., Trost, M. R., & Sundie, J. M. (2004). Sex roles as adaptations: An evolutionary perspective on gender differences and similarities. In A. H. Eagly, A. E. Beall, & R. J. Sternberg (Eds.), *The Psychology of Gender* (Second ed.) (pp. 65–91). New York: Guilford Press.

Kent, R. L., & Moss, S. E. (1994). Effects of sex and gender role on leader emergence. *Academy of Management Journal, 37*(5), 1335–1346.

Keogh, E., & Eccleston, C. (2006). Sex differences in adolescent chronic pain and pain-related coping. *Pain, 123*, 275–284.

Kephart, W. M. (1967). Some correlates of romantic love. *Journal of Marriage and the Family, 29*, 470–474.

Kessler, R. C. (2000). Gender differences in major depression. In E. Frank (Ed.), *Gender and its effects on psychopathology* (pp. 61–84). Washington, DC: American Psychiatric Press, Inc.

Kessler, R. C., & McLeod, J. D. (1984). Sex differences in vulnerability to undesirable life events. *American Sociological Review, 49*, 620–631.

Kessler, R. C., McGonagle, K. A., Nelson, C. B., Hughes, M., Swartz, M., & Blazer, D. G. (1994). Sex and depression in the National Comorbidity Survey. II: Cohort effects. *Journal of Affective Disorders, 30,* 15–26.

Kessler, R. C., McGonagle, K. A., Swartz, M., Blazer, D. G., & Nelson, C. B. (1993). Sex and depression in the National Comorbidity Survey. I: Lifetime prevalence, chronicity and recurrence. *Journal of Affective Disorders, 29,* 85–96.

Kessler, R. C., McGonagle, K. A., Zhao, S., Nelson, C. B., Hughes, M., Eshleman, S., et al. (1994). Lifetime and 12-month prevalence of DSM-III-R psychiatric disorders in the United States. *Archives of General Psychiatry, 51,* 8–19.

Khan, A. A., Gardner, C. O., Prescott, C. A., & Kendler, K. S. (2002). Gender differences in the symptoms of major depression in opposite-sex dizygotic twin pairs. *American Journal of Psychiatry, 159,* 1427–1429.

Khlat, M., Sermet, C., & Le Pape, A. (2000). Women's health in relation with their family and work roles: France in the early 1900s. *Social Science & Medicine, 50,* 1807–1825.

Kiecolt-Glaser, J. K., & Newton, T. L. (2001). Marriage and health: His and hers. *Psychological Bulletin, 127,* 472–503.

Kiecolt-Glaser, J. K., Malarkey, W. B., Chee, M., Newton, T., Cacioppo, J. T., Mao, H-Y., & Glaser, R. (1993). Negative behavior during marital conflict is associated with immunological down-regulation. *Psychosomatic Medicine, 55,* 395–409.

Kiecolt-Glaser, J. K., Newton, T., Cacioppo, J. T., MacCallum, R. C., Glaser, R., & Malarkey, W. B. (1996). Marital conflict and endocrine function: Are men really more physiologically affected than women? *Journal of Consulting and Clinical Psychology, 64*(2), 324–332.

Killeen, L. A., Lopez-Zafra, E., & Eagly, A. H. (2006). Envisioning oneself as a leader: Comparisons of women and men in Spain and the United States. *Psychology of Women Quarterly, 30,* 312–322.

Kim, H. K., & McKenry, P. C. (2002). The relationship between marriage and psychological well-being: A longitudinal analysis. *Journal of Family Issues, 23,* 885–911.

Kimura, D. (1987). Are men's and women's brains really different? *Canadian Psychology, 28,* 133–147.

Kimura, D. (1992). Sex differences in the brain. *Scientific American, 267*(3), 119–125.

Kimura, D. (1999). *Sex and cognition.* Cambridge, MA: MIT Press.

Kimura, D. (2004). Human sex differences in cognition, fact, not predicament. *Sexualities, Evolution & Gender, 6,* 45–53.

Kindlon, D. J., Thompson, M., & Barker, T. (1999). *Raising Cain: Protecting the emotional life of boys.* New York: Ballantine Books.

Kite, M. E., & Whitley, B. E., Jr. (2003). Do heterosexual women and men differ in their attitudes toward homosexuality? A conceptual and methodological analysis. In L. D. Garnets & D. C. Kimmel (Eds.), *Psychological perspectives on lesbian, gay, and bisexual experiences* (Second ed.), (pp. 165–187). New York: Columbia University Press.

Kite, M. E., Stockdale, G. D., Whitley, B. E., Jr., & Johnson, B. T. (2005). Attitudes toward younger and older adults:

An updated meta-analytic review. *Journal of Social Issues, 61,* 241–266.

Klein, E., Campbell, J., Soler, E., & Ghez, M. (1997). *Ending domestic violence: Changing public perceptions/halting the epidemic.* Thousand Oaks, CA: Sage.

Klein, L. C., Corwin, E. J., & Ceballos, R. M. (2006). The social costs of stress: How sex differences in stress responses can lead to social stress vulnerability and depression in women. In C. L. M. Keyes & S. H. Goodman (Eds.), *Women and depression: A handbook for the social, behavioral, and biomedical sciences* (pp. 199–218). New York: Cambridge University Press.

Klerman, G. K., & Weissman, M. M. (1989). Increasing rates of depression. *Journal of the American Medical Association, 261,* 2229–2235.

Kline, G. H., Stanley, S. M., Markman, H. J., Olmos-Gallo, P. A., St. Peters, M., Whitton, S. W., et al. (2004). Timing is everything: Pre-engagement cohabitation and increased risk for poor marital outcomes. *Journal of Family Psychology, 18,* 311–318.

Kling, K. C., Hyde, J. S., Showers, C. J., & Buswell, B. N. (1999). Gender differences in self-esteem: A meta-analysis. *Psychological Bulletin, 125,* 470–500.

Klinger, L. J., Hamilton, J. A., & Cantrell, P. J. (2001). Children's perception of aggressive and gender-specific content in toy commercials. *Social Behavior and Personality, 29*(1), 11–20.

Klinkenberg, D., & Rose, S. (1994). Dating scripts of gay men and lesbians. *Journal of Homosexuality, 26*(4), 23–35.

Klonoff, E. A., & Landrine, H. (1992). Sex roles, occupational roles, and symptom-reporting: A test of competing hypotheses on sex differences. *Journal of Behavioral Medicine, 15*(4), 355–364.

Klumb, P. L., & Lampert, T. (2004). Women, work, and well-being 1950–2000: A review and methodological critique. *Social Science & Medicine, 58,* 1007–1024.

Klump, K. L., Kaye, W. H., & Strober, M. (2001). The evolving genetic foundations of eating disorders. *Eating Disorders, 24,* 215–225.

Kneidinger, L. M., Maple, T. L., & Tross, S. A. (2001). Touching behavior in sport: Functional components, analysis of sex differences, and ethological considerations. *Journal of Nonverbal Behavior, 25*(1), 43–62.

Knight, G. P., Fabes, R. A., & Higgins, D. A. (1996). Concerns about drawing causal inferences from meta-analyses: An example in the study of gender differences in aggression. *Psychological Bulletin, 119,* 410–421.

Knight, G. P., Guthrie, I. K., Page, M. C., & Fabes, R. A. (2002). Emotional arousal and gender differences in aggression: A meta-analysis. *Aggressive Behavior, 28,* 366–393.

Koch, S. C. (2004). Constructing gender: A lens-model inspired gender communication approach. *Sex Roles, 51,* 171–186.

Koenig, A. M., & Eagly, A. H. (2005). Stereotype threat in men on a test of social sensitivity. *Sex Roles, 52,* 489–496.

Koerner, B. I. (1999, April 5). A study on the status of woman faculty in science of MIT. *U.S. News and World Report.* Retrieved April 5, 2006.

Kohlberg, L. (1963). The development of children's orientations toward a moral order: Sequence in the development of moral thought. *Vita Humana, 6,* 11–33.

Kohlberg, L. (1966). A cognitive-developmental analysis of children's sex-role concepts and attitudes. In E. E. Maccoby (Ed.), *The development of sex differences* (pp. 82–173). Stanford, CA: Stanford University Press.

Kohlberg, L. (Ed.). (1981). *The psychology of moral development* (Vol. 2). San Francisco: Harper & Row.

Kolaric, G. C., & Galambos, N. L. (1995). Face-to-face interactions in unacquainted female-male adolescent dyads: How do girls and boys behave? *Journal of Early Adolescence, 15*(3), 363–382.

Konrad, A. M., & Harris, C. (2002). Desirability of the Bem Sex-Role Inventory items for women and men: A comparison between African Americans and European Americans. *Sex Roles, 47,* 259–271.

Konrad, A. M., Ritchie, J., J.E., Lieb, P., & Corrigall, E. (2000). Sex differences and similarities in job attribute preferences: A meta-analysis. *Psychological Bulletin, 126,* 593–641.

Kopp, M. S., Skrabski, A., Kawachi, I., & Adler, N. E. (2005). Low socioeconomic status of the opposite sex is a risk factor for middle aged mortality. *Journal of Epidemiology and Community Health, 59,* 675–678.

Kopper, B. A. (1996). Gender, gender identity, rape myth acceptance, and time of initial resistance on the perception of acquaintance rape blame and avoidability. *Sex Roles, 34,* 81–93.

Kornstein, S. G., Schatzberg, A. F., Yonkers, K. A., Thase, M. E., Keitner, G. I., Ryan, C. E., et al. (1995). Gender differences in presentation of chronic major depression. *Psychopharmacology Bulletin, 31,* 711–718.

Koss, M. P. (1993). Detecting the scope of rape: A review of prevalence research methods. *Journal of Interpersonal Violence, 8*(2), 198–222.

Koss, M. P., Bailey, J. A., Yuan, N. P., Herrera, V. M., & Lichter, E. L. (2003). Depression and PTSD in survivors of male violence: Research and training initiatives to facilitate recovery. *Psychology of Women Quarterly, 27,* 130–142.

Koutantji, M., Pearce, S. A., & Oakley, D. A. (1998). The relationship between gender and family history of pain with current pain experience and awareness of pain in others. *Pain, 77,* 25–31.

Kraft, P., & Rise, J. (1994). The relationship between sensation seeking and smoking, alcohol consumption and sexual behavior among Norwegian adolescents. *Health Education Research: Theory and Practice, 9*(2), 193–200.

Krahé, B. (2000). Sexual scripts and heterosexual aggression. In T. Eckes & H. M. Trautner (Eds.), *The developmental social psychology of gender* (pp. 273–292). Mahwah, NJ: Erlbaum.

Krane, J. E. (1996). Violence against women in intimate relations: Insights from cross-cultural analyses. *Transcultural Psychiatric Research Review, 33,* 435–465.

Kravitz, R. L., Epstein, R. M., Feldman, M. D., Franz, C. E., Azari, R., Wilkes, S., et al. (2005). Influence of patients' requests for direct-to-consumer advertised antidepressants: A randomized controlled trial. *Journal of the American Medical Association, 293,* 1995–2002.

Kring, A. M., & Gordon, A. H. (1998). Sex differences in emotion: Expression, experience, and physiology. *Journal of Personality and Social Psychology, 74,* 686–703.

Krishnan, V. (1998). Premarital cohabitation and marital disruption. *Journal of Divorce & Remarriage, 28,* 157–170.

Kuebli, J., & Fivush, R. (1992). Gender differences in parent-child conversations about past emotions. *Sex Roles, 27,* 683–698.

Kuebli, J., Butler, S., & Fivush, R. (1995). Mother-child talk about past emotions: Relations of maternal language and child gender over time. *Cognition and Emotion, 9*(2/3), 265–283.

Kunz, M., Gruber, A., & Lautenbacher, S. (2006). Sex differences in facial encoding of pain. *The Journal of Pain, 7,* 915–928.

Kurdek, L. A. (1992). Relationship stability and relationship satisfaction in cohabitating gay and lesbian couples: A prospective longitudinal test of the contextual and interdependence models. *Journal of Social and Personal Relationships, 9,* 125–142.

Kurdek, L. A. (1993). The allocation of household labor in gay, lesbian, and heterosexual married couples. *Journal of Social Issues, 49*(3), 127–139.

Kurdek, L. A. (1996). The deterioration of relationship quality for gay and lesbian cohabitating couples: A five-year prospective longitudinal study. *Personal Relationships, 3,* 417–442.

Kurdek, L. A. (1998). Relationship outcomes and their predictors: Longitudinal evidence from heterosexual married, gay cohabiting, and lesbian cohabiting couples. *Journal of Marriage and the Family, 60,* 553–568.

Kurdek, L. A. (2003). Differences between gay and lesbian cohabiting couples. *Journal of Social and Personal Relationships, 20,* 411–436.

Kurdek, L. A. (2004). Are gay and lesbian cohabiting couples *really* different from heterosexual married couples? *Journal of Marriage and Family, 66,* 880–900.

Kurdek, L. A. (2005). Gender and marital satisfaction early in marriage: A growth curve approach. *Journal of Marriage and Family, 67,* 68–84.

Kurdek, L. A. (2006). Differences between partners from heterosexual, gay, and lesbian cohabiting couples. *Journal of Marriage and Family, 68,* 509–528.

Kurdek, L. A. (2007). The allocation of household labor by partners in gay and lesbian couples. *Journal of Family Issues, 28,* 132–148.

Kurdek, L. A., & Schmitt, J. P. (1986). Relationship quality of partners in heterosexual married, heterosexual cohabitating, and gay and lesbian relationships. *Journal of Personality and Social Psychology, 51,* 711–720.

Kurz, D. (1998). Old problems and new directions in the study of violence against women. In R. K. Bergen (Ed.), *Issues in intimate violence* (pp. 197–208). Thousand Oaks, CA: Sage.

Kuttler, A. F., LaGreca, A. M., & Prinstein, M. J. (1999). Friendship qualities and social-emotional functioning of adolescents with close, cross-sex friendships. *Journal of Research on Adolescence, 9,* 339–366.

Lacayo, R. (1995, August 28). To hell week and back: A woman's long fight to enter the Citadel withers in the heat, but the controversy marches on. *Time,* pp. 1–3.

Lacey, R. S., Reifman, A., Scott, J. P., Harris, S. M., & Fitzpatrick, J. (2004). Sexual-moral attitudes, love styles, and mate selection. *The Journal of Sex Research, 41,* 121–128.

Lach, D. H., & Gwartney-Gibbs, P. A. (1993). Sociological perspectives on sexual harassment and workplace dispute recognition. *Journal of Vocational Behavior, 42*(1), 102–115.

Lachance, J. A., & Mazzocco, M. M. M. (2006). A longitudinal analysis of sex differences in math and spatial skills in primary school age children. *Learning and Individual Differences, 16,* 195–216.

Lackie, L., & de Man, A. F. (1997). Correlates of sexual aggression among male university students. *Sex Roles, 37,* 451–457.

Lacombe, A. C., & Gay, J. (1998). The role of gender in adolescent identity and intimacy decisions. *Journal of Youth and Adolescence, 27*(6), 795–802.

Ladwig, K.-H., Mühlberger, N., Walter, H., Schumacher, K., Popp, K., Holle, R., et al. (2000). Gender differences in emotional disability and negative health perception in cardiac patients 6 months after stent implantation. *Journal of Psychosomatic Research, 48,* 501–508.

LaFrance, M., & Banaji, M. (1992). Toward a reconsideration of the gender-emotion relationship. In M. S. Clark (Ed.), *Review of personality and social psychology* (Vol. 14, pp. 178–201). Newbury Park, CA: Sage.

LaFrance, M., & Hecht, M. A. (2000). Gender and smiling: A meta-analysis. In A. H. Fischer (Ed.), *Gender and emotion: Social psychological perspectives* (pp. 118–142). New York: Cambridge University Press.

LaFrance, M., Hecht, M. A., & Paluck, E. L. (2003). The contingent smile: A meta-analysis of sex differences in smiling. *Psychological Bulletin, 129,* 305–334.

Lahelma, E., Arber, S., Kivelä, K., & Roos, E. (2002). Multiple roles and health among British and Finnish women: The influence of socioeconomic circumstances. *Social Science and Medicine, 54,* 727–740.

Lakkis, J., Ricciardelli, L. A., & Williams, R. J. (1999). Role of sexual orientation and gender-related traits in disordered eating. *Sex Roles, 41,* 1–16.

Lamke, L. K., Sollie, D. L., Durbin, R. G., & Fitzpatrick, J. A. (1994). Masculinity, femininity, and relationship satisfaction: The mediating role of interpersonal competence. *Journal of Social and Personal Relationships, 11,* 535–554.

Landrine, H. (1985). Race x class stereotypes of women. *Sex Roles, 13,* 65–75.

Lang, S. (1996). The procreative and ritual constitution of female, male and other androgynous beings in the cultural imagination of the Bimin-Kuskusmin of Papual New Guinea. In S. P. Ramet (Ed.), *Gender reversals and gender cultures: Anthropological and historical perspectives* (pp. 183–196). London: Routledge.

Langhinrichsen-Rohling, J., Lewinsohn, P., Rohde, P., Seeley, J., Monson, C. M., Meyer, K. A., & Langford, R. (1998). Gender differences in the suicide-related behaviors of adolescents and young adults. *Sex Roles, 39,* 839–854.

Langhout, R. D., Bergman, M. E., Cortina, L. M., Fitzgerald, L. F., Drasgow, F., & Williams, J. H. (2005). Sexual harassment severity: Assessing situational and personal determinants and outcomes. *Journal of Applied Social Psychology, 35,* 975–1007.

Larche, D. W. (1985). *Father Gander nursery rhymes.* Santa Barbara, CA: Advocacy Press.

Larson, R. W., & Almeida, D. M. (1999). Emotional transmission in the daily lives of families: A new paradigm for studying family process. *Journal of Marriage and the Family, 61,* 5–20.

Larson, R., & Pleck, J. (1999). Hidden feelings: Emotionality in boys and men. In D. Bernstein (Ed.), *Gender and motivation* (Vol. 45, pp. 25–74). Lincoln: University of Nebraska Press.

Larson, R., & Richards, M. H. (1991). Daily companionship in late childhood and early adolescence: Changing developmental contexts. *Child Development, 62,* 284–300.

Larson, R., & Wilson, S. (2004). Adolescence across place and time: Globalization and the changing pathways to adulthood. In R. M. Lerner & L. Steinberg (Eds.), *Handbook of adolescent psychology* (Second ed.) (pp. 299–330). Hoboken, NJ: John Wiley & Sons.

Laumann, E. O., Gagnon, J. H., Michael, R. T., & Michaels, S. (1994). *The social organization of sexuality: Sexual practices in the United States.* Chicago: University of Chicago Press.

Laumann, E. O., & Michael, R. T. (Eds.). (2000). *Sex, love, and health in America: Private choices and public policies.* Chicago: The University of Chicago Press.

Laumann, E. O., Paik, A., Glasser, D. B., Kang, J. H., Wang, T., Levinson, B., et al. (2006). A cross-national study of subjective sexual well-being among older women and men: Findings from the global study of sexual attitudes and behaviors. *Archives of Sexual Behavior, 35,* 145–161.

Lawlor, D. A., Smith, G. D., & Ebrahim, S. (2004). Socioeconomic position and hormone replacement therapy use: Explaining the discrepancy in evidence from observational and randomized controlled trials. *American Journal of Public Health, 94,* 2149–2154.

Lawton, C. A. (2001). Gender and regional differences in spatial referents used in direction giving. *Sex Roles, 44,* 321–337.

Lazarus, R. S., & Folkman, S. (1984). Stress, appraisal and coping. *Journal of Adolescence, 14,* 119–133.

Leadbeater, B. J., Kuperminc, G. P., Blatt, S. J., & Hertzog, C. (1999). A multivariate model of gender differences in adolescents' internalizing and externalizing problems. *Developmental Psychology, 35,* 1268–1282.

Leahey, E., & Guo, G. (2001). Gender differences in mathematical trajectories. *Social Forces, 80,* 713–732.

Leaper, C. (1987). Agency, communion, and gender as predictors of communication style and being liked in adult male-female dyads. *Sex Roles, 16,* 137–149.

Leaper, C., & Smith, T. E. (2004). A meta-analytic review of gender variations in children's language use: Talkativeness, affiliative speech, and assertive speech. *Developmental Psychology, 40,* 993–1027.

Leaper, C., Breed, L., Hoffman, L., & Perlman, C. A. (2002). Variations in the gender-stereotyped content of children's television cartoons across genres. *Journal of Applied Social Psychology, 32,* 1653–1662.

Leaper, C., Carson, M., Baker, C., Holliday, H., & Myers, S. (1995). Self-disclosure and listener verbal support in same-gender and cross-gender friends' conversations. *Sex Roles, 33,* 387–404.

Leary, M. R., Tambor, E. S., Terdal, S. K., & Downs, D. L. (1995). Self-esteem as an interpersonal monitor: The sociometer hypothesis. *Journal of Personality and Social Psychology, 68,* 518–530.

Leary, M. R., Tchividjian, L. R., & Kraxberger, B. E. (1994). Self-presentation can be hazardous to your health: Impression management and health risk. *Health Psychology, 13,* 461–470.

Lease, A. M., & Blake, J. J. (2005). A comparison of majority-race children with and without a minority-race friend. *Social Development, 14,* 20–41.

Lee, G. R., Willetts, M. C., & Seccombe, K. (1998). Widowhood and depression: Gender differences. *Research on Aging, 20,* 611–630.

Lee, J. A. (1973). *The colors of love: An exploration of the ways of loving.* Don Mills, Ontario, Canada: New Press.

Lee, T. M. C., & Chan, C. C. H. (1998). Vulnerability by sex to seasonal affective disorder. *Perceptual and Motor Skills, 87,* 1120–1122.

Lees, H. (1957). *Help your husband stay alive!* New York: Appleton-Century-Crofts.

Leff, S. S., Kupersmidt, J. B., & Power, T. J. (2003). An initial examination of girls' cognitions of their relationally aggressive peers as a function of their own social standing. *Merrill-Palmer Quarterly, 49,* 28–54.

Lehman, S. J., & Koerner, S. S. (2004). Adolescent women's sports involvement and sexual behavior/health: A process-level investigation. *Journal of Youth and Adolescence, 33,* 443–455.

Leigh, B. C. (1989). Reasons for having and avoiding sex: Gender, sexual orientation, and relationship to sexual behavior. *Journal of Sex Research, 26*(2), 199–209.

Lempers, J. D., & Clark-Lempers, D. S. (1993). A functional comparison of same-sex and opposite-sex friendships during adolescence. *Journal of Adolescent Research, 8*(1), 89–108.

Lenney, E., Gold, J., & Browning, C. (1983). Sex differences in self-confidence: The influence of comparison to others' ability level. *Sex Roles, 9,* 925–942.

Lennon, M. C. (1994). Women, work, and well-being: The importance of work conditions. *Journal of Health and Social Behavior, 35,* 235–247.

Lennon, M. C., & Rosenfield, S. (1992). Women and mental health: The interaction of job and family conditions. *Journal of Health and Social Behavior, 33,* 316–327.

Leone, J. M., Johnson, M. P., Cohan, C. L., & Lloyd, S. E. (2004). Consequences of male partner violence for low-income minority women. *Journal of Marriage and Family, 66,* 472–490.

Lepore, S. J., Allen, K. M., & Evans, G. W. (1993). Social support lowers cardiovascular reactivity to an acute stressor. *Psychosomatic Medicine, 55,* 518–524.

LeResche, L. (2000). Epidemiologic perspectives on sex differences in pain. In R. B. Fillingim (Ed.), *Sex, gender, and pain* (Vol. 17). Seattle, WA: IASP Press.

Lesko, A. C., & Corpus, J. H. (2006). Discounting the difficult: How high math-identified women respond to stereotype threat. *Sex Roles, 54,* 113–125.

Lester, D., & Yang, B. (1998). *Suicide and homicide in the twentieth century: Changes over time.* Commack, AL: Nova Science.

Levenson, R. W., Carstensen, L. L., & Gottman, J. M. (1993). Long-term marriage: Age, gender, and satisfaction. *Psychology and Aging, 8*(2), 301–313.

Levenson, R. W., Carstensen, L. L., & Gottman, J. M. (1994). The influence of age and gender on affect, physiology, and their interrelations: A study of long-term marriages. *Journal of Personality and Social Psychology, 67,* 56–68.

Leveroni, C. L., & Berenbaum, S. A. (1998). Early androgen effects on interest in infants: Evidence from children with congenital adrenal hyperplasia. *Developmental Neuropsychology, 14*(2/3), 321–340.

Leviatan, U., & Cohen, J. (1985). Gender differences in life expectancy among Kibbutz members. *Social Science and Medicine, 21*(5), 545–551.

Levin, S. (2000). Plum man plans for 13,000 at Promise Keepers gathering. *Pittsburgh Post-Gazette,* p. B–2. June 23, 2000.

Levine, F. M., & de Simone, L. L. (1991). The effects of experimenter gender on pain report in male and female subjects. *Pain, 44*(1), 69–72.

Levine, M. P., & Smolak, L. (1996). Media as a context for the development of disordered eating. In L. Smolak, M. P. Levine, & R. Striegel-Moore (Eds.), *The developmental psychopathology of eating disorders* (pp. 235–257). Mahwah, NJ: Erlbaum.

Levinson, D. (1989). *Family violence in cross-cultural perspective.* Newbury Park, CA: Sage.

Levinson, D. J. (1978). *The seasons of a man's life.* New York: Ballantine Books.

Lev-Wiesel, R., & Besser, A. (2006). Male definitions of sexual assault: The role of the perpetrator's gender. *Individual Differences Research, 4,* 47–50.

Levy, P. E., & Baumgardner, A. H. (1991). Effects of self-esteem and gender on goal choice. *Journal of Organizational Behavior, 12,* 529–541.

Lewin, E. (2002). "You'll never walk alone": Lesbian and gay weddings and the authenticity of the same-sex couple. In M. Yalom & L. L. Carstensen (Eds.), *Inside the American couple: New thinking/new challenges* (pp. 87–107). Berkeley, CA: University of California Press.

Lewine, R. R. J., & Seeman, M. V. (1995). Gender, brain, and schizophrenia: Anatomy of differences/differences of anatomy. In M. V. Seeman (Ed.), *Gender and psychopathology* (pp. 131–158). Washington, DC: American Psychiatric Press, Inc.

Lewinsohn, P. M., Rohde, P., & Seeley, J. R. (2001). Gender differences in suicide attempts from adolescence to young adulthood. *Journal of the American Academy of Child and Adolescent Psychiatry, 40,* 427–434.

Lex, B. W. (1991). Some gender differences in alcohol and polysubstance users. *Health Psychology, 10,* 121–132.

Li, N. P., & Kenrick, D. T. (2006). Sex similarities and differences in preferences for short-term mates: What, whether, and why. *Journal of Personality and Social Psychology, 90,* 468–489.

Light, K. C., Grewen, K. M., & Amico, J. A. (2005). More frequent partner hugs and higher oxytocin levels are linked to lower blood pressure and heart rate in premenopausal women. *Biological Psychology, 69,* 5–21.

Light, K. C., Smith, T. E., Johns, J. M., Brownley, K. A., Hofheimer, J. A., & Amico, J. A. (2000). Oxytocin responsivity in mothers of infants: A preliminary study of relationships with blood pressure during laboratory stress and normal ambulatory activity. *Health Psychology, 19,* 560–567.

Lin, Y. C., & Raghubir, P. (2005). Gender differences in unrealistic optimism about marriage and divorce: Are men more optimistic and women more realistic? *Personality and Social Psychology Bulletin, 31,* 198–207.

Lindsey, E. W., & Mize, J. (2001). Contextual differences in parent-child play: Implications for children's gender role development. *Sex Roles, 44,* 155–176.

Linn, M. C., & Petersen, A. C. (1985). Emergence and characterization of sex differences in spatial ability: A meta-analysis. *Child Development, 56,* 1479–1498.

Lippa, R. (1991). Some psychometric characteristics of gender diagnosticity measures: Reliability, validity, consistency across domains, and relationship to the Big Five. *Journal of Personality and Social Psychology, 61,* 1000–1011.

Lippa, R. (1995). Gender-related individual differences and psychological adjustment in terms of the Big Five and circumplex models. *Journal of Personality and Social Psychology, 69,* 1184–1202.

Lippa, R. A., Martin, L. R., & Friedman, H. S. (2000). Gender-related individual differences and mortality in the Terman longitudinal study: Is masculinity hazardous to your health? *Personality and Social Psychology Bulletin, 26,* 1560–1570.

Lippa, R., & Connelly, S. C. (1990). Gender diagnosticity: A new Bayesian approach to gender-related individual differences. *Journal of Personality and Social Psychology, 59,* 1051–1065.

Lippa, R., & Hershberger, S. (1999). Genetic and environmental influences on individual differences in masculinity, femininity, and gender diagnosticity: Analyzing data from a classic twin study. *Journal of Personality, 67,* 127–155.

Lisak, D. (1991). Sexual aggression, masculinity, and fathers. *Journal of Women in Culture and Society, 16*(2), 238–262.

Lisak, D., & Roth, S. (1988). Motivational factors in nonincarcerated sexually aggressive men. *Journal of Personality and Social Psychology, 55,* 795–802.

Liss, M., O'Connor, C., Morosky, E., & Crawford, M. (2001). What makes a feminist? Predictors and correlates of feminist social identity in college women. *Psychology of Women Quarterly, 25,* 124–133.

Lloyd, J. E. V., Walsh, J., & Yailagh, M. S. (2005). Sex differences in performance attributions, self-efficacy, and achievement in mathematics: If I'm so smart, why don't I know it? *Canadian Journal of Education, 28,* 384–408.

Lochhead, C. (2003, February 27). Title IX panel's proposals tossed. *San Francisco Chronicle,* p. A1.

Lockheed, M. E., & Zelditch, M., Jr. (1985). Sex and social influence: A meta-analysis guided by theory. In J. Berger & M. Zelditch, Jr. (Eds.), *Status, rewards, and influence* (pp. 406–429). San Francisco: Jossey-Bass.

Loehlin, J. C., & Martin, N. G. (2000). Dimensions of psychological masculinity-femininity in adult twins from opposite-sex and same-sex pairs. *Behavior Genetics, 30*(1), 19–28.

Loehlin, J. C., Jonsson, E. G., Gustavsson, J. P., Stallings, M. C., Gillespie, N. A., Wright, M. J., et al. (2005). Psychological masculinity-femininity via the gender diagnosticity approach: Heritability and consistency across ages and populations. *Journal of Personality, 73,* 1295–1320.

Lombardo, W. K., Cretser, G. A., Lombardo, B., & Mathis, S. L. (1983). Fer cryin' out loud: There is a sex difference. *Sex Roles, 9,* 987–995.

Love, C. (1994, June 2). A cry in the dark: Love reads Cobain's note to vigil. *Rolling Stone,* p. 40.

Lowe, G. D. O. (2004). Hormone replacement therapy and cardiovascular disease: Increased risks of venous thromboembolism and stroke, and no protection from coronary heart disease. *Journal of Internal Medicine, 256,* 361–374.

Lowe, K. B., Kroeck, K. G., & Sivasubramaniam, N. (1996). Effectiveness correlates of transformational and transactional leadership: A meta-analytic review of the MLQ literature. *Leadership Quarterly, 7,* 385–425.

Lueptow, L. B., Garovich-Szabo, L., & Lueptow, M. B. (2001). Social change and the persistence of sex typing: 1974–1997. *Social Forces, 80,* 1–36.

Lummis, M., & Stevenson, H. W. (1990). Gender differences in beliefs and achievement: A cross-cultural study. *Developmental Psychology, 26,* 254–263.

Lund, R., Due, P., Modvig, J., Holstein, B. E., Damsgaard, M. T., & Andersen, P. K. (2002). Cohabitation and marital status as predictors of mortality: An eight year follow-up study. *Social Science and Medicine, 55,* 673–679.

Lundeberg, M. A. (1997). You guys are overreacting: Teaching prospective teachers about subtle gender bias. *Journal of Teacher Education, 48*(1), 55–61.

Lundeberg, M. A., Fox, P. W., & Puncochar, J. (1994). Highly confident but wrong: Gender differences and similarities in confidence judgments. *Journal of Educational Psychology, 86*(1), 114–121.

Lundeberg, M. A., Fox, P. W., Brown, A. C., & Elbedour, S. (2000). Cultural influences on confidence: Country and gender. *Journal of Educational Psychology, 92,* 152–159.

Lupart, J. L., Cannon, E., & Telfer, J. A. (2004). Gender differences in adolescent academic achievement, interests, values and life-role expectations. *High Ability Studies, 15,* 25–42.

Lupaschuk, D., & Yewchuk, C. (1998). Student perceptions of gender roles: Implications for counsellors. *International Journal for the Advancement of Counselling, 20,* 301–318.

Luthar, S. S., & McMahon, T. J. (1996). Peer reputation among inner-city adolescents: Structure and correlates. *Journal of Research on Adolescence, 6*(4), 581–603.

Lye, D. N., & Waldron, I. (1997). Attitudes toward cohabitation, family, and gender roles: Relationships to values and political ideology. *Sociological Perspectives, 40*(2), 199–225.

Lynch, J. J. (1977). *The broken heart.* New York: Basic Books.

Lytton, H., & Romney, D. M. (1991). Parents' differential socialization of boys and girls: A meta-analysis. *Psychological Bulletin, 109,* 267–296.

Lyubomirsky, S., & Nolen-Hoeksema, S. (1993). Self-perpetuating properties of dysphoric rumination. *Journal of Personality and Social Psychology, 65,* 339–349.

MacCallum, F., & Golombok, S. (2004). Children raised in fatherless families from infancy: A follow-up of children of lesbian and single heterosexual mothers at early adolescence. *Journal of Child Psychology and Psychiatry, 45,* 1407–1419.

Maccoby, E. E. (1966). Sex differences in intellectual functioning. In E. E. Maccoby (Ed.), *The development of sex differences* (pp. 25–55). Stanford, CA: Stanford University Press.

Maccoby, E. E. (1998). *The two sexes: Growing up apart, coming together.* Cambridge, MA: Harvard University Press.

Maccoby, E. E., & Jacklin, C. N. (1974). *The psychology of sex differences.* Stanford, CA: Stanford University Press.

MacDermid, S. M., Huston, T. L., & McHale, S. M. (1990). Changes in marriage associated with the transition to parenthood: Individual differences as a function of sex-role attitudes and changes in the division of household labor. *Journal of Marriage and the Family, 52,* 475–486.

MacDowell, J. (Ed.). (1999, June 21). Personals. In *Pittsburgh Weekly,* pp. 58–59.

MacGeorge, E. L., Graves, A. R., Feng, B., Gillihan, S. J., & Burleson, B. R. (2004). The myth of gender cultures: Similarities outweigh differences in men's and women's provision of and responses to supportive communication. *Sex Roles, 50,* 143–175.

Maciejewski, P. K., Prigerson, H. G., & Mazure, C. M. (2001). Sex differences in event-related risk for major depression. *Psychological Medicine, 31,* 593–604.

Macintyre, S., Ford, G., & Hunt, K. (1999). Do women over-report morbidity? Men's and women's responses to structured prompting on a standard question on long standing illness. *Social Science & Medicine, 48,* 89–98.

Mackenzie, C. S., Gekoski, W. L., & Knox, V. J. (2006). Age, gender, and the underutilization of mental health services: The influence of help-seeking attitudes. *Aging & Mental Health, 10,* 574–582.

Madon, S. (1997). What do people believe about gay males? A study of stereotype content and strength. *Sex Roles, 37,* 663–685.

Madson, L., & Hessling, R. M. (1999). Does alternating between masculine and feminine pronouns eliminate perceived gender bias in text? *Sex Roles, 41,* 559–575.

Mahay, J., Laumann, E. O., & Michaels, S. (2001). Race, gender, and class in sexual scripts. In E. O. Laumann & R. T. Michael (Eds.), *Sex, love, and health in America: Private choices and public policies* (pp. 197–238). Chicago: The University of Chicago Press.

Major, B. (1989). Gender differences in comparisons and entitlement: Implications for comparable worth. *Journal of Social Issues, 45*(4), 99–115.

Major, B., Schmidlin, A. M., & Williams, L. (1990). Gender patterns in social touch: The impact of setting and age. *Journal of Personality and Social Psychology, 58,* 634–643.

Malatesta, C. Z., Culver, C., Tesman, J. R., & Shepard, B. (1989). The development of emotion expression during the first two years of life. *Monographs of the Society for Research in Child Development, 54*(1/2), 1–104.

Maltz, D. N., & Borker, R. A. (1982). A cultural approach to male-female miscommunication. In J. J. Gumperz (Ed.), *Language and social identity* (pp. 196–216). Cambridge, MA: Cambridge University Press.

Manheimer, R. J. (1994). *Older Americans almanac.* Washington, DC: Gale Research.

Mann, J. (1985a). Poverty after divorce. *The Washington Post,* October 4, 1985, Final Edition. Retrieved May 21, 2007, from *web.lexis-nexis.com/universe/printdoc.*

Mann, J. (1985b). Disastrous divorce results. *The Washington Post,* October 2, 1985, Final Edition. Retrieved May 21, 2007, from *web.lexis-nexis.com/universe/printdoc.*

Mann, T. (1996). Why do we need a health psychology of gender or sexual orientation? In P. M. Kato & T. Mann (Eds.), *Handbook of diversity issues in health psychology* (pp. 187–198). New York: Plenum Press.

Mann, T., Nolen-Hoeksema, S., Huang, K., & Burgard, D. (1997). Are two interventions worse than none? Joint primary and secondary prevention of eating disorders in college females. *Health Psychology, 16,* 215–225.

Manning, A. (1989). The genetic bases of aggression. In J. Groebel & R. A. Hinde (Eds.), *Aggression and war: Their biological and social bases* (pp. 48–57). New York: Cambridge University Press.

Marcia, J. E. (1993). The status of the statuses: Research review. In J. E. Marcia, D. R. Matteson, J. L. Orlofsky, A. S. Waterman, & S. L. Archer (Eds.), *Ego identity: A handbook for psychosocial research* (pp. 22–41). New York: Springer-Verlag.

Marcotte, D., Alain, M., & Gosselin, M.-J. (1999). Gender differences in adolescent depression: Gender-typed characteristics or problem-solving skills deficits? *Sex Roles, 41,* 31–48.

Marcus, A. C., & Seeman, T. E. (1981). Sex differences in reports of illness and disability: A preliminary test of the fixed role obligations hypothesis. *Journal of Health and Social Behavior, 22,* 174–182.

Marcus, A. C., & Siegel, J. M. (1982). Sex differences in the use of physician services: A preliminary test of the fixed role hypothesis. *Journal of Health and Social Behavior, 23,* 186–197.

Marecek, J. (1995). Gender, politics, and psychology's ways of knowing. *American Psychologist, 50,* 162–163.

Marecek, J., Crawford, M., & Popp, D. (2004). On the construction of gender, sex, and sexualities. In A. H. Eagly, A. E. Beall, & R. J. Sternberg (Eds.), *The Psychology of Gender* (2nd ed., pp. 192–216). New York, NY: Guilford Press.

Margolis, D. R. (1993). Women's movements around the world: Cross-cultural comparison. *Gender and Society, 7,* 379–399.

Markey, C. N., Markey, P. M., Schneider, C., & Brownlee, S. (2005). Marital status and health benefits: Different relations for men and women. *Sex Roles, 53,* 443–451.

Markiewicz, D., Devine, I., & Kausilas, D. (2000). Friendships of women and men at work: Job satisfaction and resource implications. *Journal of Managerial Psychology, 15*(2), 161–184.

Marks, N. F. (1998). Does it hurt to care? Caregiving, work-family conflict, and midlife well-being. *Journal of Marriage and the Family, 60,* 951–966.

Marks, S. R. (1994). Intimacy in the public realm: The case of co-workers. *Social Forces, 72*(3), 843–858.

Martell, R. F. (1996). Gender-based bias and discrimination. In P. J. Dubeck & K. Borman (Eds.), *Women and work: A handbook* (pp. 329–332). New York: Garland.

Martell, R. F., Lane, D. M., & Emrich, C. (1996). Male-female differences: A computer simulation. *American Psychologist, 51,* 157–158.

Martin, C. L. (1989). Children's use of gender-related information in making social judgments. *Developmental Psychology, 25,* 80–88.

Martin, C. L., & Fabes, R. A. (2001). The stability and consequences of young children's same-sex peer interactions. *Developmental Psychology, 37,* 431–446.

Martin, C. L., & Ruble, D. (2004). Children's search for gender cues. *Current Directions in Psychological Science, 13,* 67–70.

Martin, C. L., Fabes, R. A., Evans, S. M., & Wyman, H. (1999). Social cognition on the playground: Children's beliefs about playing with girls versus boys and their relations to sex segregated play. *Journal of Social and Personal Relationships, 16,* 751–771.

Martin, P. D., Specter, G., Martin, D., & Martin, M. (2003). Expressed attitudes of adolescents toward marriage and family life. *Adolescence, 38,* 359–367.

Martin, R. (1997). Girls don't talk about garages!: Perceptions of conversation in same and cross-sex friendships. *Personal Relationships, 4,* 115–130.

Martin, R., Gordon, E. E. I., & Lounsbury, P. (1998). Gender disparities in the attribution of cardiac-related symptoms: Contribution of common sense models of illness. *Health Psychology, 17,* 346–357.

Martindale, M. (1990). *Sexual harassment in the military: 1988.* Arlington, VA: Department of Defense.

Martinez-Donate, A. P., Hovell, M. F., Blumberg, E. J., Zellner, J. A., Sipan, C. L., Shillington, A. M., et al. (2004). Gender differences in condom-related behaviors and attitudes among Mexican adolescents living on the U.S.-Mexico border. *AIDS Education and Prevention, 16,* 172–186.

Marx, D. M., & Roman, J. S. (2002). Female role models: Protecting women's math test performance. *Personality and Social Psychology Bulletin, 28,* 1183–1193.

Massa, L. J., Mayer, R. E., & Bohon, L. M. (2005). Individual differences in gender role beliefs influence spatial ability test performance. *Learning and Individual Differences, 15,* 99–111.

Masser, B. M., & Abrams, D. (2004). Reinforcing the glass ceiling: The consequences of hostile sexism for female managerial candidates. *Sex Roles, 51,* 609–615.

Mastekaasa, A. (1996). Unemployment and health: Selection effects. *Journal of Community and Applied Social Psychology, 6,* 189–205.

Matschiner, M., & Murnen, S. K. (1999). Hyperfemininity and influence. *Psychology of Women Quarterly, 23,* 631–642.

Matthews, K. A., Gump, B. B., & Owens, J. F. (2001). Chronic stress influences cardiovascular and neuroendocrine responses during acute stress and recovery, especially in men. *Health Psychology, 20,* 403–410.

Matthews, R. A., Del Priore, R. E., Acitelli, L. K., & Barnes-Farrell, J. L. (2006). Work-to-relationship conflict: Crossover effects in dual-earner couples. *Journal of Occupational Health Psychology, 11,* 228–240.

Matthews, S., Manor, O., & Power, C. (1999). Social inequalities in health: Are there gender differences? *Social Science and Medicine, 48,* 49–60.

Matthews, S., & Power, C. (2002). Socio-economic gradients in psychological distress: A focus on women, social roles and work-home characteristics. *Social Science & Medicine, 54,* 799–810.

Matthews, S., Hertzman, C., Ostry, A., & Power, C. (1998). Gender, work roles and psychosocial work characteristics as determinants of health. *Social Science & Medicine, 46*(11), 1417–1424.

Matthews, S., Stansfeld, S., & Power, C. (1999). Social support at age 33: The influence of gender, employment status and social class. *Social Science & Medicine, 49,* 133–142.

Matthews, T. J., & Hamilton, B. E. (2005). *Trend analysis of the sex ratio at birth in the United States.* National Vital Statistics Reports, Vol. 53, Number 20, pp.1–20.

Mau, W. C. (2003). Factors that influence persistence in science and engineering career aspirations. *Career Development Quarterly, 51,* 234–243.

Mays, V. M., & Cochran, S. D. (2001). Mental health correlates of perceived discrimination among lesbian, gay, and bisexual adults in the United States. *American Journal of Public Health, 91,* 1869–1876.

Mazur, E., & Olver, R. R. (1987). Intimacy and structure: Sex differences in imagery of same-sex relationships. *Sex Roles, 16,* 539–558.

McBride, A. B. (1990). Mental health effects of women's multiple roles. *American Psychologist, 45,* 381–384.

McBurney, D. H., Gaulin, S. J. C., Devineni, T., & Adams, C. (1997). Superior spatial memory of women: Stronger evidence for the gathering hypothesis. *Evolution and Human Behavior, 18,* 165–174.

McClelland, D. C., Atkinson, J. W., Clark, R. A., & Lowell, E. L. (1953). *The achievement motive.* New York: Appleton-Century-Crofts.

McCloskey, L. A. (1996). Gender and the expression of status in children's mixed-age conversations. *Journal of Applied Developmental Psychology, 17,* 117–133.

McClure, E. B. (2000). A meta-analytic review of sex differences in facial expression processing and their development in infants, children, and adolescents. *Psychological Bulletin, 126,* 424–453.

McConnell, A. R., & Fazio, R. H. (1996). Women as men and people: Effects of gender-marked language. *Personality and Social Psychology Bulletin, 22,* 1004–1013.

McCreary, D. R., Newcomb, M. D., & Sadava, S. W. (1999). The male role, alcohol use, and alcohol problems: A structural modeling examination in adult women and men. *Journal of Counseling Psychology, 46*(1), 109–124.

McCreary, D. R., Wong, F. Y., Wiener, W., Carpenter, K. M., Engle, A., & Nelson, P. (1996). The relationship between masculine gender role stress and psychological adjustment: A question of construct validity? *Sex Roles, 34,* 507–516.

McDonough, P., Williams, D. R., House, J. S., & Duncan, G. J. (1999). Gender and the socioeconomic gradient in mortality. *Journal of Health and Social Behavior, 40,* 17–31.

McDougall, J., DeWit, D. J., & Ebanks, G. E. (1999). Parental preferences for sex of children in Canada. *Sex Roles, 41,* 615–626.

McGlone, M. S., Aronson, J., & Kobrynowicz, D. (2006). Stereotype threat and the gender gap in political knowledge. *Psychology of Women Quarterly, 30,* 392–398.

McGlothlin, H., & Killen, M. (2005). Children's perceptions of intergroup and intragroup similarity and the role of social experience. *Applied Developmental Psychology, 26,* 680–698.

McGlothlin, H., Killen, M., & Edmonds, C. (2005). European-American children's intergroup attitudes about peer relationships. *British Journal of Developmental Psychology, 23,* 227–249.

McHale, S. M., Kim, J. Y., Whiteman, S., & Crouter, A. C. (2004). Links between sex-typed time use in middle childhood and gender development in early adolescence. *Developmental Psychology, 40,* 868–881.

McHugh, M. C., Koeske, R. D., & Frieze, I. H. (1986). Issues to consider in conducting nonsexist psychological research: A guide for researchers. *American Psychologist, 41,* 879–890.

McIntosh, D. N., Keywell, J., Reifman, A., & Ellsworth, P. C. (1994). Stress and health in first-year law students: Women fare worse? *Journal of Applied Social Psychology, 24*(16), 1474–1499.

McKenna, W., & Kessler, S. J. (1977). Experimental design as a source of sex bias in social psychology. *Sex Roles, 3,* 117–128.

McKinlay, J. B. (1996). Some contributions from the social system to gender inequalities in heart disease. *Journal of Health and Social Behavior, 37,* 1–26.

McLendon, K., Foley, L. A., Hall, J., Sloan, L., Wesley, A., & Perry, L. (1994). Male and female perceptions of date rape. *Journal of Social Behavior and Personality, 9*(3), 421–428.

McLeod, J. D. (1991). Childhood parental loss and adult depression. *Journal of Health and Social Behavior, 32*, 205–220.

McMunn, A., Bartley, M., & Kuh, D. (2006). Women's health in mid-life: Life course social roles and agency as quality. *Social Science & Medicine, 63*, 1561–1572.

McNelles, L. R., & Connolly, J. A. (1999). Intimacy between adolescent friends: Age and gender differences in intimate affect and intimate behaviors. *Journal of Research on Adolescence, 9*(2), 143–159.

McWilliams, S., & Howard, J. (1993). Solidarity and hierarchy in cross-sex friendships. *Journal of Social Issues, 49*(3), 191–202.

Mechanic, M. B., Weaver, T. L., & Resick, P. A. (2002). Intimate partner violence and stalking behavior: Exploration of patterns and correlates in a sample of acutely battered women. In K. E. Davis, I. H. Frieze, & R. D. Maiuro (Eds.), *Stalking: Perspectives on victims and perpetrators* (pp. 62–88). New York: Springer.

Messman, S. J., Canary, D. J., & Hause, K. S. (2000). Motives to remain platonic, equity, and the use of maintenance strategies in opposite-sex friendships. *Journal of Social and Personal Relationships, 17*, 67–94.

Messner, M. A. (1997). *Politics of masculinities: Men in movements.* London: Sage.

Metha, A., Chen, E., Mulvenon, S., & Dode, I. (1998). A theoretical model of adolescent suicide risk. *Archives of Suicide Research, 4*, 115–133.

Metts, S. (2004). First sexual involvement in romantic relationships: An empirical investigation of communicative framing, romantic beliefs, and attachment orientation in the passion turning point. In J. H. Harvey, A. Wenzel, & S. Sprecher (Eds.), *The handbook of sexuality in close relationships* (pp. 135–158). Mahwah, NJ: Lawrence Erlbaum Associates.

Mezulis, A. H., Abramson, L. Y., Hyde, J. S., & Hankin, B. L. (2004). Is there a universal positivity bias in attributions? A meta-analytic review of individual, developmental, and cultural differences in the self-serving attributional bias. *Psychological Bulletin, 130*, 711–747.

Michell, L., & Amos, A. (1997). Girls, pecking order and smoking. *Social Science and Medicine, 44*(12), 1861–1869.

Mickelson, K. D., Helgeson, V. S., & Weiner, E. (1995). Gender effects on social support provision and receipt. *Personal Relationships, 2*, 221–224.

Miedzian, M. (1991). *Boys will be boys: Breaking the link between masculinity and violence.* Thousand Oaks, CA: Sage.

Milkie, M. A., Bianchi, S. M., Mattingly, M. J., & Robinson, J. P. (2002). Gendered division of childrearing: Ideals, realities, and the relationship to parental well-being. *Sex Roles, 47*, 21–38.

Miller, C. T., & Downey, K. T. (1999). A meta-analysis of heavyweight and self-esteem. *Personality and Social Psychology Review, 3*, 68–84.

Miller, C., & Swift, K. (1980). *The handbook of nonsexist writing.* New York: Harper & Row.

Miller, C., Swift, K., & Maggio, R. (1997, September/October). Liberating language. *Ms.*, pp. 51–54.

Miller, J. B. (1991). The development of women's sense of self. In J. V. Jordan, A. G. Kaplan, J. B. Miller, I. P. Stiver, & J. L. Surrey (Eds.), *Women's growth in connection: Writings from the Stone Center* (pp. 11–26). New York: Guilford Press.

Miller, K. E., Sabo, D. F., Farrell, M. P., Barnes, G. M., & Melnick, M. J. (1998). Athletic participation and sexual behavior in adolescents: The different worlds of boys and girls. *Journal of Health and Social Behavior, 39*, 108–123.

Miller, R., Willis, E., & Wyn, J. (1993). *Gender and compliance in the management of a medical regimen for young people with cystic fibrosis.* Paper presented at the BSA Medical Sociology Conference, University of York, UK.

Mischel, W. (1966). A social-learning view of sex differences in behavior. In E. E. Maccoby (Ed.), *The development of sex differences* (pp. 56–81). Stanford, CA: Stanford University Press.

Mitchell, J. E., Baker, L. A., & Jackson, C. N. (1989). Masculinity and femininity in twin children: Genetic and environmental factors. *Child Development, 60*, 1475–1485.

Moen, P., Kim, J. E., & Hofmeister, H. (2001). Couples' work/retirement transitions, gender, and marital quality. *Social Psychology Quarterly, 64*, 55–71.

Molidor, C., & Tolman, R. M. (1998). Gender and contextual factors in adolescent dating violence. *Violence Against Women, 4*, 180–194.

Möller-Leimkühler, A. M. (2003). The gender gap in suicide and premature death or: Why are men so vulnerable? *European Archives of Psychiatry and Clinical Neuroscience, 253*, 1–8.

Molloy, B. L., & Herzberger, S. D. (1998). Body image and self-esteem: A comparison of African-American and Caucasian women. *Sex Roles, 38*, 631–643.

Mongeau, P. A., Serewicz, M. C. M., Henningsen, M. L. M., & Davis, K. L. (2006). Sex differences in the transition to a heterosexual romantic relationship. In K. Dindia & D. J. Canary (Eds.), *Sex differences and similarities in communication* (Second ed.) (pp. 337–358). Mahwah, NJ: Lawrence Erlbaum Associates.

Monk, D., & Ricciardelli, L. A. (2003). Three dimensions of the male gender role as correlates of alcohol and cannabis involvement in young Australian men. *Psychology of Men & Masculinity, 4*(1), 57–69.

Monsour, M. (1992). Meanings of intimacy in cross- and same-sex friendships. *Journal of Social and Personal Relationships, 9*, 277–295.

Monsour, M. (2002). *Women and men as friends: Relationships across the life span in the 21st century*. Mahwah, NJ: Erlbaum.

Monsour, M., Harris, B., Kurzweil, N., & Beard, C. (1994). Challenges confronting cross-sex friendships: Much ado about nothing? *Sex Roles, 31*, 55–77.

Montgomery, M. J. (2005). Psychosocial intimacy and identity: From early adolescence to emerging adulthood. *Journal of Adolescent Research, 20*, 346–374.

Moore, D. W. (2005). Gender stereotypes prevail on working outside the home. Retrieved January 30, 2007, from *www.galluppoll.com/content/Default.aspx?ci=17896&pg=1&VERSION=p.*

Morabia, A., Fabre, J., & Dunand, J.-P. (1992). The influence of patient and physician gender on prescription of psychotropic drugs. *Journal of Clinical Epidemiology, 45*(2), 111–116.

Morano, C. D., Cisler, R. A., & Lemerond, J. (1993). Risk factors for adolescent suicidal behavior: Loss, insufficient familial support, and hopelessness. *Adolescence, 28*(112), 851–865.

Morgan, B. L. (1996). Putting the feminism into feminism scales: Introduction of a Liberal Feminist Attitude and Ideology Scale (LFAIS). *Sex Roles, 34*, 359–390.

Morgan, C. (2001). The effects of negative managerial feedback on student motivation: Implications for gender differences in teacher-student relations. *Sex Roles, 44*, 513–535.

Morgan, C., Isaac, J. D., & Sansone, C. (2001). The role of interest in understanding the career choices of female and male college students. *Sex Roles, 44*, 295–320.

Morokoff, P. J., Harlow, L. L., & Quina, K. (1995). Women and AIDS. In A. L. Stanton & S. J. Gallant (Eds.), *The psychology of women's health: Progress and challenges in research and application* (pp. 117–169). Washington, D.C.: American Psychological Association.

Morrongiello, B. A., & Dawber, T. (1999). Parental influences on toddlers' injury-risk behaviors: Are sons and daughters socialized differently? *Journal of Applied Developmental Psychology, 20*, 227–251.

Morrongiello, B. A., & Dawber, T. (2000). Mothers' reponses to sons and daughters engaging in injury-risk behaviors on a playground: Implications for sex differences in injury rates. *Journal of Experimental Child Psychology, 76*, 89–103.

Morrongiello, B. A., Midgett, C., & Stanton, K.-L. (2000). Gender biases in children's appraisals of injury risk and other children's risk-taking behaviors. *Journal of Experimental Child Psychology, 77*, 317–336.

Morry, M. M. (2007). The attraction-similarity hypothesis among cross-sex friends: Relationship satisfaction, perceived similarities, and self-serving perceptions. *Journal of Social and Personal Relationships, 24*, 117–138.

Morse, J. (1999, February 15). Make time for daddy. *Time*. Retrieved November 13, 2007 from *www.time.com/t?zine/article/0,9171,990197,00.html.*

Moscucci, M., Smith, D. E., Jani, S. M., Montoye, C. K., Defranco, A. C., Chandra, H., Karve, M., Share, D. (2004, November). *Gender differences in time to treatment for patients undergoing primary percutaneous coronary intervention for acute ST segment elevation myocardial infarction: An important target for quality improvement*. Paper presented at the American Heart Association's Scientific Sessions, 2004. New Orleans.

Mosher, W. D., Martinez, G. M., Chandra, A., Abma, J. C., & Wilson, S. J. (2004). *Use of contraception and use of family planning services in the United States, 1982–2002. Advance data from vital and health statistics* (No. 350). Hyattsville, MD: National Center for Health Statistics.

Moskowitz, D. S., Suh, E. J., & Desaulniers, J. (1994). Situational influences on gender differences in agency and communion. *Journal of Personality and Social Psychology, 66*, 753–761.

Moss, P., & Deven, F. (2006). Leave policies and research: A cross-national overview. *Marriage and Family Review, 39*, 255–285.

Muehlenhard, C. L., & Cook, S. W. (1988). Men's self reports of unwanted sexual activity. *Journal of Sex Research, 24*, 58–72.

Muennig, P., Lubetkin, E., Jia, H., & Franks, P. (2006). Gender and the burden of disease attributable to obesity. *American Journal of Public Health, 96*, 1662–1668.

Muhonen, T., & Torkelson, E. (2004). Work locus of control and its relationship to health and job satisfaction from a gender perspective. *Stress and Health, 20*, 21–28.

Mukai, T., Kambara, A., & Sasaki, Y. (1998). Body dissatisfaction, need for social approval, and eating disturbances among Japanese and American college women. *Sex Roles, 39*, 751–763.

Mulac, A. (1998). The gender-linked language effect: Do language differences really make a difference? In D. J. Canary & K. Dindia (Eds.), *Sex differences and similarities in communication* (pp. 127–153). Mahwah, NJ: Erlbaum.

Mulac, A. (2006). The gender-linked language effect: Do language differences really make a difference? In K. Dindia & D. J. Canary (Eds.), *Sex differences and similarities in communication* (Second ed.) (pp. 195–215). Mahwah, NJ: Lawrence Erlbaum Associates.

Mulac, A., Bradac, J. J., & Gibbons, P. (2001). Empirical support for the gender-as-culture hypothesis: An intercultural analysis of male/female language differences. *Human Communication Research, 27*, 121–152.

Multiple Risk Factor Intervention Trial Research Group. (1983). Multiple Risk Factor Intervention Trial: Risk factor changes and mortality results. *Journal of the American Medical Association, 248*, 1465–1477.

Munroe, R. L., & Romney, A. K. (2006). Gender and age differences in same-sex aggregation and social behavior. A four-culture study. *Journal of Cross-Cultural Psychology, 37*, 3–19.

Munroe, R. L., Hulefeld, R., Rodgers, J. M., Tomeo, D. L., & Yamazaki, S. K. (2000). Aggression among children in four cultures. *Cross-Cultural Research, 34,* 3–25.

Murberg, T. A., & Bru, E. (2004). Social support, negative life events and emotional problems among Norwegian adolescents. *School Psychology International, 25,* 387–403.

Murberg, T. A., Bru, E., Aarsland, T., & Svebak, S. (1998). Functional status and depression among men and women with congestive heart failure. *International Journal of Psychiatry in Medicine, 28*(3), 273–291.

Murnen, S. K., & Smolak, L. (1997). Femininity, masculinity, and disordered eating: A meta-analytic review. *International Journal of Eating Disorders, 22,* 231–242.

Murnen, S. K., Wright, C., & Kaluzny, G. (2002). If "boys will be boys," then girls will be victims? A meta-analytic review of the research that relates masculine ideology to sexual aggression. *Sex Roles, 46,* 359–375.

Murphy, E. M. (2003). Being born female is dangerous for your health. *American Psychologist, 58,* 205–210.

Murphy, G. C., & Athanasou, J. A. (1999). The effect of unemployment on mental health. *Journal of Occupational and Organizational Psychology, 72,* 83–99.

Murray-Close, D., Crick, N. R., & Galotti, K. M. (2006). Children's moral reasoning regarding physical and relational aggression. *Social Development, 15,* 345–372.

Murray-Close, D., Ostrov, J. M., & Crick, N. R. (2007). A short-term longitudinal study of growth of relational aggression during middle childhood: Associations with gender, friendship intimacy, and internalizing problems. *Development and Psychopathology, 19,* 187–203.

Murstein, B. I. (1974). *Love, sex, and marriage through the ages.* New York: Springer.

Myers, A. M., & Gonda, G. (1982). Utility of the masculinity-femininity construct: Comparison of traditional and androgyny approaches. *Journal of Personality and Social Psychology, 43,* 514–522.

Myers, S. M., & Booth, A. (1996). Men's retirement and marital quality. *Journal of Family Issues, 17*(3), 336–357.

Myhill, D., & Jones, S. (2006). She doesn't shout at no girls': Pupils' perceptions of gender equity in the classroom. *Cambridge Journal of Education, 36,* 99–113.

Nagel, B., Matsuo, H., McIntyre, K. P., & Morrison, N. (2005). Attitudes toward victims of rape: Effects of gender, race, religion, and social status. *Journal of Interpersonal Violence, 20,* 725–737.

Naifeh, S., & Smith, G. W. (1984). *Why can't men open up?* New York: Warner Books.

Nansel, T. R., Overpeck, M. D., Haynie, D. L., Ruan, W. J., & Scheidt, P. C. (2003). Relationships between bullying and violence among US youth. *Archives of Pediatrics and Adolescent Medicine, 157,* 348–352.

Nardi, P. M. (1992). Sex, friendship, and gender roles among gay men. In P. M. Nardi (Ed.), *Men's friendships* (pp. 173–185). Newbury Park, CA: Sage.

Nardi, P. M., & Sherrod, D. (1994). Friendship in the lives of gay men and lesbians. *Journal of Social and Personal Relationships, 11,* 185–199.

Nathanson, C. A. (1978). Sex roles as variables in the interpretation of morbidity data: A methodological critique. *International Journal of Epidemiology, 7*(3), 253–262.

National Association for Single Sex Public Education. (2003, June 5). *What is Title IX?* Retrieved November 9, 2007, from *www.singlesexschools.org/links-articles.htm.*

National Center for Education Statistics. (2001). *Outcomes of Learning: Results from the 2000 Program for International Student Assessment of 15-year-olds in reading, mathematics, and science literacy.* Organization for Economic Cooperation and Development, Program for International Student Assessment (PISA) 2000.

National Center for Education Statistics. (2005). First-professional degrees conferred by degree-granting institutions in dentistry, medicine, and law, by sex of student, and number of institutions conferring degrees: Selected years, 1949–50 through 2003–04. Retrieved November 9, 2007, from *nces.ed.gov/programs/digest/d05/tables/dt05_256.asp.*

National Center for Health Statistics. (2005). *Suicidal ideation, suicide attempts, and injurious suicide attempts among students in grades 9–12, by sex, grade level, race, and Hispanic origin: United States, selected years 1991–2003 (with Chartbook on trends in the health of Americans).* Hyattsville, MD: Public Health Service.

National Center for Health Statistics. (2006a). *Death rates for suicide, by sex, race, Hispanic origin, and age: United States, selected years 1950–2004.* Retrieved November 9, 2007, from *www.cdc.gov/nchs/datawh/statab/unpubd/mortabs.htm.*

National Center for Health Statistics. (2006b). *Health, United States, 2006 With chartbook on trends in the health of Americans.* Hyattsville, MD: Public Health Service.

National Federation of State High School Associations. (2006). *2005–06 High school athletics participation survey.* Retrieved November 9, 2007, from *www.nfhs.org/core/contentmanager/upload/2005-06NFHSparticipationsurvey.pdf.*

National Institute of Justice. (1993). *Project to develop a model anti-stalking code for states, final summary report.* Washington, DC: National Institute of Justice, U.S. Department of Justice.

National Institute of Mental Health. (2001). *Eating disorders: Facts about eating disorders and the search for solutions.* (NIH Publication No. 01-4901). Bethesda, MD: National Institue of Mental Health.

National Institute of Mental Health. (2003). *Eating disorder statistics.* National Association of Anorexia Nervosa and Associated Disorders. Philadelphia: Chelsea House Publishers.

National Institute on Alcohol Abuse and Alcoholism. (1997). Alcohol alert. *Alcohol, Violence, and Aggression, 38,* 1–6.

National Institutes of Health. (2006). *Fact book fiscal year 2005* (pp. 37–55). National Institutes of Health. National Heart, Lung, and Blood Institute. Washington, D.C.: U.S. Department of Health & Human Service.

National Organization for Women. (2004). *NOW Acts: March for women's lives inspired a flurry of activity.* Retrieved January 12, 2007, from *www.now.org/organization/conference/resolutions/2006.html.*

National Public Radio Morning Edition. (2001). Money in marriage and divorce. Retrieved January 15, 2007, from *www.equalityinmarriage.org/d/Pressroom/art_6.html.*

National Public Radio. (1999, November 29). *Fresh Air.* Interview with Hugh Hefner by Terry Gross.

National Science Foundation, Division of Science Resources Statisitics. (2004). *Women, minorities, and persons with disabilities in science and engineering.* Arlington, VA: NSF 04-317.

Nazroo, J. Y., Edwards, A. C., & Brown, G. W. (1997). Gender differences in the onset of depression following a shared life event: A study of couples. *Psychological Medicine, 27,* 9–19.

Neff, L. A., & Karney, B. R. (2005). Gender differences in social support: A question of skill or responsiveness? *Journal of Personality and Social Psychology, 88,* 79–90.

Nehls, N. (1998). Borderline personality disorder: Gender stereotypes, stigma, and limited system of care. *Issues in Mental Health Nursing, 19,* 97–112.

Nelson, D. L., & Burke, R. J. (2000). Women executives: Health, stress and success. *Academy of Management Executive, 14,* 107–121.

Nelson, D. L., & Burke, R. J. (Eds.). (2002). *Gender, work stress, and health.* Washington, DC: American Psychological Association.

Newcombe, N., & Arnkoff, D. B. (1979). Effects of speech style and sex of speaker on person perception. *Journal of Personality and Social Psychology, 37,* 1293–1303.

Newell, C. E., Rosenfeld, P., & Culbertson, A. L. (1995). Sexual harassment experiences and equal opportunity perceptions of navy women. *Sex Roles, 32,* 159–168.

Newport, F. (2006). American teenagers split on gay marriage: Majority believe homosexuality is due to upbringing and environment, not genes. Retrieved January 30, 2007, from *www.galluppoll.com/content/Default.aspx?ci=21829&pg=1&VERSION=p.*

Newport, F., & Carroll, J. (2007). Analysis: Impact of personal characteristics on candidate support: Americans most comfortable voting for a black or female candidate. Retrieved July 10, 2007, from *www.galluppoll.com/content/Default.aspx?ci=26857&pg=1&VERSION=p.*

New York Times. (1980). Are boys better at math? Retrieved July 6, 2000, from *web.lexis-nexis.com/universe/docu . . .*

Nichols, J. (1975). *Men's liberation: A new definition of masculinity.* New York: Penguin Books.

Nichols, T. R., Graber, J. A., Brooks-Gunn, J., & Botvin, G. J. (2006). Sex differences in overt aggression and delinquency among urban minority middle school students. *Applied Developmental Psychology, 27,* 78–91.

Nichter, M. (2000). *Fat talk: What girls and their parents say about dieting.* Cambridge, MA: Harvard University Press.

Nielsen, S. J., Siega-Riz, A. M., & Popkin, B. M. (2002). Trends in energy intake in U.S. between 1977 and 1996: Similar shifts seen across age groups. *Obesity Research, 10,* 370–378.

Niemann, Y. F., Jennings, L., Rozelle, R. M., Baxter, J. C., & Sullivan, E. (1994). Use of free responses and cluster analysis to determine stereotypes of eight groups. *Personality and Social Psychology Bulletin, 20,* 379–390.

Noel, C. (1997, February 12). Springer school students offer definitions of love. *Los Altos Town Crier,* p. 26.

Nolen-Hoeksema, S. (1987). Sex differences in unipolar depression: Evidence and theory. *Psychological Bulletin, 101,* 259–282.

Nolen-Hoeksema, S. (1990). *Sex differences in depression.* Stanford, CA: Stanford University Press.

Nolen-Hoeksema, S. (1994). An interactive model for the emergence of gender differences in depression in adolescence. *Journal of Research on Adolescence, 4,* 519–534.

Nolen-Hoeksema, S. (2004). The etiology of gender: Differences in depression. In C. M. Mazure & G. Puryear (Eds.), *Understanding depression in women: Applying empirical research to practice and policy.* Washington, DC: American Psychological Association.

Nolen-Hoeksema, S., & Davis, C. G. (1999). "Thanks for sharing that": Ruminators and their social support network. *Journal of Personality and Social Psychology, 77,* 801–814.

Nolen-Hoeksema, S., & Girgus, J. S. (1994). The emergence of gender differences in depression during adolescence. *Psychological Bulletin, 115,* 424–443.

Nolen-Hoeksema, S., & Hilt, L. (2006). Possible contributors to the gender differences in alcohol use and problems. *The Journal of General Psychology, 133,* 357–374.

Nolen-Hoeksema, S., & Keita, G. P. (2003). Women and depression: Introduction. *Psychology of Women Quarterly, 27,* 89–90.

Nolen-Hoeksema, S., & Morrow, J. (1991). A prospective study of depression and distress following a natural disaster: The 1989 Loma Prieta earthquake. *Journal of Personality and Social Psychology, 61,* 105–121.

Nolen-Hoeksema, S., Larson, J., & Grayson, C. (1999). Explaining the gender difference in depressive symptoms. *Journal of Personality and Social Psychology, 77,* 1061–1072.

Nolen-Hoeksema, S., Morrow, J., & Fredrickson, B. L. (1993). Response styles and the duration of episodes of depressed mood. *Journal of Abnormal Psychology, 102*(1), 20–28.

Nolen-Hoeksema, S., Parker, L. E., & Larson, J. (1994). Personality processes and individual differences: Ruminative coping with depressed mood following loss. *Journal of Personality and Social Psychology, 67*, 92–104.

Noller, P. (1993). Gender and emotional communication in marriage: Different cultures or differential social power? *Journal of Language and Social Psychology, 12*, 132–152.

Nomaguchi, K. M., & Bianchi, S. M. (2004). Exercise time: Gender differences in the effects of marriage, parenthood, and employment. *Journal of Marriage and Family, 66*, 413–430.

Norcross, W. A., Ramirez, C., & Palinkas, L. A. (1996). The influence of women on the health care-seeking behavior of men. *Journal of Family Practice, 43*(5), 475–480.

Nordenmark, M. (2004). Multiple social roles and well-being: A longitudinal test of the role stress theory and the role expansion theory. *Acta Sociologica, 47*, 115–126.

Nordvik, H., & Amponsah, B. (1998). Gender differences in spatial abilities and spatial activity among university students in an egalitarian educational system. *Sex Roles, 38*, 1009–1023.

Norton, K. I., Olds, T. S., Olive, S., & Dank, S. (1996). Ken and Barbie at life size. *Sex Roles, 34*, 287–294.

Notarius, C. I., Benson, P. R., Sloane, D., Vanzetti, N. A., & Hornyak, L. M. (1989). Exploring the interface between perception and behavior: An analysis of marital interaction in distressed and nondistressed couples. *Behavioral Assessment, 11*, 39–64.

Notzon, F. C., Komarov, Y. M., Ermakov, S. P., Sempos, C. T., Marks, J. S., & Sempos, E. V. (1998). Causes of declining life expectancy in Russia. *Journal of the American Medical Association, 279*(10), 793–800.

Nuttall, R. L., Casey, M. B., & Pezaris, E. (2005). Spatial ability as a mediator of gender differences on mathematics tests. In A. M. Gallagher & J. C. Kaufman (Eds.), *Gender differences in mathematics: An integrative psychological approach* (pp. 121–142). New York Cambridge University Press.

Nyquist, L. V., & Spence, J. T. (1986). Effects of dispositional dominance and sex role expectations on leadership behaviors. *Journal of Personality and Social Psychology, 50*, 87–93.

O'Barr, W. M. (2006). Representations of masculinity and femininity in advertisements. *Advertising & Society Review.* Retrieved November 12, 2007, from *www.aef.com/on-campus/asr/contents.*

O'Brien, L. T., & Crandall, C. S. (2003). Stereotype threat and arousal: Effects on women's math performance. *Personality and Social Psychology Bulletin, 29*, 782–789.

O'Brien, M., Peyton, V., Mistry, R., Hruda, L., Jacobs, A., Caldera, Y., Huston, A., & Roy, C. (2000). Gender-role cognition in three-year-old boys and girls. *Sex Roles, 42*, 1007–1025.

Ochman, J. M. (1996). The effects of nongender-role stereotyped, same-sex role models in storybooks on the self-esteem of children in grade three. *Sex Roles, 35*, 711–735.

Ogden, C. L., Carroll, M. D., Curtin, L. R., McDowell, M. A., Tabak, C. J., & Flegal, K. M. (2006). Prevalence of overweight and obesity in the United States, 1999–2004. *Journal of the American Medical Association, 295*, 1549–1555.

Ogden, C. L., Flegal, K. M., Carroll, M. D., & Johnson, C. L. (2002). Prevalence and trends in overweight among U.S. children and adolescents, 1999–2000. *Journal of the American Medical Association, 288*, 1728–1732.

Oggins, J., Veroff, J., & Leber, D. (1993). Perceptions of marital interaction among Black and White newlyweds. *Journal of Personality and Social Psychology, 65*, 494–511.

Ohannessian, C. M., Lerner, R. M., Lerner, J. V., & von Eye, A. (1999). Does self-competence predict gender differences in adolescent depression and anxiety? *Journal of Adolescence, 22*, 1–15.

Okamoto, K., & Tanaka, Y. (2004). Gender differences in the relationship between social support and subjective health among elderly persons in Japan. *Preventive Medicine, 38*, 318–322.

O'Leary, V. E. (1988). Women's relationships with women in the workplace. In B. A. Gutek, A. H. Stromberg, & L. Larwood (Eds.), *Women and work: An annual review* (Vol. 3, pp. 189–213). Newbury Park, CA: Sage.

Olff, M., Langeland, W., Draijer, N., & Gersons, B. P. R. (2007). Gender differences in posttraumatic stress disorder. *Psychological Bulletin, 133*, 183–204.

Olfson, M., Zarin, D. A., Mittman, B. S., & McIntyre, J. S. (2001). Is gender a factor in psychiatrists' evaluation and treatment of patients with major depression? *Journal of Affective Disorders, 63*, 149–157.

Oliver, M. B., & Hyde, J. S. (1993). Gender differences in sexuality: A meta-analysis. *Psychological Bulletin, 114*, 29–51.

Olson, B., & Douglas, W. (1997). The family on television: Evaluation of gender roles in situation comedy. *Sex Roles, 36*, 409–427.

Olson, J. E., Frieze, I. H., & Detlefson, E. G. (1990). Having it all? Combining work and family in a male and a female profession. *Sex Roles, 23*, 515–533.

O'Meara, J. D. (1989). Cross-sex friendship: Four basic challenges of an ignored relationship. *Sex Roles, 21*, 525–543.

O'Neil, J. M., Helms, B. J., Gable, R. K., David, L., & Wrightsman, L. S. (1986). Gender-role conflict scale: College men's fear of femininity. *Sex Roles, 14*, 335–350.

Oriña, M. M., Wood, W., & Simpson, J. A. (2002). Strategies of influence in close relationships. *Journal of Experimental Social Psychology, 38*, 459–472.

Orlofsky, J. L. (1993). Intimacy status: Theory and research. In J. E. Marcia, D. R. Matteson, J. L. Orlofsky, A. S. Waterman, & S. L. Archer (Eds.), *Ego identity: A handbook for psychosocial research* (pp. 111–133). New York: Springer-Verlag.

Orth-Gomer, K., & Johnson, J. (1987). Social network interaction and mortality: A six-year follow-up of a random sample of the Swedish population. *Journal of Chronic Diseases, 4*, 944–957.

Ostenson, R. S. (1996). Who's in and who's out: The results of oppression. In J. C. Chrisler, C. Golden & P. D. Rozee (Eds.), *Lectures on the psychology of women* (pp. 23–31). New York: McGraw-Hill.

Ostrov, J. M., Crick, N. R., & Stauffacher, K. (2006). Relational aggression in sibling and peer relationships during early childhood. *Applied Developmental Psychology, 27*, 241–253.

Ostrov, J. M., Gentile, D. A., & Crick, N. R. (2006). Media exposure, aggression and prosocial behavior during early childhood: A longitudinal study. *Social Development, 15*, 612–627.

Otis, M. D., Riggle, E. D. B., & Rostosky, S. S. (2006). Impact of mental health on perceptions of relationship satisfaction and quality among female same-sex couples. *Journal of Lesbian Studies, 10*, 267–283.

Oyserman, D., Gant, L., & Ager, J. (1995). A socially contextualized model of African American identity: Possible selves and school persistence. *Journal of Personality and Social Psychology, 69*, 1216–1232.

Ozer, E. M. (1995). The impact of childcare responsibility and self-efficacy on the psychological health of professional working mothers. *Psychology of Women Quarterly, 19*, 315–335.

Ozer, E. M., Barnett, R. C., Brennan, R. T., & Sperling, J. (1998). Does child care involvement increase or decrease distress among dual-earner couples? *Women's Health: Research on Gender, Behavior, and Policy, 4*(4), 285–311.

Page, R. M., & Cole, G. E. (1992). Demoralization and living alone: Outcomes from an urban community study. *Psychological Reports, 70*, 275–280.

Page, S., & Bennesch, S. (1993). Gender and reporting differences in measures of depression. *Canadian Journal of Behavioural Science, 25*, 579–589.

Palomares, N. A. (2004). Gender schematicity, gender identity salience, and gender-linked language use. *Human Communication Research, 30*, 556–588.

Paludi, M. A., & Barickman, R. B. (1998). *Sexual harassment, work, and education.* New York: State University of New York Press.

Pampel, F. C. (1998). National context, social change and sex differences in suicide rates. *American Sociological Review, 63*, 744–758.

Parker, S., & de Vries, B. (1993). Patterns of friendship for women and men in same and cross-sex relationships. *Journal of Social and Personal Relationships, 10*, 617–626.

Parks, M. R., & Floyd, K. (1996). Meanings for closeness and intimacy in friendship. *Journal of Social and Personal Relationships, 13*, 85–107.

Parra, E. B., Arkowitz, H., Hannah, M. T., & Vasquez, A. M. (1995). Coping strategies and emotional reactions to separation and divorce in Anglo, Chicana, and Mexicana women. *Journal of Divorce and Remarriage, 23*(1/2), 117–129.

Parsons, T., & Bales, R. F. (1955). *Family, socialization and interaction process.* Glencoe, IL: Free Press.

Pasch, L. A., Bradbury, T. N., & Davila, J. (1997). Gender, negative affectivity, and observed social support behavior in marital interaction. *Personal Relationships, 4*, 361–378.

Patterson, C. J. (2000). Family relationships of lesbians and gay men. *Journal of Marriage and the Family, 62*, 1052–1069.

Patterson, C. J. (2003). Children of lesbian and gay parents. In L. D. Garnets & D. C. Kimmel (Eds.), *Psychological perspectives on lesbian, gay, and bisexual experiences* (Second ed.) (pp. 497–548). New York: Columbia University Press.

Pavalko, E. K., & Woodbury, S. (2000). Social roles as process: Caregiving careers and women's health. *Journal of Health and Social Behavior, 41*, 91–105.

Paxton, S. J., & Sculthorpe, A. (1991). Disordered eating and sex role characteristics in young women: Implications for sociocultural theories of disturbed eating. *Sex Roles, 24*, 587–598.

Pedersen, W. C., Miller, L. C., Putcha-Bhagavatula, A. D., & Yang, Y. (2002). Evolved sex differences in the number of partners desired? The long and the short of it. *Psychological Science, 13*, 157–160.

Peirce, K. (2001). What if the Energizer bunny were female? Importance of gender in perceptions of advertising spokescharacter effectiveness. *Sex Roles, 45*, 845–858.

Pence, E., & Paymar, M. (1993). *Education groups for men who batter: The Duluth model.* New York: Springer.

Pennebaker, J. W., & Roberts, T.-A. (1992). Toward a his and hers theory of emotion: Gender differences in visceral perception. *Journal of Social and Clinical Psychology, 11*, 199–212.

Pennebaker, J. W., & Watson, D. (1988). Blood pressure estimation and beliefs among normotensives and hypertensives. *Health Psychology, 7*, 309–328.

Peplau, L. A. (1991). Lesbian and gay relationships. In J. C. Gonsiorek & J. D. Weinrich (Eds.), *Homosexuality: Research implications for public policy* (pp. 177–196). Newbury Park, CA: Sage.

Peplau, L. A. (1994). Men and women in love. In D. L. Sollie & L. A. Leslie (Eds.), *Gender, families, and close relationships: Feminist research journeys* (pp. 19–49). Thousand Oaks, CA: Sage.

Peplau, L. A., & Beals, K. P. (2001). Lesbians, gay men, and bisexuals in relationships. In J. Worrell (Ed.), *Encyclopedia of women and gender: Sex similarities and differences and the impact of society on gender* (pp. 657–666). San Diego: Academic

Peplau, L. A., & Fingerhut, A. (2004). The paradox of the lesbian worker. *Journal of Social Issues, 60*, 719–735.

Peplau, L. A., & Garnets, L. D. (2000). A new paradigm for understanding women's sexuality and sexual orientation. *Journal of Social Issues, 56*,(2), 329–350.

Peplau, L. A., & Spalding, L. R. (2000). The close relationships of lesbians, gay men, and bisexuals. In C. Hendrick & S. S. Hendrick (Eds.), *Close relationships: A sourcebook* (pp. 111–123). Thousand Oaks, CA: Sage.

Peplau, L. A., Cochran, S. D., & Mays, V. M. (1997). A national survey of the intimate relationships of African American lesbians and gay men: A look at commitment, satisfaction, sexual behavior, and HIV disease. In B. Greene (Ed.), *Ethnic and cultural diversity among lesbians and gay men* (Vol. 3, pp. 11–38). Thousand Oaks, CA: Sage.

Perenboom, R. J. M., van Herten, L. M., Boshuizen, H. C., & van den Bos, G. A. M. (2005). Life expectancy without chronic morbidity: Trends in gender and socioeconomic disparities. *Public Health Reports, 120,* 46–54.

Perkins, K. A. (1996). Sex differences in nicotine versus non-nicotine reinforcement as determinants of tobacco smoking. *Experimental and Clinical Psychopharmacology, 4*(2), 166–177.

Perkins, K. A. (1999). Nicotine discrimination in men and women. *Pharmacology, Biochemistry and Behavior, 64*(2), 295–299.

Perkins, K. A., Donny, E., & Caggiula, A. R. (1999). Sex differences in nicotine effects and self-administration: Review of human and animal evidence. *Nicotine and Tobacco Research, 1,* 301–315.

Perkins, K. A., Doyle, T., Ciccocioppo, M., Conklin, C., Sayette, M., & Caggiula, A. (2006). Sex differences in the influence of nicotine dose instructions on the reinforcing and self-reported rewarding effects of smoking. *Psychopharmacology, 184,* 600–607.

Perkins, K. A., Marcus, M. D., Levine, M. D., D'Amico, D., Miller, A., Broge, M., et al. (2001). Cognitive-behavioral therapy to reduce weight concerns improves smoking cessation outcome in weight-concerned women. *Journal of Consulting and Clinical Psychology, 69,* 604–613.

Perry, D. G., & Bussey, K. (1979). The social learning theory of sex differences: Imitation is alive and well. *Journal of Personality and Social Psychology, 37,* 1699– 1712.

Perry-Jenkins, M., & Folk, K. (1994). Class, couples, and conflict: Effects of the division of labor on assessment of marriage in dual-earner families. *Journal of Marriage and the Family, 56,* 165–180.

Perry-Jenkins, M., Seery, B., & Crouter, A. C. (1992). Linkages between women's provider-role attitudes, psychological well-being, and family relationships. *Psychology of Women Quarterly, 16,* 311–329.

Peterson, A. L. (1999). Inaccurate estimation of body weight prior to smoking cessation: Implications for quitting and weight gain. *Journal of Applied Biobehavioral Research, 4*(2), 79–84.

Peterson, C., & Villanova, P. (1988). An expanded attributional style questionnaire. *Journal of Abnormal Psychology, 97*(1), 87–89.

Peterson, Z. D., & Muehlenhard, C. L. (2004). Was it rape? The function of women's rape myth acceptance and definitions of sex in labeling their own experiences. *Sex Roles, 51,* 129–144.

Pfaff, L. (1999). *Gender differences in leadership skills.* Unpublished data.

Pfizer. (2002). *The Pfizer global study of sexual attitudes & behaviors.* Retrieved November 12, 2007, from *www.pfizerglobalstudy.com/study/study-results.asp.*

Philpott, S., Boynton, P. M., Feder, G., & Hemingway, H. (2001). Gender differences in descriptions of angina symptoms and health problems immediately prior to angiography: The ACRE study. *Social Science & Medicine, 52,* 1565–1575.

Pike, J. J., & Jennings, N. A. (2005). The effects of commercials on children's perceptions of gender appropriate toy use. *Sex Roles, 52,* 83–91.

Pike, K. M., & Striegel-Moore, R. H. (1997). Disordered eating and eating disorders. In S. J. Gallant, G. P. Keita, & R. Royak-Schaler (Eds.), *Health care for women: Psychological, social, and behavioral influences* (pp. 97–114). Washington, DC: American Psychological Association.

Pina, D. L., & Bengtson, V. L. (1993). The division of household labor and wives' happiness: Ideology, employment, and perceptions of support. *Journal of Marriage and the Family, 55,* 901–912.

Pines, A. M. (2001). The role of gender and culture in romantic attraction. *European Psychologist, 6,* 96–102.

Pinquart, M. (2003). Loneliness in married, widowed, divorced, and never-married older adults. *Journal of Social and Personal Relationships, 20,* 31–53.

Pinquart, M., & Sorensen, S. (2006). Gender differences in caregiver stressors, social resources, and health: An updated meta-analysis. *Journal of Gerontology, 61B,* P33-P45.

Pirie, P. L., Murray, D. M., & Luepker, R. V. (1991). Gender differences in cigarette smoking and quitting in a cohort of young adults. *American Journal of Public Health, 81*(3), 324–327.

Pleck, J. H. (1987). Men in domestic settings: American fathering in historical perspective. In M. S. Kimmel (Ed.), *Changing men: New directions in research on men and masculinity* (pp. 83–97). Newbury Park, CA: Sage.

Pleck, J. H. (1993). Are family-supportive employer policies relevant to men? In J. C. Hood (Ed.), *Men, work, and family* (pp. 217–237). Newbury Park, CA: Sage.

Pleck, J. H. (1995). The gender role strain paradigm: An update. In R. F. Levant & W. S. Pollack (Eds.), *A new psychology of men* (pp. 11–32). New York: Basic Books.

Pleck, J. H., Sonenstein, F. L., & Ku, L. C. (1993). Masculinity ideology: Its impact on adolescent males' heterosexual relationships. *Journal of Social Issues, 49*(3), 11–29.

Polce-Lynch, M., Myers, B. J., Kilmartin, C. T., Forssmann-Falck, R., & Kliewer, W. (1998). Gender and age patterns in emotional expression, body image, and self-esteem: A qualitative analysis. *Sex Roles, 38,* 1025–1048.

Polce-Lynch, M., Myers, B. J., Kliewer, W., & Kilmartin, C. (2001). Adolescent self-esteem and gender: Exploring relations to sexual harassment, body image, media influence, and emotional expression. *Journal of Youth and Adolescence, 30,* 225–244.

Pollack, W. S. (1998). *Real boys: Rescuing our sons from the myths of boyhood.* New York: Henry Holt.

Pollak, S., & Gilligan, C. (1982). Images of violence in Thematic Apperception Test stories. *Journal of Personality and Social Psychology, 42,* 159–167.

Pomerantz, E. M., & Ruble, D. N. (1998). The multidimensional nature of control: Implications for the development of sex differences in self-evaluation. In J. Heckhausen & C. S. Dweck (Eds.), *Motivation and self-regulation across the life span* (pp. 159–184). Cambridge: Cambridge University Press.

Pomerleau, A., Bolduc, D., Malcuit, G., & Cossette, L. (1990). Pink or blue: Environmental gender stereotypes in the first two years of life. *Sex Roles, 22,* 359–367.

Pomerleau, C. S., Tate, J. C., Lumley, M. A., & Pomerleau, O. F. (1994). Gender differences in prospectively versus retrospectively assessed smoking withdrawal symptoms. *Journal of Substance Abuse, 6,* 433–440.

Pope, H. G., Jr., Olivardia, R., Gruber, A., & Borowiecki, J. (1999). Evolving ideals of male body image as seen through action toys. *International Journal of Eating Disorders, 26*(1), 65–72.

Pope, J. H., Aufderheide, T. P., Ruthazer, R., Woolard, R. H., Feldman, J. A., Beshansky, J. R., et al. (2000). Missed diagnoses of acute cardiac ischemia in the emergency department. *New England Journal of Medicine, 16,* 1163–1170.

Popenoe, D., & Whitehead, B. D. (1999). *The state of our unions. The social health of marriage in America.* Retrieved November 12, 2007, from *marriage.rutgers.edu.*

Poulin Dubois, D., Serbin, L. A., Eichstedt, J. A., & Sen, M. G. (2002). Men don't put on make-up: Toddlers' knowledge of the gender stereotyping of household activities. *Social Development, 11,* 166–181.

Poulin, F., & Boivin, M. (2000a). Reactive and proactive aggression: Evidence of a two-factor model. *Psychological Assessment, 12*(2), 115–122.

Poulin, F., & Boivin, M. (2000b). The role of proactive and reactive aggression in the formation and development of boys' friendships. *Developmental Psychology, 36,* 233–240.

Poulin, F., Cillessen, A. H. N., Hubbard, J. A., Coie, J. D., Dodge, K. A., & Schwartz, D. (1997). Children's friends and behavioral similarity in two social contexts. *Behavioral Similarity and Friendship, 6*(2), 224–235.

Powell, G. N., & Graves, L. M. (2006). Gender and leadership: Perceptions and realities. In K. Dindia & D. J. Canary (Eds.), *Sex differences and similarities in communication* (Second ed.) (pp. 83–97). Mahwah, NJ: Lawrence Erlbaum Associates.

Pratt, M. W., Golding, G., Hunter, W., & Sampson, R. (1988). Sex differences in adult moral orientations. *Journal of Personality, 56,* 373–391.

Prescott, E., Hippe, M., Schnohr, P., Hein, H. O., & Vestbo, J. (1998). Smoking and risk of myocardial infarction in women and men: Longitudinal population study. *British Medical Journal, 316,* 1043–1047.

Prigerson, H. G., & Slimack, M. J. (1999). Gender differences in clinical correlates of suicidality among young adults. *Journal of Nervous and Mental Disease, 187*(1), 23–31.

Prout, A. (1989). Sickness as a dominant symbol in life course transitions: An illustrated theoretical framework. *Sociology of Health and Illness, 11*(4), 336–359.

Pryor, J. B. (1998). The Likelihood to Sexually Harass Scale. In C. M. Davis, W. H. Yarber, R. Bauserman, G. Schreer, & S. L. Davis (Eds.), *Sexuality-related measures: A compendium* (pp. 295–298). Beverly Hills, CA: Sage.

Pryor, J. B., DeSouza, E. R., Fitness, J., Hutz, C., Kumpf, M., Lubbert, K., Pesonen, O., & Erber, M. W. (1997). Gender differences in the interpretation of social-sexual behavior: A cross-cultural perspective on sexual harassment. *Journal of Cross-Cultural Psychology, 28*(5), 509–534.

Pryor, J. B., Giedd, J. L., & Williams, K. B. (1995). A social psychological model for predicting sexual harassment. *Journal of Social Issues, 51*(1), 69–84.

Pryor, J. B., Hesson-McInnis, M. S., Hitlan, R. T., Olson, M., & Hahn, E. J. (2000). *Antecedents of gender harassment: An analysis of person and situation factors.* Unpublished manuscript.

Pugliesi, K., & Shook, S. L. (1998). Gender, ethnicity, and network characteristics: Variation in social support resources. *Sex Roles, 38,* 215–238.

Purcell, D. W., Lewine, R. R. J., Caudle, J., & Price, L. R. (1998). Sex differences in verbal IQ - Performance IQ discrepancies among patients with schizophrenia and normal volunteers. *Journal of Abnormal Psychology, 107,* 161–165.

Purnine, D. M., & Carey, M. P. (1997). Interpersonal communication and sexual adjustment: The roles of understanding and agreement. *Journal of Consulting and Clinical Psychology, 65,* 1017–1025.

Quatman, T., & Watson, C. M. (2001). Gender differences in adolescent self-esteem: An exploration of domains. *Journal of Genetic Psychology, 162,* 93–117.

Quick, H. E., & Moen, P. (1998). Gender, employment, and retirement quality: A life course approach to the differential experiences of men and women. *Journal of Occupational Health Psychology, 3*(1), 44–64.

Quillian, L., & Campbell, M. E. (2003). Beyond black and white: The present and future of multiracial friendship segregation. *American Sociological Review, 68,* 540–566.

Quirouette, C., & Gold, D. P. (1992). Spousal characteristics as predictors of well-being in older couples. *International Journal of Aging and Human Development, 34*(4), 257–269.

Raag, T., & Rackliff, C. L. (1998). Preschoolers' awareness of social expectations of gender: Relationships to toy choices. *Sex Roles, 38,* 685–700.

Rabin, C. (1998). Gender and intimacy in the treatment of couples in the 1990s. *Sexual and Marital Therapy, 13*(2), 179–190.

Rabin, C., & Shapira-Berman, O. (1997). Egalitarianism and marital happiness: Israeli wives and husbands on a collision course? *American Journal of Family Therapy, 25*(4), 319–329.

Radloff, L. S. (1977). The CES-D scale: A self-report depression scale for research in the general population. *Journal of Applied Psychological Measurement, 1,* 385–401.

Radloff, L. S., & Rae, D. S. (1979). Susceptibility and precipitating factors in depression: Sex differences and similarities. *Journal of Abnormal Psychology, 88,* 174–181.

Radmacher, K., & Azmitia, M. (2006). Are there gendered pathways to intimacy in early adolescents' and emerging adults' friendships? *Journal of Adolescent Research, 21,* 415–448.

Raffaelli, M., & Duckett, E. (1989). "We were just talking . . .": Conversations in early adolescence. *Journal of Youth and Adolescence, 18,* 567–582.

Rajecki, D. W., Dame, J. A., Creek, K. J., Barrickman, P. J., & Reid, C. A. (1993). Gender casting in television toy advertisements: Distributions, message content analysis, and evaluations. *Journal of Consumer Psychology, 2*(3), 307–327.

Rakowski, W., Julius, M., Hickey, T., Verbrugge, L. M., & Halter, J. B. (1988). Daily symptoms and behavioral responses: Results of a health diary with older adults. *Medical Care, 26*(3), 278–297.

Raley, R. K. (1996). A shortage of marriageable men? A note on the role of cohabitation in Black-White differences in marriage rates. *American Sociological Review, 61,* 973–983.

Ramet, S. P. (1996). *Gender reversals and gender cultures.* New York: Pointing-Green.

Rankow, E. J., & Tessaro, I. (1998a). Cervical cancer risk and papanicolaou screening in a sample of lesbian and bisexual women. *Journal of Family Practice, 47*(2), 139–143.

Rankow, E. J., & Tessaro, I. (1998b). Mammography and risk factors for breast cancer in lesbian and bisexual women. *American Journal of Health Behavior, 22*(6), 403–410.

Rath, T. (2006). *Vital Friends.* New York: Gallup Press.

Rathore, S. S., Chen, J., Wang, Y., Radford, M. J., Vaccarino, V., & Krumholz, H. M. (2001). Sex differences in cardiac catheterization: The role of physician gender. *Journal of the American Medical Association, 286,* 2849–2856.

Räty, H., Vänskä, J., Kasanen, K., & Kärkkäinen, R. (2002). Parents' explanations of their child's performance in mathematics and reading: A replication and extension of Yee and Eccles. *Sex Roles, 46,* 121–128.

Rawe, J. (2007). Women's pay: Lagging from the start [Electronic Version]. Time in partnership with CNN. Retrieved May 1, 2007, from *www.time.com/time/nation/article/0,8599,1613829,00.html.*

Rawlins, W. K. (2004). Friendships in later life. In J. F. Nussbaum (Ed.), *Handbook of communication and aging research* (Second ed.) (pp. 273–299). Mahwah, NJ: Lawrence Erlbaum Associates Publishers.

Rederstorff, J. C., Buchanan, N. T., & Settles, I. H. (2007). The moderating roles of race and gender-role attitudes in the relationship between sexual harassment and psychological well-being. *Psychology of Women Quarterly, 31,* 50–61.

Reed, G. M., Kemeny, M. E., Taylor, S. E., & Visscher, B. R. (1999). Negative HIV-specific expectancies and AIDS-related bereavement as predictors of symptom onset in asymptomatic HIV-positive gay men. *Health Psychology, 18,* 354–363.

Reeder, H. M. (2000). "I like you...as a friend": The role of attraction in cross-sex friendship. *Journal of Social and Personal Relationships, 17,* 329–348.

Reeder, H. M. (2003). The effect of gender role orientation on same- and cross-sex friendship formation. *Sex Roles, 49,* 143–152.

Reevy, G. M., & Maslach, C. (2001). Use of social support: Gender and personality differences. *Sex Roles, 44,* 437–459.

Regan, P. C., & Berscheid, E. (1999). *Lust: What we know about human sexual desire.* Thousand Oaks, CA: Sage.

Rehman, U. S., & Holtzworth-Munroe, A. (2006). A cross-cultural analysis of the demand-withdraw marital interaction: Observing couples from a developing country. *Journal of Consulting and Clinical Psychology, 74,* 755–766.

Reid, S. A., Keerie, N., & Palomares, N. A. (2003). Language, gender salience, and social influence. *Journal of Language and Social Psychology, 22,* 210–233.

Reis, H. T. (1998). Gender differences in intimacy and related behaviors: Context and process. In D. J. Canary & K. Dindia (Eds.), *Sex differences and similarities in communication.* (pp. 203–231). Mahwah, NJ: Erlbaum.

Reis, H. T., & Shaver, P. (1988). Intimacy as an interpersonal process. In S. Duck (Ed.), *Handbook of personal relationships: Theory, relationships, and interventions* (pp. 367–389). Chichester, England: Wiley.

Reis, H. T., Senchak, M., & Solomon, B. (1985). Sex differences in the intimacy of social interaction: Further examination of potential explanations. *Journal of Personality and Social Psychology, 48,* 1204–1217.

Reisman, J. M. (1990). Intimacy in same-sex friendships. *Sex Roles, 23,* 65–82.

Reitzes, D. C., & Mutran, E. J. (1994). Multiple roles and identities: Factors influencing self-esteem among middle-aged working men and women. *Social Psychology Quarterly, 57*(4), 313–325.

Reitzes, D. C., & Mutran, E. J. (2004). The transition to retirement: Stages and factors that influence retirement adjustment. *International Journal of Aging and Human Development, 59,* 63–84.

Rejeski, W. J., Parker, P. E., Gagne, M., & Koritnik, D. R. (1990). Cardiovascular and testosterone responses to contested dominance in women. *Health Psychology, 9,* 35–47.

Renzulli, L. A., Grant, L., & Kathuria, S. (2006). Race, gender, and the wage gap: Comparing faculty salaries in predominately white and historically black colleges and universities. *Gender & Society, 20,* 491–510.

Resnick, M. D., Bearman, P. S., Blum, R. W., Bauman, K. E., Harris, K. M., Jones, J., et al. (1997). Protecting adolescents from harm. *Journal of the American Medical Association, 278,* 823–832.

Reuss, P., & Erickson, J. (2006). *Access for all? Reclaiming women's contraceptive options one pharmacy at a time* [Electronic Version]. National Organization for Women. Retrieved January 12, 2007, from *www.now.org/issues/ reproductive/ec_action_plan.html.*

Revenson, T. A. (1994). Social support and marital coping with chronic illness. *Annals of Behavioral Medicine, 16*(2), 122–130.

Revenson, T. A., Abraido-Lanza, A. F., Majerovitz, S. D., & Jordan, C. (2005). Couples coping with chronic illness: What's gender got to do with it? In T. A. Revenson, K. Kayser, & G. Bodenmann (Eds.), *Couples coping with stress: Emerging perspectives on dyadic coping* (pp. 137–156). Washington, DC: American Psychological Association.

Reynolds, K. A., Helgeson, V. S., Seltman, H., Janicki, D., Page-Gould, E., & Wardle, M. (2006). Impact of interpersonal conflict on individuals high in unmitigated communion. *Journal of Applied Social Psychology, 36,* 1595–1616.

Reynolds, P., & Kaplan, G. A. (1990). Social connections and risk for cancer: Prospective evidence for the Alameda County Study. *Behavioral Medicine, 16,* 101–110.

Rhee, S. H., & Waldman, I. D. (2002). Genetic and environmental influences on antisocial behavior: A meta-analysis of twin and adoption studies. *Psychological Bulletin, 128,* 490–529.

Rhoades, G. K., Petralla, J. N., Stanley, S. M., & Markman, H. J. (2006). Premarital cohabitation, husbands' commitment, and wives' satisfaction with the division of household contributions. *Marriage and Family Review, 40,* 5–22.

Rhoades, G. K., Stanley, S. M., & Markman, H. J. (2006). Pre-engagement cohabitation and gender asymmetry in marital commitment. *Journal of Family Psychology, 20,* 553–560.

Ricciardelli, L. A., & McCabe, M. P. (2004). A biopsychosocial model of disordered eating and the pursuit of muscularity in adolescent boys. *Psychological Bulletin, 130,* 179–205.

Rice, T. T. (1957). *The sythians* (Second ed.). New York: Praeger.

Rich, A. R., Kirkpatrick-Smith, J., Bonner, R. L., & Jans, F. (1992). Gender differences in the psychosocial correlates of suicidal ideation among adolescents. *Suicide and Life-Threatening Behavior, 22*(3), 364–373.

Richards, J. M., & Gross, J. J. (2000). Emotion regulation and memory: The cognitive costs of keeping one's cool. *Journal of Personality and Social Psychology, 79,* 410–424.

Richards, M. H., Boxer, A. M., Petersen, A. C., & Albrecht, R. (1990). Relation of weight to body image in pubertal girls and boys from two communities. *Developmental Psychology, 26,* 313–321.

Richardson, J. T. (1997). Introduction to the study of gender differences in cognition. In P. J. Caplan & M. Crawford (Eds.), *Gender differences in human cognition* (pp. 3–29). New York: Oxford University Press.

Rich-Edwards, J. W., Manson, J. E., Hennekens, C. H., & Buring, J. E. (1995). Medical progress: The primary prevention of coronary heart disease in women. *New England Journal of Medicine, 332*(26), 1758–1766.

Ridgeway, C. L., & Correll, S. J. (2004). Motherhood as a status characteristic. *Journal of Social Issues, 60,* 683–700.

Rieker, P. P., & Bird, C. E. (2005). Rethinking gender differences in health: Why we need to integrate social and biological perspectives. *The Journal of Gerontology, 60B,* 40–47.

Rivadeneyra, R., & Ward, L. M. (2005). From *Ally McBeal* to *Sabado Gigante:* Contributions of television viewing to the gender role attitudes of Latino adolescents. *Journal of Adolescent Research, 20,* 453–475.

Robb, J. C., Young, L. T., Cooke, R. G., & Joffe, R. T. (1998). Gender differences in patients with bipolar disorder influence outcomes in the Medical Outcomes Survey (SF-20) subscale scores. *Journal of Affective Disorders, 49*(3), 189–193.

Roberts, L. R., & Petersen, A. C. (1992). The relationship between academic achievement and social self-image during early adolescence. *Journal of Early Adolescence, 12,* 197–219.

Roberts, L. R., Sarigiani, P. A., Petersen, A. C., & Newman, J. L. (1990). Gender differences in the relationship between achievement and self-image during early adolescence. *Journal of Early Adolescence, 10,* 159–175.

Roberts, S. J., Patsdaughter, C. A., Grindel, C. G., & Tarmina, M. S. (2004). Health related behaviors and cancer screening of lesbians: Results of the Boston Lesbian Health Project II. *Women & Health, 39,* 41–55.

Roberts, T.-A. (1991). Gender and the influence of evaluations on self-assessments in achievement settings. *Psychological Bulletin, 109,* 297–308.

Roberts, T.-A., & Gettman, J. Y. (2004). Mere exposure: Gender differences in the negative effects of priming a state of self-objectification. *Sex Roles, 51,* 17–27.

Roberts, T.-A., & Nolen-Hoeksema, S. (1989). Sex differences in reactions to evaluative feedback. *Sex Roles, 21,* 725–747.

Roberts, T.-A., & Nolen-Hoeksema, S. (1994). Gender comparisons in responsiveness to others' evaluations in achievement settings. *Psychology of Women Quarterly, 18,* 221–240.

Robertson, J., & Fitzgerald, L. F. (1990). The (mis)treatment of men: Effects of client gender role and life-style on diagnosis and attribution of pathology. *Journal of Counseling Psychology, 37,* 3–9.

Robinson, J. P., & Godbey, G. (1999). *Time for life: The surprising ways Americans use their time.* University Park: Pennsylvania State University Press.

Robinson, M. E., Dannecker, E. A., George, S. Z., Otis, J., Atchison, J. W., & Fillingim, R. B. (2005). Sex differences in the associations among psychological factors and pain report: A novel psychophysical study of patients with chronic low back pain. *The Journal of Pain, 6,* 463–470.

Robinson, M. E., Wise, E. A., Gagnon, C., Fillingim, R. B., & Price, D. D. (2004). Influences of gender role and anxiety on sex differences in temporal summation of pain. *The Journal of Pain, 5,* 77–82.

Robson, K., & Wallace, J. E. (2001). Gendered inequalities in earnings: A study of Canadian lawyers. *Canadian Review of Sociology and Anthropology, 38,* 75–95.

Rodin, J., & Ickovics, J. R. (1990). Women's health: Review and research agenda as we approach the 21st century. *American Psychologist, 45,* 1018–1034.

Rogers, S. J. (1996). Mothers' work hours and marital quality: Variations by family structure and family size. *Journal of Marriage and the Family, 58,* 606–617.

Rogers, S. J., & DeBoer, D. D. (2001). Changes in wives' income: Effects on marital happiness, psychological well-being, and the risk of divorce. *Journal of Marriage and the Family, 63,* 458–472.

Rogers, S. J., & White, L. K. (1998). Satisfaction with parenting: The role of marital happiness, family structure, and parents' gender. *Journal of Marriage and the Family, 60,* 293–308.

Rose, A. J. (2002). Co-rumination in the friendships of girls and boys. *Child Development, 73,* 1830–1843.

Rose, A. J., & Asher, S. R. (1999). Children's goals and strategies in response to conflicts within a friendship. *Developmental Psychology, 35,* 69–79.

Rose, A. J., & Rudolph, K. D. (2006). A review of sex differences in peer relationship processes: Potential trade-offs for the emotional and behavioral development of girls and boys. *Psychological Bulletin, 132,* 98–131.

Rose, G. L., Suls, J., Green, P. J., Lounsbury, P., & Gordon, E. (1996). Comparison of adjustment, activity, and tangible social support in men and women patients and their spouses during the six months post-myocardial infarction. *Annals of Behavioral Medicine, 18*(4), 264–272.

Rose, S. (1996). Who to let in: Women in cross-race friendships. In J. C. Chrisler, C. Golden, & P. D. Rozee (Eds.), *Lectures on the psychology of women* (pp. 211–226). New York: McGraw-Hill.

Rose, S., & Frieze, I. H. (1993). Young singles' contemporary dating scripts. *Sex Roles, 28,* 499–509.

Rose, S., Zand, D., & Cini, M. A. (1993). Lesbian courtships scripts. In E. D. Rothblum & K. A. Brehony (Eds.), *Boston marriages* (pp. 70–85). Amherst: University of Massachusetts Press.

Rosen, B. R., & Peterson, L. (1990). Gender differences in children's outdoor play injuries: A review and an integration. *Clinical Psychology Review, 10,* 187–205.

Rosenberg, M. (1989). *Society and the adolescent self-image.* Middletown, CT: Wesleyan University Press.

Rosenbloom, A. (2000, April 16). Only a generation ago, the marathon banned women. *Boston Globe,* p. D1.

Rosenfield, S. (1989). The effects of women's employment: Personal control and sex differences in mental health. *Journal of Health and Social Behavior, 30,* 77–91.

Rosenfield, S. (1992). The costs of sharing: Wives' employment and husbands' mental health. *Journal of Health and Social Behavior, 33,* 213–225.

Rosenthal, R. (1966). *Experimenter effects in behavioral research.* New York: Appleton-Century-Crofts.

Rosenthal, R. (1994). Parametric measures of effect size. In H. Cooper & L. V. Hedges (Eds.), *The handbook of research synthesis* (pp. 231–244). New York: Russell Sage Foundation.

Rosip, J. C., & Hall, J. A. (2004). Knowledge of nonverbal cues, gender, and nonverbal decoding accuracy. *Journal of Nonverbal Behavior, 28,* 267–286.

Ross, C. E. (1995). Reconceptualizing marital status as a continuum of social attachment. *Journal of Marriage and the Family, 57,* 129–140.

Ross, C. E., & Mirowsky, J. (1995). Does employment affect health? *Journal of Health and Social Behavior, 36,* 230–243.

Ross, C. E., Mirowsky, J., & Goldsteen, K. (1990). The impact of the family on health: The decade in review. *Journal of Marriage and the Family, 52,* 1059–1078.

Ross, C., & Mirowsky, J. (2006). Sex differences in the effect of education on depression: Resource multiplication or resource substitution? *Social Science & Medicine, 63,* 1400–1413.

Roter, D. L., Hall, J. A., & Aoki, Y. (2002). Physician gender effects in medical communication: A meta-analytic review. *Journal of the American Medical Association, 288,* 756–764.

Roth, C. (2006). High court overturns injunction that curbed clinic violence [Electronic Version]. National NOW Times. Retrieved January 12, 2007, from *www.now.org/press/02-06/02-28.html.*

Roth, M. E., Cosgrove, K. P., & Carroll, M. E. (2004). Sex differences in the vulnerability to drug abuse: A review of preclinical studies. *Neuroscience and Biobehavioral Reviews, 28,* 533–546.

Rothbart, M., & John, O. P. (1985). Social categorization and behavior episodes: A cognitive analysis of the effects of intergroup contact. *Journal of Social Issues, 41*(3), 81–104.

Rothblum, E. D. (2002). "Boston marriage" among lesbians. In M. Yalom & L. L. Carstensen (Eds.), *Inside the American couple: New thinking/new challenges* (pp. 74–86). Berkeley, CA: University of California Press.

Royce, J. M., Corbett, K., Sorensen, G., & Ockene, J. (1997). Gender, social pressure, and smoking cessations: The community intervention trial for smoking cessation (commit) at baseline. *Social Science and Medicine, 44*(3), 359–370.

Royer, J. M., & Garofoli, L. M. (2005). Cognitive contributions to sex differences in math performance. In A. M. Gallagher & J. C. Kaufman (Eds.), *Gender differences in mathematics* (pp. 99–120). New York: Cambridge University Press.

Rozee, P. D., & Koss, M. P. (2001). Rape: A century of resistance. *Psychology of Women Quarterly, 25,* 295–311.

Rubin, J. Z., Provenzano, F. J., & Luria, Z. (1974). The eye of the beholder: Parents' views on sex of newborns. *American Journal of Orthopsychiatry, 44*(4), 512–519.

Rubin, K. H., Dwyer, K. M., Booth-LaForce, C., Kim, A. H., Burgess, K. B., & Rose-Krasnor, L. (2004). Attachment, friendship, and psychological functioning in early adolescence. *Journal of Early Adolescence, 24,* 326–356.

Rubin, L. B. (1983). *Intimate strangers.* New York: Harper & Row.

Rudman, L. A., & Fairchild, K. (2004). Reactions to counter-stereotypic behavior: The role of backlash in cultural stereotype maintenance. *Journal of Personality and Social Psychology, 87,* 157–176.

Rudman, L. A., & Glick, P. (2001). Prescriptive gender stereotypes and backlash toward agentic women. *Journal of Social Issues, 57,* 743–762.

Rudolph, K. D., & Hammen, C. (1999). Age and gender as determinants of stress exposure, generation, and reactions in youngsters: A transactional perspective. *Child Development, 70,* 660–677.

Rueda, B., & Perez-Garcia, A. M. (2006). Gender and social support in the context of cardiovascular disease. *Women & Health, 43,* 59–73.

Rushton, J. P. (1986). Altruism and aggression: The heritability of individual differences. *Journal of Personality and Social Psychology, 50,* 1192–1198.

Russell, A., & Owens, L. (1999). Peer estimates of school-aged boys' and girls' aggression to same- and cross-sex targets. *Social Development, 8*(3), 364–379.

Russell, B. L., & Trigg, K. Y. (2004). Tolerance of sexual harassment: An examination of gender differences, ambivalent sexism, social dominance, and gender roles. *Sex Roles, 50,* 565–573.

Russell, C. J., & Keel, P. K. (2002). Homosexuality as a specific risk factor for eating disorders in men. *International Journal of Eating Disorders, 31,* 300–306.

Russell, D. (1990). *Rape in marriage.* Bloomington: Indiana University Press.

Rust, J., Golombok, S., Hines, M., Johnston, K., Golding, J., & ALSPAC Study Team. (2000). The role of brothers and sisters in the gender development of preschool children. *Journal of Experimental Child Psychology, 77*(4), 292–303.

Ryckman, R. M., Libby, C. R., van den Borne, B., Gold, J. A., & Lindner, M. A. (1997). Values of hypercompetitive and personal development competitive individuals. *Journal of Personality Assessment, 69,* 271–283.

Saad, L. (2003). Husbands bring home most of the bacon: Men are the primary earners in most working married households. Retrieved January 30, 2007, from *www.galluppoll.com/content/Default.aspx?ci=8464&pg=1&VERSION=p.*

Saad, L. (2005). Giving thanks for a steady scale: Americans still overweight, but no increase in average weight. Retrieved August 3, 2007, from *www.galluppoll.com/ content/Default.aspx?ci=20104&pg=1VERSION=p.*

Saad, L. (2006a). Americans still oppose gay marriage but only half favor a constitutional amendment to bar it. Retrieved January 30, 2007, from *www.galluppoll .com/content/Default.aspx?ci=22882&pg=1&VERSION=p.*

Saad, L. (2006b). Blacks committed to the idea of marriage: More likely than whites to say it is very important for couples to marry. Retrieved January 30, 2007, from *www.galluppoll.com/content/Default.aspx?ci=23767&pg=1&VERSION=p.*

Saal, F. E. (1996). Men's misperceptions of women's interpersonal behaviors and sexual harassment. In M. S. Stockdale (Ed.), *Sexual harassment in the workplace: Perspectives, frontiers, and response strategies* (Vol. 5, pp. 67–84). Thousand Oaks, CA: Sage.

Sachs-Ericsson, N., & Ciarlo, J. A. (2000). Gender, social roles, and mental health: An epidemiological perspective. *Sex Roles, 43,* 605–628.

Sack, K. (1999, July 30). Gunman kills 9, self in Atlanta shootings at 2 brokerages; His wife, 2 children also found dead. *Pittsburgh Post-Gazette,* p. A–1.

Sadar, N. C. (2006). Work-family arrangements in organisations. In I. Svetlik & B. Iiac (Eds.), *HRM's contribution to hard work: A comparative analysis of human resource management.* New York: Peter Lang Publishing.

Sadker, M., & Sadker, D. (1994). *Failing at fairness: How America's schools cheat girls.* New York: Charles Scribner's Sons.

Safir, M. P., Flaisher-Kellner, S., & Rosenmann, A. (2005). When gender differences surpass cultural differences in personal satisfaction with body shape in Israeli college students. *Sex Roles, 52,* 369–378.

Sagrestano, L. M. (1992). Power strategies in interpersonal relationships: The effects of expertise and gender. *Psychology of Women Quarterly, 16,* 481–495.

Samter, W., Whaley, B. B., Mortenson, S. T., & Burleson, B. R. (1997). Ethnicity and emotional support in same-sex friendship: A comparison of Asian-Americans, African-Americans, and Euro-Americans. *Personal Relationships, 4,* 413–430.

Sanchez-Hucles, J. V. (1997). Jeopardy not bonus status for African American women in the work force: Why does the myth of advantage persist? *American Journal of Community Psychology, 25*(5), 565–580.

Sanderson, S., & Thompson, V. L. (2002). Factors associated with perceived parental involvement in childrearing. *Sex Roles, 46,* 99–111.

Sandler, B. R., & Shoop, R. J. (1997). What is sexual harassment? In B. R. Sandler & R. J. Shoop (Eds.), *Sexual harassment on campus: A guide for administrators, faculty, and students* (pp. 1–21). Boston: Allyn & Bacon.

Sandstrom, M. J., & Coie, J. D. (1999). A developmental perspective on peer rejection: Mechanisms of stability and change. *Child Development, 70,* 955–966.

Santos, S. J., Bohon, L. M., & Sanchez-Sosa, J. J. (1998). Childhood family relationships, marital and work conflict, and mental health distress in Mexican immigrants. *Journal of Community Psychology, 26*(5), 491–508.

Sastry, J. (1999). Household structure, satisfaction and distress in India and the United States: A comparative cultural examination. *Journal of Comparative Family Studies, 30*(1), 135–152.

Satterfield, A. T., & Muehlenhard, C. L. (1997). The effects of an authority figure's flirtatiousness on women's and men's self-related creativity. *Psychology of Women Quarterly, 21,* 395–416.

Sayers, S. L., Baucom, D. H., & Tierney, A. M. (1993). Sex roles, interpersonal control, and depression: Who can get their way? *Journal of Research in Personality, 27,* 377–395.

Scaramella, T. J., & Brown, W. A. (1978). Serum testosterone and aggressiveness in hockey players. *Psychosomatic Medicine, 40*(3), 262–265.

Schein, V. E. (2001). A global look at psychological barriers to women's progress in management. *Journal of Social Issues, 57,* 675–688.

Schiedel, D. G., & Marcia, J. E. (1985). Ego identity, intimacy, sex role orientation, and gender. *Developmental Psychology, 21,* 149–160.

Schmitt, D. P. (2003). Universal sex differences in the desire for sexual variety: Tests from 52 nations, 6 continents, and 13 islands. *Journal of Personality and Social Psychology, 85,* 85–104.

Schmitt, D. P., & 121 Members of the International Sexuality Description Project. (2004). Patterns and universals of mate poaching across 53 nations: The effects of sex, culture, and personality on romantically attracting another person's partner. *Journal of Personality and Social Psychology, 86,* 560–584.

Schnarch, B. (1992). Neither man nor woman: Berdache—A case for non-dichotomoous gender construction. *Anthropologica, 34*(1), 105–121.

Schneer, J. A., & Reitman, F. (1993). Effects of alternate family structures on managerial career paths. *Academy of Management Journal, 36,* 830–843.

Schneider, B. H., Woodburn, S., del Toro, M., & Udvari, S. J. (2005). Cultural and gender differences in the implications

of competition for early adolescent friendship. *Merrill-Palmer Quarterly, 51,* 163–191.

Schnittker, J. (2000). Gender and reactions to psychological problems: An examination of social tolerance and perceived dangerousness. *Journal of Health and Social Behavior, 44,* 224–240.

Schoenbach, V. J., Kaplan, B. H., Fredman, L., & Kleinbaum, D. G. (1986). Social ties and mortality in Evans County, Georgia. *American Journal of Epidemiology, 123*(4), 577–591.

Schone, B. S., & Weinick, R. M. (1998). Health-related behaviors and the benefits of marriage for elderly persons. *Gerontologist, 38*(5), 618–627.

Schulz, M. S., Cowan, P. A., Cowan, C. P., & Brennan, R. T. (2004). Coming home upset: Gender, marital satisfaction, and the daily spillover of workday experience into couple interactions. *Journal of Family Psychology, 18,* 250–263.

Schuurs, A. H., & Verheul, H. A. (1990). Effects of gender and sex steroids on the immune response. *Journal of Steroid and Biochemistry, 35*(2), 157–172.

Schwalbe, M. L., & Staples, C. L. (1991). Gender differences in sources of self-esteem. *Social Psychology Quarterly, 54*(2), 158–168.

Schweinle, W. E., Ickes, W., & Bernstein, I. H. (2002). Empathic inaccuracy in husband to wife aggression: The overattribution bias. *Personal Relationships, 9,* 141–158.

Scott, K. A. (2004). African-American-White girls' friendships. *Feminism & Psychology, 14,* 383–388.

Sebanc, A. M. (2003). The friendship features of preschool children: Links with prosocial behavior and aggression. *Social Development, 12,* 249–268.

Sebanc, A. M., Pierce, S. L., Cheatham, C. L., & Gunnar, M. R. (2003). Gendered social worlds in preschool: Dominance, peer acceptance and assertive social skills in boys' and girls' peer groups. *Social Development, 12,* 91–106.

Seelau, S. M., & Seelau, E. P. (2005). Gender-role stereotypes and perceptions of heterosexual, gay and lesbian domestic violence. *Journal of Family Violence, 20,* 363–371.

Seeman, T. E., Berkman, L. F., Blazer, D., & Rowe, J. W. (1994). Social ties and support and neuroendocrine function: The MacArthur studies of successful aging. *Annals of Behavioral Medicine, 16*(2), 95–106.

Segar, M., Spruijt-Metz, D., & Nolen-Hoeksema, S. (2006). Go figure? Body-shape motives are associated with decreased physical activity participation among midlife women. *Sex Roles, 54,* 175–187.

Seidlitz, L., & Diener, E. (1998). Sex differences in the recall of affective experiences. *Journal of Personality and Social Psychology, 74,* 262–271.

Seligman, M. E. P. (1992). *Helplessness: On depression, development, and death.* New York: Freeman.

Seltzer, J. A. (2000). Families formed outside of marriage. *Journal of Marriage and the Family, 62,* 1247–1268.

Serbin, L. A., Poulin-Dubois, D., Colburne, K. A., Sen, M. G., & Eichstedt, J. A. (2001). Gender stereotyping in infancy: Visual preferences for and knowledge of gender-stereotyped toys in the second year. *International Journal of Behavioral Development, 25,* 7–15.

Sethi, S., & Nolen-Hoeksema, S. (1997). Gender differences in internal and external focusing among adolescents. *Sex Roles, 37,* 687–700.

Sevcik, K. (2007). She's turning him into a girl. *Marie Claire,* 121–127.

Seward, R. R., Yeatts, D. E., & Zottarelli, L. K. (2002). Parental leave and father involvement in child care: Sweden and the United States. *Journal of Comparative Family Studies, 33,* 387–399.

Seymour, E. (1995). The loss of women from science, mathematics, and engineering undergraduate majors: An explanatory account. *Science Education, 79*(4), 437–473.

Shackelford, T. K., Schmitt, D. P., & Buss, D. M. (2005). Universal dimensions of human mate preferences. *Personality and Individual Differences, 39,* 447–458.

Shaffer, D. R., Pegalis, L. J., & Bazzini, D. G. (1996). When boy meets girl (revisited): Gender, gender-role orientation, and prospect of future interaction as determinants of self-disclosure among same- and opposite-sex acquaintances. *Personality and Social Psychology Bulletin, 22,* 495–506.

Shajahan, P. M., & Cavanagh, J. T. O. (1998). Admission for depression among men in Scotland, 1980–95: Retrospective study. *British Medical Journal, 316,* 1496–1497.

Sharps, M. J., Welton, A. L., & Price, J. L. (1993). Gender and task in the determination of spatial cognitive performance. *Psychology of Women Quarterly, 17,* 71–83.

Shaw, W. S., Patterson, T. L., Semple, S., & Grant, I. (1998). Health and well-being in retirement: A summary of theories and their implications. In M. Herson & V. B. V. Hasselt (Eds.), *Handbook of clinical geropsychology* (pp. 383–409). New York: Plenum Press.

Shaywitz, B. A., Shaywitz, S. E., Pugh, K. R., Constable, R. T., Skudlarski, P., Fulbright, R. K., et al. (1995). Sex differences in the functional organization of the brain for language. *Nature, 373,* 607–608.

Shaywitz, S. E., Shaywitz, B. A., Fletcher, J. M., & Escobar, M. D. (1990). Prevalence of reading disability in boys and girls: Results of the Connecticut longitudinal study. *Journal of the American Medical Association, 264,* 998–1002.

Shearer, C. L., Hosterman, S. J., Gillen, M. M., & Lefkowitz, E. S. (2005). Are traditional gender role attitudes associated with risky behavior and condom-related beliefs? *Sex Roles, 52,* 311–324.

Sheeran, P., Abraham, C., & Orbell, S. (1999). Psychosocial correlates of heterosexual condom use: A meta-analysis. *Psychological Bulletin, 125,* 90–132.

Sheets, V. L., & Braver, S. L. (1999). Organizational status and perceived sexual harassment: Detecting the mediators of a null effect. *Personality and Social Psychology Bulletin, 25,* 1159–1171.

Sheets, V. L., & Lugar, R. (2005). Friendship and gender in Russia and the United States. *Sex Roles, 52,* 131–140.

Sheets, V. L., & Wolfe, M. D. (2001). Sexual jealousy in heterosexuals, lesbians, and gays. *Sex Roles, 44,* 255–276.

Sheriff releases time line of Columbine shooting: The report from the 13-month investigation seems to counter claims that police officers could have saved lives had they acted more quickly. (2000, May 16). *Star Tribune,* Minneapolis, MN. p. 06A.

Shields, S. A. (1975). Functionalism, Darwinism, and the psychology of women: A study in social myth. *American Psychologist, 30,* 739–754.

Shih, J. H., Eberhart, N. K., Hammen, C. L., & Brennan, P. A. (2006). Differential exposure and reactivity to interpersonal stress predict sex differences in adolescent depression. *Journal of Clinical Child and Adolescent Psychology, 35,* 103–115.

Shih, M., Pittinsky, T. L., & Ambady, N. (1999). Stereotype susceptibility: Identity salience and shifts in quantitative performance. *Psychological Science, 10*(1), 80–83.

Shippy, R. A., Cantor, M. H., & Brennan, M. (2004). Social networks of aging gay men. *Journal of Men's Studies, 13,* 107–120.

Shriver, S. P., Bourdeau, H. A., Gubish, C. T., Tirpak, D. L., Gaither Davis, A. L., Luketich, J. D., & Siegfried, J. M. (2000). Sex-specific expression of gastrin-releasing peptied receptor: Relationship to smoking history and risk of lung cancer. *Journal of the National Cancer Institute, 92,* 24–33.

Shupe, E. I., Cortina, L. M., Ramos, A., Fitzgerald, L. F., & Salisbury, J. (2002). The incidence and outcomes of sexual harassment among Hispanic and non-Hispanic white women: A comparison across levels of cultural affiliation. *Psychology of Women Quarterly, 26,* 298–308.

Shye, D., Mullooly, J. P., Freeborn, D. K., & Pope, C. R. (1995). Gender differences in the relationship between social network support and mortality: A longitudinal study of an elderly cohort. *Social Science & Medicine, 41*(7), 935–947.

Siddiqui, O., Mott, J., Anderson, T., & Flay, B. (1999). The application of Poisson random-effects regression models to the analyses of adolescents' current level of smoking. *Preventive Medicine, 29,* 92–101.

Siegal, M. (1987). Are sons and daughters treated more differently by fathers than by mothers? *Developmental Review, 7,* 183–209.

Siegel, J. M., & Kuykendall, D. H. (1990). Loss, widowhood, and psychological distress among the elderly. *Journal of Consulting and Clinical Psychology, 58,* 519–524.

Siegel, S. J., & Alloy, L. B. (1990). Interpersonal perceptions and consequences of depressive-significant other relationships: A naturalistic study of college roommates. *Journal of Abnormal Psychology, 99*(4), 361–373.

Siegel-Hinson, R. J., & McKeever, W. F. (2002). Hemispheric specialisation, spatial activity experience, and sex differences on tests of mental rotation ability. *Laterality, 7*(1), 59–74.

Siegfried, J. (2000, January 5). Pitt study links gene to cancer in women. *Pittsburgh Post-Gazette,* p. A–1.

Siever, M. D. (1996). The perils of sexual objectification: Sexual orientation, gender, and socioculturally acquired vulnerability to body dissatisfaction and eating disorders. In C. J. Alexander (Ed.), *Gay and lesbian mental health: A sourcebook for practitioners* (pp. 223–247). New York: Harrington Park Press.

Sigal, J., Gibbs, M. S., Goodrich, C., Rashid, T., Anjum, A., Hsu, D., et al. (2005). Cross-cultural reactions to academic sexual harassment: Effects of individualist vs. collectivist culture and gender of participants. *Sex Roles, 52,* 201–215.

Signorielli, N., & Lears, M. (1992). Children, television, and the conceptions about chores: Attitudes and behaviors. *Sex Roles, 27,* 157–170.

Silberg, J., Pickles, A., Rutter, M., Hewitt, J., Simonoff, E., Maes, H., et al. (1999). The influence of genetic factors and life stress on depression among adolescent girls. *Archives of General Psychiatry, 56,* 225–232.

Silverman, I., & Eals, M. (1992). Sex differences in spatial abilities: Evolutionary theory and data. In J. H. Barkow, L. Cosmides, & J. Tooby (Eds.), *The adapted mind: Evolutionary psychology and the generation of culture* (pp. 533–549). New York: Oxford University Press.

Silverstein, B., & Perlick, D. (1995). *The cost of competence: Why inequality causes depression, eating disorders, and illness in women.* New York: Oxford University Press.

Silverstein, L. B., Auerbach, C. F., Grieco, L., & Dunkel, F. (1999). Do Promise Keepers dream of feminist sheep? *Sex Roles, 40,* 665–688.

Simmons, W. W. (2001). *Majority of Americans say more women in political office would be positive for the country.* The Gallup Organization. Retrieved August 21, 2003, from *www.gallup.com.*

Simms, K. B., Knight, D. M., Jr., & Dawes, K. I. (1993). Institutional factors that influence the academic success of African-American men. *Journal of Men's Studies, 1*(3), 253–266.

Simon, R. W. (1995). Gender, multiple roles, role meaning, and mental health. *Journal of Health and Social Behavior, 36,* 182–194.

Simon, R. W., & Nath, L. E. (2004). Gender and emotion in the United States: Do men and women differ in self-reports of feelings and expressive behavior? *American Journal of Sociology, 109,* 1137–1176.

Simoni-Wastila, L. (1998). Gender and psychotropic drug use. *Medical Care, 36*(1), 88–94.

Simons, A. D., Angell, K. L., Monroe, S. M., & Thase, M. E. (1993). Cognition and life stress in depression: Cognitive factors and the definition, rating, and generation of negative life events. *Journal of Abnormal Psychology, 102,* 584–591.

Simons-Morton, B., Crump, A. D., Haynie, D. L., Saylor, K. E., Eitel, P., & Yu, K. (1999). Psychosocial, school, and parent factors associated with recent smoking among early-adolescent boys and girls. *Preventive Medicine, 28,* 138–148.

Simpkins, S. D., Davis-Kean, P. E., & Eccles, J. S. (2005). Parents' socializing behavior and children's participation in math, science, and computer out-of-school activities. *Applied Developmental Science, 9,* 14–30.

Simpkins, S. D., Davis-Kean, P. E., & Eccles, J. S. (2006). Math and science motivation: A longitudinal examination of the links between choices and beliefs. *Developmental Psychology, 42,* 70–83.

Simpkins, S. D., Parke, R. D., Flyr, M. L., & Wild, M. N. (2006). Similarities in children's and early adolescents' perceptions of friendship qualities across development, gender, and friendship qualities. *Journal of Early Adolescence, 26,* 491–508.

Six, B., & Eckes, T. (1991). A closer look at the complex structure of gender stereotypes. *Sex Roles, 24,* 57–71.

Skaff, M. M., Finney, J. W., & Moos, R. H. (1999). Gender differences in problem drinking and depression: Different "vulnerabilities?" *American Journal of Community Psychology, 27,* 25–54.

Skogman, K., Alsen, M., & Ojehagen, A. (2004). Sex differences in risk factors for suicide after attempted suicide: A follow-up study of 1052 suicide attempters. *Social Psychiatry and Psychiatric Epidemiology, 39,* 113–120.

Skrypnek, B. J., & Snyder, M. (1982). On the self-perpetuating nature of stereotypes about women and men. *Journal of Experimental Social Psychology, 18,* 277–291.

Slesinski, M. J., Subar, A. F., & Kahle, L. L. (1996). Dietary intake of fat, fiber and other nutrients is related to the use of vitamin and mineral supplements in the United States: The 1992 National Health Interview Survey. *Community and International Nutrition, 126,* 3001–3009.

Smith, B. W., & Zautra, A. J. (2002). The role of personality in exposure and reactivity to interpersonal stress in relation to arthritis disease activity and negative affect in women. *Health Psychology, 21,* 81–88.

Smith, C. A., & Stillman, S. (2002). What do women want? The effects of gender and sexual orientation on the desirability of physical attributes in the personal ads of women. *Sex Roles, 46,* 337–341.

Smith, D. B., & Moen, P. (2004). Retirement satisfaction for retirees and their spouses: Do gender and the retirement decision-making process matter? *Journal of Family Issues, 25,* 262–285.

Smith, P. A., & Midlarsky, E. (1985). Empirically derived conceptions of femaleness and maleness: A current view. *Sex Roles, 12,* 313–328.

Smith, T. W., Gallo, L. C., Goble, L., Ngu, L. Q., & Stark, K. A. (1998). Agency, communion, and cardiovascular reactivity during marital interaction. *Health Psychcology, 17*, 537–545.

Smith, T. W., Limon, J. P., Gallo, L. C., & Ngu, L. Q. (1996). Interpersonal control and cardiovascular reactivity: Goals, behavioral expression, and the moderating effects of sex. *Journal of Personality and Social Psychology, 70*, 1012–1024.

Smith, T. W., Ruiz, J. M., & Uchino, B. N. (2004). Mental activation of supportive ties, hostility, and cardiovascular reactivity to laboratory stress in young men and women. *Health Psychology, 23*, 476–485.

Smith-Lovin, L., & Robinson, D. T. (1992). Gender and conversational dynamics. In C. Ridgeway (Ed.), *Gender, interaction, and inequality* (pp. 122–156). New York: Springer-Verlag.

Smolak, L., & Levine, M. P. (1996). Adolescent transitions and the development of eating problems. In L. Smolak, M. P. Levine, & R. Striegel-Moore (Eds.), *The developmental psychopathology of eating disorders* (pp. 207–233). Mahwah, NJ: Erlbaum.

Smolak, L., & Striegel-Moore, R. (1996). The implications of developmental research for eating disorders. In L. Smolak & M. P. Levine (Eds.), *The developmental psychopathology of eating disorders: Implications for research, prevention, and treatment* (pp. 183–203). Mahwah, NJ: Erlbaum.

Snell, W. E., Jr. (1986). The Masculine Role Inventory: Components and correlates. *Sex Roles, 15*, 443–455.

Snell, W. E., Jr., Miller, R. S., Belk, S. S., Garcia-Falconi, R., & Hernandez-Sanchez, J. E. (1989). Men's and women's emotional disclosures: The impact of disclosure recipient, culture, and the masculine role. *Sex Roles, 21*, 467–486.

Snodgrass, S. E., Hecht, M. A., & Ploutz-Snyder, R. (1998). Interpersonal sensitivity: Expressivity or perceptivity? *Journal of Personality and Social Psychology, 74*, 238–249.

Snyder, M. (1979). Self-monitoring processes. In L. Berkowitz (Ed.), *Advances in experimental social psychology* (Vol. 12, pp. 85–128). New York: Academic Press.

Snyder, M., Tanke, E. D., & Berscheid, E. (1977). Social perception and interpersonal behavior: On the self-fulfilling nature of social stereotypes. *Journal of Personality and Social Psychology, 35*, 656–666.

Sobieraj, S. (1998). Taking control: Toy commercials and the social construction of patriarchy. In L. H. Bowker (Ed.), *Masculinities and violence* (pp. 15–28). Thousand Oaks, CA: Sage.

Sochting, I., Skoe, E. E., & Marcia, J. E. (1994). Care-oriented moral reasoning and prosocial behavior: A question of gender or sex role orientation. *Sex Roles, 31*, 131–147.

Some state. (2003). Some state constitutions are going gender-neutral. *nytimes.com* Retrieved October 30, 2007, from *querry.nytimes.com/gst/fullpage.html.*

Sommer, I. E. C., Aleman, A., Bouma, A., & Kahn, R. S. (2004). Do women really have more bilateral language representation than men? A meta-analysis of functional imaging studies. *Brain, 127*, 1845–1852.

Sorenson, S. B., & Siegel, J. M. (1992). Gender, ethnicity, and sexual assault: Findings from a Los Angeles study. *Journal of Social Issues, 48*(1), 93–104.

South, S. J., & Spitze, G. (1994). Housework in marital and nonmarital households. *American Sociological Review, 59*, 327–347.

Special Issue of American Psychologist. (2007). Special Issue: Eating Disorders. *62.*

Spence, J. T., & Buckner, C. E. (2000). Instrumental and expressive traits, trait stereotypes, and sexist attitudes: What do they signify? *Psychology of Women Quarterly, 24*, 44–62.

Spence, J. T., & Helmreich, R. L. (1972). The Attitudes Toward Women Scale: An objective instrument to measure attitudes toward the rights and roles of women in contemporary society. *JSAS Catalog of Selected Documents in Psychology, 2*, 667–668.

Spence, J. T., & Helmreich, R. L. (1978). *Masculinity and femininity: The psychological dimensions, correlates, and antecedents.* Austin: University of Texas Press.

Spence, J. T., Helmreich, R. L., & Holahan, C. K. (1979). Negative and positive components of psychological masculinity and femininity and their relationships to self-reports of neurotic and acting out behaviors. *Journal of Personality and Social Psychology, 37*, 1673–1682.

Spence, J. T., Helmreich, R. L., & Stapp, J. (1974). The Personal Attributes Questionnaire: A measure of sex role stereotypes and masculinity-femininity. *JSAS Catalog of Selected Documents in Psychology, 43*, Ms. no. 617.

Spence, J. T., & Sawin, L. L. (1985). Images of masculinity and femininity: A reconceptualization. In V. E. O'Leary, R. K. Unger & B. S. Wallston (Eds.), *Women, gender, and social psychology* (pp. 35–66). Hillsdale, NJ: Lawrence Erlbaum.

Spencer, S. J., Steele, C. M., & Quinn, D. M. (1999). Stereotype threat and women's math performance. *Journal of Experimental Social Psychology, 35*, 4–28.

Spitzberg, B. H., & Cupach, W. R. (2007). The state of the art of stalking: Taking stock of the emerging literature. *Aggression and Violent Behavior, 12*, 64–86.

Sprague, J., & Quadagno, D. (1989). Gender and sexual motivation: An exploration of two assumptions. *Journal of Psychology and Human Sexuality, 2*(1), 57–76.

Sprecher, S. (2006). Sexuality in close relationships. In P. Noller & J. A. Feeney (Eds.), *Close relationships: Functions, forms and processes* (pp. 267–284). New York: Pychology Press.

Sprecher, S., Barbee, A., & Schwartz, P. (1995). Was it good for you, too?: Gender differences in first sexual intercourse experiences. *Journal of Sex Research, 32*, 3–15.

Sprecher, S., & Felmlee, D. (1997). The balance of power in romantic heterosexual couples over time from "his" and "her" perspectives. *Sex Roles, 37,* 361–379.

Sprecher, S., & Hatfield, E. (1996). Premarital sexual standards among U.S. college students: Comparison with Russian and Japanese students. *Archives of Sexual Behavior, 25*(3), 261–288.

Sprecher, S., & Metts, S. (1989). Development of the Romantic Beliefs Scale and examination of the effects of gender and gender-role orientation. *Journal of Social and Personal Relationships, 6,* 387–411.

Sprecher, S., & Regan, P. C. (1996). College virgins: How men and women perceive their sexual status. *Journal of Sex Research, 33*(10), 3–15.

Sprecher, S., Aron, A., Hatfield, E., Cortese, A., Potapova, E., & Levitskaya, A. (1994). Love: American style, Russian style, and Japanese style. *Personal Relationships, 1,* 349–369.

Sprecher, S., Regan, P. C., & McKinney, K. (1998). Beliefs about the outcomes of extramarital sexual relationships as a function of the gender of the cheating spouse. *Sex Roles, 38,* 301–311.

Sprecher, S., Regan, P. C., McKinney, K., Maxwell, K., & Wazienski, R. (1997). Preferred level of sexual experience in a date or mate: The merger of two methodologies. *Journal of Sex Research, 34*(4), 327–337.

Sprecher, S., Sullivan, Q., & Hatfield, E. (1994). Mate selection preferences: Gender differences examined in a national sample. *Journal of Personality and Social Psychology, 66,* 1074–1080.

Springer, S. P., & Deutsch, G. (1981). *Left brain, right brain.* New York: Freeman.

Sprock, J., Crosby, J. P., & Nielsen, B. A. (2001). Effects of sex and sex roles on the perceived maladaptiveness of DSM-IV personality disorder symptoms. *Journal of Personality Disorders, 15,* 41–59.

Stack, C. B. (1997). Different voices, different visions: Gender, culture, and moral reasoning. In M. B. Zinn, P. Hondagneu-Sotelo, & M. A. Messner (Eds.), *Through the prism of difference: Readings on sex and gender* (pp. 51–57). Boston: Allyn & Bacon.

Stack, S. (1998a). Gender, marriage, and suicide acceptability: A comparative analysis. *Sex Roles, 38,* 501–520.

Stack, S. (1998b). Marriage, family, and loneliness: A cross-national study. *Sociological Perspectives, 41*(2), 415–432.

Stack, S., & Eshleman, J. R. (1998). Marital status and happiness: A 17-nation study. *Journal of Marriage and the Family, 60,* 527–536.

Stangor, C., & McMillan, D. (1992). Memory for expectancy-congruent and expectancy-incongruent information: A review of the social and social developmental literatures. *Psychological Bulletin, 111,* 42–61.

Stanley, S. M., Rhoades, G. K., & Markman, H. J. (2006). Sliding versus deciding: Inertia and the premarital cohabitation effect. *Family Relations, 55,* 499–509.

Stanley, S. M., Whitton, S. W., & Markman, H. J. (2004). Maybe I do. *Journal of Family Issues, 25,* 496–519.

Stanley, T. D., & Jarrell, S. B. (1998). Gender wage discrimination bias? A meta-regression analysis. *Journal of Human Resources, 33*(4), 947–973.

Staples, R. (1978). Masculinity and race: The dual dilemma of Black men. *Journal of Social Issues, 34*(1), 169–183.

Staples, R. (1995). Health among Afro-American males. In D. F. Sabo & D. F. Gordon (Eds.), *Research on men and masculinities series* (Vol. 8, pp. 121–138). Thousand Oaks, CA: Sage Publications, Inc.

Stateline. (2007). *State policies on same-sex marriage.* Retrieved February 1, 2007, from *www.stateline.org/live/digitalassets/4883_social_policy.pdf.*

Steele, J. R., & Ambady, N. (2006). "Math is hard!" The effect of gender priming on women's attitudes. *Journal of Experimental Psychology, 42,* 428–436.

Steele, J., & Barling, J. (1996). Influence of maternal gender-role beliefs and role satisfaction on daughters' vocational interests. *Sex Roles, 34,* 637–648.

Steele, J., James, J. B., & Barnett, R. C. (2002). Learning in a man's world: Examining the perceptions of undergraduate women in male-dominated academic areas. *Psychology of Women Quarterly, 26,* 46–50.

Steering Committee of the Physicians' Health Study Research Group. (1988). Preliminary report: Findings from the aspirin component of the ongoing physicians' health study. *New England Journal of Medicine, 318*(4), 262–264.

Steil, J. M., & Hillman, J. L. (1993). The perceived value of direct and indirect influence strategies: A cross-cultural comparison. *Psychology of Women Quarterly, 17,* 457–462.

Steil, J. M., & Weltman, K. (1992). Influence strategies at home and at work: A study of sixty dual career couples. *Journal of Social and Personal Relationships, 9,* 65–88.

Stein, J. A., Newcomb, M. D., & Bentler, P. M. (1992). The effect of agency and communality on self-esteem: Gender differences in longitudinal data. *Sex Roles, 26,* 465–483.

Stein, M. B., & Barrett-Connor, E. (2000). Sexual assault and physical health: Findings from a population-based study of older adults. *Psychosomatic Medicine, 62,* 838–843.

Steinberg, M. B., Akincigil, A., Delnevo, C. D., Crystal, S., & Carson, J. L. (2006). Gender and age disparities for smoking-cessation treatment. *American Journal of Preventive Medicine, 30,* 405–412.

Steinberg, N. (1998, February 8). Class of 2001 has confidence, computer skills. *Chicago Sun-Times,* p. 6.

Steiner-Pappalardo, N. L., & Gurung, R. A. R. (2002). The femininity effect: Relationship quality, sex, gender, attachment, and significant-other concepts. *Personal Relationships, 9,* 313–325.

Steingart, R. M., Packer, M., Hamm, P., Coglianese, M. E., Gersh, B., Geltman, E. M., et al. (1991). Sex differences in the management of coronary artery disease. *New England Journal of Medicine, 325,* 226–230.

Stephan, W. G., & Stephan, C. W. (1993). Cognition and affect in stereotyping: Parallel interactive network. In D. M. Mackie & D. L. Hamilton (Eds.), *Affect, cognition, and stereotyping: Interactive processes in group perception* (pp. 111–136). Santa Barbara, CA: Academic Press.

Stephan, W. G., Ageyev, V., Coates-Shrider, L., Stephan, C. W., & Abalakina, M. (1994). On the relationship between stereotypes and prejudice: An international study. *Personality and Social Psychology Bulletin, 20,* 277–284.

Stephens, M. A. P., Martire, L. M., Cremeans-Smith, J. K., Druley, J. A., & Wojno, W. C. (2006). Older women with osteoarthritis and their caregiving husbands: Effects of pain and pain expression on husbands' well-being and support. *Rehabilitation Psychology, 51,* 3–12.

Stern, S. R., & Mastro, D. E. (2004). Gender portrayals across the life span: A content analytic look at broadcast commercials. *Mass Communication & Society, 7,* 215–236.

Stets, J. E., & Straus, M. A. (1990). Gender differences in reporting marital violence and its medical and psychological consequences. In M. A. Straus, R. J. Gelles, & C. Smith (Eds.), *Physical violence in American families: Risk factors and adaptations to violence in 8,145 families* (pp. 151–165). New Brunswick, NJ: Transaction.

Stevens, D. P., Minnotte, K. L., Mannon, S. E., & Kiger, G. (2006). Family work performance and satisfaction: Gender ideology, relative resources, and emotion work. *Marriage and Family Review, 40,* 47–74.

Stevens, G., Owens, D., & Schaefer, E. C. (1990). Education and attractiveness in marriage choices. *Social Psychology Quarterly, 53*(1), 62–70.

Stewart, T. L., Berkvens, M., Engels, W. A. E. W., & Pass, J. A. (2003). Status *and* likability: Can the "mindful" woman have it all? *Journal of Applied Social Psychology, 33,* 2040–2059.

Stillion, J. M. (1995). Premature death among males. In D. Sabo & D. F. Gordon (Eds.), *Men's health and illness: Gender, power, and the body* (pp. 46–67). Thousand Oaks, CA: Sage.

Stipek, D. J., & Gralinski, J. H. (1991). Gender differences in children's achievement-related beliefs and emotional responses to success and failure in mathematics. *Journal of Educational Psychology, 83*(3), 361–371.

Straus, M. A. (1979). Measuring intrafamily conflict and violence: The conflict tactics (CT) scales. *Journal of Marriage and the Family, 41,* 75–88.

Straus, M. A. (1990a). Ordinary violence, child abuse, and wife beating: What do they have in common? In M. A. Straus, R. J. Gelles, & C. Smith (Eds.), *Physical violence in American families: Risk factors and adaptations to violence in 8,145 families* (pp. 403–424). New Brunswick, NJ: Transaction.

Straus, M. A. (1990b). Social stress and marital violence in a national sample of American families. In M. A. Straus, R. J. Gelles, & C. Smith (Eds.), *Physical violence in*

American families: Risk factors and adaptations to violence in 8,145 families (pp. 181–201). New Brunswick, NJ: Transaction.

Straus, M. A. (1995). Trends in cultural norms and rates of partner violence: An update to 1992. In S. M. Stith & M. A. Straus (Eds.), *Understanding partner violence: Prevalence, causes, consequences and solutions* (pp. 30–33). Minneapolis: National Council on Family Relations.

Straus, M. A. (2004). Prevalence of violence against dating partners by male and female university students worldwide. *Violence Against Women, 10,* 790–811.

Straus, M. A., & Gelles, R. J. (1990a). How violent are American families? Estimates from the national family violence resurveyed and other studies. In M. A. Straus, R. J. Gelles, & C. Smith (Eds.), *Physical violence in American families: Risk factors and adaptations to violence in 8,145 families* (pp. 95–112). New Brunswick, NJ: Transaction.

Straus, M. A., & Gelles, R. J. (1990b). Societal change and change in family violence from 1975 to 1985 as revealed by two national surveys. In M. A. Straus, R. J. Gelles, & C. Smith (Eds.), *Physical violence in American families: Risk factors and adaptations to violence in 8,145 families* (pp. 113–131). New Brunswick, NJ: Transaction.

Straus, M. A., & Smith, C. (1990). Violence in Hispanic families in the United States: Incidence rates and structural interpretation. In M. A. Straus, R. J. Gelles, & C. Smith (Eds.), *Physical violence in American families: Risk factors and adaptations to violence in 8,145 families* (pp. 341–367). New Brunswick, NJ: Transaction.

Straus, M. A., Gelles, R. J., & Steinmetz, S. K. (1980). *Behind closed doors: Violence in the American family.* Garden City, NY: Anchor Books.

Strauss, J., Muday, T., McNall, K., & Wong, M. (1997). Response style theory revisited: Gender differences and stereotypes in rumination and distraction. *Sex Roles, 36,* 771–792.

Striegel-Moore, R. H., & Cachelin, F. M. (1999). Body image concerns and disordered eating in adolescent girls: Risk and protective factors. In N. G. Johnson, M. C. Roberts, & J. Worell (Eds.), *Beyond appearance: A new look at adolescent girls* (pp. 85–108). Washington, DC: American Psychological Association.

Striegel-Moore, R. H., Dohm, F. A., Kraemer, H. C., Taylor, C. B., Daniels, S., Crawford, P. B., & Schreiber, G. B. (2003). Eating disorders in white and black women. *American Journal of Psychiatry, 160,* 1326–1331.

Strober, M. H. (2002). What's a wife worth? In M. Yalom & L. L. Carstensen (Eds.), *Inside the American Couple* (pp. 174–188). Berkeley: University of California Press.

Stroebe, M. S., & Stroebe, W. (1983). Who suffers more? Sex differences in health risks of the widowed. *Psychological Bulletin, 93,* 279–301.

Strohschein, L., McDonough, P., Monette, G., & Shao, Q. (2005). Marital transitions and mental health: Are there gender differences in the short-term effects of marital status change? *Social Science & Medicine, 61,* 2293–2303.

Stroud, L. R., Niaura, R. S., & Salovey, P. (2000, March). *Stressor type and oral contraceptive use influence males' and females' cardiovascular responses to stress.* Paper presented at the American Psychosomatic Society, Savannah, GA.

Stroud, L. R., Papandonatos, G. D., Williamson, D. E., & Dahl, R. E. (2004). Sex differences in the effects of pubertal development on responses to a corticotropin-releasing hormone challenge: The Pittsburgh Psychobiologic Studies. *Annals of the New York Academy of the Sciences, 1021,* 348–351.

Stroud, L. R., Salovey, P., & Epel, E. S. (2002). Sex differences in stress responses: Social rejection versus achievement stress. *Biological Psychiatry, 52,* 318–327.

Struckman-Johnson, C., & Struckman-Johnson, D. (1994). Men pressured and forced into sexual experience. *Archives of Sexual Behavior, 23*(1), 93–114.

Stuhlmacher, A. F., & Walters, A. E. (1999). Gender differences in negotiation outcome: A meta-analysis. *Personnel Psychology, 52,* 653–677.

Substance Abuse and Mental Health Services Administration. (2006). *Results from the 2005 National Survey on Drug Use and Health: National Findings.* Office of Applied Studies (NSDUH Series H-30, DHHS Publication No. SMA 06-4194). National Clearinghouse for Alcohol and Drug Information (NCADI), Rockville, MD.

Sullivan, O. (2004). Changing gender practices within the household: A theoretical perspective. *Gender & Society 18,* 207–222.

Summers, L. H. (2005). Remarks at NBER conference on diversifying the science & engineering workforce. Retrieved January 31, 2007, from *www.president.harvard.edu/speeches/2005/nber.html.*

Sundaram, V., Helweg-Larsen, K., Laursen, B., & Bjerregaard, P. (2004). Physical violence, self rated health, and morbidity: Is gender significant for victimisation? *Journal of Epidemiology and Community Health, 58,* 65–70.

Susman, E. J., & Pajer, K. (2004). Biology-behavior integration and antisocial behavior in girls. In M. Putallaz & K. L. Bierman (Eds.), *Aggression, antisocial behavior, and violence among girls* (pp. 23–47). New York: Guilford Publications.

Sussman, S., Dent, C. W., Nezami, E., Stacy, A. W., Burton, D., & Flay, B. R. (1998). Reasons for quitting and smoking temptation among adolescent smokers: Gender differences. *Substance Use and Misuse, 33*(14), 2703–2720.

Suter, E. A., & Toller, P. W. (2006). Gender role and feminism revisited: A follow-up study. *Sex Roles, 55,* 135–146.

Swain, S. (1989). Covert intimacy: Closeness in men's friendships. In B. J. Risman & P. Schwartz (Eds.), *Gender in intimate relationships: A microstructural approach* (pp. 71–86). Belmont, CA: Wadsworth.

Swann, W. B., Jr., Langlois, J. H., & Gilbert, L. A. (Eds.). (1999). *Sexism and stereotypes in modern society: The gender science of Janet Taylor Spence.* Washington, DC: American Psychological Association.

Sweeting, H. (1995). Reversals of fortune? Sex differences in health in childhood and adolescence. *Social Science & Medicine, 40*(1), 77–90.

Sweeting, H., & West, P. (2003). Sex differences in health at ages 11, 13 and 15. *Social Science & Medicine, 56,* 31–39.

Swerczek, M. (1999). Copycat killing suit is facing test. *Times-Picayune.* Retrieved from *proquest.umi.com.*

Swim, J. K. (1994). Perceived versus meta-analytic effect sizes: An assessment of the accuracy of gender stereotypes. *Journal of Personality and Social Psychology, 66,* 21–36.

Swim, J. K., & Sanna, L. J. (1996). He's skilled, she's lucky: A meta-analysis of observers' attributions for women's and men's successes and failures. *Personality and Social Psychology Bulletin, 22,* 507–519.

Swim, J. K., Aikin, K. J., Hall, W. S., & Hunter, B. A. (1995). Sexism and racism: Old-fashioned and modern prejudices. *Journal of Personality and Social Psychology, 68,* 199–214.

Swim, J. K., Mallett, R., & Stangor, C. (2004). Understanding subtle sexism: Detection and use of sexist language. *Sex Roles, 51,* 117–128.

Szinovacz, M. (1987). Preferred retirement timing and retirement satisfaction in women. *International Journal of Aging and Human Development, 24*(4), 301–317.

Szinovacz, M. E., & Davey, A. (2004). Retirement transitions and spouse disability: Effects on depressive symptoms. *Journal of Gerontology: Social Sciences, 59B,* S333-S342.

Szinovacz, M., & Washo, C. (1992). Gender differences in exposure to life events and adaptation to retirement. *Journal of Gerontology Social Sciences, 47*(4), S191– S196.

Takiff, H. A., Sanchez, D. T., & Stewart, T. L. (2001). What's in a name? The status implications of students' terms of address for male and female professors. *Psychology of Women Quarterly, 25,* 134–144.

Takkinen, S., Gold, C., Pedersen, N. L., Malmberg, B., Nilsson, S., & Rovine, M. (2004). Gender differences in depression: A study of older unlike-sex twins. *Aging & Mental Health, 8,* 187–195.

Tamres, L. K., Janicki, D., & Helgeson, V. S. (2002). Sex difference in coping behavior: A meta-analytic review. *Personality and Social Psychology Review, 6,* 2–30.

Tanasescu, M., Leitzmann, M. F., Rimm, E. B., Willett, W. C., Stampfer, M. J., & Hu, F. B. (2002). Exercise type and intensity in relation to coronary heart disease in men. *Journal of the American Medical Association, 288,* 1994–2000.

Tangri, S. S., & Hayes, S. M. (1997). Theories of sexual harassment. In W. O'Donohue (Ed.), *Sexual harassment: Theory, research, and treatment* (pp. 112–128). Needham Heights, MA: Allyn & Bacon.

Tangri, S. S., Burt, M. R., & Johnson, L. B. (1982). Sexual harassment at work: Three explanatory models. *Journal of Social Issues, 38*(4), 33–54.

Tannen, D. (1990). *You just don't understand: Women and men in conversation.* New York: William Morrow.

Tasker, F. (2005). Lesbian mothers, gay fathers, and their children: A review. *Journal of Developmental & Behavioral Pediatrics, 26,* 224–240.

Tavris, C. (1999). The science and politics of gender research: The meanings of difference. In D. Berstein (Ed.), *Gender and motivation* (Vol. 45, pp. 1–23). Lincoln: University of Nebraska Press.

Tavris, C., & Wade, C. (1984). *The longest war: Sex differences in perspective.* San Diego: Harcourt Brace Jovanovich.

Taylor, S. E., & Hall, J. A. (1982). Psychological androgyny: Theories, methods, and conclusions. *Psychological Bulletin, 92,* 347–366.

Taylor, S. E., Gonzaga, G. C., Klein, L. C., Hu, P., Greendale, G. A., & Seeman, T. E. (2006). Relation of oxytocin to psychological stress responses and hypothalamic-pituitary-adrenocortical axis activity in older women. *Psychosomatic Medicine, 68,* 238–245.

Taylor, S. E., Klein, L. C., Lewis, B. P., Gruenewald, T. L., Gurung, R. A. R., & Updegraff, J. A. (2000). Biobehavioral responses to stress in females: Tend-and-befriend, not fight-or-flight. *Psychological Review, 107,* 411–429.

Taylor, W. C., Ayars, C. L., Gladney, A. P., Peters, R. J., Jr., Roy, J. R., Prokhorov, A. V., Chamberlain, R. M., & Gritz, E. R. (1999). Beliefs about smoking among adolescents—gender and ethnic differences. *Journal of Child and Adolescent Substance Abuse, 8*(3), 37–54.

Teachman, J. (2003). Premarital sex, premarital cohabitation, and the risk of subsequent marital dissolution among women. *Journal of Marriage and Family, 65,* 444–455.

Templer, D. I., & Tomeo, M. E. (2002). Mean graduate record examination (GRE) score and gender distribution as a function of academic discipline. *Personality and Individual Differences, 32,* 175–179.

Tenenbaum, H. R., & Leaper, C. (2002). Are parents' gender schemas related to their children's gender-related cognitions? A meta-analysis. *Developmental Psychology, 38,* 615–630.

Tenenbaum, H. R., & Leaper, C. (2003). Parent-child conversations about science: The socialization of gender inequities? *Developmental Psychology, 39,* 34–47.

Terman, L. M., & Miles, C. C. (1936). *Sex and personality: Studies in masculinity and femininity.* New York: McGraw-Hill.

Testa, M., VanZile-Tamsen, C., Livingston, J. A., & Koss, M. P. (2004). Assessing women's experiences of sexual aggression using the Sexual Experiences Survey: Evidence for validity and implications for research. *Psychology of Women, 28,* 256–265.

Tevlin, J. (1998, November 29). The Eveleth Mines case. *Star Tribune.* Retrieved August 8, 2007, from *web.lexis-nexis.com/universe/docu.*

Thoits, P. A. (1992). Identity structures and psychological well-being: Gender and marital status comparisons. *Social Psychology Quarterly, 55*(3), 236–256.

Thomas, J. J., & Daubman, K. A. (2001). The relationship between friendship quality and self-esteem in adolescent girls and boys. *Sex Roles, 45,* 53–65.

Thomas-Hunt, M. C., & Phillips, K. W. (2004). When what you know is not enough: Expertise and gender dynamics in task groups. *Personality and Social Psychology Bulletin, 30,* 1585–1598.

Thompson, C. A., Klopf, D. W., & Ishii, S. (1991). A comparison of social style between Japanese and Americans. *Communication Research Reports, 8,* 165–172.

Thompson, E. H., Jr., & Pleck, J. H. (1995). Masculine ideologies: A review of research instrumentation on men and masculinities. In R. F. Levant & W. S. Pollack (Eds.), *A new psychology of men* (pp. 129–163). New York: Basic Books.

Thompson, J. M., Whiffen, V. E., & Blain, M. D. (1995). Depressive symptoms, sex and perceptions of intimate relationships. *Journal of Social and Personal Relationships, 12*(1), 49–66.

Thompson, L. (1991). Family work: Women's sense of fairness. *Journal of Family Issues, 12*(2), 181–196.

Thompson, R. A. (1998). The last word. *Eating Disorders, 6,* 207–210.

Thompson, R. A., & Sherman, R. T. (1999). Athletes, athletic performance, and eating disorders: Healthier alternatives. *Journal of Social Issues, 55*(2), 317–337.

Thomson, R., Murachver, T., & Green, J. (2001). Where is the gender in gendered language? *Psychological Science, 12,* 171–175.

Thornton, A., & Young-DeMarco, L. (2001). Four decades of trends in attitudes toward family issues in the United States: The 1960s through the 1990s. *Journal of Marriage and Family, 63,* 1009–1037.

Thunberg, M., & Dimberg, U. (2000). Gender differences in facial reactions to fear-relevant stimuli. *Journal of Nonverbal Behavior, 24,* 45–51.

Tiedemann, J. (2000). Parents' gender stereotypes and teachers' beliefs as predictors of children's concept of their mathematical ability in elementary school. *Journal of Educational Psychology, 92,* 144–151.

Tiger, L. (1969). *Men in groups.* New York: Random House.

Time. (1973, January 8). Biological Imperatives (pp. 34).

Timmers, M., Fischer, A. H., & Manstead, A. S. R. (1998). Gender differences in motives for regulating emotions. *Personality and Social Psychology Bulletin, 24,* 974–985.

Tjaden, P., & Thoennes, N. (2000). Extent, nature, and consequences of intimate partner violence: Findings from the National Violence against Women Survey. Retrieved November 12, 2007, from *www.ojp.usdoj.gov/nij.*

Tjaden, P., Thoennes, N., & Allison, C. J. (1999). Comparing violence over the life span in samples of same-sex and opposite-sex cohabitants. *Violence and Victims, 14,* 413–425.

Tolin, D. F., & Foa, E. B. (2006). Sex differences in trauma and posttraumatic stress disorder: A quantitative review of 25 years of research. *Psychological Bulletin, 132,* 959–992.

Tolman, D. L., Impett, E. A., Tracy, A. J., & Michael, A. (2006). Looking good, sounding good: Femininity ideology and adolescent girls' mental health. *Psychology of Women Quarterly, 30,* 85–95.

Tolson, A. (1977). *The limits of masculinity.* New York: Harper & Row.

Tornstam, L. (1992). Loneliness in marriage. *Journal of Social and Personal Relationships, 9,* 197–217.

Toro-Morn, M., & Sprecher, S. (2003). A cross-cultural comparison of mate preferences among university students; The United States vs. The People's Republic of China (PRC). *Journal of Comparative Family Studies, 34,* 151–170.

Toronto Star. (1986). Male hormones linked to math ability in junior high school boys, study finds. Retrieved June 9, 2000, from *web.lexis-nexis.com/universe/docu. . .*

Torsheim, T., Ravens-Sieberer, U., Hetland, J., Valimaa, R., Danielson, M., & Overpeck, M. (2006). Cross-national variation of gender differences in adolescent subjective health in Europe and North America. *Social Science & Medicine, 62,* 815–827.

Tower, R. B., & Kasl, S. V. (1996). Gender, marital closeness, and depressive symptoms in elderly couples. *Journal of Gerontology, 51B*(3), 115–129.

Trautner, H. M., Ruble, D. N., Cyphers, L., Kirsten, B., Behrendt, R., & Hartmann, P. (2005). Rigidity and flexibility of gender stereotypes in childhood: Developmental of differential? *Infant and Child Development, 14,* 365–381.

Travis, C. B. (2005). 2004 Carolyn Sherif award address: Heart disease and gender inequity. *Psychology of Women Quarterly, 29,* 15–23.

Treiber, F. A., Kamarck, T., Schneiderman, N., Sheffield, D., Kapuku, G., & Taylor, T. (2003). Cardiovascular reactivity and development of preclinical and clinical disease states. *Psychosomatic Medicine, 65,* 46–62.

Trenholm, C., Devaney, B., Fortson, K., Quay, L., Wheeler, J., & Clark, M. (2007). Impacts of Four Title V, Section 510 abstinence education programs. Retrieved June 7, 2007, from *aspe.hhs.gov/hsp/abstinence07/.*

Treynor, W., Gonzalez, R., & Nolen-Hoeksema, S. (2003). Rumination reconsidered: A psychometric analysis. *Cognitive Therapy and Research, 27,* 247–259.

Trudeau, K. J., Danoff-Burg, S., Revenson, T. A., Paget, S. A. (2003). Agency and communion in people with rheumatoid arthritis. *Sex Roles, 49,* 303–311.

Tschann, J. M. (1988). Self-disclosure in adult friendship: Gender and marital status differences. *Journal of Social and Personal Relationships, 5,* 65–81.

Tsui, L. (1998). The effects of gender, education, and personal skills self-confidence on income in business management. *Sex Roles, 38,* 363–373.

Tucker, J. S., Wingard, D. L., Friedman, H. S., & Schwartz, J. E. (1996). Marital history at midlife as a predictor of longevity: Alternative explanations to protective effect of marriage. *Health Psychology, 15,* 94–101.

Turner, R. A., Altemus, M., Enos, T., Cooper, B., & McGuinness, T. (1999). Preliminary research on plasma oxytocin in normal cycling women: Investigating emotion and interpersonal distress. *Psychiatry, 62*(2), 97–113.

Turner, R. J., & Avison, W. R. (1989). Gender and depression: Assessing exposure and vulnerability to life events in a chronically strained population. *Journal of Nervous and Mental Disease, 177*(8), 443–455.

Turner, T. (with Loder, K.). (1986). *I, Tina: My life story.* New York: Morrow.

Twenge, J. M. (1997). Attitudes toward women, 1970– 1995. *Psychology of Women Quarterly, 21,* 35–51.

Twenge, J. M., & Campbell, W. K. (2001). Age and birth cohort differences in self-esteem: A cross-temporal meta-analysis. *Personality and Social Psychology Review, 5,* 321–344.

Twenge, J. M., & Nolen-Hoeksema, S. (2002). Age, gender, race, socioeconomic status, and birth cohort differences on the Children's Depression Inventory: A meta-analysis. *Journal of Abnormal Psychology, 11,* 578–588.

Twenge, J. M., Campbell, W. K., & Foster, C. A. (2003). Parenthood and marital satisfaction: A meta-analytic review. *Journal of Marriage and Family, 65,* 574–583.

Tyrka, A. R., Waldron, I., Graber, J. A., & Brooks-Gunn, J. (2002). Prospective predictors of the onset of anorexic and bulimic syndromes. *International Journal of Eating Disorders, 32,* 282–290.

U.S. Bureau of Labor Statistics. (2003). *Median weekly earnings of full-time wage and salary workers by detailed occupation and sex.* Retrieved November 12, 2007, from *www.bls.gov/cps/cpsaat39.pdf.*

U.S. Bureau of the Census. (1991). *Current Population Reports, Series P-70, No.23, Family Division and Economic Hardship: The Short-Run Picture for Children.* Washington, DC: U.S. Government Printing Office.

U.S. Bureau of the Census. (1993). *Current Population Reports.* Washington, DC: U.S. Government Printing Office.

U.S. Bureau of the Census. (2003). *Median age at first marriage.* U.S. Census Bureau. Retrieved July 18, 2003, from *www.infoplease.com/ipa/A0005061.html.*

U.S. Census Bureau. (1998). *Statistical abstracts of the United States: 1998.* Washington, DC: United States Government Printing Office.

U.S. Census Bureau. (2003). *Statistical abstracts of the United States (Expectation of life at birth, 1970 to 2000, and projections, 2005 and 2010).* Retrieved November 12, 2007, from *www.census.gov/prod/2003pubs/02statab/vitstat. pdf.*

U.S. Census Bureau. (2004a). *Educational attainment in the United States: 2003. Current Population Reports*

(P20-550, 2-3). Retrieved January 12, 2007, from *www.census.gov/prod/2004pubs/p20-550.pdf*.

U.S. Census Bureau. (2004b). *Unmarried-partner households by sex of partners: 2004.* Retrieved February 21, 2007, from *www.census.gov/prod/2006pubs/07status/pop.pdf*.

U.S. Census Bureau. (2004c). *America's families and living arrangements: 2003. Current Population Reports* (P20-553). Retrieved November 12, 2007, from *www.census.gov/prod/2004pubs/p.20-553.pdf*.

U.S. Census Bureau. (2005a). *Median age at first marriage.* Retrieved February 21, 2007, from *factfinder.census.gov/servlet/DTTable?_bm=y&-geo_id=0100*.

U.S. Census Bureau. (2005b). *Number, timing, and duration of marriages and divorces: 2001.* Current population reports (P70-97). Retrieved November 12, 2007, from *www.sipp.census.gov/sipp/*.

U.S. Census Bureau. (2006a). *All parent/child situations, by type, race, and Hispanic origin of householder or reference person: 1970 to present.* Retrieved November 12, 2007, from *www.census.gov/population/socdemo/hh-fam/fm2.pdf*.

U.S. Census Bureau. (2006b). *Marital status of the population 15 years old and over, by sex and race: 1950 to present.* Retrieved November 12, 2007, from *www.census.gov/population/socdemo/hh-fam/ms1.pdf*.

U.S. Census Bureau. (2007a). *Participation in NCAA Sports: 2004 to 2005.* Retrieved November 12, 2007 from *www.census.gov/compendia/statab/2007edition.html*.

U.S. Census Bureau. (2007b). *Death rates by age, sex, and race: 1950 to 2004.* Retrieved November 12, 2007, from *www.census.gov/prod/2006pubs/07statab/vitstat.pdf*.

U.S. Census Bureau. (2007c). *Expectations of life at birth, 1970 to 2004, and projections, 2010 and 2015.* Retrieved November 12, 2007, from *www.census.gov/prod/2006pubs/07statab/vitstats.pdf*.

U.S. Census Bureau. (2007d). *Unemployed and unemployment rates by educational attainment, sex, race, and Hispanic origin: 1992 to 2005.* Retrieved November 12, 2007, from *www.census.gov/compendia/statab/labor_force_employment_earnings*.

U.S. Census Bureau. (2007e). *Employed civilians by occupation, sex, race, and Hispanic origin: 2005.* Retrieved November 12, 2007, from *www.census.gov/prod/2006pubs/07statab/labor.pdf*.

U.S. Census Bureau. (2007f). *Labor force participation rates for wives, husband present by age of own youngest child: 1975 to 2005.* Retrieved November 12, 2007, from *www.census.gov/prod/2006pubs/07statab/labor.pdf*.

U.S. Department of Education, National Center for Educational Statistics. (2004). *Mini-digest of education statistics, 2003* (NCES 2005-017). Retrieved January 12, 2007, from *nces.ed.gov/pubs2003/2003061.pdf*.

U.S. Department of Education. (2000). *Educational equity for girls and women* (NCES 2000-030). Washington, DC: National Center for Education Statistics.

U.S. Department of Education. (2003). *Postsecondary institutions in the United States: Fall 2002 and degrees and other awards conferred: 2001–02*: Institute of Education Sciences Washington, DC: National Center for Education Statistics (NCES 2004-154).

U.S. Department of Education. (2005). *Single-sex versus coeducational schooling: A systematic review.* Retrieved November 12, 2007, from *www.ed.gov/rschstat/eval/other/single-sex/single-sex.pdf*.

U.S. Department of Health and Human Services. (1996). *Physical activity and health: A report of the Surgeon General.* Atlanta, GA: U.S. Department of Health and Human Services.

U.S. Department of Health and Human Services. (2004). *The health consequences of smoking: A report of the Surgeon General.* Atlanta, GA: Department of Health and Human Services.

U.S. Department of Health and Human Services. (2005a). *Middle School youth risk behavior survey 2003.* Retrieved November 12, 2007, from *www.cdc.gov/HealthyYouth/yrbs/middleschool2003/pdf/fullreport.pdf*.

U.S. Department of Health and Human Services. (2005b). *Fertility, family planning, and reproductive health of U.S. women: Data from the 2002 national survey of family growth.* Retrieved November 12, 2007, from *www.cdc.gov/nchs/data/series/sr_23/sr23_025.pdf*.

U.S. Department of Labor. (2006). *Women in the labor force: A databook.* Retrieved November 13, 2007, from *www.bls.gov/cps/wlf-databook-2006.pdf*.

U.S. Department of Labor. (2007a). *The employment situation: June 2007* (No. USDL 07-1015). Washington, DC: Bureau of Labor Statistics.

U.S. Department of Labor. (2007b). *Labor force statistics from the current population survey.* Retrieved November 13, 2007, from *www.bls.gov/cps*.

U.S. Department of Transportation. (2005a). *Safety belt use in 2004—demographic results.* Retrieved November 13, 2007, from *www-nrd.nhtsa.dot.gov/Pubs/809848.pdf*.

U.S. Department of Transportation. (2005b). *Traffic Safety Facts 2005.* Retrieved November 13, 2007, from *www.nrd.nhtsa.dot.gov/pdf/nrd-30/NCSA/TSFAnn/TSF2005.pdf*.

Udry, J. R., Morris, N. M., & Kovenock, J. (1995). Androgen effects on women's gendered behaviour. *Journal of Biosocial Science, 27,* 359–368.

Ulin, P. R., Cayemittes, M., & Metellus, E. (1993). Haitian women's role in sexual decision-making: The gap between AIDS knowledge and behavior change. Retrieved July 13, 2007, from *www.FHI.org/en/RH/Pubs/booksReports/haiti-wom/haitpres4.htm*.

Ullman, S. E. (1997). Review and critique of empirical studies of rape avoidance. *Criminal Justice and Behavior, 24*(2), 177–204.

Ullman, S. E., Karabatsos, G., & Koss, M. P. (1999). Alcohol and sexual assault in a national sample of college women. *Journal of Interpersonal Violence, 14*(6), 603–625.

Umberson, D. (1987). Family status and health behaviors: Social control as a dimension of social integration. *Journal of Health and Social Behavior, 28*, 306–319.

Umberson, D., & Williams, K. (2005). Marital quality, health, and aging: Gender equity? *Journals of Gerontology, 60B*, 109–112.

Umberson, D., Williams, K., Powers, D. A., Liu, H., & Needham, B. (2006). You make me sick: Marital quality and health over the life course. *Journal of Health and Social Behavior, 47*, 1–16.

Umberson, D., Wortman, C. B., & Kessler, R. C. (1992). Widowhood and depression: Explaining long-term gender differences in vulnerability. *Journal of Health and Social Behavior, 33*, 10–24.

Underwood, M. K. (2003). *Social aggression among girls.* New York: The Guilford Press.

Unger, R. K. (1990). Imperfect reflections on reality: Psychology constructs gender. In R. T. Hare-Mustin & J. Marecek (Eds.), *Making a difference: Psychology and the construction of gender* (pp. 102–149). New Haven, CT: Yale University Press.

United States Merit Systems Protection Board. (1981). *Sexual harassment in the federal workplace: Is it a problem?* Washington, DC: U.S. Government Printing Office.

United States Merit Systems Protection Board. (1988). *Sexual harassment in the federal workplace: An update.* Washington, DC: U.S. Government Printing Office.

United States Merit Systems Protection Board. (1995). *Sexual harassment in the federal workplace: Trends, progress, continuing challenges.* Washington, DC: U.S. Government Printing Office.

Updegraff, K. A., Eccles, J. S., Barber, B. L., & O'Brien, K. M. (1996). Course enrollment as self-regulatory behavior: Who takes optional high school math courses? *Learning and Individual Differences, 8*(3), 239–259.

Urberg, K. A., Degirmencioglu, S. M., Tolson, J. M., & Halliday-Scher, K. (1995). The structure of adolescent peer networks. *Developmental Psychology, 31*, 540–547.

Uvnas-Moberg, K. (1997). Oxytocin linked antistress effects—the relaxation and growth response. *Acta Physiologica Scandinavica, 640*, 38–42.

Valentine, S. (1998). Self-esteem and men's negative stereotypes of women who work. *Psychological Reports, 83*, 920–922.

Valian, V. (1998). *Why so slow? The advancement of women.* Cambridge, MA: The MIT Press.

van Beek, Y., van Dolderen, M. S. M., & Dubas, J. J. S. D. (2006). Gender-specific development of nonverbal behaviours and mild depression in adolescence. *Journal of Child Psychology and Psychiatry, 47*, 1272–1283.

van den Berg, P., Neumark-Sztainer, D., Hannan, P. J., & Haines, J. (2007). Is dieting advice from magazines helpful or harmful? Five-year associations with weight- control behaviors and psychological outcomes in adolescents. *Pediatrics, 119*, e30–e37.

van Engen, M. L., & Willemsen, T. M. (2004). Sex and leadership styles: A meta-analysis of research published in the 1990's. *Psychological Reports, 94*, 3–18.

van Grootheest, D. S., Beekman, A. T. F., van Groenou, M. I. B., & Deeg, D. J. H. (1999). Sex differences in depression after widowhood: Do men suffer more? *Social Psychiatry and Psychiatric Epidemiology, 34*, 391–398.

van Middendorp, H., Geenen, R., Sorbi, M. J., Hox, J. J., Vingerhoets, A. J. J. M., Doornen, L. J. P., et al. (2005). Gender differences in emotion regulation and relationships with perceived health in patients with rheumatoid arthritis. *Women & Health, 42*, 75–97.

Vangelisti, A. L., & Daly, J. A. (1997). Gender differences in standards for romantic relationships. *Personal Relationships, 4*, 203–219.

Vazquez-Nuttall, E., Romero-Garcia, I., & de Leon, B. (1987). Sex roles and perceptions of femininity and masculinity of Hispanic women. *Psychology of Women Quarterly, 11*, 409–425.

Veiel, H. O. F., Kuhner, C., Brill, G., & Ihle, W. (1992). Psychosocial correlates of clinical depression after psychiatric inpatient treatment: Methodological issues and baseline differences between recovered and non-recovered patients. *Psychological Medicine, 22*, 415–427.

Veniegas, R. C., & Conley, T. D. (2000). Biological research on women's sexual orientations: Evaluating the scientific evidence. *Journal of Social Issues, 56*(2), 267–282.

Veniegas, R. C., & Peplau, L. A. (1997). Power and the quality of same-sex friendships. *Psychology of Women Quarterly, 21*, 279–297.

Verbrugge, L. M. (1985). Gender and health: An update on hypotheses and evidence. *Journal of Health and Social Behavior, 26*, 156–182.

Verbrugge, L. M. (1989). The twain meet: Empirical explanations of sex differences in health and mortality. *Journal of Health and Social Behavior, 30*, 282–304.

Verkuyten, M., & Masson, K. (1996). Culture and gender differences in the perception of friendship by adolescents. *International Journal of Psychology, 31*(5), 207–217.

Viki, G. T., Abrams, D., & Masser, B. (2004). Evaluating stranger and acquaintance rape: The role of benevolent sexism in perpetrator blame and recommended sentence length. *Law and Human Behavior, 28*, 295–303.

Viki, G. T., Massey, K., & Masser, B. (2005). When chivalry backfires: Benevolent sexism and attitudes toward Myra Hindley. *Legal and Criminological Psychology, 10*, 109–120.

Vitaro, F., Brendgen, M., & Tremblay, R. E. (2002). Reactively and proactively aggressive children: Antecedent and subsequent characteristics. *Journal of Child Psychology and Psychiatry, 43*(4), 495–506.

Vogel, D. L., & Karney, B. R. (2002). Demands and withdrawal in newlyweds: Elaborating on the social structure hypothesis. *Journal of Social and Personal Relationships, 19,* 685–701.

Vohs, K. D., & Baumeister, R. F. (2004). Sexual passion, intimacy, and gender. In D. J. Mashek & A. Aron (Eds.), *Handbook of closeness and intimacy* (pp. 189–199). Mahwah, NJ: Lawrence Erlbaum Associates.

Vonk, R., & van Nobelen, D. (1993). Masculinity and femininity in the self with an intimate partner: Men are not always men in the company of women. *Journal of Social and Personal Relationships, 10,* 627–630.

Voyer, D., Voyer, S., & Bryden, M. P. (1995). Magnitude of sex differences in spatial abilities: A meta-analysis and consideration of critical variables. *Psychological Bulletin, 117,* 250–270.

Wade, M. E. (2001). Women and salary negotiation: The costs of self-advocacy. *Psychology of Women Quarterly, 25,* 65–76.

Wade, T. J., & Pevalin, D. J. (2004). Marital transitions and mental health. *Journal of Health and Social Behavior, 45,* 155–170.

Wadsworth, M. E. J., Montgomery, S. M., & Bartley, M. J. (1999). The persisting effect of unemployment on health and social well-being in men early in working life. *Social Science & Medicine, 48,* 1491–1499.

Wagner, W., Kirchler, E., Clack, F., Tekarslan, E., & Verma, J. (1990). Male dominance, role segregation, and spouses' interdependence in conflict. *Journal of Cross-Cultural Psychology, 21*(1), 48–70.

Wainright, J. L., Russell, S. T., & Patterson, C. J. (2004). Psychosocial adjustment, school outcomes, and romantic relationships of adolescents with same-sex parents. *Child Development, 75,* 1886–1898.

Wainright, N. W. J., & Surtees, P. G. (2002). Childhood adversity, gender and depression over the life-course. *Journal of Affective Disorders, 72,* 33–44.

Waldfogel, J. (1997). The effect of children on women's wages. *American Sociological Review, 62,* 209–217.

Waldron, I. (1983). Sex differences in illness incidence, prognosis and mortality: Issues and evidence. *Social Science & Medicine, 17*(16), 1107–1123.

Waldron, I. (1995). Contributions of changing gender differences in behavior and social roles to changing gender differences in mortality. In D. Sabo (Ed.), *Men's health and illness: Gender, power, and the body* (pp. 22–45). Thousand Oaks, CA: Sage.

Waldron, I. (1997). Changing gender roles and gender differences in health behavior. In D. S. Gochman (Ed.), *Handbook of health behavior research: I. Personal and social determinants* (pp. 303–328). New York: Plenum Press.

Waldron, I. (1998). Factors determining the sex ratio at birth. In Department of Economic and Social Affairs Population Division (Ed.), *Too young to die: Genes or gender?* (pp. 53–63). New York: United Nations.

Waldron, I. (2000). Trends in gender differences in mortality: Relationships to changing gender differences in behaviour

and other causal factors. In E. Annandale & K. Hunt (Eds.), *Gender inequalities in health* (pp. 150–181). Philadelphia: Open University Press.

Waldron, I., Hughes, M. E., & Brooks, T. L. (1996). Marriage protection and marriage selection: Prospective evidence for reciprocal effects of marital status and health. *Social Science & Medicine, 43*(1), 113–123.

Waldron, I., Weiss, C. C., & Hughes, M. E. (1998). Interacting effects of multiple roles on women's health. *Journal of Health and Social Behavior, 39,* 216–236.

Waldron, V. R., & DiMare, L. (1998). Gender as a culturally determined construct: Communication styles in Japan and the United States. In D. J. Canary & K. Dindia (Eds.), *Sex differences and similarities in communication* (pp. 179–201). Mahwah, NJ: Erlbaum.

Walker, K. (1994). Men, women, and friendship: What they say, what they do. *Gender & Society, 8,* 246–265.

Walker, L. E. (1979). *The battered woman.* New York: Harper & Row.

Walker, L. S., & Green, J. W. (1986). The social context of adolescent self-esteem. *Journal of Youth and Adolescence, 15,* 315–322.

Walker, L. S., & Zeman, J. L. (1992). Parental response to child illness behavior. *Journal of Pediatric Psychology, 17*(1), 49–71.

Wallace, H. (1999). *Family violence: Legal, medical, and social perspectives.* Boston: Allyn & Bacon.

Walters, A. E., Stuhlmacher, A. F., & Meyer, L. L. (1998). Gender and negotiator competitiveness: A meta-analysis. *Organizational Behavior and Human Decision Processes, 76,* 1–29.

Walters, E. E., & Kendler, K. S. (1995). Anorexia nervosa and anorexic-like syndromes in a population based female twin sample. *American Journal of Psychiatry, 152*(1), 64–71.

Walumbwa, F. O., Wu, C., & Ojode, L. A. (2004). Gender and instructional outcomes: The mediating role of leadership style. *Journal of Management Development, 23,* 124–140.

Wang, T. H., & Creedon, C. F. (1989). Sex role orientations, attributions for achievement, and personal goals of Chinese youth. *Sex Roles, 20,* 473–485.

Wannan, G., & Fombonne, E. (1998). Gender differences in rates and correlates of suicidal behavior amongst child psychiatric outpatients. *Journal of Adolescence, 21,* 371–381.

Ward, C. A. (1995). *Attitudes toward rape.* Thousand Oaks, CA: Sage.

Wardle, J., Haase, A. M., Steptoe, A., Nillapun, M., Jonwutiwes, K., & Bellisle, F. (2004). Gender differences in food choice: The contribution of health beliefs and dieting. *Annals of Behavioral Medicine, 27,* 107–116.

Watkins, D., & Yu, J. (1993). Gender differences in the source and level of self-esteem of Chinese college students. *Journal of Social Psychology, 133*(3), 347–352.

Watson, C. M., Quatman, T., & Edler, E. (2002). Career aspirations of adolescent girls: Effects of achievement level, grade, and single-sex school environment. *Sex Roles, 46,* 323–335.

Way, N., & Greene, M. L. (2006). Trajectories of perceived friendship quality during adolescence: The patterns and contextual predictors. *Journal of Research on Adolescence, 16,* 293–319.

Way, N., Becker, B. E., & Greene, M. L. (2006). Friendships among Black, Latino, and Asian American adolescents in an urban context. In L. Balter & C. S. Tamis-LeMonda (Eds.), *Child psychology: A handbook of contemporary issues* (pp. 415–443). New York: Psychology Press.

Weich, S., Sloggett, A., & Lewis, G. (1998). Social roles and gender difference in the prevalence of common mental disorders. *British Journal of Psychiatry, 173,* 489–493.

Weiner, B., Frieze, I. H. Kukla, A., Reed, L., Rest, S., & Rosenbaum, R. M. (1971). *Perceiving the causes of success and failure.* Morristown, NJ: General Learning Press.

Weiner, R. L., & Gutek, B. A. (1999). Advances in sexual harassment research, theory, and policy. *Psychology, Public Policy and Law, 5,* 507–518.

Weinstock, J. S. (1998). Lesbian, gay, bisexual, and transgender friendships in adulthood. In C. J. Patterson & A. R. D'Augelli (Eds.), *Lesbian, gay, and bisexual identities in families: Psychological perspectives* (pp. 122–153). London: Oxford University Press.

Weisbuch, M., Beal, D., & O'Neal, E. C. (1999). How masculine ought I be? Men's masculinity and aggression. *Sex Roles, 40,* 583–592.

Weissman, M. M., Bland, R. C., Canino, G. J., Faravelli, C., Greenwald, S., Hwu, H-G., et al. (1996). Cross-national epidemiology of major depression and bipolar disorder. *Journal of the American Medical Association, 276,* 293–299.

Weitzman, L. J. (1985). *The divorce revolution: The unexpected social and economic consequences for women and children in America.* New York: The Free Press.

Wellman, B. (1992). Men in networks: Private communities, domestic friendships. In P. M. Nardi (Ed.), *Men's friendships* (pp. 74–114). Newbury Park, CA: Sage.

Wells, B. E., & Twenge, J. M. (2005). Changes in young people's sexual behavior and attitudes, 1943–1999: A cross-temporal meta-analysis. *Review of General Psychology, 9,* 249–261.

Wenger, N. K. (1998). Coronary heart disease in women: Evolution of our knowledge. In K. Orth-Gomer, M. Chesney, & N. K. Wenger (Eds.), *Women, stress, and heart disease* (pp. 1–15). Mahwah, NJ: Erlbaum.

Werking, K. J. (1997a). Cross-sex friendship research as idealogical practice. In S. Duck (Ed.), *Handbook of personal relationships: Theory, research, and interventions* (Second ed., pp. 391–410). West Sussex, England: Wiley.

Werking, K. J. (1997b). *We're just good friends: Women and men in nonromantic relationships.* New York: Guilford Press.

Werner, N. E., & Crick, N. R. (1999). Relational aggression and social-psychological adjustment in a college sample. *Journal of Abnormal Psychology, 108,* 615–623.

Wethington, E., & Kessler, R. C. (1989). Employment, parental responsibility, and psychological distress. *Journal of Family Issues, 10*(4), 527–546.

Wethington, E., McLeod, J. D., & Kessler, R. S. (1987). The importance of life events for explaining sex differences in psychological distress. In R. C. Barnett, L. Biener, & G. K. Baruch (Eds.), *Gender and stress* (pp. 144–156). New York: Free Press.

Wetter, D. W., Fiore, M. C., Young, T. B., McClure, J. B., de Moor, C. A., & Baker, T. B. (1999a). Gender differences in response to nicotine replacement therapy: Objective and subjective indexes of tobacco withdrawal. *Experimental and Clinical Psychopharmacology, 7*(2), 135–144.

Wetter, D. W., Kenford, S. L., Smith, S. S., Fiore, M. C., Jorenby, D. E., & Baker, T. B. (1999b). Gender differences in smoking cessation. *Journal of Consulting and Clinical Psychology, 67,* 555–562.

Wetzel, P. J. (1988). Are powerless communication strategies the Japanese norm? *Language and Society, 17,* 555–564.

Whatley, M. A. (1996). Victim characteristics influencing attributions of responsibility to rape victims: A meta-analysis. *Aggression and Violent Behavior, 1*(2), 81–95.

Wheelan, S. A., & Verdi, A. F. (1992). Differences in male and female patterns of communication in groups: A methodological artifact? *Sex Roles, 27,* 1–15.

Wheeler, L., Reis, H., & Nezlek, J. (1983). Loneliness, social interaction, and sex roles. *Journal of Personality and Social Psychology, 45,* 943–953.

Whisman, M. A., & Uebelacker, L. A. (2006). Impairment and distress associated with relationship discord in a national sample of married or cohabiting adults. *Journal of Family Psychology, 20,* 369–377.

Whisman, M. A., Weinstock, L. M., & Tolejko, N. (2006). Marriage and depression. In C. L. Keyes & S. H. Goodman (Eds.), *Women and depression: A handbook for the social, behavioral, and biomedical sciences* (pp. 219–240). New York: Cambridge University Press.

Whitacre, C. C., Reingold, S. C., O'Looney, P. A., & the Task Force on Gender, M. S. A. A. (1999). Biomedicine: A gender gap in autoimmunity. *Science, 283,* 1277–1278.

White, J. W., & Kowalski, R. M. (1998). Male violence toward women: An integrated perspective. In R. G. Geen & E. Donnerstein (Eds.), *Human aggression: Theories, research, and implications for social policy* (pp. 203–228). San Diego, CA: Academic Press.

White, P. G., Young, K., & McTeer, W. G. (1995). Sport, masculinity and the injured body. In D. F. Sabo & D. F. Gordon (Eds.), *Men's health and illness: Gender, power, and the body* (pp. 158–182). Thousand Oaks, CA: Sage.

Whitehead, B. D., & Popenoe, D. (2001, June 27). Singles seek soul mates for marriage. *Gallup News Service.*

Whiting, B. B., & Edwards, C. P. (1988). *Children of different worlds.* Cambridge, MA: Harvard University Press.

Whitley, B. E., Jr. (1984). Sex role orientation and psychological well-being: Two meta-analyses. *Sex Roles, 12,* 207–225.

Whitley, B. E., Jr. (1991). A short form of the expanded attributional style questionnaire. *Journal of Personality Assessment, 56,* 365–369.

Whitley, B. E., Jr. (2001). Gender-role variables and attitudes toward homosexuality. *Sex Roles, 45,* 691–721.

Whitley, B. E., Jr., & Gridley, B. E. (1993). Sex role orientation, self-esteem, and depression: A latent variables analysis. *Personality and Social Psychology Bulletin, 19,* 363–369.

Whitley, B. E., Jr., & Kite, M. E. (1995). Sex differences in attitudes toward homosexuality: A comment on Oliver and Hyde (1993). *Psychological Bulletin, 117,* 146–154.

Whitley, B. E., Jr., Michael, S. T., & Tremont, G. (1991). Testing for sex differences in the relationship between attributional style and depression. *Sex Roles, 24,* 753–758.

Whitley, J., B. E., & Egisdottir, S. (2000). The gender belief system, authoritarianism, social dominance orientation, and heterosexuals' attitudes toward lesbians and gay men. *Sex Roles, 42,* 947–967.

Wiener, R. L., & Gutek, B. A. (1999). Advances in sexual harassment research, theory, and policy. *Psychology, Public Policy and Law, 5*(3), 507–518.

Wigfield, A., & Eccles, J. S. (2002). The development of competence beliefs, expectancies for success, and achievement values from childhood through adolescence. In A. Wigfield & J. S. Eccles (Eds.), *Development of achievement motivation* (pp. 91–120). San Diego, CA: Academic Press.

Wilcox, S., Aragaki, A., Mouton, C. P., Evenson, K. R., Wassertheil-Smoller, S., & Loevinger, B. L. (2003). The effects of widowhood on physical and mental health, health behaviors, and health outcomes: The women's health initiative. *Health Psychology, 22,* 513–522.

Willen, H., & Montgomery, H. (1996). The impact of wish for children and having children on attainment and importance of life values. *Journal of Comparative Family Studies, 27*(3), 499–518.

Williams, C. (2000). Doing health, doing gender: Teenagers, diabetes and asthma. *Social Science & Medicine, 50,* 387–396.

Williams, C. L. (1998). The glass escalator: Hidden advantages for men in the female professions. In M. S. Kimmel & M. A. Messner (Eds.), *Men's lives* (pp. 285–299). Boston: Allyn & Bacon.

Williams, C., & Bybee, J. (1994). What do children feel guilty about? Developmental and gender differences. *Developmental Psychology, 30,* 617–623.

Williams, D. R. (2003). The health of men: Structured inequalities and opportunities. *American Journal of Public Health, 93,* 724–731.

Williams, J. (1999). *Unbending gender: Why family and work conflict and what to do about it.* New York: Oxford University Press.

Williams, J. E., & Best, D. L. (1990). *Measuring sex stereotypes: A multination study* (Rev. ed.). Thousand Oaks, CA: Sage.

Williams, K., & Umberson, D. (2004). Marital status, marital transitions, and health: A gendered life course perspective. *Journal of Health and Social Behavior, 45,* 81–98.

Williams, S. L., & Frieze, I. H. (2005). Patterns of violent relationships, psychological distress, and marital satisfaction in a national sample of men and women. *Sex Roles, 52,* 771–784.

Williams, S. P., Gardos, P. S., Ortiz-Torres, B., Tross, S., & Ehrhardt, A. A. (2001). Urban women's negotiation strategies for safer sex with their male partners. *Women & Health, 33,* 133–148.

Williams, W. L. (1993). Persistence and change in the Berdache tradition among contemporary Lakota Indians. In L. D. Garnets & D. C. Kimmel (Eds.), *Psychological perspectives on lesbian and gay male experiences* (pp. 339–347). New York: Columbia University Press.

Williamson, B. F. (1985). Victims of reform. *The New York Times* October 13, 1985, Sunday, Late City Final Edition. Retrieved May 21, 2007, from *web.lexis-nexis.com/universe/printdoc.*

Williamson, I. (1999). Why are gay men a high risk group for eating disturbance? *European Eating Disorders Review, 7*(1), 1–4.

Williamson, I., & Hartley, P. (1998). British research into the increased vulnerability of young gay men to eating disturbance and body dissatisfaction. *European Eating Disorders Review, 6*(3), 160–170.

Willis, F. N., Jr., & Briggs, L. F. (1992). Relationship and touch in public settings. *Journal of Nonverbal Behavior, 16*(1), 55–63.

Wilsnack, R. W., Vogeltanz, N. D., Wilsnack, S. C., & Harris, T. R. (2000). Gender differences in alcohol consumption and adverse drinking consequences: Cross-cultural patterns. *Addiction, 95*(2), 251–265.

Wilson, D. K., & Ampey-Thornhill, G. (2001). The role of gender and family support on dietary compliance in an African American adolescent hypertension prevention study. *Annals of Behavioral Medicine, 23,* 59–67.

Wilson, D. K., Kliewer, W., Bayer, L., Jones, D., Welleford, A., Heiney, M. et al. (1999). The influence of gender and emotional versus instrumental support on cardiovascular reactivity in African-American adolescents. *Annals of Behavioral Medicine, 21,* 235–243.

Wilson, M., & Daly, M. (1985). Competitiveness, risk taking and violence: The young male syndrome. *Ethology and Sociobiology, 6,* 59–73.

Wing, R. R., & Klem, M. L. (1997). Obesity. In S. J. Gallant, G. P. Keita, & R. Royak-Schaler (Eds.), *Health care for women: Psychological, social, and behavioral influences* (pp. 115–131). Washington, DC: American Psychological Association.

Winstead, B. A., Derlega, V. J., & Rose, S. (1997). *Gender and close relationships.* Thousand Oaks, CA: Sage.

Winstead, B. A., Derlega, V. J., Montgomery, M. J., & Pilkington, C. (1995). The quality of friendships at work and job satisfaction. *Journal of Social and Personal Relationships, 12,* 199–215.

Winstead, B., & Sanchez, J. (2005). Gender and psychopathology. In J. E. Maddux & B. A. Winstead (Eds.), *Psychopathology: Foundations for a contemporary understanding* (pp. 39–61). Mahwah, NJ: Lawrence Erlbaum Associates.

Wise, E. A., Price, D. D., Myers, C. D., Heft, M. W., & Robinson, M. E. (2002). Gender role expectations of pain: Relationship to experimental pain perception. *Pain, 96,* 335–342.

Women and Girls Foundation. (2006). *The girlcott story.* Retrieved January 23, 2007, from *www.girl12girlgrants.com/section_girlsOurVoices/girlcott.htm.*

Wong, F. Y., McCreary, D. R., Carpenter, K. M., Engle, A., & Korchynsky, R. (1999). Gender-related factors influencing perceptions of homosexuality. *Journal of Homosexuality, 37,* 19–31.

Woo, M., & Oei, T. P. S. (2006). The MMPI-2 gender-masculine and gender-feminine scales: Gender roles as predictors of psychological health in clinical patients. *International Journal of Psychology, 41,* 413–422.

Wood, E., Desmarais, S., & Gugula, S. (2002). The impact of parenting experience on gender stereotyped toy play of children. *Sex Roles, 47,* 39–49.

Wood, R. G., Corcoran, M. E., & Courant, P. N. (1993). Pay differences among the highly paid: The male-female earnings gap in lawyers' salaries. *Journal of Labor Economics, 11*(3), 417–441.

Wood, W., & Eagly, A. H. (2002). A cross-cultural analysis of the behavior of women and men: Implications for the origins of sex differences. *Psychological Bulletin, 128,* 699–727.

Wood, W., & Karten, S. J. (1986). Sex differences in interaction style as a product of perceived sex differences in competence. *Journal of Personality and Social Psychology, 50,* 341–347.

Wood, W., & Rhodes, N. (1992). Sex differences in interaction style in task groups. In C. L. Ridgeway (Ed.), *Gender, interaction, and inequality* (pp. 97–121). New York: Springer-Verlag.

Woodside, D. B., Garfinkel, P. E., Lin, E., Goering, P., Kaplan, A. S., Goldbloom, D. S., et al. (2001). Comparisons of men with full or partial eating disorders, men without eating disorders, and women with eating disorders in the community. *American Journal of Psychiatry, 158,* 570–574.

Woodzicka, J. A., & LaFrance, M. (2005). The effects of subtle sexual harassment on women's performance in a job interview. *Sex Roles, 53,* 67–77.

Worell, J., & Goodheart, C. D. (Eds.). (2006). *Handbook of girls' and womens' psychological health.* New York: Oxford University Press.

Workman, J. E., & Freeburg, E. W. (1999). An examination of date rape, victim dress, and perceiver variables within the context of attribution theory. *Sex Roles, 41,* 261–277.

World Factbook. (2007). Field listing: Life expectancy at birth. Retrieved February 26, 2007, from *www.cia.gov/cia/publications/factbook/fields/2102.html.*

World Health Organization. (2005). *Suicide rates per 100,000 by country, year and sex.* Retrieved March 7, 2007, from *www.who.int/mental_health/prevention/suicide_rates/en/index.html.*

Wright, D. E. (1999). *Personal relationships: An interdisciplinary approach.* Mountain View, CA: Mayfield.

Wright, P. H. (1982). Men's friendships, women's friendships and the alleged inferiority of the latter. *Sex Roles, 8,* 1–20.

Wright, P. H. (1985). The acquaintance description form. In S. Duck & D. Perlman (Eds.), *Understanding personal relationships: An interdisciplinary approach* (pp. 39–62). Beverly Hills, CA: Sage.

Wright, P. H. (1989). Gender differences in adults' same- and cross-gender friendships. In R. G. Adams & R. Blieszner (Eds.), *Older adult friendship: Structure and process* (pp. 197–221). Newbury Park, CA: Sage.

Wright, P. H. (2006). Toward an expanded orientation to the comparative study of women's and men's same-sex friendships. In K. Dindia & D. J. Canary (Eds.), *Sex differences and similarities in communication* (Second ed.) (pp. 37–57). Mahwah, NJ: Lawrence Erlbaum Associates Publishers.

Wright, P. H., & Scanlon, M. B. (1991). Gender role orientation and friendship: Some attenuation, but gender differences abound. *Sex Roles, 24,* 551–566.

Wright, R. A., Murray, J. B., Storey, P. L., & Williams, B. J. (1997). Ability analysis of gender relevance and sex differences in cardiovascular response to behavioral challenge. *Journal of Personality and Social Psychology, 73,* 405–417.

Writing Group for the Women's Health Initiative Investigators. (2002). Risks and benefits of estrogen plus progestin in healthy postmenopausal women: Principal results from the Women's Health Initiative randomized controlled trial. *Journal of the American Medical Association, 288,* 321–333.

Wu, T. Y., Rose, S. E., & Bancroft, J. M. (2006). Gender differences in health risk behaviors and physical activity among middle school students. *The Journal of School Nursing, 22,* 25–30.

Wyke, S., Hunt, K., & Ford, G. (1998). Gender differences in consulting a general practitioner for common symptoms of minor illness. *Social Science & Medicine, 46*(7), 901–906.

Xu, X., Hudspeth, C. D., & Bartkowski, J. P. (2006). The role of cohabitation in remarriage. *Journal of Marriage and Family, 68,* 261–274.

Yee, D. K., & Eccles, J. S. (1988). Parent perceptions and attributions for children's math achievement. *Sex Roles, 19,* 317–333.

Yee, J. L., & Schulz, R. (2000). Gender differences in psychiatric morbidity among family caregivers: A review and analysis. *Gerontologist, 40*(2), 147–164.

Yoder, C. Y., Shute, G. E., & Tryban, G. M. (1990). Community recognition of objective and subjective characteristics of depression. *American Journal of Community Psychology, 18*(4), 547–566.

Young, R. F., & Kahana, E. (1993). Gender, recovery from late life heart attack and medical care. *Women and Health, 20*(1), 11–31.

Zaharias, G., Piterman, L., & Liddell, M. (2004). Doctors and patients: Gender interaction in the consultation. *Academic Medicine, 79,* 148–155.

Zahn-Waxler, C., & Polanichka, N. (2004). All things interpersonal. In M. Putallaz & K. L. Bierman (Eds.), *Aggression, antisocial behavior, and violence among girls: A developmental perspective* (pp. 48–70). New York: Guilford Publications.

Zandbelt, L. C., Smets, E. M. A., Oort, F. J., Godfried, M. H., & de Haes, H. C. J. M. (2006). Determinants of physicians' patient-centred behaviour in the medical specialist encounter. *Social Science & Medicine, 63,* 899–891.

Zarbatany, L., Conley, R., & Pepper, S. (2004). Personality and gender differences in friendship needs and experiences in preadolescence and young adulthood. *International Journal of Behavioral Development, 28,* 299–310.

Zarbatany, L., McDougall, P., & Hymel, S. (2000). Gender-differentiated experience in the peer culture: Links to intimacy in preadolescence. *Social Development, 9,* 62–79.

Zemore, S. E., Fiske, S. T., & Kim, H.-J. (2000). Gender stereotypes and the dynamics of social interaction. In T. Eckes & H. M. Trautner (Eds.), *The developmental social psychology of gender* (pp. 207–241). Mahwah, NJ: Erlbaum.

Zhang, Q., & Wang, Y. (2004). Socioeconomic inequality of obesity in the United States: Do gender, age, and ethnicity matter? *Social Science & Medicine, 58,* 1171–1180.

Zhu, S. H., Sun, J., Billings, S. C., Choi, W. S., & Malarcher, A. (1999). Predictors of smoking cessation in U.S. adolescents. *American Journal of Preventive Medicine, 16*(3), 202–207.

Zimmerman, R. S., Sprecher, S., Langer, L. M., & Holloway, C. D. (1995). Adolescents' perceived ability to say no to unwanted sex. *Journal of Adolescent Research, 10*(3), 383–399.

Zlotnick, C., Rothschild, L., & Zimmerman, M. (2002). The role of gender in the clinical presentation of patients with borderline personality disorder. *Journal of Personality Disorders, 16,* 277–282.

Zuckerman, M. (1994). *Behavioral expressions and biosocial bases of sensation seeking.* New York: Cambridge University Press.

Zuckerman, M., & Wheeler, L. (1975). To dispel fantasies about the fantasy-based measure of fear of success. *Psychological Bulletin, 82,* 932–946.

Zurbriggen, E. L., & Morgan, E. M. (2006). Who wants to marry a millionaire? Reality dating television programs, attitudes toward sex, and sexual behaviors. *Sex Roles, 54,* 1–17.

NAME INDEX

A

Aarestad, S., 130
Aarsland, T., 582
Abbey, A., 478
Abbott, M., 334
Abdelrahman, A.I., 410–411
Aboud, F.E., 316, 317
Abraham, C., 421
Abraham, K., 498, 500
Abrahams, M.F., 336
Abraido-Lanza, A.F., 581
Abrams, D., 75–76, 474
Abramson, L.Y., 215–216, 558, 559
Achenbach, T.M., 546
Acitelli, L.K., 352, 536
Ackerman, D., 409
Adams, C., 108
Adams, P.J., 506, 523
Adams, R.B., JR., 276
Adams, S., 163
Adams-Curtis, L.E., 465
Aday, R.H., 310
Addlesperger, E., 547
Adelson, J., 135
Adesso, V.J., 411
Adler, N.E., 394
Afifi, W.A., 314
Agras, W.S., 450
Agyei, Y., 368, 372
Ahmed, S.F., 144
Ai, A.L., 581
Aikin, K.J., 73
Akincigil, A., 404
Akiyama, H., 309
Alain, M., 569
Alansari, B.M., 547
Albert, B., 348
Albrecht, R., 417
Alegria, M., 550
Aleman, A., 146
Alfeld, C.J., 200
Ali, A., 564
Alkire, M. T., 146
Allan, K., 172
Allen, K.M., 489
Allen, M., 301
Allender, D., 65
Allgood-Merten, B., 565, 574
Allison, C.J., 464
Alloy, L.B., 550
Allred, L.J., 72
Almeida, D.M., 355, 485, 572
Alonzo, A.A., 401, 428
Alsen, M., 596
Altemus, M., 556
Altermatt, E.R., 225
Amaro, H., 420
Amateau, L.M., 489

Ambady, N., 88, 208
Ambrosini, P.J., 552
Amico, J., 556
Amico, J.A., 556
Amos, A., 411
Ampey-Thornhill, G., 489–490
Amponsah, B., 106
Andersen, A.E., 589
Andersen, B.L., 130
Andersen, P.A., 254, 260, 363
Andersen, P.K., 437
Andersen, R.E., 416
Anderson, K.G., 578
Anderson, T., 411
Andrade, C., 498–499, 500
Andreou, E., 239
Andrews, J.A., 597
Angell, K.L., 559
Angleitner, A., 334, 357, 363
Angold, A., 574
Anjum, A., 527
Annunziato, B., 489
Anson, O., 418
Antill, J.K., 352, 374, 375–376
Antonucci, T.C., 309
Aoki, Y., 250
Appelberg, K., 508
Appleyard, K., 239
Aragaki, A., 443
Arber, S., 393, 535
Arbreton, A., 219
Archer, J., 143
Aries, E., 88, 243, 248, 268
Arikian, N., 327
Arkowitz, H., 446
Arnkoff, D.B., 88
Aron, A., 339–340, 342
Aronson, J., 208
Arrighi, B.A., 456, 500
Arseneau, J.R., 410
Artazcoz, L., 498–499, 503
Arthur, H., 584
Asher, S.R., 307
Asherian, A, 334
Ashmore, R.D., 48
Atchison, J.W., 426
Athanasou, J.A., 503
Atkins, D.C., 447
Atkinson, J.W., 195
Attie, I., 587, 589, 592
Atwater, L., 271
Audesse, R.J., 299
Auerbach, C.F., 24
Aufderheide, T.P., 395
Augustson, E., 426
Aukett, R., 290, 293
Auster, C.J., 55
Avellar, S., 446

Avison, W.R., 568–569, 575
Avolio, B.J., 271
Ayars, C.L., 404
Ayers, M., 291, 298, 317
Azari, R., 549
Azmitia, M., 305

B

Babcock, L., 514–515
Bachman, J.G., 408–409
Bacon, P.L., 211
Badr, H., 352
Baenninger, M., 155
Bailey, J.A., 471
Bailey, J.M., 368, 372
Bailey, N., 525–526
Baillargeon, R.H., 123
Bakan, D., 56–57
Baker, C., 280
Baker, L., 164
Baker, L.A., 140
Baker, L.C., 131, 513
Baker, N.L., 20
Baker, T.B., 404–405
Baldassano, C.F., 546
Bales, R.F., 53, 266
Ballingrud, D., 524
Balsam, K.F., 597
Banaji, M., 273–274, 276–277
Bancroft, J.M., 399
Bandura, A., 152–153, 177–178
Bank, B.J., 288, 300
Barbeau, E.M., 409–410
Barbee, A., 349
Barbee, A.P., 301, 487
Barber, B., 219–220
Barber, B.L., 200, 219
Barboza, D., 122
Barickman, R.B., 530–531
Barker, M., 512
Barker, T., 123
Barling, J., 224
Barnes, G.M., 417
Barnes-Farrell, J., 91
Barnes-Farrell, J.L., 536
Barnett, R.C., 200, 449, 452, 480, 485, 503, 507–508, 536–537
Barreto, M., 75
Barrett-Connor, E., 471
Barron, L.A., 515
Barta, W.D., 347
Bartkowski, J.P., 375
Bartlett, M.Y., 364
Bartlett, S.J., 416
Bartley, M., 534
Bartley, M.J., 503
Bartley, S.J., 452
Barton, B.K., 231

Baruch, G.K., 507
Basow, S.A., 279, 281
Bass, B.M., 271
Bassoff, E., 569
Baucom, D.H., 357, 557
Bauman, K.E., 410–411
Baumeister, R.F., 20, 127, 129–130, 142–143, 213, 338, 370
Baumgardner, A.H., 218
Baumgarte, R., 314
Baxter, J.C., 83–84
Baxter, L.A., 318
Bayer, L., 489–490
Bazzini, D.G., 302, 312
Beach, S.R.H., 449
Beadnell, B., 420
Beals, K.P., 371, 457
Bean, J.A., 206–207
Beard, C., 313
Bearman, P., 349
Bearman, P.S., 410–411
Beauchaine, T.P., 597
Beaver, S.K., 395–396
Becker, B.E., 290
Becker, D., 590
Becker, D.V., 333
Beekman, A.T.F., 443
Behrendt, R., 86
Belcher, C., 230
Belk, S.S., 304
Bell, L.A., 198–199
Belle, D., 101, 286, 486–488
Bellgowan, P.S.F., 146
Bellisle, F., 399
Bem, S.L., 53–54, 56, 179–182
Benach, J., 498–499, 503
Benbow, C.P., 111–112, 223
Ben-David, S., 472, 474
Benenson, J.F., 296–298
Bengtson, V.L., 459
Bennesch, S., 550–551
Bennett, D.S., 552
Benson, P.R., 358
Benson, S., 327
Bentler, P.M., 211
Berenbaum, S.A., 143
Bergen, D.J., 92
Berger, B.D., 411
Bergman, M.E., 529
Berkey, C.S., 414
Berkman, L.F., 436, 486–487
Berkvens, M., 263
Berman, B.A., 401
Bern, P., 320
Bernard, J., 435, 440
Berns, S.B., 362
Bernstein, I.H., 469
Berscheid, E., 69, 346
Bersoff, D.N., 95
Beshansky, J.R., 395
Besser, A., 478
Best, D.L., 82
Bettencourt, B.A., 123–124
Beyer, S., 202, 215–216
Bhanot, R., 222
Biaggio, M.K., 44, 276
Bianchi, S.M., 455, 535
Bickel, J., 398
Biederman, J., 578
Bielby, D.D., 515
Bielby, W.T., 515
Biener, L., 507
Biernat, M., 91, 519
Billings, S.C., 404, 410

Binder, J.R., 146
Binion, V.J., 72
Bird, C.E., 382, 385, 390, 460, 489
Birns, B., 468, 469
Biro, F.M., 206–207
Bjerregaard, P., 386
Bjornson, W., 404
Black, D.A., 519–520
Blain, M.D., 355
Blair, S.L., 452–453, 456–457
Blake, J.J., 317
Blakemore, J.E.O., 167
Bland, M., 246
Bland, R.C., 445, 547
Blanks, V., 482
Blanton, P.W., 452
Blatt, S.J., 576
Blazer, D., 486
Blazer, D.G., 472, 476, 547
Blee, K.M., 72
Bleske, A.L., 313–314
Bleske-Rechek, A.L., 312, 313
Block, J., 576
Block, J.H., 103–104, 573, 576
Bloesch, E., 465
Blow, F.C., 549
Blum, J.S., 355
Blum, M.C., 597
Blum, R.W., 410–411
Blumberg, E.J., 420
Blumenfeld, P., 219
Blumenthal, J.A., 526–527
Blumenthal, L., 122
Blumstein, P., 372
Bly, R., 24
Boeringer, S.B., 476
Bohan, J.S., 21, 60–61
Bohner, G., 474
Bohon, L.M., 158–159, 536
Boivin, M., 165, 239
Bolduc, D., 162
Bolling, S.F., 581
Bombardieri, M., 193
Bond, C.F., Jr., 407
Bond, J.T., 480, 500
Bond, M.A., 506, 508
Bond, M.H., 253
Bondurant, B., 478, 530–531
Bonneh, D.Y., 418
Bonner, R.L., 595
Bookwala, J., 464
Booth, A., 375–376, 504, 555
Booth-LaForce, C., 292
Borch, C., 239
Borger, D., 143
Borgida, E., 95–96, 532
Borker, R.A., 247, 260
Boroughs, M., 589
Borowiecki, J., 591
Borowsky, S.J., 549
Borrell, C., 498–499, 503
Borrelli, B., 406
Boshuizen, H.C., 387
Bosson, J.K., 210
Botvin, G.J., 411
Bouma, A., 146
Bouman, A., 390
Bourdeau, H.A., 401
Bowen, C.-C., 510
Boxer, A.M., 417
Boydell, J., 546
Boyle, P.A., 163
Boynton, P.M., 396
Boysen, G.A., 82

Braaten, E., 578
Bradac, J.J., 247
Bradbury, T.N., 280, 353
Brady, K.L., 226
Brain, M., 170
Bramlett, M.D., 375, 435
Bramon-Bosch, E., 589
Brand, R.J., 487
Branscombe, N.R., 211
Braslow, A., 401, 428
Braver, S.L., 527
Braverman, J., 364
Breed, L., 171
Brehm, J.W., 583
Brendgen, M., 165, 239
Brennan, M., 321
Brennan, P.A., 567, 569
Brennan, R.T., 449, 452, 480, 485, 503, 508, 536
Brent, D.A., 597
Brescoll, V., 42
Bresnahan, M.J., 171
Brewer, D.D., 129
Brezinka, V., 580
Bridge, K., 318
Bridgeman, B., 112
Bridges, J.S., 91
Briere, J., 471, 476
Briggs, L.F., 254
Brill, G., 574
Bringle, R.G., 370–371
Briton, N.J., 252
Broderick, P.C., 564
Brody, L.R., 163–164, 276
Broge, M., 406
Bromberger, J.T., 565, 569
Brooks, D., 584
Brooks, T.L., 439, 441
Brooks-Gunn, J., 555, 574, 587, 589, 592
Brotherstone, H., 429
Broverman, D.M., 79–81
Broverman, I.K., 79–81
Brown, A.C., 202
Brown, C., 512
Brown, G.W., 449, 486–487, 569
Brown, L.M., 286, 288
Brown, S., 348
Brown, S.L., 373, 375–376, 436
Brown, W.A., 143
Browne, A., 469
Browne, B.A., 172
Browne, D.C., 574
Brownell, K.D., 428
Brownlee, S., 440
Brownmiller, S., 475, 478
Bru, E., 567, 576, 582
Bruckner, H., 349
Brunot, S., 211
Bryden, M.P., 106
Buchanan, N.T., 529–530
Buchtel, H.A., 581
Buckner, C.E., 55
Bugay, G., 555
Buhrmester, D., 288
Buist, A. S., 404
Buist, A.S., 404
Bukowski, W.M., 296
Bulanda, J.R., 373, 436
Bullock, H.E., 87
Bumpass, L.L., 374–376
Burckle, M.A., 299
Burgard, D., 592
Burgess, D., 532
Burgess, K.B., 292

Buring, J.E., 401
Burk-Braxton, C., 206
Burke, M.J., 95, 510
Burke, R.J., 506
Burleson, B.R., 279–280, 287, 290
Burnett, C.K., 357
Burr, J.E., 238–239
Burstein, N.R., 373
Burston, A., 481–482
Burt, M.R., 475–476
Burton, D., 404
Buschman, J.K., 8
Bush, E., 597
Bushman, S., 23
Buss, A.H., 565
Buss, D.M., 148–150, 312–314, 330, 333–334, 349, 357, 363–364
Bussey, K., 154, 177–178
Buston, P.M., 334
Buswell, B.N., 206
Butler, S., 163
Buttner, E.H., 257
Buunk, B.P., 330, 363
Bybee, J., 134
Bylsma, W.H., 522
Byrne, B.M., 219

C

Cachelin, F.M., 589, 592
Cacioppo, J.T., 391, 450
Caggiula, A.R., 405–406
Cahalan, C., 113
Cahill, L., 146
Cahn, D.D., 354, 357
Caldera, Y., 86
Cale, E.M., 577–578
Califf, R.M., 385, 389–390, 396
Calvert, S.L., 240
Camarena, P.M., 289, 305–306
Camargo, C.A.J., 414
Camp, P., 549
Campbell, A., 124
Campbell, J., 462
Campbell, M.E., 316–317
Campbell, S.M., 353
Campbell, W.K., 206
Campos, B., 556
Canary, D.J., 314, 350–352, 458
Canetto, S.S., 594–596
Canino, G.J., 445, 547
Cannon, E., 219–220
Cantor, M.H., 321
Cantrell, P.J., 172
Cantrill, J.G., 336
Capaldi, D.M., 468
Carey, M.P., 355
Carli, L.L., 243–244, 247, 250, 255, 257–258, 266–267
Carlson, C.L., 578
Carlson, M.B., 95, 593
Carpenter, K.M., 64, 82
Carr, D., 516
Carr, T.S., 143
Carrere, S., 358–359
Carroll, J., 14, 272, 434, 471
Carroll, M.E., 409
Carson, J.L., 404
Carson, M., 280
Carstensen, L.L., 358, 361, 447
Carter, J.D., 91, 251–253, 264
Casas, J.F., 238–239
Case, A., 387
Casey, M.B., 113
Cashdan, E., 267

Cassidy, K.W., 578
Castro, Y.R., 77
Catanese, K.R., 127, 142
Catania, J.A., 420
Catta-Preta, A.B., 362
Caudle, J., 577
Caughlin, J.P., 362
Cavanagh, J.T.O., 548
Cayemittes, M., 420
Cazeca, D., 506, 508
Ceballos, R.M., 556
Celentano, D.D., 427–428
Centers, R.E., 167
Chabassol, D.J., 198
Chaikin, A.L., 304
Chamberlain, R.M., 404
Chan, A.C.M., 489
Chan, C.C.H., 443, 546
Chan, L., 395–396
Chance, S.E., 143
Chandler, A.L., 485
Chandra, A., 550
Chang, C., 85
Chang, E-L., 108
Chapman, K.R., 397
Charmaz, K., 582
Chatard, A., 210–211
Chavez, A.M., 314
Cheatham, C.L., 258
Chee, M., 450
Chen, C., 165
Chen, E., 597
Chen, J., 395
Cheng, S.T., 489
Cherlin, A., 374–376
Cherpitel, C.J., 407
Cheskin, L.J., 416
Chesley, N., 571
Chesney, M.A., 402
Chesney-Lind, M., 125
Chevan, A., 374
Chia, R.C., 72
Chiaramonte, G.R., 397
Chisholm, J.F., 13
Cho, M.H., 574–575
Chodorow, N., 152, 356, 359
Choe, J., 330
Choi, W.S., 404, 410
Choo, P., 444
Chrisler, J.C., 398
Christakos, A., 296–297
Christenfeld, N., 449, 489
Christensen, A., 358–360, 362, 447
Church, A.T., 131
Ciabattari, T., 458
Ciarlo, J.A., 436, 535
Cillessen, A.H.N., 165, 239
Cini, M.A., 369–370
Cisler, R.A., 597
Clack, F., 353
Clancy, S.M., 210
Clark, C.L., 336
Clark, M., 348
Clark, M.L., 291, 298, 317
Clark, R.A., 195
Clarkberg, M., 375
Clarke, W.L., 278, 425
Clark-Lempers, D.S., 288, 310
Clarkson, F.E., 79–81
Clearfield, M.W., 162
Cleveland, H.H., 474
Coates, T.J., 420
Coats, E.J., 264
Cobb-Clark, D.A., 519
Cochran, C.C., 525

Cochran, S.D., 357, 366, 368, 370, 409, 597
Cogan, J.C., 590
Coglianese, M.E., 395
Cohan, C.L., 466, 468
Cohen, E., 544
Cohen, J., 104, 418
Cohen, R, 231
Cohen, R.D., 487
Cohen, R.Y., 428
Cohen, S., 437
Cohen, T.F., 309
Cohler, B.J., 488
Coie, J.D., 165
Colapinto, J., 145
Colburne, K. A., 86
Colditz, G.A., 414
Cole, G.E., 488
Cole, N.S., 110, 114, 116–118
Cole, S.S., 6
Collaer, M.L., 106, 142, 144–145, 155
Colley, A., 246
Collins, N.L., 304
Collis, B., 201
Colman, G.J., 407
Colten, M.E., 576
Coltrane, S., 171–172, 453, 457, 460
Compas, B.E., 546
Condry, J., 41
Condry, S., 41
Conger, J.J., 366
Conger, R.D., 568, 576
Conley, R., 297
Conley, T.D., 144–145
Connell, R.W., 58
Connelly, S.C., 61–62
Conner, M., 589
Connett, J.E., 404
Connolly, J.A., 288
Connor, J.K., 546
Constantinople, A., 53
Cook, S.W., 472
Cooke, R.G., 546
Cooper, B., 556
Cooper, M.L., 411
Cooperman, M., 506, 508
Copenhaver, M.M., 469
Corbett, K., 404
Corcoran, M., 512
Corcoran, M.E., 519
Cordova, J.V., 355
Coren, S., 596
Corpus, J.H., 208
Correll, S.J., 203, 219, 519
Corrigall, E., 506
Cortes, I., 498–499, 503
Cortese, A., 339–340, 342
Cortina, L.M., 529, 532
Corwin, E.J., 556
Coryell, W., 574
Cosenzo, K.A., 392
Cosgrove, K.P., 409
Cossette, L., 162
Costa, P.T., Jr., 131
Costanza, R., 300
Costello, E.J., 574
Costin, S.E., 297
Cote, S., 123
Cotliar, S., 122
Cotter, D.A., 512
Counts, D.A., 596
Courant, P.N., 519
Courtenay, W.H., 398–399
Covey, L.S., 404
Cowan, C.P., 536
Cowan, G.A., 300

Cowan, P.A., 536
Cox, D.J., 278, 425
Cox, R.W., 146
Coyne, J.C., 448
Craig, T.Y., 530
Crandall, C.S., 210, 592
Crawford, M., 8, 20
Crawford, P.B., 589
Creedon, C.F., 198
Cremeans-Smith, J.K., 581
Crespo, C.J., 416
Cretser, G.A., 276
Crick, N.R., 238–239
Crisp, R.J., 210
Crissey, S.R., 435
Crittenden, A., 516
Crocker, J., 207
Crombie, G., 219
Crosby, F., 8, 521–522
Crosby, F. J., 9
Crosby, J.P., 578
Cross, S.E., 210–211
Crouter, A.C, 155
Crouter, A.C., 503
Crowley, M., 121, 213
Crown, N., 395
Cruet, D., 565–566
Crump, A.D., 404, 410
Crystal, S., 404
Cuddy, A.J.C., 519
Culbertson, A.L., 528
Culbertson, F.M., 546
Cullerton-Sen, C., 238–239
Culver, C., 163
Cunningham, J.D., 374–376
Cunningham, M., 164, 455
Cunningham, M.R., 487
Cupach, W.R., 470
Currie, D.H., 465
Curtis, J., 522
Cutrona, C.E., 438
Cyphers, L., 86
Cyranowski, J.M., 130, 572

D

Dabbs, J.M., Jr., 108, 143
Dahl, G.B., 13
Dahl, R.E., 555
Dakof, G.A., 411
Daly, J.A., 328–329
Daly, M., 149–150
D'Amico, D., 406
Damsgaard, M.T., 437
Daniels, S., 589
Danielson, M., 387
Dank, S., 591
Dannecker, E.A., 426
Danoff-Burg, S., 424, 584
Darrow, W.W., 129
Datnow, A., 230
Daubman, K.A., 202, 206, 293, 311
Davey, A., 504
David, L, 64
Davidson, K., 444
Davidson, W., 226–228
Davies, P.G., 208–209
Davila, J., 280
Davis, B., 410–411
Davis, B.M., 268
Davis, C.G., 563
Davis, K.E, 89
Davis, K.L., 336
Davis, M.C., 392, 566
Davis-Kean, P.E., 219, 223

Davison, H.K., 95, 510
Dawber, T., 422
Dawes, K.I., 229
de Man, A.F., 476
de Moor, C.A., 405
De Ruijter, J.M.P., 512
de Simone, L.L., 426
de Souza, M.A., 467
de Vries, B., 287, 291, 293, 295
Dear, G.E., 570
Deaux, K., 25, 60, 83, 95–96, 140, 183, 186–188, 215–216, 519, 531
DeBoer, D.D., 501
Deeg, D.J.H., 443
DeFiore, J., 512
Deford, F., 382
Degirmencioglu, S.M., 286, 291
Del Priore, R.E., 536
del Toro, M., 298
DeLamater, J., 346
DeLamater, J.D., 348, 503
DeLisi, R., 112
Delnevo, C.D., 404
D'Emilio, J., 477–478
Denny, D., 6
Dent, C.W., 404
Denton, M., 429, 489
Deptula, D.P., 344
Derbyshire, S.W.G., 425
Derlega, V.J., 300, 301, 304, 315, 319
Desaulniers, J., 262
Desmarais, S., 161, 522
DeSouza, E.R., 526
Dessens, A.B., 144
DeSteno, D., 364
Detlefson, E.G., 537
Devaney, B., 348
Deven, F., 517
Devine, I., 319
Devineni, T, 108
Devlin, P.K., 300
DeVore, C.J., 357
DeWit, D.J., 13
Dey, J.G., 513, 516–517
Diamond, M., 145
Diaz, T., 411
Dickhauser, O., 215–216
Diehl, M., 92
Diekman, A.B., 92, 134, 169, 173
Diener, E., 274, 436
Dietz, T.L., 154
Dietz, W.H., 412, 414
Dijkstra, P., 330
DiMare, L., 250
Dimberg, U., 276
Dindia, K., 235–237, 301
Dionne, G., 239
Dishman, R.K., 417
Dittmann, R.W., 143–144
Dockwell, B., 482
Dodd, D.K., 252
Dode, I., 597
Dodge, K.A., 165
Dohm, F.A., 589
Dolgin, K.G., 301
Dollinger, S.J., 210
Donat, P.L.N., 477–478
Done, R.S., 529, 531, 533
Dong, Q., 165
Donkin, A., 419
Donny, E., 405–406
Doornen, L.J.P., 273
Doss, B.D., 447
Douglas, W., 170

Douvan, E., 135
Dowling-Guyer, S., 15
Downey, K.T., 206
Downs, D.L., 214
Doyle, A., 578
Doyle, J.A., 65
Doyle, M.M., 411
Dracup, K., 401, 428
Draijer, N., 566
Drakich, J., 245–246
Drasgow, F., 525–526
Driscoll, D.M., 530
Drop, S.L.S., 144
Droste, H.E., 506, 523
Druen, P.B., 487
Druley, J.A., 581
DuBois, D.L., 206, 219
Dubas, J.J.S.D., 550
Dubow, E.F., 597
Duck, S., 287, 293
Duckett, E., 573
Due, P., 437
Duff, J.L., 286, 288
Duffy, J., 225
Dunand, J-P., 398
Duncan, G.J., 29, 393–394
Dunkel, F., 24
Dunkle, R.E., 581
Dunlop, Y., 519
Dunn, D., 512
Dunning, D., 201
Durbin, R.G., 353
Durik, A.M., 130
Durndell, A., 246
Dweck, C.S., 226–228
Dwyer, K.M., 292
Dye, J.L., 480
Dyer, M., 307–308, 337–338, 357
Dziech, B.W., 529

E

Eagly, A.H., 20, 41, 81, 92, 121, 134, 149, 173–174, 176, 208, 210, 213, 265, 267–271, 334
Eals, M., 108
Eastwick, P.W., 334
Eaton, W.O., 130
Ebanks, G.E., 13
Eberhart, N.K., 567, 569
Ebrahim, S., 390
Eccles, J., 415
Eccles, J.S., 112, 200, 219–220, 222–224, 228, 417
Eccleston, C., 425
Eckes, T., 85
Ecuyer-Dab, I., 150
Edler, E., 230
Edmonds, C., 317
Edmundowicz, D., 449
Edwards, A.C., 449, 486–487, 569
Edwards, C.P., 174–176, 238, 242
Edwards, R.R., 425–426
Egeland, J.A., 547
Egisdottir, S., 127
Ehrlich, C.M., 248
Ehrlinger, J., 201
Eichstedt, J.A., 86
Eisenberg, M., 401, 428
Eisenberg, N., 120
Eiser, C., 581
Eiser, J.R., 581
Eisler, R.M., 64, 65, 226, 392, 469
Eitel, P., 404, 410
Eker, E., 555

Ekman, P., 273
Elasmar, M., 170
Elbedour, S., 202
Elder, G.H., Jr., 568, 576
Eldridge, K., 362
Eldridge, N.S., 366
Elkins, L.E., 294
Ell, K., 489
Ellemers, N., 75
Elliott, D.M., 471, 476
Elliott, K., 309
Elliott, S., 445
Ellis, H., 48
Ellis, J.B., 55
Ellis, L., 260
Ellsworth, P.C., 65–66
Eloy, S.V., 363
Else-Quest, N.M., 348
Elsesser, K., 317–318
Emlen, S.T., 334
Emrich, C., 105
Endicott, J., 574
Engels, W.A.E.W., 263
Engle, A., 64, 82
Enna, B., 226–228
Enns, L.R., 130
Enos, T., 556
Epel, E.S., 391
Epstein, J.A., 411
Epstein, R.M., 549
Erber, M.W., 526
Erdincler, D., 555
Erickson, J., 23
Erickson, R.J., 456–458
Erikson, E.H., 134
Ermakov, S.P., 383
Ernsberger, P., 590
Ernst, S.B., 169
Ernster, V.L., 401
Ertan, T., 555
Escobar, M.D., 114–115
Escobar, O., 590
Eshleman, J.R., 436
Eshleman, S., 547
Esterly, E., 341
Estioko-Griffen, A.A., 12
Etaugh, C., 91
Evans, G.W., 489
Evans, R.E.C., 429
Evans, S.M., 237
Evenson, K.R., 443
Evenson, R.J., 436, 483
Ewart, C.K., 450
Exline, J.J., 201
Eyler, A.E, 6

F

Faas, M.M., 390
Fabes, R.A., 120, 123–124, 237, 239–241, 312
Fabre, J., 398
Fagerstrom, K-O., 404–405
Fairchild, K., 90
Faith, M.S., 412
Faludi, S., 42
Faraone, S.V., 578
Faravelli, C., 445, 547
Farney, L.A., 310
Farrell, M.P., 417
Farrell, W., 24, 25
Fassinger, R.E., 410
Faulkner, S.L., 314, 343–344
Fazio, R.H., 15
Fearon, P., 546

Feder, G., 396
Fehr, B., 288, 305
Fein, D.J., 373
Fein, G.G., 373
Feinauer, L.L., 503
Feingold, A., 131, 298, 330, 335
Fejfar, M.C., 565
Feldman, J.A., 395
Feldman, M.D., 549
Feldman, R., 275, 517
Feldman, R.S., 253
Feldman, S.S., 357
Felix, M.R.J., 428
Felmlee, D., 353
Felton, G., 417
Feng, B., 279–280
Fenigstein, A., 565
Fennema, E., 110–113
Fernald, J.L., 87
Ferreira, M.C., 92
Feshbach, S., 155, 158
Fetters, J.K., 385, 389–390, 396
Ficher, I., 481
Field, A.E., 414
Fife, B.L., 581, 586
Fillingim, R., 426
Fillingim, R.B., 425–426
Fincham, F.D., 353, 449
Fingerhut, A., 519–520
Finney, J.W., 411, 568
Fiore, M.C., 404–405
Firestone, L., 425
Fischer, A.H., 159–160, 275–276
Fischer, A.R., 76
Fischer, C.S., 308
Fishbaugh, L., 41
Fiske, S.T., 2, 74–77, 79, 85, 95–96, 334, 519
Fitness, J., 526
Fitzgerald, L.F., 525–526, 529, 532, 549
Fitzgibbon, M., 413–414
Fitzpatrick, J., 341
Fitzpatrick, J.A., 353
Fivush, R., 163, 286
Flaisher-Kellner, S., 574
Flaks, D.K., 481
Flanigan, C., 348
Flay, B., 411
Flay, B.R., 404, 410–411
Flegal, K.M., 414
Fletcher, G.J.O., 333
Fletcher, J.M., 114–115
Flory, J.D., 565
Floyd, F.J., 358, 450
Floyd, K., 305, 312–313
Flynn, F.J., 317
Flynn, K.J., 413–414
Flyr, M.L., 288
Foa, E.B., 566
Fokkema, T., 498, 500, 535
Foley, L.A., 472
Folk, K., 458
Folkman, S., 559
Fombonne, E., 597
Fontaine, K.R., 412
Foote, C., 228
Forbes, G. B., 465
Ford, G., 424, 428
Forrest, J.A., 253
Forssmann-Falck, R., 206, 573
Forsterlee, L., 76
Forsterlee, R., 76
Fortson, K., 348
Foschi, M., 509

Fox, G.B., 76
Fox, M., 167
Fox, P.W., 202
Frady, R.L., 143
Franchina, J.J., 392, 469
Franck, K., 52
Frank, E., 556, 572
Frankenhaeuser, M., 392
Franklin, C.W., Jr., 291
Franko, D.L., 206–207
Franks, P., 412
Franz, C.E., 549
Frazier, A.L., 414
Frazier, P., 327
Frazier, P.A., 341, 525
Frecker, R.C., 404–405
Frederickson, B.L., 371
Fredman, L., 487–488
Fredricks, J.A., 223, 417
Fredrickson, B.L., 207, 563, 575
Fredrikson, M., 392
Freeborn, D.K., 436
Freeburg, E.W., 472
Freedman-Doan, C., 219, 223
Freeman, C.E., 194
Freeman, E.W., 555
French, D.C., 238, 307
French, J.F., 410–411
Freud, S., 151
Frey, A., 230
Friedan, B., 21–22
Fried-Buchalter, S., 198
Friedman, G.B., 267
Friedman, H.S., 424, 446
Friend, R., 397
Friesen, M., 333
Frieze, I.H., 20, 214–215, 336, 369, 464, 537
Frings, L., 146
Frisco, M. L., 458
Fritch, A., 426
Fritz, H.L., 56–57, 280–281, 424, 486, 570, 584–585
Frome, P., 223
Frome, P.M., 200
Frost, J.A., 146
Fuchs, D., 163
Fuegen, K., 519
Fujimoto, T., 460
Furman, W., 288
Furnham, A., 171
Fuwa, M., 455

G

Gabay, R., 131
Gable, R.K., 64
Gabriel, S., 213
Gager, C.T., 459
Gagnon, C., 426
Gagnon, J.H., 128–129, 346
Gaither Davis, A.L., 401
Galambos, N.L., 252, 572
Galinsky, E., 480, 500, 506–507, 536
Gallagher, A., 113
Gallagher, A.M., 112
Gallaher, P.E., 252
Gallo, L.C., 391, 423–424, 449, 451
Gallup, G.H., Jr., 344
Galotti, K.M., 239
Galupo, M.P., 321
Gan, S.C., 395–396
Garbarino, J., 123
Garber, J., 425, 597
Garcia, D.M., 211

Garcia-Falconi, R., 304
Gardiner, M., 506
Gardner, C.O., 552
Gardner, W.L., 213
Gareis, K.C., 502–503, 537
Garfinkel, P.E., 589, 591
Garner, D.M., 587–588, 591
Garnets, L.D., 372
Garofoli, L.M., 111
Garovich-Szabo, L., 55, 92–93
Garrett, S.B., 129
Gary, T.L., 574
Gastil, J., 15
Gaub, M., 578
Gaulin, S., 368, 372
Gaulin, S.J.C., 108
Gay, J., 136
Ge, X., 568, 576
Gear, R.W., 425
Gee, C.B., 355
Geenen, R., 273
Geer, J.H., 344
Geiger, H.J., 383
Gekoski, W.L., 550
Gelfand, M.J., 525–526
Gelles, R.J., 462–463, 468–469
Geltman, E.M., 395
Gentile, D.A, 239
George, L.K., 472, 476
George, S.Z., 426
Gerhardstein, R., 208–209
Gerhardt, C.A., 546
Gerhart, B., 514
Gerin, W., 449, 489
Germsen, J.M., 512
Gerreira, M.C., 467
Gersh, B., 395
Gersons, B.P.R., 566
Gettman, J.Y., 575
Ghaed, S.G., 423–424
Ghaemi, S.N., 546
Ghez, M., 462
Gibbons, J.L., 71
Gibbons, P., 247
Gibbs, M.S., 527
Giedd, J.L., 531, 532
Gijsbers van Wijk, C.M.T., 387, 427
Gilbert, L.A, 268, 366
Gillen, M.M., 421
Gillespie, B.L., 65
Gillespie, N.A., 62
Gilliard, J.L., 452
Gilligan, C., 61, 133, 297
Gillihan, S.J., 279–280
Gillman, M.W., 414
Gilmore, D.D., 12
Ginn, J., 393
Giordano, P.C., 336
Girard, A., 239
Girdler, S.S., 556
Girgus, J.S., 553–555
Gjerberg, E., 200
Gjerde, P.F., 573, 576
Gladney, A.P., 404
Gladue, B.A., 368, 372
Glaser, R., 391, 450
Glass, G., 569
Glass, J., 460
Glass, R.M., 404
Glass, S.P., 346
Glasser, D.B., 343
Glick, P., 74–77, 97, 271, 334, 467, 519
Glynn, L.M., 449, 489
Goble, L., 451

Godbey, G., 453, 512
Goering, P., 589
Gohm, C.L., 436
Gold, C., 555
Gold, D.P., 450
Gold, J.A., 299
Gold, Y., 525–526
Goldbaum, S., 298
Goldberg, A.E., 458
Goldberg, H., 63
Goldblatt, P., 419
Goldbloom, D.S., 589
Golding, G., 134
Golding, J., 164, 481–482
Goldner, V., 469
Goldsteen, K., 480, 482, 485, 497, 503, 507, 537
Golombek, S., 164, 286, 481–482
Golombok, S.E., 141
Gonder-Frederick, L.A., 278, 425
Gondolf, E.W., 468
Gonzaga, G.C., 556
Gonzales, M.H., 367–368
Gonzalez, A.Q., 14
Gonzalez, J.M., 550
Gonzalez, R., 563
Gooden, A.M., 169
Gooden, M.A., 169
Goodman, M.J., 12
Goodrich, C., 527
Gordon, A.H., 276
Gordon, E., 585
Gordon, E.E.I., 397
Gordon, N.C., 425
Gore, S., 576
Gorman, B.K., 387
Gorman, E.H., 95
Gornemann, I., 420
Gortmaker, S.L., 412, 414
Gortner, S.R., 580
Gosselin, M.-J., 569
Gotlib, I.H., 575
Gottman, J.M., 358–359, 361–362, 371, 447, 450–451, 487
Gove, W.R., 423, 427, 436, 440, 497, 534
Gowen, L.K., 357
Grabe, M.E., 76
Grabe, S., 574
Graber, J.A., 574, 592
Grace, S.L., 584
Gradman, T.J., 505
Gralinski, J.H., 218
Grammer, K., 149
Granger, D.A., 555
Grant, C.A., 424
Grant, I., 504
Grant, K., 547, 574–575
Grant, L., 514
Graves, A.R., 279–280
Graves, L.M., 269
Gray, J., 30, 101, 139, 356
Grayson, C., 557
Green, B.L., 352
Green, C.A., 388, 422
Green, J., 249
Green, M.C., 365
Green, P.J., 585
Greenberger, E., 165
Greendale, G.A., 556
Greene, K., 343–344
Greene, M.L., 290
Greenwald, S., 445, 547
Grewen, K.M., 556
Grieco, L., 24
Griffin, C.M., 506, 523

Griffin, K.W., 411
Griffin, M.L., 409
Griffin, P.B., 12
Griffin, S., 473
Grindel, C.G., 400
Gritz, E.R., 401, 404
Groesz, L.M., 591
Grogan, S., 589
Gross, J., 371
Gross, J.J., 275
Gross, S.M., 574
Grossman, R.J., 509
Groth, G.E., 332
Grotpeter, J.K., 238–239
Grove, J.S., 12
Gruber, A., 426, 591
Gruber, J.E., 527–528
Gruenewald, T.L., 561
Gubish, C.T., 401
Guerguerian, R., 577
Guerin, S., 333
Guerrero, L.K., 146, 254, 275, 314, 363
Gugula, S., 161
Guiller, J., 246
Guimond, S., 210–211
Guite, J.W., 425
Gulley, M.R., 487
Gump, B.B., 390
Gunderson, J., 426
Gunnar, M.R., 258
Guo, G., 110–111
Guo, M-S., 165
Gupta, S., 457
Gupta, V., 394
Gurian, M., 123
Gurung, R.A.R., 352, 561
Gustavsson, J.P., 62
Gutek, B.A., 509, 523, 525–526, 528–529, 530–531, 533
Guthrie, I.K., 123
Gwartney-Gibbs, P.A., 532
Gyulai, L., 546

H

Haase, A.M., 399
Haavio-Mannila, E., 318, 428
Haefner, P., 357
Hagedoorn, M., 448
Hahn, E.J., 532
Haines, E., 519
Haines, J., 591
Hales, D.P., 417
Hall, J., 472
Hall, J.A., 91, 163–164, 248, 250–254, 264, 267, 276
Hall, W.S., 73
Halliday-Scher, K., 286, 291
Halpern, C.T., 464
Halpern, D.F., 106, 113, 147, 155
Halsband, U., 146
Hamby, S.L., 472
Hamilton, B.E., 376, 380
Hamilton, J.A., 172
Hamilton, M.C., 15
Hamm, P., 395
Hammeke, T.A., 146
Hammen, C., 546, 567
Hammen, C.L., 569
Hamovitch, M., 489
Hampton, R.L., 468
Han, W.J., 518
Hanish, L.D., 240–241, 312
Hankin, B.L., 215–216, 559, 575
Hannah, M.T., 446

Hannan, P.J., 591
Hanneken, J., 468
Hansford, S.L., 288, 300
Harai, Y., 131
Hardesty, J.L., 206
Hardy, C.L., 296
Hare-Mustin, R. T., 189
Harlow, L.L., 420
Harned, M.S., 529
Harnish, R.J., 478
Harold, G.T., 449
Harold, R.D., 219–220, 222
Harris, B., 313
Harris, C., 55
Harris, C.R., 365
Harris, H., 165, 271
Harris, I., 65
Harris, J.A., 143
Harris, J.R., 164
Harris, K.M., 410–411
Harris, M.B., 124, 126
Harris, S.M., 65, 341
Harris, T.R., 408
Harrison, S., 300
Hartley, P., 592
Hartmann, P., 86
Hartung, C.M., 551–552
Hartup, W.W., 307
Hasegawa, K., 170
Haselton, M.G., 349, 357
Hatala, M.N., 368
Hatfield, E., 330–332, 339–340, 342, 344–345, 444
Hathaway, S.R., 51
Hause, K.S., 314
Havermans, T., 581
Hawkins, A.J., 459
Hawkins, M.W., 529
Hayes, S.M., 532–533
Haymovitz, E.L., 210
Haynie, D.L., 123, 126, 404, 410
Haythornthwaite, J.A., 425
Healy, B., 396
Hearst, N., 420
Heatherton, T.F., 404–405
Heaton, T.B., 434
Heavey, C.L., 358–360, 362
Hecht, M.A., 252, 263–264
Heckert, T.M., 506, 523
Hedges, L.V., 110, 114, 116–117
Heft, M.W., 426
Heikkilä, K., 508
Heilman, M.E., 95–96, 271
Hein, H.O., 401
Heineman, M.J., 390
Heiney, M., 489–490
Helgeson, V.S., 56–57, 59, 205, 207, 280–281, 297, 307–308, 337–338, 357, 423–424, 444–445, 447, 486, 560, 570–571, 584–586, 590
Heller, P.H., 425
Helmreich, R.L., 53–57, 70–71
Helms, B.J., 64
Helweg-Larsen, K., 386
Helwig, A.A., 154
Hemingway, H., 396
Hendrick, C., 340–342
Hendrick, S.S., 338, 340–342
Henley, N.M., 15, 263
Hennekens, C.H., 401
Henningsen, M.L.M., 336
Hennrikus, D.J., 406
Henry, D.B., 344
Heo, M., 412

Hepp, U., 590
Herbert, J., 143, 220, 223
Herek, G.M., 370–371
Hernandez-Sanchez, J.E., 304
Herold, A.L., 262
Heron, M.P., 384
Herrera, V.M., 471
Hershberger, S., 140
Hertzman, C., 506–507
Hertzog, C., 576
Herzberger, S.D., 207
Hess, U., 276
Hessini, L., 11–12
Hessling, R. M., 15
Hesson-McInnis, M.S., 532
Hetland, J., 387
Heuveline, P., 373
Hewitt, E.C., 503
Hewitt, J., 555
Hewitt, P.L., 596
H.G., 588–589
Hibbard, J.H., 507
Higgins, D.A., 124
Hill, C., 513, 516–517, 529
Hill, C.T., 375, 444
Hill, J.P., 572
Hillman, J.L., 265
Hilsman, R., 597
Hilt, L., 407–408
Hinden, B.R., 546
Hines, M., 141–145, 164
Hippe, M., 401
Hippisley-Cox, J., 395
Hiripi, E., 588–589
Hiscock, M., 146
Hiscock-Kalil, C., 146
Hitchon, J.C.B., 85
Hitlan, R.T., 532
Hitsman, B., 406
Ho, J.E., 385
Ho, R., 76
Hochschild, A.R., 7, 70, 452, 458, 460, 539
Hoffman, L., 171
Hoffman, L.W., 458
Hoffman, S.D., 29
Hoffmann, M.L., 239
Hofmeister, H., 504
Hohmann, A.A., 398
Hohmann-Marriott, B., 459
Hohmann-Marriott, B.E., 458
Holahan, C.K., 54, 56–57
Holle, R., 580
Holliday, H., 280
Holloway, C.D., 474
Holmes, M., 246
Holmes-Lonergan, H.A., 240
Holstein, B.E., 437
Holt, C.L., 55
Holt, C.L., 55
Holt, J.L., 357
Holtzworth-Munroe, A., 362
Honeycutt, H.G., 469
Honeycutt, J.M., 336
Honkasalo, M.-L., 508
Hoover, C., 278, 425
Hope, S., 439, 441, 445–446
Hoppe, M., 420
Hoppe-Ryan, C., 404
Hops, H., 410, 411, 565, 574
Horgan, T.G., 251–253, 264
Horner, M.S., 196–199
Horney, K., 151–152
Hornyak, L.M., 358
Horwitz, A.V., 411, 436–437, 445, 449
Hosterman, S.J., 421

Hostetter, A.M., 547
Houck, P.M., 395–396
House, J.S., 393–394, 436, 487
Houts, R.M., 352
Hovell, M.F., 420
Howard, J., 281
Howard, J.A., 372
Howell-White, S., 445
Hox, J.J., 273
Hoyert, D.L., 384
Hoyle, R.H., 565
Hruda, L., 86
Hsu, D., 527
Hu, F.B., 410–411, 415
Hu, P., 556
Huang, K., 592
Huang, L., 77
Hubbard, J.A., 165
Hubbard, L., 230
Hudson, J.I., 588–589
Hudspeth, C.D., 375
Huerta, M., 529
Hughes, D.L., 506–507, 536
Hughes, F.P., 167
Hughes, I.A., 144
Hughes, M., 423, 547
Hughes, M.E., 439, 441, 535
Huisman, H., 387, 427
Hulefeld, R., 123
Hull, J.G., 407
Hunt, K., 424–428
Hunter, B.A., 73
Hunter, W., 134
Huselid, R.F., 411
Huston, A., 86
Huston, T.L., 352, 362, 453, 459, 485
Hutson-Comeaux, S.L., 244
Hutz, C., 526
Huyck, M.H., 92
Hwu, H-G., 445, 547
Hyde, J.S., 105, 110–114, 126, 130, 133, 136, 140, 148, 206, 215–216, 503, 518, 559, 574
Hymel, S., 292

I

Ibarra, H., 319
Ickes, W., 352, 469
Iervolino, A.C., 141
Iezzi, T., 426
Ignacio, R.V., 549
Ihle, W., 574
Impett, E.A., 476, 575
Inaba, A., 436
Inch, R., 146
Ingram, R.E., 565–566
Inoue, Y., 171
Irish, J.T., 248
Isaac, J.D., 506
Ishii, S., 250
Ishiyama, F.I., 198
Israelian, M., 146

J

Jacek, C., 146
Jacklin, C.N., 102–104, 131, 154, 164
Jackman, M.R., 75
Jackson, C., 230, 426
Jackson, C.N., 140
Jackson, T., 426, 489
Jackson-Triche, M., 549
Jacobs, A., 86
Jacobs, J.E., 112, 219–220, 222–224, 415

Jacobs, R.R., 510
Jacobson, N.S., 362
Jaffee, S., 133
Jambekar, S., 207
James, A.N., 231
James, D., 245–246
James, J.B., 200
Janicki, D., 560, 571
Jans, F., 595
Jansen, E.A., 238–239
Jansen-Yeh, E., 238–239
Janssen, A., 248
Jarrell, S.B., 510
J.E., 506
Jeffery, R.W., 406
Jenkins, A., 240
Jenkins, C., 252
Jenkins, L.S., 580
Jennings, L., 83–84
Jennings, N.A., 173
Jerzak, P.A., 72
Jezova, D., 561
Jia, H., 412
Jobe, R.L., 465
Joffe, H., 546
Joffe, R.T., 546
Johannesen-Schmidt, M.C., 134,
    269, 334
John, D., 455
John, O.P., 90
Johns, M., 209
Johnson, B.R., 565–566
Johnson, B.T., 82, 269
Johnson, C., 262, 267, 589
Johnson, D., 376
Johnson, D.R., 555
Johnson, E.M., 352
Johnson, H., 462
Johnson, H.D., 296–297
Johnson, M., 205
Johnson, M.E., 15
Johnson, M.P., 293, 311, 465–466, 468–469
Johnston, K., 164
Johnston, L.D., 408–409
Johnston, M.K., 307
Jones, A.K.P., 425
Jones, D., 317, 489–490
Jones, D.C., 297
Jones, E.E., 89
Jones, J., 410–411
Jones, P.B., 546
Jones, S., 226
Jonsson, E.G., 62
Jonwutiwes, K., 399
Jordan, C., 581
Jorenby, D.E., 404
Jorgensen, P.F., 363
Joseph, G., 481
Josephs, R.A., 211–213
Jost, J.T., 75, 87
Jovanovic, J., 222, 225
Joyce, T., 407
Joyner, K., 576
Jozefowicz, D., 219–220
Jula, A., 395
Jurankova, E., 561
Jussim, L., 228

K

Kahana, E., 385, 585
Kahle, L.L., 399
Kahn, R.S., 146
Kahonen, M., 395

Kalbfleisch, P.J., 262
Kales, H.C., 549
Kalidindi, S., 546
Kalmijn, M., 352, 485
Kaluzny, G., 475
Kamarck, T., 390
Kamarck, T.W., 489
Kambara, A., 590
Kanazawa, S., 521
Kandolin, I., 318
Kane, E.W., 500
Kang, J.H., 343
Kaplan, A.S., 589
Kaplan, B.H., 487–488
Kaplan, G.A., 487, 489
Kaplan, R.M., 436
Kappes, M.E., 143
Kappes, M.H., 143
Kapuku, G., 390
Karabatsos, G., 473
Karau, S.J., 268, 270–271
Kärkkäinen, R, 222
Karney, B.R., 359–360, 438
Karniol, R., 131
Karraker, K.H., 161
Karten, S.J., 261
Kasanen, K., 222
Kasl, S.V., 438
Kasprzyk, D., 129
Kathuria, S., 514
Kattainen, A., 395
Katzman, D.K., 589
Kauppinen-Toropainen, K., 318
Kausch, D.F., 597
Kausilas, D., 319
Kawachi, I., 394
Kay, A.C., 75, 87
Kaye, W.H., 589
Keel, P.K., 589
Keenan, K., 123
Keerie, N., 249
Kehoe, G.C., 310
Keita, G.P., 568
Keitner, G.I., 553
Keller, J., 88, 208
Keller, M., 574
Kelly, H.A., 460
Kelly, J.R., 244, 530
Keltner, D., 556
Kemeny, M.E., 442
Kemper, T.D., 143
Kendler, K.S., 486, 489, 552, 589, 592
Kenford, S.L., 404
Kennedy, B.P., 394
Kennedy, N., 546
Kennedy, V.N., 581, 586
Kenrick, D.T., 148–149, 150, 332–333, 352
Kent, R.L., 268
Keogh, E., 425
Kephart, W.M., 339
Kesaniemi, Y.A., 395
Kessler, R.C., 443, 500, 547–548, 551, 568–569,
    588–589
Kessler, R.S., 487–488
Kessler, S.J., 39
Keywell, J., 65–66
Khan, A.A., 552
Khanom, N., 246
Khlat, M., 498, 500, 535
Kiecolt-Glaser, J.K., 391, 449, 450
Kiene, S.M., 347
Kiger, G., 454–456, 458
Killeen, L.A., 267
Killen, M., 316–317

Kilmartin, C.T., 206, 573
Kilpatrick, L., 146
Kim, A.H., 292
Kim, D.R., 546
Kim, H.-J., 2
Kim, H.K., 437, 468
Kim, J.E., 504
Kim, J.Y., 155
Kimura, D., 106, 108, 110, 142, 146
Kindlon, D.J., 123
Kinzler, M.H., 547
Kirchler, E., 353
Kirkpatrick-Smith, J., 595
Kirsten, B., 86
Kite, M.E., 81–82, 127
Kittel, F., 580
Kivelä, K., 535
Kleck, R.E., 276
Klein, E., 462
Klein, L.C., 556, 561
Kleinbaum, D.G., 487–488
Klem, M.L., 412, 414, 590
Klerman, G.K., 547
Kliewer, W., 206, 489–490, 573
Kline, G.H., 376
Kling, K.C., 206
Klinger, L.J., 172
Klinkenberg, D., 369
Klonoff, E.A., 427
Klonsky, B.G., 271
Klopf, D.W., 250
Klumb, P.L., 498
Klump, K.L., 589
Kneidinger, L.M., 254
Knight, D.M., Jr., 229
Knight, G.P., 123, 124
Knight-Bohnhoff, K., 124
Knox, V.J., 550
Kobrynowicz, D., 208
Koch, S.C., 271
Koenig, A.M., 134, 208, 210
Koerner, B.I., 509
Koerner, S.S., 417
Koeske, R.D., 20
Koestner, R., 14
Kohlberg, L., 132–135, 177–178
Kolaric, G.C., 252
Kolk, A.M., 387, 427
Komarov, Y.M., 383
Konrad, A.M., 55, 506
Kopp, M.S., 394
Kopper, B.A., 476
Korchynsky, R., 82
Kornstein, S.G., 553
Korteland, C., 564
Koskenvou, M., 508
Koss, M.P., 471–474, 477
Koutantji, M., 426
Kovenock, J., 143
Kowalewski, B.M., 512
Kowalski, R.M., 462, 528
Kozlowski, L.T., 404–405
Kraemer, H.C., 450, 589
Kraft, P., 421
Krahé, B., 478
Krane, J.E., 461
Kravitz, R.L., 549
Kraxberger, B.E., 421, 592
Krebs, D., 392
Kremen, A.M., 573
Krepostman, S., 584
Krieger, N., 409–410
Kring, A.M., 276
Krishnan, V., 375

Kriska, M., 561
Kroeck, K.G., 270
Kronick, R.G., 436
Krumholz, H.M., 395
Ku, L.C., 64, 411, 421
Kudes, D., 552
Kuebli, J., 163
Kuh, D., 534
Kuhner, C., 574
Kukkonen-Harjula, K., 395
Kukla, A., 214–215
Kuller, L.H., 449
Kumpf, M., 526
Kung, H.C., 384
Kunkel, A.W., 287
Kunz, M., 426
Kuperminc, G.P., 576
Kupersmidt, J.B., 239
Kupper, L.L., 464
Kurdek, L.A., 352, 366, 368–372, 376, 440, 457–458
Kurz, D., 461–462, 468
Kurzweil, N., 313
Kuttler, A.F., 288, 311, 315
Kuykendall, D.H., 439

L

Lacayo, R., 94
Lacey, R.S., 341
Lach, D.H., 532
Lachance, J.A., 110
Lackie, L., 476
Lacombe, A.C., 136
Ladwig, K.-H., 580
LaFleur, S.J., 258
LaFrance, M., 42, 183, 252, 264, 273–274, 276–277, 530–531
LaGreca, A.M., 288, 311, 315
Lahelma, E., 535
Lake, M.A., 161
Lakkis, J., 590, 592
Lambe, E.K., 589
Lamke, L.K., 353
Lamon, S.J., 110–113
Lampert, T., 498
Landis, D., 574–575
Lando, H.A., 406
Landrine, H., 427
Lane, D.M., 105
Lang, S., 10, 11
Langeland, W., 566
Langer, L.M., 474
Langford, R., 420
Langhinrichsen-Rohling, J., 420
Langhout, R.D., 529
Lanza, S., 219
Larsen, R.J., 363–364
Larson, J., 557, 561
Larson, R., 174, 274, 355–356, 573
Larson, R.W., 355
Laschever, S., 514–515
Lash, S.J., 469
Laumann, E.O., 128–129, 343, 346
Laursen, B., 307, 386
Lautenbacher, S., 426
LaVeist, T.A., 574
Lawlor, D.A., 390
Lawson, H.W., 395–396
Lawton, C.A., 108
Layne, C., 359, 362
Lazarus, R.S., 559
Le Pape, A., 498, 500, 535
Leadbeater, B.J., 576

Leahey, E., 110–111
Leaper, C., 164, 171, 221, 223, 245, 247, 280
Lear, M., 76
Lears, M., 170
Leary, M.R., 214, 421, 592
Lease, A.M., 317
LeBeau, L.S., 264
Lee, G.R., 373, 436, 443
Lee, J.A., 341–342
Lee, M.S., 240
Lee, T.M.C., 443, 546
Lees, H., 435
Leff, S.S., 239
Lefkowitz, E.S., 421
Lehman, S.J., 417
Leigh, B.C., 347
Leitzmann, M.F., 415
Lemerond, J., 597
Lempers, J.D., 288, 310
Lenart, S., 8
Lennon, M.C., 508
Leone, J.M., 465–466, 468
Lepore, S.J., 489, 584
LeResche, L., 387, 425
Lerner, J.V., 575
Lerner, R.M., 575
Lesko, A.C., 208
Lester, D., 594–597
Lester, J., 165
Levenson, A., 418
Levenson, R.W., 358, 361, 371, 447, 450
Leveroni, C.L., 143
Leviatan, U., 418
Levin, J., 113
Levin, S., 24
Levine, F.M., 426
Levine, J.D., 425
Levine, M.D., 406
Levine, M.P., 591
Levine, T., 444
Levinson, B., 343
Levitskaya, A., 339–340, 342
Lev-Wiesel, R., 478
Levy, P.E., 218
Lewin, E., 366
Lewin, L.M., 410, 411
Lewine, R.R.J., 577
Lewinsohn, P.M., 565, 574, 597
Lewis, B.P., 561
Lewis, G., 571
Lewis, L.L., 83
Lewis, R.J., 300
Lewinsohn, P., 420
Lex, B.W., 410
Li, N.P., 333
Libby, C.R., 299
Lichter, D.T., 452–453, 456–457
Lichter, E.L., 471
Liddell, M., 251
Lieb, P., 506
Lieberman, M.A., 488
Light, K.C., 556
Lilienfeld, S.O., 577–578
Lim, V.R., 362
Limon, J.P., 391
Lin, E., 589
Lin, H., 555
Lin, Y.C., 440
Lindberg, L.D., 373
Linders, L., 298
Lindgren, P., 404
Lindner, M.A., 299
Lindsey, E.W., 162

Linet, M.S., 427–428
Linn, M.C., 107, 113
Lippa, R., 61–62, 140
Lippa, R.A., 424
Lisak, D., 475
Liss, M., 8
Little, S., 597
Liu, H., 449
Liu, J.W., 406
Liu, W.Y., 171
Lloyd, J.E.V., 203
Lloyd, S.E., 466, 468
Lobel, M., 201
Lochhead, C., 221
Lochman, J., 165
Lockheed, M.E., 264
Loeber, C.C., 258
Loehlin, J.C., 62
Loevinger, B.L., 443
Lombardo, B., 276
Lombardo, W.K., 276
Longmore, M.A., 336
Lopez-Zafra, E., 267
Lorenz, F.O., 568, 576
Losoff, A., 327
Lounsbury, P., 397, 585
Lowe, G.D.O., 389
Lowe, K.B., 270
Lowell, E.L., 195
Lu, H., 374
Lubbert, K., 526
Lubetkin, E., 412
Luepker, R.V., 406
Lueptow, L.B., 55, 92–93
Lueptow, M.B., 55, 92–93
Lugar, R., 289, 310
Luketich, J.D., 401
Lumley, M.A., 406
Lummis, M., 222
Lund, R., 437
Lundberg, U., 392
Lundberg, M.A., 202, 226
Lupart, J.L., 219–220
Lupaschuk, D., 17, 18
Luria, Z., 161
Luschen, K., 455
Luthar, S.S., 165
Lye, D.N., 374
Lynch, J.J., 433
Lynch, K., 419
Lynch, M.E., 572
Lyons, A., 574–575
Lyons, J., 474
Lytton, H., 44, 161–162
Lyubomirsky, S., 564

M

MacCallum, F., 482
MacCallum, R.C., 391, 450
Maccoby, E.E., 53, 102–104, 131, 154, 236, 240–242, 260
MacDermid, S.M., 453, 459, 485
MacDowell, J., 329
MacGeorge, E.L., 279–281
Maciejewski, P.K., 569
Macintyre, S., 424
Mackenzie, C.S., 550
MacLehose, R.F., 395–396
Madon, S., 82
Madson, L., 15, 210
Maes, H., 555
Maggio, R., 15
Magley, V.J., 529

Mahay, J., 129
Mahler, B.A., 240
Majerovitz, S.D., 581
Major, B., 60, 140, 183, 186–188, 253–254, 522
Majors, R., 65
Mak, T, 171
Makar, H.R., 519–520
Makhijani, M.G., 270–271
Malamuth, N.M., 362
Malarcher, A., 404, 410
Malarkey, W.B., 391, 450
Malatesta, C.Z., 163
Malcuit, G., 162
Mallett, R., 73
Malmberg, B., 555
Maltz, D.N., 247, 260
Maner, J.K., 333
Manganelli, A.M., 77
Mann, T., 400, 592
Manning, A., 141
Manning, W.D., 336
Mannon, S.E., 454–456, 458
Manor, O., 393
Manson, J.E., 401
Manstead, A.S.R., 159–160, 275, 276
Mantell, J., 489
Mao, H-Y., 450
Maple, T.L., 254
Marangell, L.B., 546
Marcia, J.E., 134, 136
Marcotte, D., 569
Marcus, A.C., 427
Marcus, M.D., 406
Marecek, J., 20, 189
Margolis, D.R., 23
Markey, C.N., 440
Markey, P.M., 440
Markiewicz, D., 319
Markman, H.J., 358, 375–376, 450, 458
Markon, K., 238–239
Marks, J.S., 383
Marks, N.F., 571
Marks, S.R., 318
Markus, H.R., 211–213
Marsh, P., 547
Marshall, C.M., 459
Marshall, N.L., 449, 452, 480, 508, 536
Martell, R.F., 105, 508
Martens, A., 209
Martin, C.L., 86, 177, 237, 239–240, 241, 312
Martin, D., 374
Martin, L.R., 424
Martin, M., 374
Martin, P.D., 374
Martin, R., 248, 397
Martin, S.L., 464
Martindale, M., 531–532
Martinez-Donate, A.P., 420
Martinot, D., 210–211
Martire, L.M., 581
Marx, D.M., 209
Massa, L.J., 158–159
Masser, B., 75–77, 474
Masser, B.M., 75
Massey, K., 76
Masson, K., 288
Mastekaasa, A., 503
Masterpasqua, F., 481
Mastro, D.E., 171
Mathis, S.L., 276
Matschiner, M., 258
Matsuo, H., 475
Matthews, K.A., 390, 392, 449, 565–566, 569
Matthews, R.A., 536

Matthews, S., 393, 486, 506–507
Matthews, T.J., 376, 380
Mattingly, M.J., 455
Mau, W.C., 200
Maume, D.J., Jr., 456, 500
Maurer, S., 327
Mayer, R.E., 158–159
Mays, V.M., 366, 368, 370, 409, 597
Mazure, C.M., 569
Mazzocco, M.M.M., 110
McAlpine, D.D., 575
McBride, A.B., 484
McBurney, D.H., 108
McCabe, M.P., 591
McCarthy, J.F., 549
McClelland, D.C., 195
McCloskey, L.A., 237
McClure, E.B., 253
McClure, J.B., 405
McConnell, A.R., 15
McCoy, K., 371
McCrae, R.R., 131
McCreary, D.R., 64, 82, 399, 411
McDonough, P., 393–394, 443
McDougall, J., 13
McDougall, P., 292
McEnally, M., 257
McGlone, M.S., 208
McGlothlin, H., 316–317
McGonagle, K.A., 547
McGuinness, T., 556
McHale, S.M., 155, 453, 459, 485
McHugh, M.C., 20
McIntosh, D.N., 65–66
McIntyre, J.S., 550
McIntyre, K.P., 475
McKeever, W.F., 146
McKenna, W., 39
McKenry, P.C., 437
McKinlay, J.B., 395, 397
McKinley, J.C., 51
McKinley, N.M., 105, 114
McKinney, K., 346
McLaughlin, J., 449
McLendon, K., 472
McLeod, J.D., 487–488, 569
McMahon, T.J., 165
McMillan, D., 101
McMunn, A., 534
McNall, K., 563–564
McNelles, L.R., 288
McTeer, W.G., 421
McWilliams, S., 281
Meal, A., 395
Mechanic, M.B., 470
Mediansky, L., 489
Mehrabian, A., 355
Meiners, K.M., 459
Meischke, H., 401, 428
Melin, B., 392
Melnick, M.J., 417
Mendelson, M.J., 316–317
Meredith, L.S., 549
Merighi, J.R., 399
Messerschmidt, J.W., 58
Messineo, M., 171–172
Messman, S.J., 314
Messner, M.A., 25
Metellus, E., 420
Metha, A., 597
Metts, S., 338, 340–341
Metz, C., 552
Metzner, H.L., 436, 487
Meyer, K.A., 420

Meyer, L., 301
Meyer, L.L., 514
Meyer, W.U., 215–216
Meyers, S.A., 367–368
Mezulis, A.H., 215–216, 559
Miaskowski, C., 425
Michael, A., 575
Michael, R.T., 128–129, 346
Michael, S.T., 559
Michaels, S., 128–129, 346
Michell, L., 411
Mick, E., 578
Mickelson, K.D., 280, 584
Mickey, R.M., 597
Midgett, C., 421
Miedzian, M., 143, 157–158
Mikulis, D.J., 589
Miles, A., 429
Miles, C.C., 49–51
Milkie, M.A., 455
Mill, K., 290, 293
Miller, A., 406
Miller, C., 15–16
Miller, C.T., 206
Miller, J.B., 211
Miller, K.E., 417
Miller, L.C., 148, 304
Miller, L.H., 248
Miller, N., 123–124
Miller, R., 585–586
Miller, R.S., 304
Milos, G., 590
Milun, R., 108
Minkovitz, C.S., 550
Minnotte, K.L., 456, 458
Mirin, S.M., 409
Mirowsky, J., 480, 483, 485, 497–498, 503, 537, 557–558
Mischel, W., 152–153
Mistry, R., 86
Mitchell, J.E., 140
Mittman, B.S., 550
Mize, J., 162
Mladinic, A., 75–76, 92
Modvig, J., 437
Moen, P., 504–505, 571
Mok, D.S., 471, 476
Molidor, C., 464
Möller-Leimkühler, A.M., 594
Molloy, B.L., 207
Monette, G., 443
Mongeau, P.A., 336
Monk, D., 64
Monroe, S.M., 559
Monson, C.M., 420
Monsour, M., 310, 312–313, 315
Montano, D.E., 129
Montgomery, H., 483
Montgomery, M.J., 136, 319
Montgomery, S.M., 503
Mooney-Somers, J., 481–482
Moore, D.W., 534
Moore, T.M., 469
Moos, R.H., 411, 568
Morabia, A., 398
Morano, C.D., 597
Moretti, E., 13
Morgan, B.L., 71
Morgan, C., 228, 506
Morgan, E.M., 170
Morokoff, P.J., 420
Morosky, E., 8
Morris, M.L., 210–211
Morris, N.M., 143

Morrison, D.M., 420
Morrison, N., 475
Morrongiello, B.A., 421–422
Morrow, J., 562–563
Morry, M.M., 311
Morse, J., 518
Mortenson, S.T., 290
Mosca, L., 385
Moscucci, M., 428
Moser, D.K., 401, 428
Mosher, C.E., 424
Mosher, W.D., 375, 435
Moskowitz, D.S., 262
Mosnarova, A., 561
Mosquera, P.M.R., 275
Moss, P., 517
Moss, S.E., 268
Mott, J., 411
Mouton, C.P., 443
Muday, T., 563–564
Muehlenhard, C.L., 228, 472, 476
Mueller, M.A., 506, 523
Muennig, P., 412
Mühlberger, N., 580
Muhonen, T., 508
Mukai, T., 590
Mulac, A., 246–247
Mullooly, J.P., 436
Mulvenon, S., 597
Munroe, R.L., 123, 236
Murachver, T., 248–249
Murberg, T.A., 567, 576, 582
Murnen, S.K., 169, 258, 475, 590–591
Murowchick, E., 420
Murphy, E.M., 383
Murphy, G.C., 503
Murphy, J.D., 530
Murphy, S.L., 384
Murray, C., 481–482
Murray, D.M., 406
Murray, J.B., 392
Murray-Close, D., 239
Murstein, B.I., 21, 326
Must, A., 412, 414
Muth, S.Q., 129
Mutran, E.J., 504
Myers, B.J., 206, 573
Myers, C.D., 426
Myers, J., 486, 489
Myers, S., 280
Myers, S.M., 504
Myhill, D., 226
Mystern, A.-L., 392

N

Nagasaka, T., 426
Nagel, B., 475
Nagurney, A., 280–281
Naifeh, S., 63
Nansel, T.R., 123, 126
Nardi, P.M., 321–322
Nath, L.E., 273, 275
Nathanson, C.A., 426
Nazroo, J.Y., 449, 486–487, 569
Nealey, J.B., 402
Needham, B., 449
Neff, L.A., 438
Nehls, N., 578
Neighbors, H.W., 549
Nelson, C., 97
Nelson, C.B., 547
Nelson, D.A., 238–239
Nelson, D.B., 555
Nelson, D.L., 506

Nelson, N.M., 162
Nelson, P., 64
Nelson, S., 226–228
Neumark-Sztainer, D., 591
Newby, K., 385, 389–390, 396
Newcomb, M.D., 211, 411
Newcombe, N., 88, 155
Newell, C.E., 528
Newman, J.L., 199
Newport, F., 14, 367
Newton, T., 391, 450
Newton, T.L., 449
Nezami, E., 404
Nezlek, J., 294–296
Ngu, L.Q., 391, 451
Niaura, R.S., 391, 406
Nichols, J., 63
Nichols, T.E., 425
Nichter, M., 591
Nides, M., 404
Nielsen, B.A., 578
Nielsen, S.J., 414
Niemann, Y.F., 83–84
Nillapun, M., 399
Nilsson, S., 555
Nishida, T., 171
Nishimoto, R., 489
Noel, C., 339
Nolen-Hoeksema, S., 163, 204–205, 407–408,
    415, 547–548, 553–555, 557, 561–563,
    564–565, 567–568, 570, 572, 592
Noll, S.M., 207
Noller, P., 361
Nomaguchi, K.M., 535
Norcross, W.A., 439
Nordenmark, M., 535
Nordvik, H., 106
Norton, K.I., 591
Notarius, C.I., 357–358
Notzon, F.C., 383
Nowell, A., 110, 114, 116–117
Nuttall, R.L., 113
Nyquist, L.V., 268

O

Oakley, D.A., 426
O'Barr, W.M., 171
O'Brien, K.M., 219, 238–239
O'Brien, L.T., 210
O'Brien, M., 86
Ochion, Y., 131
Ochman, J.M., 169
Ockene, J., 404
O'Connor, C., 8
O'Connor, M., 526
Oei, T.P.S., 56
Ogawa, J.R., 307
Ohannessian, C.M., 575
O'Hara, P., 404
O'Hea, E.L., 398
Ohm, S.C., 55
Oishi, S., 436
Ojehagen, A., 596
Ojode, L.A., 270
Okamoto, K., 486, 489
Olds, T.S., 591
O'Leary, V.E., 320
Olff, M., 565–566
Olfson, M., 550
Olivardia, R., 591
Olive, S., 591
Oliver, M.B., 126, 148
Olmos-Gallo, P.A., 376
Olmstead, M.P., 587–588

O'Looney, P.A., 390
O'Loughlin, C., 333
Olson, A.M., 525
Olson, B., 170
Olson, J.E., 537
Olson, M., 532
O'Malley, P.M., 408–409
O'Meara, J.D., 312, 315
O'Neil, J.M., 64
Oppedisano, G., 546
Orbell, S., 421
Oriña, M.M., 259
Orlofsky, J.L., 136
Osborne, L.N., 449
Osgood, D.W., 219
Ostenson, R.S., 14
Ostrov, J.M., 238–239
Ostry, A., 506, 507
Otis, J., 426
Otis, M.D., 449
Oubaid, V., 357, 363
Overall, N., 333
Overpeck, M., 387
Overpeck, M.D., 123, 126
Owen, S.K., 92
Owens, D., 334–335
Owens, J.F., 390, 565
Owens, L., 126
Ozer, E.M., 485, 537

P

Packer, M., 395
Padgett, J., 206–207
Page, M.C., 123
Page, R.M., 488
Page, S., 550–551
Page-Gould, E., 571
Paget, S.A., 584
Paik, A., 343
Palinkas, L.A., 439
Palmieri, P.A., 529
Palomares, N.A., 249
Paluck, E.L., 252
Paludi, M.A., 530–531
Pancer, M., 581
Pang, J.S., 529
Papandonatos, G., 406
Papandonatos, G.D., 555
Parke, R.D., 288
Parker, L.E., 561
Parker, S., 287, 291, 293, 295
Parks, M.R., 305, 312–313
Parra, E.B., 446
Parsons, T., 53, 266
Pasch, L.A., 280
Pasko, L., 125
Pass, J.A., 263
Patsdaughter, C.A., 400
Patterson, C.J., 457, 481–482
Patterson, T.L., 504
Paul, S.M., 425
Paultre, F., 385
Pavalko, E.K., 536, 571
Paxson, C., 387
Paxton, S.J., 590
Pearce, S.A., 426
Pedersen, N.L., 555
Pedersen, W.C., 148
Pegalis, L.J., 302, 312
Penn, P., 469
Pennebaker, J.W., 277–278, 425
Peplau, L.A., 288, 293, 313, 317–318, 357, 366,
    368, 370–372, 375, 444, 457, 476, 519–520
Pepper, S., 297

Perenboom, R.J.M., 387
Perez-Garcia, A.M., 489
Perkins, K.A., 405–406
Perlick, D., 592
Perlman, C.A., 171
Perrin, J.M., 412
Perry, B., 481–482
Perry, D.G., 154
Perry, L., 472
Perry, M., 225
Perry-Jenkins, M., 458, 503
Perusse, D., 123, 239
Pesonen, O., 526
Peters, R.J., Jr., 404
Petersen, A.C., 107, 199, 289, 305–306, 417, 572, 587, 589, 592
Peterson, A.L., 407
Peterson, C., 294, 559, 581
Peterson, E.D., 385, 389–390, 396
Peterson, J., 420
Peterson, K., 414
Peterson, L., 421
Peterson, Z.D., 476
Pevalin, D.J., 447
Peyton, V., 86
Pezaris, E., 113
Pfaff, L., 271
Pfeiffer, K.A., 417
Pfizer, 128
Phillips, K.W., 258–259
Philpott, S., 396
Pickles, A., 555
Pidada, S., 238
Pierce, S.L., 258
Pietrobelli, A., 412
Pike, H., 246
Pike, J.J., 173
Pike, K.M., 587–588
Pilkington, C., 319
Pina, D.L., 459
Pinel, E.C., 210
Pines, A.M., 335
Pinquart, M., 436, 571
Pirie, P.L., 406
Piterman, L., 251
Pittinsky, T.L., 88
Pleck, J., 274, 355–356
Pleck, J.H., 62–64, 411, 421, 449, 479–480, 508, 517–518
Plomin, R., 141
Ploutz-Snyder, R, 263
Pohl, S., 278, 425
Polanichka, N., 161, 163
Polce-Lynch, M., 206, 573
Polivy, J., 587–588
Pollack, W.S., 123
Pollak, S., 297
Pomerantz, E.M., 222
Pomerleau, A., 162
Pomerleau, C.S., 406
Pomerleau, O.F., 406
Pope, C.R., 388, 422, 436, 507
Pope, F., 404
Pope, H.G., Jr., 591
Pope, J., 588–589
Pope, J.H., 395
Popenoe, D., 326, 331, 374, 376
Popkin, B.M., 414
Popp, D., 20
Popp, K., 580
Postma, K., 498, 500
Potapova, E., 339–340, 342
Potterat, J.J., 129
Poulin, F., 165
Poulin-Dubois, D., 86

Powell, G.N., 269
Power, C., 393, 439, 441, 445–446, 486, 506–507
Power, T.J., 239
Powers, D.A., 449
Powlishta, K.K., 239
Pratt, M., 416
Pratt, M.W., 134
Prehodka, J., 368
Prescott, C.A., 486, 489, 552
Prescott, E., 401
Price, D.D., 426
Price, L.R., 577
Prigerson, H.G., 569, 597
Prihoda, T.J., 550
Pringle, M., 395
Prinstein, M.J., 288, 311, 315
Prokhorov, A.V., 404
Prothrow-Stith, D., 394
Prout, A., 582, 586
Provenzano, F.J., 161
Pryor, J.B., 526, 530–532
Pugliesi, K., 486
Puncochar, J., 202
Punnett, L., 506, 508
Purcell, D.W., 577
Purdy, K.T., 316–317
Purnine, D.M., 355
Puska, P., 487
Putcha-Bhagavatula, A.D., 148
Pye, D.J., 397
Pyle, J.L., 506, 508

Q

Quadagno, D., 347
Quatman, T., 207, 230
Quay, L., 348
Quick, H.E., 504–505
Quillian, L., 316–317
Quina, K., 420
Quinn, D.M., 207–209
Quirouette, C., 450

R

Raag, T., 162
Rabin, C., 456, 458
Rabinovich, H., 552
Rackliff, C.L., 162
Radford, M.J., 395
Radloff, L.S., 544, 553
Radmacher, K., 305
Rae, D.S., 553
Raffaelli, M., 573
Raghubir, P., 440
Räikkönen, K., 565
Raley, R.K., 373
Ralston, P., 238–239
Ramet, S.P., 10
Ramirez, C., 439
Ramos, A., 532
Ranchor, A.V., 448
Rand, C., 404
Rankow, E.J., 400
Rao, S.M., 146
Rashid, T., 527
Rath, T., 317
Rathore, S.S., 395
Räty, H., 222
Rauch, J., 76
Raudenbush, S.W., 449, 452, 480, 508, 536
Ravens-Sieberer, U., 387
Rawlins, W.K., 309, 315
Read, J.G., 387
Redersdorff, S., 210

Rederstorff, J.C., 529–530
Reed, G.M., 442
Reed, J., 597
Reed, L., 214–215
Reeder, H.M., 311–313
Regan, P.C., 346, 348
Rehman, U.S., 362
Reid, S.A., 249
Reifman, A., 65–66, 341
Reingold, S.C., 390
Reis, H., 294–296
Reis, H.T., 295–297, 306
Reisman, J.M., 287, 290, 293, 303
Reiter, R.L., 146, 275
Reitman, F., 519
Reitzes, D.C., 504
Renzulli, L.A., 514
Resick, P.A., 470
Resnick, M.D., 410, 411
Rest, S., 214–215
Reuss, P., 23
Revenson, T.A., 488, 581, 584
Reynolds, K.A., 571
Reynolds, L., 574–575
Reynolds, P., 489
Rhatigan, D.L., 469
Rhee, S.H., 141
Rhoades, G.K., 375–376, 458
Rhodes, N., 243
Riad, J.K., 143
Ricciardelli, L.A., 64, 590–592
Rich, A.R., 595
Richards, H.C., 231
Richards, J.M., 275
Richards, M., 525–526
Richards, M.H., 417, 573
Richardson, J., 410–411
Rich-Edwards, J.W., 401
Ridgeway, C.L., 519
Rieker, P.P., 382, 385, 390
Riggle, E.D.B., 449
Rimm, E.B., 415
Rise, J., 421
Ritchie, J., 290, 293, 506
Rivadeneyra, R., 170
Robb, J.C., 546
Robbins, C., 436, 487
Robert, M., 150
Roberts, C.M., 570
Roberts, J., 575
Roberts, J.M., Jr., 129
Roberts, L.L., 506, 523
Roberts, L.R., 199
Roberts, S.J., 400
Roberts, T-A., 203–205, 207, 277–278, 575
Robertson, G.G., 344
Robertson, J., 549
Robinson, D.T., 243, 261
Robinson, J.P., 453, 455, 512
Robinson, L., 581, 586
Robinson, M.E., 426
Robson, K., 514, 519
Rockett, H.R., 414
Rodgers, B., 439, 441, 445–446
Rodgers, J.M., 123
Rodriguez, G., 410–411
Rogers, S.J., 485, 501–502
Rohde, P., 420, 597
Rohlfs, I., 498–499
Roman, J.S., 209
Romanov, K., 508
Romney, A.K., 236
Romney, D.M., 44, 161–162
Roos, E., 535
Rose, A.J., 237, 301, 307

Rose, G.L., 585
Rose, S., 315, 317, 336, 369–370
Rose, S.E., 399
Rose-Krasnor, L., 292
Rosen, B.R., 421
Rosen, E., 52
Rosenbaum, R.M., 214–215
Rosenberg, M., 211
Rosenbloom, A., 14
Rosenfeld, P., 528
Rosenfield, S., 498, 500–501
Rosenkrantz, P.S., 79–81
Rosenmann, A., 574
Rosenthal, L., 371
Rosenthal, R., 40, 104
Rosip, J.C., 253
Ross, C., 498, 557–558
Ross, C.E., 480, 483, 485, 497, 503, 507, 537
Ross, M.W., 409
Rostosky, S.S., 449
Roter, D.L., 248, 250–251
Roth, C., 23
Roth, M.E., 409
Roth, S., 475
Rothbart, M., 90
Rothblum, E.D., 370, 597
Rothschild, L., 577
Rovine, M., 555
Rowe, J.W., 486
Roy, C., 86
Roy, J.R., 404
Roy, R., 298
Royce, J.M., 404
Royer, J.M., 111
Rozee, P.D., 477
Rozelle, R.M., 83–84
Ruan, W.J., 123, 126
Rubenfeld, K., 279, 281
Rubenstein, L.V., 549
Rubin, J.Z., 161
Rubin, K.H., 292
Rubin, L.B., 356, 359
Rubin, Z., 444
Ruble, D., 177
Ruble, D.N., 86, 222
Rudman, L.A., 90, 271
Rudolph, K.D., 237, 567
Rueda, B., 489
Ruiz, J.M., 489
Rushton, J.P., 143
Russell, A., 126
Russell, B.L., 252, 530
Russell, C.J., 589
Russell, D., 471–473, 476
Russell, S.T., 481
Rust, J., 141, 164
Ruthazer, R., 395
Rutter, M., 555
Ryan, C.E., 553
Ryan, J.A., 410–411
Ryckman, R.M., 299
Rynes, S., 514

S

Saad, L., 367, 502, 590
Saal, F.E., 531
Sabini, J., 365
Sabo, D.F., 417
Sacco, V.F., 462
Sachs-Ericsson, N., 436, 535
Sack, K., 122
Sadalla, E.K., 332
Sadar, N.C., 517

Sadava, S.W., 411
Sadker, D., 167, 225
Sadker, M., 167, 225
Safir, M.P., 574
Sagrestano, L.M., 265
Saiz, J.L., 75–76
Sakalli-Ugurlu, N., 467
Sakinofsky, I., 595
Salisbury, J., 532
Salomaa, V., 395
Salonen, J. T., 487
Salovey, P., 364, 391
Sammel, M.D., 555
Sampson, R., 134
Samter, W., 287, 290
Sanchez, D.T., 263
Sanchez, J., 551–552, 577
Sanchez, L., 500
Sanchez-Hucles, J.V., 72–74
Sanchez-Sosa, J.J., 536
Sanders, S.G., 519–520
Sanderson, S., 455
Sandler, B.R., 532
Sandstrom, M.J., 165
Sankis, L.M., 578
Sanna, L.J., 215–216
Sansone, C., 506
Santagata, R, 362
Santos, S.J., 536
Sarigiani, P.A., 199, 289, 305–306
Sasaki, Y., 590
Sastry, J., 436, 483
Satterfield, A.T., 228
Saunders, D.G., 581
Saunders, R., 417
Saw, A., 147
Sawin, L.L., 58
Sayers, S.L., 557
Saylor, K.E., 404, 410
Scanlon, M.B., 311, 313
Scaramella, T.J., 143
Schaefer, E.C., 334–335
Schatzberg, A.F., 553
Scheidt, P.C., 123, 126
Scheier, M.F., 565
Schein, V.E., 270
Schipper, M., 390
Schippers, J.J., 512
Schmader, T., 209
Schmidlin, A.M., 253–254
Schmitt, D.P., 330, 344
Schmitt, J.P., 352, 376
Schnarch, B., 10
Schneer, J.A., 519
Schneider, B.H., 298
Schneider, C., 440
Schneider, O., 472, 474
Schneiderman, N., 390
Schnittker, J., 550
Schnohr, P., 401
Schoenbach, V.J., 487–488
Scholey, P., 584
Schone, B.S., 439
Schreiber, G.B., 589
Schulenberg, J.E., 408, 409
Schulz, M.S., 536
Schulz, R., 571
Schulze-Bonhage, A., 146
Schumacher, K., 532
Schuurs, A.H., 390
Schwalbe, M.L., 212
Schwartz, D., 165, 591
Schwartz, J., 301
Schwartz, J.E., 446

Schwartz, P., 349, 372
Schweinle, W.E., 469
Scott, J.P., 341
Scott, K.A., 317
Scudiero, M., 574–575
Sculthorpe, A., 590
Sebanc, A.M., 239, 258
Seccombe, K., 443
Seelau, E.P., 464
Seelau, S.M., 464
Seeley, J., 420
Seeley, J.R., 597
Seeman, M.V., 577
Seeman, T., 486–487
Seeman, T.E., 427, 486, 556
Seery, B., 503
Segar, M., 415
Seidlitz, L., 274
Seligman, M.E.P., 556, 558
Seltman, H., 571
Seltzer, J.A., 374–376
Semmelroth, J., 363–364
Semple, S., 504
Sempos, C.T., 383
Sempos, E.V., 383
Sen, M.G., 86
Senchak, M., 295–296
Serbin, L.A., 86
Serewicz, M.C.M., 336
Sermet, C., 498, 500, 535
Sethi, S., 565
Settles, I.H., 529–530
Sevcik, K., 11
Seward, R.R., 518
Seymour, E., 200
Shackelford, T.K., 330
Shaffer, D.R., 302, 312
Shajahan, P.M., 548
Shao, Q., 443
Shapira-Berman, O., 458
Shaver, P., 306–308, 337–338, 357
Shaver, P.R., 336
Shaw, L.J., 385, 389–390, 396
Shaw, W.S., 504
Shaywitz, B.A., 114–115
Shaywitz, S.E., 114–115
Shear, M.K., 572
Shearer, C.L., 421
Sheeran, P., 421
Sheets, V.L., 289, 310, 371, 527
Sheffield, D., 390
Sheinberg, M., 469
Shelton, B.A., 455
Shepard, B., 163
Sherman, R.T., 589
Sherrod, D., 321–322
Shibley Hyde, J., 348
Shields, S.A., 48
Shih, J.H., 567, 569
Shih, M., 88
Shillington, A.M., 420
Shippy, R.A., 321
Shkodriani, G.M., 71
Shoeny, M.E., 344
Shook, S.L., 486
Shoop, R.J., 532
Shortt, J.W., 468
Showers, C.J., 206
Shriver, S.P., 401
Shullman, S.L., 525–526
Shupe, E.I., 532
Shute, G.E., 551
Shye, D., 436
Siddiqui, O., 411

Siega-Riz, A.M., 414
Siegel, J.M., 427, 439, 472
Siegel, S.J., 550
Siegel-Hinson, R.J., 146
Siegfried, J. M., 401
Siegfried, J.M., 401
Siever, M.D., 591
Sigal, J., 527
Sigall, H., 202
Sigmundson, H.K., 145
Signorielli, N., 170
Silberg, J., 555
Silva, E., 529
Silverman, I., 108
Silverstein, B., 592
Silverstein, L.B., 24
Silverthorn, N., 219
Siminerio, L., 590
Simmons, W.W., 14
Simms, K.B., 229
Simon, R.W., 273, 275, 483, 537–538
Simoni-Wastila, L., 549
Simonoff, E., 555
Simons, A.D., 559
Simons, R.L., 568, 576
Simons-Morton, B., 404, 410
Simpkins, S., 223
Simpkins, S.D., 219, 223, 288
Simpson, A., 298
Simpson, J.A., 259
Sinclair, N., 219
Singer, J.D., 536
Sipan, C.L., 420
Sippola, L.K., 296
Sirey, J.A., 412
Sivasubramaniam, N., 270
Six, B., 85
Skaff, M.M., 411, 568
Skidmore, J.R., 64
Skoe, E.E., 134
Skogman, K., 596
Skrabski, A., 394
Skultetyova, I., 561
Slater, P.E., 266
Slavick, J.T., 344
Slesinski, M.J., 399
Slijper, F.M.E., 144
Slimack, M.J., 597
Sloan, L., 472
Sloan, M., 436
Sloane, D., 358
Sloggett, A., 571
Smith, B.W., 571
Smith, C., 468
Smith, C.A., 368, 425
Smith, D.B., 504
Smith, G.D., 390
Smith, G.W., 63
Smith, S.S., 404
Smith, T.E., 245, 247
Smith, T.W., 391, 451, 489
Smith-Lovin, L., 243, 261
Smock, P.J., 446
Smolak, L., 590–591
Snell, W.E., Jr., 304
Snodgrass, S.E., 263
Snyder, A., 278, 425
Snyder, M., 69, 185
Sobieraj, S., 154
Sobin, J., 464
Sobol, A.M., 412, 414
Sochting, I., 134
Soler, E., 462
Sollie, D.L., 353

Solomon, B., 295–296
Sommer, I.E.C., 146
Sommer, K.L., 213
Sonenstein, F.L., 64, 411, 421
Soobader, M.J., 409–410
Sorbi, M.J., 273
Sorensen, G., 404
Sorensen, S., 571
Sorenson, S. B., 472
South, S.J., 454
Spalding, L.R., 366, 368, 370–371
Specter, G., 374
Spence, J.T., 53–58, 70–71, 268
Spencer, S.J., 208–209
Spencer, T., 578
Sperling, J., 485
Spindler, A., 590
Spitzberg, B.H., 470
Spitze, G., 454
Sprague, J., 347
Sprecher, S., 330–332, 335, 339–342, 344–346,
     348–349, 353, 474
Spreer, J., 146
Spring, B., 406
Springer, J.A., 146
Springer, S.P., 146
Sprock, J., 578
Spruijt-Metz, D., 415
St. Peters, M., 376
Stack, C.B., 134
Stack, S., 436, 483, 596
Stacy, A.W., 404
Stafford, L., 350–351, 458
Stall, R., 420
Stallings, M.C., 62
Stampfer, M.J., 415
Stangor, C., 73, 101
Stanley, J.C., 111–112, 223
Stanley, S.M., 375–376, 458
Stanley, T.D., 510
Stansfeld, S., 486, 507
Stanton, K.-L., 421
Staples, C.L., 212
Staples, R., 65, 158
Stapp, J., 53, 55–56
Stark, K.A., 451
Stauffacher, K., 239
Steele, C.M., 208
Steele, J., 200, 224
Steele, J.R., 208
Stegner, H., 143
Steil, J.M., 265, 267
Stein, J.A., 211
Stein, M.B., 471
Steinberg, M.B., 404
Steinberg, N., 326, 344
Steiner-Pappalardo, N.L., 352
Steingart, R.M., 395
Steinmetz, S.K., 462–463, 468–469
Stephens, M.A.P., 581
Steptoe, A., 399
Stern, S.R., 171
Stets, J.E., 464
Stevens, D.P., 454–456, 458
Stevens, G., 334–335
Stevens, K., 123
Stevens, L.E., 79, 85, 95
Stevens, M., 481–482
Stevenson, H.W., 222
Stewart, T.L., 263
Stewart, W.F., 427–428
Stiles, D.A., 71
Stillman, S., 368
Stipek, D., 220, 223

Stipek, D.J., 218
Stockdale, G.D., 82
Stolzenberg, R.M., 375
Storey, P.L., 392
Straus, M.A., 462–465, 468–469
Strauss, J., 563–564
Striegel-Moore, R.H., 206–207, 587–589, 592
Strober, M., 589
Stroebe, M.S., 442–443
Stroebe, W., 442–443
Strohschein, L., 443
Strong, R.A., 108
Stroud, L.R., 391, 555
Struckman-Johnson, C., 472–474
Struckman-Johnson, D., 472–474
Stuhlmacher, A.F., 514
Subar, A.F., 399
Suh, E., 436
Suh, E.J., 262
Sullivan, E., 83, 84
Sullivan, J.G., 366
Sullivan, M.J., 425
Sullivan, O., 455
Sullivan, Q., 330–331
Suls, J., 585
Summers, L.H., 193
Sun, J., 404, 410
Sundaram, V., 386
Sundie, J.M., 148
Surtees, P.G., 548
Suskin, N., 584
Sussman, A.L., 275, 517
Sussman, S., 404
Suter, E.A., 8
Sutton-Tyrrell, K., 449
Svebak, S., 582
Swain, S., 305
Swanberg, J.E., 480, 500
Swanson, C., 371
Swanson, K., 371
Swartz, M., 547
Swecker, J., 525–526
Sweet, J.A., 374–376
Sweeting, H., 388
Swenson, L.P., 206
Swerczek, M., 154
Swift, K., 15–16
Swim, J.K., 73, 91, 215–216, 510
Syme, S.L., 436, 487
Syniar, G., 547
Szinovacz, M., 505
Szinovacz, M.E., 504

T

Tafarodi, R.W., 211–213
Takiff, H.A., 263
Takkinen, S., 555
Tambor, E.S., 214
Tamres, L.K., 560
Tanaka, Y., 486, 489
Tanasescu, M., 415
Tangri, S.S., 532–533
Tanke, E.D., 69
Tannen, D., 30, 278–279
Tarmina, M.S., 400
Tashkin, D.P., 397
Tasker, F., 481
Tate, J.C., 406
Tavris, C., 60
Taylor, C.B., 450, 589
Taylor, L., 519–520
Taylor, S.E., 442, 556, 561
Taylor, T., 390

Taylor, W.C., 404
Tchividjian, L.R., 421, 592
Teachman, J., 376
Teasdale, J.D., 558
Tekarslan, E., 353
Telfer, J.A., 219–220
Templer, D.I., 195
Tenenbaum, H.R., 164, 221, 223
Terdal, S.K., 214
Terman, L.M., 49–51
Terracciano, A., 131
Terry, R., 165
Tesman, J.R., 163
Tessaro, I., 400
Tevendale, H.D., 206
Tevlin, J., 524
Thase, M.E., 553, 559
Thelen, M.H., 163
Thoennes, N., 462, 464
Thoits, P.A., 436, 535
Thomas, J.J., 206, 293, 311
Thomas-Hunt, M.C., 258–259
Thompson, C.A., 250
Thompson, J.K., 589
Thompson, J.M., 355
Thompson, L., 459, 523
Thompson, M., 123, 591
Thompson, R.A., 589
Thompson, V.L., 455
Thomson, R., 249
Thornton, A., 346
Thornton, B., 299
Thunberg, M., 276
Tickamyer, A.R., 72
Tiedemann, J., 223
Tierney, A.M., 557
Tiger, L., 292
Tiggemann, M., 506
Timberlake, J.M., 373
Timmers, M., 159, 276
Tirpak, D.L., 401
Tither, J.M., 333
Tjaden, P., 462, 464
Todd, J., 9
Todd, Z., 246
Tolejko, N., 446
Tolin, D.F., 566
Toller, P.W., 8
Tolman, D.L., 575
Tolman, R.M., 464
Tolson, A., 63
Tolson, J.M., 286, 291
Tomeo, D.L., 123
Tomeo, M.E., 195
Toner, B.B., 564
Torges, C.M., 529
Torkelson, E., 508
Tornstam, L., 327–328
Toro-Morn, M., 335
Torres, J. B., 65
Torsheim, T., 387
Tower, R.B., 438
Townsend, D.W., 425
Tracy, A.J., 575
Trager, K.D., 76
Trautner, H.M., 86
Travis, C.B., 396
Treasure, J.L., 589
Treiber, F.A., 390
Tremblay, R.E., 165
Tremont, G., 559
Trenholm, C., 348
Treynor, W., 563
Trigg, K.Y., 530

Trinneer, A., 219
Troiano, R.P., 414
Troop, N.A., 589
Tross, S.A., 254
Trost, M.R., 148, 332
Troxel, W.M., 449
Trudeau, K.J., 301, 584–585
Tryban, G.M., 551
Tschann, J.M., 303
Tsui, L., 513
Tucker, J.S., 446
Tudor, J.F., 440, 497, 534
Tuomisto, M., 392
Turner, H., 420
Turner, J., 146
Turner, R.A., 556
Turner, R.J., 568–569
Twamley, E.W., 566
Twenge, J.M., 71, 130, 206–207, 343, 347, 552, 572
Tyrka, A.R., 592
Tyson, R, 371

U

Uchino, B.N., 489
Udry, J.R., 143, 576
Udvari, S.J., 298
Uebelacker, L.A., 448
Ueno, K., 436
Ulin, P.R., 420
Ullman, S.E., 473, 476–477
Umberson, D., 439, 443, 445–446, 449
Uncapher, M., 146
Unterrainer, J., 146
Updegraff, J.A., 561
Updegraff, K.A., 219
Urberg, K.A., 286–287, 291
Uvnas-Moberg, K., 561

V

Vaccarino, V., 395, 486, 487
Valenstein, M., 549
Valentine, S., 500
Valian, V., 539
Valimaa, R., 387
van Beek, Y., 550
van den Berg, P., 591
van den Borne, B., 299
van den Bos, G.A.M., 387
van Dolderen, M.S.M., 550
Van Doorne-Huiskes, A., 512
van Engen, M.L., 38, 270
van Groenou, M.I.B., 443
van Grootheest, D.S., 443
van Herten, L.M., 387
van Jaarsveld, C.H.M., 448
van Middendorp, H., 273
van Nobelen, D., 352
van Os, J., 546
van Sonderen, E., 448
van Vianen, A.E.M., 275
Van Yperen, N.W., 448
Vangelisti, A.L., 328–329
Vanneman, R., 512
Vänskä, J., 222
Vanzetti, N.A., 358
Vasquez, A.M., 446
Veccia, E.M., 254
Veiel, H.O.F., 574
Veniegas, R.C., 144–145, 288, 293, 313
Verbrugge, L.M., 429
Verdi, A.F., 249

Verheul, H.A., 390
Verkuyten, M., 288
Verma, J., 353
Vernon, M.K., 223, 415
Vescio, T.K., 91
Vestbo, J., 401
Viki, G.T., 76, 474
Villanova, P., 559
Vingerhoets, A.J.J.M., 273
Visscher, B.R., 442
Vitaro, F., 165, 239
Vogel, D.A., 161
Vogel, D.L., 82, 359–360
Vogel, S.R., 79–81
Vogeltanz, N.D., 408
Vohs, K.D., 127, 142, 338, 370
von Eye, A., 575
Vonk, R., 352
Voyer, D., 106
Voyer, S., 106

W

Wade, M.E., 515
Wade, T.J., 447
Wadsworth, M.E.J., 503
Wagner, K., 146
Wagner, W., 353
Wahba, J., 351–352
Wai, J., 147
Wainright, J.L., 481
Wainwright, N.W.J., 548
Waite, A., 298
Waite, L.J., 375
Waldfogel, J., 518
Waldman, I.D., 141
Waldron, I., 374, 381–382, 399, 401–402, 407, 409, 415, 419, 422, 428, 439, 441, 535, 592
Waldron, V.R., 250
Walker, G., 469
Walker, K., 292
Walker, L.E., 467
Walker, L.S., 425, 428
Wallace, H., 461–462, 467–469, 471, 478
Wallace, J.E., 514, 519
Wallance, G.J., 482
Waller, M.W., 464
Wallis, H, 143
Wallis, H.A., 506, 523
Walsh, J., 203
Walsh, M., 225
Walter, H., 580
Walters, A.E., 514
Walters, E.E., 589, 592
Walters, R., 152–153
Walters, V., 429, 489
Walumbwa, F.O., 270
Wang, T., 343
Wang, T.H., 198
Wang, Y., 395, 413
Wannan, G., 597
Ward, C.A., 474
Ward, D.S., 417
Ward, L.M., 170
Wardle, J., 399, 429
Wardle, M., 571
Warren, K., 225
Warren, L.Z., 355
Warren, M.P., 555, 574
Washo, C., 505
Wassertheil-Smoller, S., 443
Watkins, D., 214
Watson, C.M., 207, 230

Watson, D., 277, 425
Way, N., 286, 288, 290
Weaver, K.R., 597
Weaver, T.L., 470
Weich, S., 571
Weinbaum, D., 410–411
Weiner, B., 214–215
Weiner, E., 280
Weiner, R.L., 525
Weinick, R.M., 439
Weinstock, J.S., 321
Weinstock, L.M., 446
Weiss, C.C., 535
Weiss, R.D., 409
Weissman, M.M., 445, 547
Weitzman, L.J., 29
Welleford, A., 489–490
Wellman, B., 308
Wells, B.E., 130, 343, 347
Wells, E.A., 420
Wells, K.B., 549
Weltman, K., 267
Wendler, C., 112
Wenger, N.K., 396
Werking, K.J., 287, 310–312, 314
Werner, N.E., 238–239
Wesley, A., 472
West, P., 388
Westen, D., 363–364
Wester, S.R., 82
Wethington, E., 485, 487–488, 500
Wetter, D.W., 404–405
Wetzel, P.J., 250
Whaley, B.B., 290
Whatley, M.A., 478
Wheelan, S.A., 249
Wheeler, J., 348
Wheeler, L., 198, 294–296
Whiffen, V.E., 355
Whisman, M.A., 446, 448
Whitacre, C.C., 390
White, H.R., 411, 436–437, 445, 449
White, J.W., 462, 528, 530–531
White, K.B., 465
White, L.K., 485
White, P.G., 421
Whitehead, B.D., 326, 331, 374, 376
Whiteman, S., 155
Whiting, B.B., 174–176, 238, 242
Whitley, B.E., Jr., 82, 127, 559, 569
Whitton, S. W., 376
Whitton, S.W., 375
Widiger, T.A., 551, 552, 578
Wiener, W., 64
Wigfield, A., 219, 220
Wilcox, S., 443
Wild, M.N., 288
Wilkes, S., 549
Willemsen, T.M., 38, 270
Willen, H., 483
Willett, W.C., 415
Willetts, M.C., 443
Williams, B.J., 392
Williams, C., 134, 581–582, 584–585

Williams, C.L., 509
Williams, D.R., 382, 393–394
Williams, J., 516
Williams, J.E., 82, 92
Williams, K., 443, 446, 449, 458
Williams, K.B., 531–532
Williams, K.R., 469
Williams, L., 253–254
Williams, M., 547
Williams, R.J., 590, 592
Williams, S.L., 464
Williams, W.L., 10
Williams-Evans, L., 503
Williamson, D.E., 555
Williamson, I., 592
Willig, R.F., 143
Willis, E., 585–586
Willis, F.N., Jr., 254
Wills, T.A., 437
Wilsdon, A., 420
Wilsnack, R.W., 408
Wilsnack, S.C., 408
Wilson, D.K., 489–490
Wilson, M., 149–150
Wilson, S., 174
Winfield, I., 472, 476
Wing, R.R., 412, 414, 590
Wingard, D.L., 446
Winstead, B., 551–552, 577
Winstead, B.A., 300–301, 315, 319, 487
Wise, E.A., 426
Wisnicki, K.S., 565–566
Wojno, W.C., 581
Wolfe, M.D., 371
Wong, F.Y., 64, 82
Wong, M., 563–564
Woo, M., 56
Wood, E., 161
Wood, R.G., 518
Wood, W., 41, 149, 173, 176, 243, 259,
    261, 265, 334
Woodburn, S., 298
Woodbury, S., 536, 571
Woodside, D.B., 589
Woody, E., 230
Woodzicka, J.A., 530
Woolard, R.H., 395
Worell, J., 9
Workman, J.E., 472
Worthman, C.M., 574
Wortman, C.B., 443
Wright, C., 475
Wright, D.E., 293, 320, 362
Wright, M.J., 62
Wright, P.H., 285, 287, 289, 293, 305,
    309–311, 313
Wright, R.A., 392
Wright, T.L., 346
Wrightsman, L.S., 64
Wu, C, 270
Wu, H.X., 123
Wu, T.Y., 399
Wyke, S., 428
Wyman, H., 237

Wyn, J., 585–586
Wynn, A., 395

X

Xu, X., 375

Y

Yailagh, M.S., 203
Yamazaki, S.K., 123
Yang, B., 596–597
Yang, Y., 148
Yankeelov, P., 230
Yankeelov, P.A., 487
Yeatts, D.E., 518
Yee, D.K., 220
Yee, J.L., 571
Yewchuk, C., 17–18
Yoder, C.Y., 551
Yonkers, K.A., 553
Yoon, K.S., 223
Yoshimoto, D., 371
Young, E., 556, 572
Young, K., 421
Young, L.T., 546
Young, M.L., 464
Young, R.F., 385, 585
Young, T.B., 405
Young Ho, H., 253
Youngblade, L.M., 92, 458
Young-DeMarco, L., 346
Yu, J., 214
Yu, K., 404, 410
Yuan, N.P., 471

Z

Zaharias, G., 251
Zahn-Waxler, C., 161, 163
Zakriski, A, 165
Zand, D., 369, 370
Zarbatany, L., 292, 297
Zarin, D.A., 550
Zautra, A.J., 571
Zdaniuk, B., 464
Zehnder, S.M., 240
Zelditch, M., Jr., 264
Zellner, J.A., 420
Zeman, J., 428
Zemore, S.E, 2
Zhang, Q., 413
Zhao, S., 547
Zhu, S.H., 404, 410
Zigler, E., 275, 517
Zimmerman, M., 577
Zimmerman, R.S., 474
Zion, C., 97
Zipursky, R.B., 589
Zlotnick, C., 577
Zoccolillo, M., 123
Zottarelli, L.K., 518
Zuckerman, M., 198, 421
Zurbriggen, E.L., 170

SUBJECT INDEX

A

Abercrombie & Fitch, 171
Ability, self-perception of, 219
Abstinence only sex education, 348–349
Abusive relationships, demand/withdraw
    pattern in, 362. *See also* Domestic abuse
Access discrimination, 508
Accidents
  alcohol-related, 407
  death from, 384–385
  motor vehicle, 419
  risk-taking behavior and, 419
Achievement, 193–234
  fear of, 196–200
  individual difference factors, 195–218
    achievement motive, 195–196
    attributions for performance, 214–218
    conceptions of self, 210–214
    response to evaluative feedback, 203–205
    self-confidence, 201–203
    self-esteem, 206–207
    stereotype threat, 207–210
  mental health and, 573–574
  sex differences in higher education, 194–195
  social factors, 218–232
    expectancy/value model of achievement,
     219–220
    influence of parents, 220–224
    influence of teachers, 225–231
Achievement motive, 195
Achievement orientation, 64
Acquaintance Description Form (ADF),
  293–294, 311
Active coping, 560
Active management by exception, 269–270
Activist, feminist, 8
Activity, sex differences in, 130–131
Addiction, 404–406. *See also* Substance abuse
Adolescence
  depression in, 553, 572–576
    body image and, 574–575
    manifestations of, 576
    puberty and, 574
    relations with parents and
     friends, 576
    self-esteem and, 575–576
  eating disorders during, 590
  gender intensification in, 572–574
  interpersonal stress and, 567
  problem behaviors in, 410–411
  self-esteem, 206–207
  suicide in, 595, 597
Adulthood, interaction styles in, 255–256
Adult stereotype, 78–81
Advertisements, 597
  gender-role stereotypes in, 171–173
  toys, 172–173

Affiliation, fear of, 198–199, 297–298.
    See also Intimacy
African Americans, 85. *See also* Blacks;
    Ethnicity; Race
  body image of, 207
  divorce rate among, 435
  friendships among, 290
  gender attitudes of, 72
  gender-role stereotypes among, 83, 84
  gender-role strain among, 65
  health issues and, 383, 402
  modern sexism against women, 73–74
Against Our Will: Men, Women, and Rape
    (Brownmiller), 478
Agape (pure) love, 341–342
Age
  friendships and, 290–291
  gender intensification and, 572–573
  as moderating variable, 105
  self-disclosure and, 291
Age bias, 103
Age effects, 37
Agency
  adjusting to chronic illnesses and, 584.
    See also Agency
  coping strategies and, 560–561
  depression and, 569
  eating disorders and, 589
  health and, 423–424
  problem-solving orientation and, 569
  status theory and, 262
  unmitigated, 56–57, 197–198, 423–424, 584
Agentic orientation, 55
Aggression, 64
  biological theories of, 140–147
    brain, 145–147
    genes, 140–142
    hormones, 142–145
  crime statistics, 126
  domestic abuse, 460–469
    among homosexuals, 464
    characteristics of perpetrator, 467–468
    characteristics of victim, 468
    incidence, 461–467
    indicators, 462
    myths about, 461
    theories of, 468–470
  emotions and, 123
  gender-role theories of, 154–156
  guilt and, 134
  hostile, 121–123
  proactive, 165
  provocation to, 123
  rape and other forms of sexual coercion,
    470–478
    characteristics of perpetrator, 474–476
    characteristics of victim, 476–477
    definitions of, 471–472

    incidence of, 472–474
    myths about, 475–476
    studies of college students, 473–474
    theories of, 477–478
  reactive, 165
  relational, 124, 238–239
  research on, 123–126
    sex of perpetrator, 123–126
    sex of victim, 126
  sex differences in, 89, 124–126
  sex-related comparisons, 121–126, 149–150
  sexual harassment, 524–533
    characteristics of perpetrator, 530–531
    characteristics of victim, 531–532
    definitions of, 524–527
    incidence of, 527–529
    levels of, 525
    outcomes of, 529–530
    perceptions of, 526–527, 530
    theories of, 532–533
  social learning theory of, 152–156
    modeling, 153–155
    peer influence, 165
    reinforcement, 155–156
  sociobiology, 149–150
  toward homosexuals, 127
  verbal, 154
  women and, 125
Agreement, influence through, 255–256
Agta Negrito, 12
AIDS, 348, 367, 420–421
Alcohol use, 407–408
  cohabitation and, 436–437
  depression and, 553
  domestic violence and, 467
  health issues and, 407–408
  marriage and, 436–437
  motor vehicle accidents and, 419
  prediction of, 410–411
  rape and, 473
  suicide and, 596, 597
  violence and, 467
Alpha bias, 189
Alzheimer's disease, 384
Ambivalence Toward Men Inventory, 77–78
Ambivalent Sexism Inventory, 74, 76
Amenorrhea, 587
American Association of University Women
    (AAUW), 225, 229–231
American Psychological Association, 4
Amish, depression among, 547
Amish schoolhouse massacre, 122
Analgesic, 425
Androgens, 142
Androgyny, 7, 55–56, 182
  emotional expression and, 276–277
  friendships and, 312
  gender schematicity and, 180–181

relationship satisfaction and, 352
self and other-orientation, 134
Android obesity, 411–412
Anger, 160, 164–165, 276. *See also* Aggression
Anger rape, 475
Anglo-Americans, gender-role stereotypes
among, 84
Anorexia nervosa, 587, 589
Antianxiety drugs, 398, 549
Antidepressants, 544
Antisocial behavior, 555
Antisocial personality disorder, 577, 579
Anxiety disorders, 366, 404
Appearance, 3
Artifacts, 388
Ashe, Arthur, 395
Asian Americans
friendships among, 290
gender-role stereotypes among, 84
Asian women, quantitative skills among, 88
Aspirin, 104, 395
Assertiveness, 65, 89
Athletes, 589
Athleticism, judgment of, 91
Athletics, Title IX and, 221
Attention deficit hyperactivity disorder
(ADHD), 578
Attitude, gender-role, 7
Attitude Interest Analysis Survey
(AIAS), 49–51
Attitudes Toward Women Scale
(ATWS), 70–71
Attractiveness, physical, 552, 590
Attribution, definition of, 214
Attributional styles of depression, 557–559
Attributions
depression and, 557–559
dispositional, 89
external, 215
for failure, 217
in gender-role stereotypes, 89
internal, 215
for performance, 214–218
dimensions of causality, 214–215
expectancy model of, 216
implications for achievement, 217–218
sex comparisons, 215–217
situational, 89
stable, 215
trait, 89
unstable, 215
Audience challenge, as obstacle to cross-sex
friendships, 313
Augusta National Golf Club, 14
Autonomy. *See also* Independence
conflict over, 319
eating disorders and, 592
personal, 357
Autonomy vs. connectedness, 319
Autophotographical essays, 210–211
Avoidance, 560

B

Back-channel responses, 262
Backlash effect, 89–90
*Backlash: The Undeclared War Against American
Women* (Faludi), 42
Balkans, multiple genders in, 10
Barton, Mark, 122
Battered woman. *See* Domestic abuse
Behavior, risky, 419–422
Behavior, toys and, 167
Behavioral confirmation, 183

Behavioral constraints, 45–46, 186–187
Bem Sex Role Inventory (BSRI),
53–55, 180
Benevolent discrimination, 75
Benevolent sexism, 72, 74–76, 474
Berdache, 10
Bereavement, health effect of, 441–444
evidence of, 442–443
explanation of, 443–444
studies of, 441–442
Beta bias, 189
Bias(es)
age, 103
alpha, 189
beta, 189
clinician, 549–550
fundamental attribution error, 131
language, 15
physician, 394
recall, 551
in research, 20
response, 43, 550–551
selection, 14, 17
self-serving, 214, 559
social desirability response, 43, 56
Binge eating disorder, 587
Biological theories
of aggression, 140–147
brain, 145–147
genes, 140–142
hormones, 142–145
sociobiology, 149–150
of depression, 554–556
genes, 554–555
hormones, 555–556
of health, 389–393
cardiovascular reactivity, 390–393
genes, 389
hormones, 389
immune system, 390
of play style, 240–241
of sex differences, 140–147
brain, 145–147
genes, 140–142
hormones, 142–145
stress response and, 561
Biosocial theory, 176
Bipolar disorder, 546
Bisexuals, 7, 130
Black communities, violence in, 158
Blacks. *See also* African Americans;
Ethnicity; Race
cross-race friendships among, 317
domestic violence, 468
smoking among, 403
suicide among, 595
unemployment among, 496–497
Blended friendships, 318
Blood pressure, conflict discussions and,
450–451
Body image, 574–575
Body mass index (BMI), 412
Body objectification, 575
Books, gender-role behavior and,
167–170
Borderline personality disorder, 577, 579
Boston Couples Study, 444
Boys. *See also* Children
differential treatment of boys and girls,
161–162
girls' difficulty in influencing boys, 240
*Boys Will Be Boys: Breaking the Link Between
Masculinity and Violence*
(Miedzian), 157

Brain, sex differences and, 48–49
Brain studies, 48–49
Breast cancer, 389–390, 401, 407
Broken Heart, The (Lynch), 433
Buffering effects of marriage on health,
437–438
Bulimia nervosa, 587, 588, 589
Bush, George H., 157
Bush, George W., 157, 231
Buss, Timothy, 122
Bypass surgery, 396

C

Cancer, 384
adjustment to, 581
breast, 389–390, 401, 407
colon, 415
lung, 401
Capital, family, 514
Cardiac catheterization, 395, 396
Cardiovascular disease, 385
Cardiovascular reactivity, 390–393
Career choices of parents, 224
Caregiving role
adjustment to chronic illness, 581
depression and, 571
retirement due to life events and, 505
Cartoons, 153
Castration anxiety, 151
Catastrophic thinking, 425
Category-based expectancies, 85, 269
Caucasians. *See also* Race
gender attitude of, 72
gender-role stereotypes among, 82, 83
Causality
correlational studies and, 35–36
dimensions of, 214–215
longitudinal study and, 36–37
Center for Epidemiological Studies in
Depression (CES-D) scale, 545
Cerebrovascular disease, 384
Childbearing, preference for child's
sex, 13
Child care
concessions at work for, 516–517
division of labor and, 500
among homosexuals, 457
family-supportive workplace and, 517
father's involvement in, 455, 480
working mothers and access to, 537
Childless couples, 480
Children
adjustment to chronic illness by, 581
custody of, 479, 481
effects of homosexual parents on,
481–482
gender aschematic, 182
gender-role stereotypes in, 86
interaction styles among, 236–245, 255–256
girls' difficulty in influencing
boys, 240
play styles, 237–242
maternal wall and, 516
obesity and, 412–413
parenting and health of, 480–484
pay disparity and, 516–519
physical activity among, 415–417
women as primary caretakers of, 152
Chinese, gender role attitudes
among, 72
Chodorow, Nancy, 19, 152
Chores, household. *See* Household chores
Cho Seung-Hui, 121, 122

Chronic illness
  adjustment to, 580–586
    cancer, 581
    of children, 581
    gender roles and, 581–586
    heart disease, 580–581
  defined, 386
  gender roles and, 581
    female, 584–586
    male, 582–584
Chronic lower respiratory disease, 384
Church/synagogue attendance, 135
Cirrhosis of liver, 407
Citadel, 14, 94
Civil unions, same-sex, 367
Class, masculine mystique and, 158. *See also*
    Socioeconomic status (SES)
Clinical depression (major depressive disorder),
    544–601
Clinician bias, 549–550
Clinton, Bill, 518
Clinton, Hillary, 14
Cobain, Kurt, 593
Coercion (egoistic dominance),
    174–176, 238
Cognition
  hunter-gatherer society and, 150
  social learning theory, 180
  toys and, 167
Cognitive abilities, 106–119
  hormones and, 142
  mathematical ability, 19, 88, 110–113, 217
    parents' attributions for, 220–222
    stereotype threat and, 208–209
  spatial ability, 106–109, 142
    social learning theory, 155,
      158–159
    testosterone and, 142
  two studies in, 116–119
  verbal ability, 113–115
Cognitive confirmation, 183
Cognitive development theory, 177–178
Cognitive differences, play styles and, 242
Cohabitation, 372–376
  candidates for, 374
  outcomes of, 374–376
Cohort effects
  age effects distinguished from, 37
  defined, 37
Collective interdependence, 213
Collective lifestyle, 418
Collectivist cultures, 160–161, 527
College students
  addressing professors by, 263
  perceptions of sexual harassment, 526–527
  rape and other forms of sexual coercion,
    473–474
  as research subjects, 45
  self-confidence in, 202
  sexual harassment, 529, 530
Colon cancer, 415
Columbine High School massacre, 122
Commercials, 171–173
  toy, 154, 172–173
Common couple violence, 465
Communal orientation, 55
Communication. *See also* Language
  explanations for sex differences in, 260–267
    sex-segregated interactions in early life,
      260–261
    social role theory, 265–267
    status theory, 261–265
  influenceability in, 255–260, 264–265
    influential individuals, 256–259

interaction styles and, 255–256
  party influenced, 255–256
  social role theory of, 267
  status theory of, 264–265
  strategies for, 259
interaction styles in adulthood, 242–245
  performance implications, 244–245
  sex differences qualifiers, 243–244
interaction styles in childhood, 236–242
  girls' difficulty in influencing boys, 240
  play styles, 237–242
leadership, 267–273
  emergent leaders, 267–269
  styles of, 269–270
  views of, 270–272
nonverbal behavior, 251–255, 263–264, 267
  decoding, 253
  gazing, 252–253, 267
  sending, 253
  smiling, 252, 263–264, 267
  social role theory of, 267
  status theory of, 263–264
  touching, 253–254
of research results, 41–43
support provision in, 278–281
Communion. *See also* Femininity
  age and, 572–573
  depression and, 569
  health and, 424
  status theory and, 262
  support interactions and, 281–282
  unmitigated, 57, 197–198
    depression and, 570–571
    eating disorders and, 590
    rumination and, 570–571
    stress and, 570–571
Comparable worth policy, 512–513
Comparison referents, satisfaction with division
    of labor, 459
Competition (egoistic dominance), 174–176
  as barrier to male friendships, 298–299
Competitiveness, 3, 63
Complete androgen insensitivity syndrome
    (CAIS), 144–145
Computer science, 194
Computer usage, 223, 414
Condoms, 130, 420–421
Confidant, choice of other sex as, 487
Confirmatory hypotheses testing, 101
Conflict
  in friendships, 307–308
  interrole, 5
  intrarole, 4
  physiological reactivity, 450–451
  role, 534
    in working mothers, 537
  in romantic relationships, 356–365
    areas of, 356–357
    demand/withdraw pattern, 358–362
    gay and lesbian, 371
    jealousy and, 362–365
    management of, 357–358
Conflict management, 357–358
Conflict Tactics Scale (CTS), 462
Conformity, 133, 184
  sex differences in, 26, 41
Confucian doctrine, 72
Congenital adrenal hyperplasia
    (CAH), 142–144
Connection self-concepts, 134
Constructionist perspectives, 20–21,
    189–190
Construct validity, 103
Context, 183–188

  perceiver, 183–185
  situation, 185–188
  social, 20–21, 60–61
  target, 185
Contraceptives, 23, 148
  condoms, 130, 420–421
  oral, 390
Control
  emotional expression and, 63
  spousal abuse and, 469
  women's health and job control, 498–499
Convenience samples, 128
Conventional stages of moral development,
    132–133
Conversational style, childhood, 237–238
Coping, 559–565
  distraction, 559
  emotion-focused, 559–560
  gender roles and, 559–560
  private self-consciousness, 565
  problem-focused, 559–560
  relative, 560–561
  rumination, 561–564
  tend and befriend, 561
Coronary angioplasty, 396
Coronary artery bypass surgery, 396
Correlation
  negative, 32
  positive, 32
Correlational study, 31–33
  causality and, 36
  experimental vs., 35–36
Correspondent inference theory, 89
Cortisol, 391, 489
Co-rumination, 301
Cosby Show, The (TV show), 92, 495
Country, stereotype of, 82–83
Couric, Katie, 170
Covert intimacy, 305
Creationism, 30
Credibility, influence and, 256–258
Crimes, violent, 385–386
Crime statistics, 385–386
Cross-cultural studies. *See also* Culture(s)
  of depression, 547–548
  of domestic violence, 464, 469
  eating disorders and, 590
  on effects of separation and divorce, 445–446
  of experience of emotion, 275
  of friendships, 290–291
  of gender-role stereotypes, 82–83
  on health benefits of marriage, 436–437
  on health benefits of parental role, 483
  of influence strategies, 265
  of intimacy, 297
  of mate selection, 330
  of the perceptions of sexual harassment, 527
  of relational aggression, 238–239
Cross-sectional studies, 36–37
Cross-sex typed individuals, 7, 55
Crying, 276, 552
Cues
  nonverbal, 253
  situational, 186–187
Culture(s)
  aggression in
    domestic violence, 463
    peer support of, 165
    relational, 238
  Agta Negrito, 12
  collectivist, 160–161, 527
  demand/withdraw pattern and, 361–362
  egoistic dominance and, 174–175
  emotional expression and, 160–161

fear of success and, 198
gender roles and, 82, 83
individualistic, 160–161, 527
intimacy and, 297
jealousy and, 363–364
language and, 249–250
marriage and
    mate selection and, 149, 334–335
    power distribution, 353–354
Morocco, 11–12
mortality and, 134
with multiple genders, 10–13
obesity and, 412
patriarchal, 354
play styles and, 241–242
power and, 265
self-esteem and, 214
sexual harassment, 526–527
sexual standards, 344–345
social learning theory of sex differences
    and, 154
status and, 13–14
suicide and, 593–594
Tahiti, 12–13
traditional, 72, 160–161
Custody of children, 479, 481
Cystic fibrosis, 585–586

D

Dads and Daughters, 166–167
Data, 30, 31
Data collection, 40
Data interpretation, 40–41
Date scripts, 336, 369, 478
Dating relationships
    cross-sex friendships and, 314
    health effects of breaking up, 444–445
    women initiating breakup of, 447
d statistic, 396
Death. *See* Mortality
Decoding, 253
Demand characteristics, 43–44
Demand-side theory, 512
    gender ideology and, 72
Demand/withdraw pattern, 358–362
    explanation for, 359–362
    implications for relationships, 362
    links to gender, 358–359
Democratic leader, 269
Demographics, eating disorders and,
    589–590
Denial of disadvantage, 521
Denial of discrimination, 521–523
Dependent personality disorder, 578, 579
Dependent variable, 33–34, 36
Depression
    in adolescence, 572–576
        body image and, 574–575
        gender intensification, 572–574
        manifestations of, 576
        puberty and, 574
        relations with parents and friends, 576
        self-esteem and, 575–576
    alcohol and drug problems and, 553
    among homosexuals, 366
    attributional styles and, 557–559
    biology and, 554–556
    bipolar disorder, 546
    clinical depression (major depressive
        disorder), 544–601
    coping strategies, 559–565
        distraction, 559
        emotion-focused, 559–560

gender roles and, 559–560
    private self-consciousness, 565
    problem-focused, 559–560
    relative, 560–561
    rumination, 561–564
    tend and befriend, 561
cross-cultural studies of, 547–548
different cause theory, 553–554
female gender role and, 569–571
    caregiving, 571
    communion and agency, 569
    unmitigated communion, 570–571
heart disease and, 580
hormones and, 555–556
interactive theory of, 554
learned helplessness and, 556–557
methodological artifacts in findings
    on, 549–553
    clinician bias, 549–550
    different manifestations, 551–553
    recall bias, 551
    response bias, 550–551
pessimistic (depressive) style and, 558–559
precipitating factors, 553
same cause theory, 553
stressful life events and, 566–569
    differential exposure vs. differential
        vulnerability, 568–569
    interpersonal vs. noninterpersonal
        stressors, 567–568
suicide and, 593
susceptibility factors, 553
after widowhood, 548
Development, psychosexual stages of, 151
Development of Sex Differences,
    The (Maccoby), 53
Diabetes, 278, 411–413
Diabetes mellitus, 384
*Diagnostic and Statistical Manual of Mental
    Disorders (DSM-IV-TR)*, 545, 577
Diana, Princes of Wales, 544
Diethylstilbestrol (DES), 145
Dieting, 590–591
Different cause theory of depression, 553–554
Differential exposure hypothesis, 496, 568–569
Differential item functioning, 552
Differential vulnerability hypotheses, 496,
    568–569
Disabilities, reading, 114
Disagreement, physiological responsiveness, 451
Discomfort, denial of discrimination
    to avoid, 521
Discrimination
    benevolent, 75
    defined, 95
    health and, 508–523
        access discrimination, 508
        denial of discrimination, 521–523
        pay disparity, 510–521
        treatment discrimination, 508
    sex, 7, 70, 94–97
Diseases, communicable, 349, 423. *See also*
    Morbidity
Dispositional, attributions, 89
Dispositional level of analysis, 285
Distance, conceptions of, 307
Distraction, as coping strategy, 559
Disturbed eating behavior, 587–588
Division of labor, 452–460
    for child care, 455
        among homosexuals, 457
    in dual-earner couples, 500
    health and, 455–460
        effects on well-being, 459–460

gender-role attitudes, 455–456
    household labor and, 459–460
    power and, 456–457
    satisfaction with, 458–459
    sexual orientation and, 457–458
    work outside the home and, 457
    marriage and, 452–460
    parenthood and shift in family, 484–485
    women's employment and, 452
Divorce
    cohabitation and, 375
    custody of children and, 479
    health effects of, 445–446
    strains from, 446–447
    suicide and, 596
*Divorce Revolution, the Unexpected Social
    and Economic Consequences for
    Women and Children in America,
    The* (Weitzman), 29
Dizygotic twins (fraternal twins), 140–141
Djellaba, 11–12
Domestic abuse, 460–469
    among homosexuals, 464
    incidence of, 461–467
    indicators of, 462
    myths about, 461
    perpetrator characteristics, 467–468
    theories of, 468–470
    victim characteristics, 468
Dominance
    egoistic, 174–176, 238
    leadership and, 268–269
    prosocial, 238
    relationships and, 64
    spousal abuse and, 469
"Do not resuscitate" (DNR) orders, 396
Driving behavior, health and, 419
Drug therapy, 395
Drug use, 408–411
    prediction of, 410–411
    prevalence of, 409
Dual-earner couples
    division of labor within home and, 500
    father's participation in caregiving and, 571
    job role quality and health in, 508
    marital quality and health in, 448–449, 452
    multiple roles and, 536
    parenthood and health in, 480
Duke University Lacrosse players, 470–471
Duluth model, 466

E

Eating disorder inventory, 587–588
Eating disorders, 586–593
    during adolescence, 590
    consequences of, 588–589
    definitions and prevalence of, 586–587
    etiology of, 589–593
        demographics, 589–590
        female gender role, 590
        genes, 589
        psychological factors, 592–593
        societal factors, 590–592
Education, 194–195
    division of labor in family and, 457
    mortality and, 382
    physical attractiveness and, 329
    smoking and, 410–411
Educational Testing Service, 110, 114, 116
Effect size, 104
Egalitarian couples, devalue of family
    responsibilities by, 538–539
Egalitarian gender ideology, 70

Egalitarianism, 7, 70–71, 376
  in friendships, 288
  relationship satisfaction and, 352, 354
Egoistic dominance (coercion, competition), 174–176, 238
Elderly, labor force participation among, 504
Electra complex, 151
Electromyography (EMG) responses, 277
Emotional bond challenge, as obstacle to cross-sex friendships, 312, 313
Emotional infidelity, 363–365
Emotional inhibitions, 63
Emotionality, 3
Emotional transmission, 355
Emotion-focused coping, 559–560
Emotion(s), 273–278
  basis of, 277–278
  brain lateralization and, 146
  encoding of, 274–275
  experience of, 273–275
  expression of, 275–277
    lack of, 300
  parents' responses to, 163–164
  physiological measures of, 277
  suppression of, 275
Emotion words, 163
Empathy, sex differences in, 120–121
Empirical method, 20
Empiricism, 30
Employment
  division of labor and, 452
  effects on women's health, 498–500
  time spent on household chores, 500–502
  women's employment effects on marriage, 502–503
Empty nest, 309–310
Endocrine function, conflict discussion and, 450
Entitlement to pay, perceptions of, 522
Environment
  gender-role socialization and, 165–173
    advertisements, 171–173
    books, 167–170
    television, 170–171
    toys, 165–167
  hostile, 524–525, 530, 532
  of identical twins, 140–141
Environmental cues, 277–278
Equal Employment Opportunity Commission (EEOC), 524–525
Equality
  cross-sex friendships and, 313
  in homosexual relationships, 371
Equality challenge, as obstacle to cross-sex friendships, 312
Equal Rights Amendment (ERA), 22
Equity in relationships, 354–355
Eros (romantic) love, 341–342
Erotic plasticity, 129
Essays, autophotographical, 466
Essentialists, 60
Estrogen, 142, 389–390
Ethnicity
  cohabitation and, 373
  division of labor and, 455
  divorce and, 434
  domestic abuse and, 468
  gender attitude and, 72
  gender-role stereotypes and, 82–83
  mortality and, 134
  obesity and, 412
  power distribution in marriage, 353–354
  religiosity and, 135
  self-esteem and, 207
  sexual harassment, 527

single parent families and, 480
  smoking, 402
Eveleth Mines case, 524
Everybody Loves Raymond (TV show), 93
Evolutionary psychology, 148
Evolutionary Psychology (Buss), 148
Evolutionary theory
  of aggression, 149–150
  of jealousy, 363–364
  of sex differences, 147–150, 520–521
Evolutionary theory and sociobiology
  of hunter-gatherer society, 150
  of mate selection, 148–149
  of sexual behavior, 148
Exercise, 415–417, 484, 535–536
Expectancies, target-based vs. category-based, 85
Expectancy/value model, 216
Expectations states theory, 261–262
Experimental method, 33
Experimental study, 33–36
  correlational vs., 35–36
Experimenter biases, 37–38
Experimenter effects, 38–43
  communication of results, 41–43
  data collection, 40–41
  data interpretation, 40–41
  questions asked, 38–39
  study design, 38–40
Expressive behavior, 53–55
Extension of the Personal Attributes Questionnaire (EPAQ), 57
External attribution, 215
Externalizing behavior, 576
External validity, 35

F

Facts, 30, 31
Fagerstrom Tolerance Questionnaire, 404–405
Failing at Fairness: How America's Schools Cheat Girls (Sadker and Sadker), 225
Failure, attributions for, 217
Failure feedback, 203–205
Fairy tales, 167–168
Family and Medical Leave Act (FMLA), 517–518
Family capital, 514
Family(ies). *See also* Marriage; Parenting
  eating disorders and, 591
  friendships and, 308–309
  problem behaviors and, 410–411
  violence in, 149–150
  women's employment and demands of, 500–503
  work role and stress on, 536
Family role
  interrelations between roles, 537–539
  quality of, 534–535
  work stress and, 537–538
Family-supportive work environment, 517–518
Family Ties (TV show), 92
Father Gander (Larche), 168
Father Knows Best (TV show), 495
Faulkner, Shannon, 14, 94
Fear
  of achievement, 196–200
  of affiliation (intimacy), 198–199, 297–298. *See also* Intimacy
  and gender-role strain, 65
  of success, 196–199
Feedback
  achievement and, 203–205
  negative management, 227–228
  about performance, 203–204
  from teachers, 226–228

Female criminals, 76
Female gender category, 3–4
Female gender role, 4–6, 569–571, 584–586
Female gender-role strain, 65–66
Female Offender, The (Chesnery-Lind & Pasko), 125
Feminine, defined, 4
Feminine Mystique, The (Friedan), 21
Femininity, 4, 59–60. *See also* Communion
  cardiovascular reactivity, 392
  friendships closeness and, 296–297
  intimacy achievement and, 136
  other-orientation and, 134
  problem behaviors and, 411
  relationship maintenance and, 352
  relationship satisfaction, 352–353
  self-disclosure and, 304
  self-esteem and, 140
  twin studies, 140
Feminism, 8–9
  gender-role stereotypes in, 87
Field experiments, 36
Field setting, laboratory vs., 44–45
"Fight or flight," 531
File drawer problem, 105
Film, depictions of women in, 25
First date scripts, 336, 369
Fixed role obligations, 427
Flextime, 517
Flirting, 228
Foster, Vince, 593
Fraternities, 476
Freedom of Access to Clinic Entrances Act, 23
Friends (TV show), 93
Friendship (storge) love, 341–342
Friendship(s), 285–325
  blended, 318
  changes over the life span, 308–310
  closeness of, 292–297
    barriers to, in male friendship, 297–300
  conflict in, 307–308
  cross-race, 316–317
  cross-sex, 310–316
    changes over the life span, 315–316
    equality amount, 313
    obstacles to, 312–315
    same-sex friendship vs., 310–312
    intimacy, 297, 305–307
    definition of, 305–307
  of lesbians and gay men, 321–322
  levels of analyses, 285–286
  nature of, 287–292
    differences, 288–292
    similarities, 287–288
  network size, 286–287
  quality of, 286
  quantity of, 286
  self-disclosure, 300–304
    barriers to, 303–304
    sex of discloser, 301
    sex of recipient, 301
    situational variables, 301–303
  at work, 317–321
    role conflict, 318–319
Functional indexes, health and, 488–490
Functional measures of support, 486
Fundamental attribution error, 131

G

Gay men. *See also* Homosexuals
  friendships among, 321–322
  gender-role characteristics and, 82
  health care system and, 400

hegemonic masculinity and, 58
National Organization for Men Against
    Sexism (NOMAS), 24
pay disparity and, 519–520
prospective studies of bereavement, 442
Gazing, 252–253, 267
Gender
    defined, 3
    as legitimate domain of study, 20
    role, 4, 6
    sex vs., 3
    as social category, 58–66
    social construction of gender, 20–21
Gender aschematic, 178
Gender constancy, 177
Gender culture, 10
Gender diagnosticity (GD), 61–62
Gender differentiation, 74, 77
Gender identity, 6, 177
Gender ideologies, 70
Gender inequality, indices of, 13
Gender intensification, 103, 572–574
Gender-role attitude, 7
    division of labor and, 455–456
    marital satisfaction with women working
        and, 501–503
Gender-Role Conflict (GRC) scale, 64
Gender-role identity, 6
Gender role(s). See also History of gender
        psychology
    attitudes toward, 69–97
        men's and women's roles, 70–72
        sex discrimination, 94–97
        sexism, 73–78
        stereotyping, 78–94
    chronic illness, 581–586
    depression and, 569–571
        caregiving, 571
        communion and agency, 569
        unmitigated communion, 570–571
    eating disorders and, 590
    Freud on, 151–152
    gay men and, 82
    in kibbutz, 418
    as multifaceted, 58–60
    self-esteem and, 207
    suicide and, 596–597
    twin studies of, 140–141
Gender-role socialization
    depression and, 544–545
    environment and, 165–173
        advertisements, 171–173
        books, 167–170
        television, 170–171
        toys, 165–167
    other people's influence, 164–165
    parents' influence, 161–164
Gender-role stereotype(s), 7, 70, 78–94
    altering views on, 89–90
    in children, 86
    components of, 79–81
    contemporary status of, 92–93
    ethnic and cultural factors in, 82–83
    of feminism, 87
    function of, 86–88
    homosexuals, 82
    older people, 82
    prototype approach to, 90
    reality and, 91–92
    self-fulfilling prophecy and, 88
    structure of, 83–85
    subcategories of, 85
    views based on ethnicity or culture, 83
    views based on race and ethnicity, 82–83

Gender-role strain, 62–66
    female, 65–66
    male, 63–65
        among African Americans, 65
Gender schema theory, 56, 178–183
Gender schematic, 178
Gender tension line, 456
Genes. See also Biological theories
    depression and, 554–555
    eating disorders and, 589
    health and, 389
Genetic component of schizophrenia, 577
Gilligan, Carol, 19
Girlcott, 171
Girls. See also Children
    differential treatment of boys and
        girls, 161–162
    girls' difficulty in influencing boys, 240
Glass ceiling, 509
Glass escalator, 509
GodMen, 24
Gore, Tipper, 544
GPA, sex difference in estimating, 201–202
Grace Under Fire (TV show), 495
Graduation ceremony, 45–46
Grand Canyon (film), 65
Gross, Terry, 355
Group interactions, 266
Group performance, 244
Group socialization, 164
Growing Pains (TV show), 92, 495
Guilt, aggression and, 134
Gynoid obesity, 412

H

Harris, Eric, 122
Hasbro Toys, 167
Hazards of Being Male, The (Goldberg), 63
Health
    alcohol, 407–408
        prediction of, 410–411
        prevalence of, 408
    artifacts and, 388, 393–399
        heart disease and, 394–399
        mental health, 398–399
        physician bias, 394
        proxy responses, 394
        socioeconomic status, 393–394
    biology and, 389–393
        cardiovascular reactivity, 390–393
        genes, 389
        hormones, 389
        immune system, 390
    division of labor, 455–460
        effects on well-being, 459–460
        gender-role attitudes, 455–456
        household labor and, 459–460
        power and, 456–457
        satisfaction with, 458–459
        sexual orientation and, 457–458
        work outside the home and, 457
    drug use, 408–411
        depression and, 553
        prediction of, 410–411
        prevalence of, 409
    evidence, 435–437
    exercise, 415–417
    explanations, 437–438
    illness behavior and, 387, 426–429
        implications for morbidity, 426–428
        implications for mortality, 428–429
    marriage and, 434–441
    morbidity, 380

mortality, 380–386
    leading cause of death, 383–385
    life span and, 380–383
    multiple role(s) and, 533–539
        differential exposure vs. differential
            vulnerability, 496–497
        difficulties in combining roles, 537–539
        role buffering and role exacerbation
            effects, 536–537
        role expansion hypothesis, 534
        role scarcity hypothesis, 534
        stress-buffering hypothesis, 534
    overweight and obesity, 411–414
        definition of, 412
        etiology of, 414
        prevalence of, 412–414
    parenting and
        effect of parenting on marriage,
            484–485
        quality of parent role, 480
    preventive health care, 399–401
    quality of, 448–452
    relationship dissolution and, 444–448
        dating relationship, breakup of,
            444–445
        explanation of, 446–448
        marriage breakup of, 445–446
    smoking, 401–407
        cessation, 404–407
        prediction of, 410–411
        prevalence among adolescents and
            children, 402–404
        prevalence among adults, 402
    social roles and, 418–424
        concerns with health, 422
        driving, 419
        gender-related traits, 423–424
        job characteristics, 418–419
        nurturant roles, 422–423
        risky behavior, 419–422
    social support and, 486–490
        evidence, 487–490
        sex comparisons in, 486–487
    socioeconomic status and, 393–394
    symptom perception, 424–426
        evidence of, 424–425
        explanation of, 425–426
Health behaviors, 399–417
    marriage and, 439–440
Health care services, 387–388
Heart attacks, 385, 424
Heart disease, 384, 385, 394–399
    adjustment to, 580–581
    alcohol intake and, 407
    depression and, 580
    physician bias in treating, 394–398
    smoking and, 401
Hefner, Hugh, 355
Hegemonic masculinity, 58
Heinz dilemma, 132
Helping behavior, 121
Helplessness, learned, 556–557
Help-seeking behavior, 428
Heterosexuals, 7
Hijab, 11–12
Hispanics
    cohabitation and, 375
    exercise, 416
    life span and, 381, 385
    overweight and obesity, 384, 412
    preventive health care, 399
    sexual harassment, 532
    smoking, 402–403
    substance abuse, 409

History of gender psychology
    gender as social category, 58–66
        gender diagnosticity, 61–62
        gender-role strain, 62–66
        multifaceted, 58–60
        social context, 60–61
    masculinity-femininity (M/F) as global per-
        sonality trait, 49–52
    sex differences in intelligence, 48–49
    sex typing and androgyny, 53–57
Histrionic personality disorder, 577–578, 579
Homicide, 384
Homophobia, 63, 299–300
Homosexuals, 7, 82, 128–130. *See also* Gay men;
        Lesbians
    attitudes toward, 127
    child adoption status and, 482
    depression among, 366
    division of labor within home and, 371,
        457–458
    domestic abuse among, 464
    eating disorders and, 589
    heritability of, 140
    mate selection and, 367–368
    monogamy among, 370
    parenting among, 481–482
    romantic relationships, 366–372
        conflict in, 371
        development of, 367–369
        intimacy and sexuality in, 369–370
        jealousy in, 371–372
        satisfaction in, 370–371
        sex versus status in, 372
    social exchange theory, 370–371
    violence among, 464
Hopkins, Ann, 95
Hopkins v. Price Waterhouse, 95–96
Hormone replacement therapy (HRT), 389
Hormones
    depression and, 555–556
    health and, 389–390
    play styles and, 241
    schizophrenia and, 577
    sex differences and, 142–145
Hostile environment, sexual harassment,
        524–525
Hostile sexism, 74–77
Household chores
    division of labor and, 452–453, 457–459
    gender-role attitudes and, 32
    power and, 456
    strains after widowhood from, 443
    working women and help with, 500–502
Housewives
    health of working women compared to, 498
    work environments of working women vs.,
        507–508
How Schools Shortchange Girls (AAUW), 225
How to Help Your Husband Stay Alive (Lees),
        435–437
How to Work for a Woman Boss (Bern), 320
Hugging, 300
Human capital accumulation theory,
        519–521
Human capital theory, 512, 520
Hunter-gatherer society, 16, 150
Hypertension and renal disease, 384
Hypothesis, 30–31

I

Identity, gender. *See* Gender identity
Identity development, 136
Illness, 386. *See also* Chronic illness; Morbidity

Illness behavior, 387, 426–429
    implications for morbidity, 426–428
    implications for mortality, 428–429
Immune function changes, during conflict
        discussion, 450–451
Immune system, 390
Immunoglobulin M, 390
Impartiality vs. favoritism, 318–319
In a Different Voice (Gilligan), 19
Indecisiveness., 546
Independence, 54, 64. *See also* Autonomy
Independent variable, 33–34, 36
India
    friendships in, 303
    marriage and health in, 436
    parenting and satisfaction with home life, 483
Indian marriages, 326, 436
Individualistic cultures, 160–161, 527
Individuating information, 85, 86
Individuation self concepts, 134
Infidelity, 363–365
Influenceability, 255–260, 264–265
    influential individuals, 256–259
    interaction styles and, 255–256
    party influenced, 255–256
    social role theory of, 267
    status theory of, 264–265
    strategies for, 259
Informational support, 486
In-group social comparisons, 522–523
Injuries, risk-taking behavior and, 421
Institute for Equality of Marriage, 96
Instrumental/expressive distinctions to
        gender, 53–55
Instrumental orientation, 55
Instrumental support, 486, 489–490
Intelligence, sex differences in, 48–49
Intelligent design, 30
Interactions, support provision in, 278–281
Interaction styles
    in adulthood, 242–245
    in childhood, 236–242
        girls' difficulty in influencing boys, 240
        play styles, 237–242
    influenceability and, 255–256
    social role theory of, 266
    status theory of, 261–262
Interactive theory of depression, 554
Interdependence
    kinds of, 214
    self-esteem and, 211–212
    voluntary, 311, 593
Interest surveys, 221
Internal attribution, 215
Internalizing behavior, 576
Internal validity, 35
Interpersonal influence, 255. *See also*
        Influenceability
Interpersonal protection theory, 443
    of breakup of dating relationships, 444–445
    explanation, 446–447
    of marriage breakup, 445–446
Interpersonal skills, 95–96, 353
Interrole conflict, 5
Intimacy
    covert, 305
    cultural comparisons in, 297
    development of, 135–136
    fear of affiliation, 198–199, 297–298
    friendship(s), 296, 297, 300, 305–307
        definition of, 305–307
    in romantic relationships, 337–338
        among homosexuals, 369–370
    self-disclosure and, 302–303, 305–306

Intimate Strangers (Rubin), 356
Intrarole conflict, 4
Iron John: A Book About Men (Bly), 24
Israel-Palestinian conflict, 122

J

Jealousy, 362–365
    sexual, 371–372
Job advertisements, sexist, 22
Job attributes
    health and, 497
    housewife role and, 507–508
    valuation of, 506–507
Job burnout, family role as a buffer for, 536
Job control, women's health and, 498–499
Jordan, Michael, 85
Judgment vs. acceptance, 319

K

Keller, Helen, 339
Kennedy, Edward, 22
Kibbutz, 418
Kidney disease, 384
Klebold, Dylan, 122
Knussman, Kevin, 518
Koop, C. Everett, 461

L

Labor, division of. *See* Division of labor
Laboratory setting, vs. field, 44–45
Laboratory studies of marital quality and health,
        448, 450–452
Language, 245–247, 260–261, 262–263, 266–267
    culture and, 250, 260–261
    direct vs. indirect, 247
    effects on perception, 250–251
    features of, 247
    gender roles and, 247–250
    influenceability and, 256–258
    interruptions in, 247–248
    lateralization of, 145
    power and, 262
    qualifiers of sex differences, 247–250
    relationship maintenance and, 281–282
    during same-sex play, 260–261
    sexist, 15, 73
    social role theory of, 266–267
    status theory of, 262–263
Lateralization, brain, 146
Lateralization of language, 145
Lawyers, pay disparity among, 514, 518
Leadership
    emergent leaders, 267–272
    styles of, 38, 269–270
    views of, 270–272
Learned helplessness, 556–557
Learning, observational, 153–155
Leave It to Beaver (TV show), 495
Leisure activities, risky, 419–420
Leisure exercise, 415
Lesbians. *See also* Homosexuals
    friendships among, 321–322
    pay disparity and, 519–520
Liberal Feminist Attitude and Ideology Scale
        (LFAIS), 71
Life events, friendships and, 308
Life expectancy, 380–383
Likelihood to Sexually Harass (LSH) scale,
        530–531
Limits of Masculinity, The (Tolson), 63

Liver
  cirrhosis of, 407, 408
  disease, 384
Logic, as influence strategy, 259
Loneliness
  in marriage, 328, 436–437
  parenthood and, 483
  social interaction, 295
Longitudinal studies, 36–37
*Lost Boys: Why Our Sons Turn Violent and How
    We Can Save Them*
    (Garbarino), 123
Love, 338–342
  romanticism and, 339–341
  styles of, 341–342
Ludus (game-playing) love, 341–342
Lung cancer, 401

M

Main effects of marriage on health, 437
Major depressive disorder (clinical depression),
    544–601
Majors, switching, 198
Male gender role, 4–6, 582–584
Male gender-role strain, 63–65
Male privilege, 14
Maloney, Carolyn, 22
Malvo, John Lee, 122
Man and Woman (Ellis), 48
"Manhood hustle," 65
Mania (manic) love, 341–342
Manic-depressive illness, 546
Marital bonus, 519
Marital rape exemption clause, 472
Marital satisfaction. *See under* Marriage
Marital selection hypothesis, 440–441
Marriage. *See also* Romantic relationships
  breakup of, health effects of, 445–446
  cohabitation prior to, 372–376
  demand/withdraw pattern in, 358–362
  effect of parenthood on, 484–485
  friendships and, 308–309
  health effects of, 434–441
    evidence, 435–437
    explanations, 437–438
    marital quality and, 448–452
  same-sex, 367
  satisfaction with, 352
    demand/withdraw pattern and, 362
    division of labor and, 452–460
    health and, 440
    parenthood and, 484–485
Marshall, J. Howard, 149
Marital status
  cross-sex friendship and, 311
  job promotions and, 515–516
  self-disclosure and, 303
  suicide and, 596
Masculine, defined, 4
Masculine Gender Role Stress (MGRS)
    scale, 64
Masculine identity, 151
Masculine ideology, sexual aggression and, 475
Masculine mystique, 157
Masculinity. *See also* Agency; Gender role(s)
  cardiovascular reactivity, 392
  condom use and, 420–421
  eating disorders and, 589
  identity achievement and, 136
  leadership and, 268
  mortality and, 424
  pain tolerance, 426
  playing sports, 421

problem behaviors and, 411
relationship satisfaction and, 353
retirement and, 505
self-disclosure and, 303
self-esteem and, 140
self-orientation and, 134
twin studies, 140
Masculinity-femininity (M/F) construct, 49–52
  AIAS scale, 49–51
  BSRI scale, 53–55
  MMPI scale, 51–52
  PAQ scale, 53–55
  prototypes of, 59–60
  self-report methodology, 43, 52
  undesirable aspects of, 56–58
Masochism, 151
Massachusetts, same-sex marriage, 367
Massachusetts Institute of Technology,
    treatment discrimination at, 509
Masturbation, 126–127, 128
Maternal wall, 516
Mate selection. *See also* Romantic relationships
  among homosexuals, 367–368
  sex differences in, 148–149, 329–335
Math performance, 19, 88, 100, 110–113
Mattel Corporation, 166–167
Maximalists, 19
Media attention to thinness, 591
Media reports vs. scientific reports, 43
Medical care utilization, 387–388
Memory, spatial location, 389
Men Are from Mars, Women Are from Venus
    (Gray), 30, 101, 139, 356
Menopause, 389
*Men's Liberation: A New Definition of
    Masculinity* (Nichols), 63
Men's movements, 23–25
Mental health, 398–399, 544–601
  adjustment to chronic illness, 580–586
    cancer, 581
    of children, 581
    gender roles and, 581–586
    heart disease, 580–581
  depression. *See* Depression
  eating disorders, 586–593
    during adolescence, 590
    consequences of, 588–589
    definitions and prevalence of, 586–587
    etiology of, 589–593
  multiple roles and, 536
  personality disorders, 577–578, 579
  physician bias in treating, 398–399
  schizophrenia, 577
Mental rotation, 106–108, 113
Mentors, glass ceiling and women's lack of, 509
Meta-analysis of sex differences, 104–105
Methodology, self-report of withdrawal
    symptoms, 406
Mexican Americans
  gender-role stereotypes among, 84
  physical activity among children, 416–417
*Minds of Boys: Saving Our Sons From Falling
    Behind in School and Life, The* (Gurian
    & Stevens), 123
Minimalists, 19
Minimal response, 247
Minnesota Multiphasic Personality Inventory
    (MMPI), 51–52
Minorities, homosexual, 368. *See also*
    Ethnicity; Race
Modeling (observational learning), 153–155
Moderating variable, 105
Monitoring the Future Study, 408–410
Monogamy among homosexuals, 370

Monozygotic twins (identical twins), 140–141
Moral development, sex differences in, 132–135
Morality of responsibility, 133
Morality of rights, 133
Morbidity, 380, 386–388. *See also* Health
  illness behavior and, 387–388
Morocco, 11–12
Mortality, 380–386. *See also* Health
  leading cause of death, 383–385
  life span and, 380–383
Mothers
  parenting and health of, 498, 535
  working, role conflict in, 537
Motor vehicle accidents, 419
Muhammed, John Allen, 122
Multiple masculinities, 58
Multiple Risk Factor Intervention Trial Research
    Group, 394–395
Multiple role(s), 533–539
  differential exposure vs. differential
    vulnerability, 496–497
  difficulties in combining roles, 537–539
  role buffering and role exacerbation effects,
    536–537
    family role and work stress, 536–537
    work role and family stress, 536
  role expansion hypothesis and, 534
  role scarcity hypothesis, 534
  stress-buffering hypothesis, 534
Murder, 149–150
Muxe, 11
Myocardial infraction, 385
My Religion (Keller), 339
Myth of Male Power, The (Farrell), 24
Mythopoetic movement, 24

N

Narcissistic personality disorder, 578, 579
Narrative review, 103
National Health and Nutrition Examination
    Survey, 412
National Health and Social Life Survey, 128
National Household Survey on Drug Abuse, 409
National Institutes of Health, 395
National Organization for Changing Men, 24
National Organization for Men Against Sexism
    (NOMAS), 24
National Organization for Women
    (NOW), 21–23
National Violence Against Women, 464
National Wrestling Coaches' Association, 221
Native American cultures, multiple genders
    in, 10
Natural Born Killers (film), 154
Navratilova, Martina, 90
Negative correlation, 32
Negative femininity, 590
Negative management feedback, 269–270
Negative social behavior, 243
Negotiations, salary, 514–515
Networks, to maintain relationship, 286–287
Nicotine, addition to, 404–407
Nicotine replacement therapy, 405
No Child Left Behind Act, 231
Nonpurging bulimia, 587
Nonverbal behavior, 251–255, 263–264, 267
  decoding, 253
  gazing, 252–253, 267
  sending, 253
  smiling, 252, 263–264, 267
  social role theory of, 267
  status theory of, 263–264
  touching, 253–254

Norms, 495
   violation of, 5–6
Nuclear family, television depiction of
   traditional, 495
Nursery rhymes, 168
Nurturance (helping), 31, 174–176
Nurturant role hypothesis, 422–423
Nurturant roles, 422–423
*Nurture Assumption: Why Children Turn Out the
   Way They Do: Parents Matter Less Than
   You Think and Peers Matter More, The*
   (Harris), 164

O

Obesity. *See* Overweight and obesity
Object location game, 108
Object-relations theory, 152
Observational learning (modeling), 153–155
Observations of behavior, 124
Occupational aspirations, 154–155
Occupation(s)
   segregated by sex, 512–514
   women's employment by, 505–506
Oedipal complex, 151
Oglebay Norton Corp, 524
Openness vs. closedness, 319
Opportunity challenge, as obstacle to cross-sex
   friendships, 313
Oral contraceptives, 390
Osteoarthritis, 390, 571, 581
Outgroup homogeneity effect, 317
Out-group social comparisons, 522–523
Overweight and obesity, 411–414
   definition of, 412
   etiology of, 414
   prevalence of, 412–414
Oxytocin, 555–556, 561

P

Pain perception, 425
Pain research, 425–426
Parental leaves, 189
Parental status, pay disparity and, 516–519
Parent-child relationship, marital satisfaction
   and, 485
Parenting
   among homosexuals, 481–482
   effect on marriage, 484–485
   health and, 479–485
     effects of parent role, 480, 483–484
Parents
   abuse by, 150
   differential treatment of boys and girls,
     161–162
   gender-role beliefs, 164
   influence of, 161–164
   play styles and, 161–162
   responses to children's emotions, 163–164
Parietal lobes, 48
Parkinson's disease, 384
Participant effects, 43–44
Participants, experimenter effects in
   selection of, 33
Passive management by exception, 269–270
Paternity leave, 517–518
Patient-physician interactions, 250–251
Patriarchal cultures, 354
Patriarchal terrorism, 33–34, 465–467, 491–492
Patriarchy, 74, 77
Pay disparity, 510–521
   evolutionary theory, 520–521
   family ties, 515–520

negotiation, 514–515
   sex segregation and comparable
     worth, 512–514
Peers
   aggression and, 165
   eating disorders and, 591–592
   problem behaviors and, 410–411
   sex differences and, 164–165
Pelosi, Nancy, 14, 509
Penis envy, 151
Perceiver, 183–185
Perception(s)
   language effects on, 250–251
   of leaders, 270–272
   of pain, 425
   postmodern, 189–190
   of sexual harassment, 526–527, 530
Percutaneous transluminal coronary angioplasty
   (PTCA), 396
Perfect correlations, 32
Performance
   attributions for, 214–218
     dimensions of causality, 214–215
     expectancy model of, 216
     implications for achievement, 217–218
     sex comparisons, 215–217
   stereotype threat and, 207–210
   teachers(s) effects on, 228–231
   treatment discrimination in evaluating,
     509–510
Personal Attributes Questionnaire (PAQ),
   53–55
Personal autonomy, 357
Personality
   influence strategies and, 267
   sexual harassment, 531
   testosterone and, 143
   traits, 59–60
Personality disorders, 577–578, 579
Pessimistic (depressive) attributional style of
   depression, 558–559
Pfizer Global Study of Sexual Attitudes and
   Behavior, 128
Phallic stage, 151
Philosophical and political issues, 19–26
   gender as legitimate domain of study, 20
   men's movements, 23–25
   sex difference debate, 19
   social construction of gender, 20–21
   women's movements, 21–23
Physical appearance, 59–60
Physical attractiveness, 298, 330–334
   education and, 329
Physical strength, 64
Physical unattractiveness, fear of, 65
Physician, pay disparity among, 513–514
Physician bias, 394–399
Physician-patient interactions, 250–251
Physicians Health Study, 394–395
Physiological reactivity, 277
   during conflict discussions, 450–452
   to stress, 392–393
Play
   biological theories of, 240–241
   cognitive differences, 242
   communication differences and, 237–242
   socialization and, 241–242
   styles of, 237–242
Pneumonia and influenza, 384
Political climate, sex differences and, 118
Political issues. *See* Philosophical and political
   issues
Positive correlation, 32
Positive reappraisal, 560

Positive social behavior, 243
Postconventional stages of moral
   development, 133
Postmodern perspectives on sex differences,
   189–190
Power
   in cross-sex friendships, 312–313
   cultures and, 265
   division of labor and, 456–457
   domestic abuse and, 466
   influence strategies and, 265
   language and, 262
   in marriage, 353–354
   in romantic relationships, 353–354
Power rape, 475
Pragma (practical) love, 341–342
Precipitating factors in depression, 553
Preconventional moral development,
   132–133
Preferential treatment in job selection, 523
Pregnancy, 148
Prejudice against female leaders, 271. *See also*
   Bias(es); Discrimination; Sex
   discrimination
Premarital sex, 128–129
Pretend play, 162
Preventive health care, 399–401
*Price of Motherhood: Why the Most Important Job
   in the World Is Still the Least Valued*
   (Crittenden), 516
Price Waterhouse, 95
Priming, 75
Private self-consciousness, 565
Proactive aggression, 165
Problem drinking. *See* Alcohol use
Problem-focused coping, 559–560
Problem-solving
   agency and, 569
   rumination, 561–564
Projective storytelling method, 197
Promise Keepers, 24
Promotions
   martial status and, 515–516
   sex discrimination in, 105
Prosocial dominance, 238
Prospective design, 442
Prototype, 59–60
Prototype approach to gender-role
   stereotype s, 90
Prototypes of masculinity and
   femininity, 59–60
Provocation, 123
Proxy responses, 394
Psychoanalytic theory
   conflict and, 356–357
   on parenting by homosexuals, 482
   on sex differences, 151–152
Psychobiosocial models, 147
Psychological health. *See* Mental health
Psychological reactance, 583
Psychology of Sex Differences (Maccoby &
   Jacklin), 102
Psychosexual stages of development, 151
Psychotropic drugs, 398
Puberty, depression and, 555–556
Publication year, as moderator variable, 121
Pure (agape) love, 341
Purging bulimia, 587

Q

Questions, experimenter effects on
   research, 38–40
Quid pro quo, sexual harassment, 524–525

R

Race. *See also* African Americans; Blacks; Ethnicity
body image and, 207
cohabitation and, 373
divorce and, 434–435
drug use and, 409
gender-role conceptions and, 64–65
life expectancies/mortality and, 381–385
obesity and, 412, 413
pay disparity and, 514
smoking and, 402
unemployment rate and, 496–497
Raising Cain: Protecting the Emotional Life of Boys (Kindlon, Thompson, & Barker), 123
Random assignment, 34
Random selection/random sampling, 33
Rape and other forms of sexual coercion, 470–478
anger rape, 475
definitions of, 471–472
incidence of, 472–474
myths about, 475–476
perpetrator characteristics, 474–476
power rape, 475
prevention strategies, 477
spousal rape, 473
studies of, 472–474
theories of, 477–478
victim characteristics, 476–477
Reactance, psychological, 583
Reactive aggression, 165
Reading disabilities, 114
Real boys: Rescuing Our Sons from the Myths of Boyhood (Pollack), 123
Referents, comparison, 459
Reimer, Bruce, 144–145
Reinforcement, 155–156
Relational aggression, 238–239
Relational interdependence, 213
Relationships, 444
dissolution of, 444–446
explanation of, 446–448
marriage, 445–446
women in initiating, 447–448
marriage, 445–446
reciprocal, 291
unemotional, 65
women's concerns with, 159–160
Relative coping, 560–561
Religion
gender-role conceptions and, 83–84
schematicity and, 179
Remarriage after widowhood, health benefits of, 443–444
Rent-A-Center, sex discrimination case against, 509
Replication, 39, 43
Reproduction, sexual, 148
Reproduction of Mothering, The (Chodorow), 152
Reproductive issues, preventive care and, 400
Research methods, 30–37
correlational study, 31–33
cross-sectional vs. longitudinal designs, 36–37
experimental study, 33–36
field experiment, 36
Research on gender
biases, 37–38
experimenter effects in, 38–43
communication of results, 41–43

data collection, 40–41
data interpretation, 40–41
questions asked, 38–39
study design, 38–40
laboratory vs. field setting, 45
participant effects, 43–44
replication, 39
situational influences, 45–46
variables confounded with sex, 45
Respiratory disease, 384
Response bias, 43, 550–551
Responses to Depression Questionnaire, 561–562
Responsibility, morality of, 133
Retirement, 309–310
health and, 504–505
Reverse psychology, 584
Review, narrative, 103
Rights, morality of, 133
Risky behavior, 419–422
Roberts, Charles Carl IV, 122
Roberts, David, 518
Rochester Interaction Record, 294–296
Role conflict, 318–319, 534
Role expansion hypothesis, 534
Role models, 154
Role obligations, health problems and, 427
Role overload, 534
Role reversal, retirement and, 504
Role(s). *See also* Gender role(s); Marriage; Parenting; Work role(s)
defined, 4, 495
differential exposure vs. differential vulnerability hypothesis, 496, 568–569
multiple role(s), 533–539
role buffering and role exacerbation effects, 536–537
family role and work stress, 536–537
work role and family stress, 536
Role scarcity hypothesis, 534
Role spillover, 533
Rolland, Kayla, 122
Romantic (eros) love, 341–342
Romantic Beliefs Scale, 340–341
Romanticism, 339–342
Romantic relationships, 380–432
characteristics desired in a mate, 329–337, 367–368
evidence for, 329–333
explanation for, 333–335
cohabitation, 372–376
candidates for, 374
outcomes of, 374–376
commitment to, 458
conflict in, 356–365
areas of, 356–357
demand/withdraw pattern, 358–362
jealousy and, 362–365
management of, 357–358
gay and lesbian, 366–372
conflict in, 371
development of, 367–369
intimacy and sexuality in, 369–370
jealousy in, 371–372
satisfaction in, 370–371
sex versus status in, 372
initiation of, 336–337, 368–369
intimacy, 337–338
love in, 338–342
romanticism and, 339–341
styles of, 341–342
maintaining, 350–356
characteristics of him but not her, 354–356
gender roles, 352–353

marital satisfaction, 352
power distribution, 353–354
strategies for, 350–352
sexuality in, 343–350
attitudes toward, 343–346
first sexual experiences, 347–349
motives for, 346–347
standards for, 327–329
"Rule of thumb," 460
Rumination
depression cycle, 561–564
interpersonal resources and, 563
problem-solving, 561–564
unmitigated communion and, 570–571
Russia, life expectancy, 383

S

Salary negotiations, 514–515
Same cause theory of depression, 553
Same-sex civil unions, 367
Same-sex marriage, 367
Samples, convenience, 128
Satisfaction with division of labor and health, 458–459
Schema, 178
Schizophrenia, 577
Scientific method, 30–37
Scream (film), 154
Scripts, dating, 336, 478
Second shift, women's, 452, 460
Segregation, occupational, 512–514
Selection bias, 33
Selection effect, 498
on health of working women vs. housewives, 498
marital selection hypothesis, 440–441
on parental status and health, 483
on parenthood and martial quality, 484
Self-blame, 560
Self-confidence, 201–203
feedback and, 204–205
Self-consciousness, private, 565
Self-construal, relational-interdependent, 210–211
Self-disclosure, 40
in friendships, 300–304
barriers to, 303–304
sex of discloser, 301
sex of recipient, 301
situational variables, 301–303
Self-esteem, 206–207
of abusers, 467–468
achievement and, 199, 205
in adolescents, 206–207
attributions and, 214–215
depression and, 575–576
evaluative feedback and, 205
leadership and, 268
men's attitude toward women working and, 500
perception of others' academic and social ability, 212
self-definitions and, 211
sex similarities in, 213–214
women's employment and, 498
word recollection and, 212–213
Self-fulfilling prophecy, 40, 69, 88
Self-image, achievement and, 199
Self monitoring, 185
Self-perception, preferential treatment in job selection, 523
Self-presentation, 185
Self-reliance, 64

Self-report measures, 120
Self-role discrepancy theory, 62
Self-serving bias, 214, 559
Self-verification, 185
Sensation seeking, 421
Sensitivity, interpersonal, 263, 571
Separation
    health effects of, 445–446
    strains from, 446–447
September 11, 2001 terrorist
    attacks, 122
Septicemia, 384
Sex
    defined, 3
    gender vs., 3
    as social category, 2
    variables confounded with sex, 45
Sex and Personality (Terman & Miles), 49
Sex difference debate, 19
Sex discrimination, 7, 70, 94–97
    behavioral components, 94–97
Sex hormones, 142
Sexism, 7, 70, 73–78
    benevolent, 72, 74–76, 474
    defined, 73
    hostile, 74–77
    modern, 73–74
    negative and positive, 74
    toward men, 77–78
    traditional, 73–74
Sexist language, 15, 73
Sex-related behavior, 4
Sex-related comparisons
    biology of, 140–147
        brain, 145–147
        genes, 140–142
        hormones, 142–145
        psychobiosocial models, 147
    in cognitive abilities, 106–119
        mathematical ability, 110–113
        spatial ability, 106–109
        two studies in, 116–119
        verbal ability, 113–115
    cognitive development theory, 177–178
    constructionist and postmodern perspectives,
        189–190
    in context, 183–188
        perceiver, 183–185
        situation, 185–188
        target, 185
    evolutionary theory and sociobiology,
        147–150
        aggression, 149–150
        hunter-gatherer society, 150
        mate selection, 148–149
        sexual behavior, 148
    gender-role socialization, 157–173
        environment and, 165–173
        other people's influence, 164–165
        parents' influence, 161–164
    gender schema theory, 56, 178–183
    in higher education, 194–195
    in intelligence, 48–49
    Maccoby and Jacklin's *Psychology of Sex
        Differences,* 102–104
    meta-analysis of, 104–105
    in moral development, 132–135
    psychoanalytic theory, 151–152
    similarities hypotheses, 136–137
    in social development, 135–136
    in social domains, 120–132
        in activity, 130–131
        in aggression, 121–126
        empathy, 120–121

    in general personality attributes, 131
    in helping behavior, 121
    in sexuality, 126–130
    social learning theory of, 152–156
        observational learning or modeling,
            153–155
        reinforcement, 155–156
    social role theory, 173–176
Sex role, 6
Sex-role spillover theory, 533
Sex segregation, pay disparity and, 512–514
Sex stereotype/gender-role stereotype, 7
Sex-typed individuals, 7, 55–56
Sex typing, 7, 53–55, 56
Sexual behavior
    overinterpretation, 478
    sex differences in, 148
Sexual challenge, as obstacle to cross-sex
    friendships, 312, 313
Sexual coercion. *See* Rape and other forms
    of sexual coercion
Sexual exclusivity, 337, 371
Sexual Experiences Survey, 526
Sexual functioning, 502–503
Sexual harassment, 524–533
    definitions of, 524–527
    incidence of, 527–529
    levels of, 525
    outcomes of, 529–530
    perceptions of, 526–527, 530
    perpetrator characteristics, 530–531
    theories of, 532–533
    victim characteristics, 531–532
Sexual infidelity, 363–365
Sexual intercourse, premarital, 344–345,
    347–348
Sexuality, 343–350
    attitudes toward, 343–346
    first sexual experiences, 347–349
    motives for, 346–347
    research problems, 129
    sex differences in, 126–130
Sexually transmitted diseases (STD), 349
Sexual orientation, 7. *See also* Homosexuals
    child care skills and, 210
    division of labor and, 457–458
    friendships and, 321
    prenatal androgens and, 144
Sexual proposition, 526
Sexual reproduction, 74, 77
Sexual satisfaction, 355–356
Shifting standard, 91
Sick role behavior, 426–428
Sick role hypothesis, 426–427
Simpson, Nicole Brown, 461
Simpson, O. J., 461
Single-parent families, 480
Single-parent families, television depiction
    of, 495
Single-sex classroom debate, 229–231
"Sissies," 6
Sitcoms, 92–93
Situational influences, 45–46
Situations, as context variable, 185–188
Smiling, 35, 251–252, 263–264, 267
Smith, Anna Nicole, 149
Smoking, 401–407
    cessation, 404–407
    prediction of, 410–411
    prevalence
        in adolescents and children, 402–404
        in adults, 402
Social behavior
    hormones, 142–143

    interaction styles, 243
    negative, 243
    positive, 243
Social class, friendship and. *See also*
    Socioeconomic status (SES)
Social cognitive theory, 178
Social comparison theory, 522–523
Social constructionists approach, 60–61
Social construction of gender, 20–21
Social desirability response bias, 43, 56
Social exchange theory, 370–371
Social factors in achievement, 218–232
    expectancy/value model of achievement,
        219–220
    influence of parents, 220–224
    influence of teachers, 225–231
Socialization
    language and, 250–251
    play style and, 241–242
Socialized dysfunctional characteristic theory,
    62–63
Social leadership, 268
Social learning theory
    of aggression, 154
        modeling, 152–156
        peer influence, 165
        reinforcement, 155–156
    observational learning or modeling, 153–155
    reinforcement, 155–156
Social network
    adverse effects on women's health, 488
    size of, 308, 309, 486
Social network index, 488
Social regulation, 293
Social role theory, 30–31
    of communications, 265–267
    cross-cultural evidence for, 174–175
    of influenceability, 267
    of interaction styles, 266
    of language, 266–267
    of leadership styles, 270–272
    of nonverbal behavior, 267
    sex-related comparisons in,
        173–176
Social support, 560
    health and, 486–490
    laboratory studies of, 489–490
    marriage as source of, 438–439
Social withdrawal, 577
Sociobiology, 147–150
    of aggression, 149–150
    rate of, 434
    of sex differences
        hunter-gatherer society, 150
        mate selection, 148–149
        sexual behavior, 148
Socioeconomic status (SES)
    division of labor and, 458
    eating disorders and, 589
    gender-role conceptions and, 82
    health and, 393–394
    obesity and, 413
    single-sex schools and, 229–230
Socioemotional leader, 269
Sorenstam, Annika, 14
Spatial ability, 106–109, 142, 146
    social learning theory of, 155
Spatial location memory, 109
Spatial perception, 106–107
Spatial visualization, 106–107
Spillover role, 533
Sports
    participation in, 415–417
    violent, 421

Spousal abuse. *See also* Domestic abuse
　rape, 473
Stable attribution, 215
Stalking, 470
Standardized tests, 111–112, 118
Status. *See also* Socioeconomic status (SES)
　culture and, 13–14
　gender role violations and, 5–6
　sex effects and, 13
　suicide and, 596
Status theory
　and agency, 262
　of communications, 261–265
　　explanations for sex differences, 261–265
　　influenceability, 264–265
　　interaction styles, 261–262
　　language, 262–263
　　nonverbal behavior, 263–264
　and communion, 262
　of interaction styles, 261–262
Stereotype. *See also* Gender-role stereotype(s)
　of adults, 78–81
　children's books, 167–170
　in commercials, 171–173
　confirmatory hypothesis testing and, 101–102
　of country, 82–83
Stereotype threat, 207–210
Stewart, Martha, 125
Stimulus/target variable(s), 26, 35
Stone, Oliver, 154
Storge (friendship) love, 341–342
Strains
　multiple roles and, 536–537
　of parenting, 483–484
　from separation and divorce, 446–447
　from widowhood, 443
Stress
　communion and, 570
　marriage and coping with, 439
　social networks and, 486–487
　social support and reactivity to, 489–490
Stress-buffering hypothesis, 534
　effects on marriage, 438
　family role and work stress, 536–537
　work role and family stress, 536
Stress exposure, 566
Stressful life events, depression and, 566–569
　differential exposure vs. differential
　　vulnerability, 568–569
　interpersonal vs. noninterpersonal stressors,
　　567–568
Stress impact, 566
Stressors, 390–393
Structural indexes, health related, 487–488
Structural level of analysis, 286
Structural measures of support, 486
Structural support, 486–487
　health and, 487–488
Study design, experimenter effects on research,
　38–40
Study of Mathematically Precocious Youth
　(SMPY), 111, 223
Subject variable(s), 34
Substance abuse, 408–411
　prediction of, 410–411
　prevalence of, 409–410
Subtyping, 85
Success, fear of, 196–199
Suicide, 384, 593–597
　attempts, 595
　domestic abuse and, 461
　factors associated with, 595–597
　　among adolescents, 597
　　among adults, 595–597

gender paradox of, 595
　incidence of, 593–595
　widowhood and, 442
Suicide bombings, 122
Superwoman, 459
Supply-side theory, 512
Support interactions, 280–281
Support provision in interactions,
　278–281
Supreme Court, 95–96
Surveys, 32–33
Susceptibility factors in depression, 553
Sweden, paternity leave in, 518
Symptom perception, 424–426
　evidence of, 424–425
　explanation of, 425–426

T

Tahiti, 12–13
Tailhook Association, 524
Target (stimulus) variable(s), 26, 35
Target-based expectancies, 85–86, 224
Target variable, 185
Task behavior, 243
Task-oriented leader, 269
Task(s)
　influenceability and, 255–256
　interaction styles and, 256, 261, 266
　interaction styles during, 242–243
　leadership in, 268–269
　self-confidence and, 201, 202–203
Teachers(s)
　achievement and, 225–231
　effects on performance, 228–231
Technology, sedentary lifestyle and, 416–417
Television
　aggression and, 154
　families depicted on, 92–93
　gender-role socialization from, 170–171
　lack of exercise and, 415–417
　men and women depicted on, 92–93
Temperament, marital satisfaction and, 355–356
Tend and befriend strategy, 561
Terrorism, patriarchal, 33–34, 465–467, 491–492
Testosterone
　aggression and, 143
　depression and, 555
　personality and, 143
Tests, standardized, 111–112, 118
Thatcher, Margaret, 78
Thematic Apperception Test (TAT), 195–196
Theory, 30, 31
Thinness, media attention to, 591
Thomas, Edward, 339
Thrombolytic therapy, 395
Title IX, 221
Token resistance, 479
"Tomboys," 6
Touching, 253–254, 264
　as sexual harassment, 525
Toy advertisements, 172–173
Toy commercials, 154, 172–173
Toys
　advertisements of, 172–173
　cognition, behavior and, 167
　sex-typed, 165–167
Traditional gender ideology, 70
Transactional leadership style, 269–270
Transformational leadership style, 269–270
Transgendered individuals, 6
Transitional attitude, 70
Transitional gender ideology, 70
Transsexual, 6

Treatment discrimination, 508
Trump, Donald, 334
Turkish marriages, 354
Turner, Tina, 544
Twin studies
　of eating disorders, 589
　of gender roles, 140–141
　of hormonal effects on gender-role behavior,
　　144–145
Type 2 diabetes, 413

U

Unattractiveness, physical, 65
Unconscious, the, 151–152
Undifferentiated individual, 56
Unemotional relationships, fear of, 65
Unemployment
　health and, 503–504
　labor force participation rate for men
　　and, 496–497
　suicide rates and, 596
Unmitigated agency, 56–57, 197–198
　adjusting to chronic illnesses and, 584
　health and, 441
Unmitigated communion, 57, 197–198
　depression and, 570–571
　eating disorders and, 590
　rumination and, 570–571
　stress and, 570–571
Unstable attribution, 215
U.S. Congress, women in, 495, 509
U.S. Merit System Protection Board
　surveys, 528

V

Validity
　construct, 103
　external, 35
　internal, 35
Variable(s)
　confounded with sex, 45
　dependent, 33–34, 36
　experimenter effects in use of, 39–40
　independent, 33–34, 36
　moderating, 105
　stimulus/target, 26, 35
　subject, 34
Verbal ability, 113–115
Verbal skills, 91
Vermont, civil unions, 367
Victimization, fear of, 65
Violence. *See also* Aggression; Domestic abuse
　among homosexuals, 464
　crime statistics, 385–386
　in families, 149–150
　against men vs. women, 25
　research on, 123–126
　　sex of perpetrator, 123–126
　　sex of victim, 126
Virginia Military Institute (VMI), 95
Virginia Polytechnic Institute, 121
Virginity, 348–349
Voluntary interdependence, 311, 593

W

Wage gap. *See* Pay disparity
War, 156–157
War on terrorism, 122
"We can but I can't" paradox, 201
Weddings, 46

Weight
    marriage and, 414
    smoking cessation and, 406–407
Wendt, Gary, 96
Wendt, Lorna, 96
Wendt vs. Wendt, 96
When Harry Met Sally (film), 310, 312
Why Can't Men Open Up? (Naifeh &
    Smith), 63
Widowhood
    health effects of, 441–444
        depression, 548
        suicide, 442
Wife beating, 460
Wishful thinking, 560
Withdrawal, social, 577
Withdrawal symptoms, self-reports of, 406
Woman-man, 10
Women
    denial of discrimination, 521–523
    employment of, 496–503, 533–534
        effects on marriage, 502–503
        effects on men's health, 500–502
        effects on women's health, 498–500
        full-time vs. part-time, 499–500, 502–503
        labor force participation, 533–534
        men's support of, 500–501
        occupations of, 505–506
        reasons for increase in, 533
    participation in labor force, 496

    relationship breakups initiated by, 447–448
    on television, 495
    unemployment rate, 496–497
*Women Don't Ask: Negotiation and the Gender
    Divide* (Babcock & Laschever), 514–515
Women's Health Initiative, 395
Women's language, 88
Women's movements, 21–23
Woods, Tiger, 85
Work
    discrimination, 508–523
        access discrimination, 508
        denial of discrimination, 521–523
        pay disparity, 510–521
        treatment discrimination, 508
    division of labor and, 457
    family-supportive environment at,
        517–518
    friendships at, 317–321
        role conflict, 318–319
Working mothers, role conflict in, 537
Work role(s), 496–508, 536
    family stress and, 536
    interrelations between family and, 537–538
    multiple roles question, 533–539
        differential exposure vs. differential
            vulnerability, 496–497
        difficulties in combining roles, 537–539
        role expansion hypothesis and, 534
        role scarcity hypothesis, 534

    quality of, 505–508
        characteristics of work, 506–508
        health effects of, 508
    role buffering and role exacerbation, 536–537
        family role and work stress, 536–537
        work role and family stress, 536
    unemployment, 503–504
    women's employment, 497–503
        effects on marriage, 502–503
        effects on men's health, 500–502
        effects on women's health,
            498–500
    women's entitlement to pay and perception
        of, 522
Writing, nonsexist construction in, 16
Writing, sex differences in, 114

X

X chromosome, 389, 554–555
XYY chromosome configuration,
    141–142

Y

Y chromosome, 3, 141–142
Yentl syndrome, 396
*You Just Don't Understand: Women and Men
    in conversation* (Tannen), 30, 235,
    260–261